TENTH EDITION

Managing Human Resources

SUSAN E. JACKSON

Rutgers University
GSBA Zürich

RANDALL S. SCHULER

Rutgers University
GSBA Zürich

STEVE WERNER

University of Houston

SOUTH-WESTERN
CENGAGE Learning

Australia · Brazil · Japan · Korea · Mexico · Singapore · Spain · United Kingdom · United States

SOUTH-WESTERN
CENGAGE Learning™

Managing Human Resources, 10E
Susan E. Jackson, Randall S. Schuler,
Steve Werner

Vice President of Editorial, Business:
Jack W. Calhoun

Editor-in-Chief: Melissa Acuna

Executive Editor: Joe Sabatino

Developmental Editor: Elizabeth Lowry

Editorial Assistant: Ruth Belanger

Executive Marketing Manager:
Kimberly Kanakes

Marketing Manager: Clint Kernen

Marketing Coordinator: Sarah Rose

Senior Content Project Manager:
Kim Kusnerak

Technology Project Manager: Kristin Meere

Manufacturing Coordinator: Doug Wilke

Production Service: ICC Macmillan Inc.

Senior Art Director: Tippy McIntosh

Internal Designer: Craig Ramsdell,
Ramsdell Design

Cover Designer: Craig Ramsdell,
Ramsdell Design

Cover Image: Image Source, Getty

Photography Manager:
Deanna Ettinger

For product information and technology assistance, contact us at
Cengage Learning Customer & Sales Support, 1-800-354-9706

For permission to use material from this text or product,
submit all requests online at **cengage.com/permissions**
Further permissions questions can be emailed to
permissionrequest@cengage.com

Exam*View*® and Exam*View* Pro® are registered trademarks of FSCreations, Inc. Windows is a registered trademark of the Microsoft Corporation used herein under license. Macintosh and Power Macintosh are registered trademarks of Apple Computer, Inc. used herein under license.

© 2009 Cengage Learning. All Rights Reserved.

Library of Congress Control Number: 2007908811

ISBN-13: 978-0-324-56839-4

ISBN-10: 0-324-56839-8

Instructor's Edition ISBN 13: 978-0-324-57967-3

Instructor's Edition ISBN 10: 0-324-57967-5

South-Western Cengage Learning
5191 Natorp Boulevard
Mason, OH 45040
USA

Cengage Learning products are represented in Canada
by Nelson Education, Ltd.

For your course and learning solutions, visit **academic.cengage.com**

Purchase any of our products at your local college store or at our preferred online store **www.ichapters.com**

Printed in Canada
1 2 3 4 5 11 10 09 08

BRIEF CONTENTS

Preface, xvii

1. Managing Human Resources, 3

2. Understanding the External and Organizational Environments, 35

3. HR Planning for Alignment and Change, 73

4. Ensuring Fair Treatment and Legal Compliance, 113

5. Using Job Analysis and Competency Modeling, 153

6. Recruiting and Retaining Qualified Employees, 189

7. Selecting Employees to Fit the Job and the Organization, 229

8. Training and Developing a Competitive Workforce, 269

9. Conducting Performance Management, 313

10. Developing an Approach to Total Compensation, 355

11. Using Performance-Based Pay to Achieve Strategic Objectives, 395

12. Providing Benefits and Services, 435

13. Promoting Workplace Safety and Health, 473

14. Understanding Unionization and Collective Bargaining, 507

Integrative Case: Southwest Airlines, 544

Integrative Case: The Lincoln Electric Company, 560

Endnotes, 576

Name Index, 622

Subject Index, 633

Getty Images

CONTENTS

Preface	xvii

Chapter 1: Managing Human Resources	**3**
Managing Human Resources at Cisco Systems	3
The Strategic Importance of Managing Human Resources	4

Satisfying Multiple Stakeholders, 4 • Owners and Investors, 4 • Customers, 6 • Society, 7 • Other Organizations, 9 • Organizational Members (The Employees), 10 • Creating Win-Win Situations, 11

Gaining and Sustaining a Competitive Advantage	11

Employees Who Are a Source of Added Value, 12 • Employees Who Are Rare, 12 • A Culture That Can't Be Copied, 13

A Framework for Managing Human Resources	14

The Importance of the External and Organizational Environments, 14 • Activities for Managing Human Resources, 16

The HR Triad	19

Line Managers Have Always Been Responsible, 20 • HR Professionals Provide Special Expertise, 20 • Employees Share Responsibility, 24

Looking Ahead: Five Special Themes	24
The HR Triad: Roles and Responsibilities for Managing Human Resources	25

Managing Teams, 25 • Managing the Multicultural Workforce, 26 • Managing Globalization, 26 • Managing Ethics, 27 • Managing with Metrics, 27

Current Issues	28

eHR, 28 • Managing Complexity, 28

Chapter Summary with Learning Goals	29
Terms to Remember	30
Questions for Discussion and Reflective Thinking	30
Projects to Extend Your Learning	30
Case Study: Aligning HR with the Business at SBC	32

Chapter 2: Understanding the External and Organizational Environments	**35**
Managing Human Resources at Deere & Company	35
The Strategic Importance of Understanding the External and Organizational Environments	36

Elements of the Environment, 37 • The HR Triad, 37

The HR Triad: Roles and Responsibilities for Understanding the External and
Organizational Environments   38

Economic Globalization   39

*Competing on Cost versus Competing on Knowledge, 39 •
Worldwide Operations, 39 • Regional Trade Zones, 40*

The Political Landscape   42

*International Labor Organization, 42 • Social Accountability
International, 42 • World Trade Organization, 42*

Industry Dynamics   43

Industry Life Cycles, 43 • Mergers and Acquisitions, 45

Labor Markets   46

U.S. Labor Market, 46 • Global Labor Market, 48

Country Cultures   50

Managing Globalization: Mercedes-Benz Sets Up in Alabama   51

*Dimensions of Country Cultures, 52 •
Consequences of Country Cultures, 53*

Technologies   53

*Factories and Mass Production Technologies, 53 •
Computer Technologies, 54 • Virtual Workforce, 54 •
Human Resource Information Management, 55*

Managing with Metrics: You Change What You Measure   56

Company Culture   56

*Leadership, 56 • Vision, 57 • Mission, 57 •
Values, 58 • Company Subcultures, 58*

Business Strategies   60

Total Quality, 61 • Low Cost, 61 • Customer Service, 61

Managing Teams: Sabre's Virtual Teams   62

Innovation, 63

Current Issues   63

The Aging Workforce, 63 • Global Realities of MNCs for HRM, 64

Chapter Summary with Learning Goals   65
Terms to Remember   67
Questions for Discussion and Reflective Thinking   67
Projects to Extend Your Learning   67
Case Study: Levi Strauss & Company   70

Chapter 3: HR Planning for Alignment and Change   73
Managing Human Resources at Weyerhaeuser Company   73
The Strategic Importance of HR Planning for Alignment and Change   74

*Alignment, 74 • Types of Organizational Change, 75 •
Learning Organizations, 77*

Overview of the HR Planning and Change Process   78

*The Elements of Human Resource Planning, 78 •
Aligning Business Planning and HR Planning, 81 •
The HR Triad, 82*

Scanning and Assessing the External and Organizational Environments   82

The HR Triad: Roles and Responsibilities for HR Planning, Alignment, and Change   83

    Organizational Analysis, 84 • HR Forecasts, 85 • Employees' Opinions, 87

Managing Globalization: Building Global Leaders at Unilever   89

    Behavioral Cause-and-Effect Models, 90

Determining HR Objectives and Metrics   91

    Linking HR Objectives to Strategic Business Objectives, 91 •
    Developing Metrics to Match the Objectives, 92

Developing HR Plans and Timetables   94

    Considering Alternatives, 95 • Building a Complete HR Plan, 97 •
    Timetables, 99

Implementing HR Action Plans and Facilitating Change   101

    Involving Employees, 101 • Establishing Accountability, 101 •
    Change Has Already Started, 101

Managing Teams: Mill Improvement Process Teams at Georgia-Pacific   102

    Managing Resistance to Change, 103 • Showing Respect in Difficult
    Times, 104 • Review, Revise, and Refocus, 104

Current Issues   105

    Global Workforce Planning, 105 •
    The Wholly Sustainable Enterprise, 105

Managing Ethics: HR and Supply Chain Management at HP   106

Chapter Summary with Learning Goals   106
Terms to Remember   107
Questions for Discussion and Reflective Thinking   108
Projects to Extend Your Learning   108
Case Study: Managing Human Resources at Barden Bearings   110

Chapter 4: Ensuring Fair Treatment and Legal Compliance   **113**
Managing Human Resources at Wal-Mart   113

The Strategic Importance of Fairness and Legal Compliance   114

    Society and the Law, 114 • Concerns of the Labor Force, 114 •
    Customers Win When Employers Treat Employees Fairly, 114

The HR Triad: Roles and Responsibilities to Ensure Fair Treatment and
Legal Compliance   115

    The HR Triad, 115

What Fairness Means to Employees   116

    Distributive Justice, 117 • Procedural Justice, 117 •
    Interactional Justice, 118 •
    Reactions to Unjust Treatment, 119

Legal Means to Ensure Fair Treatment   120

    Federal Laws, 121 • State Laws, 123 • Executive Orders, 125 •
    Administrative Agencies, 125 • Legal Precedents, 128

Employment-at-Will   128

    Limits to Employment-at-Will, 129 • Employment Contracts, 129 •
    Layoffs, 130 • International Operations, 130

Settling Disputes 131

Company Grievance Procedures, 131 ⊙ Mediation and Arbitration, 132 ⊙ Resolving Disputes Online, 133 ⊙ Using the Courts to Settle Disputes, 133

Proactive Approaches to Ensuring Fair Treatment 134

Creating a Culture of Fairness, 134 ⊙ Diversity Management Initiatives, 135

Managing the Multicultural Workforce: Diversity at Darden Restaurants 138

Managing with Metrics: Montgomery Watson Harza 139

Harassment Policies, 139 ⊙ Fairness Must Be Reciprocated, 142

Current Issues 143

Privacy in the United States, 143

Managing Globalization: Privacy in the European Union 145

Privacy in the Global Context, 145

Chapter Summary with Learning Goals 146
Answers to the Quiz about Older Workers on Page 122 147
Terms to Remember 147
Discussion Questions 148
Projects to Extend Your Learning 148
Case Study: United Way and the Boy Scouts of America 150

Chapter 5: Using Job Analysis and Competency Modeling 153

Managing Human Resources at Fairchild Semiconductor 153

The Strategic Importance of Job Analysis and Competency Modeling 154

Strategic Change, 155 ⊙ Legal Protection, 156 ⊙ HR Triad Roles and Responsibilities, 158

The HR Triad: Partnership Roles in Job Analysis and Competency Modeling 159

Basic Terminology 159

Positions, Jobs, and Occupations, 159 ⊙ Job Analysis, 160 ⊙ Competency Modeling, 161 ⊙ Job Descriptions, 161 ⊙ Career Paths, 162

Sources of Information Used in Job Analysis and Competency Modeling 163

Job Incumbents, 164 ⊙ Supervisors, 164 ⊙ Trained Job Analysts, 164 ⊙ Customers, 165

Methods of Collecting Information 165

Observations, 165 ⊙ Individual and Group Interviews, 166 ⊙ Questionnaires, 166

Standardized Approaches to Job Analysis 166

Time-and-Motion Studies, 166 ⊙ Ergonomic Analysis, 167 ⊙ Occupational Information Network (O*NET), 167 ⊙ Position Analysis Questionnaire, 169 ⊙ Management Position Description Questionnaire, 170

Customized Job Analysis 171

Developing a Customized Inventory, 171 ⊙ Analyzing and Interpreting the Data, 172 ⊙ Advantages and Disadvantages, 173

Analyzing Needed Competencies   173

Standardized Approach, 174 • Customized Approach, 177

Managing Globalization: Modeling Leadership Competencies at 3M   178

Competency Inventories, 179

Current Issues   179

Managing with Metrics: Schlumberger   180

The Decline of Job Analysis?, 180 • From "My Job" to "My Role", 181

Chapter Summary with Learning Goals   182
Terms to Remember   183
Questions for Discussion and Reflective Thinking   183
Projects to Extend Your Learning   183
Case Study: Job Descriptions at HITEK   184

Chapter 6: Recruiting and Retaining Qualified Employees   189

Managing Human Resources at SAS Institute   189

The Strategic Importance of Recruiting and Retaining Talented Employees   190

Supporting Strategies, 190 • Reducing Expenses and Improving Productivity, 191

Managing with Metrics: Valero Energy   192

Retaining the Best Employees, 193

The HR Triad: Roles and Responsibilities for Recruiting and Retaining Employees   194

Addressing Societal Concerns through Legal Compliance, 194 • The HR Triad, 194

Recruitment and Retention within an Integrated HRM System   196

Links to Other HR Activities, 196 • Labor Markets, 197 • Technology, 198

Managing Ethics: Honeywell's Bloggers   198

Legal Trends, 199 • Company Reputation, 199

Recruiting Sources and Methods   199

Internal Labor Market, 200 • External Labor Market, 201

Managing Globalization: Deloitte Touche Tohmatsu   203

Contingent Workers, Rehires, and Recalls, 207

Recruiting from the Applicant's Perspective   208

Building a Corporate Reputation, 209 • The Recruitment Experience, 210 • Perceptions of Fit, 211 • HR Practices, 211

Recruiting Ethics   211

Honesty Pays, 212 • Rejecting Applicants, 212

Equal Opportunity and Nondiscrimination   213

EEO-1 Reports, 213 • Affirmative Action Programs, 213

Managing the Multicultural Workforce: IBM's Project View   215

Breaking the Glass Ceiling, 216

Retaining Employees   217

Understanding the Reasons for Turnover, 217 • HR Practices Can Reduce Unwanted Turnover, 218 • Managing Layoffs, 220

Current Issues   221

    The Global Labor Shortage, 221 • *Immigration Reform and Foreign*
    Workers in the United States, 222

Chapter Summary with Learning Goals   223
Terms to Remember   224
Questions for Discussion and Reflective Thinking   224
Projects to Extend Your Learning   225
Case Study: Downsizing: Anathema to Corporate Loyalty?   226

Chapter 7: Selecting Employees to Fit the Job and the Organization   229

Managing Human Resources at Outback Steakhouse   229

The Strategic Importance of Selection   230

    Obtaining a Capable Workforce, 230 • *Maximizing the Economic Utility*
    of Selection Practices, 230 • *The HR Triad, 232*

The HR Triad: Roles and Responsibilities in Selecting Applicants   233

    Selection within an Integrated HRM System, 234

Designing the Selection Process   236

    Establishing the Criteria of Interest, 236 • *Choosing the Predictors and*
    Assessment Techniques, 237

Managing Teams: Selecting the Walt Disney Cast   238

    Deciding When to Measure Each Predictor, 242 • *Synthesizing*
    Information to Choose Appropriate Candidates, 242

Techniques for Assessing Job Applicants   244

    Personal History Assessments, 244 • *Background Verification and*
    Reference Checks, 245 • *Written Tests, 246*

Managing Ethics: Assessment of the Twenty-First-Century Workforce   248

    Work Simulations, 249 • *Assessment Centers, 249* • *Interviews, 250* •
    Medical Tests, 252

The Perspective of Job Applicants   254

    Fair Content?, 255 • *Fair Process?, 256* • *Fair Results?, 256*

Legal Considerations in Selection   256

    Laws and Regulations That Prohibit Discrimination, 256 •
    Federal Guidelines and Professional Standards, 257 •
    Detecting Unfair Discrimination, 257 •
    Defending Discriminatory Practices, 259

Managing with Metrics: The 80% Rule   259

    Legal Considerations for Global Selection, 260

Current Issues   261

    Selecting Expatriates, 261 • *Selecting Host-Country Nationals (HCNs), 261*

Chapter Summary with Learning Goals   263
Terms to Remember   263
Questions for Discussion and Reflective Thinking   264
Projects to Extend Your Learning   264
Case Study: Selecting Patient Escorts   266
Answers to Experiential Activity: Application Blanks   267

Chapter 8: Training and Developing a Competitive Workforce — 269

Managing Human Resources at Ritz-Carlton Hotel Company — 269

Strategic Importance of Training and Development — 270

*Improving Recruitment and Retention, 270 * Improving Competitiveness, 270 * Implementing New Technology, 271 * Improving Customer Service, 271 * Ethics Training, 272 * Knowledge Management and Learning Organizations, 272*

Managing Ethics: J. M. Smucker & Co. — 273

Mergers and Acquisitions, 274

Training and Development within an Integrated HRM System — 275

*Training, Development, and Socialization, 275 * Links to Other HR Activities, 276 * Evaluating Training and Development, 278*

Managing with Metrics: IBM Evaluates Its Training — 279

The HR Triad — 280

*Managers, 280 * Employees, 280*

The HR Triad: Roles and Responsibilities in Training and Development — 281

HR Professionals, 281

Determining Training and Development Needs — 281

*Organizational Needs Analysis, 282 * Job Needs Analysis, 283 * Person Needs Analysis, 283 * Demographic Needs Analysis, 285*

Conditions for Effective Training and Development — 286

*Create the Right Conditions, 286 * Decide Who Provides, 287*

Stating the Learning Objectives — 288

*Cognitive Knowledge, 288 * Skills, 289 * Affective Outcomes, 290 * Ethical Behavior, 291*

Choosing the Program Format — 291

*e-Learning, 292 * On the Job, 293*

Managing the Multicultural Workforce: John W. Thompson, CEO and Mentor — 295

*On-Site but Not On the Job, 296 * Typically-Off-Site, 297*

Maximizing Learning — 299

*Setting the Stage for Learning, 299 * Increasing Learning during Training, 300 * Maintaining Performance after Training, 301*

Team Training and Development — 302

*Training to Develop Team Cohesiveness, 302 * Training in Team Procedures, 302 * Training for Team Leaders, 303*

Current Issues — 304

*Diversity Training for Employees in the United States, 304 * Global Leadership Training and Development, 305*

Managing Globalization: PricewaterhouseCoopers — 307

Chapter Summary with Learning Goals — 307
Terms to Remember — 308
Questions for Discussion and Reflective Thinking — 309
Projects to Extend Your Learning — 309
Case Study: Seeing the Forest *and* the Trees — 311

Chapter 9: Conducting Performance Management   313

Managing Human Resources at TRW   313

The Strategic Importance of Performance Management   314

Enhancing Motivation and Productivity, 315 •
Supporting Strategic Goals, 317 •
Strategic Planning, Alignment, and Change, 318

Performance Management within an Integrated HRM System   319

The Internal and External Environment, 319

Managing with Metrics: Setpoint's Public Performance   321

Other HR Activities, 323

The HR Triad   323

Managers, 323

The HR Triad: Roles and Responsibilities for Measuring Performance and
Providing Feedback   324

Employees, 324 • HR Professionals, 324

What to Measure   326

Personal Traits, 326 • Behaviors, 326 •
Objective Results, 327 • Multiple Criteria, 328 •
Weighting the Criteria, 328

Managing with Ethics: Measuring Values at Payless ShoeSource   328

Timing   329

Focal-Point Approach, 330 • Anniversary Approach, 331 •
Natural Time Span of the Job, 331

Participants   331

Supervisors, 332 • Self-Appraisal, 332 • Peers, 333 •
Subordinates, 333 • Customers, 334 •
360-Degree Appraisals, 334

Performance Appraisal Formats   335

Norm-Referenced Formats, 335 • Absolute Standards Formats, 336 •
Results-Based Formats, 338

The Rating Process   340

Rating Errors, 341 • Improving Rater Accuracy, 341

Providing Feedback   343

Differing Perspectives, 343 • Timing, 344 •
Preparation, 344 • Content of the Discussion, 344 •
Follow-Up, 345 • When Nothing Else Works, 346

Current Issues   347

Automated Performance Management, 347 •
Monitoring through Technology, 348

Chapter Summary with Learning Goals   348
Terms to Remember   350
Discussion Questions   350
Projects to Extend Your Learning   350
Case Study: 360-Degree Appraisals   352

Chapter 10: Developing an Approach to Total Compensation   **355**

Managing Human Resources at Synapse Group, Inc.   355

The Strategic Importance of Total Compensation   356

Attracting, Motivating, and Retaining Talent, 356 ● Implementing the Business Strategy, 360 ● Productivity Improvement, 361

Total Compensation within the Integrated HRM System   361

Monetary and Nonmonetary Compensation, 361 ● Pay Mix, 362 ● Other HR Practices, 363 ● The External Environment, 364 ● Legal Constraints and Social Considerations, 365

Managing the Multicultural Workforce: Wal-Mart's Woes   369

The Organizational Environment, 369

The HR Triad   370

The HR Triad: Roles and Responsibilities for Total Compensation   371

HR Professionals, 371 ● Managers, 371 ● Employees, 372

Establishing the Internal Value of Jobs   372

Objectives of Job Evaluation, 372 ● Job Ranking Method, 373 ● Job Classification Method, 373 ● Point Factor Rating Method, 374 ● Competency-Based Job Evaluation, 377 ● Skill-Based Pay, 378 ● Single versus Multiple Pay Structures, 378

Using External Market Rates to Set Pay Levels   379

Step 1: Determine External Market Pay Rates, 379 ● Step 2: Establish the Market Pay Policy, 382 ● Step 3: Set the Organization Pay Policy, 383

Designing the Internal Pay Structure   384

Job-Based Pay Grades and Ranges, 384 ● Competency-Based Pay Structure, 385 ● Skill-Based Pay Structure, 385

Adjustments   385

Balancing Internal and External Equity, 385 ● Changes over Time, 386 ● Achieving Individual Pay Equity, 386

Compensation in the Context of Globalization   387

Managing Globalization: Global Pay at McDonald's   388

Current Issues   389

Work/Life Balance, 389 ● Automation of Benefits and Compensation, 389

Chapter Summary with Learning Goals   389
Terms to Remember   390
Questions for Reflective Thinking and Discussion   391
Projects to Extend Your Learning   391
Case Study: The Overpaid Bank Tellers   393

Chapter 11: Using Performance-Based Pay to Achieve Strategic Objectives   **395**

Managing Human Resources at the United States Postal Service   395

The Strategic Importance of Using Performance-Based Pay   396

Supporting Strategic Objectives, 396 ● Managing Labor Costs, 397 ● Attracting, Retaining, and Motivating Talent, 398

Performance-Based Pay within an Integrated HRM System   399

*Other HR Activities, 400 * Organizational Environment, 401*

Managing a Multicultural Workforce: Rewarding Managers Who Achieve
Diversity Goals   401

External Environment, 402

The HR Triad   402

Design Choices for Performance-Based Pay   402

The HR Triad: Roles and Responsibilities for Using Performance-Based Pay
to Achieve Strategic Objectives   403

*Types of Performance-Based Pay, 403 * Rewards, 404 *
Performance Measures, 406 *
Linking Performance to Rewards, 409*

Implementation Issues   410

*Gaining Employee Acceptance, 410 * Legal Considerations, 411 *
Evaluating Effectiveness, 412*

Recognition Awards   412

*Spot Awards, 413 * Awards for Suggestions, 414 *
Multiple Awards, 415*

Managing with Metrics: Rackspace Rewards Fanatical Customer Service   415

Merit Pay   416

*Performance Measures, 416 * Rewards, 416 *
Linking Performance to Pay, 417*

Incentive Pay   418

*Individual Incentives, 418 * Team Incentives, 420*

Managing Teams: Performance-Based Pay at Children's Hospital Boston   420

Unit and Companywide Incentives, 421

Pay That Puts Earnings at Risk   422

*Commissions, 423 * Stock Ownership, 424*

Global Pay for Performance   426

Current Issues   427

*Ethical Considerations, 427 * The Shift toward Variable Pay, 429*

Chapter Summary with Learning Goals   429
Terms to Remember   430
Questions for Discussion and Reflective Thinking   431
Projects to Extend Your Learning   431
Case Study: Evaluating Nontraditional Incentives: Howe 2 Ski Stores   432

Chapter 12: Providing Benefits and Services   435
Managing Human Resources at Steelcase   435

The Strategic Importance of Employee Benefits and Services   436

*Controlling Costs, 436 * Recruiting and Retaining Talent, 437 *
Achieving Business Objectives, 438*

Employee Benefits and Services within an Integrated HRM System   439

*Links with Other HR Practices, 440 * The External Environment, 441 *
The Organizational Environment, 442*

The HR Triad: Roles and Responsibilities for Employee Benefits and Services   444

The HR Triad   444

Mandatory Protection Programs   445

*Social Security Insurance, 445 * Unemployment Compensation, 445 *
Workers' Compensation and Disability Insurance, 446 * Family and
Medical Leave, 446*

Voluntary Protection Programs   447

*Defined Benefit Plans, 447 * Defined Contribution Plans, 448*

Managing Ethics: Ethical Implications of Defined Contribution Plans   449

*Cash Balance Plans, 451 * Legal Considerations, 451*

Health Care Benefits and Services   453

*Medical Care, 453 * Wellness Programs, 456 *
Employee Assistance Programs, 457*

Paid Leave   457

Off-the-Job Paid Leave, 457

Managing Globalization: Vacationing around the World   458

On-the-Job Paid Leave, 459

Work/Life Benefits and Services   459

*Scheduling, 460 * Child Care Services, 460 * Elder Care Services, 461 *
Domestic Partner Benefits and Services, 461*

Other Benefits and Services   462

*Developmental Benefits and Services, 463 * Personal Services, 463 *
Business Travel and Relocation Assistance, 463*

Administrative Issues   463

*Determining the Benefits and Services Package, 463 * Determining the
Level of Flexibility, 464 * Communication, 464*

Current Issues   465

*Health Care Benefits and Services, 465 *
Benefits and Services for Retirees, 466*

Chapter Summary with Learning Goals   467
Terms to Remember   468
Questions for Discussion and Reflective Thinking   468
Projects to Extend Your Learning   469
Case Study: Who's Benefiting?   471

Chapter 13: Promoting Workplace Safety and Health   473

Managing Human Resources at Deere & Company   473

The Strategic Importance of Workplace Safety and Health   474

*Benefits of a Safe and Healthy Workplace, 474 * Consequences of an
Unsafe and Unhealthy Workplace, 474*

Managing with Metrics: CTS Is Reduced at Ben & Jerry's   475

Promoting Safety and Health within an Integrated HRM System   476

*Links to Other HR Activities, 477 * The Organizational
Environment, 479 * The External Environment, 480 * Global
Considerations, 483*

The HR Triad: Roles and Responsibilities in Promoting Workplace Safety and Health   485

The HR Triad, 485

Safety and Health Hazards in the Workplace   486

Occupational Accidents, 486

Managing the Multicultural Workforce: Safety Issues and the Aging Workforce   487

*Violent Employees, 488 • Occupational Diseases, 489 •
Poorly Designed Jobs, 489 • Workplace Stressors, 491 •
Job Burnout, 492*

Strategies for Improving Workplace Safety and Health   494

*Monitoring Safety and Health Rates, 494 • Accident Prevention, 494 •
Disease Prevention, 497 • Stress Management, 497 •
Wellness Programs, 499*

Current Issues   501

*Preparation for and Recovery from Diseases and Disasters, 501 •
Safety around the World, 501*

Chapter Summary with Learning Goals   502
Terms to Remember   502
Questions for Discussion and Reflective Thinking   503
Projects to Extend Your Learning   503
Case Study: Who's There on the Line?   505

**Chapter 14: Understanding Unionization and
Collective Bargaining**   **507**

Managing Human Resources at United Parcel Service   507

The Strategic Importance of Unionization and Collective Bargaining   508

Managing with Metrics: Unions' Involvement Enhances Competitiveness   509

*Unionization and Collective Bargaining within the Integrated HRM
System, 509*

The Historical Context and Unions Today   510

A Brief History, 510

The HR Triad—EXTENDED: Roles and Responsibilities in Unionization and
Collective Bargaining   511

*Decline in Membership, 512 • Distribution of Membership, 514 •
Structure of American Unions, 514 • How Unions Operate, 515*

Managing Globalization: Unionization in Mexico and Canada   516

The Organizing Campaign   516

*Soliciting Employee Support, 517 • Determination of the Bargaining
Unit, 519 • Preelection Campaign, 519 • Election, Certification, and
Decertification, 519 • Deciding to Join a Union, 520*

The Collective Bargaining Process   521

*Adversarial Relationship, 522 • Cooperative Relationship, 523 •
Bargaining Processes, 523*

Negotiating the Agreement   525

*Negotiating Committees, 526 • The Negotiating Structure, 526 •
Preparation for Bargaining, 527 • Issues for Negotiation, 528 • Factors
Affecting Bargaining, 530*

Conflict Resolution   531

   Strikes and Lockouts, 531 • *Mediation, 533* • *Arbitration, 534*

Contract Administration   534

   Grievance Procedures, 534 • *Grievance Issues, 536* • *Management
Procedures, 536* • *Union Procedures, 537* • *Metrics for Assessing the
Collective Bargaining Process, 537*

Current Issues   538

   Global Unions, 538 • *Social Accountability, 538*

Chapter Summary with Learning Goals   540
Terms to Remember   541
Questions for Discussion and Reflective Thinking   541
Projects to Extend Your Learning   542
Case Study: The Union's Strategic Choice   543

Integrative Case: Southwest Airlines, 544

Integrative Case: The Lincoln Electric Company, 560

Endnotes, 576

Name Index, 622
Subject Index, 633

PREFACE

The tenth edition of *Managing Human Resources* explains how successful companies manage human resources to compete effectively in a dynamic, global environment. Because organizations differ from each other in so many ways—including their locations, competitive strategies, products and services, and corporate cultures—we use many different companies in many different industries to illustrate how employers address the challenge of managing human resources effectively. The list of such companies includes Southwest Airlines, Deere & Company, Wegmans, Lincoln Electric, McDonald's, TRW, Steelcase, Google, Novartis, Johnson & Johnson, SAS, Outback Steakhouses, the United States Postal Service, UPS, IBM, 3M, Alberto Culver Weyerhaeuser, The Ritz-Carlton, and others. By combining a respect for established principles of human resource management with a willingness to experiment and try new approaches, these companies succeed year after year.

The Importance of Managing Human Resources Effectively

Managers from the very largest multinational firms to the smallest domestic firms claim that managing people effectively is vital to success in today's highly competitive marketplace. "The relationship we have with our people and the culture of our company is our most sustainable competitive advantage," says Howard Schultz, chair of Starbucks. According to Mike Eskew, former CEO of UPS, "Our business model is based largely on driving efficiencies and economies of scale while encouraging our people."

The task of managing human resources effectively includes all the activities that organizations use to influence the competencies, behaviors, and motivations of all the people who work for them. Because the competencies, behaviors, and motivations of employees influence profitability, customer satisfaction, and a variety of other important measures of organizational effectiveness, managing human resources is a key strategic challenge. Doing it well is important to everyone in the organization.

Meeting the challenge of managing people effectively requires the involvement of everyone in the organization. Of particular importance are managers, human resource (HR) professionals, and the employees themselves. We refer to these three groups of key players as the HR Triad. Together, the HR Triad is responsible for a number of activities.

HR activities include both the formal policies of the organization and the actual daily practices that people experience. Most chapters in this book focus on specific activities, such as recruitment, training, performance management, safety and health, and so on. Together, these activities form the organization's human resource management (HRM) system. An effective HRM system supports the organization's efforts to satisfy its key stakeholders. However, not all HRM systems are alike. Each organization's approach to managing human resources reflects its own history and the external environment in which it operates.

Aligning HR Practices with the External and Organizational Environments

If you have worked in more than one organization, you know from experience that there are many different approaches to managing human resources. Some employers are highly selective in whom they hire, while others seem to hire anyone who walks in the door. Some employers provide extensive training to their employees, while others let new hires sink or swim. Some employers pay well and offer large bonuses; others don't.

Many of the differences in how organizations manage people are due to differences in their external environments. Rapid changes in technology, as well as economic, political, and social conditions, mean that few organizations can effectively compete today by just using the old tried-and-true approaches of yesterday. Nor can they simply copy other organizations. The best organizations are changing and learning continuously.

Increasingly, the great companies—the "100 Most Admired Companies" and the "100 Best Companies to Work for in America"—manage their human resources based on an understanding of the company and its environment. To recruit the right people with the right competencies and to keep these people motivated to do their best work, managers and HR professionals alike need to understand the demands and nature of the business. A computer company that competes by continually offering innovative products and services is likely to manage people differently than a retailer that competes by offering low-cost goods or a manufacturer that competes by offering the best quality possible. Furthermore, each of these companies may change its approach to managing human resources as economic and social conditions change. Therefore, understanding the nature of the organizational and external environments is central to managing human resources strategically.

Satisfying Multiple Stakeholders

Ultimately, an organization is effective only if it satisfies its major stakeholders. Effective organizations recognize that there's more to "success" than just a good bottom line (profits). The best companies balance their concerns over short-term, bottom-line results with the recognition that long-term success requires satisfying a variety of stakeholders. In addition to satisfying the demands of shareholders, the best organizations also address the concerns of employees and their families, customers, members of the local community, government regulators, unions, public interest groups, and other organizations that they do business with—suppliers, distributors, alliance partners, and so on. These various stakeholders care deeply about how businesses conduct themselves and in particular how they treat their employees.

Throughout this textbook, we consider how different approaches to managing human resources can influence the way stakeholders view an organization—for better or for worse. Although it's not always possible to satisfy all stakeholders equally well, effective organizations make a habit of analyzing the available alternatives from multiple perspectives and seeking solutions that meet as many concerns as possible. The approach of developing human resource management policies and practices that are responsive to the concerns of an organization's key stakeholders is central to the strategic partnerships perspective adopted throughout this book.

The HR Triad: Managers, Employees, and HR Professionals

Given the importance of addressing the concerns of many stakeholders, it is not surprising that another quality shared by successful companies is their recognition that managing human resources is everyone's responsibility. Naturally, HR professionals carry much of the responsibility for ensuring that the organization is applying the best knowledge available and conforming to legal requirements. But day in and day out, line managers and the employees themselves carry most of the responsibility for managing human resources. Managers translate the formal policies of the organization into daily practice. Employees, in turn, may be asked to participate in many HR practices, such as interviewing potential new hires, assisting with training, providing feedback on the performance of colleagues, suggesting improvements, and so on. This view—that managing human resources is a shared responsibility—is highlighted throughout this book in a feature called The HR Triad. Within each chapter, it details the roles and responsibilities of HR professionals, managers, and employees.

Five Special Themes

As organizations strive to manage employees effectively, they face many challenges. And as times and conditions change, these challenges also change. Throughout this textbook, we highlight and discuss five current challenges that influence how organizations manage human resources:

1. Managing teams.
2. Managing the multicultural workforce.
3. Managing globalization.
4. Managing ethics.
5. Managing with metrics.

Managing Teams. Many managers now believe that improving the teamwork processes in their organization is essential for ensuring their organization's success. Using team-based organizational structures, employers hope to achieve outcomes that could not be achieved by individuals working in isolation. But the payoff from teams isn't automatic. To create and orchestrate teams, people need to be selected, appraised, compensated, and trained in ways that reflect the unique relationships that develop among employees who work together. Examples of how organizations use HR practices to maximize team effectiveness are highlighted in the Managing Teams feature.

Managing the Multicultural Workforce. Just as organizations have come to realize the benefits of teamwork, they have also discovered that the people who were being put into teams are more diverse than ever before. Today, organizations are finding that their management practices must be sensitive to issues of gender, ethnicity, personality, nationality, religion, sexual orientation, marital and family status, age, and various other life experiences. The Managing the Multicultural Workforce feature describes how effective organizations use HR practices to leverage their multicultural workforces and create competitive advantage.

Managing Globalization. Throughout the twenty-first century, technological advances in transportation and communications will continue to support the growth of international commerce. As firms evolve from domestic to global, they face several challenges related to managing human resources. One challenge is learning how to manage people in different countries effectively. Due to differences in employment laws, labor market conditions, and national cultures, companies cannot assume that HR practices that work in the United States will be equally effective in other countries. Another challenge is to learn how to help employees around the world work together. Although a detailed treatment of the issues raised by globalization is beyond the scope of this book, the Managing Globalization feature provides a glimpse of how some companies are addressing these challenges.

Managing Ethics. Organizations have also discovered the importance of ethics. Corporate financial scandals, questionable CEO pay practices, and public lawsuits have hurt the reputation of numerous organizations over the last few years. Managers have come to realize that serious ethical breaches can sully the good name of their companies and perhaps even put the survival of the organization in jeopardy. Many organizations want to instill a culture of ethics in their workforce, and HR practices can play an important role. HR professionals can support the successful implementation of a culture of ethics by developing HR practices that inform employees of what the organization expects from them and by rewarding ethical behavior. The Managing Ethics feature describes how effective organizations use HR practices to motivate the ethical behavior of employees for the benefit of the organization as well as society.

Managing with Metrics. Measuring the performance of employees and the organization has always been a central responsibility of managers. Nevertheless, we are only just realizing some of the numerous ways that the effective use of metrics can benefit organizations. Today, HR professionals use a wide variety of metrics to systematically measure the contributions of employees, teams, and departments. Metrics also are used to evaluate the effectiveness of the organization's many HR policies and practices. Metrics are now a critical aspect of most HR activities. Examples of how human resource practices incorporate metrics to help the organization achieve its goals are highlighted in the Managing with Metrics feature.

ORGANIZATION OF THIS BOOK

The many topics discussed in this book are organized according to the perspective illustrated in Exhibit 1.3 on page 15. We begin by discussing the "big picture," then we discuss each of the HR activities listed at the center of the exhibit.

The Big Picture

Chapter 1 describes our overarching framework for managing human resources, shown in Exhibit 1.3. This essential chapter provides an orientation for thinking about why it is so important—and difficult—for organizations to develop an effective HRM system. Then Chapter 2 describes in more detail several elements of the external environment and the internal organizational environment, which shape how organizations manage their human resources. The topics covered include globalization, the changing labor market, competitive strategies, internal structures, and corporate cultures. Chapter 4 returns to a discussion of one particularly important aspect of the external environment: the laws and social views that employers must pay attention to in order to comply with relevant laws and to address employees' concerns about being treated fairly. As these chapters make clear, managing human resources effectively starts at the top of the organization with leaders who understand the importance of people and who are committed to addressing the needs of their employees.

Specific HR Activities

Having described the environment that shapes how companies manage their human resources, we then turn to descriptions of the specific HR policies and practices that organizations use to manage their workforces. An effective HRM system requires planning and coordination as well as continual evaluation and readjustment. Chapter 3 describes how strategic planning and HR planning together can be used to align HR practices with conditions in the global and organizational environments. HR planning also serves to align the various activities with each other. Chapter 5 describes how job analysis and competency modeling can be used to understand the work and the competencies employees need to maximize their performance in current jobs as well as their longer-term success.

To get work done, organizations need to attract people to apply for jobs and retain those who do their jobs well. Chapter 6 describes how employers recruit applicants to apply for job openings and some of the ways they can reduce unwanted turnover. After applicants have applied for a position, but before they are made a job offer, the process of selection occurs. As described in Chapter 7, employers want to select employees who will be able and willing to learn new tasks and continually adapt to changing conditions. They also want employees who fit well with the organizational culture.

With rapid changes in job requirements, existing employees must be willing and able to develop new competencies, become proficient in new jobs, and even change their occupations. Chapter 8 describes training and development practices that enable employees to develop themselves and remain employable despite rapid changes in the working world. To ensure that employees perform satisfactorily, performance must be measured and employees must receive usable feedback so that they can correct performance deficiencies. Chapter 9 describes principles for performance management, measurement, and feedback, setting the stage for a discussion of using rewards to further motivate employees.

Employees work in exchange for compensation, monetary or otherwise. Chapter 10 describes how organizations design the total compensation package, which typically includes base wages or salary, some form of incentive pay, and various types of benefits. Chapter 11 describes the use of incentives, bonuses, and other forms of rewards that employers offer to motivate employees to perform at their peak.

The best companies often become targets for recruitment by competitors. Offering innovative benefits packages and employee services that address a wide array of employees' concerns is one tactic for warding off such poaching, as described in Chapter 12. In addition to the benefits that employers offer voluntarily, Chapter 12 describes benefits required by law.

Chapter 13 focuses on what employers can do to ensure that the workplace is safe and that employees are healthy. Exposure to toxic chemicals and dangerous equipment remains a concern in some work environments, but more often air quality and ergonomic concerns top the agenda. Increasing concern about violence in the workplace is another unfortunate development described in Chapter 13.

Chapter 14 addresses the current state of unionization and collective bargaining. Because unions have maintained their strength in many other countries, they play a vital role in companies that strive to be globally competitive and profitable.

HR Professionals

The design and implementation of effective HRM systems require substantial expertise. Although line managers from all areas of an organization must also be involved in the process, professional HR knowledge is essential. Some readers may wish to pursue a career in human resource management, working either as an HR staff member in an organization or as an external consultant. For readers interested in becoming an HR professional, we provide supplemental materials on the Web site for this textbook, at academic.cengage.com/management/jackson. Included is a description of the competencies you will need, along with the professional and ethical standards that you will need to meet. These materials are based on information provided by the Society for Human Resource Management, which is the largest professional organization in the United States for HR professionals. On the Web site you will also find information about the salaries, bonuses, and incentives received by HR professionals who work in a variety of jobs.

FEATURES OF THIS EDITION

We have already referred to a few features that appear throughout this book, but others have yet to be mentioned. Following are descriptions of all the special features that we use to reinforce key ideas and bring the topic of managing human resources to life.

Company Examples

As an introduction to each chapter, we provide a brief company example that illustrates the strategic importance of the HR activity to be discussed in the chapter. This opening example and many other company examples are used throughout the chapter to illustrate basic principles and to show how companies use HR activities to gain a competitive advantage. Also in each chapter you will see many examples that illustrate how some of the best and most admired companies manage human resources to deal with the challenges in the special themes of today—Managing Teams, Managing the Multicultural Workforce, Managing Globalization, Managing Ethics, and Managing with Metrics. By the end of each chapter, you will come to know, in some detail, many companies and how they manage their human resources.

The company examples reinforce two important lessons. First, successful companies follow well established principles for managing human resources; second, they also are willing to experiment with new ideas to improve on what they know. Through these examples, we hope to convince readers that managing human resources effectively requires mastering what is known and then having the confidence to venture into the unknown.

The HR Triad

The HR Triad feature highlights the role that each member of the triad plays in designing and implementing effective HR policies and practices. It appears near the beginning of each chapter and provides a quick preview of the chapter's key topics. It also serves to reinforce the need for HR professionals, managers, and all other employees to work together to ensure the effectiveness of an organization's HRM system.

Margin Notes

Throughout the chapters, margin notes reinforce and extend key ideas. The Fast Facts offer tidbits of information that may be particularly interesting and useful. The quotations illustrate the perspectives of real managers, HR professionals, and other employees. We selected some quotes because the people who spoke them are well-known executives or public figures. Other quotes come from typical employees, who may not be well-known, but they know what organizational life is like and are willing to tell it like it is. You may not recognize all the names, but we think you'll agree that their insights are worth remembering.

Current Issues

Because the organizational environment is constantly changing, human resource management is constantly changing in response. Thus, important new issues frequently emerge that HR must address. A *new* feature of this tenth addition is a section at the end of each chapter titled Current Issues. Here we briefly comment on issues that are currently being discussed extensively by HR professionals, managers, and academics. By reading about these current issues, you will become familiar with some of the most pressing challenges that confront human resource professionals, managers, and employees.

Chapter Summary with Learning Goals

Each chapter begins with a list of learning goals to focus on as you read through the chapter material. We then use these learning goals to summarize the key ideas in the chapter. Of course, our summary is brief: Your own summary of what you have learned for each learning goal should be much longer and more detailed.

Terms to Remember

Throughout the chapters, key terms to remember are shown in bold and defined in italics. A complete list of all the key terms described in the chapter is provided at the end of the chapter. The Terms to Remember feature makes it easy for you to check whether you recall and understand the key vocabulary associated with the content of the chapter. If you see a term you aren't sure about, you may want to go back and review that section of the chapter or ask the instructor to clarify its meaning for you.

Questions for Discussion and Reflective Thinking

The discussion questions at the end of each chapter seek to determine your understanding of the material found in the chapter. Questions for Discussion and Reflective Thinking challenge you to think critically about the material and consider its implications for managing human resources. By the time you finish reading and studying all the chapters, you should know a great deal about basic principles for managing human resources, about what particular companies are doing today, and about what companies should be preparing to do as they face the future.

Projects to Extend Your Learning

To further enrich your understanding, each chapter includes supplemental projects:

- Integration and Application.
- Using the Internet.
- Experiential Activity.

Integration and Application. The Integration and Application project focuses your attention on the human resource management activities used by the two companies portrayed in the end-of-text integrative cases: Southwest Airlines and Lincoln Electric. By comparing and contrasting how these two companies manage their human resources, you will gain a deeper understanding of how the characteristics of an organization and the organization's external environment influence its approach to managing human resources.

Using the Internet. The project called Using the Internet directs you to explore several useful online resources. Use this feature to investigate companies, become familiar with relevant professional associations and the services they offer, find out about the products and services offered by HR consultants and vendors, and in many other ways enrich your understanding of managing human resources effectively.

Experiential Activity. The Experiential Activity at the end of each chapter asks you to extend your learning about the topics covered in the chapter. Some experiential activities require you to complete a short questionnaire that can be used to gauge your own knowledge and improve your understanding of your own attitudes about current issues. Some activities provide interview questions that you can use to learn more about the perspectives of managers and employees in various types of work settings. Some activities provide suggestions for discussions to hold with classmates as a means for learning from them. Other activities require you to develop a personal action plan. In all activities, the goal is to challenge you to grapple with the practical implications of the material presented in the chapter.

End-of-Chapter Cases

A case at the end of each chapter offers challenge and variety. It is up to you to analyze what is going on and suggest improvements. In some instances, discussion questions are presented to guide your thinking; in other instances, you are on your own to determine the issues most relevant to the material in the chapter. Many of the companies in these cases are disguised, but their problems and challenges are real and they are likely to be familiar to many experienced managers.

Endnotes

At the end of the book, you will find an extensive list of endnotes, which provide full citations to the materials used in preparing each chapter. For anyone wishing to dig deeper into the content of a chapter, the endnotes are an excellent starting point. Included are citations to the latest academic research as well as citations for coverage that has appeared in the public press and relevant Internet addresses (which, of course, are subject to be taken down at any time).

End-of-Text Integrative Cases

At the end of the textbook we present two relatively long cases that describe various human resource activities at Southwest Airlines and Lincoln Electric. By studying each case, you should gain an appreciation for how the many aspects of human resource management described throughout the text work together as a total system. By necessity, any particular chapter focuses on only one small piece of the total HR puzzle. In the real world, the pieces must fit together into a meaningful whole. The two integrative cases at the end of this book illustrate two very different total HRM systems found in two successful organizations. These cases provide detailed examples of how two firms are meeting the challenges of managing human resources through strategic partnership.

SUPPORT MATERIALS

We have designed a comprehensive set of support materials to guide instructors and students through the many issues involved in managing human resources effectively. Supplementary materials for *Managing Human Resources*, 10th edition, include the following components.

Instructor's Manual with Test Bank (ISBN: 0-324-57972-1)

The instructor's manual and test bank were prepared by Charlie Cook, University of West Alabama. The instructor's manual includes recapped learning objectives, chapter overviews, and lecture material that is enhanced with summaries of company vignettes and other special features, including end-of-chapter case notes. Answers to all review and discussion questions are included. Most chapters in the Instructor's Manual also include additional experiential and skill-building exercises. The test bank includes approximately 40 multiple-choice questions, 25 true/false questions, and 5 essay questions for each chapter.

Instructor's Resource CD-ROM (IRCD) (ISBN: 0-324-57973-X)

The instructor's resource CD-ROM includes the instructor's manual, test bank, PowerPoint presentations, and ExamView electronic test bank. ExamView is a computerized version of the printed test bank that you find in combination with the Instructor's Manual in the print guide, that allows instructors to easily create customized tests for their students. The PowerPoint slides, also prepared by Charlie Cook, University of West Alabama, greatly enhance classroom lectures. The slides are designed to hold students' interest and prompt questions that will help them learn.

DVD Package (ISBN: 0-324-57969-1)

A brand-new DVD features companies with innovative HR practices, many of which are Optimas Award winners, recognized for their excellence in HR practices. All video content is closely tied to contemporary HR management issues and concepts in the text. Featured companies include Xerox, BuyCostumes .com, Texas Instruments, and Allstate Insurance.

Textbook Web Site

The URL for the textbook Web site is academic.cengage.com/management/ jackson. When you adopt *Managing Human Resources*, 10th edition, you and your students will have access to a rich array of teaching and learning resources that you won't find anywhere else. This outstanding site features

Appendices A and B, chapter-by-chapter online tutorial quizzes, chapter-by-chapter Web links, flashcards, and more!

ACKNOWLEDGMENTS

As with the previous editions, many fine individuals were critical to the completion of the final product. They include Tojo Eapan at Nokia; Paul Buller at Gonzaga University; Ibraiz Tarique at Pace University; Jane Barnes at Meredith College; Aparna Joshi at University of Illinois; Mila Lazarova at Simon Fraser University; Yunhyung Chung at University of Idaho; Paul Adler at University of Southern California; Hugh Scullion at the National University of Ireland in Galway, Ireland; Paul Sparrow at Lancaster Business School in England; Shimon Dolan at ESADE; Stuart Youngblood at Texas Christian University; Gary Florkowski at the University of Pittsburgh; Pawan Budhwar at Aston Business School; Lynn Shore at San Diego State University; Gerold Frick at Fachhochschule Aalen; Lynda Gratton and Nigel Nicholson at London Business School; Chris Brewster at Henley Management College; Shaun Tyson and Emma Perry at Cranfield Management School; Michael Poole at Cardiff Business School; Paul Stonham at European School of Management; Jan Krulis-Randa and Bruno Staffelbach at University of Zürich; Albert Stähli, Julia Schirbach and Beat Herren at GSBA Zürich; Dennis Briscoe at University of San Diego; Mark Mendenhall at University of Tennessee; Helen De Cieri at Monash University; Yoram Zeira at Tel Aviv University; Moshe Banai at Baruch College; Christian Scholz at University of Saarlandes; Reijo Luostarinen at Helsinki School of Economics and Business Administration; Mickey Kavanagh at SUNY-Albany; Peter Dowling at Victoria University of Wellington; David Epstein, Hyun-Gyu Kim and Teri Elkins at University of Houston; and Dean David Finegold, Barbara Lee, Charles Fay, Mark Huselid, Paula Caliguiri, Steve Director, Hui Liao, and Ashe Husein at Rutgers University.

In their roles as reviewers and evaluators, the following individuals provided many valuable ideas and suggestions for changes and alterations, all of which we very much appreciated: Timothy Barnett, Mississippi State University; Richard Churchman, Belmont University; Dorothy J. Smith, Golden Gate University; Joe Martelli, The University of Findlay; Tracy K. Miller, University of Dayton; Meredith Rentz Cook, North Central Texas College; Dorris Ferrer Roach, Northeastern University School of Continuing and Professional Education; TerryLynn Smith, New York University; and Dr. Jeffrey L. Walls, Indiana Institute of Technology.

Several human resource managers and practicing line managers also contributed in many important ways to this tenth edition, particularly with examples and insights from their work experiences. They include Ed Schuler (my brother), Johan Julin, Mark Saxer, Libby Child, Manfred Stania, Tom Kroeger, Georges Bächthold, Ann Howard, Don Bohl, Bob Kenny, Jack Berry, Paul Beddia, John Fulkerson, Cal Reynolds, Jon Wendenhof, Deb Cohen, Nick Blauweikel, Mike Loomans, Sandy Daemmrich, Jeffery Maynard, Lyle Steele, Rowland Stichweh, Bill Maki, Rick Sabo, Bruce Cable, Gil Fry, Bill Reffett, Richard Hagan, Jeff Lamb, Joe Harris, and Horace Parker.

The following individuals graciously provided case and exercise materials: Donald Brush, Stuart Youngblood, Michael Mitchell, Marcia Miceli, Stella Nkomo, Arthur Sharplin, and Kay Stratton, and Richie Freedman.

Also, several people at Cengage Learning deserve our special thanks for their help and support: Joe Sabatino, executive editor; Elizabeth Lowry, developmental editor; Kelly Hoard, content project manager; Kimberly Kanakes, executive marketing manager; Tippy McIntosh, senior art director; and Kristen Meere, technology project manager. Without their professional dedication and competence, this book would not have been possible. We thank them all for making the completion of this tenth edition both possible and enjoyable. We also thank Charu Khanna, the project manager, and her team for their careful work in producing an attractive and highly readable textbook. Their responsiveness and professionalism are much appreciated.

We also thank Charlie Cook at University of West Alabama, who prepared the instructor's manual, test bank, PowerPoint slides, and Web site material. His dedication to student learning has been essential to the development of an excellent package of support materials.

Finally, we thank the many students who have used prior editions of this book. Their reactions to the book and related course materials, their unique insights into how employers treat employees, and their suggestions for improvements to prior editions of this book have helped us develop our approach to teaching and to writing *Managing Human Resources,* 10th edition.

Susan E. Jackson, Rutgers University and GSBA Zürich
Randall S. Schuler, Rutgers University and GSBA Zürich
Steve Werner, University of Houston

Managing Human Resources

Learning Goals

After reading this chapter, you should be able to:

1 Describe the strategic importance of managing human resources.

2 Explain how to gain and sustain a competitive advantage through human resources.

3 Use a framework for managing human resources.

4 Describe the HR Triad.

5 Describe five special themes in managing human resources.

6 Discuss two current issues in managing human resources.

MANAGING HUMAN RESOURCES AT CISCO SYSTEMS

Cisco Systems was founded in 1984 by Leonard Bosack and Sandy K. Lerner, a husband and wife team who invented a technology to link separate computer systems at Stanford University. With venture funding from Don Valentine at Sequoia Capital and a new chief executive officer (CEO) in John Morridge, Cisco went public in 1990. By 2001, the company was ranked third on *Fortune*'s list of the "100 Best Companies to Work for in America." It had more than 30,000 employees.

Then the market for its products collapsed. The value of its stock decreased almost 80%! The value of the stock options held by many of the employees had been decimated. Cisco laid off 6,000 employees in 2001, yet voluntary turnover was only 8% in an industry that averages 30%. Despite a weak economy, slow sales, and virtually no hiring in 2003, its turnover rate declined to 2% and more than 50,000 applicants applied for jobs. Then in 2006, Cisco saw record sales and its stock increased 60%. And while new job growth was only 3%, the company received 222,082 job applications. Apparently Cisco is doing something that employees like.

As part of its approach to managing human resources, Cisco espouses five core values: (1) a dedication to customer success; (2) innovation and learning; (3) openness; (4) teamwork; and (5) doing more with less. These values are continually articulated by the current chief executive officer (CEO) John Chambers and reinforced—in the mission statement, in human resource (HR) policies and practices, and in the company culture. Signaling the importance of customer satisfaction as a core value, Chambers personally reviews up to 15 critical accounts per day and often calls on customers himself. When it comes to openness and teamwork, employees applaud the company for giving them the straight scoop. Says account manager Kim Fisher, who passed up medical school to work for Cisco, "You have a say in where the company's going and the vision. Where else can you have an impact at 25?" The way jobs are structured and managed reinforces culture and values. At the company's sales offices, no one "owns" a workspace: It is all "hot desks" or "nonterritorial" office space. The HR group ensures that these and other HR policies and practices are aligned with the business strategy and continually reinforced.[1] ▲

> *It's all about people. Everybody can buy coffee beans and open stores. So when it comes to being successful, it's all about how you manage your people.*
>
> Howard Schultz
> *Chair and Chief Global Strategist*
> *Starbucks*

THE STRATEGIC IMPORTANCE OF MANAGING HUMAN RESOURCES

Leaders such as John Chambers of Cisco Systems and Howard Schultz of Starbucks™ see human resources as assets that need to be managed conscientiously and in tune with their organizations' needs. Today's most competitive organizations are working to ensure that—now and a decade from now—they have employees available who are eager and able to address key competitive challenges. Increasingly this means attracting and retaining superior talent and stimulating employees to perform at peak levels. When brainpower drives the business, as it does at Cisco Systems, attracting and keeping great intellectual talent become a necessity. When customer service is important to the business, as it is with Starbucks, a key challenge is attracting and keeping employees who deliver ever better service day in and day out even to the most difficult customers. Thus, while many factors influence the success of a company, it is very difficult to succeed without managing human resources effectively.

Satisfying Multiple Stakeholders

Today, companies and society are saying that the success of an organization is determined by the evaluations of its stakeholders. An organization's approach to managing human resources is central to its ability to satisfy its many stakeholders.

Stakeholders are *individuals or groups with interests, rights, or ownership in an organization and its activities.* Stakeholders who have similar interests and rights are said to belong to the same stakeholder group.[2] Customers, owners, organizational members, society and other organizations are examples of stakeholders, as illustrated in Exhibit 1.1.

Stakeholders benefit from the organization's successes and can be harmed by its failures and mistakes. Conversely, the organization has an interest in maintaining the general well-being and effectiveness of key stakeholders. If some of the stakeholder groups break off their relationships with the organization, the organization may suffer.

> *I think corporate social responsibility has taken a much more important role than it used to.*
>
> Daniel Vasella
> *Chief Executive Officer*
> *Novartis*

For any particular organization, some stakeholder groups may be more important than others. The most important groups—the primary stakeholders—are those whose concerns the organization must address to ensure its own survival. Success means effectively serving the interests of the primary stakeholders, whose needs define the firm's fundamental objectives. These objectives, in turn, drive the organization's approach to managing employees.

The principle that effective management requires attending to all relevant stakeholders is as true for managing human resources as for other managerial tasks. Thus, organizations that manage their human resources effectively ensure that their policies and practices support the goals of providing good products and services to customers, creating financial returns on the investments of owners and shareholders, contributing to society, and meeting the needs of employees. To develop a stakeholder-friendly approach to managing human resources, management must understand the concerns of each stakeholder group.

Owners and Investors

Most owners and investors invest their money in companies for financial reasons. At a minimum, owners want to preserve their capital for later use, and ideally they want to see growth in their capital. To achieve these goals, they should invest their capital primarily in profitable companies.

EXHIBIT 1.1 Stakeholders and Examples of Their Concerns

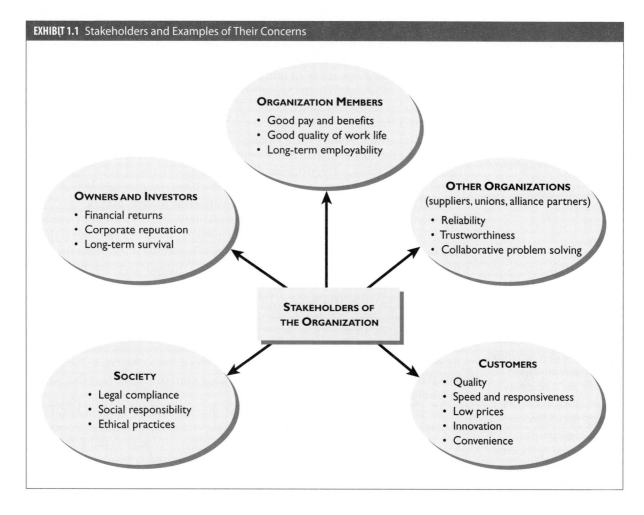

ORGANIZATION MEMBERS
- Good pay and benefits
- Good quality of work life
- Long-term employability

OWNERS AND INVESTORS
- Financial returns
- Corporate reputation
- Long-term survival

OTHER ORGANIZATIONS
(suppliers, unions, alliance partners)
- Reliability
- Trustworthiness
- Collaborative problem solving

STAKEHOLDERS OF THE ORGANIZATION

SOCIETY
- Legal compliance
- Social responsibility
- Ethical practices

CUSTOMERS
- Quality
- Speed and responsiveness
- Low prices
- Innovation
- Convenience

The job of institutional investors, which is to make money by choosing companies to investment in, has become increasingly complex as difficult-to-measure assets have become more important. To determine a firm's value in the old economy, investors focused on measuring tangible assets. **Tangible assets** *are relatively easy to measure and include such assets as inventory, equipment, real estate, and financial assets.* In the new economy, investors also recognize that many intangible assets can be just as valuable as tangible assets. **Intangible human assets** *are comparatively social in nature and include such organizational characteristics as an employer-of-choice reputation, the depth of employee talent and loyalty, and the ability to innovate and change.*

Intangible assets affect an organization's bottom line through complex chains of causes and effects. For example, suppose a chemical manufacturing firm treats its employees well and so develops a talented and loyal workforce. As a result, absenteeism and turnover are low, and so overall labor costs are also low, which means greater productivity. Through this complex chain of causes and effects, the firm's talented and loyal workforce contributes to the firm's bottom-line financial performance.[3] In this case, the cause-and-effect chain begins with an approach to managing human resources that attracts talented employees and ensures that they feel well treated. The value of the firm's approach to managing human resources eventually shows in the company's bottom line.

> " *The notion that the corporation should apply its assets for social purposes rather than for the profit of its owners—the shareholders—is an irresponsible use of assets.* "
>
> *Betsy S. Atkins*
> *Chief Executive Officer*
> *Baja Ventures, a Venture Capital Firm*

Some organizations, such as consulting firms and advertising agencies, have nothing except intangible human assets to offer. Investing in such companies often means hoping that the best employees will continue working at and for the company.[4] As one study of initial public offerings showed, companies that attend to human resource management issues are rewarded with more favorable initial investor reactions as well as longer-term survival.[5] Accountants may have difficulty attaching monetary values to a firm's human resources, but this doesn't stop investors from paying attention.

Because intangible human assets—such as how employees feel and behave—can influence financial performance, business analysts pay attention to how people are managed. For 20 years, the staff at *Fortune* magazine has conducted extensive interviews with employees to create their annual lists of "100 Best Companies to Work For."[6] To determine just how important happy workers were for achieving heightened shareholder returns, *Fortune*'s research staff led one of the earliest efforts to look at this issue. They studied the publicly traded firms on their 1987 list of "100 Best Companies." Shareholder returns for these 100 companies were compared to those of the Russell 3000®, an index that includes comparable companies. The bottom line: If you had invested $1,000 in the Russell 3000, you would have had $3,976 10 years later; but if you had invested $1,000 in the "100 Best Companies to Work for in America," you would have had $8,188 10 years later. You could earn more than twice as much by investing in the "100 Best Companies to Work for in America."[7] Research like this shows that organizations can manage employees in ways that satisfy investors as well as employees.

Several other studies have shown that the approaches companies take to managing their human resources can increase profitability, annual sales per employee (productivity), market value, and earnings-per-share growth.[8] Exhibit 1.2 illustrates the results from a study of several hundred companies. A survey was used to measure the companies' human resource (HR) practices. These responses were then used to create a score of 0 to 100, representing the extent to which the company's HR practices represented state-of-the-art knowledge. Then the performance of these companies was measured using financial accounting data. As the graph shows, companies with better HR practices experienced greater increases in market value per employee. Firms with the best human resource management systems were rewarded the most by investors.[9]

Customers

As in Cisco Systems, Amazon.com, and many other firms, improving customer satisfaction is a primary means through which HR activities affect success. Creating new products, reducing costs, improving product quality, and improving service quality are all ways to improve customer satisfaction.[10] Whatever approach is used to satisfy customers, success depends on how employees are managed. Human resource executives understand this, and so do chief financial officers (CFOs). In fact, a survey of 200 CFOs revealed that 92% believed managing employees effectively can improve customer satisfaction.[11]

To meet customers' demands for high quality, companies such as Weyerhaeuser, Deere & Company, Google, Wegmans Food Market, Boeing, Lincoln Electric, Southwest Airlines, and FedEx maintain an environment conducive to full participation by their employees, as well as to their personal and organizational growth. When the internal climate of the organization is positive, with employees generally getting along well and not leaving the company at a rapid pace, customers report they're more satisfied and intend to return.[12]

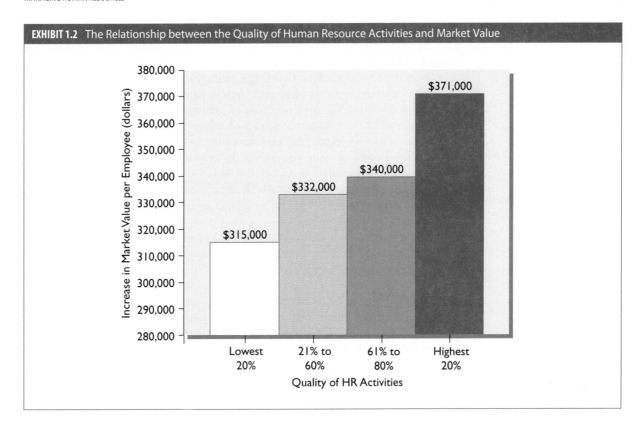

EXHIBIT 1.2 The Relationship between the Quality of Human Resource Activities and Market Value

Improving customer satisfaction often requires finding ways to improve the company's ability to understand the customer's perspective. For example, through its hiring practices, a company can make sure that its employees are demographically similar to customers. The assumption is that communication improves when employees and customers share similar experiences. Such reasoning led American Express to recruit gay and lesbian financial advisers to improve service for gay and lesbian customers. They also sought to improve customer satisfaction among this group by educating financial advisers about the special financial needs of the gay and lesbian market.[13]

For Saks Fifth Avenue, the luxury retailer, giving customers excellent service means keeping sales employees engaged in their work. Saks conducted an employee survey to measure the importance of employee engagement and found that stores with greater employee engagement also had more satisfied customers. Vice president Jay Redman was convinced by the results of the study, "There absolutely is a correlation between employee engagement and customer engagement. We've seen 20 to 25% improvement in stores with great engagement." To engage employees, managers at Saks Fifth Avenue make a point of asking employees what they need to do their jobs, then following up with initiatives to address employees' concerns. "We've probably done 100 things over three years," explained Redman. As employee engagement went up, Saks saw increases in customer loyalty and sales.[14]

> " *Historically, corporations thought keeping an eye on the environment also meant taking an eye off shareholders. That has changed dramatically in the past few years. Now there are reminders everywhere that a growing number of companies see the interests of investors and those of the environment as closely aligned.* "
>
> *Todd S. Thomson*
> *Chief Executive Officer*
> *Citigroup Global Wealth Management*

Society

For organizations such as public schools, nonprofit foundations, and government agencies, the concerns of owners—that is, taxpayers and contributors—are essentially those of society at large. But for both privately owned and publicly traded companies, the concerns of owners—that is, investors—may be quite different from those of society in general.

Under free market capitalism, the primary managerial obligation is to maximize shareholders' profits and their long-term interests. Nobel Prize–winning economist Milton Friedman is probably the best-known advocate of this approach.[15] Friedman argued that using resources in ways that do not clearly maximize investor interests amounts to spending the owners' money without their consent—the equivalent to stealing. According to Friedman, a manager can judge whether a decision is right or wrong by considering its consequences for the company's economic needs and financial well-being. If it improves the bottom line, it's right; if it detracts from the bottom line, it's wrong. For example, a company might be justified in hiring long-term welfare recipients if an analysis showed that hiring them paid off financially in terms of government tax incentives and wage subsidies. But the firm could not justify the hiring simply on the basis that it's the right thing to do for society.

Unlike Friedman, the average American does not believe that making money is the only role of business or the only responsibility of managers. In fact, socially responsible corporations are attractive alternatives to prospective employees—simply being profitable is not enough to attract the best talent. To meet the concerns of employees and of society in general, the best employers obey the law and go beyond what is minimally required; they seek to have a positive impact on society. Increasingly, the best companies are striving to serve society and shareholders at the same time.[16]

Legal Compliance. Codes of conduct for some aspects of business behavior take the form of formal laws, and many such laws have implications for managing human resources. In addition, businesses are subject to regulation through several federal agencies, as well as through various state and city equal employment commissions and civil rights commissions. Finally, **multinational corporations (MNCs)**, *which are firms with operations in multiple countries,* must be aware of the employment laws in other countries.

By complying with legal regulations, firms establish their legitimacy and gain acceptance and support from the community. Ultimately, they increase their chances for long-term survival.[17] Because they affect virtually all human resource management activities, many different laws, regulations, and court decisions are described throughout this book, beginning with an overview in Chapter 4.

FAST FACT

When Cisco laid off 6,000 employees, it offered a unique severance package. Pink-slipped employees who agreed to work for one year at a local nonprofit organization were paid one-third of their salary plus benefits and stock options, and they had the right to be first in line for rehiring in the future.

Community Relations. Formal laws and regulations establish relatively clear guidelines for how society expects a company to behave, but effective companies respond to more than these formal statements. They understand that the enactment of formal laws and regulations often lags behind public opinion by several years.

Long before legislation is agreed to, communities communicate their expectations and attempt to hold organizations accountable for violations of those expectations. Proactive organizations stay attuned to public opinion and use it as a source of information that shapes their own management practices. With heightened public interest in corporate social responsibility, many companies are discovering that they can't avoid having people evaluate how well they perform in this respect.[18]

A commitment to community involvement and development can have major implications for managing human resources. Voluntary labor is often a community's biggest need, and organizations that encourage employees to participate as volunteers help communities meet this need. UPS has sponsored its Community Internship Program for nearly 40 years. As part of this four-week program, managers live in poor neighborhoods while working in soup kitchens and women's shelters. Being socially responsive in these and other ways has many implications for managing human resources, including

- The type of employees the company chooses to hire.
- The criteria used to evaluate their performance.
- The scheduling and coordinating of activities within work units.
- Compensation practices associated with paying employees for time spent in the community.

Other Organizations

Companies of all types are becoming increasingly interdependent with other organizations. Other entities that can be considered major stakeholders include suppliers, unions, and alliance partners.

Suppliers. Suppliers provide the resources a company needs to conduct its business. In addition to the capital of owners and investors, the resources needed by most companies include material and equipment, information, and people. Other companies usually supply material and equipment. Suppliers of people might include schools, the professional associations that serve specific occupational groups, state employment agencies, and companies that offer electronic recruiting services.

Unions. Unions may also serve as suppliers of people, but they also play a much greater role. When employees are represented by a union, the employer involves the union in joint discussions on issues such as improving productivity; outsourcing policies; and improving safety, compensation, benefits, and various other conditions of work. In recent years, leaders of unions, such as Andrew ("Andy") Stern of the Service Employees International Union (SEIU), and union members have moved away from their traditional adversarial relationship with management to a collaborative, problem-solving relationship. Despite this general trend, work slowdowns and strikes remain threats to companies in which unions represent the employees. Such work disruptions often reach far beyond the firm itself. When strikes involve transportation or communications workers, the entire country feels their effects.

> **We need to help companies be more competitive.**
>
> *Andrew Stern*
> *President*
> *Service Employees International Union*

Alliance Partners. Through cooperative alliances with other firms, a company seeks to achieve goals that are common to all members of the alliance. Some alliances are formed to influence government actions. Research and development needs are another common reason for alliance formations. International Sematech, for example, is a multilateral alliance that supports learning through collaborative research. Through joint participation, 15 semiconductor manufacturers from 7 countries share knowledge and expertise in ways that ultimately influence the entire industry.

Joint ventures between two or more companies represent yet another basis for forming alliances. When a bottle maker learned how to recycle plastic, it recognized the commercial opportunities of the technology. Subsequent discussions with suppliers, customers, and competitors about a collaborative venture eventually helped all the partners realize that recycling would require a substantial investment in research and development. Out of such talks, a collaborative research network was born. Each company paid toward the research at a university and participated in quarterly board meetings. The research output became the venture's property, and all interested parties were assured licensing rights for a nominal fee.

Organizational Members (The Employees)

Organizational members make up another key stakeholder group. Unlike the other stakeholders discussed previously, organizational members reside within the organization. Included in this group are *all* of the employees who hold positions within the organization, including the CEO and top-level executives, other managers and supervisors, professionals and administrative specialists, line employees, part-time employees, and so on. Because they are such a diverse stakeholder group, they have a great variety of concerns. Nevertheless, most members of this stakeholder group share concerns about pay and benefits, quality of work life, and employability.

Pay and Benefits. Most organizational members want to be paid well and they want to be paid fairly. Nevertheless, many employees feel that their employers don't live up to this expectation. Also important are the desire for secure and affordable health insurance, paid sick leave, vacation time, and the ability to balance work and family.[19] To stay abreast of what employees care about most, progressive companies use surveys to monitor the concerns of organizational members. Human resource policies and practices can then be developed to address the most important concerns. At Starbucks, for example, all employees (called "partners") are eligible for full benefits.[20]

Quality of Work Life. Besides earning a good living, most employees also want to enjoy a good quality of life while on the job. Starbucks' Howard Schultz grew up knowing his father felt beaten down by his work. At Starbucks, Schultz strives to make sure that workers have self-esteem no matter what the nature of their jobs. Providing generous health insurance benefits for everyone—even part-timers—is part of that aim. Many aspects of human resource management contribute to a good quality of working life, including

- Training and development to improve employees' skills and knowledge.
- Job designs that allow employees to really use their knowledge and skills.
- Management practices that give employees responsibility for important decisions.
- Selection and promotion systems that ensure fair and equitable treatment.
- Safe and healthy physical and psychological environments.
- Work organized around teams.

Such practices increase employee commitment, satisfaction, and feelings of empowerment, which in turn increase customer satisfaction.[21] In general, corporate cultures characterized by heightened employee involvement and participation enhance returns on sales and investments in subsequent years.[22]

Employability. In recent years, the changing economy and its effects on the workplace have introduced tremendous uncertainty, creating feelings of insecurity and anxiety for employees and their families. When IBM restructured its organization in the early 1990s, it terminated more than 100,000 employees. The company had long been known for its policy of job security; so employees were shocked when IBM replaced some of its managers with temporary people hired to finish ongoing projects.

Today, downsizing and layoffs are an accepted part of life in most large companies. Employees are no longer surprised when they occur. Nevertheless, security remains a concern. To address employees' security concerns, companies like IBM now strive to develop a sense of *employment* security, not job security. Employment security increases when employees develop skills and knowledge that they need to be employable should they lose their current job. Feelings of employment security also improve when employers provide outplacement assistance as part of the severance package offered to laid-off workers.

Creating Win-Win Situations

Clearly, the primary concerns of the stakeholder groups differ, and conflict among stakeholders is common. But shared interests aren't unusual either. Effective managers determine the interests of their multiple stakeholders and work with them to find a solution that addresses each set of objectives.

More and more managers are beginning to understand that a company's human resource practices can either exacerbate apparent conflicts among their multiple stakeholders or create synergies. Consider what happens during restructuring and downsizing. Decisions to reduce layers of management, sell off a poorly performing division, or outsource work to an overseas location usually are made to improve efficiency and profitability in order to satisfy shareholders. The employees who lose their jobs in the process are victims of the conflict between their need for employment and the shareholders' desire for financial gain. However, when the compensation system is used to ensure that employees are owners themselves, managers and other employees may put more effort into finding a solution that minimizes employee displacements while meeting the organization's financial goals.

In the chapters that follow, we argue that approaches to managing human resources can provide organizations with effective solutions to the challenge of how best to satisfy the objectives of its multiple stakeholders, even when the objectives of different stakeholders seem to conflict. In more cases than not, appropriate HR practices make it possible to create win-win situations.

Creating a human resource management system that satisfies a company's multiple stakeholders is very challenging, to say the least. It takes a great deal of knowledge and the involvement of many employees. This situation is both positive and negative. It is negative because it takes so much time and understanding. It is positive because the few companies that succeed will gain a competitive advantage.

GAINING AND SUSTAINING A COMPETITIVE ADVANTAGE

Some firms use their approach to managing human resources to gain a sustainable competitive advantage. A company has a competitive advantage when all or some of its customers prefer its products and/or services. *If a company's advantage is difficult for competitors to understand and copy, the company has a* **sustainable competitive advantage.**[23]

Firms attempt to gain a sustainable competitive advantage in many ways: Southwest Airlines coordinates all of its operations to ensure that customers get excellent service at the lowest possible price. Oracle constantly innovates to provide new information technologies. Starbucks negotiates special supplier arrangements to ensure that they receive the best coffee beans. Management practices such as these can all help a firm gain a competitive advantage. But no strategy can create a sustainable advantage unless the company also has the human resources it needs to successfully implement the strategy.

Employees Who Are a Source of Added Value

Employees add value by using their skills and knowledge to transform the organization's other resources (e.g., raw materials, component parts, equipment, real estate, information, etc.) to produce and deliver products and services that generate profits or other valued forms of return.

Employees who are most closely associated with the activities that generate valued returns usually have the most opportunity to add value. Sometimes referred to as "core" employees, they are closest to the essential work of the organization. In software development firms, for example, programmers are core employees. In pharmaceutical firms, scientists and researchers are core employees. In orchestras, musicians are core employees. In health care institutions, doctors and nurses are core employees.

Core employees can add value to an organization in a variety of ways: through research and new product development, production, problem diagnosis, service delivery, and in other ways. In most organizations, many other employees working in staff and managerial jobs support the work of the core employees. They can improve the organization's efficiency by keeping costs low, analyzing the environment to identify new market opportunities, carrying out necessary administrative tasks, and facilitating coordination among core employees.

Regardless of the specific work being done, the objective of effective human resource management is to maximize the value added by all employees. To achieve this objective, the organization must be staffed with the right employees doing the right things, at the right time and place, and under the right conditions.

Employees Who Are Rare

To sustain a competitive advantage, a firm's human resources must be rare. If competitors have employees with the same talents, then the firm's talent provides no advantage over competitors. By being an employer of choice, organizations can gain access to the best available talent. Books, articles, and Web sites that purport to identify the "best" places to work are especially popular among students graduating from college, who view firms high in the rankings as desirable places to land their first postgraduation jobs. In other words, "the best get the best," as Google, J. M. Smucker, and Southwest Airlines have learned. Dissatisfied workers who are looking for better employment situations read these lists too. Over time, a reputation for attracting, developing, and keeping good talent acts like a magnet, drawing the best talent to the firm and keeping it.

When Lincoln Electric Company in Cleveland, Ohio, announced it was planning to hire 200 production workers, it received more than 20,000 responses. When BMW Incorporated announced that it had selected Spartanburg, South Carolina, as the site for its first U.S. production facility, it received more than 25,000 unsolicited requests for employment. Numbers this large make it more feasible for Lincoln Electric and BMW to hire applicants who are two to three times more productive than their counterparts in other manufacturing firms.

A Culture That Can't Be Copied

Getting the best people into the firm is just a first step. Keeping the best people happy and productive is equally important. Proper business practices and an effective approach to managing human resources can create a strong company culture that keeps employees happy and productive and is also difficult for other companies to copy. Business practices that are easy for competitors to copy are not sources of sustained competitive advantage. Similarly, a company culture that's easily copied provides little advantage. Southwest Airlines and FedEx are two companies with strong company cultures that contribute to business success and that are difficult for competitors to copy because they have developed over a long period of time and are unique to each company's overall approach to doing business.

Southwest Airlines. The customer-oriented culture of Southwest Airlines is unique in the airline industry, which is known for disruptive strikes and low customer satisfaction. Besides hiring the best people, Southwest Airlines maintains a company culture that keeps employees happy and motivates them to achieve peak performance. Employees at Southwest Airlines understand the company's strategy and do everything possible to achieve outstanding company success. When a gate supervisor was asked what makes Southwest different from other airlines, she said, "We're empowered to make on-the-spot decisions. For example, if a customer misses a flight, it's no sweat. We have the latitude to take care of the problem. There's no need for approvals."

A profit-sharing program is one aspect of Southwest Airlines' approach to managing human resources that keeps employees focused on the company's performance. An incident in Los Angeles illustrates the point: An agent from another airline asked to borrow a stapler. The Southwest agent went over with the stapler, waited for it to be used, and brought it back. The other agent asked, "Do you always follow staplers around?" The Southwest agent replied, "I want to make sure we get it back. It affects our profit sharing." Setting goals and targets for the performance of the company as a whole and never setting separate departmental goals is another approach to managing people to ensure that employees all pull together. At Southwest, the philosophy is that everyone should share common goals and that setting up different goals for different areas would be likely to create schisms within the company.[24]

FedEx. Since day one, its basic philosophy of doing business, as stated by Chair, CEO, and President Frederick W. Smith, has been "People, Service, and Profit." Its motto is "100% Customer Satisfaction." In a business that relies on individuals delivering packages overnight to customers anywhere, 100% customer satisfaction comes only from managing human resources as if they really matter. The FedEx philosophy of managing people is represented in the following policies:

- Achieve no layoffs.
- Guarantee fair treatment.
- Use surveys to obtain feedback and guide action.
- Promote from within.
- Share profits.
- Maintain an open-door policy.

Like Southwest Airlines, FedEx has developed a complex and integrated system of human resource policies and practices designed to keep employees focused on the needs of customers and the business. Its system was not copied intact from another company, nor did the firm develop it by applying a formula that could guarantee a correct solution. Rather, through a systematic process of analysis over many years, FedEx developed its own unique human resource management system. As a consequence, its company culture is difficult for outsiders to fully understand and impossible to copy.

LEARNING GOAL

" *With its critical role in hiring, appraising, and developing people, HR is so central to success that it's practically criminal if the department doesn't report directly to the CEO.* "

Jack and Suzy Welch
Authors and Consultants

A FRAMEWORK FOR MANAGING HUMAN RESOURCES

When you hear the words *human resources*, what do you think they mean? For many they are just another phrase to describe employees. But in this book, the term has a specific definition. **Human resources** *are all of the people who currently contribute to doing the work of the organization, as well as those people who potentially could contribute in the future, and those who have contributed in the recent past.*

The best organizations understand that managing human resources effectively involves more than focusing only on current employees; it requires a long-term perspective that is responsive to the concerns of current employees, potential future employees, and recent employees who no longer work for the organization. Together, past employees, current employees, and potential future employees are responsible for the creation and realization of the organization's vision, mission, goals, and objectives.

Exhibit 1.3 illustrates our overall framework for managing human resources effectively. At the center of the framework are activities for managing human resources—recruitment, selection, compensation, performance measurement, training, and so on. Human resource management activities are important because they partly determine how well a company satisfies the concerns of its multiple stakeholders, as described earlier. These activities do not occur in a vacuum, however. They are shaped by various forces in the external environment and by several organizational factors.

The Importance of the External and Organizational Environments

If you have worked for more than one employer, you know from experience that there are many approaches to managing human resources. Some employers are highly selective in whom they hire, and others seem to hire anyone who walks in the door. Some provide extensive training, and others let new hires sink or swim. Some pay well and offer large bonuses; others don't. Many of these differences in how organizations manage people are due to differences in the environments of the organizations.

The External Environment. The external environment affects all organizations, but its effects are not the same for all organizations. Small businesses do not have to comply with the same employment laws that apply to large organizations. Labor market conditions for businesses in high-tech industries can be very different from those in the retail industry. Global businesses face a stronger imperative to respond to differences in country cultures than do most domestic businesses.

Chapter 2 describes in detail several aspects of the external environment that can influence an organization's approach to managing human resources.[25]

EXHIBIT 1.3 A Framework for Managing Human Resources

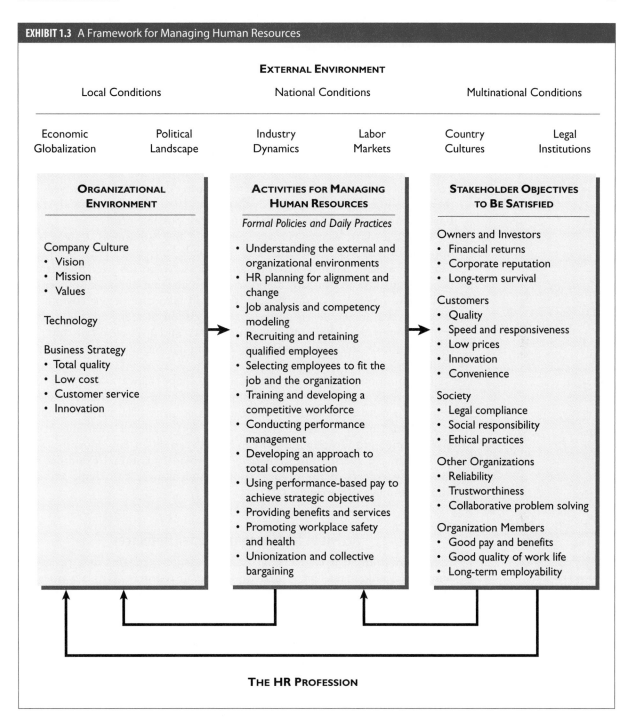

EXTERNAL ENVIRONMENT

Local Conditions   National Conditions   Multinational Conditions

Economic   Political   Industry   Labor   Country   Legal
Globalization   Landscape   Dynamics   Markets   Cultures   Institutions

ORGANIZATIONAL ENVIRONMENT

Company Culture
• Vision
• Mission
• Values

Technology

Business Strategy
• Total quality
• Low cost
• Customer service
• Innovation

ACTIVITIES FOR MANAGING HUMAN RESOURCES

Formal Policies and Daily Practices

• Understanding the external and organizational environments
• HR planning for alignment and change
• Job analysis and competency modeling
• Recruiting and retaining qualified employees
• Selecting employees to fit the job and the organization
• Training and developing a competitive workforce
• Conducting performance management
• Developing an approach to total compensation
• Using performance-based pay to achieve strategic objectives
• Providing benefits and services
• Promoting workplace safety and health
• Unionization and collective bargaining

STAKEHOLDER OBJECTIVES TO BE SATISFIED

Owners and Investors
• Financial returns
• Corporate reputation
• Long-term survival

Customers
• Quality
• Speed and responsiveness
• Low prices
• Innovation
• Convenience

Society
• Legal compliance
• Social responsibility
• Ethical practices

Other Organizations
• Reliability
• Trustworthiness
• Collaborative problem solving

Organization Members
• Good pay and benefits
• Good quality of work life
• Long-term employability

THE HR PROFESSION

In addition to the globalization of business, it reviews the important role of economic conditions, the political landscape, industry dynamics, labor markets, and cultural differences among countries.

U.S. employment laws and regulations and employees' evolving attitudes about what constitutes fairness are also important aspects of the external environment. Chapter 4 describes legal definitions of fairness, such as those provided by equal opportunity laws and various other regulations; it provides a foundation for other discussions of fairness and legal considerations that appear in subsequent chapters.

The Organizational Environment. Organizational characteristics often explain why companies in the same industry treat employees so differently. Consider the policies and practices for managing people used by two retail chains: Wal-Mart and Wegmans Food Markets.

Wal-Mart's leaders say that people matter, but their approach to managing human resources doesn't always show it. Hourly wages are low, the health benefits are minimal, the annual employee turnover rates are in the range of 50% (which is near the average for the industry), and many employees feel they have little opportunity for advancement. These practices fit Wal-Mart's business strategy of offering goods at the lowest possible price.[26]

Like Wal-Mart, Wegmans is very profitable. But its business strategy is the opposite of Wal-Mart's. Wegmans is an upscale store that offers top-quality foods for which customers pay premium prices. Wegmans' vice president of people sums up the company's approach to managing human resources like this: "If we take care of our people, they will take care of our customers." Wegmans sets its pay levels above the competition. It seeks out the highest-caliber employees (hiring only 8% of applicants) and gives most full- and part-time employees free health coverage. The annual turnover among full-time employees is 7%.[27]

Organizational characteristics that tend to shape the way a company manages its people include the leadership approach of top-level managers and the company's culture, technology, and business strategy. Chapter 2 provides a general description of these elements of an organizational environment and gives examples to illustrate how organizations can differ. Subsequently, when we explain the specific HR activities, we provide additional examples that show how aspects of the organizational environment can shape the way human resources are managed.

Activities for Managing Human Resources

Every organization, from the smallest to the largest, engages in a variety of human resource management activities. **Human resource (HR) activities** *include the formal HR policies developed by the company as well as the actual ways these policies are implemented in the daily practices of supervisors and managers.*

In some organizations, the formal HR policies and daily practices are closely aligned. In many organizations, however, the formal policies are regarded as statements of expectations and aspirations, but they are not implemented in actual daily practices. Consequently, the actual practices that evolve are not aligned with the formal policies. The more that policies and practices are aligned and the more systematic companies are in creating HR activities to fit the organization and its environment, the more effective the organization is likely to be.[28]

The many human resource policies and practices that companies need to understand and create include

- HR planning for alignment and change.
- Job analysis and competency modeling.
- Recruiting and retaining qualified employees.

- Selecting employees to fit the job and the organization.
- Training and developing a competitive workforce.
- Conducting performance management.
- Developing an approach to total compensation.
- Using performance-based pay to achieve strategic objectives.
- Providing benefits and services.
- Promoting workplace safety and health.
- Unionization and collective bargaining.

When an organization systematically understands, creates, coordinates, aligns, and integrates all of their policies and practices, it creates a **human resource management (HRM) system.**

HR Planning for Alignment and Change. An effective HRM system requires planning and coordination as well as continual evaluation and readjustment. Chapter 3 describes how strategic planning and HR planning together can be used to align and realign HR practices with conditions in the external and organizational environments.

Human resource planning also serves to align the various HR activities with each other. For example, if a company decides to offer employees a relatively low rate of pay, it can anticipate that employees may not stay for a long time. If the turnover rate is high, then recruitment will always be ongoing. Also, if employees have short careers with the organization, the company may decide not to invest heavily in training. Throughout this book, we provide you with several examples that illustrate how organizations create alignment among the many specific activities that comprise a total HRM system.

Job Analysis and Competency Modeling. Most organizations divide the work to be done into jobs, which comprise a set of task and role responsibilities. Effective HRM systems are grounded in a clear understanding of the way work is allocated among jobs, the competencies needed by employees who work in those jobs, and a long-term view of how these are likely to change in the future. Chapter 5 describes how job analysis and competency modeling can be used to develop an understanding of jobs in the organization and the competencies that employees need to maximize their performance in those jobs.

Recruiting and Retaining Qualified Employees. To get jobs done, organizations need to attract talented people and retain those who perform well. When job openings occur, recruitment may involve looking outside the organization for new employees. Alternatively, employees may be recruited to move from their current jobs to new ones. Regardless of whether recruits come from outside or inside the organization, retaining the best employees is usually desirable. Chapter 6 describes how companies recruit applicants to apply for job openings and some of the ways they can reduce unwanted turnover. An understanding of why excellent employees voluntarily leave reveals the important role of HR practices in retaining the best talent.

Selecting Employees to Fit the Job and the Organization. After applicants have applied for a position but before they are made a job offer, the process of selection occurs. Selection involves sorting and ranking employees using a standard

> **❝** *We needed a planning process that would enable us to anticipate all the different workforce changes necessary for HP to deliver our business strategies. The only way to achieve an adaptive workforce is to have a strategic workforce plan that's integral to the business plan.* **❞**
>
> Gerard Brossard
> Vice President, Global
> Workforce Planning
> Hewlett-Packard

set of criteria. As described in Chapter 7, the criteria used to select employees flow from the results of job analysis and competency modeling. Increasingly, employers want to select employees who will be able and willing to learn new tasks and continually to adapt to changing conditions. They also want employees who fit well with the organizational culture.

Training and Developing a Competitive Workforce. To ensure that people know what they're supposed to do, employers often provide instruction and training. With rapid changes in job requirements, existing employees must be both willing and able to develop new competencies, become proficient in new jobs, and even change their occupations. Chapter 8 describes the socialization, training, and development practices that enable employees to develop themselves and remain employable despite rapid changes in the world of work.

Conducting Performance Management. To ensure that employees perform satisfactorily, employers may use a variety of practices aimed at performance management. Ensuring that employees receive appropriate recognition is one aspect of performance management. For this to occur, employees need fair and clearly stated performance standards. That means performance must be measured in some way. Employees also deserve usable feedback and the support needed to identify and correct performance deficiencies. When appropriate performance standards, measures, and feedback are provided, capable employees become a high-performance workforce. Chapter 9 describes these activities and sets the stage for a discussion about using rewards to motivate employees and achieve strategic objectives.

Developing an Approach to Total Compensation. Employees work in exchange for compensation, whether monetary or otherwise. A total compensation package typically includes base wages or salaries, some form of incentive pay, and various types of benefits. Chapter 10 describes how organizations design the total compensation package. It also details the process used to set the level of compensation to be offered for specific jobs.

Using Performance-Based Pay to Achieve Strategic Objectives. During the past decade, employers have been changing the design of total compensation. An overarching objective has been to increase the extent to which performance is a key driver of the pay that people receive. In the long run, creating a stronger linkage between performance and pay should improve motivation and productivity, which in turn helps to control labor costs. Chapter 11 describes the use of incentives, bonuses, and other forms of rewards that employers offer.

Providing Benefits and Services. As many organizations have discovered, the best companies often become targets for recruitment by competitors. Offering innovative benefits packages and employee services that address a wide array of employees' concerns is one tactic for warding off such poaching. As described in Chapter 12, such benefits that employees appreciate include those with obvious monetary value, such as health insurance, as well as others whose monetary value is more difficult to quantify, such as flexible work arrangements and telecommuting options. In addition to the benefits that employers offer voluntarily, Chapter 12 describes mandatory benefits required by law.

Promoting Workplace Safety and Health. Chapter 13 focuses on what employers can do to ensure that the workplace is safe and that employees are healthy. As

> ❝ *The industrial revolution was about economies of scale. The internet revolution will be about economies of skill and how you empower people.* ❞
>
> *John Chambers*
> *Chief Executive Officer*
> *Cisco Systems*

jobs in the United States have shifted out of manufacturing, and even manufacturing jobs have become less labor-intensive, issues of workplace safety and health also have changed. Exposure to toxic chemicals and dangerous equipment remains a concern in some work environments, but more often air quality and ergonomic concerns top the agenda. Increasing concern about violence in the workplace is another unfortunate development described in Chapter 13.

Unionization and Collective Bargaining. Chapter 14 addresses the current state of unionization and collective bargaining activity. Although union membership has been shrinking steadily in the United States for many years, firms such as GE, Southwest Airlines, Continental Airlines, AT&T, and the major U.S. auto companies all hold joint discussions with the unions on issues such as productivity gains, the quality of working life, and outsourcing. Because unions have maintained their strength in many other countries, they play a vital role in companies that strive to be globally competitive and profitable.

THE HR TRIAD

Used systematically and correctly, human resource management policies and practices can transform a lackluster company into a star performer. Used without a systematic and informed approach, they create havoc. In some companies, existing approaches to managing human resources reflect chance and happenstance. Instead of analyzing how their HRM systems affect all aspects of the business, some organizations continue to do things the same way year after year. Ask why salespeople in the shoe section are paid on commission and people in toys are not, and you are likely to be told, "That's just the way we've always done it." When companies do change the way they manage people, they may do so for the wrong reason. Why did that small retail food chain just send all its middle managers to off-site wilderness training? "Everybody in the industry's doing it—we can't be the only ones who don't." Why did your insurance company start randomly listening in on calls from customers? "The new telecommunications system we installed last year included it as a no-cost feature, so we decided we should use it."

Whether a company chooses its human resource policies and practices systematically or somewhat haphazardly, those policies and practices can have powerful effects. Ensuring that those effects are *positive* rather than destructive requires the involvement of three key players, who we refer to as the **HR Triad,** *which consists of:*

- *HR professionals.*
- *Line managers.*
- *All the other employees who are affected by HR policies and practices.*

No department can, by itself, effectively manage a company's human resources. That's why there's a saying at Merck that goes like this, "Human resources are too important to be left to the HR department." Companies like Cisco Systems, Lincoln Electric, and Southwest Airlines have developed approaches to managing people that reflect all three perspectives in the HR Triad. The special expertise of HR professionals is used by, and in cooperation with, the expertise of line managers, other administrative staff, and all first-line employees in every department. So regardless of whether line managers ever hold formal positions in human resource management, they are held accountable for the task of managing people.

Line Managers Have Always Been Responsible

In small businesses, owners must have HR expertise as they build the company from the ground up. Usually, the founder makes all of the hiring and pay decisions when the company is first getting started. In small companies, performance appraisals are likely to occur on the spot whenever there seems to be a performance problem. Formal policies may not exist at all. This reality is clearly reflected in the various popular magazines targeted to small business owners—for example, *Inc., Money, Success,* and *Entrepreneurship*. These publications devote a great deal of space to discussing issues related to managing people in a small company.

Eventually, as a company grows, the owner may contract out some of the administrative aspects related to managing people (e.g., payroll), delegate some of the responsibilities to a specialist, or do both. If the company continues to grow, more specialists may be hired, either as permanent staff or on a contract basis to work on special projects, such as designing a new pay system. As with other business activities, these specialists assist the company, but responsibility for the work remains with the company managers.

HR Professionals Provide Special Expertise

Human resource (HR) professionals *are people with substantial specialized and technical knowledge of HR issues, laws, policies, and practices.* The leaders of HR units and the people who work in the department usually are HR professionals, although not always. Sometimes organizations fill the top-level HR position with a person who has a history of line experience but no special expertise in the area of human resources. Line managers who are doing a "tour of duty" in the HR department are appropriately referred to as HR managers, but they may not be considered HR professionals—at least not until they gain substantial experience and perhaps take a few executive development courses devoted to human resource management.

External experts who serve as HR consultants or vendors for the organization *may* be HR professionals, but don't assume that consultants or vendors are HR professionals just because they offer HR products or services. In addition to a record of substantial HR experience, other things indicating that a consultant or vendor has the specialized expertise of a professional include a college-level degree in the field and accreditation from a professional association. Human resource professionals of all types have many roles and responsibilities.

Exhibit 1.4 describes in more detail the several roles played by HR professionals who work as high-level managers and executives with responsibility for managing an organization's human resource activities.[29]

Key HR Competencies. To be effective, HR professionals need many competencies and a great deal of knowledge. Research conducted at the University of Michigan Business School during the past two decades has identified five major types of competencies that HR professionals need to be effective. These competencies and their weighted impact on business performance are

1. Strategic understanding and contribution (43%).

2. Personal credibility (23%).

3. HR delivery (18%).

4. Business acumen (11%).

5. HR technology (5%).[30]

EXHIBIT 1.4 Key Roles for HR Professionals	
Key Roles	**What Is Expected on the Job**
Business Partner	Shows concern for objectives of all stakeholders
	Understands the external and organizational environment
	Assists with strategy formulation and implementation
	Assists with mergers, acquisitions, and international joint ventures
	Shows how human resource management activities can affect the bottom line
Consultant	Views line managers and other employees as customers and works as partner to meet their needs
	Develops HR practices and policies with input from other members of the HR Triad
Innovator	Initiates—does not wait for others to call attention to the need for action
	Uses e-learning, the Internet, and other newly evolving technologies to improve HR services
	Continually revises and updates HR policies and practices
Monitor	Ensures employment laws are known and observed
	Evaluates the effectiveness of the organization's HR policies and practices
	Coaches and encourages line managers to practice the HR policies as intended
	Works with line managers and other employees in the HR Triad to revise policies as needed
Change Manager	Is guided by a long-term vision of where the business is headed
	Understands what talent is needed for executing future strategies
	Anticipates the concerns of employees and creates solutions to address them

As is true in other professions, an HR examination and certification process is available to assess competencies. The best-known certification process is conducted by the **Society for Human Resource Management (SHRM),** *which is a professional association with several thousand HR professionals as members.* Certification is provided by SHRM for two levels of expertise for HR professionals: Professional in Human Resources (PHR) and Senior Professional in Human Resources (SPHR). The test specifications for PHR and SPHR, along with jobs and compensation levels, are described at the Web site of the Human Resource Certification Institute (www.hrci.org). The contents of this book provide a good preparation for the PHR and SPHR certification examination programs.

At Weyerhaeuser, each major division, led by its human resources director, is responsible for developing a list of the specific competencies required by members of the HR staff. The HR directors work with their staff to generate a slate of competencies. The HR leaders interview their internal "customers"—those inside the organization—and also use their own knowledge of what the staff will be doing in their jobs. The corporation is aiming to predict future HR issues so that they can describe the future competency requirements for HR staff. The senior HR professionals at Deutsche Bank (DB) went through a similar process. In their efforts to increase DB's global competitiveness, the HR department realized it had to display more competencies and play more roles.

HR Competencies for Global Firms. The globalization of business is putting HR professionals from around the world in almost daily contact with each other and with line managers representing many different countries and cultures.

Coinciding with this globalization of business is the globalization of the HR profession. The World Federation of Personnel Management Associations (WFPMA) links country- and region-specific professional associations around the world, including SHRM. Another member of WFPMA is the United Kingdom's Chartered Institute for Personnel Development (CIPD).

A study conducted for the CIPD found that the competencies of HR professionals around the world reflect the roles they play, which are determined in part by their environment.[31] HR leaders and departments around the world have many of the same roles and responsibilities, but the specifics of what they do reflect the culture, laws, and economy of each country. Because SHRM now recognizes the unique and extensive body of professional knowledge needed by HR professionals to be successful in a global environment, there is now a third exam for HR professionals: the Global Professional in Human Resources (GPHR). The content areas of this exam are also found at the HRCI Web site.

Ethical Behavior. Human resource professionals are guided in their work by the **HR profession's code of ethics,** *which states that HR professionals must regard the obligation to implement public objectives and protect the public interest as more important than blind loyalty to an employer's preferences.* More specifically, in daily practice, HR professionals are expected to

- Thoroughly understand the problems assigned to them and undertake whatever study and research are required to ensure continuing competence and the best of professional attention.
- Maintain a high standard of personal honesty and integrity in every phase of daily practice.
- Give thoughtful consideration to the personal interest, welfare, and dignity of all employees who are affected by their prescriptions, recommendations, and actions.
- Make sure that the organizations representing them maintain a high regard and respect for the public interest and that they never overlook the importance of the personal interests and dignity of employees.

Ethical organizations have an edge in their ability to hire and retain the best people, and this edge ensures that the best workforce possible is working to achieve the organization's objectives. SHRM's code of ethics for HR professionals is shown in Exhibit 1.5. A manual that HR professionals can use as a guide to developing and instituting an employer's code of ethics for their total workforce is also available from SHRM. Ethical human resource management requires managers to eliminate such things as favoritism, friendship, sex bias, race bias, and age bias from promotion and pay decisions (it is, of course, also unlawful to take sex, race, or age into account). For more information on SHRM's code of ethics visit their home page (www.shrm.org).

Because HR professionals share responsibility for designing training and reward systems, they can encourage ethical behavior. A good starting point is to encourage the top-level executives to critically examine reward systems to ensure that they do not encourage the achievement of organizational goals at almost any cost. Other HR activities that professionals can use to encourage ethical business practices include developing standards and guidelines that employees can consult when they face difficult decisions, and setting up an easy-to-use hotline for reporting behavior that doesn't meet ethical standards.

" HR is growing significantly more involved in the implementation of ethics programs. . . . Ethics and compliance issues are becoming increasingly important to the welfare of global companies. "

Ron Berenbeim
Director, Business Ethics
The Conference Board

" It's comforting to know that ethical issues are out there and I'm not alone. But it's disheartening to know that they're so commonplace. "

Participant
Online Ethics
Bulletin Board

EXHIBIT 1.5 Excerpts from SHRM's Code of Ethical and Professional Standards for Human Resource Professionals

Professional Responsibility

Core Principle: As HR professionals, we are responsible for adding value to the organizations we serve and contributing to the ethical success of those organizations. We accept professional responsibility for our individual decisions and actions. We are also advocates for the profession by engaging in activities that enhance its credibility and value.

Guidelines

1. Adhere to the highest standards of ethical and professional behavior.
2. Measure the effectiveness of HR in contributing to or achieving organizational goals.
3. Comply with the law.
4. Work consistent with the values of the profession.
5. Strive to achieve the highest levels of service, performance and social responsibility.
6. Advocate for the appropriate use and appreciation of human beings as employees.
7. Advocate openly and within the established forums for debate in order to influence decision-making and results.

Professional Development

Core Principle: As professionals we must strive to meet the highest standards of competence and commit to strengthen our competencies on a continuous basis.

Guidelines

1. Pursue formal academic opportunities.
2. Commit to continuous learning, skills development and application of new knowledge related to both human resource management and the organizations we serve.
3. Contribute to the body of knowledge, the evolution of the profession and the growth of individuals through teaching, research and dissemination of knowledge.
4. Pursue certification such as CCP, CEBS, PHR, SPHR, etc. where available, or comparable measures of competencies and knowledge.

Ethical Leadership

Core Principle: HR professionals are expected to exhibit individual leadership as a role model for maintaining the highest standards of ethical conduct.

Guidelines

1. Be ethical; act ethically in every professional interaction.
2. Question pending individual and group actions when necessary to ensure that decisions are ethical and are implemented in an ethical manner.
3. Seek expert guidance if ever in doubt about the ethical propriety of a situation.
4. Through teaching and mentoring, champion the development of others as ethical leaders in the profession and in organizations.

Fairness and Justice

Core Principle: As human resource professionals, we are ethically responsible for promoting and fostering fairness and justice for all employees and their organizations.

Guidelines

1. Respect the uniqueness and intrinsic worth of every individual.
2. Treat people with dignity, respect and compassion to foster a trusting work environment free of harassment, intimidation and unlawful discrimination.
3. Ensure that everyone has the opportunity to develop their skills and new competencies.
4. Assure an environment of inclusiveness and a commitment to diversity in the organizations we serve.
5. Develop, administer and advocate policies and procedures that foster fair, consistent and equitable treatment for all.
6. Regardless of personal interests, support decisions made by our organizations that are both ethical and legal.
7. Act in a responsible manner and practice sound management in the country(ies) in which the organizations we serve operate.

Conflicts of Interest

Core Principle: As HR professionals, we must maintain a high level of trust with our stakeholders. We must protect the interests of our stakeholders as well as our professional integrity and should not engage in activities that create actual, apparent, or potential conflicts of interest.

Guidelines

1. Adhere to and advocate the use of published policies on conflicts of interest within your organization.
2. Refrain from using your position for personal, material or financial gain or the appearance of such.
3. Refrain from giving or seeking preferential treatment in the human resources processes.
4. Prioritize your obligations to identify conflicts of interest or the appearance thereof; when conflicts arise, disclose them to relevant stakeholders.

(continued)

EXHIBIT 1.5 *(continued)*

Use of Information
Core Principle: HR professionals consider and protect the rights of individuals, especially in the acquisition and dissemination of information while ensuring truthful communications and facilitating informed decision-making.

Guidelines

1. Acquire and disseminate information through ethical and responsible means.
2. Ensure only appropriate information is used in decisions affecting the employment relationship.
3. Investigate the accuracy and source of information before allowing it to be used in employment related decisions.
4. Maintain current and accurate HR information.
5. Safeguard restricted or confidential information.
6. Take appropriate steps to ensure the accuracy and completeness of all communicated information about HR policies and practices.
7. Take appropriate steps to ensure the accuracy and completeness of all communicated information used in HR-related training.

Employees Share Responsibility

The responsibilities of line managers and HR professionals are especially great; nevertheless, they share responsibility with the third key player in the HR Triad, namely, all the other employees who are affected by HR policies and practices. Regardless of their particular jobs, all employees in an organization share some of the responsibility for effective human resource management. Some employees write their own job descriptions and even design their own jobs. Many employees provide input for the appraisal of their own performance, the performance of their colleagues and supervisors, or both. Many organizations ask employees to participate in annual surveys in which they can express their likes and dislikes about the organization's approach to managing people. Employees should also assess their own needs and values and manage their own careers in accordance with these. As we move forward, we all need to position ourselves for the future. Learning about how effective organizations are managing human resources is an essential step for getting into position.

To help readers understand the role of the three key players in the HR Triad, each chapter includes a feature called The HR Triad. In this chapter, the feature entitled, "The HR Triad: Roles and Responsibilities for Managing Human Resources," describes some of the general roles and responsibilities of the three key players in the Triad. In subsequent chapters, the HR Triad focuses on roles and responsibilities that are relevant to the specific HR activities described in the chapter.

LOOKING AHEAD: FIVE SPECIAL THEMES

In managing people and organizations today, many common themes seem to pop up all the time. These themes are important because they help shape and influence human resource management policies and practices, and thus how companies manage their employees. In subsequent chapters, we pay attention to five special themes:

1. Managing teams.
2. Managing the multicultural workforce.
3. Managing globalization.
4. Managing ethics.
5. Managing with metrics.

LINE MANAGERS	HR PROFESSIONALS	EMPLOYEES
• Work closely with HR professionals and employees to develop HR policies.	• Work closely with line managers and employees to develop HR policies.	• Work closely with line managers and HR professionals to develop and implement HR policies and practices.
• Engage in HR practices consistent with HR policies.	• Help line managers and employees practice HRM consistent with HR policies.	• Accept responsibility for managing their own behavior and careers in organizations.
• Include HR professionals in the formulation and implementation of business strategy and discussions of its HR implications.	• Stay informed of the latest technical principles for managing human resources.	• Recognize the need for personal flexibility and adaptability.
• On a daily basis, consider the implications of business decisions for managing human resources.	• Develop the skills and competencies needed to support change processes.	• Be committed to learning and changing continuously throughout one's career.
• Accept shared responsibility for managing human resources strategically and work to reduce barriers to this objective.	• On a daily basis, consider how well the organization's approaches to managing human resources fit with the current global and organizational environment.	• Learn about and apply basic accepted principles for managing human resources for HR activities in which they participate (e.g., selecting team members, appraising supervisors, and training coworkers).
• Learn about and apply basic accepted principles for managing human resources.	• Be proactive in learning about how leading companies are managing human resources, and what they're learning from their experiences.	• Be willing to share ideas that might help the company manage its people better.
• Seek input from employees and HR professionals in order to improve own competency for managing human resources.	• Work with employees to help them voice their concerns effectively, and serve as their advocate when appropriate.	

As you will see, the human resource management activities discussed in subsequent chapters reflect these special themes, in addition to addressing the ever present issues of attracting, retaining, motivating, and improving a competitive workforce.

Managing Teams

The popularity of team-based organizational structures reflects the belief that teamwork can achieve outcomes that cannot be achieved by the same number of individuals working in isolation. Exhibit 1.6 lists several reasons for organizing employees into work teams instead of having them work on small tasks that they can complete alone.

As many organizations are discovering, the payoff from teams isn't automatic. Although teams offer great potential for increased innovation, quality, and speed, the potential isn't always realized. Even when teams fulfill their potential in these areas, team members and their organizations may experience unanticipated negative side effects, such as lingering unproductive conflicts and turnover.

Human resource management practices can make the difference between success and failure for organizations using teams. To create and orchestrate teams, people need to be selected, appraised, compensated, and trained in ways

---

EXHIBIT 1.6 Why Organizations Use Work Teams

The Most Common Reasons for Having Employees Work in Teams

To Satisfy Customers

✔ Improve on-time delivery of results

✔ Improve customer relations

✔ Facilitate innovation in products and services

✔ Improve quality

✔ Reduce costs and improve efficiency

To Satisfy Employees

✔ Facilitate management development and career growth

✔ Reinforce or expand informal networks in the organization

✔ Improve employees' understanding of the business

✔ Increase employee ownership, commitment, and motivation

---

that reflect the unique relationships that develop between employees who work together. Most companies realize that people working in teams should not be managed in the same way as people who work more independently. Nevertheless, teamwork really is a somewhat new phenomenon in the American workplace, so considerable experimentation in how best to manage teams is still taking place around the country. Some practices now viewed as experimental will undoubtedly become commonplace in the next decade. Examples of how organizations are using human resource practices to maximize team effectiveness are highlighted throughout this book in the Managing Teams feature.

Managing the Multicultural Workforce

At about the same time that organizations began to recognize the benefits of teamwork, they discovered that the people who were being put into teams were more culturally diverse than ever before. More and more women are working, for example, resulting in a new gender mix that's nearly balanced instead of being male-dominated. Throughout the twentieth century, immigration patterns also changed, resulting in more cultural diversity. In addition, employees differ with a wide variety of values and lifestyles. Thus organizations are finding that multicultural management practices must be sensitive to issues of religion, sexual orientation, marital and family status, age, and various other unifying life experiences.[32]

For organizations that are committed to fully utilizing their human resources, having a workforce that is diverse in terms of gender, ethnicity, country, culture, lifestyle, religion, sexual orientation, age, and many other characteristics requires finding new ways of managing. The increasing diversity of the workforce, combined with changing attitudes about differences that may have been ignored in the past, presents both challenges and opportunities for organizations and their employees. Throughout this book, the feature called Managing the Multicultural Workforce describes how effective organizations use HR practices to leverage employee multiculturalism and create competitive advantage.

Managing Globalization

Globalization *refers to a process in which companies in countries around the world are increasingly linked by their activities and the opportunities they provide each other.* Globalization requires changes and adaptation, some of major proportions, in a relatively short time period. It creates some winners and perhaps some losers.

During the past 50 years, technological advances in transportation and communications have spurred the pace of globalization. Many firms evolved from being purely domestic to becoming truly global. The first step in this evolution is simply exporting goods for sale in one or two foreign markets. The next step is to manufacture those goods overseas because it is more efficient than shipping products thousands of miles to markets. Setting up operations close to foreign markets also helps a company better understand its customers. Eventually, a company may evolve into a transnational firm that has "headquarters" in several nations, and no single dominant national culture.[33]

One of the most difficult challenges for truly global organizations is developing an HRM system that works at home as well as abroad.[34] When Lincoln Electric began to globalize, they assumed that their American approach to managing employees would work just as effectively in other countries as it worked in Cleveland, Ohio. They soon discovered that exporting their approach to managing human resources wouldn't work. In fact, some of their practices were illegal in other countries, just as some practices that are common in other countries may be illegal in the United States. A firm's decisions about which HR practices will be used universally and which will be adapted to reflect local conditions may ultimately determine its success or failure.

Throughout this book, we return repeatedly to issues of how globalization influences the way organizations manage their human resources. Although detailed treatment of this topic is beyond the scope of this text, many of the issues that global organizations face are illustrated in the feature called Managing Globalization. Readers who are particularly interested in cross-cultural and international human resource management should consult the relevant sources referenced throughout the chapters.

Managing Ethics

Earlier in this chapter, we described the Society for Human Resource Management's Code of Ethics for HR Professionals. That code serves as a guide to HR professionals regarding their own behaviors and their interactions with others in the organization, including senior management. For other members of the organization, a chief ethics officer or chief compliance officer may be responsible for developing and enforcing a code of ethics, and often HR professionals assist with these efforts. HR professionals may support the successful implementation of a code of ethics by developing HR activities that encourage employees to do the right things—that is, to act in the best interests of society and the company.[35] For example, at J. M. Smucker Company, employees attend ethics training programs every three to five years. And every year they read and sign a nine-page ethics statement that explains what the company means by ethical behavior.[36] Because concerns about ethical behavior are so important to employers,[37] we provide several examples throughout this text to illustrate how HR policies and practices can be used to address ethical concerns in the Managing Ethics feature.

Managing with Metrics

Some people use the expression, "If you can't measure it, it doesn't exist!" This is a rather strong statement perhaps, and one you may disagree with, but many managers take it pretty seriously. As a consequence, they need/want/demand metrics (data) that they can use to determine how well the company is doing. In turn, the results reflected in these metrics can be used to determine such things as a manager's salary increase, bonus, or promotion. For many top-level executives, the metric of most concern is the price of the company's stock![38] Metrics are very important to managers and companies, and they are important

FAST FACT

Ethics and compliance programs are found at more than 90% of the Fortune 500 companies.

" *We found that a manager of an office with a below-average overall score will produce $1 million less revenue than his counterpart with an above-average score on our Human Capital Capability Scorecard.* "

John Conover
President
Trane's Commercial Systems Distribution

to HR professionals as well because HR professionals also must measure their success and their contributions to the organization.[39]

Of course, metrics aren't new. Companies have used measures of financial performance and operating efficiency for years. More recently, companies have sought out customer opinions to measure the quality of products and services. Likewise, HR professionals are interested in employee satisfaction rates, performance ratings and accident and injury rates. Today, HR professionals are using a wide variety of metrics to systematically measure their contributions and demonstrate the contributions of HR activities to the success or "bottom line" of the company. In the following chapters, we will provide descriptions of what some HR professionals are doing with metrics in the feature called "Managing with Metrics."[40]

CURRENT ISSUES

The five broad themes we just described—teams, the multicultural workforce, globalization, ethics, and metrics—are relevant to almost every part of the HRM system. In addition, some current issues are especially relevant to particular chapters. Thus at the end of each chapter, we include a Current Issues section where we briefly comment on issues that are being discussed extensively by HR professionals, managers, and academics. While several current issues may be relevant to each chapter, we generally describe only two. For example, of the several issues that could be discussed here in more detail, we selected eHR and complexity. Each of the remaining chapters presents different current issues.

eHR

Consistent with much of what is described in Chapter 1, and especially "Managing with Metrics," is the use of eHR in all HR activities. **eHR** *refers to the practice of managing human resources through the use of various forms of hardware and software technology including databases, mainframes, laptops, use of materials online, DVDs and CDs, accessibility, confidentiality, privacy, ownership, and the Internet as applied to all HR activities.*[41] The human resource information system is one important component of eHR.

The development and application of eHR can significantly facilitate the work of the HR Triad. Databases and computer software that connect employee performance information with compensation alternatives can help line managers see the implications of hypothetical performance appraisal decisions. Employees can more easily provide and be asked to respond to surveys about their supervisors. While all this information may be helpful, it needs to be used ethically to produce its maximum value.[42] Because eHR can be such a powerful tool in enhancing the effective management of human resources, HR professionals need to be actively involved in its development and application.

Managing Complexity

For many managers, doing their job effectively is much more challenging than ever before.[43] Complexity is created by the rapidly evolving competition from around the world, the constant innovations in products and services, the changing organizational structure and strategies, the political and economic dynamics, and the continuous introduction of new technologies. For managers, complexity makes it more challenging to make the right decisions because there is so much information to process and so many factors influencing the organization's performance. HR professionals can assist in part by making the process of managing human resources as efficient and effective as possible. They also can contribute by designing management development programs that bring managers together to share their experiences with each other and learn how others are addressing the challenge of complexity. HR professionals can help line managers by making sure that complexity is always a topic for discussion; even if it cannot be reduced, it can be managed effectively.[44]

> 66 *The most common question asked by managers in management development programs today is 'How can you help me manage complexity better?'* 99
>
> *Vlado Pucik*
> *Professor*
> *IMD, Lausanne, Switzerland*

CHAPTER SUMMARY WITH LEARNING GOALS

1 STRATEGIC IMPORTANCE OF MANAGING HUMAN RESOURCES. Managing human resources is critical to the success of all companies, large and small, regardless of industry. The more effectively a firm manages its human resources, the more successful the firm is likely to be. Organizations define success by how well they serve their stakeholders. Stakeholders include those who have a claim on the resources, services, and products of the companies. The primary stakeholders who shape the typical organization's approach to managing human resources include (but aren't limited to) the shareholders and owners, society, customers, other organizations, and organization members. Addressing the concerns of these powerful stakeholders makes managing human resources a challenging and important task.

2 COMPETITIVE ADVANTAGE THROUGH HUMAN RESOURCES. Companies can gain and sustain a competitive advantage over other companies by managing their people in ways that add value to the organization but that are difficult for other companies to duplicate. Because managing human resources effectively is complex and difficult, only a few organizations gain and sustain a competitive advantage through people.

3 A FRAMEWORK FOR MANAGING HUMAN RESOURCES. Managing human resources involves many policies and practices, which, taken together, form an organization's human resource management system. Some approaches to managing human resources are more effective than other approaches. Nevertheless, there is no one best way to manage employees. Organizations need to manage human resources to fit the external environment and the organizational environment. A strategic approach to managing human resources involves systematically and correctly creating HR policies and practices that are consistent with each other and aligned with the external and organizational environments.

4 THE HR TRIAD. Managing human resources is the responsibility of line managers, HR professionals, and all other employees in the organization. These three key players—whom we refer to as the HR Triad—must work together in a way that is appropriate to each of their roles. Nearly all midsized to large-sized companies employ human resource professionals—as full-time employees, as vendors with long-term contracts, and/or as consultants who work on short-term projects. Regardless of how HR activities are structured, companies that are most concerned with HR management seek professionals who have the competencies needed for their work and who are guided by the HR profession's code of ethical conduct.

5 FIVE SPECIAL THEMES. Looking ahead, organizations face many challenges. Five themes described throughout the chapters of this book are managing teams, managing the multicultural workforce, managing globalization, managing ethics, and managing with metrics. In developing their human resource management policies and practices, the best organizations consider these themes.

⚠ **CURRENT ISSUES.** Current issues in managing human resources include eHR and complexity. eHR refers to the use of various information technologies for managing human resources. Complexity refers to enormous amount of information and the variety of options we face everyday. By making good use of eHR and helping managers learn to cope with complexity, HR professionals can contribute to an organization's effectiveness.

TERMS TO REMEMBER

eHR

Globalization

HR profession's code of ethics

HR triad

Human resource (HR) activities

Human resource management (HRM) system

Human resource (HR) professionals

Human resources

Intangible human assets

Multinational corporations (MNCs)

Society for Human Resource Management (SHRM)

Stakeholders

Sustainable competitive advantage

Tangible assets

QUESTIONS FOR DISCUSSION AND REFLECTIVE THINKING

1. What has Cisco Systems been doing that demonstrates the value of managing human resources effectively? Why have employees stayed with Cisco during the tough times?

2. Refer to the list of stakeholders and their objectives in Exhibit 1.1. For each stakeholder group, state at least one *additional* concern that you think might shape how organizations manage human resources. Then, for each stakeholder group, give one specific example of how each stakeholder's concerns could affect a major HR activity (e.g., planning, staffing, appraisal, compensation, or training).

3. Is it realistic to expect organizations to be strategic in managing human resources? What organizational and individual barriers are likely to make it difficult to adopt a strategic approach?

4. Give some examples to illustrate the possible consequences that occur when the daily HR practices of managers are inconsistent with the organization's formal HR policies.

5. Which member of the HR Triad has the most responsibility for ensuring that organizations effectively manage their human resources? Explain your answer.

6. Why are the themes of managing teams, managing multiculturalism, managing globalization, managing ethics, and managing with metrics so important today? Are these challenges likely to decrease in importance over the next decade? Why or why not?

7. Describe the two current issues discussed in this chapter and what they mean for your career.

PROJECTS TO EXTEND YOUR LEARNING

1. **Integration and Application.** Before continuing, review the cases of Southwest Airlines and Lincoln Electric at the end of this book. Then, using Exhibit 1.1 as a guide, make an illustration that identifies the stakeholders of each company and shows the relative importance of each stakeholder to each company. Here, as in the chapters to follow, you

can gather your information from materials in the chapter, the cases at the end of the text, and from other sources including newspapers, magazines, the Internet, and your experience. If you are unable to obtain information you feel is relevant, make assumptions based on your best judgment. Note any major assumptions you make.

2. **Using the Internet.** Managing human resources effectively is a topic that you can learn more about by using the Internet. Begin discovering the many online resources that are available now.

   a. Find out about this year's "100 Best Companies to Work for in America" according to *Fortune* magazine (http://money.cnn.com/magazines/fortune/bestcompanies/full_list/).

   b. Visit several professional associations in the United States whose members are experts in managing human resources, including
      * The Human Resources Division of the Academy of Management (www.aom.pace.edu).
      * WorldatWork (www.worldatwork.org).
      * Society for Industrial and Organizational Psychology (www.siop.org).
      * The Society for Human Resource Management (www.shrm.org).

      You can find links to associations in other countries at the home page of the World Federation of Personnel Management Associations (www.wfpma.com).

   c. Learn about procedures and requirements for obtaining HR certification from the Human Resource Certification Institute (www.hrci.org).

   d. Compare the HR code of ethics provided by the Society for Human Resource Management (www.shrm.org/ethics/code-of-ethics.asp) with the code of ethics for another profession of interest to you (e.g., physician, accountant, lawyer, psychologist).

   e. Begin to learn more about the two companies featured in the cases at the end of this book, Lincoln Electric (www.lincolnelectric.com) and Southwest Airlines (www.southwest.com). You'll want to visit the home pages of these companies often.

   f. Learn more about some of the consulting firms in HR including Mercer (www.mercerhr.com), Deloitte (www.deloitte.com), AON (www.aon.com), Watson Wyatt (www.watsonwyatt.com), Towers Perrin (www.towersperrin.com), Pricewaterhousecoopers (www.pwc.com), Hewitt (www.hewitt.com), and the Hay Group (www.haygroup.com).

3. **Experiential Activity.** Locate an HR professional who is willing to be interviewed for about 15 minutes. You can do this by visiting an organization, attending a meeting or conference where there are likely to be HR professionals present, or speaking to a friend or relative who works in the HR field. Ask the HR professional the questions listed below. Take notes and be prepared to report what you learn to your classmates.

   a. *Questions to ask an HR professional during your individual interview:*
      * What are your most important roles and responsibilities?
      * Describe the most difficult challenges that you face as an HR professional.
      * In your current job, how important are issues of managing teams, managing the multicultural workforce, managing globalization, managing ethics, and managing with metrics?
      * What are the most difficult ethical issues that you face as an HR professional?

   b. *Questions to discuss with your classmates:* After the interview, meet with several classmates and discuss the following questions:
      * What similarities do you see in the comments of the several HR professionals you interviewed?
      * How do the answers given by the HR professionals seem to differ? What accounts for the differences in the answers?
      * What do you feel is the single biggest challenge in managing human resources effectively?

Mike Mitchell left the Bank of Montreal to become vice president of human resources at the North American branch of the Swiss Bank Corporation (SBC). It was a move up for him in terms of status, responsibility, monetary compensation, and challenge. Of these, the challenge was the most intriguing element for Mitchell. In his mid-thirties, he saw this as perfect time to take a risk in his career. He realized that if he succeeded, he would establish a prototype that could be marketed to other firms. In addition, success could lead to further career opportunities and challenges. While he had a general idea of what he wanted to do and had gotten verbal support from his superiors, the senior vice president of human resources and the president of SBC, North America, the details of exactly what he was going to do and how he was going to do it were yet to unfold.

In the preceding year, the parent company of SBC (a $110-billion universal bank headquartered in Basel, Switzerland) decided it needed a clearer statement of its intentions to focus its energies and resources in light of the growing international competition. Accordingly, it crafted a vision statement to the effect that the bank was going to better serve its customers with high-quality products that met their needs rather than just those of the institution. While the North American operation was relatively autonomous, it was still expected to embrace this vision. The details of its implementation, however, were in local hands. For the human resource side, the local hands were Mitchell's.

While Mitchell had spent some time in human resources at the Bank of Montreal in New York, the bulk of his work experience was as an entrepreneur in Montreal, Canada. It was this experience that affected his thinking the most. Thus, when he came to the SBC, his self-image was a businessperson who happened to be working in human resources. It was in part because of this image that his stay at the Bank of Montreal was brief: The idea of human resources was a bit too conservative for his style. Too many of his ideas "just couldn't be done." In interviewing with the top managers at SBC, they warned him of the same general environment. So he knew change would be slow among the 1,000 employees, including his own department of 10 employees. He knew, however, that he wanted to reposition and "customerize" the HR department at SBC. He also understood the importance of connecting the HR department to the business.

Mitchell identified four major aspects for his program to reposition and customerize the HR department. The four aspects included (1) gathering information, (2) developing action agendas, (3) implementing those agendas, and (4) evaluating and revising the agendas.

Gathering Information

To gather information about the current environment, Mitchell asked questions of customers, diagnosed the environment, and consulted with the HR department itself. From the customers, Mitchell learned the nature of the business strategy and how HR currently fit with or helped that strategy. Customers discussed what they were getting from the HR department, what their ideal would be, and how the ideal could best be delivered. Each HR activity, as well as the entire department and the staff, was discussed. From the environment, Mitchell learned what other companies were doing with their HR departments and HR practices. He examined competitors and those in other industries to gather ideas for the entire department and for each HR activity. From the HR department, he learned about how they saw themselves in relation to servicing their customers, their knowledge of strategy, how they thought the customers perceived the department, and their desire to improve and change.

Developing Agendas

Making agendas based upon this information was the second aspect of Mitchell's plan. As the HR staff analyzed the information, they were asked to develop plans (agendas) for resolving any discrepancies between what they were currently doing and what their customers wanted. As the staff worked, they began to recognize a need to determine a vision for themselves—to formulate a statement of who they were and how they interacted with the rest of the organization. They also began to examine whether their current ways of operating and the department's current structure were sufficiently suited to moving ahead. The need to reorganize became apparent. Once the vision began to take shape and the agendas were developed, the HR department established a game plan to implement their agendas. Approval by top management and the line managers who were immediately affected was seen as critical to successful implementation.

Implementing the Agendas

To begin the implementation phase, the HR staff met with the customers to discuss the agendas. In addition to responding to the specific needs of the line managers, the HR department also had to sell the line managers on other activities. With a new focus that was more strategic and customer-oriented than in the past, the HR department began to develop programs that went beyond the regular administrative activities and services that it had provided to the line managers. Because these services were new, they had to be sold to their customers, at least at first. So in addition to implementing the specifically agreed-upon agendas and contracts, this aspect included developing, selling, and implementing new programs.

Evaluating and Revising

Developed along with the agendas were contracts that specified what would be delivered to the customer. The customer was given the right to appraise the work delivered. Based on these appraisals by the customers (the line managers), the agendas were evaluated. Revisions and adjustments were then made for continual improvement. In addition to such contracts, the work of the HR department was reviewed internally using such criteria as the reduction in turnover resulting from better selection procedures and an increase in the number of new ideas or innovations resulting from a change in the HR practices to facilitate the innovative strategy of the business.

Implications for the HR Department

There were several implications for the HR department (Mitchell and his staff) in their efforts to reposition and customerize:

- The HR department was reoriented to be strategic and customer-oriented.
- The HR department became a constant gatherer of information from the internal and external environments. By knowing the competition, the business strategy, and the current assets of the company, the HR staff could develop new HR activities, implement new ideas, and work to maintain the company's competitive advantage.
- The HR department identified the level of excellence it wanted to attain. The staff worked to make the department a strategic player while fulfilling their managerial and operational roles.
- HR managers and staff worked closely with the line managers to design systems to gather the needed services and information. They also worked with the line managers to develop contracts by which the HR department would be evaluated by the line managers.
- The HR department was changing so that there was more of a generalist than a specialist orientation. A greater team orientation was also built.
- Things would never be the same. The HR professionals in the department would now be gathering, servicing, evaluating, revising, and most of all listening. And because the business is always changing, the HR department will continue to evolve and change.

Implications for the Line Managers

There were also several implications in the repositioning and customerization program for the line managers:

- The line managers needed to cooperate with Mitchell and his staff as they gathered information and implemented new ideas and practices. Together, they became partners in the business. The line managers had to accept the new role being played by Mitchell and his HR staff.

- The line managers needed to work closely with the HR staff in developing the action agendas.
- The line managers had to continue working with the HR staff in appraising the success of the HR efforts.

Benefits from the Partnership

From Mitchell's perspective, several outcomes resulted from the repositioning and customerization program, including:

- Enhancing the quality and responsiveness of the HR department.
- Developing the HR department in terms of new jobs (skill-wise), providing new excitement, and building commitment to the company's mission, goals, and strategies.
- Linking HR with the business and integrating HR with the corporate strategy.
- Becoming market or customer oriented, with flexibility to respond to and anticipate changes.
- Developing criteria by which the behaviors of the HR department can be evaluated and changed.
- Gaining an ability to develop and use HR practices to gain competitive advantage.
- Developing an awareness of the potential ways different HR practices can be done by constantly monitoring what other successful companies are doing.
- Becoming more keenly aware of the internal and external environments.
- Providing standard HR products more efficiently.
- Developing new products and services.
- Developing technology to deliver the new products and services.
- Selling new services and products outside the company.
- Changing the HR department dramatically and consequently becoming a catalyst for change with the company.
- Becoming a department where everyone wants to work.

CASE QUESTIONS

1. Who were the customers of Mitchell and his HR staff?
2. What did Mitchell have to do so that his staff could do the things necessary to reposition and customerize?
3. Do you think the line managers would cooperate with Mitchell and his staff? What would it take to get their cooperation? Why might they resist a partnership with the HR department?
4. Develop a matrix with projects, dates, milestones, and people involved (i.e., HR, line managers, and employees) for Mitchell and his staff.

Source: Prepared by Randall S. Schuler, who expresses his appreciation for the cooperation of Michael Mitchell who moved subsequently from SBC to Tiffany and Company. SBC has merged with UBS (www.ubs.com).

Understanding the External and Organizational Environments

Learning Goals

After reading this chapter, you should be able to:

1. Explain the strategic importance of understanding the external and organizational environments.
2. Describe some aspects of economic globalization.
3. Discuss three aspects of the political landscape that influence the managing of human resources.
4. Describe how industry dynamics influence the managing of human resources.
5. Describe the U.S. and global labor markets.
6. Describe some dimensions and consequences of country culture.
7. Discuss the relationship between technologies and managing human resources.
8. Explain the components of company culture.
9. Describe how business strategies influence the managing of human resources.
10. Discuss two current issues in understanding the external and organizational environments.

MANAGING HUMAN RESOURCES AT DEERE & COMPANY

When Bob Lane became chairman and CEO of Deere & Company in August 2000, he took charge of a leading producer of agricultural, construction, forestry, and turf care equipment that enjoyed loyal customers, a strong dealer network, and a rich heritage spanning 164 years. He also inherited a company that was, in his words, "asset heavy and [profit] margin lean." Deere was not prepared to compete in a changing and demanding global environment.

With his leadership team, Lane created an ambitious plan to manage assets more efficiently, cut costs, and manufacture a new generation of products to fit the new demands of its external environment. The plan aimed to reduce Deere's vulnerability to the cyclical swings and unpredictability of the agriculture and construction markets. With the support of the board, Deere management divided the company into four divisions. With the new structure, each division was to operate on a global basis. For example, in the agricultural division—which deals with machinery such as combine harvesters, cotton pickers, tractors, and implements—managers around the world who are part of this division must all collaborate to achieve the success of their business unit, regardless of which country they work in. Now all of the combine factories—in Zweibrucken, Germany; Jiamusi, China; Horizontina, Brazil; and East Moline, Illinois—must work together as one worldwide product team.

When Deere's management team decided to reorganize the company, they realized that success would not be automatic. The company's employees also had to change so that their behaviors were aligned with the new global vision. First, the management team had to communicate the changes being made and the reasons for those changes. Then, with the involvement of the HR professionals, the performance appraisal process was altered. New training programs also were created to help employees develop the new skills they needed to work effectively in the new organization. And a new compensation plan was eventually put in place to focus attention on the company's new business objectives. In the new global agriculture division, managers now cooperate more and try to learn from each other's successes, and they all use the same financial metrics to measure their performance.[1] ▲

THE STRATEGIC IMPORTANCE OF UNDERSTANDING THE EXTERNAL AND ORGANIZATIONAL ENVIRONMENTS

For Deere & Company, a poor understanding of its changing environment led to inefficiency and less than desirable profit margins. Fortunately, it found a new CEO who understood the environment and who had the leadership skills needed to help the company thrive in its new environment. Lane's role in Deere's turnaround shouldn't be underestimated. He realized that the company's employees would ultimately determine whether the company would survive. He also understood that the people doing the work were taking their cues from the behaviors they saw from him and other company leaders.

Unfortunately, not all CEOs share Lane's views of the important role of managing human resources in the successful transition of a company. As Exhibit 2.1 shows, many leaders view people as a cost rather than as valuable assets.[2] As you read this chapter, think about how a CEO's view of employees is likely to affect the way she or he deals with the changing business environment.

In Chapter 1, we presented our guiding framework for managing human resources, illustrated in Exhibit 1.3 (see page 15). Look again at Exhibit 1.3 and you will see that it highlights the importance of the many elements of an organization's external and organizational environments. Economic globalization and changing industry dynamics forced Deere & Company to change the way they operated. These are just two of several external conditions that can create threats and opportunities for businesses and influence the way employees are managed. In this chapter, we briefly describe how globalization, industry dynamics and several other elements of the environment can influence how companies manage their human resources. In subsequent chapters, we elaborate on this discussion by describing how these elements can influence specific

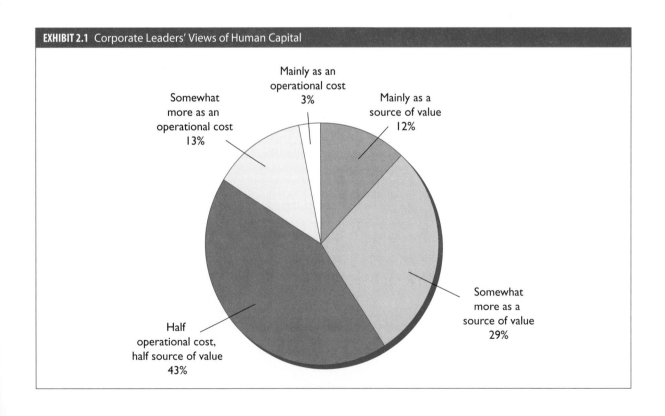

EXHIBIT 2.1 Corporate Leaders' Views of Human Capital

HR activities (HR planning, recruiting, training, performance management, compensation, and so on).

Elements of the Environment

As shown in Exhibit 1.3, organizations can be thought of as existing in an external environment. The organization itself can also be thought of as having an environment in which individual employees are embedded. Notice that we do not include stakeholders when we refer to elements of the external and organizational environments. Instead, we treat stakeholders as distinct groups of people whom the organization seeks to satisfy.

External Environment. The **external environment** *encompasses local, national, and multinational conditions that confront an organization.* The specific elements of the external environment described in this chapter are

- Economic globalization.
- The political landscape.
- Industry dynamics.
- Labor markets.
- Country cultures.

Two other important aspects of the external environment—legal institutions and unions—are discussed later in Chapters 4 and 14, respectively.

Although the external environment clearly influences how organizations manage their workforce, it does not fully determine their approach. A more accurate portrayal is to think of the external environment as a set of constraints and opportunities that can influence the way an organization manages its human resources.

Organizational Environment. The **organizational environment** *refers to conditions within the organization itself.* These are sometimes referred to as the internal environment. Effective organizations seek to create an organizational environment that fits the current external environment yet is flexible enough to change as new conditions arise. Because the external environment changes constantly, adjustments in the organizational environment often are needed, as illustrated in the experiences of Deere & Company.

Organizations are complex systems that include many elements. We will not attempt to describe *all* of these in this chapter. Instead, we focus on a few elements that have particular relevance for managing human resources:

- Technology.
- Company culture.
- Business strategy.

These organizational elements provide an immediate context for managing human resources. As is true of the external environment, components of the organizational environment are highly interdependent.

The HR Triad

Forces in the external environment constantly stimulate companies to reassess elements of the organizational environment. Because the external environment changes continually, successful companies continually evolve. Ultimately, the

> " *HR professionals need to scan the environment every day—whether by Internet, newspapers, or magazines. Everything has the potential to impact everything we do.* "
>
> *Charles Tharp*
> *Vice President of Human Resources*
> *Saks Fifth Avenue*

LINE MANAGERS	HR PROFESSIONALS	EMPLOYEES
UNDERSTANDING THE EXTERNAL ENVIRONMENT		
• Stay informed about economic and political conditions and their possible implications for the organization. • Investigate potential new markets for products and services. Encourage discussion of the potential implications. • Develop an understanding of the culture of selected countries of likely importance to the business.	• Stay informed about economic and political conditions and their possible implications for the organization. • Investigate foreign labor market qualifications and conditions. Encourage discussion of the potential implications. • Educate the organization about the new issues to be addressed as the organization expands beyond domestic borders. • Provide resources for managers and other employees to learn about cultural differences and to develop skills in cross-cultural interaction.	• Stay informed about economic and political conditions and their possible implications for the organization. • Develop a basic understanding of how global conditions are likely to affect your organization and career. • Develop an understanding of at least one culture other than your own. • Develop an understanding of the unique aspects of your own culture and how people from other cultures view it.
ALIGNING THE ORGANIZATIONAL ENVIRONMENT: TECHNOLOGY, CULTURE, AND STRATEGY		
• Investigate new technologies to learn how they can be used to gain competitive advantage. • Understand, communicate, and behave in line with the vision, mission, and values. • Recognize elements of the company's desired culture and set a positive example through your own behavior. • Assist HR professionals in determining the competencies and behaviors needed to implement the firm's strategy, and encourage these behaviors among employees.	• Learn to use advanced human resource information management technologies and apply them to gain competitive advantage. • Align the HRM system with the vision, mission, and values. • Develop HR policies that send a clear and consistent message about the desired company culture. • With line managers, determine the behaviors needed to implement the firm's strategy and develop policies and practices to support the needed behaviors.	• Take responsibility for continuously developing skills needed to use new technologies. • Focus efforts on contributing to the mission; behave consistently with the values. • Seek to understand the company culture and its implications for your own behavior. • Learn the behaviors needed to implement the firm's strategy; develop the skills needed for strategy implementation; assist other employees with the needed behaviors and skills.

success of an organization depends on its ability to adapt and change over time. Managers, HR professionals, and all other employees contribute to the organization's ability to adapt by monitoring the environment, interpreting events that occur in the environment, and making adjustments as needed, as explained in Chapter 3. Specific examples of actions that members of the HR Triad can take to improve a company's chances of success in the context of continual change are summarized in "The HR Triad: Roles and Responsibilities for Understanding the External and Organizational Environments."

Next, we describe several elements of the external and organizational environments and provide examples of their implications for managing human resources. As you learn more about specific HR activities (e.g., selection, training, compensation), you will also learn more about how a firm's external and organizational environments can influence the effectiveness of specific approaches to managing the workforce.

ECONOMIC GLOBALIZATION

Broadly speaking, globalization is about movement and change: the movement of goods, knowledge, information, people, and services across borders, facilitated and accelerated by changes in economic, financial, social, legal, political, cultural, technological, educational, and workforce conditions that require constant adjustment. Because globalization is such a broad concept, we cannot discuss all of its implications here. Instead we focus primarily on the HR implications of economic globalization.

Depending on your perspective, you may believe that the United States is either too open to foreign competition or not open enough. Regardless of your perspective, clearly the size and wealth of the U.S. market make it a desirable target for foreign competitors. In comparison with other markets of similar size, it has remained relatively open regardless of the political party in power.

An open market means that U.S. domestic firms such as Deere & Company face fierce competition in the United States from foreign firms such as Mahindra and Mahindra of India and Kubota of Japan. Imports of shoes, textiles, electronics, and farm equipment continue to increase. The intense pressure from foreign competitors threatens to put domestic producers out of business. Less than 10 years ago, U.S. companies dominated the office copier business here and abroad; today their share of the domestic market is less than 50%. Toyota has raced ahead of General Motors to become the largest automobile company in the world. We look at some of the implications of economic globalization for managing human resources later in this chapter.

FAST FACT

The economic output of all countries is almost $40 trillion. The share taken by the United States is about one-third of the total—and shrinking.

Competing on Cost versus Competing on Knowledge

Finding it difficult to compete in their established areas of expertise, some U.S. manufacturers are surviving by diversifying their product and service offerings so as to compete in industries where cost pressures are less severe. The 150-year-old Menasha Corporation, which makes containers and packaging, diversified into logistics and information technology to increase profitability. One new product is a label with an embedded computer chip that uses radio frequencies to transmit data about the package being shipped. To develop this new product, Menasha capitalized on its knowledge about logistics, which it had developed to efficiently manage its own operations.

Malden Mills, the textile company that makes Polartec®, is also counting on its knowledge resources. Located in Massachusetts, its factory employees can't compete with the low-cost labor in other countries. Instead, it needs to leverage research capabilities to develop new products and production methods. As these and other factories evolve, low-skilled jobs will be replaced by jobs requiring much higher skills. Employers and employees alike will be required to adapt accordingly.[3]

FAST FACT

Of college students in China, 50% major in engineering compared to 5% in the United States.

Worldwide Operations

Just as many foreign firms are expanding into the United States, many American companies are expanding to serve a rapidly growing global market. Examples of U.S. companies that generate substantial sales in other countries include

UPS, FedEx, EDS, and IBM. At Hewlett-Packard, providing service to a global market meant creating worldwide sales and marketing groups so that multinational clients could meet all their worldwide needs with a single source.[4]

When Harry Newman was the director of employee relations at IBM, he saw clearly how these changes are shaping human resource management practices. "It [globalization] is rapidly accelerating," he observed, "and it means shifting a lot of jobs, opening a lot of locations in places we had never dreamt of before, going where there's low-cost labor, low-cost competition, shifting jobs offshore."

Whether economic globalization is ultimately good or bad for employees is a matter of considerable debate.[5] One thing that no one disputes, however, is that it is changing the way companies manage their human resources. These changes, in turn, will have significant implications for employees, owners and investors, customers, and the community. Exactly how each group of stakeholders is affected will depend on a variety of factors, one of which is how governmental and nongovernmental agencies choose to regulate business activity, as we discuss next.

Regional Trade Zones

Trade relations often are strongest among countries that are geographically close to each other. Besides shared trade, countries within geographic regions often share similar languages, cultures, and environmental concerns. Thus, the development of regional cooperation seems only natural as a strategy for survival amid global competition. By forming regional trade zones, smaller countries can reap the benefits of economies of scale in consumer markets and gain easier access to a large labor pool.

Many attempts at regionalism have not yet fully succeeded—for example, those of Africa and Latin America. Others, such as the Association of Southeast Asian Nations (ASEAN), have been effective in promoting greater cooperation but do not yet have formal, binding treaties or agreements. The North American Free Trade Agreement (NAFTA) and the European Union (EU) are examples of regionalism that have succeeded to the point of creating free trade zones and permanently changing the competitive landscape.

North American Free Trade Agreement. *In 1993, the Canadian Parliament, the U.S. Congress, and the Mexican Congress approved a historic agreement designed to allow for eventual free trade among these three countries: the* **North American Free Trade Agreement (NAFTA).** NAFTA immediately removed all tariffs for some classes of goods (e.g., computers, telecommunications, and aerospace and medical equipment) as well as for all new services. Tariffs for other goods and services were decreased gradually over subsequent years. Now, nearly all tariffs have been eliminated.

Following the passage of NAFTA, dozens of major U.S. manufacturing companies set up factories along the U.S.–Mexico border in plants referred to as **maquiladoras.** In many cases, low-skilled, low-paying jobs moved from the U.S. side of the border to the Mexican side, where wages are substantially lower. Predictably, unemployment levels in U.S. border towns went up, often to levels that were two and three times higher than the national average for the United States. What was perhaps less predictable was that the average wages in the area also rose on both sides of the border. Wages for maquiladora workers remain much lower than they would be in the United States, yet their average wage is five times Mexico's minimum wage.[6]

Wage differences between Canada and the United States have quite different consequences. Typically, employees who hold lower-level jobs are paid more in Canada than in the United States. On the other hand, health care costs are much lower for employers.[7] In contrast, Canadian professionals and managers typically earn one-third less than their U.S. counterparts. Feeling underpaid, some Canadian managers and professionals seek employment across the border. As more Canadian professionals and managers seek employment in the United States, Canadian companies face the possibility of a brain drain.

Nearly a decade after NAFTA took effect, observers disagree about whether the economic benefits of NAFTA outweigh its negative social consequences. Supporters seem to be in the majority, however, and they are in favor of expanding NAFTA to cover the entire Western Hemisphere. As a step in this direction, the **Central American Free Trade Agreement** (**CAFTA**) *establishes free trade among the United States, El Salvador, Guatemala, Honduras, Nicaragua, and Costa Rica.*

European Union. The **European Union** (**EU**) *describes itself as "an institutional framework for the construction of a united Europe."* The EU developed out of a desire to reduce conflict in the region and to prevent another devastating event like World War II. The EU now encompasses more than 27 countries. A primary goal is to create a single market through the removal of trade barriers, such as tariffs.

Prior to the establishment of the euro (€), which most EU countries have adopted, each EU country had its own currency. Through monetary union and the trade agreements that the EU can make with other countries, EU members expect to reduce costs associated with currency conversions and increase economic stability within the region.

The EU also establishes free movement of people across its members' borders, creating a more mobile workforce. Directives of the EU address numerous issues relevant to employment. For example, EU policies provide employees with considerable privacy protection; compared to U.S. regulations, they make it much more difficult for employers to use personal data about employees and to engage in electronic monitoring of employees. Policies of the EU also provide protection from several forms of discrimination, require employers to conduct wage audits to ensure fair pay, and give employees the right to access the wage audit results if they suspect they are victims of pay discrimination. These and a variety of other employment directives seek to create fair and uniform employment conditions throughout EU member countries.[8]

Association of Southeast Asian Nations. The **Association of Southeast Asian Nations** (**ASEAN**), *in its own words, strives to "accelerate the economic growth, social progress, and cultural development in the regions through joint endeavors in the spirit of equality and partnership in order to strengthen the foundation for a prosperous and peaceful community of Southeast Asian nations."* When ASEAN was established in 1967, intrapartner trade among its 10 members accounted for less than 15% of the region's total trade. Since then the percentage has more than tripled.

Historically, labor and employment issues have not been central to ASEAN's concerns, but this seems to be changing. At a meeting in 2007, several specific policy areas related to employment were identified for future discussion, including creating a framework for labor laws and regulations, wages, productivity improvement, and harmony of industrial relations with technological

FAST FACT

Canada was an attractive place for Toyota to locate a new plant because of its national health care system.

and economic integration. As ASEAN develops new policies in these areas, it is calling on its neighbors (e.g., China, Japan, Republic of Korea) for advice and inclusion.

ASEAN also works to promote the integration of employment policies throughout the region through collaboration with the **Asia-Pacific Economic Cooperation (APEC),** *which has 21 member countries, including the United States, Japan, and China (but not India) all bordering on the Pacific Ocean.* Improved and more consistent labor practices are expected to stimulate economic growth, for both ASEAN and APEC member countries.[9]

THE POLITICAL LANDSCAPE

The globalization of business operations is unfolding against a complex and changing political landscape. As government administrations come and go, businesses must constantly analyze the implications of their philosophies and policies. Trade policies and military conflicts can obviously have enormous consequences. Also important among the many aspects of the political landscape are international nongovernmental organizations (NGOs), whose concerns often include labor issues.

Members of nongovernmental organizations generally have no official authority to impose rules of business conduct. The force of their appeals to business is determined by the support they receive in the social realm. Among the most influential of such organizations are the International Labor Organization (ILO), Social Accountability International (SAI), and the World Trade Organization (WTO).

International Labor Organization

The **International Labor Organization (ILO)** *is housed within the United Nations and its mandate is to promote "social justice and internationally recognized human and labor rights."* Representatives within the ILO include workers, employers, and governments. Together, these stakeholders formulate international labor standards regarding the right to organize, collective bargaining, forced labor, equality of opportunity and treatment, safety and health, and an array of other working conditions. The ILO also encourages multinational corporations (MNCs) to be more socially sensitive when they move operations from one country to another.[10]

Social Accountability International

Social Accountability International (SAI) *promotes socially responsible approaches to conducting business and administers a certification process called Social Accountability 8000 (SA 8000).* Companies that wish to be considered for SA 8000 certification volunteer to undergo an intensive audit and to permit additional scheduled and unscheduled inspections. To obtain certification, the company must satisfy standards in the areas of child labor, forced labor, health and safety, collective bargaining, discrimination, disciplinary action, working hours, and compensation. By satisfying these standards, employers also address the broader issues of corporate social responsibility, ethics, and sustainability.[11]

World Trade Organization

With almost 150 member countries, the **World Trade Organization (WTO)** *is the most inclusive international trade organization, and it is the only global* *body able to enforce its decisions through its own court.* Established in 1995, the WTO promotes global harmonization through the agreements it negotiates among member countries. For example, the WTO requires that taxes and tariffs applied to imported goods and services must be applied equally to their domestic equivalents, unless a concession is negotiated and approved. Based on the most-favored-nation principle, businesses operating in WTO countries know that concessions offered to one WTO member country automatically apply to all other WTO members. The WTO also promotes global harmonization of trade policies by establishing cooperative relationships with other international trade and economic organizations, including major regional ones such as NAFTA, the EU, and an expanded version of ASEAN that includes China, India, Japan, and South Korea, and other members of APEC.

INDUSTRY DYNAMICS

Economic and political events often have varying implications for different industries. Changes in national policies regarding tariffs or wages may be viewed as favorable for one industry and unfavorable for another. An overall trend in the direction of increasing productivity at the national level can mask the fact that some industries are enjoying substantial gains while other industries may actually be declining.

Because industry boundaries are fuzzy and unstable, it isn't always easy to answer the question, "What industry are we in?" Nevertheless, companies in the same industry—those that offer similar products and services—typically experience similar patterns of growth and may also share a common industry culture. Generally, companies in the same industry are a firm's most significant competitors, its most likely partners in strategic alliances, and its most likely targets for mergers and acquisitions. In addition, companies in the same industry tend to draw on the same labor pool for people working in the technical areas that define the industry. Thus, common approaches to managing human resources tend to evolve within industries.

Industry Life Cycles

Like people and the organizations they work in, industries have life cycles.[12] Companies in the same industry may experience these life cycles in tandem. An **industry life cycle** *can be thought of as a series of stages that create certain similarities in the issues that industry members face and the solutions they adopt.* When there are many opportunities for growth (e.g., because of strong demand or government deregulation), many firms can thrive within the industry. Eventually, however, competition is likely to intensify, and growth of the industry levels off or even contracts.[13]

Nascent. During the nascent stage of an industry's life cycle, firms are competing to establish a distinctive reputation and to create customer loyalty. Because the industry isn't yet well established, there is a great deal of risk associated with this stage of an industry's life cycle. Simply surviving is the primary concern. A major HR challenge is finding highly qualified employees who accept the high risk of working in an industry that is not yet well established and in which the future opportunities are unclear.

Rapid Growth. Companies that survive the early phase of an industry's creation usually enjoy a period of rapid growth. Now acquiring new talent and retaining employees become more central than before. The competition for talent intensifies among firms in the growing industry, and job-hopping becomes more common as employees seek the best deal. Unless staffing can be maintained at adequate levels, opportunities for growth may be missed.

Mature Stage. In most industries, the rate of growth eventually slows and the industry moves into a mature stage. In this phase, a few large firms all strive to increase efficiency while improving the quality of their products. Employers begin to seek every way possible to reduce labor costs. A common approach is to shrink the size of the firm's core workforce and then hire contingent employees. Often referred to as free agents, contingent employees work on an as-needed basis. This staffing approach can reduce the costs associated with paying for benefits like medical insurance and vacation time. For employees, working on a contingent basis may have some advantages, such as more flexibility to take time off and often better hourly pay. But these advantages may be gained at the cost of decreased health care coverage and lessened employment security. The number of contingent workers has been increasing in recent years, as shown in Exhibit 2.2. Another response to increased pressures on profits is to reduce labor costs by outsourcing work to another company that is willing to do it for a lower cost. Yet another approach is to offshore the work to another country.[14] These alternative approaches to managing human resources are discussed throughout the next several chapters. As you will see, these options for managing the workforce are available to companies in virtually all life cycle stages.[15]

Decline and Renewal. Finally, an industry may go into decline as its products and services become obsolete. During this stage, companies in the industry may go through repeated downsizings before they eventually go out of

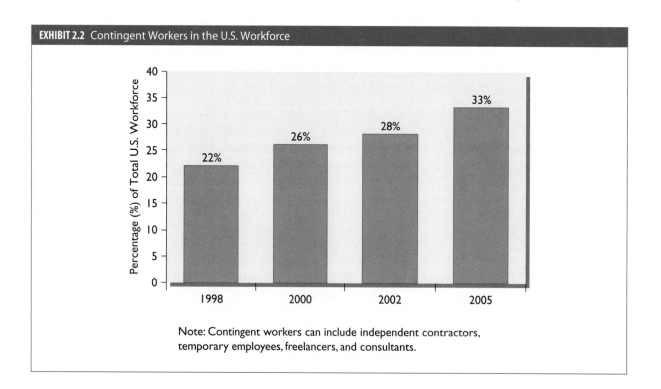

EXHIBIT 2.2 Contingent Workers in the U.S. Workforce

Note: Contingent workers can include independent contractors, temporary employees, freelancers, and consultants.

business. For employees who have spent many years in the industry, being laid off means the beginning of long-term unemployment. If their skills are not easily transferred to other industries, laid-off employees may have to accept lower-paying jobs while they develop the new skills needed in growing industries.

Mergers and Acquisitions

Companies today need to be fast growing, efficient, profitable, flexible, adaptable, future-ready, and dominant in market position. Without these qualities, being competitive in today's global economy is virtually impossible. To compete in this environment, many firms evolve and grow through mergers or acquisitions (M&As).[16]

In the computer and biotech industries, a major objective of M&As is to gain access to the skills and talents of people employed by another company. Any technological or pharmaceutical discovery that a company owns will quickly become outdated. But if the people who created that technology or drug stay and remain energized, they're likely to create new products that will continue to succeed in the marketplace.

HR Issues in M&As. Mergers and acquisitions unfold in many stages. At each stage, success requires effectively managing specific human resource issues.[17] Through experience, some companies have learned that M&As are more successful when human resource issues are addressed early and often. Exhibit 2.3 describes the stages of M&A implementation and the key HR issues to be addressed at each stage, along with the related HR activities.[18]

EXHIBIT 2.3 Key HR Issues and Activities in the Implementation of Mergers and Acquisitions

HR Issues	Key HR Activities
Stage 1—Precombination	
• Identify reasons for the M&A • Form M&A team/leader • Search for potential partners • Select a partner • Plan for managing the process • Plan to learn from the process	• Participate in preselection assessment of target firm • Assist in conducting thorough due diligence assessment • Participate in planning for combination • Assist in developing HR practices that support rapid learning and knowledge transfer
Stage 2—Combination	
• Select the integration manager(s) • Design/implement transition teams • Create the new structure/strategies/leadership • Retain key employees • Manage the change process • Communicate and involve stakeholders • Develop new policies and practices	• Assist in recruiting and selecting integration manager(s) • Assist with transition team design and staffing • Develop retention strategies and communicate to top talent • Assist in deciding who goes • Facilitate establishment of a new culture • Provide assistance to ensure implementation of HR policies and practices
Stage 3—Solidification and Assessment	
• Solidify leadership and staffing • Assess the new strategies and structures • Assess the new culture • Assess the concerns of stakeholders • Revise as needed • Learn from the process	• Participate in establishing criteria and procedures for assessing staff effectiveness • Monitor the new culture and recommend approaches to strengthen it • Participate in stakeholder satisfaction • Assist in developing and implementing plans for continuous adjustment and learning

Companies that have made many acquisitions usually recognize the complexity of M&A implementation. To manage the process, they may have sophisticated procedures designed to minimize the problems that can arise, such as developing extensive checklists of things to look for in managing mergers or acquisitions.

Reasons for M&A Failures. As the importance of and need for mergers and acquisitions grows, and as the base of experience expands, it may seem reasonable to assume that these types of combinations are more likely to succeed than fail. In fact, the opposite is true. Most M&As in the United States fail to achieve their financial objectives, as measured by share value, return on investment, and profitability. In Europe, a study of deals valued at $500 million or more showed that 50% destroyed shareholder value, 30% had minimal impact, and only 17% created shareholder returns.[19]

Mergers and acquisitions fail for a variety of reasons. Among the reasons most often cited are culture clashes, incompatibility, and loss of key talent—all human resource issues.[20] Plans that looked logical on paper often fall apart when managers try to implement them. People, it seems, get in the way. Clashes between company cultures can be so severe that the financial benefits of a merger can't be realized. Thus many companies thinking about a merger or acquisition seek to assess the cultures of all the companies involved to see if there is a fit.[21]

5
LEARNING GOAL

LABOR MARKETS

Just as firms must compete for customers, so must they compete for employees. Organizations can seek employees in the domestic labor market only, or they can broaden their horizons to include the global labor market.[22]

U.S. Labor Market

It is believed that the U.S. labor market will experience dramatic changes over the next 20 years. The anticipated changes include slowed growth, a decrease in skills availability, greater competition for employees, and an increased dependence on immigrants.

Slow Growth. With a population of more than 305 million today, projections indicate that the U.S. population will continue to grow, reaching 383 million by 2050. Despite this change, the rate of growth in the working population (typically people 18 and 65 years old)—the domestic labor market—is expected to slow each year between now and 2020.[23] The biggest reason for the slowing growth in the size of the workforce is the impending retirement of Baby Boomers (those born between 1946 and 1964). Another reason is that much of the growth during the last 30 years was due to the influx of women. Now that so many women are already working, their entry into the workforce is no longer a source of labor market growth. Thus, by 2010, the Bureau of Labor Statistics (BLS) predicts a shortfall of 3 million workers. Because this topic is so important, it is described in more detail at the end of this chapter under Current Issues.

Skills Shortage. The slow growth of the labor market means that in many industries employers cannot find workers with the needed skills. After installing millions of dollars worth of computers in its Burlington, Vermont factories,

EXHIBIT 2.4 Fastest-Growing Occupations Requiring a Bachelor's or Higher Degree for the Next 10 Years	
Network systems and data communications analysts	Medical and health services managers
Physician's assistants	Elementary school teachers, except special education
Computer software engineers, applications	Accountants and auditors
Computer software engineers, systems software	Computer systems analysts
Network and computer systems administrators	Secondary school teachers, except special and vocational education
Education administrators, preschool and child care center/program	General and operations managers
Computer and information system managers	Management analysts
Training and development managers	Financial managers
Actuaries	Sales managers

the IBM Corporation discovered that it had to teach high school algebra to thousands of workers before they could use the equipment. Labor shortages are severe for so-called new economy and high-tech jobs.[24] Projections indicate that some of the fastest job growth during the next 10 years will be in computer-related jobs, as shown in Exhibit 2.4. Given that enrollments in college science and engineering programs have been dropping steadily during the past two decades, it is clear that the people needed to fill these jobs will not come from the U.S. workforce alone.[25]

The construction industry provides another example of the looming skills shortages that can be expected during the next decade. A recent study by the Construction Industry Institute revealed that there are too few project engineers available in the industry's talent pipeline, given the projected number of engineers who are likely to be retiring in the near future. For the industry, the talent shortage may limit the level of possible growth. For individual firms, the rapid retirement of experienced engineers, combined with too few replacements, may mean that valuable knowledge gained through years of experience is lost.

The Construction Industry Institute's research has several implications for managing human resources in that industry. One implication is that employers in the industry should be proactive in recruiting students into the field, for example, by partnering with local universities. Another implication suggested by the Institute is that the demographics of this workforce (which is now predominantly male and mostly Caucasian) are likely to change. So the industry should learn to manage diversity effectively. A third predictable implication of the talent shortage is that compensation costs will increase, putting more pressure on firms to find new ways to maintain their current levels of profitability.[26]

Competition. When people and skills are in short supply, competition among employers heats up as they seek to attract and retain the human resources they need. In Des Moines, Iowa, 68% of children under six years of age have no stay-at-home parent. For the Principal Financial Group, Des Moines' largest employer, this means that there is no untapped labor pool to draw on as the firm grows. According to the firm's vice president of human resources, "The goal then becomes to make jobs attractive enough to keep those spouses in the workforce and keep our turnover as low as possible." Even during a recent recession, this was a key concern for Principal Financial. And how does the

> *" The U.S. is now No. 3 in the world and quickly falling farther behind No. 1 [India] and No. 2 [China] in terms of computer science graduates. "*
>
> Steven A. Balmer
> Chief Executive Officer
> Microsoft

company make itself attractive? Among the benefits they offer are these:

- Free financial counseling.
- Free parking (which is quite valuable in a downtown location).
- Lactation centers for new mothers.
- A Muslim prayer room.
- Subsidized WeightWatchers® programs.
- On-site childbirth classes.
- Elevated skyways that connect the building to a nearby school, so employees can easily visit it during the workday.
- Daddy Boot Camp (where dads-to-be learn to care for their newborns).
- A state-of-the-art athletic facility, which offers tai chi, Pilates, spinning, volleyball, and more![27]

> " At the height of the conflict [in Yugoslavia], we had fund-raising going on on one floor of the factory, and clothing and food collection going on on another floor for the opposite sides, and we still made pianos every day. "
>
> *Michael A. Anesta*
> *Personnel Director*
> *Steinway & Sons*

Immigrants. In recent years, foreign-born workers have constituted nearly half of the net labor force increase in the United States. These workers are less likely to be employed in professional specialty occupations and are overrepresented in occupations that do not require a high school education.[28]

In New York City, immigrants from numerous countries work together to produce pianos for Steinway & Sons. Steinway pianos are still crafted mostly by hand using traditional methods. As U.S. immigration patterns have changed, so have the faces of Steinway's employees. For generations after it was founded in 1853, Steinway hired mostly immigrants from Germany, Austria, Italy, and Ireland. By the 1980s, the immigrants they hired were mostly from Haiti and the Dominican Republic. During the 1990s, they began hiring refugees from the war in Yugoslavia—from Croatia, Serbia, and Bosnia. This practice continues to this day. While their relatives at home fought against each other in war, these immigrants worked side by side making Steinways.[29]

Global Labor Market

FAST FACT

The world's labor supply has increased by 1.5 billion in the last 10 years. More than 1 billion people are expected to enter the labor force in the next 10 years.

Currently there are more than 6.5 billion people on this planet. While the labor force in Europe and Japan will continue to decline, it will continue to expand in Africa, Latin America, North America, and Asia. Projections indicate that the labor force in developing nations alone will expand by about 700 million people by the year 2010. Asia's share of the global labor market will reach 65% in 2025, up from 57% in 1990.[30]

When employers make decisions about where to place their operations and where to locate their workers, they begin by considering where people live, but they also consider many other factors, including costs, skills, and health issues.

Labor Costs. It is well-known that the lower cost of labor in other counties is one reason that U.S. employees have moved some operations offshore. When IBM disclosed that it was shifting U.S. jobs overseas, the influence of labor costs was apparent: In the United States, it cost $56.00 per hour to employ a programmer with three to five years of experience. In China, it costs only $12.60 an hour. (Both figures include salary and benefits.)[31] More details about the relative cost of labor in several counties can be seen in Exhibit 2.5.[32]

Where the Skills Are. The high cost of U.S. labor is certainly one reason many U.S. jobs have been relocated to other countries. But, as some people are surprised to learn, the lack of skilled labor in the domestic labor market is another factor.

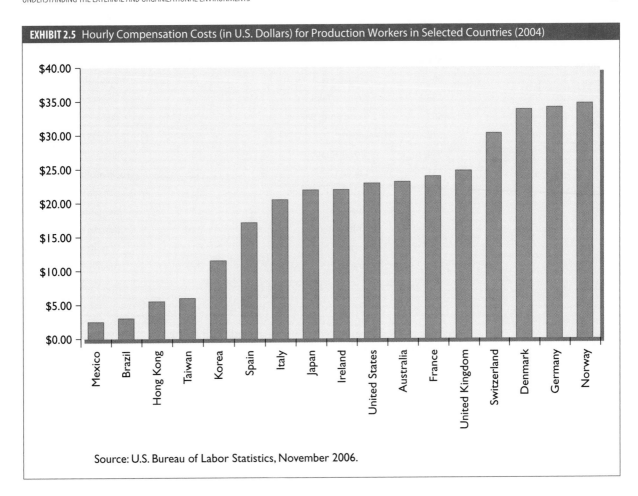

EXHIBIT 2.5 Hourly Compensation Costs (in U.S. Dollars) for Production Workers in Selected Countries (2004)

Source: U.S. Bureau of Labor Statistics, November 2006.

Consider the data shown in Exhibit 2.6, which shows the math and science scores of eighth graders in several countries.[33] Increasingly, well educated, entry-level workers can be found in developing countries. Furthermore, educational gains are being made more rapidly in developing countries. In 1970, fewer than 25% of all college students were in developing countries; today the figure has risen to about 50%.

For U.S. companies that require high skill levels in areas such as science and engineering, adopting a global approach is no longer questioned. India is a particularly desirable labor market for U.S. employers due to the prevalence of English language and various technical skills. The successes experienced by companies like GE and American Express have convinced other companies that India is an excellent location for information technology (IT)–enabled jobs. When planning for their staffing needs, employers must weigh carefully the costs and benefits of employing labor in a variety of countries to fill jobs as diverse as customer service, medical transcription, finance and accounting services, and media publications.

Health Issues. According to a report by the United Nations, more people have now died from HIV/AIDS than from any of the world's other large catastrophes, including the bubonic plague and a more recent influenza epidemic, which both killed about 20 million people. In some African countries (including South Africa, Zimbabwe, and Zambia), one in five working-age adults is infected with HIV. Epidemiologists warn that India and China may be on the verge of similar

FAST FACT

Today, there are 33 million educated professionals in the developing nations, and their number is growing by 5% per year, compared to only 1% per year in the developed nations.

FAST FACT

In Zambia, an estimated 66% of manager mortality is attributable to HIV/AIDS.

EXHIBIT 2.6 A Sampling of Test Scores for Eighth Graders Around the World

Math		Science	
604	Singapore	569	Chinese Taipei
585	Chinese Taipei	568	Singapore
582	Hong Kong SAR	550	Japan
579	Japan	540	Australia
534	Slovak Republic	538	England
531	Canada	535	Slovak Republic
526	Russian Federation	533	Canada
525	Australia	530	Hong Kong SAR
502	United States	529	Russian Federation
496	England	515	United States
466	Israel	468	Israel

disease rates. For employers who are evaluating whether to rely on these populations as part of their future workforce, the cost of AIDS may outweigh any other benefits. The costs to employers of sick employees include

- Medical care for affected employees.
- Benefits payments to employees and their families.
- Higher recruitment and training costs due to the loss of severely ill and dying workers.
- Higher insurance premiums throughout the region.
- Accidents due to ill workers and inexperienced replacements.
- Increased litigation over benefits and other issues.
- Lower productivity due to workers who are ill while at work, absenteeism, unpredictable job vacancies, and loss of experienced workers.
- Depressed morale.
- Costs associated with employer-sponsored prevention programs.
- More management time devoted to dealing with health issues.[34]

Unless this epidemic is brought under control, it threatens to choke economic development in regions of the world that would otherwise be expected to grow rapidly during the twenty-first century. The role to be played by employers in the region is now under debate, but it is likely that a consensus will gradually be reached that employers must adopt a code of behavior to ensure humane and economically sustainable HR practices.[35] HIV/AIDS is discussed again in Chapter 13, which focuses on safety and health.

LEARNING GOAL 6

COUNTRY CULTURES

Entire volumes have been devoted to describing differences in country cultures and the space here isn't in any way sufficient to summarize this work. Nevertheless, it is important to recognize that managing in a global environment requires developing new approaches to managing people.[36]

MANAGING GLOBALIZATION
Mercedes-Benz Sets Up in Alabama

Mercedes-Benz is one of the world's most widely recognized brands. It stands for quality and luxury. Some people are surprised to learn that Mercedes-Benz manufactures some of its automobiles in Vance, Alabama. That's where Mercedes-Benz U.S. International (MBUSI) is located, and it's where the award-winning M-Class SUV was born. A team of executives and workers who came from three countries—Germany, the United States, and Japan—created the facility. Each country has its own approach to designing and building automobiles.

In Germany, engineers are highly trained experts who develop their skills by working as apprentices to a meister (a master in the profession). Workers accept the authority of meisters and don't expect to be treated as their equals. Once they learn the skills they need, they expect to carry out their tasks without close supervision. This is a sign that they are respected and can be trusted to do a good job. Strong norms exist concerning the importance of producing automobiles of superior quality.

In traditional U.S. automobile plants, managers control workers through the division of labor and narrow spans of control. Henry's Ford's assembly line approach still dominates many production plants. At the Jeep plant in Ohio, relationships between managers and subordinates are relatively informal. People are quite direct in saying what they think. Americans tend to be driven to get things done, and they are more willing to begin production before working through every problem.

In Japan, strong norms concerning the importance of quality are similar to those in Germany. However, quality is achieved using a system of team-based production and continuous improvement. Employees are generalists rather than specialists and it is important to reach consensus. At MBUSI, elements of all three cultures have been blended together. How did they do it?

The creation of MBUSI began with U.S. executives spending 18 months in Germany, where they worked with German engineers to design the plant. When the Vance plant was built, German engineers spent two years there helping to train the Americans. Following the Japanese model, multidisciplinary teams are used to manage the operation. Each team is autonomous and self-managing. They are held accountable for meeting quality standards, controlling costs, and meeting production schedules. Relationships between managers and their subordinates are egalitarian and open. Apparently the new hybrid organizational culture is a success. Demand for the M-Class SUV was so robust that the company has created the second generation M-Class, and added the R-Class and the GL-Class!

Cultural differences have many far-reaching consequences for managing organizations. As described in the feature "Managing Globalization: Mercedes-Benz Sets Up in Alabama," cultural differences often show up in how companies are managed.[37] Cultural differences in how work is designed, employees' expectations for how they will be treated, and even management styles must all be bridged as a company expands beyond its borders.

Differences among country cultures can be significant even when comparing cultures that we may think of as similar (e.g., because they share the same language). For example, compared with those in the United States, companies in Australia place much less emphasis on merit, and they tend to adopt a more top-down approach with a command-and-control management style.[38] In Japan, the country culture and values go hand in hand with HR practices that reflect a long-term perspective. Employees typically expect to stay at the same firm for many years. Even in difficult economic times, Japanese firms are less likely to use large-scale layoffs as a means of reducing costs. Employees, in turn, often feel more loyalty toward their employers.[39] Managers working in a culture that they don't understand are likely to make poor decisions about how to staff their organizations and motivate employees.[40]

Dimensions of Country Cultures

Geert Hofstede developed the best-known framework for comparing and contrasting country cultures, based on research conducted at IBM several decades ago. Hofstede's work continues to serve as a foundation for describing cultural differences, although in recent years more complex frameworks have been developed. We use results from the Global Leadership and Organizational Behavior Effectiveness (GLOBE) research project to describe cultural differences. The GLOBE is a team of 150 researchers who have collected data on cultural values from 18,000 managers in 62 countries. The GLOBE results indicate that cultural comparisons are best described using the dimensions

---

EXHIBIT 2.7 Dimensions for Comparing National Cultures

Cultural Dimension	Sample Countries	Sample Countries
Behaviors That Society Encourages and Rewards	**Low-Scoring Countries or Regions**	**High-Scoring Countries or Regions**
Assertiveness Toughness, confrontation, competitiveness (vs. modesty, tenderness)	Sweden Switzerland Kuwait	Spain United States Greece
Future Orientation Planning, investing in future, delaying gratification	Russia Argentina Poland	Netherlands Switzerland Singapore
Gender Differentiation Males and females expected to behave differently and be treated differently (vs. accepting gender neutral behavior)	Hungary Poland Slovenia	South Korea Egypt Morocco
Uncertainty Avoidance Orderliness, consistency, following formal procedures and laws	Russia Hungary Bolivia	Germany Sweden Switzerland
Power Distance Recognizing and showing respect for people and groups with greater authority, prestige, status, material possessions than oneself	Denmark Netherlands South African (blacks)	Thailand Argentina Morocco
Institutional Collectivism Participating in legislative, economic, and political processes (vs. personal autonomy). Behaviors that support the collective good are encouraged through formal institutions, taxes, etc.	Greece Hungary Germany	Japan South Korea Sweden
In-Group Collectivism Taking pride in one's membership in smaller groups such as family, circle of close friends, employer	Denmark Sweden New Zealand	China India Iran
Performance Orientation Performance improvements and excellence, acceptance of feedback	Russia Argentina Greece	New Zealand Hong Kong Singapore
Humane Orientation Being fair, generous, altruistic, kind toward others	Germany Spain France	Malaysia Ireland Philippines

shown in Exhibit 2.7. Examples of countries that are high and low on each dimension are also shown in Exhibit 2.7.[41]

Consequences of Country Cultures

Associated with differences in country cultures are differences in the HR policies that employers are likely to adopt.[42] As one example, U.S. employers make much more use of incentive pay compared to employers in many European countries. Of course, culture also shapes how employees relate to work. Compared to many other cultures, Americans tend to view work as more central to their lives and they are more willing to make personal sacrifices to perform well on the job.[43]

U.S. employers cannot simply impose their domestic HR practices on employees around the world and expect them to be effective. For example, one study found that workers in the United States, Mexico, and Poland responded well to being empowered to make work-related decisions, but employees in India responded negatively to empowerment. On the other hand, employees in all of these countries responded well to HR policies that supported continuous improvement.[44] Using data from 18 countries, another study showed that European and Asian work units had better financial performance when HR policies in the units were congruent with the country culture.[45] The key in a global environment is finding a balance that respects local differences while enabling global success.

TECHNOLOGIES

Technology *refers to the process of making and using tools and equipment plus the knowledge used in this process.* Technology has been evolving for thousands of years. In early civilization, the available technology was limited to simple tools—hammers, levels, pulleys, shovels, picks—and the related knowledge about how to use them.

The rate of technological evolution greatly accelerated after reliable technology was created for generating power. The steam engine, introduced in the late 1700s, was a revolutionary technology. By powering ships and trains, it greatly expanded the speed and reach of trade and commerce. By powering machines such as the "spinning jenny," it lowered production costs, lowered prices, and in doing so expanded markets for the goods produced. The expanding demand required more workers, more machines, and a larger scale of production, and soon another fundamentally new technology evolved: the factory.

Factories and Mass Production Technologies

With the factory system came myriad new challenges related to managing human resources. The first challenge was recruiting talent. People had to be convinced to leave their farms or small workshops and move near the factory, usually in a large city and often far away. Once recruited to the factory, people had to be convinced to accept the authority of factory owners and their agents, and they had to accept standardized procedures for doing their work. Workers who had enjoyed personal autonomy and who had felt pride in their work were now asked to accept work that was routine and depersonalized. Factory owners, in turn, had to address the issue of skills. Most laborers had little education. They were unable to read instruction sheets or manuals. They knew little about planning large-scale production processes

FAST FACT

Years it took for each new technology to reach an audience of 50 million people:

Telephone 74 years

Television 13 years

World Wide Web 4 years

or managing other workers. Their skills simply didn't match those needed in the factory.[46]

Computer Technologies

More recently, computers have revolutionized how people work and how they are managed. Employees who work in factories have robots as coworkers. At the New Balance athletic shoe factory in Maine, skilled employees use sophisticated computer technology to produce shoes similar to those that most competitors are producing overseas using low-tech workers. A computer runs 20 sewing machine heads at once. A camera-guided automated stitcher sews six times faster than a person. A shoe that takes three hours to produce in China can be made in 24 minutes in Maine. Finding workers to operate their high-tech factories is just one of the challenges New Balance faces. Another is keeping labor costs at the factory low enough to make it competitive with the alternative means of production—low-wage workers in China who use traditional sewing equipment. By managing their human resources effectively, New Balance can continue operating in Maine to produce shoes for its American market.[47]

For U.S. workers who don't work in factories, information technology (IT) is more relevant to their daily lives than robotics. As customers, we often must negotiate an electronic menu before speaking with a person. When we do speak with a customer service employee, it is likely to be someone working in a call center, and the call center might be located anywhere in the world. The same technologies make it possible for accountants in India to process U.S. tax returns for Ernst & Young. Technology also makes it possible for physicians around the country to simultaneously view an x-ray and discuss its implications. In Bangalore, India, radiologists now analyze computer tomography (CT) scans and chest x-rays for American physicians. By making such innovations possible, IT promises to improve patient care and customer service, at the same time reducing their costs.[48]

Sophisticated technologies are central to implementing Yellow Freight's customer-focused strategy. Customers—who are located throughout the United States, Canada, Mexico, and Puerto Rico—can place their orders online, track shipments, and review their accounts. Dockworkers and drivers can communicate instantly with each other and easily access schedule and delivery information using wireless, mobile data terminals. A sophisticated information system also allows sales representatives to instantly learn about a customer's company, the type of loading dock it has, and who needs to sign for deliveries, among other things. Of course, changing to this high-tech approach has required tremendous change on the part of managers and employees. Managers had to learn to support a more empowered workforce. Employees had to learn to use the new technologies and completely change the way they work with customers. The company's success requires that everyone understands how the business works. Their weekly company newsletter provides honest assessments of how Yellow is performing and explains important trends in the industry.[49]

Virtual Workforce

Perhaps the most dramatic consequence of the IT revolution is that it makes it possible for an organization to employ a virtual workforce, with employees located all over the world. Members of the **virtual workforce** *perform their jobs anywhere and anytime, often on an as-needed basis.* By eliminating the need for office space for employees who telecommute, IBM reduced its real estate expenses by about 50% per office site. Hewlett-Packard reported that it doubled revenue per salesperson after adopting virtual work arrangements.[50]

Of course, the benefits of a virtual workforce are not won without overcoming significant challenges. Employees working under such arrangements may feel isolated and detached from their employer. If their actions are closely monitored electronically, their morale may suffer. If they have not been properly trained in the use of IT, their insensitive electronic interactions with others may create misunderstandings or resentment among coworkers or even clients. As discussed in subsequent chapters, a variety of human resource activities can be used to address these challenges and enable organizations and their employees alike to enjoy the benefits of a virtual workforce.

Human Resource Information Management

Just as technology influences jobs and the design of organizations, it influences how employers manage their human resources. Virtually all employers post job openings on the Internet, and almost all large employers accept electronic applications. Many companies conduct employee surveys using the Internet, and some companies require their employees to use a Web site to manage their benefits packages.

When computer technologies are used to gather, analyze, and distribute information about job applicants and employees, the resulting system is referred to as a **human resource information management (HRIM)** system (also referred to as HRIS, for human resource information system). Low-level HRIM systems merely allow employees to access general information (e.g., policies, procedures, company events) using a company intranet. A sophisticated HRIM architecture allows employees and managers to enter performance data, display and analyze it for trends over time, and use the data as input for both the employee's personal development plan and the organization's longer-term workforce and succession planning.

HRIM systems make it easy to communicate a company's values and strategy to all employees, regardless of their location. They also make it easy for firms to design and implement HR policies and practices that are common across different cultures. Dow's HRIM system facilitates worldwide coordination among its employees. Managers working from any workstation in the company can get information about any employee. Conversely, employees around the world can access

- Information about the performance expectations and competencies required for all types of jobs in the company.
- Personal development plans and tools for managing their own development.
- Descriptions of job openings and employment opportunities everywhere in the company.
- Compensation information—including benefits—for all jobs on a country-by-country basis.

At Dow, employees are expected to take a proactive approach to managing their careers. If they are interested in possibly changing jobs, they can keep informed of the jobs that become available in a typical year. If they are considering an international move, they can study the compensation and benefits likely to be available to them before deciding which country to target and prepare themselves accordingly. Managers, in turn, serve as coaches and mentors to employees, while also being proactive in identifying potential internal hires for open positions.

▲8
LEARNING GOAL

" We have a killer culture. People work hard and play hard. They are here because they want to change the world. "

Jerry Yang
Cofounder and Chief
Yahoo!

COMPANY CULTURE

A **company culture** *is the unique pattern of shared assumptions, values, and norms that shape the socialization activities, language, symbols, and ceremonies of people in the organization.* Assumptions, values, and norms form the base of a culture, but they can't be observed directly. They can only be inferred from a culture's more visible elements: its socialization activities, language, symbols, and ceremonies.[51]

Like personality, a company's culture affects in predictable ways how people behave when no one is telling them what to do. As the best CEOs understand, human resource policies and practices contribute to the development of a strong company culture when they are aligned with and support a firm's strategic direction. This is illustrated in the feature, "Managing with Metrics: You Change What You Measure."[52]

Leadership

Effective leadership ensures that people are generally working to achieve the same results. By formulating a vision, mission, and values, company leaders

---

MANAGING WITH METRICS
You Change What You Measure

Alberto-Culver Company may be best-known for its VO5 hair care products, but the company also manufactures and markets many other personal care, specialty grocery, and household products worldwide. When Carol Lavin Bernick and her husband took over the leadership roles in the company founded by her parents, the company needed a makeover. To help show the urgency of the situation, she used hard financial data. Sales were flat, margins were slipping, and the competitive environment was getting tougher due to the emergence of power retailers (such as Wal-Mart). Bernick believed the best way to change the company's performance was to change its culture.

Like other companies, most Alberto-Culver employees understood little about how the company made money or how their job performance affected sales and profits. To change this, the company named 70 growth development leaders (GDLs) and charged them with creating cultural change. Each GDL mentors about a dozen people. As mentors, GDLs help employees understand how their work is related to achieving company goals, participate in performance reviews, and make sure employees understand and

take advantage of the company's family-friendly benefits. The GDLs also meet with the CEO every six weeks or so. They bring their people's questions to the meeting and work with the top management team to develop solutions. Four years after the GDLs were established, the company introduced an award to recognize those who were most successful, again based on financial indicators of success. A year later, two other change initiatives were introduced: A formal statement of the company's cultural values was published, and new employee performance measures were developed, again based on objective evidence of success.

To assess whether the changes are working, Bernick examines data such as sales and pretax profits. The company also conducts annual employee surveys to assess its progress in changing the corporate culture. "I'm a firm believer that you change what you measure," says Carol Lavin Bernick, chairperson of the board of directors. Her analyses have convinced her that the cultural changes made in the past several years are responsible for the large increases in sales and pretax profits that have accumulated during that time, and she has the metrics to prove it!

convey answers to questions such as, "Where are we going?" and "Why are we going there?" Together, an organization's vision, mission, and values create a framework that points people in one direction. They state the firm's aspirations for what it would like to be, though few organizations fully live up to these expectations.

Leaders also shape the culture by how they treat employees. At The Container Store, the founders support the culture by sending handwritten notes to employees and personally offering their praise for work that is well done.

Human resource professionals help organizations build strong cultures by developing HR practices to ensure that everyone behaves in ways that are consistent with the corporate vision, mission, and values. In their first year on the job, full-time employees at The Container Store attend more than 200 hours of training to learn about the company's philosophy, culture, and products. At Adobe Systems in San Jose, California, the company culture is preserved by recruiting and selecting new hires who share the same values. Adobe also weaves the values into the company's reward and recognition programs. Each year, six Adobe employees receive the Founders Award, to honor them for upholding the company's core values of integrity, respect, innovation, leadership, operational excellence, customer focus, and community involvement.[53]

> " There's a family mentality here as opposed to just being another member. That trickles down from the top. He [the CEO] knows everyone's name and says 'hi' everyday when I see him during morning workouts at the gym. "
>
> *Andrew Smith*
> *Accountant*
> *Analytic Graphics, Inc.*

Vision

A **vision** *is top management's view of the kind of company it is trying to create. It can be thought of as a best-case scenario of where the company will be in the future.*[54] At the 54,000-employee Weyerhaeuser lumber and paper company, the vision is "to be the Best Forest Products Company in the World and a Global Leader Among All Industries." At American Express, the vision is "to become the world's most respected service brand." Southwest Airlines' vision is "to be the airline of choice." The vision of The Ritz-Carlton states, "We want to be the world's No. 1 hospitality provider." The success of each company in pursuit of its vision rests in part on employees: For Southwest to be the airline of choice, employees (i.e., associates) have to be treated well enough to satisfy their customers.

Mission

A **mission statement** *defines a company's business and provides a clear view of what the company is trying to accomplish.* A mission statement is more specific than the vision. It provides more guidance for developing plans that can be implemented to fulfill the vision. Often the mission statement addresses issues that more directly reflect the interests of the organization's different stakeholders, including employees. For Merck Pharmaceuticals, the mission is to

- Provide society with superior products and services—innovations that improve the quality of life and satisfy customer needs.
- Provide employees with meaningful work and advancement opportunities.
- Provide investors with a superior rate of return.

Bill Gates, founder and chair of Microsoft, believes a company's mission is ultimately what inspires employees to do their best at work. According to Gates, "When people come to work, it's important that they be connected to a dream." When Gates founded Microsoft, the mission was, "A computer on every desk in every home." By 2003, that mission had been largely accomplished—at least

FAST FACT

The mission of the Bill & Melinda Gates Foundation is to increase opportunity and equity for those most in need.

EXHIBIT 2.8 Excerpts of the Core Values in the Principles of Global Citizenship at Deere & Company

Core Values
Our efforts are guided by our core values—integrity, quality, commitment, and innovation.

Corporate Governance
Review our governance guidelines, executive biographies, and committee charters.

Environment, Health, & Safety
Every day, we strive to safeguard our employees, customers, and the environment.

Community Involvement
We strive to improve the quality of life in the communities where we live and work.

Diversity/Inclusion
We support and encourage diversity and inclusion throughout our global operations.

---

in developed countries. So the company developed a new mission: "To enable people and businesses throughout the world to realize their full potential."[55]

Values

> *In this new economic order, at a time when the very concept of globalization is under scrutiny, it is only through responsible action that positive outcomes will be achieved.*
>
> Lea Soupata
> Senior Vice President of
> Human Resources
> UPS

Values *are the strong enduring beliefs and tenets that the company holds dear and that help to define the company and differentiate it from other companies.* Value statements have a direct impact on managing human resources because they state how employees are expected to behave—toward each other, toward customers, toward suppliers, and toward the community. The core values at Deere & Company include integrity, quality, commitment, and innovation. Reflecting the global nature of its business, these values are incorporated into a broader concept called global citizenship. The principles of its global citizenship are shown in Exhibit 2.8.[56]

At UPS, which is known as the Brown company, sustainable development is an important value that does not mean just protecting the physical environment. It also means being a socially responsible partner with local communities all around the world. And it means making decisions with a long-term view—for the next quarter century instead of the next quarter. How does this value influence the company's approach to managing human resources? Actually, it has many consequences, of which these are just a few:

- Having citizens of the local community run the Brown company in each country, instead of using expatriates to run the local businesses.
- Investing about $300 million annually in global training programs.
- Including the senior vice president for human resources as a member of the board of directors.[57]

Timberland also values its community partnerships. Planning analyst Anthony Gow knows that Timberland's actions are consistent with their values. As a way of contributing, Timberland allows employees to take off up to 40 hours of paid leave for community service. Gow was granted a six-month sabbatical to help a local food pantry.[58]

Company Subcultures

A **company subculture** *exists when assumptions, values, and norms are shared by some—but not all—organizational members.* It's not unusual to find several subcultures within a single organization.

Company subcultures occur for a variety of reasons. Organizational subcultures are common in international firms, where country and company cultures

EXHIBIT 2.9 Generations Present in the U.S. Workforce

When They Were Born	Label Used	Characteristics
1945 or before	Traditionalists	Prize loyalty. Prefer top-down management approach and information provided on a need-to-know basis.
1946–1964	Baby Boomers	Optimistic and idealistic. Achieve success by challenging authority and creating open lines of communication.
1965–1977	Generation X	More skeptical than other generations. Often distrust institutions and prize individualism. Value work-life balance.
1978–1989	Generation Y	Approach work with realization that they will change employers many times and may also change the type of work they do.
1990–2000	Internet Generation	Just entering the workforce with the most early-life exposure to interactive video games and the Internet.
2001–2020	New Silent Generation	Comfortable with activities that allow for deeply personal interactions over the Internet.

combine to create distinct subcultures. After a merger or acquisition, subcultures are likely to exist as the two established organizations come together to form a new one. Subcultures may also emerge among employees working in different divisions or occupations, and among employees from different demographic groups, as Exhibit 2.9 illustrates.[59] People of different ages share many experiences and values. Of course, not all members of each generation are exactly alike. Nevertheless, age-based subcultures are found in many societies around the world.

Managers have many different views about whether subcultures are "good" or "bad" for business. Sometimes organizational subcultures coexist peacefully within an overall organizational culture; at other times subcultures are a major source of continuing conflict.[60]

Benefits. Some managers believe that the presence of distinct subcultures can be beneficial. Former Disney CEO Michael Eisner expressed a similar view: "We believe in diversity because the more diverse you are as an organization, the more diverse are the opinions that get expressed. That will make us more creative."[61] At Ford Motor Company, the rationale for valuing the perspectives present in different subcultures focuses on customers. The design and marketing teams for Ford's minivan, which is bought mostly by women, included many women.

Challenges. The presence of subcultures sometimes creates problems for employees and employers. After an acquisition, employees in the acquired firm may now be expected to give up the culture of their old company and adopt the culture of the acquiring company. Suddenly, the old ways of doing things are unacceptable. Often, managers in the acquired firm feel that their level of status and influence has been reduced.

Like employees of an acquired firm, members of demographic minority groups often feel that their subculture is not valued as highly as the subculture of the majority group. Consider the experience of Eula Adams, who was the first African American to become a partner at Touche (which is now Deloitte). When Adams began working at Touche in the 1970s, none of the 800 partners was African American. He remembers "the loneliness, especially in the early days."[62] Despite the early challenges, Adams was very successful and eventually became a partner in the firm. *Fortune* magazine included him on its list of "The Most Powerful Black Executives in America."

In general, research shows that employees who are part of a minority subculture often perceive the existence of a glass ceiling that limits their career opportunities.[63] Even employees who work for companies that have been recognized as among America's Best Companies for Minorities often feel dominated and undervalued by members of the majority.[64] Worries about possible cultural clashes also play a role in the decisions gay and lesbian employees make about whether to be open about their sexual orientation.[65]

To reduce the negative consequences of clashes between subcultures, many organizations are in the process of transforming themselves into multicultural organizations. A **multicultural organization** *has a workforce representing the full mix of cultures found in the population at large, along with a commitment to utilize fully these human resources.* Multicultural organizations strive to permit many subcultures, including those represented by employees around the world, to coexist while ensuring that no one subculture dominates the others.

LEARNING GOAL

BUSINESS STRATEGIES

A **business strategy** *is a set of integrated and coordinated commitments and actions intended to achieve stated business goals.* Like its vision, mission, and values, a firm's business strategy serves as a guide for action, but it is much more closely linked to the nature of the company's business.[66] When well chosen business strategies are effectively implemented, they generate profits and improve the firm's competitiveness.

Business strategies influence the types of employees who must be recruited to work at the company, the behaviors needed from those employees, the conditions in which employees are expected to work, and so on. At ExxonMobil and many other companies, managers articulate the implications of their strategy using a strategy map. A **strategy map** *shows the cause-and-effect relationships that ultimately determine firm performance.*[67] ExxonMobil's managers created a strategy map to understand the causes of return on capital—an important financial indicator of their success. Their strategy map helped them see that three HR practices could help improve their return on capital. They realized they needed to (a) help employees develop expertise in several key functional areas, (b) develop everyone's leadership skills, and (c) develop an integrated view of the company among all employees. Achieving these HR objectives would contribute to operational excellence, which in turn would improve ExxonMobil's ability to satisfy its customers (dealers) and establish win-win relationships with them. Through win-win relationships with dealers, ExxonMobil would improve both the performance of the dealers and their own performance, which would ultimately generate more available capital.[68]

A full description of a business strategy can be complicated, especially if the organization is large and complex. Throughout this book, when we discuss business strategies, we usually are interested in how the HRM system can be used to implement the competitive strategy of a specific business. A **competitive strategy** *describes how a particular business or business unit competes against direct rivals who offer the same products and services.* The competitive strategy states how the business will attract and retain customers: What value will the business offer that its competitors will find difficult to match? Large corporations develop different competitive strategies for each business unit. Time Warner has competitive strategies for AOL, HBO, Time Warner Cable, Turner Broadcasting, and its various other lines of business. Most small and medium-sized businesses have one competitive strategy for the entire company.

Total Quality

One way firms can differentiate their products and services from those of others is to offer outstanding quality. Delivering total quality depends on all parts of the organization working together. Increasingly, these efforts are guided by feedback from customers, because quality is in the customers' eyes—and ears and hands and taste buds! Firms such as 3M and GE that compete on quality adopt practices such as Total Quality Management (TQM), ISO 9000, and Six Sigma to ensure that their products and services meet the highest possible quality standards.

Many firms pursuing total quality rely heavily on employee empowerment.[69] Empowering employees is critical to getting them involved and committed to finding ways to continuously improve the quality of products and services. Empowered employees have the autonomy and responsibility to make key decisions about how work gets done, without seeking approval from their supervisors.

Mabe is a Mexican company that cares deeply about the quality of its products. Mabe manufactures refrigerators, ranges, heating elements, and compressors for companies such as GE, which then sell those products to consumers. Numerous HR practices help to ensure Mabe's success in satisfying the quality standards set by GE and others. For example, Mabe invests heavily in training. At least 6% of an employee's working hours are spent in training. Thus, at its plants in Mexico, the average employee receives about three weeks of training per year. Training programs teach employees how to set production objectives and how to assume responsibility for Six Sigma–level quality. Training also teaches employees the skills they need to work in self-managed teams, where they are responsible for measuring defects, reducing the amount of scrap, and maintaining their equipment. These training efforts are successful because the employees Mabe hires have been carefully selected; they all have the reading and math skills as well as the attitudes that are needed in this empowered factory setting.[70]

Low Cost

Competing on the basis of cost is another common competitive strategy. A firm pursuing a cost leadership strategy seeks to generate a high volume of sales to make up for the low margin associated with each sale. Efficient production systems, tight cost monitoring and controls, low investment in research and development (R&D), and a minimal sales force are characteristic of this strategy.

The HRM system also must support the goal of maximizing efficiency. This usually implies keeping labor costs low. To succeed in keeping labor costs as low as possible, the company may need employees who will accept part-time and shift work, perform repetitive behaviors efficiently and accept the boredom this often engenders, work in a no-frills facility, and accept minimal fringe benefits.

Customer Service

As most companies within an industry learn to produce excellent-quality products and reduce their costs, the basis for competing may change. For many industries, providing excellent customer service has become increasingly important as a way to differentiate themselves from competitors. And research shows that customer service quality can be improved by using appropriate HR policies and practices. For example, some companies use personality tests when screening job applicants in order to find employees who will relate well to customers. In addition, training programs and rewards can reinforce the message that satisfying customers is a top priority.[71]

FAST FACT

Deere & Company serves its customers well using "aligned high-performance teamwork."

Sabre Holdings is an example of a company that competes by offering excellent service to customers all over the world. You may have never heard of Sabre Holdings, but if you ever booked a reservation through Travelocity.com, you've done business with them. Sabre's North American division relies heavily on multidisciplinary virtual teams, each with about eight members located all over the continent. The challenges that these virtual teams face and Sabre's solutions to them are described in the feature "Managing Teams: Sabre's Virtual Teams."[72]

MANAGING TEAMS
Sabre's Virtual Teams

Sabre, the company that invented electronic commerce for the travel industry, processes more than 500 million travel bookings annually; that's 40% of the world's travel reservations. Sabre's customers include millions of people who use Travelocity.com, as well as more than 50,000 travel agencies and more than 200 airlines. Account executives sell the company's reservation system, field service technicians install it, training representatives teach customers how to use it, and so on. Members of Sabre's virtual teams occasionally work alongside each other at a location, but most of the time they work in isolation. To coordinate their activities, the teams use e-mail, telephones, videoconferencing, and Web-based conferencing. Interviews with members of Sabre's virtual teams revealed that they encountered some unique challenges. The following chart describes these challenges and shows the HR actions that Sabre has used to address them.

Challenges	HR Actions
Building Trust: Team members are often strangers with few opportunities for personal bonding.	*Establish Norms for Reliable Performance:* Team members developed trust when they responded rapidly to each other's communications and agreed to norms for how to communicate.
Creating Synergy: Because team members do not see each other often, it's difficult to clarify roles and spot problems before they become serious.	*Team Building and Team Training:* Before a team's launch, members receive classroom training to help them develop a team mission and values statement, set objectives, clarify roles, and build relationships. They also complete 15 CD-ROM training modules.
Feeling Isolated: In face-to-face teams, people share personal stories and family pictures, take breaks together, celebrate birthdays, and so on. When such social activities don't occur, people feel detached and isolated.	*Member Selection:* Sabre uses interviews to identify people who may not enjoy virtual teamwork, provides realistic previews, and allows candidates to opt out of isolating positions if they become dissatisfied.
Balancing Technical Skills and Communication Competencies: At first, Sabre believed technical skills were almost all that mattered. They soon realized that communication competencies were much more important than they had thought.	*Member Selection:* Sabre assesses communication and teamwork competencies before hiring virtual team members. Team members and managers use teleconferencing to conduct panel interviews and assess a candidate's fit with the team.
Performance Management: Sabre discovered that traditional methods of measuring and rewarding performance didn't work when managers seldom saw the people they were managing.	*Using Multiple Performance Measures:* Sabre invested in developing new measures of team effectiveness, including customer satisfaction ratings, electronic monitoring of team discussions, and 360-degree performance assessments.

Innovation

One of the most important strategies for U.S.-based companies to compete successfully worldwide is innovation. Companies that pursue an innovation strategy and compete by developing new products often need highly educated employees from specific fields (e.g., engineering or biochemistry). Once hired, these employees must be managed in ways that encourage experimentation and risk taking. Teamwork is usually important for innovation, and frequent failures are to be expected. Because highly skilled employees are so important to the success of firms that compete through innovation, HR practices are designed to attract and retain the very best talent. Addressing the needs of employees takes priority over cost considerations.

Innovation is central to IBM's strategy. Before Sam Palmisano became CEO of IBM in 2002, Big Blue (as the company is known) spent 10 years pulling itself back from the brink. A firm that revolutionized computing earlier in the twentieth century seemed to have lost its way as that century came to a close. Now the firm is striving to become the one-stop provider of on-demand e-business computing.

IBM's new strategy assumes that companies will no longer own and house their own computing systems. Instead, they will purchase computing power directly from a provider in a way that's similar to what we now do with electrical power. Only about 10% of the technology needed for this strategy to succeed is actually available today. The rest still has to be invented.

To rev up IBM's ability to innovate, Palmisano restructured the business around teams in charge of operations, strategy, and technology. Made up of people from all levels of the company, he believed these teams would be the engines of creativity at IBM. To motivate the teamwork needed for innovation, Palmisano asked the board to cut his own bonus and set the money aside as a pool to be shared based on team performance.[73]

CURRENT ISSUES

The changing external environment creates many challenges for employers. Here we focus on the current issues that arise due to the aging workforce and globalization.

The Aging Workforce

One consequence of the aging workforce in the United States, as well as in Japan and Western Europe, is that there should be plenty of job opportunities for younger workers. While good for employees, for most employers this situation warrants major concern. Companies in virtually all industries see a labor shortage on the horizon, particularly for skilled jobs.

To cope with the expected labor shortages, companies are considering a variety of responses, including

1. Making it more attractive for employees to not retire.
2. Reducing the turnover rates of all employees.
3. Outsourcing some work.
4. Offshoring some work.
5. Encouraging more immigration of skilled workers.
6. Increasing the use of technology and automation.
7. Seeking greater involvement in educational programs to help prepare younger workers.

> " *If you want an innovative environment, hire innovative people, listen to them tell you what they want, and do it.* "
>
> *Arthur D. Levison*
> *Chairman and Chief Executive Officer*
> *Genetech, Inc.*

10 LEARNING GOAL

FAST FACT

Thirty-five million boomers in the United States will be eligible to retire between 2000 and 2020.

Due to the magnitude of the expected labor shortage, it is likely that most companies and their HR professionals will have to consider using several of these options.[74]

The global realities facing companies today mean that simply moving work offshore will not be the best solution for addressing this issue. Increasingly there are skilled labor shortages in India and China, countries where a great deal of outsourcing and offshoring have occurred in recent years. Instead, U.S. employers are beginning to get serious about keeping older American workers engaged as productive members of the workforce. Retraining older workers to update their skills, allowing more flexibility in work schedules, and designing benefits packages that appeal to older employees are among the best practices of leading firms.[75] Safety and health issues are likely to become more prevalent also, as people work longer. By managing older human resources effectively, the best firms are striving to maximize their productivity and stay ahead of their competitors.

Global Realities of MNCs for HRM

To pursue their business strategies, companies like IBM, Mercedes, and Deere have had to become global companies. As described in the opening feature, Deere found it necessary to restructure itself into four major worldwide divisions to more effectively compete against the likes of Kubota of Japan and Mahindra and Mahindra

---

EXHIBIT 2.10 Global Realities of MNCs

Economic Characteristics

- Globalization and free trade have many supporters and also many critics.
- Huge disparities in income and standards of living worldwide.
- The increasing globalization of the biggest markets for products and services.
- The increasing demands on energy, raw materials, and infrastructure.
- The concern of societies for worldwide competitiveness and job creation.
- Growth in foreign direct investment (FDI).

Social Characteristics (Geopolitical, Cultural, and Technological)

- More integration and expansion within the EU, ASEAN, WTO, NAFTA, and similar organizations.
- Increased recognition of the relationship between government efficiency and business efficiency.
- Greater concern of societies for sustainability.
- More complexity, volatility, and unpredictability.
- The persistence of many local and regional legal and cultural qualities.
- Technology's effect on the world, making it flatter, more accessible, and less costly to work in.

Strategic (Enterprise) Characteristics

- An increasingly larger number of MNCs.
- Consolidation through increased merger and acquisition activity.
- Opportunities for growth and expansion in the emerging markets.
- Global competitive advantage attained through scale, scope, local adaptation, knowledge management, and optimal relocation.
- High costs, risks, and uncertainties, with a greater need for cross-border alliances such as international joint ventures.
- The need to change business and organization models constantly.

Workforce Characteristics

- A huge potential labor force that is more highly educated and growing.
- A greater awareness of worldwide disparities in income and lifestyles.
- The potential for workers to be adaptable to workplace styles and human resource practices.
- The acceleration of emigration flows in some areas, slowdowns in others.
- The elimination of the need for workers to move by means of offshoring and outsourcing.

EXHIBIT 2.11 The HR Implications of the Global Realities of MNCs

HR Implications: Societal Level

- Globalization will open new markets and create new economies to enter.
- CEOs will be concerned about multiple stakeholders.
- There is a need to consider the issues of multiple stakeholders, such as the environment, ethics, providing jobs, the impact of relocating and restructuring as well as profits.
- When doing relocating and restructuring, there is a need to be socially sensitive.
- There is a need to think/act globally, regionally, and locally.
- There is a need to think about workforce equality worldwide.

HR Implications: Strategic Level

- Gaining global competitive advantage depends on effective HR practices.
- Consider the context of all HR policies and practices: legal, cultural, sociopolitical, religious, economic, and so on.
- Systematically link HR policies and practices horizontally and vertically to the MNC.
- To establish cross-border alliances, you need to know and manage the many HR issues in cross-border M&As.
- There is a heightened need for learning, knowledge transfer, and knowledge management.
- There is an increased need to rely more on people than structure for coordinating and controlling global operations.
- Offshoring and outsourcing will continue to be strategies for MNCs.
- MNC expansion will be greater in the developing markets than the developed markets.

HR Implications: Workforce Level

- There is a heightened need for transnational and diverse teams, global leadership, and borderless careers.
- High-quality managers, those who can motivate employees to innovate, will be in big demand.
- High-talent individuals, those who have skills and are flexible and innovative, will be in big demand.
- Global mind-sets and cross-cultural competencies will be needed.
- Think of HR policies and practices in terms of the global workforce but *also* in terms of regional and local workforces and *how* to mesh them.
- There is a need to prepare employees to deal with complexity, volatility, and change.
- The challenge of managing employees of an MNC will increase as MNCs get larger.

Implications for HR: HR Professional and MNC Level

- All companies need to think of themselves as MNCs and act accordingly.
- HR professionals (leaders and staff) can play a major role in all this.
- All employees need to think of themselves as part of the global workforce.

of India.[76] David C. Everitt, president of Deere's $10.5 billion agricultural division, concedes, "Mahindra could someday surpass Deere in global unit sales."[77]

Today, virtually all organizations, regardless of size, must adapt to the process of globalization.[78] For most MNCs, globalization presents numerous challenging realities that reflect economic, social, enterprise, and workforce conditions, as shown in Exhibit 2.10.[79]

The Society for Human Resource Management and a growing number of HR professionals recognize that these realities have many implications for managing human resources. Some of these are summarized in Exhibit 2.11.[80]

CHAPTER SUMMARY WITH LEARNING GOALS

⚠ **STRATEGIC IMPORTANCE.** Managing people effectively is a critical task for organizations that strive to achieve excellence and remain competitive. The external environment is complex and dynamic, creating a constant flow of new opportunities and challenges for organizations and their employees. Economic conditions, the political landscape, industry dynamics, labor markets, and country cultures are key elements of the external environment. Continuous change in the external environment means that adjustments often are needed in the organizational environment. Key elements of the organizational environment include the technology, the company culture, and business strategies. For a firm to gain competitive advantage, all of these elements must be aligned internally and be well suited to the conditions in the external environment.

2 ECONOMIC GLOBALIZATION. Organizations face an increasingly global marketplace for their products. Competitors as well as customers are located all over the world. Consequently, companies are becoming more global, with operations in all parts of the world. In high-wage countries such as the United States, companies find it hard to compete by keeping labor costs low. Instead they often pursue business strategies that emphasize innovation and require employees with high levels of skill and knowledge.

3 POLITICAL LANDSCAPE. The intensity of competition is one reason many U.S. companies become involved in international activities. International competition is not shaped by economic conditions alone. Regional trade alliances such as NAFTA and the EU also play important roles. Organizations such as the WTO, ILO, and SAI are also important because they all can influence the working conditions that are considered acceptable for employees around the world.

4 INDUSTRY DYNAMICS. Industries and companies evolve through a series of life cycle stages. As they evolve, the pressures on them change, as do their approaches to managing human resources. Companies also choose to expand or create new ventures with other companies. Often mergers or acquisitions bring together companies that were formerly competitors. Research shows that managing human resources effectively is important for M&A success.

5 LABOR MARKETS. Shortages of skilled labor at home and the wealth of talent and skills elsewhere in the world further contribute to globalization. Employing a global labor force is made possible, in part, by information technologies. Many types of skilled jobs can be performed anywhere in the world; no longer is it necessary for office work to be performed at a central location. There is, however, a shortage of talented employees worldwide.

6 COUNTRY CULTURE. Country cultures differ along many dimensions. HR policies that work in the United States are not always appropriate in other countries. For companies with operations in more than one country, managing human resources effectively involves adapting to the local cultures of each country.

7 TECHNOLOGIES. Besides making new forms of organizing work possible, technology is changing human resource management activities. The HRIM systems often shift HR tasks to line managers and their employees and take them out of the hands of specialized HR staff. Technology makes eHR possible.

8 COMPANY CULTURE. As an organization evolves, it develops a distinctive company culture. A strong culture provides clear guidelines for how people in the organization should behave. Leadership sets the stage for managing human resources by providing a broad set of guidelines that help people make choices and direct their energies. The organization's vision, mission, and values answer questions such as, "Where are we going? Why are we going there? And how will we get there?" Company values often suggest how employees are to be treated and what is expected from them in return.

9 BUSINESS STRATEGIES. Competitive strategies describe how firms seek to create value for customers and gain advantage over competitors. Among the competitive strategies a firm might use are ensuring high quality, keeping costs low, being innovative, and providing the best customer service. A firm's competitive strategy can have many implications for the competencies and behaviors needed from employees, so HR policies and practices should be tailored to fit the strategy.

10 CURRENT ISSUES. Working together, members of the HR Triad can identify the key business issues a company faces. Two current issues they must address are the consequences of the aging workforce and globalization.

TERMS TO REMEMBER

Asia-Pacific Economic Cooperation (APEC)

Association of Southeast Asian Nations (ASEAN)

Business strategy

Central American Free Trade Agreement (CAFTA)

Company culture

Company subculture

Competitive strategy

European Union (EU)

External environment

Human resource information management (HRIM)

Industry life cycle

International Labor Organization (ILO)

Maquiladoras

Mission statement

Multicultural organization

North American Free Trade Agreement (NAFTA)

Organizational environment

Social Accountability International (SAI)

Strategy map

Technology

Values

Virtual workforce

Vision

World Trade Organization (WTO)

QUESTIONS FOR DISCUSSION AND REFLECTIVE THINKING

1. Economic globalization has many implications for business. It also has implications for employees. From your perspective, what are the three most significant implications of economic globalization for employees of U.S. companies?

2. Imagine that you work at a local bank in a midlevel management position. You learn on the evening news that your company has agreed to a merger with a competitor. The rationale given for the merger is, "A merger will allow us to exploit many synergies and lower our costs. This merger is about becoming more efficient; this is the way of the future for our industry." Assume this statement is true. Describe three significant HR issues for the new organization.

3. Think about the most recent technological developments. What are the likely implications of these developments for employers during the next 10 years? For employees?

4. Some people argue that organizations can develop their own strong company culture and that doing so will make differences in country cultures irrelevant to effectively managing human resources. Do you agree? Explain your opinion.

5. Describe how a powerful and clear statement of an organization's vision, mission, and values can be helpful to employees of the organization.

PROJECTS TO EXTEND YOUR LEARNING

1. **Integration and Application.** Before continuing, review the cases of Southwest Airlines and Lincoln Electric at the end of this book. Then answer the following questions.

   a. Describe the relevance of the following environmental forces for Lincoln Electric's approach to managing human resources:
      - Economic globalization.
      - The country culture of the United States.
      - The competitive strategy of Lincoln Electric.

   b. Describe the relevance of the following possible events for Southwest Airlines' approach to managing human resources:
      - The U.S. unemployment rate declines, putting more pressure on wages.
      - A tax law change makes it more difficult for business travelers to treat airfare as a deductible expense.
      - A new agreement creates a regional trade zone that covers all of the Americas, and business travel throughout the region skyrockets.

2. **Using the Internet.** Many online sources provide useful information about conditions in the external environment. Begin learning more by exploring the websites listed below.

   a. Read the code of conduct that students helped develop to ensure that goods bearing university labels were produced under fair labor conditions (The National Workrights Institute, available at www.workrights.org).

   b. Go to the Web site of the International Labor Organization (www.ilo.org) for information about labor force characteristics in different countries. You may also find the country descriptions provided by the CIA useful (www.odci.gov/cia/publications/factbook).

   c. Find out what you can learn about economic conditions and trends by visiting the Bureau of Economic Analysis (www.bea.gov).

   d. Learn more about the domestic labor market from the Bureau of Labor Statistics (www.bea.gov) and the U. S. Census Bureau (www.census.gov).

   e. Learn about recent developments in HRIM technology from the International Association for Human Resource Information Management (www.ihrim.org).

Also visit the following sites:

   f. The National Council on Aging (www.ncoa.org) provides general aging news, Medicare matters, research topics, and job postings.

   g. The U.S. Department of Health and Human Services, Elderare Locator (www.eldercare.gov) provides services about adult day care, assisted living programs, critical support services, and resources such as current news.

   h. WorkingSeniors.com (www.workingseniors.com) offers senior health benefits, senior news, home care for the elderly, travel insurance, self-help for the elderly, e-mail for seniors, blogs about seniors, and life care planning.

   i. The Microsoft Accessibility home page (www.microsoft.com/enable/aging/workforce.aspx) presents the technologies available to overcome vision and hearing problems, as well as guidance on how to train older workers to use the technology.

   j. Aging Workforce (www.agingworkforcenews.com) contains current events and news, along with links to books and Internet resources on many topics (safety, productivity, etc.).

   k. The U.S. Department of Health and Human Services, Administration on Aging (www.aoa.gov/prof/notes/notes_workforce.asp) provides statistics on the aging population, trends, and forecasts.

   l. The AARP Money and Work page (www.aarp.org/money/) contains links to articles on ways to combat ageism; the Careers tab has information for employers on workplace flexibility for older workers, preparing for exiting Baby Boomers, and automation of retirement information and plans.

For more information on world events and facts, see:

   m. The World Economic Forum (www.weforum.org/en/index.htm).

   n. The World Bank (www.worldbank.org).

   o. The Doing Business project (www.doingbusiness.org).

   p. Japan Blog (www.jinjapan.org).

   q. World Federation of Personnel Management Associations (www.wfpma.com).

   r. AllAfrica.com (www.allafrica.com).

   s. Organization of American States (www.oas.org).

   t. Organization for Economic Co-operation and Development (www.oecd.org).

   u. Emabassy.org (www.embassy.org/embassies).

3. **Experiential Activity.** Professor Warren Bennis had a hunch that people who grew up during different eras are motivated by different things. To find out if he was right, he conducted

in-depth interviews with 25 "geezers" and 18 "geeks." The geezers were all 70 or older, and the geeks were all 35 or younger. Regardless of their ages, all of the people interviewed were accomplished leaders in their fields. But these two groups had very different experiences early in their lives.

Geezers. The geezers were traditionalists. They had experienced the Great Depression and World War II. These events shaped how they viewed the world and what was important to them. As children and young adults, they worried about their own security and how to satisfy their basic needs. For many of them, success meant making money and earning a steady paycheck. A successful career meant getting ahead in terms of increasing salary and rank. When they were young, geezers expected to work hard and "pay their dues" so that eventually they would get ahead. Some were entrepreneurs, of course, who built their own companies. For them, a primary motivation seemed to be gaining control over their own work lives. Balancing career and family was a matter people didn't talk about—at least not openly. Most of the geezers grew up in homes where fathers worked in an organization and the mothers managed the family and home.

Geeks. The geeks were mostly from Generation X. In the families of their childhoods, it was much more common for both parents to earn income outside the home. Also much more common were divorces, second marriages, and blended families. As the geeks entered adulthood, the economic possibilities available to many seemed almost endless. Furthermore, they saw no reason why family life should have to suffer to realize those economic possibilities. Both men and women could have it all: a great job and a fulfilling family life. When asked what motivated them in their careers, the geeks sought to make a difference in the world. They were concerned with their own identities, they wanted to develop themselves as individuals, and they wanted to maintain a healthy balance between work and other aspects of life.

Although most of the geezers interviewed by Bennis were over 70 years old, they were still employed and actively involved in their jobs. They may be a bit older than your typical manager, but they are not so different from many CEOs of large U.S. companies. In these same companies, the middle- and lower-level managers are more similar to the geeks.

Activities

a. Talk to at least two people from these different generations. Ask them whether they agree or disagree with the descriptions of their generations. Also ask them to describe other generational similarities or differences that they have observed.

b. Next, talk to at least two Baby Boomers—people born between 1946 and 1964. Ask them to describe how their generation is similar to or different from that of the geezers interviewed by Bennis.

c. Finally, talk to at least two people who are between the ages of 18 and 25. People from this generation are often called Millenials. Ask them to compare their generation to older generations and have them describe generational similarities or differences that they have observed.

d. Share this information with your classmates. As a class, discuss the similarities and differences that really seem to exist, based on the interviews conducted by everyone.

e. Given the generational differences that have been identified (by you, your classmates, and Professor Bennis), what are the implications for the types of company cultures that geeks and geezers are likely to prefer? How can organizations that want a strong company culture manage to achieve this when their employees have different perspectives about what a "good" company culture is like?

CASE STUDY
LEVI STRAUSS & COMPANY

In 1872, Levi Strauss received a letter from Jacob Davis, a Nevada tailor who had been buying bolts of fabric from Strauss's dry goods company. Davis wrote to explain how he used metal rivets to strengthen the construction of the overalls he made. Because Davis couldn't afford to file for a patent, he invited Strauss to become a partner. Strauss knew a good idea when he saw it, and the two were granted the patent in 1873.

Today, Levi Strauss & Company is still privately owned, and the company's approach to ethical management is as familiar to business leaders as its jeans are to teenagers. Its mission statement begins, "The mission of Levi Strauss & Co. is to sustain responsible commercial success as a global marketing company of branded apparel." Its aspiration statement goes on to say, "We all want a company people can be proud of . . . ," which includes "leadership that epitomizes the stated standards of ethical behavior."

At Levi Strauss, ethical leadership extends well beyond company walls to its dealings with some 500 cutting, sewing, and finishing contractors in more than 50 countries, and with customers in more than 110 countries. Despite cultural differences in what is viewed as ethical or as common business practices, the company seeks business partners "who aspire as individuals and in the conduct of all their businesses" to ethical standards compatible with those of Levi Strauss. In addition to legal compliance, the company will do business only with partners who share a commitment to the environment and who conduct their business in a manner consistent with its own Environmental Philosophy and Guiding Principles. In the area of employment, partners must pay prevailing wage rates, require less than a 60-hour week, not use workers under age 14 and not younger than the compulsory age to be in school, not use prison labor, and not use corporal punishment or other forms of coercion. Levi Strauss regularly conducts contractor evaluations to ensure compliance. It helps companies develop ethical solutions when noncompliance is discovered.

Closer to home, Levi Strauss actively promotes ethical business practices through activities such as membership in Business for Social Responsibility, an alliance of companies that share their successful strategies and practices through educational programs and materials. The company's domestic employment policies are also known for being ahead of the times. For example, during the 1950s, they were pioneers

---

CASE EXHIBIT 1 Social Audit Criteria Considered by Levi Strauss & Company

Stakeholder Group	Examples of Criteria Considered When Assessing Performance
Owners and investors	Financial soundness
	Consistency in meeting shareholder expectations
	Sustained profitability
	Average return on assets over five-year period
	Timely and accurate disclosure of financial information
	Corporate reputation and image
Customers	Product or service quality, innovativeness, and availability
	Responsible management of defective or harmful products or services
	Safety records for products or services
	Pricing policies and practices
	Honest, accurate, and responsible advertising
Organization members	Nondiscriminatory, merit-based hiring and promotion
	Diversity of the workforce
	Wage and salary levels and equitable distribution
	Availability of training and development
	Workplace safety and privacy
Community	Environmental issues
	Environmental sensitivity in packaging and product design
	Recycling efforts and use of recycled materials
	Pollution prevention
	Global application of environmental standards
	Community involvement
	Percentage of profits designated for cash contributions
	Innovation and creativity in philanthropic efforts
	Product donations
	Availability of facilities and other assets for community use
	Support for employee volunteer efforts

in integrating factories in the South. In the 1990s, they were among the first companies to offer insurance benefits to their employees' unmarried domestic partners. Through this and other policies, the company has taken a strong stance in favor of the diversity that employees bring to the workplace. That said, Levi Strauss faces a very competitive environment that requires continuous adjustments. Levi Strauss, nevertheless, retains a prominent image in the minds of shoppers worldwide.

To assess how well the company adheres to its values, the company conducts a social audit. Some of the criteria they evaluate the company against are shown in Case Exhibit 1.[81]

To learn more about the company's current activities, its values, vision, and transformation, visit the home page at www. levistrauss.com.

CASE QUESTIONS

1. Knowing that its managers are willing to trade off some economic efficiency to operate according to their collective view of what is "ethical," would you buy shares of stock in this company? Why or why not?

2. Managers at Levi Strauss believe that they run an ethical company, but some critics view their liberal employment and benefits policies as immoral. These critics object to the policies because they're inconsistent with the critics' religious views. Analyze the pros and cons of an organizational culture that includes socially liberal employment policies that are viewed by some members of society (including potential employees and potential customers) as immoral.

3. Suppose you are looking for a new job. You have two offers for similar positions: one at Nike and one at Levi Strauss. Both organizations have indicated that they would like you to work for a year in one of their offshore production plants somewhere in Southeast Asia. The two salary offers are very similar, and in both companies you would be eligible for an annual bonus. The bonus would be based largely on the productivity of the production plant where you will be located. Which offer would you accept? Explain why.

4. In recent years, Levi Strauss has not performed well financially. Sales began declining in 1996, and since then the company has closed more than 50 plants worldwide. Employment has gone from a peak of 37,000 employees to around 10,000. There is no longer any jean production in North America. Do you think the company was living up to its vision when it laid off so many workers and contracted work to suppliers in 50 countries outside the United States?

HR Planning for Alignment and Change

Learning Goals

After reading this chapter, you should be able to:

1. Explain the strategic importance of HR planning for alignment and change.
2. Describe a planning process for aligning human resources and the business.
3. Discuss how to scan and assess the environment.
4. Give examples of several possible HR objectives and metrics.
5. Explain how to develop HR plans and timetables.
6. Describe how to implement HR action plans.
7. Discuss two current issues in HR planning.

MANAGING HUMAN RESOURCES AT WEYERHAEUSER COMPANY

With yearly sales of about $25 billion and approximately 54,000 employees in the United States and 18 other countries, Weyerhaeuser Company is one of the largest paper and forest products companies in the world. Through the 1970s, it enjoyed fairly consistent success. In the 1980s, global and domestic competition roared in at the same time that the national economy went into recession, and the housing industry entered a major slump. Overcapacity plagued the paper industry. Suddenly the company's successful strategy of being a large commodity lumber and paper business was no match against the new, smaller, and speedier competitors who focused more on the customer. Faced with a do-or-die crisis, top management restructured the company into three major divisions: (1) forest products, (2) paper products, and (3) real estate. They also specified the firm's core values, which highlighted the importance of customers, people, accountability, citizenship, and financial responsibility.

To live by these values, employees had to change their behaviors. To support the new behaviors, a new human resource management (HRM) system was needed. Managers were trained to understand the new strategy and its implications for how the new business units would be managed. Performance appraisals and compensation were revised to evaluate and reward environmental responsibility, customer focus, and teamwork.

As business conditions continue to change, Weyerhaeuser's strategy and structure will continue to evolve, and further alignment of its HR policies and practices may be needed. Continuous HR planning will surely accompany the company's continuous process of systematic environmental scanning, strategic business planning, and objective setting.[1] ▲

FAST FACT

The Association of Washington Business presented Weyerhaeuser with an Environmental Excellence Award for its continuous efforts in environment innovation and resource conservation.

THE STRATEGIC IMPORTANCE OF HR PLANNING FOR ALIGNMENT AND CHANGE

At Weyerhaeuser, changes in the global environment were a major impetus for strategic change efforts. To succeed under new competitive conditions, the company changed its vision, values, structure, strategy, and even its corporate culture. All of these changes had significant implications for the behaviors and competencies needed from people in the organization. To encourage and support the behaviors required in the new organization, many of the company's HR policies and practices had to be changed. Over a period of several years, Weyerhaeuser succeeded in repositioning itself to become a highly successful global competitor. Human resource planning for (re)alignment and change—the focus of this effort—greatly aided the company's strategy for repositioning itself in the industry.

Alignment

Major environmental changes and organizational actions such as those at Weyerhaeuser are being repeated in hundreds of companies across all industries. Environmental changes that provoke major organizational actions include changing global labor market conditions, new customer demands, increased competition, revised regulations, new technologies, growth of the Internet, and fundamental changes in the structure and dynamics in the industry.

Today, events requiring major organizational actions are constant. Regardless of the type of actions an organization undertakes, success almost always requires changes in HR policies and practices. This point was illustrated in Chapter 2 using the Deere & Company example. In this chapter, we describe in more detail the interplay between changes in the environment and an organization's HRM system. Sometimes a firm's entire HRM system is transformed to align the competencies and behavior of employees with strategic business objectives. When HR policies and practices facilitate the behaviors and competencies needed for organizational success, the HRM system and the needs of organization are in a state of alignment.[2]

Creating complete alignment involves addressing two components of alignment, which are sometimes referred to as vertical alignment and horizontal alignment. Human resource planning provides a means for achieving both types of alignment.

Vertical Alignment. **Vertical alignment** *exists when the HRM system fits with all other elements of the organizational environment—the culture, strategy, structure, and so on.* When Weyerhaeuser developed a new strategy and adopted a new set of values, it also introduced new training programs and changed its approach to performance management.

When Fairchild Semiconductor was created as a spin-off from National Semiconductor, one of its first strategic business objectives was to make a transition from National's data management system to one of its own. It chose an Enterprise Resource Planning (ERP) application from Peoplesoft (now a part of Oracle) and set about adapting its processes to meet the software's requirements. The first step was to form teams of employees from all over the world to rework the company's business processes in finance, manufacturing, logistics, and human resources. By including HR professionals in these cross-functional teams, Fairchild ensured that new HR policies and practices would be vertically aligned with the business objectives. Training was then used to teach employees the new tasks they would be expected to perform, and to explain why these new tasks were important. The company felt that employees would be less likely to take shortcuts to reduce their own workloads if they understood how their own contributions affected other people in the company and the bottom line. To build employees' confidence in their ability to use the new system and to reduce their fears, training sessions provided plenty of time for people to practice using the software and receive feedback. At Fairchild, installing new ERP software was a change that resulted in employees becoming more knowledgeable about the business and more excited about their own roles within the company.[3]

Horizontal Alignment. **Horizontal alignment** *exists when all the HR policies and practices that comprise the HRM system are consistent with each other so that they present a coherent message to employees concerning how they should behave while at work.* At Weyerhaeuser, creating horizontal alignment was the responsibility of the company's HR professionals. With a full understanding of the business, they worked in partnership with the senior management team to develop new HR policies and practices. Working together, the entire top management team crafted HR policies and practices that supported and reinforced employee behaviors related to environmental responsibility, customer focus, and teamwork. As explained in Chapter 2, horizontal alignment among all HR activities is necessary to provide employees with clear and meaningful direction.

Types of Organizational Change

Organizations can undergo many types of planned change, which vary in both degree and timing. Some types of change are easier to plan for than others.

Degree of Change. *When organizations make major adjustments in the ways they do business, it usually creates the need for* **radical change**. Adopting a new organizational structure, merging with another organization, or changing from a privately held to a publicly traded company is likely to require radical organizational change. When Clayton, Dubilier & Rice, a private equity firm, took over Kinko's, the copy shop, they attempted to create radical change. Under Kinko's founder, Paul Orfalea, Kinko's had been run as a very decentralized organization. Store managers were encouraged to run their businesses as they chose, and employees were encouraged to express their individuality. Clayton, Dubilier & Rice focused on cutting costs and creating more standardization. They cut training, closed stores, and laid off workers. Eventually, Clayton, Dubilier & Rice sold Kinko's to FedEx. Today, the process of change continues at the new company, FedEx Kinko's.[4]

Radical change is relatively infrequent and generally takes a long time to complete. When managers undertake radical change, they often make huge investments in planning and implementing the change.[5] Radical change touches everyone and everything in the organization. It changes the daily lives of every employee, as well as the lives of other key stakeholders, such as customers, suppliers, and alliance partners. FedEx Kinko's, Procter & Gamble, and Ford Motor Company are just a few of the many companies that have embarked on major efforts requiring radical change.[6]

In contrast, **incremental change** *is an ongoing process of evolution over time, during which many small changes occur routinely.* Over time, the cumulative effect of many small changes may be to transform the organization

> " *I told them that our biggest asset was the sparkle in our people's eyes. But they threw away senior people like garbage.* "
>
> *Paul Orfalea*
> *Founder of Kinko's*

FAST FACT

Kaizen, the approach to Total Quality Management in Japan, is based on small, continuous improvements.

totally. Yet, while they are occurring, the changes seem to be just a normal aspect of revising and improving the way that work gets done.

Total Quality Management (TQM) is an approach that relies heavily on incremental change. Employees routinely look for ways to improve products and services, and they make suggestions for changes day in and day out. The desire to improve performance continuously to stay ahead of competitors is a common reason for small organizational changes.[7]

As chairman and CEO of MTV Networks, Judy McGrath is responsible for managing such well-known brands as Comedy Central, Nickelodeon, Spike TV, CMT, Noggin, LOGO, VH1, and, of course, MTV. When MTV celebrated its twenty-fifth year, she was one of the few people there who had been with the company since its beginning. During her years at MTV, McGrath has been involved in continuous incremental changes that have made characters like SpongeBob SquarePants and Jon Stewart part of our daily lives. The MTV culture nurtures creative talent and recognizes that good ideas can come from anywhere at any time. Spotting good ideas and implementing them—regardless of what changes may be necessary for the company—are the core of MTV's success. In the past, MTV could focus almost exclusively on developing and delivering television programming. But going forward, it will expand into and perhaps create new interactive media channels. To succeed, MTV must anticipate and exploit a rapidly expanding and ever changing media landscape. Hiring and retaining great talent will undoubtedly be a key driver of the company's continued success. As the nature and preferences of that creative talent change, MTV's approaches to managing human resources will need to evolve as well.[8] Successful organizations like MTV must be equally adept at making both radical and incremental changes, as needed.

Timing of Change. In addition to differences in the magnitude of change are differences in the timing of change. **Reactive change** *occurs when an organization is forced to change in response to an event in the external or organizational environment.* New strategic moves made by competitors, new scientific or technological discoveries, and performance problems are common reasons for reactive change. Weyerhaeuser didn't foresee the changes in the environment that would shake the paper and lumber industry, so it was forced into radical reactive change. If an organization adapts to changes in the environment without undergoing a substantial reorientation in its strategy or values, it experiences incremental reactive change.

Sometimes upcoming events are predictable, and managers can foresee that change will be needed to succeed in the future. *When an organization takes action in anticipation of upcoming events or early in the cycle of a new trend, it undergoes* **anticipatory change.** Well-run organizations are always looking for better ways to do things to stay ahead of the competition. Some companies strive to keep their costs low by continually introducing technological improvements. Others such as MTV stay ahead of their competitors by always looking for new ways to satisfy their customers. Often, anticipatory change is incremental and results from constant tinkering and improvements.

Occasionally anticipatory change is radical. Visionary leaders in the organization become convinced that major changes are needed even though there is no apparent crisis. Because there is no crisis, the changes can be planned carefully and implemented gradually.

Successful companies are adept at all types of change. They understand the need to assess whether HR policies and practices are aligned and how to

> " *The smartest thing we can do when confronted with something truly creative is get out of the way.* "
>
> *Judy McGrath*
> *Chairman and Chief Executive Officer*
> *MTV Networks*

> " *The species that survive are not the biggest but the most adaptable.* "
>
> *Charles Darwin*

make adjustments to the HRM system when needed. Increasingly, they are also adept at learning from their experiences so that they can be more effective in making future changes.[9]

Learning Organizations

During the past decade, many companies identified learning as an important core competency. A **learning organization** *continually finds new ways to satisfy customers and other stakeholders by skillfully integrating the resources of information, technology, and people to produce and then effectively use new knowledge.* Learning organizations are changing all the time. They are adept at both incremental and radical change. They make radical changes when necessary, but more often they anticipate the need to change before a crisis forces them to react.

As Exhibit 3.1 shows,[10] continuous organizational learning and change have many implications for managing human resources. Together with other elements of the organizational environment (leadership, culture, strategy),

> *❝ I want us to create an environment of continuous learning and challenge that will allow us to move from one business unit to another in engineering, or from sales to customer advocacy, or from financial to IT. ❞*
>
> John Chambers
> Chairman and Chief Executive Officer
> Cisco Systems

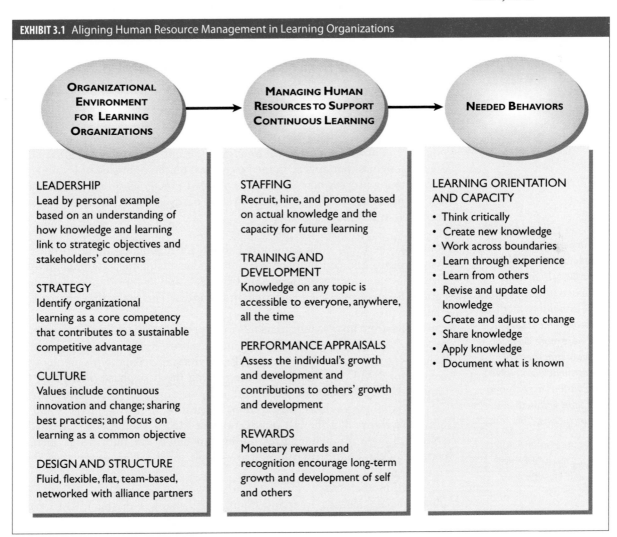

EXHIBIT 3.1 Aligning Human Resource Management in Learning Organizations

ORGANIZATIONAL ENVIRONMENT FOR LEARNING ORGANIZATIONS

LEADERSHIP
Lead by personal example based on an understanding of how knowledge and learning link to strategic objectives and stakeholders' concerns

STRATEGY
Identify organizational learning as a core competency that contributes to a sustainable competitive advantage

CULTURE
Values include continuous innovation and change; sharing best practices; and focus on learning as a common objective

DESIGN AND STRUCTURE
Fluid, flexible, flat, team-based, networked with alliance partners

MANAGING HUMAN RESOURCES TO SUPPORT CONTINUOUS LEARNING

STAFFING
Recruit, hire, and promote based on actual knowledge and the capacity for future learning

TRAINING AND DEVELOPMENT
Knowledge on any topic is accessible to everyone, anywhere, all the time

PERFORMANCE APPRAISALS
Assess the individual's growth and development and contributions to others' growth and development

REWARDS
Monetary rewards and recognition encourage long-term growth and development of self and others

NEEDED BEHAVIORS

LEARNING ORIENTATION AND CAPACITY
- Think critically
- Create new knowledge
- Work across boundaries
- Learn through experience
- Learn from others
- Revise and update old knowledge
- Create and adjust to change
- Share knowledge
- Apply knowledge
- Document what is known

HR policies and practices support the behaviors for continuous learning and change. These behaviors include experimentation, learning from others, documenting what is learned, and several others listed in Exhibit 3.1.

In learning organizations, the process of HR planning is used to ensure that the HRM system supports these needed behaviors by providing learning opportunities, building learning competencies, and keeping employees motivated and interested in learning.[11]

2
LEARNING GOAL

FAST FACT
Three-quarters of HR professionals indicate that their organizations have a strategic business plan in place.

OVERVIEW OF THE HR PLANNING AND CHANGE PROCESS

In many organizations, the process of business planning begins with a scanning of the external environment and a vision of where the organization needs to be in five (or even ten) years. Once a long-term vision and clear objectives are developed, the management team works backward to understand the near-term implications. Subsequently, the organization may then go through numerous cycles of short-term (e.g., annual) planning as it moves toward its long-term objectives.

Strategic change seldom occurs without a bit of chaos. Indeed, a few organizations seem to thrive on chaos. But most organizations strive to impose some order and keep chaos under control during strategic change by engaging in systematic planning.

The Elements of Human Resource Planning

The term **human resource (HR) planning** *refers to the activities associated with (1) scanning and assessing the environment; (2) specifying the objectives to be achieved by HR activities, along with the measures to be used to assess the achievement of those objectives; and (3) developing specific plans for HR policies and practices along with timetables for implementing the plans.* These are the activities that appear in the box shown on the right side of Exhibit 3.2. The planning process may not always proceed exactly as shown, but, regardless of the sequence, these activities are the basic components of a systematic approach to HR planning.[12]

Scanning. The framework shown in Exhibit 3.2 highlights the importance of systematically and continuously scanning and assessing the external and organizational environments described in Chapter 2 and of considering their implications for managing the firm's human resources. This is the first phase of the planning process.

To illustrate how scanning relates to a specific strategic issue, consider the process of merging with or acquiring another firm. Refer again to Exhibit 2.3 (page 45), which describes the key HR activities associated with mergers and acquisitions (M&As). As you can see, during the first phase of M&As, one way that HR professionals participate is by scanning the environment to assess potential target firms. Research on integration following mergers and acquisitions shows that the HR implications of M&As should not be treated as an afterthought. By planning for the human side of the integration, merging companies can build trust and prepare people for the changes they are about to undergo.[13]

Objectives and Metrics. In many companies, changes in the HRM system are stimulated by the company's strategic objective of improving customer

“ HR departments with a strategic plan in place were more likely than those without a strategic plan to have established methods of measurements in place and were more likely to indicate that their HR department was involved with various aspects and functions within their organizations. ”

Society for Human Resource Management (SHRM) in the "2006 Strategic HR Management Survey Report"

EXHIBIT 3.2 Phases in Strategic Business and HR Planning for Alignment and Change

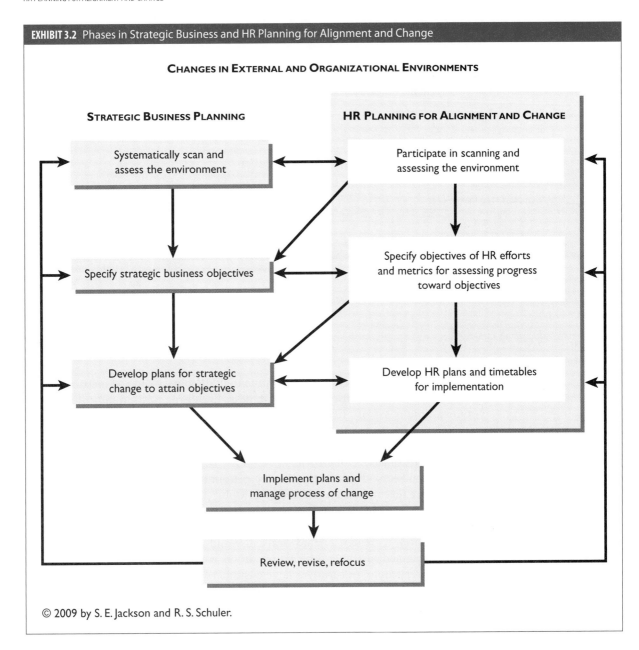

CHANGES IN EXTERNAL AND ORGANIZATIONAL ENVIRONMENTS

STRATEGIC BUSINESS PLANNING

HR PLANNING FOR ALIGNMENT AND CHANGE

Systematically scan and assess the environment

Participate in scanning and assessing the environment

Specify strategic business objectives

Specify objectives of HR efforts and metrics for assessing progress toward objectives

Develop plans for strategic change to attain objectives

Develop HR plans and timetables for implementation

Implement plans and manage process of change

Review, revise, refocus

© 2009 by S. E. Jackson and R. S. Schuler.

satisfaction. A study by The Conference Board found that customer-driven changes were common in the manufacturing and service sectors. Exhibit 3.3 summarizes some of the findings from that study.[14]

Human resource (HR) objectives *state in quantitative or qualitative terms what is to be achieved with regard to the firm's human resources.* Ideally, if the stated HR objectives are met, the firm will meet its overall strategic objectives. For the objectives listed in Exhibit 3.3, how would *you* measure the organization's progress?

To evaluate whether their objectives are being met, organizations need to identify the measures they will use to assess progress. *The measurements that are used to assess progress against HR objectives are often referred to as* **human**

FAST FACT

Common HR metrics can include employee satisfaction, turnover rate, turnover costs, absenteeism, productivity cost per hire, and revenue per employee.

EXHIBIT 3.3 The Most Common Objectives When Changing HR Practices

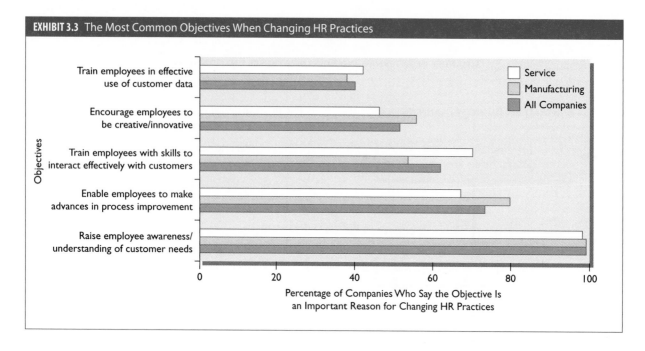

resource (HR) metrics. The list of potential HR objectives and metrics that an organization might use is almost limitless. Each organization must develop its own unique set of HR objectives and metrics to fit its specific situation. For example, as described in Chapter 2, at Alberto-Culver, Carol Lavin Bernick uses the results of annual employee surveys to monitor the company's progress against its objective of creating a cultural change.

When Sears, the department store, set out to improve customer satisfaction and store revenues, it established an HR objective of increasing employee commitment. Sears had conducted a study to improve its understanding of the factors that lead to customer satisfaction. Using data from all of its stores around the country, it created a behavioral cause-and-effect model showing the factors that explained customer satisfaction. Stores with higher employee commitment and lower employee turnover have customers who were more satisfied. Thus, Sears began using measures of employee attitudes (such as satisfaction) and retention as key HR metrics.[15]

Plans and Timetables. Once the objectives are clearly specified, HR plans for achieving the objectives can be developed. **Human resource (HR) plans** *can be thought of as blueprints for action; they specify who needs to do what, where, and how.* **Timetables** *specify when each planned activity will be completed.* At this stage, HR plans need to address two key issues:

1. What procedures will be used to design new HR policies and practices that will be aligned with the new business plans?

2. How will the new HR policies and practices be introduced to the workforce?

Developing plans and timetables requires close coordination between the HR professionals and the line managers involved in creating business plans. Whatever time frame is adopted, HR planning should parallel the business planning process.[16]

> 66 *In many companies, traditional workforce planning was an onerous process that HR imposed on management. Too often, the net result was a humongous report blending spreadsheets and a dizzying amount of data that provided little value to the business.* 99
>
> Mary B. Young
> Senior Research Associate
> The Conference Board

Aligning Business Planning and HR Planning

Historically, in times of heightened environmental stability, HR planning focused almost exclusively on matching human resource demand with human resource supply. Its primary purpose was ensuring that the right number and type of people were available at the right time and place to serve relatively predictable business needs that resulted from business plans created in relatively stable environmental conditions. If the business was growing at a rate of 10%, for example, top management would continue to add to the workforce by 10%: It worked before; it would work again. Today, environmental conditions seldom remain stable for long. As a consequence, HR planning that anticipates the need for future changes is of greater strategic value.[17]

The double-headed arrows in Exhibit 3.2 show that close coordination and collaboration between line managers and HR professionals are desirable during strategic business planning and HR planning. At Weyerhaeuser, close coordination and collaboration helped the company achieve its strategic business objectives during its changes in strategy and structure. As Weyerhaeuser did, managers and HR professionals should systematically consider changes in HR policies and practices in the context of issues related to other tangible and intangible resources, including finances, technology, physical resources, and the firm's current and desired reputation.

Research by the Society for Human Resource Management indicates that the alignment of business and HR planning has been improving in recent years. To achieve alignment, HR professionals become involved in many aspects of their organization's strategic business planning process, as shown in Exhibit 3.4.[18] In companies that have a strategic HR plan, members of the senior HR team often participate in the development and review of the strategic business plan. Not surprisingly, HR professionals are less often involved in developing the business goals.

At Hewlett-Packard (HP), the computer company, the alignment of business and human resource planning became a top priority after the firm acquired

> " *HP operates in a rapidly changing environment. It's critical to be agile and respond to change faster than our competition. A new set of products [digital entertainment] and a new set of customers required radical workforce change.* "
>
> *Gerard Boussard*
> *Vice President of Global Workforce Planning*
> *Hewlett-Packard*

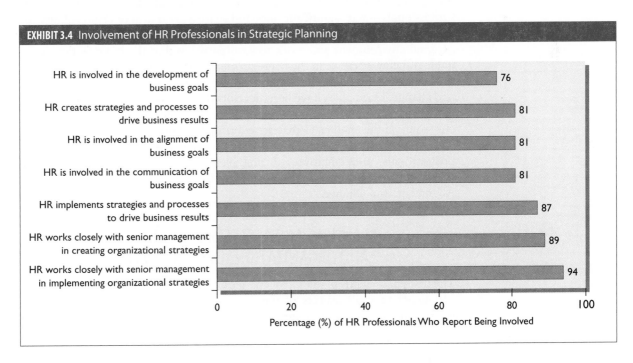

EXHIBIT 3.4 Involvement of HR Professionals in Strategic Planning

Category	Percentage
HR is involved in the development of business goals	76
HR creates strategies and processes to drive business results	81
HR is involved in the alignment of business goals	81
HR is involved in the communication of business goals	81
HR implements strategies and processes to drive business results	87
HR works closely with senior management in creating organizational strategies	89
HR works closely with senior management in implementing organizational strategies	94

Percentage (%) of HR Professionals Who Report Being Involved

EXHIBIT 3.5 HP's Workforce Planning Process

Step 1. Business leaders scan the environment to detect business trends, and HR professionals scan the environment to learn about demographic changes, workforce trends, and political trends.

Step 2. Business leaders describe the high-level workforce implications of business strategies. For example, if the strategy calls for growing the market in China, this step reveals that the company will have to have a sales force in place in China and it identifies the regions of China where growth will occur.

Step 3. Business leaders describe in general terms their current workforce. What types of competencies do they have in place today? Where are these competencies located?

Step 4. The next task is to understand the implications of the projected trends. Given the business strategies and an understanding of the current workforce, what changes are needed by HP in the next three years? Where will the company find new talent? What new competencies are needed? Where are new competencies needed?

Step 5. Here the focus shifts to operational issues. Now the big picture trends that were identified in earlier steps are quantified with specific numbers and dates. Questions about how to achieve the changes (e.g., retraining current employees, hiring new employees, conducting layoffs, and so on) also are addressed.

Step 6. The final step involves focusing on the short term. Given the three-year plan, what needs to get done in the next six months? If hiring is needed, who will be used for recruiting and where will the applicants come from? If layoffs are expected, how will this be communicated to employees?

Compaq. Through planning, HP determined which employees would stay in the new HP and who would have to leave. More recently, HP has been focusing on how its move into the digital entertainment market will influence the types of employees it will need. To plan for its future workforce needs, HP uses the six-step process shown in Exhibit 3.5.[19]

HP relies on its own managers to forecast the company's future needs. Boussard knows he and his colleagues can't predict the future perfectly. Any long-term plan is likely to change. But the planning process is valuable nevertheless because it keeps everyone thinking about how human resource management contributes to the firm's long-term success.

The HR Triad

As Exhibit 3.2 suggests, two members of the HR Triad—line managers and HR professionals—play significant roles and share a great deal of responsibility for the HR planning processes. Working together, their goal is to understand the external environment and work toward ensuring that the organization is capable of being effective in the context of a changing environment.

Of course, planning is only the initial phase of organizational alignment and change. Once plans have been developed, implementation can begin. Later in this chapter, the role of employees will become more apparent when we discuss some of the challenges that arise during the implementation phase.

The primary opportunities for collaboration among line managers, HR professionals, and employees during planning, alignment, and change are described in "The HR Triad: Roles and Responsibilities for HR Planning, Alignment, and Change."

SCANNING AND ASSESSING THE EXTERNAL AND ORGANIZATIONAL ENVIRONMENTS

The first phase of HR planning for change involves gathering data to learn about and understand all aspects of the environment. As described in Chapter 2, important elements of the external environment are

- Economic globalization.
- Political landscape.

LINE MANAGERS	HR PROFESSIONALS	EMPLOYEES
• Systematically scan and assess the environment to help establish specific strategic objectives.	• Participate in environmental scanning and assessment to gain an understanding of specific strategic objectives.	• Monitor and seek to understand the environment and its potential implications for the company.
• In early phases of planned change, provide information about the current external and organizational environments and help forecast likely changes.	• Manage HR planning activities, including forecasting of labor needs and supplies, and identification of the HR implications of planned changes.	• Provide input during early phases of planning for change as needed (e.g., by providing opinions for use during organizational assessment and forecasting).
• Share information with and involve HR professionals during development of plans, including development of metrics and timetables for evaluating change.	• Develop detailed HR objectives, plans, metrics, and timetables for strategic change. Facilitate the change process as it unfolds.	• Provide input during the development of HR plans. Approach change with a positive attitude rather than resistance.
• Collaborate in the collection and interpretation of data to assess progress toward strategic and HR objectives.	• Develop, collect, and analyze data to assess progress toward strategic and HR objectives.	• Collaborate in the collection and interpretation of data to assess progress toward strategic and HR objectives.
• Learn about effective change processes and act as a role model for effective learning and change.	• Serve as the facilitator of change; help line managers and other employees develop an enhanced capacity for leading and accepting change.	• Recognize that change is constant and develop a personal capacity for frequent change.
• Communicate constantly with employees concerning planned changes using formal and informal means.	• Work with line managers to develop and disseminate formal communications about planned changes in HR activities; respond promptly and candidly to questions about planned changes in HR activities.	• Take personal responsibility for ensuring own understanding of planned changes and their implications.
• Participate in the process of evaluating and revising change initiatives.	• Assist in conducting evaluations of change initiatives, interpreting the results, and revising plans accordingly.	• Participate in the process of evaluating change and making adjustments as needed.

- Industry dynamics.
- Labor markets.
- Country cultures.
- Legal institutions.
- Unionization.

Chapter 2 also described the elements of the organizational environment, which include technology, company culture, and business strategy. The likely and possible changes in customers' needs and preferences also must be considered.[20]

During this early phase of HR planning, the expertise of HR professionals is especially relevant for assessing labor market conditions, making predictions about how new employment laws and regulations might affect the organization, alerting managers to relevant trends in union activity and labor relations, and assessing the organizational culture.

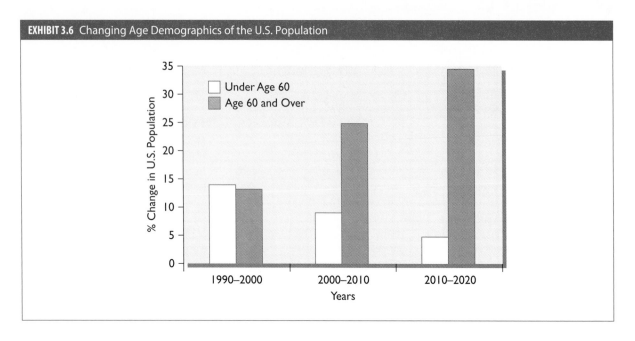

EXHIBIT 3.6 Changing Age Demographics of the U.S. Population

The specific implications of changes in the external and organizational environments depend on each company's situation. Consider the age trends depicted in Exhibit 3.6. For some firms, the aging workforce may mean that older workers will experience increasing frustration as they realize that a glut of senior talent means that fewer of them will be able to continue their climb up the corporate ladder. For other firms, like Chevron, having a glut of workers nearing retirement has made downsizing easier; generous buyout packages can be used to encourage voluntary early retirement, eliminating the need for layoffs.

For Deloitte, these age trends mean that the number of partners over age 50 will double in five years, to make up 25% of the total. Partners are highly paid, and they become vested in the firm's pension plan at age 50. Retirement at age 50 is likely to be financially feasible for most partners. Whereas some companies might welcome mass retirements, they could be disastrous for Deloitte, because partners are a very valuable source of experience and talent. Unless the firm does something to keep these people, they may begin leaving the firm at a very high cost. Of course, these same conditions are being faced by many other U.S. companies today.[21]

Organizational Analysis

An assessment of the external and internal environments is often referred to as **organizational analysis.** The aim is to fully understand the current environment before taking action. The idea that organizational analysis should precede any actions taken to create change may seem obvious, but its importance is often underestimated.[22]

> **" The assets at P&G are what? Our people and our brands. "**
>
> *A. G. Lafley*
> *Chief Executive Officer*
> *Procter & Gamble*

When A. G. Lafley took the helm as CEO of Procter & Gamble (P&G), half of the company's top brands were losing market share.[23] A major corporate restructuring had recently taken place and employees seemed demoralized by its effects. To make things worse, the company's stock price had fallen dramatically. An organizational analysis was the first step to getting things back on track. The organizational analysis of P&G was not limited to addressing HR issues; it turned out, however, that people issues were at the center of many of the company's problems.[24]

When the market share of P&G brands fell, rebuilding the company's marketing strength became a top priority. The job fell to Chief Marketing Officer Jim Stengel. With the help of two marketing professors, Stengel began the change process by conducting an in-depth organizational analysis. After talking with other executives, Stengel concluded that P&G's leaders really didn't understand the problems confronting the company's core talent: its marketers. To develop a clearer picture of the problems, Stengel's team used its own marketing methods to understand employees' concerns.

The marketing professors began by shadowing a cross-section of marketing directors, brand managers, and brand assistants as they went about their work. After people got comfortable with the "shadows," they opened up and began expressing their frustrations. At the same time, the shadows were able to observe the positive behaviors employees engaged in (e.g., using face-to-face communication for some tasks instead of relying on e-mail). These would later become the basis for new training programs.

After several days of shadowing, the next step was to conduct focus groups. Six to eight marketing employees met for two to three hours to discuss a variety of issues. In addition, several one-on-one interviews were conducted with marketing managers. The focus groups were confidential, but the interviews with managers were taped. One manager observed that "there is a real need to get back to the basics of people development. No one even understands . . . how to evaluate people anymore." Another recalled, "When I came to P&G 15 years ago, you got your 15 minutes of coaching from your boss every day. We now have nothing. Coaching is a skill we have lost."

Stengel was beginning to get it. To create action plans, he convened a task force headed by the director of human resources for global marketing. The task force understood that a systematic change effort was needed. The company couldn't solve all of its problems with a few new training courses; it would have to rethink its compensation and rewards practices, career paths, and every aspect of its management approach that sent signals to employees about what was important. It has taken several years, but today P&G is considered a success story. As one manager from a major competitor put it, "Things are getting tougher for us [the competing company]. P&G has come roaring back!" Many of the tools that Stengel used were HR tools for planning and change.

HR Forecasts

Human resource (HR) forecasts *estimate the firm's future human resource needs.* Historically, in times of environmental stability, forecasting human resource needs and planning the steps necessary to meet those needs consisted largely of a numbers game. Forecasting efforts focused on (1) developing estimates of how many people with which competencies would be needed, (2) forecasting the likely supply of people and skills, and (3) implementing plans to ensure that the right number and type of people would be available at the right time and place. If the supply of people was expected to exceed the projected needs, downsizing plans might be developed. If the projected needs were greater than the anticipated supply, aggressive recruiting plans might be developed.

In many organizations, quantitative forecasts of future human resource needs continue to be an important ingredient in an organizational analysis.

At Chevron, for example, all operating units must conduct a demographic analysis each year to identify where talent shortages or surpluses are likely to occur. In addition to information about the supply and productivity of employees, data about skills, competencies, educational levels, turnover and absenteeism rates, and attitudes may be used to forecast future human resource needs.

The quality of any forecast depends on the accuracy of information used and the predictability of events. The shorter the time horizon, the more predictable the events and the more accurate the information. For example, organizations are generally able to predict how many graduates they need for the coming year, but they are less able to predict how many they will need for the next five years. Predicting the behavior of new college graduates is easier than predicting the behavior of people at the other end of their employment cycle. You can count on new graduates to be looking for jobs, but at what age should you expect older workers to be thinking about retirement?[25]

Forecasting involves approximations, not absolutes or certainties. A variety of forecasting methods—some simple, some complex—can be used to predict an organization's demand for human resources and the likely supply that will be available to meet the demand. Two commonly used methods are judgmental forecasts and statistical forecasts.

Judgmental Forecasts. **Judgmental forecasts** *rely on the opinions of informed experts (usually managers), who provide their estimates of current and projected productivity levels, market demand, and sales, as well as current staffing levels and mobility information.* One way to arrive at an agreement about what estimates to use is the Delphi technique. At a Delphi meeting, experts take turns at presenting their forecasts and assumptions to the others, who then make revisions in their own forecasts. This collaborative process continues until a viable composite forecast emerges. The composite may represent specific projections or a range of projections, depending on the experts' positions. Although judgmental forecasts rely on less data than those based on statistical methods, they tend to dominate in practice.

> **The railroad took a punitive attitude toward people who had already worked to exhaustion. You're threatening people who have already worked too much to get them to go to work more.**
>
> *James Brunkenhoefer*
> *National Legislative Director*
> *United Transportation Union*

Union Pacific, the railroad company, used judgmental forecasting to estimate how many employees it needed to hire to meet the demands of its new customer, United Parcel Service (UPS). UPS provided Union Pacific with fairly accurate predictions of how much they would need the railroad to ship for them. But Union Pacific had a difficult time estimating how this new customer's demands would influence the railroad's hiring needs. The problem was that Union Pacific had not anticipated how many of its employees would retire when the Railroad Retirement Board changed the rules to make earlier retirement more attractive to railroad employees. To predict that number, Union Pacific conducted focus groups, conducted employee surveys, and even hired the Gallup organization to take a poll. Despite these efforts, the railroad was surprised by how many employees chose to retire when the new rules took effect. "We admit we got caught short of people," said Robert Turner, a senior vice president at Union Pacific. The staff shortages soon led to overworked crews. Managers pushed people to work harder and punished those who tried to take time off. Poor labor relations developed, and people who could retire decided it was a good time to do so. Due to Union Pacific's staff shortage, shipments for UPS were delayed, but so were agricultural shipments. Some observers worried that the delays would affect international trade. Meanwhile, to correct the problem, Union Pacific was rushing to hire and train nearly 4,000 new employees and worrying about how they would cope when the holiday shipping season kicked in.[26]

Statistical Forecasts. In contrast to judgmental methods, **statistical forecasts** *rely heavily on objective data and formal models*. For example, statistical methods might be used to predict labor needs under various conditions of business growth or decline. As another example, statistical forecasting could be used to determine how long it would take to reduce the workforce by 15% through normal attrition. Fairly accurate statistical forecasts are possible when large amounts of historical data are available for analysis, and when past conditions are similar to those during which the forecast is to apply. Statistical projections often are used to estimate the likely supply of labor in the external labor market, for example. In that case, data about birth rates, typical retirement ages, and educational trends can be used to forecast future labor supplies.

Statistical forecasts also can be used to predict future labor supply and demand given changes in demand for the products and services provided by the organization. Again, making such forecasts is possible only if the organization keeps track of the information needed to make such forecasts. For this example, an organization would need a well specified model of how changes in demand for products and services translate into changes in the company's operations and thus into changes in the number, types, and locations of employees needed.

Regardless of the method used, forecasts of future labor needs and supplies should be considered rough estimates at best. Accurate forecasts depend on the ability to predict changing conditions in the external labor market, the impact of new technologies, current employees' future employment competencies, employee attitudes, and employee behaviors.

Employees' Opinions

Employees' opinions are another of the many sources of information that can be useful when conducting an organizational analysis. Opinions about both problems and potential solutions can be helpful when HR professionals are planning for change.

Employee Surveys. Employee surveys are one method for finding out employees' opinions. The content of the survey depends on the areas of greatest concern to the organization.

A firm interested in implementing Total Quality Management (TQM) may want to assess the organizational environment to determine whether the company culture is aligned with TQM principles. For this type of assessment, a survey tool for assessing employees' views is available from the National Institute of Standards and Technology. As shown in Exhibit 3.7, the survey asks the organization's leaders to indicate their degree of agreement with statements that describe the culture of effective TQM organizations. Items are grouped into categories that reflect the criteria used to evaluate organizations for the Malcolm Baldrige Award. Analysis of responses to these items can be used in the development of plans for creating a strong TQM company culture. Then, after changes have been implemented, the survey can be administered again to assess the success of the organization's efforts.[27]

Yum! restaurant uses an employee survey to assess the state of the organization's culture in order to determine whether managerial actions are needed to improve it. Items in the employee survey ask people to assess their commitment to the company's core values, which include customer focus, teamwork, recognition, and excellence. The results are broken out for each functional area and each level. Managers receive the results for their areas of responsibility. If the survey results are unsatisfactory, a manager is required to develop an action plan to improve the situation.[28]

FAST FACT

The global labor market is predicted to expand by 1 billion people over the next 10 years.

FAST FACT

The Malcolm Baldrige National Quality Award was created by the Malcolm Baldrige National Quality Improvement Act of 1987. It is awarded annually to companies that meet the highest standards for quality and performance excellence.

EXHIBIT 3.7 Baldrige Application Self-Analysis Worksheet (Optional)

Purpose: This worksheet can be used by companies interested in competing for the Malcolm Baldrige National Quality Award. The worksheet is to be completed by managers after they have evaluated the organization using the Baldrige criteria questions. The assumption is that members of the organization are able to identify their organization's key strengths and key opportunities for improvement (OFIs). Shown here are criteria for five of the seven categories of criteria considered when making the award. For OFIs of high importance, the organization should establish a goal and a plan of action.

Criteria Category	Importance High, Medium, Low	Stretch (Strength) or Improvement (OFI) Goal	For High-Importance Areas		
			What Action Is Planned?	By When?	Who Is Responsible?
Category 1—Leadership: Includes establishing and communicating vision and values.					
Strength					
1. 2. OFI 1. 2.					
Category 2—Strategic Planning: Includes action plan development and deployment.					
Strength					
1. 2. OFI 1. 2.					
Category 4—Measurement, Analysis, and Knowledge Management: Includes decisions about what performance data to collect and how to make use of the data.					
Strength					
1. 2. OFI 1. 2.					
Category 5—Workforce Focus: Includes practices used to engage the workforce and practices for building an effective and supportive workforce environment.					
Strength					
1. 2. OFI 1. 2.					
Category 7—Results					
Strength					
1. 2. OFI 1. 2.					

Focus Groups. A focus group brings together a small number of employees to discuss a specific issue in a conversation guided by a trained facilitator. Texas Instruments (TI) used focus groups when it launched an effort to revise its HRM system. Over time, TI had developed a cumbersome set of HR policies that prevented the company from responding quickly to a rapidly changing environment. It set an objective of developing a new HRM system around a small set of application guidelines that would reflect TI's core values. But what were these core values? To find out, HR professionals conducted 30 focus group discussions with employees from all around the world. These conversations revealed three core values that were shared throughout the company: integrity, innovation, and commitment. These values became the foundation of TI's new application guidelines, around which they built a new HRM system.[29]

Involving Employees in Developing Plans. Another way to ensure that employees' views are taken into consideration is by involving employees directly in the development of the HR plans. As described in the feature "Managing Globalization: Building Global Leaders at Unilever," employees' opinions can be more than a source of diagnostic information; they may also form the basis of a plan to address strategic business issues.[30]

In the example of Unilever, employees' opinions were the primary method of organizational analysis as well as the basis for a large-scale plan to ensure that the company's top leadership understood and became connected to its key customer base: women around the world.

MANAGING GLOBALIZATION
Building Global Leaders at Unilever

U.S. Unilever, a Dutch-Anglo company, is one of the largest consumer products companies in the world with sales of $50 billion. Its products include Hellmann's® Real Mayonnaise, Mazola® corn oil, Skippy® peanut butter, and Thomas'® English Muffins. Unilever operates in more than 150 countries and employs more than 200,000 workers. The company's projections are that future growth will come primarily from Africa, Asia, Eastern Europe, the Middle East, and the countries of the former Soviet Union.

When the company learned that women made more than 80% of purchasing decisions for its products, it decided it was time to develop and promote more women to senior leadership positions in the company. To begin to address this strategic issue, the CEO worked with the Corporate Strategy Council to convene a weeklong Women's Global Leadership Forum. Attended by 55 women from 25 countries, the event was an intensive work session that sought to document women's beliefs about the current situation, identify barriers to advancement, and provide suggestions for an action plan that the company could implement. To inform discussions at the forum, the company conducted a survey of its 20 corporate officers and its 125 senior executives. The survey results were presented by the CEO at his kickoff address to the forum. The results documented top management's perceptions of the benefits associated with having more women in leadership positions and provided suggestions for what the company could do to increase the number of high-ranking women leaders.

Throughout the week, global teams met to develop recommendations on how the company could begin to create change. These fell into three categories: enhancing career opportunities, increasing women's representation in senior positions, and addressing issues of work/life balance to enable women to perform at their highest capabilities. For each category, suggestions were made for implementation at both global and local levels within the company. In two months, the company's Strategic Council had reviewed and approved the suggestions and launched a companywide change effort based on the recommendations received.

Behavioral Cause-and-Effect Models

As explained in Chapter 1, behavioral cause-and-effect models and strategy maps can be used to provide a more detailed understanding of how employee attitudes and behaviors influence organizational outcomes of interest. When these models include business outcomes that reflect the perspective of shareholders and investors, they make it easy for managers to see the linkages between how human resources are managed and the firm's success at implementing its strategy. For example, if a pharmaceutical company's strategic business objective is growing revenues, a behavioral cause-and-effect model would probably show that revenues are determined, in part, by the ability of the firm to develop innovative drugs and marshal them through the regulatory approval process. Developing innovative drugs, in turn, requires managing research and development (R&D) teams effectively. A behavioral cause-and-effect model could be used to understand the attitudes and behaviors that contribute to the success of R&D teams that develop new products and that obtain approval for them from the Federal Drug Administration.[31]

FAST FACT

Most managers believe that employees do what's rewarded and avoid almost everything else.

Cause-and-effect models can also show direct links between specific HR practices and organizational performance metrics. For example, a study of 61 hospitals in England found that the HR practices used in the hospitals predicted patient mortality rates. Mortality rates—a key performance metric—were lower in hospitals that relied more on teams and in those with more sophisticated training and more rigorous performance appraisal.[32]

Procter & Gamble used employee opinions to construct a behavioral cause-and-effect model as part of its organizational analysis. Based on the qualitative

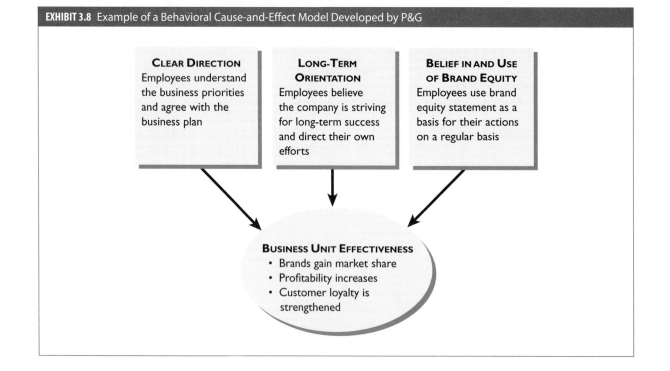

EXHIBIT 3.8 Example of a Behavioral Cause-and-Effect Model Developed by P&G

CLEAR DIRECTION
Employees understand the business priorities and agree with the business plan

LONG-TERM ORIENTATION
Employees believe the company is striving for long-term success and direct their own efforts

BELIEF IN AND USE OF BRAND EQUITY
Employees use brand equity statement as a basis for their actions on a regular basis

BUSINESS UNIT EFFECTIVENESS
• Brands gain market share
• Profitability increases
• Customer loyalty is strengthened

information from its shadowing, focus groups, and interviews, Stengel's team created an employee survey and used it to gather systematic data from its worldwide marketing workforce of 3,500 people. The survey contained 300 questions and covered 10 major issues. By analyzing the responses, P&G determined three major drivers of business unit effectiveness. The basic cause-and-effect model created by P&G is illustrated in Exhibit 3.8. This cause-and-effect model captures the employees' views about what drives business unit effectiveness.

DETERMINING HR OBJECTIVES AND METRICS

Organizations must keep two things in mind when determining HR objectives and metrics.

1.   The HR objectives must be tied to strategic business goals.
2.   The metrics must be well aligned with the specified HR objectives.

Linking HR Objectives to Strategic Business Objectives

Strategic business objectives help focus attention on several important aspects of managing employees, including (1) the number of employees that will be needed as a consequence of anticipated growth or decline, (2) new competencies and behaviors that will be needed as a consequence of aspiring to provide higher-quality customer service, and (3) higher levels of productivity needed as a consequence of identifying the reduction of operating costs as an objective.

Once the strategic business objectives of a change effort have been specified, the implications for managing human resources become clearer. If strategic business objectives call for involvement in mergers and acquisitions, an HR objective might be developing competencies needed for involvement in "soft" due diligence activities. **Soft due diligence** *describes the activities that firms use to assess the compatibility of potential new partners, taking into consideration the corporate cultures and specific HR policies and practices in the organizations being combined.* If the strategic objectives call for improving the organization's learning capacity, an HR objective might be to help the various businesses learn from each other and derive more synergies from their common membership in the larger corporate entity. If strategic objectives call for implementing a customer service strategy, all HR policies and practices may have to be changed to ensure that employees exhibit the behaviors consistent with customer service.

Successful strategic changes are guided by clear objectives. The strategic business objectives of a major change effort typically flow directly from an analysis of the environment and what the company needs to do in the time period ahead. At Unilever, the company's international growth strategy stimulated a discussion about how to ensure the company would have the global leaders it would need to succeed in the future. At P&G, one of the strategic business objectives that drove change efforts was rebuilding market share for its leading brands.

Another example of how an organization's strategic business objectives can set the stage for change is provided by Continental Airlines. When former CEO Gordon Bethune took over beleaguered Continental Airlines, he was charged with turning around a losing operation. Bethune, CEO during the transformation, initiated the change effort by setting out the following strategic objectives and specific metrics for assessing success:

1. *Fly to win.* The goal was to achieve top-quartile industry profit margins.
2. *Fund the future.* To do so required reducing interest expense by owning more hub real estate.
3. *Make reliability a reality.* Specific goals included ranking among the top airlines on the four metrics used by the U.S. Department of Transportation (DOT).
4. *Work together.* The goal was to have a company in which employees would enjoy working and would be valued for their contributions.

Bethune realized early on that achieving the company's strategic objectives would require several changes in the company's HR policies and practices to better align them with the needs of the business. Employees were given specific, companywide goals, and incentives were offered to reward them for achieving the goals. When the specific goals were met, specific rewards followed. For example, one goal was to be ranked in the top five of the DOT on-time performance ratings. For each month the goal was achieved, employees would earn an extra $65. Two months later, Continental was in first place. Goals and rewards were developed for executives, too. For example, employees regularly rated their managers on an employee survey, reporting on how well they communicated, set goals, and treated employees. Executives' bonuses reflected their performance as measured by the survey. Besides improving the bottom line, the changes resulted in higher pay for employees, while the rates of sick leave, turnover, workers' compensation claims, and on-the-job injuries all went down.[33]

Going forward it appears likely that many of these HR practices will remain in place, with some modification, under the new CEO Larry Kellner. When Gordon Bethune announced this transition in CEOs in early 2004, he called Mr. Kellner a "strong leader with tremendous people, operational marketing and analytical skills."

> " *We measure everything around here, except how high the grass grows.* "
>
> *Dave Sanchez*
> *Plant Manager*
> *Ford Factory, Kansas City*

Developing Metrics to Match the Objectives

To track the effectiveness of their change efforts, the best organizations develop clear metrics for assessing progress. Measurement makes assessing improvement possible. The best HR metrics are accepted by managers as legitimate, they are relatively easy to use, and they have an obvious connection to the stated business and HR objectives.[34] Continental Airlines made sure managers accepted its metrics by linking rewards to the achievement of goals that the metrics defined.

Bottom-Line HR Metrics. One way to gain managers' acceptance of the HR metrics used to track the success of change efforts is to use HR metrics that are similar to other so-called bottom-line measures.[35] A human capital return-on-investment (HC ROI) metric is an example of this approach. One way to calculate such an index is with the following formula:

$$\text{HC ROI} = \frac{\text{Revenue} - (\text{Operating expense} - [\text{Compensation cost} + \text{Benefit cost}])}{\text{Compensation cost} + \text{Benefit cost}}$$

An alternative is to calculate a human capital value-added index, as follows:

$$\text{HR value added} = \frac{\text{Revenue} - (\text{Operating expense} - [\text{Compensation cost} + \text{Benefit cost}])}{\text{Total number of full-time equivalent employees (FTEs)}}$$

In organizations that are focused on keeping costs low, a simple index of HR expenses might be appropriate:

$$\text{HR expense ratio} = \frac{\text{Total of all HR expenses}}{\text{Total operating expenses}}$$

Compare the information provided by an expense ratio to the following index, which focuses on revenues. This index might be used by a company whose strategy emphasizes the importance of growth:

$$\text{HR revenue ratio} = \frac{\text{Total revenue}}{\text{Total number of full-time equivalent employees (FTEs)}}$$

HR metrics such as these are gaining popularity because they provide a simple index for tracking changes in an organization's effectiveness in managing its human capital. Nevertheless, such HR metrics must be used with caution. Currently, there are no widely accepted accounting rules to guide an organization's choice of HR metrics. Over a period of time, changes in HR metrics such as these can be caused by many factors that have nothing to do with how well an organization manages its human resources. Nevertheless, indices such as these may prove helpful as a means of tracking general trends over the course of several years.

HR Metrics for SunTrust Bank. When SunTrust Bank adopted the OneBank concept as a principle for its new business strategy, the implications for managing human resources were huge. Until then, there were 28 different HR departments serving 1,200 branches spread across 6 southeastern states. One of the objectives was to develop a single, centralized approach for recruiting, evaluating, and hiring new employees. Besides adhering to professional HR standards for effective staffing, the new approach would have to meet the needs of all the branch managers for it to be accepted and used. To evaluate the effectiveness of the new staffing approach, SunTrust used the HR metrics shown in Exhibit 3.9. As this exhibit shows, the plans that SunTrust developed and implemented helped speed up the hiring process and also reduced costs.[36]

HR Metrics for Deutsche Bank. At Deutsche Bank, the concept of risk management is central to the business strategy, and the HR metrics used by the firm reflect this concern. The firm's research established the following HR risk factors that required careful management: employee motivation, adaptability, qualification, and resignations (departures). Within these domains of

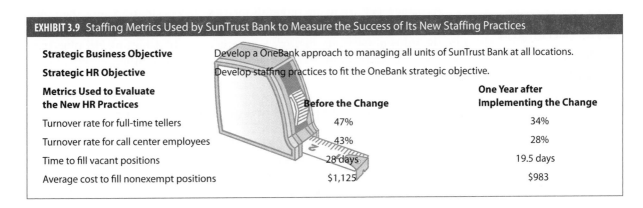

EXHIBIT 3.9 Staffing Metrics Used by SunTrust Bank to Measure the Success of Its New Staffing Practices

Strategic Business Objective	Develop a OneBank approach to managing all units of SunTrust Bank at all locations.	
Strategic HR Objective	Develop staffing practices to fit the OneBank strategic objective.	
Metrics Used to Evaluate the New HR Practices	**Before the Change**	**One Year after Implementing the Change**
Turnover rate for full-time tellers	47%	34%
Turnover rate for call center employees	43%	28%
Time to fill vacant positions	28 days	19.5 days
Average cost to fill nonexempt positions	$1,125	$983

EXHIBIT 3.10 HR Metrics for Risk Management at Deutsche Bank

HR Objective: Maintain strong employee commitment and minimize turnover of key employees.

Metrics

1. Three times a year, conduct a survey of at least 1,000 employees and analyze their responses to survey items that assess:
   - Willingness to stay
   - Attitudes about the labor market
   - Emotional involvement with the organization
   - Early warning signs

2. Focusing on recent hires, assess the extent to which their expectations upon joining the firm have been met, exceeded, or disappointed.

3. Focusing on key leavers, record the reasons for departure, using both managers' judgments and data from exit interviews.

HR Objective: Maintain strong corporate identity by living a set of shared values.

Metrics

Annually conduct a survey of approximately 4,000 employees to assess their attitudes toward the values of
   - Teamwork
   - Trust
   - Innovation
   - Customer focus
   - Performance

Responses are broken out by departments and fed back to managers.

(Based on responses from manager director reports, managers are given suggestions for specific actions they should take to improve employees' attitudes toward the values.)

HR Objective: Maintain status as an employer of choice.

Metrics

At least every three years, conduct a survey of all employees to assess their perceptions of the organization's image, their feelings about their individual job situation, and the corporate culture. Measures include perceptions of:
   - Coordination and integration
   - Strategic direction and intention
   - Organizational learning
   - Recognition
   - Responsibility and empowerment
   - Performance
   - Compensation
   - Leadership

FAST FACT

Of Fortune's Most Admired Companies, 40% track progress on retention, career development, and other employee-oriented measures—more than triple the percentage for companies that didn't make the list.

risk, the company also determined that losing high performers in key areas of the business was the most significant risk. In fact, the cost of losing a key employee was estimated to be 1.5 times the person's annual salary. Deutsche Bank's HR metrics, described in Exhibit 3.10, were designed to help the firm manage these risks.[37]

As managers learn to interpret HR metrics, they begin to see how their own actions can support or impede progress. Over time, they are likely to appreciate the value of measures that track progress toward achieving HR objectives and other precursors of business success instead of focusing exclusively on financial measures.

DEVELOPING HR PLANS AND TIMETABLES

For major change efforts, an organization's strategic plan can be quite complex, with specific plans for all levels and all units involved in the change effort.[38] If an organization is structured along functional departments, then each department develops a strategic plan; if it is organized by region, then plans for each region are developed; and so on.

At P&G and Weyerhaeuser, a cross-functional team of HR and line managers planned many of the changes. The changes that were eventually implemented required a great deal of HR expertise during the planning and design phase, but for the plans to be implemented effectively, line managers had to be committed to the changes and be actively involved in making them happen. The human resource component was fully integrated with the business component of the overall plan.

Regardless of how the HR plan is structured, its development begins with a full consideration of alternatives. After evaluating the pros and cons associated with each alternative, choices are made about which HR activities and policies will change.

Considering Alternatives

After the attack on the World Trade Center and the Pentagon sent the airline industry into a tailspin in the autumn of 2001, most major airlines soon began announcing plans to cut their workforces by as much as 20%. But Southwest Airlines' Chair Herb Kelleher was determined to do everything possible to avoid layoffs. Instead of cutting costs through layoffs, the company scrapped its growth plans, delayed deliveries of new aircraft, and prepared for possible damage to its stock price. This approach to dealing with the economic downturn was possible in part because the company was debt-free and had $1 billion in cash.

In choosing to adopt a no-layoffs policy, some companies have decided that the costs associated with maintaining their workforce are justified to avoid the hidden costs associated with layoffs. These costs include:

- Severance payments made to departing employees.
- Fees paid to consultants who assist with the downsizing process.
- Litigation from aggrieved workers.
- Loss of trust in management.
- Lack of staff needed to grow when the economy rebounds.
- Loss of reputation in the labor market, making future hiring more difficult.
- Cynical and paranoid behaviors among layoff survivors.
- Declining customer satisfaction resulting from low employee morale.[39]

For most strategic business objectives, the list of alternative ways to achieve them can be quite long. The same is true for most HR objectives. For example, some of the alternatives available to employers who face an HR objective of coping with the shortage of skilled workers are listed in Exhibit 3.11. As Exhibit 3.11 reveals, the available alternatives have both potential advantages and potential disadvantages. Solutions that might work in the short term may create new problems in the long term. Solutions that might work in the long term may do little to address short-term needs. Different alternatives have different advantages.

Suppose an organization has the goal of reducing labor costs. Following are several alternatives the firm might consider. Under what conditions would each of these be appropriate?

Layoffs. An analysis of the average size of U.S. firms revealed that the average size of companies grew at a fairly steady pace from 1935 until about 1985. After that, average firm size began to decline rapidly. The reasons that led firms to shrink in size are many, but the approach they used was often the same: massive layoffs. Layoffs can be used to reduce costs relatively quickly and thereby achieve a short-term gain in profits. This appears to explain their popularity. Layoffs have been especially common in the manufacturing sector.[40]

EXHIBIT 3.11 Alternatives for the HR Objective of Coping with Shortages of Skilled Workers

Possible Solutions to a Labor Shortage	Possible Negative Consequences
• Raise base wages to attract more applicants	• May attract more applicants, but new applicants may not be any more qualified. Recruiting costs per hire go up as number of applicants to be screened goes up.
• Offer more financial incentives in an effort to motivate employees to boost their productivity	• If productivity increases don't keep up with increased labor costs, margins will shrink unless consumers are willing to pay higher prices.
• Reduce turnover rates to lessen the need for new hires	• May drive up labor costs if wages tend to increase with time at the company. Too little turnover may stifle creativity. Obsolete skills may become a problem.
• Hire people without the skills needed and train them	• Productivity of new hires is low. Increased supervision of new workers is required, which raises costs. Can be costly, takes time, and workers, once trained, may leave to work for competitors.
• Buy up other companies to acquire their workforce	• The challenge of integrating the acquired company may cause productivity declines in the short term. Success rates for mergers and acquisitions are only about 50%.
• Buy new technologies that reduce the number of people needed	• Major changes in technology require major organizational changes, which take time. New technologies may require even higher levels of skill to operate.
• Utilize foreign labor markets	• The organizational learning curve is steep for domestic firms with no prior international experience. Competition for labor in the global market may be just as stiff as in the domestic market.
• Make business decisions that will reduce the need for more skilled workers	• May be possible, but would probably involve major changes in strategy and even changing the businesses in which the company competes.

Facing the threat of job loss and seeing others lose their jobs can be a traumatic and bitter experience for employees.[41] Furthermore, the long-term economic benefits of downsizing are not well established. These are among the reasons why many excellent companies do everything possible to avoid layoffs.[42] Despite their best efforts, however, even the most employee-friendly companies may deal with difficult economic conditions by reducing their workforces.

FAST FACT

Financial services companies in the United States transferred about 500,000 jobs—8% of industry employment—to foreign countries between 2003 and 2008. The next five years are expected to be similar.

Reducing Turnover. When large and immediate cost reduction is not necessary, an alternative may be to cut costs by reducing employee turnover. As discussed in Chapter 6, the costs of turnover are significant, especially when top performers leave. Reducing turnover may be an effective way to reduce costs if a company has a relatively high turnover rate and it is willing to invest in making the changes that would be needed to retain workers longer.

Outsourcing. In **outsourcing**, *work that had been performed inside the company is contracted out to another company.* For example, a retailer located in the United States may decide to let IBM manage all its computer operations and thereby reduce the total number of employees the firm needs to employ. IBM has much greater expertise than retailers when it comes to managing computer operations, so its employees can do this work more efficiently and with higher quality than the kind of employees who work for large department stores. Retailers can thus reduce the total number of their employees and focus their energies on what they do best. In this example, jobs may be lost at one company (the retailer), but they are not lost to the U.S. economy; they are simply shifted to another employer. If a U.S. firm outsources work to a company in the Philippines to do its payroll, then some jobs may be lost in the United States. The same may also happen in offshoring.[43]

Offshoring. In **offshoring,** *a company decides to continue to do the work itself but moves the work to another country.* Since its founding, Levi Strauss was proud of its American-made jeans, but eventually the pressure to reduce its labor costs grew too great. To survive, it decided to close its U.S. plants and move the work to China and other lower-wage countries. In recent years, many U.S. companies have relocated their software design work and call center operations to India, where talent is plentiful and wages are far below those in the United States.[44] Indeed, the use of offshoring has become so widespread that it has begun to raise concerns about the long-term economic prospects of the American workforce.[45]

Still More Alternatives. The 3M company, based in St. Paul, Minnesota, works hard to keep employees even when the company needs to eliminate jobs. Instead of being fired, displaced employees are given first consideration for other job openings within their unit. If no suitable placement can be found, they are put on the Unassigned List, which makes them eligible for jobs in other units. They can stay on the list for six months. During that time, finding employment is the employee's responsibility, but the company supports their efforts. Before recruiting externally to fill open positions, managers first check the qualifications of people on the Unassigned List. The company also sponsors an optional three-day workshop that covers topics such as outplacement services, coping with job loss, resume writing, and interviewing skills. For the first four months that they are on the Unassigned List, employees have the option of taking a severance package and leaving the company. Approximately 50% of the people on the list find other jobs at 3M within the four-month window. When that happens, both employees and the company are winners.

Internal transfers are just one of many alternatives to massive layoffs. Others include:

- Restricting overtime.
- Reducing the hours in a standard workweek.
- Not renewing contracts for temporary and part-time workers.
- Offering temporary leaves.
- Job sharing.
- Retraining.
- Providing seed funds and entrepreneurship training and encouraging employees to start their own businesses.
- Transferring staff to other companies (e.g., suppliers, customers).
- Giving early retirement with preferential conditions.
- Reducing executive salaries and incentive pay.
- Partnering with government agencies and professional societies to find jobs for displaced employees.
- Managing an employee buyout of the company.[46]

Building a Complete HR Plan

Addressing strategic business objectives such as the need to reduce costs usually requires multipronged solutions. Thus, a comprehensive HR plan for change is likely to have many components, just as a companywide plan for change has many components. To illustrate what some of the components of an HR plan might be, we briefly describe examples of the HR activities of staffing, training, leadership development, and managing benefits.

Staffing Plans. The plans for staffing arise from forecasts about future labor demand and supply. Earlier in this chapter, we described how domestic skilled labor shortages and the age demographics in an organization make staffing a strategic issue. For growing businesses, HR objectives often focus on ensuring that new people are available to support the projected growth. For businesses undergoing global expansion, the HR plan may include developing new approaches to evaluating the ability of new hires and of current employees to work in multicultural settings, as well as their effectiveness while working on projects completed by virtual teams.[47]

Talent Management Plans. Forecasting human resource demand and supply is essential for succession planning and the development of replacement charts. The objective of **succession planning** *is to ensure that the organization is prepared to fill key positions when the incumbents leave for any reason.* For employees, succession planning provides useful information about the direction their career is likely to take if they continue to work in the organization.

Succession planning for CEOs often receives attention in the business press, because staffing for this position is so important to shareholders. Up to a year prior to the CEO's planned retirement, a successor may be named so that there is no uncertainty about the company's plans. Or several possible successors may be identified, with the understanding that their performance will be closely monitored during the next year and used as a basis for making a final decision when the CEO steps down.

Although less public, many organizations conduct similar succession planning for all executive positions, and some also engage in succession planning for all managerial positions. Often, these succession plans involve formal procedures for tracking talent and preparing replacement charts. To keep track of their top talent, many organizations maintain a talent pool. A **talent pool** *is a list of employees who have been identified as having high potential for advancement, usually because they are top performers in their current positions.* The employees in a talent pool are the people whom the organization is especially interested in retaining and developing. Ensuring that employees in the talent pool are considered when job openings occur is one tactic for successful long-term staffing of the organization.

A replacement chart is used to keep track of opportunities for people in the talent pool. In a **replacement chart,** *the titles of key jobs in the organization are displayed along with the names of the incumbents.* Also included are the names of current employees who might be used to fill potential vacancies (i.e., the most appropriate employees from the talent pool). Besides serving the career objectives of employees in the talent pool, replacement charts also alert the organization to possible areas of vulnerability, in the event of an unexpected departure.

Identifying a talent pool and maintaining replacement charts are not the only steps that go into effective succession planning. According to a recent study of exemplary practices in succession planning, the best companies also use the HR practices shown in Exhibit 3.12.

Training Plans. At United Stationers, the HR objectives of clarifying managerial accountability and helping employees see how they fit into the big picture led to HR plans that emphasized training activities. To help managers perform in their new roles, the HR group developed a leadership framework and offered to train interested managers. (Note that it was up to the managers to decide whether to receive training in the leadership framework.) To help employees see how they fit into the picture, HR professionals worked with line managers to develop business awareness training modules for employees. The HR experts made sure the training

EXHIBIT 3.12 Best Practices in Succession Planning

- The process is simple, with minimal paperwork.
- The process is decentralized and owned by local managers.
- Information technology makes it easy to give employees feedback.
- The process fits with the corporate culture.
- Employees receive a variety of job assignments early in their careers.
- Bosses are trained to hold good career discussions.
- Bosses are held accountable for ensuring that developmental action plans are implemented.
- One-on-one mentoring and mentoring networks are supported by the company.

modules met professional-quality standards, but line managers were responsible for the actual business content and for delivering the training to employees.

At P&G, the need for better skills among marketers was met with a plan to develop a marketing university. Now employees can attend several one-week "colleges" that focus on developing the competencies needed for new job assignments. Also available are refresher courses to help employees improve skills such as interviewing and coaching. Opportunities for learning also are available through newly instituted centers of expertise—networks of employees linked in a virtual community led by a "master" who organizes learning forums for the group.

Leadership Development Plans. At Weyerhaeuser and P&G, HR plans for achieving strategic objectives emphasize leadership development activities. Leadership development activities are likely to be important for firms whose strategic objectives include evolving to become a multinational corporation. As organizations globalize, meeting the leadership challenge is often a top priority. In addition to answering the question of who will be available for the senior leadership roles, HR plans should provide a means to ensure that the available people have the competencies required to do the work.

Unfortunately, many global firms do not have the global leadership talent they need. According to one study of 1,500 executives in 50 global companies, only 8% of their top 100 executives were from other countries, even though the companies generated 40% of their business overseas. Furthermore, only one-third of the executives in the study reported having any expatriate experience. Clearly, to begin developing a strong talent pool for the future, such firms must develop new practices to encourage and support the development of global leaders.[48]

Timetables

Change is tough work that often involves making difficult and sometimes painful decisions. If people can put it off, they will. Building in deadlines and scheduling checkpoints is one way to keep the change process moving ahead. The best deadlines are both challenging and achievable.[49]

Realistic expectations about how quickly change will occur are important to the long-term success of change efforts. Changes designed to help employees balance their work and nonwork commitments might be effective in only a year or two. More fundamental changes can take much longer. Usually even changes that seem relatively simple occur more slowly than expected. Xerox began changing its culture to be more receptive of diversity more than 30 years ago and continues to do so. It is doubtful that managers anticipated how long this change effort would continue to evolve.

At Weyerhaeuser, the process of change unfolded over several years. Continuity in the company's senior management ranks facilitated this long-term

FAST FACT

Less than 20% of executives in global companies speak a second language.

realignment of the business. From the beginning, top-level managers understood that they were embarking on a long journey that would require patience and persistence. Over the years, they learned from their mistakes, and because most managers stayed at the company, the lessons they learned were retained and used as new challenges arose.

Timelines for Developing Talent. When a computer manufacturing company that produced leading-edge specialty products for business decided to change its strategy to include the consumer market, it knew it would need managers with a different set of skills. The company estimated it would need five years to build the talent pool. The first year was spent analyzing the environment, developing a model of the skills that would be needed, and developing a strategy for building the talent pool. The initiatives taken during the next four years included

- Assessing their current managers to determine who had the skills needed for the new business strategy.
- Training managers on the meaning of the new strategy.
- Externally recruiting new managers with the needed skills.
- Meeting quarterly with senior executives to keep them informed of progress.

As these planned initiatives were rolled out, it became clear that changes were needed in most other aspects of the HRM system, including the development of a variety of additional training programs and changes in the compensation system.

Timelines for Layoffs and Plant Closings. Often, the process of establishing timetables reveals the full complexity of a change effort. Consider the planning process for layoffs and plant closings. For employers with 100 or more employees, some elements of the HR timetable are specified by legal regulations. According to the **Worker Adjustment and Retraining Act of 1988 (WARN)**, *employers are required to provide workers with 60 days' notice of a plant or office closing.* For plant closings and layoffs covered under the WARN act, employers must describe their planned actions to

- Employees (or their union representatives, if applicable).
- The mayor or other chief elected official of the local government.
- The top official of the state's dislocated workers program.

The WARN act specifies that these notices be given in writing, but few employers rely only on written notices. Instead, they set timetables for meetings with managers and employees to explain what will happen at each site, when, and how.

Often employees experience shock and confusion when layoffs are first announced. The result is that they retain little of the information presented at the early meetings. Consequently, HR professionals must make plans to follow up with additional meetings. They may also establish hotlines, provide counseling services, and furnish other services to assist those who are laid off. Because some employees may react violently, additional security measures may be needed for several months after the announcement. The HR timetable for a layoff or plant closing may also include dates by which

- Decisions will be made about the status of individual employees.
- Offers will be made to encourage voluntary employee departures.
- Employees must sign a separation agreement.
- Meetings will be held to explain the implications for employees' benefits.

- Media announcements will be released.
- Negotiations with unions will be initiated and completed.
- Service contracts will end for relevant outside vendors (e.g., recruiters, outplacement counselors).[50]

IMPLEMENTING HR ACTION PLANS AND FACILITATING CHANGE

Organizations can do a number of things when implementing HR action plans to improve their effectiveness. These include involving employees, establishing accountability, managing resistance to change, and showing respect in difficult times.

Involving Employees

An important role for HR professionals when creating and implementing a plan of action is finding ways to involve people throughout the organization. For a change effort to be effective, those who are affected by it must buy into it. The best way to ensure that they do is through early involvement.[51] It seems obvious that employees should be involved when planning change, but often even experienced managers forget this principle. Task forces, focus groups, surveys, hotlines, and informal conversations are just a few of the ways managers can involve employees and other stakeholders in planning change efforts.[52]

To involve managers in developing plans for meeting strategic business objectives, Siemens uses its university. Its in-house corporate training gives responsibility for solving real business problems to analysts and engineers from around the world, who work together in "student" teams. Students share their analyses with business units and debate the benefits and costs of their plans.

At Georgia-Pacific, employee teams take responsibility for creating change. This company's approach to involving employees in the change process is described in the feature "Managing Teams: Mill Improvement Process Teams at Georgia-Pacific."[53]

Establishing Accountability

When specifying objectives, it is important to state not only what is to be achieved, but also who is responsible for making the needed changes. If the change is a success, will only managers reap the rewards? If things don't go well, will the lower-level employees be the ones who suffer? Involvement is likely to be most effective when people also have a stake in the outcomes.

Holding people accountable for achieving the objectives of a change can have a variety of implications for human resource management practices. Typically, accountability translates into new approaches to awarding incentive pay and bonuses. Depending on the nature of the strategic objectives and on whether they are qualitatively different from those of the past, new performance management practices may be required. Procedures for deciding on future promotions may also be affected. At Unilever, for example, the compensation system was changed as part of the HR plan to improve the representation of women in leadership positions. Senior managers were given goals for developing and retaining high-performing women, and incentive pay was linked to the managers' success in achieving the goals.

Change Has Already Started

If the people who are responsible for drawing up the blueprint for strategic change efforts have followed the principle of involvement, the implementation stage is

FAST FACT

To align employees' self-interests with the goals of Mercedes-Benz, the president, Georg Bauer, offered the security of a new—and probably better—job to anyone bold enough to eliminate his or her own current position.

" **Communications: Everybody needs to hear the same message and know what it means and what they need to do and what they are accountable for.** "

Rodger L. Boehm
Former Chief Executive Officer
Deere & Company

MANAGING TEAMS
Mill Improvement Process Teams at Georgia-Pacific

Georgia-Pacific, which is based in Atlanta, manufactures and markets tissue, packaging, paper, and building products. Founded 80 years ago as a lumber company, it is now a division of Koch Industries and employs 55,000 people in 300 locations throughout North America and Europe. With Wal-Mart as its biggest customer, it must continually improve to retain that account and stay competitive.

Georgia-Pacific relies heavily on teamwork in order to continuously change for the better. The goal is to create targeted incremental change quickly and continuously. A Mill Improvement Process team, located in the engineering department, coordinates all of the change projects going on throughout the company. To initiate a change, this group conducts some preliminary diagnostic work. The diagnosis helps the group make decisions about the particular types of changes needed in specific mills. Then the group works with the managers of each mill to initiate a change effort. If a mill is targeted for change, the process begins with the formation of a mill steering committee. At the container-board mill, for example, the steering committee might include five section heads who understand all aspects of manufacturing in that mill. The first task of this committee is to conduct a thorough diagnosis of the mill. After talking to employees to get ideas, the steering committee selects about a dozen specific changes that are needed.

For each needed change at a mill, a special project team is created. Each project team focuses on making a targeted change in a period of 10 weeks. A team leader is appointed to each team and the project becomes that person's full-time responsibility. The 10-week periods of targeted change are called *waves*. A wave begins with each project team conducting an all-day kickoff meeting to set a specific goal, establish the metrics they will use to track changes, and set up a work plan to achieve the goal. After setting their goals, project teams review them with the mill steering committee. Then project teams work on their own to implement specific changes. As an example, at the Lehigh Valley Dixie plant, where they manufacture paper cups and plastic lids, a team set a goal of finding new equipment that could produce products more efficiently at a cost that was affordable for the plant. The team investigated all of the requirements the new equipment would have to meet, discussed the implications of using a new technology, and conducted an analysis to determine if the required investment was justified.

At the end of 10 weeks, the wave concludes with teams reporting their results to the steering committee. Then, the whole cycle starts over with a new set of project teams working on a new set of issues. To ensure that the same people are not always called on for these intensive projects, the company has a set of rules to ensure rotating involvement in the process.

At Georgia-Pacific, the basic process for creating change is highly structured, but each mill has a great deal of independence to implement the process in its own unique way. Often project teams create logos for their projects, print identifying t-shirts, and in general find ways to take ownership of the process. At the end of each wave, rewards and recognition may be given to celebrate the achievements of the project teams. During the past decade, thousands of change projects have been carried out, and the Mill Improvement Process has contributed hundreds of thousands of dollars to the company's bottom line. Just as important, the process has helped Georgia-Pacific become a learning organization that is capable of thriving in a highly competitive industry.

actually already well underway by the time the plans have been fully developed. People already have a good grasp of the vision; they had to understand it to be involved in the planning process. Although a leadership team may have been responsible for putting the plan together, many details (e.g., goals and timetables) were developed using substantial input from the people who will be expected to implement the plan. If honest two-way communication has occurred throughout the planning process, major obstacles to implementing change are already identified and removed. If empowered employees have been energized by the challenges identified, some are already experimenting with new approaches to their work. To the extent this is true, problems of resistance—the major barrier to implementing change—will be lessened. Even in the best of circumstances, however, pockets of resistance will be found.

Managing Resistance to Change

Few planned organizational change efforts of any kind proceed smoothly. Most run into some amount of resistance. The various forms of resistance include immediate criticism, malicious compliance, sabotage, insincere agreement, silence, deflection, and in-your-face defiance.[54] The reasons for such resistance include fear, misunderstanding, and cynicism.[55]

Fear. Some people resist change because they fear that they'll be unable to develop the competencies required to be effective in the new situation. When Mercedes-Benz Credit Corporation set out to restructure its operations in the United States, employees seemed to have good reason to be fearful of the future. Weren't layoffs sure to follow? The company's president, Georg Bauer, knew that fear could be a problem and that it would make getting needed help from employees difficult. "It was absolutely essential to establish a no-fear element in this whole change process," he said. Rather than resist change, he wanted employees to help create a new, more efficient organization by expressing their ideas about where to cut and how to do work differently. Besides empowering employees to make decisions about how to change their work, he offered an incentive to convince employees that even cutting their own jobs wouldn't harm them financially.[56]

Misunderstandings. People resist change when they don't understand its implications. Unless quickly addressed, misunderstandings and lack of trust build resistance. When wide-ranging changes are planned, managers and HR professionals should anticipate that misunderstandings will develop and take steps to minimize them. Top managers must be visible during the change process to spell out clearly the new direction for the organization and what it will mean for everyone involved. Getting employees to discuss their problems openly is crucial to overcoming resistance to change.[57] Senior managers at Weyerhaeuser provided frequent, clear, and precise communications throughout that company's restructuring efforts. The communications helped keep employees informed about what was happening and why.

At Prudential Insurance, a specially designed game was used to help employees understand the implications of the company's impending change from a mutual association to a public company. Small groups of employees at all levels and in all types of jobs throughout the company were brought together to play the game, which was both informative and fun. Top management was convinced that this approach to informing the workforce about the implications of the change they were about to experience would enable the change process to go smoothly—and it did.

Cynicism. In some organizations, initiating change efforts is seen simply as something that new managers do to make their mark.[58] Over time, employees see change efforts come and go, much like the seasons of the year, as managers implement one fad after the other. Eventually, cynicism sets in and employees refuse to support yet another change "program." Without employee support, the change efforts fail, further contributing to cynicism.[59] Cynicism is difficult to combat once it sets in. Perhaps the best approach is to prevent it from developing by avoiding the temptation to adopt the latest management fad. Organizations that take a strategic and systematic approach to developing and implementing change efforts are less likely to initiate a change effort simply because it is the latest craze.

> *The top team, and there are only six of us, so it's a very small management team, must be ambassadors of change.*
>
> Peter Gossas
> Chief Executive Officer
> Sandvik Materials Technology

> *My biggest challenge was change management. Poor communication will cause a re-org to fail. If people understand and accept the change and the ups and downs that come with it, they will make it work. If they don't accept the change, it will disintegrate on you.*
>
> Ken Troyan
> Senior Vice President
> SunTrust Bank

Showing Respect in Difficult Times

Sometimes, employees' fears are justified. When a firm's strategic plan calls for substantial reductions in the size of its workforce, some employees will lose their jobs. When employees must be let go, the process by which jobs are eliminated can make a difference—for those who remain as well as for those who are terminated. Feelings of loss, lack of information, and a perception of apparent managerial capriciousness as the basis for decisions about who will be terminated cause anxiety and an obsession with personal survival.[60] They also result in a loss of trust, without which organizations can't be very effective.

The negative cycle of reactions may not be inevitable. If survivors feel that the process used to decide whom to let go was fair, their productivity and the quality of their job performance may not suffer as much. It's not the terminations themselves that create bitterness; it's the manner in which terminations are handled.

Survivors often express feelings of disgust and anger when their friends and colleagues have been fired. If they believe their own performance is no better than those who have been let go, survivors may feel guilty that they have kept their jobs.[61] Statistics show that older displaced workers who find new work earn about one-third less than they did in their old job. This contributes to survivors' angst.[62] Thus, in developing human resource policies, procedures, and practices for effective downsizing and layoffs, even the needs of survivors require attention.

As with any major organizational change, the steps of diagnosing the current situation and developing a careful plan to implement change are essential during downsizing. But the process of downsizing isn't just about strategies and plans; it's also about relationships between the people in a company, and it's about personal character. The greatest challenges for companies and their managers are maintaining employee morale and regaining employee trust while the actions of the company seem to say, "You are not valuable."[63]

Review, Revise, and Refocus

When a company offers a product to the external marketplace, it almost certainly reviews and evaluates the success of the product using objective indicators. Likewise, the success of products and services offered in the company's internal marketplace should be monitored. At this point, the measures developed to track the progress of change efforts come into play. The measures define the criteria for evaluating whether a program or initiative is successful or is in need of revision. For example, if personal self-development is the only goal one hopes to achieve from holding diversity awareness workshops, then asking employees whether the workshop experience was valuable may be the only data that should be collected. However, when large investments are made for the purposes of reducing turnover, of attracting new or different employees to the firm, or of improving team functioning (or all three), then data relevant to these objectives should be examined.

A human resource information management (HRIM) system facilitates evaluation by allowing for the thorough, rapid, and frequent collection and dissemination of data. Based on what is learned, people can make informed decisions about whether to stay the course as planned, or revisit and perhaps revise the original plan. Overall objectives for the change effort are not likely to be changed at this point, but new goals might be added and timetables might be adjusted.

Change expert John Kotter believes that change can be facilitated by virtually guaranteeing that the review and evaluation process produces some positive results, which can then be used as a cause for celebration. He calls these "short-term wins." The slowness of change can be demotivating. After several months of all-out effort, employees will almost certainly be asked to rededicate themselves for another several months of effort. Without some evidence that the new ways

FAST FACT

Many companies use outplacement firms, such as Lee Hecht Harrison, Manchester, and Challenger, Gray and Christmas, to ensure that the separation process is done professionally.

of doing things are paying off, too many people may give up and join the ranks of the resisters. Rather than leave to chance the question of whether there will be anything to celebrate after a year or two of effort, Kotter suggests specifically assigning a few excellent people to the task of creating a short-term win. And when they meet the challenge, be sure to involve everyone in the celebration.[64]

Whether or not the evaluation of progress against goals is accompanied by celebration, pausing to reflect on how the evaluation process is an essential part of any effective change process is valuable. This ensures that the change process will be self-correcting and should prevent most misjudgments made during the planning process from turning into major fiascoes.

CURRENT ISSUES

Of the several issues related to HR planning that are currently being discussed, the two noted here are global workforce planning and the wholly sustainable enterprise.

Global Workforce Planning

Increasingly companies, regardless of size, are being impacted by the realities of globalization, as described in Chapter 2. Managers must always think about where their competition is and where their customers are or might be. They realize, in many cases, that they may have to be in markets around the world to survive in the long run. They may also have to outsource or offshore some of their production or service activities for cost and for skill reasons.[65] HR professionals, in turn, need to think in terms of planning and managing a global workforce. For example, IBM, Cisco, and Intel are increasingly moving operations to India, China, and Vietnam. As a consequence, the HR professionals in those companies need to develop plans for where and how to get the necessary employees. Do the HR professionals in the United States hire local HR professionals to do all the local hiring overseas? Are the senior managers of these operations going to be sent over from the United States? If yes, who will do their jobs at home? If these companies send operations abroad, what do they do with U.S. employees who may no longer be needed? Can the HR activities in use in their U.S. locations be transferred to their overseas locations, or is it better to develop them to fit local conditions? These are just a few of the many important questions facing HR professionals as they engage in planning for the global workforce.

The Wholly Sustainable Enterprise

Just as companies more than ever need to think and act in local and global ways in planning for their global workforces, they also need to think about the impact (footprint) they have on the environments in which they operate. In a recent report on the growing importance of sustainable business practices, Deloitte, the consulting firm, put it this way:

> The Industrial Revolution sparked a relationship between growth and profitability and the conversion of resources, namely human, capital, and natural, to revenue and profit. This resulted in the corresponding expansion of the required "global footprint" related to employees, facilities, technologies, organizations, capital, and natural resources. Today there is a clear and growing support for the idea that companies can transform themselves into environmentally and socially responsible enterprises that deliver measurable benefits to their host communities, while still providing solid earnings.[66]

LEARNING GOAL 7

FAST FACT
Over 1.5 billion people have entered the global labor market in the past ten years, thanks in large part to technology.

FAST FACT
Companies are thinking more about their impact on the communities in which they operate. This is referred to as their footprint.

MANAGING ETHICS
HR and Supply Chain Management at HP

As with many MNCs today, HP uses suppliers from around the world to produce parts for its final products, many of which are also assembled abroad. To achieve the desired quality and cost, HP is concerned about how these suppliers manage their operations. HP is also concerned about how the employees are managed. These concerns are reflected in HP's approach to supply chain social and environmental responsibility.

In 2002, HP released its Supply Chain Social and Environmental Responsibility (SER) Policy, which built on its own internal Human Rights and Labor Policy. When developing the HP Supplier Code of Conduct, it benchmarked against the codes that had been established in the footwear, apparel, and telecommunication industries. HP's approach is founded on the supplier requirements stated in the HP Supplier Code of Conduct and their General Specification for the Environment, which address product and operational environmental issues such as restrictions on materials used in HP products.

Human rights, or the standards of treatment to which all people are entitled, are a central focus of HP's SER approach. The most widely recognized definition is the Universal Declaration of Human Rights, adopted by the United Nations in 1948. HP's Global Citizenship Policy states its commitment to the Universal Declaration of Human Rights and includes specific policies on Human Rights and Labor. HP supports and respects the protection of international human rights within its sphere of influence and ensures that it is not complicit in human rights abuses. HP believes that its suppliers should observe the same policies. Making progress on human rights, therefore, requires a multistakeholder approach. To support their suppliers in meeting HP's SER standards, HP has collaborated with the United Nations and other firms to create a "human rights starter kit" for employers around the world.

If companies are operating in an environmentally and socially responsible manner, trying to minimize their footprint and thus becoming wholly sustainable enterprises, is there a role for HR professionals? Many HR professionals are saying yes. The Code of Ethics of SHRM suggests that HR professionals have an ethical responsibility to be involved in the company's effort to become a wholly sustainable enterprise.

Hewlett Packard's (HP's) company practices for social responsibility illustrate just how extensively HR's role in corporate sustainability can go. This is described further in the feature "Managing Ethics: HR and Supply Chain Management at HP."[67] As the HP example shows, the HR implications of a company's sustainability efforts can be significant.[68] If you think about it, virtually every HRM activity can be utilized to improve sustainability: for example, how the individuals are selected, how they are trained, how they are paid, and how their performance is evaluated.

CHAPTER SUMMARY WITH LEARNING GOALS

⚠ **STRATEGIC IMPORTANCE.** The dynamic external environment often creates the need for organizations to do things differently, requiring new strategies and new strategic objectives. To achieve their strategic objectives, organizations may need to focus on a new vision, restructure their operations, expand, downsize, or otherwise transform who they are and what they do. A new competitive strategy may require new employee behaviors and competencies, and as a result new HR policies and practices may be needed. Thus, as the environment changes, HR activities need to be correctly aligned with these changing conditions.

2 HR PLANNING PROCESS. Human resource planning refers to the systematic efforts of firms and HR professionals to identify and respond to the short- and long-term human resource implications of a company's strategic business objectives created by the changing environment. The HR planning phases include assessing the global and organizational environment, specifying HR objectives and metrics for change, and developing specific HR plans and timetables. A comprehensive HR plan for strategic change is likely to address a variety of HR activities, including staffing, training, leadership development, and benefits.

3 SCANNING AND ASSESSING. To make sure that the HR actions for change and/or alignment are appropriate, it is necessary to determine what needs to be done. Essential in this determination is scanning and assessing the qualities of the external and organizational environments, as described in Chapter 2.

4 HR OBJECTIVES AND METRICS. Significant change almost always involves unforeseeable sources of resistance and unintended consequences. Although these cannot be avoided, their detrimental effects can be minimized by involving the entire organization in planning for and evaluating the change process. Managers and other employees who will be affected by strategic changes should be involved in developing the objectives and the metrics used to evaluate success. Monitoring key metrics of success throughout the change process makes it possible for an organization to quickly detect when corrective action is needed, as well as when key milestones have been reached and can be celebrated.

5 HR PLANS AND TIMETABLES. As in the determination of HR objectives and metrics, developing HR plans and timetables benefits from the participation of all members of the HR Triad. All members bring an important perspective and body of knowledge that enhances the quality of the HR plans and the accuracy of the timetables.

6 HR ACTION PLANS. Effective HR planning, aligning, and changing improve the ability of organizations to satisfy customers while addressing the concerns of other stakeholders. HR planning, aligning, and changing, in turn, require an understanding of specific HR policies and practices and their impact on employees. By studying the remaining chapters, you will begin to gain the insight and understanding required to design and implement an HRM system that is aligned with and appropriate for an organization's specific strategic objectives and its environment.

7 CURRENT ISSUES. Two current issues of increasing concern today are global workforce planning and sustainability. Both reflect the reality of the global environment for organizations and employees, and we all have a stake in how well they are managed.

TERMS TO REMEMBER

Anticipatory change
Horizontal alignment
Human capital (HC) ROI expense ratio
Human resource (HR) expense ratio
Human resource (HR) forecasts
Human resource (HR) metrics
Human resource (HR) objectives
Human resource (HR) planning
Human resource (HR) plans
Human resource (HR) revenue ratio
Human resource (HR) value added
Incremental change
Judgmental forecasts
Learning organization

Offshoring
Organizational analysis
Outsourcing
Radical change
Reactive change
Replacement chart
Soft due diligence
Statistical forecasts
Succession planning
Talent pool
Timetables
Vertical alignment
Worker Adjustment and Retraining Act of 1988 (WARN)

QUESTIONS FOR DISCUSSION AND REFLECTIVE THINKING

1. Review Chapter 2, which describes several aspects of the external and organizational environments. Which aspects of the external environment will be most likely to stimulate change in the next 10 years? Do you think these changes will be incremental or radical? Explain.

2. Now consider the HR implications of the changes you identified in question 1: Which HR policies and practices are most likely to be affected by these changes (e.g., recruitment, training, performance management, etc.)? Describe the consequences you think are the most likely.

3. Deutsche Bank relies heavily on employee surveys to create its HR metrics. What are some advantages and disadvantages of employee surveys as a method for assessing progress toward HR objectives? For each HR objective shown in Exhibit 3.9, describe one HR metric of actual employee behavior that could be used.

4. Is it inevitable that employees will respond to change with feelings of fear? If you believe the answer is yes, state the implications of this for managing strategic change. If you believe the answer is no, describe what managers can do to minimize such feelings during change.

5. A thorough approach to planning for change can take a great deal of time. When time is short, which steps in the planning process can be eliminated the most readily? What are the potential risks of skipping these steps? Explain your logic.

6. Throughout your career you will often be expected to lead and facilitate radical change initiatives. What can you personally do now to become better prepared to be an effective change leader and facilitator?

PROJECTS TO EXTEND YOUR LEARNING

1. **Integration and Application.** Before continuing, review the case of Southwest Airlines at the end of this book. Then consider how changing from a regional carrier to a national carrier is likely to affect the company. Suppose you were assigned to a task force charged with planning for the addition of service to a new hub location in Vermont. Assume the new hub will be open for operation in six months.

    a. Establish a timetable and indicate the major HR objectives that will have to be achieved in the next six months.

    b. Prioritize the top five HR objectives associated with expanding operations into a new state.

    c. For the top five HR objectives, list at least five HR metrics that could be used to measure progress toward meeting them.

2. **Using the Internet.** Many useful online resources are available to help organizations plan for and deal with change.

    a. Learn about assessment tools that can be used during organizational analysis, including
       - KEYS, a survey published by the Center for Creative Leadership that is designed to assess the organization's climate for creativity (www.ccl.org).
       - An expert system (OrgCon) intended to identify strategic misalignments that was developed by EcoMerc (www.ecomerc.com).

    b. Visit the home pages of several professional organizations whose members have special expertise in the area of strategic change, including
       - The Academy of Management's Division of Organizational Change and Development (http://division.aomonline.org/odc/).
       - The Tavistock Institute (www.tavistockinstitute.org/index.php).

    c. For more information on the wholly sustainable enterprise, visit
       - Business for Social Responsibility (www.bsr.org).
       - Social Accountability International (www.sa-intl.org).

- Sustainable Culture: Evolution of Humanity (www.sustainability.org).
- Society for Human Resource Management (www.shrm.org).
- Ethics Resource Center (www.ethics.org).
- Oxfam International (www.oxfam.org).

d. Learn the details of Hewlett-Packard's Supply Chain Social and Environmental Responsibility (SER) at www.hp.com.

3. **Experiential Activity.** This activity involves developing metrics for a company to evaluate progress against their objective of becoming an employer of choice. Your instructor will assign students to small groups. Before you meet with your group, you need to prepare individually. Your group will be asked to meet for a few minutes to make a final recommendation. Here is the situation:

You just started in your new job at the Farma Pharmaceuticals firm. You are serving on a task force charged with developing HR metrics that can be used to track the firm's progress toward becoming an employer of choice. Members of the task force are all recent hires because Farma Pharmaceuticals believes new hires are in the best position to understand the implications of being an employer of choice. The task force has met several times and now has a list of specific HR metrics that it is considering. Today, the task force is meeting to make its final decision about which HR metrics it will recommend to top management.

Activities

Below are descriptions of the most-favored metrics. Rank-order these choices using 1 to indicate the measure you think is best, 2 for the second-best measure, and so on. Be sure to make notes to justify your reasoning so that you can explain your rationale to the other members of your task force.

Rank	Metric Being Considered	Your Notes
☐	Cost per hire (includes advertising, external recruiter fees, employee referral bonuses, candidate travel expenses, and product giveaways)	
☐	Number of positions that remain open for ___ days before being filled. Metrics are kept for each of the following times: <ul><li>0–50 days</li><li>51–100 days</li><li>101–150 days</li><li>151–200 days</li><li>200+ days</li></ul> Separate metrics are kept for four categories: <ul><li>Entry level</li><li>Middle level</li><li>Executives</li><li>Technical and professional</li></ul>	
☐	Year-to-date accept/decline ratio: Number of offers accepted divided by number of offers made, averaged across all positions	
☐	Intern conversion ratio: Percentage of interns who are subsequently hired for full-time positions	
☐	Offer acceptance rate: Percentage of offers for full-time work that are accepted	
☐	Retention ratios: Percentage of employees who remain with the company for: <ul><li>Less than one year</li><li>1–2 years</li><li>More than two years</li></ul>	

(continued)

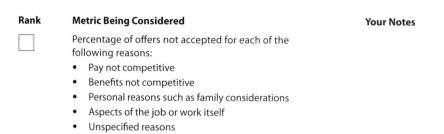

Rank	Metric Being Considered	Your Notes
☐	Percentage of offers not accepted for each of the following reasons: • Pay not competitive • Benefits not competitive • Personal reasons such as family considerations • Aspects of the job or work itself • Unspecified reasons	

CASE STUDY

MANAGING HUMAN RESOURCES AT BARDEN BEARINGS

The Barden Bearings Corporation manufactures high-precision ball bearings for machine tools, aircraft instruments and accessories, aircraft engines, computer peripherals, textile spindles, and medical and dental equipment. Currently, it employs about 1,000 people and includes a marketing department and a small corporate staff. It was founded during World War II to manufacture the special bearings needed for the Norden bombsight and has been nonunion since the beginning. Mr. Donald Brush, vice president and general manager of the precision bearings division, gave the following description of his division:

"Reporting directly to me is a small staff comprising a manufacturing manager, a quality manager, an engineering manager, a director of manufacturing planning, and a manager of human resources (see Case Exhibit 1). We meet several times a week to discuss current problems, as well as short- and long-range opportunities and needs. On alternate weeks, we augment this group by including the supervisors who report to the senior managers listed in Case Exhibit 1. I might interject here that all supervisors meet with hourly employees on either a weekly or biweekly basis to review specific departmental successes and failures, and to otherwise keep employees informed about the business and to encourage ownership of their jobs. The managers themselves meet on call as the Employee Relations Committee to discuss and recommend the approval of a wide range of issues that include the evaluation and audit of hourly and salaried positions, as well as the creation and modification of all divisional HR policies.

"A few words about our Human Resource Department: There are six employees who together provide the basic services of employment, affirmative action, employee activity support, labor relations, interpretation of the federal and state laws, benefits administration, wage and salary administration, records preparation and maintenance, cafeteria supervision, and so on. There are, in addition, two people who coordinate our rather extensive training activities.

"As currently organized, the Medical Department comes under the supervision of the manager of human resources. Its authorized staff includes a medical director, the manager of employee health and safety (who is an occupational health nurse), a staff nurse, a safety specialist, and a secretary/clerk.

"The development and execution of plans and programs, including those of a strategic nature, almost invariably involve the active participation of HR. And that's how we want it to be. On the other hand, the HR department doesn't run the business. By this I mean they don't hire or fire, promote or demote. They don't write job descriptions or determine salaries or wages. All these things are done by the line managers with the HR department providing a framework to ensure that all actions are consistent with and appropriate to company goals. You might say that HR is our 'Jiminy Cricket'—they're there for advice, consent, and, importantly, as a conscience.

HR Objectives

"During the past several months, we have been running into many issues that affect the very essence of our business objectives: growth, profits, survival, and competitiveness. Because the issues involve our human resources, these must be our major focus. The following briefly describes the nature of each of the four HR objectives.

Recruiting and Training New Hourly Employees

"The need to recruit and train approximately 125 new hourly workers to respond to a surge in business is very challenging. By midyear, it became evident that we had an opportunity to significantly increase our business. To achieve otherwise attainable goals, we need to increase our hourly workforce by a net of about 125 employees (that is, in addition to normal turnover, retirements, etc.) in one year. I have asked HR to test the waters, recognizing that the unemployment in the Danbury labor market for skilled workers has reached an unprecedented low of about 2.6%.

Safety and Occupational Health Improvement

"The need to create a heightened awareness by the workforce for safety and occupational health considerations is very important. This is an evolving mission born of a dissatisfaction on our part about 'safety as usual.' Over the years, Barden employees have assumed that, because we are a metalworking shop, people were just going to get hurt. But we cannot afford

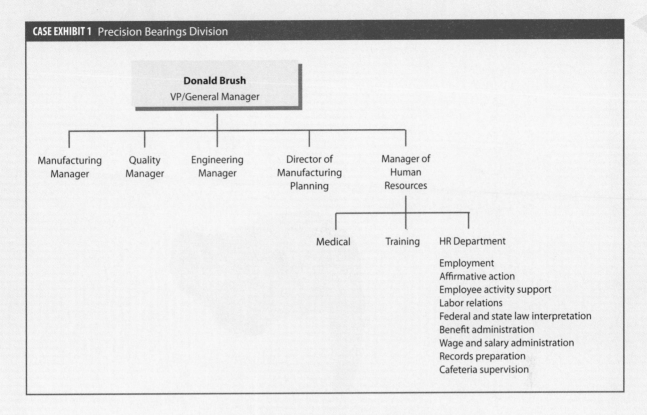

CASE EXHIBIT 1 Precision Bearings Division

Donald Brush — VP/General Manager

- Manufacturing Manager
- Quality Manager
- Engineering Manager
- Director of Manufacturing Planning
- Manager of Human Resources
  - Medical
  - Training
  - HR Department
    - Employment
    - Affirmative action
    - Employee activity support
    - Labor relations
    - Federal and state law interpretation
    - Benefit administration
    - Wage and salary administration
    - Records preparation
    - Cafeteria supervision

to have people get hurt and miss work anymore. Yet, as our workforce ages, the employees seem to get out of shape and become more injury- and illness-prone.

Managing Health Costs of an Aging Workforce

"The spiraling health costs of an aging and sometimes out-of-shape workforce are very costly. All employers face this. Barden's problem is a little unique in that hourly employees tend to stay with the company and retire from the company. For example, we still have several employees whose careers began with us 45 years ago. Our average age approaches 45 for employees and their dependent spouses. Generally, our jobs do not require much physical effort, and it's easy to become out of shape. As a consequence, employees get sick, use hospitals, and have accidents.

New Machines and the Development of Qualified Workers

"The technological evolution of increasingly complex machinery and related manufacturing equipment, and the development of trained workers to operate and maintain this equipment, are important facts of life. This process is unceasing and requires a good deal of planning for both the short and the long run. For example, what should we do in the next year, or five years out, to remain competitive in terms of cost, quality, and service? Buying and rebuilding machines is part of the story. Running them efficiently is quite another. As you know, modern equipment of this

sort requires operational people who are not only knowledgeable about the turning or grinding of metals, but also conversant with computerized numerical controls. The employee who sets up and operates a $500,000 machine must be well trained. Yet finding trained people is getting more difficult."

Mr. Brush knows that these HR objectives all reflect the increasing multiculturalism of the workforce. He also knows these issues will be around for a long time. He requests that you provide him with your general ideas and suggestions. He doesn't want details at this time.

CASE QUESTIONS

1. Which of the HR objectives facing Mr. Brush are really the most important to the success of the business? Prioritize them and justify your list.

2. Now consider this list of objectives from the perspective of employees. Using the employees' perspective, how would you prioritize the list? What are the implications of any differences in the two lists of priorities for Mr. Brush?

3. Choose two objectives. For each, describe the key roles and responsibilities of the HR manager, the line managers, and other employees.

This case was prepared by Randall S. Schuler, who expresses his appreciation for the cooperation of Donald Brush.

Ensuring Fair Treatment and Legal Compliance

Learning Goals

After reading this chapter, you should be able to:

1 Describe the strategic importance of fairness and legal compliance.

2 Explain three factors that influence perceptions of fairness.

3 Describe several employment laws intended to ensure fair treatment.

4 Understand the primary procedures for settling disputes between employees and employers.

5 Recognize the proactive approaches employers use to ensure fair treatment.

6 Describe two current issues in ensuring fair treatment and legal compliance.

MANAGING HUMAN RESOURCES AT WAL-MART

Tom Coughlin, chief of Wal-Mart's U.S. stores, found himself explaining in court how he tried to encourage store managers to bring more women and minorities up to higher levels in the company: "I've rearranged rooms by ethnicity and gender to try to drive home that we're not all recognizing what our opportunities are relative to finding people in the organization that better represent both the gender and race issue." Apparently, this approach to managing workforce diversity—dubbed "managing by musical chairs" by one reporter—did not work. Coughlin was in court that day because a female employee named Stephanie Odle had filed a complaint with the Equal Employment Opportunity Commission (EEOC). The complaint led to a class action lawsuit against Wal-Mart. Odle's complaint claimed that she was fired for protesting how she was treated when she asked for a raise. Odle was an assistant manager at the time. One day she learned that her pay was $10,000 less than that of a male assistant manager. When she inquired about the pay difference, she was told that her coworker was paid more because he had "a wife and kids to support." Odle, who was a single mother, protested. She was told to submit a household budget to support her request for a pay raise, which she did. The result? She was granted a pay raise of $40 per week. At the time, Odle didn't know that throughout Wal-Mart, female assistant managers earned $16,402 less, on average, than male assistant managers.

It turns out that Stepanie Odle wasn't the only woman who felt mistreated. Betty Dukes also believed she experienced discrimination at Wal-Mart. An African American, Dukes had worked for Wal-Mart for six years before she encountered a supervisor who treated her badly. After she was promoted to the position of customer service manager, her new supervisor denied her the training that many younger men were offered. When she complained to the company, she was demoted back to her old job. Within two years, testimony from at least 100 other Wal-Mart employees in California was used as the basis for a class action lawsuit. The case is referred to as *Dukes v. Wal-Mart*. Today, more than 1.6 million women are part of the lawsuit. If Wal-Mart loses, it could cost as much as $11 billion. It is the largest discrimination case in U.S. history. One issue is pay: The plaintiffs claim that women are paid less than men in every job category. Another issue is promotions: Whereas 66% of hourly employees are women, only 14% of store managers are women.

Wal-Mart is the nation's largest employer, and its executives admit that it has some work to do to improve how managers treat employees. As one spokeswoman put it, "When you have one million people working for you, there are always going to be a couple of knuckleheads who do dumb things." Unfortunately, these knuckleheads are detracting from Wal-Mart's reputation and profits.[1] ▲

LEARNING GOAL

THE STRATEGIC IMPORTANCE OF FAIRNESS AND LEGAL COMPLIANCE

In an idealized capitalistic economic system, managers on behalf of shareholders seek to maximize profits free of noneconomic external constraints—that is, without constraints other than those imposed by consumers and competitors. In the real world, however, effective businesses address the concerns of many stakeholders. They go beyond codified laws and regulations in order to live up to society's ethical principles and address the concerns of their employees.

Society and the Law

Society's view of what constitutes fair treatment of employees is in constant flux. Practices that were considered fair at the beginning of the twentieth century are now illegal. Practices considered fair today may no longer be legal in five or ten years.

In the United States, the legal system helps define and interpret the meaning of fair treatment in employment settings. Members of the labor force initiate and ultimately create federal and state laws. They pay taxes to cover the costs of a vast array of government agencies and courts that are responsible for interpreting and enforcing the laws. Thus, employment laws reflect the issues that employees are likely to be thinking about as they decide whether to join or leave an organization. Nevertheless, complying with laws and regulations is seldom enough to ensure that employees feel they are treated fairly.

Concerns of the Labor Force

> *Treat people fairly and give them an environment that they can work in and trust. If you do that, you can take care of your business objectives and your employees and everybody can win.*
>
> *Joe R. Lee*
> *Former Chairman and Chief Executive Officer and Member of Founding Management Team*
> *Darden Restaurants*

People believe that fairness is a desirable social condition: We want to be treated fairly, and we want others to view us as being fair.[2] Fairness creates the feeling of trust that's needed to "hold a good workplace together."[3] Companies that rank high as the best places to work generally emphasize fairness as part of their corporate culture.

Members of the labor force communicate their fairness concerns to employers in many ways. Job applicants evaluate whether a company pays a fair wage, whether it offers desirable benefits, whether the corporate culture is appealing, and so on. As free agents, they decide where to work. When making these evaluations, perceptions of what is fair, desirable, and appealing reflect the applicant's fairness concerns.

Once hired, employees continue to express their concerns about fairness. They voice their concerns informally and indirectly through daily conversations at work. If they feel unfairly treated, they "vote with their feet" and seek employment elsewhere.[4] Or, like Kim Miller, who says she complained more than a dozen times about her treatment at Wal-Mart, they may eventually file a lawsuit.[5]

To avoid having their employees vote with their feet and to surface problems before they become severe, many companies conduct employee surveys to track employees' feelings about fairness. Employee grievance systems are another proactive approach that employers can use to address employees' concerns. Employees who belong to unions voice their concerns directly when they collectively bargain over working conditions and compensation.

Customers Win When Employers Treat Employees Fairly

Clearly, treating employees fairly is good for employees. Fairness is also good for business. When employees are treated fairly, they treat customers better.

LINE MANAGERS	HR PROFESSIONALS	EMPLOYEES
• Proactively seek to understand and respond to employees' fairness concerns.	• Encourage the use of societal views of fairness rather than adopting a narrow legalistic model.	• Accept and fulfill responsibilities to behave fairly toward your colleagues and employer.
• Stay informed about laws and regulations protecting employees' rights and behave in accordance with them.	• Stay up-to-date about new legal developments in employment law; consult with legal experts as needed.	• Be informed about laws and regulations protecting employees' rights and behave in accordance with them.
• Establish and review policies to ensure fair treatment of employees in collaboration with HR professionals.	• Develop and help implement policies that support fair and ethical behavior by everyone in the organization.	• Work with HR professionals to establish procedures for dealing fairly with workplace issues.
• Learn the steps involved in the organization's grievance procedures and follow them.	• Administer grievance procedures and participate in alternative dispute resolution activities.	• Report discriminatory or other illegal behavior among subordinates, colleagues, or superiors to an HR professional.
• Participate in diversity training programs and other diversity management initiatives.	• Design, deliver, and evaluate diversity training and other diversity management initiatives.	• Participate in diversity training and provide feedback on its effectiveness and other diversity initiatives.
• Intervene if you observe discriminatory or other illegal or unethical behavior among subordinates, colleagues, or superiors.	• Help keep employer and employee rights and responsibilities in balance.	• Help educate employees from other cultures about U.S. employment law; learn about employment laws in other countries.

Employees who feel mistreated at work can drive away customers. One hotel chain discovered this after agreeing to participate in a large research project. Nearly 9,000 hotel employees at 111 different locations completed surveys about their fairness perceptions. Employees indicated whether the employer showed concern for their rights, whether they could appeal management decisions, whether employees' concerns were listened to, and so on. Customer satisfaction data were available from 84 of the locations. Analysis of these data showed that customer satisfaction ratings were higher in locations where employees felt they were treated more fairly. Both the formal procedures followed by managers and the way individual supervisors treated employees proved to be important.[6]

In this chapter, we explain how employees evaluate whether they are treated fairly and how this affects their behavior at work. Then we describe the legal rights and responsibilities of employers and employees, and explain how legal disputes are settled. We conclude by describing the proactive approaches employers can use to ensure that employees are treated fairly.

The HR Triad

Fair treatment and legal compliance are complex issues that involve all three members of the HR Triad, as shown in the feature "The HR Triad: Roles and Responsibilities to Ensure Fair Treatment and Legal Compliance." Human resource professionals, with the assistance of legal experts, share responsibility for enforcing the legal obligations of employers and protecting the legal rights of employees. They participate in policy development, monitor HR actions and their consequences, provide training, and serve as mediators when conflicts arise. Managers carry out their responsibility for ensuring fair treatment and legal compliance through daily interactions with employees. Managers set a tone that communicates what behaviors the company endorses and tolerates. They play a key role in determining whether the workplace is hostile or welcoming to members of a diverse workforce. Finally, all employees share responsibility for reporting illegal workplace behaviors, respecting the property rights of employers, and safeguarding the company's intellectual capital.

WHAT FAIRNESS MEANS TO EMPLOYEES

Imagine that you are the employees involved in the following two situations. How do you feel? What will you do?

A. A Missed Promotion. Michelle Chang graduated with her master's of business administration (MBA) five years ago. Since then, she has worked for a large financial services company as an industry analyst. Her performance reviews have always been positive. She and her peers assumed she was on the company's informal fast track, but recently, she has begun to wonder. After the manager of her unit left last month for a better opportunity at another firm, Michelle applied for the job. She didn't get the promotion. To her surprise, the person chosen to be the new boss for her unit was Jim Johnson, a 10-year veteran of the firm who was transferred from another unit. After three weeks at his new job, it has become obvious that Jim does not have the knowledge and skills needed for the job. Michelle feels that the company's decision to give Jim the job is a signal that her future is not as bright as everyone thought. Perhaps it's time to look into possibilities at other companies.

B. An Unexpected Layoff. Bill Markham works for the same firm as Michelle and Jim. He has been with the organization for about seven years. As manager of the information services department, he has been responsible for managing all of the company's computer specialists. Last week, the firm unexpectedly disclosed plans for a major reorganization of information services. To "improve efficiency," the company will decentralize several staff activities. In the new structure, the activities of information services will be carried out by generalists who will work in each of the firm's several divisions. Of course, everyone knows that the words *improve efficiency* are a code, meaning the size of the information services staff will be reduced.

Bill was not worried when he heard the announcement; he expected to be assigned to the largest division and had already begun discussing the idea of a major move with his family. He was shocked when he learned that he was going to be let go. He appreciated the firm's offer to pay for outplacement counseling, but he wondered whether he should accept its decision as final. As a 50-something white male, he imagined that finding a new job would be pretty tough. Maybe he should put up a fight.

How much do Michelle and Bill trust their employer? Has each person been treated fairly?

It's a given that people prefer favorable outcomes for themselves. In the case of Michelle, a promotion would have been better than no promotion. For Bill, a transfer would have been better than being let go. No one likes such negative outcomes, but we do not necessarily feel that we have been treated unfairly when we do not get the best possible outcome. What other information might you want to obtain before deciding whether this company is treating employees fairly?

Since the mid-1970s, social and organizational scientists have conducted numerous studies designed to improve our understanding of fairness and justice. This research shows that perceptions of fairness reflect at least three features of the situations in which people find themselves: the actual *outcomes*, the *procedures* used in arriving at these outcomes, and the *interactions* the employees have with their managers. These features are referred to as distributive justice, procedural justice, and interactional justice, respectively.[7]

Distributive Justice

Perceptions of fairness reflect our perceptions of how our own outcomes compare with the outcomes of other people. In evaluating the fairness of her situation, Michelle may compare her outcome with Bill's. Generally, people judge outcomes such as pay and promotions as fair when they believe that the distribution of the outcomes corresponds to their judgments of what people deserve.[8] When the relative sizes of raises correspond to the relative performance levels of people in the unit, people tend to accept the system as fair. When promotions are given to people who seem to be the most qualified, the decision seems fair. In general, *when employees believe that the outcomes they experience are fair in comparison to the outcomes of others, they feel a sense of* distributive justice.

The principle of distributive justice means that employees who do not get the best outcomes may nevertheless feel they are treated fairly. For example, if Michelle believed that Jim's qualifications were better than her qualifications, then Michelle would probably accept the situation as fair even though she didn't get promoted. Michelle's and Jim's coworkers would use similar heuristics in evaluating their employer. If their coworkers believe that Michelle deserved the promotion more than Jim, they will feel bad about what happened to Michelle and they might conclude that their employer generally treats employees unfairly.[9]

At Wal-Mart, many women felt that their outcomes (pay, promotions, training opportunities) were generally of less value than what men received and for no appropriate reason. Outcomes that were important to women at Wal-Mart seemed to be distributed according to one's gender, not based purely on merit.

Cultural Differences. Employees in the United States typically experience distributive justice under conditions of equity, or merit-based decision making.[10] However, employees from other countries and cultures may see things quite differently. American culture is individualistic, whereas many other cultures are relatively collectivistic. In collectivistic cultures—like many of those found throughout Asia—concern for social cohesion is greater than in the United States. People from collectivistic cultures value *equality* of treatment or treatment based on *need,* and they allocate rewards accordingly.[11] In a country with a collectivistic culture, the decision to promote Jim instead of Michelle might be viewed as fair because Jim *needed* the job more than did Michelle.

Procedural Justice

Perceptions of justice depend on more than the final distribution of outcomes, or the end result. Also important are beliefs about the process used to determine outcomes. For example, Michelle and Bill might wonder *how* their company made its decisions.

> **❝I worked there longer than most people are married these days and I never got a promotion.❞**
>
> *Kim Miller*
> *Greeter*
> *Wal-Mart*

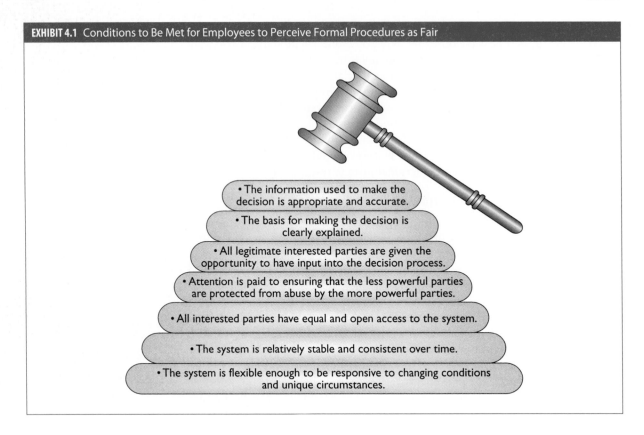

EXHIBIT 4.1 Conditions to Be Met for Employees to Perceive Formal Procedures as Fair

- The information used to make the decision is appropriate and accurate.
- The basis for making the decision is clearly explained.
- All legitimate interested parties are given the opportunity to have input into the decision process.
- Attention is paid to ensuring that the less powerful parties are protected from abuse by the more powerful parties.
- All interested parties have equal and open access to the system.
- The system is relatively stable and consistent over time.
- The system is flexible enough to be responsive to changing conditions and unique circumstances.

Procedural justice *refers to perceptions about fairness in the process used to make decisions.* American employees consider a formal procedure to be fair if it meets the conditions shown in Exhibit 4.1.[12]

At Costco, some women are concerned about the procedures used to staff management jobs. Women make up nearly half of Costco's workforce, but only 13% of store managers are women. In a lawsuit against Costco, female employees have argued that the highest-paid management positions are filled by word of mouth. They claim that the system favors men and shuts out women because most managers are men. Female employees of Costco have emphasized procedural justice. Costco's CEO James Sinegal has argued that the outcomes of the company's process are fair. He says the explanation for the low number of female managers is due to the fact that "women have a tendency to be caretakers and have the responsibility for the children and for the family."[13] Apparently, he believes this means that women are not able to perform management jobs as well as men.

When employers attend to procedural justice, employees are more productive and less likely to be absent.[14] According to one study, fair HR practices give employees confidence that they will be treated well. Employees feel they can trust their managers even if they experience conflict. As a result, employees are more willing to "go the extra mile" for the company.[15]

Interactional Justice

Inevitably, employees sometimes feel that a decision or procedure is unfair. Under these circumstances, how managers behave in their one-on-one meetings and conversations with employees can make a difference. When evaluating how fairly they are treated, employees take into account how they personally are treated in their interactions with managers. Perceptions of **interactional justice** *reflect employees' feelings about whether managers are sensitive to their situations and treat them politely and respectfully.*[16]

Sensitive managers may provide encouragement to employees who are not promoted, and they offer emotional support to employees who are laid off. Managers who acknowledge these negative situations and express concern can minimize the disruptive effects of the situations. When Bill is laid off, his manager could make the layoff seem at least a little less unfair by treating Bill with respect and showing compassion for his situation. If Bill's manager is callous or demeaning, Bill will feel the situation is even more unfair. When employees feel that their managers care about their personal situation, it helps reduce anger. Later in this chapter, we describe diversity initiatives aimed at ensuring that managers are equally effective when dealing with employees from a wide range of diverse backgrounds. Many of the diversity management initiatives we describe are aimed at increasing employees' feelings of interactional justice.

Reactions to Unjust Treatment

Consider again the situation of Michelle and the actions she might take. If you were Michelle, you might

1. Quit and put the incident behind you.
2. Stay and simply accept the situation.
3. Stay but engage in negative behaviors that help you restore your sense of fairness.
4. Talk to people inside the organization, such as a mentor or someone in the employee relations office.
5. Complain to external authorities, such as a lawyer or the press.[17]

Quit? For high performers like Michelle, quitting may be the best alternative. From the organization's perspective, however, having Michelle leave and perhaps join the competition may be the least desirable alternative. It will cost money to replace her. Her coworkers may feel demoralized. And her manager may have to pick up Michelle's job duties while looking for her replacement.

Stay and Accept the Situation? Alternative 2 may seem to be better for Michelle's employer, but would she really be productive if she stayed? Few people easily shrug off injustices suffered at the hands of their employers. Employees who stay in situations that they believe are unfair lose confidence in the competence of management and feel they cannot trust management.[18] Employees who feel unfairly treated also report feeling more distressed, dissatisfied, and uncommitted to both their employers and the goals their employers set for them.[19] In other words, they develop a bad attitude.

Stay and Seek Revenge? Feelings of injustice affect behavior, not just attitudes. Therefore, reactions that fall into categories 3 and 4 are possible. If a legal issue is involved, employees may seek legal solutions. Often, however, feelings of unfairness arise in response to perfectly legal management behavior. In such situations, employees may try to even things out by taking longer breaks, calling in sick so they can work less, or even stealing supplies from the company. Michelle might seek revenge by trying to undermine Jim.

Talk to Others in the Organization? When employers inspire feelings of loyalty in employees, unhappy employees are less likely to seek revenge. Instead, they will use informal communication channels to voice their dissatisfaction.[20] Wal-Mart employees have a reputation for being loyal to the company, so it is not surprising that Stephanie Odle and Betty Dukes first talked to people inside the company about their concerns. Wal-Mart might have avoided a lawsuit if the managers of these women were more responsive to their concerns. By fully explaining *how* decisions are made and by offering employees opportunities to voice their concerns and have their questions answered, employers can minimize negative employee reactions.

In well managed companies, employees' feelings of dissatisfaction are intentionally surfaced and used to stimulate positive changes that actually benefit both employees and employers. Unfortunately, Wal-Mart didn't have a system in place to ensure that Stephanie's and Betty's concerns were addressed.

Complain to External Authorities? Employees who feel they have been treated unfairly can seek redress through the legal system. Like Stephanie Odle and Betty Dukes, they can file a complaint with the EEOC, or they can hire a lawyer to pursue their case. Depending on their circumstances, employees may sue their employer claiming unfair discrimination, wrongful termination, failure to comply with laws regulating pay, and so on. For example, as an older worker, Bill might suspect he was laid off because of his age, which would be illegal. Regardless of whether the employee wins or loses, litigating and settling such lawsuits can end up costing employers millions of dollars as well as immeasurable reputational loss in the eyes of the public.[21]

LEARNING GOAL

LEGAL MEANS TO ENSURE FAIR TREATMENT

Issues of fairness and legal compliance pervade almost every area of human resource management. In Chapters 5 and 6, for example, you will learn about laws governing staffing procedures and the means that employers can use to ensure that job applicants are treated fairly. In Chapters 10, 11, and 12 you will learn about laws governing compensation and practices that improve employees' perceptions of pay fairness. In those and other chapters, the laws, policies, and practices that are especially important to the activities will be described in more detail.[22] Here we set the stage for our discussions in subsequent chapters by describing some of the most sweeping legislation and the agencies that enforce it.

Laws are simply society's values and standards that are enforceable in the courts. In general, the legal system is designed to encourage socially responsible behavior.[23] The legal system considers the outcomes of all parties concerned and attempts to impose decisions and remedies that balance the perspectives of employees, employers, and other stakeholders.[24]

As society's concerns change, so do employees' legal rights. At one time, U.S. employers could legally discriminate against women and minorities in hiring and promotions. As a consensus developed that such discriminatory practices were unethical, laws were passed to stop the practices and ensure equal employment opportunities for all citizens. In addition, the federal government issued regulations requiring government agencies and federal contractors to work at correcting the effects of past discrimination. Today, society's views concerning gay, lesbian, bisexual, and transgender (GLBT) employees are in flux, and so are employers' legal responsibilities. As shown in Exhibit 4.2,

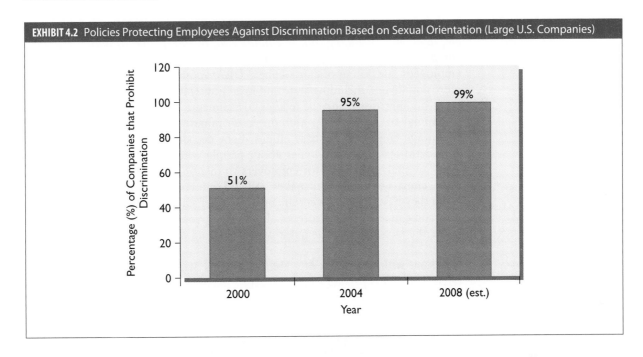

EXHIBIT 4.2 Policies Protecting Employees Against Discrimination Based on Sexual Orientation (Large U.S. Companies)

most large employers in the U.S. now have policies that prohibit discrimination based on sexual orientation.[25] Such policies were extremely rare just 20 years ago.

Federal Laws

To understand how the legal environment affects the way companies manage human resources, it's necessary to understand several major federal employment laws and regulations that are pervasive and enforced by our legal system.[26] Next we describe a few laws and regulations that have significant consequences for human resource management.

Title VII of the Civil Rights Act of 1964. One especially important federal employment law is Title VII of the Civil Rights Act of 1964. Originally enacted in 1964, the Civil Rights Act has since been revised twice, in 1978 and 1991. The 1991 law reinforces the intent of the Civil Rights Acts of 1964 but states more specifically how cases brought under the act should proceed.[27] **Title VII of the Civil Rights Act of 1964** *prohibits discrimination by employers, employment agencies, and unions on the basis of race, color, religion, sex, national origin, or pregnancy.* The original protections of the Civil Rights Act have remained unchanged during the past several decades.

Title VII of the Civil Rights Act is one of several key statutory laws that affect the employment relationship. When you see headlines about employment discrimination lawsuits, Title VII of the Civil Rights Act is usually relevant. For example, when Morgan Stanley agreed to pay $54 million to settle a lawsuit involving 300 women, the lawsuit claimed that the firm was biased against women. Similar lawsuits have been filed by women at several other Wall Street firms in recent years, including Citigroup and UBS, which is based in Switzerland.[28]

Age Discrimination in Employment Act. The **Age Discrimination in Employment Act of 1967 (ADEA)** *protects people 40 years of age or older from employment*

FAST FACT

Citizens of the United States employed elsewhere by a firm that's controlled or owned by an American parent are protected by Title VII of the Civil Rights Act, the Age Discrimination in Employment Act (ADEA), and the Americans with Disabilities Act (ADA).

discrimination based on age with respect to any term, condition, or privilege of employment—including, but not limited to, hiring, firing, promotion, layoff, compensation, benefits, job assignments, and training. The law protects both employees and job applicants. The ADEA applies to employers with 20 or more employees, including state and local governments, employment agencies, labor organizations, and the federal government.

Similar to other laws prohibiting discrimination, the ADEA is intended to encourage employers to base employment decisions on performance-related considerations, not stereotypes about people who belong to various groups. This law makes it illegal for employers to mention age preferences in job announcements and generally makes it illegal to force persons to retire simply because they have reached a certain age. Whether you are young or old, you may hold some inaccurate stereotypes about older people. To find out how well you know the facts, answer the questions in the quiz shown in Exhibit 4.3.[29]

Americans with Disabilities Act. The **Americans with Disabilities Act of 1990 (ADA)** *prohibits private employers, state and local governments, employment agencies, and labor unions from discriminating against qualified individuals*

EXHIBIT 4.3

What Do You Know about Aging?
How informed are you about older workers? To get a sense of how well you are able to separate myth from fact, take the knowledge quiz presented here.

Quiz about Older Workers
Instructions: Indicate whether each of the following statements is true (by circling "T") or false (by circling "F"). Correct answers are given on page 147.

1.	T	F	Physical strength declines with age.
2.	T	F	It's almost impossible for older people to learn.
3.	T	F	The majority of older people are working/want work to do.
4.	T	F	All five senses decline with age.
5.	T	F	Older people react more slowly than younger people.
6.	T	F	Over three-fourths of older people say they are healthy.
7.	T	F	The majority of older people are senile.
8.	T	F	The majority of older people say they are miserable.
9.	T	F	Older people tend to be pretty much alike.
10.	T	F	The majority of older people have no capacity for sex.
11.	T	F	Lung capacity declines with age.
12.	T	F	Older workers aren't as effective as younger workers.
13.	T	F	Older people take longer to learn something new.
14.	T	F	The majority of older people cannot adapt to change.
15.	T	F	Older workers have fewer accidents than younger workers.
16.	T	F	The majority of older people are below the poverty line.
17.	T	F	The majority of older people say they are seldom bored.
18.	T	F	Drivers 65 years of age and over have fewer accidents compared to those under 65.
19.	T	F	Medical personnel give lower priority to older people.
20.	T	F	The majority of older people are seldom angry or irritated.
21.	T	F	The majority of older people say they are lonely.
22.	T	F	The health and economic status of older people will not get better.
23.	T	F	Older people become more religious as they age.
24.	T	F	At least one-tenth of older people live in institutions.
25.	T	F	Over 20% of the population is age 65 or older.

with disabilities in job application procedures, hiring, firing, advancement, compensation, job training, and other terms conditions, and privileges of employment. A qualified employee or applicant is someone who can perform the essential functions of the job in question either with or without accommodations being made by the employer. Employers with 15 or more employees, including state and local governments, are covered by this law. For the purposes of this law, a person has a disability if she or he

- Has a physical or mental impairment that substantially limits one or more major life activities.
- Has a record of such an impairment.
- Is regarded as having such an impairment.[30]

The ADA requires employers to make "reasonable" accommodations to the known disabilities of qualified applicants and employee. A reasonable accommodation is one that does not require significant difficulty or expense given the employer's size, financial resources, and the nature of its operation. Employers are *not* required to lower quality or production standards to make an accommodation. Examples of reasonable accommodations include

- Making the work facilities readily accessible to and usable by persons with disabilities.
- Restructuring the way a job is performed.
- Modifying the work schedule.
- Acquiring or modifying equipment or devices.
- Adjusting or modifying examinations, training materials, or policies.
- Providing qualified readers or interpreters.

The ADA does not hold employers responsible for accommodating a disability that they do not know about. Furthermore, an employee with a disability does not have to disclose it if it does not affect job performance. People with "hidden" disabilities (e.g., learning disabilities, seizure disorders, psychiatric conditions) may be afraid to tell their employer about their condition. If an employee does not disclose a disability, he or she should not expect the employer to accommodate it. As we explain in Chapter 6, however, a job applicant should wait to tell a potential employer about a disability until after the job offer is received.

Several other important federal laws are summarized in Exhibit 4.4. We cannot fully discuss all of these laws here, but you should familiarize yourself with them in preparation for future chapters, where they are referred to again.

State Laws

State laws must be consistent with federal law, but this does not mean that state and federal laws must be the same. In fact, state laws often offer employees better protection from unfair treatment by employers.

State laws often cover companies that are not covered by federal laws. For example, federal employment laws such as Title VII of the Civil Rights Act often apply only to businesses with 15 or more employees; similar state laws may apply to even smaller businesses. State laws may also offer different types of protection. For example, state laws in California, Vermont, Connecticut, and New Jersey require employers to treat same-sex couples the same as married couples. One implication for employers is that same-sex partners must have equal access to benefits such as health insurance and family leave time.[31]

EXHIBIT 4.4 Major Federal Employment Laws and Regulations

ACT	JURISDICTION	BASIC PROVISIONS
National Labor Relations Act (Wagner Act, 1935)	Most nonmanagerial employees in private industry	Provides right to organize; provides for collective bargaining; requires employers to bargain; requires unions to represent all members equally.
Fair Labor Standards Act (FLSA, 1938)	Most nonmanagerial employees in private industry	Establishes a minimum wage; controls hours through premium pay for overtime; controls working hours for children.
Equal Pay Act (1963)	Most employers	Prohibits unequal pay for males and females with equal skill, effort, and responsibility working under similar working conditions.
Title VII of the Civil Rights Act (1964,1991)	Employers with 15 or more employees; employment agencies; unions	Prevents discrimination on the basis of race, color, religion, sex, or national origin; establishes EEOC; provides reinstatement, back pay, and compensatory and punitive damages; permits jury trials.
Executive Order 11246 (1965), Executive Order 11375 (1966), and Executive Order 11478 (1969)	Federal contractors with large contracts and 50 or more employees	Prevents discrimination on the basis of race, color, religion, national origin, sex, political affiliation, marital status, or physical disability; establishes Office of Federal Contract Compliance (OFCC).
Age Discrimination in Employment Act (ADEA, 1967)	Employers with more than 20 employees	Prevents discrimination against persons age 40 and over; states compulsory retirement for some employees.
Occupational Safety and Health Act (OSHA, 1970)	Most employers involved in interstate commerce	Ensures, as far as possible, safe and healthy working conditions and the preservation of our human resources.
Rehabilitation Act (1973)	Government contractors and federal agencies	Prevents discrimination against persons with physical and mental disabilities.
Employee Retirement Income Security Act (ERISA,1974)	Most employers with pension plans	Protects employees covered by a pension plan from losses in benefits due to mismanagement, job changes, plant closings, and bankruptcies.
Pregnancy Discrimination Act (1978)	Employers with 15 or more employees	Identifies pregnancy as a disability and entitles the woman to the same benefits as any other disability.
Worker Adjustment and Retraining Notification Act (WARN, 1988)	Employers with more than 100 employees	Requires 60 days' notice of plant or office closing or substantial layoffs.
Americans with Disabilities Act (ADA, 1990)	Employers with 15 or more employees	Prohibits discrimination against individuals with disabilities.
Family and Medical Leave Act (FMLA, 1993)	Employers with 50 or more employees	Allows workers to take up to 12 weeks unpaid leave for childbirth, adoption, or illness of employee or a close family member; employees who have worked for the employer 12 months or 1,250 hours become eligible.
Uniformed Services Employment and Reemployment Rights Act (USERRA, 1994)	All employers in the public and private sectors, including federal employers	Prevents discrimination against employees who take leave to meet military service obligations.
Health Insurance Portability and Accountability Act (HIPAA, 1996)	Health plans, health care clearinghouses, health care providers, and employers to the extent that they operate in one or more of those capacities	Allows an employee with an existing illness to transfer existing insurance coverage to a new employer.
Sarbanes-Oxley Act (2002)	Most publicly held companies	Imposes strict rules intended to reduce wrongdoing in public by corporations and strengthens protections for employees who report wrongdoing.

At this time no federal law prevents discrimination based on sexual orientation, however.

Family leave laws provide another example of how state laws may offer greater protection than federal laws. The federal Family and Medical Leave Act of 1993 (FMLA) requires employers to provide time off for family care, but does not require employers to pay employees while they are on leave. California's state laws provide greater protection. Eligible workers in California receive half pay for six weeks while they tend to a newborn, move a parent to a nursing home, or in other ways care for family members. Unlike the federal law, which applies only to employers with 50 or more workers, California's leave plan—called Family Temporary Disability Insurance—applies to all employers regardless of size.[32]

State laws often anticipate federal laws. In this sense, they tell us what to expect in the future at the federal level. For example, New York had adopted a fair employment law in 1945 and about half the states had adopted similar laws by the time the Civil Rights Act of 1964 was passed at the federal level. Florida, Maine, and the District of Columbia had all adopted family leave legislation before the federal Family and Medical Leave Act was enacted in 1993.

More recently, states have been acting to increase the minimum wage rates employers must pay their employees to levels far above the federal minimum wage. In early 2007, the federal minimum wage was $5.15 an hour. At the time, 29 states had higher minimums, ranging from $6.15 to $7.63 an hour. In May of 2007, the Fair Minimum Wage Act raised the federal minimum wage to $5.85 as of July 24th, 2007, to $6.55 as of July 24th, 2008, and to $7.25 as of July 24th, 2009.[33] Do you know the minimum wage rate in your home state?

Executive Orders

United States presidents shape the legal environment by approving and vetoing bills passed by Congress and by influencing how vigorously administrative agencies carry out their duties and responsibilities. In addition, the president can create law by issuing an executive order. An executive order can, among other purposes, specify the rules and conditions for conducting government business and for contractors who do business with the government.

The actions of government contractors that do work for the federal government are primarily affected by three executive orders.

1. Issued in 1965 by President Lyndon B. Johnson, Executive Order 11246 prohibits discrimination by federal contractors and subcontractors on the basis of race, color, religion, or national origin.

2. In 1967, President Johnson issued Executive Order 11375 to prohibit discrimination based on sex by these employers.

3. In 1969, President Richard Nixon expanded these. Executive Order 11478 prohibits discrimination based on race, color, religion, national origin, sex, and political affiliation, marital status, and physical disability.

Administrative Agencies

At both the federal and state levels, the government can delegate authority for rule making and enforcement to an administrative agency. In carrying out their duties, administrative agencies make rules (often called standards or guidelines), conduct investigations, make judgments about guilt, and impose sanctions. These agencies have the responsibility and authority to prosecute companies they believe are violating the law.

FAST FACT

In 2005, the Texas State Labor Code was amended to require that juveniles be at least 11 years old to engage in the delivery of newspapers on a paper route.

FAST FACT

Approximately 70,000 companies are federal government contractors.

FAST FACT

In most states, employees have up to 300 days after an alleged discriminatory event to file a charge with the EEOC.

Three federal administrative agencies of particular importance for managing human resources are the

- Equal Employment Opportunity Commission (EEOC).
- Occupational Safety and Health Administration (OSHA).
- National Labor Relations Board (NLRB).

EEOC. The **Equal Employment Opportunity Commission (EEOC)** *administers Title VII of the Civil Rights Act as well as the Equal Pay Act and the Age Discrimination in Employment Act.* For each of these acts, the EEOC has produced regulations that inform employers of how the agency assesses whether a legal violation has occurred. The EEOC is one of the most influential agencies responsible for enforcing employment laws. As you read subsequent chapters, you will see that EEOC regulations have implications for nearly every area of HR activity—recruitment, selection, training, promotions, performance management, compensation, termination, and so forth.

As an enforcer of laws, the EEOC can prosecute employers who engage in illegal discrimination. Each year, the EEOC receives approximately 80,000 complaints from employees. Exhibit 4.5 shows the types of discrimination charges filed in a recent year.[34] As Exhibit 4.6 shows, the number of claims has been declining in recent years.

When the EEOC files a class action suit against an employer, it is likely to be resolved with a large monetary settlement. In a **class action lawsuit,** *a group of similar employees (i.e., a "class") asserts that all members of the employee class suffered due to an employer's unfair policies and practices.* In the case of *Dukes v. Wal-Mart,* the class of employees covered by the lawsuit includes about 1.6 million women who worked in the company's U.S. stores any time since December 26, 1998. As Exhibit 4.7 shows, the monetary awards that the EEOC won for employees grew substantially during the 1990s.

The size of awards may go down in future years, however, because the number of claims filed is decreasing. According to the EEOC, a decline in the awards won by the EEOC may be a good sign. Fewer cases and lower

FAST FACT

Wal-Mart employs about 800,000 women in more than 3,700 U.S. stores—more than any other employer in the country and more than the total number of people who live in the states of Vermont or Wyoming or North Dakota.

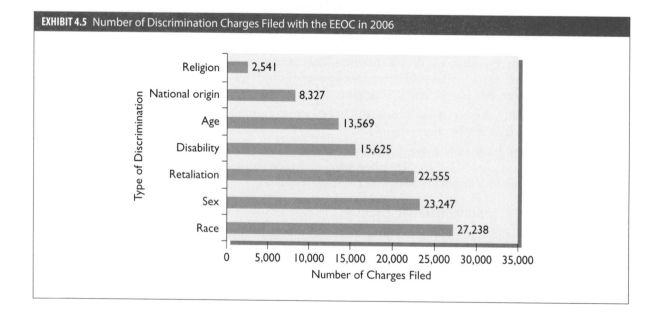

EXHIBIT 4.5 Number of Discrimination Charges Filed with the EEOC in 2006

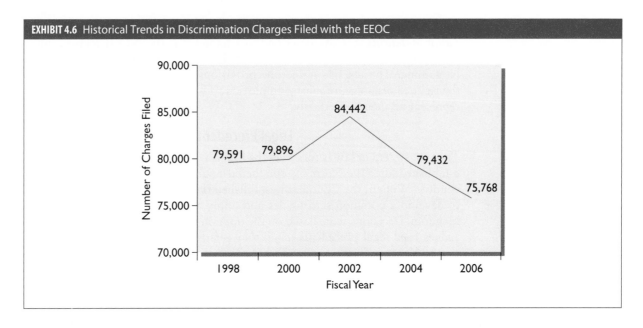

EXHIBIT 4.6 Historical Trends in Discrimination Charges Filed with the EEOC

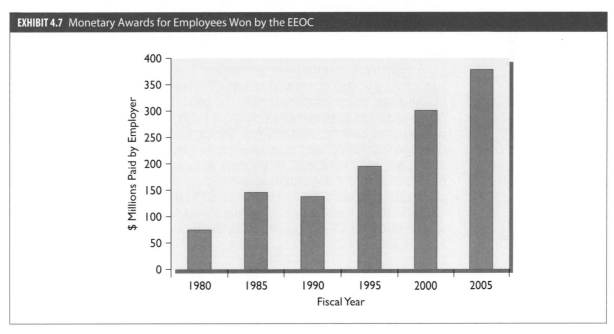

EXHIBIT 4.7 Monetary Awards for Employees Won by the EEOC

monetary awards may indicate that employers are discriminating less. Another possibility is that the EEOC has been less aggressive in pursuing cases against employers.[35]

OSHA. The **Occupational Safety and Health Administration (OSHA)** *administers the Occupational Safety and Health Act.* As described in Chapter 13, OSHA conducts safety and health inspections, investigates accidents and alleged hazardous conditions, issues citations for violations, levies fines, collects mandatory reports prepared by employers, and compiles statistics on work injuries and illnesses.

NLRB. The **National Labor Relations Board (NLRB)** *administers the National Labor Relations Act.* As described in Chapter 14, the NLRB focuses much of its attention on group activities related to union organizing and collective bargaining. The act has numerous provisions, such as providing employees the right to organize, requiring employers to bargain, and requiring unions to represent all members equally.

Legal Precedents

The U.S. system of law is rooted in the English common law system, which was established after the Normans conquered England in 1066. To help unify the country, William the Conqueror established the King's Court. Its purpose was to develop a common set of rules and apply them uniformly throughout the kingdom. Decisions were based on the opinions of judges and legal precedents. Judges used **legal precedents** *when they referred back to important decisions that were made in the past and used these as the basis for making a decision in a new case.* When new types of disputes arose, judges created new law to resolve them. This system is still in effect today in England.

In the United States, judges do not make laws; they only interpret and apply them. Nevertheless, the interpretations of judges continue to be very important. When judges explain the reasons for their decisions, they reveal how they are likely to treat related cases in the future. Rulings made by the Supreme Court carry the most weight because many of the decisions made by federal and state courts are subject to review by the Supreme Court.

A Supreme Court decision involving a claim of age discrimination illustrates how precedents work. A group of police officers sued their employer claiming age discrimination in pay. The employer was the City of Jackson, Mississippi. The City had given raises to lower-ranking younger officers but not to higher-ranking older officers. The City argued that they based the pay decisions on factors other than age. Specifically, The City said that it offered higher pay to new recruits to compete with nearby cities. In this case, the Supreme Court decided that differences in pay caused by market forces were not illegal, and they dismissed the lawsuit. The decision set an important precedent for future cases involving age discrimination and pay by clarifying that market forces are a legally valid reason for paying younger workers more than older workers.[36]

EMPLOYMENT-AT-WILL

One of the most significant common law principles is the **employment-at-will rule,** *which is the assumption that employers have the right to terminate employees for (almost) any reason.* During the 1800s, as the industrial era was beginning, employers and employees alike assumed that a person held a job at the will of the employer. Employers were allowed great freedom to decide whether an employee would be hired and fired. A Tennessee court explained the employment-at-will rule as follows:

> All may dismiss their employee(s) at will, be they many or few, for good cause, for no cause, or even for cause morally wrong without being thereby guilty of legal wrong. (*Payne v. Western & A.R.R Co.,* 1884)

Counterbalancing the employer's right to dismiss employees is the right of employees to leave their employers at any time and for any reason.

Limits to Employment-at-Will

The courts still recognize the force of at-will employment. Nevertheless, over the years, there has been a shift in the balance of power between employers and employees. The courts give employers wide latitude, but employers do not have absolute autonomy to end a person's employment. Giving employers too much freedom would be harmful to employees and essentially nullify all employee rights.

Since 1884 many laws have been enacted to limit the rights of employers. The Civil Rights Act, the Age Discrimination in Employment Act, and the Americans with Disabilities Act all curtail employers' rights to do whatever they want to do. In addition, the National Labor Relations Act (NLRA) prohibits discharge for union-organizing activities or for asserting rights under a union contract, even if the employee in question has a record of poor performance. Other acceptable and unacceptable reasons for terminating employees are listed in Exhibit 4.8.[37]

Employment Contracts

In an effort to avoid wrongful termination lawsuits, many employers have developed written employment contracts, which state that accepting employment with the company carries no guarantee of security and employees may be terminated at the employer's option. To further protect themselves, many employers require employees to sign agreements in which they waive their rights to sue as a condition for accepting severance packages during layoffs.

Critics of such contracts argue that employees have little choice when they sign such agreements and that they may be giving up too many rights. They

---

EXHIBIT 4.8 Acceptable and Unacceptable Reasons to Terminate Employees

ACCEPTABLE REASONS FOR DISMISSAL

- Incompetence in performance that does not respond to training or to accommodation
- Gross or repeated insubordination
- Civil rights violations such as engaging in harassment
- Too many unexcused absences
- Illegal behavior such as theft
- Repeated lateness
- Drug activity on the job
- Verbal abuse
- Physical violence
- Falsification of records
- Drunkenness on the job

UNACCEPTABLE REASONS FOR DISMISSAL

- Blowing the whistle about illegal conduct by employers (e.g., opposing and publicizing employer policies or practices that violate laws such as antitrust, consumer protection, or environmental protection laws)
- Cooperating in the investigation of a charge against the company
- Reporting Occupational Safety and Health Administration violations
- Filing discrimination charges with the Equal Employment Opportunity Commission or a state or municipal fair employment agency
- Filing unfair labor practice charges with the National Labor Relations Board or a state agency
- Filing a workers' compensation claim
- Engaging in concerted activity to protest wages, working conditions, or safety hazards
- Engaging in union activities, provided there is no violence or unlawful behavior
- Complaining or testifying about violations of equal pay or wage and hour laws
- Complaining or testifying about safety hazards or refusing an assignment because of the belief that it's dangerous

argue that employees do not enter into such agreements voluntarily. Instead, they sign under duress when threatened with the loss of an employment opportunity or of a large severance package. Because employers wield so much power, employees feel they have little choice but to sign away rights that they would otherwise have under current law.

Layoffs

Most court decisions regarding an employer's right to terminate employees emphasize the value of procedural justice. Termination of employment should be the last step in a series of documented steps designed to ensure that an employee understood that performance problems existed and had the opportunity to improve. Even though an employer may have the right to discharge an employee, the employer may be required to show evidence indicating that none of the protections against wrongful termination were violated. All evidence and material relevant to each step should be documented and filed.

Employers may also terminate an entire workforce in a plant or location, if proper procedures are followed. Employers also may be required to offer training programs to assist workers in adjusting to new employment conditions elsewhere.

International Operations

Among the many challenges that U.S. employers face as they expand their operations into other countries is dealing with the varying protections given to employees in different countries. The right of an employer to fire employees is taken for granted in the United States. In many other countries it is much more difficult for employers to fire employees or conduct layoffs. As a result, it is often more difficult for employers to use layoffs as a tactic for adapting to changing business conditions in their non-U.S. operations.

In many countries, termination of employment is viewed as a harsh action that's potentially harmful to employees. In fairness to employees, it should occur only for good cause, and employers are held responsible for minimizing its negative consequences. Most countries have some traditional or legally required practices that come into play in the event of a plant closing or a substantial reduction of the workforce.[38] In general, laws and regulations regarding layoffs and terminations in other countries create more extensive and costlier employer obligations than do laws regarding layoffs in the United States and Canada.

In many countries, a company that wishes to close down or curtail operations must develop a "social plan" or its equivalent, typically in concert with unions and other interested stakeholders. The plan may cover the continuation of pay, benefit plan coverage, retraining allowances, relocation expenses, and supplementation of statutory unemployment compensation.[39] Frequently, a company planning a partial or total plant closing must present its case to a government agency. In the Netherlands, for example, authorities may deny permission for a substantial workforce reduction unless management is able to demonstrate that the cutback is absolutely necessary for economic reasons and that the company has an approved social plan.

For employers that wish to compare the difficulty of firing employees in different countries, the World Bank provides an index, or rating. In countries with a high value, regulations provide stronger protections for workers, so firing employees is more difficult. Exhibit 4.9 shows the index values for several countries, along with how many weeks of wages employers must pay to employees whom they fire.[40]

EXHIBIT 4.9 Consequences of Labor Regulations on Workforce Flexibility in Selected Countries

Country	Difficulty of Firing Index (Zero = Least Difficult)	Firing Cost (Weeks of Wages)
United States	0	0.0
Canada	0	28.0
Brazil	0	36.8
Hong Kong	0	62.1
United Kingdom	10	22.1
Argentina	20	138.7
Ireland	30	49.0
Turkey	30	94.7
Poland	40	13.0
Russia	40	17.3
South Africa	40	24.0
Germany	40	69.3
Mexico	40	74.3
China	40	91.0
India	70	55.9

Note: For information about other countries, go to www.worldbank.org.

SETTLING DISPUTES

Even the best companies occasionally experience disputes over the treatment of employees. In the extreme cases, such disputes end up in court, where they are eventually resolved by a legal decision or settlement.[41] More often, however, disputes are resolved through a company's grievance procedure or using alternative dispute resolution procedures before they reach a court.

Company Grievance Procedures

Grievance procedures *(also referred to as complaint resolution procedures) encourage employees to voice their concerns to the company instead of to the courts, and they encourage employees to seek constructive resolutions without litigation.* Almost all public and private unionized employees are covered by contracts that specify formal written grievance procedures.[42] More than half of America's largest corporations also have some type of formal complaint resolution system covering nonunion employees.[43] The growing popularity of formal grievance procedures is consistent with managers' beliefs that employees have a right to fair treatment.

Pinellas County in Florida has a grievance procedure that is much like those found in private and public organizations. Employees who feel they have experienced discrimination can go through the following steps to resolve the issue:

- *Step 1: Informal Discussion.* When a problem arises, the first step is talking it over with your immediate supervisor. Sometimes this is all that's needed to clear the air and establish a positive working relationship. If the supervisor is the source of the problem, step 1 may be skipped. Or if the supervisor's response is not satisfactory, the employee may move to Step 2.

- *Step 2: Written Complaint.* Next is filing a formal written complaint with the department director, using forms provided by the employer. The director must send a written response to the formal complaint. The employee and his or her supervisor are expected to discuss this written response from management.

- *Step 3: Grievance Hearing.* If the employee is not satisfied with management's response, she or he may request a grievance hearing with a company committee that includes both nonmanagerial and managerial representatives. The committee reaches and issues a written decision.
- *Step 4: Appeal.* Finally, if either the employee or management is not satisfied with the informal committee's decision, they can appeal to the personnel board, which is made up of appointed citizens who are not employed by the county. The board's decision is final.[44]

As is true of most administrative systems, the specific details of a grievance procedure policy are not as important as how the policy is carried out on a daily basis. When they work well, grievance procedures help lower the legal costs associated with resolving disputes in the courts. They also increase employee loyalty and commitment.[45]

Mediation and Arbitration

When disputes cannot be resolved through a company's internal process, another option can be tried before resorting to the courts. Because the courts are a slow, expensive, and difficult way to resolve serious disputes, a growing number of businesses are using alternative dispute resolution when employees make charges of unfair treatment.

Alternative dispute resolution (ADR) *involves making an agreement to forego litigation and instead resolve disputes by either internal or external mediation or arbitration.* Working out a dispute before it reaches litigation can promote goodwill between management and employees and reduce the adverse publicity often associated with legal disputes.[46] It can also reduce legal costs to both employers and society. Mediation and arbitration are the two most common forms of alternative dispute resolution.

Mediation. In **mediation,** *all concerned parties present their case to a third-party neutral: the mediator.* Mediators may be appointed by a judge, selected by the parties or their representatives, or recommended by agencies such as the EEOC. Often, the disputing parties are required to prepare a confidential written statement of their case and a statement of the resolutions they would find acceptable. Each side then presents its arguments in a private meeting with the mediator.

Like a diplomat shuttling between warring parties, the mediator's role is to help the parties understand each other's views. The mediator also helps each party understand the strengths and weaknesses in its own case. The ultimate goal is to steer the parties toward compromise and to construct a fair settlement.[47] Mediation is the most popular form of ADR.

Arbitration. Compared to mediation, **arbitration** *is a more formal process for alternative dispute resolution, yet not so formal that the rules of a court must be followed.* Employees must be permitted to have a representative for their case (usually an attorney), and representatives must present their cases in a formal manner. Typically, decisions are rendered by a panel of arbitrators. Unlike court judges, arbitrators do not need to provide written decisions or use previous cases in rendering their decisions.

Many employers ask employees to sign contracts upon being hired, stating that they'll accept arbitration as a means to settle any potential future discrimination complaint. Usually employees are asked to agree to *binding*

EXHIBIT 4.10 Weighing the Pros and Cons of Using Mandatory Arbitration to Settle Disputes

PROS	CONS
Quick dispute resolution	Relinquishment of employees' statutory rights to a trial as a condition of employment
Lower personal, professional, and financial costs for both parties	Availability of "user-friendly" arbitration may stimulate a flood of claims
Reduction in employers' advantage in litigation by outspending and outlasting an employee	May prevent better guidance for future action since courts are better able to provide consistent and clear interpretations of law
More business-related experience and expertise of professional arbitrators	Arbitrators may not be competent or impartial
Reduction in exposure to unpredictable jury awards for emotional distress and punitive damages	Small monetary penalties may reduce their effectiveness as remedies in the case of a wronged employee
Permits disputes to remain private	Confidentiality of the process may reduce its deterrent effect; conversely, confidentiality isn't guaranteed
May improve communication and employee relations	May deter some talented employees from accepting employment

arbitration in which the arbitrator's decision is final, subject to a very limited right of appeal. In most cases, employees who sign arbitration agreements give up their right to a court hearing.[48]

Exhibit 4.10 summarizes the arguments for and against mandatory arbitration practices.[49] Before signing an arbitration agreement, job applicants should investigate the details of an employer's arbitration process and be sure that they fully understand and are willing to accept the consequences of signing such an agreement.

Resolving Disputes Online

The newest approaches to alternative dispute resolution take advantage of Web-based technology to prevent, manage, and resolve employment grievances. Online dispute resolution initially evolved to address e-commerce disputes, but the technology has since migrated to employment disputes. Among the pioneers in this area were mediators working for the Federal Mediation and Conciliation Service (FMCS). They began experimenting with software that allows parties in a dispute to view a mediator's proposals for resolution, see notes submitted by each party, keep track of open issues, and participate in a chat line.[50] Because this approach to employment dispute resolution is new, little is known about its effectiveness in comparison to traditional face-to-face approaches.

Using the Courts to Settle Disputes

Despite these alternative means for solving disputes, some disputes result in a lawsuit. As we have already noted, often the EEOC becomes involved and files a lawsuit on behalf of an employee or a group of employees. For employment cases that are resolved in court, two common remedies to violations are monetary damages and settlement agreements.

Monetary Damages. If the court determines that an employee's legal right has been violated and that this has resulted in injury, the defendant (employer) may be required to pay monetary damages to the plaintiff (employee). Compensatory monetary damages are intended to help victims retrieve what they have lost (e.g., back pay and attorneys' fees). Punitive monetary damages are intended specifically to punish wrongdoers and deter future wrongdoing.

Settlement Agreements. Often, lawsuits are resolved by a **settlement agreement,** in which *the defendant does not admit to wrongdoing but nevertheless agrees to pay money to the plaintiff or plaintiffs.* For example, when Coca-Cola settled a racial discrimination lawsuit brought against it on behalf of African American employees, it denied any wrongdoing. At the same time, it agreed to pay an average of $40,000 to each of the company's 2,000 black employees. The company also set aside $59 million for a fund to cover claims of emotional distress, and it set aside nearly $67 million to be used to correct past pay disparities and to eliminate pay disparities in the future.[51] As is common in settlement agreements, Coca-Cola also agreed to make significant changes to its HR management policies and practices, as directed by the court.

Texaco is another example of a company that agreed to change its management practices as part of a settlement agreement. In 1990, in the process of its normal monitoring activities, the Department of Labor found that Texaco was deficient in its minority representation, and in 1995 the EEOC issued a similar finding. The company's employment numbers indicated that it had been making some progress in terms of hiring a more diverse workforce, but promotion and pay rates lagged behind those of other companies in the industry. Evidence presented during the case revealed that it was common for supervisors to refer to members of racial subgroups in derogatory terms. Many employees did nothing to protest such treatment for fear of losing their jobs. Others quit. Eventually, some took their evidence to the EEOC and the EEOC took Texaco to court. As part of the lawsuit settlement, Texaco agreed to implement wide-ranging diversity management initiatives like those described in Exhibit 4.11.[52]

LEARNING GOAL 5

> *We [women] have all had hurdles we've had to overcome, but I also believe you can take control of your own destiny. I've always tried to align myself with companies that had good positive cultures that supported both men and women.*

Maggie Wildertrotter
Chief Executive Officer
Citizens Communications

PROACTIVE APPROACHES TO ENSURING FAIR TREATMENT

When employees resort to grievance procedures, alternative dispute resolution, or litigation, it indicates that the organization is not succeeding in the goal of treating all employees in ways that they consider to be fair. An effective means for resolving disputes quickly will always be needed, but many employers realize that these reactive measures alone are not sufficient. Proactive measures that reduce the occurrence of disputes are also needed.

Creating a Culture of Fairness

Because employees' perceptions of fairness can have such far-reaching consequences, employers use a variety of policies and practices to ensure fairness. A proactive approach to managing fairness reduces the need for employees to go to court to assert their right to fairness. Perhaps if Wal-Mart had been more proactive in its effort to ensure fair treatment, its employees would not have gone to court. According to one person familiar with the

---

EXHIBIT 4.11 Changes a Firm May Agree To in Order to Settle a Discrimination Lawsuit

Recruiting and Hiring

- Ask search firms to identify widened arrays of candidates.
- Enhance the interviewing, selection, and hiring skills of managers.
- Expand college recruitment at historically minority colleges.

Identifying and Developing Talent

- Form a partnership with nationwide internship programs that target minority students for management careers.
- Establish a mentoring process.
- Refine the company's global succession planning system to improve the identification of talent.
- Improve the selection and development of managers and leaders to help ensure that they're capable of maximizing team performance.

Ensuring Fair Treatment

- Conduct extensive diversity training.
- Implement an alternative dispute resolution process.
- Include women and minorities on all HR committees throughout the company.

Holding Managers Accountable

- Link managers' compensation to their success in creating "openness and inclusion in the workplace."
- Implement 360-degree feedback for all managers and supervisors.
- Redesign the company's employee attitude survey and begin using it annually to monitor employee attitudes.

Improving Relationships with External Stakeholders

- Broaden the company's base of vendors and suppliers to incorporate more minority- and women-owned businesses.
- Increase banking, investment, and insurance business with minority- and women-owned firms.
- Add more independent, minority retailers and increase the number of minority managers.

---

situation, the lawsuit was "the end of a long journey for a lot of people. Many, many people had been complaining for a long time—even some senior executives had acknowledged the absences of women and lamented it for a decade or more."[53] Diversity management initiatives and harassment training are two proactive approaches that might have benefited Wal-Mart and its employees.

Diversity Management Initiatives

Many companies proactively address employees' fairness concerns by initiating a variety of diversity management policies and practices. **Diversity management initiatives** *are policies and practices that the organization adopts voluntarily (not because of legal requirements) for the purpose of ensuring that all members of a diverse workforce feel they are treated fairly.* A recent survey of HR professionals indicated that 75% of organizations in the United States have some policies and practices in place to address workplace diversity.[54]

McDonald's has been proactively managing diversity since 1980 when it established its affirmative action department. Back then, informal networking groups provided people of color with opportunities for casual discussions and social support. Over time, these networking groups became more formal, and the company began to offer seminars on career management and leadership skills. In recognition of the company's diversity initiatives, they received the EEOC's Freedom to Compete award. As an indication of how times have changed, today employee networks at McDonald's focus most of their energy on business issues.[56]

FAST FACT

Of the Fortune 500 firms, 8 had a female CEO in the year 2000. Based on the current pipeline, this number could reach 30 by 2016.[55]

Wal-Mart introduced diversity initiatives more recently than McDonald's. In 2007, it introduced an initiative called the Supplier Diversity Program. The objective is to put pressure on their suppliers to hire more women and minorities. If suppliers fail to meet the diversity goals that Wal-Mart sets for them, Wal-Mart says it will quit doing business with them.[57]

> **" Diversity has so many dimensions. It means different things to different countries. "**
>
> *Patricia Harris*
> *Global Chief Diversity Officer*
> *McDonald's Corporation*

Who Is Covered by Diversity Initiatives? When they first appeared, diversity management initiatives targeted the issues of fairness among women and minority employees. Today, it's increasingly evident that members of many demographic groups are sometimes victims of unfair discrimination. Diversity initiatives generally address the concerns of groups that are protected legally, but they may also address the concerns of some groups that enjoy no legal protections. Federated Department Stores, parent of Macy's and Bloomingdales, provides a typical example. In 1996, their diversity initiatives covered only two employee groups: women and minorities. Today, Federated's diversity initiatives cover more than two dozen employee groups, including seniors, people with disabilities, homosexuals, atheists, the devout, and many others.[58] Critics of a broad approach to diversity management argue that all-inclusive diversity initiatives dilute the impact of the organization's efforts. According to this view, a broad approach robs women and ethnic minorities of the resources and of the attention required to address persistent problems rooted in long histories of systemic sex and race discrimination. Supporters of a broad approach argue that focusing on the concerns of only a few groups ignores the legitimate concerns of many other groups and may also stimulate backlash and feelings of ill will among some employees. Exhibit 4.12 shows the diversity topics typically covered in corporate diversity training programs.[59]

EXHIBIT 4.12 Areas Typically Covered in Corporate Diversity Training Programs

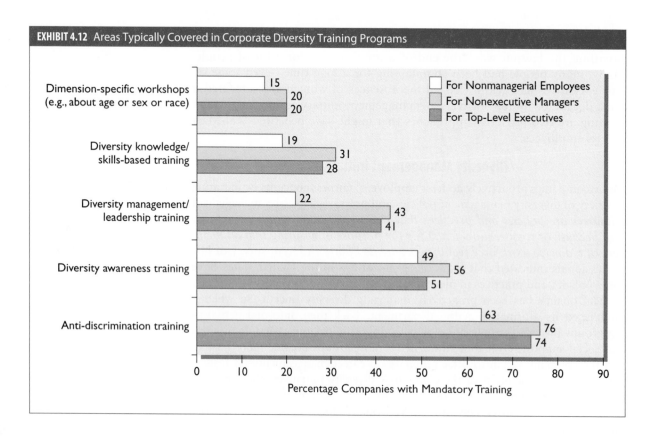

A Culture of Inclusion. What has become increasingly apparent is that simply trying to "obey the law" is not a very effective way for employers to ensure that they treat employees fairly. A better approach to meeting employees' and society's concerns about fairness is to create a company culture in which all employees respect each other and everyone feels included.

By using diversity initiatives to create a **culture of inclusion**, employers strive to create a company culture in which everyone feels equally integrated into the larger system. Members of majority and minority subcultures feel respected; everyone has an equal chance to express views and influence decisions, and everyone has similar access to both formal and informal networks within the organization. When all members of the workforce feel they have equal opportunities and access within the company, they are less likely to resort to legal means for ensuring fair treatment. Respect for all employees is shown when employment decisions are made on the basis of merit rather than personal or demographic attributes.

Darden Restaurants is one company that has been working hard to establish a culture of inclusion, as described in "Managing the Multicultural Workforce: Diversity at Darden Restaurants"[60] (page 138). Their success in managing diversity has been recognized by *Fortune, Black Enterprise,* and *Hispanic Business.*

Evaluating the Effectiveness of Diversity Initiatives. Diversity initiatives are most likely to be effective when they are developed to meet clear objectives and then monitored to ensure that those objectives are met.

For Credit Suisse, customer satisfaction is a key objective. The firm's largest customers include companies such as Coca-Cola, Pepsi, and Starbucks. Those companies demand diversity in the companies they hire for investment banking and other services.[61] According to Freda Campbell, an assistant vice president at Credit Suisse, the company's customers "want to know that the companies they are giving their money to have the same level of concern for diversity as they do."

When Montgomery Watson Harza (MWH) launched its first diversity initiative, the goal was to create a more harmonious and productive workplace through the improvement of individual awareness and group effectiveness. They wanted to create a culture of inclusion, but how would they know if they succeeded in achieving their goal? As described in the feature, "Managing with Metrics: Montgomery Watson Harza" (page 139), they developed a scorecard to keep track of their results.

Economic Benefits of Diversity. To date, little research is available publicly to document the economic benefits of a diverse workforce and positive organizational culture.[63] Some managers use proprietary information to establish the economic benefits of diversity. Others simply believe that there is a link and don't require research evidence to support their view.

New Jersey radio station NJ 101.5 learned the hard way how costly it can be to ignore issues of diversity. After a DJ made several comments that were offensive to Asians, Hyundai Motor America and Cingular Wireless immediately suspended their advertising. The comments also touched off a wave of protests against the radio station, including a campaign to pressure elected officials and the Federal Communications Commission to take legal action against the station.[64]

Undoubtedly, personal experiences with customers and clients have convinced some CEOs that managing diversity poorly is risky business. Multimillion-dollar legal penalties and the negative effects of penalties on stock prices also grab the attention of CEOs. For Wal-Mart, the costs of not

> *We establish diversity goals to create accountability and drive our success. By weaving diversity into the fabric of our company, we create a mind-set in every employee and manager that will allow them to think consciously about diversity and inclusion in everything they do.*
>
> Emily Duncan
> Vice President, Culture and Diversity
> Hewlett-Packard

FAST FACT

After radio talk show host Don Imus made a sexist and racist comment against the Rutgers University women's basketball team, the public's disgust resulted in the 30-year veteran being fired.

MANAGING THE MULTICULTURAL WORKFORCE
Diversity at Darden Restaurants

You may not recognize the corporate name of Darden Restaurants, but you probably know the restaurants that fall under their umbrella: Olive Garden, Red Lobster, Bahama Breeze, and Smokey Bones Barbeque and Grill. Founded by Bill Darden nearly 70 years ago, today Darden Restaurants is the world's largest casual dining company. It employs more than 140,000 people and serves about 300 million guests annually. In a company this large, diversity is a fact of life. At Darden, diversity and inclusion are core values that support the company's core purpose, which is "To nourish and delight everyone we serve."

Like many U.S. organizations, Darden's approach to managing diversity has evolved over time. For many years, their headquarters buildings, located in Orlando, Florida, were decorated to celebrate the Christmas season. Managers thought the decorations were appropriate because they were secular and not religious in nature (e.g., Christmas trees and Santa, not a nativity scene). Then some employees began to complain that the secular Christmas decorations failed to recognize the importance of other non-Christian holidays. And some Christians complained that "Christ was being taken out of Christmas." This was a difficult situation for Darden. Should they stop celebrating holidays altogether, as one consultant recommended? Should they try to celebrate all holidays that were important to their employees, as another consultant recommended? After surveying employees, Darden decided to celebrate the holidays that employees said they wanted to celebrate. In one recent year, they celebrated 12 holidays between October and February. Employees are encouraged to celebrate their own religious and/or cultural heritage by putting up decorations for the holidays they care about. The goal is to support a culture that is inclusive of the wide variety of backgrounds present in the company's multicultural workforce.

Darden's approach is grounded in a firm understanding of its customers. Strong brands like Red Lobster and Olive Garden take decades to build but their reputations can be quickly tarnished. Emerging brands like Bahama Breeze and Smokey Bones will grow only if guests leave feeling satisfied and they tell their friends about the experience.

In stating that diversity is a core value, Darden's management understands that they are inviting scrutiny from all of their stakeholders. Their actions in all arenas must reflect this value. To show their commitment to diversity and inclusion as core values, managers strive to

- Achieve minority and female representation at all levels in the company.
- "Nourish and delight" guests from all backgrounds.
- Increase supplier diversity.
- Partner with the communities from which they draw employees and guests.
- Evaluate leaders' performance against diversity objectives.

As an example of how valuing diversity influences Darden's relationships with its stakeholders, consider its Community Alliance Project (CAP). CAP operates in 10 large cities (e.g., Atlanta, Cincinnati, Orlando, Miami), striving to ensure that Darden is considered a "neighbor of choice." Restaurant directors and managers serve as ambassadors to local organizations focused on race, gender, disability, age, and the gay and lesbian community. One of their tasks is to stay abreast of community needs and opportunities and to pass along relevant information to the company's Diversity Affairs team. Through CAP, Darden sponsors activities such as

- Nulites, a youth development project of the National Urban League.
- LINC TELACU, a college scholarship program for Hispanic students in East Los Angeles and Chicago.
- Sphinx, a music program for inner-city schools in Detroit.
- Bit Thought, a music appreciation and performance program in Dallas.

From the dining room to the boardroom, Darden promotes and celebrates diversity because it makes good business sense, and the people there also believe it is the right thing to do.

managing diversity include poor public relations and lost sales to customers who have decided to boycott the company. For radio stations and other media, the loss of advertising by major sponsors can cost millions of dollars. In the long run, employers such as these will also find it more difficult to recruit and retain the best employees available.

MANAGING WITH METRICS
MANAGING WITH METRICS
Montgomery Watson Harza

Montgomery Watson Harza (MWH) is a global engineering company that offers services in environmental engineering, power generation, construction, information technology (IT), and other areas. Its 6,100 employees include scientists, lawyers, architects, and a wide variety of other knowledge workers. A global company that thrives on teamwork, it considers diversity an "essential element to achieving success." To help employees use their differences for creative problem solving, MWH launched an initiative to improve the company's culture.

The senior leadership team participated in diversity training sessions. Network groups were established for employees with common backgrounds and interests. The quarterly newsletter carried stories describing the contributions made by diverse employees in the company. Numerous courses were offered at MWH's corporate university. And a diversity council was established to advise management on the effectiveness of diversity policies and behaviors.

To measure the effectiveness of their diversity management initiative, the senior managers at MWH created a balanced scorecard. Some of the items in the scorecard were

- Responses on the company's employee survey.

- The number of employees who attended the diversity courses offered by the company.
- Being named as one of the best companies for women and minorities to work for.
- The number of "diverse" new hires throughout the company.
- The number of "diverse" candidates who achieved the level of vice president or above.

At many other companies, measures used to assess the effectiveness of diversity initiatives also include

- Comparing turnover patterns for employees belonging to different demographic groups.
- Comparing pay and promotion rates for employees in different demographic groups.[62]
- Reducing complaints, grievances, and lawsuits related to discrimination.

By having such metrics in place, employers can evaluate the effectiveness of their diversity initiatives and judge whether the costs of such practices are paying off.

Harassment Policies

Under EEOC regulations, employers have a duty to maintain a working environment free of harassment based on sex, race, color, religion, national origin, age, or disability.[65] Like diversity management initiatives, policies and practices aimed at reducing the problem of workplace harassment focus on improving relationships among employees from differing demographic groups. Despite this similarity, companies often manage these two issues—diversity and harassment—as if they were separate from each other. One reason for this separation of the issues is historical. Most modern-day diversity initiatives grew out of concerns about inequality in access to jobs and upward career progress. In contrast, the issue of harassment deals with the daily interactions among coworkers and the consequences of those interactions for how coworkers *feel*.

What Is Harassment? **Harassment** *is conduct that creates a hostile, intimidating, or offensive work environment; that unreasonably interferes with the individual's work; or that adversely affects the individual's employment opportunities.* Harassing conduct includes racist epithets, raunchy jokes, and ethnic slurs. Usually, though not always, the conduct has to be repetitive or systematic.

Harassment creates an offensive, hostile, and stressful work environment that prohibits effective performance; often it leads to expensive financial settlements and negative publicity as well. Ultimately, harassment interferes with the ability of the organization to attract and retain the best talent. Indeed, whole industries can be hurt when the public learns about unfavorable work-place climates.[66]

Following the terrorist attacks on September 11, 2001, many American Muslims were harassed at work. They were called names; graffiti was written in their work areas; and bosses subjected them to questions about their family members. Several Muslims eventually took their cases to court, but it may be years before those cases are settled.[67]

According to a *Wall Street Journal*/NBC poll, 31% of American women experience workplace harassment. Other research indicates that minority women are the most frequent targets of harassment.[68] In several cases, the offending behavior has taken the form of inappropriate e-mail or Internet messages.[69] For example, in one well publicized case, Salomon Smith Barney discharged two managing directors for sharing X-rated material on their office computers. A month earlier, Morgan Stanley settled a lawsuit brought against them by two black employees who charged that they lost out on promotions because they had complained about the distribution of e-mail messages containing racist jokes.[70]

The perpetrators of harassment often feel that people who complain about it are overreacting to coworkers who are just having a little fun and trying to relieve some of the stress that builds up in high-pressure environments. But such explanations carry little weight. The standard for evaluating harassment is whether a "reasonable person" in the same or similar circumstances would find the conduct intimidating, hostile, or abusive. The perspective of the victim—reflecting her or his race, gender, age, place of origin, and so forth—has an important place in the evaluation. This is an expansion of the "reasonable woman" standard articulated in *Ellison v. Brady* (1991), in which the court said that "unsolicited love letters and unwanted attention . . . might appear inoffensive to the average man, but might be so offensive to the average woman as to create a hostile working environment." The "average woman" in this case became the "reasonable woman."[71] In 1998, in the case of *Oncale v. Sundown Offshore Service Inc.*, the court further clarified the rules by stating that employers also could be held liable for same-sex harassment.[72]

Reactions to Being Harassed. No one enjoys being harassed, but people respond in many different ways to the experience. Some victims lash out against the perpetrator, which may escalate the situation. Other victims blame themselves and simply suffer in silence. Regardless of differences in how they behave when harassed, most victims feel bad and report lower job satisfaction. Many people experience physical symptoms, anxiety, and depression. If such reactions are strong, the employee is likely to quit or perhaps file a lawsuit.[73] For employers, all of these reactions are problematic, of course, because they are harmful to the employee and to productivity.

Sexual Harrassment. Over the last decade, more than half of the harassment charges filed with the EEOC allege sexual harassment. **Sexual harassment** *is unwelcome conduct of a sexual nature.* It is a form of sex discrimination that is prohibited by the Civil Rights Act of 1964. There are two types of sexual harassment.

The first is **quid pro quo harassment,** *which occurs when submission to or rejection of sexual conduct by an individual is used as the basis for employment decisions affecting the employee.* An example is a supervisor firing a subordinate for refusing to grant a sexual favor. In such cases, the harasser must be someone with supervisory authority and the employer is usually responsible for the harasser's actions.

The second type of sexual harassment is **hostile work environment harassment,** *which occurs when unwelcome sexual conduct creates a hostile, intimidating, or offensive work environment.* The legal definition requires that the conduct must be sufficiently severe or pervasive to negatively affect the employee's performance or the nature of the work environment. The harasser can be the victim's supervisor, an agent of the employer, a supervisor in another area, a peer, a subordinate, or a nonemployee.

Preventing Harassment. The EEOC guidelines clearly state that an employer is liable for the acts of its workers if the employer knew or should have known about the conduct and took no immediate, appropriate corrective action. Employers who fail to develop explicit, detailed antiharassment policies and grievance procedures may put themselves at special risk.

One way to reduce the incidence of harassment is by having and enforcing a zero tolerance policy. For a zero tolerance policy to have meaning, companies need clear procedures for dealing with complaints about harassment, effective training to teach employees about what is and isn't acceptable, and strong enforcement. Awareness training programs help employees understand the pain and indignity of harassment. If they're comprehensive and used aggressively, such programs can be highly effective. Being willing to dismiss problem employees is also part of a zero tolerance approach. When Salomon Smith Barney discharged two top executives for their offensive behavior, it signaled that the firm was serious about adopting a zero tolerance approach to dealing with harassment.

Exhibit 4.13 describes the components that should be part of a sexual harassment policy.[74] Such policies may not eliminate harassment, but they do

FAST FACT

If an outside contractor's employees sexually harass the on-site workers, the workers can sue their employer, who hired the outside contractor.

EXHIBIT 4.13 Preventing Harassment in the Workplace

✔ Clearly Inform Employees of the Rules
- Raise affirmatively the issue of harassment. Acknowledge that it may be present in the organization, and make all employees aware of the company's position on harassment.
- Provide a clear and broad statement defining what constitutes harassment.
- Specify that offenders will be subject to appropriate discipline, up to and including discharge.

✔ Establish Procedures to Detect Harassment and Handle Complaints
- Build in checkpoints designed to detect harassment. For example, review all discharges to ensure that the employee was clearly performing poorly and had been given adequate opportunity to improve.
- Set up a list of names and positions to whom complaints can be made. The list should make it clear that employees who are harassed by supervisors have alternative reporting options.
- State that employees who experience or witness harassment are required to report it.
- Establish procedures for investigating and corroborating a harassment charge.

✔ Provide Protection to Those Involved in Harassment Investigations
- Give the person accused of harassment the opportunity to respond immediately after charges are made. Due process must be provided to the alleged perpetrator as well as the alleged victim.
- Assure employees that they won't be subjected to retaliation for reporting incidents of harassment.

✔ Provide a Fair System for Discipline and Punishment
- Specify a set of steps in a framework of progressive discipline for perpetrators of harassment. These could be the same steps used by the organization in treating any violation of organizational policies.

help communicate the company's expectations and provide a fair means for enforcing appropriate behavior.

Research shows that female employees appreciate it when company leaders make honest efforts to stop harassment. When they know the leaders are sincere, women who experience harassment not only are more likely to report it, but also are more satisfied with the process for resolving their complaints and feel more committed to the organization.[75]

Fairness Must Be Reciprocated

It's easy to emphasize the responsibility of employers to treat employees fairly, but fairness is a two-sided coin. The other side is the responsibility of employees to treat their employers fairly. Unfortunately, employee misconduct is as much a problem as employer misconduct. A National Business Ethics Survey identified the following types of prevalent misconduct: lying, withholding needed information, misreporting actual time or hours worked, and abusive or intimidating behavior. A similar survey conducted by the Society for Human Resource Management found that employees are quite aware that such behaviors occur. Although they may not report it, the following figures indicate that they see it happen:

- Twenty-seven percent of employees observed stealing or theft.
- Thirty-six percent of employees observed lying on reports or falsifying records.
- Forty-five percent of employees observed lying to supervisors.[76]

Also troubling are data showing that employees who see misconduct often don't report it. The National Business Ethics Survey found that younger employees are much less likely to report misconduct; only 43% reported it when they saw it. The main reason many younger workers gave for not reporting misconduct was that they believed no corrective action would be taken.[77]

The prevalence of workplace misconduct reflects, and at the same time contributes to, the fraying of trust between employers and employees. Of increasing concern to employers is another violation of trust: leaking or failing to keep secure valuable information about the firm's products, services, competitive strategies, and intellectual property.

In many firms, the responsibilities of employees are spelled out in a code of ethics. **A code of ethics** *informs employees that they are expected to conduct business in a way that upholds high standards of integrity.* Typically, a code of ethics communicates that employees are expected to

- Act with personal and professional integrity.
- Understand and comply fully with the letter and spirit of laws and regulations, as well as with the firm's rules and policies.
- Safeguard the firm's reputation.
- Preserve the confidentiality of information about clients, colleagues, and the firm.

In exchange, the company often agrees to:

- Engage in business activities that are consistent with its reputation for integrity.
- Articulate its standards and rules clearly.

> " *Most smoking guns are found in e-mail.* "
>
> Sharon Nelson
> Lawyer and President
> Sensei Enterprises Inc.

- Provide support in making legal and ethical decisions.
- Refuse to tolerate illegal, unethical, or unprofessional conduct.

Perhaps the best indicator of how fairly employees feel they're being treated is the degree to which they're willing to accept responsibility for behaving fairly in all dealings with their employers.

CURRENT ISSUES

6
LEARNING GOAL

Managers will always need to be alert to employees' concerns about fairness. Yet, at particular times in history and in particular organizations or industries, specific fairness issues are especially salient and in need of attention. Today, a significant concern is employee privacy, at home as well as abroad.

Privacy in the United States

Simply stated, the right to privacy is the right to keep information about ourselves to ourselves. Early in U.S. history, Henry Ford faced no resistance from the government when he sent social workers to the homes of employees to investigate their personal habits and family finances. Such invasions of privacy went hand in hand with the doctrine of employment-at-will. This changed in 1965, when the U.S. Supreme Court concluded that various guarantees stated in the Constitution (e.g., the Fourth Amendment's protection against illegal search and seizure) have the effect of creating zones of privacy. Since then, new state and federal legislation has begun to address employee privacy rights more explicitly.[78]

The **Privacy Act of 1974** *was the first major statute to address issues of privacy directly; it gives individuals the right to verify information collected about them and used by federal agencies (not private employers) in selection and employment decisions.* It allows individuals to

- Determine which records pertaining to them are collected, used, and maintained.
- Review and amend such records.
- Prevent unspecified use of such records.
- Pursue civil suit for damages against those intentionally violating the rights specified in the act.

What many employees don't understand is that electronic documents can be considered business records, which employers may be obligated to preserve.[79] Which of the following do you think could become a business record that must be retained and perhaps become evidence in a legal case?

- Personal e-mails sent on a company computer.
- E-mail messages typed on a company computer but never sent.
- Personal Web searches conducted on a company computer.
- Personal IMs sent to friends on a company computer.
- Text entered into a Word document that you later deleted.

If you answered that *all* of these can be treated as business records, you are correct.[80]

As issues of privacy continue to be debated, two issues of particular concern are employer access to medical information and employee monitoring.[81]

> " *Anyone who turns on an employer's computer has no right to expect privacy.* "
>
> *Marion Walker*
> *Senior Counsel*
> *Ford & Mathiason (law firm)*

Access to Medical and Lifestyle Information. Health insurance costs are growing so dramatically that many employers feel pressure to do whatever is necessary to reduce them. One way to lower costs is to employ people who make little use of health care services, because insurance for such employees is less expensive. Information about lifestyles and genetic makeup could help an employer determine who is likely to need extensive and expensive health care.

Like insurance companies, employers can predict how much health care a person is likely to need if they have information about factors that put people into high health-risk categories: Does she smoke? Is he overweight? Does she abuse alcohol? Other drugs? Does he exercise regularly? Does she participate in "extreme" sports? Does he often drive too fast? Employers can penalize, refuse to hire, or even terminate employees because of some conditions associated with high health care costs.

Data about the link between behaviors such as these and a person's use of health care support General Mills's policy of lowering workers' insurance premiums if they lead healthy lives. Insurance costs also help explain why drug testing has quickly gone from a rare to a routine practice: Twenty years ago, only about 20% of employers conducted drug testing; now more than 90% do so. Research indicates that about 2 million employees use marijuana while at work or shortly before going to work.[83]

Access to Genetic Information. Some employers also conduct on-site *blood* tests as a way to monitor employee health. Snap-On, the power tool manufacturer, offers voluntary blood testing to screen for cholesterol, diabetes, body fat, liver function, and nicotine. Employees who agree to participate get a $20-per-month discount on health care premiums. At Westell Technologies, employees who choose not to participate in the company's "voluntary" blood testing program must pay 10% more for their health insurance, and they also have their paychecks reduced by $10. Some Westell employees may be concerned about their privacy, but 90% agreed to have their blood tested.[84]

Advances in our understanding of the link between genetics and disease susceptibility raise new concerns about medical privacy. Should a 25-year-old applying for a sales job be required to undergo genetic screening for diseases that may be experienced in middle age? Is it fair to penalize workers with high cholesterol, given that genes as well as diet affect cholesterol levels? Federal legislation that would prohibit employers from using genetic testing for staffing decisions has been proposed, and it has been approved by the House of Representatives. As of 2007, it was not passed by the Senate or signed into law.[85]

Electronic Monitors. A relatively new concern over privacy is being raised now due to the ability to implant electronic monitoring devices directly into our bodies. The size of a grain of rice, the devices are based on the same technology used by UPS to track the movement of packages and by Wal-Mart to manage their inventories. In 2003, the Baja Beach Club in Barcelona, Spain implanted chips with credit card information into their VIP club members, which made it easier for them to process charges for drinks. In the United States, companies have begun experimenting with implanting chips into employees. For example, Citywatcher.com implanted chips into two employees who needed to frequently enter secure areas. The chips meant that the employees could just wave their arms over a sensor instead of having to carry around a special identification card.[86]

FAST FACT

About 40 million workers are drug-tested each year in the United States.[82]

66 *There is a clear need for us to pass a law to protect genetic information from discriminatory uses.* 99

George Miller
Chairman of the Labor Committee
U.S. House of Representatives

FAST FACT

In 2007, the Wisconsin legislature voted to make it illegal for anyone, including employers and the government, to implant radio frequency identification microchips into people without their consent.

MANAGING GLOBALIZATION
Privacy in the European Union

The goals of the European Union's Data Protection Directive are to protect the personal privacy of citizens of the European Union (EU) and to standardize privacy regulations across the EU countries. It has four basic provisions:

- Personal data may be collected for "specified, explicit and legitimate purposes."
- Any person on whom data is kept is to receive information about who is processing that information and for what purposes.
- Any person has the right to access any data that is being kept and to change or delete information that is not correct.
- People who believe their data are being misused have the right to pursue remedies through the court system.

United States companies with operations in the European Union must comply with the directive in those operations. Compliance typically requires that an employer submit a plan to the Data Protection Authority before it collects, processes, or analyzes any employee information.

Because the directive regulates the flow of information, U.S. companies must be concerned with the law's restrictions on data transfers between European locations and operations in other countries, including an HR office in a U.S. headquarters location. The directive forbids companies from sending any data in any form to any country that the European Union judges to have inadequate privacy protection laws.

Companies that demonstrate they are in compliance with the directive can be certified by the U.S. Department of Commerce. To receive such certification, companies must state that they adhere to the following principles:

Notice. Individuals are notified about what information is collected, how it is used, who receives the information, and whom to contact with questions or complaints.

Choice. Individuals must be able to refuse to have their data disclosed to third parties or used for purposes other than those for which it was originally collected.

Transfer. Data must be sent only to other organizations that satisfy the certification principles.

Access. Individuals can access their information, and correct or delete inaccurate information.

Security. The organization must take adequate measures to protect the information against loss, destruction, or misuse.

Integrity. The information must be relevant, accurate, complete, and current.

Enforcement. The company must have an acceptable process for complaint resolution.

Privacy in the Global Context

Laws and regulations intended to protect employee privacy vary from country to country. For example, the **Data Protection Directive** is a European regulation that *sets restrictions on what personal information can be collected and stored; it applies to all areas of everyday activity and to all European Union (EU) countries.* Each member country decides how to implement the directive. Failure to comply with the directive can result in civil penalties (up to $500,000 in Spain) and criminal penalties (up to three years in France).

Details of the Data Protection Directive are described in the feature "Managing Globalization: Privacy in the European Union." Compared to U.S. laws and regulations, the EU is much more restrictive.[87]

When operating abroad, as when operating at home, complying with legal regulations is one step toward managing fairly. To be truly effective, however, managers need to realize that perceptions of fairness reflect cultural assumptions and values, not just legal realities. Managers who are insensitive to the broader social fabric will find it difficult to anticipate employees' reactions to how they're treated. Unenlightened managers run the risk of triggering negative employee reactions.[88]

CHAPTER SUMMARY WITH LEARNING GOALS

1 STRATEGIC IMPORTANCE. Treating employees fairly and legally is a strategic challenge faced by all employers. Failure to meet this challenge can result in litigation, legal penalties and fines, consumer boycotts, employee turnover, reduced numbers of new job applications, lower productivity, and poor service quality, among other negative consequences. Managers and HR professionals may find the question "What is fair?" difficult to answer. Historically, the power to determine workplace conditions rested largely in employers' hands. Gradually, society recognized that this was unfair and that a shift in the power balance was needed. Numerous laws now sanction some employer actions because they're clearly unfair to employees. A first step toward ensuring workplace fairness, therefore, is legal compliance.

2 PERCEPTIONS OF FAIRNESS. Workplace fairness is more than an issue of legal compliance. Individual feelings and perceptions as well as societal norms also come into play. Even legal actions by an employer may be considered unfair by employees. Managing human resources fairly requires an understanding of how employees evaluate fairness. Managing in ways that meet the principles of distributive, procedural, and interactional justice is one approach to creating fair employment conditions. Managers need to understand that the same policy and the same outcome can be perceived as relatively fair or unfair depending on the attitudes they display and the amount of respect they show personally for the concerns of employees.

3 LEGAL MEANS. Companies in the United States must act in accordance with different types of laws, which include constitutional laws, statutory laws, administrative regulations, executive orders, and common law rules. All members of the HR Triad can benefit from an understanding of the major employment laws and regulations in our legal system.

4 SETTLING DISPUTES. An organization's grievance procedures should encourage employees to voice their concerns to the company so that they can be resolved quickly. Alternative dispute resolution may be used when disputes cannot be resolved through a company's internal process. Mediation and arbitration are the two most common forms of alternative dispute resolution. Online dispute resolution is a new approach to alternative dispute resolution. When none of these approaches succeeds, employees may seek justice by taking their cases to court. For employment law cases that are resolved by court decisions, two common remedies to violations are monetary damages and settlement agreements.

5 PROACTIVE APPROACHES. Diversity management initiatives are a proactive approach to improving perceptions of fairness among members of a diverse workforce. When effective, diversity initiatives help to create a culture of inclusion, where all employees in an organization feel they are treated equally. Training programs to deter harassment are also useful. Harassment policies and practices, including zero tolerance policies, aim at reducing the problem of workplace harassment.

6 CURRENT ISSUES. As technologies evolve, they pose another fairness challenge: balancing employees' right to privacy and employers' right to information. Three current issues in ensuring fair treatment and legal compliance are (1) privacy, (2) access to medical and lifestyle information, and (3) access to genetic information. Genetic information and medical records may be useful to employers, but is it fair to require employees to share such private information? How members of the HR Triad answer this question may depend on which country they are in. In general, employees receive better privacy protection in Europe than they do, for example, in the United States.

ANSWERS TO THE QUIZ ABOUT OLDER WORKERS ON PAGE 122

1. T
2. F
3. T
4. T
5. T
6. T
} Most people answer these items correctly.

7. F
8. F
9. F
10. F
11. T
} About 2 out of 3 people answer these correctly.

12. F
13. T
14. F
} About half the people answer these correctly.

15. T
16. F
17. T
18. T
19. T
} About 2 out of 3 people do not answer these correctly.

20. T
21. F
22. F
23. F
24. F
25. F
} Most people do not answer these correctly.

TERMS TO REMEMBER

Age Discrimination in Employment Act of 1967 (ADEA)

Alternative dispute resolution (ADR)

Americans with Disabilities Act of 1990 (ADA)

Arbitration

Class action lawsuit

Code of ethics

Culture of inclusion

Data Protection Directive

Distributive justice

Diversity management initiatives

Employment-at-will rule

Equal Employment Opportunity Commission (EEOC)

Grievance procedures

Harassment

Hostile work environment

Interactional justice

Legal precedents

Mediation

National Labor Relations Board (NLRB)

Occupational Safety and Health Administration (OSHA)

Privacy Act of 1974

Procedural justice

Quid pro quo harassment

Settlement agreement

Sexual harassment

Title VII of the Civil Rights Act of 1964

DISCUSSION QUESTIONS

1. Describe an incident of when you felt you (or someone you know) were treated unfairly. Did the incident occur due to a lack of procedural, distributive, and/or interactional justice?

2. Describe some of the key federal regulatory agencies, as well as the employment laws and regulations that they administer and enforce.

3. Some people feel there are simply too many laws and regulations governing how companies may manage their employees. These people believe everyone would be better off if we let the free market system work without so much government interference. Other people believe that employees are not sufficiently protected against unfair treatment by employers. They believe employers would treat employees poorly if our laws didn't forbid them from doing so. Which position do you agree with more? Explain why.

4. Suppose a coworker harassed you. Would you prefer to resolve it using mediation, arbitration, or the court system? Would your answer change if the harasser were your boss? Why or why not?

5. Develop counterarguments for the following arguments in support of the employment-at-will doctrine:
   a. If the employee can quit for any reason, the employer can fire for any reason.
   b. Discharged employees are always free to find other employment.
   c. Employers have economic incentives not to discharge employees unjustly; therefore, their power to terminate should not be restricted by laws.

6. Health care costs keep increasing, and technology is making it possible, such as through blood testing, for employers to determine which employees are most likely to require expensive health care. What are the pros and cons of allowing employers to collect medical information about their employees?

PROJECTS TO EXTEND YOUR LEARNING

1. **Integration and Application.** Before continuing, review the cases of Southwest Airlines and Lincoln Electric at the end of this book. Then answer the following questions.

   a. What evidence exists to demonstrate that each company manages employees fairly and legally? Are there company practices that you would consider unfair? Which ones? Why?

   b. Describe what management appears to expect from employees in each company. What does Lincoln agree to give employees in return? How do the expectations and responsibilities of management relate to the notions of distributive, procedural, and interactional justice?

2. **Using the Internet.** Keeping up with changes in employment law is a challenge, but there are many online resources that employers can use to meet this challenge.

   a. Visit the home page of the EEOC (www.eeoc.gov). Learn more about the laws prohibiting discrimination, and also read about the procedures employees should follow to file a claim with the EEOC.

   b. Visit the home page for a field office of the EEOC near you. For example, if you live in Minnesota, you may want to visit the Minneapolis field office: www.eeoc.gov/minneapolis/index.html. Links to local, area, and district EEOC field offices can be found by going to the federal EEOC home page (www.eeoc.gov/offices.html).

   c. Learn more about the Electronics Industry Code of Conduct by visiting www.eicc.info. After reading about what is expected of its members, consider how adopting this code might affect the operation of a small manufacturing company based in the United States. Assume the company purchases some of its supplies from China and is not currently monitoring its foreign suppliers in any way. Do you think it would be wise for a small U.S. company to voluntarily adopt the code? If the company did adopt the code, would it be likely to require radical or incremental change? Explain your reasoning.

d. The Catalyst Award honors innovative approaches with proven results taken by companies to address the recruitment, development, and advancement of all managerial women, including women of color. Learn more about the Catalyst Award and the companies that have been recognized by Catalyst for excellence in managing gender diversity at work (www.catalyst.org/award/whatis.shtml).

e. Visit the Privacy Rights Clearinghouse for facts and additional resources related to privacy in the workplace (www.privacyrights.org).

f. NATLEX is the database of national labor, social security, and related legislation maintained by the International Labour Standards Department of the International Labour Organization (ILO). Visit NATLEX and learn more about employment laws around the world (www.ilo.org/dyn/natlex).

3. **Experiential Activity.** This exercise is designed to help you reflect on the role that culture has played in your life.

Activities

a. First, take a few minutes to write out answers to the following questions.

b. Describe the earliest experience you can think of when you became aware of your cultural background. What happened?

c. What is the most important way that your cultural background has shaped you into the person you are today?

d. Do you have any negative feelings about your cultural background? If so, what are they?

e. Do you think other people you know have any negative feelings about your cultural background? Explain.

f. Have you ever felt discriminated against because of your cultural background? If yes, what happened?

g. How do you think employers should address issues of cultural diversity?

h. Next, share your answers with one or more members of your class. In this step, your objective is simply to describe yourselves to each other. Share as much information as you feel comfortable doing, but you don't have to read everything you wrote.

i. Finally, after sharing your answers, discuss these questions:

- What seem to be the most significant differences in your cultural backgrounds?
- How have your differing cultural backgrounds shaped who you are as individuals and your life experiences—for example, what you value, your interests, your goals, your experiences with your family and in school?
- How are your cultural backgrounds likely to influence your experiences in the workplace? For example, will you feel like an insider or an outsider? Will your culture present any special opportunities or challenges?
- How can understanding cultural backgrounds help you become a more effective team member or manager?

UNITED WAY AND THE BOY SCOUTS OF AMERICA [89]

James Dale spent 12 years of his life working with the Boy Scouts of America (BSA). As an assistant scoutmaster, he was proud of the work he was doing and the organization itself. In 1990, the Scouts learned he was gay and expelled him from the organization. In an interview with *The Advocate*, Dale was quoted as saying, "I think what the scouting program teaches is self-reliance and leadership. Giving your best to society. Leaving things better than you found them. Standing up for what's right. That's one of the ironies of this whole story—that when they found out that I was gay, suddenly I wasn't good enough anymore."

Searching for help, Dale turned to the courts. A state court ruled that the BSA's restriction was illegal and Dale should be allowed to serve as a scoutmaster. The court further concluded that there was no evidence that a gay scoutmaster could not care for or impart the BSA's values to his Scouts. When the BSA appealed this decision, the U.S. Supreme Court reversed the state supreme court's decision and ruled against Dale and for the Boy Scouts of America. In essence, the decision allowed the BSA to continue to be able to determine who could or could not join their organization.

The United Way realized that their antidiscrimination policies were in conflict with the national BSA policy that allowed discrimination against avowed gays. The national United Way organization issued a statement emphasizing that local United Way chapters determined their own antidiscrimination policies. Several independent United Way agencies had funding policies requiring agencies wishing to receive funds over which the United Way has discretion to agree to provide services without discriminating on the basis of age, gender, race, religion, sexual orientation, ethnicity, national origin, or disability.

United Way of Columbia-Willamette

Larry Norvell, the local head of the United Way of Columbia-Willamette (UWCW), knew that the time had come for his agency to face the issue of allocations to the local BSA organization, the Cascade Pacific Council of the Boy Scouts of America (CPCBSA). By this time, three board members had spoken to the media accusing the BSA of teaching hatred and intolerance. Besides these board members, Norvell had to work with several other groups of stakeholders (agency heads, UWCW personnel, donors, board members, community people, etc.) who strongly felt that the agency's antidiscrimination policy should be applied to the local Boy Scout organization.

Norvell experienced his own personal struggles over the matter. He realized that, as the head of the local United Way, his task was to obtain donations for the numerous agencies in the Portland area that served the needy, not to pursue a personal agenda over an issue that could be construed as divisive.

Larry Norvell's Perspective

Larry Norvell stated his perspective in an interview:

"Long before the Dale case, our allocation volunteers had raised questions about the Scouts' outreach to minorities and gays. We have an antidiscrimination policy within the United Way but don't impose it on agencies. It originated in 1984 when one of our board members became very concerned about the Boy Scouts and the gay issue. I wasn't here at the time, but I was told that the board didn't want lots of negative publicity during the campaign. They came up with a policy statement strongly encouraging agencies to have policies of antidiscrimination, including sexual orientation.

"When the Dale story broke in the paper last summer [2000], my board chair told me to get on it. One board member, in particular, was very concerned. Other board members were equally concerned about the possibility of negative publicity occurring during our campaign.

"There are a couple of board members who are particularly conflicted about this issue. I know it is going to be a difficult decision for them as well as the other board members, but I am convinced everyone will go into this with an open mind and make the best decision for us. We have to put aside any personal agenda. The central issue is, 'How can the United Way best serve the community?' We have to look beyond the immediate situation. We can decide to not fund the Scouts because of our policy against any kind of discrimination, but we have to weigh the consequences for all of our stakeholders.

"We have to consider the future implications of any decision that we make. If we adopt a policy that precludes allocation of United Way funds to any agency that discriminates, we might lose $2 million in contributions, which is about 10% of our total campaign.

"A bigger issue is future controversy; how does a decision today set us up for the next controversial issue to affect our community? Several years ago we had a controversy over allocations to Planned Parenthood. Catholic Charities withdrew from the United Way in opposition to Planned Parenthood's stance on abortion. Should we take stances on community issues and run the risk of losing agencies, funding, and other types of support? And yet these are exactly the types of agencies we are pledged to help.

"Others argue that we represent 83,000 contributors in this community and those contributors do not speak with one voice. People make contributions to the United Way without advocating a particular moral set or philosophy. They're saying we want the United Way to be the big umbrella that makes decisions based on where the dollars can have the greatest impact.

"Another thing to consider is that we have one of the most progressive donor-directed giving programs in the nation.

Donors have the ability to direct their gifts to a specific agency or away from a specific agency. If people feel an agency such as the Boy Scouts is unacceptable to them, they can [tell us to] send their gift where they choose.

"This past year we only had 11 agencies that were negatively designated and the Scouts were one. I believe they were negatively designated to the tune of about $380,000, most of which were corporate funds. In particular, Wells Fargo Bank and Portland General Electric asked us to withhold funds from the local BSA because of their companies' nondiscrimination policies. In addition, we had 140 companies that told us they would not conduct their United Way campaigns until we resolve this Scout issue.

"We also met with 30 to 40 key business leaders who told us, 'United Way, why are you into this mess? We are not supporting you to weigh in on political or controversial issues.'

"Personally I don't want anyone discriminated against. I believe that people don't choose to be gay. I spoke with several ethicists about our situation. Does discrimination against gays fall in the context of a moral issue? Both said it did. But one told me that at least half of the energy devoted to the gay issue would be feelings-oriented rather than rational. He said I wouldn't be likely to persuade people with reason.

"I also spoke with African American leaders and several Jewish leaders and asked for their advice. One advisor told me to look at how the United Way can serve the greater good. If the United Way weighed in for gays, who would be helped? Who would be hurt? Would it change the public's feelings about gays? What about the poor elderly lady who lives in isolation and needs assistance—what if she isn't able to receive help from an agency because our contributions fall? Is taking a moral stance worth it? Can we really change the Scouts?"

Larry Otto's Perspective

Larry Otto is the executive director of the CPCBSA. Otto also met with one of the case authors and provided numerous insights on the Boy Scouts' position:

"I worry about the 30-year-old mother who may not send her son to Cub Scouts because of this controversy. I don't want her to keep her son out of Scouting. We're not homophobic. We don't sit around making cracks about gays. In fact, many of our people disagree with the BSA's national policy. We don't ask people about their sexual preference—it's inappropriate.

"There was one individual—a young man who was registered in Scouting as an adult volunteer leader. When he insisted on presenting me with his document declaring his homosexuality, I was required by BSA policy to deny his volunteer status with the BSA and sent him a letter stating this. He wasn't in our employ so we didn't fire him but simply denied him registration.

"I'm Catholic. For decades Catholics have been told about approved birth control methods, which some follow and some ignore. The fact that someone uses pills doesn't mean that they're going to leave the Church. We can't let specific issues blow communities apart. Look at the agencies that have strong ties to religious denominations—they don't welcome gays either yet they haven't been singled out for media attention or pressure from the United Way.

"Look at all the positive things the Scouts do. For example, we annually serve more than 53,000 youth, operate nine summer camps that served nearly 13,000 boys, and operate three winter lodges serving 6,000 youth and a Sea Scout base serving 200 young men and women. Our outreach programs serve 16,000 boys and girls in 'at-risk' neighborhoods. Our members contributed more than 1.3 million hours of service to the local communities in the Cascade Pacific Council. We planted more than two million trees and collected 500,000 pounds of usable clothing and household goods for Goodwill Industries and more than 361,000 pounds of food for local relief agencies.

"What we're most proud of is that the Scouts have clearly had a positive impact on the lives of so many young people. We're here to help kids grow up to be good citizens.

"You know, this all began when a *New York Times* article that was full of errors came out after the Supreme Court decision. . . . The gay issue just doesn't play in Middle America. Only a dozen or so United Way agencies, out of 1,400, have pressured the Scouts. Only around 30% of the public question what we did. The Mormons clearly line up behind us. Some of the other church groups are ambivalent but generally supportive. It's unfair to single the Scouts out."

CASE QUESTIONS

1. In your opinion, does Larry Norvell face an ethical challenge? Or can he simply handle this situation as a business decision? Explain.

2. If you were Larry Norvell, how would you prepare for your meeting with the United Way board to discuss the issue of whether to continue providing funds to the Boy Scouts? Identify the three *key* points that you would make and your rationale for each point.

3. If you were a board member, what would *your* position be on the question of whether the Columbia-Willamette United Way should continue to provide funds to the local Boy Scouts? Explain your thinking.

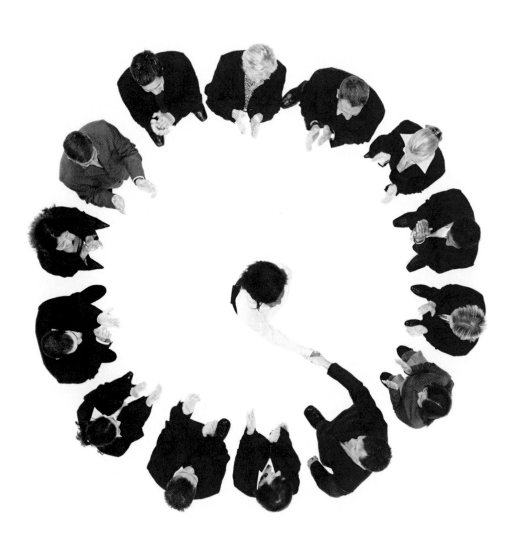

5

Using Job Analysis and Competency Modeling

Learning Goals

After reading this chapter, you should be able to:

1 Explain the strategic importance of job analysis and competency modeling in managing human resources.

2 Describe the specific terminology in job analysis and competency modeling.

3 Identify the various sources of information used in job analysis and competency modeling.

4 Report the methods used to collect job and organizational analysis information.

5 Describe several standardized techniques used for job analysis.

6 Describe the customized approach to competency modeling.

7 Explain the different approaches to analyzing needed competencies.

8 Discuss two current issues in job analysis and competency modeling.

MANAGING HUMAN RESOURCES AT FAIRCHILD SEMICONDUCTOR

When Fairchild Semiconductor introduced the first integrated circuit back in the 1960s, it began a revolution in information technology. Since its founding, the company has undergone many transformations, including being acquired by National Semiconductor and subsequently being spun off again. After it was spun off from National, one of its first goals was to transition from National's data management system to one of its own. It chose an enterprise resource planning (ERP) application from PeopleSoft, then set about adapting its processes to meet the software's requirements. The first step was to form teams of employees from all over the world to rework the company's business processes in finance, manufacturing, logistics, and human resources. The goal was to replace all of the customized business processes throughout the company with "plain vanilla" processes that fit the generic software system.

Once new processes were designed, extensive training was needed before and after the rollout of the new system. Besides teaching employees the new tasks they would be expected to perform, the training sessions explained why these new tasks were important. The goal was to ensure that employees understood how their own work was related to the overall business processes. The company felt that employees would be less likely to take shortcuts to reduce their own workloads if they understood how their own contributions affected other people in the company and the bottom line. To build employees' confidence in their ability to use the new system, training sessions provided plenty of time for people to practice using the software and to receive feedback.

Fairchild's installation of ERP software turned out to be the first step in an ongoing and long-term process of change. Once they had software in place to manage day-to-day activities, the company began another major change effort. This time the goal was to design and deploy a comprehensive solution for forecasting demand and managing their supply chain. Fairchild needed to reengineer its core business processes and implement world-class supply chain management practices for all plants and divisions. Working with IBM as their strategic partner, Fairchild used a similar approach for managing this change effort. To build on its past achievements, the new system would not introduce new data sources. Instead it would use data captured by the existing ERP system. When completed, the new system would change the company's methods of demand forecasting, supply and demand matching, strategic capacity planning, factory loading, allocation management, inventory transfers, warehouse management, and order promising. Throughout the organization, employees were required to approach their work in new ways. HR professionals supported these strategic changes by helping managers understand precisely how jobs were changing and the implications of these changes for how employees should be recruited, trained, and compensated.[1] ▲

THE STRATEGIC IMPORTANCE OF JOB ANALYSIS AND COMPETENCY MODELING

Job analysis and competency modeling are procedures for systematically understanding the work that gets done in an organization. Among HR practitioners, there is some disagreement about whether job analysis and competency modeling are two different procedures or just two variations on the same theme.[2] Our view is that competency modeling represents one approach to job analysis. In other words, job analysis is a broad and general term, with competency modeling being a type of job analysis.[3] This chapter describes traditional approaches to job analysis as well as the competency modeling approach, which currently enjoys increased popularity.

The strategic importance of job analysis and competency modeling is grounded first and foremost in their usefulness as systematic procedures that provide a rational foundation on which to build a coherent approach to managing human resources. These procedures can be used to ensure that an organization's entire system for managing people is internally consistent and appropriate for the organization's context, as shown in Exhibit 5.1.

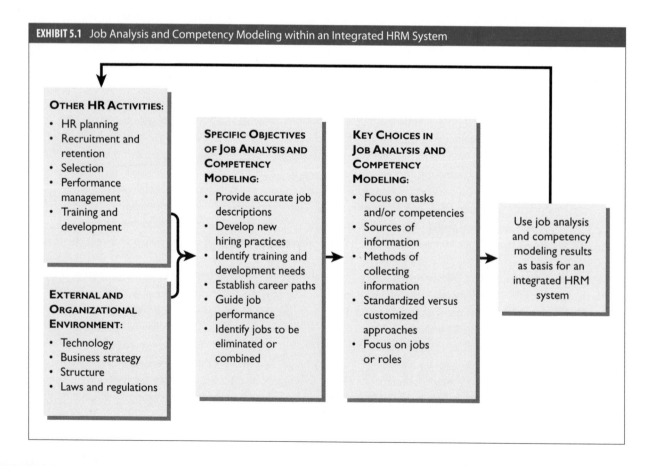

EXHIBIT 5.1 Job Analysis and Competency Modeling within an Integrated HRM System

OTHER HR ACTIVITIES:
- HR planning
- Recruitment and retention
- Selection
- Performance management
- Training and development

EXTERNAL AND ORGANIZATIONAL ENVIRONMENT:
- Technology
- Business strategy
- Structure
- Laws and regulations

SPECIFIC OBJECTIVES OF JOB ANALYSIS AND COMPETENCY MODELING:
- Provide accurate job descriptions
- Develop new hiring practices
- Identify training and development needs
- Establish career paths
- Guide job performance
- Identify jobs to be eliminated or combined

KEY CHOICES IN JOB ANALYSIS AND COMPETENCY MODELING:
- Focus on tasks and/or competencies
- Sources of information
- Methods of collecting information
- Standardized versus customized approaches
- Focus on jobs or roles

Use job analysis and competency modeling results as basis for an integrated HRM system

This role for job analysis and competency modeling becomes especially obvious during periods of strategic change. According to research by William M. Mercer, Inc., driving strategic change is one of the key reasons that organizations are turning to competency-based job analyses. When a company moves into a new market or a new business area, job analysis can be used to identify the new skills and competencies that will be needed to succeed in the new venture.[4] Legal considerations also contribute to the strategic importance of job analysis. As described in Chapters 1 and 4, compliance with various employment laws and regulations is one of the many objectives of effective organizations.

Strategic Change

The desire to improve organizational performance and to stay ahead of competitors is a common reason for strategic change. New technologies, restructuring, downsizing, merging with another organization, and expansion into new markets are all examples of strategic moves that may change the design of employees' jobs.

New Technologies. At Fairchild Semiconductor, the installation of ERP software changed the way people worked in jobs throughout the organization. YRC (formerly Yellow Roadway Corporation) is another organization that underwent a strategic change resulting in the redesign of employees' jobs. When Bill Zollars became CEO, the company had just finished one of its worst years in its 70-year history. It had suffered losses of $30 million, two rounds of layoffs, and a major strike by the teamsters. Zollars was hired to help save the company. From a company that used to think of itself as just delivering goods, Zollars transformed YRC into a high-tech, customer-focused delivery and service business. A sophisticated information system was introduced to implement YRC's new customer-focused strategy. Now customers place their orders, track shipments, and review their accounts online. Dockworkers and drivers communicate instantly with each other and easily access schedule and delivery information using wireless, mobile data terminals. Using these same means of communications, sales representatives can learn instantly about a customer's company, the type of loading dock it has, and who needs to sign for deliveries, among other things. YRC employees are now expected to quickly spot and solve problems as they strive to satisfy customers.[5]

At Fairchild Semiconductor and YRC, strategic changes and new technologies meant that employees had to give up old ways of thinking and learn new ways of working. Newly hired employees needed a different set of skills to do the new jobs. Training programs were needed to teach people about the new strategy and how to use the new technology. New standards were needed to evaluate employees' job performance. Job analysis and competency modeling are tools that can help organizations like Fairchild and YRC understand precisely what types of people to hire, what specific training is needed for the redesigned jobs, and what new performance standards should be used when making decisions about pay and promotions.

Organizational Redesign. Job analysis and competency modeling can also be helpful when organizations undergo an **organizational redesign**, *which may involve realigning departments, changing who makes decisions, and merging or reorganizing departments.* At Emerson, an electronics business based in St. Louis, Missouri, an organizational redesign involved setting up account teams to deal with big customers who buy from several of the company's different divisions.

The new organizational design resulted in changes in how sales people did their jobs, which had implications for the types of skills needed, and the types of people the company wanted to hire.[6]

Reengineering, *which refers to the radical redesigning of an organization's functions and business processes,* is a common reason for redesigning an organization. The goal of reengineering is to design the most effective process for making and delivering a product or service.[7] Effective processes are those that cost the least while rapidly producing goods and providing services of excellent quality. Reengineering requires employees to think across functions. It can reduce the number of handoffs between departments by increasing the resources that are brought together simultaneously to meet customers' needs. By reengineering its insurance claims processes, National Grange Mutual & Insurance Company, a subsidiary of Main Street America Group, was able to reduce its response time by 55%. These improvements were achieved by making significant changes in employees' jobs.[8]

Job Redesign. Organizational redesigns almost always create changes in employees' jobs. Although the design of a job might change for many reasons, generally only two basic types of changes are experienced by an employee: One's job is either simplified or enriched. In most modern organizations, jobs are being enriched, not simplified. Most competitive challenges require a committed and involved workforce that is able to make decisions and experiment with new ways of doing things.

Job enrichment *involves changing jobs to broaden and to add challenge to the tasks required.* Enriched jobs typically require increased teamwork and allow employees to have heightened autonomy. Enriched jobs tend to be more interesting and challenging than before, leading to increased employee satisfaction, engagement, and performance. When organizational change results in jobs being enriched, employees doing the new jobs may need different competencies, which has implications for hiring and training. If the enriched jobs require higher levels of skill, the changes may also have implications for compensation.

Mergers and Acquisitions. For many organizations, the process of restructuring occurs in the context of a merger or acquisition. During a merger or acquisition, job analysis helps provide a systematic basis for comparing the content of jobs that existed in the separate companies, which is essential when deciding where jobs can be eliminated. The comparison can reveal whether two jobs with similar job titles are in fact the same and therefore potentially redundant. The comparison might lead to combining the best parts of two jobs into one new one. Job analysis can also ensure that two people who were doing essentially the same work, perhaps with different but similar job titles, are paid essentially the same following the merger.

Regardless of the type of changes an organization undergoes, job analysis and competency modeling provide the information needed to develop new HR policies and practices that are appropriate for the organization's new jobs. Other uses of job analysis and competency modeling include developing new hiring procedures, redesigning jobs to accommodate employees with disabilities, and determining which jobs to eliminate or outsource.[9]

Legal Protection

Because it serves as the basis for selection decisions, performance appraisals, compensation, and training, job analysis has received considerable attention from legal and regulatory bodies. Regularly conducting job analysis studies and documenting the results in formal job descriptions help employers protect themselves against claims of unfair treatment. Principles for conducting appropriate job analyses have been articulated in federal regulatory guidelines and several court decisions.[10]

Nondiscrimination. During the past three decades, the courts have clearly indicated that employers should conduct thorough job analyses for all jobs in the organization and use the results of those job analyses as the basis for a variety of personnel decisions. For example, in *Rowe v. General Motors* (1972), the court ruled that to prevent discriminatory practices in promotion decisions, a company should have written objective standards for promotion. In *United States v. City of Chicago* (1978), the court stated that employers should have objective standards for promotion and that these standards should describe the job to which the person is being considered for promotion. Objective standards for promotion can be determined using job analysis.[11] By conducting job analyses and documenting job requirements, employers can reduce the role of stereotypes and uninformed opinions about the skills needed to perform a job.

As described in Chapter 4, The Americans with Disabilities Act of 1990 (ADA) makes it unlawful to discriminate against a qualified individual who has a disability. A person is considered qualified for a job if she or he can perform the job's essential functions, although some accommodation may be necessary on the part of the employer. Job analysis procedures help employers establish a job's essential functions and the competencies needed to perform those functions. For example, a hearing-impaired employee may be able to perform the essential functions of a proofreading job, provided the employer makes reasonable accommodations in the procedures used to assign work to the individual. In this example, it would not be legal for the employer to use the hearing disability of applicants as a basis for refusing to allow them to work as proofreaders.[12]

Independent Contractors. As described in Chapter 2, many organizations employ workers who are not full-time members of their workforce. For purposes of compensation and taxation, the law treats contingent workers and regular employees differently. For regular workers only, employers must withhold and pay Social Security and Medicare taxes and pay for unemployment insurance. None of these is required for contingent employees who work as independent contractors. Another major difference is that regular workers enjoy the right to certain benefits and overtime pay, to which independent contractors are not entitled.

Thoroughly documenting workers' job duties is a good approach to determining whether they should be treated as regular employees.[13] During a period of rapid growth, Microsoft hired thousands of workers through local personnel agencies and *treated* them as "temps"—paying them no company benefits and clearly stating that full-time employment in the future was not guaranteed. The temps (who wore orange badges) stayed around so long that they acquired the nickname "permatemps." Eventually, the permatemps filed a class action lawsuit. They claimed they had been denied benefits (including the opportunity to purchase company stock) that they were entitled to receive. After eight years of legal battles, the courts ruled in favor of Microsoft's permatemps, agreeing that these employees did not forfeit the rights ordinarily granted to regular

---

EXHIBIT 5.2 Using Job Analysis to Accurately Classify Permanent Employees and Independent Contractors

Questions to Be Answered Using Job Analysis

1. Does the job description tell the worker *how* to do the job, or indicate that a supervisor will tell the person *how* to do the job?
2. Does the job description state that the work performed on the job is an essential part of the business?
3. Does the job description state that the worker must do the work him- or herself?
4. Does the job description specify the hours to be worked?
5. Does the job description indicate that the worker is expected to work full-time?
6. Does the job description specify that the work is to be performed at the company's facilities?

Practical Guidelines

1. An employer should not tell independent contractors how to do their jobs.
2. Independent contractors should not be hired to perform essential tasks or services.
3. An independent contractor should be allowed to hire someone else to do the work.
4. An independent contractor should be allowed to determine the hours of work needed to complete the job.
5. An independent contractor should not be prevented from doing work for other employers.
6. An independent contractor chooses where to do the work.

---

employees (who wore blue badges) just because they had signed a waiver stating that they understood their "temporary" status.[14] The court ruled that they should be classified as regular employees and were entitled to back pay and the value of stocks they had not received. Microsoft was ordered to reimburse these workers at an estimated cost of $97 million. In addition to the financial costs, Microsoft's image as an employer of choice took a beating in the public press. Today, Microsoft continues to employ several thousand independent contractors, but now the company is much more careful to ensure that these contractors are truly temporary.[15]

Employers can use job analysis to assess whether a worker who has been classified as an independent contractor should be reclassified and treated as a regular employee. Some of the key questions regarding how to classify employees that a job analysis can resolve are shown in Exhibit 5.2.[16]

HR Triad Roles and Responsibilities

As this chapter explains, the process of conducting a thorough job analysis or competency study can involve many different people. Human resource professionals almost always have the primary responsibility for overseeing the process, but they cannot conduct an adequate analysis on their own. The people who work in a job and the people who observe a job being done day in and day out are the experts when it comes to describing the job; so their involvement in job analysis is essential. The feature "The HR Triad: Partnership Roles in Job Analysis and Competency Modeling" summarizes the major ways that HR professionals, managers, and other employees get involved in job analysis. In the remainder of this chapter, we describe these roles in more detail.

Automobile Club d'Italia (ACI) is a nonprofit organization in Italy that provides information and road services to motorists. In recent years, the competitive environment for such service organizations has changed, so Club d'Italia needed to change too. When ACI's top management decided to transform the organization, the change process required the involvement of all members of the HR Triad. HR professionals took responsibility for replacing the existing very bureaucratic approach that had been used for many years with a new, competency-based management system. A design team that included HR professional and line managers coordinated all of the activities required

LINE MANAGERS	HR PROFESSIONALS	EMPLOYEES
• With knowledge of strategic business plans, work with HR managers to determine whether jobs need to be analyzed or reanalyzed.	• Ensure that job analysis information is up-to-date and that it is used as the foundation for the organization's entire HRM system.	• Help line managers recognize when major changes in a job indicate the need for job analysis or reanalysis.
• Participate in job analysis through interviews and questionnaires.	• Serve as a job analysis expert, or help to select an external vendor to conduct job analysis.	• Provide accurate information for the job analysis process.
• Facilitate job incumbents' participation in job analysis.	• Ensure that line managers and employees are aware of legal considerations.	• Use job analysis results for career planning and job choice decisions.
• Understand the relationship among job analysis and other HR practices.	• Prepare and update job descriptions with line managers and employees.	
• Understand the differences between permanent employees and independent contractors.	• Keep up-to-date on new techniques and changing trends in job analysis.	

to develop this new system. Employees throughout the organization as well as trade union representatives also participated throughout the process. For example, to understand the competencies needed to perform three front office jobs, the design team held interviews with top managers as well as 214 employees located in seven offices around the country. After the key competencies had been identified and new HR practices were developed (e.g., a new performance evaluation process, new training programs), managers and employees were actively involved in testing out the new practices and providing feedback about what worked well and what could be done to make further improvements. By involving people throughout the organization to develop a new competency-based integrated HRM system, ACI achieved its goal of developing a new management approach that fit the needs of the organization, its customers, and its employees.[17]

BASIC TERMINOLOGY

In everyday conversations, people often use the word *job* whenever they refer to an employment situation. But when an entire system for managing human resources depends on understanding the jobs in an organization, specific terminology is needed. The precise use of several related terms facilitates clear communication.

Positions, Jobs, and Occupations

Human resource professionals use the term **position** *to refer to the activities carried out by any single person.* Each employee holds one position in an organization. The term **job** *refers to positions that are functionally interchangeable in the organization.* In small organizations, each job may have only one position associated with it; no two employees would be expected to do the

EXHIBIT 5.3 Standard Occupational Categories Used by the Federal Government

Architecture and engineering	Education, training, and library	Management
Arts, design, entertainment, sports, and media	Farming, fishing, and forestry	Military
Building and grounds cleaning and maintenance	Food preparation and service	Office and administrative support
Business and financial operations	Health care practitioner and technical occupations	Personal care and service
Community and social services	Health care support	Production
Computer and mathematical	Installation, maintenance, and repair	Protective services
Construction and extraction	Legal	Sales and related occupations
	Life—physical and social science	Transportation and material moving

same thing. An example of this situation would occur if Ray's position is account manager and only Ray holds the job of account manager.

As organizations grow, the number of positions associated with some jobs increases. A family bakery may eventually hire more people to work as bakers as well as more people to work at the sales counter. The bakery's growth requires adding positions without increasing the number of jobs. If the bakery continues to expand, new jobs may eventually be added. The bakery may add seating and coffee service for customers; so the job of waiter might be added. Additional jobs could also be created through increased specialization. In a small bakery, the job of baker includes baking breads as well as pies and cakes, but as the organization grows, the baker's job is split into two jobs: bread baker and pastry maker.

An **occupation** *refers to a group of jobs that involve similar work and requires similar competencies, training, and credentials.*[18] The U.S. government categorizes jobs into approximately 1,000 occupations, which can be grouped into the categories listed in Exhibit 5.3. Which occupational category do you think the jobs in the bakery fit into?

Job Analysis

Job analysis *is a systematic process of describing and recording information about job behaviors, activities, and worker specifications.*[19] Typically, the information described and recorded includes the

- Purposes of a job.
- Major duties or activities required of job holders.
- Conditions under which the job is performed.
- Competencies (i.e., skills, knowledge, abilities, and other attributes) that enable and enhance performance in the job.

> *"Friendly and caring personality. Competent in handling difficult situations. Able to communicate effectively with people from all parts of the world. Supportive of colleagues. Able to remain calm and efficient under pressure. Self-reliant and independent. Willing to treat everyone as an individual."*
>
> *From British Airways Vacancy Announcement*

Human resource experts have devoted a great deal of attention to developing systematic job analysis techniques, and many different techniques are available. In fact, there are at least 15 major job analysis approaches.[20] Some techniques are task focused and others are worker focused. Traditional job analysis often focuses on tasks. **Task-focused job analysis** *describes what the job involves in terms of work activities and outcomes.*

Worker-focused job analysis *identifies the characteristics of job incumbents that are required to perform the job well.* The objective is to provide a description of the skills, abilities, attitudes, and personality characteristics that lead to successful performance. The question is *who* can do the job. Competency modeling is worker focused.

Each job analysis technique has strengths and weaknesses. No one technique is perfect. The usefulness of a particular technique often depends on the purpose for conducting the job analysis. If the results of a job analysis will be used to design a new recruitment plan, a worker-focused approach that identifies needed competencies may be desirable. On the other hand, the results of a task-focused approach may be more useful for designing a training or coaching program. HR professionals often rely on a combination of job analysis techniques when developing an organization's total HRM system.

Competency Modeling

A **competency** *is a measurable pattern of knowledge, skills, abilities, behaviors, and other characteristics that an individual needs to perform work roles or occupational functions successfully.*[21] As already noted, we consider competency modeling to be a specific approach to conducting a job analysis. Some consultants prefer to use the new language of competency modeling to describe the services they offer. Nevertheless, the basic procedures and objectives of competency modeling are firmly grounded in traditional job analysis procedures. What distinguishes the competency modeling approach is that it places more emphasis on specifying the individual characteristics associated with effective performance.

For **competency modeling,** *the objective is to describe the skills, knowledge, abilities, values, interests, and personality of successful employees.* The objective is similar to that of worker-focused job analysis. Ideally, a competency model describes both competencies that are necessary for successful performance and behavioral indicators that can be used to assess an individual's proficiency on each competency.[22] Competency models are particularly useful when an organization is developing career paths and developmental or training experiences that enable employees to progress along those career paths.[23] For employees, competency models provide information about which skills to develop to be qualified for particular jobs.

Job Descriptions

Often, the most immediate use of job analysis and competency modeling results in writing job descriptions that detail what the jobholder is expected to do and the competencies needed for the job. Job descriptions are part of the written contract that governs the employment relationship. A **job description** *spells out essential job functions or duties, describes the conditions in which the job is performed, and states special training or certification requirements for the job.* Exhibit 5.4 shows portions of a job description for a job at a hospital.

During recruitment, clear job descriptions provide job applicants with accurate information. For employees, a job description serves as a guide to work behavior. Well written job descriptions help employees direct their energies to the most important aspects of the job. For supervisors and managers, a job description serves as a guide to performance management. Job descriptions also serve as the basic building blocks for designing pay policies and training programs. In other words, job analysis provides the foundation upon which to build virtually all components of an integrated human resource management

EXHIBIT 5.4 Medical Center Job Description

Job Title	Worker Participation Developer (management)
Job Designation	Nonsupervisory
Department	Human resources
Reports to	Employment supervisor
Positions Supervised	None

Job Summary

Facilitates the Labor-Management Partnership effort through planning and implementing changes in the Medical Center to improve patient care and services, enhances management/worker relationships, controls costs and increases revenues with the full involvement of management. The Developer serves as trainer, group facilitator, informal mediator, change agent, and internal organizational development consultant.

Essential Job Functions

- Supports labor-management effort (champions the process) in the institution; including overseeing the development of project team charters; provides orientation, training, and coaching of team members; facilitates team meetings; verifies workforce input and involvement in projects; and assists in monitoring the implementation and institutionalization of changes.
- Coordinates communications about Labor-Management Collaboration projects through the Communications Committee and other sources. Assists in developing and maintaining forums for two-way dialogue in the hospital, where news, information, and issues can be shared and discussed.
- Serves as facilitator to the Labor-Management Collaboration; assists the cochairs with the development of goals, projects, and work plans with timelines; and evaluates processes for the partnership each year.
- Oversees work plans and progress on joint projects. Provides necessary administrative support including coordination of resources and follow-up training, information, and facilitation of project team meetings.
- Organizes training to support strategic alliance work, as necessary.
- Responsible for keeping abreast of industry news, both health care and union, for self and Medical Center.
- Maintains established Medical Center policies and procedures, objectives, continuous quality improvement standards, safety, environmental, and infection control standards.

Other Job Duties

Performs other related duties as required.

Basic Competencies

Education: Bachelor's degree required.
Experience: Minimum of five years experience in a hospital setting required.
Skills: The applicant must possess
Leadership skills.
Good analytical/mathematical skills.
Good interpersonal skills.
Proven change and consulting skills.
Good communication skills.
Proven project management skills.

Job Setting and Physical Demands

Contact within the human resource department and with all levels of staff. Mobility required.

Potential Exposures (Category I, II, III)

Blood	III
Body fluid	III
EthO	III
Formaldehyde	III
Radiation	III
Glutaraldehyde	III

system. To meet all of these uses, a well written job description includes the elements listed in Exhibit 5.5.[24]

Career Paths

The initial results of job analyses are typically many separate and unique job descriptions and employee specifications—as many as there are unique jobs. Often, however, these unique jobs do not differ greatly from each other. That is, employees

EXHIBIT 5.5 Elements of a Job Description

Element	What Should Be Specified
Job title	• Defines a group of positions that are interchangeable (identical) with regard to their significant duties.
Department or division	• Indicates where in the organization the job is located.
Date the job was analyzed	• Indicates when the description was prepared and perhaps whether it should be updated. A job description based on a job analysis conducted prior to any major changes in the job is of little use.
Job summary	• An abstract of the job, often used during recruitment to create job postings or employment announcements and to set the pay levels.
Supervision	• Identifies reporting relationships. If supervision is given, the duties associated with that supervision should be detailed under work performed.
Work performed	• Identifies the duties and underlying tasks that make up a job. A *task* is something that workers perform or an action they take to produce a product or service. A *duty* is a collection of related, recurring tasks. Duties should be ranked in terms of the time spent on them as well as their importance. Specified duties are used to determine whether job accommodations for individuals protected under the Americans with Disabilities Act are reasonable, whether the job is exempt from overtime provisions of the Fair Labor Standards Act, and whether two jobs with different titles should be treated as equal for purposes of compliance with the Equal Pay Act.
Job context	• Describes the physical environment that surrounds the job (e.g., outdoors, in close quarters, in remote areas, in extremely high or low temperatures, exposed to dangerous conditions such as fumes and diseases) as well as the social environment in which work is performed (e.g., teamwork, flexibility, and continuous learning). Increasingly, the degree of change and uncertainty associated with the job, the corporate culture, and elements of the organizational mission or vision statement are specified.

who perform one job may be able to perform several others. And, increasingly, flexibility is what employers need.[25] By identifying jobs that require similar competencies, a company can help employees see the logical progression that their careers might take if they stay with the company for a period of years.[26]

When the career path is quite clear, competency modeling can help determine the level of performance that should be achieved to be considered for a promotion. For example, the career ladder for Royal Canadian Mounted Police (RCMP) is quite clear: It begins with the job of constable, then corporal, then sergeant, and then staff sergeant. The core competencies needed for all of these jobs is the same, including leadership, flexibility, and communication among others. Using competency modeling, the RCMP was able to establish the level of each competency that should be exhibited before promotion to the next job in the career path.[27]

SOURCES OF INFORMATION USED IN JOB ANALYSIS AND COMPETENCY MODELING

LEARNING GOAL 3

The information needed to write job descriptions can be obtained from anyone who has specific information about what the work involves. *The people used as sources of information about specific jobs are often referred to as* **subject matter experts (SMEs)**, and they can include current job incumbents, supervisors, trained job analysts, and/or customers.

Each of these sources sees the job from a different perspective. Associated with each source of information about a job are some advantages and disadvantages. By using several sources, there is less chance of error in the final result. To conduct the most comprehensive analysis, the best strategy is to include as many different sources as possible.[28]

Job Incumbents

Job incumbents, *the people who are currently doing the job,* have the most direct knowledge about the tasks, duties, and competencies associated with the job. Incumbents usually provide input into job analysis by participating in an interview or responding to a questionnaire.

One concern in job analysis is selecting the particular job incumbents to include. If your restaurant employs 30 waiters, do you need to obtain information from them all to understand the job of a waiter? Many companies feel that it is inefficient to survey all employees, so they survey only a sample of them. When a sample is used, it must be representative. That is, it should include men and women, members of different ethnic groups and nationalities, younger people as well as older ones, people who work in different divisions or regions, and so on.[29] A representative sample helps capture the full variety of perspectives among job incumbents.

Line managers and job incumbents usually agree about whether an incumbent performs specific tasks and duties. However, incumbents tend to see their jobs as requiring greater skill and knowledge than do line managers or outside job analysts.[30] One reason for this difference may be self-enhancement. Because job analysis is related to many human resource outcomes—including compensation—incumbents may exaggerate job duties to maximize organizational rewards.[31]

Although incumbents may inflate the difficulty of their jobs, there are still good reasons to include them in the job analysis process. First, they're the source of the most current and accurate information about the job. Second, their inclusion allows line managers and incumbents to gain a shared perspective about job expectations. Third, including incumbents can increase perceptions of procedural fairness and reduce resistance to changes that might be introduced on the basis of job analysis results.

Supervisors

Like incumbents, supervisors (line managers) have direct information about the duties associated with a job. Therefore, they're also used as SMEs. Yet, because they're not currently performing the job, supervisors may find it more difficult to explain all the tasks involved in it. This is especially true of tasks the supervisors cannot observe directly, such as mental tasks or tasks performed out in the field. On the other hand, supervisors who have seen more than one job incumbent perform a job broaden the perspective of the analysis. Supervisors also may be in a better position to evaluate which tasks *should* be included in the job and which tasks could be included or excluded if the job is redesigned.[32]

Trained Job Analysts

Some methods of job analysis require input from trained job analysts. Supervisors or incumbents can be trained to serve as job analysts, but usually outside consultants or members of the company's HR staff perform this role.

An advantage of enlisting the help of trained job analysts is that they can observe many different incumbents working under different supervisors and in different locations. Trained job analysts also can read through organizational records and technical documentation and provide information culled from these indirect sources. Furthermore, trained experts are more likely to appreciate fully the legal issues associated with conducting job analysis. Trained job analysts may also provide more reliable ratings.[33]

Like every other source of information, trained job analysts are imperfect. One drawback to using their skills is that they cannot observe all aspects of a job. They can see the physical aspects, but not the mental and emotional demands. Also, they may rely too much on their own stereotypes about what a job involves, based on the job title, rather than attending to all the available information. Finally, especially in the case of outside consultants, their services may be expensive.

Customers

If satisfying customers is a strategic imperative, it seems obvious that customers should also be used as SMEs. In actuality, this is seldom done. Collecting information from customers is usually considered to be a marketing activity rather than an HR activity. Yet, in some jobs, customers are clearly an excellent source of information. For example, cashiers spend 78% of their time interacting with customers and only 13% of their time interacting with managers.[34] For jobs like these, using customers as SMEs is likely to become more common as organizations increasingly incorporate the perspectives of customers when designing jobs and assessing employee performance.

METHODS OF COLLECTING INFORMATION

Just as many sources provide information about jobs and the organization as whole, many methods are used to obtain that information. The three most common methods are

1. Observations.

2. Individual and group interviews.

3. Questionnaires.

Observations

Observing workers as they perform their work provides rich information about the tasks involved. Observation may mean simply watching people do their jobs, or it may include videotaping, audiotaping, and computer monitoring. By watching someone doing the filler job in the original Ben & Jerry's Homemade Ice Cream factory, an observer could learn that the job involved a series of basic tasks: holding a pint container under a pipe that exuded ice cream and pulling the container away at just the moment it was filled. At the same time, the filler moved another container under the pipe. As the second container filled, the free hand was used to print a production code on the bottom of the filled container and slide it along a table to the next workstation. Fillers did this over and over again, all day long.[35] Today, employees monitor machines that do this job.

Observation can be very time-consuming, especially if the work tasks and conditions change depending on the time of day or on a seasonal basis. For example, the work of a landscaper looks very different during the winter planning season, the spring planting season, the summer maintenance season, and the autumn cleanup season. For national homebuilding companies, the jobs of landscapers also vary across different types of locations—for example, townhouses in cities versus single-family homes in the suburbs.

To be practical, the use of observation generally requires sampling. **Work sampling** *refers to the process of taking instantaneous samples of the work activities of individuals or groups of individuals.* A haphazard work sampling approach—which yields equally haphazard results—is simply to observe the work being performed when it's convenient for the job analyst. Systematic

work sampling yields better information. To be systematic, a job analyst should observe incumbents at several predetermined times and places.[36]

Individual and Group Interviews

For jobs involving tasks that are difficult to observe, observations may not be an appropriate method of job analysis. A better way to understand some jobs and their organizational context may be to conduct interviews with the various people touched by them. For example, to really understand the job of a software designer who develops customized graphics programs for commercial printers, you might interview job incumbents, their supervisors, members of their product design teams, staff members who write the computer codes to implement their designs, and the customers who ultimately define their objectives.

Interviews can be conducted individually, or a number of employees can be interviewed all at once in a focus group. Individual interviews are useful because there is less chance that social pressures will distort the responses of employees. On the other hand, focus groups are useful because employees tend to stimulate each other to think of more ideas. Again, combining multiple approaches to obtaining information is usually the best solution.

Questionnaires

Questionnaires are useful for collecting information from many different people because they're more economical, especially when they are administered electronically. Many employers use standardized questionnaires, which can be purchased from external vendors. Often an added benefit of purchasing a vendor's questionnaires is that the vendor can provide useful information from a larger database. On the other hand, customized questionnaires usually yield information that is more specific to the company's particular situation.

STANDARDIZED APPROACHES TO JOB ANALYSIS

Next, we describe several standardized approaches that can be used to conduct job analysis. Standardized approaches can be used across many types of jobs and organizations. HR professionals should understand the advantages and disadvantages of each technique. For line managers and other employees, the different techniques yield different types of information.

Time-and-Motion Studies

A **time-and-motion study** *involves identifying and measuring a worker's physical movements when performing tasks and then analyzing the results to determine whether some motions can be eliminated or performed more efficiently.* Time-and-motion studies were popularized at the dawn of the industrial revolution by a team of engineers named Frank and Lillian Gilbreth. The Gilbreths used the newly invented motion camera to study the motions of workers and make recommendations for how their work could be carried out with fewer movements that required less physical effort.

At UPS, time-and-motion studies have helped the company thrive. In the business where "a package is a package," UPS has always understood that the way people do their work has direct consequences for the company's profitability. In the 1920s, UPS engineers cut away the sides of UPS trucks to study the drivers. Changes in equipment and procedures were then made to enhance workers' efficiency. Today, the study of workers' behavior on the job continues. In one project, a time-and-motion study was used to discover how drivers naturally carried packages and how they handled money received from customers. Job design experts then determined the best way to carry packages (under the left arm) and how to handle money (place it face up before folding it). Training programs now incorporate this information.

As jobs have become more knowledge intensive and less labor intensive, many organizations have shifted away from the time-and-motion study. Nevertheless, it's still used by companies that rely heavily on human labor to carry out repetitive and routine tasks accurately and efficiently.

Ergonomic Analysis

The objective of the **ergonomic analysis** *is to minimize the amount of stress and fatigue experienced as a result of doing work; the focus is on understanding how job tasks affect physical movements and physiological responses.*[37] For example, with an understanding of the biomechanics of the wrist, arm, and shoulder, ergonomic analysis of office jobs can be used to identify sources of unnecessary strain. Office equipment that causes unnecessary strain might then be replaced, workers may be trained to operate the equipment in ways that minimize strain, or other accommodations may be made to safeguard employees' health.

The human factors approach to job analysis and redesign has proved useful in automobile factories, where the physical capabilities of the workforce members have changed as they have aged. On average, U.S. autoworkers are now more than a decade older than their counterparts in Japan. Ergonomic analysis of these jobs has helped U.S. auto companies identify the sources of strain that affect older workers and has guided the auto industry's efforts to redesign plants and install equipment to ease the strain. Overhead conveyor belts tilt auto bodies at angles that make assembly work less physically demanding, and the air guns used to drive screws are designed to reduce the stresses that cause carpal tunnel syndrome. Gyms have been installed, and workers have taken "back classes" to learn how to lift without injuring themselves. More discussion of ergonomics is found in Chapter 13, which covers health and safety.

Occupational Information Network (O*NET)

Organizations with limited resources to invest in job analysis can turn to the U.S. Department of Labor's job analysis service. Titled the Occupational Information Network (O*NET), it is available on the Internet. **O*NET** *provides a comprehensive database system for collecting, organizing, describing, and disseminating data on job characteristics and worker attributes.*[38] O*NET describes jobs using the six content areas shown in Exhibit 5.6.[39]

Perhaps the most innovative aspect of O*NET is that it places information about jobs and the people who fill those jobs into an organizational and economic context. O*NET provides descriptions of the labor market conditions, wages, and the future occupational outlook for the jobs included in it. O*NET also describes the typical organizational context in which a job is likely to be found. Such information is useful to HR professionals interested in projecting future labor supplies and recruitment strategies. It is also useful to high school and college students choosing their future careers.

Employees Use O*NET. O*NET is a useful resource for anyone who seeks to make informed employment decisions. Employees can get facts about occupations and jobs by visiting O*NET's home page and searching the database. For example,

> "They do everything through computers. The supervisor says you have to do 20.2 stops an hour and you can only do 15. Next day the supervisor tells you it took you two hours longer than the computer says it should take; it's terrible."

Edward Martin
Package Truck Driver
UPS

FAST FACT

Eighty percent of us will sustain a back injury during our lifetime.

EXHIBIT 5.6 O*NET Content Model for Describing Jobs

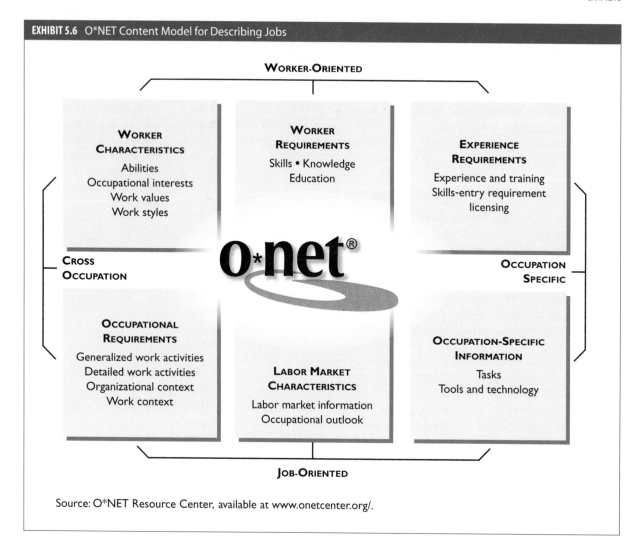

Source: O*NET Resource Center, available at www.onetcenter.org/.

a search for information about actuaries yielded details about the

- Specific tasks actuaries perform.
- Work conditions of typical jobs.
- Education needed to become an actuary (including recommendations that can be used when selecting college courses).
- Examinations and occupational certifications required for advancement in the profession.
- Average salaries for actuaries at different stages of their careers.
- Typical work values of people in this occupation.

Managers Use O*NET. Suppose you're a line manager in a small business, and you want to provide job descriptions for all of your employees. How can you do this given your limited resources? O*NET offers a solution. You can find a detailed job description and then adapt it to fit the specific conditions in your company. O*NET can be consulted quickly, and it's essentially free. Furthermore, the job descriptions available through O*NET are based on hundreds of observations.

HR Professionals Use O*NET. For HR professionals, O*NET provides a wealth of information at a very low cost. However, O*NET is a work in progress; it does not include all types of jobs. Fortunately, O*NET is not the only resource of this kind. HR professionals can purchase commercial software products that include hundreds of job descriptions, ready for them to edit and tailor to their needs. Quick and relatively inexpensive, commercial software packages may be a good alternative to O*NET. But before deciding whether to purchase commercial software, HR professionals need to know whether the procedures used to generate the job descriptions were rigorous. What sources of information were used to generate the job descriptions? Were acceptable job analysis procedures followed, or are the job descriptions just convenient examples? Unless systematic job analysis procedures were applied to very large samples of incumbents in the jobs of interest, O*NET is probably the best solution for use in small organizations.

Position Analysis Questionnaire

The **Position Analysis Questionnaire (PAQ)** *is a widely used questionnaire that measures the work behaviors required by a job and relates them to worker characteristics.* It can be used to analyze a wide variety of jobs that involve many different types of tasks, technologies, and duties.

The creator of the PAQ, Ernest J. McCormick, started with two assumptions: (1) A relatively small set of work behaviors are common to all jobs, and (2) all jobs can be described in terms of how much they involve each of these behaviors. Based on these assumptions, he developed a structured questionnaire containing statements that describe worker behaviors. Each statement is rated on scales such as extent of use, importance to the job, and amount of time spent performing the job. The statements are organized into the six divisions shown in Exhibit 5.7.[40]

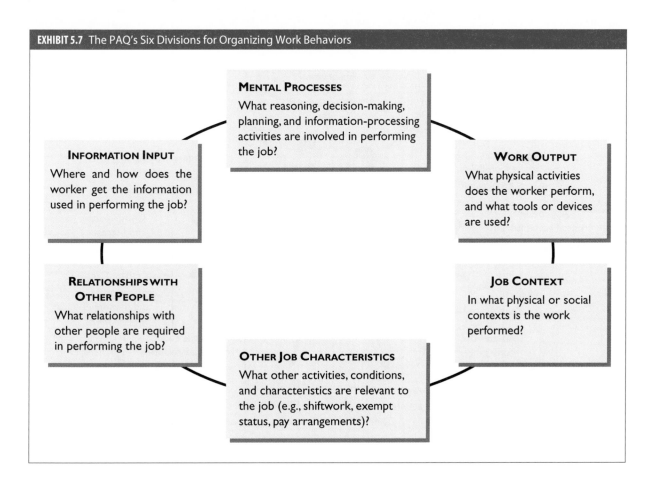

EXHIBIT 5.7 The PAQ's Six Divisions for Organizing Work Behaviors

MENTAL PROCESSES
What reasoning, decision-making, planning, and information-processing activities are involved in performing the job?

INFORMATION INPUT
Where and how does the worker get the information used in performing the job?

WORK OUTPUT
What physical activities does the worker perform, and what tools or devices are used?

RELATIONSHIPS WITH OTHER PEOPLE
What relationships with other people are required in performing the job?

JOB CONTEXT
In what physical or social contexts is the work performed?

OTHER JOB CHARACTERISTICS
What other activities, conditions, and characteristics are relevant to the job (e.g., shiftwork, exempt status, pay arrangements)?

The PAQ has been used to analyze hundreds of jobs held by thousands of people. The results from many of these job analyses have been centrally stored in a database to allow comparisons among similar jobs in different organizations. The PAQ database also contains information about the relationships between PAQ responses, job aptitudes, and pay rates for the labor market. Thus, the PAQ can be used to decide the selection criteria to use when making hiring decisions, and it can be used to design pay packages. However, the PAQ must be bought from a consulting firm; consequently, direct costs appear to be high. Another potential drawback to using the PAQ is that it requires a postcollege reading comprehension level. The PAQ shouldn't be given to raters who have lower levels of reading skill or language fluency.[41]

Management Position Description Questionnaire

The **Management Position Description Questionnaire (MPDQ)** *is a standardized questionnaire for analyzing the concerns, responsibilities, demands, restrictions, and miscellaneous characteristics of managerial jobs.*[42] These items capture the essential components of managerial jobs, as illustrated in Exhibit 5.8.

Because the MPDQ is designed for analyzing all managerial positions, responses are expected to vary by managerial level in any organization and also across different organizations. The MPDQ can be used to develop selection procedures and performance appraisal forms, to determine the training needs of employees moving into managerial jobs, and to design managerial pay systems.

EXHIBIT 5.8 Components of Managerial Jobs Assessed by the MPDQ

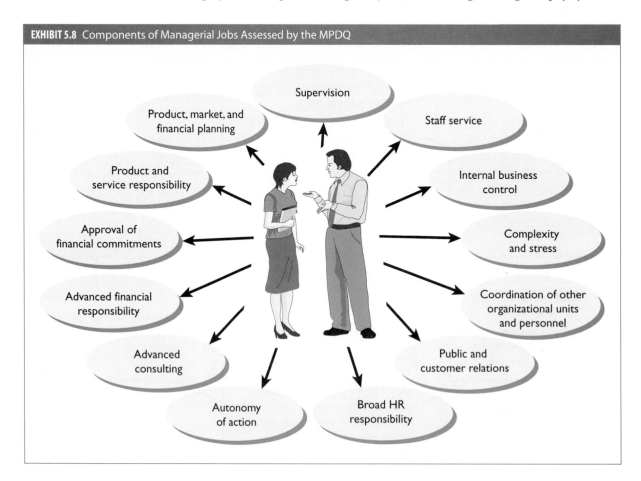

CUSTOMIZED JOB ANALYSIS

Whereas standardized approaches to job analysis are generic, customized approaches are unique to each situation. Instead of relying on a standard list of task items or job components, the customized approach begins with the development of the measurement tools to be used for the job analysis. Usually, the customized approach begins with the development of a **customized task inventory,** *which is a listing of tasks, work behaviors, or worker characteristics (called items) that has been created specifically for the jobs or group of jobs being analyzed.* The items in the inventory are unique to the jobs being studied.

Customized inventories are developed from the ground up for each new customer, such as a company, a unit within a company, or a manager.[43] If the job of human resource analyst was analyzed using a customized task inventory, a part of the inventory might look like Exhibit 5.9.

The development of customized task inventories depends heavily on the cooperation of employees. Usually, they must be willing to have their behavior observed, participate in interviews, and respond to lengthy questionnaires. Furthermore, analyzing the results from this method requires complex statistical analysis. Consequently, the use of these instruments is usually limited to organizations that employ many people in the same job or occupation (such as police, firefighters, and data entry clerks).

Using a customized inventory involves using multiple sources of information and multiple methods for collecting information. Usually, observations and interviews are used to learn about the basic activities involved in the jobs being analyzed. Then questionnaires are developed and used to systematically collect more detailed information. In the end, the payoff for this effort is a very detailed understanding of the jobs being studied.

Developing a Customized Inventory

The items that appear in a customized inventory can be generated in a variety of ways. The basic procedures are always the same, however: First, items are generated for the jobs of interest; then a questionnaire is created and used to collect job ratings.

Generating Items. Usually, a job analyst begins by observing the job being performed by incumbents and reviewing samples of the materials, forms, and equipment used in the job. Brief, informal interviews may be conducted during this phase, if needed, to clarify observations and identify the purpose of employee activities. This step familiarizes job analysts with various aspects of the job.

During this phase, some job analysts ask job incumbents and supervisors to describe critical incidents that represent effective or ineffective performance.[44] Those describing the incidents are asked to describe what led up to the incidents, what the consequences of the behavior were, and whether the behavior was under the incumbent's control.

Creating a Questionnaire. Based on observations, interviews, and reports about critical incidents, the job analyst writes task statements. For example, items developed for a job analysis of librarians included items like these:

- Handles serious disturbances created by users of the library.
- Represents the library to members of the news media (e.g., reporters).

EXHIBIT 5.9 Portions of a Job Analysis Questionnaire for Human Resource Analyst I

Work Behaviors	A. Is the work behavior performed in the position? 1 = Yes 0 = No (circle one)	B. Indicate the percentage of time spent performing it. The percentages must total exactly 100. (fill in)	C. How important is it that this work behavior be performed acceptably? 4 = Critical 3 = Very important 2 = Moderately important 1 = Slightly important 0 = Of no importance (circle one)	D. Is it necessary that employees new to the position be able to perform this work behavior? 1 = Yes 0 = No (circle one)
1. *Counsels employees* on various matters (career opportunities, insurance and retirement options, personal problems relating to employment, etc.) by listening, asking relevant questions, and noting alternative courses of action.	1 0	____%	4 3 2 1 0	1 0
2. *Disseminates information* (job vacancies and requirements, insurance and retirement programs, merit system rules, etc.) to applicants, employees, and the public verbally through written materials and/or using electronic means.	1 0	____%	4 3 2 1 0	1 0
3. *Prepares reports* (e.g., management reports, HUD reports) by collecting, organizing, and summarizing statistical data, historical documents, or verbal records, or all three.	1 0	____%	4 3 2 1 0	1 0
4. *Interviews applicants or employees* in a structured or unstructured manner to investigate applicant or employee complaints, grievances, or adverse action appeal cases and to identify qualified applicants for specific job vacancies.	1 0	____%	4 3 2 1 0	1 0
5 *Conducts job analyses* by reviewing written records (e.g., job descriptions, class specifications), observing and interviewing job experts, and administering questionnaires.	1 0	____% ____%	4 3 2 1 0	1 0
		Total = 100%		

The items generated from critical incidents are used to create a job analysis questionnaire like the one shown in Exhibit 5.9.

Analyzing and Interpreting the Data

Ratings from customized questionnaires are arithmetically combined to arrive at a description of the job. Finally, work behaviors included in the job description are screened based on the combined ratings. A work behavior must meet several minimum criteria to be a qualifying work behavior that goes into the job description. A qualifying work behavior is one performed by the majority of job incumbents.

EXHIBIT 5.10 Partial Job Analysis Results for Human Resource Analyst I

Work Behavior Ratings

Item	Work Behavior	Percentage Who Perform	Mean Percentage of Time Spent	Median Importance Rating*
1	Counsels employees	100	5	2
2	Disseminates information	100	20	3
3	Prepares reports	100	33	3
4	Interviews applicants	100	14	2
5	Conducts job analyses	10	8	0

Note: Importance ratings are based on the responses of only SMEs who perform the task.
*Scale for median importance rating:
3 = Critical
2 = Very important
1 = Moderately important
0 = Of slight or no importance

Exhibit 5.10 shows the partial results of work behavior ratings for the job of HR analyst. Item 5 ("Conduct Job Analyses") would be eliminated at this step in the process because it doesn't qualify as being part of the job for the majority of people in the job.

After the data have been analyzed and interpreted, the results need to be summarized in a way that employees can easily understand. Exhibit 5.11 illustrates how the job of an administrative assistant was described following a job analysis that used a customized inventory.

Advantages and Disadvantages

A major advantage of customized task inventories is that they generate vivid job descriptions. When reading a job description developed with this method, it's easy to picture the tasks required. This advantage makes it easier to develop training programs for the people who will do the job.[45]

The major disadvantages of customized inventories are the time required to develop the task statements and the complex data analysis required after the ratings have been obtained. One job analysis conducted for an organization with 120 positions (i.e., 120 employees) involved 106,000 task ratings; another job analysis for an organization with 3,600 positions involved 1.8 million ratings. Desktop software, computers, and even artificial intelligence systems can ease the task of collecting and analyzing data.[46] Nevertheless, most organizations rely on consultants who specialize in this work rather than perform the complex analyses required.

ANALYZING NEEDED COMPETENCIES

Information about required competencies is essential if job analysis results are going to be used to develop procedures for selecting people to perform jobs effectively and to design training programs. Competency information also can be obtained using either a standardized or customized approach.

EXHIBIT 5.11 Partial Job Analysis Results from a Customized Inventory

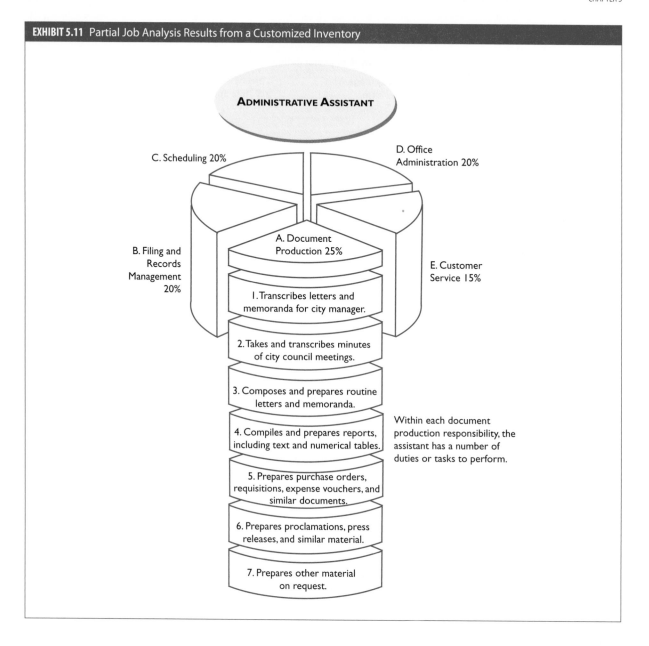

Standardized Approach

Many consulting firms that perform job analysis collect competency information using fairly standardized procedures.[47] For example, Personnel Decisions
Inc. developed a taxonomy of managerial competencies that includes the basic
domains of

- Thinking.
- Communications.
- Intrapersonal skills.
- Leadership.
- Motivation.
- Self-management.

- General operations management.
- Functional business knowledge.[48]

Another popular standardized approach to competency modeling focuses on personality dimensions that are related to performance in particular jobs. The **Personality-Related Position Requirements Form (PPRF)** *is designed to measure the importance of 12 personality characteristics for job performance:*

1. General leadership.
2. Interest in negotiation.
3. Achievement striving.
4. Friendly disposition
5. Sensitivity to others.
6. Cooperative or collaborative work tendency.
7. General trustworthiness.
8. Adherence to a work ethic.
9. Thoroughness and attentiveness to details.
10. Emotional stability.
11. Desire to generate ideas.
12. Tendency to think things through.

Exhibit 5.12 illustrates some of the items from the PPRF.[49]

The PPRF approach to competency modeling asks SMEs to rate the importance of the personal characteristics described. For example, suppose a consulting company wanted to develop an understanding of the personalities associated with

EXHIBIT 5.12 Sample Items in the PPRF			
Effective Performance in This Position Requires the Person to (Sample Items)	**Not Required**	**Helpful**	**Essential**
Set 1 Sample items from Set 1 assess the importance of "general leadership competencies."			
1) Lead group activities through exercise of power or authority.	☐	X	☐
2) Take control in group situations.	☐	X	☐
3) Initiate change within the person's work group or area to enhance productivity or performance.	☐	☐	X
4) Motivate people to accept change.	☐	X	☐
Set 2 Sample items from Set 2 assess the importance of "interest in negotiations."			
5) Negotiate on behalf of the work unit for a fair share of organizational resources.	☐	☐	X
6) Work with dissatisfied customers or clients to achieve a mutually agreeable solution.	☐	☐	X
7) Help people in work groups settle interpersonal conflicts that interface with group functioning.	☐	X	☐
8) Help settle work-related problems, complaints, or disputes among employees or organizational units.	X	☐	☐

effective performance for junior associates. The company would ask experienced consultants and those who supervise junior associates to be the SMEs and complete the PPRF. With the duties of a junior associate clearly in mind, the SMEs would rate the extent to which they believe the personality descriptions contribute to an associate's effective performance.

EXHIBIT 5.13 Questionnaire to Identify Competencies Needed for Human Resource Analyst I

Competencies	1. Is the competency used in the position? 1 = Yes 0 = No	2. How important is this competency to acceptable job performance? 4 = Critical 3 = Very important 2 = Moderately important 1 = Slightly important 0 = Of no importance	3. Is it necessary that employees new to the position possess this competency? 1 = Yes 0 = No	4. To what extent does this distinguish between superior and adequate new employees? 3 = To a great extent 2 = Considerably 1 = Moderately 0 = Not at all
	(circle one)	(circle one)	(circle one)	(circle one)
1. *Knowledge of HR procedures:* Knowledge of the working rules and regulations. Included are policies on overtime, absences, vacations, holidays, sick leave, court leave, selection, promotion, reassignment, disciplinary actions, terminations, grievance procedures, performance appraisals, and so forth, as outlined in relevant manuals.	1 0	4 3 2 1 0	1 0	3 2 1 0
2. *Knowledge of organizational structure:* Knowledge of whom to contact when various situations arise. Included is the knowledge of interrelationships between organizational units, lines of authority, and responsibility within organizational units.	1 0	4 3 2 1 0	1 0	3 2 1 0
3. *Knowledge of laws and ethics:* Knowledge of legal and ethical standards to be maintained in HR work. Included are ethical considerations governing general professional practice (e.g., confidentiality of records) as well as state and federal regulations governing fair employment practices (e.g., EEO legislation and the *Uniform Guidelines on Employee Selection Procedures*).	1 0	4 3 2 1 0	1 0	3 2 1 0
4. *Computer skill:* Skill in the use of a computer. Included is a basic knowledge of the keyboard and of computer terminology.	1 0	4 3 2 1 0	1 0	3 2 1 0

The supervisors' responses to the PPRF would yield a picture of the type of person who is likely to succeed as a junior associate. With this information, HR professionals could more effectively screen job applicants and make better selection decisions when they hire junior associates. If the consulting company also wanted to understand the competencies associated with high-performing managers, they could ask high-ranking partners to be the SMEs. They would use the PPRF to describe the characteristics that they believe are needed to succeed as a manager in the company. The results could then be used to make promotion decisions and develop succession plans.

Customized Approach

The example analysis questionnaire shown in Exhibit 5.13 illustrates a customized method to assess the competencies needed for a job. The questionnaire in the exhibit was developed by asking SMEs (incumbents and supervisors) to identify all the skills, knowledge, attitudes, values, and other characteristics that they thought were needed to be an effective HR Analyst. A group interview meeting was held to create the list of possible competencies. Based on the results of the group interview meeting, a competency rating questionnaire was created and distributed to the SMEs, who rated (a) whether the competency is used at all; (b) its importance; (c) whether a new incumbent needs the competency upon entry to the job; and (d) the extent to which the competency distinguishes a highly effective incumbent from an adequate one.

Exhibit 5.14 shows the results of the SMEs' competency ratings. The results indicate that the organization should ensure that new hires have a good knowl-

FAST FACT

When the Royal Canadian Mounted Police recently revised their performance appraisal system, they used a customized competency model to determine the key competencies needed.

EXHIBIT 5.14 Competency Rating Results for Human Resource Analyst I

Competency Ratings

Item	Competency	Percentage Who Use It	Median Importance Rating*	Percentage Rating It as Necessary at Entry	Median Rating for Distinguishing Superior Employees**
1	Knowledge of HR procedures	100	2.5	70	3.0
2	Knowledge of organizational structure	100	2.0	0	2.0
3	Knowledge of laws and ethics	100	2.0	60	2.5
4	Computer skill	100	2.5	80	0.5

Note: Ratings provided by job incumbents. Results are shown only for SMEs who reported they use the competency.

*Scale for importance ratings:

4 = Critical
3 = Very important
2 = Moderately important
1 = Slightly important
0 = Of no importance

**Scale for extent to which competency distinguishes superior from average employees in the job:

3 = To a great extent
2 = Considerably
1 = Moderately
0 = Slightly or not at all

edge of HR procedures and good computer skills, as well as some familiarity with relevant laws and ethical standards. To maximize performance, the organization may want to offer additional training in both HR procedures and legal and ethical standards. Investing in computer training for new hires may not pay off as much, however. While computer skills are necessary, they do not contribute much to outstanding performance.

MANAGING GLOBALIZATION
Modeling Leadership Competencies at 3M

Due to the breadth of businesses and technologies within 3M, it takes years of experience before executives learn to function effectively in the company. Thoughtful succession planning efforts would ensure that the occasional managerial and executive job openings were leveraged as opportunities for leadership development.

Customized Approach
The decision to use a customized approach to developing a leadership competency model for the company fit well with this company's culture. Innovation is a core competence for 3M, and employees are constantly tinkering with products and systems to improve them.

Partnership Perspective
The customized approach also served the objective of involving all key players in the process. Human resource professionals worked hand in hand with a team of key executives. The process of developing the leadership competency model required getting input from the CEO, from executives who report directly to the CEO, and from representatives in Europe, Asia, Latin America, Canada, and the United States.

Rather than simply hand the executives an off-the-shelf competency model, the HR professionals held meetings and discussions with the executives to solicit their ideas, craft the language used in describing the competencies, and so on. After all, the leadership competency model would have important implications for the careers of key talent in the company. Involving executives early in the process contributed to the validity of the model and enhanced their acceptance of it.

Strategic Importance
The 12 dimensions of 3M's global leadership competency model reflect the company's corporate values and business strategy. At 3M, the stated values are as follows:

- We satisfy customers with superior quality, value, and service.

- We provide our investors with a fair rate of return through sustained quality growth.
- We respect our social and physical environment.
- We work to make 3M a company employees are proud to be a part of.

These values are apparent in competency dimensions such as customer orientation, ethics and integrity, and developing people.

Behavioral Anchors
Associated with each of 3M's global leadership competencies are specific behaviors that illustrate exemplary levels of competency. Information about the specific behaviors displayed by top-level executives is used by the CEO during his annual review of these executives. Elsewhere in the company, executives and managers refer to the specific behaviors when setting performance expectations, judging performance, and discussing the development needs of their employees. As an example, specific behaviors associated with the competency of global perspective include

- Respects, values, and leverages other customs, cultures, and values.
- Uses global management team to understand and grow the total business.
- Able to leverage the benefits from working in multicultural environments.
- Optimizes and integrates resources on a global basis, including manufacturing, research, and businesses across countries, and functions to increase 3M's growth and profitability.
- Satisfies global customers and markets from anywhere in the world.
- Actively stays current on world economies, trade issues, international market trends, and opportunities.

At 3M, two forces put pressure on the organization to invest in conducting a customized competency-based job analysis. As was true at many other companies, the decade of the 1990s brought increased global competition. The fierce competition, in turn, highlighted the need for highly effective leaders who could steer the company through a period of shrinking margins, pressures on pricing, and the ever present demand for innovation. This environment highlighted the importance of succession planning as an activity that could promote the company's long-term viability. As described in the feature "Managing Globalization: Modeling Leadership Competencies at 3M," a customized competency model helped this company address this long-term strategic issue. At 3M, the belief is that the specific desired behaviors and the leadership competencies can be developed.[50]

Competency Inventories

One way to keep track of the skills present in a company's workforce is to use competency inventories. A **competency inventory** *is a detailed file maintained for each employee that documents a person's competencies.* The inventory may include scores from a standard instrument such as the PPRF, and/or it may include more general information that can be used to estimate employee competencies. For example, managers can use information about an employee's level of education, training, experience, length of service, current job title, and performance history to judge how well an employee is likely to perform in a new job if he or she is promoted.[51]

Schlumberger is an energy company that uses complex technologies to search for and retrieve the petroleum. Its core values are simple: *people* who thrive on the challenge of excelling in any environment and who are dedicated to safety and customer service worldwide, a commitment to *technology,* and a determination to produce superior *profits.* To ensure that it has the people it needs to succeed, Schlumberger uses a competency inventory that helps the company keep track of its talent around the world. As described in the feature, "Managing with Metrics: Schlumberger," it has invested significant resources in developing its talent pool. It strives to use that talent wisely and to retain the people whose development it has invested in. Employees document their competencies by filling out a Career Networking Profile. Schlumberger's engineers appreciate having opportunities to develop and move up throughout their careers, and CEO Andrew Gould seems to understand the value of keeping the people pipeline filled.

Focusing on developing and tracking the competencies of their workforce, as is done at Schlumberger, can pay off in the long run. According to recent studies, the best-performing firms are much more likely to have homegrown CEOs. In poor-performing firms, CEOs are more likely to have been hired externally. Schlumberger has returned 240% to shareholders during the past decade, beating the S&P 500 and most of its competitors.[52]

> 66 *The capacity to develop talent from anywhere in the world is one of our key strengths. We treat attrition, especially if someone has high potential, as a catastrophic incident.* 99
>
> *Andrew Gould*
> *Chief Executive Officer*
> *Schlumberger*

CURRENT ISSUES

8
LEARNING GOAL

At organizations such as AT&T and Microsoft, technological changes occur so rapidly that traditional job analysis is all but impossible. And increasingly, job requirements are hard to specify because companies expect employees to do whatever the customer wants.

MANAGING WITH METRICS
Schlumberger

What types of people does this high-tech company need to reach its goals? Mostly engineers, researchers, and scientists, but also electrical and mechanical technicians and equipment operators—and they're needed all around the world. With only 1,500 petroleum engineers enrolled in U.S. colleges, Schlumberger must win in a fierce war for the talent it needs.

To get the talent it needs, high-level Schlumberger executives serve as "ambassadors" to 44 of the best engineering programs around the world. As ambassadors, these executives develop relationships with faculty and their students. When the Nigeria University of Ibadan was struggling, a Schlumberger ambassador saw to it that the university received several million dollars to create a petroleum learning center. As a result of that investment, Schlumberger now has more Nigerian-trained engineers working around the world than it has employees in Nigeria itself.

When it comes to finding talent, Schlumberger is in better shape than most oil companies these days. Many competitors hired and fired talent as the industry went through earlier cycles of boom and bust. Schlumberger focused on keeping its talent and developing people to build up its bench strength. According to CEO Gould, "The capacity to develop talent from anywhere in the world is one of our key strengths."

The task of keeping track of employees with specific competencies is aided by a sophisticated information system. HR professionals can search the database of career networking profiles as well as performance and salary data for employees working in dozens of countries. Written by each employee, a career networking profile describes career goals, past assignments, professional affiliations, skills, patents, hobbies, and so on. If a country manager is needed in Brazil, for example, the system can immediately identify current employees who have the competencies needed for the job and who might be interested in making the move.

In the short run, developing the employee competencies that Schlumberger needs seems costly. For example, engineers must first complete three years of on-the-job training and classroom education in the company before they can be sent to work in the oil fields. In the third year, they must demonstrate their competencies by completing and presenting a major project of their own. The education is not a cakewalk—about 40% who start the process drop out before completing it. But those who do finish have the competencies Schlumberger needs and are grateful for the experience. Of the company's top managers today, 80% were recruited right out of school and have remained loyal employees throughout their entire careers.

The Decline of Job Analysis?

Decreased job specialization, increased job sharing, and the increased prevalence of work teams are just a few of the reasons people have begun to question the usefulness of traditional job analysis techniques. Traditional techniques force boundaries to be drawn between jobs and are inconsistent with the trend toward increased sharing of responsibilities across jobs and across levels in the organization.[53]

The apparent inconsistency between the assumptions of traditional job analysis and new approaches to managing employees is so great that it has led some HR professionals to raise the question, "Do we need job analysis anymore?" We think the answer to this question is clearly yes. Unless employers understand the work employees are expected to do, they cannot possibly develop an integrated HRM system to support the work. As we stated at the beginning of this chapter, job analysis and competency modeling can be valuable tools during strategic change. Also, job analysis is essential to any organization concerned about legal compliance and its ability to defend its employment practices (the legal status of competency modeling is not as well established, however). Clearly, organizations will continue to use job analysis in some form as a foundation on which to build integrated HRM systems.

From "My Job" to "My Role"

Traditional job analysis techniques were developed during a time when organizations and jobs were more stable and predictable. People could be hired to do a particular job, and they could expect to do basically the same job in the same way for many months or even years. This arrangement was convenient for management and workers, except when management wanted the workers to change or do something "not in their job descriptions."

Flexibility. Today's environment requires adaptable organizations and flexible individuals. Organizations focus on how they can get flexibility without worker resistance, while satisfying workers' needs for comfort. Many Japanese firms such as Nissan and Honda hire applicants to work for the company rather than to do a specific job. Many companies agree that it is better to focus the employee's attention on doing whatever is necessary to accomplish the organization's work.[54] Corresponding to this, some HR professionals have argued that the term *role analysis* should be used in place of the term *job analysis*.[55] Focusing on roles is consistent with the philosophy of emphasizing results over procedures, and it works well in organizations that allow employees to use flexible work arrangements, such as telecommuting and flextime, to adapt work requirements to their personal needs.[56]

Teamwork. This shift of focus from "the job" to work roles is almost inevitable in organizations where work is organized around teams instead of individuals. In a team environment, the tasks performed by a particular individual may depend on the talents and interests of the other people in the team. The team as a whole is assigned duties and may be held accountable for specific tasks. If the team is self-managed, the members can organize the team's work in any way they wish.

When Wilbert L. Gore founded his company in 1958, he believed teams were the best way to successfully innovate. Today, W. L. Gore & Associates is famous for products such as Gore-Tex fabrics, Glide dental floss, and Elixir guitar strings. W. L. Gore & Associates still feels like a small company; its team-based culture is one reason for its reputation as one of the best companies to work for. When new associates are hired, they're chosen to work in general areas, not in specific jobs. Their sponsors (not bosses) help them identify opportunities to use their talents to help meet team objectives. There are no standard job descriptions, and employees decide for themselves what "commitments" they take on in their teams. In such situations, the HRM system is designed to support teams; it is not built around individual jobs or the competencies of individual employees. In situations like this, individual-focused job analysis and competency modeling techniques are not very useful.[57]

While job analysis will not disappear, the procedures used are likely to evolve and change to meet the new needs of organizations. The increasing popularity of competency modeling (instead of task-focused job analysis) is one example of how job analysis is evolving. Part of the appeal of competency modeling seems to be that it is more useful for identifying the core competencies and behaviors that are *similar* across all jobs in a department, business unit, or organization. When these are included in employees' job descriptions, competency modeling serves as a tool for defining and communicating a consistent corporate culture.

> " *The job is just a social artifact. Most societies since the beginning of time have done fine without jobs. In the preindustrial past, people worked very hard, but they did not have jobs.* "
>
> *William Bridges*
> Author of Job Shift

> " *When I arrived at Gore, I didn't know who did what. Who was my boss? Then I realized your team is your boss, because you don't want to let them down. Everyone is your boss and no one is your boss.* "
>
> *Diane Davidson*
> *Sales Executive*
> *W. L. Gore & Associates*

CHAPTER SUMMARY WITH LEARNING GOALS

1 **STRATEGIC IMPORTANCE.** The creation and maintenance of effective organizations require a comprehensive understanding of the work that needs to be done and the way that work is structured into jobs. Job analysis and competency modeling provide systematic information about the duties associated with jobs, the behaviors required to fulfill those duties, and the competencies needed by job holders. In turn, this information is helpful for determining hiring criteria, designing training programs, developing measures of performance, creating career paths, and setting pay policies. Job analysis and competency modeling results serve as a basis for linking all human resource activities and also linking these activities to the needs of the business.

2 **SPECIFIC TERMINOLOGY.** Specific terminology is needed because the entire system for managing human resources depends on understanding the jobs in an organization. Some of the important terms to know are *position, job, occupation, job analysis, competency modeling, job description,* and *career path.*

3 **SOURCES OF INFORMATION.** Subject matter experts are the people who are sources of information about specific job requirements. They can include job incumbents, supervisors, trained job analysts, and/or customers. The best way to conduct a comprehensive job analysis is to include as many different sources of information as possible.

4 **METHODS OF COLLECTING INFORMATION.** The three most common ways to collect job and organizational analysis information are (1) observations, (2) individual and group interviews, and (3) questionnaires. Two types of methods analysis that focus on analyzing job elements are time-and-motion studies and the human factors approach.

5 **STANDARDIZED JOB ANALYSIS TECHNIQUES.** Standardized job analysis techniques include time-and-motion studies, ergonomic analysis, the federal government's Occupational Information Network (O*NET), the Position Analysis Questionnaire, and the Management Position Description Questionnaire. Standardized job analysis techniques make it easy to compare the results for a job with the results found for many other similar or dissimilar jobs—including those in other organizations.

6 **CUSTOMIZED APPROACHES.** With a customized approach, information is collected using an inventory that lists the tasks, work behaviors, or worker characteristics that are specific to the jobs or groups of jobs being analyzed. A customized questionnaire is developed from the ground up for each new organizational setting. Compared to standardized approaches, a customized job analysis provides more job-specific details. Such details are particularly useful for designing training programs and creating performance measurement and feedback systems.

7 **ANALYZING NEEDED COMPETENCIES.** Like job tasks, the competencies needed to perform a job can be analyzed using either a standardized or customized approach. The Personality-Related Position Requirements Form is an example of a standardized approach; it assesses the importance of several personality characteristics for job performance. The customized approach to identifying needed competencies is similar to the customized approach to measuring key job tasks.

8 **CURRENT ISSUES.** Changes in the nature of organizations and in the way work is done mean that approaches to job analysis and competency modeling also need to change. Organizations want to hire employees who can perform a variety of different jobs and who are effective workers in teams. Traditional approaches to job analysis were developed when people were hired for a specific job that often was performed alone. The growing use of competency models reflects these changes in the work place.

TERMS TO REMEMBER

Competency
Competency inventory
Competency modeling
Customized task inventory
Ergonomic analysis
Job
Job analysis
Job enrichment
Job description
Job incumbents
Management Position Description Questionnaire (MPDQ)
Occupation

O*NET
Organizational redesign
Personality-Related Position Requirements Form (PPRF)
Position
Position Analysis Questionnaire (PAQ)
Reengineering
Subject matter experts (SMEs)
Task-focused job analysis
Time-and-motion study
Worker-focused job analysis
Work sampling

QUESTIONS FOR DISCUSSION AND REFLECTIVE THINKING

1. Describe how job analysis and competency modeling can be useful during times of strategic change (e.g., after a merger, prior to downsizing, or during rapid growth).
2. What does it mean to say that job analysis serves as a foundation for an organization's integrated HRM system?
3. What are the advantages and disadvantages of standardized and customized approaches to job analysis and competency modeling?
4. The courts have recognized task-based job analysis as useful for preventing unfair discrimination. Some HR professionals worry that competency-based approaches are more susceptible to stereotyping and bias. From an employee's perspective, would you prefer to have a job description and performance appraisal based on a task-focused job analysis or on a competency modeling study? Explain why.
5. Describe how job analysis results can be used by managers.
6. As an employee, why is it useful to understand the competencies required in specific jobs?

PROJECTS TO EXTEND YOUR LEARNING

1. **Integration and Application.** Before continuing, review the cases of Southwest Airlines and Lincoln Electric at the end of this book. Then answer the following questions.

    a. Explain how job analysis can help each organization meet its strategic objectives.
    b. For each company, describe how managers and employees could make use of the results of competency modeling.

2. **Using the Internet.** Several useful online resources are available to help you learn more about job analysis and competency modeling.

    a. Study the *Uniform Guidelines*, which are available online from the U.S. Department of Labor (www.dol.gov), to learn more about the legal reasons for conducting a job analysis.
    b. Job-analysis.net (www.job-analysis.net) provides online assistance for creating a job description. Visit their home page and try creating a job description for a job you have held.
    c. The Society for Industrial and Organizational Psychology (www.siop.org) has many members who are experts in job analysis and competency modeling. Visit their home page to search for experts and learn about the services they offer.

3. **Experiential Activity.** This chapter described some of the useful information that is available from the Employment and Training Administration's O*NET services (www.doleta.gov/programs/onet). Choose a job that you are interested in and then visit O*NET. See what you can learn about the job, including answers to the following questions:

a. What are the educational requirements for the job?

b. If you want to be hired for this job, what types of prior experience would be useful?

c. How much do people in this job typically get paid?

d. What other jobs in the same occupation look interesting to you?

e. What is the long-term outlook for this occupation? Is the demand for people likely to increase or decrease over the next few years?

CASE STUDY

JOB DESCRIPTIONS AT HITEK

Jennifer Hill was excited about joining HITEK Information Services after receiving her bachelor of arts degree. Her job involved examining compensation practice, and her first assignment was to review HITEK's job descriptions. She was to document her work and make recommended changes, which would include reducing more than 600 job descriptions to a manageable number.

Background

To its stockholders and the rest of the outside world, HITEK is a highly profitable, highly aggressive company in the computer business. In addition to its numerous government contracts, it provides software and hardware to businesses and individuals. From its inception in the late 1970s, it has maintained its position on the leading edge by remaining flexible and adaptable to the turbulent environment in which it operates. It's a people-intensive organization that relies enormously on its human resources; therefore, it's in HITEK's best interests to establish policies and procedures that nurture productivity and enhance the satisfaction of its employees.

Because the computer industry is growing at an incredible pace, opportunities for placement are abundant, and the competition for high-quality human resources is tremendous. HITEK has grown about 30% in the last three years, and its management knows that, as easily as it attracts new employees, it can lose them. Its turnover rate (14%) is about average for its industry.

HITEK remains relatively small at 1,000 employees, and it prides itself on its small-team company culture. This culture is maintained partly by extensive use of the company's intranet and by the utilization of open office spaces. The relatively flat, lean organizational structure (shown in Case Exhibit 1) and the easy accessibility of all corporate levels also support an open-door policy. All in all, employees enjoy working for HITEK, and management is in touch with the organization's pulse.

With the notable exception of the HR department, there are few rules at HITEK. In other departments, employees at all levels share the work, and positions are redefined to match the specific competencies and the interests of the incumbent so that "over-qualified" and "overachieving" individuals are often hired but are then promoted rapidly. Nothing is written down; if newcomers want to know why something is done a certain way, they must ask the person(s) who created the procedure. There is extensive horizontal linkage between departments, perpetuating the blurring of distinctions between departments.

The HR Department

The HR department stands in stark contrast to the rest of HITEK. About 30 people are employed in the department, including the support staff members, or about one HR employee per 33 HITEK employees. The vice president for human resources, Isabel Rains, rules the department with an iron fist. Employees are careful to mold their ideas to match Rains's perspective. When newcomers suggest changes, they're told, "This is the way things have always been done because it's our culture." Written rules and standard operating procedures guide all behavior. Department employees know their own job descriptions well, and there is little overlap in their duties.

With the exception of one recruiter, all 12 of the incumbents whose positions are represented in Case Exhibit 2 are women. Only half of them have degrees in industrial relations or HRM, and only one-fourth have related experience with another company. Most of them have been promoted from clerical positions. In fact, some employees view the vice president position as a "gift" that was given to Rains, a former executive secretary, the day after she received her bachelor's degree from a local college. In other departments, it's widely believed that gaining professional degrees and related experience leads to expertise.

One incident that conveyed the department's image to Hill occurred during her second week on the job. While preparing a job description with Dave Pruitt, Hill explained that she would submit the job description to Janet Voris for final approval. Pruitt became confused and asked, "But Janet is only a clerical person; why would she be involved?"

CASE EXHIBIT 1 HITEK's Organizational Chart

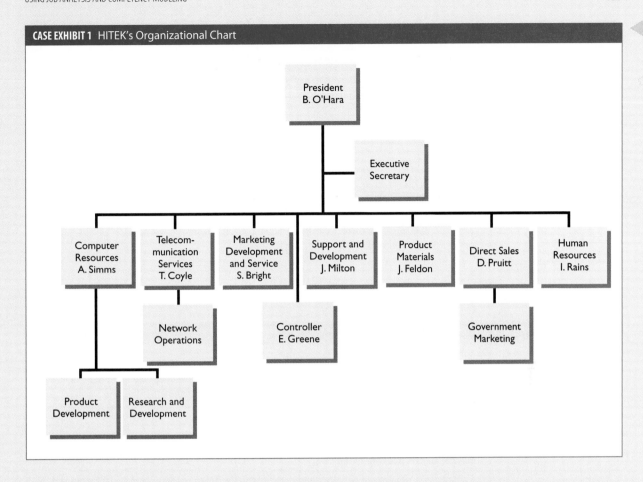

CASE EXHIBIT 2 The Structure of the Human Resource Department at HITEK

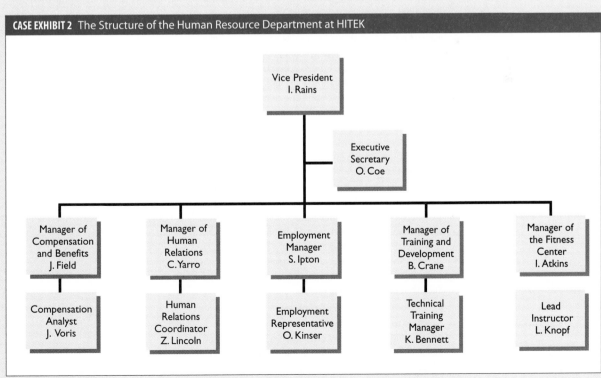

CASE EXHIBIT 3 An Old Job Description

Associate Programmer

Basic Objective	Perform coding, testing, and documentation of programs, under the supervision of a project leader.
Specific Tasks	• Perform coding, debugging, and testing of a program when given general program specifications.
	• Develop documentation of the program.
	• Assist in the implementation and training of the users in the usage of the system.
	• Report to the manager of Management Information Services.
Job Qualifications	Minimum:
	• BA/BS degree in relevant field or equivalent experience/knowledge.
	• Programming knowledge in Java or C++.
	• Good working knowledge of business and financial applications.
	Desirable:
	• Computer programming experience in a time-sharing environment.
	• Some training or education in XML, UML, and HTML.

CASE EXHIBIT 4 A New Job Description

Associate Programmer

General Statement of Duties	Performs coding, debugging, testing, and documentation of software under the supervision of a technical superior or manager. Involves some use of independent judgment.
Supervision Received	Works under close supervision of a technical superior or manager.
Supervision Exercised	No supervisory duties required.
Examples of Duties	(Any one position may not include all the duties listed, nor do listed examples include all duties that may be found in positions of this class.)
	• Confers with analysts, supervisors, and/or representatives of the departments to clarify software intent and programming requirements.
	• Performs coding, debugging, and testing of software when given program specifications for a particular task or problem.
	• Writes documentation for the program.
	• Seeks advice and assistance from supervisor when problems outside the realm of understanding arise.
	• Communicates any program specification deficiencies back to supervisor.
	• Reports ideas concerning design and development back to supervisor.
	• Assists in the implementation of the system and training of end users.
	• Provides some support and assistance to users.
	• Develops product knowledge and personal expertise and proficiency in system usage.
	• Assumes progressively complex and independent duties as experience permits.
	• Performs all duties in accordance with corporate and departmental standards.
Minimum Qualifications	• Education: BA/BS degree in relevant field or equivalent experience/knowledge in computer science, math, or other closely related field.
	• Experience: No prior computer programming work experience necessary.
	• Knowledge, skills, ability to exercise initiative, and sound judgment.
	• Knowledge of a structured language.
	• Working knowledge in operating systems.
	• Ability to maintain open working relationship with supervisor.
	• Logic and problem-solving skills.
	• System flowchart development skills.
Desirable Qualifications	• Exposure to Java, C++, and data transfer languages.
	• Some training in general accounting practices and controls.
	• Effective written and communication skills.

Jennifer Hill's Duties

At HITEK, the pool of job descriptions had grown almost daily as newcomers were hired, but many of the old job descriptions were not discarded, even when obsolete. Other job descriptions needed updating. Hill spent some time thinking about how to proceed. She considered the uses of the job descriptions and what steps she would need to take to accomplish all that was expected of her. Support from within the department was scarce because other employees were busy gathering materials for the annual review of HITEK's hiring, promotion, and development practices conducted by the Equal Employment Opportunity Commission.

After six harried months on the job and much frustration, Hill had revised all the descriptions that were still needed (examples of "old" and "new" job descriptions appear in Case Exhibits 3 and 4). She was also beginning to develop some strong opinions about how the HR department functioned at HITEK and what needed to be done to improve its effectiveness and its image. She decided to arrange a confidential lunch with Billy O'Hara, HITEK's president.

CASE QUESTIONS

1. Based on what you know about high-tech companies, what are some likely strategic objectives for HITEK? Given these, what should be the objectives of HITEK's HR department? Do you think these are the objectives that guide the behaviors of Rains? Explain.

2. Jobs change frequently at HITEK. What approach to job analysis makes the most sense in such a fast-changing environment? Customized? Standardized? Task-focused? Competency modeling? Evaluate the strengths and weaknesses of the alternative approaches and make recommendations to Hill about how to proceed.

3. Is the new job description (Case Exhibit 4) better than the old one (Case Exhibit 3)? Why or why not? Consider the perspective of employees as well as the perspective of the person supervising this job. Does your answer change depending on the way the job description is being used?

Source: Written by M. P. Miceli and Karen Wijta.

Recruiting and Retaining Qualified Employees

Learning Goals

After reading this chapter, you should be able to:

1 Explain the strategic importance of recruiting and retaining talented employees.

2 Show how recruiting and retention activities are shaped by other aspects of the HRM system and the environment.

3 Specify several recruiting methods and sources.

4 Describe recruiting activities from the applicant's perspective.

5 Discuss some ethical issues associated with recruiting.

6 Describe how the objectives of equal opportunity and nondiscrimination influence the recruiting and hiring process.

7 Explain how retention practices influence recruiting needs.

8 Discuss two current issues in recruiting and retaining qualified employees.

MANAGING HUMAN RESOURCES AT SAS INSTITUTE

SAS Institute is the largest private software company in the world. It has about 10,000 employees and revenues exceeding $1.3 billion. Headquartered in Cary, North Carolina, it is always highly ranked on the *Fortune* list of "100 Best Companies to Work For." According to Jim Goodnight, CEO of SAS Institute, "attracting and retaining the best people is crucial to our success." In an industry where turnover averages about 20%, employee turnover at SAS has always been 5% or less. Their low turnover rate saves the company an estimated $75 million a year in recruiting, training, and other turnover-related costs.

Surprisingly, SAS Institute was a late adopter of automated online recruiting. Jeff Chambers, director of human resources, acknowledged that this was an activity "that we don't do as progressively as other companies."

The company was slow to adopt new recruiting technologies because the technology wasn't necessary. With its low turnover rate, an informal recruiting method worked well, according to Chambers: "A lot of our people will recommend friends, neighbors, and family members because they think we are such a good place to work. We have been known as an employer of choice for a long time." Even without online recruiting, the company received 20,000 applications for 200 job openings.

Today, the SAS Web site describes the company's current needs and accepts electronic resumes from people who have some interest in working at the company. It doesn't require candidates to apply solely for open positions. Current employees also can let the company know that they may be interested in changing jobs if there is an opportunity to advance. Information about both current employees and applicants is stored in a database along with descriptions of their competencies. The database makes it possible for HR managers to scan for critical job skills and keep track of individual candidates. Typically, the HR staff prequalifies candidates, saving time for managers and giving them a higher-quality pool of choices. In addition to its electronic recruiting from current employees, SAS uses a more personal recruiting method. It employs people to work as "networkers," whose job is to help connect people in the firm to the projects in need of their skills. To keep employees satisfied and retain them, SAS offers generous benefits, including three weeks vacation after only one year, unlimited sick leave, and an on-site medical facility.[1] ▲

THE STRATEGIC IMPORTANCE OF RECRUITING AND RETAINING TALENTED EMPLOYEES

Recruitment *involves searching for and obtaining qualified applicants for the organization to consider when filling job openings.* Recruitment stops short of deciding which individuals should be hired from the pool of applicants. The methods used to select whom to hire will be explained in Chapter 7.

Research conducted by Ernst & Young shows that the stock purchasing decisions of institutional investors take into account a company's ability to attract talented people. At SAS and many other companies, getting good people into the organization is so important that the chairperson gets personally involved in the firm's recruiting and selection. SAS managers devote time and attention to recruiting because they know it's vital to the company's long-term business success.

We also discuss the issue of retention in this chapter. **Retention** *includes all the activities an employer does to encourage qualified and productive employees to continue working for the organization.* The objective of retention activities is to reduce the unwanted voluntary turnover by people the organization would like to keep in its workforce. Effective recruitment and retention practices attract individuals to the organization *and* increase the chances of retaining them.

FAST FACT

At ManTech, a company that operates military surveillance systems, managers who succeed in reducing voluntary departures can earn bonuses of 10% or more.

Supporting Strategies

Effective recruitment and retention practices grow out of the strategic planning process described in Chapter 3. Recruiting efforts should be consistent with the organization's strategy, vision, and values. Consequently, recruiting activities vary across companies, even in the same industry. Exhibit 6.1 illustrates how different strategic business objectives can result in varying HR implications for recruitment and retention.

EXHIBIT 6.1 Examples of How Strategic Business Objectives Create HR Implications for Recruitment and Retention

Strategic Objective	Examples of Implications for Recruitment and Retention Objectives
Increase Market Share by Offering Lowest-Cost Service	• Important to retain current talent as company grows. • Need to predict rate of growth and translate changes in market share to increases needed in size of workforce. • Continuously improve efficiency of recruitment practices needed to keep costs down. • Low-cost strategy puts pressure on compensation and benefits costs, so need to be creative in finding low-cost ways to attract and retain talent.
Increase Return on Investment by Offering Innovative Products and Maintaining High Margins	• Recruiting practices need to focus on attracting highly qualified applicants at the cutting edge of their fields. • Best talent not likely to be looking for jobs, so need to go to them (not wait for them to come to us). • Excellent retention strategy for top talent needed, as workforce will be an attractive pool that other companies will try to raid. Knowledge retention is a key strategic concern, also.
Respond to Declining Industry Trends by Diversifying into New Businesses	• May need to develop and implement layoff plans, creating the challenge of how to attract new talent and retain best talent at the same time. • Recruiting efforts for new business areas should include plan for lateral transfers from declining business areas, to minimize need for layoffs. • For new businesses, HR will need to develop strategies for recruiting key talent in those industries.

Questions to be addressed during strategic HR planning might include

- How many new hires do we need in the near term and three to five years from now?
- Do we want to recruit people who are motivated to stay with the company for a long time, or are we looking for a short-term commitment?
- Are we prepared to pay top dollar, or should we look for people who will be attracted to our company despite the modest compensation we offer?
- Are we interested in finding people who are different from our current employees to bring in new perspectives, or is it important to find people who will fit well in our culture and help maintain the status quo?
- What competencies do we need from our employees, and how rapidly will these needs change?

Strategic discussions focus on the general needs of the organization. Once those needs are understood, the focus turns to defining the needs of specific units or departments and the requirements for specific positions. At this stage, job analysis results become relevant. Described in Chapter 5, job analysis supports recruitment activities by answering relevant questions:

- Which competencies must people have when they first enter the organization?
- How important is it that new hires be eager to learn new competencies?
- What long-term career opportunities can we discuss with applicants?

In manufacturing firms, supply chain management is a well-known management technique. Typically, the term is used to refer to procedures for coordinating all aspects of the production process. One goal of supply chain management is keeping costs as low as possible. Valero Energy was one of the first companies to recognize that this concept could be applied to their labor supply. As described in the feature, "Managing with Metrics: Valero Energy," creating a labor supply chain was an excellent way to support their strategies.[2]

Reducing Expenses and Improving Productivity

Today, concerns about recruiting and retaining talented employees are salient for many employers. Even as some companies continue to downsize, finding the talent that's needed remains a concern. The combination of strong competitive business pressures and tight labor market conditions for the most talented employees means that employers must find a way to keep costs under control and at the same time ensure that the organization has the workforce it needs to grow, diversify into new areas of business, expand internationally, and be otherwise effective.

At JPS Health Network in Fort Worth, Texas, a shortage of nurses was hampering the health center's ability to deliver high-quality patient care. Ineffective recruiting meant that 17% of nursing jobs were vacant. If a nurse resigned, it usually took six or seven weeks to hire a new nurse. When JPS set out to redesign its recruiting process, it started with three goals:

1. Reduce the vacancy rate to below 12%, which was the average for the local area.
2. Shorten the time needed to fill vacancies.
3. Improve the quality of applicants who applied for open positions.

> *" Companies are spending hundreds of thousands of dollars on advertisements, career fairs and recruiters, and they want to know what they're getting for it. Recruiting continues to be more bottom line–oriented. It's a good trend. "*
>
> *Mark Mehler*
> *Cofounder*
> *Career Xroads*

MANAGING WITH METRICS
Valero Energy

Valero Energy, an oil refiner, experienced explosive growth in the early 2000s. In just five years, it went from 5,000 employees to 22,000, with some of that growth due to its strategy of making acquisitions. To support its rapid growth, Valero created a labor supply chain and closely monitors all steps in the recruitment and hiring process.

Valero's supply chain model was developed by Dan Hilbert, an employment manager who also had strong project management skills. Dan's first step was to map out the staffing department's processes. Next, he developed a way to quantify the results of each step in the process. "To me, it's just Accounting 101," he explained.

At Valero, the staffing process begins with predictions of the company's labor needs. As described in Chapter 3, this step ensures that business objectives and HR objectives are in alignment. Posting announcements, screening resumes, contacting candidates, scheduling and conducting interviews, making formal offers, and all the things that happen along the way are monitored. Quantitative measures are used to track the volume, speed, and cost of recruiting activities. The metrics make it possible to compare results against recruiting goals. To evaluate how well they are performing, the HR professionals consult a labor supply chain "dashboard." Indicators on the dashboard are shown in green, yellow, or red, which makes it easy to spot and fix problems quickly. Because the supply chain system keeps track of everything that happens, HR managers can analyze the data to correctly diagnose the cause of problems. When they make changes in how they recruit—for example, using a new job board or altering their method of screening resumes—they have data to evaluate whether the changes were effective.

With their new supply chain approach, Valero has eliminated most of the paperwork that was involved in the old hiring process. More importantly, it has reduced the average time needed to fill openings from 120 days to 40 days. Just four years after the labor supply chain was introduced, the average cost per hire dropped nearly $10,000, from $12,000 to $2,300. Another indication of the effectiveness of the new labor supply chain is that the people being hired like their work. Valero is consistently included on *Fortune*'s list of "100 Best Companies to Work for in America."[3]

To achieve these goals, JPS upgraded its existing online recruiting efforts. An internal study of recruiting problems found that most nurses who applied for jobs at JPS had visited the organization's Web site but then applied using the traditional paper-and-pencil approach. A study of the Web sites of competing hospitals suggested many ways to improve: JPS added more pictures to convey the organization's culture and show what the work environment was like; it made it easier for nurses to apply online; and it enabled applicants to contact the hiring managers directly with questions about the open positions. Managers also saw improvements. Completed applications were sent immediately to both the nurse recruiter and the hiring manager, so no one was lost in the shuffle. To shorten processing time, the nurse recruiter conducted telephone interviews to screen applicants instead of arranging on-site interviews.

How successful were JPS's change efforts? Consider these results:

- Applications increased by more than 60%.
- The time needed to fill vacancies was reduced to about 2.5 weeks.
- The vacancy rate dropped to 7.6%.
- Advertising costs went down 31%.

Although more difficult to measure, JPS believes that their patients and the doctors who care for them benefited from these changes. With fewer vacancies and a reduced workload, the quality of work life for JPS's nursing staff improved.[4]

Retaining the Best Employees

Recruiting people to meet the organization's human resource needs is only half the battle in the war for talent. The other half is keeping good employees. Organizations that keep employee turnover rates low gain an advantage against competitors by reducing overall labor costs and improving competitiveness.

Reducing Labor Costs. The true cost of turnover includes easy-to-quantify, out-of-pocket expenses and intangible opportunity costs associated with lost productivity. The out-of-pocket costs associated with hiring an employee are substantial.[5] But these out-of-pocket costs are just a portion of the total costs. At Saint Francis Medical Center in Grand Island, Nebraska, staff shortages meant that fewer patients could be treated for their illnesses and injuries.[6] In supermarkets, the costs include the expenses associated with filling the empty positions, as well as the costs created by inexperienced employees, such as errors in making change, paperwork mistakes, and damaged products. For professional work, turnover hurts productivity because projects are lost when employees who were favored by a client leave. Staffing shortages among a firm's professional staff may also mean that the firm cannot bid on projects because it simply can't meet the deadlines. Other costs associated with turnover include lower morale among overworked employees who must pick up the extra work created when a colleague leaves, lost knowledge that only the departing employee has, and the business contacts that the departing employee may have been able to use to build the business.

Staying Competitive. For some organizations, high turnover threatens the firm's strategic competitiveness. At Schering Plough, high turnover apparently contributed to the firm's repeated failure to meet governmental manufacturing standards for its prescription drugs. The quality of the company's manufacturing process was so unreliable that the Food and Drug Administration would not grant approval for a new allergy drug until the manufacturing problem was fixed. The company was forced to order several large recalls of products after discovering they had been contaminated during the manufacturing process. What was causing these problems? According to an auditor's report, excessive turnover created a staffing shortage, which meant that the company had many new and inexperienced supervisors with inadequate training. There were simply too few experienced supervisors to achieve adequate oversight of subordinates and manufacturing operations. The costs of turnover at Schering Plough included significant damage to the firm's reputation and brand image.

When the original Jack in the Box® restaurant opened in San Diego in 1951, a hamburger cost just 18 cents and McDonald's was unknown. Like most employers at the time, Jack in the Box offered its employees good health insurance coverage as well as other benefits that were considered standard. As competitors entered the market, Jack in the Box had to look for ways to reduce its costs. Competitors like McDonald's and Burger King generally did not offer health insurance, so Jack in the Box decided to stop offering it to its newly hired crew members. During the next 15 years, the company found that the turnover rate for crew members without health insurance was 10 times the rate for insured crew members! An analysis of the cost of turnover versus the cost of insurance revealed that it would actually be cheaper to offer insurance. Today Jack in the Box is again offering medical, dental, and vision insurance. As an indication of the success of its new approach, Jack in the Box was named

> *We had physicians not able to admit their patients because we didn't have adequate staffing. When the doctors started screaming, we started paying attention.*
>
> *Lee Elliot*
> *Vice President of Human Resources*
> *Saint Francis Medical Center*

> *Spirit Award winners have developed outstanding recruitment and retention programs that can serve as a model for operators in every segment as restaurateurs throughout the industry constantly seek ways to enhance employee satisfaction. We commend these restaurant companies for their inspiring commitment to their people.*
>
> *Mary M. Adolf*
> *President and Chief Executive Officer*
> *National Restaurant Association Educational Foundation*

LINE MANAGERS	HR PROFESSIONALS	EMPLOYEES
• Work with HR staff to develop recruiting objectives and plans that meet the organization's strategic needs and address employees' concerns.	• Work with line managers to develop recruiting objectives and plans that meet the organization's strategic needs and address employees' concerns.	• Openly discuss your short-term and long-term goals in order to facilitate the development of recruiting plans that address your concerns.
• Develop an understanding of the linkages that exist between recruiting activities, other aspects of the HRM system, and longer-term employee retention.	• Design recruitment and retention activities that contribute to the development of an integrated, internally consistent HRM system.	• When searching for work, consider all aspects of the HRM system before making a decision about where to work.
• Help disseminate information about open positions to all potentially qualified internal candidates.	• Develop recruiting plans that meet legal guidelines and generate a diverse pool of qualified internal and external candidates.	• Participate in recruiting efforts such as referring others to the company and answering questions about what it is like to work there.
• Stay informed of labor market trends in order to anticipate the implications for recruiting and retaining talent.	• Evaluate recruiting outcomes and be innovative in developing practices to ensure a sufficient number of qualified applicants.	• Use knowledge of competitors' recruiting approaches to help your employer develop innovative and more effective practices.
• Understand and abide by relevant legal regulations.	• Provide training as needed to line managers and employees involved in recruitment activities.	• Work with HR professionals and line managers in the organization's efforts to effectively manage workforce diversity.
• Facilitate retention efforts by being supportive of employees and facilitating their development.	• Monitor retention patterns to diagnose potential problems. Use exit interviews, employee surveys, etc. to identify needed improvements.	• Seek out information about openings within the company and actively pursue those that fit your personal career objectives.

the winner of the National Restaurant Association Educational Foundation's Spirit Award for the category of quick service restaurants.[7]

Addressing Societal Concerns through Legal Compliance

Obtaining a pool of qualified applicants is the primary objective of recruiting, but legal compliance is very important too. As described later in this chapter, legal compliance requires careful record keeping. Managers sometimes deride such record keeping as a bureaucratic nuisance, but these same records can be used to evaluate the effectiveness of the organization's recruiting efforts.[8]

The HR Triad

As you will see, recruiting activities truly can involve everyone in an organization. Several of the ways that managers, HR professionals, and other employees get involved in recruiting and retaining employees are summarized in "The HR Triad: Roles and Responsibilities for Recruiting and Retaining Employees."

HR Professionals. HR professionals usually take the lead in designing a systematic and integrated approach to recruiting and retaining employees. When Designer Blinds was experiencing production problems, managers were asked to come up with a solution. The production problems were putting the company at risk. High turnover among employees was the source of the problem. Without a stable and experienced workforce in the factory, orders were going unfilled and quality suffered. HR Manager Deb Franklin embarked on an all-out campaign to improve the company's recruiting and to retain its new hires. Her efforts included increased community outreach, improved orientation for new hires, and the training of managers.

HR professionals also take responsibility for filling the organization's staffing needs efficiently. The cost of Web-based recruiting software, time spent at job fairs, the salaries and benefits paid to recruiters, and/or the fees paid to headhunters must all be justified by recruitment and retention results.

Line Managers. Line managers can help promote the company and make it attractive to employees, or they can be the cause of high turnover. Managers often are less directly involved in the early recruiting stages, and they usually become more actively involved as the selection process gets underway. Once an employee is onboard, the manager plays a key role in determining whether a good employee stays with the company or leaves.

As a result of Designer Blinds' new recruiting efforts, the company began hiring many more members of Omaha's Sudanese and Hispanic populations. To ensure that these employees felt welcome, managers were trained to improve their understanding of these cultures. Managers were also taught leadership skills, and they began attending weekly meetings to learn about issues such as attitudes and sexual harassment.[9]

Other Employees. A company's current employees may be involved directly in recruiting applicants—for example, when they encourage friends and family to apply. Employees also become involved when they apply for other jobs in the organization. At this point, employees learn how the organization handles recruiting from its own workforce. Such experiences with the organization's recruiting activities may be especially important in determining whether talented employees are retained. Of course, employees also are central to retention. When other employees are talented and fun to work with, the company finds it easier to retain top talent.

At Advanced Financial Solutions, the involvement of employees is an essential aspect of its recruiting and retention strategy. Located in Oklahoma City, Advanced Financial Solutions must compete with the glamour of cities like New York, San Francisco, Boston, and even Paris, Brussels, and Tokyo when hiring software technicians. Yet employee turnover averages only about 1% annually. How does AFS make sure that the professionals it hires will like Oklahoma City and their new jobs well enough to stay? It invests heavily in recruitment. Applicants participate in lengthy telephone interviews, and detailed reference checks are conducted. When the company thinks it has found a good candidate, he or she is invited to spend one week visiting the company. Spouses are invited too. Prospective employees visit all departments and meet everyone from the CEO to the support staff. Spouses are shown around the town and company volunteers make an effort to answer their questions about life in Oklahoma City: How are the schools? What religious organizations are there? How good are the sports facilities? And so on. No job offers are made until the applicants complete their one-week visit. The approach costs AFS about $7,500 per hire and the company feels the investment is well worth it.[10]

RECRUITMENT AND RETENTION WITHIN AN INTEGRATED HRM SYSTEM

Organizations differ greatly in their efforts to recruit and retain top talent, and job applicants vary greatly in how attracted they are to job openings in different organizations. To understand a particular organization's approach to recruiting and retaining employees, it helps to consider how these activities are shaped by other aspects of the HRM system as well as by the forces in the external and organizational environments.

Links to Other HR Activities

In a fully integrated, strategically aligned HRM system, activities for recruiting and retaining employees are developed with a full appreciation for how they influence other parts of the system and how other parts of the system influence those activities.

Clearly, recruitment and retention should be firmly grounded in the strategic planning process, as described in Chapter 3. Effective planning minimizes unexpected labor shortages created by managerial actions, such as excessive layoffs and failing to develop succession plans. The results of job analysis and competency modeling activities also provide direction to recruiting activities; they identify the types of talent needed by the company and thus suggest which populations should be targeted (e.g., high school graduates, college graduates, experienced managers). As we explain in this chapter, an applicant's decision about whether to accept a job offer is affected by the company's compensation practices, benefits, work arrangements, and approach to career development. For applicants, it is clear that the effectiveness of world-class recruiting practices will be limited if other HR Policies are not world-class also.

Infosys Technologies is a software company based in Bangalore, India. It is considered one of India's best companies to work for. Its low turnover rate of 10% is an indicator of how well its HRM system works. With more than 40,000 employees, it's a challenge to keep a family feeling at the company, but that's the goal of the Employee Relations Program. The program includes counseling services, health fairs, athletic events, and celebrations that are open to employees' families. Employees' parents and other relatives are welcome to visit the company's campus. The average age of Infosys employees is 26, so the company headquarters really does feel like a university campus. A gym, swimming pool, and movie screenings are all part of the experience, as are occasional late hours and "crunch" times. So far, the approach seems to be working.[12]

Experienced managers understand the connections between recruiting activities and other aspects of the HRM system. However, inexperienced managers may not appreciate the importance of effective recruiting activities. They often focus on speed when evaluating recruiting activities. They want jobs filled quickly and with as little effort as possible. While speed is important, the quality of people hired is ultimately more important. If the hiring process does not succeed in getting qualified employees, managers then need to provide more training to new employees. Similarly, if qualified people are found and convinced to accept job offers, they are productive and stay only as long as the organization addresses their desire for rewards, work flexibility, career advancement, and so on. Managers at Infosys Technologies appreciate these realities. They know that their best employees will be welcomed with open arms at IBM, Oracle, and the other employers in Bangalore.[13]

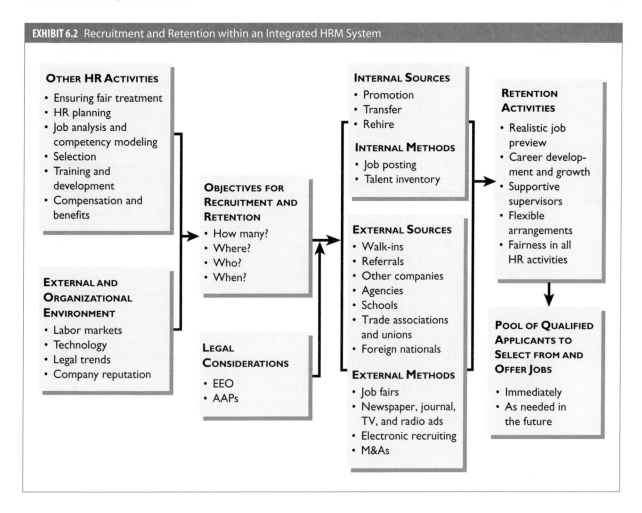

EXHIBIT 6.2 Recruitment and Retention within an Integrated HRM System

OTHER HR ACTIVITIES
- Ensuring fair treatment
- HR planning
- Job analysis and competency modeling
- Selection
- Training and development
- Compensation and benefits

EXTERNAL AND ORGANIZATIONAL ENVIRONMENT
- Labor markets
- Technology
- Legal trends
- Company reputation

OBJECTIVES FOR RECRUITMENT AND RETENTION
- How many?
- Where?
- Who?
- When?

LEGAL CONSIDERATIONS
- EEO
- AAPs

INTERNAL SOURCES
- Promotion
- Transfer
- Rehire

INTERNAL METHODS
- Job posting
- Talent inventory

EXTERNAL SOURCES
- Walk-ins
- Referrals
- Other companies
- Agencies
- Schools
- Trade associations and unions
- Foreign nationals

EXTERNAL METHODS
- Job fairs
- Newspaper, journal, TV, and radio ads
- Electronic recruiting
- M&As

RETENTION ACTIVITIES
- Realistic job preview
- Career development and growth
- Supportive supervisors
- Flexible arrangements
- Fairness in all HR activities

POOL OF QUALIFIED APPLICANTS TO SELECT FROM AND OFFER JOBS
- Immediately
- As needed in the future

Exhibit 6.2 illustrates the relationship between recruiting activities and other aspects of the HRM system. Also shown in Exhibit 6.2 are several aspects of the external and organizational environments that influence recruitment and retention. The most significant forces influencing recruitment and retention are labor markets, technology, legal trends, and company reputation.

Labor Markets

Clearly, labor market conditions and competitive pressures can be powerful determinants of the resources companies invest to attract and retain top talent. During the high-tech boom of the 1990s, employers spared no expense to recruit talented programmers. By 2004, demand for programmers had cooled off, the average starting salaries for computer programmers were declining, and employers were flooded with applicants. By 2007, demand had begun to pick up again and salaries were moving up too.

Almost all biotech firms anticipate hiring additional employees during the next several years. To attract the talent it needs, Genetech promotes an open and friendly workplace where new ideas are welcome. It is also known for holding plenty of parties that encourage everyone to celebrate successes. By keeping excellent talent in the company, Genentech hopes to attract the best new talent.

FAST FACT

A survey of 2,600 employers found that 40% of the employers had job openings for which they could not find qualified candidates.

Technology

New technologies also influence the design and implementation of a company's recruiting activities. Employers encourage applicants to apply online because this reduces recruiting costs and may increase the applicant pool.

When Citigroup studied the cost of electronic recruiting, it found that the average cost per hire was in the range of $300–$400—similar to the cost of employee referrals and about one-tenth of the cost for employment agencies. When a global publishing company adopted electronic recruiting, it found that this reduced its recruiting and hiring costs by 50%. The savings were due to improved efficiency in several areas: The electronic system was able to screen applicants to assess their basic qualifications, thereby reducing the time hiring managers spent interviewing candidates. By using less of the managers' time, the company saved money. Also, the electronic system automated the interview scheduling process. Instead of paying a staff member to call applicants to arrange an interview, applicants used the company Web site to schedule their own interviews. The improved efficiency of the electronic recruiting process yielded an estimated return on investment of $6 for every $1 invested in the new system.[14]

Job applicants can learn about job openings in most large companies by visiting the company Web site or using job boards. Podcasting and blogs are two new trends in recruiting. Cadbury Schweppes uses podcasting to let listeners hear snippets of interviews with recent hires who speak enthusiastically about their experiences with the company.[15] Blogs are another new recruiting tool. Some employers worry that employee bloggers might harm their company's reputation, especially if employees use blogging to vent their work-related frustrations. But do employers have the right to censor their employees to prevent this? The legal rights of employee bloggers are not well established at this time, so how a company manages bloggers is likely to reflect its corporate culture. As described in the feature "Managing Ethics: Honeywell's Bloggers," Honeywell is trusting employees to blog responsibly.[16]

MANAGING ETHICS
Honeywell's Bloggers

Honeywell manufactures aerospace and specialty materials, supplying the U.S. government as well as corporations such as Shell Global Manufacturing, Amgen, Samsung Semiconductor, and Infineon. As part of an overhaul of its campus recruiting practices, Honeywell recently unveiled its newest recruiting tool: a blog. Honeywell enlisted people from information technology (IT), human resources, and the supply chain to be the first bloggers. They were asked to write three entries per week for about three months. Then new bloggers would take over. Being a blogger is voluntary. The company doesn't try to control what bloggers do, but the hope is that they will produce content that attracts qualified college students.

Each year, Honeywell hires about 300 students from colleges and universities. How will Honeywell ensure that the bloggers comply with corporate governance standards and decency? After all, the culture of the blogging community seems to be that "anything goes." Kevin Gill, director of global staffing, says responsibility for behaving ethically rests with the bloggers themselves. How well this experiment works will depend on their using good judgment in deciding what to share and how. Ideally, the blogs will become sites that recruiters can talk up during their campus recruiting visits.

Legal Trends

As described later in this chapter, a dynamic and changing legal environment is another important factor that organizations must take into account. In particular, recent court decisions have caused some employers to wonder whether long established affirmative action recruiting might suddenly be under legal attack.

Federal contractors must keep records of the race, gender, and ethnicity of job applicants. These data are used to monitor hiring decisions and to ensure the decisions are nondiscriminatory. Before Internet recruiting, it was easy to identify job applicants: They were people who filled out a job application. But the Internet changed the recruiting process. People can now submit their resume in a matter of seconds. They may apply for hundreds of jobs without being serious applicants. Must federal contractors collect background data on all these people? To answer this question, a new regulation (70 Fed. Reg. 58946) clarified employers' record keeping requirements by defining who qualifies as an "Internet applicant" for federal contractors.[17]

Company Reputation

This chapter also discusses the important consequences that an organization's reputation has on recruitment and retention. SAS Institute is an example of a company that enjoys a reputation for being an unusually great place to work. Because of that reputation, SAS has an easier time attracting applicants and retaining its best talent. Once an offer is extended, SAS's reputation increases the likelihood that the best applicants will accept an offer of employment. To compete for talent to work at its satellite campus in New York City, Google offers employees free food, including a sushi bar and espresso bar. The company's dynamic feel helps it retain its employees. "Google is about as interesting as starting your own company," according to employee Richard Burdon. Exploring new ideas and being rewarded if they succeed is what excites Burdon and his coworkers.[19]

RECRUITING SOURCES AND METHODS

In designing recruiting activities, two central issues to address are the sources to target and the methods to use. Effective organizations choose recruiting sources and methods based on the company's specific hiring needs and objectives.

Different sources of applicants can be reached using different methods of recruiting. *The company's current employees are one source of applicants; they are called the* **internal labor market.** Posting announcements in a company newsletter is a good way to recruit applicants who are already employees of the company. Usually, current employees apply for positions that offer higher pay or more interesting work. *Another source of potential applicants are people who don't work for the organization; they are called the* **external labor market.** Using electronic media and referrals from employees are common methods used to reach those in the external labor market.

Many studies have considered whether recruiting from these different sources results in different employee outcomes (e.g., performance, turnover, loyalty, and job satisfaction). If different sources of applicants were found to have different outcomes, companies could target their recruiting efforts to the most appropriate sources, given their strategic needs. Overall, however, research has shown no clear differences in the employment experiences of new employees recruited from different sources.[20]

FAST FACT

Chiquita, the banana producer, employs 30,000 workers in seven Latin American countries. In the past ten years, it spent $20 million to overhaul its environmental and employment standards, earning it certification by the Rainforest Alliance.[18]

LEARNING GOAL **3**

FAST FACT

The U.S. Postal Service starts recruiting in August for the 40,000+ temporary workers it needs to handle the holiday mail in December.

Instead of targeting one source of applicants, most employers recruit from multiple sources using more than one method. This approach helps the organization generate a large applicant pool. In addition, recruiting from multiple sources is a good way to increase the diversity of the applicant pool. Next, we describe the most common methods used for recruiting applicants from internal and external labor markets.

Internal Labor Market

Especially when labor shortages are constantly in the news, a natural tendency may be to assume that recruiting efforts should focus on finding *new* employees to hire. But wise employers understand the value of first looking for candidates inside the organization. SAS Institute and Valero Energy place a high value on recruiting from their internal labor markets. For jobs other than those at entry level, current employees should be considered a primary source of applicants for any job opening.

Internal applicants for job vacancies can be located using several methods. Some (e.g., the grapevine and job postings) assume that potential applicants should take most of the responsibility for learning about open positions and applying for those they find interesting. Others (e.g., using talent inventories) place more responsibility on the HR staff and line managers. Whichever methods they choose, employers should be particularly careful to manage how internal candidates experience recruiting activities. If they have negative experiences when they apply for jobs within the organization, it may trigger them to look outside the organization for other opportunities.

Job Postings. **Job postings** *prominently display current job openings to all employees in an organization.* They are usually found on bulletin boards (historically made from cork, but today more likely to be electronic). Other than word of mouth, job postings are the most commonly used method for generating a pool of internal applicants.

Job postings usually provide complete job descriptions. A well constructed job description communicates competencies needed as well as organizational goals and objectives. By also including information about compensation and performance standards, job postings send signals to employees about what is valued. Astute employees realize that observing postings over time yields information about turnover rates in various departments. When a department has high turnover, it may indicate a problem that causes employees to be dissatisfied. Paying attention to job postings also provides information about the competencies that are most in demand.

FAST FACT

Adecco, the giant staffing agency, sets up Job Shop Kiosks in shopping malls so that companies can post job openings.

Posting jobs that are available in the organization can reduce turnover by communicating to employees that they don't have to go elsewhere to find opportunities for advancement and development. Posting jobs creates an open recruitment process, which helps to provide equal opportunity for advancement to all employees.

Job posting has many advantages, but it's not foolproof. If hiring decisions are already made by the time a job is posted, the system soon loses credibility. Managers who merely go through the motions of posting jobs generate ill will and cynicism.

Talent Inventories. A **talent inventory** *is a database that contains information about the pool of current employees.* Talent inventories usually include employees' names, prior jobs and experiences, performance and compensation histories, and demonstrated competencies. The employees' work-related interests, geographic preferences, and career goals also should be included.

Almost every organization has a reservoir of qualified employees that it can tap when recruiting to fill open positions. Like savings accounts, these reservoirs of internal talent contain easily accessed resources that can be "withdrawn" as needed. In addition, the future value of the organization's reservoir pool can be enhanced through investments in selection procedures, training programs, and retention efforts.

SAS Institute keeps track of its entire reservoir of talent at all levels and in all positions. SAS uses its talent inventory to systematically monitor its internal talent and match internal applicants to suitable opportunities. With an up-to-date talent inventory to consult, there is no need to rely on employees to nominate themselves for job openings. Instead, qualified potential applicants can be identified and encouraged to apply when jobs become available. By being proactive, employers can ensure that they consider *all* internal candidates with the necessary qualifications, regardless of whether taking the open position would involve a promotion, transfer, or temporary job rotation.

Citibank uses its talent inventory to identify suitable positions for staff members who wish to transfer or who are seeking another job because of technological displacement or reorganization. With this system, Citibank makes sure it considers suitable internal candidates before recruiting from outside the organization.

A promotion generally involves moving into a position that's recognized as having higher status—and often higher pay. Understandably, current employees often feel they should be given priority as applicants for jobs that represent opportunities for promotion. When this doesn't happen, it creates dissatisfaction. A transfer or lateral move involves moving into a position that's of similar status, often with no increase in pay. After several transfers, employees develop a broader perspective and can better understand how the entire organization functions as a system. Lateral transfers play an important role in the long-term development of employees. Thus, it is important that the company's recruitment procedures alert employees to such opportunities when they arise.

Pros and Cons of Internal Recruitment. Several potential benefits are associated with recruiting applicants who are eligible for promotions and transfers. Employees appreciate internal recruiting because it provides opportunities for personal development and career advancement without the disruption of switching to another employer. Gaining a reputation for excellent employee development is one of the best ways to become an employer of choice.[22]

Employers also benefit from internal recruitment because it typically is less costly. Outside recruits tend to receive higher salaries. In addition, when talent is in short supply, the organization may have to offer a one-time signing bonus to external recruits.

Counterbalancing the advantages of internal recruitment are several disadvantages. If internal recruitment is used in place of external recruitment, the most qualified candidates may never be considered because they don't work for the company. Other disadvantages include infighting between candidates vying for a position and inbreeding. Inbreeding results when someone who is familiar with the organization has come to accept its ways of doing things. Such people are less likely to come up with creative and innovative ideas for improvement.

External Labor Market

Rapidly growing organizations and those that require large numbers of highly skilled professionals and managers seldom can meet their labor needs without

FAST FACT

At Hallmark, 90% of management positions are filled internally.

FAST FACT

A survey by the consulting firm Watson Wyatt found that 86% of employers believed their organization treated employees well, but only 55% of employees felt this way.[21]

recruiting from the external labor market. Internal recruitment simply can't produce the numbers of people needed to sustain continued growth. During one of its growth spurts, for example, Cisco Systems was taking on about 1,000 new hires each quarter, which amounted to nearly 10% of the total job growth in Silicon Valley. Later, when there was a downturn in the industry, Cisco switched its philosophy to emphasize internal recruitment and promotion from within the organization.

At Scana, a gas and electric company, the challenge will be replacing the Baby Boomers who expect to retire in the next 5 to 10 years. The company estimates that half its workforce is in this group. Eventually, Scana will be forced to recruit externally. For now, however, the company is looking for ways to encourage people to stay around.[23]

Even when companies have enough people inside, they may not have enough internal applicants with the right competencies. If internal candidates require training to be qualified, it may be cheaper, easier, and quicker to go outside the firm and hire people who already have the needed competencies.

Methods for recruiting from the external labor market include walk-ins; electronic recruiting; employee referrals; the use of private search firms, public agencies, and school placement services; and staffing with foreign nationals. Regardless of how external applicants are recruited, the goal should be to attract *qualified* applicants, not just a large number of applicants.[24]

Walk-in Applicants. Some individuals become applicants simply by walking into an organization's employment office and declaring their interest in working for the organization. They may be motivated by a recruiting advertisement, or they may simply have a good impression of the organization and want to explore the possibility of working there.

Most small companies rely heavily on walk-ins, as do the local sites of large franchise companies. At almost every fast-food restaurant and coffee shop, customers can fill out a job application if they are interested in being considered for a job.

Holding an open house is another excellent way to attract walk-in applicants. An open house can serve to introduce the organization to the community and attract individuals who might not otherwise become applicants. Such events give the firm a chance to look at potential applicants in a fairly informal setting.

Before the Internet explosion, managerial, professional, and sales applicants were seldom walk-ins.[25] New technology is quickly changing that, however. Now, applicants for almost any type of job can "walk in" to an organization through its electronic, cyberspace doors.

Electronic Media. Virtually every large and medium-sized company now has a Web site where applicants can learn about the company. Many of these sites have specific information about job openings, required competencies, career progression programs, mentoring, diversity initiatives, and benefits. Well-designed Web sites (e.g., those that are playful or aesthetically appealing) increase an applicant's desire to apply for jobs at the company.[26]

As companies expand their global operations, Web-based technologies make it possible for a company to coordinate its recruitment activities around the world. Barclaycard International was the United Kingdom's first credit card. Today, it's one of the world's largest global credit card businesses, with operations in the United States, Europe, Africa, and Asia. As it continues to

---

> " *We found [that] the types of people we get from walk-ins and newspaper ads turned over 2.5 times faster than referrals from employees.* "
>
> Walter Kalinowski
> Executive Director of Human Resources
> Petro Stopping Centers

FAST FACT

A study of **Fortune** 500 companies found that recruiting online cut the average hiring time from 43 to 37 days.

expand, international talent acquisition is one of its key issues. Internal transfers of talent within the company are essential to Barclaycard. As a global firm, its top leadership positions require managers who have had international experience and an understanding of the global market. The company's intranet recruiting platform supports the challenge of coordinating short-term staffing needs with its long-term leadership development goals. It makes it easy for managers to fill jobs quickly, and it makes it easy for employees to find opportunities that will allow them to advance in their careers.[27]

Deloitte Touche Tohmatsu uses a Web site to recruit talent from the external global market. As described in the feature "Managing Globalization: Deloitte Touche Tohmatsu," a single centralized Web site serves managers in 15 countries.[28]

Like any recruiting method, Web-based recruiting is no panacea. According to a study of business school graduates who were looking for jobs, poorly designed electronic recruiting causes frustration and turns some applicants off to the company. Exhibit 6.3 describes some of the most common problems encountered by electronic applicants. How many of these problems would you put up with before deciding not to submit a job application?[29]

Employee Referrals. **Employee referrals** *occur when current employees inform their acquaintances about openings and encourage them to apply.* Companies such as New York Life Insurance facilitate employee referrals by supporting online alumni networks. Other companies make it easy for their employees to send electronic job announcements to their friends. When labor shortages are severe, some companies offer rewards to employees who refer qualified applicants. The financial incentives may be linked to a recruit's completion of an application, acceptance of employment, or completion of work for a specified time period.

FAST FACT

The EEOC's compliance manual warns that word-of-mouth recruiting—including employee referrals—may generate applicant pools that do not reflect the diversity of the labor market.

MANAGING GLOBALIZATION
Deloitte Touche Tohmatsu

At a meeting of recruitment managers from 15 countries, Maryanne West discovered that she wasn't the only one having difficulty with recruitment. Located in Australia, West had a difficult time filling all of the vacant positions created by the firm's rapid growth. At the time, the company maintained 35 separate local Web sites. The sites didn't generate much traffic, however, because they were often difficult for job applicants to locate. To address the problem, Deloitte established the Global Recruitment Council. Their charge was to devise a plan to meet the company's global recruitment and staffing challenges. "We literally started with a blank piece of paper," explained the global director of recruitment, Kent Kirch. Within a year, a new centralized Web site was launched to serve the entire company. But that first Web

site wasn't effective. The site provided a single location for applicants to learn about the company's global vision, but it didn't allow country-level leaders to communicate their unique message or address applicants in their particular region of the world. Recruitment manager Maryanne West didn't like the initial design because it didn't describe all of the various activities in Australia and it didn't appeal to the different interests of new graduates and experienced professionals. Eventually, a new site was developed to address these and other concerns raised by recruiting managers. Shortly after the new site was launched, applications increased 20%. The global recruiting site is currently saving the company $1.5 million per year, and the savings are expected to be even greater as more and more applicants discover it.

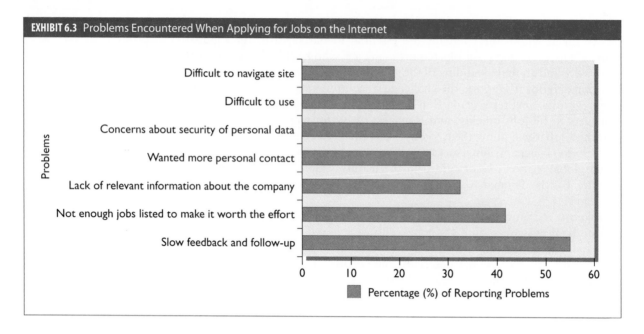

EXHIBIT 6.3 Problems Encountered When Applying for Jobs on the Internet

Compared with other external recruiting methods, employee referrals result in the highest one-year survival rates for most occupations. Employees provide a balanced view of organizational life, and the people they refer generally have more information available to them; so a better decision is likely. In addition, employees tend to recruit applicants who are similar to them in interests and motivations. Since employees are already adjusted to the organizational culture, this matching process increases the likelihood that referrals will fit into the environment.[30] At Citibank, referral applicants submit more appropriate resumes, are more likely to apply under favorable market conditions, perform better in interviews, and are more likely to get hired.[31]

A potential disadvantage of referrals is that employees tend to refer others who are similar in age, gender, ethnicity, and religion. If relied on too heavily, this recruiting method may be detrimental to equal employment opportunity goals. Minority employees may refer only minority candidates and nonminorities may refer only other nonminorities. That's what got Carl Buddig & Company in trouble. Located in Chicago, Carl Buddig is a meat processor. The employee referral approach resulted in very few African Americans being hired; so the EEOC sued the company. After two years of litigation, the company paid a $2.5 million fine and agreed to revamp their recruiting practices.[32]

Public Employment Agencies. Public employment agencies are good sources of both temporary employees and permanent employees. American public employment agencies operate under the umbrella of the U.S. Training and Employment Service; it sets national policies and oversees the operations of state employment agencies, which have branch offices in many cities.

State employment agencies offer counseling, testing, and placement services to everyone and provide special services to military veterans, members of some minority groups, colleges, and technical and professional people. Their services are supported by employer contributions to state unemployment funds. The Social

Security Act provides that, in general, workers who have been laid off from a job must register with the state employment agency to be eligible for unemployment benefits. Thus, most state agencies have long rosters of potential applicants.

Private Employment Agencies. Private employment agencies—sometimes called headhunter, placement, or search firms—serve professional, managerial, and unskilled job applicants. Agencies dealing with unskilled applicants often provide job candidates whom employers would have a difficult time finding otherwise. Many employers looking for unskilled workers do not have the resources to do their own recruiting or have only temporary or seasonal demands for these workers.

Founded in Milwaukee, Wisconsin, in 1948, Manpower employs 27,000 people in 73 countries. It is one of the world's leading employment services firms. Many employers rely on Manpower for temporary workers. Demand for temporary workers is strong in France because labor regulations make it very difficult to fire full-time workers. But in China, employer needs are different. In that country, Manpower hopes to grow its business by placing people into full-time jobs.[33]

Search firms such as Korn/Ferry, Spencer Stuart, and Heidrick & Struggles play a major role in recruiting professional and managerial candidates. Executive search firms can be an expensive recruitment method. Employers pay fees as high as one-third of the first year's total salary and bonus package for a job that's filled. More troublesome are the hidden intangible costs. A search firm generally cannot approach executives it has recently placed, and it may have agreements with its clients that limit its ability to approach the clients' employees. This restricts the pool of applicants a search firm can consider and runs counter to the objective of creating a large pool of qualified applicants. In addition, search firms typically prescreen heavily before letting the employer and applicant meet. This protects applicants' privacy and saves the employer time. But it also places a great deal of weight on the judgment of the search firm. Finally, search firms have much less information about the needs of the organization than its managers do; so they are more likely to err by rejecting a candidate who would do well. To minimize such hidden costs, close monitoring of the search firm's activities is necessary.

In spite of the drawbacks, headhunter firms are doing well, especially when it comes to helping talented employees of troubled companies find new positions. Exhibit 6.4 offers suggestions for how to select a search firm when one is needed.[34]

Job Fairs. *At a* **job fair,** *usually several employers are present to provide information about employment opportunities at their companies.* The setting is often somewhat informal, and the public is invited to attend to gather information and ask questions. School job fairs are an important method of recruiting for most organizations, although their importance varies depending on the type of applicants sought. If an organization is recruiting managerial, technical, or professional applicants, then participating in job fairs at colleges and universities is useful. These institutions become less important when an organization is seeking production, service, office, and clerical employees.

Many trade and professional associations also provide recruiting opportunities. Often jobs can be announced through their newsletters and/or through links to the association's Web site. Job fairs at annual trade conferences provide a more personal forum where employers and potential job

FAST FACT

France is Manpower's biggest market, generating one-third of the company's revenue.

FAST FACT

The U.S. Department of Labor lists hundreds of officially approved recruiting agencies on its Web site.

EXHIBIT 6.4 Tips for Selecting an Executive Search Firm

- Learn about the search industry; be sure to understand its weaknesses.
- Investigate the firm's "completion" rate. Some firms fill the positions they are hired for more than 90% of the time. Others fill the positions less than 70% of the time.
- Be sure you know how many restrictions the firm is under. If a firm you want to use is obligated to not recruit from a long list of clients, you may need to hire more than one firm.
- Determine the ratio of "lions" (the partners who often are essential to arranging a meeting and closing a deal) to "squirrels" (researchers and recruiters who help put together a list of possibilities). Be sure you meet the squirrels before hiring the lions.
- Understand and carefully consider the fee structure. Most fee structures are designed to benefit the search firm making few performance commitments to clients. Negotiate a flat fee rather than a fee based on the new hire's compensation and insist on a refundable retainer.
- Understand the search process used by the firm and evaluate how likely it is that the process will yield candidates who meet your recruitment objectives.

---

applicants can meet. Some communities also sponsor job fairs. Participating in community job fairs is a good way for a company to build goodwill and meet its obligations to society.

Foreign Nationals. In professions with domestic labor shortages, employers often recruit foreign nationals. Foreign nationals may be employed in operations in the United States or abroad. When they work abroad, they serve as **host-country nationals** (*persons working in their own country, not the country of the parent company*) or **third-country nationals** (*persons working in a country that's neither their own nor that of the parent company*). Increasingly U.S. companies are using host-country nationals to fill newly created jobs that have been offshored from the United States to substantially reduce their labor costs. Software programmers in India or Bulgaria or Romania may work at wage levels that are 50–75% less than their U.S. counterparts.[35]

Recruiting foreign employees to work in the United States is a useful approach to dealing with labor shortages, but it involves some extra administrative work and planning. Under the Immigration Reform and Control Act of 1986, the Immigration Act of 1990, and the American Competitiveness in the Twenty-First Century Act of 2000, it's unlawful for employers to hire foreign nationals to work in the United States unless they are authorized to do so. Those hired must be paid the prevailing wage. For professional-level workers, employers typically spend an additional $100,000 to $200,000 in relocation costs.[36] Several of the activities associated with recruiting foreign workers are summarized in Exhibit 6.5.

Recruiting foreign nationals successfully requires making an extra effort to understand other cultures from which applicants are sought. For example, whereas U.S. applicants can be expected to recognize the names of many large companies, the names of those companies may be very unfamiliar to applicants outside the United States. Even if foreign applicants recognize the company's name, they may know little about what it would be like to work in a U.S. city. Many French students recognize Coca-Cola's brand name, but few are likely to have a clear image of what it would be like to work in the Atlanta headquarters.

FAST FACT

Labormex Foreign Labor Solutions is a staffing agency that offers to help employers recruit "hardworking people acclimated to tough physical labor and who have worked under severe warm weather conditions."

FAST FACT

More than half a million Americans work for Japanese companies located in the United States.

EXHIBIT 6.5 Employing Foreign Workers

Complying with federal regulations and facilitating the successful relocation of foreign workers are two responsibilities that must be accepted by employers of foreign workers. Specific activities include the following:

✓ Publicize job openings in foreign labor markets using methods that are culturally appropriate to the location (as well as legally acceptable in the United States).

✓ Document domestic recruiting efforts and their lack of success to meet Department of Labor regulations governing the employment of foreign workers.

✓ Monitor the salaries and benefits of foreign and domestic workers to ensure that foreign workers are treated equally to domestic workers, as required by H1-B visa regulations.

✓ Monitor the percentage of employees holding various types of visas to ensure that legal limits are not exceeded within the company.

✓ Provide relocation support to foreign employees, including assistance with immigration, travel, permanent residence applications, visa renewals, bank accounts, credit cards, drivers' licenses, and so on.

✓ Develop and provide training and acculturation programs for both domestic and foreign employees.

✓ Develop a long-term strategy on how to handle visa expirations.

✓ Assist foreign employees with the process of repatriation into their home country at the end of their employment assignment.

Contingent Workers, Rehires, and Recalls

To cope with unexpected or temporary fluctuations in their staffing needs, companies often hire contingent workers. When fluctuating demand is more predictable (e.g., due to seasonal patterns that affect the industry), rehires and recalls can be used as a strategic approach to maintaining workforce flexibility.

Contingent Workers. **Contingent workers** *are people hired with no implicit or explicit contract for long-term employment, including "free agents," independent contractors, and temporary workers.* Contingent workers understand that they'll be frequently entering into and exiting from employment relationships. The temporary assignments generally last three months to a year. Therefore, even when they are working on temporary assignments, they nurture their connections to a wide range of possible future employers. In effect, contingent workers must continually maintain their status as a member of the applicant pool to ensure their continued employment.[37]

Usually, employers hire contingent workers from the external labor market. Firms like Manpower and Adecco often serve as brokers for matching available workers to employers' temporary staffing needs.

Getting short-term employees without an extensive search is an obvious advantage of temporary help agencies. Agencies serve both temporary workers and employers by helping establish rates of pay, contract terms, standardized billing, and other arrangements.[38] For some employees, working on short-term projects and assignments is preferred over regular full-time employment because it gives them more flexibility. They can work intensively on a project for a while knowing that they can easily take a break from work when the project is finished, without having to get their employers' permission.

Recalls and Rehires. Many employers recruit workers for temporary employment as part of a planned strategy for dealing with seasonal fluctuations. Department stores, canneries, construction companies, and ski resorts often rely on recalls and rehires during their peak seasons. Each summer and fall during the apple harvest, canneries in eastern Washington State recall large numbers of employees, some of whom have been on the payroll for more than 20 years. Mail-order companies like L.L.Bean continually bring back a large share of their laid-off workforces between September and December, the busiest months of the year.

FAST FACT

According to the American Staffing Association, every day about 2.5 million people are working as temporary or contract employees.

FAST FACT

Lehman Brothers, Goldman Sachs, JPMorgan Chase, and Deutsche Bank all have return-to-work recruitment programs targeted at women who left Wall Street for one reason or another.

Wall Street is known as a place where 70-hour weeks are expected from all employees who take their work seriously. Many women have found this and other aspects of Wall Street firms to be a poor fit with their personal needs; so after a few years they quit to do something else: raise a family or even pursue other passions, like playing the cello. One result is that Wall Street firms have fewer women than they would like. To lure women back, some companies are trying to change the Street's culture and give people more flexibility to have a healthy work/life balance. Programs such as Encore (Lehman Brothers) and New Directions (Goldman Sachs) seek to find and rehire women with Wall Street experience, often as part-time employees.[39]

Advantages and Disadvantages. Rehiring former or laid-off employees is a relatively inexpensive and effective method of recruiting. The organization already has information about the performance, attendance, and safety records of these employees. Rehires are already familiar with job responsibilities; so they need less time to settle in (*unless* the job has changed substantially while they were away).

However, the growing reliance on contingent employment is often considered a negative trend for employees. Contingent workers lead uncertain lives, and they almost never receive benefits. Nevertheless, some employees prefer contingent arrangements because it allows them to work on a schedule of their own choosing. Highly skilled temporary workers often earn more per hour than permanent employees doing similar work. Temporary employment also provides a way to preview different jobs and work in a variety of organizations. For employees, temporary work is a good way to learn about possible new careers. Good temporary employees often receive permanent job offers. Contingent employment also serves the needs of core employees because it facilitates implementation of temporary leave policies.

Yet recalls, rehires, and contingent employees have unique disadvantages. The commitment of rehires who would have preferred to keep their steady, full-time jobs may be low. Permanent employees who know they are being paid less per hour than comparable temporary hires may feel resentful. On Wall Street, some employees who are expected to work 24/7 resent the freedom enjoyed by the returning part-timers. For these and other reasons, conflict between permanent and temporary employees is common. L.L.Bean is very aware of these possible disadvantages and realizes that relying on rehires would backfire if all employees weren't fully committed to providing high-quality service. To prevent this, it works very hard to recruit employees who prefer seasonal employment and then seeks to establish positive employment relationships. Lehman Brothers addressed this problem by offering the more flexible arrangements to all current employees, not just to rehires.

LEARNING GOAL 4

RECRUITING FROM THE APPLICANT'S PERSPECTIVE

Regardless of who the applicants are or how they became applicants for positions, events that occur during recruitment can determine whether they accept or reject an organization's employment offer. Exhibit 6.6 illustrates the factors that influence applicants' job search and job choices.[40]

Recruiting activities should create positive experiences for all applicants—even those who aren't offered positions. If the firm's recruitment methods promote a favorable image of the company, rejected applicants may try again in the future and encourage their friends to view the company as an employer of

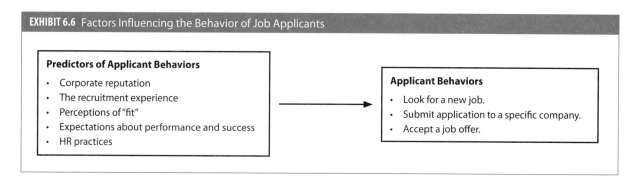

EXHIBIT 6.6 Factors Influencing the Behavior of Job Applicants

Predictors of Applicant Behaviors
- Corporate reputation
- The recruitment experience
- Perceptions of "fit"
- Expectations about performance and success
- HR practices

Applicant Behaviors
- Look for a new job.
- Submit application to a specific company.
- Accept a job offer.

choice. In other words, recruitment addresses current labor needs while antici-pating future labor needs.

To effectively attract *and* retain potentially qualified candidates, employers need to understand the behaviors and preferences of the diverse workforce. What do candidates consider when searching for and choosing a new job? How do candidates differ in their job search activities? Where do they get their information regarding job availability, and what do they react to the most?

Building a Corporate Reputation

For many applicants, the reputation of the organization they work for is an important consideration. Generally, people prefer to work for an organization that they can be proud of. That often means finding a company with values that match your own.[41] Research shows that applicants' images of potential employers are shaped by recent publicity and the company's own advertis-ing.[42] Organizations with more positive corporate reputations attract more, and somewhat more qualified, applicants.[43]

Wendy Kopp, the founder of Teach for America, knows all about the value of a good reputation. She dreamed up the idea for this organization when she was a senior at Princeton. Since then, Teach for America has become one of the top picks for graduating college students. Out of about 19,000 applicants, only 2,400 are selected each year to participate in this unique program. Successful applicants receive five months of intensive training and then take positions as teachers in some of the country's most impoverished and challenging school districts. Their goal is to help build tomorrow's leaders. Many of these teachers work 80 to 90 hours a week for modest pay. Few of these recruits plan to stay in teaching as their career, but many believe the experience will make them more attractive as applicants for future employers regardless of what types of jobs they later apply for. The appeal of working for Teach for America is also about idealism and a desire to do something that makes a significant contribu-tion to society. Why else would nearly 10% of seniors at Ivy League schools like Yale, Dartmouth, and Columbia be attracted to this organization? So far, Teach for America's teachers have taught 2.5 million students in more than 1,000 schools.[44]

With all the talk about becoming an employer of choice, it's worth pointing out that organizations should think carefully about whether to mount a public campaign to raise public awareness. Unless a company really is a great place to work, employers should not claim that it is. And if managers aren't ready to make significant investments to make their firm a great place to work, the company is better off not jumping on this bandwagon. After Merrill Lynch made *Working Woman*'s list of best companies in one year, a group of female

> **"** *We're one of the few companies where employees identify themselves by the company name—here you're not just an IBM employee—you're an IBMer.* **"**
>
> *Randy MacDonald*
> *Senior Vice President of Human Resources*
> *IBM*

> **"** *One of the few jobs that people pass up Goldman Sachs offers for is Teach for America.* **"**
>
> *Edie Hunt*
> *Co–chief Operating Officer of Human Capital Management*
> *Goldman Sachs*

stockbrokers started a writing campaign to have the company removed from the list. They also hired an airplane to fly banners at sporting events, informing spectators that the group had sued the company for sex discrimination. To be successful, organizations that seek to be employers of choice should address the concerns of all of their employees, not just the majority of them.

The Recruitment Experience

Attracting applicants by establishing a good reputation and getting people to apply for jobs are the first elements of recruitment. But if too many applicants decline job offers, the investments in these activities have been wasted. Starbucks knows that it pays to make the recruiting experience positive for applicants, and strives to treat its job applicants as well as it treats its customers.

Easy and Fast. User-friendly online application software that accepts applicants' resumes is one way to create a positive experience. Timing is also important. Slow or late decisions by employers are a major reason for negative impressions.

Allstate Insurance makes it easy for independent contractors to apply by using software that instantly conducts the initial screening process and gives immediate feedback to the applicant. Successful applicants are told on the spot that an interview will be scheduled as the next step. There is literally no waiting required for the applicant to learn whether the company is a good prospect. JPMorgan Chase went one step further. The firm made it *fun* to apply online by creating a job-hunting game that helps applicants match their interests to job alternatives in the company.[45]

Behavior of Recruiters. Effective recruiters show sincere interest in applicants, and, in return, applicants show more interest in the job.[46] Research indicates that the behavior of recruiters influences how job applicants react to the experiences they have during the hiring process. In one study, a team of researchers asked placement directors from four colleges of a large university to identify job seekers who were as different from each other as possible in terms of sex, race, grade point average, and so on. Forty-one job seekers were interviewed early in the recruiting season and again near the end, 8 to 10 weeks later. The results showed that job seekers' early perceptions of how well they fit a job were affected most by job and company characteristics, then by contacts with recruiters, and then by contacts with people in the company other than recruiters.

In many instances, recruiters made jobs that initially appeared unattractive seem attractive. Positive impressions were created by the status of recruiters and whether recruiters made applicants feel specially treated. Another interesting finding was that the best applicants were more likely than weaker applicants to interpret recruiting practices as indications of what the employing organization was like rather than assuming the practices were just a poor reflection on the particular recruiter involved. In other words, a poor recruiter had the most negative impact on the best applicants.[47]

In the study just described, almost all job seekers reported that some recruiters or recruiting practices, or both, created poor impressions and made some jobs seem less attractive. Training recruiters is one way to improve the impressions they make on applicants. Training programs should teach recruiters to spend less time talking about topics that are irrelevant to the job, be receptive to questions from applicants, not be overly aggressive in trying to sell the job, and in general convey a professional image of the organization.[48] Recruiters also need to

> " I was impressed that these women executives would take the time out to interview me, a mid-level person. I was delighted to find people that embrace the same values I embrace. "
>
> *Teri Robinson*
> *Vice President*
> *Darden Restaurants*

understand the jobs to be filled. This appears to be especially true when recruiting highly skilled professionals. At Chiron, a biopharmaceutical firm, recruiters regularly sit in on the business meetings to learn about the company and issues in the industry. The goal is to make sure that recruiters can relate to the concerns of job applicants.[49]

Perceptions of Fit

Recruiters and the recruiting process help create a good (or bad) impression, but other things matter too. Especially for younger applicants, deciding whether to accept an employment offer may be entangled with choosing an occupation. Economic issues, including the realities of the labor market, also have some impact on what applicants pay attention to. Individual needs, interests, and abilities all play a role, as do sociological factors such as one's prior exposure to the occupation through parents and relatives.[50] Contrary to what many people believe, the differences between what attracts men and women to jobs are quite small.[51]

Applicants want jobs that fit their skills. Important job characteristics include the status of the functional area the job is in, as well as the nature of the work itself.[52] In their efforts to attract a large pool of applicants, many employers oversell their virtues and cover up their flaws. Just as applicants work to create the best possible impression,[53] so do employers. Some recruiters tell job applicants only about the positive aspects of a job. This tactic follows from a desire to increase offer acceptances. In the short run, this tactic may work,[54] but in the longer term it's counterproductive. When applicants take jobs that don't fit their skills or meet their expectations for career advancement, their performance and morale are likely to suffer.

HR Practices

Salary is often the most important consideration for job applicants, but benefits and flexible work arrangements are important too. Men and women alike prefer companies that offer more flexibility and opportunities to learn quickly.[55] With the exception of workers under age 30, almost everyone agrees that benefits such as health insurance are among the most important factors to consider. For those at the bottom of the earnings scale, job security is one of the most important concerns.[56]

As the number of older applicants grows, HR practices that appeal to older workers are becoming more important. Some job boards specialize in servicing employers with work environments that appeal to this older population. Many older workers prefer part-time work and are looking for employers who will give them plenty of flexibility. They are not as likely to be interested in relocating, and they want to be assured that they won't be subjected to age discrimination once they are hired.[57]

RECRUITING ETHICS

Accepting a job offer can have far-reaching implications for a person's life: It can influence where a person lives, how much stress a person experiences commuting to work, where a person's children attend school, where a partner works, how much income a person can earn, and so on. Viewed in this light, persuading someone to take a job becomes a big responsibility. At the same time, recruiters may be under pressure to fill jobs quickly. Indeed, their pay may depend on how many jobs they fill and how quickly they do it.

FAST FACT

A survey of 400 employees in 80 companies who were on international assignments around the world revealed that 40% wouldn't take another international assignment after learning what it was like.

FAST FACT

When JigZaw Inc. places job ads, they include the phrase "people interested in flextime are encouraged to apply."

FAST FACT

According to the Bureau of Labor Statistics, the number of workers aged 55 and older is growing at over twice the rate of the overall employment level.

5 LEARNING GOAL

Honesty Pays

In fairness to applicants, the only ethical approach to recruitment is to engage in an honest exchange of information with job applicants. Applicants appreciate the concern shown by employers who provide negative as well as positive information.[58]

Realistic Previews. **Realistic job previews** *occur when the organization is careful to describe both the positive and negative aspects of a job and organization.* Research shows that using realistic job previews actually increases the number of eventual recruits. In addition, recruits who receive both types of information are more committed and slightly less likely to quit once they accept the job.[59]

Employees share in the responsibility of acquiring a realistic job preview. To make sure they know what they are getting into, applicants should ask questions until they get detailed answers about things such as the expected results, the timetable available to achieve the results, and the resources available to employees.

Multiple Sources of Information. If the only source of information about a company is a single recruiter who is paid to fill job openings, applicants may be at risk of being oversold on a job's desirability. To avoid this potential problem, employers can be sure to give applicants information from many sources, including advertisements, formal job descriptions, video presentations, Web casts, blogs, and samples of the actual work.

In general, more information is better, and informal means of communicating about the job often produce more accurate perceptions.[60] A study involving several large companies found that potential applicants are attracted to companies that provide more information in their ads. When ads tell about the company, the job, and the job benefits, job seekers are more likely to follow up and apply for the job.[61] Another study found that applicants who obtained information through both formal and informal means had more knowledge about the job than those who relied on only one type of information.[62]

Rejecting Applicants

When Mirage Resorts received 84,000 applications for 9,600 job openings, it had to tell thousands of applicants they wouldn't be hired. Southwest Airlines sends the same message to thousands of applicants year after year. Teach for America rejects about 10,000 applicants annually. If rejected candidates feel angry, it tarnishes the organization's reputation. If recruiting procedures are viewed as unfair, too lengthy, or too impersonal, rejected candidates may share their dissatisfaction with friends and associates. For applicants and employers alike, managing rejections is an extremely important step in the entire recruitment process.

With the large numbers of applicants generated by Internet recruiting, many companies adopt an attitude best described as, "Don't call us, we'll contact you." Applicants sometimes wonder if anyone really looked seriously at their application materials. Sending a *personalized* response to every applicant is the best way to head off this concern. Whether it's a traditional letter or an e-mail message, the same basic principles apply. To leave a positive impression, a rejection letter should include statements that are friendly. The letter should include a correct salutation, and acknowledge the applicant's job qualifications. Including statements about the size and excellence of the application pool can reduce disappointment and increase perceptions of fairness.

Applicants also appreciate *timely* rejection notices. A recruitment and selection timetable should be specified for applicants, and the organization should meet its self-imposed deadlines. If applicants who have no chance of getting a job are not informed promptly, they may take the risk of rejecting other opportunities. Ethical recruitment practices reduce the likelihood of this unfortunate scenario.

EQUAL OPPORTUNITY AND NONDISCRIMINATION

6 LEARNING GOAL

As described in Chapter 4, U.S. employment laws prohibit discrimination in recruiting. Many other countries also have regulations that influence the hiring process. Thus, legal considerations play a critical role in the recruiting and hiring processes of most companies.

EEO-1 Reports

The federal government requires most employers with more than 100 employees to file an annual Employer Information Report (EEO-1). These reports are used to monitor compliance with nondiscrimination laws. Each year, about 45,000 employers file EEO-1 reports. An **EEO-1 report** *gives an accounting of the composition of the workforce using four factors: job family (9 categories), sex (2 categories), race/ethnicity (8 categories), and employment status (5 categories)*. The reports are confidential, but the Equal Employment Opportunity Commission (EEOC) uses them to investigate discrimination complaints.

Affirmative Action Programs

The U.S. employment laws that are most directly relevant to recruitment are those describing affirmative action programs. **Affirmative action programs (AAPs)** *are intended to reduce employment discrimination or to correct underutilization of qualified members of protected groups in an organization's relevant labor market*. Title VII of the Civil Rights Act identifies the following as protected groups: women, African Americans, Hispanics, Native Americans, Asian Americans, and Pacific Islander Americans.

AAPs are required when the company is a federal contractor. They may also be required as part of a settlement to resolve a discrimination lawsuit. However, many AAPs are simply voluntary efforts intended to guard against intentional or unintentional discrimination. Regardless of why an AAP is developed, regulatory guidelines and subsequent Supreme Court decisions make it clear that AAPs must not include strong preferential treatment or strict quotas. They should emphasize recruiting activities that increase the representation of protected groups and employment practices that eliminate bias.

Federal Contractors. If a company has a federal contract greater than $50,000 and has 50 or more employees, it's referred to as a federal contractor. In addition to protecting members of the groups identified in Title VII, federal contractors are required to take affirmative action to employ and advance qualified individuals with disabilities. Executive Order 11246, which became effective in 1965, requires federal contractors to

1. Have and abide by an equal employment policy.
2. Analyze their workforces to assess possible underutilization of women and ethnic minorities.
3. When underutilization is revealed, develop a plan of action to eliminate it and make a good faith effort to implement the plan.

FAST FACT

Approximately 65,000 companies are federal contractors.

Federal contractors are required to file written affirmative action plans with the **Office of Federal Contract Compliance Programs (OFCCP),** *which is the agency responsible for overseeing the employment practices of federal contractors and enforcing relevant federal regulations.* The Department of Labor specifies the following required components of a federal contractor's AAP:

1. **Utilization analysis,** *which determines the number of minorities and women employed (utilized) in each type of job in the organization.*

2. **Availability analysis,** *which measures how many members of minorities and women are available to work in the relevant labor market of an organization.* The relevant labor market is generally defined as the geographic area from which come a substantial majority of job applicants and employees. If an organization employs proportionately fewer members of protected groups than are available, a state of underutilization exists.

3. **Goals and timetables** *specify how the organization plans to correct any underutilization of protected groups.* Because goals and timetables become the organization's commitment to equal employment, they must be realistic and attainable. When a protected group is found to be underutilized, the timetable for addressing the problem is likely to stretch over several years.

AAPs may not completely eliminate discrimination by federal contractors, but the representation of black males and black females has grown rapidly since they became mandatory.[63]

Consent Decrees. Employers that are not federal contractors may nevertheless be subject to a government-regulated affirmative action plan if they have had a history of discrimination complaints. As part of a legal settlement of a discrimination lawsuit, a federal court may issue a consent decree. A **consent decree** *is a legally enforced court ruling that specifies the affirmative action steps an organization must take to remedy the effects of past discrimination.* The evidence that leads the courts to require AAPs often comes from utilization analyses conducted by the EEOC. Since the 1960s, hundreds of consent degrees have put AAPs into place.

Voluntary Affirmative Action. Driven by their own desire to treat job applicants fairly, many U.S employers take a proactive approach to recruiting a diverse pool of applicants. IBM is just one example of many that could be described. Its approach is explained in the feature "Managing the Multicultural Workforce: IBM's Project View."[64]

The EEOC publishes guidelines for organizations that wish to establish voluntary AAPs, and it offers an annual Exemplary Voluntary Efforts Award to recognize companies with the best voluntary programs. Winning the award appears to have value beyond simply good public relations. A study of firms that have won this award showed that investors bid up the stock prices of the winning companies after the award was announced. By comparison, stock prices fell following announcements of discrimination settlements.[65]

Public Opinion. Views about affirmative action vary greatly in the United States. When a lawsuit against the University of Michigan questioned whether AAPs were legal, several of the nation's largest employers—including Microsoft,

MANAGING THE MULTICULTURAL WORKFORCE
IBM's Project View

An IBM motto is, "None of us is as strong as all of us." In a company that values teamwork, it's important that all employees feel that their employer meets their personal needs and the needs of their communities. IBM's commitment to workforce diversity is one way that the company satisfies the needs of all employees. Project View is one program that supports the company's diverse workforce.

Project View was started about 20 years ago as a way to bring candidates in for summer positions. Today, it is a core element of IBM's recruiting strategy for regular full-time hires. Project View is a series of multiday events that bring underrepresented minority students who have hardware, software, and business backgrounds to the company for an extended visit, during which they see the facilities, obtain information, and participate in interviews. For example, each year, a three-day Native American Project View event is held in the Southwest to recruit qualified applicants from some of this country's 32 tribal colleges. As another example, IBM has held a two-day Project View for People with Disabilities. The company's extensive network of relationships with colleges and universities is central to the event's success.

Line managers with available job openings and HR professionals work together to host Project View events. Managers from all over the organization come to the Project View recruiting events. During the two or three days of the event, managers have plenty of opportunity to talk with talented college students who will soon be entering the job market, and they identify those who have the skills and geographic preferences that fit the anticipated job openings. Project View also provides an opportunity for recruits to learn about IBM's other diversity-friendly HR Policies. For example, Leadership Development for Asia Pacific (LEAP) is a five-day program designed to promote the professional development of high-potential employees of Asian Pacific heritage, and IBM has 15 Hispanic/Latin diversity groups. Thus, Project View is just one element of IBM's total strategy for recruiting and retaining a diverse workforce.

Bank One, General Motors, Steelcase, and two dozen others—prepared a formal statement of their opinion and sent it to the U.S. Court of Appeals. Their statement, called an *amicus brief*, argued that campus diversity was essential to developing the type of workforce that employers need. Diversity was good for business, the CEOs argued. Unless colleges educated a diverse workforce, their companies would not be able to benefit from the advantages that diversity can bring. Increasingly, multinational companies are expanding their affirmative action programs overseas.[66]

Unlike these CEOs, many people oppose affirmative action efforts. Even if they agree that it is unfair to discriminate, opponents of affirmative action argue that preferential treatment often backfires, causing harm to the intended beneficiaries of AAPs. Consistent with this argument, studies have shown that affirmative action hires are *perceived* as being less competent than equally qualified employees not hired under an AAP.[67] Nevertheless, minority applicants tend to be more attracted to firms that advertise the importance of diversity than to those that don't.[68]

According to numerous opinion polls, Americans strongly support efforts designed to ensure equal opportunity and eliminate bias, and they oppose practices that they believe involve giving any group preferential treatment.[69] Research also shows that affirmative action efforts are more acceptable when merit is emphasized as being central to the decision-making process.[70] Furthermore, people who have recently experienced workplace discrimination tend to have more favorable views of affirmative action practices.[71] Exhibit 6.7 summarizes some of the arguments made for and against affirmative action activities.

> " *Our success as a global company is a direct result of our diverse and talented workforce. Our ability to develop new consumer insights and ideas and to execute in a superior way across the world is the best possible testimony to the power of diversity any organization could ever have.* "
>
> John E. Pepper
> Chairman
> Procter & Gamble Co.

EXHIBIT 6.7 Two Sides of the Affirmative Action Debate

ARGUMENTS SUPPORTING AFFIRMATIVE ACTION	ARGUMENTS AGAINST AFFIRMATIVE ACTION
• Historical inequities in the treatment of members of protected groups cannot be corrected unless affirmative efforts are made to bring these groups up to parity. • Affirmative action efforts that are appropriately designed and implemented do not result in reverse discrimination. • They increase the diversity of the applicant pool; they do not involve lowering standards for making hiring decisions. • Affirmative action efforts benefit society as a whole by ensuring that the country's human resources are not squandered. Without such efforts, significant portions of the population will be caught in a vicious cycle of low economic achievement. • Some groups may have to suffer temporary reverse discrimination due to affirmative action efforts, but the greater good that such efforts serve justify this.	• Affirmative action efforts inadvertently harm those who are intended to be the beneficiaries by lowering their self-esteem and causing others to view them as less qualified. • Affirmative action efforts result in reverse discrimination. • Any efforts to help one group necessarily mean discrimination occurs against the groups that do not receive such help. • By classifying employees into protected and unprotected groups, affirmative action efforts create polarization and separation between men and women and between majority and minority ethnic groups. Pitting groups against each other leads to greater racism and prejudice. • Affirmative action efforts create innocent victims. The males and nonminorities who experience reverse discrimination today are not the same individuals who are responsible for the historical events that resulted in present-day inequities.

Breaking the Glass Ceiling

Regardless of why organizations develop AAPs, the presence of such programs often stimulates people to think more systematically about their recruiting efforts. Until recently, the disciplined approach associated with AAPs—that is, defining the relevant labor market and tracking how recruiting efforts affect both who is offered a position and who accepts job offers—was used only for lower-level positions and external recruitment efforts. In recent years, however, similar monitoring approaches have been used to evaluate promotion patterns, which reflect internal recruiting processes.

Many companies found that a decade or two of affirmative action recruiting at lower levels meant that by the late 1980s, plenty of women were in the pipeline for higher-level positions. Yet women still seem to be trapped below a glass ceiling. Based on its intensive study of nine large corporations, the Department of Labor concluded that the recruiting methods typically used to hire managerial

---

EXHIBIT 6.8 Recruiting Practices That May Create a Glass Ceiling

Reliance on Networking—Word-of-Mouth: Middle- and upper-level positions often are filled through word-of-mouth referrals. Corporate executives may learn of individuals, interview them casually at luncheons or dinners, and make them an offer, without a formal recruitment process. People not in the executive network experience diminished opportunities.

Reliance on Networking—Employee Referrals: In some companies, elaborate employee referral systems are in place. If employees in the company do not represent the full diversity of the labor force, the pool of applicants created by their referrals also will not reflect this diversity.

Executive Search Firms: Employers are responsible for obtaining a diverse pool of applicants. Companies may not make executive recruitment firms aware of their equal employment and affirmative action obligations and objectives, or they may not use success in this area in deciding which search firm to hire.

Job Postings: Some companies post job notices for lower-level jobs, but not for mid- to upper-level jobs. At the higher levels, employees learn about openings only through their informal networks. Informal communications tend to flow more intensely among people who are demographically similar, which means that members of many protected groups are less likely to hear about openings for higher-level positions.

Recruiting Venues: Recruiting often occurs at conferences for trade and professional associations and interviews often are scheduled to take place in a hotel room. A study by the Wellesley College Center for Research on Women found that holding job interviews in hotel rooms can be intimidating for many women and reduces the possibility of finding qualified women applicants.

---

talent contributed to the problem of the glass ceiling.[72] Exhibit 6.8 summarizes how several common recruiting practices can contribute to this problem. The challenge for companies is to balance their desire to recruit the best available talent with their desire to break the glass ceiling.

RETAINING EMPLOYEES

7
LEARNING GOAL

For some organizations, rapid growth is the primary reason that new employees must be recruited. But the need to replace workers who leave is a far more common force driving most recruiting activities. Turnover, not growth, creates most recruitment pressures.

Understanding the Reasons for Turnover

Some employee turnover is unavoidable, even in the best organizations. People retire or move for non-job-related reasons. As described earlier, in Chapter 2, turnover due to the upcoming retirement of Baby Boomers is expected to have major implications for future recruiting activities.

Not all turnover is bad. Research suggests that too little turnover can actually harm firm performance.[73] Sometimes organizations encourage employees to leave. The objective may be to shrink the size of the workforce overall or simply to help unproductive workers realize that they may be better off finding alternative employment. But the lion's share of turnover—that caused by dissatisfied employees—is not desirable. Reducing turnover among the best performing employees can contribute to improved firm performance.[74]

Exhibit 6.9 shows some of the known causes of voluntary turnover, based on hundreds of research studies conducted over many years.[75] The exhibit illustrates the most common causes of turnover. Of course, each employee and each organization is unique. In some organizations, job dissatisfaction may be a big problem, whereas in other companies poor pay might be a major concern to employees. Sometimes employees leave for personal reasons that

FAST FACT

In the fast-food industry, the annual turnover of hourly workers averages 140%.

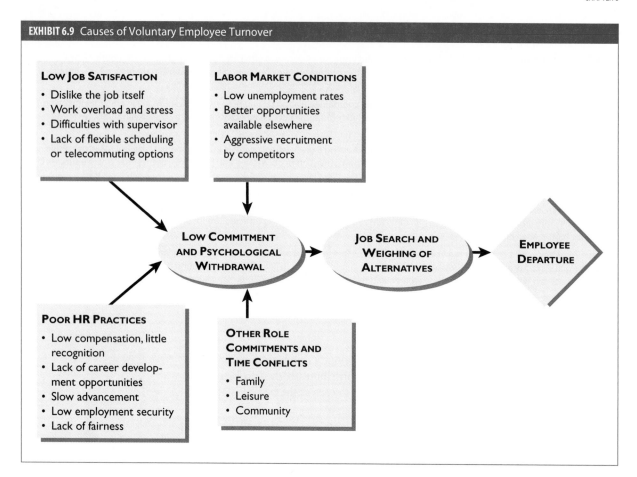

EXHIBIT 6.9 Causes of Voluntary Employee Turnover

LOW JOB SATISFACTION
- Dislike the job itself
- Work overload and stress
- Difficulties with supervisor
- Lack of flexible scheduling or telecommuting options

LABOR MARKET CONDITIONS
- Low unemployment rates
- Better opportunities available elsewhere
- Aggressive recruitment by competitors

POOR HR PRACTICES
- Low compensation, little recognition
- Lack of career development opportunities
- Slow advancement
- Low employment security
- Lack of fairness

OTHER ROLE COMMITMENTS AND TIME CONFLICTS
- Family
- Leisure
- Community

LOW COMMITMENT AND PSYCHOLOGICAL WITHDRAWAL → JOB SEARCH AND WEIGHING OF ALTERNATIVES → EMPLOYEE DEPARTURE

have nothing to do with their employer, perhaps because a spouse is moving to another city.[76] To reduce turnover, each organization should diagnose the reasons that good talent voluntarily decides to look elsewhere for employment.

The reasons employees quit their jobs may seem obvious, yet many employers simply don't have a good understanding about what's most important to their top-performing employees. An analysis by Watson Wyatt Worldwide revealed the disconnect between employers and employees. HR professionals at 262 large U.S. companies indicated what they thought was important. These opinions were compared to the responses of 1,100 top performers at similar companies. Exhibit 6.10 shows some of the results.[77]

To understand the reasons behind their own employees' decisions to seek other employment, some organizations conduct exit surveys. About the time employees leave the organization, they are asked several questions that usually focus on assessing the employees' satisfaction with things such as benefits, work conditions, career advancement and development, supervision, and pay. Such information may be gathered using an interview, a paper-and-pencil survey, or an online survey. Regardless of the method used, the information gathered will not be useful to the employer unless the employee is candid.

> 66 *We bend over backwards to make part-time schedules work. We think it keeps a lot of good people from quitting.* 99
>
> Ken Bottoms
> Compensation Chief
> First Horizon

HR Practices Can Reduce Unwanted Turnover

From Exhibits 6.9 and 6.10, it's easy to see that many causes of turnover are under the employer's control. By improving their HR practices, employers can often make changes that reduce the rate at which the best employees leave. Plante & Moran,

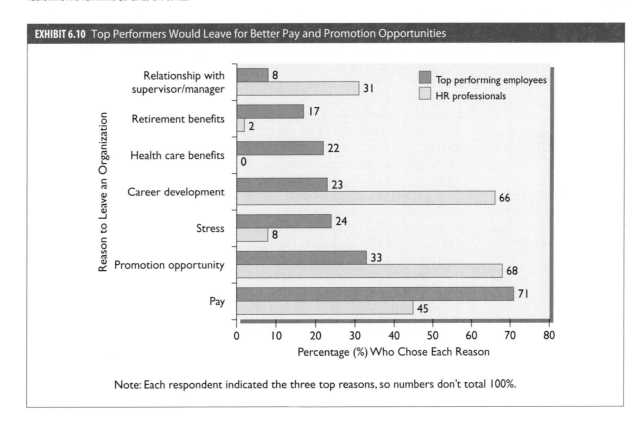

EXHIBIT 6.10 Top Performers Would Leave for Better Pay and Promotion Opportunities

Note: Each respondent indicated the three top reasons, so numbers don't total 100%.

a large accounting firm, has been successful in keeping its annual turnover rate at 1.4%. The company estimates that it costs $75,000 to replace an accountant who leaves—about one year's salary. By keeping its accountants satisfied, Plante & Moran not only reduces these expenses, but also retains its most talented employees and improves its productivity.

If you walked into a Plante & Moran office on a Saturday morning in early April, you might expect to find harried CPAs hunched over their desks and focused only on getting through the brutal realities of the income tax season. In fact, what you are more likely to find are CPAs working alongside a roomful of their tots and toddlers. The family-friendly culture at Plante & Moran is part of what makes this company attractive to the growing number of women entering the accounting profession. Cofounder Frank Moran was a philosophy major before he became an accountant. His personal philosophy was that professionals should be allowed considerable autonomy in doing their work. Instead of working set hours, he believed employees should come and go as needed to serve the needs of clients. At the same time, he understood that serving clients could put tremendous pressure on family life. His company's culture reflects his view that work should allow employees to meet the needs of their clients without sacrificing their personal needs or the needs of family members. Besides child-friendly work sites, other HR practices that keep accountants at this firm include generous vacations, a sabbatical leave program for partners, six months of parental leave for both mothers and fathers, performance evaluations that emphasize results rather than face time, and a breakfast club that ensures that the firm's five managing partners get to know all 1,200 of its employees. [78]

FAST FACT

An analysis of 25 years of Gallup interviews with more than a million employees found that employees' relationships with their supervisors were a major determinant of whether they stayed in a job.

Managing Layoffs

Employers also can reduce the need to recruit new employees by the way they manage layoffs. Layoffs are typically a short-term solution to difficult economic conditions. During business downturns, companies may lay off 5%, 10%, or even 15% of their employees in a matter of weeks.[79] Often sooner than they expected, companies that have conducted layoffs find that they need to rehire the same people. According to one large study, approximately 25% of the companies that had trimmed their workforces were rehiring people the next year—either for their former jobs or for new permanent jobs.

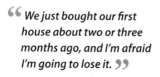

" We just bought our first house about two or three months ago, and I'm afraid I'm going to lose it. "

Car Stereo Installer
Laid Off from Circuit City

In 2007, the electronics store Circuit City announced it would lay off 3,400 employees, mostly people who worked in the warehouses or in the stores. The workers to be laid off were the ones with the longest tenure in the company and therefore cost the most. For example, a salesperson with seven years of experience cost the company 55% more than a salesperson with only one year of experience. The company apparently expected to rehire some of the people being fired; when it announced the layoffs, it also announced a policy stating that the fired employees could reapply for a job after 10 weeks.[80]

Managers use layoffs as a quick method of cost cutting, but the approach often backfires. In the long term, layoffs create problems because the overall trend is that the size of the labor force is growing very slowly.[81] Therefore, as soon as business conditions improve, employers who have conducted layoffs quickly find that they must compete even harder to find new workers. Applicants generally shun companies that are known to have conducted large layoffs.[82]

Investors often view layoffs as an indication of mismanagement. A four-year study of companies that conducted layoffs found that companies with no layoffs or only small reductions in the workforce (less than 3%) posted share price gains

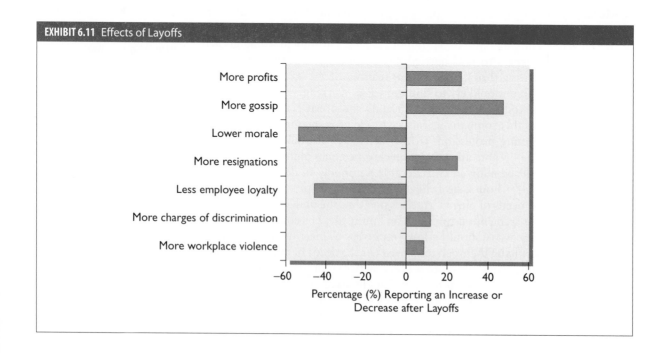

EXHIBIT 6.11 Effects of Layoffs

of 9%. During the same time, companies that laid off 3–9% of their workforces showed no gains, and those that cut 10% or more had prices plunge by 38%.[83]

Avoiding Layoffs. Wise managers understand that layoffs have many consequences. After a layoff, profits may improve in the short term, but these come at a longer-term cost. As shown in Exhibit 6.11, morale and loyalty often plunge among the survivors. Some of the best employees may look elsewhere for employment and resign rather than live in fear of what's to come.[84] For these and other reasons, facing the threat of job loss and seeing others lose their jobs can be a traumatic and bitter experience. This is one reason why excellent companies do everything possible to avoid layoffs. A good example is Southwest Airlines, which has never laid off an employee.

At The Vanguard Group, a money management and mutual fund company, there is no policy statement that guarantees employees that layoffs will never happen, but the company behaves as if they have such a policy. With 10,000 employees, the economic pressures that hit their industry put pressure on Vanguard's bottom line. The company responded by redeploying people to wherever they could be most useful. This approach fits with the firm's basic hiring philosophy. When Vanguard hires people, it doesn't hire them for specific positions. It hires them for careers.[85]

Assisting Displaced Employees. When downsizing is unavoidable, some companies act as if they have little responsibility to the downsized employees. After all, downsizing has become an accepted business practice in America.[86] Shouldn't employees be prepared for a layoff to happen to them? When layoffs are unavoidable, the best companies keep the longer-term view in mind. They understand that they may one day want to rehire some of their laid-off workers. By treating people respectfully during a layoff, employers increase their ability to recruit and rehire experienced employees later.[87]

> 66 *I'm hurt mainly because I loved this company. I've taken very good care of them. I can't believe they did this.* 99
>
> *Laid-Off Employee*

CURRENT ISSUES

An organization that fails to recruit and retain the talent it needs will ultimately fail. Thriving organizations beat the competition by attracting the best workers and by motivating them to perform their best for as long as they are needed. New technologies and the changing concerns of a diverse and increasingly older workforce can pose recruitment and retention challenges, as explained in this chapter. Two additional challenges companies face are a looming global labor shortage and uncertainties over how new legislation may affect the supply of immigrants.

> 66 *One challenge that has to be on our radar is the impending labor shortage. You can't be a large organization today and not have it on your radar.* 99
>
> *Jeff Lamb*
> *Vice President, People and Leadership Development*
> *Southwest Airlines*

The Global Labor Shortage

For years, American employers have been hearing warnings about an impending labor shortage, but few seem to really appreciate the magnitude of this issue. One reason for this may be that employers believe there is a vast supply of labor in other countries that can be easily tapped when needed. Surely the problem is not that there are not enough people to do the work. Is the problem simply getting the work to where the people are? With more than 6 billion people on the planet, is it really possible to have a labor shortage?

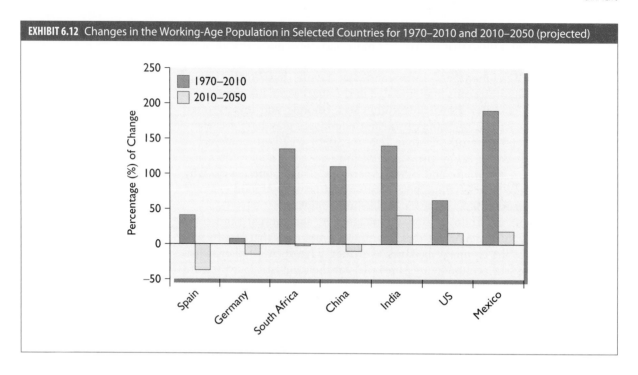

EXHIBIT 6.12 Changes in the Working-Age Population in Selected Countries for 1970–2010 and 2010–2050 (projected)

Data compiled by the United Nations indicates that labor shortages are likely to be a very real issue in the coming years, especially for high-skill jobs. Population growth has been slowing down in most countries while economic development has been speeding up. Exhibit 6.12 illustrates the problem. As labor supplies tighten, the ability to recruit and retain highly talented employees will become increasingly important to an organization's ability to achieve its strategic goals.[88]

Immigration Reform and Foreign Workers in the United States

America's history has been one of constant and large-scale immigration. But in recent years, attitudes toward immigrants seem to have become increasingly unfriendly. Congress has pondered the question of what to do with immigration reform for years. Meanwhile, the states are moving ahead with their own plans. It appears that many states are likely to adopt a system called Basic Pilot, which was developed by the federal government. The Basic Pilot System is currently a voluntary program through which employers can verify the employment eligibility of job applicants by electronically cross-checking Social Security numbers. Administered by the Department of Homeland Security, one of its objectives is protecting the public from terrorists. For employers, the Basic Pilot system adds new regulations and requirements for recruitment and hiring. In the short term, it almost certainly will slow down hiring. If it achieves its goals, the Basic Pilot program may also substantially reduce the supply of low-cost labor available to U.S. employers.

Supporters of tightened immigration and employment controls argue that plenty of Americans are ready to take the jobs currently done by illegal immigrants. Opponents point out that the U.S. unemployment level is very low by historical standards. They also claim that even if Americans are willing to take the jobs that illegal immigrants are forced to abandon, labor costs will soar. Regardless of the laws eventually enacted by Congress and the states, employers must develop a recruitment strategy that allows them to secure the employees they need while meeting their legal obligations.[89]

CHAPTER SUMMARY WITH LEARNING GOALS

1. **STRATEGIC IMPORTANCE.** When done effectively, recruiting and retaining employees can support organizational strategies, reduce expenses and labor costs, improve competitiveness, and ensure legal compliance. Effective recruiting efforts are consistent with the organization's strategy, vision, and values. Practices that help the organization retain the best employees reduce overall labor costs and improve the firm's competitiveness.

2. **AN INTEGRATED HRM SYSTEM.** In a fully integrated, strategically aligned system for managing human resources, recruiting activities are developed with a full appreciation for how they may affect other parts of the system, and how other parts of the system may affect recruiting activities. The most significant forces in the external environment influencing the recruitment and retention of employees are the labor market, technology, and legal trends.

3. **RECRUITING METHODS AND SOURCES.** Recruiting involves internal and external searches. For both internal and external recruiting, organizations weigh the costs and benefits of various methods to choose the most effective ones. The choice of recruitment methods and the implementation of a recruiting plan should take into account the perspective of applicants, as well as the needs of the organization.

4. **THE APPLICANT'S PERSPECTIVE.** Events that occur during recruitment could determine whether the applicant accepts or rejects an employment offer. Recruiting activities should create positive experiences for all applicants. To effectively attract and retain potentially qualified candidates, organizations need to understand the behaviors and preferences of the diverse workforce. Organizations can build a positive corporate reputation by making it easy for applicants to apply, making a good personal impression, giving applicants the information they need, and making rejections with tact. For applicants, the process of searching for employment is fundamentally a search for information.

5. **RECRUITING ETHICS.** Hiring managers may be tempted to make a job seem better than it really is in an effort to convince applicants to accept an offer. Being dishonest is unethical and likely to backfire. Ethical managers provide realistic job previews and respect applicants' need for timely information when they've been rejected.

6. **EQUAL OPPORTUNITY AND NONDISCRIMINATION.** Recruiting activities take place in a dynamic legal environment. While the objectives of nondiscrimination legislation are clear, the means that society finds acceptable for creating equal employment opportunities are under debate. Sharply different opinions prevail concerning the best ways to use and design affirmative action programs. It is increasingly difficult for employers to simply "follow the law" when recruiting; they must consider the strategic and social objectives to be achieved, and they must design recruitment strategies to meet those objectives.

▲ **RETAINING EMPLOYEES.** Retaining employees is one way to reduce the need for extensive recruiting and its associated costs. To retain top-performing employees, employers must first understand what's important to them. Only with this understanding can employers succeed at retaining their top talent. Employers that plan and manage well can also avoid layoffs, which damage the organization's reputation and make it more difficult to recruit in the future.

▲ **CURRENT ISSUES.** Two current issues in recruiting and retaining qualified employees are (1) the global labor shortage for skilled workers due to slowing population growth and speeding economic development in many countries and (2) the immigration of foreign workers into the United States.

TERMS TO REMEMBER

Affirmative action programs (AAPs)
Availability analysis
Consent decree
Contingent workers
EEO-1 report
Employee referrals
External labor market
Goals and timetables
Host-country nationals
Internal labor market

Job fair
Job postings
Office of Federal Contract Compliance Programs (OFCCP)
Realistic job preview
Recruitment
Retention
Talent inventory
Third-country nationals
Utilization analysis

QUESTIONS FOR DISCUSSION AND REFLECTIVE THINKING

1. How can blogs and Web casts enable companies like Honeywell to improve the effectiveness of their recruiting activities? What are the possible disadvantages of using these new technologies for recruiting?

2. Describe the recruiting and retention implications that might follow from a strategic business objective of offering low-cost products to a broad consumer market. Compare these implications to those that might follow from a strategic objective of offering innovative business services to owners of small businesses.

3. What information should be contained in a realistic job preview by a firm seeking to attract the best college graduates? Does your answer depend on the type of industry? On the geographic location of the job? On whether it involves an overseas assignment?

4. Does the age of the applicants an employer hopes to attract affect the methods that are most likely to be effective? Visit the American Association of Retired Persons Web site at www.aarp.org for ideas. Explain your reasoning.

5. Do you think firms such as Colgate-Palmolive, American Express, and General Mills should address the glass ceiling problem by explicitly stating on their Web site that they want to fill a specific percentage of managerial positions with females? Why or why not?

6. Job applicants typically want to find a job that is a "good fit." For you personally, what is a good fit? Describe how you will decide whether a job you are offered is a good fit.

7. Assume that the projected global shortage of labor is in fact likely to occur. What are the implications for recruitment and retention at firms such as Deloitte Touche Tohmatsu and SAS Institute? Be specific.

8. What does/will an employer need to do to keep *you* from looking for a job elsewhere? List the three most important considerations in their order of importance for you personally.

PROJECTS TO EXTEND YOUR LEARNING

1. **Integration and Application.** Before continuing, review the cases of Southwest Airlines and Lincoln Electric at the end of this book. Then answer the following questions.

    a. Which company do you think needs to be more concerned about recruiting? Why?
    b. What should be the objectives of each company's recruiting efforts? Relate the recruiting objectives to each company's strategic objectives.
    c. Which company is likely to have the most difficult time creating a large pool of qualified applicants? Explain your reasoning.
    d. For each company, describe the practices that are most likely to influence employee turnover. Does low turnover contribute to the success of these companies? Explain.

2. **Using the Internet.** All members of the HR Triad can find many online resources that are useful for recruiting and retaining qualified employees.

    a. Evaluate the possible advantages of aggressively recruiting from the growing ranks of senior citizens by learning more about this population and their work habits. Information is available from
        *   American Association of Retired Persons (AARP, www.aarp.org).
        *   Senior Community Service Employment Program (www.doleta.gov/seniors).
        *   Senior Job Bank (www.seniorjobbank.org).
    b. Evaluate the possible advantages of aggressively recruiting people with disabilities. Learn more about the Able to Work consortium and read about best practices related to the employment of people with disabilities at DisabilityInfo.gov (www.disabilityinfo.gov).
    c. Learn about the services of executive search firms and employment agencies by visiting the company home pages of
        *   Adecco (www.adecco.com).
        *   Kelly Services (www.kellyservices.com).
        *   Manpower (www.manpower.com).
        *   East West Consulting (www.ewc.co.jp/en/).
    d. Learn more about affirmative action plans from the Office of Federal Contract Compliance Programs (OFCCP, www.dol.gov/elaws/ofccp.htm).
    e. Learn more about the glass ceiling and what companies are doing to reduce its negative consequences by visiting Catalyst (www.catalystwomen.org).

3. **Experiential Activity.** We know much less about the consequences of voluntary turnover than we do about its causes. To improve your understanding of the consequences of turnover for employers and employees, interview four people who are currently employed or were employed until recently. All four people should be familiar with a particular industry (e.g., if you are interested in retailing, select four people with experience in the retail industry). The four interviews can be conducted with class members, family members, coworkers, or anyone you choose.

    Your goal in conducting the four interviews is to generate a list of all the ways turnover affects employers and employees in a particular industry. Working individually or in small teams, prepare a brief presentation that summarizes all the consequences of turnover (both positive and negative) that you identify during the interviews. Use a template like the following one to organize your results.

The Consequences of Turnover

Type of industry: _____

Backgrounds of people interviewed (e.g., job title, years of experience in the industry, company)

1. _____   3. _____

2. _____   4. _____

Affected Stakeholders	**Consequences of Voluntary Employee Turnover**	
	Positive	**Negative**
Customers		
Owners and investors		
Departing employee (DE)		
DE's direct supervisor		
DE's coworkers		
DE's subordinates		
HR professionals		
Other: _____		
Other: _____		

CASE STUDY

DOWNSIZING: ANATHEMA TO CORPORATE LOYALTY?

Jim Daniels was unprepared for the dilemma facing Defense Systems, Inc. (DSI). Daniels, vice president of human resources, joined the company one year ago when he was pirated away from one of the company's major competitors. DSI manufactures electronic components used in weapons supplied to the Air Force and many other firms. In addition, DSI makes semiconductors used in many of the weapons systems as well as in personal computers and automotive computers.

When Daniels joined DSI, a major drive to build up the staff in engineering was undertaken in anticipation of a major upturn in the semiconductor market. Unfortunately, industry analysts' projections were overoptimistic, and the semiconductor market failed to pick up. DSI recently completed an aggressive hiring policy at the major universities around the United States, wherein the company had selected 1,000 engineers who were among the cream of the crop with an average GPA of 3.4. Without a pickup in business, however, DSI is confronted with some fairly unpleasant alternatives.

From one point of view, potential cost reduction measures at DSI fit the overall pattern of cutbacks, restructuring, and downsizing that many major U.S. companies face. The motives among firms who have trimmed their workforces vary—some to please Wall Street and the stockholders, others to keep pace with foreign competitors or to shrink an unwieldy organizational structure. To Daniels, DSI layoffs or terminations are poor alternatives to dealing with a turbulent environment.

The major problem, as Daniels sees it, is to preserve as many jobs as possible until business picks up. To terminate the new hires would irreparably harm DSI's future recruitment efforts. On the other hand, underutilizing these talented recruits for very long would certainly lead to major dissatisfaction. Although terminations would improve the balance sheet in the short run, Daniels worried about the impact of such a move on corporate loyalty, a fragile and rare commodity at other major firms that have had to cut their white-collar workforce.

Daniels is scheduled to meet with the executive committee of DSI in three days to discuss the overstaffing problems and to generate alternatives. In preparation for this meeting, Daniels is trying to draw on his experience with his past employer to generate some ideas. A number of differences between DSI and Daniels's old employer, though, make comparisons difficult. For one, DSI does not employ nearly the number of temporaries or student interns as did his former employer. Nor does DSI rely on subcontractors to produce parts needed in its assembly operation. Because of extra capacity, DSI can currently produce 50% of the parts it purchases, whereas Daniels's ex-employer could produce only 5%.

Another major difference is the degree of training provided by DSI. At Daniels's last employer, each employee could expect a minimum of 40 hours of additional training a year; at DSI, however, training consists of about 10 hours per year, much of it orientation training.

Daniels wondered whether there might be some additional ways to remove slack from the system and at the same time preserve as many jobs as possible. For example, overtime hours are still paid to quite a few technicians. Would the engineers be willing to assume some of these duties in the interim until business picked up? Some older employees have accumulated several weeks of unused vacation. Could employees be encouraged to take unpaid leaves of absence? Perhaps early retirement incentives could be offered to make room for some of the bright young engineers. DSI also has 14 other geographic locations, some in need of additional workers.

Could a recruiting plan for internal transfers address this problem?

As Daniels thinks about these options, one thing is clear: He needs to organize and prioritize these ideas concisely if he is to be prepared for his upcoming meeting.

CASE QUESTIONS

1. Why is Daniels sensitive to DSI's recruitment efforts?
2. What are some potential problems for the current class of engineers recruited at DSI?
3. How could the use of temporaries, student interns, or subcontractors potentially help DSI?
4. Evaluate Daniels's alternatives for reducing DSI's labor surplus. What do you recommend? Why?

Selecting Employees to Fit the Job and the Organization

Learning Goals

After reading this chapter, you should be able to:

1. Describe the strategic importance of selection.
2. Discuss the choices to be made when designing the selection process.
3. Explain the techniques used for assessing job applicants.
4. Describe the perspective of job applicants.
5. Report the legal considerations in selection.
6. Describe two current issues in selection.

MANAGING HUMAN RESOURCES AT OUTBACK STEAKHOUSE

In the restaurant business, employee turnover can be a big problem. It averages about 200% per year across the industry for hourly employees. Across the 700 Outback Steakhouses, turnover for hourly employees is only about 50%. Many employees have been with the company for six or more years, and 95% of the company's managers were promoted internally from hourly staff jobs.

President Paul Avery believes that the company's low turnover is due to the procedures it uses to select new employees. In its first two years of existence, when the company was small, Outback hired solely on the basis of interviews. As the company grew, it became more important to control turnover costs and hire people who fit the image that the company wanted to be known for. The strategy was to get employees who would indulge customers a bit more than they would expect from a chain restaurant. According to Avery, Outback's culture calls for people who are "fun, spirited, gregarious and team players." When selecting new hires, Outback uses a personality test to find people who are adaptable, highly social, and meticulous. Avery knows that the personality test is better than interviews at identifying candidates with the appropriate personality. Outback keeps data about the test scores of all of its employees. The company analyzes these data to set the cutoff scores used when hiring new staff members. Applicants who fall below specified cutoff scores on important traits are dropped from consideration, even if they have a great resume and do well when interviewed. Managers conduct the interviews, asking a series of behavioral questions. For example, one question is, "What would you do if a customer asked for a side dish we don't have on the menu?" Because almost all managers began working as waiters, they are good judges of how likely it is that an applicant will treat customers well.[1] ▲

THE STRATEGIC IMPORTANCE OF SELECTION

Selection *is the process of obtaining and using information about job applicants to determine who should be hired for long- or short-term positions.* It begins with an assessment of the requirements to be met by the new hire, including the technical aspects of a job and the more difficult to quantify organizational needs. Applicants are then assessed to determine their competencies, preferences, interests, and personality.

Typically, the objective of selection is to predict the likely future performance of applicants—in the job that is open, as well as in other jobs that the new hire might hold at the company in the future. The decision about when to promote or transfer a current employee—and in which job—is a selection decision. When a special task force is created and a manager decides whom to recommend or appoint, the manager makes a selection decision. In organizations with mentoring programs, participating mentors make selection decisions when they decide whom to mentor, if anyone. When managers develop replacement charts and succession plans (as described in Chapter 3), they make selection decisions.

Obtaining a Capable Workforce

Done well, selection practices ensure that employees are (1) capable of high productivity, (2) motivated to stay with the organization for as long as the organization wants to employ them, (3) able to engage in behaviors that result in customer satisfaction, and (4) capable of implementing the strategy of the company. The strategic importance of selecting the right people for key roles is especially clear. Hiring a scientist who invents or discovers a new product may be worth millions or even billions of dollars to a company. Conversely, hiring a person who engages in fraud or illegal activity may end up costing the company millions.

At Lincoln Electric, the selection of production workers is so important that new hires are put on probation for six months, after which coworkers decide whether they can stay. By selecting the right people, Lincoln Electric keeps its productivity level high, maintains high-quality production, and delivers a product that satisfies its customers at a reasonable cost. At Southwest Airlines, it's important to hire employees with a fun-loving attitude who work well in a team-oriented culture. Effective selection practices at Southwest Airlines help the company stay on schedule, maintain an excellent safety record, and maintain a positive company culture. As a result, customers, employees, and investors all reap benefits.

Maximizing the Economic Utility of Selection Practices

The **economic utility** *of a selection procedure refers to the net monetary value associated with using it.* In general, economic utility is a function of the costs incurred to design and use the selection practices and the value of outcomes gained by doing so. Thus, economic utility is essentially a measure of return on investment (ROI).

Cost. The cost of selection decisions includes the value of all the time and resources used to collect information about job applicants. Gleaning information from resumes and brief screening interviews costs relatively little; conducting multiple interviews, conducting background investigations, and paying for medical exams usually costs a great deal. The time used by highly paid employees in the organization (e.g., the CEO) costs more than the time used by those who are paid less (e.g., a product manager). The goal is not simply to reduce these costs. Expensive means of acquiring information may be worthwhile if they enable the organization to make better decisions *and* if substantial consequences are attached to making better decisions. Generally, more expensive procedures may be justified when

- Tenure in the job is expected to be relatively long, so that return on the investment accrues for several years.
- Incremental increases in performance reap large rewards for the organization, so getting someone who performs better is worth a lot.
- The procedure used is very effective in assessing which applicants will perform best and screening out those who will perform poorly.

Expensive procedures might not be justified if

- Progressively higher tax bites are associated with increased company profits, which means that increasing performance is less valuable.
- Labor costs are variable and rise with productivity gains.
- Labor markets are tight, which makes it less likely that the best candidates, once identified, can be enticed to take the position.[2]

Each of these conditions reduces the value to be gained by selecting better employees.

In the past 20 years, numerous studies have demonstrated that well designed selection practices pay off handsomely.[3] The value of using several selection methods in combination was demonstrated in a study of 201 companies from several industries. Companies reported their use of practices such as conducting validation studies, using structured interviews, and administering cognitive tests. The researchers showed that companies that used these practices had higher levels of annual profit, profit growth, and overall performance. The relationship between the use of these practices and bottom-line performance was especially strong in the service and financial sectors.[4] In these industries, the quality of employees hired clearly had an effect on the company's bottom line.

Value. When the job being filled is CEO, the value of making a good selection decision can be in the millions, even billions, of dollars. Some of the economic gains are returned to the CEO as compensation, but usually most of the gains are returned to shareholders, employees, and the government.

Clearly, the potential value of a good CEO selection decision is the exception. The economic value of any single selection decision is usually not so large. Nevertheless, it is important to realize that the potential to reap large economic gains from effective selection is not limited to selecting people for a few key positions. When good decisions are made in the hiring of people at low levels in the organization, small gains for each of those decisions accumulate across large numbers of people. In large organizations like Outback Steakhouse, the accumulated benefits of making thousands of good selection decisions add up quickly. Effective selection also minimizes the risk of harm and the costs of lawsuits brought by victims of criminal, violent, or negligent acts perpetrated by employees who shouldn't have been hired or kept in their jobs.

Calculating Utility. Calculating the economic value of any HR practice is extremely difficult. It is fairly easy to add up all the costs of interviewing, administering and scoring tests, conducting background checks, and so on. But it is very difficult to put dollar values on all the potentially important positive and negative consequences of a selection decision.

FAST FACT

To assess the value of their hiring practices, Dell Computer uses information on performance, retention, surveys by the hiring managers, new hire surveys, and productivity.

EXHIBIT 7.1 The Consequences of Correct and Incorrect Selection Decisions

	Do Not Offer Applicant the Open Position	Offer Applicant the Open Position
High Performance	• Applicant and employer continue to pay costs of continued searching, unnecessarily. • Applicant may decide to accept alternative job that's less well suited to his or her competencies and interests. • Applicants may remain unemployed unnecessarily and forgo rewards they could have earned. • Applicant may file discrimination lawsuit. • Employees may be required to carry an overload until job is filled. • Customers' expectations may not be met while employer is understaffed.	• Employee performs well. • Employee receives rewards associated with good performance. • Employee enjoys work. • Peers benefit from employee's good performance and high morale. • Managers achieve their objectives. • Customers receive products and services that meet their expectations.
	Reject a Qualified Candidate (Incorrect decision)	**Accept a Qualified Candidate (Correct decision)**
	Reject an Unqualified Candidate (Correct decision)	**Accept an Unqualified Candidate (Incorrect decision)**
How Employee Does/Would Perform	• Applicant continues to look for more suitable work. • Employer continues to search for more suitable employee. • Applicant may decide to get more training. • Employer may decide to offer more training so that more applicants can be accepted. • Customers do not suffer from the mistakes of a poor performer. • Employees may continue to carry an overload while search continues, but they do not suffer from the errors produced by an ineffective peer.	• Employee performs poorly. • Employee loses self-esteem due to poor performance, and forgoes the rewards associated with good performance. • Peers suffer consequences of poorly performing employee. • Customers' expectations aren't met due to employee's poor performance. • Managers fail to meet their objectives. • Injuries, accidents, and other serious problems may occur due to employee's poor job performance. • Employee eventually must find new job, creating additional costs associated with turnover.
Low Performance		

Employer's Selection Decision

Exhibit 7.1 summarizes several of the consequences that result from making correct versus incorrect selection decisions. To be accurate, estimates of economic utility should attach dollar values to all of these consequences. In reality, however, the formulas used typically take into account only the costs and benefits that are easily quantified. Thus, most estimates of economic utility probably underestimate the true value of the procedure being evaluated.[5]

The HR Triad

Job applicants are among the key partners in the selection process. Effective selection practices recognize and respect the applicant's concerns and sensitivities. In addition, they actively involve line managers, HR professionals, and other employees, as summarized in the feature "HR Triad: Roles and Responsibilities for Selecting Employees."

LINE MANAGERS	HR PROFESSIONALS	EMPLOYEES
• Identify staffing needs through articulating business strategies, along with strategic business issues and objectives.	• Coordinate the administrative aspects of the selection process.	• May participate as applicants for internal transfers, promotions, and other opportunities.
• Help HR professionals identify appropriate criteria for evaluating the performance of new hires and new placements.	• Develop a selection process that fits the organizational environment and that yields reliable and valid results that job applicants accept as fair.	• May participate by identifying appropriate criteria for evaluating performance.
• Help HR professionals develop selection tools.	• Participate in the selection, monitoring, and evaluation of external vendors that provide selection services.	• May interview candidates to work in the team or work unit.
• Coordinate the selection process with applicants and HR professionals.	• Schedule applicant interviews with managers and other employees.	• May be involved in selecting new group members.
• Interview applicants. May administer and score some selection tests. May make final hiring decision.	• Provide education and training to everyone involved in the selection process.	• Attend training programs put on for employees involved in selection processes.
• Understand and comply with relevant legal regulations; provide accurate information to other organizations when they conduct reference checks.	• Monitor selection outcomes and keep complete and accurate records for possible use in defending the organization against lawsuits.	• When considering whether to accept a new position, accept responsibility for self-selecting into jobs that fit you and out of jobs in which you aren't likely to perform well.
• Facilitate the organization's accommodation to the ADA.	• Articulate and oversee organizational compliance with the ADA.	• Inform managers of any disabilities requiring accommodation.

Line Managers. To achieve its strategic objectives, selection must be aligned with the external environment, as well as with the organizational environment. The involvement of line managers helps to ensure alignment. Achieving alignment is one reason that Outback Steakhouse has two managers interview an applicant before making a hiring decision. During strategic planning, line managers identify the jobs to be filled and perhaps the jobs to be eliminated. Line managers also participate in the job analysis and competency modeling activities used to identify the behaviors needed from employees. Eventually managers evaluate employee performance, and these evaluations serve as a basis for promotions, transfers, and dismissals. In many companies, immediate supervisors have almost total control over these selection decisions.

Line managers from other units also play a role. Whether acting as formal mentors or informal sponsors, managers in other units can help to ensure that their protégé's strengths get noticed. They can also withhold information about poor performance of an employee in their unit to increase the likelihood of that person's being moved to another unit. Managers who control selection decisions should accept responsibility for making such decisions wisely.

HR Professionals. In very small organizations, there may be no HR professionals to be involved in selection decisions. But as small organizations experience rapid growth, they often turn to HR professionals to assist with selection processes. In large organizations, human resource professionals usually gather detailed information about applicants and arrange interviews between job applicants and

> " *I'd rather interview 50 people and not hire anyone than hire the wrong person.* "
>
> *Jeff Bezos*
> *Chief Executive Officer*
> *Amazon.com*

EXHIBIT 7.2 How Centralizing Selection and Placement Activities Can Benefit Job Applicants and Employers

Benefits for Applicants

✔ **Convenient:** Applicants go to only one place to apply for all jobs in the company.

✔ **Good Match to Job:** Specialists trained in staffing techniques do hiring, so the selection decisions are often better, resulting in personal success.

✔ **Fair:** People who know about the many legal regulations relevant to selection handle a major part of the hiring process, which improves legal compliance.

Benefits for Employers

✔ **Efficient:** The company can consider each applicant for a variety of jobs, which is efficient.

✔ **Effective:** Specialists trained in staffing techniques do hiring, so the selection decisions are often better, resulting in better business performance.

✔ **Consistent:** Common selection standards are used throughout the company, making it easier to maintain a workforce of consistent quality, which facilitates employee mobility between business units.

---

line managers. They may also administer standardized tests to assess the applicants' competencies and to select the most qualified applicants for managers to interview. As detailed in Exhibit 7.2, centralization of some aspects of selection benefits both the organization and the applicants.

Multibusiness companies often have several human resource departments, with each serving the unique needs of its own business. The decentralization is intended to produce a closer congruence between HR activities, such as selection, and the strategy and culture of each business unit. However, decentralization has potential disadvantages. If each division or unit operates independently, each is likely to select only from among its own employees and not from the whole workforce. Decentralization may also mean that each unit relies on its own performance appraisal system; so even if candidates from other divisions become internal applicants, they may be difficult to evaluate.

Fundamentally, the role of a company's HR professionals is to help ensure that the best candidates available are identified and placed into open positions. Besides ensuring that selection decisions are based only on relevant information, HR professionals should continually evaluate the effectiveness of the practices in use and look for ways to improve them.[6]

> ❝ *Peers need an opportunity to weigh in on a candidate. They need a chance to ask whether they want to split the pie with a particular individual.* ❞
>
> *Eric Smolenski*
> *Vice President of Human Resources*
> *Worthington Industries*

Other Employees. As organizations rely more and more on teamwork, they are likely to involve more and more employees in selecting new coworkers. Coworkers often help determine how well an applicant is likely to fit into the company's culture. At Rosenbluth International, a travel management company in Philadelphia, applicants for managerial jobs might be asked to play a game of softball with the company team or help repair a broken fence. The objective isn't to test the applicant's skill at softball or fence mending; it's to learn whether the applicant is able and willing to be nice.

Involving employees in the selection process is generally a good idea and is a practice that seems to be growing. When employees are involved in the selection of new team members, they seem to become more committed to making sure the new hires succeed. As employees become more involved in this important decision process, it's essential that they understand the process and receive training about how to make appropriate decisions. Just as managers can be influenced by many factors other than an applicant's ability to perform well, so too are employees susceptible to making decisions for the wrong reasons.

Selection within an Integrated HRM System

Exhibit 7.3 shows how selection practices fit within an integrated HRM system. The example of Cirent, a computer chip manufacturer, illustrates some of the relationships between selection practices and other aspects of the HRM system.

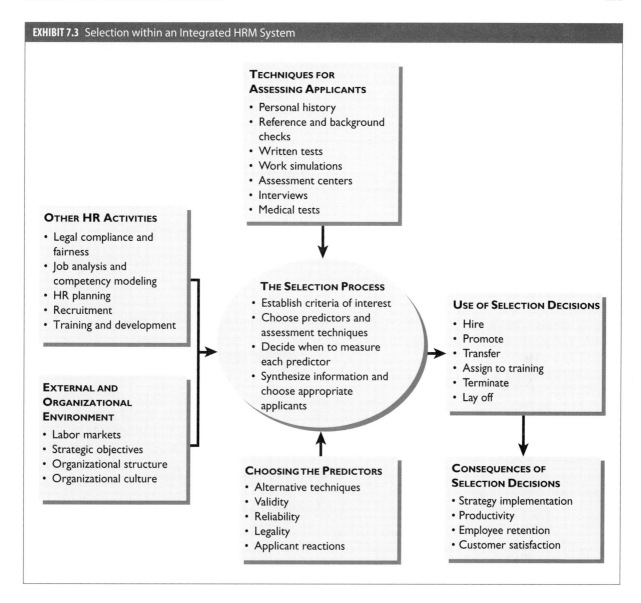

EXHIBIT 7.3 Selection within an Integrated HRM System

TECHNIQUES FOR ASSESSING APPLICANTS
- Personal history
- Reference and background checks
- Written tests
- Work simulations
- Assessment centers
- Interviews
- Medical tests

OTHER HR ACTIVITIES
- Legal compliance and fairness
- Job analysis and competency modeling
- HR planning
- Recruitment
- Training and development

EXTERNAL AND ORGANIZATIONAL ENVIRONMENT
- Labor markets
- Strategic objectives
- Organizational structure
- Organizational culture

THE SELECTION PROCESS
- Establish criteria of interest
- Choose predictors and assessment techniques
- Decide when to measure each predictor
- Synthesize information and choose appropriate applicants

USE OF SELECTION DECISIONS
- Hire
- Promote
- Transfer
- Assign to training
- Terminate
- Lay off

CHOOSING THE PREDICTORS
- Alternative techniques
- Validity
- Reliability
- Legality
- Applicant reactions

CONSEQUENCES OF SELECTION DECISIONS
- Strategy implementation
- Productivity
- Employee retention
- Customer satisfaction

Cirent was created as a joint venture between Lucent Technologies and Cirrus Logic. When Cirent built a new $600 million clean room in Orlando, Florida, it needed to fill many new jobs, and often those jobs required the skills of trained technicians. Cirent's job analysis for the new jobs indicated that the technicians would need expertise in robotics, pneumatics, vacuum technology, silicon processing, as well as interpersonal communications, writing, and teaching. Of course, they also would need to continuously learn and adapt to change.

To assess applicants for these qualifications, Cirent developed a selection procedure that included written tests to assess knowledge and cognitive ability, as well as interviews to assess interpersonal and communication skills. But Cirent encountered a problem: The company could not find the skills it needed in the local labor market. There simply weren't enough people who had these skills. To address this problem, Cirent developed a training curriculum. For the short term, the company offered a series of courses to newly hired employees, giving them time off from their jobs to attend classes. But the company's longer-term objective was to develop a larger pool of local labor from which it could select trained technicians. Toward that end, the company collaborated with a local community college. Cirent helped the college design the curriculum for an associate degree program that would give technicians the skills Cirent needed.[7]

Recruitment is also closely linked to selection. Unless the organization attracts a pool of qualified applicants, there is little need to invest time and energy in making a selection decision. A firm's choice of recruiting methods influences the quality of applicants who apply for jobs. If your firm needs creative talent with great computer skills, where should you recruit? For Semper International, IBM, and Advanced Micro Devices, the answer was Second Life. Second Life is an online virtual community where members create avatars to represent themselves and then "live" a variety of experiences.[8]

②
LEARNING GOAL

66 *We are a grow-from-within organization. When we hire somebody, we don't hire them for a position. We hire them for a career. We look not only at the position they're in today, but the position they could be in 5, 10, or 20 years down the road.* 99

*Kathleen C. Gubanich
Managing Director of Human Resources
The Vanguard Group*

DESIGNING THE SELECTION PROCESS

The selection process generally involves several steps. Designing the entire process involves making choices:

1.   What are the criteria of interest?

2.   What predictors and assessment techniques will be used?

3.   What sequence will be used to measure the predictors?

4.   How will the information collected be combined to make the selection decision?

Selection does not end when the organization makes its decision about someone to fill an open position. The candidate also makes a decision about whether to accept the new position and under what conditions. As the person enters the new position, accommodation, socialization, and training activities may all be involved. As time passes, both the organization and the new job incumbent will reevaluate their decisions.[9]

Establishing the Criteria of Interest

The outcomes that selection decisions are intended to predict are referred to as **criteria.** As described in Chapter 5, job analysis results provide descriptions of the specific tasks involved in a job. Predicting who will perform these tasks well is the goal of selection. Understanding what comprises effective performance also requires knowledge of the company's culture, values, business strategy, and structure. As described in Chapter 3, this information can be determined by conducting an organizational analysis. Ideally, all selection decisions are guided by rigorous job and organizational analyses.

Often, the primary criteria of interest are job performance and organizational citizenship. For a corporate loan assistant, speed and accuracy in documenting decisions would probably be important job performance criteria, and a willingness to help out colleagues during times of work overload would be an example of good organizational citizenship. Increasingly, employers also consider other criteria. As described in Chapter 6, organizations seeking to lower their voluntary turnover rates may use the selection process as one tool for achieving that objective. In such situations, turnover is a criterion for selection. Employers also are looking for employees who will adapt quickly in an organization that is continually changing.[10] Companies like W. L. Gore, the makers of Gore-Tex®, and Patagonia, which makes sports apparel, seek to hire people who will fit into the corporate culture and embrace the philosophy of the organization.

66 *When people are not successful, more times than not it's because of the inability to work effectively within the culture as much as it is a lack of technical skills.* 99

*Jackie Brinton (no job title—no one at the company has one)
W. L. Gore & Associates*

Choosing the Predictors and Assessment Techniques

When making selection decisions, employers are making predictions about how people will perform in the future, how long they are likely to stay, whether they will be good organizational citizens, and so on. This is why *the various pieces of information used to make selection decisions are referred to as* **predictors.** Generally, organizations assess skill, ability, knowledge, personality, and behavioral styles, and they use these as predictors—that is, they use competencies as predictors.[11]

The characteristics needed in an employee depend on the type of work as well as the work setting. Different characteristics are useful for predicting the performance of nurses, waiters, accountants, and retail clerks, for example. Within jobs, different characteristics may be useful for predicting the performance of a person who works in relative isolation versus someone working in a team. For people who work alone, technical skills and abilities are likely to be the most useful predictors. The performance of people who work in teams is likely to also be predicted by personality and interpersonal skills.[12]

In work teams, the personality traits of *agreeableness* and *conscientiousness* seem to be especially important.[13] People with agreeable personalities seek to find areas of common understanding with the members of the team. When areas of agreement are known, team members may also be able to accept their differences relatively easily. People who are conscientious tend to stay focused on the task and seem to be good at organizing and coordinating activities.

At Worthington Industries, a steel company, the personalities of new team members are evaluated by the employees already on the team. New hires must have the necessary skills to get a job. But when hired, they are put on probation for 90 days. Their teammates use this probation period to evaluate the new hire's personality and teamwork competencies, and *they* decide whether the new hire is allowed to stay on the team.[14]

Personalities are difficult to change, and interpersonal skills develop slowly over time. For these reasons, team-based organizations often prefer to hire people who already have such skills. To assess such skills, some team-based organizations use very intensive and sophisticated selection procedures when hiring new employees. GE's airline engine plant in Durham, North Carolina, illustrates this point. When the plant was started, management decided that all job candidates would have to be FAA-certified mechanics. FAA certification requires two years of training and is something that no other GE plant requires of all job candidates. First-rate mechanical skills are just one of the 11 areas that job applicants must possess to get a job. Others include helping skills, teamwork, communication, coaching, and flexibility. As one current employee remembers, the interview process—lasting eight hours—was especially grueling: "That was one heck of an experience. I talked to five different people. I participated in three group activities with job candidates. I even had to do a presentation: I had 15 minutes to prepare a 5-minute presentation." Through these activities, GE assessed the teamwork and communication competencies that these mechanics would have to rely on day in and day out in doing their new jobs.

Paying attention to predictors of effective teamwork pays off even for jobs involving very high levels of technical skill. A study of cardiac surgery teams found that the process used to select members of the team predicted the team's subsequent performance. When team members participated more in the selection of new members, and when they took both teamwork competency and technical skills into account, cardiac surgery teams were more effective.[15]

Ranked by *Business Week* as the Number 1 Best Place to Launch a Career, success at Walt Disney's theme parks requires the right personality

Selecting the Walt Disney Cast

The next time you visit Walt Disney World in Florida or Disneyland in California, consider the complexity of finding more than 25,000 people needed to fill more than 1,000 types of jobs that make the entertainment complexes so effective. With over 50 million visitors to Disney World and Disneyland yearly, the company is a major player in the entertainment business.

The managers and employees of the Walt Disney Company view themselves as members of a team whose job is to produce a very large show. This is reflected in how they speak of themselves, their activities, and the process of selecting new members. Eager applicants to the firm are cast for a role, rather than hired for a job. Rather than being employees, applicants who join the firm become cast members in a major entertainment production. A casting director interviews applicants.

For hourly jobs, a casting director spends about 10 minutes interviewing every applicant. The interviewer's (casting director's) major objective is to evaluate the applicant's ability to adapt to the firm's very strong culture. Does the applicant understand and accept the fact that Disney has strict grooming requirements (no facial hair for men, little makeup for women)? Is the applicant willing to work on holidays—even ones that almost everyone else has off? After the first screening, the remaining applicants are assessed as they interact with each other and judged as to how well they might fit with the show. Current employees who are experts in their roles participate in this entire process: They assess applicants' behaviors and attitudes while providing firsthand information about the role the successful applicant will have in the production.

Once people join the firm, they become cast members whose inputs and talents are highly valued by the Walt Disney Company. The company fills 60 to 80% of its managerial positions by promoting existing cast members. In addition, the firm draws on suggested referrals from current cast members for help in hiring the 1,500 to 2,000 temporary employees required during particularly busy periods: Easter, Christmas, and summers.

and interpersonal skills to fit the company's highly collaborative culture. To select people to work in their theme parks, Walt Disney's employees judge the personalities of applicants and assess their ability to fit into the Disney culture.[16]

FAST FACT

A national survey of employers revealed that 66% screened applicants by grade point average (GPA).

Assessment Techniques. For each predictor of interest—each competency, personality characteristic, and the like—many different techniques can be used to assess applicants. Information can be obtained from application forms, resumes, reference checks, written tests, interviews, physical examinations, and other measurement approaches. Thus, an important step in designing a selection practice is choosing how to measure the predictors of interest. Many employers use a grade point average from high school or college as a predictor of future job performance. Usually, however, this information is just one of several items considered.[17] Exhibit 7.4 illustrates how a company might use several different techniques to capture all the information it wishes to use in selecting a corporate loan assistant. We describe several of these techniques in more detail later in the chapter.

Valid Predictors. A great deal of information often *can* be gathered and used to evaluate candidates; whether that information *should* be gathered and used depends on the likelihood that it will lead to better selection decisions. Put simply, information that predicts the criteria of concern should be used, and information that doesn't predict these outcomes should be avoided. The term

EXHIBIT 7.4 Possible Assessment Techniques for Several Competencies

Corporate Loan Assistant

Assessment Techniques

Code	Competencies	Used to Rank?	SAF	WKT	WS	PCD	SPI	DMI	BI/REF	PAF
MA	1. Communication	Yes	X				X	X	X	X
MQ	2. Math		X		X					
MQ	3. Writing		X							X
MQ	4. Reading		X		X					X
MQ	5. Researching		X							
MQ	6. Organizing	Yes	X							X
MQ	7. Listening	Yes	X				X			X
MQ	8. Social skills		X				X			X
MQ	9. Sales	Yes								X
MQ	10. Interpreting	Yes					X			
WT	11. Bank policy									
WT	12. Bank services	Yes	X	X				X		X
MT	13. Computer				X					

MQ = Minimum Qualification
MT = May Train for this, but preference may be given to those who possess this competency
MA = May Accommodate for lack of this, within reason
WT = Will Train for this; not evaluated in the selection process
SAF = Supplemental Application Form
WKT = Written Knowledge Test
WS = Work Sample
PCD = Physical Capability Demonstration
SPI = Structured Panel Interview
DMI = Departmental Manager Interview
BI/REF = Background Investigation/Reference Check
PAF = Performance Appraisal Form (internal hires only)

validity *refers to the usefulness of information for predicting job applicants' job-related and organizational outcomes.*

High validity is present when low predictor scores translate into low scores on the specified criteria and when high predictor scores translate into high scores on the criteria. For most predictors, validity depends on what you want to predict. A personality test that assesses gregariousness might be valid for predicting performance as a fund-raiser for the city ballet company, but it's probably useless for predicting performance as a highway landscape designer.

How can you be sure that a given measure is valid for the situation of interest? Three basic strategies are used to ascertain whether inferences based on predictor scores will be valid:

1. Content validation.
2. Criterion-related validation.
3. Validity generalization.

All these strategies begin with job and organizational analyses. Then the three strategies diverge.

Content validation *involves using job analysis or competency modeling results to build a rational argument for why a predictor should be useful.* In the simplest case, an expert consults the results of a competency modeling study and makes judgments about which predictors are likely to be associated with the competencies that are identified as important. Suppose competency modeling reveals that senior managers should be able to effectively manage relationships with the firm's strategic partners—suppliers, customers, members of an alliance network, and others. The job analyst might conclude that it would be logical to assess applicants' past experience in managing such relationships. This basic content validation strategy can be substantially improved by involving a widened range of people in judging whether a predictor is likely to be useful. Although such judgments are necessarily subjective, confidence is increased when several experts agree that a particular predictor is likely to be useful. When an organization is creating new jobs and experiencing major organizational change, a content validation strategy may be the only feasible validation approach.

Criterion-related validation *uses statistical data to establish a relationship between predictor scores and outcome criteria.* It involves assessing people in terms of the predictor and also assessing actual outcomes, such as performance in the job. If a ballet company wanted to decide whether gregarious people are better fund-raisers, it could ask all its current fund-raisers to take a personality test (the predictor). Then it could correlate the fund-raisers' scores on gregariousness with their performance as fund-raisers (criteria). If gregariousness and fundraising performance were correlated, criterion-related validity would be established.

Criterion-related validity replaces judgments about which predictors are the most useful with quantitative analyses that demonstrate the predictive usefulness of criteria. CapOne, a credit card and financial services firm, used criterion-related validity to establish the usefulness of the online tests it uses to select call center representatives. After choosing the test to be given and developing the online technology to be used, the company had their current call center reps take the tests. Then they developed statistical models to show that the test results were correlated with the performance of reps currently in the job. In this example, the criteria used included sales rates and dollars collected per hour. The predictors included scores on math tests and scores on a simulated over-the-phone interaction, among other things.[18]

Validity generalization *assumes that the results of criterion-related validity studies conducted in other companies can be generalized to the situation in your company.* This is a relatively new approach that has been gaining acceptance during the past decade and may continue to gain popularity in the twenty-first century.[19] To illustrate, suppose you are the HR professional at the ballet company referred to earlier. You know that 10 other institutions of the cultural arts have already shown that gregarious people tend to be more successful fund-raisers. Even if the correlation between this personality characteristic and fund-raising performance was not strong in all those organizations, and even if the type of fund-raising was quite different, you might nevertheless conclude that gregariousness is likely to be a valid predictor of fund-raising success for your ballet company. If you accept this conclusion, then your company should evaluate gregariousness and use it as a criterion for selecting people whose roles include fund-raising.[20]

Validity generalization analyses have been conducted for a large number of applicant characteristics that an employer might assess during the selection process. The results indicate that each of the techniques described in this chapter *can* be

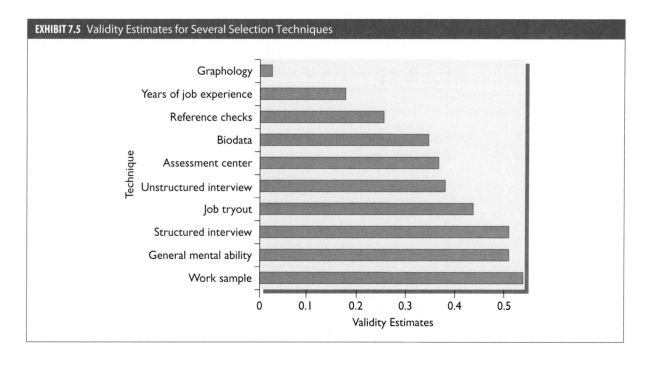

EXHIBIT 7.5 Validity Estimates for Several Selection Techniques

effective predictors of performance across a variety of jobs.[21] Exhibit 7.5 shows the results of validity generalization estimates for several commonly used selection procedures.[22] Note that these estimates describe the average relationship between the selection procedure and performance in a variety of jobs.

Each validation strategy has advantages and disadvantages. The criterion-related strategy has the advantage of documenting empirically that a predictor is correlated with the criteria of interest in a particular job in a particular organization. CapOne can be very sure that its new automated selection tests will help the company select better call center reps. However, this strategy can be costly and is not applicable for jobs that have only a few incumbents (e.g., CEO). The content validation strategy is more feasible, but it also depends more on subjective judgment. Finally, validity generalization is a low-cost strategy, but you won't know whether results from other organizations will hold in your organization until after you make a selection decision. Furthermore, whereas the legal credibility of the other strategies is well established, validity generalization has not been sufficiently tested in the courts. Ultimately, employers must weigh the costs and benefits of each approach to establishing the validity of the predictors to be used in making selection decisions.

Reliable Predictors. Each bit of information contributes to the final selection decision; so the quality of information used determines the quality of the final outcome. One aspect of information quality that's especially important is reliability. The **reliability** *of a predictor (e.g., an interview, a mathematical reasoning test, or a work simulation) is the degree to which it yields dependable, consistent results.* Unreliable predictors produce different results depending on the circumstances. Different circumstances could include having different people administer and score the measure (e.g., having several interviewers screen applicants) or administering the measure while different events are occurring (e.g., giving a mathematical reasoning test in August versus during the week immediately after everyone files a tax return). When purchasing a test of any sort, information about reliability should be requested. Reputable test developers will be able to demonstrate that they have performed and documented all the steps needed to create a reliable and valid test.[23]

Deciding When to Measure Each Predictor

Often, selection decisions progress through several steps, with each progression to a new step based on some information about how the candidate scored in the prior step. Because more people go through the earlier steps, employers generally try to use less expensive procedures early in the process. This reduces the costs of selection because fewer applicants go through the more expensive stages of the process. Clearly, each piece of information used throughout this process has the potential to determine the final outcome. Perhaps less clearly, information used early in the process is, in effect, weighted the most heavily: Applicants who fail to do well early in the process fail by default on all the later steps.

Synthesizing Information to Choose Appropriate Candidates

Closely related to the sequencing of steps in the selection process is the decision about how to combine all the information gathered. A large amount of information of many types—some of it easily quantified and some of it very "soft"—may be available for a large number of applicants. To complicate things further, some applicants might be considered simultaneously for more than one job opening. Combining and synthesizing all available information to yield a yes-or-no decision for each possible applicant–job match can be a fairly complex task. Alternative approaches to combining and synthesizing information might lead to very different final decisions, so this step takes on great significance for both applicants and the organization. When multiple predictors are used, the information can be combined using three approaches:

1. Multiple hurdles.
2. Compensatory.
3. Combined.

Multiple Hurdles. In the **multiple-hurdles approach**, *an applicant must exceed fixed levels of proficiency on all the predictors to be accepted.* A higher-than-necessary score on one predictor doesn't compensate for a low score on another predictor. This approach assumes that some skills or competencies are essential; so if an applicant does not have the needed level of competency, the person simply cannot be successful on the job.

Compensatory. For jobs that do not have absolute requirements, the compensatory approach is commonly used. With the **compensatory approach**, *a high score on one predictor can compensate for a low score on another predictor.* For example, the excellent math skills of an applicant for the job of corporate loan officer may compensate for the person's weak sales skills. When hiring engineers to work in nuclear power plants, educational qualifications may offset lack of experience.[24] With a compensatory approach, no selection decisions are made until the entire process is completed. Then a composite index that considers performance on all predictors is developed.

Combined. Many organizations combine the multiple-hurdles and compensatory approaches. With the **combined approach,** *the employer first screens out everyone who does not meet one or more specific requirements, then uses a compensatory approach in comparing the applicants who have passed the required hurdle.* Kinko's, the copy shop, uses a combined approach. The first hurdle assesses basic experience and availability using a short screening test, which is completed by calling a toll-free number and answering some simple questions using automated procedures. Applicants who pass this hurdle enter a second phase, in which they are asked questions designed to assess their fit with Kinko's culture and business strategy. This is also done using automated telephone technology. Applicants who make it past the second hurdle (about 50%) are invited for interviews. The results of interviews and other selection information are then combined into a composite score that determines the final selection decision.[25]

Companies that are trying to enhance their competitiveness by improving quality seem to agree that the employees at the front line are key to improving and delivering quality. Thus, they devote considerable time and effort to selecting frontline production workers. In high-quality manufacturing environments, work is organized around teams; so selecting people who can be effective as team players is essential. The same is true in many service organizations, where employees work in teams that serve specific customers. To assess these competencies, some organizations use very sophisticated selection procedures, like the one shown in Exhibit 7.6. In this exhibit, each box

FAST FACT

Automated online testing of applicants has quickly become popular due to its convenience and low cost. But verifying who actually takes an online test remains difficult.

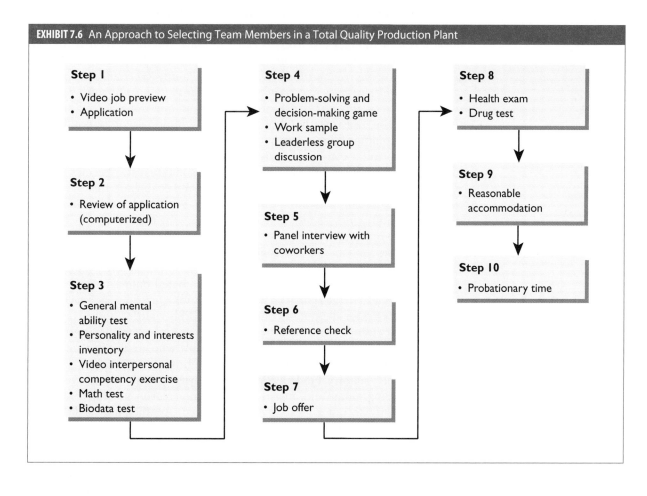

EXHIBIT 7.6 An Approach to Selecting Team Members in a Total Quality Production Plant

Step 1
- Video job preview
- Application

Step 2
- Review of application (computerized)

Step 3
- General mental ability test
- Personality and interests inventory
- Video interpersonal competency exercise
- Math test
- Biodata test

Step 4
- Problem-solving and decision-making game
- Work sample
- Leaderless group discussion

Step 5
- Panel interview with coworkers

Step 6
- Reference check

Step 7
- Job offer

Step 8
- Health exam
- Drug test

Step 9
- Reasonable accommodation

Step 10
- Probationary time

represents one step in a series of hurdles. A compensatory approach is used to combine the information within each step and decide whether to involve the applicant in the next step.

LEARNING GOAL

TECHNIQUES FOR ASSESSING JOB APPLICANTS

Clearly, employers have many techniques available to them for making selection decisions.[26] Next we describe some of the most commonly used techniques in more detail.

Personal History Assessments

Premised on the assumption that past behavior is a good predictor of future performance, personal history assessments seek information about the applicant's background. Application blanks and biodata tests are two commonly used methods of assessing personal histories.

Application Blank. An **application blank** *is usually a short form that asks applicants to provide basic information about educational achievements and work experience.* It is often the first hurdle applicants must clear. Both educational and experience requirements may be useful in selecting individuals for high-level, complex jobs that cannot be easily learned.[27] Application blanks may also request the applicant's willingness to work split shifts, work on weekends, or work alone. If the job requires split-shift work, items that inquire about shift preferences tend to be good predictors of turnover.[28]

Biodata Test. A **biodata test** *asks autobiographical questions related to such subjects as extracurricular activities (e.g., "Over the past five years, how much have you enjoyed outdoor recreation?"), family experiences as a child, and recent and current work activities (e.g., "How long were you employed in your most recent job?").* Responses to these questions are empirically keyed based on research that usually involves hundreds of respondents.[29] Biodata information alone can be quite effective as a predictor of overall performance, and it can also be effective when used in combination with an interview, a general mental ability test, or a personality test.[30] Besides overall performance, other criteria that biodata can predict include turnover, customer service, coping with stress, learning rate, teamwork, and promotability.[31] The validity of these tests is a major reason why they tend to be used in the insurance industry.[32]

Google uses biodata to select engineers and sales representatives. The company receives applications from more than 100,000 people every month. To sort out applicants to hire, Google uses an automated online survey that assesses biographical details going back to high school. Questions include, "Have you ever set a regional-, state-, country-, or world-record?" and "Have you ever started a club or recreational group?" In the longer term, Google hopes that questions like these will help them hire people who are not just smart but also likely to fit the entrepreneurial company culture.[33]

Despite their validity, biodata tests have a downside: Applicants often react to them as being unfair and invasive.[34] The major reason for this reaction is that some items do not appear to be job related. Another downside is that these tests often are quite long, frequently including 200–300 items. Finally, experts must design these tests to ensure that they do not include items that create legal risks.

Background Verification and Reference Checks

The information obtained from application blanks, interviews, and biodata tests has proven to be useful in a variety of settings. But increasingly, employers question the accuracy of background information supplied by applicants. To supplement information provided by applicants, many employers hire outside vendors to conduct applicant screening.[35] At a minimum, however, employers should always conduct reference checks.

Background Verification. ADP Screening and Selection Services performs millions of background checks for employers. Their experience is that about 40% of applicants lie about their work histories and educational backgrounds, and about 20% present false credentials and licenses. Nationwide, an estimated 30% of job applicants make material misrepresentations on their resumes.[36] Distortions vary from a wrong starting date for a prior job to inflated college grades to actual lies involving degrees, types of jobs, and former employers. The most common distortions relate to the length of employment and previous salary. Exhibit 7.7 shows that the problem is widespread across a number of different industries.

Reference Checks. The large numbers of job applicants who falsify their qualifications and misrepresent their past are one reason employers have stepped up efforts to check references thoroughly. Another reason is that employers have a legal duty not to hire an unfit individual who poses a threat of harm to others. If an employer hires someone who injures others and the employer did not make an adequate effort to discover relevant facts about the applicant, the employer may be found guilty of negligent hiring. Finally, a third reason to check references and conduct background checks is to avoid bad publicity. It can be embarrassing when a company's top executives are found to have lied about their

FAST FACT

Within the first year of operation, the Transportation Security Administration discovered that it had inadvertently hired 1,208 airport security screeners with criminal backgrounds.

FAST FACT

American Eagle hired M. P. Hillis as a pilot without checking his job reference. When his plane crashed four years later, killing him and 14 others, an investigation revealed a record of poor performance at his previous employer.

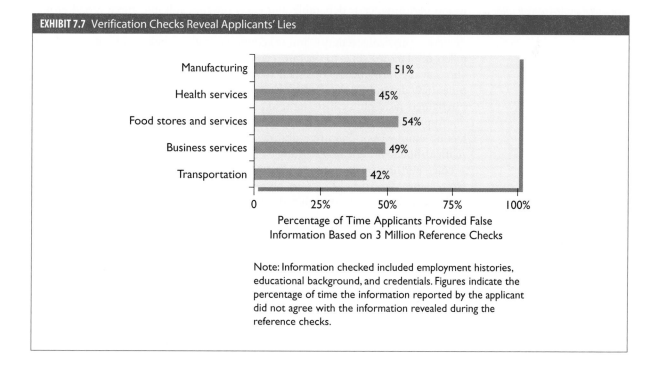

EXHIBIT 7.7 Verification Checks Reveal Applicants' Lies

Manufacturing 51%
Health services 45%
Food stores and services 54%
Business services 49%
Transportation 42%

Percentage of Time Applicants Provided False Information Based on 3 Million Reference Checks

Note: Information checked included employment histories, educational background, and credentials. Figures indicate the percentage of time the information reported by the applicant did not agree with the information revealed during the reference checks.

credentials, as Ron Zarrella did. After he was hired as CEO of Bausch & Lomb, the company discovered Zarrella did not posses the MBA he said he had earned. A simple phone call could have determined that fact and prevented the negative image the company suffered when the press later reported the lie.

Unfortunately, the potential for defamation of character suits has made getting information from past employers more and more difficult. Reference checks of an applicant's prior employment record aren't an infringement on privacy if the information provided relates specifically to work behavior and to the reasons for leaving a previous job. Nevertheless, to avoid possible lawsuits, many employers strictly limit the type of information they provide about former employees.[37]

Even if applicants tell the truth when they apply for a position, screening may reveal information that eliminates them from further consideration. Increasingly, applicant screening includes doing an electronic search for information on the Internet. Such searches can locate pictures, opinions expressed on a blog, news stories, and so on. Execunet is a firm that conducts electronic screening for executive applicants. Their research indicates that about 35% of firms that used the Internet for electronic screening had eliminated some candidates based on "Internet dirt" found online.[38]

Written Tests

Due to the widespread use of computer testing technology, the term *written test* is becoming outdated. Nevertheless, it continues to be used to describe tests that originally involved traditional paper-and-pencil testing measures. The most common types of written tests measure ability and personality.

Ability. An **ability test** *measures the potential of an individual to perform, given the opportunity.* Widely used in the United States and Europe since the turn of the twentieth century, numerous studies document the usefulness of such tests for a wide variety of jobs.[39] The number of distinct abilities of potential relevance to job performance is debatable, but generally they fall into three broad groupings: (1) psychomotor (perceptual speed and accuracy), (2) physical (e.g., manual dexterity, physical strength), and (3) cognitive (e.g., verbal, quantitative).[40] Bank tellers need motor skills to operate a computer and finger dexterity to manipulate currency. Performance in jobs such as wine taster, coffee bean selector, and piano tuner may depend on the acuity of a person's senses, such as vision and hearing. Firefighters need physical strength to perform their jobs effectively.

Approximately 30% of employers use tests of cognitive abilities when selecting employees. Cognitive abilities include verbal comprehension, mathematical fluency, logical reasoning, memory, and many others. These abilities predict performance in many jobs. Nevertheless, many employers shy away from using cognitive ability tests because they create adverse impact. When deciding whether to use cognitive ability tests, employers must weigh their value in predicting job performance against the fact that they are very likely to have an adverse impact on some ethnic groups.[41]

Knowledge. A **knowledge test** *assesses what a person knows at the time of taking the test.* There is no attempt to assess the applicant's future potential; that is, a knowledge test can inform employers about what applicants know, but not what they are likely to learn or learn quickly in the future. Knowledge tests can be useful for jobs that require specialized or technical knowledge that takes a long time to acquire. For example, selection practices for hiring and promoting law enforcement officers usually include a test for knowledge about laws and the appropriate means for enforcing laws.

Personality. A **personality test** *assesses the unique blend of characteristics that define an individual and determine her or his pattern of interactions with the environment.* A variety of psychological assessment tools can be used to measure personality. Written tests are the most common.[42]

Most people believe that personality plays an important role in job success or failure, but for many years U.S. employers shied away from measuring it, largely because research indicated that personality seldom predicted performance. This early conclusion may have been inaccurate. Recent advances in the academic community's understanding of the nature of personality suggest that employers may have abandoned personality measures too early. The most significant advance has been the realization that most aspects of personality can be captured using only a few basic dimensions. Often referred to as the Big Five, these are

1. Extraversion (sociable, talkative, assertive).

2. Agreeableness (good-natured, cooperative, trusting).

3. Conscientiousness (responsible, dependable, persistent, achievement-oriented).

4. Emotional stability (not being overly tense, insecure, or nervous).

5. Openness to experience (imaginative, artistically sensitive, intellectual).[43]

In general, conscientious people perform better, and this seems to hold true even more in managerial jobs characterized by high levels of autonomy. Not surprisingly, extraversion is somewhat predictive of performance in jobs that involve social interaction, such as sales and management, but these linkages are actually not very strong.[44]

Personality tests are helpful, but employers must choose the tests they use carefully. One popular personality test—The Minnesota Multiphasic Personality Inventory (MMPI)—was used by Rent-a-Center, Inc. to evaluate applicants for promotion. The MMPI was developed to measure psychological characteristics that are related to mental illnesses. It was not designed to predict job performance. In a court case, Rent-a-Center's use of the MMPI was considered problematic in part because it was not clear how the test results could be used to evaluate future job performance.[45]

Integrity Tests. Personal integrity (honesty) is another personality characteristic that's attracting a lot of attention among employers. Employee theft is often cited as a primary reason for small business failures, with some estimates suggesting it's the cause of up to 30% of all failures and bankruptcies. In retailing, inventory shrinkage (unexplained losses in cash, tools, merchandise, and supplies) is a major problem, requiring companies to invest large amounts in security systems. In a survey of 9,000 employees by the Justice Department, one-third admitted to stealing from their employers.

White-collar crime involving millions of dollars regularly makes the news. Discovering that an executive has integrity problems can cost a company millions. When the CEO of Bausch & Lomb was found to have not earned an MBA from New York University as he had claimed, shares in the company dropped 3%.[46] Problems of this scope and magnitude help to explain why employers administer millions of integrity tests annually.[47]

Assessment of the Twenty-First-Century Workforce

The Conference Board is an organization that creates and disseminates knowledge about management for the purpose of helping employers improve the performance of their organizations and better serve society. In 2006, it conducted a large-scale study to determine the skills and abilities that employers were looking for when hiring new employees for entry-level jobs. A sample of 431 employers representing a workforce of more than 2 million U.S. employees provided their views. One type of applied skill included in the study was ethics/social responsibility. Applicants with this skill demonstrate integrity and ethical behavior, and act responsibly with the interests of the larger community in mind. How important is this skill? Exhibit A shows the percentage of employers who indicated that ethics/social responsibility is important to them.

Ron Halligan of Great River Health Systems explained what his organization is looking for when screening for ethical people: "The vast majority of housekeepers may never come in direct contact with patients, but they have to understand that the patient rooms they are cleaning have to be absolutely infection-free… the young people we hire have to understand that helping patients is a way of life here." In this health care setting, cleanliness may mean the difference between life and death for a patient. The employer must be able to trust housekeepers to have the personal integrity to put patients' health first under all circumstances and never to cut corners in their work.

Clearly, employers want to select new hires who will behave ethically. Is this a difficult problem for them? The study revealed that employers believe many people in the workforce are "deficient" in this aspect. Exhibit B summarizes these results from the study.

These levels of deficiency in ethics/social responsibility are worrisome for employers, and the problem may be worse in the future. When asked whether the importance of ethical and social responsibly is expected to increase in importance over the next five years, 64% of employers said yes.

EXHIBIT A

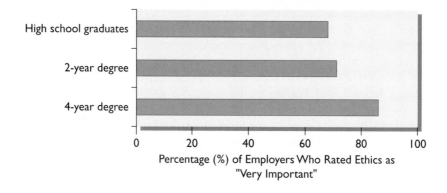

Percentage (%) of Employers Who Rated Ethics as "Very Important"

EXHIBIT B

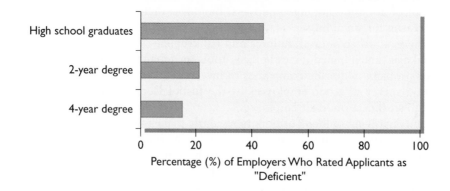

Percentage (%) of Employers Who Rated Applicants as "Deficient"

A recent study by The Conference Board revealed that employers view ethical and socially responsible behavior as among the most important competencies needed in employees. The feature "Managing Ethics: Assessment of the Twenty-First-Century Workforce" describes some of the results from a national study of employers' views.[48]

Work Simulations

Work simulations *(also referred to as work samples) require applicants to perform activities similar to those required on the job under structured "testing" conditions.* For example, applicants for the job of retail associate at a department store might be asked to watch a videotape that shows a typical customer behavior and then role-play how they would handle the situation. Interactive video assessments of conflict resolution skills can be used to predict the performance of managers.[49]

Work simulations are very difficult to fake and they are good predictors of job performance, performance in training programs, and career advancement. They tend to be more valid than other types of selection devices, and they are less likely to result in unfair discrimination. However, they can be expensive to develop; so they may not be cost-effective unless large numbers of applicants are to be examined. The total price of work simulations is lower if they're placed at the end of a selection process, when the number of applicants tested has been reduced.[50]

Assessment Centers

Assessment centers *evaluate how well applicants or current employees might perform in a managerial or higher-level position.* Some organizations use assessment centers only for developmental purposes. That is, they assess employees' strengths and weaknesses and then provide feedback to employees for use in creating their personal career development plans. When assessment centers are used only for developmental purposes, no selection decision is involved. When they are used for selection purposes, the objective is to rank-order applicants and choose the best for placement in a new job.

Assessment centers usually involve 6 to 12 attendees, although they can involve more. Customarily, they're conducted off the premises for one to three days. Usually managers from throughout the organization are trained to assess the employees or job applicants. Increasingly, team members who will work with new hires also assess the participants.[51] Assessment centers can be particularly effective for selecting team-oriented candidates, and their use grows each year.[52]

At a typical assessment center, candidates are evaluated using a wide range of techniques. One activity, the in-basket exercise, presents applicants with a variety of situations and problems that they must prioritize and to which they must decide how to respond. To simulate a typical day, the in-basket exercise may be performed under time pressure. Business games are another way to simulate organizational situations. Business games are living cases that require individuals to play assigned roles, make decisions, and deal with the consequences of those decisions. Usually, business games involve several people and several rounds of play, which unfold over several hours or days.

In a leaderless group discussion, a group of individuals is asked to discuss a topic for a given period of time. For example, participants might each be asked to make a five-minute oral presentation about the qualifications of a candidate for promotion and to defend their nomination in a group discussion with several other participants. Participants may be rated on their selling ability, oral communication skill, self-confidence, energy level, interpersonal competency, aggressiveness, and tolerance for stress.

FAST FACT

When hiring managers for its stores in China, McDonald's requires potential management candidates to work in a restaurant for three days before a final selection decision is made.

FAST FACT

Assessment centers were developed in the 1950s at AT&T under the direction of Doug Bray. By the time he retired, about 200,000 AT&T employees had been assessed.

" *Teams spend a lot of energy on the hiring process, and they want the new person to succeed.* "

Deborah Harrington-Mackin
President
New Directions Corporate
Consulting Group

Assessment centers appear to work because they reflect the actual job environment and measure performance on multiple job dimensions. Although they are expensive to operate, the cost seems to be justified. The annual productivity gains that are realized by selecting managers through assessment centers average well above the administrative costs.[53] In addition, assessment centers appear to be nondiscriminatory and valid across cultures.[54]

Interviews

The job interview is the most widely used procedure for determining who gets a job offer. Interviews that follow sound procedures can be quite useful. Poorly conducted interviews may yield very little useful information and may even damage the organization's image.

Candidates for flight attendant jobs at Southwest Airlines are first interviewed by a panel of representatives from the People Department and the Inflight Department. Before the selection process is finished, they also have one-on-one interviews with a recruiter, a supervisor from the hiring department, and a peer. Southwest Airlines' interview process was developed in collaboration with a consulting firm that specializes in designing sound selection practices. Thus, the procedures at Southwest Airlines adhere to the basic principles of good interview design: structured questions, a focus on behavior, systematic scoring, multiple interviewers, and interviewer training.[55]

Structure. In an **unstructured job interview**, *the interviewer merely prepares a list of possible topics to cover and, depending on how the conversation proceeds, asks or does not ask questions about them.* Although this provides for flexibility, the resulting digressions, discontinuity, and lack of focus may be frustrating to the interviewer and interviewee. Unstructured interviews provide unreliable results and generally have low validity.

In a **structured job interview**, *all the applicants are asked the same questions in the same order.* Usually, the interviewer has a prepared guide that suggests which types of answers are considered good or poor. Although structuring the interview restricts the topics that can be covered, it ensures that the same information is collected on all candidates.[56] In a semistructured job interview, the same questions are asked of all candidates and responses are recorded, but the interviewer also asks follow-up questions to probe specific areas in depth. In general, structured and semistructured interviews are more valid than unstructured interviews.[57] Structured interviews also appear to be less likely to unfairly discriminate against members of ethnic minority groups.[58]

Focus on Behavior. A **behavioral job interview** *uses a structured or semistructured approach to asking questions that focus on behavior.* There are two basic approaches to asking behavioral questions.[59] One popular approach is to ask the candidate to describe specific instances of past behavior that reflect a competency for which the employer is looking. The assumption behind this approach is that past behavior is the best predictor of future behavior—an assumption that is well supported by research.

CORE is a consulting firm that specializes in the design and implementation of human resource systems. When designing interview questions for clients to use in their selection process, CORE writes questions that focus the interview on past job-related behavior. Based on job analyses conducted in many different companies, CORE has identified relationship building as one of several important competencies required of managers. Exhibit 7.8 lists

---

EXHIBIT 7.8 Examples of Questions to Use in a Structured Interview

Competency Being Assessed: Relationship Building

Interview Questions Designed to Focus on Behavioral Descriptions

1. Sketch out two or three key strengths you have in dealing with people. Can you illustrate the first strength with a recent example? [Repeat same probes for other strengths.]

   Probes:
   - When did this example take place?
   - What possible negative outcomes were avoided by the way you handled this incident?
   - How often has this situation arisen?
   - What happened the next time this came up?

2. Tell me about a time when you effectively used your people skills to solve a customer problem.

   Probes:
   - When did this take place?
   - What did the customer say?
   - What did you say in response?
   - How did the customer react?
   - Was the customer satisfied?

3. Maintaining a network of personal contacts helps a manager keep on top of developments. Describe some of your most useful personal contacts.

   Probes:
   - Tell me about a time when a personal contact helped you solve a problem or avoid a major blunder.
   - How did you develop the contact in the first place?
   - What did you do to obtain the useful information from your contact?
   - When was the next time this contact was useful?
   - What was the situation at that time?
   - How often in the past six months have personal contacts been useful to you?

---

some of the types of questions CORE designed to assess an applicant's competency in the area of relationship building.[60]

An alternative approach to conducting behavioral interviews is to pose hypothetical situations that might arise on the job. Interviewees are then asked to describe or role-play what they would do. This approach assumes that behavior on the job can be predicted by an applicant's intentions; this assumption is also supported by research. Questions that ask about behavioral intentions are more appropriate when applicants do not have experience in a job like the one they have applied for. For example, newly promoted managers usually face a variety of new situations associated with coaching, providing performance feedback, discipline, dismissals, and other areas of interaction with people.[61]

Systematic Scoring. Job interviews vary in the degree to which results are scored. At one extreme, an interviewer merely listens to responses, forms an impression, and makes a decision. Alternatively, raters may use a detailed scoring key to score the response to each question. Systematic scoring procedures improve the reliability and validity of interviews because all applicants are evaluated against the same criteria, regardless of who conducts the interview.

Multiple Interviewers. Typically, interviewers meet with applicants one person at a time. This is true around the world, as shown in Exhibit 7.9.[62] But one-on-one meetings are time-consuming, and the interviewer's impressions vary, depending on what was discussed. These problems can be overcome by using a panel interview, in which several individuals (typically two, three, or four) simultaneously interview one applicant. Because all interviewers hear the same responses, panel interviews produce more consistent results. They may also be less susceptible to the biases and prejudices of the interviewers, especially if panel members come

> *If you're being considered as a pilot, one of your interviews is with a pilot. The interviewers keep notes and the interview is scored. The pilot, along with the recruiter and someone from the line leadership, all put their scores together and, as a group, decide if a person is going to be hired or take the next step. Our posture in this is to help [employees] get people [they] would want to work with.*
>
> Vincent Stabile
> Vice President of People
> JetBlue Airways

from diverse backgrounds.[63] If applicants are to be interviewed by more than one person anyway, panel interviewing can be efficient, reliable, and cost-effective.[64]

Trained Interviewers. Left on their own, interviewers tend to form their impressions based on whatever information is important or salient to them. One interviewer might reject an applicant for being "too aggressive," whereas another might choose the applicant as being appropriately "assertive." In fact, an interviewer's recommendations about whether to hire an applicant are strongly influenced by how much the interviewer likes the applicant and by the applicant's physical attractiveness.[65] Consequently, interviewers must be trained to use job-relevant information and to apply it consistently across applicants.[66] According to a study of 1,302 large organizations, about two-thirds offer formal interview training to hiring managers.[67]

For companies that conduct video interviews, training is especially important because video interviews may be stored and looked at again in the future. Even if the company does not keep a copy, job applicants may make an electronic copy. If a dispute later arises about the hiring decision, such a video could be used as evidence in court.[68]

Medical Tests

Although not all organizations require medical tests, these are being given in increasing numbers. Three types of medical tests that employers sometimes use when making selection decisions are

1. General health examinations.
2. Genetic screening.
3. Drug and alcohol tests.

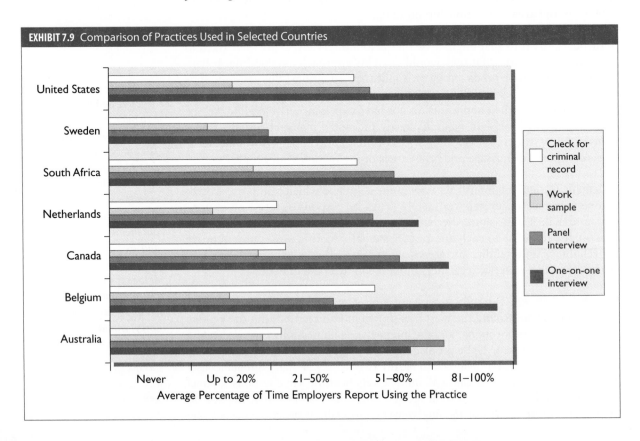

EXHIBIT 7.9 Comparison of Practices Used in Selected Countries

Legend:
- Check for criminal record
- Work sample
- Panel interview
- One-on-one interview

Countries (top to bottom): United States, Sweden, South Africa, Netherlands, Canada, Belgium, Australia

X-axis: Never | Up to 20% | 21–50% | 51–80% | 81–100%
Average Percentage of Time Employers Report Using the Practice

General Health Examinations. Since the enactment in 1990 of the Americans with Disabilities Act (ADA), general health examinations may be given only after a job offer has been made.[69] Before the offer is made, employers may only describe the job's functions and ask if the applicant is capable of performing the job. Prior to making an initial job offer, which may be contingent on the results of a medical exam, it is illegal to inquire about any disabilities. If a medical exam subsequently determines that the person is not able to perform the job for medical reasons, the employer may then revoke the job offer. In other words, disabilities may be used in making selection decisions only when they are job related.

After Ozark Airlines refused to hire Gary Frey due to a nonfunctioning left ear, the Office of Federal Contract Compliance Programs (OFCCP) sued the airline on Frey's behalf. Ozark acknowledged that Frey was capable of performing the required job duties. Their defense for not hiring him claimed that the decision was justified because he did not prove that he could do the job without endangering himself and others. The court ruled in favor of Frey, stating that it was Ozark's duty to show that Frey's condition would be a source of danger; Frey did not have to prove that the disability was not a source of endangerment. In this landmark decision, the court also stated that a disabled person is "qualified for employment if he [or she] is capable of performing a particular job with reasonable accommodation to his [or her] handicap" (*OFCCP v. Ozark Airlines*).

Many jobs—including police officer, firefighter, electrical power plant worker, telephone line worker, steel mill laborer, paramedic, maintenance worker, and numerous mechanical jobs—require particular physical, sensory, perceptual, and psychomotor abilities. When a job analysis (something Ozark Airlines did not have) documents that these are needed to perform a job, employers may be justified in not hiring applicants without the required abilities. The exception is when the employer could make reasonable accommodations that would enable the applicant to perform the job despite the disability.[70] Even when accommodation is possible, however, the courts have made it clear that employers are not obligated to hire a person with a disability over a more qualified nondisabled applicant.[71]

Genetic Testing and Screening. Each year, hundreds of thousands of job-related illnesses and deaths occur. The recent completion of a map of the human genome provides hope for reducing this number substantially. It creates almost endless possibilities for the development of medical tests to assess a person's genetically determined risks of experiencing various medical problems. For example, genetic testing and screening can identify individuals who are hypersensitive to harmful pollutants in the workplace. Once identified, these individuals can be screened out of chemically dangerous jobs and placed in positions in which environmental toxins do not present specific hazards.

Genetic testing and screening are not prohibited by the ADA or other federal legislation. However, numerous state laws restrict their use in employment, particularly in hiring and termination decisions.

Drug and Alcohol Testing. When employers first introduced drug and alcohol testing in the 1980s, the practice was very controversial, but today this practice is common in the United States. In fact, pre-employment drug and alcohol testing is mandatory for federal jobs that are safety sensitive, such as truck drivers, airline pilots, and railroad workers. Drug and alcohol abuse costs U.S. industry more than $100 billion annually, which helps explain why more than 15 million applicants and employees are tested for drugs annually. As shown in Exhibit 7.10, the percentage of applicants who test positive for some drugs is quite high, despite the fact that people usually know in advance that they will be subjected to the tests.[72]

FAST FACT

Able to Work is a strategic alliance among a consortium of 22 companies that are working to develop assistive technologies to enable people with disabilities to see a computer screen better, hear a telephone call better, talk to others when they lack speech, and do word processing when they cannot type.

FAST FACT

The ADA provides protection only for physical or mental impairments that substantially limit one or more major life activities.

FAST FACT

A survey by the American Management Association found that 61% of companies administer drug tests to job applicants.

A recent study of the selection practices used around the world revealed that some of the selection techniques commonly used in the United States are also used in many other countries (e.g., drug testing and medical exams). On the other hand, the popularity of other techniques varies among countries. Exhibit 7.11 illustrates some of the country differences identified by this study.[73]

LEARNING GOAL

4

> 66 *I want to stay in this job a long time, so I'm actually glad they care enough to determine if I'm a good match.* 99
>
> *Thuy Pham*
> *Data Analyst*
> *Kelly Blue Book*

THE PERSPECTIVE OF JOB APPLICANTS

Job applicants almost always care deeply about the outcomes of selection decisions and can have strong reactions to their experiences as they go through the selection process. Applicants' reactions influence their decisions about whether to pursue job opportunities in a company. For applicants already employed in the organization, such as those seeking a promotion, reactions to selection practices can influence their decisions about whether to remain with the company, and perhaps even their levels of work motivation.[74] Equally important, these early experiences serve as an organization's first steps in a socialization process that will continue for several months after an applicant is eventually hired.[75]

At the heart of applicants' concerns is the desire to be treated fairly. Applicants judge fairness by the

1. Content of the measures used to select people.
2. The administration of the process.
3. The results of the process.

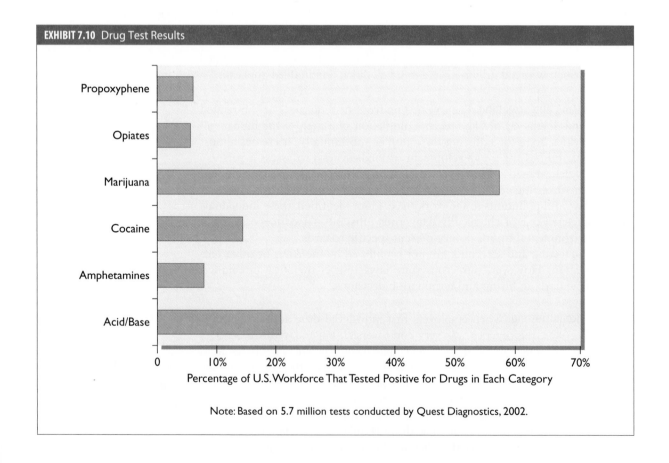

EXHIBIT 7.10 Drug Test Results

Percentage of U.S. Workforce That Tested Positive for Drugs in Each Category

Note: Based on 5.7 million tests conducted by Quest Diagnostics, 2002.

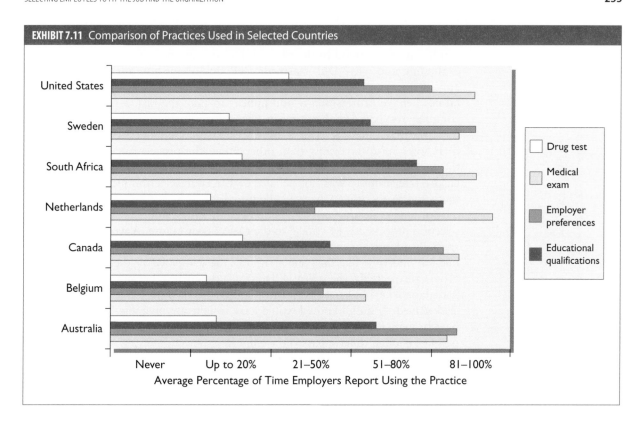

EXHIBIT 7.11 Comparison of Practices Used in Selected Countries

Fair Content?

Applicants prefer a process that involves them in activities that have obvious relevance to the available job. For example, work simulations usually seem more relevant to applicants than written tests and handwriting analysis. Perhaps for this reason, applicants view work simulations as relatively fair.[76] Applicants react negatively to poorly conducted interviews. Offensive or discriminatory questions obviously send negative messages, but so do questions that appear to be superficial or not clearly related to the job.[77] The best way to ensure that applicants experience a fair process is to train managers in how to select and hire their employees. Unfortunately, untrained managers often "talk too much and ask the wrong questions," according to Jennifer Sandberg, an employment attorney. "They also don't know how to respond to questions from candidates." To teach managers how to ask appropriate questions, role-playing is a useful training technique.[78]

PSE&G, a public utility company, wants to be sure its employees know what type of content to expect when they apply for a job in the company. The company has prepared a detailed manual that describes the various types of tests used in the company. The manual describes specific jobs and provides sample items that might appear on tests used to select people for those jobs. Meter readers, for example, must be able to work with figures quickly and accurately. The manual provides an example of a test question that could be used to test this ability. The manual also provides helpful advice on preparing a professional-looking resume and conducting oneself professionally during interviews.

FAST FACT

At Universal Pictures, a candidate for the position of assistant director was asked in a telephone interview, "What color are you, are you black?" The interviewer was the production manager.

Fair Process?

Applicants also attend to the process: Did the company tell them what it was evaluating and why? Did it provide feedback about how they scored? Did it appear to respect their desire for confidentiality? Did the company representatives behave professionally and appear to take the task seriously? Was the company respectful of their time and need for information about their chances for a positive outcome? Did it seem to treat all candidates equally, or did it treat some more favorably than others? Did the process appear to recognize the potential for applicants to misrepresent themselves and include steps to ensure that honesty was not penalized? Effective selection includes managing these and many other aspects of the process.[79]

For job applicants with disabilities, getting information in advance about the selection process can be critical to their success or failure. A woman who uses a specially adapted keyboard to do computer work described her experience with one job interview like this: She arrived at the company for the scheduled interview. Unexpectedly, she was asked to take a typing test. Because she did not have her adapted keyboard, she performed poorly. "I failed the typing test miserably," she recalled. "I didn't know I would have to take a typing test. If I had, I would have brought my keyboard." Using it, she could type 40 words per minute, which was fast enough to have passed the employer's selection test.[80]

Fair Results?

The content and administrative features of many selection procedures are visible primarily to applicants, but the results are visible to a broader array of people. Selection decisions are usually known by the acquaintances and coworkers of applicants who tell stories about the process, by the new coworkers of successful applicants, by the managers inside an organization who participated in the process, and by people who served as references for applicants. Based on who is selected and who is rejected, all these constituencies form opinions about whether a company uses fair procedures and makes wise choices about whom to hire or promote.

The news media also may evaluate the results of an organization's selection procedures. In reporting on companies that made its list of the 50 best places for minorities to work, *Fortune* applauded the fact that 60% of Marriott's new hires were minorities. It also observed that senior management had a different complexion from the overall workforce, stating: "Heady minority representation in the workplace has not yet shown gains in the executive ranks." The news story stimulated the company to set a three-year objective of doubling representation of women and minorities in the senior management ranks.[81]

LEARNING GOAL **5**

LEGAL CONSIDERATIONS IN SELECTION

Like all HR practices, selection practices must be designed with legal regulations and social norms clearly in mind.[82] These can vary greatly from one country to the next, from state to state within the United States, and from year to year. For example, California prohibits discrimination against people who have a genetic tendency toward disease.[83] Thirteen states have laws prohibiting employers from using information about home ownership. A dozen states prohibit the use of questions that probe into whether an applicant "resides with parents or relatives."[84]

Laws and Regulations That Prohibit Discrimination

As described in Chapter 4, numerous acts and executive orders prohibit employers from discriminating against employees and job applicants on the basis of various personal characteristics (see Exhibit 4.4 on page 124 to review these laws). Recall that Title VII of the Civil Rights Act and Executive Order 11246 prohibit discrimination on the basis of race, color, religion, sex, or national origin. The Age Discrimination in Employment Act prohibits age discrimination. And the Rehabilitation Act and the Americans with Disabilities Act prohibit discrimination against persons with disabilities.

Federal Guidelines and Professional Standards

Several federal guidelines and documents explain how to develop and use selection tools and how to determine whether a selection procedure discriminates unfairly.

Federal Guidelines. The *Uniform Guidelines on Employee Selection Procedures (1978)* is generally considered the most complete and useful legal document relevant to selection practices. It provides many specific do's and don'ts, as well as questions and answers regarding hiring and promotion. The Equal Employment Opportunity Commission (EEOC) also has published many guidelines relevant to selection, including *The Guidelines on Discrimination Because of National Origin* and *The Guidelines on Discrimination Because of Religion.* To determine how to comply with the Americans with Disabilities Act, employers can refer to the EEOC's *Technical Assistance Manual on Employment Provisions.*

Professional Standards. Selection processes are monitored by the American Psychological Association (APA), which includes among its members many experts in testing and individual assessment. In collaboration with other professional associations, the APA publishes *Standards for Education and Psychological Tests,* which is updated regularly to reflect changes in scientific knowledge as well as changing legal conditions. Another useful set of professional standards is the *Principles for the Validation and Use of Personnel Selection Procedures,* published by the Society for Industrial and Organizational Psychology (SIOP). HR professionals should be familiar with all of these documents and the standards they set forth.[85]

Detecting Unfair Discrimination

In a typical discrimination lawsuit, a person alleges discrimination due to unlawful employment practices. The person may first go to the EEOC office. The EEOC may seek out the facts of the case from both sides and attempt to facilitate a resolution. Failing a resolution, the person may continue the case and file a suit. In the first phase of the suit, the person filing it (the plaintiff) must establish a prima facie case of discrimination by showing disparate treatment or adverse impact.

Disparate Treatment. Disparate treatment *is a legal term used to describe illegal discrimination against an individual.* A prima facie case of disparate treatment exists when an individual can demonstrate all of the following:

- The individual belongs to a protected group.
- The individual applied for a job for which the employer was seeking applicants.
- Despite being qualified, the individual was rejected.
- After the individual's rejection, the employer kept looking for people with the applicant's qualifications.

> *" Video resumes allow future employers to make hiring decisions [about the video applicants] based on race and looks, which is not what should be part of the decision process. "*
>
> Anonymous respondent in a survey of attitudes about the use of video resumes

Demonstrating a case of disparate treatment can be difficult. One reason is that discrimination can be subtle. Unless someone makes a very blatant statement during the selection process (e.g., "I don't think women can do this job"), the applicant may never realize that a decision was made on the basis of personal characteristics.[86] Also, most of the decision processes aren't visible to applicants. Rejected applicants, especially external ones, seldom know how other applicants performed or even who was eventually hired. For these reasons, the law provides another means for establishing a case of illegal discrimination: demonstrating adverse impact.

Adverse Impact. **Adverse impact** *(or disparate impact) is a legal term used to refer to discrimination against an entire protected group.* Statistics that reflect the consequences of a large number of hiring decisions made by an employer are used to show adverse impact. Based on the statistics, a judgment is made concerning whether the employer *appears* to have discriminated against members of a protected subgroup. If the statistics show that selection practices resulted in adverse impact against a protected group, then the burden is on the employer to prove that the selection techniques used assessed job-related predictors.

Showing adverse impact generally requires the involvement of the EEOC, which has authority to audit the EEO-1 reports that employers file. As described in Chapter 6, employers file EEO-1 forms with the EEOC to report the demographic characteristics of job applicants—their sex, race, religion, and so on. Without access to such information, it would be nearly impossible for an individual to show that an employer's selection practices have had an adverse impact.[87] The two most common approaches to assessing adverse impact are

1. Making comparisons to labor market data.
2. The 80% rule.[88]

Labor Market Comparisons. Comparing the representation of a group in an organization's workforce to the representation of that group in the relevant labor market is one way to document adverse impact. Selection practices have had an adverse impact if an employer's workforce does not reflect parity with the composition of the relevant labor market. For example, if the relevant labor market for a job is 50% male and 50% female, the people an employer hires for that job also should be approximately split evenly on gender. The key to this approach is determining the relevant labor market. The approach preferred by the EEOC is to identify where potentially qualified applicants reside and to consider this population as the relevant labor market. Employers may be able to successfully defend themselves against discrimination claims if they can show that the proportions of protected group members in their workforce mirror the proportions in the relevant labor market.

The 80% Rule. The **80% rule** *(also called the four-fifths rule) evaluates adverse impact by comparing the representation of a group in the applicant pool to the representation of that group among those who have been hired, fired, promoted, transferred, or demoted.* The *Uniform Guidelines* state that adverse impact is demonstrated when the selection rate "for any racial, ethnic, or sex subgroup is less than four-fifths or 80% of the highest selection rate for any group." The rule applies to *each part* of the selection process as well as to the process as a *whole* (*Connecticut v. Teal*, 1982). So, if the hiring process contains multiple tests, the 80% rule should be used to evaluate the discriminatory effects of each one.

The 80% rule provides employers with a simple metric to evaluate whether their selection practices unfairly discriminate against some groups of applicants. This rule is explained in more detail in "Managing with Metrics: The 80% Rule."

Defending Discriminatory Practices

Once a prima facie case of disparate treatment or disparate impact has been established, the employer is given the opportunity to defend itself. An organization accused of illegal discrimination may be able to successfully defend its employment practices by showing that the demonstrated discrimination is legally justified. Discriminatory employment practices can be acceptable if they're used on the basis of

- Job-relatedness.
- Business necessity.
- Bona fide occupational qualifications.
- Bona fide seniority systems.
- Voluntary affirmative action programs.

Job-Relatedness. To demonstrate **job-relatedness,** *the company must show that the information used in selection decisions is related to success on the job.* Job-relatedness can be demonstrated using any of the methods for establishing validity that were described earlier in this chapter.

Business Necessity. Showing the job-relatedness of a selection practice isn't always possible. The law recognizes this and allows companies to defend their selection practices in other ways. To defend a procedure that is discriminatory on the

MANAGING WITH METRICS
The 80% Rule

To illustrate how the 80% rule works, consider the use of a physical ability test for selecting firefighters. The test assesses whether an applicant can drag a 220-pound weight a distance of 100 feet in 3 minutes or less. Does this test have adverse impact against women?

Using the 80% rule, compare the percentage of female applicants who passed the test to the percentage of male applicants who passed the test. Suppose 2 out 20 female applicants passed the test and 30 out of 100 male applicants passed the test. The 80% rule compares these pass rates as follows:

$$\frac{0.10 \text{ (pass rate for females)}}{0.30 \text{ (pass rate for males)}} = 0.33 \text{ (relative success of females compared to males)}$$

In this example, the pass rate for females is only 33% of the pass rate for males. So, according to the 80% rule, this test has adverse impact against women.

One way the firefighters could deal with this apparent problem would be to change the way they score the test. For example, they could make it easier to pass the test by allowing more time, by using a lighter weight, and/or by shortening the distance involved. Suppose they made some changes, and the next time the test was given, 7 out of 10 females passed and 80 out of 100 males passed. Using the 80% rule, the pass rate for females compared to males would now be

$$\frac{0.70 \text{ (pass rate for females)}}{0.80 \text{ (pass rate for males)}} = 0.88 \text{ (relative success of females compared to males)}$$

Using the new test, the employer could successfully argue that the test does not unfairly discriminate against women because, according to the 80% rule, the pass rates for females is sufficiently similar to the pass rate for males.

basis of **business necessity,** *an employer must show that the selection decision was based on a factor that is essential to the safe operation of the business.* The courts and the language of the Civil Rights Act of 1991 define job necessity in very narrow terms. For example, employers cannot argue that business necessity exists because customers prefer employees from certain demographic groups or because not hiring members of certain groups reduces the cost of doing business.

Bona Fide Occupational Qualifications. To use the defense of a **bona fide occupational qualification (BFOQ),** *the employer must show that the discriminatory practice is "reasonably necessary to the normal operation of that particular business or enterprise."* The BFOQ defense is sometimes used to justify hiring based on sex or religion. For example, sex is considered a BFOQ for jobs such as restroom attendants, and religion is considered a BFOQ for some jobs in religious institutions.

Bona Fide Seniority Systems. A **bona fide seniority system** *is one that a company establishes and maintains without the intent to discriminate illegally.* When a bona fide seniority system is in place, decisions regarding promotions, job assignments, and layoffs can be made on the basis of seniority. For many occupations, women and members of ethnic minority groups are more likely to be recent hires, so often using seniority results in adverse impact. Nevertheless, using seniority as a basis for selection decisions may be legal.

Voluntary Affirmative Action Programs. As described in Chapter 6, the legal and social status of voluntary affirmative action programs is currently a topic of much discussion. Nevertheless, past court decisions have held that voluntary affirmative action programs can be a defense against illegal (reverse) discrimination. Voluntary affirmative action programs are legally defensible if they are

- Remedial in purpose.
- Limited in duration.
- Restricted in effect.
- Flexible in implementation.
- Minimal in harm to innocent parties.

Legal Considerations for Global Selection

By enacting the Civil Rights Act of 1991, Congress affirmed its policy that American civil rights laws cover U.S. citizens employed outside the country by American multinationals. Sometimes this puts American employers in the position of having to violate local practices to comply with American law. The United States also holds foreign companies operating in the United States accountable for adhering to U.S. employment laws. However, there are some exceptions to this general rule. For example, a treaty between the United States and Japan permits companies of either country to prefer their own citizens for executive positions in subsidiaries based in the other country. Japanese firms usually select parent-country (i.e., Japanese) executives to run their American subsidiaries, and they provide few opportunities for promotion to the top management slots for their American managers.[89] United States employees often consider this practice to be discrimination based on national origin. But according to the ruling in *Fortino v. Quasar Co.,* Title VII of the Civil Rights Act was preempted by a subsequent trade treaty. As these examples illustrate, managing human resources effectively in a global organization is not as simple as following the advice offered by one sage: "When in Rome, do as the Romans do."

CURRENT ISSUES

When an organization's strategic plans call for expanding into the global market, the selection of employees becomes a key determinant of success. Globalization strategy requires operating facilities overseas, and the plan may call for building new facilities or acquiring existing operations. Either way, decisions about how to staff the facilities are among the first strategic choices made. For example, suppose an American music production company decides to open a new recording studio in India. How should it fill the job of studio director? Should the company send an expatriate (a parent-country national, or PCN)? Should it hire a host-country national (HCN)? Or should it hire a third-country national (TCN)? The pros and cons of selecting these three types of individuals are listed in Exhibit 7.12.[90] Here we briefly discuss selecting expatriates or selecting host-country nationals to work in U.S. firms abroad.

Selecting Expatriates

United States companies have generally sent expatriates to their locations abroad. Yet it is common knowledge that U.S. expatriates and their families often do not perform well in such assignments and they are very costly for the company.

An organization's decision to fill a job by hiring an expatriate is likely to reflect a concern that the individual knows the organization and its values, as well as having the competencies to do the job. Their selection decision takes into consideration both the nature of the job and the competencies of people in the two talent pools (at home and abroad). Expatriate managers must be able to carry out daily activities with the concerns of the parent company clearly in focus, while also responding to the host country's societal concerns and a local culture that's often quite different from their home culture. In addition, expatriate managers typically operate in a culture with a different language—a major obstacle for many of them.[91]

For expatriate managers to succeed, they need to perform their specific job and also effectively manage many types of relationships, including those with:

- Their coworkers.
- Their families.
- The host government.
- Their home government.
- The local clients, customers, and business partners.
- The company's headquarters.

Selecting Host-Country Nationals (HCNs)

Because it is so difficult to find expatriates with the competencies needed to be successful in foreign assignments, many companies prefer to rely on the local labor market. In the case of opening a new recording studio in India, it is unlikely that a U.S. employee would be as well connected to the local music scene as someone from the host country. The competencies needed for a particular job are the same regardless of whether the person filling the job is an expatriate or a host-country national. However, the selection procedures used are likely to be different depending on whether they are used to assess U.S. applicants who will become expatriates or applicants from the local labor market who will become HCNs. Expatriates are usually selected using U.S practices, while HCNs are usually selected using host-country practices.[92]

> " We prefer to recruit country nationals [HCNs] for each new location simply because they have the local language and culture in their blood. They know the local market, customs, and how to motivate other local talent. [But] we are increasingly importing and exporting nationals of different countries . . . so we get international experience into each center. "
>
> *Mark Dixon*
> *Chief Executive Officer*
> *Regus*

EXHIBIT 7.12 Selecting Managers: Pros and Cons of PCNs, HCNs, and TCNs

Parent-Country Nationals (PCNs)

Advantages

- Organizational control and coordination is maintained and facilitated.
- Promising managers are given international experience.
- PCNs are the best people for the job.
- The subsidiary will likely comply with the company objectives, policies, and so forth.

Disadvantages

- The promotional opportunities of HCNs are limited.
- Adaptation to the host country may take a long time.
- PCNs may impose an inappropriate headquarters style.
- Compensation for PCNs and HCNs may differ.

Host-Country Nationals (HCNs)

Advantages

- Language and other barriers are eliminated.
- Hiring costs are reduced, and no work permit is required.
- Continuity of management improves, since HCNs stay longer in positions.
- Government policy may dictate the hiring of HCNs.
- Morale among HCNs may improve as they see the career potentials.

Disadvantages

- Control and coordination of headquarters may be impeded.
- HCNs have limited career opportunities outside the subsidiary.
- Hiring HCNs limits opportunities for PCNs to gain overseas experience.
- Hiring HCNs could encourage a federation of national rather than global units.

Third-Country Nationals (TCNs)

Advantages

- Salary and benefit requirements may be lower than for PCNs.
- TCNs may be better informed than PCNs about the host-country environment.

Disadvantages

- Transfers must consider possible national animosities.
- The host government may resent the hiring of TCNs.
- TCNs may not want to return to their own countries after assignment.

Cirque du Soleil is a company that hires large numbers of HCNs to work in their shows. When making hiring decisions in various parts of the world, Cirque du Soleil must understand the legal constraints as well as the cultural factors that apply in each country. Perhaps you've seen a performance of Cirque du Soleil—one of the most unusual acts in the world. With corporate headquarters in Montreal and offices in Las Vegas, Nevada, and in Amsterdam, The Netherlands, Cirque du Soleil is an international entertainment company that employs more than 1,200 people representing 17 nationalities and speaking at least 13 different languages. Its main products include a permanent show that runs in Las Vegas and several touring shows that run in countries around the world. People are clearly the company's most important asset. Success is possible only with careful planning, recruitment, and selection.

For its tours, Cirque relies heavily on temporary staff (temps) hired in each city—people who work as ushers, ticket sellers and takers, and security personnel. For a year of tours, that adds up to some 1,800 temps. Although Cirque employs them for only a few days, good temps are essential to the company's reputation because they have the most direct personal contact with customers. To be hired, applicants must conduct themselves well during an interview designed to assess attitude, experience, and skills. For positions in the touring groups, the selection process is more intensive. Throughout these selection processes, the company must ensure that it adheres to all local labor laws. Ideally, Cirque will also be sensitive enough to avoid practices that, although legal, are considered undesirable in local cultures.

CHAPTER SUMMARY WITH LEARNING GOALS

▲1 STRATEGIC IMPORTANCE. Through selection procedures, organizations strive to fill job openings with the most appropriate people. By the same token, job applicants strive to obtain jobs that are appropriate to their personal objectives. Effective selection practices result in the assignment of individuals to jobs (and even career paths) that match the individuals' technical competencies, personalities, behavioral styles, and preferences.

▲2 DESIGNING THE SELECTION PROCESS. The selection process generally involves establishing the criteria of interest, choosing predictors and assessment techniques, deciding when to measure each predictor, and synthesizing the information collected and making the final decision. To achieve an effective match between individuals and job situations, organizations need to obtain information about the applicant and clearly communicate information about the job and the work setting. Typically, employers gather several types of information using a variety of methods.

▲3 ASSESSING JOB APPLICANTS. Building on the results of job analysis and competency modeling, employers can develop valid selection practices that enable them to make job offers to the applicants who are most likely to perform well in the jobs, be good corporate citizens, and not leave the organization prematurely. Application forms, written and physical tests, work simulations, assessment centers, interviews, and medical tests are among the selection techniques that organizations use for selection purposes.

▲4 PERSPECTIVE OF JOB APPLICANTS. Most applicants care deeply about the outcomes of selection decisions. Both internal and external applicants could have strong reactions to their experiences as they go through the selection process. If either the content or the process of selection seems unfair, applicants who are well qualified may decide not to accept a job offer.

▲5 LEGAL CONSIDERATIONS. An extensive framework of U.S. legal regulations, court decisions, and guidelines provides U.S. organizations with advice for how to conduct the selection process in a manner that enhances the performance of the workforce while avoiding unfair discrimination.

▲6 CURRENT ISSUES. The selection of international employees becomes a key determinant of success for organizations expanding into the global market. One of the first strategic decisions to be made is how to staff the new international facilities. Two choices were discussed: sending an expatriate or hiring a host-country national. Each option has some advantages and some disadvantages. The best choice depends on the specific needs of the organization.

TERMS TO REMEMBER

Ability test

Adverse impact

Application blank

Assessment centers

Behavioral job interviews

Biodata test

Bona fide occupational qualification (BFOQ)

Bona fide seniority system

Business necessity

Combined approach

Compensatory approach

Content validation

Criteria

Criterion-related validation

Disparate treatment

Economic utility

80% rule

Job-relatedness

Knowledge test

Multiple-hurdles approach

Personality test

Predictors

Reliability

Selection

Structured job interview

Unstructured job interview

Validity

Validity generalization

Work simulations

QUESTIONS FOR DISCUSSION AND REFLECTIVE THINKING

1. Describe the selection methods used by Outback Steakhouse. Then explain why this company considers employee selection to be an important strategic practice.
2. A frequent diagnosis of an observed performance problem in an organization is, "This person was a selection mistake." What are the short- and long-term consequences of so-called selection mistakes? If possible, relate this question to your own experiences with organizations.
3. Describe how selection practices are related to other human resource activities.
4. Given all the weaknesses identified with unstructured interviews, why do they remain so popular? What can employers do to improve the usefulness of job interviews?
5. What are the costs and benefits to employers of being responsive to the applicant's perspective throughout the selection process? Are the concerns of applicants who are eventually accepted different from those of applicants who are eventually rejected? Explain.
6. How does the unethical behavior of job applicants affect an organization? Describe the consequences of unethical job applicants for each member of the HR Triad.
7. Some people feel the government should not get involved in regulating business practices. To what extent do you think legal regulations affecting selection practices hinder or facilitate running an effective company?

PROJECTS TO EXTEND YOUR LEARNING

1. **Integration and Application.** Before continuing, review the cases of Southwest Airlines and Lincoln Electric at the end of this book. Describe, evaluate, and compare the selection procedures used at these two companies. In preparing your answer, consider the following issues:

   a. The objectives of the selection process.
   b. The criteria used.
   c. The techniques used to assess the competencies of job applicants.
   d. The apparent effectiveness of the selection process.
   e. The roles and responsibilities of managers, HR professionals, and other employees in each company.

2. **Using the Internet.** Improve your understanding of selection practices by exploring the online resources listed here.

   a. Assess the potential usefulness of having a third-party vendor conduct reference checks at
      - Verified Credentials (www.verifiedcredentials.com).
      - VTS Investigations (www.pichicago.com).
      - Access Background Checks (www.accesschecks.com/employmentpackage.htm).
   b. Take a popular test for assessing personality style at AdvisorTeam (www.advisorteam.org) or PsychTests.com (www.psychtests.com).
   c. Find out everything you ever wanted to know about the Federal Civil Service Exam (www.federaljobs.net/exams.htm), which is taken by most applicants for federal jobs.
   d. Get advice about how to handle yourself well during job interviews at job-interview.net (www.job-interview.net).
   e. Learn more about genetic testing and screening at the Occupational Health and Safety Administration (www.osha.gov); search for key words "genetic testing."
   f. Learn how employers can establish a drug-free workplace from the U.S. Department of Labor (www.dol.gov); search for "Drug-Free Workplace Adviser."
   g. Learn how to file a discrimination charge and what it takes to prove a case of discrimination at the U.S. Equal Employment Opportunity Commission (www.eeoc.gov).

3. **Experiential Activities.** Use the two activities described here to develop interview skills for selecting new employees.

a. Focusing on Behavior. You are responsible for interviewing candidates for an entry-level job. Your employer has provided you with very little information about how to proceed. You know that the job does not require a great deal of skill, but it is important to select someone who will fit the company culture. Following is a list of questions you have used in the past during similar interviews. After reading this chapter, you realize that these questions need to be reworded to focus more on behavior. Rewrite each question to show two alternatives to what is listed. First rewrite the questions to ask the interviewees about their behavior in the past. Then rewrite the questions to ask the interviewees how they would likely behave in a specific situation. Use situations that would be relevant to the available job, which is assistant animal keeper at the Cleveland Zoo. The job involves cleaning cages in the bird and small animal exhibits and putting out food for the birds and animals.

EXHIBIT Writing Behaviorally Focused Questions

Old Version	New Question, Focusing on Past Behavior in Other Jobs	New Question, Focusing on Future Behavior in This Job
1. Are you an introvert or an extrovert?		
2. How important is it to follow the rules?		
3. Do you believe that a person should have fun at work?		
4. How important is a sense of humor at work?		
5. What values are important to you at work?		
6. Describe your problem-solving style.		

After you have completed rewriting the interview questions, list the pros and cons associated with the new questions you have developed.

Advantages of New Questions Focused on Past Behavior in Other Jobs	Disadvantages of New Questions Focused on Future Behavior in This Job
1.	1.
2.	2.
3.	3.
4.	4.
5.	5.
6.	6.

b. Avoiding Illegal Questions. What information may employers request during interviews? Check "Legal and Low Risk" or "Legal but Risky," or "Illegal" in the chart to indicate your understanding of which topics are acceptable. (The answers appear on page 267.)

Item	Legal and Low Risk It's generally OK to ask without legal concerns.	Legal but Risky It's legal, but rarely should be asked.	Illegal Never ask.
1. Marital status			
2. Number of children			
3. Skills to do the job			
4. A woman's maiden name			

(continued)

Item	Legal and Low Risk It's generally OK to ask without legal concerns.	Legal but Risky It's legal, but rarely should be asked.	Illegal Never ask.
5. Age of applicant			
6. Driver's license			
7. Religious affiliation			
8. Birthplace of applicant			
9. Club memberships			
10. Whether applicant plans to have children			
11. Preferred hours of work			
12. Whether applicant has disabilities			
13. Other names applicant has used			
14. Arrest record			
15. Applicant's height and weight			
16. Nature of military discharge			
17. Friends or relatives employed by the firm			
18. Clergy members as references			
19. Credit questions			
20. Whether applicant is willing to travel			

CASE STUDY
SELECTING PATIENT ESCORTS

City Hospital is located in the heart of a large Midwestern city. It is one of five major hospitals in the area and has recently built a small addition for treating well-known patients such as professional football players, top company executives, and stage performers. Visiting or local celebrities always choose City Hospital if they need treatment.

City Hospital has about 1,200 hospital beds and employs 4,500 individuals, including about 40 patient escorts. The job of patient escort is a simple one, requiring only minimal training and no special physical talents. When patients need to be moved from one location to another, patient escorts are summoned to assist in the move. If the move is only a short distance, however, a nurse or orderly can move the patient. Of particular importance is the fact that patient escorts almost always take patients who are being discharged from their hospital room to the front door of the hospital. A wheelchair is always used, even if the patient is able to walk unassisted. Thus, the typical procedure is for the nurse to call for a patient escort, and then the escort gets a wheelchair, goes to the patient's room, assists the patient into the wheelchair, picks up the patient's belongings, wheels the patient down to the hospital's front door or to a car in the parking lot, and returns to the workstation.

The job of patient escort is critical to the hospital, since the escort is always the last hospital representative the patient sees and hence has a considerable influence on the patient's perception of the hospital. Of the approximately 40 escorts, about three-fourths are men, and

one-fourth are women. Most are high school graduates in their early twenties. Some, particularly those on the early morning shift, are attending college at night and working for the hospital to earn money to pay college expenses. Four of the escorts are older women who previously served as hospital volunteers and then decided to become full-time employees. Turnover among patient escorts is quite high and has averaged 25% in recent years. In addition, upward mobility in the hospital is quite good, and as a result another 25% of the escorts typically transfer to other jobs in the hospital each year. Thus, about half of the patient escorts need to be replaced annually.

The hospital follows a standard procedure when hiring patient escorts. When a vacancy occurs, the Personnel Department reviews the file of applications of individuals who have applied for the patient escort job. Usually the file contains at least 20 applications because the pay for the job is good, the work easy, and few skills are required. The top two or three applicants are asked to come to the hospital for interviews. Typically, the applicants are interviewed first by Personnel and then by the patient escort supervisor. The majority of those interviewed know some other employees of the hospital, so the only reference check is a call to these employees. Before being hired, applicants are required to take physical examinations given by hospital doctors.

Every new escort attends an orientation program the first day on the job. This is conducted by a member of the hospital's Personnel Department. The program consists of a complete tour of the hospital; a review of all the hospital's personnel policies, including a description of its promotion, compensation, and disciplinary policies; and a presentation of the hospital's mission and philosophy. During this orientation session, employees are told that the hospital's image in the community is of major importance and that all employees should strive to maintain and enhance this image by their conduct. After orientation, all patient escorts receive on-the-job training from their immediate supervisor.

During the last two-year period, the hospital has experienced a number of problems with patient escorts that have had an adverse effect on the hospital's image. Several patients have complained to the hospital administration that they have been treated rudely, or in some cases roughly, by one or more patient escorts. Some complained that they had been ordered around or scolded by an escort during the discharge process. Others stated that the escort had been careless when wheeling them out of the hospital to their cars. One person, in fact, reported that an escort had carelessly tipped him over. All escorts are required to wear identification tags, but patients usually can't remember the escort's name when complaining to the hospital. Additionally, the hospital usually has difficulty determining which escort served which patient because escorts often trade patients. Finally, even when the hospital can identify the offending escort, the employee can easily deny any wrongdoing. Such an employee often counters that patients are generally irritable as a result of their illness and hence are prone to complain at even the slightest provocation.

At the hospital administrator's request, the personnel manager asked the chief supervisor of patient escorts, the head of the Staffing Section in the Personnel Department, and the assistant personnel director to meet with her to review the entire procedure used to select patient escorts. It was hoped that a new procedure could be devised that would eliminate the hiring of rude, insulting, or careless patient escorts.

During the meeting, a number of suggestions were made about how the selection procedure might be improved. Criticisms of the present system were also voiced. The chief supervisor of patient escorts argued that the problem with the hospital's present system is that the application blank is void of any truly useful information. He stated that the questions that really give insights into the employee's personality are no longer on the application blank. He suggested that applicants be asked about their hobbies, outside activities, and their personal likes and dislikes on the application blank. He also suggested that each applicant be asked to submit three letters of recommendation from people who know the applicant well. He wanted these letters to focus on the prospective employee's personality, particularly the applicant's ability to remain friendly and polite at all times.

The assistant personnel director contended that the hospital's interviewing procedure should be modified. He observed that, during the typical interview, little attempt is made to determine how the applicant reacts under stress. He suggested that if applicants were asked four or five stress-producing questions, the hospital might be in a better position to judge their ability to work with irritable patients.

The head of the Staffing Section noted that patient escorts require little mental or physical talent and agreed that the crucial attribute escorts need is the ability to be always courteous and polite. He wondered whether an "attitude" test could be developed that would measure the applicant's predisposition toward being friendly. He suggested that a job analysis could be done on the patient escort position to determine the attitudes that are critical to being a successful patient escort. When the job analysis was complete, questions could be developed that would measure these critical attributes. The test questions could be given to the hospital's present patient escorts to determine whether the test accurately distinguishes the best from the worst escorts. The head of the Staffing Section realized that many of the questions might need to be eliminated or changed, and, if the test appeared to show promise, it would probably need to be revalidated to meet government requirements. He felt, however, that a well designed test might be worth the effort and should at least be considered.

The meeting ended with all four participants agreeing that the suggestion of trying to develop an "attitude test" was probably the most promising. The assistant personnel director and chief supervisor of patient escorts stated that they would conduct a thorough job analysis covering the patient escort position and develop a list of attitudes that are critical to its success. A second meeting would then be scheduled to prepare the actual items to be included in the attitude test.

ANSWERS TO EXPERIENTIAL ACTIVITY: APPLICATION BLANKS

In most situations, it's probably fine to ask:

- Questions 3 and 6 when driving is required on the job.
- Questions 11 and 20 if the job requires travel.

Question 12 is clearly illegal since the ADA specifically forbids inquiring about any disabilities before making a job offer.

The rest of the questions create legal risk (and thus are legal but risky) because they could be used as evidence against the firm in a discrimination claim. Unless the company can demonstrate that they are job related, they should not be asked.

8

Training and Developing a Competitive Workforce

Learning Goals

After reading this chapter, you should be able to:

1 Discuss the strategic importance of training and development.

2 Explain how the training and development activities relate to other elements of the HRM system.

3 Describe the roles and responsibilities of the HR Triad in training and developing a competitive workforce.

4 Show how training and development needs are determined.

5 Identify the conditions for effective training and development.

6 Report the three types of learning objectives for a training or development program.

7 Describe the different program formats that can be used for training and development activities.

8 Show how to create conditions to maximize learning during a training or development program.

9 Explain three main goals of team training programs.

10 Discuss two current issues in training and development.

MANAGING HUMAN RESOURCES AT RITZ-CARLTON HOTEL COMPANY

Employees who work for the Ritz-Carlton Hotel Company are proud that the company is a two-time winner of the Baldrige National Quality Award and consistently earns top ratings in the travel and leisure industry. The awards and the excellent customer service they represent don't happen by accident. The company knows what types of people perform well in each job, and it is careful to hire only the right people. Then it uses intensive training to turn newly hired employees into a staff of stellar award-winning service providers.

Orientation begins the process; it's a key practice for creating a team of employees who all share the same vision and goals. Orientation infuses new employees with the company's "soul." Company executives tell new employees the story of how the hotel began and explain the firm's credo—three paragraphs that capture the firm's most important values and principles.

After the general orientation program, employees receive more specific training. Some principles of conduct all employees must learn. For example, when a guest asks for directions, always escort them rather than just pointing, and answer the phone with a "smile."

Employees also are trained for specific jobs. Emphasis is placed on how people do their jobs, not just getting the job done. Job-specific training is designed and delivered by the five best employees in each job category. Working together, those who are best at doing each job develop a set of principles that everyone in that job needs to understand to perform it well. For example, room service waiters attend formal training sessions and learn on the job by working with veteran waiters who serve as coaches. New waiters are taught how to use language that fits the Ritz-Carlton's image (e.g., "Please accept my apologies," rather than "I'm sorry," and "Certainly, my pleasure," instead of "Okay"). Coaches also teach new hires to think about situations from the customer's perspective, to imagine the customer's emotional reactions, and to anticipate (rather than respond to) each customer's concerns. Ultimately, the hotel's goal is to create a workforce whose attitudes and habits are perfectly aligned with the hotel's values.[1] ▲

STRATEGIC IMPORTANCE OF TRAINING AND DEVELOPMENT

The best competitors use training and development practices to improve the ability of the workforce to implement their business strategy. At the Ritz-Carlton Hotel Company, training teaches new employees about the company's values, and it helps experienced employees continually improve the quality of their service. The Ritz-Carlton Hotel Company has become so widely recognized for its ability to use HR practices to support quality service that it decided to teach other companies how they can improve. Interested managers and executives can attend classes and presentations at the firm's leadership training center and buy consulting services.

Improving the competence of the workforce is one way that training and development can create a competitive advantage, but it is not the only way. Training and development activities also contribute to organizational success in less direct ways. For example, they can provide shared experiences that promote understanding among employees with many different histories and so help speed the development of organizational cohesiveness and employee commitment. Training and development activities also are a means for employers to address employees' needs. By offering training and development opportunities, employers help employees develop their own personal competitive advantage and ensure their long-term employability.[2]

Improving Recruitment and Retention

> " At Toyota, we have a really tough time finding good people. Training is important. "
>
> *Jim Wiseman*
> *President of External Affairs*
> *Toyota Engineering &*
> *Manufacturing North America*

Chapter 6 described in detail the strategic importance of being able to attract and retain qualified employees. You may recall from that discussion that a common source of employee dissatisfaction is the lack of career advancement opportunities. For most employees, making a significant career move involves taking a job that requires competencies not needed in their current job. How can employees acquire these competencies? One way is by seeking out educational opportunities on their own—for example, by attending classes at night or on weekends. But a more appealing way for most people is through participation in training and development activities offered by their employer. Many people seek out employers who provide training and development activities that facilitate career advancement. When they receive such opportunities, employees are likely to feel more committed to the organization and are less likely to leave. Offering job training to employees whose jobs are lost to offshoring or outsourcing is also a means of creating loyalty among employees.

Improving Competitiveness

> " When you're in a business like ours, the HR dynamic is incredibly important. Education—training and teaching others—are key elements of our culture. It's a consistent theme. If our organization doesn't continue to evolve, it will fail. "
>
> *Richard Mott*
> *Chief Executive Officer*
> *Kyphon, Inc.*

United States corporations spend more than $60 billion annually on formal employee training and development programs that use an estimated 1.5 billion hours of time for the more than 56 million employees who participate.[3] Often, large investments in training and development are justified by a belief that training and development will enhance the organization's ability to compete effectively.

At Kyphon, Inc., effective training can make the difference between life and death. Kyphon produces and sells a patented device that is used to correct painful spinal conditions. The firm's salespeople teach surgeons how to use it in the operating room. So, in addition to offering the more common types of training to people in accounting, operations, and other areas, Kyphon provides medical training to its sales force. Kyphon's zeal for training doesn't stop there, however. They view learning as the lifeblood of the company. Employees are encouraged to pursue training in any form that suits them—from technical and business courses to lifestyle management. The philosophy is that everyone needs to be continuously learning and developing to support a company that is evolving and changing as new technologies become available.[4]

In highly competitive industries, training for immediate performance improvement is particularly important to organizations with stagnant or declining rates of productivity or customer satisfaction. Training for performance improvement is also important to organizations that are rapidly incorporating new technologies and consequently increasing the likelihood of employee obsolescence. According to Pat Galagan, executive director for the American Society for Training & Development, "Companies are getting better at linking learning efforts to strategy and business. Before, training was done across the board, without thinking about how it supports a specific business goal."[5]

Implementing New Technology

New technologies account for much of the enhanced levels of productivity achieved in recent years. But new technology seldom can be introduced without also providing training in its use. When Health Partners installed a major upgrade to its data processing system, employees needed to upgrade their skills to use it. The training program was made up of numerous 45-minute sessions that could easily be scheduled into any workday. Employees were encouraged to retake sessions as many times as they needed to develop a sense of mastery. Besides technical training, employees were taught about the longer-term benefits that would be realized once they all could use the new technology. Discussions about the inevitable stresses that accompany major change were also included. Soon employees were speeding through the program, and customer complaints dropped to nearly none.[6]

Improving Customer Service

Training can improve customer service in a number of ways. Training can help employees understand customer needs while creating a customer-oriented culture. Further, training customers can help meet their needs.

Understanding Customer Needs. Providing excellent customer service is important to Infosys BPO, a business process outsourcing firm in Bangalore, India. Every six months, hundreds of new employees converge on Infosys BPO to learn how to improve their customer service and communication skills. These skills are essential to providing support to the global clients of Infosys BPO, which include firms in banking, telecommunication, and financial services. The firm's employees handle home mortgage information, overdraft issues, telephone repair problems, and other customer service tasks. They are hired to answer the phone as well as communicate via e-mail. To prepare for these jobs, employees attend a boot camp training program. One objective of the training is to master accent "neutralization." English accents in India vary tremendously depending on one's native language; at least 18 different languages are spoken in India. Language is not the only concern, however. Training addresses general communication and selling skills too. According to Nandita Gurjar, vice president and head of human resources, "In terms of their ability to interact with people from different cultures, they have absolutely no experience." In addition, new hires learn about their client's business. For some employees who handle sophisticated transactions, training can last as long as eight weeks. They immerse themselves in their client's world, learning their history, their jargon, and the latest news in order to better connect with customers and develop their own knowledge.[7]

Training for Customers. Increasingly, training activities are crossing organizational boundaries. Besides training their own workforce, many organizations help their customers train and develop *their* workforces. Siemens USA—one of the world's leading manufacturers of high-technology equipment—conducts a variety of training programs to meet the special needs of customers and their markets. Training for customers ensures that all the capabilities of the company's technologically advanced systems are fully utilized and that all their benefits are fully realized.

When Chesterton, a company that makes sealing devices, developed a training program for its sales force, it never intended to offer it to customers. But the course proved to be very effective within the company, even among managers who initially thought it was unnecessary. Before long, Chesterton realized the training could also benefit customers by educating them on the uses and operation of their new equipment. Chesterton doesn't give the training away, however; they preferring using it to generate additional revenue.[8]

Ethics Training

Workforce Management magazine sponsors the Ethical Practice Award to recognize companies with world-class HR practices aimed at ensuring that employees meet high ethical standards. J. M. Smucker & Co. is one of the award winners. The approach used by Smucker's is described in the feature "Managing Ethics: J. M. Smucker & Co."[9]

Knowledge Management and Learning Organizations

In recent years, some companies have elevated the importance of learning and related activities, recognizing them as potential sources of sustained competitive advantage. Organizations that strive to make learning an activity that occurs in many ways every day throughout all parts of the organization have been referred to as learning organizations.[10]

Knowledge Management Technologies. To support their learning agendas, companies such as Xerox, Booz Allen and Hamilton Consulting, General Electric, JPMorgan Chase, and many others have adopted various types of knowledge management technology. Knowledge management is about making sure that knowledge from employees, teams, and units in an organization is captured, remembered, stored, and shared with others.

Knowledge management technologies provide software that makes it possible for people to share knowledge electronically. The systems, which usually operate on the organization's intranet, can capture and distribute "soft" knowledge as well as quantitative data. For example, employees might enter narrative information about their successes and failures during a project. Later, people working on similar projects can read these entries and learn from the experiences of others. Typically, knowledge management software organizes the stored knowledge and provides a means to search and retrieve it using key words that reflect the everyday language and jargon used in an organization.

For knowledge management technology to facilitate learning, employees must be willing to share their knowledge and experiences, and they must be willing to use the ideas and knowledge of others. Neither of these behaviors is

---

FAST FACT

Toyota University offers free training in continuous process improvement to the police and U.S. military as a public service.

" *How we get results is as important as the results we get.* "

Robert W. Lane
Chairman and Chief Executive Officer
Deere & Company

FAST FACT

To help ensure that a company's knowledge management technology is fully integrated with other learning activities, many learning organizations have created a position titled chief learning officer or chief knowledge officer.

MANAGING ETHICS
J. M. Smucker & Co.

J. M. Smucker is a fourth-generation family business in Orville, Ohio, that wants its name to stand for integrity. When James Monroe Smucker started the company in 1897, he personally inspected every jar of apple butter he produced. Today, with nearly 4,000 employees making jams, peanut butter, fruit spreads, shortening, and ice cream toppings in 45 countries, that level of personal involvement by the co-CEOs, Timothy and Richard Smucker, isn't possible. Instead, they rely on an integrated HRM system of practices to ensure ethical conduct. During job interviews, applicants hear Smucker executives refer frequently to the company's basic beliefs: ethics, quality, people, independence, and growth. In the interview, applicants hear specific information about how ethics relates to the job they want. For applicants who do well in the interview, the next stage is reference checking. Here too, the company asks prior employers and other people serving as references to specifically address the applicant's ethical conduct.

Those who pass these selection hurdles are hired and then they immediately attend a training session that includes executive presentations, videos, and group discussions on moral awareness, moral courage, and values. Smucker's training programs present employees with examples of the choices they may have to make, such as making decisions that are good in the short term versus the long term, being honest versus being loyal, and doing what's best for an individual versus doing what's best for the community.

Throughout the training, employees learn about different approaches they can use to address the ethical dilemmas they face at work: the utilitarian approach, which involves seeking to do the greatest good for the greatest number of people; a rules-based approach, which involves making decisions based on rules others have created; and the Golden Rule, which means treating others as you would want them to treat you. After completing their initial training and once a year thereafter, employees sign a nine-page ethics contract. Needless to say, ethical violations are all it takes to get fired from this company. To ensure that employees remember the lessons they learn as new hires, they also take refresher ethics training every three to five years.

Employees seem to respond well to the company's ethical commitment. According to *Fortune*, Smucker has consistently been ranked as one of the "100 Best Companies to Work for in America." By using effective HR practices, this company hopes to prevent unethical employee behaviors that will harm the company.

automatic. As is true for all of the training and development opportunities that employers provide, a variety of other practices should be used to encourage, support, and reward the learning process. Managers may need to reward employees for sharing their knowledge so that others can benefit. They also may need to reward employees for using information and knowledge in a common stored database, the knowledge management library.[11]

Communities-of-Practice. The Hewlett-Packard Company strives to be a learning organization. Learning is especially important at HP Labs, the company's central research unit. To promote learning, HP Labs uses communities-of-practice. A **community-of-practice** *is a social network of people who share a common interest and who are committed to collaborating on projects related to their shared interest.*

HP Labs is the innovation engine of the Hewlett-Packard Company. Its 900 engineers and scientists are charged with discovering and developing products that will fuel the company's long-term growth. To ensure that HP Labs can deliver what the company needs, HP's top managers challenged the lab to implement whatever changes were needed for it to become the world's leading R&D facility.

The change process began with an organizational needs analysis, which was a comprehensive discussion that involved everyone in the lab—managers and technical professionals as well as support staff. Using a variety of communication technologies, including surveys, electronic groupware, and face-to-face discussions, HP Labs employees assessed their current situation and agreed on a set of metrics to measure progress toward their goal of becoming the best lab in the world. Among these indicators were the behaviors of the people in the lab. Behaviors that they wanted to see more of in the lab included listening to each other's suggestions, questioning each other to explore how people's ideas differ, encouraging others to think outside the box, encouraging risk taking, and collaborating across traditional functional boundaries.

The needs analysis resulted in a decision to use communities-of-practice to promote changes in how employees behaved. Initially, 36 communities-of-practice were formed. One community-of-practice addressed the problem of poor communications between engineers. Their goal was to solve a problem that the engineers themselves identified: the tendency of people to focus on their own work and "never talk to each other." The solution to this problem was something called Chalk Talks, which would take place on Friday afternoons, when time was set aside for people to meet and talk about the projects they were working on that week. Another community-of-practice tackled the issue of work/life quality. This group included mostly secretaries, who felt that they could be performing many tasks more effectively and that doing things differently would make their work more enjoyable. During the course of a year, this community-of-practice rewrote the corporate shipping manual, reduced the number of forms needed to enroll employees in the company's benefits plans from 13 to 1, and started a self-development seminar program for the secretarial staff. Four years after this change process began at HP Labs, several significant results have been documented by the company, including a substantial increase in collaborative work, stepped-up use of lateral communication instead of vertical communication, the creation of more than 100 results-oriented improvement programs, and agreement on a clear vision for the lab.[12]

Mergers and Acquisitions

Following mergers and acquisitions, training that focuses on helping employees understand the new culture is probably the most common. But promoting cultural harmony need not be the only objective of postmerger training. Retaining key talent is another objective served by postmerger training.

When Gates Energy Products purchased a battery division from GE, the company's managers worried about how difficult it might be to integrate the plant into their existing company culture. According to Robin Kane, an HR manager at Gates, "the GE management philosophy was very strong, and deeply embedded in each manager, through extensive training and leadership classes at GE's corporate university." At Gates, on the other hand, managers had received only informal training. This caused Gates' managers to worry that the experienced GE managers would abandon the division, choosing instead to seek other employment within GE. Retaining the managerial talent was a key strategic issue that Gates needed to address for their acquisition to pay off. Kane attacked the problem by developing a training program that emphasized the need for trust and teamwork among managers in the merged facilities. Gates wanted GE managers to see that their expertise was needed and appreciated. The company also wanted to convince these managers that they could continue to grow and develop if they remained with Gates. The training seemed to work. Turnover was low among the managers who participated, and their feedback indicated that they learned just as much from the Gates training as they had at GE.[13]

TRAINING AND DEVELOPMENT WITHIN AN INTEGRATED HRM SYSTEM

The activities of training, developing, and socializing employees are so closely related that it is difficult, and perhaps impossible, to make a clear distinction among them. Instead, the entire system of activities usually is referred to simply as training and development (T&D). In general, an organization's training and development practices are its *intentional* efforts to improve current and future performance by helping employees acquire the skills, knowledge, and attitudes required of a competitive workforce.

Training, Development, and Socialization

Usually, **training** *has as its main objective improving performance in the near term and in a specific job by increasing employees' competencies.* Most training for job knowledge and skills is completed in a matter of hours or days.

Depending on an organization's recruitment and selection practices, new hires may have insufficient skills and require training before being placed in a job. For current employees, technological changes, loss of current jobs, and job redesign may create the need for new job skills. Employees may also need new skills or knowledge because they have been transferred or promoted. And in some cases, employees may need training to freshen skills that they don't use very much, such as those used in emergencies.

In comparison to the near-term focus of most training efforts, **development** *refers to activities intended to improve competencies over a longer period of time in anticipation of the organization's future needs.* Development activities may improve performance in one's current job, but that is not typically the main objective. In fact, a common approach to development is giving people "stretch" assignments. Often the expectation for a stretch assignment is that the employee's performance may not be optimal, but a great deal of valuable learning will occur that should prove useful in the future. For this reason, development activities often are referred to as career development and/or leadership development.[14]

Upon entry into a new job or a new organization, all employees initially need to "learn the ropes." **Socialization** *has the major objective of teaching employees about the organization's history, culture, and management practices.* Through socialization, or "onboarding," new employees learn how things are done in the new environment, including things that are not written down in any policy or procedures manual.[15] Intentional efforts to socialize employees usually occur near the time of initial hiring, but merger and acquisition activity in the firm or other major changes may stimulate socialization efforts at other times as well.

Analytical Graphics, chosen in 2006 as the Best Medium Company to Work for in America, uses socialization to maintain its company culture. The tone is set by CEO Paul Graziani and Human Resources Director Lisa Velte. For Velte, maintaining the company's friendly and open atmosphere is a key area of responsibility. New hires are socialized through a long process of orientation, which includes having long lunches in small groups that include new hires, the founders, and the COO and CFO. These lunches are used to pass along this software company's history and teach new hires about the company's markets,

" Fulfilling the grow-from-within policy involves a substantial commitment to training. About 60% of Vanguard's 250-strong HR staff is involved in training activities. "

Kathleen C. Gubanich
Managing Director of Human
Resources
The Vanguard Group

" When people walk in the door, they want to know: What do you expect out of me? What's in this deal for me? What do I have to do to get ahead? "

Fred Smith
Founder and Chief Executive
Officer
FedEx

products (navigation systems), and plans. They also serve to establish open lines of communication so that employees feel free to participate actively once they know their way around. On Fridays, everyone meets for a buffet lunch to receive updates about company performance. Employees working in the field join these buffet meetings via teleconferencing.[16]

Links to Other HR Activities

The objectives of specific training and development activities vary greatly, as will become apparent in this chapter. The differing objectives, in turn, often determine which other aspects of the HRM system should be more tightly integrated with a particular training and development activity. When the objective of training is improving job performance, the training should be designed using job analysis information about what is required to do the work. If the objective is developing employees for future promotion and advancement, the activities should be aligned with the selection criteria used when hiring people into those higher-level positions. If the objective of training is to create a culture change, it may be appropriate to link performance evaluations and rewards to the completion of the training.

Exhibit 8.1 provides a general overview of training and development activities, as well as the relationships they have to other HR activities. Because training and development has so many possible objectives, all the other areas of HR activities are shown in the exhibit. Here we comment on just a few of the many possible linkages.

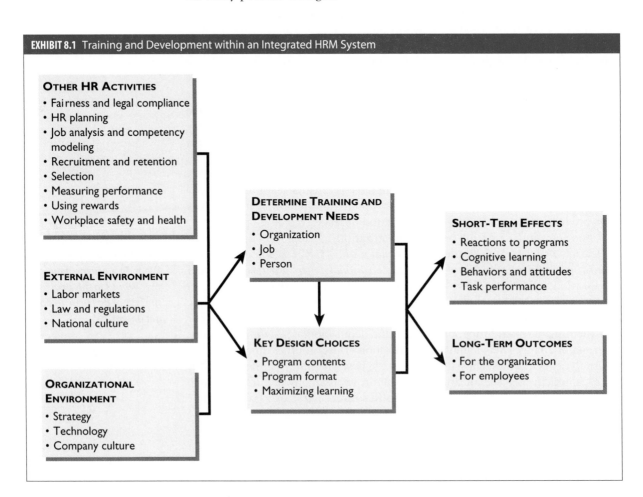

EXHIBIT 8.1 Training and Development within an Integrated HRM System

OTHER HR ACTIVITIES
- Fairness and legal compliance
- HR planning
- Job analysis and competency modeling
- Recruitment and retention
- Selection
- Measuring performance
- Using rewards
- Workplace safety and health

EXTERNAL ENVIRONMENT
- Labor markets
- Law and regulations
- National culture

ORGANIZATIONAL ENVIRONMENT
- Strategy
- Technology
- Company culture

DETERMINE TRAINING AND DEVELOPMENT NEEDS
- Organization
- Job
- Person

KEY DESIGN CHOICES
- Program contents
- Program format
- Maximizing learning

SHORT-TERM EFFECTS
- Reactions to programs
- Cognitive learning
- Behaviors and attitudes
- Task performance

LONG-TERM OUTCOMES
- For the organization
- For employees

Legal Compliance. For some jobs in some industries, federal regulations require employers to provide training. The Occupational Safety and Health Administration (OSHA), the Food and Drug Administration (FDA), and the Federal Aviation Administration (FAA) are examples of agencies that monitor and enforce training requirements. In many other industries, such as financial services and real estate, employees must have a license or be certified to hold particular jobs. When licenses and certification are required, employers may provide the needed training as part of their staffing strategy. In many professions, periodic training is required to update the knowledge acquired earlier.

Recent Supreme Court rulings are expected to spur employers to provide training even when it is not required. These decisions established that an employer may not be held liable for discriminatory behavior by its employees if it can show that (a) it acted reasonably to prevent the behavior and (b) the victim acted unreasonably by not using the company's available procedures for preventing harm. Companies that can prove they offered training to inform employees of their policies and procedures should be able to provide the evidence they need to defend themselves. Exhibit 8.2 summarizes several principles that employers should follow to meet the court's standards for appropriate antidiscrimination training.[17]

Job Analysis, Competency Modeling, and HR Planning. Together, job analysis and competency modeling establish the tasks performed in a job and the competencies required for effective job performance. Such information should serve

FAST FACT

Seventy percent of Delta Air Lines' customer service workforce gets required FAA training via the Internet annually.

EXHIBIT 8.2 Antidiscrimination Training Principles

The following principles are based on statements in several court rulings. These principles represent the suggestions of an informed legal expert. They are not formal regulatory guidelines.

What Are the Objectives?

✔ Inform employees of their rights, duties, and responsibilities regarding nondiscriminatory behavior.
✔ Create a sense of accountability and shared responsibility for creating a harassment-free workplace.

Who Is To Be Trained?

✔ All employees should be trained, with additional training for supervisors to ensure they understand their duties and responsibilities.

When Does Training Occur?

✔ Antidiscrimination training should be offered upon hiring and periodically (e.g., annually) thereafter. Additional training may be appropriate if a complaint is filed.

What Is the Course Content?

✔ Communicate the company policy, which should include a statement prohibiting all forms of harassment, disciplinary action, procedures for reporting incidents of harassment, safeguards to prevent retaliation against those who report such incidents, and assurance of confidentiality.
✔ The legal meaning of harassment should be explained, and employees should be taught which behaviors constitute harassment. Practical examples should be discussed.
✔ The negative consequences of workplace discrimination and harassment should be explained. In addition to legal issues, explain the negative effects on morale and productivity.
✔ Supervisors should receive additional training. It should inform them of their duties and explain that the standards for their behavior are more stringent. Disrespectful behavior by rank-and-file employees may not be unlawful, while the same behavior by a supervisor is clearly illegal.

What To Document?

✔ In order to provide protection against a lawsuit, keep records of all of the previous information. It may also be useful for employees to sign a document acknowledging that they completed the training.

as the foundation for the design of training programs aimed at improving job performance. Competency models, along with HR planning, also can guide the design of career development activities. For many companies, the impending wave of retirements among Baby Boomers has created anxiety about whether the next generation will be ready to fill the high-level jobs that Baby Boomers will soon vacate. With an understanding of the competencies that will be needed by future leaders, companies can begin now to develop the large pools of managerial and executive talent they will soon need.[18]

For Hovnanian Enterprises, one of the nation's largest homebuilders, rapid growth during the recent housing boom created the need for leadership development. The company's succession plan identified candidates for top-level positions about two years in advance of when an opening was expected. When a candidate for future promotion was identified, a committee evaluated the candidate's competency profile to determine which technical or managerial skills the candidate needed to improve. Working with an HR professional, the candidate then developed a personal plan of action. For the next one to two years, candidates were expected to spend 10 to 20% of their work time in personal development activities. The success rate for candidates who completed the development program was twice the success rate for external hires placed into similar positions.[19]

Recruitment and Selection. Disney begins the socialization process during recruitment as a way to discourage applicants who may not fit the corporate culture.[20] To be sure everyone knows what to expect, one of the first steps in the hiring process involves showing applicants a video that details dress codes and rules of grooming and discipline.

Procter & Gamble (P&G) also begins socializing employees during recruitment and selection. Applicants meet with an elite cadre of line managers who have been trained in interviewing skills. Through the interviewers' questions, applicants begin to learn about the organization's culture. After successfully completing at least two interviews and a test of general knowledge, applicants are flown to P&G headquarters in Cincinnati, Ohio, where they undergo a daylong series of interviews. These interviews are two-way communications that continue the socialization process at the same time that selection decisions are being made. If applicants pass the extensive screening process, they then confront a series of rigorous job experiences calculated to induce acceptance of and openness to new ways of doing things. Throughout this phase, new employees learn transcendent company values and organizational folklore, including the importance of product quality and stories about the dedication and commitment of employees long since retired. Intense socialization such as this increases employees' commitment to the success of the company. Commitment, in turn, translates into a greater willingness to work long hours, less absenteeism, and lower turnover rates.

Evaluating Training and Development

Because training and development programs have many different objectives, various measures can be used to evaluate their effectiveness.[21] The major components that can be included in the evaluation of training and development activities are shown in Exhibit 8.3.

Exhibit 8.3 divides the many possible measures of T&D effectiveness into two broad categories: short-term effects and long-term consequences. Usually, employers offer training and development in hopes of reaping the long-term consequences. When it comes to evaluating the effectiveness of their efforts, however, they usually assess only short-term effects. Furthermore, evaluations

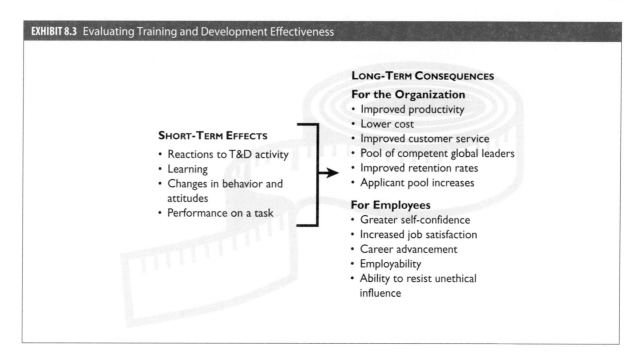

EXHIBIT 8.3 Evaluating Training and Development Effectiveness

SHORT-TERM EFFECTS
- Reactions to T&D activity
- Learning
- Changes in behavior and attitudes
- Performance on a task

LONG-TERM CONSEQUENCES

For the Organization
- Improved productivity
- Lower cost
- Improved customer service
- Pool of competent global leaders
- Improved retention rates
- Applicant pool increases

For Employees
- Greater self-confidence
- Increased job satisfaction
- Career advancement
- Employability
- Ability to resist unethical influence

usually focus on the achievement of the organization's objectives and pay less attention to the objectives of individual employees.

IBM uses metrics to evaluate a wide range of its HR practices, including training. Its approach is described in the feature "Managing with Metrics: IBM Evaluates Its Training."[22]

MANAGING WITH METRICS
IBM Evaluates Its Training

IBM is an information technology (IT) giant with 330,000 employees who generate approximately $90 billion in revenues annually. Senior Vice President for HR Randy McDonald is responsible for ensuring that the IBM workforce is capable of delivering on the company's promise to provide customers around the world with IT products and services whenever and wherever customers need them. According to McDonald, at IBM, managers are expected to demonstrate their success with metrics that businesspeople understand. For HR professionals at IBM, this means showing that HR practices such as training programs produce the desired results.

Ted Hoff is IBM's vice president of learning. He views the development of HR metrics for his activities as a difficult intellectual challenge: "If you can figure out how to do them [metric-based analyses], they'll give you guidance about what's working, and equally important, they'll help you demonstrate your value," says Hoff. The biggest challenges according to Hoff are

- Clearly stating the goals for your training activities.

- Figuring out what metrics you can use to evaluate progress against those goals.
- Getting reasonably good data to use for your analysis.

One example of an analysis Hoff performed was designed to assess the effectiveness of an online learning program. Some executives took advantage of the training program and others didn't. Hoff compared executives who completed 15 or more modules to those who completed 5 or fewer. He found that those who completed 15 or more training modules improved their performance 107% over one quarter, while those who completed 5 or fewer modules improved only 95%. This difference in performance was worth $500 million to the company. Taking into account various other factors, including the investment cost to create the modules, Hoff estimated that IBM earned $150 million in gross margin returns against a learning investment of $12 million.

THE HR TRIAD

Training and development activities can be very expensive, requiring both time and money. Much of the expense is due to employees taking time off from work to participate. Perhaps the most important role of top-level executives is recognizing the value of training investments and supporting such activities. As an organization begins to embrace a philosophy of continuous learning and improvement, more active participation in the design and delivery of the organization's training system by all stakeholders is seen as both desirable and necessary.

At Health Partners, HR professionals sit in on meetings held throughout the company so that they can anticipate future training needs. Their training goal is to be prepared to deliver programs within a week or two from the time a manager makes a request. After several successful training initiatives, managers at Health Partners have learned to rely on the in-house training function. Health Partners also believes in the power of using its own employees as trainers whenever possible. The HR staff is constantly on the lookout for quick learners who can be recruited to serve as volunteer instructors. Employees at Health Partners respond well to having coworkers as instructors. Communication seems to be easier because everyone has the same daily frustrations and challenges. And when a question comes up outside of training sessions, it's easy to catch an instructor in the hallway or at lunch to get advice. The feature "The HR Triad: Roles and Responsibilities in Training and Development" shows some of the training activities that line managers, HR professionals, and other employees engage in.

Managers

FAST FACT

According to a five-year study of 20,000 managers in 40 organizations, continuous personal and professional development is a key characteristic of executives who make a positive difference in their organizations.

Besides providing the financial resources and time needed for training and development, managers can improve the effectiveness of their organization's efforts by participating as trainers, coaches, and mentors. Without top management involvement and commitment, the major focus of an organization is likely to be on other activities. This is particularly true in organizations that focus on short-term goals and getting immediate results, allowing too little time to wait for the benefits of training and development. Top managers at GE, The Container Store, Toyota, Gillette, Ritz-Carlton, Hilton, the Four Seasons, and PepsiCo began to emphasize training and development at the same time they recognized that they had to develop their people and businesses to be effective.[23]

Employees

FAST FACT

Employees hired to work at a new Container Store that opened in New York City spent 230 hours in training before the store opened for business.

The effectiveness of an organization's training system requires the support and cooperation of all employees in the system—top management's support alone isn't sufficient. Although most employees aren't actively involved in designing and delivering training systems, most organizations depend heavily on employees' seeking opportunities to use the available system to their advantage. Research indicates that training and development opportunities are more likely to be used by employees who acknowledge their own needs for improvement and who have developed a specific career plan.[24]

Formal training is often mandatory, but some training may be offered to employees on a voluntary basis. Companies also sponsor informal events designed to provide opportunities for employees to meet other people in the company, develop informal networks and support groups, and even establish mentoring relationships. Career-planning workshops, tuition reimbursement for job-related coursework, and support for attending professional conferences

LINE MANAGERS	HR PROFESSIONALS	EMPLOYEES
• Cooperate with HR professionals in identifying the implications of business plans for training and development.	• Identify training and development needs in cooperation with line managers.	• Seek to understand the objectives of training and development opportunities and accept responsibility for lifelong learning.
• Work with employees to determine their individual training and development needs.	• Assist employees in identifying their individual training and development needs.	• Identify your own training and development needs with HR professionals and line managers.
• Participate in the delivery of training and development programs.	• Communicate with employees regarding training and development opportunities and the consequences of participating in them.	• Consider employment opportunities that will contribute to your own personal development and long-term employability.
• Support employees' participation in training and development opportunities and reinforce the transfer of newly learned behaviors to the job.	• Develop and administer training and development activities.	• Actively participate in training and development opportunities.
• Do much of the on-the-job socialization and training.	• Train the line managers and employees in how to socialize; train and develop employees.	• Assist with the socialization, training, and development of coworkers.
• Participate in efforts to assess the effectiveness of training and development activities.	• Evaluate the effectiveness of training and development activities.	• Participate in efforts to assess the effectiveness of training and development activities.

also may be offered. By participating in such activities, employees facilitate their own socialization into the organization, potentially reaping longer-term benefits such as greater income and job satisfaction, as well as a better sense of personal identity.[25]

HR Professionals

HR professionals usually are heavily involved in the design of the training and development system and the delivery of formal training programs. As this chapter explains, a vast array of training techniques is available to employers, and new technologies continually increase the possibilities. Human resource professionals take responsibility for identifying the objectives to be achieved through training and development and then for choosing or designing appropriate training and development activities, given the objectives. In the best organizations, HR professionals also ensure that investments in training and development result in the desired outcomes.

DETERMINING TRAINING AND DEVELOPMENT NEEDS

Training is usually offered on the basis of need—to rectify skill deficiencies, to provide employees with job-specific competencies, to prepare employees for future roles they may be given, and so on.[26] Sometimes, however, employees receive training and development for reasons other than need. In some organizations, attendance at an executive training program serves as a reward for past performance. In other organizations, participation in training programs is a ritual that signals to newly promoted employees as well as to members of

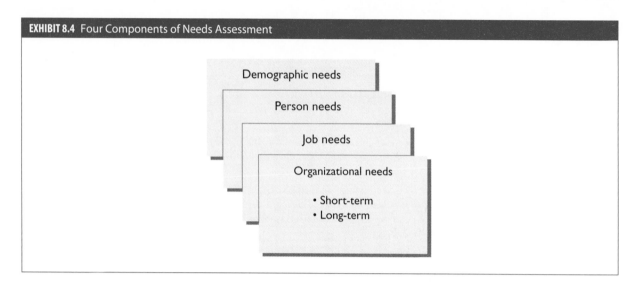

EXHIBIT 8.4 Four Components of Needs Assessment

Demographic needs

Person needs

Job needs

Organizational needs

- Short-term
- Long-term

their former work groups that a change in status has occurred (e.g., a rank-and-file employee is now a manager).

Although training and development can serve these and other purposes, a formal needs assessment is a vital part of a training system.[27] The four primary components of the needs assessment process are shown in Exhibit 8.4.[28]

Organizational Needs Analysis

Organizational needs analysis *begins with an assessment of the short- and long-term strategy and strategic business objectives of the company.* This step is essentially the same as the organizational assessment, described in Chapter 3, except that the focus is specifically on identifying the implications for future training and development activities.

Goals. The organizational needs analysis should produce a clear statement of the goals to be achieved by the organization's training and development activities. At USA Bank, the results of an employee survey led the company to conclude that it needed to improve its career development activities. The survey, which was conducted following a merger, revealed that employees felt pessimistic about their prospects at the company. The company's Opportunity Knocks program was subsequently developed to respond to the concerns that employees had expressed.[29]

Climate for Training. An organizational needs analysis may also include an assessment of the organization's current climate for training. A supportive training climate improves the chances that employees will successfully transfer what they learn from training programs to the job. Some indicators of a supportive training climate are

- Incentives are offered to encourage employees to participate in T&D activities.

- Managers make it easy for those who report directly to them to attend T&D programs.

- Employees encourage each other to practice newly learned skills and do not ridicule each other.

66 We already had a sense that career development...was an issue. The survey really threw it in our faces, and made us realize we had to do something about it. 99

Jeff Brown
Assistant Vice President
USA Bank

- Employees who successfully use their new competencies are recognized and rewarded with special assignments and promotions.

- There are no hidden punishments for participating in T&D (e.g., T&D activities are not scheduled to conflict with other important events; participation doesn't limit access to overtime pay).

- Managers and others who are effective providers of T&D are recognized and rewarded.

These conditions are most likely to be found in learning organizations.[30]

Resources and Constraints. Finally, the organizational needs analysis should identify the available resources and any constraints that need to be considered when designing T&D programs and activities. Can employees be taken off their jobs to participate in training? If so, for how long? Will training needs differ across locations, for example, in different states or different countries? If computer-based technology is to be used to deliver T&D, do employees have access to the specific technology they will need? By addressing such questions, an organizational needs analysis can help ensure that T&D activities are practical in a specific context.

Job Needs Analysis

A **job (or task) needs analysis** *identifies the specific skills, knowledge, and behavior needed to perform the tasks required by present or future jobs.* A thorough job analysis with competency modeling, discussed in Chapter 5, provides the information required for job needs analysis. If training is to be provided for existing jobs, traditional job analysis and competency modeling are appropriate. If training and development are intended to address future needs, future-oriented job analysis and competency modeling should be used for the needs analysis.

As described in Chapter 5, 3M has been very systematic in developing global leaders. They have done this through specifying global leadership competencies and developmental activities that can develop them.[31] The global leadership competency model at 3M specifies the major competencies required for success as a leader in this global corporation. Leadership development and other HR practices at 3M help ensure that future leaders will be prepared for their responsibilities. Exhibit 8.5 shows the global leadership competencies that 3M identified through needs analysis.

Person Needs Analysis

After information about the job has been collected, the analysis shifts to the person. A **person needs analysis** *identifies gaps between a person's current competencies and those identified as necessary or desirable.* Person needs analysis can be either broad or narrow in scope. The broad approach compares actual performance with the minimum acceptable standards of performance, and it can be used to determine the training needs for the current job. The narrower approach compares an evaluation of employee proficiency on each required skill dimension with the proficiency level required for each skill. This approach is useful for identifying development needs for future jobs that will require a specific competency. Whether the focus is on performance of the job as a whole or on particular skill dimensions, several different approaches can be used to identify the training needs of individuals.[32]

EXHIBIT 8.5 Global Leadership Competencies at 3M

Fundamental Leadership Competencies

New employees should possess these when hired and refine them through experience in successive managerial assignments.

- Ethics and integrity
- Intellectual capacity
- Maturity and judgment

Essential Leadership Competencies

These competencies are developed through experience leading a function or department, and they set the stage for more complex executive positions.

- Customer orientation
- Developing people
- Inspiring others
- Business health and results

Visionary Leadership Competencies

These competencies develop as executives take on responsibilities that require them to operate beyond the boundaries of a particular organizational unit, and they are used extensively in higher-level positions.

- Global perspective
- Vision and strategy
- Nurturing innovation
- Building alliances
- Organizational agility

Output Measures. Performance data (e.g., productivity, accidents, and customer complaints), as well as performance appraisal ratings, can provide evidence of performance deficiencies. Person needs analysis can also consist of work sample and job knowledge tests that measure performance capability and knowledge. The major advantages of such measures are that

- They can be selected according to their strategic importance.
- They often are easily quantified.
- When they show improvements, the value of training investments is readily apparent.

A major disadvantage is that such indicators reflect the past and may not be useful for anticipating future needs.

Self-Assessed Training Needs. The self-assessment of training needs is growing in popularity. At Motorola, for example, top managers require employees and their supervisors to identify the business needs for both the department and the business, as well as the skill needs and deficiencies of the individuals. Many major U.S. firms allow managers to nominate themselves to attend short-term or company-sponsored training or education programs. Self-assessment can be as informal as posting a list of company-sponsored courses and asking who wants to attend, or as formal as conducting surveys regarding training needs. For the growing ranks of contract employees and temporary workers, self-assessments are essential to career development. Unlike most employees, these workers must accept full responsibility for assessing their training and development needs. They can then select job assignments that allow them to learn by doing.[33]

Surveys and worksheets are convenient tools for self-assessment.[34] At Colgate-Palmolive, high-potential employees are expected to conduct a self-assessment

> **❝ *People instinctively want to learn.* ❞**
>
> *Kent C. Nelson*
> *Former Chair and Chief*
> *Executive Officer*
> *UPS*

EXHIBIT 8.6 Components of a Tool Kit for Individual Career Development

I. Overview of the Individual Development Process

- Assess individual competencies and values
- Define personal strengths, development needs, and options for career growth
- Identify developmental actions
- Craft individual development plan
- Meet with manager to decide a course of action (based on preceding analysis)
- Accept the challenge of implementing the plan

II. Worksheets for Individual Assessment

- Competency assessment worksheet: assesses strengths and weaknesses for a specified set of competencies
- Personal values survey: assesses preferences for types of work environments, work relationships, work tasks, lifestyle needs, and personal needs
- Development activities chart: describes on-the-job and off-the-job learning opportunities that can be used to develop key competencies
- Global training grid: lists all formal training programs offered by the company and explains how each relates to key competencies
- Individual development plan: developed by the employee, this describes specific development goals and a course of action to be taken to achieve the goals

III. Defining and Understanding Global Competencies

- This section of the tool kit is like a dictionary. It lists all the competencies considered to be important for various types of jobs throughout the company and describes the meaning of each competency. This section serves as a reference guide and encourages people across the company to use a common set of terms when discussing competencies and career development issues.

---

and use it to develop a career plan.[35] The components of this development activity are shown in Exhibit 8.6.

Career Planning Discussions. To assist employees in identifying their strengths and weaknesses, some companies make sure that managers hold career planning discussions with employees. At Eli Lily, "high potentials" discuss their strengths and weaknesses with their managers. Prior to the conversation, the managers hold conversations with other executives to get their input. The managers then communicate the key points raised in those discussions. Afterward, the employees prepare a career plan and review it with their managers.[36]

Attitude Surveys. Attitude surveys completed by a supervisor's subordinates and/or customers can provide information about the training needs of the supervisor. A supervisor who receives relatively low scores regarding fairness in the treatment of subordinates may need training in that area. Similarly, if the customers of a particular unit seem to be more dissatisfied than the customers of other units, training may be needed in that unit. Thus, customer surveys can serve a dual role: providing information to management about service and pinpointing employee deficiencies.

Demographic Needs Analysis

The objective of a **demographic needs analysis** *is to determine the training needs of specific populations of workers.* A demographic needs analysis also can be used to assess whether all employees are given equal access to growth experiences and developmental challenges, which are known to be useful on-the-job methods for promoting skill development. For example, one large study of managers compared the developmental career experiences of men and women. In general, men were more likely to have been assigned to jobs that presented difficult task-related challenges (e.g., operation start-ups and "fix-it" assignments). Women were more likely to have been assigned to jobs that presented challenges caused by obstacles to performance (e.g., a difficult boss or a lack of support from top management).[37] If a company finds demographic differences such as these, it might conclude that an intervention is needed to ensure that men and women have equal access to valuable developmental challenges, along with equal exposure to debilitating obstacles. Such demographic differences may also suggest the need for diversity training.[38]

CONDITIONS FOR EFFECTIVE TRAINING AND DEVELOPMENT

The successful implementation of training and development depends on offering the right programs under the right conditions. Before discussing issues to consider when designing programs, we first look at the importance of creating the right conditions.

Create the Right Conditions

> **You have to hit the executives over the head at the very beginning of an education program and somehow cause failure. Get them to realize they don't know how to do it and confront them with feedback that says, 'You're not as good as you think you are.'**
>
> *Jim Moore*
> *Director of Workforce Planning and Development*
> *Sun Microsystems*

To guide the design of training and development programs, Personnel Decisions International (PDI), a large and successful HR consulting firm, developed a simple framework with five components. By attending to each of these components, organizations can ensure that the right conditions are in place. Both the design of the T&D activities and a consideration of how T&D activities are integrated into the HRM system contribute to ensuring that they are in place.[39]

The five components identified by PDI are as follows:

1. *Insight:* People need to know what it is they need to learn. Employees gain insight into what they need by participating in person needs analysis and receiving feedback about their current skills and competencies.

2. *Motivation:* To put in the required effort, people need to be motivated by internal or external means. Some employees may be eager to learn simply for the sake of learning, but most are likely to become motivated when they believe that participation in training and development activities will lead to positive benefits. Thus, motivation to participate can be increased by integrating training and development activities with other facets of the HRM system (e.g., performance measurement, promotions, incentives, and rewards), as described previously.[40]

   Even when explicit rewards are not directly tied to participation in training and development activities, motivation can be enhanced by clearly communicating that participation is valued by the organization. One way to send the message is by involving everyone—including top-level managers. When everyone has been targeted as needing training, as is often the case with major corporate change efforts, top managers often participate first, and other employee groups are scheduled in hierarchical sequence.

3. *New skills and knowledge acquisition:* People must be shown how to acquire the needed competencies. The design and content of the training and development activities themselves address this issue. Alternatives to consider when developing the content are described in detail later in this chapter.

4. *Real-world practice:* Programs that engage participants in realistic activities improve the likelihood that they will apply their learning. Similarly, when

at their jobs, employees should have the opportunity to practice what they learned. The program design can ensure that training and development activities are realistic, but, as already noted, managers and coworkers share responsibility for encouraging people to apply their new competencies while on the job. The discussion in this chapter about choosing a learning format illustrates the advantages of some formats for providing real-world experience.

5. *Accountability:* Of course, the responsibility for applying new learning is not carried by managers and peers alone. All employees need to feel personally accountable for using what they have learned. The most direct approach to holding employees accountable is to include assessments of improvement as part of the performance appraisal process. However, less formal approaches to providing feedback also can be effective.

Decide Who Provides

Another key question to be addressed when setting up training and development activities is, "Who provides the required guidance?" Training and development activities may be provided by any of several people, including

- Supervisors and other managers.
- A coworker.
- An internal or external subject matter expert.
- The employee.

The selection of the person or people to teach often depends on where the program is held and what skills or competencies are taught. A member of the HR staff usually handles basic orientation sessions. Literacy and technical competencies are usually taught by the immediate job supervisor or a coworker, although technical competencies may also be taught by internal or external subject matter experts. Interpersonal, conceptual, and integrative competencies for management are often taught by training specialists, university professors, or consultants.

Supervisors and Other Managers. In many organizations, on-the-job training is the only form of training offered. In these circumstances, supervisors almost always are the providers of whatever training employees receive. For development activities that involve mentoring, supervisors and managers are appropriate also, because they are in the best position to assess their employees' career needs.[41] Furthermore, because of their position in the organization, supervisors and managers are accessible to employees and have control over the employees' work assignments, which facilitates their effectiveness.[42] Supervisors and managers may also be effective as trainers in off-the-job programs.

At Goldman Sachs, using executives to deliver training is a key principle.[43] According to Goldman Sachs executive Mark Schwartz, "When the division heads ended up teaching . . . , it was a lot easier to persuade vice presidents and younger managing directors in those divisions that they should be participating thoughtfully. Over time it became really inspirational. People wanted to participate in the program and thought it might be pretty neat to teach in the program."[44]

Coworkers. When Disney trains new hires, the company's message is delivered by some of the best "cast" members in the company. Dressed in full costume, they show through example how to create happiness—the most important aspect of their

FAST FACT

Many line managers spend up to 50% of their time giving and clarifying instructions to new employees.

" *Nobody wants to work for someone they can't learn from.* "

Steve Jobs
Chief Executive Officer
Apple

FAST FACT

More than 2,000 employees and 2,000 clients have taken courses at Goldman Sachs University.

role. After the initial training session, new cast members are paired with experienced employees for 16 to 38 hours of paired-training, which is essentially one-on-one coaching. As the Disney example illustrates, coworkers can be very effective trainers. Often, coworkers are more knowledgeable about the work than anyone else.

Coworkers also play an important role in many management development programs. For management development programs, it is common to bring together employees from different parts of the organization for several days of training. Participants in such programs often report that the most valuable learning occurs through conversations with their colleagues. Furthermore, exposure to the perspectives of colleagues working around the world helps employees develop more sophisticated "mental maps" of how business is conducted in different locations. ExxonMobil's Global Leadership Workshop takes advantage of this phenomenon. Twice a year, about 30 participants from around the world participate in the workshop. IBM uses a similar model for its eight-day global leadership training program.[45]

Clearly, coworkers can be valuable providers of training. Nevertheless, their effectiveness as trainers or mentors should not be assumed. A concern with relying on coworkers as trainers is that they may not be able to instruct others. They may also teach others their own shortcuts rather than correct procedures. If coworkers are to be trainers, they should receive instruction on how to train and should be given sufficient time on the job to work with trainees.

Experts. Subject matter experts may not be familiar with procedures in a specific organizational culture. As a result, they may be respected for their expertise but mistrusted because they aren't members of the work group. Still, if no one in the immediate work environment possesses the knowledge needed, or if large numbers of individuals need to be trained, the only option may be to hire experts. Experts who are expressive when delivering training and well organized are especially effective.[46]

Employee. Self-paced instruction is also an option. With the growing popularity of computer-based training, self-paced instruction is becoming more common. Trainees benefit from this method by learning at a speed that maximizes retention. However, if they aren't given incentives to complete the instruction in a specified period of time, they may place it on the back burner.

6

LEARNING GOAL

STATING THE LEARNING OBJECTIVES

A training or development program must have content congruent with its learning objectives. Typical learning objectives include improving cognitive knowledge, developing employees' skills, influencing affective responses, and encouraging ethical behavior.[47]

Cognitive Knowledge

Cognitive knowledge includes the information people have available (what they know), the way they organize this information, and their strategies for using this information. Of these components, what people know is by far the primary type of cognitive knowledge that most organizations try to address through training systems.

Company Policies and Practices. **Orientation programs** *brief new employees on benefit programs and options, advise them of rules and regulations, and explain the policies and practices of the organization.* Typically, orientation programs inform new employees about equal employment opportunity practices, safety regulations, work times, coffee breaks, the structure and history of the organization, and perhaps the products or services of the organization. For the Ritz-Carlton Hotel, orientation helps instill core values that are central to realizing its strategic vision.[48]

Basic Knowledge and the Three Rs. Increasingly, organizations are concerned about cognitive knowledge of a more basic nature: the three Rs (reading, writing, and arithmetic). Training programs designed to correct basic skill deficiencies in grammar, mathematics, safety, reading, listening, and writing are still necessary in today's organization. In particular, Total Quality Management (TQM) requires basic math and statistical knowledge that many high school graduates haven't mastered. Statistical tools are fundamental to W. Edwards Deming's approach to quality, which is improvement by the numbers. Almost every job that is done using information technology requires basic reading and writing skills. Unfortunately, many recent high school graduates lack these basic skills. In a recent survey, 40% of employers said that many high school graduates are unprepared for entry level jobs.[49]

The Big Picture. Employees striving for or currently in managerial positions may need knowledge about the organizational structure, the organization's products and services, the organization's business strategies, and changing conditions in the environment. Much of this type of knowledge is learned through standard job assignments as well as through temporary developmental learning experiences, such as serving on a task force or taking an overseas assignment. Adapting to complex and changing environments is often a responsibility for top and middle managers, and conceptual training helps employees make new associations.

Skills

Whereas cognitive knowledge is essentially inside the head, skills are evident in behaviors. Skill-based learning generally involves practicing desired behaviors, such as those that demonstrate technical, interpersonal, or language skills.

Technical. Owing to rapid changes in technology and the nature of jobs, as well as the implementation of automated office, industrial, and managerial systems, technological updating and skill building have become a major thrust in training.[50]

Six Sigma is a management process that is used for high-impact improvement efforts. It is grounded in systematic measurement and statistical analysis, and it requires that employees use several specific problem-solving skills. Invented at Motorola in the 1980s, Six Sigma has become a centerpiece of the management systems in companies like GE, Dupont, Ford, Allied Signal, and Dow. When a company decides to adopt Six Sigma, senior leaders typically are the first to go through the training. After they understand the system, they set goals and often agree to a new compensation package that links their pay to the goals. Next, the entire workforce must be trained in statistical process control techniques. Often a few employees are trained first, and then they serve as trainers for the others. In many companies, employees are awarded the status of "black belts" for achieving high levels of proficiency in Six Sigma techniques.[51]

Interpersonal. Skills in communication, conducting performance appraisals, team building, leadership, and negotiation are increasingly in demand. The development of interpersonal skills is essential for lower- and middle-level managers as well as for employees who have direct contact with the public

" The future workforce is here, and it is ill-prepared. "

Conclusion from "Are They Really Ready to Work?" (a report on the 21st Century Workforce Initiative)

" Certification for a maid? Absolutely. 'Room attendants,' as we call them, have a most important job in our organization. "

Debra Phillips
Training Manager and Quality Adviser
The Ritz-Carlton, New York

(e.g., sales associates). Can you describe your experiences with salespeople? What is a good salesperson like? What is a bad one like? Usually, good interpersonal skills are what make the difference.

Language. For employers who hire large numbers of immigrants, providing language training is an effective way to reduce errors and improve job performance, at the same time enhancing employee loyalty. Bob Chinn's Crabhouse in Wheeling, Illinois, offers English as a second language (ESL) training as a way to maximize customer satisfaction. About half of the 350 employees at this restaurant didn't speak fluent English when they were hired. Most of these employees work in the "back" of the establishment as cooks, food preparation staff, bus persons, and dishwashers. Lack of English fluency often meant mistakes in preparing food orders and lack of responsiveness to customers who made requests to buspersons that should have been directed to the wait staff. To improve their English, now employees can take classes twice a week, beginning at 7:00 a.m. (a time chosen based on employees' preferences!). Part of the training is funded by the Welfare to Work Partnership, a nationwide program that supports efforts to improve work and life skills. In this case, the English classes help employees cope with life outside work in addition to improving their job performance. With improved English skills, they find it easier to apply for drivers' licenses, attend PTA meetings, and be effective members of their communities. The training also seems to have enhanced employee loyalty. Since the ESL training began, annual turnover has dropped to 38%—much lower than 100% turnover rate that had been considered normal in the past.[52]

Affective Outcomes

> **"** *Our staff was excited we were taking the time to learn their language.* **"**
>
> Patricia Hutcherson
> Executive Vice President and
> Chief Financial Officer
> Casa Rio Mexican Foods

When the desired result of socialization, training, or developmental experiences is a change in motivation, attitudes, or values (or all three), the learning objectives of interest are affective outcomes. The Disney company's orientation and training programs are clearly intended to influence the affect of cast members. They learn about the key Disney "product"—happiness—and their roles in helping to provide it.[53]

The objectives of building team spirit and socializing employees into the corporate culture aren't the only affective outcomes of a training system. In fact, training activities often are designed in part to develop employees' feelings of mastery and self-confidence. For example, mentoring programs provide not only information but also the feedback and supportive encouragement that give employees confidence in their ability to take on new tasks and to make decisions that might otherwise seem risky. Self-confidence enhances task performance. This is a point not lost on athletes, their coaches, or sportscasters—nor, apparently, is it lost on the many companies now providing wilderness training. Although the evidence is sparse, testimonials and some research indicate that participating in outdoor group adventures boosts self-confidence.[54]

Training programs designed to enhance employees' emotional intelligence are another example of efforts that target affective outcomes. **Emotional intelligence** *involves recognizing and regulating emotions in ourselves and in others. It includes self-awareness, self-management, social awareness, and relationship management.* One objective of emotional intelligence training is to teach people techniques to deal with emotions in the workplace. For example, people who work in customer service jobs may benefit from training that teaches them to keep their emotions in check when dealing with customers who are upset and angry. For people in many other jobs that create stress, emotional intelligence training can help lower the experience of stress and may contribute to overall improvements in health.[55]

Ethical Behavior

There has been much discussion and concern about unethical business behavior in recent years, and business is starting to get the point. Simply relying on employees to use their best judgment does not seem to be enough to ensure that people in leadership positions behave ethically. In fact, a recent survey of more than 3,000 U.S. workers revealed that a variety of unethical behaviors still occur frequently: At least one out of six workers reported that they observed managers who were abusive or intimidating, lied to customers and employees, and/or tolerated safety violations that could result in harm.

Weyerhaeuser Co. doesn't want its leaders—or any other employees—engaging in unethical behaviors. Founded in 1900, Weyerhaeuser is a $25 billion producer of forest products and services with employees in 19 countries. Developing ethical leaders is a top priority at Weyerhaeuser. To achieve its objective, the company offers leadership assessments and training through its corporate university. For years, it has included ethics training as part of its formal leadership training program. The company's philosophy is that remarkable leaders can inspire and motivate others to accomplish great tasks. From the beginning, effective leadership has meant ethical leadership.

To help managers spot and think through tough ethical situations, Weyerhaeuser's top executives serve as the teachers. During training programs, managers are asked to read and discuss several case studies that present realistic ethical challenges. Leaders present several choices for managers to consider, including one or two good ones. A group discussion gives managers a chance to explain what they think about the situation, how they would behave, and why.

"Pulp Fiction" is the title of one case that Weyerhaeuser uses to teach ethics. In this case, Lena is an employee at a pulp mill. When the maintenance contractor employed by the plant begins to do shoddy work, her boss, Donna, asks her to recommend another contractor to perform the needed maintenance tasks. Lena hears that the current maintenance contractor employs the son-in-law of Donna, the mill's maintenance manager. What would you do? Here are some options:

1. Ask a coworker if she has the correct information: Is the man really Donna's son-in-law?
2. Tell the plant manager about the potential conflict.
3. Ask the contractor about the situation.
4. Ask Donna whether her son-in-law works for the maintenance contractor.

Leaders and managers discuss how each choice might affect the various people involved as well as the company. Very few managers will ever face this particular situation; that's not the point. The point is to help managers develop an approach to thinking about the ethical issues they might face. What would you do if you were Lena, and why?[56]

CHOOSING THE PROGRAM FORMAT

Many different formats can be used for training and development activities. Three general categories of formats are on-the-job, on-site but not on-the-job, and typically-off-site. Choices about format may be constrained by the type of learning that's to occur—cognitive, skill-based, or affective—as well as by cost

EXHIBIT 8.7 Advantages and Disadvantages of Several Learning Formats

Type of Program	Advantages	Disadvantages
On-the-Job		
e-Learning and video teleconferencing	• Bring employees together from many locations • Speed up communications • May reduce costs • May be done on or off the job	• Start-up and equipment costs are high • Require adaptation to a new learning format
Apprenticeship training	• Does not interfere with real job performance • Provides extensive training	• Takes a long time • Is expensive • May not be related to job
Internships and assistantships	• Facilitate transfer of learning • Give exposure to real job	• Are not really full jobs • Provide vicarious learning
Job rotation	• Gives exposure to many jobs • Allows real learning	• Involves no sense of full responsibility • Provides too short a stay in a job
Supervisory assistance and mentoring	• Is often informal • Is integrated into job • Is expensive	• Means effectiveness rests with the supervisor • May not be done by all supervisors
On-Site, but Not On-the-Job		
Corporate universities	• Tailored to company needs • Support company vision and culture	• Can be costly • Require skilled management
Programmed instruction on an intranet or the Internet	• Reduces travel costs • Can be just-in-time • Provides for individualized learning and feedback • Provides for fast learning	• Not appropriate for some skills • Is time-consuming to develop • Is cost-effective only for large groups • Often no support to assist when trainee faces learning problems
Interactive videos	• Convey consistent information to employees in diverse locations	• Costly to develop • Do not provide for individual feedback
Typically-off-site		
Formal courses	• Are inexpensive for many • Do not interfere with job	• Require verbal skills • Inhibit transfer of learning
Simulation	• Helps transfer of learning • Creates lifelike situations	• Cannot always duplicate real situations exactly • Costly to develop
Assessment centers and board games	• Provide a realistic job preview • Create lifelike situations	• Costly to develop • Take time to administer
Role-playing	• Is good for interpersonal skills • Gives insights into others	• Cannot create real situations exactly; is still playing
Sensitivity training	• Is good for self-awareness • Gives insights into others	• May not transfer to job • May not relate to job
Wilderness trips	• Can build teams • Can build self-esteem	• Costly to administer • Physically challenging

and time considerations. Exhibit 8.7 summarizes the advantages and disadvantages of several learning formats.

FAST FACT

An estimated 30% of all company training is now delivered using e-learning technologies.

e-Learning

Note that the three major categories of training and development formats do not depend on using a specific type of technology. Before the computer, film, and communications industries began to merge, the technology used was often what most clearly distinguished one training format from another. Today, however, *technology makes it possible to combine many formats and deliver them as an integrated learning system that combines, for example, Web-based learning, virtual classrooms, computerized learning modules, interactive TV, satellite broadcasts, and other vehicles. When such technologies are used for training and development, they often are referred to as **e-learning.**[57] Many people are skeptical about e-learning technologies, but recent research shows that such concerns may not be justified. A review of nearly 100 studies that compared classroom instruction to Web-based instruction found that Web-based instruction can be more effective than traditional classroom training methods for teaching basic knowledge.[58]

On the Job

On-the-job training (OJT) *occurs when employees learn their jobs under direct supervision.* Trainees learn by observing experienced employees and by working with the actual materials, personnel, or machinery (or all three) that constitute the job. An experienced employee trainer is expected to provide a favorable role model and to take time from regular job responsibilities to provide job-related instruction and guidance. Assuming the trainer works in the same area, the trainee receives immediate feedback about performance. As described earlier in this chapter, on-the-job training is central to developing the skills of employees who work for the Ritz-Carlton Hotel Company.

One advantage of OJT is that the transfer of training is high. Because trainees learn job skills in the environment in which they will actually work, they readily apply these skills on the job. However, on-site training is appropriate only when a small number of individuals need to be trained and when the consequence of error is low. Also, the quality of the training hinges on the skill of the manager or lead employee conducting it. OJT is most likely to be effective when it is designed carefully and treated as a formal process for managing workforce performance.[59]

Apprenticeships, Internships, and Assistantships. A method for minimizing the disadvantages of on-the-job training is combining it with off-the-job training. Apprenticeship training, internships, and assistantships are based on this combination.

Apprenticeship training is mandatory for admission to many skilled trades, such as plumbing, electronics, and carpentry. These programs are formally defined by the U.S. Department of Labor's Bureau of Apprenticeship and Training and involve a written agreement "providing for not less than 4,000 hours of reasonably continuous employment . . . and supplemented by a recommended minimum of 144 hours per year of related classroom instruction." The Equal Employment Opportunity Commission (EEOC) allows the 48,000 skilled trade (apprenticeship) training programs in the United States to exclude individuals aged 40 to 70 because these programs are part of the educational system aimed at youth.[60]

Somewhat less formalized and extensive are internship and assistantship programs. Internships are often part of an agreement between schools or colleges and local organizations. As with apprenticeship training, individuals earn while they learn, but usually the pay rate is lower than that paid to full-time employees or master crafts workers. Internships also provide a realistic preview of the job and the organizational conditions in which an employee is likely to work. Assistantships involve full-time employment and expose an individual to a wide range of jobs. However, because the individual only assists other workers, the learning experience is often vicarious. Assistantship programs that combine job or position rotation with active mentoring and career management avoid this problem.

Job Experiences. When development is the objective, employers may put people into jobs to facilitate their learning and development. **Job rotation programs** *involve rotating employees through jobs at a similar level of difficulty to train them in a variety of jobs and decision-making situations.* Job rotation programs often are useful for helping employees see the bigger picture. However, usually employees aren't in a single job long enough to learn very much, and they may not be motivated to work hard since they know they will soon move on.

The philosophy of having employees learn while doing also underlies the use of developmental job assignments. **Developmental job assignments** *are those that place employees in jobs that present difficult new challenges and hurdles.* The assumption is that employees develop new competencies by learning to deal with the new challenges. Components of a developmental job assignment include

- Unfamiliar responsibilities.
- Responsibility for creating change (e.g., to start something new, fix a problem, deal with problem employees).
- High levels of responsibility (e.g., high-stakes and high-visibility assignments; jobs involving many stakeholders, products, or units).
- Boundary-spanning requirements (e.g., working with important stakeholders outside the organization).
- Dealing with diversity (working with people from multiple cultures or demographic backgrounds).[61]

Supervisory Assistance and Mentoring. Often the most informal program of training and development is supervisory assistance or mentoring. Supervisory assistance is a regular part of the supervisor's job. It includes day-to-day coaching, counseling, and monitoring of workers on how to do the job and how to get along in the organization. The effectiveness of these techniques depends in part on whether the supervisor creates feelings of mutual confidence, provides opportunities for growth, and effectively delegates tasks.

With **mentoring**, *an established employee guides the development of a less experienced worker, or protégé.* Mentoring can increase employees' competencies, achievement, and understanding of the organization.[62] Usually, mentors counsel their protégés on how to advance and network in the company, and they sometimes offer personal advice.

John Thompson, CEO of Symantec, has mentored dozens of people. As a very successful African American, his mentorship is especially valued by young people of color. Thompson's mentoring style is described in the feature "Managing the Multicultural Workforce: John W. Thompson, CEO and Mentor."[63]

Grace Lieblein, a chief engineer at GM, is a mentor who is especially interested in helping female engineers manage their careers. As a mentor, she helps them find assignments that develop their potential for long-term advancement to become either technical leaders or CEOs. "I strongly encourage folks I mentor to get a very strong foundation of experiences that help you find your career potential. I definitely think a broad foundation of experiences is really important," she said.[64]

FAST FACT

In the United States, IBM is using Second Life, a 3D virtual world, to create a mentoring community.

FAST FACT

At American Express, a leadership competency model is used to set expectations and coach managers on key elements of leadership, including diversity.

FAST FACT

When Avon's CEO Andrea Jung began working at Bloomingdale's, she sought out executive Joan Vass to act as her mentor because Vass had a fast-paced career, was tactfully aggressive, and successfully balanced her job with a quiet family life.

MANAGING THE MULTICULTURAL WORKFORCE
John W. Thompson, CEO and Mentor

Operating in more than 40 countries, Symantec provides a broad range of information security and storage products that facilitate companies' management of their IT infrastructure. Under the leadership of CEO and Chairman John W. Thompson, Symantec has grown from a $632-million consumer antivirus company to an enterprise security player with $4.1 billion in annual sales. Today, almost every *Fortune* 500 firm uses Symantec products.

John W. Thompson grew up in Florida, where his mother was a teacher and his father was a postal worker. "My mom and dad believed very much in the concepts of working hard for what you want and making sure you're properly prepared for what your pursuits are," he recalls. After college, he went to work as a salesman for IBM. By the time he left—28 years later—people were thinking he might someday be CEO of IBM. Thompson didn't think that was likely to ever happen, however. Instead, he chose to become CEO of Symantec.

Thompson quickly refocused Symantec on its data security business. He sold or shut down several units and replaced more than half of the company's original 2,300 employees, including most top managers. Within three years, he was being recognized as one of the country's best managers, and BlackEngineer.com listed him as one of the 50 Most Important African Americans in Technology. During this challenging time, Thompson's confidence and resolve served him well. "He did not back off [for] one moment on everything he said about Veritas and the need and the value of that acquisition, despite the pressure that he was under," observed Bruce Chizen, CEO of Adobe in San Jose, who met Thompson through a Silicon Valley CEO peer group. "He did not cave. The leadership he demonstrated under difficult circumstances was admirable." In fact, Chizen was so impressed with Thompson's leadership skills that he later sought Thompson's advice and support. "I continue to ask him to share with me his experience, and that has helped me form my own opinions on how to move ahead with Macromedia," Chizen says. "I learned a great deal from the experiences he had."

Thompson points to the important role of mentors in his own life: "I had the belief that if I could produce good results, the rest would take care of itself. But along the way, I also was fortunate enough to have support from some really well-placed people who took an interest in my career....Success is a combination of hard work and a good support structure that helps to get you going, but it's determination along the way that keeps you moving along. I had enough of all of those to get me where I am today." With his own future secure, Thompson is spending more of his time encouraging young African Americans to pursue engineering careers. He takes this responsibility personally, inviting young talent to his home and treating them to a barbecue. Periodically he also coaches students at Florida A&M University, his alma mater.

Thompson's approach to mentoring is friendly and easygoing. He's a good storyteller, and the kind of person people describe as charismatic. Based on three decades of business experience, Thompson thinks he understands what it takes to be successful. In his mentoring, he helps people understand that besides being able to work with numbers, personal integrity is essential. He also stresses the importance of taking time to rest and reflect. "You cannot run 24/7, 365 days a year. You need to take time to enjoy the fruits of your labors." Thompson shares these views with his employees and other mentees at so-called bordeaux-and-barbecue dinners, where he might serve ribs and beans with a $500 bottle of bordeaux wine.

The U.S. Army also uses peer-to-peer mentoring. For managers and army officers, talking with mentors about how to develop more effective leader behaviors is important to career advancement. Mentors can help managers understand how others respond to their behaviors and point out weaknesses or blind spots. Mentors also serve as role models that individuals can emulate, and they provide valuable advice concerning the styles of leadership favored in the organization. Finally, mentors often assist managers in developing leadership capabilities by helping them obtain assignments that will foster on-the-job learning.[65]

If leadership skills can't be developed and improved through mentoring and other HR practices, all an organization can do is to search for good leaders and hope to find them somewhere. But most CEOs seem to believe that leadership can be improved by giving employees opportunities for development, and research supports this view. That's why CEOs invest both personal time and company resources in efforts to develop the leadership capacity of their employees.[66]

At some companies, finding enough mentors to provide such advice is getting more difficult. As companies downsize and flatten their management structures, they find that the middle managers who once served as mentors are either no longer with the company or are too busy to spend their time on mentoring. Yet another challenge for mentoring programs is that the best mentor for a particular employee may be located in another state or even another country. To solve this problem, some companies are moving to electronic mentoring, which relies heavily on telephone calls and meetings over the Internet.[67]

Coaching. For high-level executives and other employees who hold visible and unique jobs, traditional forms of on-the-job training are impractical. Yet these employees often need to develop new competencies to be fully effective. In recent years, more and more executives have turned to personal coaches to address their training needs. **Personal coaches** *typically observe the employee in action and later provide feedback and guidance for how to improve their interaction skills in the future.* Most coaches also encourage their "trainees" to discuss difficult situations as they arise and to work through alternative scenarios for dealing with them. Although coaching is rapidly growing in popularity, it's a relatively new technique, and few guidelines are available to evaluate whether a potential coaching relationship is likely to succeed.[68] Nevertheless, the evidence of its effectiveness is beginning to accumulate. An effective coaching program appears to help managers change themselves and, in the process, change their organizations.[69]

On-Site but Not On the Job

When the consequence of error is high, it's usually more appropriate to conduct training off the job. Most airline passengers would readily agree that it's preferable to train pilots in flight simulators rather than have them apprentice in the cockpit of a plane. Similarly, it's typically useful to have a bus driver practice on an obstacle course before taking to the roads with a load of school children. Training at the work site but not on the job is appropriate for required after-hours programs and for programs in which contact needs to be maintained with work units but OJT would be too distracting or harmful. It's also appropriate for voluntary after-hours programs and for programs that update employees' competencies while allowing them to attend to their regular duties.

For example, when a major Northeast grocery store chain switched to computerized scanners, it faced the problem of training thousands of checkers spread out across three states. The cost of training them off-site was prohibitive. Yet management also was fearful about training employees on the job, lest their ineptitude offend customers. To solve the problem, the grocery chain developed a mobile training van that included a vestibule model of the latest scanning equipment. Checkers were trained on-site but off the job in the mobile unit. Once the basic skill of scanning was mastered, employees returned to the store, and the trainer remained on-site as a resource person. According to one store manager, the program was effective because employees could be trained rapidly and efficiently, yet no customers were lost owing to checker errors or slowness.

Corporate Universities and Executive Education Programs. A growing trend in the United States is the development of corporate universities that offer programs tailored to the needs of the company. Corporate universities focus on the education of employees and sometimes customers. McDonald's Hamburger University, begun in 1961, is among the oldest corporate universities. Started in a basement, the center now trains more than 2,500 students annually in the fine details of restaurant and franchise operations. General Electric, an advocate of training and development for years, has an up-to-date facility in Croton-on-Hudson, New York, that it uses for divisional and group training. Corporate universities have been developed by such diverse firms as 3M, Ford, General Motors, Motorola, United Airlines, Boeing, Kodak, Goldman Sachs, Dell, and Harley-Davidson.[70] In fact, research suggests that 65% of all major firms offer some form of executive education. Today, many corporate colleges offer degrees, and hundreds of corporations offer courses leading to degrees. While not always the case, the executive programs at companies may be under the direction of the chief learning officer.

Interactive Video Training. Interactive video training (IVT) *programs present a short video and narrative presentation and then require the trainee to respond to it.* This sequence—packaged program, learner response, and more programmed instruction—provides for individualized learning. FedEx has a pay-for-knowledge program that is based on interactive video training and job knowledge testing for its 35,000 customer-contact employees. Before couriers ever deliver a package, they receive at least three weeks of training. Because FedEx is constantly making changes or additions to its products and services, it also must continually update its training programs. Employees at hundreds of FedEx locations around the United States can readily access a 25-disk training curriculum that covers topics such as customer etiquette and defensive driving. Customer-contact employees take a job knowledge test every six months; the company pays each employee for four hours of study and preparation time and for two hours of test-taking time. The knowledge required to do well on the test is so job related that performance on the test essentially reflects performance on the job. As an incentive for employees to get serious about doing well on the test, the company links their compensation to performance on the test. Employees who excel in applying their knowledge to job performance become eligible for additional proficiency pay.

Typically-Off-Site

Off-site training may be appropriate when complex competencies need to be mastered or when employees need to focus on specific interpersonal competencies that might not be apparent in the normal work environment. It's difficult to build a cohesive management work team when members of the team are constantly interrupted by telephone calls and subordinate inquiries. Team building is more likely to occur during a retreat, when team members have time to focus on establishing relationships.

One disadvantage is that the costs of off-site training are high. Another cause for concern is that knowledge learned off the job may not transfer to the workplace. The issue of **transfer**—*whether employees can readily apply the knowledge and skills learned during training to their work*—is one of the most important considerations when choosing a format. Research has shown that the

FAST FACT

Dell Computer Corporation uses the computers it manufactures to educate employees at its corporate university.

FAST FACT

Research shows that the transfer of skills learned during training is improved when supervisors are involved in designing and evaluating training activities.[71]

more dissimilar the training environment is to the actual work environment, the less likely trainees will be to apply what they learn to their jobs. For example, the transfer-of-knowledge problem is minimal when trainees work with machines that are comparable to the ones in their actual work environment. However, it may be difficult to apply teamwork competencies learned during a wilderness survival program to a management job in a large service organization.[72] McDonald's Corporation wants to be sure that the money it invests in training transfers to its restaurants in 128 countries. To ensure that their training programs develop skills that transfer to the work setting, McDonald's uses mystery shoppers and review teams, which make visits for the purpose of conducting evaluations.[73]

Formal Courses. Formal courses can be directed either by the trainee—using programmed instruction, computer-assisted instruction, reading, and correspondence courses—or by others, as in formal classroom courses and lectures. Although many training programs use the lecture method because it efficiently and simultaneously conveys large amounts of information to large groups of people, it has several drawbacks. Perhaps most importantly, except for cognitive knowledge and conceptual principles, the transfer of learning to the actual job is probably limited. Also, the lecture method does not permit individualized training based on individual differences in ability, interests, and personality.

Simulation. **Simulations** *present situations that are similar to actual job conditions and allow trainees to practice how to behave in those situations.*[74] All airlines use flight simulators for pilot training. Because the simulated environment isn't real, it's generally less hectic and safer than the actual environment; as a consequence, trainees may have trouble adjusting from the training environment to the actual environment.

The arguments for using a simulated environment are compelling: It reduces the possibility of customer dissatisfaction that can result from on-the-job training; it can reduce the frustration of the trainee; and it may save the organization a great deal of money because of fewer training accidents. Not all organizations, even in the same industry, accept these arguments. Some banks, for example, train their tellers on the job, whereas others train them in a simulated bank environment.

Assessment Centers. Just as they are popular in managerial selection, assessment centers (described in Chapter 7) are an increasingly popular simulation technique for developing managers. Certain aspects of the assessment center, such as management games and in-basket exercises, are excellent for training.[75] When these are used for training purposes, however, it is essential that instructors help participants analyze what happened and what should have happened. The opportunity for improvement may be drastically reduced if the trainees are left to decide what to transfer from the games or exercises to the job.

Business Board Games. Companies are finding that it pays to have all employees know how the company makes money, the difference between revenue and profit, and how much profit the company makes on each sale. To facilitate this learning, companies such as Prudential and Sears use board games, similar in form and shape to Monopoly, that reveal the workings of the company. Employees actually play these games, and, as they do, they learn about the company and how the company runs the business and makes a profit or loss.

Wilderness Trips and Outdoor Training. To increase employees' feelings about the here and now and to raise their self-esteem, organizations sometimes use programs that involve physical feats of strength, endurance, and cooperation. These can be implemented on wilderness trips to the woods or mountains or water. Siemens, for example, dropped 60 managers from around the world onto the shores of Lake Starnberger, south of Munich, and gave them the task of building rafts using only logs, steel drums, pontoons, and rope. Among the rules for the exercise: No talking. The objective was to teach managers the importance of knowledge sharing. Back on the job, managers could earn bonuses for contributing their knowledge to ShareNet, the company's knowledge management software.[76]

Whereas firms such as Siemens use some variation of outdoor experiences in their management training with success, many others question the degree of transfer to the job that these experiences offer. Firms using outdoor experiences recognize this concern and thus articulate the link between the competencies developed in the experiences and the competencies needed by the managers on the job. At its retreat for managers, Wells Fargo uses activities specifically designed to improve teamwork skills. The firm's CFO feels the expense is justified, explaining that the managers are "very high-powered, very capable, very technically skilled, and very competitive. And they are very individualistic in their approach to work." What he wants is to get them to "see the power of acting more like a team." His view is that activities like walking a narrow plank blindfolded and crossing a river on a jerry-rigged bridge can build the sense of teamwork that Wells Fargo needs.[77]

Cooking Events. One of the fastest growing forms of off-site training may be team cooking. UBS, the financial services company, used a team cook-off to help develop employees' teamwork skills. Based on popular television shows, such training provides a comfortable, fun, and satisfying environment for employees to learn to collaborate in a nonhierarchical team. UBS brings in famous chefs for its training events, but other companies simply use the services of a cooking school or local catering company.[78]

MAXIMIZING LEARNING

Even when a training technique is appropriate, learning may not take place if the experience isn't structured appropriately. Thus, when designing a training or development program, it is important to take time to set the stage for learning, to create conditions that will maximize learning during the training or development program, and to provide conditions that will maintain performance in the longer term.

Setting the Stage for Learning

Before launching a training program, trainers or managers need to consider how information will be presented. In addition, they must consider the beliefs of trainees regarding task-specific competencies.[79]

Clear Instructions. To perform as desired, employees must know what is expected. Clear instructions establish appropriate behavioral expectations. Training expectations should be stated in specific terms. The conditions under which performance is or isn't expected should be identified, along with the behavior to be demonstrated.

To set the stage for desired performance, it's also useful to specify up front what the reward will be for performing as desired. Trainees are more likely

to be motivated if they know that successful performance can lead to positive reinforcement (e.g., promotion, pay raise, or recognition) or block the administration of negative reinforcement (e.g., supervisory criticism or firing).[80]

Behavioral Modeling. Even when instructions are clear, the desired behavior still may not occur if the trainee does not know how to perform it. This problem can be overcome through **behavioral modeling,** *which involves describing the behaviors to be learned to trainees, having a role model provide a visual demonstration of the desired behavior, allowing the trainees to imitate the desired behaviors, and giving feedback.*[81] The important thing is to show employees what needs to be done before asking them to do it. Thus, role models should show not only how to achieve desired outcomes but also how to overcome performance obstacles.

Increasing Learning during Training

Although employees should be responsible for their own learning, organizations can do much to facilitate this.

Active Participation. Individuals perform better if they're actively involved in the learning process. For example, research in behavioral modeling training shows that trainees learn more when they participate in designing the scenarios used for their role-modeling practice sessions.[82] Organizational help in this area can range from encouraging active participation in classroom discussions to establishing a set of programs to assist managers in a major strategic change. The important point is to hook the individual on learning. Through active participation, individuals stay more alert and are more likely to feel confident.

Mastery. If individuals dwell on their personal deficiencies relative to the task, potential difficulties may seem more formidable than they really are. When training experiences fail to validate fears about failure, trainees are less likely to feel threatened and more likely to develop a sense of mastery.[83]

To facilitate mastery, trainers should arrange the subject matter so that trainees experience success. Whereas this may be easy when tasks are simple, it can be quite difficult when tasks are complex. Solutions include segmenting tasks, shaping behavior, and setting proximal goals.

Task segmentation involves breaking a complex task into smaller or simpler components. For some jobs (e.g., laboratory technician), the components (e.g., drawing blood, culturing a specimen, and running a blood chemistry machine) can be taught individually and in any order. For other jobs (e.g., engineer, chauffeur, and interviewer), segments must be taught sequentially because task B builds on task A and task C builds on task B.[84]

Shaping includes rewarding closer and closer approximations to desired behavior. For example, when managers are learning how to conduct a selection interview, they can be reinforced for making eye contact and for developing situational questions.

The setting of proximal, or intermediary, goals also increases mastery perceptions. Consider a software developer with an overall objective of developing a new word processing package. Proximal goals might include meeting a project specifications deadline, developing algorithms for fonts by a set deadline, developing an algorithm for formatting paragraphs, and so on. These proximal goals all lead to the attainment of the distal, or overall, objective.[85]

Feedback. For individuals to master new concepts and acquire new competencies, they must receive accurate diagnostic feedback about their performance.

Feedback can be provided by a supervisor, coworkers, customers, computers, or the individual performing the task. It must be specific, timely, based on behavior and not personality, and practical. If a performance discrepancy exists, the feedback should be diagnostic and include instructions or modeling of how to perform better.[86] The topic of providing performance feedback is discussed in more detail in Chapter 9, where the focus is on performance management. When studying that chapter, keep in mind that feedback is an important element of training and development.[87]

Practice. The goal of skill training is to ensure that desired behavior occurs not just once but consistently. Consistency is most likely to occur when trainees are able to practice and internalize the standards of performance. Even mental practice appears to help improve performance.[88] However, because practicing the wrong behaviors is detrimental, employees should be given specific feedback about what they are doing wrong to ensure that they practice only the correct behaviors.

For some jobs, tasks must be overlearned. When a task is overlearned, the trainee does not have to think consciously about behavior before responding. For example, if a plane is losing altitude rapidly, a pilot must know immediately how to respond. The pilot has no time to think about what should be done. The emergency routine must be second nature and internalized.

Maintaining Performance after Training

Following employees' exposure to socialization, training and development experiences, the environment needs to support the transfer of new behaviors to the job and their maintenance over time. The use of goals and reinforcers can improve performance following training.

Specific Goals. Without goals that are specific and measurable, people have little basis for judging how they're doing.[89] Specific goals for subsequent performance should be challenging but not so difficult as to be perceived as impossible. They also shouldn't be set too early in the learning process. The development of a specific action plan is one goal-setting approach that relates what has been learned to the job in the near future.

Reinforcers. Learning new behaviors is difficult and threatening. To ensure that trainees continue to demonstrate the skills they have learned, behavior must be reinforced. **Reinforcement** *is a consequence that follows behavior.* It can be positive (e.g., praise and financial rewards) or negative (e.g., "If you perform as desired, I will quit screaming at you"), but the consequence must be contingent on performance. Often supervisors and coworkers can be taught to reinforce desired changes. If a supervisor or coworker responds positively to a positive change in behavior, the frequency with which the new behavior will be displayed is likely to increase.

Self-Reinforcement. Because it isn't always possible for others to reinforce an individual worker, a long-term objective should be to teach employees how to set their own goals and administer their own reinforcement. When people create self-incentives for their efforts, they're capable of making self-satisfaction contingent on their own performance. The challenge is to ensure that personal goals are congruent with organizational goals, thus leading to self-management.

FAST FACT

The average Trident employee receives special recognition 10 times per year for behaviors that fit the culture.

" *Tomorrow's leader will be a team player who will seek to decentralize leadership and work towards creating an entire organization of leaders. This is a pattern the survey found to be true across all industries and geographic borders.* "

Windle Priem
Chief Executive Officer and
President
Korn/Ferry International

TEAM TRAINING AND DEVELOPMENT

Management often rushes to form work teams without considering how the behaviors needed for effective teamwork differ from those needed for effective individual contributions. Team members may receive little or no training to ensure that they can perform the required tasks and achieve the goals set. NASA takes the opposite approach. Perhaps more than any other organization, NASA understands that training comes before effective teamwork. Before astronauts are sent into space to live in a community that relies heavily on teamwork for survival, NASA has them working together every day for a year or two to become a team. They share office space, spend countless hours together in flight simulators, and rehearse everything from stowing their flight suits to troubleshooting malfunctions. Formal training in procedures is part of the experience, but it isn't everything. NASA realizes that teamwork training also involves helping teammates get to know each other and develop confidence in each other.

Most organizations can't afford to give team members a year or two of training before teams begin working on their tasks. They look for quicker ways to achieve the same objectives that NASA has for its training program. The three main goals of most team training programs are to develop (1) team cohesiveness, (2) effective teamwork procedures, and (3) work team leaders. For some teams, such as airline flight crews, team members may also need specialized training to ensure that they respond appropriately to rare and unexpected events, such as equipment failure, when lives are at risk.[90] Organizations that invest resources to train teams can increase both team and organizational effectiveness.[91]

Training to Develop Team Cohesiveness

To develop team cohesiveness, many organizations use experientially-based adventure training. Evart Glass Plant, a division of Chrysler Group, involved its entire 250-person staff in such training as a way to prepare its employees for working in self-managed work teams. Union members and managers trained side by side during employees' normal work hours. A hi-lo driver (similar to a forklift operator), a maintenance person, a shift supervisor, and a receptionist found themselves working together as a team throughout their training. After each activity, trainers led a discussion about the experience to identify the lesson to be learned from it. Exhibit 8.8 describes a few of the activities and associated lessons from the company's specially designed one-day program.

Was the team training at Evart Glass Plant effective? Surveys and personal interviews were conducted to assess employees' reactions, and the results were positive. Employees commented that people now were going out of their way to help others and felt that people were doing a better job of seeking out opinions from employees at all levels. Employees also got to know each other. Explained one engineer, "Personally, I hadn't been on third shift very long and found there were three people on that shift that I had the wrong opinion of. I saw they were real go-getters and they stayed positive throughout the experience; I was surprised." Overall, the training helped break down personal walls that people had built around themselves and helped them see the benefits of being a contributing member of a team.[92]

Training in Team Procedures

Experiential training is an effective way to develop cohesiveness, but used alone it isn't likely to result in optimal work team effectiveness. Work teams can also benefit from more formal training.

EXHIBIT 8.8 Examples of Team Training Activities Used at the Evart Glass Plant

Challenging Activity	Teamwork Lesson
Juggle several objects simultaneously (e.g., tennis balls, hackey sacs, and koosh balls) as a team.	Although everyone has a different role, each person touches and affects the outcome.
Find the path hidden in a carpet maze and move each member through it in a limited amount of time.	Teams must find and use each individual's hidden strengths (e.g., a good memory and the ability to move quickly). Doing so allows the team as a whole to succeed.
Balance 14 nails on the head of a nail that has been pounded into a supporting block of wood, creating a free-standing structure without supports.	Things that may seem impossible can be achieved when people work together.
Draw a vehicle that represents the training teams and signify which part of the vehicle each member represents.	Each member has different strengths, and bringing these strengths together leads to task success.

Work teams of all types are being empowered to perform tasks that previously weren't employees' responsibility. The greater the degree of self-management is, the more the team has authority, responsibility, and general decision-making discretion for tasks. The more self-managing a team is, the more important it is for team members to receive training.

Training for Team Leaders

New team leaders often misunderstand their role. Good team leaders are receptive to member contributions and don't reject or promote ideas because of their own personal views. Good team leaders summarize information, stimulate discussion, create awareness of problems, and detect when the team is ready to resolve differences and agree to a unified solution. Training in how to support disagreement and manage meetings is especially useful for new work team leaders.

- *Supporting disagreement.* A skillful work team leader can create an atmosphere for disagreement that stimulates innovative solutions while minimizing the risk of bad feelings. Disagreement can be managed if the leader is receptive to differences within the team, delays the making of decisions, and separates idea generation from idea evaluation. This last technique reduces the likelihood that an alternative solution will be identified with one individual rather than with the team. The absence of disagreement on a work team may be as destructive to its proper functioning as too much disagreement. The use of decision-making aids, such as brainstorming, the nominal group technique, devil's advocacy, and dialectical inquiry, creates productive controversy and can result in better-quality decisions that are fully accepted by members of the team. Training team leaders to use these simple techniques is a good first step toward stimulating constructive controversy within teams.[93]

- *Managing meetings.* People who resist teamwork often point to time wasted in meetings as a big source of dissatisfaction. True, teams need to meet, one way or another, but team meetings should never be a waste of time. Training team leaders in the tactics of running meetings can make meetings more efficient. In addition, training can help team leaders learn how to strike a proper balance between permissiveness and control. Rushing through a team session can prevent full discussion of the problem and lead to negative feelings and poor solutions. However, unless the leader keeps the discussion moving, members will become bored and inattentive. Unfortunately, some leaders feel that pushing for an early solution is necessary because of time constraints. Such a move ends discussion before the team has had a chance to work through a problem effectively.

CURRENT ISSUES

Because training and development activities serve so many important objectives, organizations continually consider new activities. In other words, it is always a "current" issue! Here we focus on two areas that are especially challenging at this time: diversity training and developing global leaders. These two issues share the common objective of preparing people to effectively work together and be comfortable with others who come from different backgrounds and may have different values.[94] In the United States, training people from different cultures to work together is often the aim of diversity training initiatives. For global firms, long-term success requires managers and leaders who are effective working in a multinational, multicultural context.

Diversity Training for Employees in the United States

As the importance of learning to manage workforce diversity became more salient to U.S. employers, many companies looked to cross-cultural training programs as a solution. Their thinking was that diversity can be disruptive to the organization and create dissatisfaction among employees if people from different cultural backgrounds do not understand each other's cultures. The hope was that diversity training programs would improve cross-cultural understanding. Suddenly, thousands of consulting firms were offering diversity training.[95]

Cultural Awareness Training. Many diversity training programs seek to raise cultural awareness among participants. Typically, these programs are designed to teach the participants about how their own culture differs from the cultures of other employees with whom they work. In this context, the term *culture* is used to refer very broadly to the social group to which a person belongs. Ethnic background is one aspect of culture, but so are one's age, socioeconomic status, religion, and so on. Cultural awareness training also teaches people to understand how the stereotypes they hold about various groups can influence the way they treat people—often in subtle ways that they may not be conscious of. The main objective of this type of diversity training is increasing people's knowledge about their own and other cultures.

A typical cultural awareness program is conducted over the course of one or two days. Among the activities are information sharing intended to educate employees about the array of differences in the workplace. Some organizations supplement formal training sessions with informal learning opportunities such as Black History Month or Gay and Lesbian Pride Week, using the time to focus on a group's history and cultural traditions. The hope is that raising awareness about differences will lead to attitudinal and behavior changes. Although there is scant research on the effectiveness of such awareness programs, the general consensus is that awareness programs *alone* do little to create positive change.

Building Competencies. Another approach to diversity training focuses more specifically on developing the behavioral competencies needed to work effectively in organizations characterized by diversity. Training designed to develop the interpersonal competencies needed in diverse workplaces often includes role-playing and practice sessions. The interpersonal behaviors taught include showing respect and treating people as equals. Videos of leaderless group discussions also may be used to help point out inappropriate behaviors that people may engage in and not be aware of. Changing behaviors and developing interpersonal skills can improve the climate in diverse workplaces.

Supplementing Diversity Training. As companies quickly learned, diversity training alone cannot create fundamental changes in how effectively organizations manage diversity. As already discussed in earlier chapters, the issue of diversity should be considered during succession planning and when developing recruitment and selection practices. In addition, efforts may be needed to ensure that members of minority groups are included on advisory boards and as members of committees involved in compensation decisions. Tying compensation and other rewards to success in meeting goals for recruiting, hiring, developing, and promoting people from diverse backgrounds has been shown to improve the success of diversity training and development interventions.[96]

Global Leadership Training and Development

Few things seem certain, but one thing is clear: Globalization will continue to be an inescapable buzzword. Businesses will operate in an ever more interconnected world. With 91,000 employees working in 78 countries, Intel plans to invest more than $3 million to train 800 midlevel managers who are working across cultures. These managers will be flown to one-week seminars held outside their home regions. The goal is to help the managers deepen their understanding of how country-based differences influence how people do their jobs.[97]

As shown in Exhibit 8.9, the opportunities for training and development activities in global companies are many. The different groups who can benefit from training include headquarters staff, global managers, expatriates, members of expatriates' families, and members of work teams that include people from different nationalities. The times at which training and development activities

> *"People who are responsible for hundreds of millions of Intel's wealth and prosperity need to be able to understand how to work well on a global basis."*
>
> Kevin Gazzara
> Head of the Leading Through People Program
> Intel

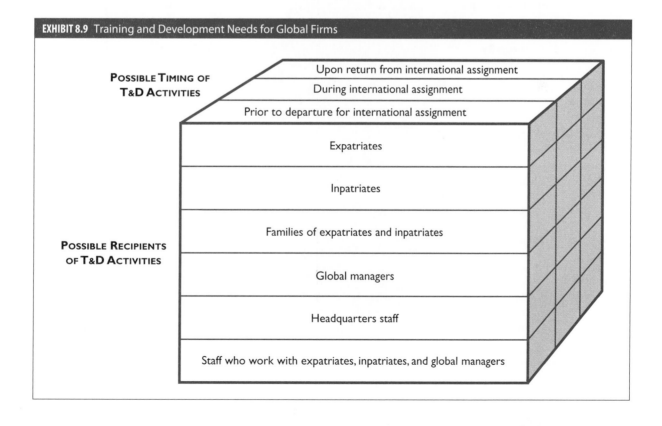

EXHIBIT 8.9 Training and Development Needs for Global Firms

POSSIBLE TIMING OF T&D ACTIVITIES

- Upon return from international assignment
- During international assignment
- Prior to departure for international assignment

POSSIBLE RECIPIENTS OF T&D ACTIVITIES

- Expatriates
- Inpatriates
- Families of expatriates and inpatriates
- Global managers
- Headquarters staff
- Staff who work with expatriates, inpatriates, and global managers

can be offered include prior to the departure of expatriates, during international assignments, and upon the return of expatriates. Clearly, a full discussion of how organizations address all these training and development needs is not feasible here. We focus instead on global leadership development, because CEOs view it as one of their most pressing concerns.[98] Global leaders need to manage operations in several different countries simultaneously. Global leadership competency is especially important in global organizations that are structured around products rather than according to geographic regions.

What does it take to be an effective global leader? The first step is understanding how employees in different cultures think about leadership; effective leadership in the United States may not be effective elsewhere. In fact, research shows that leadership takes different forms in different countries. Exhibit 8.10 summarizes a few of the research findings. As the exhibit shows, some behaviors facilitate effective leadership in almost all cultures. Other behaviors interfere with effective leadership almost anywhere. There also are behaviors that are effective in some cultures and ineffective in others.[99]

PricewaterhouseCoopers (PwC) knows that understanding these culturally contingent behaviors is essential for global leaders. To help its managers develop their global leadership skills, PwC sends them abroad in a program called Ulysses, which is described in the feature "Managing Globalization: PricewaterhouseCoopers."[100]

FAST FACT

A recent global leadership survey found that 75% of U.S. companies expected to hire 25% or more of their leaders from outside the country in the ensuing five years.

EXHIBIT 8.10 Behaviors for Global Leaders

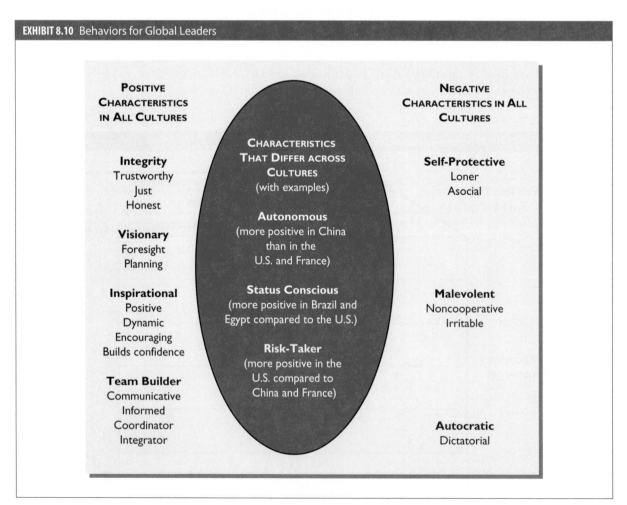

MANAGING GLOBALIZATION
PricewaterhouseCoopers

Tahir Ayub is a partner at PricewaterhouseCoopers (PwC) who needs to be able to "think global, act local." PwC helped him develop this competency by sending him to Namibia, a country being devastated by HIV/AIDS. PwC arranged for the trip and Ayub's stay there as part of their Ulysses Program to develop global leaders. Each year, as part of that program, PwC sends 17 partners to work in small teams on projects in developing countries where they "go local." Partners are stripped of all the comforts they take for granted, and they are given a specific task to complete. They must rely on their own resourcefulness to succeed. PwC believes such hands-on experience is essential to developing global leaders.

For his project, Ayub was paired up with two other PwC partners whom he had never met before: one from the Netherlands and the other from Mexico. Having grown up in the United Kingdom and having gone to college in Vancouver, British Columbia, his work in Namibia was a life-changing experience: "When you work in a [culturally diverse] place like Vancouver, you work with people from different backgrounds and you think you are culturally

aware," he recalled. But working as part of the Namibia team, he was less sure of his open-mindedness. He also learned that "perhaps the way you see things isn't necessarily the best way"—a humbling experience for someone as successful as a PwC partner.

Two years after returning from Namibia, Ayub says he can still see the faces of the orphans he met, whose parents had died from AIDS. PwC says it can see that Ayub benefited from the experience. Today, he recognizes the importance of listening to different perspectives before making decisions. "Before, when I came across an issue that I thought I knew how to deal with, I would say that I didn't have a lot of time to listen to everyone involved to make sure it was the right way to go. Now I am much more open to listening and to other people's points of view," he says. As more and more of its partners work through such experiences, the firm knows it will improve the company's global effectiveness. In 10 years, they expect to really begin to see the results of this long-term investment.

Of course, participating in a single leadership development program is not enough to fully develop all of the competencies needed to be an effective global leader. In addition to such programs, some of the other best practices for developing global leaders include working as a member of an international cross-functional team, working in a variety of longer-term international assignments, and receiving coaching and mentoring.[101] Ultimately, the goal of such activities is to develop leaders who understand a variety of cultural contexts and who are able to lead effectively in different countries and across several cultures.

CHAPTER SUMMARY WITH LEARNING GOALS

1. **STRATEGIC IMPORTANCE.** Training and development contribute to organizational effectiveness in numerous ways. Improving the competencies of the workforce and organizational competitiveness are the most direct results of well designed training activities. By offering employees opportunities to improve their skills, employers also address employees' concerns about maintaining their long-term employability. In learning organizations, employees are learning every day throughout the organization, and they help each other learn by participating in communities-of-practice.

2. **INTEGRATED HRM SYSTEM.** The entire system of activities related to training, development, and socialization are referred to as training and development (T&D). In an integrated HRM system, T&D activities are designed to ensure legal compliance, they are informed by job analysis and competency models, and they are aligned with HR planning as well as with recruitment and selection policies.

3 THE HR TRIAD. Successful training and development requires the active involvement of all members of the HR Triad. Human resource professionals take responsibility for identifying the objectives of training and development and the methods of achieving them. Effective training and development require managers to actively participate and employees to capitalize on available training opportunities.

4 DETERMINING TRAINING AND DEVELOPMENT NEEDS. Training and development are most likely to achieve the desired results when they are grounded in the results of a needs assessment. A thorough needs assessment includes organizational, job, person, and demographic needs analyses.

5 CONDITIONS FOR EFFECTIVE TRAINING AND DEVELOPMENT. Setting up training and development activities involves deciding who will be trained, who will train, where the training will occur, and what methods will be used. Organizations have to ensure that the right conditions are in place. Activities may be provided by supervisors, managers, coworkers, subject matter experts, or employees, depending on what skills or competencies are taught and where the program is held.

6 DEVELOPING PROGRAM CONTENT. The program content of a training or development program should be congruent with its learning objectives. Several types of learning objectives are cognitive knowledge, technical or interpersonal skills, affective outcomes, and ethical behavior.

7 CHOOSING THE PROGRAM FORMAT. Program formats available to employers include e-learning, on-the-job training, apprenticeships, developmental job assignments, and mentoring, and several types of off-site training. Several considerations, including cost and the amount of time available, affect the choice of format, and the types of competencies to be acquired and the format of the training affect the selection of appropriate methods.

8 MAXIMIZING LEARNING. Regardless of the method chosen, the content of training and development activities should be designed to maximize learning. Principles to consider include clear instructions, proper behavioral models, active participation, achieving mastery, providing feedback, and practice. It is also important to examine the work environment to ensure that new behaviors will be sustained, by setting goals for subsequent performance and ensuring that improvements are reinforced back on the job.

9 TEAM TRAINING AND DEVELOPMENT PROGRAMS. Training and development for teams are especially important for organizations that depend heavily on teamwork for survival and success. The three main goals of team training programs are to develop team cohesiveness, effective team procedures, and team leaders.

10 TWO CURRENT ISSUES. In the United States, diversity training aims to help people understand each other's ethnic grounds and cultures and to develop the competencies they need to work together effectively. For firms with international operations, developing the ability of managers to lead effectively in a multinational environment is an important objective of leadership and development policies and programs.

TERMS TO REMEMBER

Behavioral modeling	Interactive video training (IVT)
Community-of-practice	Job needs analysis
Demographic needs analysis	Job rotation programs
Development	Mentoring
Developmental job assignments	On-the-job training (OJT)
e-Learning	Organizational needs analysis
Emotional intelligence	Orientation programs

Person needs analysis	Socialization
Personal coaches	Training
Reinforcement	Transfer
Simulations	

QUESTIONS FOR DISCUSSION AND REFLECTIVE THINKING

1. What is the role of training and development in learning organizations? Do you think a pharmaceutical company could effectively manage knowledge without having well developed T&D activities?

2. An auto dealer has hired you to help improve the performance of its sales and service staff. Your first task is to conduct a needs analysis for the organization. Describe what you will do. Then provide examples of possible training and development activities that could be used to influence the knowledge, behavior, and attitudes of the staff.

3. Consider the various training and development formats described in this chapter. Which three do you think would be the most effective for maintaining the skills of IT engineers? Which three do you think would be the least effective? Explain your rationale.

4. Imagine that your organization—a publishing company—has decided to hire an external vendor to provide diversity training. You want to begin by having the vendor conduct the training for just a small portion of the employees to study and assess the training's effectiveness. Describe a plan for evaluating the effectiveness of the diversity training offered by the vendor. What measures will you use, and how will you design the evaluation study?

5. Discuss the strategic role of training and development activities in companies with international operations and markets.

PROJECTS TO EXTEND YOUR LEARNING

1. **Integration and Application.** Before continuing, review the cases of Southwest Airlines and Lincoln Electric at the end of this book. Then answer the following questions.

   a. For which company is training and development more important?

   b. Describe how the training and development activities in both companies are related to other HR activities.

2. **Using the Internet.** Discover the online resources that are available to help employers address the training and development needs of their employees.

   a. Read about the role of training in ensuring safety and health at work by visiting the Web page of the Occupational Safety and Health Administration (http://www.osha.gov).

   b. Customers of Siemens can receive training from the company. Learn more about the training Siemens offers to its customers (http://siemens.com).

   c. The American Society for Training & Development is an association of T&D professionals. Visit their Web site (http://www.astd.org/astd) to learn about the resources available through this organization.

   d. Learn more about corporate universities by visiting the Corporate University Xchange (http://www.corpu.com).

3. **Experiential Activity.** Training and development activities are the most effective when the people participating in them understand how they can benefit from the experience. What types of training and development activities would be helpful to you? Use the following Personal Development Plan form to list activities that would help you develop specific knowledge, skills, and insights.

Personal Development Plan

INSTRUCTIONS

A. Setting Objectives. After reviewing this chapter, list five learning objectives that you could benefit from achieving during the next year. Consider the cognitive knowledge you need to acquire, the technical and interpersonal skills from which you could benefit, and the new attitudes that would be helpful for you to develop. List these five learning objectives, being as specific as possible:

1.

2.

3.

4.

5.

B. Choosing Methods. For each objective, consider the alternative types of training and development methods that might be available (e.g., e-learning, business games, wilderness training). Several possible methods are listed in the following chart, but you may add others if you wish. For each of your five learning objectives, evaluate how effective you think each alternative method would likely be. Use this simple rating system to record your evaluations:

1	2	3	4
Not at all effective	Not sure	May be somewhat useful	Quite effective

Methods	Likely Effectiveness (1, 2, 3, or 4)				
	Objective 1	Objective 2	Objective 3	Objective 4	Objective 5
e-learning					
On-the-job training (OJT)					
Apprenticeship or internship					
Job rotation program					
Mentoring					
Personal coaching					
Corporate university program					
Executive education program at local university					
Interactive video training (IVT)					
Simulation					
Sensitivity training					
Wilderness training					

C. Developing a Specific Action Plan. Choose three objectives that are important to you. For each objective, state what you will do to develop yourself. Keep in mind that a useful plan must be feasible. Consider the potential value of the actions you listed and their feasibility for you. Are you willing to make a commitment to carry out any of these actions in the next 12 months?

My Action Plan		
Objective	Actions	Target Date for Completion
1.	a.	
	b.	
	c.	
2.	a.	
	b.	
	c.	
3.	a.	
	b.	
	c.	

CASE STUDY
SEEING THE FOREST *AND* THE TREES

The face of domestic and global competition that the leaders of the Forest Products Company (FPC) and its parent, the Weyerhaeuser Corporation, saw as they surveyed an industry on its knees in the early 1980s was a far different face from the one Weyerhaeuser and its subsidiaries had successfully competed against for so long. They knew how to compete—and win—against a large-firm, commodity lumber business. But that business was in its death throes, and what was emerging from the ashes presented an entirely new set of challenges, one that would require a radical change in Weyerhaeuser's strategy. The new competitors weren't the old monolithic organizations but were instead small mills—lean, mean, and configured so that their products could be tailored to customer demand and their product lines could change rapidly according to need. They were nonunion, owner-operated, and entrepreneurial; and in this configuration, they were running the lowest-cost, most market-oriented operations around.

Going out of business was not an alternative anyone cared to think about, but if things didn't change, it would be a definite possibility. Charley Bingham, CEO of the Forest Products Company, knew that something had to be done—and soon. He gathered his top dozen managers, and together they decided that a massive reorganization was called for, accompanied by a radical change in strategy. According to Bingham, the change in strategy went something like this: "Approximately 80% of our sales dollars in 1982 represented products sold as commodities. By 1995, we resolved that we must reverse the proportions."

The massive reorganization at FPC mirrored that occurring at its parent company. The Weyerhaeuser Corporation decided to drastically decentralize. The three operating units, of which FPC was one, were given free reign on how to do their business. Given this scenario, Bingham and his team decided they needed to create an organization capable of acting and responding just like their competitors. Thus, they created 200 profit centers with each center being largely responsible for its own bottom line.

This restructuring soon proved to be only a first step in the right direction. The ability of FPC to implement its new strategy was being undermined by low morale, which was pervasive. In addition, many middle managers, those needed to actually carry out the change, were pessimistic about the possibility of sustained future success. Silently, they even questioned their own ability to operate the profit centers.

With insights from Horace Parker, director of executive development at FPC, the rest of the top team came to realize that there would have to be a total transformation of the organization: The corporate culture, knowledge base, skill levels, style of leadership, and team orientation would all have to change, for all employees. With 18,000 employees across the United States, Parker wasn't sure where to start. The others said they would help, but he had to tell them what to do. Parker, of course, is waiting to hear what you have to tell him.

CASE QUESTIONS

1. Where does Parker start? What programs does he put in place to deal with the needs of corporate culture, knowledge, skills, leadership, and team orientation?

2. How does he go about developing the programs that he needs to put into place? Does he do it by himself? Can he buy off-the-shelf programs?

3. What time frame does Parker need to implement the programs to make the change successful? If he deals only with executive development programs, does he need to be concerned with programs for middle managers and below? How does he do this?

Source: Randall S. Schuler, Rutgers University

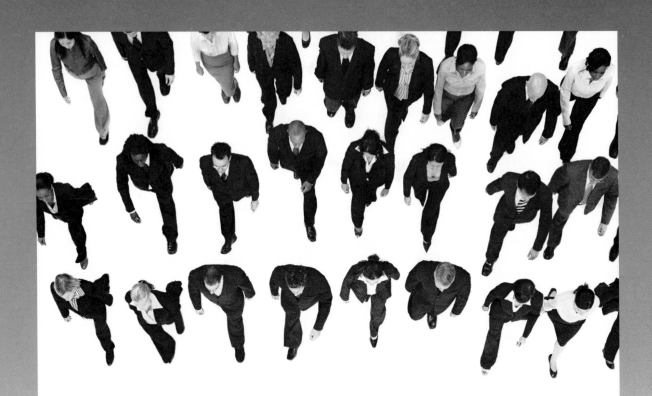

Conducting Performance Management

Learning Goals

After reading this chapter, you should be able to:

1 Explain how performance management is strategically important to firms.

2 Show how performance management fits within an integrated HRM system.

3 Detail the responsibilities of the HR Triad for performance management.

4 Describe several ways to measure performance.

5 Discuss the timing of the performance measurement and feedback.

6 Describe the participants in performance measurement and feedback.

7 Explain the features of different performance appraisal formats.

8 Discuss the rating process.

9 Describe the important factors in performance feedback.

10 Detail two current issues related to performance management.

MANAGING HUMAN RESOURCES AT TRW

TRW is a business with nearly 100,000 employees worldwide who work in four major businesses: automotive, aeronautical systems, space and electronics, and information systems. When business conditions started to decline, top-level managers sought to revitalize the company by instituting numerous change initiatives. One initiative created a companywide performance management process with two components: performance appraisal and career development. Instead of several paper-based forms that were unique to each business unit, top management wanted a single, integrated approach that communicated the behaviors needed for the company's profitability. Profit-related behaviors included creating trust, energizing people, embracing change, building teamwork, and being customer oriented. The global design team, which operated as a virtual team, recognized that delivering online performance management tools was the best solution. However, because not all employees had access to the company's e-mail hub, a parallel paper-based process was also needed.

Within three months, a new performance appraisal form was created. Managers evaluated performance against specific goals and rated their subordinates' performance-related behaviors using a four-point scale. For each point on the scale, a paragraph explained what the rating meant. For example, the highest rating was:

Far Exceeds Expectations: Organizational contributions and excellent work are widely recognized. Performance consistently exceeds all defined expectations, producing important and impactful results through superior planning, execution, and creativity. Employee consistently demonstrated the rated TRW behaviors and/or initiatives at higher levels than expected.

The lowest possible rating was:

Needs Improvement: Performance falls below expectations on one or more critical position competencies, objectives, or tasks. While some responsibilities may be executed in a generally satisfactory manner, improvement is required for performance to become fully competent. Demonstration of the TRW behaviors and/or initiatives is inconsistent or at lower levels than expected.

Another section addressed career development issues. Managers described the subordinate's performance goals and professional development activities for the upcoming year. The subordinate's perspective was recorded also. Subordinates described their strengths and areas they felt they could improve. They also assessed their own future potential and possible future positions.

A year after implementing the new performance management process, the company reported that managers and subordinates alike found the new tools to be both more efficient and more effective in achieving uniform and comprehensive performance measurement, feedback, and career planning.[1] ▲

THE STRATEGIC IMPORTANCE OF PERFORMANCE MANAGEMENT

For companies like TRW, Lincoln Electric, Cendant Mortgage, FedEx, Con-Way, and Southwest Airlines, performance management is the difference between being just OK and being the leader in the industry. **Performance management** *is a formal, structured process used to measure, evaluate, and influence employees' job-related attitudes, behaviors, and performance results.*[2] Performance management helps to *direct* and *motivate* employees to maximize their efforts on behalf of the organization.

As described in this chapter, organizations with effective performance management define clear performance goals and measures, conduct performance appraisals, and provide ongoing performance feedback. In addition, other HR practices that are central to effective performance management include linking performance results to rewards and consequences (discussed in Chapter 11) and providing employees with opportunities for career planning and development (discussed in Chapters 5 and 8).[3] As illustrated by the TRW example, performance management directs the attention of employees toward the most important tasks and behaviors. It informs employees about what's valued and provides information about whether the employees' behaviors and results meet

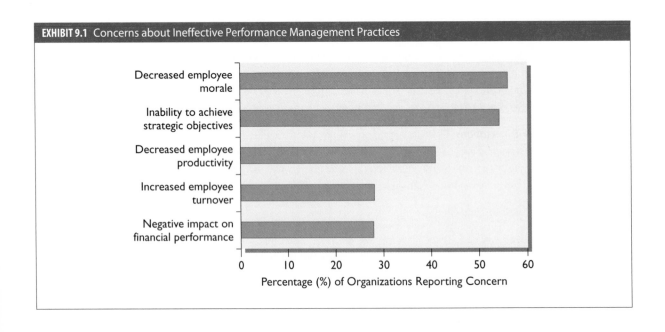

EXHIBIT 9.1 Concerns about Ineffective Performance Management Practices

the expectations of managers, colleagues, and customers. Performance management is essential for organizations to meet their strategic objectives.

Performance management serves many purposes in organizations. It can enhance employee motivation and productivity, support the achievement of the organization's strategic goals, and facilitate strategic planning and change. Conversely, ineffective performance management can have numerous negative consequences. Exhibit 9.1 reports the findings of a recent survey about the negative consequences of ineffective performance management, which include low morale, high turnover, and poor financial performance.[4]

Enhancing Motivation and Productivity

Chapter 8 described how training and developmental activities can be used to improve the knowledge and skills that employees need to perform well in their jobs. There the emphasis was on improving performance by increasing the capabilities of employees. But even the most capable employees won't perform well unless they are motivated to do so. Performance management practices address the issue of motivating employees to ensure that their capabilities are fully utilized.

Clearly, motivation is a complex phenomenon, with many factors coming into play. Exhibit 9.2 illustrates some of these factors. Notice that in this model, **motivation** *has two elements: (1) decisions about which behaviors to engage in and (2) decisions about how much effort to expend.* Usually, effective job performance requires that employees engage in the appropriate behaviors and exert relatively high levels of effort.[5]

The foundation of the model shown in Exhibit 9.2 is expectancy theory. **Expectancy theory** *states that people choose their behaviors and effort levels after considering whether their behaviors and effort will improve their performance and lead to desired consequences (e.g., recognition and rewards).* Behavioral choices related to work performance include whether to go to work or call in sick, whether to leave work at the official quitting time or stay late, and whether to exert a great deal of effort or work at a relaxed pace. Expectancy theory states that people tend to choose behaviors they believe will help them achieve outcomes they personally value (e.g., a promotion or job security), and people avoid behaviors they believe will lead to outcomes they view as undesirable (e.g., a demotion or criticism).

An employee's motivation to perform well is determined by how he or she responds to three key questions:

1. The expectancy question.
2. The instrumentality question.
3. The valence question.

As you will see, many aspects of an organization's human resource management system can influence how employees answer these questions.

Expectancy. The **expectancy** *question is, "If I make an effort, will I be able to perform as intended?"* For employees to be motivated to expend effort, they must expect that their efforts will translate into performance. Employees are more likely to expect that their efforts will lead to performance if they are confident in their own skills and abilities.[6] Effective selection and training help employees feel confident in their ability to perform. Over time, feedback about performance also can improve employees' confidence in their ability to perform.

The quality of an organization's performance measures is relevant to the expectancy question. Even when employees know that they can improve

> " *The average person puts only 25% of his energy and ability into his work. The world takes off its hat to those who put in more than 50% of their capacity, and stands on its head for those few and far between souls who devote 100%.* "
>
> *Andrew Carnegie*

> " *In the beginning, you're the lowest paid and you're trying hard to get raises. But no matter what I did, nobody reviewed my work and I never got noticed. After awhile, I stopped being so concerned about performance.* "
>
> *John Ranson*
> *Employee in the Aerospace Industry*

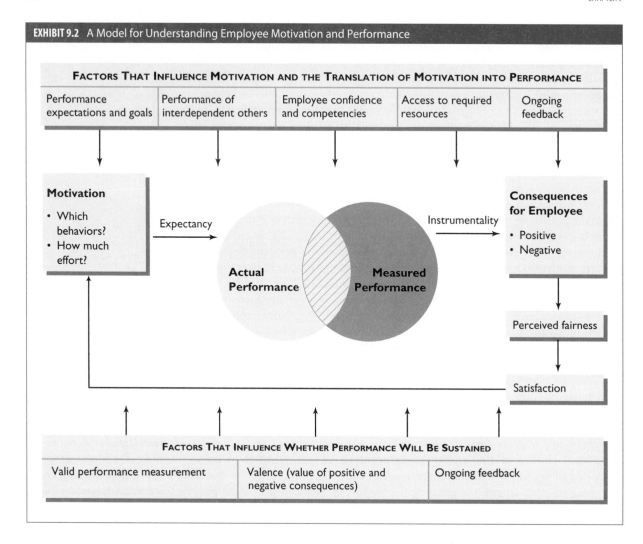

EXHIBIT 9.2 A Model for Understanding Employee Motivation and Performance

their performance, their motivation may remain low if the organization uses inadequate performance measures. In Exhibit 9.2, the degree of overlap between actual and measured performance reflects the adequacy of the organization's performance measure. In an organization where performance measures do a good job of assessing actual performance, the two circles completely overlap. In most organizations, however, the two circles do not overlap completely because some aspects of actual performance do not get measured adequately. In addition, biases and inaccuracies on the part of the people who assess an employee's performance can mean that the performance measures reflect irrelevant information, such as whether the boss likes the employee.

Instrumentality. The **instrumentality** *question is, "What consequences, if any, will follow from my decision to perform?"* The issue is whether performance is of any instrumental usefulness. An HRM system that uses performance as a basis for incentive pay, decisions about promotions, opportunities for personal development, discipline, and other actions should result in employees' believing that desirable consequences await those who perform well, and *only* those who perform well. When important consequences are influenced by factors other than performance (e.g., seniority, personal relationships, and favoritism), employees may feel that performance is of little consequence.

Medi-Health Outsourcing is a fast growing, young company that helps hospitals and other health care organizations manage patient records and documents for inclusion in national databases. For founders Paula and Ron Lawlor, highly motivated employees are essential to the growing company, which may add as many as 60 or 70 new hospitals to its roster each year. At Medi-Health, employees are held accountable for performance results and rewarded for achieving them. For example, if your job is to code documents for entry into a database, you might be given the goal of abstracting 100 records per week with 95% accuracy. If you meet the goal on Thursday, you can take the rest of the week off.[7]

Valence. The **valence** *question is, "How much do I value the consequences associated with the intended behavior?"* Even when employees believe that good performers experience different consequences than poor performers, they may not be motivated to put in the required effort if the consequences are not valued. Valences are personal; the same outcome may have a high valence for one person and a low valence for another.[8] Medi-Health strives hard to make sure employees value the rewards they receive from working at the company. The company's employee-friendly approach allows employees to work from home or from the beach, arrange their weekly schedules around their personal needs, and even take three months off without worrying about losing their jobs. When it comes to keeping good performers satisfied, the Medi-Health philosophy is pretty much that "anything goes."

Satisfaction. The model shown in Exhibit 9.2 suggests that an employee's satisfaction is determined by perceptions of whether the rewards received for performance are fair. Satisfied employees are more likely to continue to feel motivated. Dissatisfied employees exert less effort, which results in declining performance and a general downward spiral to ineffectiveness.[9]

It follows from this model of motivation that a company's prospects for attaining peak performance at the individual, team, and organizational levels depend on a performance management process that includes monitoring performance *and* giving employees useful feedback as quickly as possible on how well they're doing.

> *Sometimes I think we baby the heck out of them. But when you ask them to do something, you just don't hear a lot of complaining.*
>
> Chuck Hammond
> Manager
> Medi-Health Outsourcing

Supporting Strategic Goals

As mentioned earlier, defining goals and their measures is an important part of the performance management process. There is a large body of research showing that goal setting can enhance productivity.[10] Specifically, goals that are clearly defined, difficult but achievable, and accepted have a positive effect on productivity and performance. When goals have a direct and obvious link to strategic goals and to the firm's success factors, two benefits occur. First, employees better understand their organization's strategic focus and how their jobs fit with it. Second, the goals direct employee behaviors toward activities that are consistent and supportive of the organization's strategy.[11] It appears that most organizations make sure that individual and team goals are tied to organizational goals. A recent survey found that nearly 80% of respondents believed that their firms' individual and team goals were aligned at least to some extent with organizational goals.[12]

When PPG Industries discovered that their strategic goals had not been translated into specific behaviors and goals for employees, they took action. Meetings were held throughout the organization, with managers sharing the organization's strategy and relating it to the employees' level and function. Employees were involved in creating specific, measurable, agreed-upon, realistic, and time-bound (named SMART) goals that they could achieve within the year. Employees received feedback throughout the year in various forms. Now employees know their specific goals and how they relate to the organization's strategy, and they receive feedback so that they know how well they are progressing toward those goals.[13]

Strategic Planning, Alignment, and Change

Besides helping to support strategic goals, performance measures provide valuable information for use in strategic planning and organizational change. The performance of executives and their management teams is almost synonymous with the performance of the business. If the performance measures used to evaluate executives are designed appropriately, they illuminate the strategic shortcomings and suggest when realignment and change are needed.

Detecting Problems. The role of performance measures in detecting strategic shortcomings in the business unit is perhaps most easily illustrated by considering performance management practices for CEOs. Responsibility for managing the performance of a company's CEO rests with the board of directors. The board is expected to engage the CEO in strategic planning to identify strategic business objectives, set goals, identify the means for achieving these objectives and goals, and define how performance will be measured. The board also monitors the CEO's progress toward achieving the business objectives and goals and is responsible for staying alert to significant performance problems.

Monitoring the performance of employees at lower levels in the organization can also be useful for detecting organizational shortcomings. For example, declining sales performance may point to a deficiency in training or to a poorly designed incentive program. In service industries, poor performance of frontline employees may be an indication of poor recruitment and selection practices. When performance deficiencies persist, it should serve as an indication that the company needs to consider engaging in large-scale organizational change, as described in Chapter 3.[14]

Evaluating Change. As described in Chapter 3, the process of strategic planning, alignment, and change involves first identifying objectives and subsequently assessing results in light of those objectives. Not *all* organizational change efforts target performance improvement as an objective; for example, some change efforts are intended to attract more talent to the organization, others are intended to increase employee satisfaction, and so on. Nevertheless, improving organizational performance, and therefore the performance of at least some of the organization's employees, is the most common objective behind large-scale change efforts. Consequently, employee performance measures should be a key component of a plan for evaluating the success of a change initiative. If human resource issues aren't fully addressed during strategic planning, the performance management process evolves in isolation from strategic initiatives, rather than in anticipation of them.

PERFORMANCE MANAGEMENT WITHIN AN INTEGRATED HRM SYSTEM

To be effective, performance management activities must be aligned with the organization's internal environment, particularly its business strategy and organizational culture. Performance management activities also must be aligned with its external environment, taking into consideration the legal environment, the labor market, and national culture. And, as we have already noted, the performance management activities described in this chapter should be aligned with performance-based incentives and career development activities. The elements of performance management described in this chapter and their relationship to other aspects of the HRM system are shown in Exhibit 9.3.

The Internal and External Environment

We've already discussed how performance management can be related to a firm's business strategy. It is also important for performance management activities to be aligned with a firm's culture. A *culture that depends on effective performance management is known as a* **performance-driven culture.**

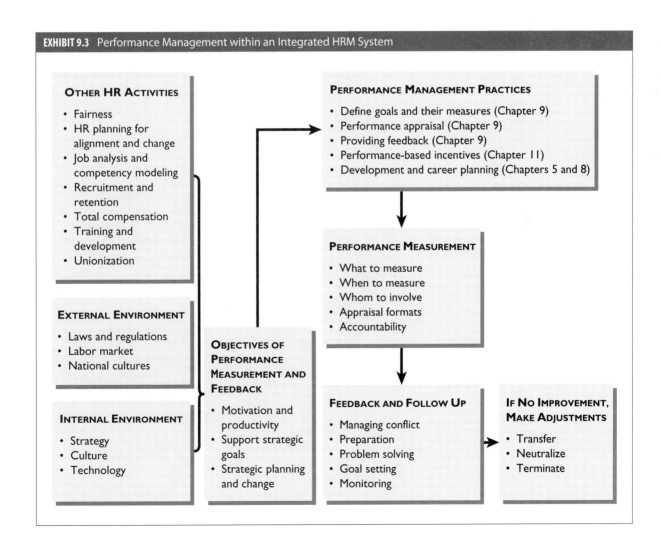

EXHIBIT 9.3 Performance Management within an Integrated HRM System

Performance-Driven Cultures. In performance-driven cultures, performance measurement and feedback are central elements of the HRM system; they're not merely annual exercises in which everyone goes through the motions and then carries on as they did before. In firms with performance-driven cultures, promotions, raises, and other financial rewards go only to employees who excel in performing all aspects of their jobs. Some regularly dismiss their lowest-performing employees (e.g., bottom 10%) simply as a matter of practice. Many people consider this approach to performance management unjust, but GE has made it a central feature of that company's approach to performance management. Even in performance-driven cultures where the lowest performers are not regularly terminated, everyone is expected to welcome feedback that points out how they can do better.

Performance-driven cultures share a common focus on monitoring and improving performance, but there are many different ways to go about these tasks. Often, the details of how a performance-driven culture goes about these tasks reflect the philosophies of the company's CEO and/or founder. Dell Inc., the computer company, has a performance-driven culture. Founder and CEO Michael Dell thinks of his company as the underdog—always in a fight for survival and always striving to improve. Some of his core principles for managing performance are described in Exhibit 9.4.[15] The performance-driven

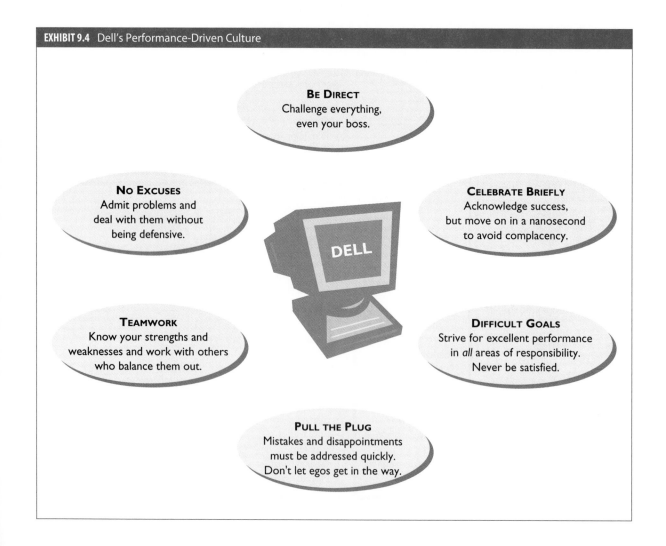

EXHIBIT 9.4 Dell's Performance-Driven Culture

BE DIRECT
Challenge everything, even your boss.

NO EXCUSES
Admit problems and deal with them without being defensive.

CELEBRATE BRIEFLY
Acknowledge success, but move on in a nanosecond to avoid complacency.

TEAMWORK
Know your strengths and weaknesses and work with others who balance them out.

DIFFICULT GOALS
Strive for excellent performance in *all* areas of responsibility. Never be satisfied.

PULL THE PLUG
Mistakes and disappointments must be addressed quickly. Don't let egos get in the way.

MANAGING WITH METRICS
Setpoint's Public Performance

If you like roller coasters, chances are you have enjoyed a product that was manufactured by Setpoint, which is in the business of producing amusement park entertainment. The Super Saturator at Paramount's Carowinds Water and Theme Park is one of their latest creations. Imagine taking a roller coaster ride and having people take aim at you with water shooters. You would get soaked as your roller car plunged through a forest of shooting water, but you would laugh and scream throughout the entire ride. Creating experiences like these is the mission of Setpoint.

For Setpoint's employees, having fun at work is as important as creating fun for others. And at this company, having fun goes hand in hand with a focus on performance. Setpoint's CEO, Joe Knight, has managed to create a culture that aligns the way employees think about their work with Setpoint's strategic objectives. Setpoint's culture embraces employee involvement. It uses an open book approach to management. Regardless of their specific jobs, employees receive financial training and are expected to participate in enhancing the firm's financial performance. During its first few years, Setpoint's practice was to distribute financial spreadsheets to employees on a monthly basis. Now the metrics are displayed on "the board." By studying the board, anyone can figure out what stage a project is at and its financial success. For each project, employees can track various metrics such as operating expenses and gross profits per hour. And because everyone understands how the company makes money, they can interpret the figures to understand how their projects are doing compared to other projects.

Every Monday morning, the board is the focus of a company "huddle"; projects are reviewed and tactics are discussed to ensure that goals are met. In most companies, understanding and monitoring the metrics and project management plans detailed on the board are the responsibility of managers. At Setpoint, everyone who works on a project shares responsibility for its success. Employees understand both their own personal role in the project and how the performance of everyone involved influences their bottom-line success. One visitor described the atmosphere at Setpoint like this: "I talked to several of them and I just couldn't get over the positive attitude they had and their understanding of the business. That openness—we started with it [but] you lose that feeling over time. We want to get it back. It's something to strive for." At Setpoint, the scoreboard that has been the focus of so much employee attention symbolizes the open and trusting relationships that managers and other employees share. At the same time, the board and the huddles that take place around it strengthen the company's performance-driven culture.

---

culture of another company, Setpoint, is described in the feature "Managing with Metrics: Setpoint's Public Performance."[16]

Legal Environment. Performance management activities must be aligned with external environmental factors. In addition to labor markets and national cultures,[17] the legal environment is an important external environmental factor that affects performance management. In almost all organizations, performance information partly determines pay, promotions, terminations, transfers, and other types of key decisions that affect the well-being of employees and the productivity of a company. Society has a vested interest in ensuring that employers use high-quality information for these important decisions, and their interests are reflected in various laws and regulations. The basic principles for ensuring the legality of performance management practices are similar to those for selection practices. In both cases, the measures used to assess employees should be nondiscriminatory, job related, and fairly used.

The numerous nondiscrimination laws discussed in Chapter 4 apply to performance-based decisions. These laws emphasize the importance of protecting employees against negative consequences in the workplace caused by unfair discrimination and the use of inappropriate information when making employment decisions. In general, the legal system makes it clear that employers will be better able to successfully defend any legally contested employment decisions if they can show that their actions were based on valid measures of employee performance. A **valid performance measure** *accurately reflects all aspects of the job, and nothing else.* In Exhibit 9.2, a valid performance measure is indicated by a high degree of overlap between the two circles. *If the performance measure does not assess all of the behaviors and results that are important and relevant to the job, it is a* **deficient performance measure.** *If the performance measure assesses anything that is unimportant or irrelevant to the job, it is a* **contaminated performance measure.** Deficient and contaminated performance measures are quite common in organizations and are among the biggest reasons for employees' complaints about performance measurement.

Valid performance measures are based on job analysis results, which identify the key areas of performance expected in a job. A condensed set of recommended actions for developing and implementing legally defensible performance measurement is detailed in Exhibit 9.5.[18] All of these recommendations are consistent with the objective of developing a performance management process that supports the business strategy and objectives. They also are consistent with creating a process that employees perceive as fair and just.

Following the guidelines in Exhibit 9.5 requires careful record keeping and may limit a manager's freedom to make unilateral evaluations. Nevertheless, research indicates that managers respond favorably to the introduction of procedurally just performance management practices. A major advantage for managers is that procedurally fair performance management improves relationships between managers and their direct reports, as well as motivation.[19] As described in Chapter 4, employees certainly echo the importance of procedural justice. The development and use of alternative dispute resolution mechanisms also attest to this importance. As Chapter 14 describes, unions can be attractive to employees when managers fail to be fair.

EXHIBIT 9.5 Prescriptions for Legally Defensible Appraisal and Feedback

1. Job analysis to identify important duties and tasks should precede development of a performance appraisal system.
2. The performance appraisal system should be standardized and formal.
3. Specific performance standards should be communicated to employees in advance of the appraisal period.
4. Objective and uncontaminated data should be used whenever possible.
5. Ratings on traits such as dependability, drive, or attitude should be avoided or operationalized in behavioral terms.
6. Employees should be evaluated on specific work dimensions rather than on a single global or overall measure.
7. If work behaviors rather than outcomes are to be evaluated, evaluators should have ample opportunity to observe ratee performance.
8. To increase the reliability of ratings, more than one independent evaluator should perform appraisals whenever possible.
9. Behavioral documentation should be prepared for extreme ratings.
10. Employees should be given an opportunity to review their appraisals.
11. A formal system of appeal should be available for appraisal disagreements.
12. Raters should be trained to prevent discrimination and to evaluate performance consistently.
13. Appraisals should be frequent, offered at least annually.

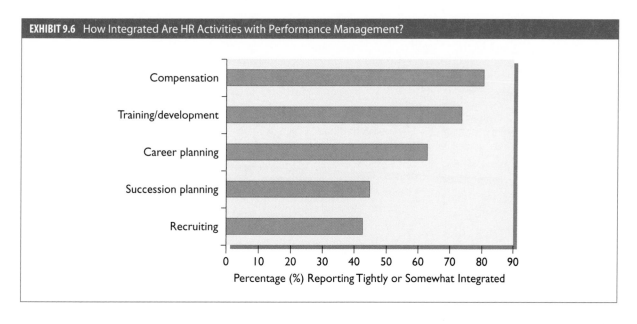

EXHIBIT 9.6 How Integrated Are HR Activities with Performance Management?

Percentage (%) Reporting Tightly or Somewhat Integrated

Other HR Activities

As already noted, effective performance management typically requires the use of performance-based incentives as well as career planning and development activities. Because performance management is so central to managing human resources, all other HR activities should also be closely aligned. For example, effective planning involves assessing past performance and setting goals for future performance. The development of appropriate performance measures involves job analysis and competency modeling. Most organizations use performance indicators when making promotion and layoff decisions. And performance measurement can reveal deficiencies that suggest the need for additional training. Of course, not every organization achieves complete alignment between performance management and other HR activities. Exhibit 9.6 reports the percentage of HR managers who believe that their HR activities are tightly or somewhat integrated with their firms' performance management process.[20]

THE HR TRIAD

Unfortunately, performance management often falls short of achieving continuous performance improvements. One reason is the ambiguity about who owns responsibility for managing the process. Does performance management fall in the domain of human resource departments or line departments? But debates about who is responsible miss the point. Line managers, HR professionals, and employees all need to work together to ensure that performance measurement and feedback are effective and fair to everyone concerned, as described in the feature "The HR Triad: Roles and Responsibilities for Measuring Performance and Providing Feedback."

Managers

Usually, managers are responsible for measuring the performance of their subordinates, communicating performance evaluations to their subordinates, and helping their subordinates improve in the future. Regardless of how performance is measured, managers are expected to review performance results

FAST FACT

Two surveys of HR professionals revealed that fewer than 10% were "very satisfied" with their company's performance management process.

LEARNING GOAL

" *Managers are solely responsible for evaluating their employees. No specific, company-wide evaluation forms are used for salespeople and managers. Rather, each manager designs his or her own evaluation system.* "

Mary Kim Stuart
Human Resources Manager
Nordstrom

LINE MANAGERS	HR PROFESSIONALS	EMPLOYEES
• Work with HR professionals and employees to develop valid performance measures that meet legal guidelines.	• Work with line managers, providing job analysis data to use in developing valid and legal performance measures.	• Work with line managers and HR professionals to set performance expectations.
• Develop an understanding of how common appraisal rating errors can be avoided.	• Train everyone who completes performance appraisals (e.g., peers, subordinates, and supervisors) in how to avoid appraisal rating errors.	• Candidly appraise the work of other employees (bosses, peers, etc.).
• Measure employee performance conscientiously and keep accurate records.	• Coordinate the administrative aspects of performance measurement and feedback.	• Participate in self-appraisal.
• Give constructive and honest feedback to employees.	• Train line managers to give and receive feedback.	• Seek and accept constructive and honest feedback.
• Seek and accept constructive feedback about own performance.	• May train self-managing teams to give feedback.	• Learn to give constructive and honest feedback to others.
• Use performance information for decision making.	• Monitor managerial decisions to ensure they're performance based.	• Develop accurate understanding of performance expectations and criteria.
• Diagnose individual and team performance deficiencies.	• May train self-managing teams to diagnose performance deficiencies.	• Learn to diagnose causes of performance deficiencies for self and team.
• Work with employees to develop performance improvement strategies.	• Ensure managers and employees are aware of all possible ways to deal with performance deficiencies.	• Work with managers to develop performance improvement strategies.
• Provide resources and remove constraints as needed for improvement.	• Provide personal assistance to employees if requested; develop and administer appeals process.	• Develop goal-setting and self-management skills.

with their employees and explain any consequences that may follow (e.g., pay raises, disciplinary action, training). Performance measurement isn't an end to be achieved. Rather, it's a means for moving into a more productive future. For performance evaluations to be useful, employees must *act* on them. Thus, one of a manager's major responsibilities is ensuring that employees accept the feedback they receive and use it as a basis for improving in the future.

Employees

The primary performance management responsibilities of employees are seeking honest feedback and using it to improve their performance. Prior to discussions about their performance, employees often are asked to participate by first providing their own assessment of their performance. In addition, all employees—even those with no managerial responsibilities—often share responsibility for evaluating the performance of others and providing them with feedback.

HR Professionals

The responsibilities of HR professionals include ensuring that the organization's performance management practices are aligned with the internal organizational contexts, reflect state-of-the-art knowledge, and meet legal standards. HR professionals also help ensure that well-designed practices are implemented appropriately. Performance management practices are more effective when HR professionals support managers, hold them accountable for their appraisals, and support employees.[21]

Support for Managers.

Organizations are not always successful in using performance measurement and feedback strategically, and one reason is that line managers do not fully understand and appreciate the basic principles. Most managers spend far more time acquiring technical competencies (e.g., in the areas of accounting, marketing, and operations management) than they do learning to manage human resources. Yet skillfully managing the performance of others is necessary for managers to achieve their corporate mandate to get things done through other people. The best managers know how to accurately assess performance and can provide feedback in ways that guide and motivate employee improvement. HR professionals can help by teaching managers about the objectives of performance management and by helping them develop the skills they need to improve the performance of subordinates. Managers should receive training in how to set clear goals and keep appropriate performance records, as well as how to accurately assess performance and provide constructive feedback.[22]

Accountability of Managers.

A common roadblock to effective performance measurement and feedback is that managers fail to see a payoff. Most organizations offer no obvious incentives for managers to do a good job of measuring employee performance and providing useful feedback to employees. Many managers so dislike these activities that they try to avoid the process entirely. As expectancy theory makes clear, this situation is not optimal! One solution to this problem is to measure how well managers perform this important aspect of their job and provide them with feedback about how to improve. HR professionals can help ensure that managers are held accountable for effective performance measurement and feedback by including this aspect of managers' jobs in the performance reviews of managers.

Support for Employees.

Through their influence on the design of an organization's performance management practices, HR professionals provide indirect support to employees. Human resource professionals also can provide direct support to employees. When employees feel their performance evaluations are unfair, HR professionals can assist them in using the organization's appeal process (described in Chapter 4). In many organizations, HR professionals are available to talk to employees about performance problems and provide informal assistance. If necessary, they can recommend other sources of professional assistance. For example, they can help employees find appropriate training opportunities and understand the organization's Employee Assistance Program (EAP). As described in Chapters 12 and 13, EAPs were originally created to battle alcoholism, and some employees still think that EAPs are relevant only for people with alcohol-related problems. But in fact, most EAPs also assist employees with family, financial, and legal problems, all of which can cause unsatisfactory work performance.

As this chapter reveals, developing effective performance management requires involvement and buy-in from everyone affected by it. Achieving this ideal takes time and determination. But for companies like Cendant Mortgage and others who want to be seen as employers of choice, there is little doubt that investing the required effort contributes to the company's success.

> " *Part of being an 'Employer of Choice' is treating our associates like valued members of the company. Giving them honest and specific feedback about their performance is a major way to do this.* "
>
> *Paris Couturiaux*
> *Senior Vice President, Human Resources*
> *Cendant Mortgage*

FAST FACT

Employees who perform well on specific job tasks also tend to be good organizational citizens.

WHAT TO MEASURE

Performance criteria *are the dimensions against which the performance of an incumbent, a team, or a work unit is evaluated.* They are the performance expectations that individuals and teams strive for in order to achieve the organization's strategy. If jobs have been designed well, with attention paid to how job demands relate to strategic business needs, then conducting a job analysis should ensure that performance measures reflect strategic concerns. The performance criteria should capture the employee's performance on specific tasks and as an organizational citizen.[23] Examples of organizational citizenship (sometimes referred to as contextual performance) include

- Volunteering to carry out task activities that are not formally a part of the job.
- Persisting with extra enthusiasm or effort when necessary to complete task activities successfully.
- Helping others.
- Following organizational rules and procedures even when doing so is inconvenient.
- Endorsing, supporting, and defending organizational objectives.[24]

When measuring task performance and organizational citizenship, organizations can use three types of performance criteria: personal traits, behaviors, and objective results.

Personal Traits

Trait-based criteria *focus on personal characteristics, such as loyalty, dependability, communication ability, and leadership.* Criteria such as these address what a person is, not what a person does or accomplishes on the job. For jobs involving work that's difficult to observe, trait-based performance measures may be easier to use than others. Unfortunately, they may not be reliable indicators of actual job performance. To one manager, "dependability" may mean showing up to work on time every day; to another manager, it may mean staying late when the boss requests it; to a third manager, it may mean coming to work and not using sick days even when the worker is really sick.

Performance evaluations should not depend on who is making the judgment. They should reflect what employees do, regardless of who is evaluating them. Because trait-based measures of performance are often unreliable, the courts have penalized employers who rely on them when making employment decisions.[25]

Do the position of the courts and the importance of meritocracy in U.S. culture mean that difficult-to-measure personal qualities should not be evaluated as part of the performance appraisal process? Can employers still build corporate cultures around having the right kinds of people as defined by personal qualities that extend beyond job skills? The answer is that personal qualities can be assessed if the measure focuses on employee behaviors.

Behaviors

Behavioral criteria *focus on how work is performed.* Behavioral criteria can include task-related behaviors or more general counterproductive behaviors such as absenteeism, tardiness, and carelessness.[26] The positive aspects of behavioral criteria include that they can be used for many different jobs, they allow raters to take into consideration factors that are beyond the employee's control that affected performance, and they allow the evaluation of the acceptability of the behaviors. Their subjectivity and susceptibility to biases are the major disadvantages of behavioral criteria.[27] Task-related behavioral criteria are particularly important for jobs that involve interpersonal contact. Customer service jobs and managerial jobs are examples that show how behavioral criteria can be used to measure performance.

Customer Service. Having friendly cashiers is critical to Au Bon Pain's customers and to the store's image. But Au Bon Pain doesn't use store managers' judgments of employees' friendliness to measure this critical aspect of performance. Instead, it measures behaviors. To assess friendliness, the company generated a list of specific behaviors that employees should engage in and that convey a friendly image to most customers. To assess friendliness, the store hires mystery shoppers to buy meals and fill out behavior-based appraisals.

Managing Multiculturalism. As organizations desire to create cultures in which multiculturalism is valued and respected, behavioral criteria are proving useful for monitoring whether managers are investing sufficient energy in the development of employees from diverse backgrounds. Imagine how difficult it would be to evaluate whether a manager achieved a trait-based criterion like "Values the diversity of subordinates." A trait-based criterion like this provides little guidance to the manager about what actually to *do*. It would be equally difficult for the manager's superior to interpret. For the purpose of performance management, more effective criteria would be *specific* behaviors, such as whether the manager has attended a diversity training program and whether the manager has formed a diversity caucus group in his or her unit.

When combined with performance feedback, behavioral measures are particularly useful for employee development. With behaviors clearly identified, an employee is more likely to exhibit the acts that lead to peak performance. The behaviors identified by TRW relate to creating trust, energizing people, embracing change, building teamwork, and being customer oriented. TRW believes that when managers exhibit such behaviors, company success will follow.

Objective Results

Results criteria *focus on what was accomplished or produced rather than on how it was accomplished or produced.* Results criteria may be appropriate if the company does not care how results are achieved, but they are not appropriate for every job. Results criteria are more common at the team and work unit level, because it is generally more difficult to identify results at the individual level that are not largely dependent on others. Results criteria are often criticized for missing critical aspects of the job that are difficult to quantify. For example, the number of cases handled annually by a lawyer can easily be counted, but this result does not indicate the quality of legal counsel, the difficulty of the cases, how the cases were resolved, or whether a lawyer helped establish any important new legal principles.

Another criticism of results criteria is that they can create unexpected problems by encouraging a results-at-all-costs mentality among employees. A collection agency used the total dollars collected by agents as its sole measure of performance. Large sums of money were collected, but the agency ended up being sued because agents used threats and punitive measures to amass collections. This issue will be further discussed in Chapter 11.

Multiple Criteria

For most jobs, performing well requires performing many tasks well using many different competencies, and job descriptions usually reflect this requirement. Just as a job description covers all aspects of the job, so should performance measures. For some duties, trait-based measures may be appropriate. For others, behavioral measures or results may be best. Payless ShoeSource uses both behavioral measures and results in evaluating not only how well their employees perform, but also whether they follow the company's ethical standards. This is described in more detail in the feature "Managing with Ethics: Measuring Values at Payless ShoeSource."[28]

Some researchers have argued that a limited set of performance domains can be used to capture all aspects of nearly any job. A taxonomy that can be used to describe all the important elements of performance in most organizations is shown in Exhibit 9.7. Notice that this taxonomy includes aspects of the job itself (the top half) as well as criteria that reflect how well an employee responds to stress and adapts to new work conditions.[29] The elements in the bottom of Exhibit 9.7 reflect the fact that many jobs and organizations are in a state of constant flux and need employees to be able to adapt and change accordingly.

Weighting the Criteria

For jobs involving multiple performance criteria, another question must be asked: "How should these separate aspects of performance be combined into

MANAGING WITH ETHICS
Measuring Values at Payless ShoeSource

Payless ShoeSource, Inc. is a footwear retailer with more than 4,500 stores. They are located in all 50 U.S. states, as well as Canada, Central America, the Caribbean, and South America. In a recent year, Payless sold nearly 180 million pairs of shoes. Shortly after Matt Rubel joined Payless as the chief executive officer and president, he and the board of directors adopted a 17-page code of ethics that specifies the ethical standards expected of managers and employees. It discusses many topics including equal opportunity and respect in the workplace, the financial integrity of books and records, avoiding conflicts of interest, payment practices, the use and protection of company assets, retaliation, and obligations to customers, competitors, and vendors.

To enforce the new ethics code, Payless ShoeSource introduced new performance management practices that direct attention both to what results are achieved and to how the results are achieved. Performance goals are set by managers in consultation with their employees. Managers are expected to make sure that their employees' goals are attainable, related to corporate strategies, linked to departmental goals, and consistent with the values of Payless ShoeSource. Together, managers and their

subordinates also are expected to ensure that the performance goals they agree to do not encourage unethical behavior. To communicate the new ethical values to employees, managers were given discussion guides that explain how to provide appropriate feedback to employees. Employees were specifically directed to incorporate the company's values into their performance plans.

Payless also developed a new performance measurement approach. In one section, managers rate the employee's performance as meeting, exceeding, or falling short of the goals. In another section, managers evaluate how the employee accomplished the results. Employees who achieve their quantitative goals but ignore company values receive lower performance scores and lower pay.

By including an evaluation of ethical behavior in their performance reviews, Payless ShoeSource is showing employees that top management is serious about running an ethical business. When ethical behavior is central to performance management, including decisions about promotions and pay, it becomes part of the company's culture— and that is what Payless ShoeSource is striving for.

EXHIBIT 9.7 A Two-Part Taxonomy of Performance Domains

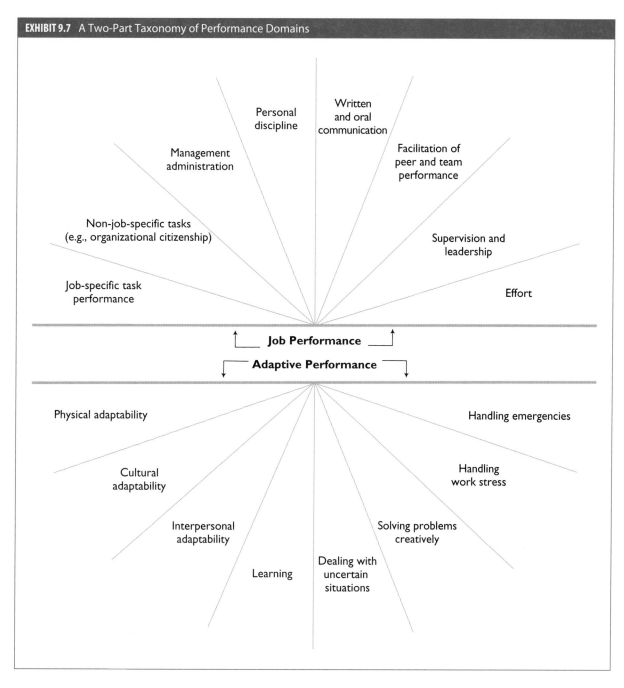

a composite score that facilitates comparisons of incumbents?" One way is to weight all the criteria equally. If some criteria are much more important than others, then weights should be assigned to reflect these differences. The simplest approach to assigning weights is to use job analysis information, such as ratings of task frequency and importance.

TIMING

The timing of performance measurement *should* reflect strategic considerations. But often the timing of performance measurement and feedback is driven by convenience and tradition. The three most common approaches to

EXHIBIT 9.8 Frequency of Performance Reviews

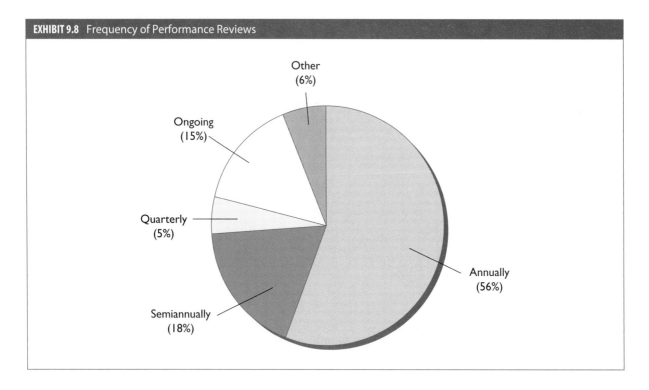

timing performance measurement and feedback are focal-point, anniversary, and natural time span. The timing of the performance review may also affect its frequency. Exhibit 9.8 shows the results of a recent survey on the frequency of performance management reviews.[30] Most firms conduct performance management annually, which is typical of the focal-point approach.

Focal-Point Approach

With the **focal-point approach,** *performance measurement for all employees occurs at approximately the same time.* The major advantage of the focal-point approach is that supervisors find it easier to make direct comparisons among employees. They consider everyone at once and get a sense of how their performances compare during the same time period. Similarly, top management can compare the performances of different strategic business units to assess how well they are meeting corporate objectives. Such comparative information is particularly important if performance information is used for compensation decisions.

At Lincoln Electric, performance measures determine the employees' bonuses, which are paid out every six months. Prior to distributing the bonus money, line managers spend up to two weeks evaluating the performance of each subordinate. The HR department spends several weeks before this making sure that the line managers have all the data they need, including attendance records, productivity figures, and information about the quality of products produced by each employee.

The focal-point approach has some disadvantages. One is that it creates a tremendous workload for a concentrated period of time, which can be burdensome. The burden can be reduced by having clear criteria against which to evaluate performance and by ensuring that subordinates share with their supervisors the responsibility for documenting accomplishments relative to performance standards. Another concern is that the focal-point approach

> *Doing annual reviews is like dieting only on your birthday and wondering why you're not losing weight.*
>
> Anne Saunier
> Principal
> Sibson & Co.

may create artificial productivity cycles that merely reflect the timing of performance measurement and feedback. Suppose a department store measures performance once a year in July. As part of the process, managers assess the customer responsiveness of each salesperson. Knowing they will be evaluated soon, sales employees are likely to be quite friendly in June. During August and the next several months, they may be less friendly. After all, by next July, their manager is not likely to remember how they behaved many months ago; in fact, they may even have a new manager by then!

Anniversary Approach

The **anniversary approach** *distributes the task of reviewing performance and providing feedback over the year.* Often, employees' performance reviews are timed to take place on the dates they joined the organization. For example, employees may receive their first review 30 to 90 days after their starting date.[31] After that, employees may receive reviews every 6 or 12 months. Assuming the organization hires throughout the year, this approach spreads out the workload for supervisors.

The anniversary approach also has some disadvantages. One problem is that it is difficult to tie individual or team performance to an overall measure of organizational performance, which detracts from the strategic value of performance measurement. The anniversary approach may also make it more difficult for managers to directly compare the performance of one subordinate to others. This is particularly likely if managers must use a forced distribution, or "curve." Early in the year, managers tend to be lenient, because they prefer to avoid giving negative evaluations. If the system is set up to permit a fixed percentage of high, medium, and low ratings, then managers who begin the year lenient must balance out the distribution by giving lower ratings later in the year.

Natural Time Span of the Job

Some experts argue that a better timing rule is to schedule reviews to correspond to the natural time span of the job. If performance is assessed too soon in the natural time span, it cannot be reasonably measured due to lack of information. If performance is measured too late, motivation and performance may suffer because the feedback comes too late to be of any use. Feedback that comes too late is particularly detrimental to a poor performer, who will likely not know how to improve performance until it's too late. In the case of some simple jobs, the time span may be only a few minutes; in the case of a senior-level management job, the appropriate time period may be as long as a year. In an advertising agency, account executives receive evaluation feedback after each presentation.

For teams working on projects, good times for performance measurement and feedback are once about midway through the project and again at the end of the project.[32] At the midway point, team members are open to suggestions for improvement because they have a good understanding of the team's strengths and weaknesses, yet enough time remains to make changes that may improve the team's performance. After the project ends is the best time to measure performance against deadlines, budget constraints, and other project goals.

> *We told employees, 'You have a right to feedback and you can ask for it [any time].'*
>
> Jeff Chambers
> Human Resources Director
> SAS

PARTICIPANTS

It should be apparent by now that there are many sources of performance data, including organizational records, supervisors, employees themselves, peers or team members, subordinates, and customers. Organizational records generally provide objective indicators of performance. All of the other sources—people—provide subjective judgments. Each source has some advantages and disadvantages.

When determining whom to involve when measuring performance, employers need to consider the amount and type of contact each source has with the person being evaluated. Team members, customers, supervisors, and subordinates all see different facets of an individual's task behavior. A customer is more likely to observe the selling behavior of a sale's representative—for instance, greeting the customer or closing the sale. Other peers and team members are in a better position to evaluate how well the sales rep cooperates with peers and whether she is a good corporate citizen. Supervisors have more information about the sales rep's objective sales results. No one—not even the employee—has complete information. Thus, rating differences among various sources can be substantial and different sources may invoke different reactions.[33] To compensate for the disadvantages of gathering data from any single source, most large organizations involve multiple participants when measuring performance and providing feedback.

Supervisors

Many companies assume that supervisors know more than anyone else about how well subordinates perform their jobs, so they give supervisors all the responsibility for measuring performance and providing feedback. Supervisors produce more reliable and useful performance judgments than other sources, perhaps because they have knowledge about several aspects of employees' performance.[34] Nevertheless, to help ensure that all aspects of performance are measured and that different perspectives are considered, supervisors should make administrative and developmental decisions based on multiple sources of information.[35] Employees view this as more fair, which creates greater openness and enhances the quality of the superior-subordinate relationship.

Self-Appraisal

When employees assess their own performance, they conduct a **self-appraisal.** Subordinates who participate in the evaluation process become more involved and committed to the goals. Subordinate participation also clarifies employees' roles and may reduce role ambiguity and conflict.[36]

Accuracy. Self-appraisals increase employees' satisfaction with the appraisal process[37] and are effective tools for self-development, personal growth, and goal commitment. However, self-appraisals are subject to systematic biases and distortions. Self-ratings often are more lenient and less accurate than those obtained from supervisors and other sources. Also, self-appraisals often reveal blind spots to employers—areas of poor performance that the employee is unaware of. High-performing employees appear to have fewer such blind spots and more accurate appraisals than do low-performing employees.[38] Providing extensive performance feedback, building a culture of trust, and including some objective performance data are ways to increase the accuracy and reduce the problem of leniency in self-appraisals.[39]

Cultural Differences. For global firms, and even domestic firms with culturally diverse workforces, self-appraisals raise another concern: Employees from different cultures approach self-appraisal differently.[40] The tendency to project a positive self-image to others is common in individualistic cultures (like that of the United

States), which stress individual achievement, self-sufficiency, and self-respect. In contrast, collectivistic cultures encourage interpersonal harmony, interdependence, solidarity, and group cohesiveness. In the interest of interpersonal harmony, people do not draw attention to their individual achievements.

Research supports the notion that workers in collectivistic cultures are more modest than their American counterparts when it comes to rating their own job performance. Thus, the use of self-ratings by multinational firms may create bias against employees from collectivist cultures, particularly young employees. Consistent with the notion that collectivistic cultures value the wisdom that comes with aging, young workers from such cultures give themselves lower ratings than older workers. Besides giving themselves lower ratings, employees from collectivist cultures may be reluctant to engage in self-promotion, which may be necessary for informing supervisors about accomplishments. As a result, supervisors may give these employees ratings that are lower than what's deserved. Unintended discrimination, unfair treatment, lower morale, and ineffective use of the best talent may be consequences of using self-appraisals in a culturally diverse workforce.[41]

Peers

Research shows that appraisals by peers are useful predictors of training success and future performance.[42] It also shows that the appraisals of peers and subordinates tend to be consistent with each other.[43] In team-based organizations, peer involvement in performance management is growing. Anonymous peer appraisals in teams increase interpersonal effectiveness, group cohesion, communication openness, and group satisfaction.[44] However, peer ratings may be biased for self-serving motives and may be inaccurate if peers have limited interaction with the employee being reviewed.[45]

Jamestown Advanced Products Incorporated, a small metal fabrication firm, relies on peers to help manage a variety of performance problems. One problem was tardiness. One person's late arrival disrupted everyone else's schedule, reduced team performance, and consequently lowered financial bonuses. Traditionally, a tardy employee lost some wages but remained eligible for the quarterly performance bonus. Team members thought this was unfair. To increase fairness, the team was encouraged to set performance standards for its members and identify consequences for low performers. The team batted around the issue of how much lateness or absenteeism it could tolerate and how punitive it should be until it reached agreement: Employees could be tardy (defined as one minute late) or absent without notice no more than five times a quarter. Beyond that, they would lose their entire bonus.

Subordinates

Few subordinates have information about all dimensions of their supervisor's performance, but most have access to information about supervisor-subordinate interactions. Organizations such as Johnson & Johnson and Sears have been surveying employees for their opinions about managers for years. *When such surveys are used to evaluate the performance of specific managers, the process is called* **upward appraisal.**

General Mills uses upward appraisal, and even the CEO is included in the process. CEO Steve Sanger understands that he can be a powerful example for the rest of the company's employees. "Just last year, my team told me that I needed to do a better job of coaching my direct reports," he explained. "I have been working on being a better coach for the past year or so. I just reviewed

FAST FACT

In a survey of executives of the nation's 1,000 largest companies, 60% said employees should be allowed to participate in a formal review of the boss.

my feedback [for this year and last year]. I'm still not doing as well as I want, but I am doing a lot better." Sanger is proud of the improvement in his coaching, and he also is proud that he got high scores on "effectively responds to feedback."[46]

Anonymity. One drawback to upward feedback is that subordinates don't always evaluate performance objectively or honestly, especially if their ratings are not anonymous.[47] To protect anonymity, evaluations need to be made by several subordinates, and someone other than the supervisor should average the subordinates' ratings.

Usefulness. For managers who do not already perform well, upward appraisal can be quite useful. One study followed managers for five years to track changes in performance following upward appraisal and feedback. The results showed that managers who initially performed poorly significantly improved after receiving the results of upward appraisals. The greatest improvements occurred for managers who met with their direct reports to discuss their own performance results.[48] Other research shows that even managers who already perform well benefit from upward feedback. Overall, managers who are confident in their own abilities seem to be the ones who are most able to accept negative feedback and use it to improve their own performance.[49] Finally, research shows that upward feedback is most effective when it is accompanied by specific suggestions about *how* to improve.[50]

Customers

At a medical clinic in Billings, Montana, patients routinely rate desk attendants and nursing personnel on behaviors such as courtesy, promptness, and quality of care. Domino's Pizza hires mystery customers who order pizzas and then evaluate the performance of the telephone operator and delivery person. The owner of a carpeting firm uses a customer checklist to monitor the on-site performance of carpet installers. When customers are used as appraisers, it is difficult for employees to discount the results because employers usually obtain the impressions of *many* customers. Nevertheless, a potential difficulty in using real customers is getting a fair sampling of customer experiences. For example, customers who have had particularly bad experiences may be more likely to complete a questionnaire.

360-Degree Appraisals

" *With 360-degree feedback, we capture input from people with whom the employee works on a regular basis. We call it their 'knowledge network.' The person who receives the evaluation views it as very accurate.* "

Ann J. Ewen
President
TEAMS, Inc.

When evaluations from supervisors, subordinates, peers, and employees themselves are all used to measure performance, it is referred to as **360-degree appraisal.** In contrast to the traditional approach, where a single person—usually a supervisor—rates employee performance, 360-degree appraisal collects performance information from a set of colleagues and internal customers who form a circle around the employee. Because it is seen as more appropriate in today's flatter, team-based work environments, many employers, including GE, Motorola, Proctor & Gamble, and UPS, have adopted 360-degree appraisal and feedback.[51]

Multiple-source evaluations are perceived as being more fair, reliable, and valid than single-source approaches. The evaluation process produces better results because it involves a group of people who interact with the employee in many different ways. For the same reason, the process should be less susceptible to gender and ethnicity biases than are single-source evaluations.[52]

Organizations must keep a number of things in mind when developing appropriate 360-degree practices. First, raters' identities should remain anonymous when possible. Second, this technique appears to work best when many sources are represented, not just a few (e.g., including only subordinates or only peers). No one rater should be able to dramatically alter the outcome. In most other respects, the principles for developing effective appraisals are the same as for single-source assessments; for example, only relevant data should be collected and raters should be trained.[53]

PERFORMANCE APPRAISAL FORMATS

Performance appraisal is a central component of performance management in most organizations. **Performance appraisal** *involves evaluating performance based on the judgments and opinions of subordinates, peers, supervisors, other managers, and even the employees themselves.* It is perhaps the most common approach to performance measurement.

When performance appraisals are used (instead of objective measures), some sort of format is provided to appraisers. Appraisals may be recorded on paper or electronically. Either way, the appraisal format provides a structure for making and recording judgments.

Norm-Referenced Formats

For many human resource decisions, employees must be compared to each other directly. Special recognition cannot be given without knowing: Who is the best performer in the group? Layoffs should not be conducted without knowing: Who are the weakest performers to let go, given that we have to cut our workforce? For these types of decisions, norm-referenced formats are appropriate. With a **norm-referenced format**, *the rater is forced to evaluate the individual or team and make comparisons to others.* The two most commonly used norm-referenced formats are straight ranking and forced distribution.

Straight Ranking. In **straight ranking,** *the appraiser lists the focal employees (or teams of employees) in order, from best to worst, usually on the basis of overall performance.* As the number of employees to be ranked grows, straight ranking becomes increasingly difficult. A problem with straight ranking is that ties usually are not allowed. Although no two subordinates perform exactly alike, many supervisors believe that some incumbents perform so similarly that making performance distinctions between them is not appropriate.

Forced Distribution. With the **forced distribution method,** *the appraiser distributes employees across several categories of performance following a set rule about the distribution of ratings that are permitted.* A typical rule specifies five categories of performance and forces most of the evaluations to fall near the middle, as illustrated in the following chart:

Lowest Performers	Next Lowest	Middle	Next Highest	Highest Performers
10%	20%	40%	20%	10%
(5 employees)	(10 employees)	(20 employees)	(10 employees)	(5 employees)

7
LEARNING GOAL

" *The system forced me to turn people who were excellent performers into people who were getting mediocre ratings.* "

*Eric Wisnefsky
Vice President for Corporate Finance
Chemtura*

" *I LOVE this company, but I hate 'The Curve.'* "

Anonymous Microsoft Employee's Blog

The forced distribution method creates problems for evaluators who believe that the performances of the people being evaluated do not conform to the fixed percentages. Further, distribution curves can hurt morale and teamwork, because they foster competitiveness rather than cooperation among employees. Nevertheless, this method seems to be gaining popularity. It is now used in one out of five *Fortune* 500 companies. One advantage of forced distribution is that it forces managers to give some employees low ratings, which can be difficult. Using forced distribution to terminate the bottom 10% of employees appears to improve firm performance, but only in the short term.[54]

Absolute Standards Formats

With the absolute standards format, appraisers assess performance in relation to specified criteria and do not make direct comparisons among employees. Three widely used formats using absolute standards are graphic rating scales, behaviorally anchored rating scales, and behavioral observation scales.

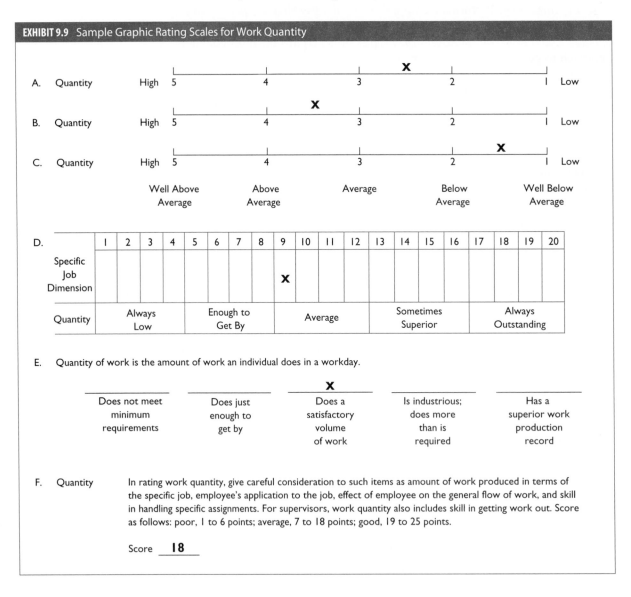

EXHIBIT 9.9 Sample Graphic Rating Scales for Work Quantity

Graphic Rating Scales. Introduced in the 1920s, graphic rating scales were touted as useful because direct output measures were not needed and the rater was free to make as fine a judgment as desired. The primary advantage of the graphic rating scale format is its simplicity. Exhibit 9.9 shows several graphic rating scales that might be used to assess the quantity of work a person completes. In this exhibit, scales A to C require the rater to define the dimension. This obviously leads to different interpretations by different raters. Scales D and E do a better job of defining work quantity, but they still provide latitude for disagreement. Scale F provides the most extensive definition of work quantity, but the rater must consider more than one aspect of quantity. In addition, scale F provides anchors for only three general groups of scale values, although 25 discrete scale values can be used. As these examples illustrate, the major disadvantage of graphic rating scales is their lack of clarity and definition. Even when raters are trained, they still might not define the performance dimensions in the same way. At TRW, four-point rating scales provide very specific descriptions of what each level of performance means on each of the five behavioral criteria described earlier.

Behaviorally Anchored Rating Scales. Dissatisfaction with graphic rating scales led to the development of formats that include more specific behavioral criteria. As shown in Exhibit 9.10, **behaviorally anchored rating scales (BARS)** *provide appraisers with specific examples of the behaviors that go along with each value that can be assigned to an employee's performance.* In this example,

> **" At Schwab, we have three possible ratings for employees. The bottom one is never assigned. "**
>
> *Maureen Hilts*
> *Vice President of Compensation*
> *Charles Schwab & Co.*

FAST FACT

A hospitality checklist reminds Red Lion Hotel employees of their company's customer service goals:

1. *Greet the guest.*
2. *Show the guest that you care.*
3. *Show the guest that you can help (by going out of your way to accommodate the guest's needs).*
4. *Appreciate the guest's business.*

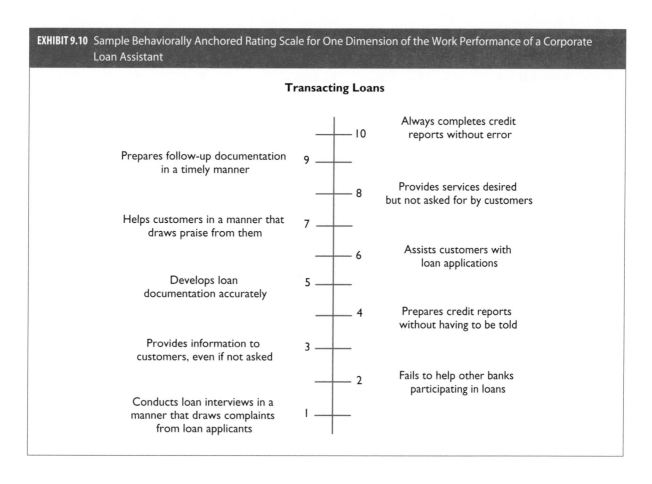

EXHIBIT 9.10 Sample Behaviorally Anchored Rating Scale for One Dimension of the Work Performance of a Corporate Loan Assistant

Transacting Loans

	10 — Always completes credit reports without error
Prepares follow-up documentation in a timely manner — 9	
	8 — Provides services desired but not asked for by customers
Helps customers in a manner that draws praise from them — 7	
	6 — Assists customers with loan applications
Develops loan documentation accurately — 5	
	4 — Prepares credit reports without having to be told
Provides information to customers, even if not asked — 3	
	2 — Fails to help other banks participating in loans
Conducts loan interviews in a manner that draws complaints from loan applicants — 1	

performance dimension measured is "transacting loans." The behavioral descriptions are intended to ensure that appraisers all use similar interpretations when assigning performance scores, thereby increasing their validity and reliability.[55]

The development of a BARS performance measure involves collecting descriptions of incidents that illustrate very competent, average, and incompetent work behaviors. These performance descriptions must be obtained in advance, often as part of a job analysis. A high scale value means high performance.

Like any format, the BARS format has limitations. Scales can be difficult and time-consuming to develop, and they become more difficult to modify as jobs change and performance expectations shift. From a cost-benefit perspective, the development of behavioral formats should be restricted to jobs that have many incumbents or for which the job *processes* (versus results) are critical to job success. In the service sector, success often depends on *how* work is performed, so it is worthwhile to invest in the effort required to develop clear behavioral standards.[56]

For raters, problems occur when the incidents shown on the form don't correspond to any behavior the rater has observed or when the rater has observed the employee displaying behaviors associated with both high and low performance. For example, a corporate loan assistant could prepare follow-up documentation in a timely manner and also receive complaints from loan applicants about rudeness and inappropriate questioning. In such situations, it is difficult to decide whether to give a high or low rating.[57]

Behavioral Observation Scales. **Behavioral observation scales (BOS)** *ask appraisers to report how frequently employees engage in specific behaviors.* As with BARS, the behaviors listed are developed using job analysis information. Because of the way points are assigned to behaviors, adding up all the ratings yields an overall measure of performance. (Items that describe ineffective performance are reverse-scored.) Exhibit 9.11 illustrates the BOS format.[58]

BOS is just as expensive and time-consuming as BARS to develop, but raters find it easier to use. Unfortunately, however, raters often don't have sufficient time or ability to accurately assess the frequency of the behaviors under observation.

Results-Based Formats

For some jobs, or some aspects of a job, the results achieved are more important than the behaviors that led to them. In such cases, measuring actual results may be appropriate. Results-based formats focus on job products as the primary criteria. As with the norm-referenced and absolute standards approaches, job analysis should guide the choice of results selected for measurement. Two widely used results-based formats are management by objectives and the direct index approach.

Direct Index Approach. The **direct index approach** *measures performance using objective, impersonal criteria, such as productivity, absenteeism, and turnover.* At Busch's Inc., a retail grocer in Michigan, managers are evaluated on the store's sales figures, profit margins, cost of supplies, employee turnover, and payroll expenses. *Using multiple objective measures that tap into numerous different dimensions of performance is referred to as the* **balanced scorecard approach.**

EXHIBIT 9.11 Sample Behavioral Observation Scale Items for a Maintenance Mechanic

In completing this form, circle
0– if you have no knowledge of the employee's behavior
1– if the employee has engaged in the behavior 0 to 64 percent of the time
2– if the employee has engaged in the behavior 65 to 74 percent of the time
3– if the employee has engaged in the behavior 75 to 84 percent of the time
4– if the employee has engaged in the behavior 85 to 94 percent of the time
5– if the employee has engaged in the behavior 95 to 100 percent of the time

	Behavior Frequency					
Customer Relations						
1. Swears in front of customers (e.g, operators and vendors) (R)	0	1	2	3	4	5
2. Blames customers for malfunction (R)	0	1	2	3	4	5
3. Refers to customers by name or asks for their names when first introduced	0	1	2	3	4	5
4. Asks operators to demonstrate what they were doing at the time of the malfunction	0	1	2	3	4	5
Teamwork						
1. Exhibits rude behavior that coworkers complain about (R)	0	1	2	3	4	5
2. Verbally shares technical knowledge with other technicians	0	1	2	3	4	5
3. As needed, consults fellow workers for their ideas on ways to solve specific problems	0	1	2	3	4	5
4. Given an incomplete assignment, leaves a clear, written tie-in for the next day shift to use	0	1	2	3	4	5
5. Works his or her share of overtime						
Planning						
1. Estimates repair time accurately	0	1	2	3	4	5
2. Completes assigned jobs on time	0	1	2	3	4	5
3. Is able to set job priorities on a daily or weekly basis	0	1	2	3	4	5
4. Even when the job is not yet complete, cleans up area at the end of the shift	0	1	2	3	4	5
5. Identifies problems or potential problems that may affect repair success or completion time						
Planned Maintenance Repairs						
1. Executes planned maintenance repair, requiring no follow-up	0	1	2	3	4	5
2. Adjusts equipment according to predetermined tolerance levels; commits no errors	0	1	2	3	4	5
3. Replaces components when necessary rather than when convenient or easy	0	1	2	3	4	5
4. Takes more time than allotted to complete a planned maintenance repair (R)	0	1	2	3	4	5

Note: "R" denotes item is reverse-scored (5 = 1, 4 = 2, 3 = 3, 2 = 4, 1 = 5, 0 = 0)

One advantage of the direct index approach is that it provides clear, unambiguous direction to employees regarding the desired job results. Another advantage is that extraneous factors—for example, prior performance, salary, and personal characteristics like gender—are less likely to bias the results.

On the other hand, important job behaviors may be ignored. This problem can be overcome by supplementing the direct indexes with other formats. For example, at Busch's Inc., the direct index approach is combined with graphic ratings scales that assess follow-through, merchandizing execution, creative problem solving, leadership, the training and development of subordinates, and the use of computers.[59]

Management by Objectives. **Management by objectives (MBO)** *begins with the establishment of performance objectives (goals) for the upcoming performance period; performance is then measured against the objectives that were set.* In some organizations, superiors and subordinates work together to establish

FAST FACT

A recent survey of executive performance management practices found that most executives have performance goals for their units, but only half translate them into personal goals.

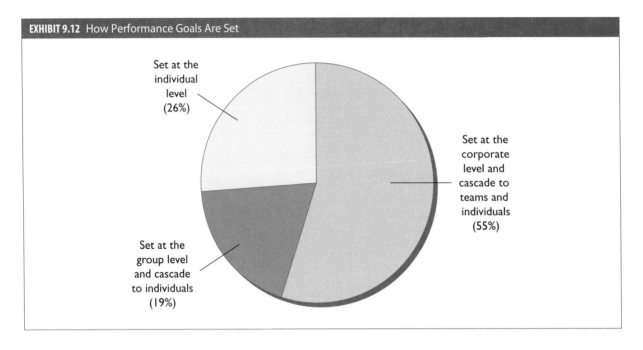

EXHIBIT 9.12 How Performance Goals Are Set

Set at the individual level (26%)

Set at the corporate level and cascade to teams and individuals (55%)

Set at the group level and cascade to individuals (19%)

goals; in others, superiors establish goals for work groups or individuals; in still others, in organizations with self-managed work teams, teams may set their own goals. Exhibit 9.12 illustrates how performance goals are typically set.[60]

Goals should be challenging, but not so difficult that employees don't believe they can be achieved. Easy goals don't give employees any reason to exert extra effort. If goals are too difficult, however, employees will reject them as impossible and won't even bother trying to achieve them.[61]

Once goals are established, the next step is to develop a strategy for goal attainment. Clearly delineating how a goal is to be attained reduces ambiguity and heightens the likelihood of goal attainment. Strategy development includes outlining the steps necessary to attain each objective, as well as addressing any constraints that may block attainment.

At the conclusion of the performance period, actual performance is evaluated relative to the preestablished goals or objectives. During the feedback session, the reasons goals were not attained or were exceeded should be explored. This step helps to determine training needs and development potential. The final step is to set new goals and possibly new strategies.

For MBO to be effective, managers must be committed to the process. Goals should cascade from the top down, which helps employees see how their efforts link back to the broader strategic business objectives and vision of the company.

> ❝ A company needs clear, elevating goals that people at all levels of the organization can understand and relate to. Whether a person is a CEO or a forklift operator in Detroit, they need to understand how what they do for their eight hours at work relates to that clear, elevating vision. ❞
>
> *Tony Rucci*
> *Executive Vice President and*
> *Chief Administrative Officer*
> *Cardinal Health*

8

LEARNING GOAL

THE RATING PROCESS

Clearly, employers can take many different approaches to measuring performance; some are objective, but most involve some subjectivity. Some use identical standards for all employees, while others allow managers to take into account individual circumstances. None is perfect and all cause some employees to feel uneasy about the problems of bias and inaccuracy.

The quality of performance judgments depends, in part, on how the person making the evaluation processes information.[62] The evaluator first attends to and recognizes relevant information. The information is stored—first in short-term memory and then in long-term memory—until a performance judgment needs to be made. Finally, before the evaluation is recorded officially, it may be revised depending on reactions of the incumbent or higher-level managers, the goals the rater hopes to achieve through the appraisal process, performance trends, and even organizational norms.[63] The fallibility of managers combines with this process to create numerous types of performance rating errors.[64]

Rating Errors

Even seemingly innocuous factors like how performance measures are expressed (e.g., percentage of time absent versus percentage of time present) and how they are communicated (e.g., e-mail versus paper and pencil) have been found to affect rating accuracy.[65] Thus, it's not surprising that when criteria aren't clearly specified and no incentives are associated with rating accuracy, a number of substantial errors occur during the rating process. These rating errors, which are described in Exhibit 9.13, can affect all stages of the process, but their effects are most clearly seen at the final stage, after ratings have actually been recorded.[66]

Improving Rater Accuracy

Even the best performance management practices may not be effective when so many extraneous errors impinge on the performance appraisal process. Fortunately, several strategies can be used to reduce appraisal errors and improve

EXHIBIT 9.13 Common Performance Rating Errors	
Halo and Horn	A tendency to think of an employee as more or less good or bad is carried over into specific performance ratings. Or stereotypes based on the employee's sex, race, or age affect performance ratings. In either case, the rater doesn't make meaningful distinctions when evaluating specific dimensions of performance. All dimensions of performance are rated either low (horn) or high (halo).
Leniency	All employees are rated higher than they should be rated. This happens when managers aren't penalized for giving high ratings to everyone, when rewards aren't part of a fixed and limited pot, and when dimensional ratings aren't required.
Strictness	All employees are rated lower than they should be. Inexperienced raters who are unfamiliar with environmental constraints on performance, raters with low self-esteem, and raters who have themselves received a low rating are most likely to rate strictly. Rater training that includes a reversal of supervisor-incumbent roles and confidence building can reduce this error.
Central Tendency	All employees are rated as average, when performance actually varies. Raters with large spans of control and little opportunity to observe behavior are likely to use this "play-it-safe" strategy. A forced distribution format requiring that most employees be rated average also may create this error.
Primacy	As a cognitive shortcut, raters may use initial information to categorize a person as either a good or a bad performer. Information that supports the initial judgment is amassed, and unconfirming information is ignored.
Recency	A rater may ignore employee performance until the appraisal date draws near. When the rater searches for cues about performance, recent behaviors or results are most salient, so recent events receive more weight than they should.
Contrast Effects	When compared with weak employees, an average employee will appear outstanding; when evaluated against outstanding employees, an average employee will be perceived as a low performer.

rater accuracy, including making the rating scale format precise, providing memory aids and rater training, rewarding accurate and timely appraisals, and using multiple raters.

Rating Scale Format. The accuracy of performance ratings tends to increase when the performance criteria and the rating scales are precise. When the correct elements are in place, evaluators are more accurate in their ratings and more confident about their ratings. Features of good rating scales include

- Each performance dimension addresses a single job activity, rather than a group of activities.
- Each performance dimension is rated separately, and the scores are then summed to determine the overall rating.
- Ambiguous terms like *average* are not used because different raters have various reactions to them.[67]

Provide Memory Aids. Everyone involved in making appraisals should regularly record behaviors or results—good or bad—that relate to an employee's or work group's performance. Reviewing these records at the time of the performance appraisal helps ensure that the rater uses all available and relevant information. Consulting a behavioral diary or a critical incident file before rating reduces recency and primacy errors, yielding more accurate measures of performance. Electronic diary keeping software makes this task easier than ever.[68]

Provide Rater Training. Rating accuracy can also be improved through training. Training may focus on improving the observation skills of raters (e.g, frame of reference training), on their judgments, and on their objectivity. Training programs often have managers evaluate videotaped actors and then provide the raters with feedback on their rating accuracy. Training should teach raters the relevant criteria, the relevant behaviors to observe, and ways to reduce rating errors.[69]

Reward Accurate and Timely Appraisals. One cause of rating inaccuracy is a lack of rater motivation. Without rewards for accurate and timely ratings (or negative outcomes for inaccurate ones), raters may find it easier to give high rather than accurate ratings.[70] A straightforward strategy for increasing rater motivation is to have supervisors' quality of performance management be part of their own appraisal, which is then related to base salary increases, promotions, and assignments to key positions. Ratings done in a timely and fair manner (as measured by employee attitude surveys) should be rewarded.

Use Multiple Raters. Often, the ratee believes that the rater is solely responsible for a poor evaluation and any subsequent loss of rewards, and the rater may also have the same belief. Research suggests that this negative effect can be minimized by relying on the judgments of multiple raters.[71] The diffusion of responsibility frees each rater to evaluate more accurately. Furthermore, employees are less likely to shrug off negative information when multiple raters are involved.[72] Multiple raters acting as a group that must come to a consensus may be especially effective in producing accurate ratings, because discussion among members of the group helps overcome the various errors and biases of individuals.[73]

PROVIDING FEEDBACK

Performance management is an ongoing process, punctuated by formal performance measurement and formal feedback sessions intended to improve future performance. In feedback sessions, supervisors and subordinates meet to exchange information, including evaluations of performance and ideas for how to improve. The feedback makes employees aware of any problems and should address the importance of change when applicable. Many managers feel uncomfortable providing feedback to employees, in part because the process often stimulates conflict.[74] Understanding the sources of conflict associated with performance feedback is the first step in providing feedback successfully.

Differing Perspectives

Performance discussions are most productive when they yield concrete suggestions for how to improve future performance. Ideally, a conversation about how to improve in the future follows naturally from a discussion of how well things have gone in the past. But this discussion becomes difficult when employees and their managers have different perspectives about the causes of past performance.

Low-performance situations accentuate a natural tendency that we all share, which is to account for performance in a self-serving manner. To protect our egos, we attribute our own poor performance to external circumstances: a difficult task, unclear instructions, lack of necessary equipment, and other situations that often implicate the supervisor. Supervisors also wish to protect their egos, so they may deny responsibility for the subordinate's poor performance and instead attribute problems to the employee's own deficiencies. These self-serving attributions, as well as the emotions involved, can make it difficult for supervisors and their employees to come to agreement about how to improve poor performance.[75]

Self-serving biases may also dampen the expected effects of positive appraisals. When we perform well, the natural tendency is to take full credit for our performance. We use positive evidence to reinforce our high opinion of ourselves, discounting the role external forces may have played. The self-interested perspective of managers, however, leads them to view our success as due to such things as chance or luck and the support we received from the manager and other employees. Add to this our general feeling that we are better-than-average performers, and the scene is set for a potentially dysfunctional cycle: Employees believe they perform well and deserve credit for having done so; their supervisors often evaluate their performance less favorably, and these evaluations are perceived as unfair. When supervisors do recognize good performance, employees may perceive the recognition as merely what they deserved, leaving supervisors to wonder why their subordinates aren't more grateful.

The attributions supervisors make to explain the poor performance of their subordinates influence the strategies they develop for performance improvement.[76] If the employee is viewed as responsible for performance problems, strategies aimed at changing the subordinate (e.g., retraining) will seem more

"What really needs to happen is an ongoing dialogue between the manager and the employee. The form won't make a difference if those ongoing conversations don't happen."

Galina Jeffrey
Executive Vice President
The Forum Corp.

FAST FACT

Merrill Lynch managers receive extensive training in how to give feedback to employees at different performance levels. Online training modules mean managers can review the principles for giving effective feedback whenever they wish.

appropriate. If performance is attributed to external circumstances, strategies that modify the environment, such as changing the job design or providing more rewards, are more likely.

Timing

The delivery of performance feedback needs to be well timed. In general, immediate feedback is most useful. Feedback also should involve only as much information as the receiver can use. Providing continuous feedback from multiple sources is the best way to avoid information overload and maximize the value of the feedback given.[77] General Electric Medical Systems encourages employees to establish their own "personal board of directors," a panel of two to four peers and managers selected by the employee to provide candid continual feedback. Half of GE Medical Systems' high-potential employees have a personal board of directors.

Preparation

> 66 *Schedule an appointment and have a meeting. Don't give important feedback in the hallway.* 99
>
> *Rick Maurer*
> *Consultant*

To signal that performance matters, feedback sessions need to be scheduled in advance. In setting up the session, the manager and employee should reach agreement regarding the purpose and content of their discussion. Allowing subordinates to voice their opinions in the session appears to increase the subordinates' satisfaction with the appraisal, their perceived accuracy of the appraisals, and their motivation to improve.[78] However, the level of their participation needs to be determined ahead of time. Issues such as "Will the subordinate provide feedback to the supervisor, or will the discussion be one-way?" need to be discussed before the actual interview, so that both participants have time to prepare.

Content of the Discussion

The most useful feedback sessions focus on solving problems and planning for the future. Problem solving involves diagnosing the causes of performance. Planning for the future involves agreeing to address problems that were revealed in the diagnosis and setting goals. The effort pays off when employees get feedback they find constructive and useful, motivating them to improve.[79]

> 66 *When people identify something that they need to work on, it's usually what everyone else wishes they'd work on too.* 99
>
> *Darcy Hitchcock*
> *Consultant*

Diagnosis. The objective of diagnosis is to understand the factors that affect an employee's performance. Diagnosis is particularly important for employees who have not performed as well as required, but it also can be useful for employees who have performed well. Usually, even the best performers run up against roadblocks whose removal allows them to do even better.

The model of motivation shown in Exhibit 9.2 suggests a number of factors that can impede performance. To determine whether any of these are causing problems for an employee, the manager and employee together can consider questions such as those listed in Exhibit 9.14. Sharing perceptions and identifying solutions should be the focus. This type of discussion is difficult for most supervisors, so prior training in problem solving and in giving and receiving feedback should be provided.

Removing Roadblocks. Based on what is learned from the diagnostic process, both the supervisor and subordinate should agree to an action plan. The specific content of the plan depends on both organizational needs and

---

EXHIBIT 9.14 Sample Checklist for Diagnosing the Causes of Performance Deficiencies

Check the determinants of performance or behavior that apply to the situation you are analyzing.

	Yes	No
I. Confidence and Competencies		
A. Does the employee have the competencies needed to perform as expected?	___	___
B. Has the employee performed as expected before?	___	___
C. Does the employee believe he or she has the competencies needed to perform as desired?	___	___
D. Does the employee have the interest to perform as desired?	___	___
II. Goals for the Employee		
A. Were the goals communicated to the employee?	___	___
B. Are the goals specific?	___	___
C. Are the goals difficult but attainable?	___	___
III. Certainty for the Employee		
A. Has desired performance been clearly specified?	___	___
B. Have rewards or consequences for good or bad performance been specified?	___	___
C. Is the employee clear about her or his level of authority?	___	___
IV. Feedback to the Employee		
A. Does the employee know when he or she has performed correctly or incorrectly?	___	___
B. Is the feedback diagnostic so that the employee can perform better in the future?	___	___
C. Is there a delay between performance and the receipt of the feedback?	___	___
D. Can performance feedback be easily interpreted?	___	___
V. Consequences to the Employee		
A. Is performing as expected punishing?	___	___
B. Is not performing poorly more rewarding than performing well?	___	___
C. Does performing as desired matter?	___	___
D. Are there positive consequences for performing as desired?	___	___
VI. Access to Resources		
A. Can the employee mobilize the resources to get the job done?	___	___
B. Does the employee have the tools and equipment to perform as desired?	___	___
C. Is performance under the control of the employee?	___	___

---

information from the diagnosis. In general, the action plan for the supervisor should address problems such as lack of resources, providing additional information and training, and improving ongoing communications and feedback. The action plan for the subordinate should address behavioral changes that may be needed, career development activities, as well as specific performance goals.

Follow-Up

Follow-up is essential to ensuring that agreements reached during the feedback session are fulfilled. Supervisors should verify that subordinates know what is expected and realize the consequences of good or poor performance. Follow-up can be as simple as a pat on the back or a compliment ("That was nice work, George") or as tangible as a note placed in the employee's file or a token reward.[80] Almost everyone appreciates positive feedback for good performance and it appears to have the benefit of causing employees to raise their future goals.[81] Employees with serious performance problems may require constant monitoring and even the use of punishment.

> *There are two things people want more than sex and money—recognition and praise.*
>
> *Mary Kay Ash*
> *Founder*
> *Mary Kay Cosmetics*

Positive reinforcement *involves the use of positive rewards to increase the occurrence of the desired performance.* Positive reinforcement focuses on the job behavior that leads to the desired results, rather than on the results directly. It uses rewards rather than punishment or the threat of punishment to influence that behavior, and it is generally a very effective method for creating behavioral changes.[82]

When behavioral problems persist, formal disciplinary action is needed. When used appropriately, **punishment** *decreases the frequency of undesirable behavior.* Punishments can include material consequences, such as a cut in pay, a disciplinary layoff without pay, a demotion, or ultimately termination. Punishment is frequently used by organizations because it can achieve relatively immediate results. Besides alerting the marginal employee to the fact that his or her low performance is unacceptable, punishment has vicarious effect. When one person is punished, it signals other employees the norms regarding expected performance and behavioral conduct. When the punishment an employee receives is viewed as appropriate by other employees, it may increase their motivation, morale, and performance.

Punishment can also have undesirable side effects. An employee reprimanded for low performance may become defensive and angry toward the supervisor and the organization. As many news reports attest, this anger may result in sabotage (destroying equipment, passing trade secrets) or retaliation (shooting the supervisor). Another concern is that control of the undesirable behavior becomes contingent on the presence of the punishing agent. When the manager isn't present, the behavior is likely to be displayed again.

When Nothing Else Works

Helping employees improve their work performance is a tough job. It's easy to get frustrated and wonder if we are just spinning our wheels. Even when we want our efforts to work, they sometimes don't. Still, when we conclude that the employee doesn't "seem to get it," we are really saying that it's no longer worth our time and energy to help the employee improve.[83] This conclusion shouldn't be made in haste, because the organization has already invested a great deal of time and money in the selection and training of its employees. Nevertheless, some situations require drastic steps, such as when

- Performance actually gets worse.
- The problem behavior changes a little, but not enough.
- The problem behavior doesn't change.
- Drastic changes in behavior occur immediately, but the improvements don't last.

If, after repeated warnings and counseling, performance doesn't improve, the supervisor may need to transfer, neutralize, or terminate the employee.

Transfer. Sometimes, an employee is just not well matched to the job. If the employee has useful skills and abilities, transferring her or him to another job may be beneficial. Transferring is appropriate if the employee's performance deficiency would have little or no effect in the new position. The requirement is that a job must be available for which the employee is qualified.

Neutralize. Neutralizing a problem employee involves restructuring the job in such a way that areas of needed improvement have as little effect as possible. Because group morale may suffer when an ineffective employee is given special treatment, neutralization should be avoided whenever possible. However, temporary neutralization may be practical and even benevolent for a valued employee who is close to retiring or suffering unusual personal distress due to illness or family problems.[84]

Terminate. Termination is generally warranted for dishonesty, habitual absenteeism, substance abuse, insubordination including flat refusals to do certain things requested, unethical behavior, and consistently low productivity that can't be corrected through training. Termination, even for legitimate reasons, is unpleasant. In addition to the administrative hassles and required documentation, supervisors often feel guilty. The thought of sitting down with an employee and delivering the bad news makes most supervisors anxious, so they put off firing and justify the delay by saying that they won't be able to find a "better" replacement. Still, when one considers the consequences of errors, drunkenness, unethical behavior, or being under the influence of drugs on the job, it is unwise to avoid firing some problem employees. To ensure that employees are not terminated unfairly, an appeal process and dispute resolution procedures should be used prior to terminating them.

CURRENT ISSUES

As with many areas of HR, changing technology is having a dramatic impact on performance management. Two current issues related to technology's effect on performance management are automated performance management and high-tech employee monitoring.

Automated Performance Management

Technological advances have changed the way many companies now handle performance management. Technology can automate the process by tracking goals, scoring and approving appraisals, and processing the data for use in determining compensation, training, succession planning, and recruiting. Attendance and other work-related data usually can be easily integrated with other performance data, such as managers' performance appraisal ratings and customer satisfaction data. The technology allows organizations to convert a great deal of data into usable information, enabling users to spot patterns and gaps and to improve analysis, particularly against defined metrics. For firms in regulated industries, the data can be easily used for reporting requirements.[85]

Automation can do more than just improve efficiency and save managers time—it also can increase the accuracy of the appraisals, making them seem more equitable to employees. Information technology also can be useful for communicating performance standards to employees. At Seagate, employees at all levels can see the connection between their goals and corporate goals through an online system. Managers also can generate a series of performance reports that show trends, strengths, and weaknesses. Although automated performance management can provide many benefits, as with any major change, it takes careful planning and collaboration among multiple areas of the firm for it to work.[86]

❝ We had people whose whole jobs came to a standstill for weeks and months at a time because of manually putting together 360-degree views on thousands of employees. ❞

Hank Jonas
Manager
Corning Inc.

❝ Performance management is more about goal management than it is about automating back-end forms to do performance evaluations. ❞

Karen Hanlon
Vice President for Human Resources
Seagate

Monitoring through Technology

Technological advances have provided employers with tremendous monitoring capabilities, which can be used for performance management. Hand scanners can track employee attendance and location with foolproof accuracy. GPS devices can monitor the location and usage of employer vehicles. Radio frequency identification tags can pinpoint the location of employees at all times. Software can scan employee e-mails and Internet activities. Employers are now able to monitor employees with a level of accuracy and precision that was not possible even a few years ago.

As discussed in Chapter 4, monitoring raises concerns about employee privacy. When New York City introduced hand scanning to track when workers come and go, employees were outraged. Several unions in the city have vowed to fight the hand scanners and other **biometric technologies,** *which are technologies using unique qualities of body parts for identification.* The unions consider the practice degrading, intrusive, and unnecessary.[87]

Employers must find a balance between the benefits of monitoring and the costs of violating employee privacy. A key to finding that balance is not violating employees' reasonable expectation of privacy. Sound company policies that communicate what employees can expect are essential. When employees are informed in advance about monitoring practices, their expectations of privacy are lowered, which may protect the employer from some of the outrage employees feel when they believe their privacy rights have been ignored. Policies should clearly communicate the employer's right to monitor and access all communication, provide examples of prohibited uses, and state that violations of policies will result in discipline. In addition, employers should make sure that any monitoring is tied to business purposes only.[88]

Although lowering privacy expectations and monitoring only business-related activities will help protect the employer from a legal standpoint, employees may still resent constant monitoring.

> " *Are these hand scanners the wave of the future, or are they unnecessary, costly, and a detriment to worker morale and productivity?* "
>
> *Joseph P. Addabbo, Jr.*
> *Councilman*
> *Queens, New York*

CHAPTER SUMMARY WITH LEARNING GOALS

Performance management is a formal, structured process used to measure, evaluate, and influence employees' job-related attitudes, behaviors, and performance results. Three critical components of performance management discussed in this chapter are goal setting, performance measurement, and feedback.

⚠ **STRATEGIC IMPORTANCE.** Performance management is strategically important because it can enhance employee motivation and productivity, support strategic goals, and facilitate strategic planning and change. Instrumentality, valence, and expectancy are key concepts in motivating employees. Effective performance management helps ensure that the organization's strategic goals are linked to the performance goals of individual employees and their work teams.

⚠ **INTEGRATED HRM SYSTEM.** Effective performance management practices are aligned with the organization's internal environment, particularly its business strategy and organizational culture. Performance management practices also should be aligned with the organization's external environment, taking into consideration the legal environment, the labor market, and national culture. Other HR activities also should be closely aligned with performance management practices, including planning, job analysis and competency modeling, and training.

3 **THE HR TRIAD.** Line managers, HR professionals, and employees all need to work together to ensure that performance management practices are effective and fair to everyone concerned. HR professionals must support employees and managers by ensuring that managers are held accountable for providing accurate and timely performance appraisals and giving useful feedback.

4 **MEASURES OF PERFORMANCE.** When measuring task performance and organizational citizenship, organizations can use three types of performance criteria: personal traits, behaviors, and objective results. Trait criteria address what a person is, not what a person does or accomplishes on the job. Behavioral criteria can include task-related behaviors or more general counterproductive behaviors such as absenteeism, tardiness, and carelessness. Results criteria may be appropriate if the company does not care how results are achieved, but they are not appropriate for every job.

5 **TIMING.** The three most common approaches to timing performance measurement and feedback are focal-point, anniversary, and natural time span. Most firms conduct performance appraisals annually using the focal point or anniversary approach.

6 **PARTICIPANTS.** Given the many sources of performance data, getting a complete and accurate assessment often requires gathering information from several sources, including supervisors, employees themselves, peers or team members, subordinates, and customers. Using many participants to assess performance is known as 360-degree appraisal.

7 **FORMATS.** The appraisal format provides a structure for raters to use when making and recording their judgments. The most common types are norm-referenced formats, absolute standards formats, and results-based formats. Straight ranking and forced distribution are the most common norm-referenced formats, and three widely used absolute standards formats are graphic rating scales, behaviorally anchored rating scales, and behavioral observation scales. Direct index and MBO are common results-based formats.

8 **THE RATING PROCESS.** Numerous rating errors can occur throughout the performance rating process. These include halo, contrast, recency, and primacy errors. Fortunately, several strategies can be used to minimize rating errors and improve accuracy, including making the rating scale format precise, providing memory aids and rater training, rewarding accurate and timely appraisals, and using multiple raters.

9 **PERFORMANCE FEEDBACK.** Performance management is an ongoing process, punctuated by formal performance measurement and formal feedback sessions intended to improve future performance. Understanding the sources of conflict associated with performance feedback is the first step in providing feedback successfully. To be effective, managers should be well prepared and feedback should be given frequently. Managers must be willing and able to diagnose any performance problems and develop strategies to improve the future performance of their employees.

10 **CURRENT ISSUES.** Changing technology is having a dramatic effect on performance management. Two current issues related to technology's effect on performance management are automated performance management and technological monitoring of employees. Automation can provide many benefits that increase the strategic value of performance management practices. Technological monitoring may prove useful for improving employee performance, but employees may feel that it invades their right to privacy. Organizations must balance the benefits of technological monitoring with the costs of possibly creating discontent among employees.

TERMS TO REMEMBER

Anniversary approach	Norm-referenced format
Balanced scorecard approach	Performance appraisal
Behavioral criteria	Performance criteria
Behavioral observation scales (BOS)	Performance-driven culture
Behaviorally anchored rating scales (BARS)	Performance management
Biometric technologies	Positive reinforcement
Contaminated performance measure	Punishment
Deficient performance measure	Results criteria
Direct index approach	Self-appraisal
Expectancy	Straight ranking
Expectancy theory	360-degree appraisal
Focal-point approach	Trait-based criteria
Forced distribution method	Upward appraisal
Instrumentality	Valence
Management by objectives (MBO)	Valid performance measure
Motivation	

DISCUSSION QUESTIONS

1. What are the advantages and disadvantages of TRW's approach to performance management?
2. Why is job analysis essential for the development of performance measures?
3. What are the advantages and disadvantages of 360-degree appraisals?
4. Explain how poorly designed performance measures can contribute to poor employee performance. Can well designed measures contribute to improving performance? Explain.
5. Assume you are supervising employees who fall into one of three categories: (1) effective performers who have lots of potential for advancement; (2) effective performers who are happy to stay where they are and who lack motivation or ability, or both, for advancement; and (3) ineffective performers. You've assessed their performance, and now it's time to have a feedback session. What are your objectives for each of these three discussions? Explain how your discussions will be similar and how they will be different.
6. Explain how the differing perspectives of employees and their supervisors can create conflicts or disagreements in performance appraisal and feedback discussions.
7. Do you think employers should be allowed to use biometric technology to track the movement of all employees? Or is such monitoring demeaning and unnecessary? Explain your opinion.

PROJECTS TO EXTEND YOUR LEARNING

1. **Integration and Application.** Before continuing, review the cases of Southwest Airlines and Lincoln Electric at the end of this book. Then answer the following questions.

    a. Compare Lincoln Electric and Southwest Airlines with respect to the major purposes of performance measurement and feedback. Which organization seems more concerned with traits? With behavior? With results? What uses does performance measurement serve in these two companies?

b. For Lincoln Electric, how well do the performance criteria fit the company's strategic objectives? Identify the potential sources of deficiency and contamination in the company's performance measures.

c. Compare the sources of performance information used at Lincoln Electric and Southwest Airlines. Would you recommend that these organizations use 360-degree appraisals? Why or why not?

2. **Using the Internet.** Many organizations provide online resources related to performance management. Start to learn about some of these by visiting the following Web sites.

a. For a broad range of useful information on performance management, visit
   - Zigon Performance Group (www.zigonperf.com).
   - HR Guide (www.hr-guide.com).

b. Learn more about Employee Assistance Programs (www.eap-sap.com/eap).

c. Visit the Web site of the American Arbitration Association to learn more about issues related to employee terminations (www.adr.org).

3. **Experiential Activity.** Develop a plan to change your own behavior and performance by taking the following steps. You may choose to focus on behavior related to your life at work, at school, or at home. Most important is that you focus on something fairly specific.

Activities

Step 1. Choose a behavior that you really would like to change (e.g., being more friendly at work, learning to use a new type of software, walking more and driving less). "I want to change this behavior":

_____

_____

Step 2. State a specific short-term goal for changing the behavior (e.g., "Within six months, I'll increase the number of times I walk to work from one to five times per week"):

_____

_____

Step 3. Develop a procedure for monitoring the behavior (e.g., "I'll make a chart and tape it to my bathroom mirror"):

_____

_____

Step 4. Create a plan to reward yourself for making progress toward your goal (e.g., "Each day I walk, I'll put $5 in a special reward fund, to be spent at the end of each month. Each day I drive, I'll remove $6"):

_____

_____

Step 5. Consider the obstacles you are likely to face as you attempt to implement your plan. Consider your own attitudes and motivations as well as the behavior of others, time constraints, resources, and so on. To what extent do these obstacles interfere with your "expectancy" and "instrumentality" beliefs? Is there anything else you can add to your plan to strengthen your expectancy and instrumentality beliefs regarding this behavior change, and increase your motivation to change? List three additional things you can do to strengthen your expectancy and/or instrumentality beliefs:

(1) _____

(2) _____

(3) _____

Step 6. Now try to implement your plan. Keep a diary of your experience and use it to write an essay describing what this experience has taught you about performance measurement and feedback.

CASE STUDY
360-DEGREE APPRAISALS

In Durham, North Carolina, 170 GE employees work in nine teams to produce the GE90 jet engines that Boeing installs in its long-range 777 aircraft. Each team "owns" the engines they build—from the beginning of the assembly process to getting them loaded onto a truck for delivery. As they begin work on each engine, these teams generally receive no instructions except for the date on which the engine is to be shipped from the plant. Getting the engine produced is the team goal, but that goal can be reached only if the teams effectively manage themselves. Besides producing an 8.5-ton jet engine out of 10,000 individual parts, team members order tools and parts; schedule their vacations, training, and overtime; make adjustments to the production process to improve their efficiency; monitor their product quality; and take responsibility for diagnosing and resolving problems that arise among members of a team.

Decisions about these and all other issues that the teams face are made by consensus, which was a founding principle for the plant. Each employee understands that living with ideas that they don't necessarily agree with is part of the job. They don't blame others when things go wrong, because they make the decisions. The process of reaching agreement on decisions is so much a way of life here that people routinely talk about "consensusing" on this or that.

The one boss in this plant—plant manager Paula Sims—keeps everyone's attention focused on the common goal: making perfect jet engines correctly, quickly, and cheaply. Her job is (1) to make sure that the efforts of all teams are coordinated so that together their decisions optimize the plant's performance and then (2) to free up resources for growth and improvement.

In her four years as the plant manager responsible for GE's jet engine production teams, Sims has learned that communicating what you intend to communicate isn't always easy. She describes her job as plant manager as "the most challenging

four years of my life—and also the most rewarding. To do it well requires a different level of listening skills—significantly different. More and more of what I do involves listening to people, to teams, to councils, to ideas, trying to find common themes."

In this culture of continuous feedback, one reason Sims has listened so carefully is to monitor her own effectiveness. She learned early that her actions can be easily misinterpreted. Recalling an incident from her early days, she explained, "An employee came to me and said, 'Paula, you realize that you don't need to follow up with us to make sure we're doing what we agreed to do. If we say we'll do something, we'll do it. You don't need to micromanage us.'" At most plants, following up is just part of a manager's job, but here it was sending the wrong message. Because she always followed up, people concluded that she didn't trust them. The real problem was that she had not yet learned the plant's norms about decision making.

Sims also listens when the plant is trying to solve a problem. At other companies, the title of manager almost means "decision maker." At GE/Durham, however, the manager actually makes only about a dozen major decisions each year. All other decisions either rely heavily on input from the other plant employees or are actually made by them. The plant manager is responsible for making sure that plant employees know about problems and for informing the GE managers that she reports to about the solutions. But to get the solutions, the plant manager is expected to listen, not decide. For major issues, such as reducing costs or improving safety, a task force is formed to decide how to address the problem. The plant manager educates the task force and everyone else about the problem and explains why it is important. Then the task force takes responsibility for finding solutions. When they have a plan for the future, the plant manager informs those above her about how the plant will proceed and makes sure the higher-ups are on board with the plan.

Sims has approached you, the HR manager for the plant, with a request: She wants you to help her install 360-degree appraisals for everyone in the plant, including her. The 360-degree appraisals will not replace the other performance measures that already are being used. They will simply be added on as a new element in the performance management process. You have expressed some concerns about the idea, but she is determined to move ahead with the plan. Describe how you will proceed.[89]

CASE QUESTIONS

Begin by analyzing the possible advantages and disadvantages of using 360-degree appraisals in this plant. Then indicate the decisions you would make regarding each of the following questions:

1. Will you use one set of performance dimensions for everyone, or will people in different jobs be evaluated on different dimensions? Explain your logic.

2. How will you determine the specific content of the 360-degree appraisal form?

3. What type of rating format will be used to make the appraisal ratings?

4. For members of the nine production teams, who will provide performance assessments? All members of the team? Members of other teams? Will Sims provide evaluations of all employees?

5. How will feedback be handled?

6. The plant is operating well right now. What steps will you take to ensure that this new activity doesn't reduce the plant's productivity?

Developing an Approach to Total Compensation

Learning Goals

After reading this chapter, you should be able to:

▲ **1** Explain the strategic importance of an organization's approach to total compensation.

▲ **2** Show how total compensation fits within an integrated HRM system.

▲ **3** Detail the roles and responsibilities of the HR Triad related to total compensation.

▲ **4** Discuss how organizations establish the internal value of jobs.

▲ **5** Describe how organizations set pay levels using external market values.

▲ **6** Explain the design of an internal pay structure.

▲ **7** Discuss the adjustments organizations make to the pay system.

▲ **8** Show how globalization affects total compensation.

▲ **9** Explain two current issues related to total compensation.

MANAGING HUMAN RESOURCES AT SYNAPSE GROUP, INC.

Synapse Group, Inc. is a marketing company with revenues of $400 million and over 300 employees. The company helps magazines attract and retain subscribers. It markets subscriptions through methods such as direct mail, credit card bill inserts, the Internet, and relationships with numerous partners, such as airline frequent flyer programs. It has introduced innovations such as the multipublisher continuous service subscription system and has developed a variety of nontraditional marketing channels. Headquartered in Stamford, Connecticut, the firm has appeared on the list of "The Best Medium Companies to Work for in America" for two years in a row. When Michael Loeb and Jay Walker founded the firm in 1991, they envisioned a financially successful company with a unique culture that would attract exceptional employees and be a fun place to work.

Having fun is not the only reason Synapse Group is one of the best places to work. Synapse Group's philosophy is to be a meritocracy first and democracy second. Thus, great performers are given great rewards. Exceptional talent is attracted to the company's total compensation practices, which include competitive wages and salaries, performance-based bonuses, and generous benefits and services. In this performance-driven organization, annual raises typically exceed those offered by other organizations competing for the same talent. In addition, all employees are eligible for bonuses tied both to individual and to company goals. To reward and recognize employees for achieving short-term goals and other excellent performance, managers often give on-the-spot awards to individuals as well as larger work teams. These special awards range from movie tickets to several thousands of dollars in cash. Loyalty is rewarded with length of service awards worth up to $1,000. All employees receive stock options. Benefits include health, dental, disability, and life insurance, as well as tuition reimbursement for continuing education courses, a fitness center, daily catered lunches and dinners, and several annual parties that frequently include new cars as prizes .[1] ▲

THE STRATEGIC IMPORTANCE OF TOTAL COMPENSATION

For Synapse Group, compensation practices are a central element in the HRM system, which is designed to help the company fulfill its vision of being an organization that creates extraordinary value and allows employees to participate in both the challenges and the rewards of success. Managers at Synapse understand that employees respond to more than just money; they are interested in the total compensation package offered to them. **Total compensation** *refers to the monetary and nonmonetary rewards offered to employees.* It includes the emotional rewards experienced from working in an organization with a fun corporate culture, all forms of financial payments, and a variety of employee benefits. In this chapter, we explain how organizations develop their total compensation policy, and then we focus more specifically on the procedures typically used to set wages and salaries. Chapter 11 continues our discussion of compensation practices by focusing on performance-based practices. Finally, we conclude our discussion of compensation with Chapter 12, which describes legally mandated and voluntary types of indirect compensation, commonly referred to as employee benefits.

There is a growing appreciation that total compensation can facilitate (or interfere with) achieving many different strategic objectives. A recent study showed that 60% of compensation professionals believe that compensation practices are more relevant to strategic business issues now than they were just two years ago. Further, those surveyed believed that strategic thinking is now the most important competency needed by HR professionals who are involved in designing and managing an organization's compensation policies and practices.[2]

A company's compensation philosophy should be tied to its strategic objectives,[3] of which three are particularly relevant to total compensation: (1) attracting, motivating, and retaining the talent required for a sustainable competitive advantage; (2) focusing the energy of employees on implementing the organization's particular competitive strategy; and (3) improving productivity. Paying competitive wages, giving better-than-market raises, rewarding performance, and providing valued benefits helps Synapse Group achieve its goals of attracting, motivating, and retaining exceptional employees, fostering an enjoyable creative culture, and being financially successful.

Attracting, Motivating, and Retaining Talent

In conjunction with an organization's recruitment and selection efforts, total compensation practices provide pay that is sufficient to attract the right people at the right time for the right jobs and to keep them motivated to perform their jobs to the best of their ability. Unless the total compensation program is perceived as internally fair and externally competitive, good employees are likely to leave.[4]

Pay fairness *refers to what people believe they deserve to be paid in relation to what others deserve to be paid.* People tend to determine the fairness of their pay by comparing what they give to and get out of the organization compared to others. If they regard this comparison as fair or equitable, they're likely to be satisfied. If they see it as unfair, they're likely to be dissatisfied.[5] Thus, pay fairness is strongly related to **pay satisfaction,** *which is the amount of positive or negative feelings employees have toward their pay.*[6]

When assessing whether their pay is fair, employees compare the ratio of their inputs and outcomes to the ratios of others. *Inputs* are what employees give to the job, such as time, effort, experience, and education. *Outcomes* are

> "To the extent that auto insurance is a commodity, our biggest differentiator is our people. We want the best people at every level of the company, and we pay at the top of the market."
>
> *Peter B. Lewis*
> *Chairman of the Board*
> *Progressive Corporation*

what people get out of doing the job, such as pay, benefits, and feelings of meaningfulness. When inputs and outcomes seem to be equitable compared to others, employees feel their pay is fair. Assessments of equity and fairness can be quite complex, involving all the elements of total compensation.[7]

As a result of equity perceptions, an employee will feel fairly rewarded, underrewarded, or overrewarded. Feelings of being overrewarded are probably rare, but when they occur they have beneficial consequences for employers. Overrewarded employees tend to perform better in their jobs and are better members of the organization than employees who haven't been well rewarded.[8]

When employees feel underrewarded, they are likely to engage in behaviors to achieve equity, and such behaviors are generally detrimental to the organization. They include leaving the organization, demanding a raise, stealing from the employer, and withholding effort to restrict output or to lower quality.[9] Feelings of inequity can also cause personal distress, resulting in individual symptoms such as insomnia or feelings of frustration, which may lead people to behave in hostile and aggressive ways.[10] A store clerk may be hostile to customers, or a factory worker may sabotage equipment. Unfortunately, such hostility can even lead to such drastic reactions as threatening or using violence against former colleagues and managers.

Most employers understand the strategic importance of pay fairness. But even when employers think they have succeeded in designing "fair" systems, employees may perceive inequities. Three culprits that contribute to perceptions of unfairness are low pay, pay secrecy, and executive compensation practices.

Low Pay. When choosing where to work, job applicants consider many aspects of the total pay package: Some focus on the predictable, guaranteed level of pay; others focus on the maximum potential pay; still others focus on the less tangible aspects of total compensation.[11] Once hired, employees continue to evaluate these aspects of their pay, although perhaps with less vigilance. Regardless of what employees attend to when evaluating their pay, they will be dissatisfied if they judge the company's total pay policy to be less generous than that offered by competitors. Employees who are compensated above or on par with the market average are more likely to feel fairly paid than those who are paid below the going rate. Exhibit 10.1 shows the results of a recent study looking at what drives worker retention. The study found that 69% of

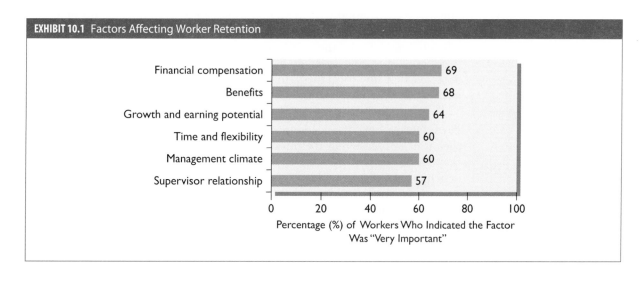

EXHIBIT 10.1 Factors Affecting Worker Retention

Financial compensation — 69
Benefits — 68
Growth and earning potential — 64
Time and flexibility — 60
Management climate — 60
Supervisor relationship — 57

Percentage (%) of Workers Who Indicated the Factor Was "Very Important" workers believed that financial compensation was a very important driver of retention: Pay was more important than any other factor.[12]

In the past, the issue of how employers dealt with external equity—fairness relative to the external market—was typically framed by a simple question that indicated their pay level strategy: "Should we pay at the market average—or above or below the market?" When a basic salary, little at-risk pay, and a few benefits were what almost everyone received, this simple view made sense. In today's highly competitive environment, however, external equity has become more complex because companies creatively mix several forms of pay. For example, Aflac Inc. generally pays below-market salaries but provides substantial profit-sharing bonuses, stock option grants for all employees, health and pension benefits, retiree health benefits, college tuition for children of employees, on-site child care, and health clinics. Employees who focus on the base salary will perceive the pay to be unfairly low.[13] Compare Aflac with Cisco Systems, which pays above-market base salaries and above-market bonuses, but doesn't provide the same level of benefits. Employees who focus on the benefits package will view this as being unfairly low.

Employees also care about the size of the raises they get. In fact, people seem to care as much about how their pay level changes from year to year as they do about how much they earn in a particular year.[14] Thus, managers must know how the base pay of their employees compares to the market *and* how the size of raises will be viewed by employees.

Pay Secrecy. Perceived pay inequities sometimes occur because employees have inaccurate and/or incomplete information. Although it is illegal for employers to forbid employee discussions of pay, keeping pay secret is the norm in many U.S. organizations.[15] According to organizational etiquette, asking others their salaries is generally considered gauche. In a study at DuPont, all employees were asked if the company should disclose more payroll information so that everyone would know everyone else's pay. Only 18% voted for an open pay system. Managers often favor pay secrecy, too. It makes their lives easier. Without knowledge of pay differentials, employees are less likely to perceive inequities and are less likely to resent those who make more. When pay is secret, managers are less likely to have to deal with these issues, and they may feel they don't have to justify pay decisions.

Although there may be benefits to pay secrecy, particularly when companies don't pay fairly, good pay communication can have numerous advantages.[16] Many believe that total compensation practices cannot motivate employees who don't understand the details. Openness and transparency about pay practices foster trust and seem to fit a high-performance culture. It is generally accepted that low awareness and poor understanding of compensation can lead to pay dissatisfaction and turnover.[17]

Pay Communication. If an employer works hard to design fair pay practices, then it makes sense that the more information employees have, the less likely they are to feel that they are treated unfairly. At MedStar Health, a hospital system in Maryland, employee satisfaction with total compensation went from 30% to 65% in five years without any meaningful increases in pay or benefits. The increase in pay satisfaction was achieved by implementing a compensation communication plan that cost about $20 per employee.[18]

When pay practices are fair, there doesn't appear to be a downside to making sure employees understand them. As described in Chapter 4, employees judge fairness using information about outcomes (distributive fairness), as well as the procedures that led to those outcomes (procedural fairness). When employees perceive the process used to determine their pay as fair, they also are substantially more likely to perceive their actual pay as fair.[19] Exactly how much to reveal about pay practices is debatable, however. Some employers worry that giving employees too much information may create destructive competition among employees. Another worry is that employees may provide sensitive pay information to competitors. Providing employees with everyone's actual pay is perhaps the most risky approach to communicating about pay because it violates social norms, raises issues of privacy, and publicizes pay inequities. Nevertheless, most government agencies disclose the pay received by their employees. In fact, such disclosure is often required by law. Whole Foods, a grocery retailer, also believes in being completely open about pay. Employees are welcome to peruse a list that includes every employee's total annual compensation. The company acknowledges that not all employees like the system; it has made some employees so uncomfortable that they quit, whereas others decided against taking a job offer.[20]

In addition to deciding *what* pay information to communicate, employers also must decide *how* to communicate the information. Face-to-face information from managers and supervisors is the preferred pay communication method. Many organizations also use electronic tools. Exhibit 10.2 shows the percentage of organizations that release compensation information to employees through online/intranet communications.[21] Using marketing principles to educate employees and promote the organization's pay practices can be an effective way to increase employee acceptance.[22] It's not enough for employees to have access to information; they must understand and trust it. As discussed in Chapter 3, involving employees in developing HR practices is a good way to promote such understanding and trust and to improve two-way communications between managers and subordinates.

Executive Compensation. CEO pay has been a hot topic for a long time, probably because of its perceived unfairness and high visibility.[23] On average, CEOs are paid more than 400 times what their average employee earns. A recent study found median CEO pay for the 200 largest American organizations to be over $8 million, an increase of 10% from the previous year. Widely publicized figures such as these have had an impact on the opinions of the public. More than 80% of Americans and 90% of institutional investors believe that CEOs are paid too much! Outrage over CEO compensation isn't limited to how much they make. Other sore points include the lack of a clear link between CEO pay and firm

> " *Whichever system an organization adopts, employees need clear, convincing, and consistent communication from leadership about how salaries are determined and excellence is rewarded.* "
>
> Deborah K. Hoover
> Director of Human Resources
> The Urban Institute

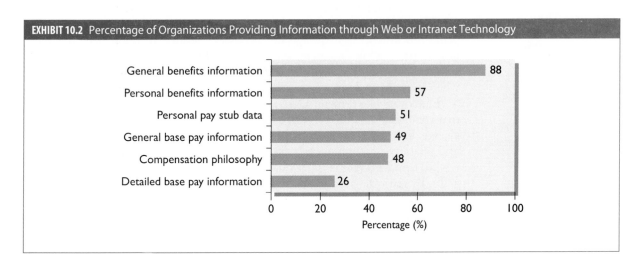

EXHIBIT 10.2 Percentage of Organizations Providing Information through Web or Intranet Technology

Category	Percentage (%)
General benefits information	88
Personal benefits information	57
Personal pay stub data	51
General base pay information	49
Compensation philosophy	48
Detailed base pay information	26

performance, lavish pensions and severance packages, and questionable stock option transactions.[24]

Public outcries about CEO pay have prompted government actions that are designed to increase its transparency and fairness. Government responses have included tax laws limiting the amount of salary that organizations can deduct, substantial revisions to financial disclosure requirements for reports filed with the Securities and Exchange Commission (SEC), and several provisions in the Sarbanes-Oxley Act of 2002 (SOX) intended to restrict some forms of CEO compensation.[25]

Apparently, some executives are finally getting the message. In fact, a few CEOs have even volunteered to take pay cuts, give their bonus money to employees, and create a tighter linkage between their own pay and company performance.[26] When Robert S. Miller, Jr., CEO of Delphi Corporation, announced that employees' salaries would be cut, he also requested that his own salary be cut to $1. Brad Anderson, CEO of Best Buy, gave some of his incentive pay to employees in the form of company stock. Jeffrey R. Immelt, CEO of General Electric, converted his $6-million cash bonus into performance-linked shares, to show that he was serious about taking responsibility for the company's future performance.[27] Despite such noble actions by a few CEOs, public concern about unfair CEO pay is still the norm.

The extent to which employee perceptions of inequity due to CEO pay affect employee behaviors is unknown, but it seems likely that there is at least a modest effect. When the bonus of Home Depot's CEO rose from $5.75 million to $7 million while the employee bonus pool dropped 49%, there were numerous complaints in Internet chat rooms frequented by Home Depot employees.[28] It is reasonable to conclude that these negative reactions affected the motivation and desire to continue working for Home Depot for at least some of these employees.

Implementing the Business Strategy

Do you regard a smile and a "Thank you for shopping" from the cashier of the local store as examples of quality customer-oriented service? Many people do and are willing to pay more for the goods in stores that have salespeople who engage in these behaviors. As we have seen, selection practices, socialization, and training help ensure that employees are *able* to engage in courteous, friendly behaviors. Compensation practices provide the supporting structure that *motivates* employees to display these behaviors even under the most trying circumstances.

Whether the focus is customer service, innovation, or ethics, effective compensation practices encourage the behaviors needed to implement the business strategy, while enhancing employees' feelings of satisfaction.[29] The role of compensation in implementing competitive strategies becomes especially clear when a company desires organizational change.

Employers like General Electric, Motorola, Sears, and IBM have discovered that compensation practices can encourage employees to embrace organizational change. Instead of handing out automatic annual pay increases based on job title and seniority—a common practice in the old economy—these companies now reward teamwork, measurable quality improvements, and the acquisition of new skills. By rewarding and reinforcing the desired employee behaviors, compensation can facilitate a change in an organization's strategy or culture.[30]

Several years ago, IBM began a major change in its strategy. Instead of designing systems and then trying to sell them, the new strategy called for designing

66 *When you have executives gouging their companies, it undermines trust. Frankly, they aren't worth that much.* 99

John P. Mackey
*Chief Executive Officer
and Chairman of the
Board of Directors
Whole Foods Market, Inc.*

FAST FACT

When the CEO of Home Depot left the organization in 2007, he received a severance package worth $210 million.

66 *Employees have a better feel about the measurement of their personal career or the development of their personal career because the company is indeed making a statement that it is important for us to make that investment.* 99

Randy MacDonald
*Senior Vice President of
Human Resources
IBM*

customized systems and providing more business services. Once the new strategy was announced, the challenge was to find a way for employees to implement and support this strategy. IBM's new strategy required new skills, so they started using skills or competencies as a partial basis for determining employees' base pay and their annual pay increases. The new compensation approach encourages employees to develop those new skills and rewards them for doing so. These changes were costly for IBM. But the cost increases were considered necessary as the company evolved into a knowledge-intensive service provider.[31]

Compensation practices also can reward and reinforce employee behaviors that support the introduction of values such as diversity and tolerance, strong ethics, safety-orientation, employee empowerment, social support, and high performance.[32] When Arbella Insurance, a medium-sized organization of 400 employees, was spun off from Kemper Insurance, its managers wanted to create a performance-driven culture like the one at Synapse Group with a greater emphasis on performance than on security and loyalty. Developing new compensation practices was a key step in creating that change in the culture. The old culture was control oriented and inflexible. To ensure that employees understood that the new culture would emphasize performance, Arbella Insurance introduced a new merit pay program that gave managers more flexibility in granting pay raises. With the new approach to merit pay, Arbella sought to establish a culture in which high performance is valued, expected, and rewarded.[33]

Productivity Improvement

Compensation practices influence productivity in numerous ways.[34] Compensation practices that link employees' pay to the company's financial performance or other indicators of productivity can help focus employees' attention on finding new ways to reduce costs and increase revenues. At Whole Foods, budget surpluses achieved through productivity gains go back into employees' pockets.[35] When pay is tied to productivity, productivity tends to go up. Whether that occurs because employees work harder or work smarter is not clear, but effective compensation practices motivate employees to spend their energy on the activities that are the most important to the organization's success.

TOTAL COMPENSATION WITHIN THE INTEGRATED HRM SYSTEM

Synapse Group uses monetary and nonmonetary forms of compensation to attract talented people and keep them motivated to perform well. Choosing the forms of compensation to offer is one of the major decisions to be made when designing a total compensation package, but it is not the only choice that must be made. As the feature about Synapse Group illustrated, companies use total compensation to influence employee behaviors and to achieve company goals.

Exhibit 10.3 summarizes the major choices to be made when designing compensation practices and shows how total compensation fits within the total HRM system.

Monetary and Nonmonetary Compensation

As we have already explained, total compensation encompasses numerous monetary and nonmonetary elements. **Monetary compensation** *includes direct payments such as salary, wages, and bonuses, and indirect payments such as payments to cover benefits and services.* **Nonmonetary compensation** *includes many forms*

FAST FACT

Labor costs account for two-thirds of the average company's expenses.

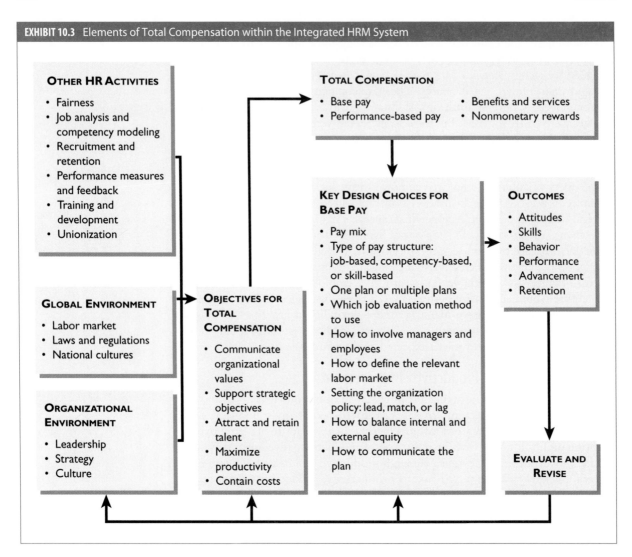

EXHIBIT 10.3 Elements of Total Compensation within the Integrated HRM System

OTHER HR ACTIVITIES
- Fairness
- Job analysis and competency modeling
- Recruitment and retention
- Performance measures and feedback
- Training and development
- Unionization

GLOBAL ENVIRONMENT
- Labor market
- Laws and regulations
- National cultures

ORGANIZATIONAL ENVIRONMENT
- Leadership
- Strategy
- Culture

OBJECTIVES FOR TOTAL COMPENSATION
- Communicate organizational values
- Support strategic objectives
- Attract and retain talent
- Maximize productivity
- Contain costs

TOTAL COMPENSATION
- Base pay
- Performance-based pay
- Benefits and services
- Nonmonetary rewards

KEY DESIGN CHOICES FOR BASE PAY
- Pay mix
- Type of pay structure: job-based, competency-based, or skill-based
- One plan or multiple plans
- Which job evaluation method to use
- How to involve managers and employees
- How to define the relevant labor market
- Setting the organization policy: lead, match, or lag
- How to balance internal and external equity
- How to communicate the plan

OUTCOMES
- Attitudes
- Skills
- Behavior
- Performance
- Advancement
- Retention

EVALUATE AND REVISE

of social and psychological rewards—recognition and respect from others, enjoyment from doing the job itself, opportunities for self-development, and so on. Kathleen C. Gubanich, managing director of human resources at The Vanguard Group, put it this way: "You always have to be clear that you'll be very competitive on pay and benefits. But at the end of the day, people come to and leave organizations not because of money. They stay because of a culture and a career opportunity. Because of the people they work with."[36] Nevertheless, people differ in the value they attach to these different types of compensation.[37]

Pay Mix

The way an organization distributes pay among all elements of total compensation, including monetary versus nonmonetary elements, is referred to as the **pay mix**. Normally, base pay is the largest pay element, and it is the pay element that we focus on in this chapter. **Base pay** *refers to the wage or salary an employee receives, exclusive of any incentive pay or benefits.* Base pay is predictable and fixed: As long as employees come to work and perform satisfactorily, they are assured of receiving the agreed-upon amount of base pay. As competitive pressures increase, many employers are striving to keep costs low by keeping base pay as low as possible. At the same time, they are striving

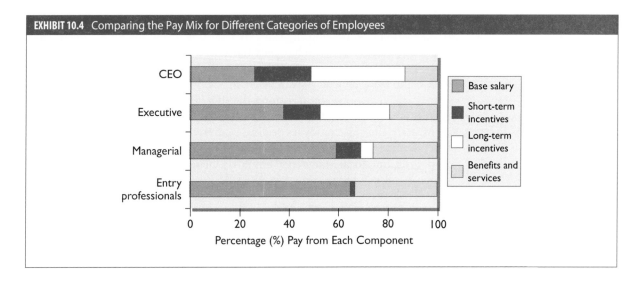

EXHIBIT 10.4 Comparing the Pay Mix for Different Categories of Employees

Percentage (%) Pay from Each Component

Legend: Base salary · Short-term incentives · Long-term incentives · Benefits and services

to ensure that any pay increases are linked to productivity gains so that costs won't increase unless the company can afford it.

Organizations differ greatly in terms of the mix of pay elements they offer their employees. Furthermore, many companies offer a different pay mix to different groups of employees. Exhibit 10.4 shows the pay mixes found in the United States.[38]

Other HR Practices

The many elements of total compensation mean that significant effort is needed to ensure that all of the elements are aligned. It can be a challenge to design a system that achieves an appropriate balance between rewards based on individual, team, and organizational performance, for example. An added challenge is designing compensation practices that are well integrated with other aspects of the total HRM system. However, combining compensation with other HR practices in logical and consistent ways is critical for good results.[39]

Recruitment and Retention. As noted in Chapter 6, the monetary and nonmonetary compensation that an organization offers partly determines the number and quality of job applications received during recruitment. Once the best applicants have been selected, their decisions about whether to join the organization are likely to be influenced by the specific salary and bonus offers they receive.

Compensation practices also influence employees' decisions about whether to stay with their employers. At Cendant Mobility, a provider of global relocation services, employee turnover was over 30% annually before it introduced its Flexible Work Options (FWO) program. With FWO, employees are offered daily start- and end-work times, consolidated four-day workweeks, and several combinations of on- and off-work days. Cendant Mobility also offers wellness programs, on-site flu shots, and educational programs on topics such as elder care and how to quit smoking. By introducing these new forms of nonmonetary compensation, the company reduced turnover to 9% and saved $8.6 million in recruitment and hiring costs.[40]

Training and Development. It should be apparent that applicants attach value to the training and development opportunities (e.g., tuition reimbursements, management development programs) offered by employers. Compensation is linked to

FAST FACT

Wal-Mart estimates that it costs $2,500 per worker to test, interview, and train a new hire.

training and development in other ways as well. For example, employers who provide training to develop the skills they need generally pay less to new hires compared to employers who hire only those who already have the needed skills.

Performance Management. As discussed in Chapter 9, a well designed performance management program requires the effective use of incentive pay. In many organizations, poor alignment between the pay practices and performance measurement results in employees feeling unmotivated. In the worst situations, poor alignment between these elements of the HRM system can result in unscrupulous, unethical, and illegal employee behaviors. We discuss this issue in greater detail in Chapter 11.

The External Environment

Perhaps more than any other aspect of the HRM system, compensation practices must be responsive to the external environment. Of particular importance are conditions in the external labor market. Especially when talent is scarce relative to demand, employers must devise compensation practices that enable them to attract and retain the people they need at a cost they can afford. Industry conditions, legal constraints, and social considerations are other external environmental factors that also influence compensation practices.

Labor Market Conditions. The term **pay level** *refers to how an organization's overall monetary pay compares to that of other organizations.* Labor market conditions affect the pay level and total compensation. Is the value of the total pay package more than what most others are offering, at about the same as the market, or below the market? Typically, the organizations of most interest for market comparison purposes are those competing for the same talent. If a company's pay level is too low, it won't be able to recruit qualified labor.

Shortages in the labor market provide qualified workers the opportunity to negotiate better terms of employment. Under conditions of low unemployment, low supply drives labor prices up. After Hurricane Katrina substantially reduced the labor force in New Orleans, jobs that had been paying as low as $6 an hour were paying as much as $11 an hour.[41] Higher pay attracts more entrants to the market—if any are available.

When wage demands become too high, employers may react by hiring fewer people.[42] High wage demands push employers to seek alternatives. Introducing new technology that reduces the need for labor is one alternative. Raising prices for products and services is another, as is simply accepting smaller profit margins.[43]

Moving work abroad, known as offshoring, is another way employers respond to high compensation costs. Recall the discussion of offshoring in Chapter 3. We are currently seeing an increased use of offshoring largely because of enabling technology and the substantial wage differential between developed and developing countries.[44] However, when moving jobs abroad, companies need to consider wage levels, taxes, productivity, and the effects on their current workforce.

Industry Conditions. Just as compensation practices differ among countries, they also differ across industries. An accountant who works for a financial services firm will probably earn more than someone doing the same job at a retail department store or hospital. Studies have consistently found large pay level differences among industries. Exhibit 10.5 shows the differences in pay level among several industries.[45]

FAST FACT

Henry Ford had to hire close to 1,000 workers just to keep 100 who would work on his demanding and numbing assembly line. This persuaded him to raise wages from the prevailing $2.30 per day to $5 per day.

" *Offshoring jobs can reduce costs and enhance service. But it can also unnerve and demotivate home country employees.* "

Jonathan Gardner
Economist
Watson Wyatt

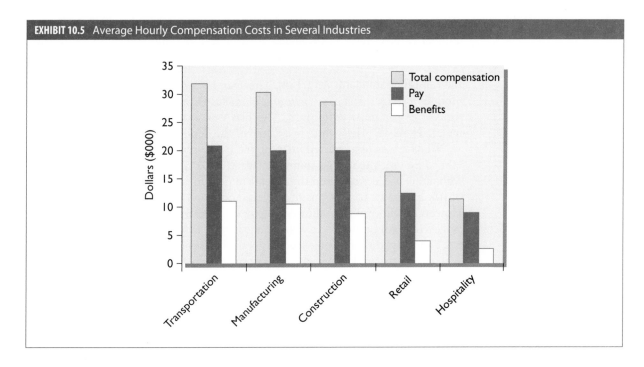

EXHIBIT 10.5 Average Hourly Compensation Costs in Several Industries

High-paying industries such as energy and automobile manufacturing pay 50–70% more than low-paying ones, such as retail and services, even when the jobs and employees are similar.[46] Two reasons for this are the industry's capital intensity and its unionization levels.[47] **Industry capital intensity** *is the ratio of capital to total expenses.* In industries where capital costs are high and labor costs are a small portion of total costs, employers can pay more because the extra expense doesn't increase total costs by very much. Examples of industries that are relatively capital intensive include energy, automated manufacturing, and construction.

Compensation practices are also influenced by the level of **industry unionization,** which *is the percentage of organizations in the industry that are unionized.* Unionized organizations tend to pay more. They also tend to have less performance-based pay, and they tend to offer better benefits. When an industry is heavily unionized, it affects the whole industry—not just the companies with unionized employees, because the nonunionized companies compete for the same employees. High-paying industries such as transportation (where 23.4% of employees are unionized), manufacturing (13.3%), and construction (13.1%) are substantially more unionized than relatively low-paying industries, such as retail (5.2%) and hospitality (3.1%).[48]

Legal Constraints and Social Considerations

Like other aspects of managing human resources, compensation activities are shaped by a plethora of laws and regulations, covering topics such as taxation, nondiscrimination, fair wages, a minimum wage, the protection of children, hardship pay for employees who work unusually long hours, and income security through pension and welfare benefits. There have been substantial changes in how society views compensation and work, including the understanding of what a normal workweek is. A standard workweek now consists of five 8-hour days. In 1840, a typical workweek was six 13-hour days. In 1913, when Henry Ford introduced the 8-hour day at a $5-a-day minimum wage, most of his competitors still expected employees to work 60 hours a week. Since then, a number of laws have been passed governing hours and wages. These include the Fair Labor Standards Act, the Equal Pay Act, and living wage laws.

FAST FACT

The worst industries for wage violations are eating and drinking establishments, apparel manufacturers, and heavy construction.

The Fair Labor Standards Act (FLSA). The **Fair Labor Standards Act (FLSA)** *sets minimum wages, maximum hours, child labor standards, and overtime pay provisions for most employees.* The FLSA is a complex law with many elements. Here we briefly note just a few of the details.

When it was first enacted in 1938, the FLSA (sometimes called the Wage and Hour Law) set the federal minimum wage at $0.25 an hour. In 2007, the Fair Minimum Wage Act raised the federal minimum wage from $5.15 to $5.85 as of July 24, 2007, to $6.55 as of July 24, 2008, and to $7.25 as of July 24, 2009. However, employers are allowed to pay wages lower than the federal minimum wage to employees under 20 years of age in their first 90 days, to "tipped employees," and to certain full-time students, student learners, apprentices, and workers with disabilities under special certificates issued by the Department of Labor.[49]

Before the new wage rates were set in 2007, the question of whether to raise the federal minimum wage had been debated by Congress for several years. Arguments made for raising it included the following:

- A higher minimum wage would reduce wage inequality between those at the top and those at the bottom of the economic ladder.
- It had been more than a decade since the minimum wage was changed.
- At $5.15/hour, the minimum wage was less than 30% of the national average hourly wage.
- People earning the minimum wage had incomes that were substantially below the government-defined poverty line.
- The public supported raising the minimum wage.

Arguments made against raising the minimum wage included:

- A higher minimum wage would lead to layoffs of low-skill workers.
- States have the right to set higher minimum wage rates (and half the states had already done so).
- Raising the minimum wage would affect very few workers (about half a million) because most people earn more already.
- Having a higher mandated minimum wage would be an imposition on the free market.[50]

Besides setting the minimum wage rate, the FLSA specifies overtime rules. Employees who are covered by the FLSA's overtime provisions must be paid time-and-a-half for all work exceeding 40 hours a week. Essentially all work-related activities must be counted when determining whether a person has worked for more than 40 hours.[51] Furthermore, compensation must be in the form of direct pay. Employers may not use a barter system. If a restaurant owner asks employees to come in on their days off and help spruce up their workplace, it's not legal to compensate them by giving them a free pizza-and-beer party instead of overtime pay. Employers can't get around this requirement simply by claiming the work wasn't required. If an employer *permits* someone to work, they're obligated to pay for that work.[52] *Employees who are protected by the FLSA are referred to as* **nonexempt employees** (because they are not exempted from the rules).

Exempt employees *are not covered by the minimum wage or overtime provisions of the FLSA.* Executives, managers, professionals, administrators, outside sales employees, and certain computer employees who are paid on a salary basis are exempt employees. To be considered exempt, salaried employees must be paid a fixed, predetermined salary, regardless of the precise number of hours they work in a given week. In addition, they must meet certain criteria regarding the content of their work and salary level.[53] Job title alone is not a sufficient basis for treating a job as exempt. A comprehensive job analysis is necessary to document the activities required for exempt jobs.

Failure to correctly classify employees as exempt or nonexempt can result in costly lawsuits. Financial services organizations have been the focus of many recent FLSA lawsuits.[54] Morgan Stanley recently agreed to pay $42.5 million to settle with their stockbrokers and financial advisers who alleged overtime violations. Similarly, Merrill Lynch paid $37 million to its brokers, and Swiss-based UBS paid $89 million to its U.S.-based financial advisors.

To prevent abuses regarding children, the FLSA prohibits minors under the age of 18 from working in hazardous occupations. For nonhazardous positions, the minimum age ranges from 14 to 16, depending on the type of work to be performed and whether the employer is the child's parent. Fourteen- and fifteen-year-olds are not permitted to work more than 3 hours on a school day and 18 hours in a school week. Also, they may not work between 7 p.m. and 7 a.m., except in the summer, when they may work until 9 p.m.[55]

Equal Pay Act. Title VII of the Civil Rights Act, with which you are now familiar, prohibits pay discrimination in any form. Prior to the passage of the Civil Rights Act in 1964, gender-based discrimination was addressed by the Equal Pay Act of 1963, which amended the Fair Labor Standards Act. The **Equal Pay Act** *prohibits an employer from discriminating "between employees on the basis of sex by paying wages to employees . . . at a rate less than the rate at which he pays wages to employees of the opposite sex . . . for equal work on jobs the performance of which requires equal skill, effort and responsibility, and which are performed under similar working conditions."* For monitoring purposes, employers submit compensation data when they file EEO-1 reports (described in Chapter 6).

Besides filing pay information with the EEOC, employers should conduct comprehensive audits of all aspects of their compensation practices to identify and correct any pay inequity problems. Such audits typically scrutinize each pay element for possible evidence of pay inequities that are based on gender and/or ethnicity. When a pay equity audit uncovers apparently discriminatory pay practices, a plan should be developed to correct the problems. The cost of pay equity adjustments usually has been between 2 and 5% of payroll. Following the lead of public employers, many private sector businesses incorporate pay equity analyses in their annual budget proposals. Interestingly, most HR professionals believe that gender-based pay gaps exist in other organizations, but they don't believe such gaps are present in their organizations; see Exhibit 10.6 for the results of a recent survey on this issue.[56]

Gender- and ethnicity-based wage inequities are pervasive in the United States, as are lawsuits related to pay discrimination. To establish a prima facie case of wage discrimination under the Equal Pay Act, the plaintiff needs to show that a disparity in pay or benefits exists for males and females performing equal jobs. If gender-based pay differences can be shown, then employers are given the opportunity to justify them as due to reasons other than illegal discrimination. Acceptable reasons for gender-based pay differences include the use of seniority and/or merit as the basis for pay decisions and the use of objective performance measures such as sales revenue or quality of production.

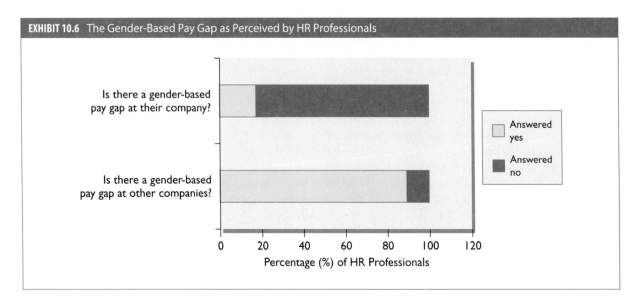

EXHIBIT 10.6 The Gender-Based Pay Gap as Perceived by HR Professionals

Wal-Mart is currently in the middle of one of the largest gender discrimination lawsuits in history. As described in the feature "Managing the Multicultural Workforce: Wal-Mart's Woes," many women at the company believe that Wal-Mart treated them unfairly by paying them less than men doing similar work.[57]

Note that the EPA does not require employers to adopt a practice of **comparable worth,** *which is based on the principle that pay for even dissimilar jobs should be equal if the jobs have a similar overall value to the organization.* (The value of the job to the organization is generally measured with a job evaluation, which is discussed later in this chapter.) In the United States, comparable worth laws cover government employees in six states and numerous local municipalities. All employees in the Canadian Province of Ontario are covered by comparable worth laws. Comparable worth laws seek to address the fact that pay rates tend to be lower in female-dominated jobs than in male-dominated jobs, even when the different jobs require similar levels of skill or experience. Comparable worth laws have been shown to be effective in reducing the male-female wage gap. Nevertheless, it is not likely that a federal comparable worth law will be passed in the near future.[58]

> " *Poverty just isn't a necessary ingredient for economic development.* "
>
> David Coss
> Mayor of Santa Fe
> New Mexico
> Commenting on the
> City's Living Wage Law

Living Wage Laws. Some employers are subject to living wage laws. These laws reflect a widespread social concern about the need to ensure that low-wage employees earn enough to live at a reasonable level of comfort. More than 140 jurisdictions have living wage laws that require some employers to pay wages high enough to raise employees above the poverty level.[59] In 2007, Maryland became the first State to adopt a living wage law that applies to all employers with State contracts.[60] Consistent with equity theory, living wage laws appear to lead to increased worker morale, greater work effort, and reduced turnover and absenteeism of covered workers.[61] Currently, almost all living wage laws apply to local government contractors, but this may be changing. Recently, Chicago's city council passed a living wage law that applied to all large retailers, including Wal-Mart, Target, and Home Depot. Chicago's living wage law required these employers to pay a starting wage of $10 per hour plus benefits valued at a minimum of $3 per hour. Although the law was vetoed by Mayor Richard J. Daley, several other cities are considering similar laws.[62]

MANAGING THE MULTICULTURAL WORKFORCE
Wal-Mart's Woes

Dukes v. Wal-Mart Stores, Inc., is a class action lawsuit filed in federal court in 2001 by six female Wal-Mart employees. The suit contends that Wal-Mart paid female employees less than men in the same jobs, promoted women less often than men, and retaliated against women who complained about the discriminatory practices. The lawsuit has been filed on behalf of all women who worked at Wal-Mart or Sam's Club stores since December 26, 1998. That's about 1.6 million women—more than the total number of people who live in states such as Alaska, Delaware, Hawaii, Maine, Montana, New Hampshire, North or South Dakota, Rhode Island, Wyoming, or Vermont! The historical audit records indicate that women who worked in Wal-Mart stores were paid less than men in every geographic region and in most job categories, and this difference increased over time. That is, the difference in pay between men and women has grown over the years.

When the lawsuit was originally filed, Wal-Mart argued that a class action lawsuit shouldn't be allowed because any pay differences that might exist were not pervasive throughout the company. Wal-Mart wanted to defend itself against each woman who believed she had experienced pay discrimination separately. Wal-Mart contended that the statistics show anomalies between men and women in only 10% of its stores and that in most of those cases there are justifications for the differences on a case-by-case basis. Because pay and promotion decisions are largely decentralized, Wal-Mart argued that its constitutional rights are being violated by not being able to defend itself against each women's claim. But in 2004, the court certified the case as a national class action lawsuit.

Beside the fact that so many women may have been paid less than they deserved, this case will be important for other employers. Already, the court has set a precedent that has implications for any organization that has decentralized pay policies. When such policies are in place, any discriminatory consequences of the policies are likely to be far-reaching and costly. Had Wal-Mart been more proactive in auditing each store's pay practices and taken steps to correct the problems it found, it might not be the defendant in one of the largest discrimination lawsuits in history.

The Organizational Environment

The organizational environment also plays a role in shaping the design of a total compensation system. Strategy, size, and corporate culture all combine to shape each organization's specific approach to compensation.

Strategy. As we have already explained, an organization's strategic objectives often have important implications for the design and implementation of its compensation system. You have read how Synapse designed its compensation practices to support the company's strategic objectives, and how IBM's strategic change affected that company's pay plan. Organizations benefit when their compensation practices are consistent with and support their strategy.[63] Thus, HR needs to play a role in developing and executing the strategy.[64]

Size. Small organizations typically offer less monetary compensation than large ones. Exhibit 10.7 illustrates the average pay and benefits of employees in the private sector.[65] The total compensation of employees in the smallest organizations (fewer than 100 employees) was $21.29 an hour, whereas employees in large organizations (more than 500 employees) earned $36.48 an hour. Despite the fact that they generally earned less, employees working in small organizations typically report being more satisfied, presumably because they receive better nonmonetary compensation.

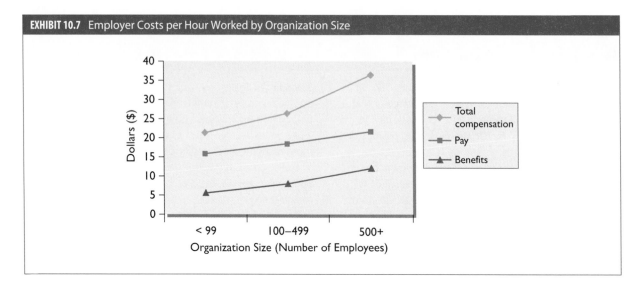

EXHIBIT 10.7 Employer Costs per Hour Worked by Organization Size

Corporate Culture. The culture of the company and the preferences of top management also have a significant impact on many aspects of a company's total compensation. A comparison of Wal-Mart's Sam's Club to Costco, a major competitor, illustrates the point. Both companies seek to offer goods at very low cost. But the two large companies have very different approaches to the way they manage employees as they strive to implement a similar business strategy. As Exhibit 10.8 shows, Costco offers relatively generous compensation in order to motivate and retain good workers. Wal-Mart pays workers much less and accepts in return a much higher rate of employee turnover. Given the wages and benefits shown in Exhibit 10.8, it is easy to understand why turnover rates are so much higher at Wal-Mart. But many people might be surprised to learn that Costco's labor costs as a percentage of sales are actually lower than Wal-Mart's. As a consequence, Costco is not only more profitable, but it has consistently outperformed Wal-Mart in the stock market.[66]

THE HR TRIAD

Effective compensation practices align the needs and characteristics of the organization with the motivation and behaviors of employees, and ultimately it addresses the concerns of both. The coordinated efforts of HR professionals,

EXHIBIT 10.8 Comparison of Compensation at Costco and Wal-Mart

Pay Elements	Costco	Wal-Mart
Average hourly wage	$17	$10.11
Annual health costs per worker	$5,735	$3,500
Annual retirement costs per worker	$1,330	$747
Results		
Annual employee turnover	17%	44%
Sales per square foot	$886	$525
Profits per employee	$21,805	$11,615

LINE MANAGERS	HR PROFESSIONALS	EMPLOYEES
• Attend training programs and stay current on legal issues relevant to pay practices. • Work with HR professionals to ensure alignment of the pay system with strategic business objectives. • Work with employees to ensure that the pay system satisfies and motivates them. • Participate in designing and conducting job evaluations. • Communicate pay system principles and abide by them. • Fairly administer all components of compensation.	• Ensure all policies and practices are consistent with legal requirements. • With line managers, ensure the alignment of the pay system with strategic business objectives. • Assess employees' preferences and reactions to the pay systematically and regularly. • Design processes for job evaluation to involve line managers and job incumbents (employees). • Work with line managers to communicate pay system. • Work closely with line managers to finalize pay decisions.	• Take responsibility for understanding total compensation practices. • May participate in designing new pay systems as the employer's strategic objectives change. • Participate in surveys designed to assess pay preferences and pay satisfaction. • May participate in conducting job evaluation of own job. • May provide input into pay decisions for others. • May register complaints about fairness of pay.

managers, and all other employees are needed to design and implement effective compensation practices. The roles and responsibilities of managers, employees, and HR professionals are summarized in "The HR Triad: Roles and Responsibilities for Total Compensation."

HR Professionals

The many roles and responsibilities of HR professionals will become apparent in this and other chapters as we describe the details of total compensation. In general, however, HR professionals take primary responsibility for ensuring the legality and fairness of compensation practices. They also take the lead on a variety of technical aspects of compensation practices, and they coordinate the involvement of managers and employees. Finally, HR professionals should ensure that compensation practices are communicated and understood by everyone who is affected by them.

Managers

Managers often participate in the design of compensation practices, and they always participate in implementing them. For compensation practices to be effective, managers need to know more than just how much the people they supervise are paid. They should understand how base pay rates are established (explained later in this chapter), the rationale for any incentives that are part of the total pay package (see Chapter 11), and the details of the benefits and services offered to employees (see Chapter 12).

Managers tend to know less about pay than they should, possibly because only about one out of six employers provide any training to teach managers about compensation practices.[67] Beyond training, HR organizations can make sure that managers are properly knowledgeable by involving them in the design of compensation practices, rewarding managers who effectively communicate pay information, and welcoming feedback from the managers.[68]

Employees

Given that managers often are not knowledgeable about compensation, it is no surprise that most other employees are in the dark, too. Surveys of employees indicate that only about one out of three employees understands how their pay is determined. Research also indicates that employee satisfaction is substantially higher among employees who understand their employers' pay decisions.[69] As is true for managers, involving employees during the development of new compensation practices helps ensure that the diverse needs of all employees are met. Several studies show that pay practices designed by a task force that includes employees produce both higher satisfaction and better performance.[70] As you read the following section, which describes the procedures that organizations use to establish the relative value of jobs, you will begin to understand how educational it would be to participate in the process of deciding how to pay people working in various jobs.

ESTABLISHING THE INTERNAL VALUE OF JOBS

The salaries and wages paid to employees are typically governed by an organization's pay structure. A **pay structure** *combines job evaluation information and information about market pay rates in order to establish a policy that specifies the base pay of employees in each job.* In general, jobs that are more important to the organization are worth more, and so employees in those jobs receive higher pay. Internal worth reflects a job's importance or its contribution to the overall attainment of organizational objectives. In this section, we describe the procedures used to establish the value of jobs in an organization. Later we describe the procedures used to assess the market pay rates for jobs, that is, what other employers typically pay people holding similar jobs. Finally, you will learn how information about the organizational value of jobs and the market prices typically paid for similar work are used to develop the organization's pay structure.

Objectives of Job Evaluation

In most organizations, the primary determinant of one's base pay (wages or salary) is the job one holds. **Job evaluation** *is a procedure for establishing the relative internal worth of jobs.* Job evaluation focuses internally and only on the job; it does not take into account market forces or individual performance.

Job evaluation is based on information provided from job analysis. As explained in Chapter 5, job analysis provides a description of job content: What tasks are performed? What are the responsibilities of the job? What competencies are required? Job evaluation then asks, "What is the relative *value* of jobs with various contents and responsibilities involving the use of various competencies?" By tying wages and salaries to job evaluation results, employers seek to create perceptions of **internal pay equity,** *that is, employees should perceive that they are paid fairly compared to others in the same organization, given the contributions that they and others make to the organization.*

Job evaluation is usually undertaken by HR professionals, who oversee the development and implementation of the process, who provide training in the use of the pay structure and in communicating pay decisions, and who administer the organization's appeals procedures.[71] Although HR professionals typically oversee job evaluation, the process invites give and take among all members of the HR Triad. Often, consensus building among job holders, managers, HR professionals, and union officials is required to resolve conflicts that inevitably arise when evaluating the relative worth of jobs. The use of group judgments throughout the job evaluation process helps ensure that these conflicts are addressed, producing an approach to compensation that is accepted by management and employees, congruent with organizational values and strategic objectives, and not based solely on external market valuations of worth.

The three major approaches to establishing the value of jobs are

1. Job ranking.
2. Job classification.
3. The point factor rating method.

Each of these conventional job evaluation methods focuses on the job as the unit of interest. In a **job-based pay structure,** *the pay people receive is determined primarily by the job they hold.* Some methods evaluate the whole job, whereas others evaluate components of jobs using **compensable factors,** *which are the dimensions of work that an organization chooses to use when establishing the relative value of jobs.*

Job Ranking Method

The simplest approach to job evaluation is the **job ranking method,** *which involves simply placing jobs into a rank order according to their perceived overall value or importance.* Job ranking is quick, easy, and cheap. It works best when only a few jobs need to be evaluated and when one person is familiar with them all. As the number of jobs increases, it becomes less likely that one person will know them all well enough to rank-order them.

The simplicity of the job ranking is also one of its disadvantages. Using perceptions of overall value to rank jobs is subjective; so the results can be difficult to justify—to employees, to managers, and in court. Another disadvantage is that the result is simply a list of jobs in hierarchical order from least valued to most valued. The rankings don't provide information about the size of the differences in job value: Is the top ranked job three times more valuable than the bottom ranked job, or ten times more valuable, or thirty times more valuable?[72]

Job Classification Method

The **job classification method** *first groups jobs into a smaller set of job classes and then the job classes (not individual jobs) are ranked according to their value of importance to the organization.* Jobs within a class are usually referred to as being in the same job grade. Jobs within the same grade are assigned the same value. Class descriptions specify the kinds and levels of responsibilities assigned to jobs in each grade, the difficulty of the work performed, the required employee qualifications, and other work factors. The description of a class (or job grade) should be specific enough that jobs can be easily classified, but general enough that numerous different jobs can be classified into the same grade.[73]

The job classification method is more structured and less subjective than job ranking because the criteria for classifying jobs must be clearly stated and specific. Another big advantage it has compared to the job ranking method is that it can be applied to a large number and a wide variety of jobs. The federal government uses the job classification method to evaluate jobs held by more than 1 million employees. The job classification method categorizes the vast majority of federal government jobs into just 15 job grades.

However, the job classification method also has some disadvantages. Like the job ranking method, the final ranking of job classes does not specify the size of the value differences between job classes. Another disadvantage is that some jobs are difficult to classify.

Point Factor Rating Method

As Exhibit 10.9 shows, the most widely used method of job evaluation is the point factor rating method.[74] The **point factor rating method** *uses a sophisticated system for assigning values to jobs based on numerical ratings of job elements.* The point method results in a hierarchy of jobs, with each job having a point value exactly specifying the differences between jobs. The federal government uses the point factor method for evaluating most nonsupervisory jobs. When you read about the five steps of this method, it may appear to be a very objective approach to valuing jobs, but like other job evaluation plans, the point factor rating method also involves subjective judgments.[75] The procedures for making and using judgments are much more rigorous, however, involving five steps.

Step 1: Select Compensable Factors. The aspects of jobs that an organization chooses to value are referred to as compensable factors. Exhibit 10.10 shows the nine factors of the Federal Government's Factor Evaluation System.[76] These nine factors are common to most nonsupervisory governmental jobs, and are typical of those used by many organizations.

When selecting compensable factors, employers can choose either to use a standardized off-the-shelf system such as the one used by the federal government or to develop their own customized set of factors. Regardless of their approach, the objective for employers is to ensure that the jobs receiving the highest values involve tasks and responsibilities that the organization considers most important.

The most widely used standardized point factor rating method is the **Hay Guide–Chart Profile.** Developed by Hay Group, an HR consulting company, it relies on three primary compensable factors: problem solving, know-how, and accountability. The Hay approach has been particularly popular for evaluating executive, managerial, and professional positions, but it's also widely used for technical, clerical, and manufacturing positions. Because organizations worldwide use the system, Hay can provide clients with comparative pay data by industry or locale. However, like any standardized system, it may not reflect a particular organization's true values. Thus, companies need to consider whether a package of standard factors is truly congruent with the

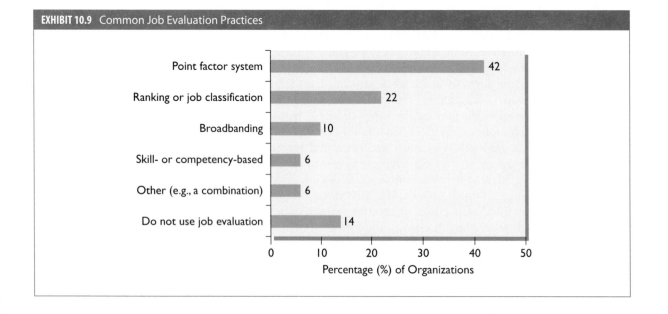

EXHIBIT 10.9 Common Job Evaluation Practices

Point factor system — 42
Ranking or job classification — 22
Broadbanding — 10
Skill- or competency-based — 6
Other (e.g., a combination) — 6
Do not use job evaluation — 14

Percentage (%) of Organizations

EXHIBIT 10.10 The Compensable Factors of the Federal Evaluation System

Factor 1: Knowledge Required by the Position

Kind or nature of knowledge and skills needed and how the knowledge and skills are used in doing the work.

Factor 2: Supervisory Controls

How the work is assigned, employee's responsibility for carrying out the work, and how the work is reviewed.

Factor 3: Guidelines

Nature of guidelines for performing the work and judgment needed to apply the guidelines or develop new guidelines.

Factor 4: Complexity

Nature of the assignment, difficulty in identifying what needs to be done, and difficulty and originality involved in performing the work.

Factor 5: Scope and Effect

Purpose of the work and impact of the work product or service.

Factor 6: Personal Contacts

People and conditions/setting under which contacts are made.

Factor 7: Purpose of Contacts

Reasons for contacts in Factor 6.

Factor 8: Physical Demands

Nature, frequency, and intensity of physical activity.

Factor 9: Work Environment

Risks and discomforts caused by physical surrounding and the safety precautions necessary to avoid accidents or discomforts.

organization's values. In recognition of the idea that different companies are likely to value different aspects of a job, Hay also works with companies to create tailored point systems that fit specific organizations.

Custom-designed factors that are tailored to an organization are more likely to reflect the organization's strategy and values. For example, a company pursuing an innovation strategy may want to include innovation as a compensable factor. This will result in the organization's paying more for jobs that require innovation, which is consistent with their strategy.

Note that assigning points to jobs that require innovation is not the same as awarding a bonus or giving raises to employees because they did something especially innovative. Compensable factors are applied to jobs, not to individual employees. All employees in the same job receive the same points. The goal is to establish the value of each job, not to evaluate the performance of particular individuals who perform the job.

Step 2: Assign Factor Weights. Regardless of whether standard or customized factors are used, the next step in valuing jobs involves assigning relative weights to the factors. How the factors are weighed substantially affects the final pay structure.[77] Although factors could be weighed equally, organizations tend to differentiate between factors, enabling the system to allocate more points to factors that are the most important to the company's success. For example, most job evaluation plans include a working condition factor, so that employees in jobs with poor working conditions (working in the heat, in hazardous conditions, etc.) are compensated for having to work in unpleasant conditions. However, this factor is generally valued at around 5%, so that working conditions are not an overwhelming determinant of the job's pay.

To illustrate the use of points and weights, consider the point system presented in Exhibit 10.11. It has six compensable factors. The total maximum number of points that can be assigned to a job using this system is 1,000, and the minimum is 225. Factor weights are built into the points, which make the system easier for managers to use. The maximum points assigned to the factors can easily be translated into weights, however. To obtain the factor weights, simply divide the maximum points for each factor by the total points possible (1,000). This yields the following weights for factors 1 to 6, respectively: 20%, 26%, 24%, 5%, 10%, and 15%.

Step 3: Define Factor Degrees. Once factors are chosen and weighted, the next step is to construct scales reflecting the different degrees within each factor. Exhibit 10.11 shows descriptions for five degrees of problem solving. Each degree is anchored by a description of the typical tasks and behaviors associated with that degree. The wording of degree definitions should be consistent with the wording of the job descriptions, but the definitions also need to be general enough to apply to a diverse array jobs.[78]

Step 4: Establish the Degree of Each Factor Present in Each Job. In this step, each job is evaluated using the point system created in Steps 1–3. Typically, a compensation committee is given the duty of assessing the degree of each factor present in each job. The compensation committee usually includes managers, union officials (if appropriate), and workers from various job categories. Committee members should be trained in the job evaluation process before they begin evaluating jobs. Then,

---

EXHIBIT 10.11 Example of a Compensable Factor and Related Degree Statements

Part A: Sample Point Evaluation System

Compensable Factor	First Degree	Second Degree	Third Degree	Fourth Degree	Fifth Degree
1. Job knowledge	50	100	150	200	NA
2. Problem solving	50	100	150	205	260
3. Impact	60	120	180	240	NA
4. Working conditions	10	30	50	NA	NA
5. Supervision needed	25	50	75	100	NA
6. Supervision given	30	60	90	120	150

Note: NA = Not Applicable, which means that this degree level is not used for the relevant compensable factor.

Part B: Example of a Compensable Factor and Related Degree Statements

Problem Solving

This factor examines the types of problems dealt with in your job. Indicate the one level that is most representative of most of your job responsibilities.

Degree 1: Actions are performed in a set order according to written or verbal instructions. Problems are referred to a supervisor.

Degree 2: Routine problems are solved and various choices are made regarding the order in which the work is performed, within standard practices. Information may be obtained from various sources.

Degree 3: Various problems are solved that require general knowledge of company policies and procedures applicable within own area of responsibility. Decisions are made based on a choice from established alternatives. Actions are expected to be within standards and established procedures.

Degree 4: Analytical judgment, initiative, or innovation is required in dealing with complex problems or situations. Evaluation is not easy because there is little precedent or information may be incomplete.

Degree 5: Complex tasks involving new or constantly changing problems or situations are planned, delegated, coordinated, or implemented, or any combination of these. Tasks involve the development of new technologies, programs, or projects. Actions are limited only by company policies and budgets.

working independently, each committee member rates the degree level for each factor for each job, based on job descriptions and other job analysis information. Then committee members usually discuss their evaluations, and debate continues until consensus is reached. At the end of the process, each job has been assigned degrees for each compensable factor, providing the data for the final step.

Step 5: Calculate Job Values. The final step in using the point factor rating method is to add up the points for each job. Software programs used for job evaluation usually do this automatically. The result is a hierarchy of jobs, with each job given a numeric score that represents its value to the organization. The job scores are relatively easy to justify because employees can be shown specific reasons for differences in point scores.

Competency-Based Job Evaluation

As Chapter 5 explained, when organizations analyze jobs, they can focus on the tasks and responsibilities required to do the job, or they can focus on the competencies required for people to perform the job. Organizations can tie competencies to pay in numerous ways, but the most common is to use **competency-based job evaluation**, *which keeps the focus on the job, but emphasizes the competencies needed to perform the job, rather than the job duties.*[79]

Domain Competencies. Competency-based job evaluation establishes the value of jobs using domain competencies instead of job factors. The most commonly used competencies are customer focus, communication, team orientation, technical expertise, results orientation, leadership, adaptability, and innovation.[80] Jobs are grouped with others of similar competency requirements. Jobs requiring greater competencies end up in higher pay grades than those requiring few competencies. Domain competencies should be chosen so as to reflect the organization's values and strategies. Further, they should be accepted by employees and management.[81]

Broadbanding. Competency-based job evaluation is often used by organizations that use broadbanding. **Broadbanding** *refers to the use of pay structures that have very few (e.g., three to five) pay grades.* When broadbanding is used, many jobs are grouped into the same grade. When employees move from one pay grade to the next, they typically receive large pay raises. However, such promotions occur less often. Broadbands provide much more flexibility to employers because it is easier to move people into and out of different jobs that require similar competencies without having to reassign them to a different pay grade.[82]

Companies often adopt broad competency-based salary bands because they promote individual development and growth through lateral moves in the organization. Growth through lateral moves is consistent with flatter, team-based structures. When Pharm Tech, a unit of GlaxoSmithKline, began shifting to a competency-based organization, it envisioned career advancement as moving through four stages. To move through the four stages, employees needed to progress through jobs that required increasing levels of seven key competencies. Consistent with this view of careers, Pharm Tech structured its jobs into four broad competency bands. Salaries were tied to the four bands rather than to the numerous pay grades previously used.[83]

Broadbanding has some drawbacks. According to a study by Hewitt and Associates, an HR consulting company, broad salary bands meet stiff cultural resistance in some countries. For example, in India work often is organized hierarchically. Promotions up through the hierarchy are a major form of reward and recognition for employee loyalty. People typically expect promotions every three or four years, and this is easy to do when there are many grades in the pay structure. But with broadbanding, promotions from one grade to the next occur less often.[84] In the United States, the corporate cultures of many organizations reflect similar cultural values; they're still hierarchical, bureaucratic, and rule driven. When companies with such corporate cultures attempt to introduce broad competency-based salary bands, the effort may ultimately fail.[85]

Skill-Based Pay

As just described, competency-based job evaluation systems begin to shift the focus of pay systems toward the competencies of employees. Skill-based pay is an even more radical approach to paying people according to their competencies. **Skill-based pay** *rewards employees for the range, depth, and types of skills they're capable of using, regardless of whether the job they currently hold requires the use of those skills.* This is a very different philosophy from the conventional job-based approaches. Skill-based pay is premised on the belief that highly skilled and knowledgeable employees are more valuable. Thus, compensation practices should encourage employees to develop their competencies; employees should not have to change jobs to get pay raises.

Paying employees based on their competencies—instead of their job assignments—is one way to develop a more highly skilled workforce. With skill-based pay, employees earn more if and when they demonstrate specific skills or knowledge at specific levels of difficulty. For machine operators, valuable skills include those needed to perform assembly, material handling, inventory, and maintenance tasks. For supervisors, valuable skills and knowledge include budget planning and analysis, employee performance management, and developing client relationships.[86]

Skill-based pay fits best with organizational cultures that support open communication, employee involvement, empowerment, and employee growth and development. It requires environments with easily measurable skill progression, capable training programs, supportive supervisors, and opportunities for job rotation.

As an organization's workforce becomes more skilled, compensation costs tend to increase. The additional cost is justified if having more skilled employees gives managers more flexibility to quickly assign people to work whenever and wherever their skills are needed. Other potential advantages of skill-based pay are improved morale and employees who develop a better understanding of how their skills can improve organizational performance. Thus, under the right conditions, skill-based pay may actually help reduce an organization's overall labor costs.

Single versus Multiple Pay Structures

Traditionally, organizations have used different pay structures for different job categories (e.g., clerical, skilled craft, and professional). This approach assumes that the work content of jobs in different families is too diverse to be captured by one pay policy. For example, manufacturing jobs may vary in terms of working conditions and physical effort. So these factors should be used in setting pay for those jobs, but they shouldn't be used for office jobs where these factors don't vary. Proponents of using multiple pay structures contend that because what's valued in the job differs across job categories, different job evaluation plans are needed for various job categories.

From a strategic perspective, using multiple systems makes it more difficult to communicate a coherent message about what the organization values. If the strategy calls for being customer focused, it may be logical to use the potential for affecting customers as a factor in determining the relative worth of *all* jobs in the company. If men and women tend to be segregated into different job categories (e.g., clerical and administrative versus skilled and technical), the use of multiple job evaluation structures may contribute to unintentional sex-based inequities. When multiple pay structures are created, different methods might be used for each of the pay structures, or a single method could be used for all of them.

USING EXTERNAL MARKET RATES TO SET PAY LEVELS

To be effective, an organization's approach to total compensation must take into account the realities of the external labor market.[87] Allowing people to negotiate their pay is one way to do this. But even when managers negotiate pay with people they are trying to hire or retain, they usually are constrained by a set of guidelines that limit what they are allowed to offer an employee. The constraints placed on managers are specified by the organization's pay structure. Using job evaluation procedures helps ensure that the pay structure addresses the issue of internal pay equity, as you have just learned. The pay structure also must address the issue of external pay equity. **External pay equity** *exists when employees feel they are being paid fairly relative to what people in similar jobs (or with similar competencies) are paid by other employers.* Creating a pay structure that achieves external pay equity involves three steps:

1. Determining pay rates in the external market.
2. Establishing the market pay policy.
3. Setting the organization pay policy.

Step 1: Determine External Market Pay Rates

A **compensation survey** *is used by employers to obtain data about pay rates in the external labor market.* Compensation surveys are usually conducted by consulting organizations, which sell the results to employers. Using independent third parties for surveys is important in helping employers avoid violating antitrust litigation.[88] Employers participating in surveys provide compensation information for selected jobs in return for getting access to the aggregated data. To properly use the data from a compensation survey, an organization needs to identify the relevant labor market and the appropriate benchmark jobs.[89]

Relevant Labor Market. Using survey data requires defining the relevant labor market. (Recall that, in Chapter 6, we discussed the concept of a relevant labor market and its role in recruitment.) When establishing pay policies, three factors are commonly used to define the relevant labor market: (1) the occupation or skill required, (2) the geographic location (the distance from which applicants would be willing to relocate or commute), and (3) the other employers competing for labor. The relevant geographic labor market for a vice president of sales for Microsoft Corporation may be the entire United States. The relevant geographic labor market for an accounts receivable clerk may be the greater Seattle area. In global companies, the relevant labor market for some jobs is the entire world.

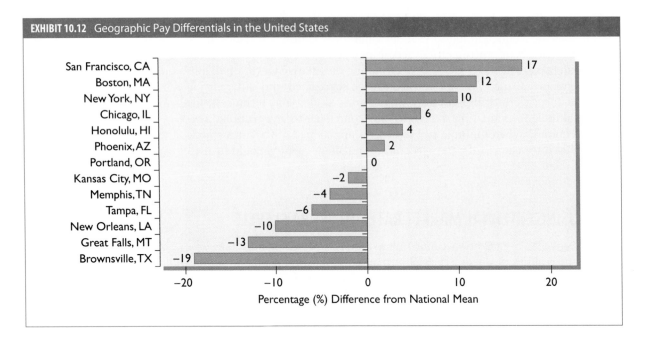

EXHIBIT 10.12 Geographic Pay Differentials in the United States

Exhibit 10.12 shows how the costs of labor vary in the United States. The data shows the average differences in pay across occupations for a metropolitan area relative to the national average.[90] For example, jobs in the San Francisco, California, area pay 17% more than the national average, while jobs in the Brownsville, Texas, area pay 19% less. These differentials tend to matter more for lower-level jobs, where the labor markets are local.[91] For global companies, it is important to understand how pay rates vary from one country to another. Thus, some compensation surveys focus on country comparisons. For example, an employer with operations throughout Asia can purchase compensation survey data describing pay rates for dozens of jobs in each of several Asian countries. To establish equity in a geographic area, employers typically use information about the actual pay rates for specific jobs, rather than more general information about cost of living differences, because employees base their judgments of pay fairness on comparisons for their specific job.[92]

Industry differences also may become evident in definitions of the relevant labor market. If industry-specific knowledge and experience are important, an employer may consider the relevant labor market to be defined by other employers in the same industry. In such cases, the company would use surveys only of organizations in their industry. As noted in the earlier discussion of industry pay effects, this could have a substantial effect on pay levels.

Benchmark Jobs. To interpret market survey data, benchmark jobs must be identified. Traditionally, **benchmarks jobs** *are jobs commonly found across a range of organizations and they involve essentially the same work and responsibilities regardless of the company.* In other words, regardless of the employer, the job description of a benchmark job should sound pretty much the same.

There are a number of things organizations look for to determine whether a job should be considered a benchmark job. They include:

- Is the job common across many different employers?
- Is the job generally accepted by other employers as a benchmark job?

- Is the job relatively stable over time?
- Is the job frequently included in compensation surveys?
- Is the job performed by a considerable number of people?

If the answer to all these questions is yes, then the organization can be confident in using this job for the purpose of setting wages.

When data are collected for a market survey, the jobs in the survey have brief job descriptions. The Clayton Wallis Company conducts market surveys for employers in numerous industries, so they have developed dozens of benchmark job descriptions. Below are examples of three benchmark job descriptions that this firm uses when it conducts market surveys. The job of photographer might be included in a market survey for jobs in publishing or entertainment. The job of carpet installer would be used for a market survey of jobs in construction. The bartender job description would be used for a market survey of jobs in the hospitality industry.[93]

Photographer. Photographers produce and preserve images that paint a picture, tell a story, or record an event. To create commercial quality photographs, photographers need both technical expertise and creativity. Producing a successful picture requires choosing and presenting a subject to achieve a particular effect and selecting the appropriate equipment. Photographers use either a traditional camera that records images on silver halide film that is developed into prints or a digital camera that electronically records images. Using computers and specialized software, photographers also can manipulate and enhance the scanned or digital image to create a desired effect. Images can be stored on portable memory devices including compact disks (CDs) or on new types of smaller storage devices.

Carpet Installer. Carpet installers inspect the surface to be covered to determine its condition then they measure the area to be carpeted and plan the layout, keeping in mind expected traffic patterns and placement of seams for best appearance and maximum wear. When installing wall-to-wall carpet without tacks, installers first fasten a tackless strip to the floor, next to the wall. They then install the padded cushion or underlay. Next, they roll out, measure, mark, and cut the carpet, allowing for 2 to 3 inches of extra carpet for the final fitting. Using a device called a knee kicker, they position the carpet, stretching it to fit evenly on the floor and snugly against each wall and door threshold. They then cut off the excess carpet. Finally, using a power stretcher, they stretch the carpet, hooking it to the tackless strip to hold it in place. The installers then finish the edges using a wall trimmer.

Bartender. Bartenders fill drink orders either taken directly from patrons at the bar or through waiters and waitresses who place drink orders for dining room customers. Bartenders check identification of customers seated at the bar to ensure they meet the minimum age requirement for the purchase of alcohol and tobacco products. They prepare mixed drinks, serve bottled or draught beer, and pour wine or other beverages. Bartenders must know a wide range of drink recipes and be able to mix drinks accurately, quickly, and without waste.

To determine whether a job is useful as a benchmark, the job description used for the survey is compared to the job description in the employer's organization. If the two descriptions are very similar, the employer can feel confident that the market wage data provided by the survey can be applied to the job in the employer's organization. Market information about the compensation levels of benchmark jobs is used to establish the market pay policy, as explained next. Note that for competency-based pay systems, the appropriate benchmarks would be competency profiles. For skill-based pay, the appropriate benchmarks would be identifiable skill levels. In practice, however, most companies still rely on benchmarking against common jobs because that is the method ordinarily used to collect market wage data.

Step 2: Establish the Market Pay Policy

The **market pay policy** *is established by plotting pay rates against the evaluation points that the company assigned to the benchmark jobs.* A regression line is calculated to describe the relationship between the job evaluation results and market pay rates.

The benchmark jobs in Exhibit 10.13 are labeled Job A, Job B, Job C, and so forth. The points that were assigned to the jobs using a point rating method are shown on the horizontal axis. Job E was assigned 290 job evaluation points; Job B was assigned 750 job evaluation points; and so on. The average market wage rates for the benchmark jobs are shown on the vertical axis. For Job E, the average market wage is $35,000. For Job B, it's $73,000. The pay policy for the external market is defined by the best-fitting line relating job evaluation points to average market pay. Typically, regression analysis is used to establish the best-fitting line.

Why does an organization need to calculate the external market's policy line? Because market data aren't available for all jobs in the organization. In Exhibit 10.13, Job X represents a job that exists in the organization. But market

EXHIBIT 10.13   Market Pay Policy Line Based on Market Survey Results for Benchmark Jobs

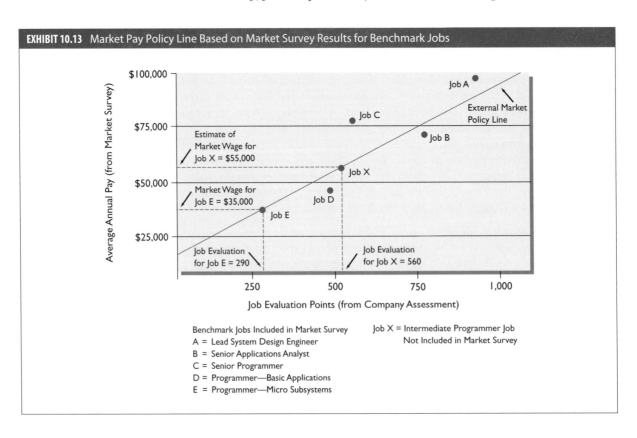

pay data were not available for Job X because no similar job was included in the market survey. The market policy line makes it possible to assign a dollar value to Job X without knowing its actual market value.

Step 3: Set the Organization Pay Policy

The **organization pay policy** *specifies the pay rates that will be used for the jobs in a particular organization.* If the company wants simply to match the market, it may set its organization pay policy line equal to the line for the external market. Alternatively, the company may choose to pay somewhat above the market or somewhat below the market. The choice of an organization pay policy is influenced by the pay rates of major competitors, the organization's profits or losses, surpluses or shortages of qualified workers, the stage of the organization's development, the role of performance-based pay, the strength of union demands, the organizational culture, and other factors.[94]

A **lead policy** *indicates that the organization intends to pay somewhat above the market rate.* Paying more than other employers maximizes the company's ability to attract and retain quality employees and helps to minimize employee pay dissatisfaction. It can increase labor costs, too, unless paying employees more results in higher productivity, lower costs due to turnover, reduced training costs, and so on.

By far the most common policy is to match the competition. A **match policy** *sets the organization's policy line at the middle of the market.* A match policy does not give an employer a competitive advantage, but it does ensure that the organization isn't at a disadvantage.

It is also possible to adopt a **lag policy,** *where the organization intentionally pays below the market.* However, a lag policy may hinder a organization's ability to attract and retain potential employees unless other considerations—such as job security, benefits, locale, and job content—compensate for the low base pay.

Exhibit 10.14 shows the pay policies reported by companies that participated in a salary survey conducted by the Hay Group. The exhibit shows the

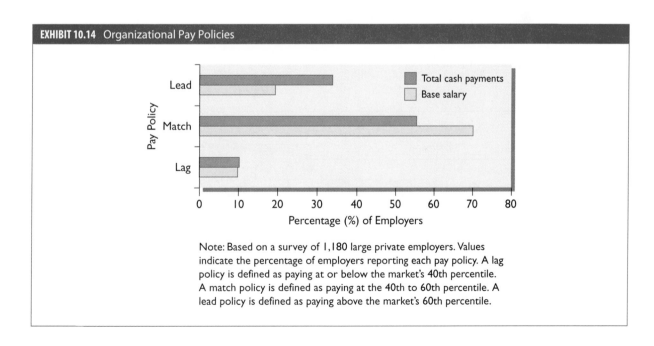

EXHIBIT 10.14 Organizational Pay Policies

Note: Based on a survey of 1,180 large private employers. Values indicate the percentage of employers reporting each pay policy. A lag policy is defined as paying at or below the market's 40th percentile. A match policy is defined as paying at the 40th to 60th percentile. A lead policy is defined as paying above the market's 60th percentile.

policies for base salaries and total cash payments, which would include annual bonuses and long-term incentive pay.

DESIGNING THE INTERNAL PAY STRUCTURE

When the organization pay policy is set, a pay structure can be developed. A pay structure helps control the rates paid for jobs in the same pay grade. It fosters internal equity by ensuring that employees who work in jobs that are of similar value to the organization are paid approximately the same.[95] It fosters external equity by ensuring that the wages paid by the organization are similar to those paid by other employers who compete for talent in the same labor market. The pay structure also provides guidance to managers and gives them a rationale to use when explaining their pay decisions to employees. The process of creating the pay structure differs somewhat depending on whether the pay is job-based, competency-based, or skill-based.

Job-Based Pay Grades and Ranges

Exhibit 10.15 shows a conventional job-based pay structure. The boxes are associated with a spread of job evaluation points (the job grade) and a range of pay (the minimum and maximum that can be earned). Usually, several different jobs are covered by one box. The jobs covered by each box have similar evaluation points, but they may have very dissimilar content. The boxes that make up the structure may be the same size or may systematically increase in width and height. They ascend from left to right, reflecting the association of higher pay levels (shown on the vertical axis) with more valued jobs (shown on the horizontal axis).

In establishing pay ranges, the organization's pay policy line generally serves as the midpoint. Maximums and minimums are generally set at a

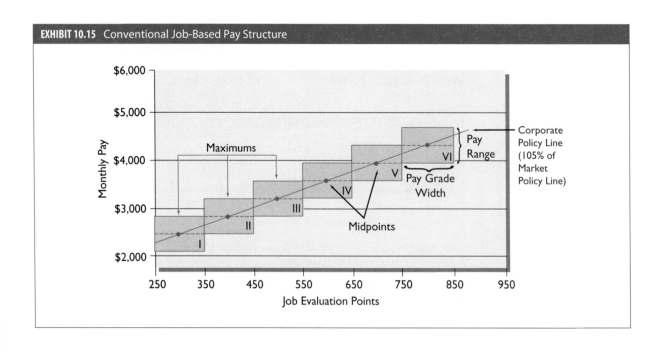

EXHIBIT 10.15 Conventional Job-Based Pay Structure

percentage above and below that amount. The difference between the maximum and minimum allowable pay rates is the pay range. Pay ranges tend to become greater as one moves to higher pay grades, with ranges of lower-level grades ranging from 10 to 25% and higher-level grades ranging from 40 to 100%. Larger pay ranges allow for greater differences in pay among those in the same grade. For the organization depicted in Exhibit 10.15, six equal-interval pay grades were established, each with a width of 100 points. Each grade has a pay range of $800. For Pay Grade II, the range goes from $2,400 (minimum) to $3,200 (maximum) a month; the midpoint is $2,800 a month. Notice that the maximum annual pay for these jobs is less than $60,000, which suggests that the plan does not cover higher-level professionals or executives.

Competency-Based Pay Structure

A competency-based pay structure is based on the results of a competency-based evaluation. Competency-based pay structures look very similar to job-based pay structures. That is, pay grades and ranges ascend upward along a continuum. In a competency-based pay structure, however, the points on the horizontal axis correspond to levels of competencies. At the lower end of the scale are jobs that require competencies of relatively less value to the organization. At the higher end of the scale are jobs that require competencies that are more valuable to the organization. In other words, the key difference between competency-based and job-based models is not in how points are used, but in how points are assigned to jobs.

Skill-Based Pay Structure

With skill-based pay, pay is tied to the skills of individuals. Pay rates reflect the value assigned to the demonstrated skills of employees, not to their job assignments. Because it is based on the person rather than the job, the structure of a skill-based system is fundamentally different from a job-based or competency-based system. Typically, everyone begins with a fixed rate of pay that is more or less equal for everyone covered by the pay structure. Over time, pay raises are earned by demonstrating proficiency in the competencies valued by the organization. The pay structure defines the competencies that are rewarded and the size of the pay increases given for each added skill.

ADJUSTMENTS

Developing a pay structure requires a major investment; so most organizations make major changes in their pay structure only when they are needed to support other major change initiatives, such as a change in the business strategy or an organizational restructuring. Nevertheless, some adjustments are needed for any pay structure to remain effective in achieving its objectives. Adjustments may be needed to balance internal and external equity, to compensate for changes in pay over time, and to achieve individual equity.

Balancing Internal and External Equity

As we have shown, both external and internal data are used to construct the pay structure. When the organizations' system for assigning points and weights to compensable factors are similar to those used by competitors, an organization's job evaluation results are likely to be closely aligned with the market wages paid to similar jobs. Nevertheless, in some cases the organization's pay structure may indicate that the value of a particular job is not well aligned with the market pay rate for that job.

To illustrate this problem, look at Exhibit 10.13 again, focusing on the job of senior programmer (Job C). The job evaluation process assigned 570 points to this job. The policy indicates that a 570-point job should be paid about $60,000. But the market survey indicated that the pay rate for senior programmers is more than $75,000. If this organization pays less than the market rate, it may have difficulty attracting and retaining excellent senior programmers. But if it pays the market rate, the organization will be spending more than it judges this job to be worth, given how it contributes to the organization's objectives.

How can this problem be resolved? Sometimes differences between market rates and job evaluation results can be resolved by reviewing the judgments that were made when evaluating the job and finding its price in the external market. If a discrepancy persists even after a check of the job evaluation and wage survey data, it often is due to a temporary labor market irregularity that causes an unusual change in the demand for labor. To address such market irregularities, the organization can create a **shadow range,** *which is a temporary readjustment that expands the size of the minimum and maximum pay rates associated with a pay grade.* Typically, shadow ranges indicate that it is OK for managers to offer somewhat higher pay to attract or retain employees during labor shortages. Shadow ranges can then be eliminated when the labor market imbalance corrects itself.

Changes over Time

Most organizations make annual adjustments to their pay structures to address changes in the overall market pay rates caused by inflation. People often refer to such changes in pay as cost-of-living adjustments.

In recent years, inflation in pay rates for most jobs has averaged about 3–4%. To stay competitive, organizations must continually adjust their pay policies using their best estimate of what changes in the market wage have occurred since the survey was taken. **Salary budget surveys,** *which estimate the amount of salary increases for the coming year,* are useful for making this type of adjustment. Typically, organizations adjust the entire structure upward by the percentage of average market increase, keeping the wages of adjusted employees equivalent in real dollars.

Achieving Individual Pay Equity

Individual pay equity *is established when the individual perceives that he or she is paid fairly compared to others in the same organization with the same job.* Organizations address individual pay equity through raises based on performance, seniority, or both, as we explain in Chapter 11. When organizations first implement a new pay structure, they almost always find that some employees are paid well above the maximum or below the minimum allowable for their jobs in the new pay structure. One way to handle this problem is simply to adjust the individual's pay to fit into the new structure. For employees who are being paid much less than the pay structure indicates they are worth, an immediate pay raise is deserved and should be offered. An employee who is being paid below the minimum is usually **green-circled,** *indicating that the* *person needs to be given a pay adjustment to bring his or her pay up to at least the pay grade's minimum.*

Individual employees who are being paid above the maximum of their pay grade require a different approach. Employers seldom tell an employee that his or her pay will be reduced to fit a new pay structure, unless they are prepared for the consequences of the employee quitting! In this situation, the employee is **red-circled,** *indicating that the person's pay is frozen and that he or she should not be offered any more pay raises.* The pay of a red-circled employee remains frozen until the annual pay structure adjustments for inflation eventually result in the employee's pay falling within the pay range.

COMPENSATION IN THE CONTEXT OF GLOBALIZATION

Most large organizations these days are multinational corporations (MNCs) that must develop compensation practices that make sense from a global perspective. A key issue when designing a global approach to total compensation is balancing global consistency with sensitivity to local conditions.[96]

Should a multinational organization like Wal-Mart or Starbucks or IBM have a centralized approach to total compensation designed to fit the company's global strategy? Should it use compensation practices as a way to help establish a consistent corporate culture that is the same for all employees around the world, regardless of which country they are in? Or should it develop compensation practices that are tailored to the unique conditions in each country? Centralizing global pay seems to be the current trend, possibly because the evidence suggests that globally consistent compensation practices can contribute to organizational effectiveness.[97] The major objectives of MNCs adopting a centralized approach to total compensation are to create consistency in the link between results and rewards, to ensure that employees doing similar jobs all around the world are paid comparably, and to achieve internal pay equity.[98]

Global consistency is more easily achieved with a centralized pay structure. The degree of centralized control exerted by the headquarters office can vary from making all decisions at headquarters to providing tools, guidelines, and technological support to country or business unit managers abroad to ensure consistency. Even when organizations take the highly centralized approach, they cannot ignore local considerations. There are clear differences in the norms around the world that influence pay decisions and perceptions of pay fairness. Exhibit 10.16 shows some of these differences for four countries.[99]

At what point are local considerations more important than a globally consistent structure? Clearly, the laws of a particular country must be respected and taken into consideration when designing pay practices. In the Netherlands, for example, stock options are taxed at the time they are given to employees. Consequently, most Dutch employees consider them to be a burden. In the United States, however, favorable tax treatment of stock options has led to their widespread use.

Cultural values should also be considered when designing a global approach to total compensation. Some managers believe that HR practices should always be consistent with a country's normal practices and culture. Other managers argue that there is so much variance among individuals in any particular country

Increasingly, pay is being managed from a global perspective—to facilitate global expansion efforts, better manage labor costs, create internal equity, or ensure effective governance.

Mark Edelsten
European Partner
Mercer in London

FAST FACT

About 50% of MNCs have a centralized global pay structure.

EXHIBIT 10.16 Country Compensation Comparisons of Nonmanagement Employees

	United States	Mexico	Japan	Germany
Average hourly compensation cost for manufacturing	$23.17	$2.50	$21.90	$32.53
Percent of labor costs taken by taxes and Social Security	29.6%	15.4%	26.6%	50.7%
Typical basis for pay	Job	Job	Person	Job
Typical basis for raises	Performance or seniority	Seniority, across-the-board raises	Seniority, skill improvement, use of merit increasing	Seniority, sometimes performance
Pay structure	Hierarchical	Hierarchical	Egalitarian	Egalitarian
Pay for performance	Common through merit system, bonuses, and profit sharing	Attendance bonuses, profit sharing	Common through group bonuses	Less common
Unique feature	The use of stock options for nonmanagerial employees	Acquired rights laws (practices in place for two years become required); high mandatory payments	Prevalent use of "wage compositions," which include housing and commuting allowances	Strong trend toward harmonization of pay across organizations

that it is not necessary to do what is "normal." Even when a company does something unusual, it will probably attract individuals with values that are consistent with the practice. As described in the feature "Managing Globalization: Global Pay at McDonald's," McDonald's has attempted to find the proper balance between global consistency and cultural adaptability while adopting a centralized global pay structure.[100]

MANAGING GLOBALIZATION
Global Pay at McDonald's

In 2003, McDonald's decided to adopt a centralized approach for compensating managers and executives, so the company developed a centralized pay structure that covers more than 400,000 managers and senior staff working in 118 countries. This new system replaced the old set of many different pay structures, which were wildly inconsistent. With the old approach, there were no standards in place for tying pay to performance, although paying for performance was central to the company's strategy and the corporate culture it wanted to establish. To correct this problem, McDonald's launched a new compensation initiative in 2004, called Plan to Win. Developed with the input of its global managers, Plan to Win provides clear principles and guidance, but also allows managers to implement them using pay practices that fit local situations. An example of a principle is to reward excellent customer service, because McDonald's considers customer service to be central to its strategy. Managers are allowed to choose a set of three to five issues to focus on in their local market and then create business targets for the year to address those issues. Annual bonuses are paid according to performance against the set targets. McDonald's believes the new approach is working, as indicated by reduced turnover and increased perceptions of pay fairness.

CURRENT ISSUES

Throughout this chapter we have mentioned several current issues in compensation, including offshoring, increased reliance on competency-based pay, and managing global pay. Two other issues that will shape how organizations handle total compensation in the near future are an increased concern for work/life balance and automation of benefits and compensation administration.[101]

Work/Life Balance

An increasing desire for a balance between home life and work is shaping the way people work and how they value rewards.[102] From an employer's standpoint, changing views of work/life balance send a signal that nonmonetary rewards will become increasingly important in the next few years. Among the reasons employers offer benefits that help employees balance their home and work life are to

Many individuals find elements such as flex schedules, telecommuting, on-site day care, or more personal time to have greater importance than cash.

Peg Buchenroth
Managing Director
Compensation and Benefits
Hudson Highland Group

- Improve morale.
- Make recruiting easier.
- Help the organization remain competitive.
- Improve the organization's image in the industry.[103]

Benefits that employers offer to address work/life balance are sometimes called family-friendly benefits. Examples of these include scheduling benefits, child care benefits, elder care benefits, and domestic partner benefits. Chapter 12 describes these in more detail.

Automation of Benefits and Compensation

Improved technology is sparking substantial changes in how employers process compensation information and how they communicate information about compensation to employees. On-demand comprehensive benefits information, easy access to market pay surveys, Web-based compensation management systems, automated benefits enrollment, and automated compensation analysis tools are just some of the ways that technology has changed the management of compensation.[104] When Nintendo of America introduced an automated Web-based system for managing compensation, it experienced significant cost savings, improved accuracy of the system, and greater access to information that could be used for strategic planning.[105] By improving communication and increasing employees' and managers' access to compensation information, automation may allow employees to become more directly and more meaningfully involved in decisions about their compensation. The improved technology may also allow HR professionals to focus more on strategic issues rather than on administrative details.

CHAPTER SUMMARY WITH LEARNING GOALS

Total compensation is critical to an organization's success. It is a major expense and a powerful tool for motivating, attracting, and retaining employees.

⚠ **STRATEGIC IMPORTANCE.** Total compensation is strategically important to organizations because it can be used to attract, retain, and motivate talent; it can be used to implement the organization's strategy; and it can improve productivity.

2 **THE INTEGRATED HRM SYSTEM.** Compensation practices should be designed to fit the organization's external and internal environment. Labor market conditions, industry conditions, and the legal environment all influence an organization's approach to total compensation. The organization's size, corporate culture, and strategy also shape its specific approach. Other HR practices that should be aligned with compensation include job analysis, recruitment, performance measurement, and training.

3 **THE HR TRIAD.** HR professionals, line managers, and employees all have substantial responsibilities with respect to total compensation. The HR Triad is responsible for aligning the needs and characteristics of the organization with the motivation and behaviors of employees. Ensuring that employees are paid fairly is another major responsibility.

4 **INTERNAL VALUE OF JOBS.** The value of a job is established with a job evaluation. The value may be based on many factors, including the level of knowledge required, the responsibilities associated with the job, or the competencies required for the job.

5 **PAY LEVELS.** Organizations establish market-based pay levels by determining external market rates, establishing the market pay policy, and setting the organization pay policy. The organization may choose a policy that leads, matches, or lags the pay offered by competitors.

6 **INTERNAL PAY STRUCTURE.** Most organizations use a job-based pay structure that specifies the minimum and maximum pay for all jobs in the organization. The pay structure should achieve the objectives of ensuring both internal and external pay equity.

7 **ADJUSTMENTS.** Adjustments to the pay structure and to individual pay may be needed to balance internal and external equity, to adjust to changes over time, and to achieve individual equity.

8 **GLOBALIZATION.** MNCs face the challenge of designing pay practices that balance the advantages of global consistency with the need for sensitivity to local conditions. Consistency can be established by centralizing the pay structure, but local conditions such as laws and cultural norms for pay should still be considered.

9 **CURRENT ISSUES.** Two current issues in compensation are the focus on work/life balance and the automation of the compensation function.

TERMS TO REMEMBER

Base pay	Job-based pay structure
Benchmark jobs	Job classification method
Broadbanding	Job evaluation
Comparable worth	Job ranking method
Compensable factors	Lag policy
Compensation survey	Lead policy
Competency-based job evaluation	Market pay policy
Equal Pay Act	Match policy
Exempt employees	Monetary compensation
External pay equity	Nonexempt employees
Fair Labor Standards Act (FLSA)	Nonmonetary compensation
Green-circled	Organization pay policy
Hay Guide–Chart Profile	Pay fairness
Individual pay equity	Pay level
Industry capital intensity	Pay mix
Industry unionization	Pay satisfaction
Internal pay equity	Pay structure

Point factor rating method

Shadow range

Red-circled

Skill-based pay

Salary budget surveys

Total compensation

QUESTIONS FOR REFLECTIVE THINKING AND DISCUSSION

1. Explain how an organization's approach to total compensation can help it be effective or prevent it from being effective.
2. How and why do the objectives of total compensation vary across organizations?
3. What are the elements of total compensation, and which ones are most important to you personally?
4. Describe the purpose of job evaluation. What are the advantages and disadvantages of using the job ranking method? What are the advantages and disadvantages of using a customized job evaluation point system?
5. List the possible negative consequences that organizations are likely to experience if employees do not understand the organization's compensation practices.
6. What are your views on pay secrecy? How much do you think employees should be told about how their pay is determined?
7. If you were considering a job offer, which elements of total compensation would be more important to you: base pay, incentives, or benefits and services? Why? What are the implications of your answer for employers seeking to attract people like you to work for them?

PROJECTS TO EXTEND YOUR LEARNING

1. **Integration and Application.** Before continuing, review the cases of Southwest Airlines and Lincoln Electric at the end of this book. Then answer the following questions.

   a. Compare and contrast the two companies on the following:
      - The objectives of their total compensation practices.
      - The role of total compensation in achieving competitive advantage.
      - The pay mix and employees' reactions to the pay mix.
   b. Which approach to compensating employees would you prefer? Explain why.

2. **Using the Internet.** Many organizations provide online resources related to total compensation. Start to learn about some of these by visiting the following websites.

   a. WorldatWork is an association of compensation professionals. Learn more about the resources available through this organization and current issues of interest to their members at www.worldatwork.org.
   b. The Society of Human Resource Management (SHRM) makes available many resources related to compensation and benefits at www.shrm.org/rewards.
   c. Learn more about pay equity, comparable worth, and exempt/nonexempt status from the
      - State of Minnesota's Department of Employee Relations (www.doer.state.mn.us).
      - Capital Research Center (www.capitalresearch.org).
      - U.S. Department of Labor (www.dol.gov/esa/regs/compliance/whd/fairpay/main.htm).
   d. Find out about the AFL-CIO's position on executive pay practices at www.aflcio.org/corporateamerica/paywatch.
   e. Learn about pay levels in the United States and discover what other compensation information is available from the Bureau of Labor Statistics at www.bls.gov. Learn about the federal government job classification at www.opm.gov.
   f. Read more about the Hay Guide–Chart Profile method by visiting the Hay Group at www.haygroup.com.
   g. Read about the current state of the Wal-Mart class action suit at www.walmartclass.com.

3. **Experiential Activity.** As domestic companies begin to expand overseas, they face many new challenges. Among these is deciding how to compensate the people who fill top-level management positions in global operations. This activity asks you to choose the approach you think is best.

    Activity

    Two basic alternatives to compensation are (a) pay managers by matching the market rate of local executives in the non-U.S. locations, or (b) pay managers by matching the compensation of their U.S. counterparts.

    a. First, make a list of the pros and cons of alternatives (a) and (b). What HR objectives might best be achieved by each approach?
    b. Next, choose your preferred approach to this strategic issue. Do you think (a) or (b) is the better way to pay managers?
    c. Finally, assume your company adopted your preferred approach a year ago when it opened a new facility in France. It is time to evaluate whether the approach was the right choice. You have been put in charge of the evaluation project. You must develop a list of interview questions to ask all of the company's American managers working abroad. There are a total of 50 American managers working in six countries outside the United States. What questions will you ask these 50 people in order to evaluate the effectiveness of their compensation? Be ready to share your list with your classmates and explain the logic that guided you in developing it.

CASE STUDY

THE OVERPAID BANK TELLERS

The State Bank is located in a Southwestern U.S. town of about 50,000 people. It is one of four banks in the area and has the reputation of being the most progressive. Russell Duncan has been the president of the bank for 15 years. Before coming to State Bank, Duncan worked for a large Detroit bank for 10 years. Duncan has implemented a number of changes that have earned him a great deal of respect and admiration from both bank employees and townspeople alike. For example, in response to a growing number of Spanish-speaking people in the area, he hired Latinos and placed them in critical bank positions. He organized and staffed the city's only agricultural loan center to meet the needs of the area's farmers. In addition, he established the state's first "uniline" system for handling customers waiting in line for a teller.

Perhaps more than anything else, Duncan is known for establishing progressive personnel practices. He strongly believes that the bank's employees are its most important asset and continually searches for ways to increase both employee satisfaction and productivity. He feels that all employees should strive to continually improve their skills and abilities, and hence he cross-trains employees and sends many of them to courses and conferences sponsored by banking groups such as the American Institute of Banking.

With regard to employee compensation, Duncan believes that employees should be paid according to their contribution to organizational success. Hence, 10 years ago, he implemented a results-based pay system under which employees could earn raises from 0 to 12% each year, depending on their job performance. Raises are typically determined by the bank's HR Committee during February and are granted to employees on March 1 of each year. In addition to granting employees merit raises, six years ago the bank also began giving cost-of-living raises. Duncan had been opposed to this idea originally but saw no alternative to it.

One February, another bank in town conducted a wage survey to determine the average compensation of bank employees in the city. The management of the State Bank received a copy of the wage survey and was surprised to learn that its 23 tellers, as a group, were being paid an average of $22 per week more than were tellers at other banks. The survey also showed that employees holding other positions in the bank (e.g., branch managers, loan officers, and file clerks) were being paid wages similar to those paid by other banks.

After receiving the report, the HR Committee of the bank met to determine what should be done regarding the tellers' raises. They knew that none of the tellers had been told how much their raises would be but that they were all expecting both merit and cost-of-living raises. They also realized that, if other employees learned that the tellers were being overpaid, friction could develop and morale might suffer. They knew that it was costing the bank more than $26,000 extra per year to pay the tellers. Finally, they knew that as a group the bank's tellers were highly competent, and they did not want to lose any of them.

Source: S. Nkomo, M. Fottler, and R. B. McAfee, *Human Resource Management Applications*, 6th ed. (Mason, OH: Thomson South-Western, 2008).

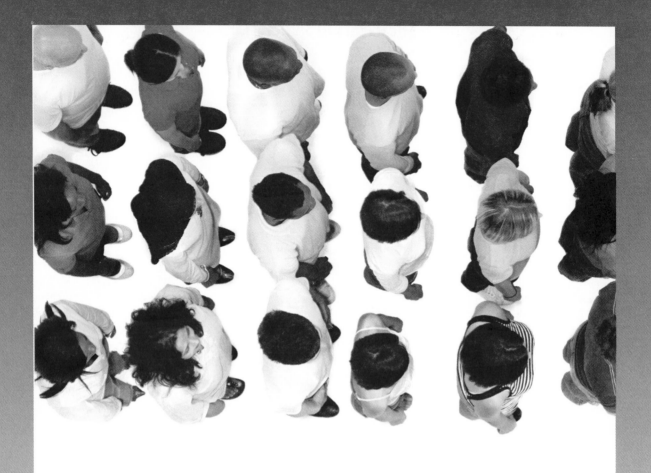

Using Performance-Based Pay to Achieve Strategic Objectives

Learning Goals

After reading this chapter, you should be able to:

1 Explain the strategic importance of performance-based pay.

2 Show how performance-based pay fits within an integrated HRM system.

3 Detail the roles and responsibilities of the HR Triad for performance-based pay.

4 Describe the design choices for performance-based pay.

5 Discuss the implementation of performance-based pay.

6 Describe the features of recognition awards.

7 Explain how merit pay works.

8 Discuss several types of incentive pay.

9 Explain the reasons and approaches for putting earnings at risk.

10 Describe some global differences in how organizations implement performance-based pay.

11 Detail two current issues related to performance-based pay.

MANAGING HUMAN RESOURCES AT THE UNITED STATES POSTAL SERVICE

Today, people can communicate and do almost every type of transaction using electronic means. Sending a handwritten letter or paper documents is becoming a thing of the past, something only your parents and grandparents do. Yet nearly all of us still have paper (snail) mail delivered daily to our homes and offices by the United States Postal Service (USPS). In fact, the USPS delivers over 200 billion pieces of mail annually.

However, the USPS's financial performance hasn't always been acceptable. From 1970 to 1994, the postal service lost $10 billion. As part of an effort to turn things around, the USPS implemented a new, market-driven and performance-based pay approach. Since implementation, the approach has helped the postal service earn more than $10 billion. In addition to improved financial performance, performance-based pay has also helped USPS achieve record high on-time delivery rates, low injury and illness rates, and substantial increases in productivity and customer service.

New technologies and changing competitive pressures have required the USPS to repeatedly change its business strategy and address new challenges. As its goals and objectives have changed, so have its performance-based pay practices. The pay practices in place at USPS today evolved over several years. Currently, 75,000 employees are rewarded for achieving corporate, unit, and individual performance targets. When setting individual performance targets, managers strive to consider each individual's specific situation. The goal is to set targets for performance that employees can control directly. Once a year, managers provide performance ratings that indicate how well employees performed against their targets.

Annual pay raises can range from 0 to 12%, with the amount determined by the performance rating received from the employee's manager. Receiving a 0% raise doesn't necessarily mean the employee's performance was poor, however. Some employees receive no raise because they are already paid the maximum amount allowed for their job. Such employees can receive a lump sum payment of several hundred dollars for excellent performance, instead of a pay raise. The USPS believes that the success of their approach to performance-based pay is due to several things, including the support it has from top-level managers, the use of clear and specific performance targets, rewards that are clearly linked to performance, pay consequences that are large enough to make a difference to employees, and effective communication.[1]▲

THE STRATEGIC IMPORTANCE OF USING PERFORMANCE-BASED PAY

New technologies and changing competitive pressures have required the USPS to repeatedly change its strategies and address new challenges. As USPS's goals and objectives have changed, so have its performance-based pay practices. **Performance-based pay** *recognizes that people working in the same job can differ greatly in terms of the value they contribute to the organization, and it seeks to provide employees with an incentive for maximizing the value they contribute.* In Chapter 10, we described how employers design and implement base pay, that is, wages and salaries. In addition to base pay, most employers offer some form of performance-based pay.

The use of performance-based pay has been increasing steadily in recent years. Its use is up 23% from a decade ago and is likely to keep increasing in the future.[2] Perhaps the most important reason for the increasing popularity of performance-based pay is the belief that it helps organizations achieve their strategic objectives. At the USPS, performance-based pay helped align the goals of employees with those of the company, which was essential to the organization's ability to execute a turnaround. At Lincoln Electric, performance-based pay supports the strategic objective of producing low-cost, high-quality products. For start-up firms, performance-based pay attracts outstanding talent. Although strategic business objectives vary among companies, the principle of using pay to drive performance toward those objectives is applicable to most firms. Exhibit 11.1 illustrates this point.[3]

Supporting Strategic Objectives

Pay for performance helps firms by linking the daily efforts, behaviors, and decisions of employees to strategic objectives.[4] When employees earn rewards for meeting specific performance goals, those goals are more likely to be achieved. Tying pay to performance goals that reflect strategic objectives is a way for employers to communicate what the organization values and boost employee

EXHIBIT 11.1 The Strategic Value of Three Types of Pay			
	Percentage (%) of Employers Who Ranked the Type of Pay as the Most Effective for Achieving the Stated Goal		
	Long-Term Incentives	**Short-Term Bonuses**	**Base Pay**
Controlling costs	53	58	52
Attracting and retaining top performers	67	76	72
Achieving key strategic goals	57	76	35
Aligning participant behavior to desired culture	50	61	39
Aligning participant behavior to business goals	61	76	38
Improving financial performance	55	70	41

motivation. Whether the goals are tied to growth, profit, cost savings, project success, customer service, environmental performance, or innovation, tying pay to achieving such goals usually improves performance in that area.[5]

When the strategic goal is growth, it's reasonable to reward employees for achieving growth targets. A recent study found that firms with long-term impressive growth had a far greater percentage of employees receiving performance-based pay than slower growing firms. Further, faster growing companies were much more likely to evaluate employees' performance using measures such as sales and revenue increases; that is, they use performance measures that were clearly related to organizational growth.[6] Unilever's Path to Growth strategy emphasizes both growth and profits. Its compensation practices reflect the achievement of both, not just one or the other. Large bonuses are rewarded to units that deliver both outstanding growth and profits, providing the motivation needed to achieve both of these strategic objectives.

A recent study identified five firms in the United Kingdom that excelled in customer service. The study found that all five used performance measures of customer service as a basis for pay. One company in the study was Impulse Leisure. They measure customer service in several different ways and then tie employee bonuses and other noncash awards to performance on these measures. Of course, employees are fully aware of the measures used and understand the relationship between performance on those measures and their own compensation.[7]

As discussed in Chapter 9, performance measurement can focus on individual, group, team, department, division, and/or corporate performance. Regardless of the performance measures used, however, they are of questionable value if they don't relate to the firm's strategic objectives. CA, the company formerly known as Computer Associates International, recently restated its earnings because it paid $70 million in unexpected sales commissions. The company stated that it had not appropriately aligned "commission payments with the company's overall performance."[8] Presumably, CA was paying for performance as measured by sales, which did not positively affect its strategic objective of profits.

Managing Labor Costs

Employers have always recognized the importance of rewarding employees for good performance. For the past several decades, most employers have relied on merit pay to achieve this objective. But in the long run, merit pay is very costly: Employees who receive a 10% merit pay raise for outstanding performance in the past year will always be paid at the higher rate, regardless of their future performance. The high cost of merit pay is one reason many companies prefer to offer incentive pay instead of merit raises. Incentives are a form of variable pay.

Cash rewards that are tied to some aspect of performance and paid in lump sums rather than as raises are known as **variable pay**. Once an employee has been hired, the employer's base pay cost is relatively fixed; it does not fluctuate as company profits rise and fall. By comparison, the cost to employers of rewarding employees by giving them a lump sum award can vary from quarter to quarter and from year to year depending on the company's financial situation. When profits are up, more money can be spent to reward employees with lump sum payments. If profits go down, the employer is not obligated to spend money on incentive pay.

Variable pay helps control costs because a reward earned this year does not carry over to future years, as merit raises do. For employees, an important

> 66 *[The shift to performance-based pay] is absolutely gut-wrenching. Some people hate it.* 99
>
> Lisa Weber
> Executive Vice President of
> Human Resources
> Metlife

FAST FACT

A survey by Hewitt Associates revealed that 8 in 10 companies had some form of variable pay in 2006. In 1990 the figure was fewer than 5 in 10.

consequence is that the financial benefits of variable pay for them can be substantially less than merit pay. Another reason employers like variable pay is that it shifts some financial risk to employees. When the company's performance is poor, labor costs go down because less is paid out in compensation. The importance of these cost savings to employers is greatest when large portions of the budget are spent on compensation. In service companies, compensation costs account for up to 80% of the operating budget. Thus, controlling compensation costs and using compensation wisely is a very high priority for banks, hospitals, and other labor-intensive service providers.

Interestingly, although variable pay can cost employees a substantial amount of money over time compared to permanent merit raises, most employees like lump sum bonuses because they get a substantial amount of money all at once. When the reward is paid in a lump sum, it seems to have more impact than when it is paid out as small additions to employees' weekly or monthly paychecks. Thus, employers are able to save money with variable pay, usually without employees getting upset about it.

Attracting, Retaining, and Motivating Talent

Performance-based pay can influence whether applicants apply for a position and whether they accept an offer of employment. By paying for performance, a company signals that it's interested in employees who want to be paid for good performance. This is more likely to attract good rather than poor performers.[9] With variable pay, the best performers reap the greatest rewards, and often their rewards are substantial.

Start-up companies attract top talent while controlling costs by using variable pay. In start-up companies, risk is high, sales growth is slow, and earnings are low, so offering a low base is almost a necessity. To compensate, start-ups typically give large bonuses based on the company's successful performance. For employees who are willing to work hard and don't mind taking the risk, working for a start-up company is attractive because it's possible to become wealthy as the company grows and succeeds.

Once employees have been hired, performance-based pay can influence employee satisfaction and their decisions to stay or leave. Recall from Chapter 10 that perceptions of equity are based on employees' comparisons of their inputs and outcomes relative to those of others. Most employees consider performance to be an input in their equity considerations, and they generally are more satisfied when performance is linked to pay.[10] When high performers believe that they contribute more (inputs) but do not receive proportionately greater rewards (outcomes), they experience feelings of inequity and become dissatisfied. Dissatisfaction, in turn, causes employees to reduce their effort and perhaps look elsewhere for employment; in either case, the organization loses. Not paying for performance is likely to demotivate and alienate the best workers, and they are the employees organizations really want to retain!

Effective performance-based pay creates strong *instrumentality* perceptions among employees. As explained in our discussion of expectancy theory in Chapter 9, instrumentality refers to the belief that your performance actually determines how much you earn. At Lincoln Electric and the United States Postal Service, the instrumentality of performance is very clear. Employees know in advance what formula the company will use to translate their performance into dollar amounts in their paychecks. Expectancy theory also states that the rewards attached to performance must have high *valence* for employees to be motivated by the rewards. At Lincoln Electric, the highest-performing factory workers often earn twice as much as the lowest performers, and the difference is due almost entirely to how people perform in their jobs. In dollar terms, the difference in annual earnings for high versus low performers may be $50,000 or more. For factory workers at Lincoln Electric (and almost anyone else), the valence of $50,000 in earnings is quite high.

PERFORMANCE-BASED PAY WITHIN AN INTEGRATED HRM SYSTEM

No one HR practice accounts for the high levels of motivation and productivity found at companies like Lincoln Electric. The HRM system as a whole produces the desired results. To be effective, performance-based pay practices must fit with other elements of the HRM system and reflect conditions in the external and organizational environments. Exhibit 11.2 shows these linkages and the major choices employers make when designing performance-based pay.

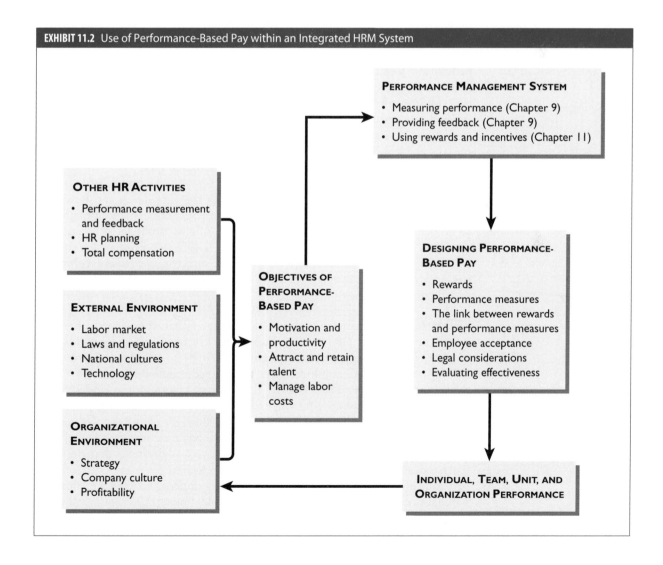

EXHIBIT 11.2 Use of Performance-Based Pay within an Integrated HRM System

PERFORMANCE MANAGEMENT SYSTEM
- Measuring performance (Chapter 9)
- Providing feedback (Chapter 9)
- Using rewards and incentives (Chapter 11)

OTHER HR ACTIVITIES
- Performance measurement and feedback
- HR planning
- Total compensation

EXTERNAL ENVIRONMENT
- Labor market
- Laws and regulations
- National cultures
- Technology

ORGANIZATIONAL ENVIRONMENT
- Strategy
- Company culture
- Profitability

OBJECTIVES OF PERFORMANCE-BASED PAY
- Motivation and productivity
- Attract and retain talent
- Manage labor costs

DESIGNING PERFORMANCE-BASED PAY
- Rewards
- Performance measures
- The link between rewards and performance measures
- Employee acceptance
- Legal considerations
- Evaluating effectiveness

INDIVIDUAL, TEAM, UNIT, AND ORGANIZATION PERFORMANCE

Other HR Activities

After studying Chapters 9 and 10, you can readily see some of the connections between performance-based pay and other HR activities. Here we discuss just three other HR activities to illustrate a few of the many possible connections:

1. Total compensation.
2. Performance measurement and feedback.
3. HR planning.

Total Compensation. As Chapter 10 explained, performance-based pay is one element of total compensation. It supplements base pay and the various benefits and services offered by employers. Recall that the pay mix refers to the way employers use all of these pay elements in combination. At Lincoln Electric, the pay mix includes a large chunk of performance-based pay. In most manufacturing companies, the pay mix includes higher base pay and much less performance-based pay. When choosing an approach to total compensation, a key question is, "What proportions of total pay costs should be spent for pay that is (1) guaranteed to employees in advance (base pay), (2) paid out based on performance, and (3) spent on various benefits and services?" The answer is discussed in more detail later in this chapter.

Performance Measurement and Feedback. For performance-based pay to be effective, it must motivate employees. People are motivated when they believe that their efforts will influence their performance as measured by their employer. Appropriate and valid performance measures help establish strong *expectancy* perceptions. When performance measures are deficient or contaminated, employees are less likely to feel that their efforts directly influence the performance measures used to determine performance-based pay.

Besides valid measures, performance-based pay works best when employees receive frequent feedback telling them how they are doing and how they can improve. At Lincoln Electric, employees receive feedback about quality as soon as a customer notifies the company of a quality problem. When quality problems arise, the employee who produced a defective product is required to fix the problem. For sales reps at Avon, the direct sales cosmetic company, feedback is even more straightforward; employees know at the end of each day exactly how much they sold.

HR Planning. Performance-based pay at Lincoln is aligned well with the company's approach to HR staffing plans. The Lincoln philosophy holds that employers should help employees achieve their personal goals by providing employment security. Employees are guaranteed employment security after three years of service. The company has not had layoffs in the United States since 1948. At Lincoln, employment security is possible because employees agree to reduce their work schedules during slow times and work overtime during the busiest times. Its performance-based pay practices are aligned with its philosophy of employment security. Employees understand that the company needs to sell the products employees produce to cover the costs of their generous bonuses. Thus, if orders decline, they understand that the company will have to cut production to remain profitable. Lower production will mean less pay, but it won't mean layoffs. Employment security is possible because Lincoln's pay practices allow the company to reduce production without laying off employees.

Avon, the cosmetics company, offers another example of how performance-based pay can influence staffing plans. Avon introduced new pay practices that rewarded sales reps not only for their own sales, but also for the sales made by the reps whom they recruited and trained. Soon the company found that many of the reps were recruiting and training new reps—that is, they were taking on more management responsibilities that previously had been done by district sales managers. When the reps began doing most of the recruiting and training, Avon was able to reduce the number of district sales managers by 20%.[11]

Organizational Environment

USPS, Unilever, and Lincoln all illustrate how companies use performance-based pay to execute their business strategies. Perhaps less apparent is the importance of aligning the design of performance-based pay with the company's culture. At Lincoln Electric, a culture of involvement, participation, and teamwork all support the use of performance-based pay. Since 1914, an elected Advisory Board has ensured that all employees have direct and open communication with senior managers. Through their participation and involvement in various aspects of the company's management activities, employees learn about the needs of the business and its implications for their pay. At the same time, the management team stays in touch with the concerns of employees.

Some companies are using performance-based pay to develop diversity-friendly company cultures. Examples of this use of performance-based pay are described in the feature "Managing a Multicultural Workforce: Rewarding Managers Who Achieve Diversity Goals."[12]

MANAGING A MULTICULTURAL WORKFORCE
Rewarding Managers Who Achieve Diversity Goals

According to a study by the Society for Human Resource Management, most *Fortune* 500 companies either do not measure performance against diversity goals or do measure it but do not use compensation to reward success. Apparently, these organizations simply hope that the use of fair hiring methods and sending managers to diversity training will produce a truly multicultural organization. But about 30% of the *Fortune* 500 companies (and about 10% of firms in general) take a more controversial approach: They pay managers to achieve diversity objectives.

Tenneco, the oil company, was one of the mavericks. Back in the mid-1980s, Tenneco was among the first organizations to link a portion of managers' bonuses to how many women and people of color they hired and moved up the ladder. The number of professional women and people of color in the company soon doubled. At the same time, some managers lost out when it came time for bonuses: "We've all had some of our bonus subtracted because of this program," explained one human resource manager. Deloitte, the big public accounting firm, also uses performance-based pay to achieve diversity goals. Within two years of tying managers' bonuses to increasing the rate at which women were promoted, the company experienced a 50% increase in the number of women partners in the firm. At Motorola, a belief in the strategic importance of managing diversity is reflected in the CEO's bonus formula, which includes goals for managing diversity, EEO, and affirmative action.

Managers who are perfectly comfortable using performance-based pay to achieve other types of strategic objectives—such as increasing ROI and improving customer satisfaction—often balk at this practice. For some critics, the practice seems misguided because it ties pay to something other than improved financial performance. Companies that link bonuses to effective diversity management are saying they value this objective even if the financial benefits of diversity can't be directly measured.

External Environment

Throughout this chapter, we emphasize the importance of designing performance-based pay that fits the organizational environment, especially its corporate culture and business strategy. It is worth noting, however, that the external environment also influences the use of performance-based pay. Throughout the past century, the shifting popularity of different approaches to performance-based pay has reflected changes in economic conditions, fluctuations in union activity, and the enactment of various laws and regulations. For global organizations, national differences in culture and other external forces also influence the design of performance-based pay.

One environmental factor that has been particularly important in pay-for-performance applications is the available technology. As described in Chapter 9, technology has made it easier for employers to track and measure the performance of some employees. Performance-based pay practices are only as good as the performance measures used. Technological improvements in performance measurement have increased the popularity of performance-based pay by making it easier to administer. Measures of performance such as delivery time for shipped products, computerized diagnostics of auto repairs, and instantaneous online customer satisfaction surveys are more accurate thanks to improved technology. Recent improvements in technology have helped integrate performance measurements and rewards so that the link is clear, consistent, and well communicated.[13]

THE HR TRIAD

Designing and administering performance-based pay requires close cooperation among all players in the HR Triad. In particular, line managers and HR professionals must work together to ensure that performance-based pay practices support the overall strategic objectives of the organization, as well as the specific strategic goals of small units and teams within the organization.

Changes in strategic objectives often cause managers to scrutinize and redesign their compensation practices. In many organizations, such efforts represent major changes in its culture. Thus, for many line managers and HR professionals, the roles and responsibilities associated with performance-based pay include those associated with managing organizational change, as described in Chapter 3.

As is true for any component of the HRM system, the ultimate effectiveness of any performance-based pay depends on employee understanding and acceptance. Seeking and using the input of the employees who will be affected by performance-based pay is an important responsibility of line managers and HR professionals. Even when employees participate in the design, however, the introduction of new performance-based pay practices often has unintended consequences, which can be disruptive if not detected quickly. Thus, continuous monitoring should be kept up to assess employee satisfaction, key behaviors, and performance results. These issues are summarized in the feature "The HR Triad: Roles and Responsibilities for Using Performance-Based Pay to Achieve Strategic Objectives."

DESIGN CHOICES FOR PERFORMANCE-BASED PAY

Although external factors provide some constraints on how employers use performance-based pay, they have a great deal of latitude in designing practices to fit their organizations. Key design choices are the type of rewards, the performance measures, and the means for linking them. The USPS, Avon, and

LINE MANAGERS	HR PROFESSIONALS	EMPLOYEES
• Work with HR professionals to establish the strategic objectives of performance-based pay (PBP). • Work with HR professionals to establish the performance measures to be linked to pay. • Assist with communicating the objectives and administrative procedures for PBP. • Assist HR in monitoring and evaluating PBP as needed. • Understand the many forms of PBP pay available and their strengths and weaknesses; learn the principles of how to use rewards effectively.	• Work with line managers to establish the strategic objectives of PBP. • Work with line managers to establish the performance measures to be linked to pay. • Work with accounting and finance staff to assess the cost implications of PBP. • Monitor the effects of PBP on employee satisfaction, behavior, and results, and recommend revisions to the PBP practices as needed. • Develop and deliver training and communications to ensure that line managers and other employees understand the PBP practices and the reasons for using them.	• Develop a comprehensive understanding of the strategic objectives of PBP. • Make sure you accurately understand the performance measures used to determine your PBP. • Perhaps assist in administering PBP for team members. • Be alert to dysfunctional attempts to "game" PBP, and work to improve PBP so that it reduces dysfunctional behaviors. • Adapt to the needed changes in the PBP practices as they are revised and modified.

Lincoln Electric all use performance-based pay, but the details of their specific practices are quite different. Each company uses an approach that fits its specific situation.

Types of Performance-Based Pay

In this chapter, we discuss four types of performance-based pay: recognition, merit pay, incentive pay, and putting employees' earnings at risk. For each of these, we describe the rewards used, the performance measures used, and how the two are linked. Before describing the details of each approach, however, we first provide a broad overview of the four approaches and the design choices to be made.

Recognition awards *are noncash rewards as an after-the-fact display of appreciation or acknowledgment of an individual's or team's desired behavior, effort, or business result that supports the organization's goals and values.*[14] The rewards tend to be modest, but are likely to include a public acknowledgment of some achievement.

With **merit pay,** *base pay (the pay to be received regardless of performance) is set at a market rate and a small pool of money is allocated for distributing annual raises that reflect the past year's performance of each employee.* The merit raises received by employees in the same job and with the same length of tenure in the job are usually quite small (e.g., 5%). **Incentive pay** *pegs base pay near the market average and employees earn additional monetary compensation for excellent performance.* With incentive pay, there is little downside risk for employees and there is more upside potential. The value of an excellent performer's incentive pay in a given year (e.g., 10–20%) is greater than the size of a typical merit payment. With incentive pay, high performers earn more but no permanent adjustment is made to an employee's base pay.

With **earnings-at-risk pay**, *base pay is set below the market average and a large portion of total earnings are paid based on performance.* The lower base pay means that employees must earn their way back to the average market rate through their performance. Thus, employees face some downside risk; they will earn significantly less than the market average if they perform poorly. Offsetting this risk is an opportunity to earn much more than the market average.

The typical features of the four types of performance-based pay are illustrated in Exhibit 11.3.

Rewards

Employees are not likely to strive to achieve rewards that don't matter to them. As stated by expectancy theory, rewards influence effort when they have a high value. As employers make decisions about the form, size, and timing of rewards, a guiding principle is to offer rewards valued by employees.

Which Rewards to Offer? Rewards for performance can be of many types, ranging from a feeling of personal satisfaction, to public recognition and small tokens, all the way to substantial monetary payments and stock ownership. Monetary rewards include cash and rewards that have a cash value such as small (gift certificates) and large prizes (e.g., all-expenses-paid vacations), direct stock awards, or stock options. The terms *performance-based pay and incentive pay* are generally *not* used to refer to rewards that consist mostly of nonmonetary rewards such as social recognition. However, no clear lines separate social rewards from those that are primarily monetary. Recent research indicates

---

EXHIBIT 11.3 Performance-Based Pay under Recognition, Merit, Incentive, and Earnings-at-Risk Pay Plans

Rewards	Recognition Plans	Merit Plans	Incentive Plans	Earnings-at-Risk Plans
Form	Noncash	Raises	Monetary	Monetary
Size	Modest	Up to 12%	Up to 100%	Limitless
Eligibility	All	Nonmanagers	All, higher-level employees	Sales, higher-level employees
Timing	Shortly after event	Yearly	Quarterly to yearly	From pay period length to the long term
Base pay level	Market	Depends on performance	Market	Below market
Total pay level	Market	Depends on performance	Market or above	Depends on performance
Employee risk	Low	Low	Medium	High
Performance Measure				
Form	Milestones, outstanding event	Supervisor's appraisal	Objective measure	Objective measure
Level	Individual, group	Individual	Individual to organization	Individual to organization
Components	Single	Depends on appraisal	Single or multiple	Single
Time frame	Varies	Year	Varies	Varies
Linking Mechanism	Policy or judgment	Merit matrix	Formula	Formula

that nonmonetary rewards may be as effective as monetary rewards in certain situations, but may not affect outcomes as quickly as monetary rewards.[15]

Because different employees value different rewards, some companies are introducing choice into their performance-based pay practices. For example, GeoEngineers, Inc., a consulting engineering firm in Redmond, Washington, lets its employees choose between cash rewards and time off.[16] This allows employees to choose the reward of greater value to them.

> **"** *I don't think there's a one-size-fits-all reward program out there that's going to work.* **"**
>
> *Susan Richards*
> *Buck Consultants*

How Big Is the Reward? Companies clearly make different decisions when choosing the mix of base pay and incentives to offer. Even within the same company, employees in different jobs usually have different percentages of their total pay coming from incentive pay. The general pattern is that proportionately more incentive pay is used for employees higher in the hierarchy. Exhibit 11.4 illustrates this pattern.

Many organizations offer several types of rewards. For example, a salesperson might be able to earn a 5% bonus based on total sales plus a 3% bonus based on customer service. It is typical for employers to offer different rewards tied to three, four, or even five different performance measures.[17] Using too many smaller rewards has some disadvantages, however. With so many rewards, no single reward matters very much; so employees are likely to focus on the aspects of performance they think are easiest.[18] Also, if there is too much complexity, fewer employees are likely to understand the details, thus reducing its effectiveness.

Valassis Communications, a marketing services firm, is an example of a company that offers several types of rewards. Valassis management views its key to success as having a fun culture in which goal-oriented individuals and teams are rewarded for achieving their goals in multiple ways. Supporting this culture is total compensation that includes profit sharing, stock purchases, "champion pay" to reward outstanding achievements, and recognition awards. Valassis uses a variety of rewards to create a performance culture where employees enjoy coming to work and are eager to brag about their employer in their community.

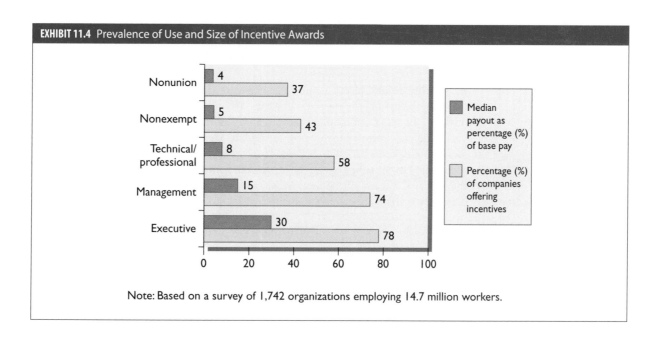

EXHIBIT 11.4 Prevalence of Use and Size of Incentive Awards

Note: Based on a survey of 1,742 organizations employing 14.7 million workers.

Who Gets the Reward? Usually, not all employees are able to receive all the rewards an employee offers. *The rules used to determine which employees are covered by the various pay practices are called* **eligibility rules**. Many of the ongoing changes in the use of performance-based pay reflect changes in the eligibility rules used by employers rather than the introduction of truly new forms of pay. When companywide profit sharing is adopted, for example, the change usually involves going from a situation in which only a limited pool of employees share the profits (top-level executives) to making all employees eligible to receive this form of pay. The same is true for other forms of performance-based pay, such as bonuses and stock options.

Whether employees are eligible for a particular reward is usually related to the employees' line-of-sight. **Line-of-sight** *is a term managers often use to refer to the amount of influence an employee has on a performance measure.* It is very similar to the concept of expectancy described in Chapter 9. Generally, the better an employee's line-of-sight for a performance measure, the more likely he or she is to be eligible for the related rewards. For employees working in jobs where individual efforts are the primary determinants of their performance, it is appropriate to base rewards on individual performance. Team rewards work well when they are tied to success in meeting team goals. For executives who are responsible for the performance of an entire business unit, companywide measures may be appropriate. Factors that affect the level of aggregation of the performance measure are discussed later in this chapter.

The organization's strategic objectives also influence eligibility. Employers use rewards to communicate corporate values and establish the desired culture. For example, to create a sense of ownership and camaraderie, some organizations offer profit sharing and stock grants to all employees. The line-of-sight may be poor for many of the eligible employees because their job performance seems to have such a small consequence for the bottom line. Thus, these practices may not be effective in motivating employees to work hard. But if the purpose of making all employees eligible is to establish a sense of ownership and camaraderie, the rewards may nevertheless be effective in achieving the strategic objectives. Resource Interactive gives each of its employees one share of stock of every firm that's a customer of theirs. The stock isn't given to provide a reward for employees who help increase the share price of their customers, but to signal to employees that the firm values its customers.[19]

When Is the Reward Given? Generally speaking, the more quickly rewards follow desirable behavior, the more potent they are in evoking subsequent desirable behavior.[20] In most companies, incentive pay is received from several weeks to a year after the performance being rewarded. Delayed rewards may not work in increasing desired behavior because the employee doesn't see an immediate consequence. On the other hand, the longer the company delays paying the incentive, the longer it has use of the money. Also, by delaying the payment of rewards, the company is less likely to reward employees who are about to leave.

Performance Measures

Valid, transparent, and accepted performance measurements are central to any effort to link pay to performance. The practice of linking pay to performance can quickly highlight and exacerbate any flaws in an organization's performance measurement practices. Organizations must make a number of decisions when choosing performance measures to use for performance-based pay. Here we focus on choices about the measure's form, level, components, and time frame.

What Gets Measured? Firms have a large range of choices when deciding what measures pay should be tied to. The one sure thing we know about performance-based pay is that employees will focus on the performance measures used to determine their pay—sometimes to the detriment of the organization. A telecommunication firm offered bonuses to call center employees based on the length of their calls. Managers thought shorter calls were an indication of more efficient performance. Employees reduced the call times, as expected. But they did it by giving out incorrect information just to end the calls quickly.[21] When choosing performance measures to use for performance-based pay, the organization's strategy, the quality of the measures, and the behavior desired by the organization should all be considered.

As discussed throughout this book, the organization's strategy and related goals should influence important HR decisions. Whether the organization desires creativity, innovation, profits, growth, or something else, the performance measures used should reflect the purpose of giving rewards. If the organization is trying to grow through outstanding customer service, then measures of both growth and customer service would be appropriate. When Continental Airlines set out to improve customer service, it offered a $100 quarterly bonus to every employee if the airline achieved 80% on-time performance.[22] It soon became one of the top-ranked airlines in on-time performance.

To be sure employees buy in, performance-based pay should be linked only to measures of the highest quality. If individual performance can be measured only with subjective appraisals, it may not be appropriate to tie performance-based pay to individual performance. The more subjective the performance measure is, the less likely it is that employees who receive a low rating will accept the measure as valid. Usually, more objective performance measures can be obtained when performance is measured at higher levels of aggregation, such as the team or strategic business unit. Such higher-level measures also tend to be seen as more relevant to business objectives.[23]

The behaviors that employers want from their employees also drive the choice of performance measures. Nordstrom's managers want their salespeople to behave like entrepreneurs; so they use individual incentive pay to stimulate competition and increase performance pressures. If individual incentive pay pits employees against each other, information sharing and other forms of coworker support may be reduced.[24] In some contexts, this may not be a problem, but usually cooperation is beneficial and direct competition is dysfunctional. Employers strive to find measures that promote positive behaviors, while not encouraging undesirable ones.

Level of Aggregation. Should rewards be based on the performance of an individual, a work team, a division, or the business as a whole? Merit pay and commissions usually tie pay to individual performance. At many companies, team performance is the basis for giving rewards. With profit sharing, the rewards employees receive depend on the performance of the company as a whole.

Higher-level measures such as division or organizational performance are more likely to directly relate to a firm's strategies, be more objective, and be more valid.[25] However, they are less likely to provide a clear line-of-sight, reducing their effect on employee behaviors. Team-based incentives are proving to be quite effective at many companies, perhaps because the midlevel of aggregation can avoid the problems that come with individual measures (such as competition among employees and subjectivity), while clearly connecting to strategic objectives and providing a clear line-of-sight. As Exhibit 11.5 reveals,

> " *If you can't measure it, you can't manage it, and if you can't do either, you sure as heck shouldn't pay for it.* "
>
> *Steven J. Berman*
> *Managing Director*
> *PricewaterhouseCoopers*

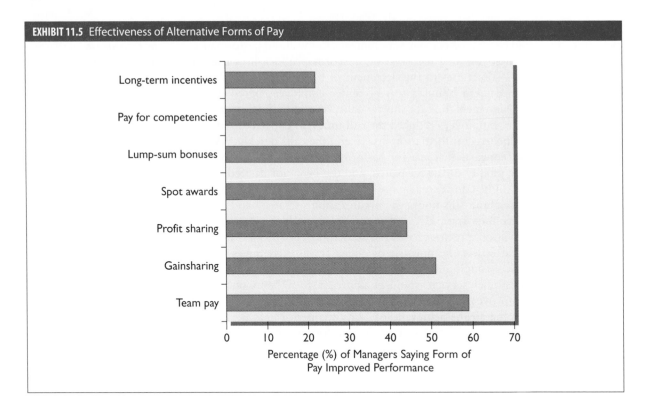

EXHIBIT 11.5 Effectiveness of Alternative Forms of Pay

team-based pay was consistently viewed as improving performance, while other approaches showed mixed results.[26]

Multiple Measures. As we noted earlier, some employers use multiple performance measures as the basis for rewards. Using multiple measures can make up for the weaknesses of any single measure and help prevent employees from ignoring important aspects of their job. In recent years, the use of the balanced scorecard approach to measuring organizational performance has put the spotlight on precisely this issue. Proponents of balanced scorecards argue that organizations should monitor their performance using measures that reflect performance in four domains: finances, customers, operations (internal processes), and employees (learning and development).[27] But when it comes to offering incentives for performance in these four domains, financial performance is the most frequently used performance metric—by far! Exhibit 11.6 shows the results of a survey of 1,742 organizations conducted by Mercer HR Consulting.[28] What do *you* think explains the results of this survey?

When it comes to paying for performance, many companies have relied heavily on financial performance measures while ignoring other performance indicators that reflect the perspectives of employees, customers, and other strategic partners. The result is a mismatch between the incentives that influence how employees behave and the company's effectiveness in the long run.[29]

Time Frame of the Measure. Finding the appropriate balance between rewarding for current performance versus rewarding for long-term performance is a difficult balancing act. Many critics of performance-based pay point to this as a common problem. Traditional commissions focus the attention of a sales staff on the short-term objective of selling goods and services, and do nothing

EXHIBIT 11.6 Metrics for Short-Term Incentives

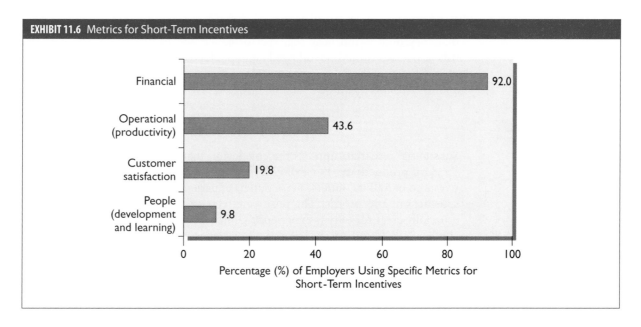

Percentage (%) of Employers Using Specific Metrics for
Short-Term Incentives

to ensure that the customer is satisfied with the purchase. Yet building customer loyalty and repeat business are important strategic objectives for most organizations. That's why performance-based pay for sales organizations increasingly includes measures of customer satisfaction.[30] Using multiple measures is one way to help employees achieve short- and long-term objectives.

As companies consider paying for knowledge or skill acquisition, they come face to face with the question of how much value they should place on performance in the current job versus behaviors that prepare employees for future jobs. Motorola discovered this conflict when it introduced pay for developing reading and mathematical skills. Team members resented it when their colleagues disappeared to school for weeks, at full pay, leaving the teams weaker. The workers complained about the mixed message they were getting and the conflict between self-development and teamwork.[31]

Linking Performance to Rewards

If the link between performance and rewards is not clear, performance-based pay won't work. The strength of the link between performance and rewards is captured by the concept of *instrumentality* in expectancy theory. When the rewards employees receive are influenced heavily by factors other than their performance, perceptions of instrumentality suffer, which reduces motivation. Imagine that you work for State University, where merit raises are used to reward performance. Usually, better performers get bigger raises, but the sizes of those raises depend on the financial condition of the university, which in turn depends on funding from the state legislature and student enrollments. In some years, the university budget may be so tight that it can afford to give raises that average only 1%; there are even years when no one gets any raise at all due to budget problems. This scenario is not unusual in state-funded universities. When raises are small and when the best performers receive raises that are nearly identical to average and poor performers, employee motivation is likely to suffer unless other valued outcomes are clearly provided.

For performance-based pay to work, there must be a strong link between rewards and performance measures, and employees must know about it. Clear

> **" It's the underlying philosophy which is the key thing. Three years ago we paid bonuses on sales. Then we moved to profit. Now we're looking for something which more accurately reflects the shareholder's position. "**
>
> *Andrew Higgins*
> *Finance Director*
> *Burton (a U.K. retailer)*

policies help. Policies should be communicated to employees in advance, so that they understand how their performance will be rewarded. Once established, policies should be followed and not changed before rewards are distributed. Changing the rules in the middle of the game is frustrating to employees, and it's considered unfair.

IMPLEMENTATION ISSUES

Substantial research supports the conclusion that performance-based pay can improve productivity. For example, when a major retailer introduced incentives into of half its outlets, those outlets experienced increased sales, customer satisfaction, and profits. The positive effects of performance-based pay were especially great for outlets experiencing intense competition.[32] Numerous other studies have found similar results. However, research also shows that under some conditions, performance-based pay has no effects or even has detrimental effects.[33] Results from these latter studies serve as ammunition for critics of performance-based pay.

Compensation specialist Alfie Kohn has been a particularly vocal critic, stating that "any incentive or pay-for-performance system tends to make people less enthusiastic about their work and therefore less likely to approach it with a commitment to excellence." Although it has been widely publicized, Kohn's assertion is not consistent with the findings of empirical research. While it's true that performance-based pay does not always improve performance, the research indicates that ineffective use of rewards is often due to poor design and implementation, not to negative psychological consequences of performance-based pay.[34]

We've already discussed how the design choices of rewards, measures, and links relate to the effectiveness of performance-based pay. Issues such as employee acceptance, legality, and evaluation of the practices also can influence the long-term success of performance-based pay, as we explain next.

Gaining Employee Acceptance

Employee opposition can be a major obstacle to the successful implementation of performance-based pay, especially pay practices that put earnings at risk. Several conditions that improve employee acceptance and thus the effectiveness of incentive pay are shown in Exhibit 11.7.[35] Particularly important for

> 66 **With better understanding comes better support. A good rule of thumb is to communicate incentive plans two to three times as often as you pay them out.** 99
>
> *Mark Stiffler*
> *Chief Executive Officer and*
> *President*
> *Synygy*

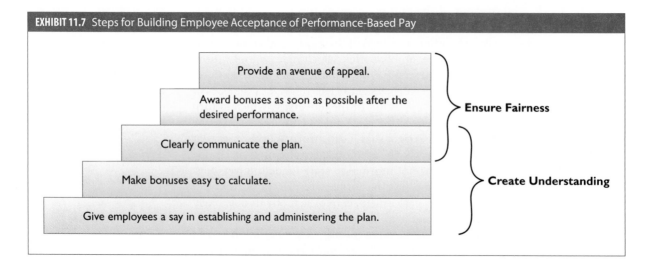

EXHIBIT 11.7 Steps for Building Employee Acceptance of Performance-Based Pay

success is effective communication, which can dispel employees' fears, enhance their trust, and improve their understanding of how performance-based pay may affect their future earnings.

For employers who use an intranet to communicate with employees about compensation and benefits, many convenient software tools can be used to improve employees' understanding of how their income might be affected. Towers Perrin, a consulting firm with expertise in designing compensation practices, recommends using software that allows employees to easily calculate and recalculate estimates of their likely annual income as often as they wish. This can be especially useful for employees who are eligible to receive (or not receive) large bonuses depending on the fluctuating performance of the firm. Sophisticated software makes it possible for employees to calculate their bonuses under various "what-if" scenarios, so that they see the earnings implications of changes in their performance and changes in the firm's performance.[36]

Legal Considerations

Even otherwise successful pay practices will be considered ineffective if they lead to large lawsuits, huge fines, and a damaged corporate reputation. Avoiding unfair discrimination and obeying relevant tax laws are particularly important.

Discrimination. Under Title VII of the Civil Rights Act and the Equal Pay Act, a supervisor may be charged with unlawful discrimination by an employee in a protected group who believes that a pay raise, bonus, or other monetary reward was denied on a basis not related to performance. Such problems are most likely to arise when performance appraisals are subjective and when the size of rewards given is left to managerial discretion rather than computed by a fixed formula.[37]

Data showing persistent pay differences between men and women and among employees from differing ethnic backgrounds lead many people to believe that unfair pay discrimination persists in many organizations today. Unfair pay discrimination is a global phenomenon.[38] The documented pay differences among demographic groups can be partly explained by years in the labor market, education, experience, and performance, but such explanations to do not fully account for differences in the earnings of men versus women and among ethnic groups.[39] Discrimination also seems to be part of the explanation. When awarding performance-based pay, applying the same decision rules to all employees is essential and is one way to reduce unfair discrimination.[40]

Taxation and Accounting Rules. Taxation and accounting rules also are worthy of some comment, although a detailed discussion is beyond the scope of this book. Changes in taxation and accounting rules can dramatically alter the methods companies use to administer performance-based pay. For example, since 2005, the Financial Accounting Standards Board (FASB) has required companies to treat stock options as an expense on their income statements. This has substantially reduced the attractiveness of stock options to companies because they now directly reduce earnings. Companies quickly reacted to the new rule: In place of stock options, many now offer other types of long-term incentives, such as time-vested restricted stock grants, performance shares, or stock appreciation rights instead of stock options.[41] These will be discussed later in the chapter.

Tax laws that affect the value of financial rewards to employees also influence how firms pay for performance. When employers spend money on

FAST FACT

Employers may prorate the production-based bonus of an employee who takes a leave under the Family and Medical Leave Act. (Sommer v. Vanguard Group, 3rd Cir., No 05-4034, August 24, 2006)

EXHIBIT 11.8 Indicators Used to Evaluate the Effectiveness of Performance-Based Pay		
High Popularity	**Moderate Popularity**	**Low Popularity**
Revenues	Labor costs	Informal opinions of employees
Employee retention	Employee productivity	Ability to recruit
	Profits	
	Employee surveys	
	Informal opinions of leaders	

pay, they want the money to go to their employees, not to the government. So, when tax rates for long-term capital gains are low relative to tax rates for ordinary income, stock options become more popular. But when the tax rates for both types of payments are the same, cash becomes more popular. Laws that require taxes to be paid at the time a stock option is granted—as is true in Norway—also discourage the use of stock as a form of reward; laws that defer taxation until the option is exercised have the opposite effect.

Evaluating Effectiveness

Performance-based pay practices should be closely monitored and evaluated to identify any problems. Even well designed practices can cause unexpected problems that need to be fixed. When USPS introduced group incentives that tied pay to team performance, it found that the financial performance measures used were too complex and employees couldn't understand them. To fix the problems, USPS developed new measures of individual performance and made sure employees could see how their individual performance was related to organizational goals.

Some of the indicators organizations use to evaluate pay practices are shown in Exhibit 11.8.[42] Revenues and employee retention are the most popular indicators. The same survey found that successful firms were three times more likely to formally evaluate their pay practices than less successful firms.

When the effectiveness indicators reveal problems, the sources must be investigated. Employee surveys and interviews can help identify specific weaknesses. Although it is not shown in Exhibit 11.8, a few employers use return on investment (ROI) to evaluate their reward practices. The ROI for rewards can be difficult to calculate, but showing a positive return on money invested in compensation provides powerful evidence of the effectiveness of pay practices.[43]

> " *Measuring incentive plan ROI is not as complicated as it sounds; you measure what you pay out and what you get in, and if there is a profit, it is a good plan.* "
>
> *Adrienne Giannone*
> *Chief Executive Officer*
> *Edge Electronics*

6
LEARNING GOAL

> " *I try to remember that people—good, intelligent, capable people—may actually need day-to-day praise and thanks for the job they do.* "
>
> *John Ball*
> *Service Training Manager*
> *Honda Motor Company*
> *United States*

RECOGNITION AWARDS

Recognition provides employees with something most of them want—a showing of appreciation—at a modest cost, which makes them very popular. Nine out of ten organizations offer recognition awards, and half are considering adding new awards in the near future. The most common reasons for offering recognition awards are creating a positive work environment, motivating high performance, and reinforcing desired behaviors. Exhibit 11.9 shows the common goals of recognition awards along with the percentage of firms that listed them.[44]

The many different types of recognition awards can be generally categorized by the "performance" measure used. Length-of-service is the most popular such measure (used by 89% of employers). Length-of-service awards recognize seniority milestones such as 10 years of service, 20 years of service,

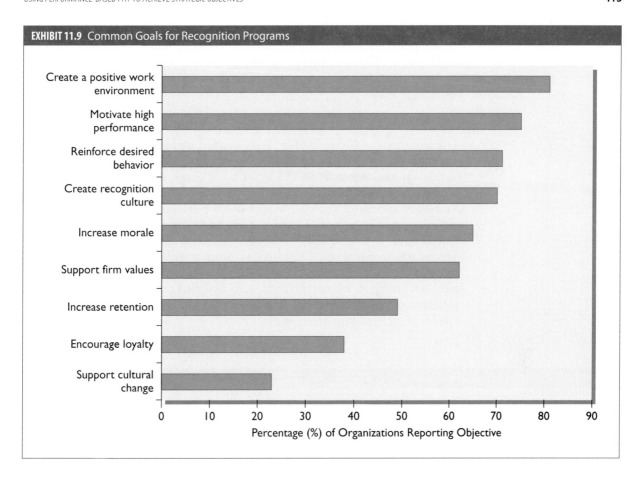

EXHIBIT 11.9 Common Goals for Recognition Programs

and so on. Awards for exceptional performance (offered by 88% of employers) are popular as well. Also known as spot awards, they reward employees for performance above and beyond expectations. Following spot awards in popularity are recognition awards for sales performance, retirement, and employees' suggestions.

Spot Awards

Spot awards *are granted on the spot to recognize employees for performing beyond the call of duty.* When spot awards are designed well, they focus attention on core values and business objectives. Typically, recipients are nominated by supervisors (and sometimes by peers) to receive recognition awards such as small gifts, company merchandise, dinner certificates, or even cash. The rationale behind spot awards is to recognize and reward employees instantly for great performance, which strengthens the link between performance and rewards. Using spot awards can be risky, however. The biggest challenge lies at the foundation of performance-based pay: measuring performance. When giving spot bonuses, managers often are free to use their own idiosyncratic criteria. Training can help prevent this.[45]

When giving spot awards, one challenge is awarding employees fairly and avoiding the potential resentment that can arise among employees who don't receive them. One way to reduce the possibility of resentment is to present spot awards to an entire team for exceptional group performance.

> **If your company creates a culture of recognition—one where people are being recognized and appreciated regularly—employees will want to work there.**
>
> *Peter Hart*
> *Chief Executive Officer*
> *Rideau Recognition Solutions*

Data I/O Corporation, an electronics manufacturing company in Redmond, Washington, awarded all members of a computer-aided electronics software development team—including engineers, technical writers, shippers, and quality assurance personnel—$60 dinner certificates when the product was successfully released.

Awards for Suggestions

To encourage employees to offer their ideas for improvement, many companies use suggestion systems and provide awards for the best suggestions. According to the National Association of Suggestion Systems, its 900 members received nearly 1 million suggestions from their employees, resulting in savings of over $2 billion annually. Crowley Maritime Corporation's Ship Us an Idea is a typical suggestion system. Crowley receives an average of 20 suggestions per month from its 1,000 employees. Employees with the best ideas earn between $50 and $150 for them. They may earn up to 10% of the cost savings for significant ideas. A presidential award of $1,000 is given annually for the best idea. According to Moon Hui Kim, who designed the Ship Us an Idea award program, the value of the suggestions is far greater than the $6,000 to $10,000 annual program administration costs.[46]

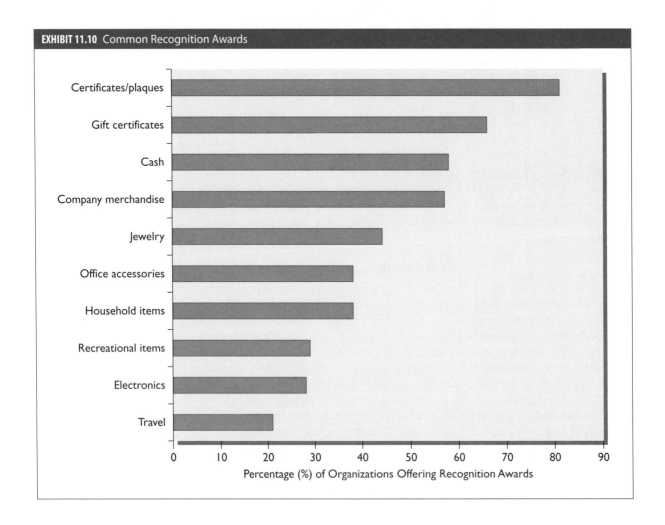

EXHIBIT 11.10 Common Recognition Awards

Percentage (%) of Organizations Offering Recognition Awards

Multiple Awards

Eligibility for recognition awards can be companywide or department specific. Most firms use a number of different types of recognition awards, with some being department specific and others being companywide. Intuit, headquartered in Silicon Valley, is the maker of well-known software programs such as Quicken and TurboTax. But one program you may not have heard about is the company's Thanks Program. Giving out small awards is part of every manager's job. The Thanks Program includes multiple types of recognition awards. Some employees get awards for going beyond the call of duty to help out their colleagues. Some get awards for making suggestions that reduce bureaucracy. Some get awards for technical programming achievements or even for outstanding service to the community.[47]

Unlike other approaches to performance-based pay, recognition awards usually provide public recognition for employees' achievements, along with modest gifts to symbolize the company's appreciation. The awards given by Intuit include gift certificates to restaurants, movie tickets, written thank-you notes, and a night on the town. The awards at Data I/O Corporation include recognition plaques, mugs, T-shirts, pen sets, and employee of the month awards, which come with a parking place by the front door, an engraved plaque, and verbal acknowledgment in a company meeting.

Exhibit 11.10 shows the percentage of firms that use a variety of recognition awards.[48] Note that certificates and plaques are the most popular recognition awards. The second most popular are gift certificates/gift cards, which are most effective when tailored to each individual employee.[49]

Most employers offer recognition awards along with other forms of performance-based pay that provide more substantial monetary compensation. That's what Rackspace does, as described in the feature "Managing with Metrics: Rackspace Rewards Fanatical Customer Service."[50]

FAST FACT

The most popular gift certificates given as recognition awards are for restaurants.

MANAGING WITH METRICS
Rackspace Rewards Fanatical Customer Service

Located in San Antonio, Texas, Rackspace is a Web-hosting company that manages Web sites for clients such as e-tailers, online ad agencies, and game sites. In this business, technical tasks make up a large part of the staff members' jobs, but good customer relations are important too. When the company realized that employees were not as customer friendly as they needed to be, they restructured the staff into customer-focused teams, introduced some simple new rules (e.g., you can be fired for criticizing a customer), and introduced new incentives. One new incentive is the Straightjacket Award, which recognizes the employee who is the best example of living the company's new motto of delivering "fanatical" customer support. Employees who win the award wow their customers by being friendly, reliable, and genuinely concerned about understanding the customer's perspective. Monthly bonuses also support fanatical customer service. Each month, employees can earn a bonus of up to 20% of their base pay for excellent team performance. Customer-focused performance metrics include speed in resolving customer problems, percentage of customers who renew or expand their business with Rackspace, and customer referrals. By linking customer service behaviors to both the recognition employees receive and their monthly earnings, Rackspace has created a culture that respects customers and keeps them satisfied. Employees get the message. As one employee put it: "At most companies, these [customer-oriented] policies are just lip service, but that's our bonus you're talking about." Customers get the message too, and they repay Rackspace by giving it more business and referring it to others.

FAST FACT

About 40% of companies boost the size of merit raises in a good financial year, while 45% reduce merit raises in a poor year.

MERIT PAY

Merit pay has been the cornerstone of public and private compensation practices for many years.[51] Merit pay typically ties an employee's performance as measured by the supervisor's appraisal to the employee's yearly raise. Well designed merit pay practices result in top performers earning substantially higher salaries than poor performers. Over time, top performers end up being paid near the top of their pay range and poor performers end up near the bottom of their pay range.

Performance Measures

A major disadvantage of merit pay is that the performance measures used are usually subjective. As described in Chapter 9, many sources of error can influence subjective performance appraisals. Because of biases, rater errors, or other measurement problems, the link between actual performance and rewards may be weak. An employer must have excellent performance appraisals in place for merit pay to be effective.

Rewards

As we have explained, a disadvantage of merit pay is that the reward is typically an increase in salary, which can be expensive for employers. One way employers can reduce the cost of merit pay is to use **lump sum merit,** *which ties performance appraisals to lump sum bonuses rather than to raises.* Exhibit 11.11 compares costs to an employer using lump sum merit pay versus traditional merit raises. The example is of a top-performing employee earning $40,000 a year with performance that justifies additional pay of 8%. Due to compounding, at the end of a decade the employee's base pay would be $86,356 in a typical merit plan versus $40,000 in a lump sum merit plan. For the employee, the traditional merit pay approach means that his or her salary increased 116% in 10 years. Over a decade, the traditional approach paid the employee $193,813 more.

You might think that employees react negatively to the lump sum merit approach because of the long-term earnings losses. This tends not to be the case! Employees are usually happy to get their entire merit pay in a lump sum all at once. Over a period of several years, however, employees begin to see that the

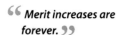 *Merit increases are forever.*

Brad Hill
Tandehill Human Capital

EXHIBIT 11.11 Merit Pay versus Merit Lump Sum

	Merit Pay			Lump Sum Merit		
	Salary	8% Raise	Annual Earnings	Salary	8% Bonus	Annual Earnings
Year 1	$ 40,000	$ 3,200	$ 43,200	$ 40,000	$ 3,200	$ 43,200
Year 2	$ 43,200	$ 3,456	$ 46,656	$ 40,000	$ 3,200	$ 43,200
Year 3	$ 46,656	$ 3,732	$ 50,388	$ 40,000	$ 3,200	$ 43,200
Year 4	$ 50,388	$ 4,031	$ 54,419	$ 40,000	$ 3,200	$ 43,200
Year 5	$ 54,419	$ 4,354	$ 58,773	$ 40,000	$ 3,200	$ 43,200
Year 6	$ 58,773	$ 4,701	$ 63,474	$ 40,000	$ 3,200	$ 43,200
Year 7	$ 63,474	$ 5,078	$ 68,552	$ 40,000	$ 3,200	$ 43,200
Year 8	$ 68,552	$ 5,484	$ 74,036	$ 40,000	$ 3,200	$ 43,200
Year 9	$ 74,036	$ 5,823	$ 79,859	$ 40,000	$ 3,200	$ 43,200
Year 10	$ 79,959	$ 6,397	$ 86,356	$ 40,000	$ 3,200	$ 43,200
Total earnings	$579,457	$46,256	$625,713	$400,000	$32,000	$432,000

real value of their salary is actually dropping due to inflation. To overcome this, some companies use a modified lump sum approach that provides all employees (or at least those with satisfactory performance) with a modest cost of living increase in addition to a merit-based lump sum bonus for the top performers.

Linking Performance to Pay

With merit pay, rewards are linked to performance using a **merit matrix**, *which is a tool used by managers and compensation professionals to determine the merit increase using information about employees' performance ratings.*[52] A single merit matrix can be used for the entire organization, or different departments and units can use a matrix tailored to their situations.

For each possible performance rating score, the merit matrix shows the percentage raise (or the value of the lump sum merit bonus) that should be given to employees. A typical matrix is designed so that poor performers get 0%, average employees who are performing their job satisfactorily get an average raise compared to the market (historically 3–5%), and top performers get the biggest raises (e.g., 10%). The merit matrix is designed to match the available budget. So, if managers follow the matrix, the average merit raise will be equal to the average raise permitted by the merit pay budget.[53] Some managers find it difficult to give a person no raise because it is likely to be upsetting for the employee, but that may be a good thing in the long term. When a financial services company revamped its merit pay practice to make sure that poor performers got nothing, many quit. This "good turnover" led to increased company performance.[54]

Because top performers can get rather large increases (e.g., 10%), merit pay increases can mean that top-performing employees get raises that move them beyond the maximum for their pay grade. To address this problem, most merit matrices also consider an employee's position in the range. Exhibit 11.12 shows a typical merit matrix, in which the raises to be given are based on performance and position in the range.

Employee equity and career progression are accomplished through raises. The merit matrix helps position employees where they belong in the pay grade: satisfactory employees at the middle, poor employees toward the bottom, and exemplary employees toward the top. Top performers who are at the bottom of the range get the biggest raises to move them toward the top quickly. Employees may perceive this approach as unfair because equally performing employees do not get equal percentage increases in pay. Although employee education may help to minimize this problem, a more practical approach is to uncouple performance-based and range-based pay adjustments and award each type of increase separately.

> *You cannot get entrepreneurial results from a communistic approach—that socialistic feeling that everybody gets something.*
>
> Chuck Coonradt
> Chief Executive Officer
> The Game of Work

EXHIBIT 11.12 Example of a Merit Matrix

	Percentage (%) Increase in Annual Salary			
Performance Rating	First Quartile	Second Quartile	Third Quartile	Fourth Quartile
1. Unacceptable	0	0	0	0
2. Below average	2	0	0	0
3. Satisfactory	7	5	3	1
4. Above average	8	6	4	3
5. Superior	10	8	6	4

LEARNING GOAL 8

Critics of merit pay contend that even the best designed merit pay practices are ineffective because of the costs, measurement problems, and lack of distinction between high and low performers. The problem of having too little distinction in the raises given to high and low performers was revealed by a recent survey, which found that the average merit raise was 3.7%, with top performers getting 5.6% and poor performers getting 2.5% on average.[55] Supporters of merit pay contend that the principles behind it are sound, but poor implementation or inadequate performance appraisals are the reasons for ineffectiveness.[56] Yet, even with sound implementation and effective performance appraisals, traditional merit pay raises are a costly approach compared to lump sum merit and other forms of incentive pay.

INCENTIVE PAY

A major difference between merit pay and incentive pay is that merit pay is a permanent pay raise whereas incentive pay is a one-time award. Also, whereas merit pay typically uses subjective performance appraisal ratings, incentive pay is usually based on objective measures. Compared to merit pay, incentive pay often gives managers more latitude to make large distinctions in the rewards given to employees. For the best performers, this provides opportunities to earn relatively large amounts of performance-based pay. In this section we review individual incentives, team incentives, gainsharing, and profit sharing.

Individual Incentives

Individual incentives are among the oldest and most popular form of incentive pay. With this approach, individual standards of performance are established and communicated in advance, and rewards are based on individual results. Unfortunately, objective measures of individual results are frequently hard to come by. Many jobs are so interdependent that it's often difficult to attribute outcomes to any single person. Nevertheless, when a good objective measure of individual performance is available, linking it to incentives tends to improve performance.

Performance Measures. Common performance measures used to award individual incentives include measures of production, sales, quality, customer service, and innovation. The measures depend on the job and on what the organization wants employees to focus on. For example, at some banks, employees can earn extra cash by persuading someone to apply for a credit card (up to $25), consumer loan ($25), or mortgage (up to $75). Medicare uses individual incentives to encourage doctors to offer top-quality medical care. In 2007, Medicare started offering 1.5% bonuses to doctors simply for providing records that can be used to evaluate the quality of care patients receive. Eventually, Medicare will use the quality data to design performance-based pay practices that reward doctors who provide the best-quality care.

Effectiveness. Whatever performance measure is used, tying incentives to it tends to get results. An example is the case of Motorola. New inventions and patents (i.e., intellectual property) are essential to Motorola's success. To encourage inventors, Motorola pays bonuses to employees when a patent application is filed and again when a patent is issued. For inventors receiving their tenth patent, another bonus is awarded. Depending on the company's estimate of the invention's value, these lump sum awards may be in the range of $10,000 to $20,000. Motorola consistently ranks among the top ten companies awarded U.S. patents each year.[57]

As mentioned earlier, two disadvantages of individual incentives is that they tend to increase competition among coworkers and they focus attention on whatever is being measured to the exclusion of other parts of their job. The Internal Revenue Service learned about the latter disadvantage when it offered bonuses to agents who closed audit cases within a specified time frame. The bonus was independent of the quality of the audit or the number of dollars collected. Audits were closed faster, but some people believe that the IRS lost billions of dollars in possible tax receipts because of rushed audits.[58]

Other possible disadvantages to using individual incentives include their inability to work on everybody, increased work for managers who need to solve problems and address complaints, increased administrative burdens for measurement and reward disbursements, and increased communication and training requirements to educate managers and employees.[59]

Types of Individual Incentives. Two common types of individual incentives are piecework plans and standard hour plans. In piecework plans, such as the one used at Lincoln Electric, employees are paid a certain rate for each unit of output. In a **straight piecework plan**, *employees are guaranteed a standard pay rate for each unit.* The standard pay rate is based on the standard output and the base wage rate. For example, if the base pay of a job is $80 a day and the employee can produce at a normal rate 20 units a day, the standard rate may be established at $4 a unit. With a **differential piece-rate plan**, *more than one rate of piecework pay is set for the same job.* Differential piece rates usually are designed to pay more for work that passes a preset threshold level. For example, employees may earn $4 per piece if they complete five or more pieces per hour, but only $3.50 per piece if they complete only four pieces per hour.

A **standard hour plan** *sets a standard time for each unit of production and uses this time unit to determine how much employees are paid.* Tasks are broken down by the amount of time it takes to complete them, which can be determined by historical records, time-and-motion studies, or both. The normal time to perform each task becomes a standard. Employees are paid for the normal time required to complete each task, not the actual time used. If you go into an automobile repair shop, you will probably see a chart indicating the labor rates associated with various types of repair. These reflect the use of standard hour plans. Each rate includes the rate paid to the mechanic who does the work plus the premium charged by the owner of the shop. The rate is fixed regardless of how long it actually takes to do the repair. Thus, the mechanic and the shop owner both have incentives to ensure that the work is completed in a shorter amount of time than that used to set the standard rate.

When used appropriately, piecework and standard hour plans increase individual performance, but like all individual incentives, they can have undesired consequences. Consider what happened when a group of bank processing operators went to a per-item-processed piecework plan. The staff of 12 operators increased the items processed from an average of 980 items per hour to more than 3,000 items per hour. Their take-home pay increased an average of 50% over their former hourly pay. The incentives seemed to be working—until the bank president made a visit to the unit. One operator cut off her conversation with the president after a brief time, telling him that he was costing her money. The president also could see that operators were unwilling to help each other out because doing so reduced their own pay. As in this case, when piece-rate incentives reward individual employees without regard to the consequences for the overall organization, their disadvantages may outweigh any benefits.[60]

Team Incentives

With team incentives, performance goals are tailored specifically to what the work team needs to accomplish. Team pay works best in contexts and cultures where cooperation among employees is necessary and valued.[61]

Advantages. When designed appropriately, team incentives offer several major advantages over individual incentives. First, the mere presence of team members who have some stake in the rewards creates social pressure and evokes more vigorous and persistent behavior than when individuals work alone. Second, the competition among coworkers is replaced by cooperation. Third, the strength of the rewards is increased, since they're now paired with social rewards, such as praise and camaraderie. Fourth, the performance of another group member (usually the high performer) can serve as a model, encouraging other team members to imitate successful behavior.[62] Team incentives have an advantage over unit and companywide incentives in that the line-of-sight to team performance is clearer. This may be why team-based pay is seen as the most effective type of incentive, as shown earlier in Exhibit 11.5.

At Children's Hospital Boston, the accounts receivable department is organized around teams. The feature "Managing Teams: Performance-Based Pay at Children's Hospital Boston" describes how team pay helped improve both employee morale and customer service.

Disadvantages. Team pay has a number of disadvantages. It may produce unintended side effects, such as competition among groups. Such competition may or may not complement goal attainment. When teams need to cooperate with each other, incentives that create team competition should be avoided. Team incentives also involve administrative responsibilities that are at least as great as those associated with individual incentive plans.

MANAGING TEAMS
Performance-Based Pay at Children's Hospital Boston

Prior to introducing team-based pay, morale and productivity were low in the accounts receivable department at Children's Hospital Boston. Employees were struggling to learn how to use a new billing system, and it took more than 100 days to receive payment after bills were sent. The hospital needed to shorten the billing cycle and improve cash flow. To motivate employees and establish a clear line of sight between their own work and the hospital's goals, hospital executives introduced team incentives. Productivity goals were set for the department, and rewards were distributed based on the department's success in achieving the goals. To meet the goals, employees had to work together to process bills efficiently. Employees could earn quarterly bonuses for achieving preset goals. Achieving the "threshold" paid $500 to each employee; achieving the "target" paid $1,000; and achieving "optimal" paid $1,500.

To explain the new pay plan to employees, the financial officer and several other managers from the Patient Financial

Services Department held two meetings with employees. They described the plan, explained why it was being introduced, and showed how it would affect each employee. Employees learned how the time that it took to collect bill payments affected cash flow and how cash flow affected the hospital. They also learned that no one in the department would receive a bonus unless the department as a whole met its targets. To help employees see how they were doing, the department received a weekly progress report. Employees got the message. Employees who weren't carrying their weight felt the heat of peer pressure. Within a year, the average number of days a bill spent in accounts receivable fell from 100 to 75, and then it decreased to about 65. According to Steve Nicholl, director of patient financial services, the team incentives also helped recruitment and retention. "We had been losing our staff to local competitors," he explained. "Now we don't lose them. An HR director just down the street told me, 'I hire and train them, then you take them.'"

Although the line-of-sight with team incentives is greater than with unit or companywide incentives, it may not be as clear as with individual incentives. Bonuses are determined by team performance measures that reflect the efforts of numerous team members. Some employees may not work hard because if the team does well anyway, they can still receive a bonus.[63] In effective teams, social pressure from the team reduces this effect.

Team incentives usually reward all team members equally. Giving different rewards within the team tends to demotivate most team members.[64] However, giving everyone in the team the same reward may create equity problems if team members contributed unequally. A final disadvantage of team pay is that mixing exempt and nonexempt employees in teams creates administrative headaches and complications resulting from overtime issues as specified by the FLSA.

Unit and Companywide Incentives

Incentives tied to unit or companywide performance are easier to relate to the firm's strategic goals, foster greater cooperation among all employees, and help create an ownership mentality in employees. Two of the most popular incentives used at these levels are gainsharing and profit sharing.

Gainsharing. Introduced in 1889, **gainsharing plans** *involve measuring a work unit's costs and productivity, then sharing future gains with employees.* Because gainsharing plans also emphasize the need for continuous improvement, they work well with currently popular quality plans such as Lean Six Sigma.[65] Gainsharing plans are premised on the assumption that employees can help continuously reduce costs and improve productivity by eliminating wasted materials and labor, developing new or better products or services, or working smarter. Typically, gainsharing plans involve all employees in a work unit or firm.

The introduction of gainsharing plans has improved productivity and decreased costs in a variety of settings. Presumably, gainsharing is effective for two reasons: First, the rewards motivate employees to work harder. Second, and more importantly, employees become actively involved in suggesting new ways to work more efficiently.[66] Although gainsharing plans tend to focus on cost savings or productivity gains, they can encompass a broad range of organizational goals and can be tailored to the specific needs of a company.[67] For example, Whole Foods Market gives employees any surpluses between actual payroll spending and what was budgeted, and the Men's Wearhouse pays incentives tied to "shrinkage," the percentage of inventory unaccounted for between audits largely due to theft.[68]

The three most common gainsharing plans are Scanlon, Rucker, and Improshare plans. Scanlon and Rucker plans, developed in the Depression Era, focus on cost savings relative to historical standards. The Scanlon Plan focuses only on labor cost savings, while the Rucker Plan ties incentives to a wide variety of savings. Both plans are appropriate in small, mature firms employing fewer than 500 workers. Because standards are based on past performance, simple and accurate measures of performance are needed. The heavy involvement of all employees requires a culture that is open, trusting, and participative.[69]

Improshare (which stands for improved production through sharing) includes nonproduction workers in the measurement of the organization's productivity and in the distribution of variable pay, realized from cost savings. It has been adopted in a wide array of firms, including service sector firms such as hospitals and financial institutions. Exhibit 11.13 compares the details of the calculations of the Scanlon, Rucker, and ImproShare plans.

> " *Individuals don't accomplish anything, teams do.* "
>
> *The late W. Edwards Deming TQM guru*

FAST FACT

Thanks to gainsharing, operators of Chick-Fil-A fast-food chicken outlets made more than $100,000 a year.

EXHIBIT 11.13 Calculations for Selected Gainsharing Plans

Scanlon Plan Base Ratio

[(Sales Dollars − Returned Goods) + Inventory] ÷ [(Cost of Work and Nonwork Time Paid + Pension + Insurance)]

Rucker Plan Base Ratio

(Cost of All Wages and Benefits) ÷ (Sales Dollar Value of Product − Goods Returned − Supplies, Services, and Material)

Improshare Plan Base Formula

[(Standard Value Hours Earned, Current Period) × (Total Actual Hours Worked, Base Period ÷ Total Standard Value Hours Earned, Base Period)] ÷ [(Total Hours Worked, Current Period)]

Profit Sharing. Introduced first at the Gallatin glasswork factory in New Geneva, Pennsylvania, in 1794, **profit-sharing plans** *include any system under which an employer pays regular employees, or makes available to them, special current or deferred sums based on the profits of the business, in addition to their regular pay.* Profit-sharing plans are designed to pay out incentives when the organization is most able to afford them. The plans fall into three categories.

1. **Current distribution plans** *provide a percentage of profits to be distributed quarterly or annually to employees.*

2. **Deferred distribution plans** *place earnings in an escrow fund for distribution upon retirement, termination, death, or disability.* These are the fastest-growing type of plan owing to tax advantages.[70]

3. **Combined distribution plans** *distribute a portion of profits immediately to employees, setting the remaining amount aside in a designated account.*

Research evidence suggests that firms with profit-sharing plans increase their profits over competitors without the plans and compared to their own previous performance.[71] However, other than sharing profits, these plans often do not have clear strategic objectives. Furthermore, the motivational power of these plans is questionable because employees may not see the relationship between their individual performance and the profitability of the firm. Critics of profit sharing argue that tying pay to achieving more specific strategic objectives is preferable to tying pay directly to profitability.

9
LEARNING GOAL

PAY THAT PUTS EARNINGS AT RISK

Merit and incentive pay usually apply to a large percentage of the workforce. Usually, only employees in particular jobs are paid with the earnings-at-risk approach. Sales personnel and high-level executives frequently have their earnings placed at risk. Because this approach creates so much uncertainty about how much total pay employees are going to receive, it is not for everybody. Employees' risk preferences, career stages, and personalities have all been shown to affect reactions to pay practices that put earnings-at-risk.[72]

Nevertheless, some companies have pushed the notion of at-risk pay throughout the organization. Nucor, a steel mill, is a well-known pioneer of this approach. Factory workers at Nucor's steel mills earn wages set at less than half the typical union rate. At year's end, the company distributes 10% of pretax earnings to employees. Bonuses based on the number of tons of acceptable quality steel produced increase total pay to about 10% more than that of comparable unionized workers. The bonuses reflect company productivity levels, but they also encourage individuals to behave responsibly. Workers who are late lose their bonus for the day; workers who are more than 30 minutes late lose their bonus for the week. Managers at Nucor earn bonuses also. The bonuses of department managers are based on return on plant assets, and those of plant managers are based on return on equity. The rewards seem to work. Compared to many other steel companies, Nucor produces more than twice as much steel per employee.[73]

Arguably, Lincoln Electric's pay practices put employees' earnings at risk, as does any incentive plan that doesn't guarantee earnings near the market average. In other words, earnings-at-risk is a matter of degree. The two most common practices that put considerable amounts of pay at risk are commissions and stock options.

Commissions

Usually, the term **commission** *refers to pay based on a percentage of the sales price of the product.* About two-thirds of all salespeople receive commissions. A key decision in establishing a sales commission plan is the choice of the sales measure. Although total sales and new sales are the most common measures, many others are used. Exhibit 11.14 shows the most common sales measures.[74]

Straight Commission. Under straight commission plans, responsibility for generating an income rests directly with the salesperson. The more sales, the greater the earnings; no sales means no income. When employees accept these as legitimate pay plans, their effect on behavior is enormous. At Nordstrom, where salespeople work entirely on commission, the salespeople earn about twice what they would at a rival's store. Unfortunately, such incentives can be so powerful that they elicit

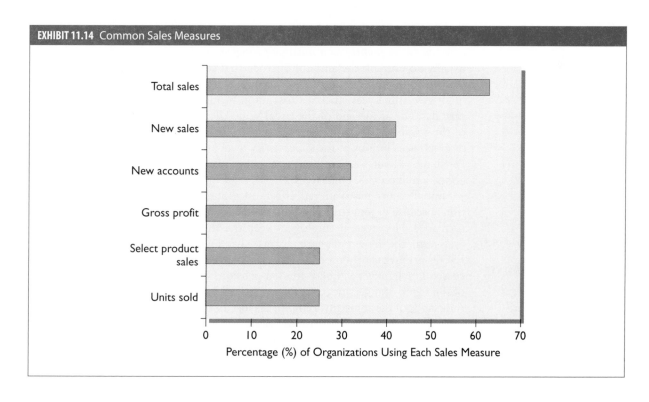

EXHIBIT 11.14 Common Sales Measures

Percentage (%) of Organizations Using Each Sales Measure

unintended behaviors. Best Buy dropped its commission plan because customers didn't like the high-pressure atmosphere it created.[75] Sears Auto Centers in California changed their plan because mechanics were caught making unnecessary repairs on customers' cars to improve their bonuses.

To curb behaviors that negatively affect the organization, organizations tie commissions to several measures. Almost nine out of ten use more than one measure as part of their sales incentive plan, and two-thirds use three or more.[76]

Combination Approach. Because of concerns about the negative effects of straight commission plans, more than half of all sales compensation plans combine base salary and commissions. In setting up a combination approach, the critical question is, "What percentage of total compensation should be salary and what percentage should be commission?" The answer depends on the availability of sales criteria (e.g., sales volume, units sold, product mix, retention of accounts, and number of new accounts) and on the number of nonsales duties in the job. For primary sales jobs, the commission portion of these plans ranges from 20 to 60%, with a 60-to-40 salary-to-commission mix being the most common. For jobs in which the sales function is secondary, the commission portion ranges from 0 to 20%, with a 90-to-10 salary-to-commission mix being the most common.[77]

Stock Ownership

Companies use many different approaches to encourage their employees to own company stock and so take part as an owner of the company. The two main approaches are stock grants, where stock is given to employees, and stock options, where employees may buy future shares at current prices. Like profit sharing, the motivational power of these plans for most employees in large firms is questionable because they may not see the relationship between their individual performance and the firm's share price. Nevertheless, many firms offer them with the belief that stock ownership will lead to beneficial employee reactions.

Stock Grants. **Employee stock ownership plans (ESOPs)** *grant shares of stock to employees, frequently as a means of long-term savings and retirement.* ESOPs usually do not link the amount of stock that can be purchased or the purchase price to individual or group performance indicators. Stock ownership plans often give employees stock awards upon being hired, on their annual anniversary date, or at the end of the fiscal year. UPS has an ESOP. Each year, 15% of the company's pretax profit is used to buy company stock for distribution to employees in jobs at the supervisory level and above. Starbucks, Whirlpool, Pepsi, and about 11,000 other companies also have ESOPs in place, covering about 9 million U.S. employees.[78]

Initially, any motivational effects of grants may be less than of stock options because grants still have some value, regardless of the firm's market performance. However, if employees keep the shares of multiple grants over the long term, the impact of share increases can be substantial. Perhaps that is why ESOPs are frequently used as a means for funding employee pensions. As discussed in Chapter 12, ESOP-funded pensions are risky for employees, because of their lack of diversification. Since the well publicized case of Enron, in which thousands of the company's employees lost all of their retirement money because Enron's stock crashed, the use of ESOPs for pensions is being scrutinized.[79]

Stock appreciation rights (SARs) *grant employees cash or stock awards based on the increase in the stock price over a specified time.* SARs don't cost firms as much as stock grants, because employees receive stock (or cash) only in the amount of stock appreciation. Like stock options, their value depends on

> 66 *The most important thing I ever did was give our partners [employees] bean stock, meaning Starbuck's stock options. That's what sets us apart and gives a higher-quality employee, an employee that cares more.* 99
>
> Howard Schultz
> Chair
> Starbucks

FAST FACT

A survey of nearly 3,000 companies revealed that more than 50% give stock grants to officers and executives, about 25% give them to exempt employees, and fewer than 10% give them to nonexempt employees.

increases in share price. Historically, SARs were not frequently used because of their accounting requirements. But recently there has been a dramatic increase in the use of SARs as a response to changes in tax law regulations mentioned earlier in the chapter.[80]

Stock Options. A **stock option** *gives an employee the right to buy stock during a specified time period or under other specified conditions.* When a company gives most of their employees the right to buy some amount of stock options, the plan is referred to as a broad-based stock option plan. Companies with broad-based stock option plans include Google, Pfizer, and Eli Lilly. Unlike stock options for executives, broad-based stock option plans seldom put earnings at risk.[81] There are numerous forms of stock options, as shown in Exhibit 11.15.[82] Note that the various plans differ in terms of the time frame for vesting, of whether vesting is contingent on attaining performance goals, and of pricing.

Many companies offer stock options only to executives on the assumption that the plans encourage executives to "think like owners." After all, employees

---

EXHIBIT 11.15 Explanation of Selected Stock-Based Pay Awards

Type of Plan	How It Works
Time-Restricted Stock Option	The basic "plain vanilla" plan: for a given period of time, employee may purchase a stock at a specified price.
Time-Based Restricted Stock	Award of shares with restrictions that require a predetermined length of service to elapse before vesting occurs. If employee leaves, stock is returned to the company.
Performance-Vested Stock Option	A stock option that vests upon the achievement of specified goals.
Performance-Vested Restricted Stock	Award of shares with restrictions that require the achievement of prespecified goals. Failure to attain goals in a specified time period may result in forfeiture.
Performance-Accelerated Stock Option	Award of shares that has a set vesting schedule but vesting may occur more rapidly if specified performance goals are met. If performance goals are not achieved, stock becomes vested with employee nevertheless.
Indexed Stock Option	Employee has the option to purchase stock at a price that fluctuates based on a specified standard index or a group of peer companies.
Premium-Priced Stock Option	Stock options with an exercise price that is above the market price at the time of the grant.
Stock Appreciation Rights	Cash or stock award based on increase in stock price over a specified time.

profit only if the stock price goes up. During the rising stock market of the 1990s, the use of stock options exploded. For senior executives, the total value of stock awards often exceeds the combined value of their base salaries and all annual bonuses. The 1990s also saw companies offer stock options to more and more employees at lower levels in the organization. The popularity of stock options was fueled partly by accounting and tax rules and partly by the belief that stock options increase employee motivation, particularly in small firms.[83]

Three factors have substantially reduced the use of stock options in the last few years. First, when the stock markets (particularly the Nasdaq) substantially declined between 2000 and 2002, many options went underwater, becoming essentially worthless. **Underwater stock options** *have an exercise price that is above the market value of a company's stocks.* Employees and employers came to realize the substantial risk in stock options.[84] Second, in 2006 and 2007, many firms received unfavorable publicity due to the widespread practice of back-dating stock options of executives. **Backdating** *involves changing the option date after the stock is issued to a date when stock prices were particularly low, which maximizes the option value.* It is generally considered unethical and illegal.[85] Finally, and most importantly, the changes in accounting regulations in 2005 ended the tax advantages of stock options over time-based restricted grants.[86]

Microsoft was a leader in the switch from options to grants. The problem of underwater stocks, along with the changes in financial reporting rules, led them to end the stock option rewards that had made many Microsoft employees millionaires. In 2002, the last year it offered them, Microsoft gave employees stock options worth $3.6 billion—nearly a third of its pretax income. Since then it has offered direct stock grants with restrictions. Steve Ballmer, CEO of Microsoft, said the change was necessary to prevent its best talent from leaving to join start-up companies. When Microsoft was thriving, its stock options appealed to talented employees, and the company needed to attract those people to continue growing. But today the company is in a stage of maturity. Growth has slowed, and attracting new talent is not as high a priority, but retaining experienced workers is still a concern. As long as Microsoft continues to perform well, the stocks employees receive should retain their value. Microsoft hopes that for those holding stock, stimulating, secure jobs are enough to keep them happy.[87]

> " I think it's a very fair deal [Microsoft's stock grants]. I've heard no one who thinks it's a bad idea. The market and the environment have changed drastically, and you can't go out and recruit with stock options anymore. "
>
> *Project Manager*
> *Microsoft*

LEARNING GOAL 10

FAST FACT

Approximately 85% of U.S.-based multinational companies grant stock options internationally. Of those, 90% use the same eligibility rules for expatriates as for U.S.-based employees.

GLOBAL PAY FOR PERFORMANCE

There is an added level of complexity in pay for performance when dealing with international pay practices. Differences in laws, tax regulations, and cultural values all affect the applicability of performance-based pay.[88] Although it appears that some convergence in international pay practices is occurring, there are still clear differences among countries. To illustrate how countries differ in their use of performance-based pay, Exhibit 11.16 shows variable pay (as a percentage of base pay) for HR executives in several different countries.[89] The range varies from 24% in Japan to 95% in the United States.

One reason for the variation in Exhibit 11.16 is the cultural differences among countries. The people of some cultures are more accepting of risk while others are more risk averse. To date, there has been relatively little systematic research investigating cultural differences in how employees react to alternative forms of performance-based pay. Thus, companies are learning as they go.

When HR professionals at Motorola conducted their research on attitudes toward pay-at-risk plans, they found that such plans were acceptable to employees in many countries—and that the pattern of findings wasn't always what

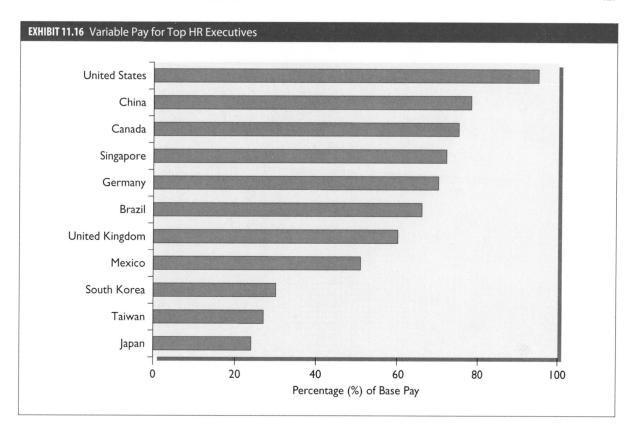

EXHIBIT 11.16 Variable Pay for Top HR Executives

they expected. Exhibit 11.17 summarizes the conclusions Motorola reached about which countries were most accepting of putting earnings at risk.[90]

CURRENT ISSUES

▲ 11 ◄ LEARNING GOAL

Two issues in performance-based pay are currently receiving considerable attention: ethical considerations and the shift toward variable pay and away from fixed pay.

Ethical Considerations

Generally targeted at executive pay, many people have expressed substantial ethical concerns about the use of performance-based pay. Because of its powerful motivating ability, performance-based pay can increase unethical behavior by employees. Poorly designed pay practices can lead to employee behaviors that maximize the performance measure but that are detrimental to the firm. The case of auto mechanics at Sears Auto Centers making unneeded repairs to maximize their bonuses is a good example. The bonuses motivated some employees to resort to fraud to increase their bonuses.

To control unethical behaviors, firms should have a clear code of ethics and enforce it through training, performance appraisals, and pay practices. That is, pay practices should be designed to motivate ethical behaviors and discourage unethical ones.[91]

Much of the concern about the ethics of performance-based pay is directed at the use of executive stock options. Critics cite stock options for the ethical

At the very least, options tended to create a short-term focus, and at worst, they promoted fraudulent activity to manipulate earnings.

Carol Bowie
Investor Responsibility
Research Center

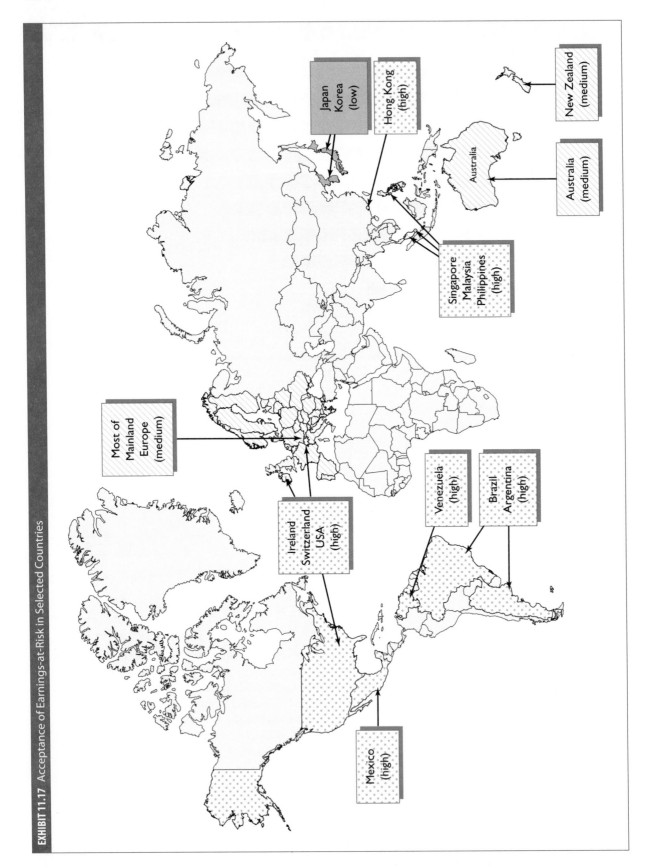

EXHIBIT 11.17 Acceptance of Earnings-at-Risk in Selected Countries

Japan
Korea
(low)

Hong Kong
(high)

New Zealand
(medium)

Australia

Australia
(medium)

Singapore
Malaysia
Philippines
(high)

Most of
Mainland
Europe
(medium)

Ireland
Switzerland
USA
(high)

Venezuela
(high)

Brazil
Argentina
(high)

Mexico
(high)

problems at companies such as Enron, Tyco, and Worldcom. They point out that too often stock options simply encourage executives to use accounting and other tricks to achieve short-term paper profits, which they can use to enrich themselves. Greater stock options for executives have been related to increased fraudulent activity that has cost investors more than $100 billion.[92] The widespread publicity of these actions have also hurt the reputation of many firms and damaged public confidence in corporate America.

On the other hand, stock options have been found to relate to greater corporate social performance and more socially responsible actions by firms. Presumably, stock options cause executives to focus on long-term outcomes, which socially responsible decisions help improve. To support this argument, firms offering more short-term incentives have been found to be less socially responsible.[93] Nevertheless, it is likely that stock options will be less widely used in the future. We think it's doubtful that eliminating the use of stock options will solve the problem of unethical behavior in business or achieve significant reform in corporate governance. Fixing such problems will require more than redesigning performance-based pay practices.[94]

The Shift toward Variable Pay

The use of stock options for executives is declining, but the use of other forms of variable pay is not. In fact, variable pay is being used for an increasing segment of the workforce. During the past several decades, we saw a shift from seniority-based pay practices to the use of merit pay. Now we are seeing a shift away from merit pay and toward incentives and pay-at-risk, which make it easier to tie pay to strategic goals and motivate employees.[95] As you have learned, the latter types of performance-based pay help control labor costs more than merit pay can.

A recent study showed that 80% of employers now offer performance-based bonuses, up from 67% a few years earlier. For nonexecutive white collar employees, variable pay now accounts for more that 11% of employees' total compensation; that figure increased 25% over a period of just three years.[96] The buzzword for this shift is *entitlement*. Managers say they want to eliminate the entitlement attitude that many employees have regarding pay. That is, employees feel that if they show up to work, they are entitled to their full pay regardless of how they perform. More and more firms are discovering, as the United States Postal Service did, that properly implemented, well designed performance-based pay benefits all stakeholders.

CHAPTER SUMMARY WITH LEARNING GOALS

Performance-based pay continues to attract the attention of many human resource managers, and line managers continue to ask whether pay can be used to achieve strategic objectives and motivate their employees.

⚠ **STRATEGIC IMPORTANCE.** Performance-based pay is strategically important to firms. It reduces labor costs while helping to attract, retain, and motivate talented employees. The challenge is to design performance-based pay to support the organization's strategic objectives while avoiding the liabilities associated with such pay.

⚠ **PERFORMANCE-BASED PAY AND THE INTEGRATED HRM SYSTEM.** Performance-based pay should be designed to fit the organization's external and internal environment. The labor market, technology, and the legal environment can affect performance-based pay practices. The organization's financial situation, corporate culture, and strategic objectives all combine to shape the specific approach that is likely to work best.

3 THE HR TRIAD. HR professionals, line managers, and employees all have substantial responsibilities with respect to performance-based pay. In particular, line managers and HR professionals must work together to ensure that performance-based pay practices are consistent with the business environment and the other HR practices in the organization.

4 DESIGN CHOICES. The major choices to be made when designing performance-based pay practices include which rewards to offer, which performance measures to use, and how to create a link between the performance measures and the rewards.

5 IMPLEMENTATION ISSUES. Issues such as employee acceptance, legality, and the evaluation of the effectiveness of the performance-based pay practices can have important consequences for their long-term success.

6 RECOGNITION AWARDS. The most popular recognition awards reward length of service and exceptional performance (with what are known as spot awards). Awards that recognize outstanding sales performance, retirement, and employee suggestions for organizational improvements round out the top five most popular types of recognition awards.

7 MERIT PAY. Merit pay ties employees' performance, as measured by supervisors' appraisal ratings, to the size of employees' yearly raises. Two major disadvantages of traditional merit pay practices are problems caused by the use of subjective appraisals to measure performance and the costs associated with giving merit raises instead of lump sum payments. Lump sum merit pay is used by some employers to address the latter disadvantage.

8 INCENTIVE PAY. Incentive pay is based on objective performance measures and typically makes larger distinctions in the rewards received by excellent versus poor performers. The major types of incentives are individual incentives, team incentives, gainsharing, and profit sharing.

9 PUTTING PAY AT RISK. With the pay-at-risk approach, employees receive base pay that is below the market average and are offered sizable incentives for excellent performance. The two most common approaches for putting pay at risk are commissions and stock options. Many employers encourage their employees to own company stock by giving stock grants and stock options.

10 GLOBAL DIFFERENCES. Differences in laws, tax regulations, and cultural values all affect the applicability of various approaches to performance-based pay. Although it appears that some convergence in international pay practices is occurring, clear differences among countries remain.

11 CURRENT ISSUES. Two important current issues being tackled by HR professionals are ethical issues associated with performance-based pay and the shift from fixed pay to the increased use of variable pay. The shift from merit raises to incentives and to putting pay-at-risk is occurring for many reasons, and the implications are significant for employees and employers alike.

TERMS TO REMEMBER

Backdating	Earnings-at-risk pay
Combined distribution plans	Eligibility rules
Commission	Employee stock ownership plans (ESOPs)
Current distribution plans	Gainsharing plans
Deferred distribution plans	Incentive pay
Differential piece-rate plan	Line-of-sight

Lump sum merit	Standard hour plan
Merit matrix	Stock appreciation rights (SARs)
Merit pay	Stock option
Performance-based pay	Straight piecework plan
Profit-sharing plans	Underwater stock options
Recognition awards	Variable pay
Spot awards	

QUESTIONS FOR DISCUSSION AND REFLECTIVE THINKING

1. Describe the strategic importance of performance-based pay. Why do employers use it?
2. From the perspective of employees, what are the major disadvantages of the four major forms of performance-based pay (recognition, merit, incentives, earnings-at-risk)?
3. Debate the following assertion: *If selection and placement decisions are made effectively, performance differences among employees should be relatively small; therefore, performance-based pay isn't needed and may even be disruptive.*
4. What does it mean to put earnings at risk? List the potential costs and benefits of placing a substantial percentage of pay at risk for *all* employees in the following types of organizations: a hospital, a restaurant, a brokerage firm, and a fashion design house.
5. Describe the challenges associated with using team incentives. Do you think these challenges differ for team bonuses versus team recognition awards? Explain your opinion.
6. Do you think performance-based pay is more likely to cause employees to behave unethically compared to paying a straight salary or wage? Why or why not?

PROJECTS TO EXTEND YOUR LEARNING

1. **Integration and Application.** Before continuing, review the cases of Southwest Airlines and Lincoln Electric at the end of this book. Then answer the following questions.

   a. Compare and contrast the approaches to performance-based pay used by Lincoln Electric and Southwest Airlines. Overall, which plan do you think is more effective? Why?

   b. Lincoln Electric is gradually moving toward using a more traditional approach to pay, putting less emphasis on earnings-at-risk. What strategic objectives would lead the company to conclude that a more traditional approach to pay may be more effective than their present practices?

2. **Using the Internet.** Designing effective performance-based pay practices can be challenging. Learn about the online resources available on this topic.

   a. The Bureau of Labor Statistics provides a wealth of information about economic conditions that influence pay policies. Learn more by visiting the BLS Editor's Desk (www.stats.bls.gov/opub/ted/).

   b. Learn more about recognition awards from Recognition Professionals International's Web site (www.recognition.org).

   c. Find out more about the services offered by consulting firms who specialize in compensation, including:
      - Pearl Meyer & Partners (www.pearlmeyer.com).
      - William M. Mercer (www.mercer.com).
      - Towers Perrin (www.towersperrin.com).

   d. Performance-based pay has been discussed at length in the field of education. Learn more about using merit pay and incentives to pay educators for excellent performance by visiting the home pages of the
      - American Federation of Teachers (www.aft.org).
      - National Education Association (www.nea.org).

e. Learn more about Scanlon Plans from Scanlon Leadership (www.scanlonleader.org). Learn about employee ownership from the National Council for Employee Ownership (www.nceo.org).

3. **Experiential Activity.** People who work in sales jobs often receive some type of performance-based pay. Learn more about the pay practices used for salespeople in the retail stores in your neighborhood.

Activity

Step 1. Visit three different retail stores, such as Sears, Wal-Mart, and Target. Choose stores that are conveniently located, but try to choose ones that have different strategies (e.g., selling at the lowest price, providing excellent customer service, offering high-end luxury goods). Talk to at least two salespeople in each store to learn about how they are paid. Try to obtain answers to the following questions (be sure to keep notes about your conversations):

a. Is the person paid a commission? If yes, what formula is used to determine the commissions earned? What percentage of the person's average paycheck is a commission award?

b. What other forms of performance-based pay, if any, does the person receive? Be sure to ask about achievement bonuses, merit pay, and stock ownership.

c. Does the performance-based pay offered focus on improving individual, team, or company performance?

d. Does the person feel there are any drawbacks to the employer's approach to pay? If yes, what are the drawbacks?

Step 2. After interviewing the salespeople, evaluate the performance-based pay offered at each of the three retail stores. Which store do you think has the most effective approach to paying its salespeople? Explain.

CASE STUDY

EVALUATING NONTRADITIONAL INCENTIVES: HOWE 2 SKI STORES

The Howe 2 Ski Stores are a chain of three ski and windsurfing shops located in the suburbs of a large Eastern U.S. city. Maria Howe, a ski enthusiast and business school major, opened a store 10 years ago after her college graduation with financial backing from her family and several friends. From its inception, the Howe 2 store was intended to provide state-of-the-art equipment and clothing for skiers at all skill levels, from beginner to champion. It was to be staffed by employees who were themselves advanced skiers and could provide expert advice on the choice of clothing and equipment, and it was intended to have a quick response time that would permit the last-minute purchase of equipment and clothing prior to a ski trip.

Howe originally drew from a pool of skiing friends and fellow students to staff the stores and still prefers to hire part-time employees with skiing expertise, who might leave in a year, over more stable, full-time employees with less expertise and interest in the sport. Whether administrative staff, cashiers, clerks, or molders (who fit bindings to skis), employees were encouraged to keep up on the latest skiing equipment and trends, attend ski vendor shows, try out demo equipment, and give feedback on the store's inventory so as to provide the highest-quality, state-of-the-art equipment and advice for the customer. Suggestion boxes were placed in the store, and Howe herself regularly collected, read, and acted on the suggestions made by the clerks and customers. To increase the market, she developed special advertising campaigns to build an image for the nearby slopes. As the business grew, Howe even added a line of rental equipment to lower the costs and encourage people to try the sport.

Although profits grew irregularly due to weather effects and the faddish nature of the sport, Howe's efforts paid off in the long term, and within four years business had grown sufficiently to permit the opening of a second Howe 2 Ski Store in another suburb about 10 miles from the first. To even out sales across the year, about six years ago Howe took a chance on the growing windsurfing market and the East Coast location and added a line of equipment for this sport. The move turned out to be a very good one. The windsurfing market increased by more than 300% in four years and continues to experience a slow but stable pattern of growth as families and older adults attempt the sport. This market has enabled her to smooth out the number of sales occurring throughout the year.

Three years ago, Howe was able to open a third store, located within 15 miles of the other two. Although managers have been hired to run each of the stores and the total number of employees has grown to 65, Howe's basic strategy has remained the same: high-quality, state-of-the-art products, a knowledgeable staff, and quick response time. Profits from the stores have continued to grow, although at a slower rate. Competition from other ski stores has also increased noticeably within the last two years.

The threat of increased competition has been exacerbated by signs that employee productivity has begun to slide. Last year, on eight occasions expensive ski orders were not delivered in time for the customer's ski vacation. Although Howe used a variety of maneuvers to retain the customers' patronage (e.g., paying for the customers to rent equipment of equivalent quality, express shipping the equipment to the customer as soon as it was delivered, and lowering the price of the equipment), the costs of these late orders were high. She realizes that word of this kind of incident could significantly damage the store's reputation. Furthermore, at least 15% of all ski orders were more than two days late, even though customers did not miss a trip or vacation as a result.

In an attempt to respond to these difficulties, Howe instituted a merit performance system for the molders (employees who fit the binding to skis). Although productivity seemed to increase for a while, waves of discontent surfaced among all the employees. The molders felt that their merit ratings were inaccurate because the store managers could not observe them much of the time. Further, they argued that their performance would have been much higher had other employees not interrupted them with questions about appropriate bindings or failed to clearly identify the appropriate equipment on the sales tickets. Other employees also complained because they were not given the opportunity for merit pay. The buyers, who visit ski shows, examine catalogs, and talk with sales representatives to decide on the inventory, argued that their work was essential for high sales figures and quality equipment. Sales clerks claimed that their in-depth familiarity with an extensive inventory and their sales skills were essential to increasing sales. They also noted their important role in negotiating a delivery date that the molders could meet. Similar arguments were made by the people in the credit office who arranged for short-term financing if necessary, and by the cashiers who verified costs and checked credit card approvals. Even the stockers noted that the store would suffer if they did not locate the correct equipment in a warehouse full of inventory and deliver it in a timely manner to the molders.

Howe had to concede that the employees were correct on many of these points, so she suspended the merit plan at the end of the ski season and promised to reevaluate its fairness. Even more convincing were several indications that productivity problems were not limited to molder employees. Complaints about customer service increased 20% during the year. Several customers noted that they were allowed to stand, merchandise in hand, waiting for a clerk to help them, while clerks engaged in deep conversations among themselves. Although Howe mentioned this to employees in the stores when she visited and asked the store managers to discuss it in staff meetings, the complaints continued. A record number of "as is" skis were sold at the end-of-season sale because they were damaged in the warehouse, the store, or by the molders. The closing inventory revealed that 20% of the rental equipment had been lost or seriously damaged without resulting charges to the renters because records were poorly maintained. Regular checks of the suggestion boxes in the store revealed fewer and fewer comments. Although less extreme, similar problems occurred during windsurfing season. Employees just didn't seem to notice these problems or, worse, didn't seem to care.

Source: S. Nkomo, M. Fottler, and R. B. McAfee, *Applications in Human Resource Management,* 5th ed. (Mason, OH: South-Western, 2005).

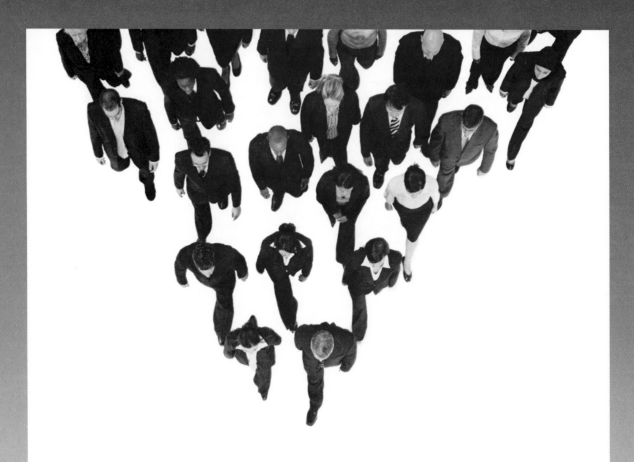

Providing Benefits and Services

Learning Goals

After reading this chapter, you should be able to:

1. Explain the strategic importance of employee benefits and services.
2. Show how benefits and services fit within an integrated HRM system.
3. Detail the roles and responsibilities of the HR Triad for employee benefits and services.
4. Describe the different forms of mandatory protection programs.
5. Discuss the types of voluntary protection programs.
6. Describe the various health care benefits and services employers offer.
7. Explain the different types of paid leave benefits employers offer.
8. Describe work/life benefits and services that may be granted by firms.
9. State other benefits and services that some companies provide.
10. Discuss the administrative issues related to employee benefits and services.
11. Detail two current issues related to employee benefits and services.

MANAGING HUMAN RESOURCES AT STEELCASE

Steelcase, headquartered in Grand Rapids, Michigan, since 1912, is the world's leading provider of high-performance workplaces. It serves virtually every country of the world. With manufacturing facilities in over 30 locations, and more than 800 dealers around the globe, its workforce of 13,000 employees is a global one.

To compete effectively, Steelcase must carefully manage its costs and strive to reduce them wherever and however it can. During the past decade, Steelcase has focused on reducing the costs of workers' compensation claims—essentially the costs associated with having people hurt, injured, and out of work. With input from medical services and the safety director, Steelcase developed and implemented a return-to-work program. The goal of the program is to have injured employees return to work as soon as they are able. The program has substantially reduced the average cost per claim and improved worker morale. Initiatives such as this one are among the reasons that Steelcase was recognized by *Industry Week* as one of the 100 best managed companies in the world. [1] ▲

THE STRATEGIC IMPORTANCE OF EMPLOYEE BENEFITS AND SERVICES

Like many other companies, Steelcase is trying to address a mounting crisis: the escalating costs of providing health-related employee benefits and services. As international competition heats up, U.S. firms are struggling to contain costs of all types. For many firms, the costs of benefits and services are a significant part of the challenge. Steelcase's approach is an excellent example of what firms can do to reduce one part of these costs, workers' compensation claims. Other firms reduce the costs of benefits and services by changing their health care coverage or retirement plans.

Employee benefits and services *are generally defined as in-kind (noncash) payments to employees for their membership or participation in the organization.* Benefits and services enable employees to enjoy a better lifestyle and to maintain a reasonable work/life balance. The term *benefits* is typically used to describe payments for protection against health and accident-related problems, payments for income protection after retirement (pensions), and pay for time not spent working (for instance, vacations, holidays, sick days and absences, breaks, and washup and cleanup). The term *services* is often used to refer to a wide arrange of auxiliary conveniences and facilities provided to employees, which generally make work life more enjoyable (some people call these "perks"). Examples of services include discounts on company products, exercise and wellness centers, on-site dry cleaning, and assistance with child and elder care. There no hard-and-fast rules for how to use the two terms *benefits* and *services;* we tend to use them together and interchangeably.

Driving the desire to offer better employee benefits and services are the pressures to attract and retain valued employees and thereby to compete effectively against other employers in the labor market. Controlling costs, on the other hand, is a major counterbalancing force. The key strategic challenge is offering benefits and services that maximize the return on the employer's investments. Exhibit 12.1 shows the most important objectives that employers hope to achieve by offering appropriate employee benefits and services, as reported in a recent survey.[2]

Included in the top five objectives is increasing employee productivity. This is somewhat surprising, because employee benefits and services are not usually tied to employee performance and are not used to increase employee effort. Most benefits and services are available on a noncontingent basis—as long as employees remain employed, they receive the same benefits and services regardless of job performance. Apparently, employers believe that providing some benefits and services will result in productivity improvements in less direct ways. For example, employee assistance programs and work/life balance programs may improve productivity by reducing employee absences. By getting insured workers to return to work as quickly as possible, Steelcase hopes to reduce the number of lost workdays, which improves productivity. Benefits and services that encourage employees to stay healthy may also translate into a workforce that is more efficient and effective. The survey also shows that cost savings and retaining, attracting, and satisfying employees are among the top objectives of benefits and services. If all of these other objectives can be achieved, productivity improvements are almost sure to follow.

Controlling Costs

In 1929, the cost of all monetary benefits and services payments averaged 5% of total compensation. By 2007, the figure had risen to an average of about 30% of total compensation, or about $17,400 a year for each employee.[3]

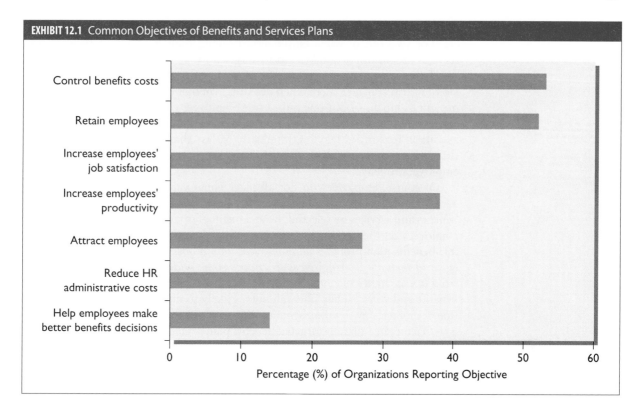

EXHIBIT 12.1 Common Objectives of Benefits and Services Plans

Although these numbers vary across industries and by type of worker, the cost of benefits and services to organizations is, in general, enormous. Wages and salaries are 40 times what they were 60 years ago; benefits and services are 500 times what they were.[4]

During the economic boom of the 1990s, employers were relatively generous—a growing economy meant that simply finding enough people to staff organizations required less focus on controlling costs. During the mid-1990s, the rate of growth for health care costs slowed a bit, as employers found more economical ways to provide health insurance (e.g., managed care). But today, controlling costs has again become a major concern.[5]

As will become apparent, some of these costs cannot easily be avoided because the protections they provide are legally mandated. Thus, cost-cutting efforts focus on benefits and services that employers offer voluntarily. Clearly, the easiest way to reduce costs would be to eliminate all benefits and services that are not required by law. But employers who offer benefits and services voluntarily do so because they believe it improves the organization's ability to succeed. The challenge for these organizations is providing benefits and services that are both effective and financially efficient.

Recruiting and Retaining Talent

Benefits and services are important for attracting and retaining talent. SAS Institute has never had turnover greater than 5% in an industry whose average is 20%. They keep turnover low by offering lavish benefits and services.[6] As we reported in Exhibit 10.1 (see page 357), 68% of workers believe that benefits and services are a very important consideration when choosing whether to stay with a company. Another survey found that 63% of employees would be more likely to stay with a company that offered good benefits and services, and 60% would be attracted to work for such a company.[7]

> **People come here for the benefits, and they stay for them. . . . Turnover is very expensive, and our benefits keep our rate down.**
>
> *Bradley Honeycut*
> *Director of Compensation and Benefits*
> *Starbucks*

Employees consider some benefits and services as more important than others. For two out of three employees, keeping their health care benefits and services are an important reason to stay with their current employer. Clearly, employees consider benefits and services when deciding whether to take a job. Do they also consider them when deciding whether to leave? The answer is yes, but not as much. About one out of five employees cite health care benefits and services as a main reason for leaving, and one out of six cite retirement benefits as a main reason for leaving. Interestingly, less than 2% of employers believe that retirement or health care benefits and services would be a main reason for employees to leave.[8]

Of course, employees do not all place equal value on the array of possible benefits and services they might receive. Allowing employees to personalize their benefits and services by selecting from a menu of options is one way to make sure employees get the benefits and services they value, while balancing costs. A **flexible benefits plan** *provides all employees with a base benefits and services package and then allows employees to choose some additional benefits and services from a wide array of options.* Giving employees the opportunity to choose the benefits and services they find valuable is likely to improve attraction and retention.[9] Another way to tailor benefits and services to the organization's workforce is with a targeted plan. A **targeted benefits plan** *provides different types and levels of benefits and services depending on an employee's location and position in the organization.*[10] Flexible and targeted benefits and services increase administrative costs and also must be carefully designed to ensure that they pass legal scrutiny.

To attract and retain talent that is in short supply, a few employers compete successfully by providing new and innovative benefits and services. Google offers free gourmet meals, all-expenses-paid annual ski trips, free flu shots, free snack stations, a climbing wall, volleyball courts, and on-site laundry facilities, car washes, and oil changes![11] Other employers provide concierge services, prepared take-home meals, pet health insurance, massage therapy services, personal tax services, foreign language lessons, and free cell phones.[12]

> " *Balancing the benefit needs of both the company and employees can certainly be a challenge, but the rewards of sound, cost-effective benefits programs, and employee understanding and appreciation are certainly worth the effort.* "
>
> *Cherly Poulson*
> *Manager of Benefits Planning*
> *GlaxoSmithKline*

Achieving Business Objectives

To capitalize on the money spent on employee benefits and services, employers must take into account their business objectives. Some employers spend money on benefits and services as a means to communicate corporate values and to establish a particular type of organizational culture. Others pay for benefits and services

---

EXHIBIT 12.2 Achieving Business Objectives Using Benefits and Services

Business Objective	Benefits Response
1. To reduce total costs of doing business by 10% yearly.	1. Contain the rise in health care costs to 2% yearly and increase employee contributions by 2% yearly.
2. To develop a working environment that is founded on integrity, open communication, and individual growth.	2. Develop an employee career counseling system that provides employees with an opportunity to assess skills and develop competencies. Establish a tuition reimbursement program.
3. To establish the division as a recognized leader in support of its community.	3. Establish a corporate-giving matching fund.
4. To complete the downsizing of the company by the end of the third quarter.	4. Develop various termination subsidies such as severance pay, outplacement assistance, and early retirement benefits.
5. To cut accident rates 10% by year-end.	5. Establish an employee assistance program by year-end. Set up a free literacy training program to ensure that all employees can read job safety signs.

that address the needs of employees hit by layoffs. Exhibit 12.2 provides several examples of strategic business objectives and the ways in which benefits and services can be used to address them.

EMPLOYEE BENEFITS AND SERVICES WITHIN AN INTEGRATED HRM SYSTEM

Exhibit 12.3 shows the major elements of employee benefits and services and their linkages with other HR practices. Also shown are the factors in the external and organizational environments that have the most influence on employee

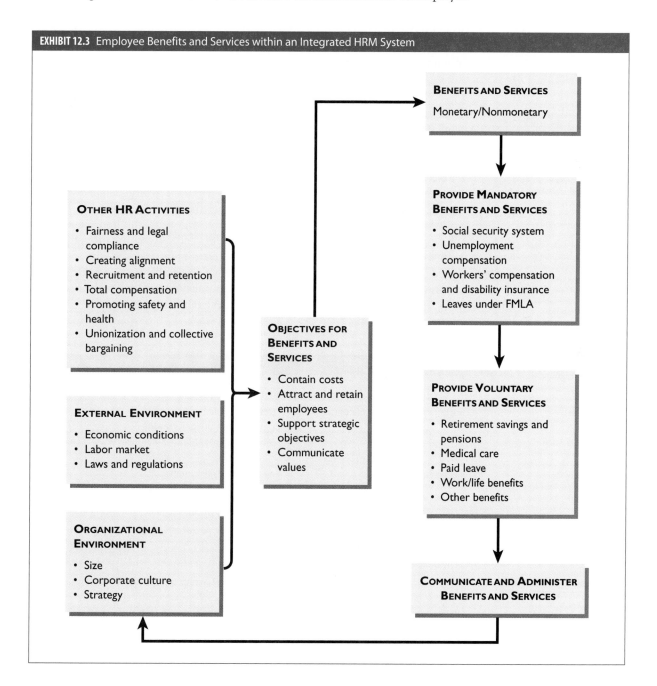

EXHIBIT 12.3 Employee Benefits and Services within an Integrated HRM System

BENEFITS AND SERVICES

Monetary/Nonmonetary

OTHER HR ACTIVITIES

- Fairness and legal compliance
- Creating alignment
- Recruitment and retention
- Total compensation
- Promoting safety and health
- Unionization and collective bargaining

EXTERNAL ENVIRONMENT

- Economic conditions
- Labor market
- Laws and regulations

ORGANIZATIONAL ENVIRONMENT

- Size
- Corporate culture
- Strategy

OBJECTIVES FOR BENEFITS AND SERVICES

- Contain costs
- Attract and retain employees
- Support strategic objectives
- Communicate values

PROVIDE MANDATORY BENEFITS AND SERVICES

- Social security system
- Unemployment compensation
- Workers' compensation and disability insurance
- Leaves under FMLA

PROVIDE VOLUNTARY BENEFITS AND SERVICES

- Retirement savings and pensions
- Medical care
- Paid leave
- Work/life benefits
- Other benefits

COMMUNICATE AND ADMINISTER BENEFITS AND SERVICES

benefits and services. In this chapter, we describe several of the most frequently offered benefits and services, which include mandatory protection programs, voluntary protection programs, and supplemental benefits and services aimed at improving the quality of employees' work and nonwork lives.

Protection programs required by the federal and state governments are referred to as **mandatory protection programs.** Also known as public protection programs, they provide insurance for employees and their families when an employee's income (direct compensation) is terminated. Mandatory protection programs grew rapidly during the Great Depression of the 1930s in response to the hardships faced by millions of unemployed Americans. The government manages mandatory protection programs, and employers support them by providing some of the funding. Many employers also pay costs associated with providing additional insurance for health care and retirement. *Protection programs that are offered by employers and that are not required by law are called* **voluntary protection programs.** Examples of each are listed in Exhibit 12.4.

Links with Other HR Practices

As described in Chapter 10, employee benefits and services are one component of total compensation. They account for approximately one-third of a company's total labor costs.[13] Base wages and performance-based pay account for the remaining costs, as illustrated in Exhibit 12.5.

We have already described how an organization's various objectives influence their use of benefits and services. Other HR practices should also be aligned with benefits and services. At Ernst & Young, the decision to expand flexible work arrangements was consistent with other efforts to recruit and retain more female employees. At Wal-Mart, minimal benefits and services are offered, which is consistent with other elements of its HR system that drive down labor costs. At United Technologies, developing the knowledge and skills of the workforce is a top priority. A generous tuition reimbursement policy complements the organization's investments in employee training and development programs.

EXHIBIT 12.4 Mandatory and Voluntary Protection Programs

Issue	Mandatory Programs	Voluntary Programs
Retirement	• Social Security old-age benefits	• Defined benefit pensions • Defined contribution pensions • Money purchase and thrift plans [401(k)s and ESOPs]
Death	• Social Security survivors' benefits • Workers' compensation	• Group term life insurance including accidental death and travel insurance • Payouts from profit-sharing, pension, or thrift plans, or any combination of these • Dependent survivors' benefits
Disability	• Workers' compensation • Social Security disability benefits • State disability benefits	• Short-term accident and sickness insurance • Long-term disability insurance
Unemployment	• Unemployment benefits	• Supplemental unemployment benefits or severance pay, or both
Medical and dental expenses	• Workers' compensation	• Hospital surgical insurance • Other medical insurance • Dental insurance

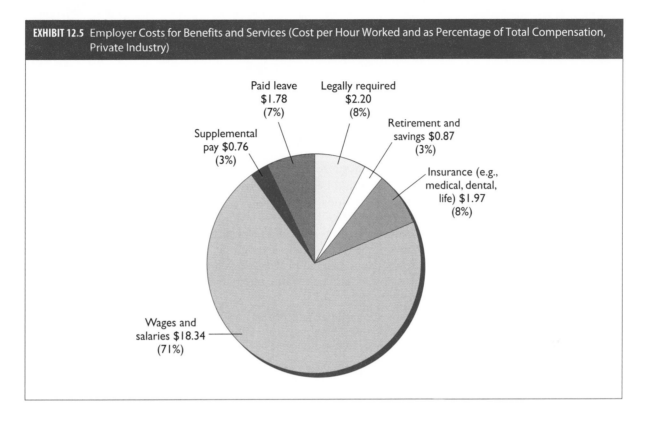

EXHIBIT 12.5 Employer Costs for Benefits and Services (Cost per Hour Worked and as Percentage of Total Compensation, Private Industry)

Two other sets of HR practices that are intertwined with benefits and services are (1) safety and health and (2) unionization and collective bargaining. These linkages will be described in more detail in Chapters 13 and 14.

The External Environment

In Chapter 10, you learned that controlling labor costs takes on heightened importance in industries that are labor intensive. Industry dynamics such as these have consequences for all components of total compensation, including benefits and services. When labor costs are a relatively minor portion of an organization's total costs, providing unusually good benefits and services may provide a competitive advantage that ensures the company is getting the best possible employees. Although cost concerns vary somewhat across industries and firms, the desire to reduce the growing costs of benefits and services is quite widespread because these costs have grown so rapidly. The growth in the costs and types of employee benefits and services can be traced to several trends in the broader business environment.

Economic Conditions. Under normal business conditions, employers compete for labor primarily through the wages they offer. During times of major crises, such as World War II and the Korean War, the government curtailed such activity to prevent runaway inflation. Throughout the twentieth century, the imposition of wage controls in times of war forced organizations to offer more and greater benefits and services in place of wage increases, to attract new employees. More recently the most important economic condition has been growth in health care costs. In 1940, U.S. health care expenses were $4 billion, which was about 4% of the GDP. By 2009, health care spending was estimated to be about $2.9 trillion, which is more than 16% of the GDP. Regardless of their causes, these increases have major consequences for employee benefits and services.[14]

Inflation and tax laws also come into play. Benefits managers must anticipate the long-term effects of inflation on medical service, education, and pensions. Tax rules for benefits and services can substantially influence both their real cost for employers and their real value to employees.

Union Bargaining. From 1935 into the 1970s, unions were able to gain steady increases in wages and benefits for their members. Practically all benefits and services are now mandatory bargaining items. That means that employers must bargain in good faith on union proposals to add them. Recent data show that companies spend more than $12 per hour on the benefits and services of unionized workers, compared to less than $7 per hour for nonunionized workers.[15] In heavily unionized industries, companies without union representation may have to offer similarly high benefits and services to remain attractive to job applicants.

The effects of unions on monetary benefits have been particularly strong for government employees. Government employers have typically been willing to agree to provide general pensions—that is, they promise to provide compensation in the future—in exchange for employees agreeing to accept somewhat lower salaries and wages in the near term. Such agreements suited politicians because they allowed city and state governments to defer these costs well into the future. It also suited employees, who believed they would have a secure retirement. Unfortunately, as the Baby Boomer generation approaches retirement, it has become clear that many state governments do not have the money required to meet their obligations to employees.[16]

Laws and Regulations. A variety of laws significantly affect the administration and offering of monetary benefits, including the Family and Medical Leave Act of 1993 (FLMA), the Employee Retirement Income Security Act of 1974 (ERISA), and the Social Security Act of 1935. When Congress initiated the Social Security Act, it covered only 60% of all workers. Subsequently, the scope of these benefits and the percentage of eligible workers have increased substantially. Today 95% of all workers are eligible for Social Security benefits, including disability benefits, health care benefits, and retirement pay. These laws and regulations are described more thoroughly later in this chapter.

The Organizational Environment

The organizational environment also plays a role in shaping the design of employee benefits and services. As with total compensation, size, corporate culture, and strategy all combine to shape each organization's specific approach. We've already discussed how a firm's strategies can shape its benefit offerings. Here we comment briefly on how size and organizational culture come into play.

FAST FACT

Pella, the window maker, takes care of its employees by giving workers' sons and daughters scholarships and first crack at summer jobs.

Size. Large firms tend to offer their employees a wider range of benefits and services, compared to small firms. This is probably because large firms have greater purchasing power and so they can afford more. Companies with fewer than 10 employees may have difficulty finding an insurance carrier. Dental and vision care insurance options aren't very good either. Disability insurance for these small companies is very restrictive and very expensive. Only after a

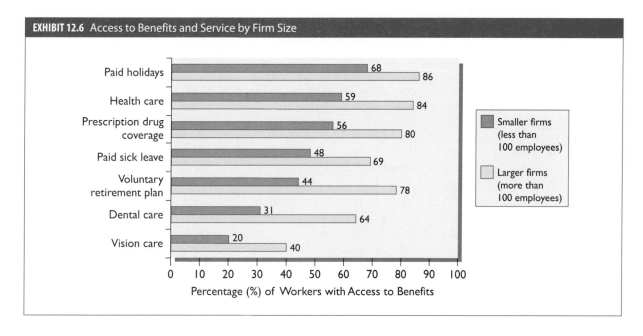

EXHIBIT 12.6 Access to Benefits and Service by Firm Size

Paid holidays — Smaller firms 68, Larger firms 86
Health care — Smaller firms 59, Larger firms 84
Prescription drug coverage — Smaller firms 56, Larger firms 80
Paid sick leave — Smaller firms 48, Larger firms 69
Voluntary retirement plan — Smaller firms 44, Larger firms 78
Dental care — Smaller firms 31, Larger firms 64
Vision care — Smaller firms 20, Larger firms 40

Percentage (%) of Workers with Access to Benefits

Smaller firms (less than 100 employees)
Larger firms (more than 100 employees)

company has at least 25 employees can it begin to offer a choice of medical insurance plans, according to some experts.

Exhibit 12.6 shows the percentage of small and large firms that offer their employees various health, retirement, and leave benefits. Large firms are more likely to provide each of the benefits and services shown. They also tend to provide greater levels of the benefit and ask employees to contribute less.[17]

The consequences of firm size seem to apply to all types of benefits and services. A recent survey compared large and small firms on 220 types of benefits and services. The results showed that large firms were more likely to offer 183 of the 220 items. Only 2 of the items—letting employees bring children to work in an emergency and having holiday parties—were much more likely to be offered by small firms.[18]

Corporate Culture. An organization's fundamental values set the stage for developing an approach to managing employee benefits and services. The benefits manager must understand the culture and the role of the HRM system in supporting that culture. Some firms adopt an egalitarian approach to benefits and services by insisting that the same ones be provided to all employees. Other firms offer targeted benefits and services. Lincoln Electric's approach is to offer only limited voluntary benefits and services, and to use the savings to fund the company's profit-sharing bonus pool. The company makes it easy for employees to participate in a group insurance plan, but doing so is completely voluntary on the part of employees.

Google provides a vast array of innovative benefits and services to reinforce its culture. Google wants its hard-driving employees to have so many amenities at work that they don't want to leave. The benefits and services are provided so that Google employees will love to work there, and so they can focus on their work, thereby increasing productivity.[19]

At Starbucks, customer service and a fun culture are critical, and the benefits and services they offer support these values. With more than 75,000 partners (employees) working in more than 7,500 locations around the world, Starbucks seeks to create a spirit of camaraderie and fun. To stay attuned

" Here I am, a guy who can afford a good meal, and every time I go to a Google board meeting, I don't leave until ten o'clock at night because I get a free dinner there. "

*Art Levinson
Chief Executive Officer of Genentech and Google Board of Directors Member*

LINE MANAGERS	HR PROFESSIONALS	EMPLOYEES
• Attend training programs and stay current on legal issues relevant to benefits and services.	• Ensure that all policies and practices are consistent with legal requirements.	• Take responsibility for understanding the available benefits and services.
• Work with HR professionals to ensure alignment of the benefits plan with strategic business objectives.	• With line managers, ensure alignment of the benefits plan with strategic business objectives.	• May participate in determining new benefits and services as the employer's strategic objectives change.
• Work with employees to ensure that the benefits and services satisfy them and encourage retention.	• Assess employees' preferences and reactions to benefits and services systematically and regularly.	• Participate in surveys designed to assess benefits preferences and benefit satisfaction.
• Recognize employees who may need certain benefits and services and communicate availability to them.	• Assist employees in technical aspects of benefits and services, such as enrollment and receiving benefits and services payments.	• Use available assistance to enroll and receive needed benefits and services.
• Provide employees with the tools to make sound benefits choices.	• Work with line managers to provide employees with the tools to make sound benefits choices.	• Use the available tools to help make sound benefit choices.
• Fairly administer all benefits and services.	• Work closely with line managers to provide valued benefits and services within organizational constraints.	• May register complaints about benefits availability or administration.

to employees' concerns, Starbucks regularly conducts surveys and solicits employees' ideas and responds to them. Through all of these efforts, Starbucks communicates that it cares about employees and their needs and respects them as members of the company's team of key players.

THE HR TRIAD

Designing and administering an effective array of benefits and services requires close cooperation among all players in the HR Triad. In particular, line managers and HR professionals must work together to ensure that the benefits and services offered support the organization's strategic objectives, fit the external environment, and are consistent with other HR practices. Seeking and using the input of all employees is an important responsibility of line managers and HR professionals, and providing honest input to such discussions is the responsibility of employees. HR professionals are also the ones who need to ensure that all employees fully understand all of the benefits and services available to them. HR professionals and managers are responsible for giving employees the tools they need to make good choices.

The HR professionals take primary responsibility for ensuring the legality and fairness of the package of benefits and services offered to employees. They also take the lead on a variety of technicalities such as enrollment and helping eligible employees receive payments.

Managers need to know the details of the benefits and services offered to employees, because they often determine how managers should treat their employees. For example, under what conditions are employees allowed to take sick leave, what are the rules governing flexible scheduling, and so on? Managers also are responsible for identifying employees who should be taking advantage of particular services and helping to direct them to sources that will provide assistance.

The ultimate value of the benefits and services package to the organization and to the employees depends on whether employees fully understand, value, and use what's available to them. Employees should provide feedback about the benefits and services they are receiving and be specific about which benefits and services they value. Employee involvement in benefits and services decisions is growing, particularly in health care. Thus, employees must accept increasing responsibility for making informed and sound choices. These roles and responsibilities are summarized in the feature "The HR Triad: Roles and Responsibilities for Benefits and Services."

The members of the HR Triad work together so that benefits and services are tailored to meet the needs of both employees and the organization. Next we describe some of the most widely offered benefits and services, beginning with those that are legally mandated.

MANDATORY PROTECTION PROGRAMS

Many of the benefits provided by employers are mandated by the **Social Security Act of 1935,** *which provides for retirement, disability, and unemployment insurance.* Health insurance, particularly Medicare, was added in 1966 to provide hospital insurance to almost everyone age 65 and older. The Medicare program was modified again in 2003 to include prescription drug coverage. The Social Security Administration has the responsibility for administering the Social Security Act.

Social Security Insurance

Social Security Insurance is a forced savings plan intended to provide older Americans with a reliable source of income during their retirement years. Funding of the Social Security system is provided by equal contributions from the employer and employee under the terms of the Federal Insurance Contributions Act (FICA).

Initially, employees and employers each paid into the Social Security system at the rate of 1% of the employee's annual income, up to a maximum income of $3,000. Today the employer and employee each pay the Social Security system 6.2% of the employee's annual income for retirement and disability, up to a specified maximum income of approximately $100,000. In addition, the employer and employee each contributes 1.45% of an employee's total income for hospital insurance through Medicare.

Upon reaching a specified age, employees become eligible to begin receiving the benefit of this forced savings plan. Currently, employees can choose to begin receiving Social Security income at age 62 or wait until they are age 65–67, depending on their date of birth. Employees who begin taking benefits at age 62 receive somewhat less per year. The annual Social Security payment to retirees ranges from 20% to 40% of their pre-retirement income, with adjustments routinely made for increases in the consumer price index.[20]

Unemployment Compensation

The Social Security Act also set up an insurance program to provide unemployment compensation as income for employees who lose their jobs. Unemployment compensation programs are jointly administered by the federal and state governments. The amount that employers contribute to

FAST FACT

For each employee, employers pay an average of $1.20 per hour for Social Security Insurance and $0.31 per hour for Medicare coverage.

unemployment compensation programs is determined by both the location of the employer and the employer's history of layoffs and dismissals. Employers with historically more employees drawing from the fund pay higher unemployment insurance premiums.

Unemployment compensation costs vary by state because income levels vary from state to state. Payments made to unemployed workers range from 50 to 70% of base salary up to a specified maximum weekly amount, which also varies by state. Critics of the current system, which has not changed substantially since 1935, believe that reforms are necessary to adapt to economic and work pattern changes.[21]

Workers' Compensation and Disability Insurance

Of the more than 4.2 million job-related injuries reported annually, about half are serious enough for the injured worker to lose work time, to experience restricted work activity, or both. Most of these injuries are associated with repetitive motions such as vibration, repeated pressure, and carpal tunnel syndrome.[22] When injuries or illnesses occur as a result of on-the-job events, workers may be eligible for workers' compensation benefits.

Workers' compensation covers medical costs, lost income or earnings capacity, and rehabilitation expenses. Survivors' benefits are provided following fatal injuries. The system is administered at the state level and fully financed by employers for most workers. As a supplement to workers' compensation, some employers also voluntarily offer disability insurance.[23] According to the Social Security Administration, workers who are 20 years old today have a 33% chance of becoming temporarily or permanently disabled before they hit retirement age.

As with unemployment insurance, employers who have historically had more employees drawing from the workers' compensation fund pay higher premiums. This provision encourages employers to minimize workers' compensation claims. Steelcase uses a variety of cost-containment strategies to reduce workers' compensation claims. Their return-to-work program, which resulted in a savings of more than $50 million, has been especially successful. By setting up therapy centers and accommodating working conditions, Steelcase reduced time away from work for most injuries by 50% in six years.[24]

Family and Medical Leave

The **Family and Medical Leave Act (FMLA)** *requires employers with 50 or more workers to grant an employee up to 12 weeks of unpaid leave annually "for the birth or adoption of a child, to care for a spouse or an immediate family member with a serious health condition, or when unable to work because of a serious health condition. Employers covered by the law are required to maintain any preexisting health coverage during the leave period."* The most common reason for taking family leave is for the arrival of a new child.

To be covered by the Family and Medical Leave Act, employees must have worked at a company for at least 12 months and have put in at least 1,250 hours in the year before the leave. The employee taking leave must be allowed to return to the same job or a job of equivalent status and pay—with the exception of some highly paid executives.[25] About one-third of employees taking FMLA leave take the full 12 weeks allowed by law.

Less than 10% of the employees who are eligible for leave under the FMLA take it. One reason for this low rate is that many employees cannot afford to take an extended unpaid leave. To keep a steady income, they may use accrued vacation time instead of taking an unpaid leave. Another reason some employees give for not taking family leave is the belief that taking such a leave has negative consequences for career advancement. Although the FMLA only requires unpaid leave, about a third of employers offer paid family leave as a benefit.[26]

VOLUNTARY PROTECTION PROGRAMS

Mandatory protection programs are intended to ensure that employees and their families have a safety net that protects them from catastrophic poverty. In contrast, most voluntary protection programs are designed to help employees achieve a greater level of comfort and security. For example, the income most people can expect to receive through Social Security is not enough to maintain their lifestyle at the time of retirement. Unless people have planned well for their retirement income needs, they may need to significantly reduce their spending after they stop working.

Voluntary protection programs encourage people to save and make it easy for them to do so. They include retirement income plans, capital accumulation plans, savings and thrift plans, supplemental unemployment benefits, and guaranteed pay.

About 60% of employees in U.S. firms are covered by some type of private retirement or capital accumulation plan, which they rely on to provide future security. The number goes up to 80% for medium-sized and large companies. Employees, through their pension funds, have become America's largest retirement bankers, lenders, and business owners.[27] The 20 largest pension funds (including those for public employees) hold 10% of the equity capital of publicly owned U.S. companies.

The various retirement income plans can be classified in terms of whether they are qualified or nonqualified, which reflects how they are treated by the IRS. A **qualified plan** *covers a broad class of employees (e.g., not just executives), meets Internal Revenue Code requirements, and consequently is qualified to receive favorable tax treatment.* Contributions to a qualified plan typically are tax deductible for employers for the current year and contain provisions for the deferment of taxes for employees until retirement. A **nonqualified plan** *doesn't adhere to the strict tax regulations, covers only select groups of employees (e.g., only senior management), and doesn't receive favorable tax treatment.*[28] Nonqualified plans are legal, but they are more costly for employers. By designing benefits and services that qualify for favorable tax treatment, employers can stretch the value of their investments considerably.

Three common types of retirement plans are defined benefit, defined contribution, and cash balance. Exhibit 12.7 reports the percentage of firms that make these available to their employees.

Defined Benefit Plans

With a defined benefit plan, the actual benefits received upon retirement are determined by the employee's age and length of service. For example, an employee who retires at age 65 might receive $50 a month for each year of company service. Unions prefer defined benefit plans because they produce predictable, secure, and continuing income.

With a defined benefit plan, funds are put aside and usually managed by the employer until they are paid out to retirees. To prevent employers from using pension funds for other purposes and to protect employees' savings, employers

FAST FACT

Only about 50% of workers have any idea how much they need to save for retirement.

FAST FACT

Institutional investors (primarily pension funds) control approximately 40% of the common stock of the largest U.S. businesses.

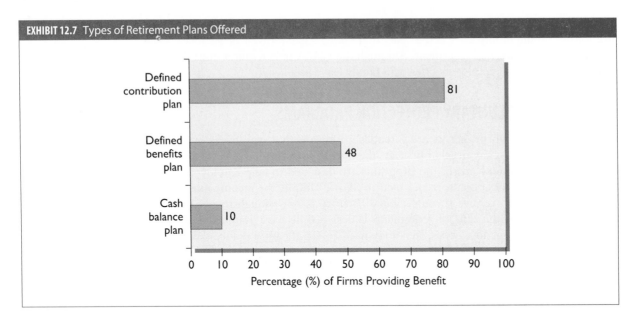

EXHIBIT 12.7 Types of Retirement Plans Offered

must adhere to stringent reporting rules, disclosure guidelines, fiduciary standards, participation rules, and vesting standards.

Defined benefit plans are often referred to as "traditional" pension plans because they had been widely offered by employers during the past several decades. Traditional pensions helped retain employees because the value of the payouts made to retirees built up with age and tenure in the organization. By design, they discouraged or penalized employee mobility. Given the reality of employee mobility in the twenty-first century, such "benefits" are no longer as desirable as they were when employees enjoyed more job security. In addition, employers have learned that defined benefit plans can be expensive. As employees live longer and investment returns decrease, the cost of funding traditional, defined benefit pensions has increased. Unfortunately, many of the companies that once promised employees a continuing source of income now find that they cannot meet their obligations. For these and other reasons, many employers are phasing out defined benefits and replacing them with defined contribution plans.

Defined Contribution Plans

With a defined contribution plan, each employee has an account to which contributions are added; the value of the account depends on how well the investment performs over time, so retirement payouts are not guaranteed. The two major types of defined contribution plans are called noncontributory plans and contributory plans. *If only the employer contributes to the retirement account, it's a* **noncontributory plan.** *When both the employee and the employer contribute to the retirement account, it's a* **contributory plan.** Most employers that offer defined contribution plans offer a contributory plan.

Typically, employees must activate a contributory plan by agreeing to contribute a set amount of money; the employer then matches the percentage contribution at a specific level. For example, the employee might contribute 5% of each paycheck, and the employer might agree to match what the employee contributes up to 3%. The most common types of defined contribution plans are 401(k)s, 403(b)s, employee stock ownership, and profit sharing.

401(k)s and 403(b)s. The most common type of defined contribution plan is a 401(k). With a 401(k), both the employer and the employee contribute to a fund, and the employee is responsible for investment decisions. For public employees, 403(b)s serve the same purpose, although slightly different rules apply.

Historically, employers sponsor these plans and make some contributions, but employees decide if they want to sign up, how much to invest, and how to invest it (e.g., putting their funds into stocks, money market accounts,

---

MANAGING ETHICS
Ethical Implications of Defined Contribution Plans

In December of 2007, IBM froze its defined benefit plan, stopping accruals for all participants. Now, employees are automatically enrolled in a 401(k) that matches employee contributions up to 6% of their base pay. This is a generous matching amount; the average match from employers is only 3%.

IBM is one of many companies, large and small, making the switch from a defined benefit plan to a defined contribution plan. As the Baby Boomer generation begins to retire, many companies have found that the costs and volatility of their defined benefit plans can be bad for a company's financial health. Defined benefit plans reduce corporate profitability, create problems with cash flow, and reduce a firm's ability to invest in new initiatives.

Switching to a 401(k) may be helpful for the company, but it usually has the opposite consequences for employees. This creates an ethical dilemma. How can firms make sure that all of their employees will be as well taken care of upon retirement as they would have been with a defined benefit plan? Will employees simply have to learn to live with having a less secure retirement future?

Participation in 401(k)s is voluntary, and not all employees want to sign up. If employees don't participate, they give up the amount their employer would match (6% of base pay for IBM employees), as well as an opportunity to take advantage of favorable tax treatment of their retirement savings. The Pension Protection Act of 2006 helps address this concern by allowing employers to automatically enroll their employees in a 401(k). This is what IBM does. Instead of having employees volunteer to participate, they automatically participate unless they specifically choose not to. Research shows that automatic enrollment dramatically increases participation rates.

Some employers also worry about their employees making poor investment choices that put their entire retirement savings at great risk. One way employers are addressing this concerns is by providing financial investment counseling to employees. Firms had been wary of providing such advice for fear of lawsuits when the advice resulted in poor plan performance, but the Pension Protection Act now provides some legal protection against such lawsuits. Employers are legally protected as long as their advisors rely on objective computer models or work under a fee arrangement that doesn't depend on the investments chosen by the participant. These provisions are designed to reduce conflicts of interest for the financial advisors and to ensure that employees get unbiased advice. About 50% of employers provide investment advice or financial planning to help employees make wise investment choices. Employers also are stepping up their communication to help educate employees about their retirement benefits.

In addition to automatic enrollment and providing financial advice, IBM has taken several additional steps to help protect its employees against the downside risk of 401(k)s. These include automatic rebalancing of their investments and an annuity income option. Other ideas under consideration include automatic step-ups that periodically increase employee contributions and a managed account feature. None of these services restores the level of security that IBM employees had when the firm offered a defined benefit retirement plan—those days are in the past. Nevertheless, IBM is setting a high standard for addressing the concerns faced by the next generation of retirees.

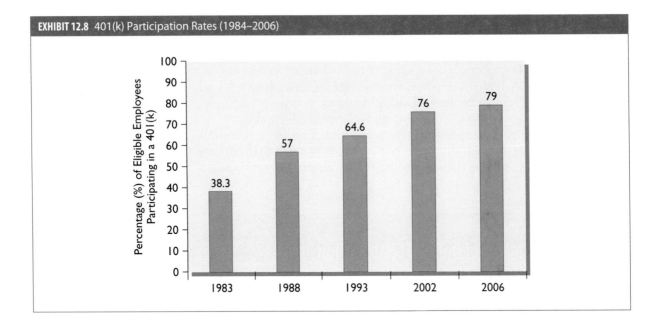

EXHIBIT 12.8 401(k) Participation Rates (1984–2006)

bonds, etc.). Employees who invest successfully can accumulate substantial funds for retirement.[29]

Many employers—including IBM, JC Penney, DuPont, and Hewlett-Packard—have recently switched from traditional retirement pension plans to 401(k)s. They are now the most popular retirement plans because they tend to save employers money and they shift the risk of poor plan performance from the employer to the employee. The shifting of risk to employees has created new concerns. One big concern is that many employees who are eligible for 401(k)s choose not to participate, which may mean they have too little money when they retire. Another concern is that many employees may not have the financial knowledge needed to invest wisely. How will society treat future retirees who do not have the money they need during retirement? These concerns raise some ethical issues for employers who offer 401(k)s, as discussed in the feature "Ethical Implications of Defined Contribution Plans."[30]

Employee participation in 401(k)s has risen steadily over the last two decades, as Exhibit 12.8 shows. Today, 80% of eligible employees participate in such plans. As automatic enrollment becomes more widespread, the number is likely to be even higher in the future. To further increase enrollments, some employers are looking for other ways to increase participation.[31] Starbucks offers a 401(k). The average employee at Starbucks is only 28 years old. Thinking clearly about retirement isn't always easy at that age; so Starbucks makes an extra effort to encourage employees to learn about and take advantage of their retirement savings account. At a company Web site called Futureroast.com, employees can play computer games that teach them about the company's retirement plan. By playing the games, employees learn about concepts such as "company match" and they also see how much the money they save today can grow in value over long periods of time.[32]

Employee Stock Option and Profit Sharing Plans. As described in Chapter 11, many corporations offer stock grants, stock options, or profit-sharing programs.

> ❝ *People spend more time planning a vacation than planning for retirement.* ❞
>
> *Dallas Salisbury*
> *Chief Executive Officer*
> *Employee Benefit Research Institute*

Some companies view stock offerings and profit-sharing programs as elements of incentive pay, which is why we discussed them in Chapter 11. However, employees often think of these forms of compensation as benefits because they affect future earnings more rather than current earnings.

When retirement contributions are paid to employees in the form of stocks, the value of the retirement plan is closely tied to the performance of a single firm: the employer. If that firm falters, employees may lose both their jobs and their retirement funds. Tying retirement plans primarily to the performance of a single firm usually violates sound financial principles for spreading risk by investing in a more diversified portfolio.[33] Due to the high risk employees face with these types of retirement programs, legal challenges are being raised. Many employers who are funding their retirement plans primarily with their own company's stock are being sued for violating fiduciary duties.[34]

Cash Balance Plans

Cash balance plans, which cover about 8.5 million workers, are another type of private pension offered by some employers. With a cash balance plan, the employer pays a specific amount into employees' accounts each year, and a lump sum of cash is later paid out to employees upon their retirement or departure from the company. Each employee's account earns a specific interest rate, typically tied to an index rate such as U.S. Treasury bonds. The IRS considers cash balance plans to be defined benefit plans because payouts are determined by a formula and they are federally insured. But many consider them to be a hybrid between a defined benefit plan and a 401(k). Like a traditional pension, employees can count on a fixed payout when they leave the firm or retire. And, as in a 401(k), the money in a cash balance account belongs to the employee as soon as it is contributed, which makes it portable.[35] **Portable benefits** *are benefits that employees can take with them when they leave the firm for a different employer.* For employees who work for several employers over the course of their careers, cash balance plans may be more desirable than traditional defined benefit plans, which penalized people who did not stay with one employer throughout their careers.

For more mobile employees, cash balance plans result in greater accrued benefits compared to traditional defined contribution plans. By age 65, a cash balance plan provides a 40% greater benefit compared to an average defined benefit plan for workers who have switched jobs often. However, a recent GAO (Government Accountability Office) report concluded that workers' benefits are often reduced when their firm switches from a defined benefit to a cash balance plan, particularly for older, longer tenured workers.[36]

Before IBM's recent switch to a 401(k), it had tried to offer a cash balance plan. Older employees were outraged and filed a lawsuit. IBM was found guilty of age discrimination by a lower court, which raised serious questions about the legality of cash balance plans. An appeals court reversed the ruling in 2006, and the Pension Protection Act of 2006 also included a provision clarifying the legality of cash balance plans. Thus, we are likely to see more use of cash balance plans in the future.[37]

Legal Considerations

No federal laws require employers to provide employees with retirement income beyond Social Security insurance. For employers who offer voluntary retirement benefits, however, many laws specify a variety of rules and standards.

The most comprehensive of these is the Employee Retirement Income Security Act (ERISA).

ERISA. *The* **Employee Retirement Income Security Act of 1974 (ERISA)** *is designed to protect the interests of workers covered by private (voluntary) retirement plans by regulating the management of pension funds.* ERISA does not require an employer to offer a pension fund, and it does not specify how much money a participant must be paid as a benefit. It only requires that those who establish retirement plans must follow certain rules and meet certain minimum standards that relate to reporting and disclosure, fiduciary duties, nondiscrimination, participation, and vesting for contribution benefit plans.

For defined benefit and cash balance plans, employers also must follow rules relating to funding and plan termination insurance.[38] Plan termination insurance is handled through the **Pension Benefit Guaranty Corporation (PBGC)**, *which administers the required insurance program and guarantees the payment of basic retirement benefits to participants if a plan is terminated.* The PBGC collects insurance premiums from employers and dispenses retirement payments to retirees if plans become insolvent. Since 2000 the number of insolvent pension funds has been rapidly increasing, due primarily to airline and steel company bankruptcies. Over 73% of all the payouts by the PBGC since 1975 have gone to employees in the airline and steel industries.

Exhibit 12.9 shows the five largest claims that the PBGC has covered since 1975. All five have occurred since 2002. The rapid rise in pension plan insolvencies and PBGC insurance payouts has put great financial pressure on the PBGC. In fact, experts worried that the PBGC itself was near the brink of insolvency. Fortunately, the Pension Protection Act of 2006 included new rules governing insurance premiums paid to the PBGC, which seem to have improved the agency's financial stability.[39]

Other Laws Related to Retirement Plans. To encourage Americans to save for retirement, the **Economic Recovery Tax Act of 1981** *allows employees to make tax-deductible contributions to (1) an employer-sponsored pension, profit-sharing, or savings account; or (2) to an individual retirement account (IRA).* By providing tax relief, this law stimulated the growth of both private protection programs and the use of stock ownership as a form of compensation (described in Chapter 11).[40] The law was later updated by the Economic Growth and Tax Relief Reconciliation Act of 2001, which raised the contribution limits for employer-sponsored retirement plans and shortened pension vesting waiting periods. Another law with far-reaching consequences is the Pension Protection Act of 2006, which makes it easier for people to participate in defined contribution plans like IRAs and 401(k)s.[41]

FAST FACT

Firms may specify a normal retirement age earlier than 65 for employees to be eligible to collect retirement benefits, but ERISA requires that the guideline refer to an age, not years of employment at the company. (Laurent v. PricewaterhouseCoopers LLP. S.D.N.Y. No. 06 Civ. 2280 (MBM), September 5, 2006)

FAST FACT

In 2000 the PBGC paid out $900 million in pension benefits to 243,000 retirees. In 2006 it paid out $4.1 billion to 612,000 retirees.

EXHIBIT 12.9 Largest PBGC Claims by Firms in Default since 1975			
Largest 5 Claims	**Year**	**Claim**	**Vested Participants**
1. United Airlines	2005	$7,093,803,951	122,541
2. Bethlehem Steel	2003	$3,654,380,116	97,015
3. US Airways	2003	$2,861,901,511	58,823
4. LTV Steel	2002	$1,959,679,993	80,961
5. National Steel	2003	$1,161,019,567	35,404

With the Baby Boomer generation nearing retirement, government regulation of employer-sponsored retirement benefits is likely to remain active. One result is that HR professionals with expertise in this area will be in great demand well into the future.

HEALTH CARE BENEFITS AND SERVICES

Health care benefits and services typically help employees pay for hospital charges, home health care, physician charges, and a variety of other medical services. Health care benefits and services also include wellness programs, employee assistance programs, and short- and long-term disability insurance beyond what is legally mandated. Employees who receive health care benefits and services, particularly medical insurance, can expect to receive adequate health care at a cost that is far less than that paid by individuals who do not have such benefits and services. Although these benefits and services are very expensive for employers, most employees underestimate their employer's costs and view coverage as an entitlement rather than a discretionary benefit.[42]

Employers pay an average of $11,500 for a health insurance plan that covers a family of four. Out of every benefits and services dollar spent, a quarter goes to health care. As a consequence, U.S. companies have been very aggressive at reducing health care expenses. Reducing these costs often means reducing the amount of choice employees have concerning which physicians they may use and increasing the amount that employees are required to pay to obtain health care coverage. Other ways employers reduce health care costs will be discussed later in this chapter.[43]

Medical Care

Employers usually provide benefits to cover medical care for employees and their dependents through payments to insurance companies or other third parties. Many employers offer employees a choice of plans. Employees who expect to have few medical needs may choose a low-cost plan with somewhat less desirable features, while those who expect to have greater needs may opt for a relatively expensive plan. Employees who prefer the expensive plan must pay toward covering the additional cost of buying into it. Exhibit 12.10 shows the percentage of workers with health insurance enrolled in each type of plan.[44]

Conventional Insurance Plans. Known as an indemnity plans, conventional health insurance plans offer a broad range of health care services from which employers can select coverage. Employees choose any provider they want. The cost premiums (fees paid to the insurance company) are set and adjusted depending on usage rates by the company's employees and projected increases in costs. The insurance company administers the plan, handling all the paperwork, approvals, and problems. An advantage of this approach is that it protects employers against wide fluctuations in claim exposure because the risk is spread across a large pool of participants. This is especially important for small and medium-sized companies. Another advantage is that insurance companies have administrative expertise related to certification reviews, claim audits, coordination of benefits, and other cost containment services.

On the downside, the insurance company, not the employer, makes decisions regarding covered benefits. Its decisions may go against the corporation's ethics and sense of social responsibility. But the biggest disadvantage is cost. Twenty years ago, the vast majority of employees with health insurance were

FAST FACT

General Motors spends about $1,500 on employee medical benefits and services for each automobile it makes in the United States.

FAST FACT

General Motors provides medical benefits and services for 1.1 million Americans.

FAST FACT

Health care costs are now rising four times faster than consumer prices and wages.

EXHIBIT 12.10 Percentage of Enrolled Workers by Type of Health Care Plan

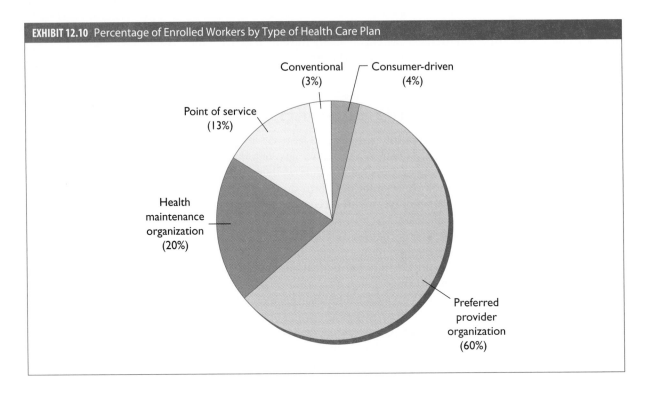

covered by a conventional plan—that's why it's called "conventional"! But today only 3% of covered workers have this type of plan.

Health Maintenance Organizations. About 20% of all eligible employees participate in health maintenance organization (HMO) plans. With HMOs, employees choose from a restrictive list of **primary care physicians (PCPs)**, *who serve as gatekeepers of the employees' health care.* An employee's PCP provides routine and preventative care and, when needed, refers the employee to specialists who are also in the restricted system. There is no coverage provided for visits to doctors who are not in the HMO's approved network.[45]

One successful HMO is operated by Deere & Company, a farm machinery manufacturer. Deere's health care costs were skyrocketing 20 years ago. To control its costs, the company brought its health insurance in-house by establishing its own HMO, called John Deere Health. Deere's HMO has been so successful that it has attracted more than 300 other company clients.[46]

Preferred Provider Organizations. About 60% of U.S. employees with health care coverage are enrolled in preferred provider organizations (PPOs), making these the most popular type of health care plan. With PPOs, employers contract directly or indirectly through an insurance company with health care providers (physicians, dentists, laboratories, hospitals, and so forth) to deliver discounted services to program participants. The rates and requirements for these plans are relatively unregulated and employers have a great deal of flexibility in structuring an arrangement.

Unlike HMOs, there is no gatekeeper approval process. Also, employees in a PPO are not required to use the plan's providers exclusively. If they need to see a specialist who is not part of the PPO network, the cost is covered. However, often PPOs use incentives to encourage employees to use providers from the PPO network. For example, the employer may cover all the costs of health care provided by a physician in the PPO's network, but only 80% of the costs of care provided by physicians outside the network. Employees in a PPO have more freedom than those in an HMO, and that tends to cost them a bit more. To cover the higher costs, employees in PPOs often pay co-pays and deductibles.[47]

Point of Service Plans. A point of service (POS) plan is a hybrid type of plan that combines some of the features of PPOs and HMOs. As with an HMO, employees have primary care physicians who serve as the gatekeepers and who make referrals to specialists. As with a PPO, employees can go out of the plan's network of physicians, and the extra cost is covered through co-pays, deductibles, and other rules. Out-of-network physicians may be covered at the same rate as in-network physicians if they are referred to by the employee's PCP. Thus, POS plans contain some of the managed care aspects of HMOs while providing the flexibility of PPOs.[48]

Consumer-Driven Plans. Consumer-driven plans are a new type of plan that requires employees to be more proactive in their health care decisions and management. Employers provide employees with a predetermined amount of money that the employee uses to choose a health care plan. Some employers offer a wide range of options to choose from, while others offer only a few.

Employers like consumer-driven plans because they cost less. One reason for this is that they tend to have higher deductibles. Some employees also like the plans because they are more efficient, which means each employee gets more of the services they value most. Most consumer-driven plans involve the use of health savings accounts, and in some plans employees get to keep any money that's left in the account because they didn't use it.[49]

Health savings accounts (HSAs) *are tax-free accounts funded by employees, employers, or both that set aside money to pay health care expenses.* For contributions to be tax exempt, the account must be part of a high-deductible health care plan, with deductibles of at least $1,000 and out-of-pocket expense limits of at least $5,000. At year-end, any unspent funds in an HSA belong to the employee. The leftover money can be rolled over for use in the following year, and it is portable; that is, the account goes with the employee if he or she changes employers. The portability of HSAs is a major advantage over the other types of health care insurance we have described. HSAs are easier to administer than other plans, which save employers money, and they encourage consumers to make cost-conscious well-informed medical choices. Furthermore, with HSAs employees can accumulate surplus funds by the time they reach retirement, and the savings can be used for other purposes. On the downside, HSAs may encourage employees to avoid spending money by not getting beneficial preventive care and even essential medical treatments; consumers are expected to make wise medical choices.[50]

Because consumer-driven plans require employees to make important choices, they must be well-informed. Companies with consumer-driven plans, such as Wendy's, Reader's Digest, and Harrah's, know that effective communication and education are necessary for HSAs to work.

Fairview Health Systems is a regional medical system in Minnesota. When they launched a new consumer-driven plan called Ultimate Choice, they made

> *Frankly, health care today is too complex, frustrating, and expensive for it to be anything but a shared responsibility.*
>
> Allen Hill
> Senior Vice President of Human Resources and Public Affairs
> United Parcel Service

FAST FACT

Health savings accounts are allowed by a provision of the Medicare Modernization Act of 2003.

sure employees were well-informed about their choices. Fairview used a comprehensive program to educate employees, who had access to online interactive software that they could use to model the costs and benefits associated with each of their alternatives. To help them determine their health risks, employees were given personalized health risk assessments. When the new plan was introduced, the company held an 18-week communication campaign that used newsletters, e-mails, fact sheets, computer training, group meetings, posters, and personalized one-on-one communication to educate employees about the plan. With the comprehensive communication program, Fairview achieved a 95% enrollment rate and an increase in employee satisfaction.[51]

Wellness Programs

Frustrated with efforts to manage health care costs for employees who already are sick, a growing number of employers are taking proactive steps to prevent health care problems. Wellness programs may include exercise classes held at on-site fitness facilities, training in stress management, assistance in quitting smoking, free health screening clinics, practices to promote healthy eating, and a variety of other programs. Consumer-driven health plans usually include these programs. Exhibit 12.11 shows the percentage of firms that offer various wellness benefits.[52]

Many firms are implementing well designed wellness programs to produce significant savings on the bottom line. United Parcel Service (UPS) has a program called UPS Healthy Connections–Informed Choices, which includes health assessments, health coaches, dieticians, Web-based health education, and weight loss, smoking cessation, and stress management programs. UPS is hoping to see lowered absenteeism, improved productivity, and lower health

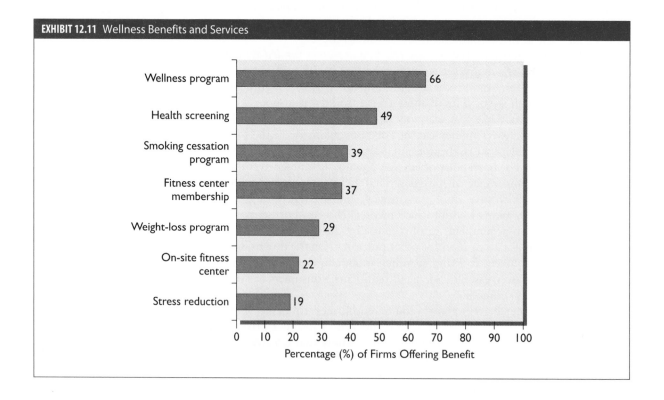

EXHIBIT 12.11 Wellness Benefits and Services

Wellness program — 66
Health screening — 49
Smoking cessation program — 39
Fitness center membership — 37
Weight-loss program — 29
On-site fitness center — 22
Stress reduction — 19

Percentage (%) of Firms Offering Benefit

care costs as a result. Of course, such programs are good for employees too. The Dow Chemical Company has a program called Backs in Action that encourages exercise, dieting, and ergonomics. Since it was implemented, on-the-job strains and sprains suffered by employees have decreased by about 90%.

Employee Assistance Programs

Whereas wellness programs attempt to prevent the development of health problems, **Employee Assistance Programs (EAPs)** *are designed to assist employees with chronic personal problems that hinder their job performance and attendance.* EAPs often serve employees with alcohol or drug dependency, or both, or those with severe domestic problems. EAPs also help employees cope with mental disorders, financial problems, stress, eating disorders, smoking cessation, dependent care, bereavement, and AIDS. EAPs and wellness programs are described in more detail in Chapter 13.

FAST FACT

Seventy percent of U.S. employers offer EAPs.

PAID LEAVE

LEARNING GOAL 7

As Exhibit 12.5 showed, paid leave accounts for about 7% of employers' total compensation costs, on average. The two major categories of paid leave are time not worked while off the job and time not worked while on the job.

Off-the-Job Paid Leave

The most common types of off-the-job paid leaves are vacations, holidays, jury duty leaves, bereavement leaves, sick leaves, and personal days. The challenge in administering these benefits and services is to contain costs while seeking better ways to tailor the benefits and services to fit employees' needs and preferences.

Holidays and Vacations. Most employees get paid leave for some holidays. The average number of paid holidays is eight; the vast majority of employees get between six and eleven paid holidays. Almost 90% of all full-time workers receive paid holidays and paid vacations, but only about a third of part-time workers do.[53]

FAST FACT

Nongovernment employers in the United States are not legally required to offer paid vacation days.

Vacations give employees time to recuperate from the physical and mental demands of work. Increased days of vacation time are often given as a reward to employees as they accumulate more years of employment tenure. Vacations are viewed as a reward for company loyalty; so this benefit can help employers retain valued workers. For employees with one year of tenure, the average number of vacation days is 9; for employees with 25 years, the average is 19 days.

In setting up vacation programs, several issues need to be addressed: (1) Will vacation pay be based on scheduled hours or on hours actually worked? (2) Under what circumstances can an employee receive cash in lieu of taking a vacation? (3) Can vacations be deferred, or will they be lost if not taken? (4) What pay rate applies if an employee works during a vacation? (5) How much choice do employees have in choosing when they take their vacation days? The trend is toward vacation banking, with employees being able to roll over a specified period of unused vacation days into a savings investment plan.[54]

In some countries, the government mandates the minimum number of vacation days per year. International differences in vacation policies are described in the feature "Managing Globalization: Vacationing around the World."[55]

MANAGING GLOBALIZATION
Vacationing around the World

For employees who work in global firms, vacation policies and practices are among the most visible differences in benefits and services enjoyed by employees around the world. Governments differ substantially in terms of what they mandate, and employees in different countries differ in how they actually use their vacation time. Many Europeans would never consider not using all of their vacation time, while Americans often take fewer days than they are entitled to. A recent survey found that Americans on average did *not* take 1.8 days of vacation they were entitled to. In effect, they chose to work for free! The following chart indicates some of the differences in vacations taken by employees around the world.

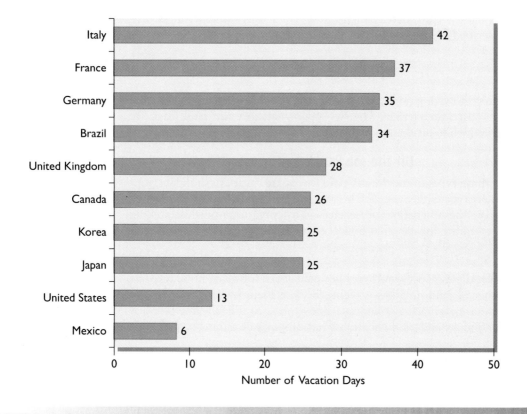

Other Paid Leaves. Employers grant many other off-the-job leaves as benefits to workers. Exhibit 12.12 shows the most popular of these. Other off-the-job leaves that are sometimes offered, but are not typical, include release time for volunteering, adoption leave, additional paternity and maternity leave beyond what is required by the FMLA, a day off for an employee's birthday, and sabbaticals.[56] Not surprisingly, as the number of paid days off increases, the number of days of actual absence increases proportionally. Thus, by providing numerous leave days, many organizations unwittingly reward absenteeism. Their policies make it easier to be absent than to come to work.

In any given day, one million American employees will be absent from work. In the United States, the daily absenteeism rate ranges from 2 to 3% of total payroll, but some organizations report absenteeism in excess of 20%.

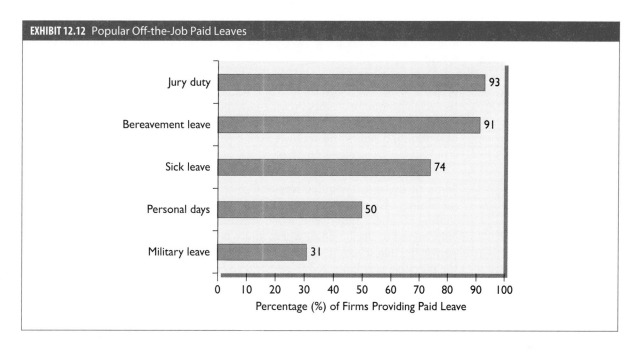

EXHIBIT 12.12 Popular Off-the-Job Paid Leaves

Jury duty — 93
Bereavement leave — 91
Sick leave — 74
Personal days — 50
Military leave — 31

Percentage (%) of Firms Providing Paid Leave

Almost two-thirds of all absences are due to something other than personal illness.[57] For most employers, unscheduled absenteeism is more disruptive than predictable absenteeism (e.g., a day off on your birthday). To help reduce unscheduled absenteeism, about half of all employers grant personal days, or personal time off. Employees can use these days during the year for any reason, but, to be eligible for pay, the employees must notify supervisors in advance that they will be absent.

Using discipline is another way employers try to reduce absenteeism. Disciplinary actions range from simple warnings for first offenses to firing workers who are absent too often. Discipline appears to be ineffective in controlling absenteeism among habitual offenders. Programs that reward attendance—with, for instance, cash prizes, bonuses, or conversion of a proportion of unused absence days to vacation days—appear to be more effective.

On-the-Job Paid Leave

On-the-job paid leave includes rest periods, lunch periods, washup times, and clothes-changing and getting-ready times. Employees are typically paid for their time in these activities, although the activities do not actually involve working at the job itself.

Another benefit that's growing in popularity is paid time for use of on-site physical fitness facilities. This is clearly pay for time not spent working. Organizations often offer it because of its on-the-job benefit: healthy workers.

WORK/LIFE BENEFITS AND SERVICES

In response to a growing number of single-parent families, two-earner families, aging parents in need of care, and nontraditional families, employers are expanding their benefits and services packages to address new priorities.[58] Also known as family-friendly benefits, some work/life benefits and services

FAST FACT

Companies in Fortune's list of "100 Best Companies to Work for in America" have significantly lower absenteeism because of their culture, leadership, and HR practices.

8

LEARNING GOAL

are offered by only a handful of firms. However, employers are realizing that a failure to address these needs may restrict their ability to compete in the future.

A recent survey of 600 U.S. companies found that the top reasons for offering work/life benefits and services were to improve morale, enhance recruitment, remain competitive, and improve the company's image in the industry. Exhibit 12.13 shows the percentage of U.S. firms offering several types of work/life benefits and services.[59]

Scheduling

Some of the most popular work/life benefits and services involve employee scheduling. Flextime, the compressed workweek, telecommuting, and job sharing all affect employees' work schedules.[60] Ernst & Young employees are empowered to decide how, when, and where to get their jobs done. The company's flexible schedule options have been in place since the mid-1990s, when the initiative was launched to respond to employees' concerns about work/life balance. Those who use the flexible work arrangement (FWA) option value it greatly. According to a survey of those using FWA at the firm, 84% say this service is the primary reason they stay at Ernst & Young.

Child Care Services

Addressing child care needs is a responsibility that must be addressed by working parents, and more and more employers are providing some assistance to their employees. Child care benefits and services include scholarships for children of employees, subsidized tutoring, care for sick children, subsidized college educations, on-site or subsidized child care, child care referrals, extended leaves, benefits for employees with children who have special needs, workplace

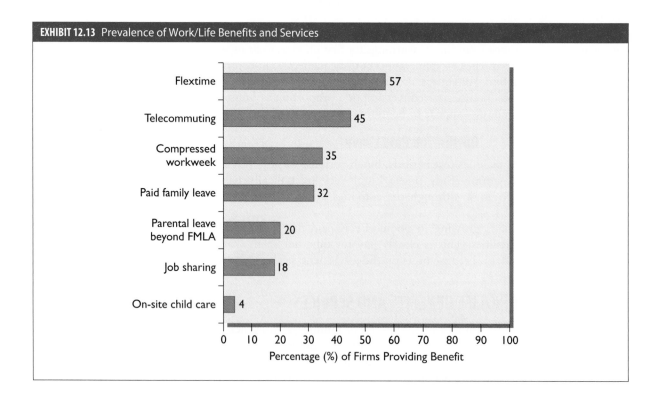

EXHIBIT 12.13 Prevalence of Work/Life Benefits and Services

schools, and employer-sponsored summer camps. To be competitive in the labor market, firms should survey their employees to find out their preferences, and then work to offer options that meet employees' needs.[61]

Currently, an estimated 10% of large employers offer on-site or near-site child care. SAS, the software company, operates four on-site child care centers. Parents can visit their children during the day and even join them for lunch. When children's activities are held outside, parents often can watch their children from their office windows. Like other corporate child care centers, the one operated by SAS offers quality care that is far above the norm for this service. The teachers who work for SAS are paid above-average salaries, and many have been on the job for a decade or more. At Procter & Gamble's child care center, most staff members are college educated, and many hold master's degrees.[62]

Elder Care Services

About 25% of the U.S. labor force has elder care responsibilities and about 35% of those also have child-care responsibilities. For a significant number of workers, providing care for older family members is equivalent to a second job. Some 12% of workers who care for aging parents are forced to quit their jobs to do so. With the aging of Baby Boomers and the parents they care for, more and more employers are considering ways to help workers who care for elderly relatives.

Employers can help their workers meet elder care responsibilities in many ways. Elder care referral services are provided by about 25% of firms, which is up from 11% in 1990. Extended leaves beyond the mandated FMLA requirement are provided by 14% of firms. Emergency elder care services or subsidies to help cover the cost of elder care are provided by around 5% of employers.[63]

The most popular elder care benefit is long-term care insurance. The insurance covers medical, social, custodial, and personal services for people who suffer from chronic physical or mental illnesses or disabling injury or disease over an extended period of time. Fewer than 15% of firms offered this benefit in the mid-1990s, and now more than 40% offer it.[64]

Some employers fear that childless employees or those without elder care responsibilities may resent some work/life policies because they do not benefit from them. Research indicates that any backlash tends to be of limited scope and does not create generalized job dissatisfaction. One study of employee attitudes found differences in the attitudes of employees with and without children, but did not find that the negative attitudes of the childless employees translated into concrete behaviors.[65] Even if some backlash occurs, the benefits and services associated with child and elder care initiatives may outweigh the disadvantages.

Domestic Partner Benefits and Services

In 1950, married couples made up 80% of all households. Today, married couples make up less than 50% of all households. Increasingly, adults are choosing to cohabitate instead of marrying.[66] In 1997, only about 10% of companies had extended "spousal" benefits and services to same-sex partners and to unmarried opposite-sex domestic partners. Today, about 35% of companies offer benefits and services to domestic partners. At Prudential Securities, cohabitants can get health benefits and services for an opposite-sex or same-sex partner as long as they've lived together for at least six months. Employers provide domestic partner benefits and services to attract and retain talent, comply with the company's nondiscrimination policy, and comply with local laws.

FAST FACT

Cisco constructed a $16-million child care center for 432 children. Web cameras give parents a real-time window for checking in on their children.

FAST FACT

About two out of three employees under age 60 say they will have elder care responsibilities in the next decade.

" **Domestic partner benefits isn't a gay and lesbian issue. It's a business issue. We believe that by providing domestic partners access, we are enhancing our ability to recruit and retain the best employees.** "

Bill Shelley
Health and Welfare Supervisor
Pacific Gas & Electric

Federal laws do not require employers to provide domestic partner benefits and services, but some local ordinances do. At Shell, providing the full range of benefits and services to both same-sex and opposite-sex partners is one of several practices that support workforce diversity. According to Ronnie Kurtin, director of corporate human resources, domestic partner benefits and services are included as "part of the overall people strategy in order to create an inclusive environment so we can be sure folks are focusing on productive efforts." Of course, not all employers adopt this approach. Some employers consider domestic partnerships to be morally unacceptable and develop their policies accordingly.[67]

OTHER BENEFITS AND SERVICES

In addition to protection, health care, leave, and work/life benefits and services, employers may offer numerous other benefits and services to their employees. Exhibit 12.14 shows the most popular ones. Many of these other benefits and services fall into one of the following categories: developmental benefits, personal services benefits, or business travel and relocation assistance.

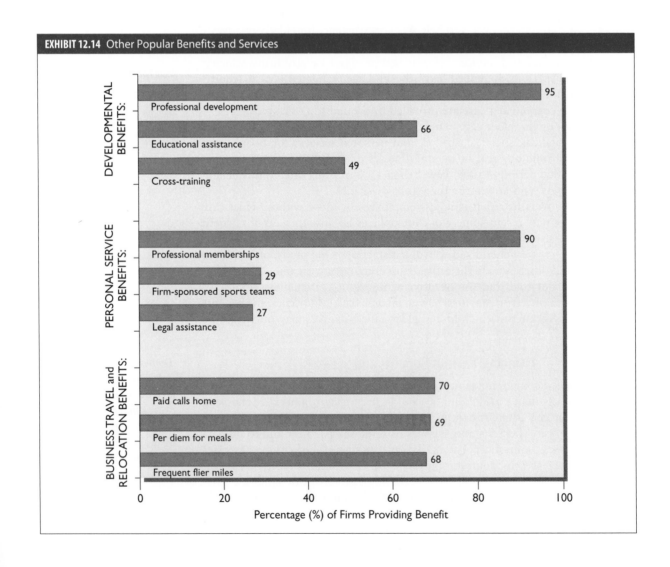

EXHIBIT 12.14 Other Popular Benefits and Services

Developmental Benefits and Services

Faced with skills obsolescence, downsizing, and retraining demands, most firms provide developmental opportunities and some form of educational expense assistance. These benefits and services help workers achieve personal goals while providing the employer with better-skilled employees.[68]

After developing employees, firms may need to reward them for their new skills or risk losing them. A study of more than 8,000 salaried employees at a large manufacturing firm found that people who participated in a tuition reimbursement program were less likely to leave the company while they were in school. But when employees earned their degrees, the likelihood of their leaving increased significantly unless they were subsequently promoted.[69]

Personal Services

The use of personal service benefits is increasing as more firms are trying to attract employees by providing employees with services that they might value. These services may be fully paid, subsidized, or made available at discounted rates negotiated by the employer.[70] Such personal services include legal assistance, career counseling, postal services, travel planning, massage therapy, food services, dry cleaning, and concierge services. When talent is in high demand, employers tend to be creative in coming up with new services that set them apart. For example, Microsoft offers free grocery delivery and valet parking at work. Quicken Loans provides its workers with company-sponsored buses to see professional sports games.[71]

Business Travel and Relocation Assistance

Business travel benefits generally pay for services and expenses that employees incur because of business travel. These can include dry cleaning, pay-per-view movies at hotels, minibar snacks, pet care arrangements, and health club fees while traveling. Almost half of all companies pay for travel accident insurance.

Relocation benefits pay for services and expenses associated with relocating because of a transfer or new hiring. These can include a relocation fee, rental assistance, mortgage assistance, home insurance assistance, assistance in selling the previous home, and spouse relocation assistance.

ADMINISTRATIVE ISSUES

Effectively administering employee benefits and services is a complicated challenge. In addition to deciding which benefits and services to offer and how much flexibility to offer employees, employers must work to ensure that people understand both the content plan and the economic cost/value of the benefits and services they receive.

Determining the Benefits and Services Package

Earlier in the chapter, we discussed how an organization's size, culture, and strategy can help shape the benefits and services package. The preferences of the firm's employees are also important in shaping the benefits and services package. Knowing employees' preferences helps organizations prioritize their spending on benefits and services; decisions about what to offer must take into account the cost for the employer relative to the value for employees.

Employee preferences can be discovered through well designed surveys and by examining benefit-related grievances and complaints. Clues that the benefit plan is not meeting employee needs can be uncovered by monitoring benefits-related metrics and by benchmarking against other firms. When NCR surveyed its employees about benefits and services, it found several that it could change to reduce costs while better meeting employee needs.[72]

Individual differences play a large role in determining which benefits and services employees prefer; one size does not fit all employees. Preferences differ based on employees' age, gender, education, marital status, and other demographic factors. For example, young employees prefer time off and money, while older employees prefer good retirement and health care plans. Those with young children are interested in flexible schedules, child care, and family leaves.[73]

Employee benefits and services preferences can also differ based on factors that are less easy to identify. A study of retirement plan options found that preferences for the different plans depended upon how much value an employee placed on various plan features. Some employees valued portability, others valued being in control of their investments, and some preferred to avoid risk.[74] These preferences were not related to demographics, such as age and gender. When employers find large differences in benefit preferences among their workers, flexible benefit plans may be the best way to meet the needs of most employees.

Determining the Level of Flexibility

As you have learned, many employees select some elements of their benefits and services package; not everyone receives a standard no-choice plan. With flexible benefits, employers typically provide basic coverage to everyone and then let employees choose additional benefits and services up to a certain cost ceiling. The options given to employees may be developed by the employees themselves, working in small discussion groups.

When employees participate in designing their own benefits and services, both they and the company can come out ahead. An advantage of flexible benefits, also known as cafeteria plans, is that employers don't have to pay for benefits and services that employees don't use. Also, employee participation in the process improves their understanding and appreciation of the benefits and services they receive.

Flexible benefits also have some disadvantages. Because employees are the primary decision makers, there is always a risk that they will make unsound decisions. Also, offering flexible benefits is more complicated, from the designing of the choices to administering the individualized packages. Depending on the mix of benefits and services offered, the tax implications may also be more complicated. Nevertheless, flexible benefit plans are now easier than ever to administer thanks to automation and the prevalence of company intranets. Technology also makes it easier to communicate benefits and services information to employees and to provide guidance as they evaluate their options and make choices.[75]

Communication

Many employers pump money into benefits and services because they believe it will enhance the organization's image among employees and in the business community. Applied wisely, this effort may work toward that end. On the other hand, ample research demonstrates that these objectives are usually not achieved. Most employees don't know which benefits and services they receive or how much they are worth. Recent surveys have shown that three out of four employees underestimate how much their company

> **The better HR professionals understand their employees and the issues they face, the better equipped they will be to respond.**
>
> *Debra Cohen*
> *Chief Knowledge Officer*
> *Society of Human Resource Management*

spends on their health insurance. More than two-thirds of employees do not view their employer's benefits communication as effective. Only 36% of employees are satisfied with their benefits and services. Yet 85% of consumers are satisfied with their new car, which is what employers could buy for them with the $18,000 that they spend on benefits and services on average.[76]

If employees don't know they receive a benefit, they won't stay with the company in order to retain that benefit. That's one reason Starbucks, Google, and many other successful firms aggressively market their benefits and services to employees; they want to be sure that their employees understand the value of this aspect of their total compensation. Hard Rock Café International makes benefit information available through an interactive CD that can be played at publicly available monitors in the employee break rooms.

Exhibit 10.2 from Chapter 10 (page 359) showed that about 88% of companies use Web-based tools to communicate general benefits information. At Oracle, Boeing, and Charles Schwab, workers can surf company intranets to learn about and self-manage 401(k)s, health care benefits and services, and even tax-withholding options. The Web and other forms of electronic communication are useful tools for providing benefits information, but small group presentations and face-to-face meetings may also be needed to reach all employees effectively.[77] By effectively communicating about benefits and services and providing flexibility, companies can do more than just improve their image and increase employee satisfaction. By ensuring that employees make sound benefits and services choices, employers may also help control their benefit costs.[78]

CURRENT ISSUES

Today, the dominant issue in benefits and services is escalating costs. In fact, HR professionals believe that the high cost of health care is the issue that will have the greatest impact on the workplace and the HR profession in the near future.[79] Employers spend enormous sums of money providing benefits and services. Yet, because many employees feel they are entitled to these benefits and services, employers do not receive much of a return on the expense. Employers are working hard to change this, especially for health care and retiree benefits and services.

Health Care Benefits and Services

A recent survey conducted by Deloitte & Touche found that 86% of benefits specialists ranked controlling the costs of health and welfare benefits as a top priority. One approach employers use to reduce their costs is to shift some health care costs to employees. Exhibit 12.15 shows some of the changes recently made by employers. Increased co-pays for doctors' visits and prescription drug purchases, employee contributions to pay for insurance premiums, and higher deductibles are all common. Workers now pay $1,094 more in premiums per year for family coverage than they did in 2000; the average employee contribution to company-provided health insurance has increased more than 143%; and employees' out-of-pocket expenses have gone up 115%.[80]

With employee costs reaching the limits of affordability, employers are looking for other ways to save on health care. We have already discussed several cost-reduction initiatives, including consumer-driven health care, wellness programs, and health savings accounts. Other tactics being used to further

FAST FACT

Health care coverage can cost employers more than $10,000 per employee—and even more in small firms.

EXHIBIT 12.15 Recent Changes to Health Care Benefits and Services by Employers Offering Them

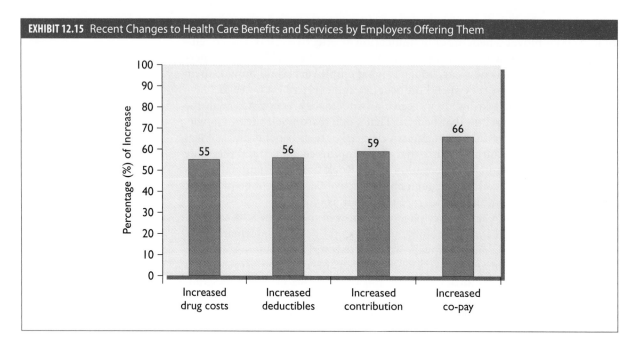

control health care costs include the following:

- *Hospital utilization programs.* Employers set up a system to review the necessity and appropriateness of hospitalization prior to admission, during a stay, or both.
- *Coordination of benefits.* Employers coordinate their benefits with those of other providers (e.g., Medicare or coverage under a spouse's plan) to prevent duplicate payment for the same health care service.
- *Data analysis.* Employers analyze the available information to determine the most viable cost management approach.
- *Prescription drug management.* Cost sharing, higher deductibles, and incentives for using mail order supplies and generics to reduce prescription drug costs.
- *Case management.* Many employers are active participants in case management. Medical procedures may include requirements for second opinions and peer reviews.
- *Auditing employee usage.* Audits of bill payments are done to determine whether ineligible family members (e.g., children above the allowed age) are using the benefits.[81]

Some firms are trying more radical approaches, such as encouraging employees to have some medical procedures done in other countries where the costs are lower, and firing workers who smoke. Scotts Miracle-Gro Company fired a worker during his probationary period because his drug test came back positive for nicotine. The fired worker sued the company; the legality of the action will eventually be decided by the federal courts.[82]

Benefits and Services for Retirees

According to HR professionals, the aging workforce is the next most important influence shaping the workplace. This issue includes the costs of benefits and services for retirees. As discussed earlier in the chapter, the risks and high costs of pensions are currently causing many firms to reevaluate and change their pension plans. Health care for retirees is also an issue.

Currently, about 16 million retirees receive health care benefits and services from their former employees. Because of increasing costs of health care during the past 20 years, half of the firms who once offered health benefits and services to retirees have stopped doing so. Usually, employers implement this change by continuing the benefits and services for people who have already retired, while dropping the benefit for new employees. Current employees may get squeezed, too—and that's where some of the biggest challenges come up.

About one out of three large firms still offer retiree health benefits and services to all. However, only 25% of employers who do so prefund retiree health benefits and services. In other words, many employers have led their employees to believe that they will have health coverage upon retirement without taking steps to ensure that the company will be able to pay the related costs. As the number of retirees rises, many firms are finding it difficult to meet their obligations to retirees. General Motors (GM) recently renegotiated changes in its retiree health care benefits and services with the United Auto Workers (UAW) union to help ensure GM's survival. The changes save GM about $15 billion in liabilities. On the other hand, GM's retirees will now have to pick up about $15 billion in additional costs that they had not planned for. As retiree expenses grow, it is likely that more firms will have to choose between providing the retiree benefits and services they had promised and remaining competitive. And employees will have to find other ways to pay for their health care after retirement.[83]

CHAPTER SUMMARY WITH LEARNING GOALS

On average, employees receive about 30% of their total compensation in the form of benefits and services. Employers make many choices when deciding which benefits and services to offer, how much control to give employees, and how much they require employees to contribute to covering their own costs.

1   **STRATEGIC IMPORTANCE.** Benefits and services are strategically important to firms because they are a substantial cost, can be used to attract and retain talent, and can be designed to support the firm's strategy. The major challenge is to be financially efficient in the strategic use of benefits and services.

2   **INTEGRATED HRM SYSTEM.** Benefits and services should be designed to fit the organization's external and internal environment. Economic conditions, union strength, and the legal environment all influence the benefits and services that an employer offers. The firm's size, corporate culture, and strategy also shape each organization's specific approach. Large firms tend to offer more benefits and services than small ones. Some employers offer benefits and services that support their corporate culture.

3   **THE HR TRIAD.** HR professionals, line managers, and employees all have substantial responsibilities with respect to benefits and services. A clear trend is to shift responsibilities from the employer to employees. These responsibilities include covering more of the costs of benefits and services and making more decisions when choosing among the available benefits and services.

4   **MANDATORY PROTECTION PROGRAMS.** Social Security, workers' compensation, and unemployment insurance are worker protection programs required by law. These mandatory benefits help employees survive financially when employees are not able to work. FMLA allows employees to take an unpaid leave when their personal lives warrant it.

5   **VOLUNTARY PROTECTION PROGRAMS.** Retirement plans and supplemental unemployment insurance are voluntary protection programs provided by many employers. Three common types of retirement plans are defined contribution plans, defined benefit plans, and cash balance plans. ERISA is the federal law that regulates the voluntary retirement plans offered by employers.

6 **HEALTH CARE.** Health care benefits and services include medical insurance, wellness programs, employee assistance programs, and short- and long-term disability insurance to supplement what is legally mandated. Most employers insure their workers with preferred provider organizations, health maintenance organizations, point-of-service plans, or consumer-driven plans.

7 **PAID LEAVE.** Firms offer both on-the-job leaves, such as lunch breaks and work breaks, as well as off-the-job leaves. Sick days, vacations, and holidays are the most common types of off-the-job leaves. Many U.S. employees give up their vacation days and instead use the time to work!

8 **WORK/LIFE.** Scheduling benefits, child care services, elder care services, and domestic partner benefits are offered by employers. The objectives of these additional benefits and services include improving employee morale, attracting and retaining talent, and increasing productivity.

9 **OTHER BENEFITS AND SERVICES.** Some employers also offer developmental benefits, various personal services, and business travel and relocation assistance. These and other innovative benefits and services are being used by employers to differentiate themselves so that they are better able to create a competitive workforce.

10 **ADMINISTRATIVE ISSUES.** Employers must decide which benefits and services to offer, how much flexibility to include in their offerings, and how to ensure that employees fully understand the benefits and services provided. Excellent benefit communications are essential for employers to get the greatest return on the money they spend.

11 **CURRENT ISSUES.** The high cost of health care and retiree benefits and services are two very important current issues. Because of rapidly rising costs, many employers are making significant changes in what they offer. As employers shift more of the burden to employees, employees and retirees will have to pay more of these costs.

TERMS TO REMEMBER

Contributory plan
Economic Recovery Tax Act of 1981
Employee Assistance Programs (EAPs)
Employee benefits and services
Employee Retirement Income Security Act of 1974 (ERISA)
Family and Medical Leave Act (FMLA)
Flexible benefits plans
Health savings accounts (HSAs)
Mandatory protection programs

Noncontributory plan
Nonqualified plan
Pension Benefit Guaranty Corporation (PBGC)
Portable benefits
Primary care physicians (PCPs)
Qualified plan
Social Security Act of 1935
Targeted benefits plan
Voluntary protection programs

QUESTIONS FOR DISCUSSION AND REFLECTIVE THINKING

1. Imagine you are the benefits and services manager for a medium-sized U.S. firm that offers consulting services. Describe how could you use benefits and services to improve your organization's productivity.
2. Do you think more companies should establish wellness programs? Why or why not?
3. As employers strive to offer benefits and services to an increasingly diverse workforce, they sometimes encounter backlash from employees who resent their policies. For example, some employees may not approve of spending on child care facilities, given that the facilities benefit some employees and not others. Or some employees may not approve

of policies that give equal treatment to spouses and domestic partners. Do you think employers should avoid offering a benefit if a substantial minority of employees object to it? Explain your rationale.

4. Make a list of the advantages and disadvantages of providing a broad range of benefits and services and then letting employees choose a few that fit their needs. Compare this approach to simply providing standardized bare-bones benefits and services. Which approach would you recommend? Why?

5. Most employers recognize the rising costs of health care and retiree benefits and services, but employees seem not to. As an employee, what benefits and services do you need to learn more about? Why?

PROJECTS TO EXTEND YOUR LEARNING

1. **Integration and Application.** Before continuing, review the cases of Southwest Airlines and Lincoln Electric at the end of this book. Then answer the following questions.

    a. What are the objectives of the company's approach to benefits and services?

    b. How well do the benefits and services packages serve the business objectives of the organization and the needs of employees? Which package would you prefer? Explain why.

    c. Could Southwest Airlines adopt the approach to benefits and services used at Lincoln Electric? What would be the advantages and disadvantages for Southwest Airlines to adopt the Lincoln Electric approach? Be sure to consider how various stakeholders would be affected by such a change.

2. **Using the Internet.** In order to provide benefits and services that are cost-effective and appealing to employees, employers must understand conditions in the labor market and be aware of what competitors are offering.

    a. Discover what information employers can get on benefits and services from the following sources:
    *   Employee Benefits Research Institute (www.ebri.org).
    *   Bureau of Labor Statistics (www.bls.gov).
    *   International Foundation of Employee Benefits Plans (www.ifebp.org/).

    b. Learn about the consulting services available to employers from several prominent consulting firms:
    *   Hay Group (www.haygroup.com).
    *   Towers Perrin (www.towers.com).
    *   Mercer (www.mercer.com).
    *   Hewitt Associates (www.hewitt.com).

    c. Find out about integrated disability management from the Integrated Benefits Institute (www.ibiweb.org).

    d. Learn more about the problem of underfunded pensions and the financial obligations of the Pension Benefit Guaranty Corporation (www.pbgc.gov).

    e. Explore the issues regarding health care, Medicare, and health savings accounts at the
    *   National Coalition on Health Care (www.nchc.org).
    *   U.S. Department of Health and Human Services (www.cms.hhs.gov).
    *   Internal Revenue Service (www.irs.gov).

    f. Get more information about long-term care from the
    *   National Clearinghouse for Long-Term Care Information (www.longtermcare.gov).
    *   U.S. Office of Personnel Management (www.opm.gov).
    *   EBRI Research (www.ebri.org).

3. **Experiential Activity.** Begin to learn about the similarities and differences in benefits and services offered by firms in an industry of interest to you.

Activity

Step 1. Choose two companies in the same industry to focus on. For example, you might choose Coca-Cola and Pepsi or Colgate-Palmolive and Procter & Gamble.

Step 2. Investigate the voluntary benefits and services offered by the two companies by exploring the companies' Web sites and, if possible, interviewing a few of the companies' employees. Then fill in the matrix below and answer the questions on p. 471.

Description of the Benefit or Service	How Important to YOU? 1 Not very 2 Somewhat 3 Extremely (Circle one number to indicate its importance to you.)	Name of Company A: _____ _____ _____ Offered by A? (Circle Y for yes or N for no.)	Name of Company B: _____ _____ _____ Offered by B? (Circle Y for yes or N for no.)	If Offered by Both Companies, Which Company's Plan Would Be Better for YOU? (Circle A or B.)
Telecommuting	1 2 3	Y N	Y N	A B
Flextime	1 2 3	Y N	Y N	A B
Subsidized child care	1 2 3	Y N	Y N	A B
Extended parental leave beyond FMLA requirement	1 2 3	Y N	Y N	A B
Paid family leave	1 2 3	Y N	Y N	A B
Tuition reimbursement	1 2 3	Y N	Y N	A B
Educational loans	1 2 3	Y N	Y N	A B
Mortgage assistance	1 2 3	Y N	Y N	A B
Dental insurance	1 2 3	Y N	Y N	A B
Vision insurance	1 2 3	Y N	Y N	A B
Prescription drug coverage	1 2 3	Y N	Y N	A B
HMO	1 2 3	Y N	Y N	A B
PPO	1 2 3	Y N	Y N	A B
On-site fitness center	1 2 3	Y N	Y N	A B
Casual dress day(s)	1 2 3	Y N	Y N	A B
Defined contribution retirement plan	1 2 3	Y N	Y N	A B
Defined benefit retirement plan	1 2 3	Y N	Y N	A B
Stock purchase plan	1 2 3	Y N	Y N	A B
Paid holidays	1 2 3	Y N	Y N	A B
Paid release time for volunteering	1 2 3	Y N	Y N	A B
Discounts on company products/services	1 2 3	Y N	Y N	A B
Flexible benefits program	1 2 3	Y N	Y N	A B
Other benefits of interest to you: _____	1 2 3	Y N	Y N	A B
Other: _____	1 2 3	Y N	Y N	A B
Other: _____	1 2 3	Y N	Y N	A B
Other: _____	1 2 3	Y N	Y N	A B

Step 3. Answer the following questions.

a. Overall, which company offers the benefits and services that you prefer—Company A or B?

b. Based on what you know about the benefits and services offered by the two companies, what conclusions can you draw about the corporate cultures of the companies? Does one company seem to be more employee friendly than the other?

c. If you were offered similar jobs with similar salaries at these two companies, would the difference in benefits and services influence which job offer you accepted? Why or why not?

d. Do you think the company with the less desirable benefits package is at a disadvantage strategically? Why or why not?

CASE STUDY
WHO'S BENEFITING?

Jack Parks is a benefits and services manager in the auto electronics division of USA Motors, a major manufacturer of audio systems and auto electronic ignition systems. After analyzing the impact of absenteeism on the division's staffing costs for the previous quarter, he is very concerned. What troubles Parks is an agreement negotiated 10 years ago between the national union and USA Motors that, in effect, pays workers for being absent.

The "paid absence" agreement was not supposed to work quite that way. The theory was that by giving workers one week of paid absence against which they could charge personal absences, the company would be encouraging workers to notify their supervisors when they would be gone, so that staffing arrangements could be made and production maintained. In practice, workers discovered that, by not charging off any "paid absences," they could receive a full week's pay in June when the company paid off the balance of unused paid absences for the previous year. This cash bonus, as workers had come to think of it, often coincided with the summer vacations taken by many of the 8,000 hourly employees when USA Motors shuts down for inventory.

As Parks learned, employees with chronic absentee records had figured out how to charge off absences using the regular categories (sick days, as well as excused and unexcused absences), and then collect the cash for the week of paid absences. In Parks's mind, USA Motors might just as well have negotiated a cash bonus for the hourly workers or given them another 10 to 15 cents per hour. After reviewing the division's absenteeism rates for controllable absences (i.e., those categories of absences believed to be of the employee's own choice), Parks concludes that the company could reduce this rate from the previous year's figure of 11%.

And then Parks has a brainstorm: What USA Motors needs to negotiate is an incentive plan for reducing absenteeism. The plan Parks has in mind entails a standard for the amount of controllable absence deemed acceptable. If a chronically absent employee exceeds the standard, then vacation, holiday, and sickness/accident pay would be cut by 10% during the next six months. If worker absence continues to exceed the allowable limits, then vacation, holiday, and sickness pay would be cut during the next six months by the actual percentage of absent days incurred by the chronic absentee. Hence, if a worker misses 15% of scheduled workdays during the first six-month period, vacation pay for the next six-month period would be reduced by 10%. If the employee continues to be absent at the 15% rate, then vacation pay would be reduced by 15% during the next six months.

Parks immediately drafted a memorandum outlining the program and submitted it to the corporate HR manager of USA Motors for inclusion in the upcoming bargaining session. To Parks's surprise and delight, the memorandum received strong corporate support and is scheduled as a high-priority bargaining topic for the fall negotiations.

CASE QUESTIONS

1. Will the incentive plan to reduce absenteeism succeed? Explain your opinion.
2. How much absenteeism is really under the employee's control?
3. Why didn't the paid absence plan work?
4. What plan would you suggest to USA Motors?

Promoting Workplace Safety and Health

Learning Goals

After reading this chapter, you should be able to:

1. Describe the strategic importance of workplace safety and health.
2. Explain how to promote workplace safety and health.
3. List the safety and health hazards often found in the workplace.
4. Present several strategies for improving workplace safety and health.
5. Discuss two current issues in workplace safety and health.

MANAGING HUMAN RESOURCES AT DEERE & COMPANY

As we described in Chapter 2, Deere & Company recently undertook a series of strategic change efforts aimed at improving the performance of this global manufacturer of agricultural, construction, forestry, and turf care equipment. In addition to all the recent strategic changes, described in Chapter 2, that Bob Lane and his management team have been making at Deere & Company, they also have been working to create a safer workplace. During the past decade, Deere's safety efforts have focused especially on reducing injuries and their related costs. As is true in many manufacturing companies, injuries due to repetitive motions are common. Such injuries can be quite painful, and they become worse and worse if not treated. Today, employees who experience significant pain while working are encouraged to summon their plant's ergonomics team. Terry Hardy works as a toolmaker at a John Deere tractor plant in Dubuque, Iowa. He's also a member of the plant's ergonomics team. As part of his duties, he carries a beeper that alerts him when a plant worker calls for help. When the beeper sounds, Hardy rushes to the scene of the latest backache or painful wrist. In addition to all the normal tasks of a toolmaker, Hardy helps develop solutions that will reduce the incidents of workplace injuries in the plant. He and other members of the team may consult with the employee to find a quick fix for the problem, or the team may take days to come up with a feasible solution. Having this safety procedure in place goes a long way toward creating an organizational environment that values employee safety and health.[1]▲

THE STRATEGIC IMPORTANCE OF WORKPLACE SAFETY AND HEALTH

Virtually all employees in an organization are affected by workplace safety and health—for better or worse.[2] Workers in factories are exposed to potentially dangerous machines. Construction workers may fall. Employees working in computer chip manufacturing plants are exposed to chemicals and fumes. White-collar workers also suffer. They are exposed to air of poor quality, which is common in closed office buildings.[3] Chemical components from sources such as carpeting and structural materials build up and are circulated through ventilation systems.[4] Infectious diseases can spread quickly through these environments, putting everyone at risk.

Benefits of a Safe and Healthy Workplace

By reducing the rates and severity of occupational accidents, diseases, workplace violence, and stress-related illnesses, and by improving the quality of work life for their employees, organizations can become significantly more effective.[5] Among the positive consequences of safe and healthy workplaces are (1) higher productivity owing to fewer lost workdays, (2) increased efficiency and quality from a healthier workforce, (3) reduced medical and insurance costs, (4) lower workers' compensation rates and direct payments because of fewer claims being filed, (5) and improved reputation as an employer of choice. Companies can thus increase their profits substantially and better serve the objectives of all their multiple stakeholders.[6]

Consequences of an Unsafe and Unhealthy Workplace

The costs of poor workplace safety and health are numerous. They include the human costs of injury and disease, mental health problems, and death, and the economic costs associated with such human suffering.

Injury and Disease. Back injuries are one the most prevalent types of workplace injuries. Every year, an estimated 10 million employees in the United States encounter back pain that impairs their job performance. Approximately 1 million employees file workers' compensation claims for back injuries, and billions of dollars are spent each year to treat back pain. Employees receive $50 billion in workers' compensation payments alone, and employers spend another $50 billion to find and train substitute workers and run employee recovery programs.[7]

Eye injuries are common too. Each day, more than 2,000 U.S. workers receive medical treatment because of work-related eye injuries. The U.S. Bureau of Labor Statistics reported that over $924 million was paid to workers as compensation for workplace eye injuries in one year alone.[8]

For office workers, carpal tunnel syndrome (CTS) has become an epidemic. Recent studies show that CTS affects more women than men by a ratio of almost three to one. CTS does not favor one hand over another and can occur in one or both hands. People who consistently use computer mice and trackballs have an increased risk of CTS, because of repetitive hand motion.[9] It now causes more lost workdays than anything else. Half of all the people who suffer from carpal tunnel syndrome miss 30 days or more of work during the year. According to the Bureau of Labor Statistics, the record number of lost days is due to the fact that so many people undergo surgery to correct the problem. On average, the annual cost of each case of carpal tunnel syndrome (CTS) is $13,000.[10]

FAST FACT

Some 2.2 million people die of work-related accidents and diseases each year.

FAST FACT

Each year 800,000 work-related eye injuries cost employers about $4 billion in lost wages and productivity.

Because CTS is so prevalent and harmful, many companies try to reduce it as much as possible. Ben and Jerry's is an example of one company that has worked hard to reduce CTS injuries. Some of its efforts are described in "Managing with Metrics: CTS Is Reduced at Ben & Jerry's."[11]

When employees suffer physical injuries, their pain is usually obvious, at least to them. But for workers exposed to dangerous chemicals, especially airborne ones, the effects often go undetected for many years. By the time a chemical, whether airborne or contained, is discovered to be dangerous, hundreds of employees may have been exposed to it for many years. Some of the most common airborne chemicals of concern are asbestos, mold, sanitation, and smoke.[12]

Mental Health. The physical injuries that employees suffer at work may be easier to count and quantify than psychological injuries, but mental health is just as important as physical health.[13] For some employees, the workplace is a source of substantial mental strain. Five of the 10 leading causes of disability worldwide are mental health problems. In the United States, it is estimated that more than 40 million people have some type of mental health disorder.

MANAGING WITH METRICS
CTS Is Reduced at Ben & Jerry's

Repetitive motion injuries were first recognized more than 200 years ago. In modern parlance, these are called cumulative trauma disorders or carpal tunnel syndrome (CTS). They result from motions that are harmless in themselves, unless they are chronically repeated. Movements that involve awkward positions or extra force can also be problematic. The results for employees can include musculoskeletal disease, pain, or injury. You don't have to work in a factory to have these problems. Office workers are at risk, and so too are tennis players and runners. But at Ben and Jerry's, the famous ice cream maker, work on the manufacturing line is the primary cause.

Injuries of this sort are the most common workplace injuries. During the working years, between ages 18 and 64, they are the most common reason for lost work time. When Ben & Jerry's compared the frequency of CTS injuries in their plants, they discovered that they had abnormally high injury rates—even higher than those found in Steelcase plants.

Based on the statistical evidence, Ben & Jerry's concluded they had a problem and their employee-friendly image was at risk if they didn't do something fast to improve their own record of workplace safety. One of the first actions they took was to discontinue a communications campaign that emphasized a long record of workdays without injuries. That great record didn't tell the whole story. Apparently, some employees who had experienced injuries chose not to report them because they didn't want to damage the company's record of injury-free days. Unfortunately, these employees may have suffered more as a consequence of not seeking treatment as soon as they began experiencing pain.

With their new approach, Ben & Jerry's became more proactive in preventing injuries. Instead of emphasizing their record of injury-free days, they encouraged employees to quickly report any pains or potential injuries. Education and training programs were used to help inform employees of what symptoms to watch for and the importance of getting treatment. The company also hired a number of consultants who specialized in ergonomics. The experts visited all of the plants and helped the company make changes that would help prevent repetitive motion injuries. In some cases, this meant using different tools or using the same tools differently. In other cases, it meant teaching employees to change their posture or seating arrangements. In the Waterbury, Vermont, production area, new equipment and improved line layouts were needed to improve the working conditions. Several material handling issues, such as palletizing, were also addressed via new equipment and improved procedures. Fortunately, these changes paid off. The number of repetitive motion injuries declined and so did the workers' compensation claims.

Depressive disorders, for example, represent one of the most common health problems of adults in the United States workforce. The estimates for national spending on depression alone are $30–40 billion, with an estimated 200 million days lost from work each year.[14] As noted in Chapter 4, for example, employees who suffer harassment at work may suffer psychological symptoms that affect not only their productivity but also the quality of their lives away from work. Mental health may also suffer when employees' jobs subject them to heavy emotional workloads or when there is simply too much work to be done.

Death and Violence. For many employees, workplace injuries result in death. Between 5,000 and 6,000 fatal work injuries are recorded yearly in the United States. Fatal highway incidents remain the most frequent type of fatal workplace event, accounting for 25% of workplace fatalities nationally. The major categories of yearly workplace deaths are approximately as follows:

- Transportation incidents   2,500
- Contact with objects and equipment   1,000
- Assaults and violent acts   800[15]

The overwhelming majority of dangerous jobs are held by men, who account for about 90% of all workplace fatalities, although they comprise only about half of the overall workforce. On a per capita basis, those who fish for a living hold the most dangerous jobs. While the profession accounts for only about 50 deaths yearly, the relatively small number of commercial fishermen put the fatality rate at 118 per 100,000, or about one of every 5,400 workers. Much of the U.S. fishing industry is concentrated in Alaska, where vessel sinking, deck falls, and people going overboard are ongoing causes of injuries and deaths. Among executives and supervisors, homicides account for the majority of workplace deaths.[16]

Economic Costs. The National Center for Health Statistics estimates the annual cost of violence (mostly physical assaults) as $13.5 billion in medical costs and 1.75 million days of lost work.[17] Although deaths have declined, the economic cost to businesses of workplace deaths and injuries remains high at an estimated $50 billion annually. Similar costs are estimated for the more than 100,000 workers who annually succumb to occupational diseases. Enormous costs are also associated with psychological conditions. For example, alcoholism and drug abuse, which can result from attempts to cope with job pressures, cost organizations and society over $250 billion annually, including about 500 million lost working days.[18] Perhaps more difficult to quantify, but just as symptomatic of stress and a poor quality of working life, are workers' feelings of lack of meaning and involvement in their work, fatigue, and loss of importance as individuals.[19]

PROMOTING SAFETY AND HEALTH WITHIN AN INTEGRATED HRM SYSTEM

The term **workplace safety and health** *refers to the physiological-physical and psychological conditions of a workforce that result from the work environment provided by the organization.* If an organization takes effective safety and health measures, fewer of its employees will have short- or long-term ill effects as a result of being employed at that organization.[20]

Physiological-physical conditions *include occupational diseases and accidents such as actual loss of life or limb, repetitive motion injuries, back pain, carpal tunnel syndrome, cardiovascular diseases, various forms of cancer such as lung cancer and leukemia, emphysema, and arthritis.* Other conditions that are known to result from an unhealthy work environment include white lung disease, brown lung disease, black lung disease, sterility, central nervous system damage, and chronic bronchitis.

Psychological conditions *encompass symptoms of poor mental health and job burnout, including apathy, emotional exhaustion, withdrawal, confusion about roles and duties, mistrust of others, inattentiveness, irritability, and a tendency to become distraught over trifles.* These conditions often are responses to workplace stress and a low quality of working life.

Links to Other HR Activities

As Exhibit 13.1 suggests, the linkages between other HR activities and workplace safety and health are many.[21]

Job Analysis and Competency Modeling. As described in Chapter 5, job analysis procedures can be used to identify aspects of a job that may contribute to

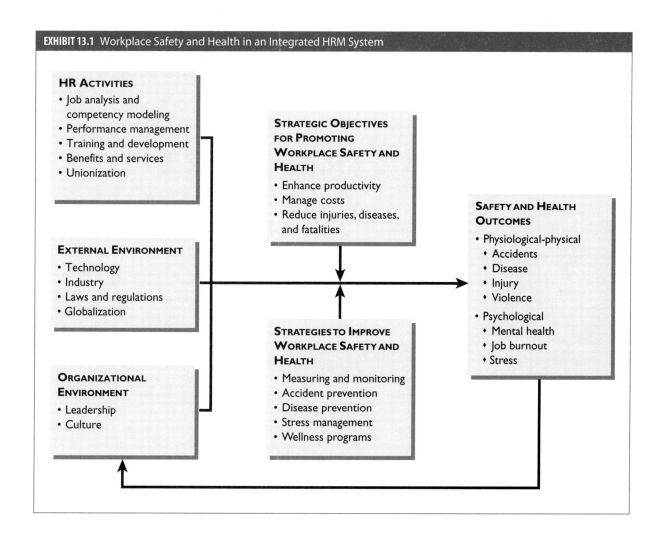

EXHIBIT 13.1 Workplace Safety and Health in an Integrated HRM System

HR ACTIVITIES
- Job analysis and competency modeling
- Performance management
- Training and development
- Benefits and services
- Unionization

EXTERNAL ENVIRONMENT
- Technology
- Industry
- Laws and regulations
- Globalization

ORGANIZATIONAL ENVIRONMENT
- Leadership
- Culture

STRATEGIC OBJECTIVES FOR PROMOTING WORKPLACE SAFETY AND HEALTH
- Enhance productivity
- Manage costs
- Reduce injuries, diseases, and fatalities

STRATEGIES TO IMPROVE WORKPLACE SAFETY AND HEALTH
- Measuring and monitoring
- Accident prevention
- Disease prevention
- Stress management
- Wellness programs

SAFETY AND HEALTH OUTCOMES
- Physiological-physical
  - Accidents
  - Disease
  - Injury
  - Violence
- Psychological
  - Mental health
  - Job burnout
  - Stress

workplace injuries, so that ergonomic principles can be applied to redesign the work environment. At some companies, job analysis and competency modeling have shown that some personality characteristics predict workplace accidents and psychological symptoms. Some employers use their selection procedures to screen out employees with tendencies that are contrary to a safe and healthy workplace.

Training. Training is another HR activity that can be effectively used to improve workplace safety and health. Employees participate in training to learn about safety policies and to learn behaviors that reduce the likelihood of accidents and injuries. Training may also be needed to teach employees how to use new equipment intended to protect them from workplace hazards. The training of managers may include detailed explanations of the relevant laws and regulations that govern workplace safety and health.[22]

Performance Management. When safety and health are viewed as issues of strategic importance, they become central to the entire performance management process. Performance measures monitor how well managers are doing against their goals. Managers and other employees also may be offered monetary incentives for reducing accidents and improving safe behaviors on the job. Providing tangible incentives to employees for achieving health and safety goals appears to be effective. However, incentives should be used cautiously. Critics of this approach worry that offering employees incentives may merely reduce their willingness to *report* accidents and injuries. Instead of offering incentives for safety outcomes, they suggest that managers use incentives to reward behaviors that are likely to *promote and improve* safety and health outcomes.[23]

Benefits and Services. Injured and unhealthy workers often require medical care and must take time off from work while they recover. Thus, there is a close alignment between managing benefits and services and managing workplace safety and health. For employers, improving safety and health is one way to reduce workers' compensation claims, medical insurance claims, and their related costs. It is also a way to reduce the number of days that employees must be paid for time not worked.[24]

At Dannon Yogurt, preventive measures are important, but the company recognizes that injuries are not completely avoidable. When employees are injured, Dannon strives to help employees return to work as quickly as possible. As part of an unusual return-to-work program, Dannon allows recovering employees to ease their way back by doing light-duty work for nonprofit organizations in the community. The program allows employees to build up their strength gradually before returning to work, while at the same time keeping them in the habit of going to work each day. Dannon pays a portion of their wages, and the community's nonprofit organizations reap the benefits. Dannon also wins: Since the program began, lost workdays and recovery time have been reduced.[25]

Unions. As will be described in Chapter 14, managing employee relationships in unionized environments often involves negotiating issues of safety. Collective bargaining agreements typically include a clause that recognizes management's duty to provide safe work conditions.[26] Specific safety provisions are often stated too. Exhibit 13.2 shows the most common safety provisions stated in collective bargaining agreements in recent years.[27]

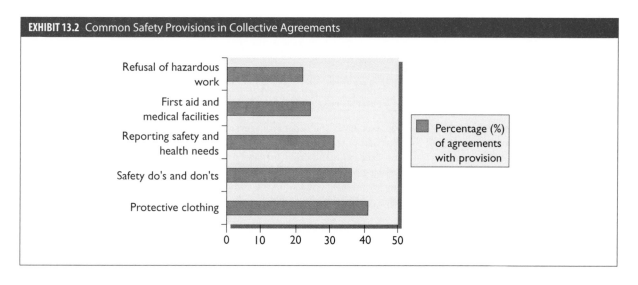

EXHIBIT 13.2 Common Safety Provisions in Collective Agreements

Despite all of these efforts, however, many employees become victims of workplace accidents, injuries, and illnesses. Thus, employers want to develop policies and practices to help reduce mishaps as much as possible.[28]

The Organizational Environment

Internal environmental factors that are important for workplace safety and health include the organization's culture and its leadership.

Company Culture. In organizations where safety is valued and embedded in the organization's culture, employees benefit by experiencing fewer injuries.[29] Developing such a culture (sometimes referred to as a positive safety climate) requires the involvement of everyone in the organization. Employees should be encouraged to identify safety and health problems and develop solutions to address them, and they do at Deere & Company. Employee involvement in improving workplace safety and health is also important in companies such as Alcan and DynMcDermott, which have been awarded the prestigious Robert W. Campbell Award for safety.[30]

In an effort to understand the conditions needed to ensure workplace safety and health, the Conference Board conducted a study to identify "best practices." Exhibit 13.3 lists the eight core elements of an organizational culture that supports workplace safety and health.[31]

Leadership. During the strategic planning process, line managers can promote safety and health through the development of policies and goals. For such policies and goals to have an effect, everyone in the organization must direct their efforts toward creating a culture where safety is valued.

Creating a safety-driven culture, such as the ones found at Ben & Jerry's, Deere & Company, Alcan, or DynMcDermott, requires visible leadership from top-level managers. Effective leaders do more than just talk about the importance of workplace safety; they explain why it is important, encourage safe behaviors, and reward safe performance. With leadership like this, employees get the message. They become more conscious of safety issues, and a climate that values safety is established.[32] A study of restaurant workers showed that these dynamics result in decreased safety incidents and occupational injuries.[33]

FAST FACT

Each year, the National Safety Council gives the Robert W. Campbell Award to companies that successfully integrate health, safety, and environmental management into their overall business operations.

" *Our clients are saying, 'If I have deficiencies in my safety programs, then I probably have deficiencies in other areas.'* "

Michael Murray
Director of Casualty Risk
Control Consulting
Aon Risk Services

FAST FACT

The National Safety Council recognized Deere & Company's CEO, Bob Lane, as a leader who "gets it" on safety issues.

EXHIBIT 13.3 Elements of an Organizational Culture That Supports Workplace Safety and Health

KEY FEATURES OF CULTURE	SPECIFIC INDICATORS OF A STRONG SAFETY CULTURE
Leadership believes safety and health are important to organizational success	• Top executives and other managers set the tone by speaking often about the importance of safety and health. • Top executives and other managers serve as role models by engaging in safe and healthy behaviors. • Employees feel confident in the company's commitment to safety and health.
Employees have ownership of safety and health issues	• Employees help develop safety and health strategies and initiatives that are tailored to the organization's specific needs. • Knowledge and information about safety and health provisions and outcomes are shared openly with employees.
Metrics are used to monitor safety and health performance	• Health and safety performance is measured systematically. • Employees at all levels of the organization are held accountable for meeting safety and health standards and goals.

Company leadership also can be blamed for creating a culture that puts profits ahead of employees' lives. That's the reputation of McWane's executive leadership. McWane is one of the world's largest makers of cast iron water and sewer pipes, and it has one of the highest injury rates in the nation. During the past decade, it has been cited 400 times for safety violations. That's four times more than the total number of safety violations received by all six of its competitors combined. Sadly, many workers have lost their lives. After one death, workers began displaying a bumper sticker that read, "Pray for me. I work at Kennedy Valve," the name of one of McWane's facilities.[34]

The External Environment

External forces that are important to workplace safety and health include evolving technologies, industry conditions, and the laws and regulations that govern this aspect of work.[35]

Technology. In manufacturing environments, the introduction of new technologies often greatly improves workplace safety and health. By introducing the latest manufacturing equipment, including robotics, employers often can eliminate the need to expose employees to unsafe conditions. At Ben & Jerry's, investments in new manufacturing technology were part of the solution for reducing repetitive motion injuries.

On the other hand, some new technologies introduce new hazards into the workplace. For example, new buildings often do not allow employees to open their windows, making them completely dependent on ventilation systems for the provision of clean air. Office equipment that makes the workplace more efficient may emit fumes that induce illness.[36] As jobs of all types become increasingly dependent on computers, employees of all types are subjected to conditions that put them at a heightened risk of repetitive motion injuries, such as carpal tunnel syndrome.

Industry. As you might expect, employees in some industries are more likely to be injured at work than others. Can you guess which types of workplaces have the highest rates of injuries?

As already explained, in Alaska's fishing industry the accident rate is extremely high; in fact, it is nearly 100 times higher than the national average. Another dangerous industry is construction, where workers face a constantly changing physical environment. Often one misstep or forgetful moment can crush a limb or end a life. When pressure mounts to finish a job quickly to meet a deadline, supervisors may push their workers to take extra risks. Add to these pressures a "macho" culture that tends to belittle safety and romanticize danger, and the stage is set for accidents and injuries. Meat packing and poultry processing are also dangerous. Some workers perform the same repetitive motion as many as 30,000 times per shift; knives are ever present too. When you consider their working environment, it's easy to understand why one of every seven poultry workers is injured on the job—a rate that is double the national average.[37] According to the Bureau of Labor Statistics, the industries with the highest numbers of worker injuries are as follows:

Nonfatal workplace injuries by industry sector:

1. Manufacturing.
2. Health care and social assistance.
3. Retail trade.
4. Construction.
5. Leisure and hospitality.

Fatal occupational injuries by industry sector:

1. Construction.
2. Transportation and warehousing.
3. Agriculture, forestry, fishing, and hunting.
4. Government.
5. Professional and business services.[38]

Working hours also affect injury rates. After adjusting for age, gender, type of industry, and job, employees working overtime were 61% more likely to sustain a work-related injury or illness than employees who did not work overtime. Working at least 12 hours a day was associated with a 37% increased risk of injury or illness, while working at least 60 hours a week was associated with a 23% increased risk, compared with those who worked fewer hours.[39]

U.S. Laws and Regulations. The federal government's primary response to the issue of safety and health in the workplace has been the **Occupational Safety and Health Act of 1970,** *which calls for safety and health inspections of organizations regardless of size, reporting by employers, and investigations of accidents and allegations of hazards.* The **Occupational Safety and Health Administration (OSHA)** *is the federal agency responsible for establishing and enforcing occupational safety and health standards and for inspecting and issuing citations to organizations that violate these standards.*

Two organizations that support the role of OSHA are the National Institute for Occupational Safety and Health (NIOSH) and the Occupational Safety and Health Review Commission (OSHRC). The **National Institute for Occupational Safety and Health (NIOSH)** *conducts research to reduce work-related illnesses and injuries and promotes safe and healthy workplaces by developing interventions and recommendations for employers.* The commission reviews appeals made by organizations that received citations from OSHA inspectors for alleged safety and health violations.[40]

Most organizations are required to keep safety and health records so that OSHA can compile accurate statistics on work injuries and illnesses. These records should cover all disabling, serious, or significant injuries and illnesses, whether or not they involve loss of time from work. Excluded are minor injuries that require only first aid and don't involve medical treatment, loss of consciousness, restriction of work or motion, or transfer to another job. Falsification of records or failure to keep adequate records can result in substantial fines.

An employee's right to know about workplace hazards is guaranteed by the Federal Hazard Communication Standard, which takes a sweeping approach to ensuring that employees know about the hazards of workplace chemicals and the precautions they should take because of those chemicals. Employers who use hazardous chemicals in their operations are required to prepare a formal inventory of the chemicals; inform and train employees on the nature of the chemicals through signs, labels, and material safety data sheets; and prepare a written program summarizing the employer's hazard communication program. This broad-based federal law has wide implications for many of the 6 million facilities that are subject to OSHA enforcement of safety and health regulations. Since 1983, the Federal Hazard Communication Standard has been the federal safety standard cited most frequently by compliance officers.

The OSHA standards can be summarized as seven key steps:

1. Prepare an inventory of chemicals used in the facility.
2. Identify drums and containers of chemicals with signs and labels.
3. Make material safety data sheets available for each chemical.
4. Provide hazard communication training to employees.
5. Prepare a written hazard communication program.
6. Devise a spill or emergency plan.
7. Develop ways to inform outside contractors of the chemical hazards to which they will be exposed in the facility.

A number of states have developed their own right-to-know laws, some of which have more stringent provisions than the federal standards. HR professionals and employees alike should check to see whether their states have hazard communication requirements.[41]

Research on employees who work with hazardous waste materials suggests that training is most effective when employees develop a deep knowledge about safety issues and specific skills to address safety concerns. Training that merely provides a broad overview of the issues appears to be less effective in reducing unsafe behaviors.[42]

In addition to OSHA, workplace safety and health are governed by workers' compensation regulations and state initiatives. As discussed in Chapter 12,

FAST FACT

Since OSHA was established, an estimated 100,000 lives have been saved, and the workplace fatality rate has decreased 62%.

workers' compensation insurance provides financial aid for those unable to work because of accidents and diseases. For many years, workers' compensation awards were granted only to workers unable to work because of physical injury or damage. Since 1955, however, court decisions have either caused or enticed numerous states to allow workers' compensation awards in job-related cases of anxiety, depression, and mental disorders.

Determining whether employers are responsible for diseases and illness is sometimes difficult because of the long time it can take for symptoms to appear. Reactions such as asbestosis or hypertension take a long time to develop. In addition, many diseases occur only in some people at a work site, which makes it difficult to establish that the work site is the cause of the disease. This point is illustrated by the development of lung disease among firefighters who worked at the World Trade Center (WTC) Ground Zero disaster site in 2001. Due to health and safety concerns about possibly dangerous chemicals that might be in the dust and rubble, the Fire Department of New York (FDNY) established a WTC Monitoring and Treatment Program. Firefighters who enrolled in the program underwent chest CT imaging, pulmonary function testing, provocative challenge, and biopsy. Researchers later compared the annual incidence rates for the firefighters for the 15 years before 2001. After five years, the results began to reveal that new-onset sarcoidosis of the lung was on the rise among Ground Zero firefighters, according to a new study. By then, an additional 26 firefighters were suffering from the inflammatory illness.[43]

Global Considerations

With globalization has come an increasing awareness of differences in national standards for workplace safety and health. Because of this, global organizations have emerged to improve workplace heath and safety worldwide.

Country Differences. There are substantial differences in national standards regarding workplace safety and health. Developing countries that attract foreign investment often have few government regulations regarding workplace safety and health. Unions in these countries often are weak, and their focus is more likely to be on issues of wages rather than safety and health.

During the 1990s, concerns about safety and health issues in Mexico became a stumbling block during congressional discussions of the North American Free Trade Agreement (NAFTA). Many people were concerned that low standards for workplace safety and health would be yet another reason for U.S. companies to move operations across the border. Thus, besides losing jobs at home, Americans could potentially be guilty of unfairly exploiting Mexico's labor force. Subsequent to the enactment of NAFTA, a new concern arose. With more and more Mexican workers coming into the United States, people began to worry that U.S. employers would be lax in enforcing safety and health standards at facilities with large numbers of immigrant employees, who were unlikely to complain to the legal authorities. The Occupational Safety and Health Administration sought to allay such concerns and assured concerned parties that they will actively enforce U.S. safety and health standards in plants that employ Mexican workers. Working with the Mexican consulates, OSHA developed a letter of agreement outlining the efforts they would make to communicate with and train Mexican workers. The goal is to ensure that all workers understand their right to a safe and healthful workplace. One example of how OSHA works to assure workplace safety and health is their alliance with the Hispanic-American Chamber of Commerce in Essex County, New Jersey, and the New Jersey Department of Labor. As part of this alliance, OSHA agreed to

- Deliver a 10-hour construction course in both Spanish and English to Hispanic employers and employees.
- Develop programs regarding hazards such as falls and electrical shocks.
- Encourage bilingual individuals to take the OSHA 30-hour construction or general industry courses in order to qualify to teach Hispanic workers.
- Promote and encourage employers to participate in other OSHA-relevant programs.[44]

FAST FACT

The ILO estimates that the HIV/AIDS epidemic will reduce the size of the available workforce in some African countries by as much as 20% in coming years.

Global Organizations. Two global organizations that strive to improve workplace safety and health throughout the world are the International Labour Organization (ILO) and the World Health Organization (WHO). As described in Chapter 2, the ILO promotes internationally recognized labor rights. Toward this end, they formulate minimum standards that employers should meet in a variety of domains, including workplace safety and health. They also conduct research and provide technical assistance to employers.

An estimated 25 million labor force participants, between 15 and 64 years of age, are living with HIV or with AIDS worldwide. The vast majority—nearly 67%—live in Africa. The ILO has demonstrated that the rate of economic growth in countries heavily affected by HIV/AIDS has been reduced by the epidemic's effects on labor supply, productivity, and investment over the last decade or more. Research by the ILO found that 43 countries lost on average 0.5 percentage points of their economic growth rate every year between 1992 and 2004. The 31 countries in Sub-Saharan Africa lost 0.7 percentage points of their average annual rate of economic growth during that time. Cumulative mortality losses to the global labor force are expected to continue to increase as a result of the impact of the HIV epidemic, from 28 million estimated for 2005 to 45 million projected by 2010, over 64 million projected for 2015, and nearly 86 million anticipated by 2020.[45]

The ILO's Code of Practice on HIV/AIDS is an example of how this organization seeks to improve workplace health. This manual contains practical advice to employers interested in HIV/AIDS prevention, training, and care. The ILO's belief is that employers have a social obligation and an economic self-interest in ridding the world's workforce of this and similar epidemics. At the same time, the organization seeks to protect affected workers from unfair treatment by employers. Its stated policy is to "oppose discrimination and promote an environment of open and constructive discussion of HIV issues."

To achieve their objectives, the ILO works cooperatively with employers to help them develop effective strategies for dealing with this monumental health crisis. For example, working with an auto manufacturer, it showed that averting one new case of HIV infection saves the company the equivalent of three to four years' worth of an employee's annual salary. Data such as these prompted the company to offer free antiretroviral treatments to infected employees. In the future, it plans to extend its efforts to include community support.[46]

The World Health Organization also provides information on global occupational safety and health, and offers technical assistance to interested

LINE MANAGERS	HR PROFESSIONALS	EMPLOYEES
• Recognize the strategic consequences of improved workplace safety and health.	• Educate managers to understand the long-term value of improved safety and health.	• Participate in the development and administration of safety and health programs (e.g., by serving on a safety and health committee).
• Proactively promote workplace safety and health as core values of the organizational culture.	• Ensure that accidents and health-related incidents are accurately monitored, reported, and recorded.	• Perform in accordance with established safety and health guidelines.
• Encourage employees to report unsafe conditions and suggest how to improve workplace safety and health.	• Work with other professionals such as medical doctors and industrial engineers to develop new programs.	• Take an active role in promoting changes that will enhance workplace safety and health, including attending training programs.
• Avoid creating incentives for unsafe behaviors.	• Create HR programs that train employees for safe and healthy behaviors and reward them for their success.	• Promote work group norms that value safety and health.
• Help train employees in health and safety procedures.	• Develop selection programs that recognize individual characteristics for safety.	• Engage in safe and healthy behaviors.

employers. The WHO's global strategy for workplace safety and health calls for it to:

- Strengthen international and national policies.
- Develop practices for improving health at work.
- Promote health at work by providing technical assistance and support.
- Develop human resources for the field of occupational health.
- Establish relevant and useful registration and data systems.
- Raise public awareness.
- Strengthen research on occupational health.

Like the ILO, the World Health Organization has no official regulatory power. It strives to improve workplace health around the world by educating employers and employees, developing knowledge about how to improve the health of workers, and establishing a shared view of the rights and responsibilities of employees and employers.

The HR Triad

As is true of all critical HR policies and practices, promoting safety and health involves everyone in the organization. The roles and responsibilities of employees, HR professionals, and managers are summarized in "The HR Triad: Roles and Responsibilities in Promoting Workplace Safety and Health."

Even when they are not directly involved in the organization's operations, managers play a key role by setting the tone and making safety and health a priority. As will become clear later in this chapter, HR professionals are responsible for monitoring and recording workplace incidents, as well as for developing HR policies that promote safety and health.

Perhaps most importantly, employees must be actively committed to creating a safe and healthy workplace. Employees can spot problems and help to develop solutions. When solutions are found, employees often must be willing to adapt and change how they do their work. Unfortunately, some employees would rather suffer in silence than admit to experiencing physical symptoms. Another problem can be that employees may not recognize how their work habits affect their own health.

Mike Rainville, owner of Maple Landmark Woodcraft in Vermont, was surprised when his woodworkers resisted job changes designed to reduce repetitive motion injuries. Before the change, employees worked at the same tasks (e.g., hammering wheels onto a toy truck) all day, every day. An expert recommended changing the line so that workers could rotate among tasks every hour. The company bought new chairs that workers could more easily move around and adjust. At first, workers thought the changes would make their work more stressful. According to Rainville, "People just wanted to do one job every day and didn't want the stress of having to do something different." Eventually, with an education program that taught workers about ergonomics and constant preaching about the need for injury prevention, the workers accepted the change. For Rainville's small one-time investment of about $7,000, he reaped an annual return of about $8,000.[47]

LEARNING GOAL 3

SAFETY AND HEALTH HAZARDS IN THE WORKPLACE

Workplace conditions and the strategies that organizations use to manage safety and health have implications for both physiological-physical and psychological employee outcomes. Traditionally, physical hazards and disease have received the most attention. Increasingly, however, employers and OSHA have come to recognize the importance of also attending to employees' psychological outcomes.[48]

Occupational Accidents

At AES, a global power company, top management is so concerned about safety that they hold everyone in the company accountable for reducing accidents. Under normal circumstances, the company may distribute as much as a 12% bonus for reaching safety-related goals. When the company experienced four fatalities worldwide, the bonus was reduced for everyone. By significantly penalizing poor safety performance, AES intends to motivate its employees to examine the causes of accidents and institute changes to prevent them in the future. At AES and elsewhere, the causes of organizational accidents are numerous, so eliminating them completely represents a major challenge.

Organizational Qualities. In general, the factors that most affect workplace accidents are (1) the working conditions and times (e.g., vehicle driving, desk work, shift work), (2) the tools and technology available to do the job (e.g., heavy machinery, ladders, personal computers), and (3) the availability of guns brought to work. However, the size of the organization has also been shown to be related to incidence rates.

Small organizations (those with fewer than 50 employees) and large organizations (those with more than 250 employees) have lower incidence rates than medium-sized organizations. This may be because supervisors in small organizations are better able to detect safety hazards and prevent accidents than those in medium-sized ones, while larger organizations have more resources to hire staff specialists who can devote all their efforts to safety and accident prevention.

Individual Qualities. Accidents result from the behaviors of people, the hazards in the work environment, and pure chance. The degree to which a person contributes to an accident can be an indication of the individual's proneness to accidents. No stable set of personal characteristics *always* contributes to accidents. Nevertheless, certain psychological and physical characteristics seem to make some people *more susceptible* to accidents. For example, employees who are emotionally "high" have fewer accidents than those who are emotionally "low." Employees who have fewer accidents are more optimistic, trusting, and concerned for others than those who have more accidents.

Employees under great stress are likely to have more accidents than those under low stress. Substance abusers also experience more job-related injuries, and this is true regardless of whether the substance abuse takes place at work or off the job. People who are quicker at recognizing visual patterns than at making muscular manipulations are less likely to have accidents than those who are just the opposite. Employees who do not control their diabetes properly risk losing their hands or feet due to workplace accidents.[49]

Last, older workers are less likely to have accidents. However, when older people do have accidents, they are more likely to suffer fatalities and they recover more slowly.[50] As a consequence, the issue of older workers in the workplace is a significant one. This is described more in the feature "Managing the Multicultural Workforce: Safety Issues and the Aging Workforce."[51]

Nevertheless, safety data give employers and society some concern. Federal studies show that older workers (above 54 years and particularly above 64 years of age) are 5.0 times more likely to die of a fatal transportation accident and 3.8 times more likely to be killed by objects and equipment than are younger workers. Significant medical differences also appear to exist between older and younger workers: As a group, older workers take nearly twice as long to mend and are more likely to die from injuries, compared to younger workers. The average annual per-person cost of health claims for workers who are 65–69 years old is more than double that for workers who are 45–59 years old.

With the number of older workers rising quickly, what can be done about this vulnerability? Research suggests that 70% of older workers who are injured in work accidents received no safety training; so providing more training is a good first step. Research also shows that it is helpful to make relatively simple workplace modifications, such as painting the steps of ladders with bright colors. With older workers, many accidents and injuries might be avoided if employees were more aware of the hazards that surround them.

FAST FACT

Older workers have better attendance and accident records than younger workers.

MANAGING THE MULTICULTURAL WORKFORCE
Safety Issues and the Aging Workforce

"I'm 51 years old, and I know for a fact that there's more risk for me to climb to the top of a rail car today than there was when I was younger and more agile," says Wayne Gordon, general manager of Farmers Cooperative Association in Jackson, Minnesota. Mr. Gordon indicates, however, that it's difficult to get other older workers to always agree with him: "Individuals have a tendency to think they can still do things they did 20 years ago."

Gordon believes that sometimes it might be in the worker's interest to be prevented from performing a specific job, but not allowing older workers to have dangerous jobs might violate age discrimination laws. The Age Discrimination in Employment Act means that employers can't automatically exclude workers from jobs solely because of age. Older workers, in fact, are among the best performers many companies have.

Violent Employees

Each year, as many as 800 homicides occur in the workplace, accounting for almost 10% of all workplace deaths.[52] About two-thirds of workplace homicides are committed during robberies (often in retail stores), but most others are committed by relatives, coworkers, or former coworkers.[53]

Homicide is the leading cause of death for women in the workplace, accounting for 40% of all workplace deaths of female workers. Workplace homicides are primarily robbery related, and they often occur in grocery or convenience stores, eating and drinking establishments, and gasoline service stations.

Female victims of workplace homicide are often assaulted by people they know (coworkers, customers, spouses, or friends). Domestic violence incidents that spill into the workplace account for 16% of job-related homicides of female victims. Female workers are also at risk for nonfatal violence. Women were the victims in nearly two-thirds of the injuries resulting from workplace assaults. Most of these assaults (70%) were directed at women employed in service occupations, such as health care, while an additional 20% of these incidents occurred in retail locations, such as restaurants and grocery stores.[54]

Homicide, as well as other less serious forms of violence, can be triggered by a number of forces, including being treated unfairly, an organizational culture that accepts aggressive behavior as normal, layoffs and downsizing, and even anger at being monitored too closely.[55] Although it may be difficult to identify the violent employee before the fact, employers are urged to be on the lookout for some common signs, such as

- *Verbal threats.* Individuals often talk about what they may do. An employee might say, "Bad things are going to happen to so-and-so" or "That propane tank in the back could blow up easily."
- *Physical actions.* Troubled employees may try to intimidate others, gain access to places where they don't belong, or flash a concealed weapon in the workplace to test reactions.
- *Frustration.* Most cases of workplace violence don't involve a panicked individual who perceives the world as falling apart. A more likely scenario involves an employee who has a frustrated sense of entitlement to a promotion, for example.
- *Obsession.* An employee may hold a grudge against a coworker or supervisor, which in some cases can stem from a romantic interest. These may be early warning signals for acts of violence, including assault against coworkers and property damage. Like other forms of unacceptable performance on the job, the options for how to deal with violent employees include employee assistance programs, training in conflict management, and termination.[56]

FAST FACT

Employers may be held liable for the violent action of an employee if they knew, or should have known, that the employee was at risk for committing violence.

For a period of several years during the 1980s and 1990s, the United States Postal Service (USPS) had "a culture that accepted a certain level of violence," according to Carl Augustinho. When employees fought with each other, they would simply be told to "shut up" and go back to work. After a dozen incidents in which coworkers were murdered, USPS decided it needed to do something to change its culture. Now supervisors are trained to handle violent situations. Employees who engage in violent behavior are immediately taken off the job while an investigation is conducted. Perhaps more importantly, USPS began efforts to ensure that supervisors treat their employees with respect. They learned the importance of providing for due process and taking employees' complaints seriously. HR professionals also improved the hiring procedures. Now applicants are interviewed more intensively to detect possible sources of problems, and background checks are more rigorous.[57]

Occupational Diseases

Potential sources of work-related diseases are as distressingly varied as the symptoms of those diseases. Several federal agencies have systematically studied the workplace environment, especially air quality and contained liquids and solids, and they have identified the following disease-causing hazards: arsenic, asbestos, benzene, bichloromethylether, coal dust, coke oven emissions, cotton dust, lead, radiation, and vinyl chloride. Workers likely to be exposed to those hazards include chemical and oil refinery workers, miners, textile workers, steelworkers, lead smelters, medical technicians, painters, shoemakers, and plastics industry workers. Continued research will no doubt uncover additional hazards that firms will want to diagnose and remedy for the future well-being of their workforces.[58]

Environmental hazards in the workplace have been linked to occupational diseases such as thyroid, liver, lung, brain, and kidney cancer; white, brown, and black lung disease; leukemia; bronchitis; emphysema; lymphoma; aplastic anemia; central nervous system damage; and reproductive disorders (e.g., sterility, genetic damage, miscarriages, and birth defects). Chronic bronchitis and emphysema are among the fastest growing diseases in the United States, doubling every five years since World War II; they account for the second highest number of disabilities covered by Social Security Insurance. Cancer tends to receive the most attention, however, because it's a leading cause of death in the United States. Many of the known causes of cancer are physical and chemical agents in the environment, which OSHA would like to see eliminated from the workplace.[59]

OSHA is also concerned with the many categories of occupational diseases and illnesses, including occupation-related skin diseases and disorders, dust diseases of the lungs, respiratory conditions due to toxic agents, poisoning (the systematic effect of toxic materials), disorders due to physical agents, disorders associated with repeated trauma, and all other occupational illnesses. OSHA requires employers to keep records of all these diseases.

Poorly Designed Jobs

For many workers, poorly designed jobs are a source of both psychological and physical stress. Job design quality, work pacing, and shift work are especially relevant to workplace safety and health.

Job Design Quality. Job characteristics theory is the most popular and extensively tested approach to designing jobs that employees enjoy and feel motivated to perform well. **Job characteristics theory** *states that employees are more satisfied and motivated when their jobs are meaningful, when jobs create a feeling of responsibility, and when jobs are designed to ensure that some feedback is available.*[60] In essence, jobs should be designed to provide work that employees enjoy doing. People who enjoy doing their jobs may not need the extra motivation of high pay and impressive job titles. In fact, according to a recent survey of 1,200 U.S. employees, the nature of the work they did was the most important factor (ahead of direct and indirect financial rewards and career concerns) in determining how people felt about staying with their current employer and how motivated they were to work hard.[61]

When jobs are poorly designed, workers feel little sense of responsibility and self-worth; they experience little job involvement and are seldom challenged; their work often feels meaningless and their good deeds seem to go unnoticed. All of these conditions contribute to poor psychological health, and some have been shown to increase accidents and injuries. A large study of Australian work sites found that workplace injuries were more likely to occur in organizations where employees received little training, worked at jobs that were highly repetitive, and had little autonomy over their work. Lower injury rates were found in organizations that offered more training and that designed jobs to include both more variety and more employee control.[62] Other studies show that job design quality affects health outcomes such as cardiovascular disease and musculoskeletal problems.[63]

Work Pacing and Control. Work pacing, the speed at which work proceeds, may be controlled by machines or people. Machine pacing gives control over the speed of the operation and of the work output to something other than the individual. Employee pacing gives that control to the individual. The negative effects of machine pacing can be severe, because the individual is unable to satisfy a crucial need for control of the situation. Employees who work at machine-paced jobs often feel exhausted at the end of their shifts and are unable to relax soon after work because of increased adrenaline secretion on the job. Giving employees more control over the pace of work reduces stress symptoms.[64]

Control over work also appears to be important in other types of jobs. Assembly line workers are not the only ones who sometimes feel unable to control their work or their work life. In fact, some workers in almost all occupations report feeling that they have less control over their work environment than they would like. Workers with relatively low control are at greater risk of developing cardiovascular disease and gastrointestinal disorders. Thus, workplace practices that provide opportunities for employees to offer their input and to participate in organizational decisions appear to also contribute to the development of a healthy workplace.[65]

Shift Work. During the past two decades, the demand for 24-hour consumer services, the prevalence of just-in-time delivery practices in manufacturing, and the globalization of business have all contributed to an increasing prevalence of shift work. **Shift work** *refers to any arrangements for daily work hours that differ significantly from the standard daylight hours.* Nonstandard shifts can be fixed or rotating and of various lengths (e.g., 8, 10, or 12 hours), but usually they involve at least some night work. Shift workers often experience sleep disruptions, and they face extra challenges in meeting the normal demands of family life and pursuing personal leisure time. Many new shift workers find these disruptions so difficult that they quit soon after they are hired, but others may spend years working on nonstandard shifts, in part because shift workers typically receive higher pay than their daytime colleagues. In exchange for their higher pay, however, shift workers often accept higher rates of recurring gastrointestinal symptoms, such as constipation, gas, and appetite disturbances. Perhaps more frightening is research showing that shift workers have a 40% greater risk for cardiovascular disease. Accidents and injuries also are more common during shift work hours.[66]

Shift work may be unavoidable, but its negative consequence might not be. Many studies have investigated the issue of how to design shift work to

> " *Being tired makes everything that much more stressful, but it's like having a baby. You get used to it. The kids sometimes ask, 'What's the deal with dad? Does he still live here?' It's kind of sad.* "
>
> *Codey Mooneyhan*
> *Shift Worker*
> *Germantown, Maryland*

minimize its negative effects. This research shows that one of the most common shift arrangements—the weekly rotating shift, in which shift workers change their schedule every week—is one of the worst schedules. Research also shows that very few employees ever fully adapt to working the night shift, even when this is a permanent arrangement. The best shift arrangement appears to be a forward-rotating shift. With this schedule, an employee rotates from the day shift to the evening shift to the night shift. Furthermore, it appears that 12-hour shift systems (i.e., a compressed workweek) have fewer negative health consequences than traditional 8-hour shifts. Research findings such as these serve as the foundation for the ILO's standards for night work and for some of the laws that protect night workers in several European countries. In the United States, shift workers are not protected by special laws or regulations.[67]

Workplace Stressors

Whereas poor-quality job designs often cause employees to feel disengaged from work and dissatisfied, workplace stressors often cause employees to become overly engaged in work. In extreme cases, the result may be feelings of exhaustion and burnout. Workplace stressors that put employees at risk for severe strain include organizational change, the physical environment, stress-prone employees, and the manager.[68]

Organizational Change. Changes made by organizations usually involve something important and are accompanied by uncertainty (e.g., the development of new HR policies that are aligned with new strategic business objectives). Often when changes are made, there is too little communication about the need for change and the nature of changes to come. Rumors may circulate that a change is coming, but the exact nature of the change is left to speculation. People become concerned about whether the change will affect them—perhaps by displacing them, changing their job duties and pay level, or by causing them to be transferred. And they wonder how those remaining will do all the work! The result is that many employees suffer stress symptoms, such as anxiety and depression at work as well as at home. To cope, employees who experience these symptoms are likely to be absent more frequently and for more total days.[69]

Physical Environment. Although office technologies can improve productivity, they may also have stress-related drawbacks, as we have already noted. In addition to contributing to disease and injuries, exposure to hazardous chemicals and dangerous tools and machinery can cause employees to feel anxious or tense. Other aspects of the physical work environment associated with stress are crowding, noise, lack of privacy, and lack of control: for example, being prohibited from moving a desk or chairs or even hanging pictures in a work area in an effort to personalize it.[70] Poor indoor air quality is another aspect of the work environment that employees report being a source of stress. About one out of three managers believes that poor air quality is a significant cause of both illness among employees and lost productivity.[71]

Stress-Prone Employees. People differ in how they respond to organizational stressors. A classic difference is referred to as Type A versus Type B behaviors. Type A people like to do things their way and are willing to exert a lot of effort to ensure that even trivial tasks are performed in the manner they prefer. They often fail to distinguish between important and unimportant situations.

FAST FACT

According to NIOSH, health care expenditures are nearly 50% greater for workers who report high levels of stress.

FAST FACT

Working in hot environments promotes accidents because of sweaty palms, dizziness, and fogging of safety glasses.

They are upset, for instance, when they have to wait 15 minutes to be seated in a restaurant, since this isn't in compliance with their idea of responsive service. In short, Type A people spend much of their time directing energy toward noncompliances in the environment. By comparison, Type B people are generally much more patient and accepting of current conditions. They aren't easily frustrated or easily angered, nor do they expend a lot of energy in response to noncompliance. Although Type A people are often "movers and shakers," some of their behaviors have the disadvantage of inducing stress in themselves and others.[72]

The Manager. A recent study found that employees working for a bad boss experienced more exhaustion, job tension, nervousness, depressed moods, and mistrust. The researchers found that a good working environment is often more important than pay and that it's no coincidence that poor morale leads to lower production. "Employees were less likely to take on additional tasks, such as working longer or on weekends, and were generally less satisfied with their job," the study found. "Also, employees were more likely to leave if involved in an abusive relationship than if dissatisfied with pay." Nearly 40% of bosses don't keep their word and more than 25% bad-mouth those they supervise to coworkers. [73]

Job Burnout

Job burnout *is a particular type of stress that seems to be experienced by people who work in jobs in health care, education, police work, customer response centers, and the airline industry.* This type of reaction to one's work includes attitudinal and emotional reactions that a person goes through as a result of job-related experiences.[74]

Emotional Exhaustion. Often the first sign of burnout is a feeling of being emotionally exhausted by work. Emotionally exhausted employees might express feelings of being drained, used up, at the end of their rope, or physically fatigued. Waking up in the morning may be accompanied by a feeling of dread at the thought of having to put in another day on the job. For someone who was once enthusiastic about the job and idealistic about what could be accomplished, feelings of emotional exhaustion may come somewhat unexpectedly, though to an outsider looking at the situation, emotional exhaustion would be seen as a natural response to an extended period of intense interaction with people and their problems. Extreme emotional exhaustion can be very debilitating both on and off the job; so people who are experiencing it must find some way to cope. Yet even mild feelings of emotional exhaustion can affect how employees perform on the job. In a study of call center employees, for example, even the most conscientious workers completed fewer calls if they were emotionally exhausted.[75]

Depersonalization. One common coping reaction is to put psychological distance between one's self and one's clients and to decrease one's personal involvement with them. In moderation, this reaction may be an effective method for creating what is called detached concern, but when it is engaged in to excess, the employee may begin to dehumanize or depersonalize the clients. People who have reached the extreme end of the depersonalization continuum report feeling they have become calloused by their jobs and that they have grown cynical about their clients.

Low Personal Accomplishment. In addition to emotional exhaustion and depersonalization, a third aspect of burnout is a feeling of low personal accomplishment. Many human service professionals begin their careers with great expectations that they will be able to improve the human condition through their work. After a year or two on the job, they begin to realize they aren't living up to their expectations.

The gap between the novice's goals and the veteran's accomplishments occurs for many reasons, including unrealistically high expectations due to a lack of exposure to the job during training, constraints placed on the worker by bureaucratic rules and regulations, inadequate resources for performing one's job, clients who are frequently uncooperative and occasionally antagonistic, and a lack of feedback about one's successes. These and other characteristics of human service organizations almost guarantee that employees will be frustrated in their attempts to reach their goals. Workers may not recognize that their workplace conditions produce this frustration. Instead, workers may feel personally responsible and begin to think of themselves as failures. When combined with emotional exhaustion, feelings of low personal accomplishment may reduce motivation to a point where performance is in fact impaired, leading to further feelings of failure.

Performance Deteriorates. Burned-out employees may perform more poorly on the job compared to their counterparts who are still "fired up." Consider as an example the job of an intake interviewer in a legal aid office. The intake interview serves as a screening device for the organization; through it all potential clients must pass. During the interview, specific information about the nature and details of a case must be assessed and an evaluation of the "appropriateness" of the case for the office must be made. As many as 40 intake interviews may be conducted per day, so it's important that the interviewer work as efficiently as possible. Here the major index of efficiency is the number of forms accurately filled out for further processing. To the extent that time is spent talking about problems not relevant for these forms, efficiency decreases.

Now consider the client's perspective. Upon arriving for an interview, the client is likely to be rehearsing the injustices done and planning for retaliation. The client does not consider the precise statutes encompassing the problem nor the essential details that make the case worthy of attention. The client's primary concern is to return emotional and physical life to normal, and the law seems to offer a solution. The intake interview may be the client's first chance to explain the problem. From this perspective, an interviewer who lends a sympathetic ear displays good job performance.

How will the interviewer handle this situation? Typically, the interviewer will be a relatively recent graduate of law school with little or no clinical experience to rely on. Law school training emphasized an objective, analytic attitude. But clearly, that training, combined with the pressure to efficiently fill out forms, does not make for the sympathetic ear the client is looking for. The objective interviewer appears unconcerned and the client becomes frustrated. The upset client becomes an obstacle to detached efficiency, which frustrates the interviewer. Whether or not open hostility erupts, both participants are aware of the antagonistic relationship they have formed.

Coworker Relations Deteriorate. Another unfortunate consequence of burnout is deteriorating relationships with coworkers. A study of mental health workers found that people who experienced calloused feelings toward their clients

FAST FACT

Poor or unfriendly customer service may result from a burned-out employee.

also complained more about their clients to their coworkers and generated a negative workplace atmosphere. These burned-out mental health workers also were absent from work more often and took more frequent work breaks. Thus, burnout can have a contagious effect, spreading throughout the organization.[76]

STRATEGIES FOR IMPROVING WORKPLACE SAFETY AND HEALTH

Once workplace hazards are identified, strategies can be developed for eliminating or reducing them. To determine whether a strategy is effective, organizations can compare the incidence, severity, and frequency of illnesses and accidents before and after the intervention. OSHA has approved methods for establishing these rates.

Monitoring Safety and Health Rates

OSHA requires employers to maintain records of their injuries and illnesses. Employers can record these by their incidence, severity, or frequency. Such records provide a basis for determining long-term trends, including improvement in or deterioration of employee health.

Incidence Rate. The **incidence rate** *is a measure that takes into account the number of injuries and illnesses in a year.* It's calculated by the following formula:

$$\text{Incidence rate} = \frac{\text{Number of injuries and illnesses} \times 200{,}000}{\text{Number of employee hours worked}}$$

The base for 100 full-time workers is 200,000 (40 hours a week times 50 weeks). Suppose an organization had 10 recorded injuries and illnesses and 500 employees. To calculate the number of employee hours worked, multiply the number of employees by 40 hours and by 50 weeks: $500 \times 40 \times 50 = 1{,}000{,}000$. Thus, the incidence rate is 2 for every 100 workers a year: $(10 \times 200{,}000)/1{,}000{,}000 = 2$.

Frequency Rate. The **frequency rate** *is a measure of the number of injuries and illnesses for every million hours worked.* It's calculated as:

$$\text{Frequency rate} = \frac{\text{Number of injuries and illnesses} \times 1{,}000{,}000 \text{ hours}}{\text{Number of employee hours worked}}$$

Severity Rate. The **severity rate** *reflects the hours actually lost owing to injury or illness.* It recognizes that not all injuries and illnesses are equal. Four categories of injuries and illnesses have been established: (1) deaths, (2) permanent total disabilities, (3) permanent partial disabilities, and (4) temporary total disabilities. An organization with the same number of injuries and illnesses as another but with more deaths would have a higher severity rate. The severity rate is calculated by this formula:

$$\text{Severity rate} = \frac{\text{Total hours charged} \times 1{,}000{,}000 \text{ hours}}{\text{Number of employee hours worked}}$$

Accident Prevention

Designing the work environment to make accidents unlikely is perhaps the best way to prevent accidents and increase safety. Among the safety features that can be designed into the physical environment are guards on machines, handrails in

FAST FACT

By creating a culture of safety at Alcoa, CEO Paul O'Neill reduced the company's rate of lost time because of injuries from one-third the U.S. average to one-twentieth.

stairways, safety goggles and helmets, warning lights, self-correcting mechanisms, and automatic shutoffs. The extent to which these features will actually reduce accidents depends on employee acceptance, company policies, and company culture (e.g., that of Alcoa, Alcan, Deere & Company, or Ben and Jerry's). For example, eye injuries will be reduced by the availability of safety goggles only if employees wear the goggles correctly.[77] This is more likely when employees accept responsibility for their own safety.

Alcoa employees understand that they bear responsibility for their safety. This responsibility has grown as the company has reduced its organizational levels, which means lessened supervision and a more participatory approach to management. With self-management and teamwork comes the burden on individuals to assume responsibility. Teams are expected to work toward common objectives, and these objectives should include excellent safety performance.[78]

Ergonomics. One way to improve safety is to make the job itself more comfortable and less fatiguing through ergonomics. **Ergonomics** *considers changes in the job environment in conjunction with the physical and physiological capabilities and limitations of the employees.*[79]

Possible ergonomic changes that employers can make to improve the health and comfort of their workforce include having employees

- Vary their tasks during the day, particularly the motions used to accomplish them.
- Take small, 10- to 30-second breaks every 30 minutes.
- Take longer breaks from the video display terminals every 2 hours.
- Employ discretion in how they work—in their posture, schedule, pace, and work processes.
- Minimize the number of keystrokes whenever possible.
- Have opportunities to learn about their job performance, what they contribute to projects, and their value.
- Become educated on the value of ergonomics.
- Reduce sources of environmental stress, such as heat, glare, or noise.
- Discover the features and functions of their workspace that enable them to adjust their environment for safety and comfort.[80]

In an effort to reduce the number of back injuries, Ford Motor Company redesigned workstations and tasks that caused musculoskeletal problems for workers. Lifting devices were introduced on the assembly line to reduce back strain, and walking and working surfaces were studied to determine how floor mats could be used to reduce body fatigue.[81]

OSHA has targeted injury-prone industries and offered to collaborate with them to develop voluntary guidelines to reduce specific types of injuries. With new initiatives, OSHA develops a set of guidelines and then asks for input from various experts, including physicians, industry representatives, and HR managers. The final guidelines are then made available to employers, who are encouraged to voluntarily adopt them as guides to improving workplace safety and health. The first industry to participate in this new program was the nursing home industry. Other industries that OSHA plans to work with include retail grocery, poultry processing, and shipyards.[82]

Health and Safety Committees. An estimated 75% of companies with 50 or more employees use health and safety committees to involve employees in improving

> " *We teach employees to look for potential issues, listen to their bodies, work with team leaders, and see if they can resolve the issues. If they can't resolve them, they call the ergonomics committee.* "
>
> *Bradley Joseph*
> *Manager of Ergonomics*
> *Ford Motor Company*

FAST FACT

Refineries can be dangerous places; of the 23 refineries designated by OSHA as having the best safety programs, 11 are units of Valero Energy. It is one of Fortune's *"Best Companies to Work for in America."*

workplace conditions, as Steelcase does. At least 16 states require certain businesses to establish permanent safety and health committees, but many businesses voluntarily establish safety committees in states where they are not required.

Health and safety committees typically take responsibility for identifying issues that need to be addressed in the workplace and for developing recommendations for how to make improvements. Often, organizations have several safety committees at the department level, for implementation and administration, and one overall committee at the organization level, for policy formulation. HR professionals often serve as coordinators for such committees, which typically include several employee representatives and several managers. In unionized settings, the committee should include union representatives as well. The available evidence indicates that such committees can be effective in reducing the frequency and severity of workplace injuries.[83]

Behavior Modification. Employers have known for a long time that a small percentage of their workforce is responsible for the majority of their health insurance claims. Originally, they tried to encourage their employees to be healthy by offering to subsidize health club memberships and building exercise facilities and jogging trails, but the results were disappointing. Now many companies are implementing incentive-based health care programs.

Using incentives to reward behaviors that reduce the likelihood of accidents can be highly successful. Incentives can range from nonmonetary rewards (e.g., positive feedback) to activity rewards (e.g., time off) to material rewards (e.g., company-purchased doughnuts during a coffee break) to financial rewards (e.g., bonuses for attaining desired levels of safety).

Caution, however, has to be exercised in the design of incentive systems. One concern of OSHA is that poorly designed incentives can cause employees to hide injuries. Safety programs often include goals for reducing accidents and injuries, with rewards linked to goal achievement. When employees are injured, they may find themselves weighing the costs of reporting the injury and getting it treated quickly against the cost to themselves and their coworkers of not achieving their safety goals.

Jenny-O Foods Turkey Store shares OSHA's concerns. Jenny-O avoids that problem by setting goals and linking rewards to safety knowledge and behavior, not to reductions in injuries and accidents. Safety audits are used to check on dozens of workplace conditions that might cause accidents. Employees are randomly interviewed to check their knowledge of safety guidelines. Small rewards are given to employees who score well on these quizzes.

Assessing Intervention Effectiveness. Regardless of the specific interventions that an organization chooses, the effectiveness of the interventions should be monitored.[84] When Maurice Myers became CEO of Waste Management, he soon realized the importance of measurement and training to improve safety. Early on, it became clear to Myers that Waste Management had problems. The company had never fully integrated the thousands of small-scale garbage operations it had acquired during the 1980s and 1990s into its system. Not only did Waste Management not know how many landfills it owned, it also didn't keep safety records. As a result, insurance costs and workers' compensation costs were high.

Waste Management had been claiming for years that it was the best in the industry and that it completely satisfied its customers, but Myers discovered this was just wishful thinking. Myers introduced rigorous measures to track all aspects of the company's performance: how long it took to answer a customer's call, how many customers reported billing problems, how many garbage pickups the company missed, and how many accidents company workers had. Executives were stunned by what they discovered. For example, they learned that 68% of the company's accidents were being caused by 12% of its drivers. Those drivers had typically worked at Waste Management for less than a year and usually were repeat offenders. The solutions were simple: The company increased training and dismissed bad drivers. As a result, the driver accident rate fell 48%.[85]

Disease Prevention

Occupational diseases can be far more costly and harmful than occupational accidents. Because diseases often take a long time to develop, dangerous working conditions may go undetected for several years. Developing strategies to reduce the incidence of disease is generally more difficult than reducing accidents and injuries.

Record Keeping. At a minimum, OSHA requires employers to measure the chemicals in the work environment and keep records on these measurements. The records must include precise information about ailments and exposures. Such information must be kept for as long as the incubation period of the specific disease, even as long as 40 years. If the organization is sold, the new owner must assume responsibility for storing the old records and continuing to gather the required data. If the company goes out of business, the administrative director of OSHA must be told where the records are. Guidelines for record keeping are given in Exhibit 13.4.

Monitoring Exposure. The obvious approach to controlling workplace illnesses is to rid the workplace of chemical agents or toxins. An alternative approach is to monitor and limit exposure to hazardous substances. Some organizations now monitor genetic changes due to exposure to carcinogens (e.g., arsenic, benzene, ether, and vinyl chloride). Samples of blood are obtained from employees at fixed intervals to determine whether the employees' chromosomes have been damaged. If damage has occurred, the affected employees are placed in different jobs, and, where feasible, conditions are modified.

Genetic Screening. Genetic screening is the most extreme, and consequently the most controversial, approach to controlling occupational disease. By using genetic testing to screen out individuals who are susceptible to certain ailments, employers can reduce the likelihood of exposing sensitive workers to conditions that some people can tolerate without harm. This strategy can be beneficial for workers' health and it reduces employers' health and insurance costs. However, opponents of genetic screening and many state laws contend that it measures a predisposition to disease, not the actual presence of disease, and therefore it violates the rights of individuals. When employees feel they really need a particular job and the income it brings, they often prefer to risk the possibility of future illness rather than go without work.[86]

Stress Management

Increasingly, organizations are offering programs designed to help employees deal with work-related stress. JPMorgan Chase offers stress management programs as part of an overall supervisory and management development curriculum. Available to supervisors, professional staff, and officers, the courses are

FAST FACT

OSHA requires organizations to

- Allow inspections.
- Keep records.
- Disclose medical records.

EXHIBIT 13.4 OSHA Guidelines for Recording Cases

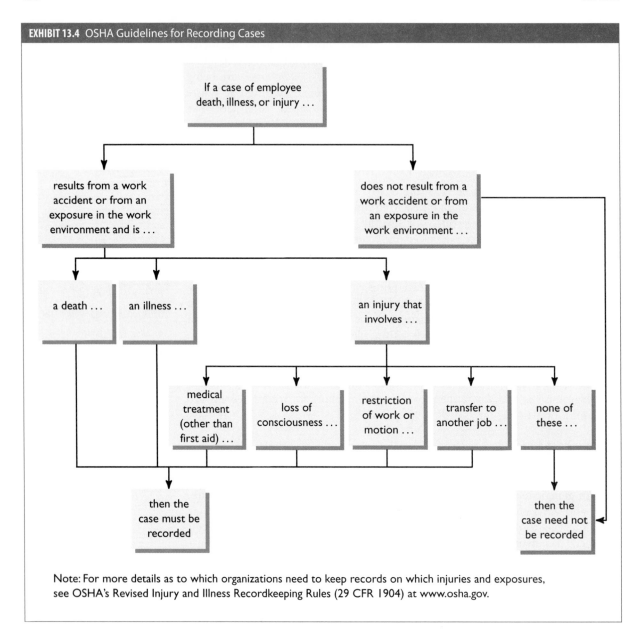

Note: For more details as to which organizations need to keep records on which injuries and exposures, see OSHA's Revised Injury and Illness Recordkeeping Rules (29 CFR 1904) at www.osha.gov.

FAST FACT

St. Luke's Episcopal Hospital in Houston has seminars on topics from career management to dealing with stress. Despite a nurse shortage, St. Luke's staffed a new facility entirely from employee referrals.

designed to introduce supervisory and management material, information skills, and role definition. The emphasis is on providing concrete information to reduce the ambiguity associated with fast-paced, changing work roles. The hope is that these programs will reduce the stress experienced by employees.[87]

Besides attempting to reduce the sources of stress at work, many employers provide training and other programs intended to help employees cope effectively with stress. Such programs recognize that workplace stressors will never be completely eliminated. By helping employees cope effectively with stress, employers can reduce the negative health consequences of long-term exposure to it.

Developing time management skills is one effective strategy for employees to use in coping with organizational stress. It's based in large part on an initial identification of an individual's personal goals. Other strategies that should be part of an individual's stress management include following a good diet, getting regular exercise, getting a good night's sleep, monitoring physical health, and building social support groups.[88]

Besides educating employees in the benefits of such strategies, some employers make it easy for workers to follow these prescriptions by designing the workplace accordingly. For example, Coors encourages employees to enroll in regular exercise programs, where their fitness and health are carefully monitored. In addition, some employers offer training in muscle relaxation techniques, meditation, self-hypnosis, and imagery.[89] Finally, encouraging employees to use, not bank, their vacation time and regular days off is another effective strategy for managing stress and burnout.[90]

Wellness Programs

Corporations are increasingly focusing on keeping employees healthy and well.[91] As Exhibit 13.5 shows, unhealthy workers increase employers' costs in several ways. By improving the health of their employees, companies can reduce these costs and increase their profitability. Often, the costs of wellness programs are small relative to the costs of disease and illness; so companies are investing in wellness programs at record rates. These investments appear to be paying off in terms of morale, performance, absentee rates, and health care costs.

Union Pacific Railroad estimated that its wellness program saved the company about $53 million during the past decade. A key element of their program is a free and voluntary health risk assessment. About two-thirds of the company's 51,000 employees went through this assessment, and up to half of those who were assessed subsequently enrolled in preventive health education and disease management programs. Union Pacific credits the program with reducing smoking, alcohol abuse, high blood pressure, and high cholesterol among employees.[92] These improvements reflect behavioral changes that employees made in their eating, drinking, smoking, and exercise habits. That is, the health improvements accrued mostly because employees changed their personal lifestyles outside of work, not because the company made changes in the work environment itself.

FAST FACT

Beginning in 2009, Clarian Health in Indianapolis charges employees a fee of $5 per pay period for each of the following: tobacco use, body mass index above 29.9, blood pressure above 140/90, blood glucose over 120, and LDL cholesterol above 130.

EXHIBIT 13.5 How Unhealthy Employees Increase Costs

Costs for Individuals

- Lower productivity while at work due to illness
- Medical care
- Benefits payments
- Recruitment and training of replacement workers

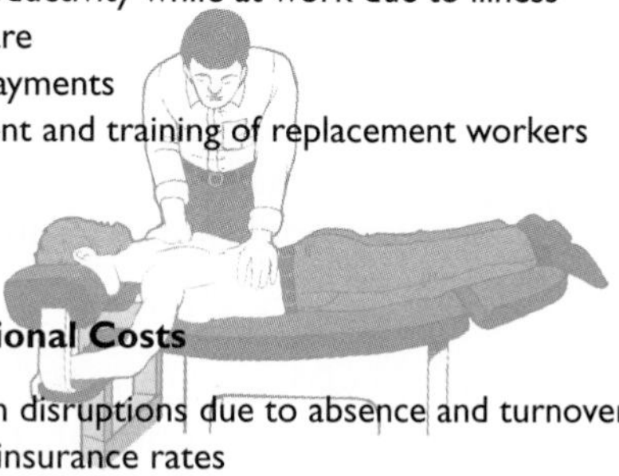

Organizational Costs

- Production disruptions due to absence and turnover
- Increased insurance rates
- Increased accidents due to inexperienced replacement workers
- End-of-service costs associated with an employee's death, such as funeral expenses and depressed morale

Weight Loss. Weight loss activities are an essential component of many employers' wellness programs. Economists with RTI International, a nonprofit think tank, and the Centers for Disease Control and Prevention, examined two national surveys that track absences and medical information on more than 20,000 full-time employees aged 18 to 64. Among the findings:

- The average medical expenditure for a normal-weight man is $1,351 a year. Men who are 30 to 60 pounds overweight cost $462 more based on added medical costs and absenteeism. Extremely obese men cost $2,027 a year more.

- Average medical expenditures for normal-weight women are $1,956. Women who are 30 to 60 pounds overweight cost $1,372 more when medical costs and missed work are included. Women who weigh 60 to 100 pounds too much cost $2,485 more.[93]

In total, obesity costs U.S. companies nearly $13 billion annually, according to recent estimates. Health care costs for obese employees are about one-third higher than for normal-weight employees, and medication costs (often covered by prescription drug benefits) are 77% higher. Furthermore, obese workers are twice as likely to be absent more than 14 days per year.[94]

At Union Pacific Railroad, 54% of the 51,000 employees are overweight. Looking at injury claims and illness records, the company estimated that reducing that percentage by one point would save $1.7 million; 5 points, $8.5 million; and 10 points, $16.9 million. As a consequence, Union Pacific Railroad has begun offering some employees the latest prescription weight-loss drugs as part of a study to determine how best to get its workers to slim down.[95] As employers become more sophisticated in their understanding of the bottom-line benefits of a healthy workforce, programs designed to actually improve employee health—not just prevent accidents and injuries—are likely to become more widespread.[96]

Smoking Cessation. The adverse health effects from cigarette smoking account for 440,000 deaths, or nearly one of every five deaths, each year in the United States. Smoking is the largest preventable cause of premature death.[97] For employers, the costs of smoking include lost productivity due to absenteeism and time spent on smoking breaks, increased health care costs and insurance premiums, and increased accidents and injuries. To reduce these costs, U.S. employers have adopted policies aimed at reducing smoking among employees. Banning smoking in the workplace and supporting employees in their efforts to quit smoking appear to be effective strategies. Research shows that banning smoking from the workplace is twice as effective in reducing tobacco consumption as permitting smoking in designated areas. Research also indicates that smokers are more likely to participate in smoking cessation programs when they receive financial incentives to do so. Thus, it appears that the workplace offers an important opportunity for improving the health of workers who wish to stop smoking.[98]

HIV/AIDS. To cope with the HIV/AIDS epidemic, many companies are investing in AIDS prevention and treatment. Experts suggest that effective prevention programs have four components: (1) educating employees, their families, and the surrounding community about how to avoid HIV infection; (2) free and voluntary testing and counseling; (3) treatment for other sexually transmitted diseases that facilitate HIV transmission; and (4) distribution of free condoms. Such programs cost relatively little and appear to be quite effective in reducing infection rates. Treatment for HIV/AIDS generally involves providing daily supplies of required drugs and close monitoring by a medical professional. Some companies simply pay for these services through medical insurance benefits, while others contract with stand-alone providers of AIDS management programs. Employees who work for some of the largest mining and agricultural companies receive treatment at company-run clinics.[99]

To date, corporate investment in HIV/AIDS prevention and treatment is focused in Africa. But experts warn that this disease is spreading rapidly in China, India, Russia, and the Ukraine. Thus, companies with operations in any of these areas should be considering how this disease affects them and the role they should play in reducing their employees' risk.

CURRENT ISSUES

Of the issues that are current in safety and health today, the two described here relate to (1) preparation for and recovery from diseases and disasters and (2) safety around the world.

Preparation for and Recovery from Diseases and Disasters

Diseases such as HIV/AIDS and diabetes have been described earlier in this chapter, but it is worth emphasizing their importance to individuals and organizations. As already described, companies can take many steps to address such disease epidemics, and the HR professional certainly has an important role to play in them. Similar consideration should also be given to protecting employees against the threat of avian flu. OSHA has developed guidance on what companies can do. The Centers for Disease Control (CDC) also provides useful information for companies as an aid in prevention, treatment, and recovery.[100] OSHA, the CDC, and NIOSH also have suggestions and guidance regarding disasters such as hurricanes, floods, and terrorism.[101] In all of these situations, the HR professional needs to work with others in the company to prepare for and recover from diseases and disasters. One of the biggest questions for the HR professional is, "How much should I get involved, especially in a proactive way?" This same question applies to the issue of safety around the world.

Safety around the World

As companies become more global, they have more employees in various locations around the world and more employees traveling to these locations. Agencies such as the United Nations and the U.S. State Department, among others, provide information related to the safety of conditions in other countries. Because companies assume responsibility for their workers around the world, HR professionals can make a very significant contribution by preparing employees and managers to work and live overseas. Of course, they can also provide employees and their families with security protection.[102] HR professionals can engage security professionals such as Kroll, to provide this security protection. Indeed Kroll's business is to "help clients reduce their exposure to global threats, seize opportunities, and protect employees and assets."[103]

Together, these two current issues highlight the growing risk employers confront as they strive to provide a safe and healthy workplace for employees. Increasingly, the management of health and safety issues is being recognized as a piece of the larger problem of risk management. As shown in Appendix A (on the Web site for this book, academic.cengage.com/management/jackson), understanding the principles of risk management is one of the requirements for certification as an HR professional.

CHAPTER SUMMARY WITH LEARNING GOALS

▲1 STRATEGIC IMPORTANCE OF WORKPLACE SAFETY AND HEALTH. By improving workplace safety and health, organizations can reduce costs and improve productivity while meeting the needs of their employees and fulfilling their obligations to the broader community. The federal government, through OSHA, monitors the performance of employers to protect workers from unnecessary harm and provides assistance to employers seeking to improve their work environments. The government's concern is primarily with occupational accidents and diseases, both aspects of the physical environment. However, organizations can choose to become involved in programs dealing with the psychological environment as well.

▲2 PROMOTING SAFETY AND HEALTH. Safety and health committees provide a forum to promote safety and health. They enable employees to inform employers about unsafe and unhealthy conditions and make recommendations for improvement. Employers can also use their safety and health records to track changes in safety and health outcomes. Records on the rate and severity of accidents and injuries can alert employers to new dangers as they arise and thus promote safety and health. These records also can provide data that can be used to determine whether interventions are having the desired effects.

▲3 SAFETY AND HEALTH HAZARDS. Many aspects of jobs and organizations can be unsafe and hazardous to health. Sometimes, jobs can be modified to reduce these hazards. Of course, some qualities of individuals can also be hazardous to safety and health.

▲4 IMPROVING WORKPLACE SAFETY AND HEALTH. Many interventions can be used to improve workplace safety and health. Among the most common are programs designed to reduce accidents and injuries, reduce disease, improve employees' ability to manage stress, and improve employees' overall health. While some of these interventions are intended to make the workplace safe and healthy, others are intended to change the lifestyles and nonwork behaviors of employees. All of these interventions can reduce the many costs associated with employee injuries, illness, and death.

▲5 CURRENT ISSUES. Designing and implementing intervention programs is more challenging to companies that have operations around the world because it is more difficult to monitor progress. Related to this is the challenge and responsibility of HR professionals and organizations in managing the conditions resulting from major disease epidemics and major disasters. Because of the magnitude of the impact of disease and disaster, organizations must be proactive in managing for their occurrence.

TERMS TO REMEMBER

Ergonomics

Frequency rate

Incidence rate

Job burnout

Job characteristics theory

National Institute for Occupational Safety and Health (NIOSH)

Occupational Safety and Health Act of 1970

Occupational Safety and Health Administration (OSHA)

Physiological-physical conditions

Psychological conditions

Severity rate

Shift work

Workplace safety and health

QUESTIONS FOR DISCUSSION AND REFLECTIVE THINKING

1. Describe the legal responsibility of employers for providing safe workplaces. Do you think employers should invest more than is legally required in workplace safety and health? Why or why not?
2. Describe the responsibilities that employees have for improving workplace safety and health.
3. Explain how each of the following HR practices can be used to maintain safe and healthy workplaces: job analysis, selection, training, performance measurement and feedback, and incentives.
4. Wellness prevention programs often target illnesses and diseases that are not caused by aspects of the workplace itself. Do you think it is appropriate for employers to intervene to improve their employees' personal health and wellness? Explain.

PROJECTS TO EXTEND YOUR LEARNING

1. **Integration and Application.** Before continuing, review the cases of Southwest Airlines and Lincoln Electric at the end of this book. Then answer the following questions.
    a. First, jot down the threats to employee health and safety at these two companies.
    b. Next, choose one company and describe the safety and health programs that you believe should be in place. Be specific about the objectives of the programs, and make sure you state who should be responsible for them.

2. **Using the Internet.** Many organizations provide useful information to help employers improve workplace safety and protect employee health. Learn more about these online resources.
    a. Find out about safety and health statistics at
        *   ILO (www.ilo.org).
        *   World Health Organization (WHO) (www.who.int/en/).
        *   National Safety Council (www.nsc.org).
        *   Bureau of Labor Statistics (www.bls.gov).
        *   OSHA (www.osha.gov).
    b. Learn about activities to promote safety and health at some of the firms discussed in this section by visiting their company home pages:
        *   Ben and Jerry's (www.benjerry.com).
        *   Deere & Co. (www.deere.com).
        *   Steelcase (www.steelcase.com).
        *   Union Pacific Railroad (www.up.com).
    c. Learn more about OSHA's record-keeping requirements at www.osha.gov.
    d. Investigate the safety issues that are most relevant to various industries on the National Safety Council Web site (www.nsc.org).
    e. Learn more about union views on safety and health at
        *   United Mine Workers of America (www.umwa.org).
        *   AFL-CIO (www.aflcio.org).
        *   Service Employees International Union (www.seiu.org).
    f. Visit fgiWorld (www.fgiworld.com) to learn more about how companies can prepare their workforces for natural disasters.

3. **Experiential Activity.** Carpal tunnel syndrome is a very common problem among employees who work in a variety of occupations. Learn more about carpal tunnel

syndrome (CTS) and how it affects employees who suffer from it by conducting several interviews. This activity can be done individually, or your class instructor may ask you to do the interviews as part of a team project.

Activity

Step 1. Locate a work site where employees seem to be at risk for this injury because their work involves a lot of repetitive motion.

Step 2. Conduct interviews with three people. Choose the following types of people to interview.

a.   A person who has suffered from carpal tunnel syndrome.
b.   A coworker of someone who has suffered from carpal tunnel syndrome.
c.   A manager or supervisor of someone who has suffered from carpal tunnel syndrome.

Step 3. Based on your interviews and what you have learned in this chapter, write a memo that makes three recommendations for reducing the effects of carpal tunnel syndrome in the workplace you visited. Use the following questions to guide your interview.

For the person with carpal tunnel syndrome:

a.   What symptoms did you experience?
b.   For how long did you experience these symptoms before seeking medical advice?
c.   How did the symptoms affect your productivity at work (e.g., making mistakes due to pain, working more slowly, taking days off to rest or get medical treatment)?
d.   How did your symptoms affect your life outside work?
e.   Did you have surgery? If so, how many days were you absent while you recovered?
f.   What did your employer do to reduce the risk of your experiencing these problems again in the future (e.g., new equipment, reassigned to different job duties, education or training)?
g.   Do you feel any different about your employer as a result of how the organization responded to your problems? Explain.

For the coworker:

a.   Did your coworker's experience with carpal tunnel syndrome have any consequences for you (e.g., disrupting your own work, creating more work for you, or causing you to worry about your own health)? If yes, for how long did you experience these consequences?
b.   Do you feel your employer treated your coworker fairly when your coworker was dealing with the problems of carpal tunnel syndrome? Why or why not?
c.   Did your employer make any changes in the workplace to reduce the risk that you and others might develop carpal tunnel syndrome? If yes, describe these changes.
d.   Do you have any suggestions for how the organization could improve the workplace to address this problem in the future? If yes, what are they?

For the supervisor or manager:

a.   How many employees with carpal tunnel syndrome have you dealt with in the past five years?
b.   Do you think the problem of injuries like this is increasing in importance? Staying the same? Becoming less important? Why?
c.   Based on your experiences, what do you see as the most significant consequence of this injury for individual employees?
d.   What are the consequences of this injury for the organization?
e.   What is your estimate of the cost of this injury to the organization, taking into account medical expenses, lost productivity, and so on? (This estimate can be the cost for one individual or for the organization as a whole.)
f.   Does the organization have a formal program for preventing the risk of carpal tunnel syndrome injuries? If yes, describe the program and explain your role in it.

CASE STUDY
WHO'S THERE ON THE LINE?

The telecommunications field continues to change very rapidly. In perhaps no other field has technology had such a significant impact on the jobs of so many workers. Mitch Fields, for example, still remembers that tragic day in November 1963 when President John F. Kennedy was assassinated while Fields was pulling the afternoon shift as a switchman for Midwest Telephone Company (MTC). As Fields described it, it sounded like 30 locomotives hammering their way through a large room filled with walls of mechanical switches putting phone calls through to their destination. Today, that room of switches has been replaced by a microchip. Fields himself has undergone extensive training to operate a computer console used to monitor and diagnose switching problems.

The job of operator has changed from sitting in long rows of operating equipment that was attached to walls of jacks and cords to individual workstations that look like command centers out of a Star Trek spaceship. In addition, the competitive environment of telephone services has changed dramatically because of deregulation and competition from other phone companies offering similar services. The new thrust now is to shift operator performance from being not just fast and friendly but profitable as well, by marketing the company ("Thank you for using MTC") and selling high-profit-margin services ("Is there someone else you would like to talk to? The person-to-person rate is only additional for the first minute").

The operator's job at MTC remains unchanged in two respects: (1) Operators will talk to nearly 600 people in a typical day, some of whom are abusive, and (2) operator job performance is monitored. Technological innovation has enabled MTC to monitor each operator by computer to produce statistics on the numbers of calls handled per shift, the speed of the calls, and the amount of revenue generated by the calls. In addition to computer monitoring, supervisors may also listen in on operators to ensure that proper operator protocol is being followed. For example, customers are never told they dialed the "wrong" number, obscene calls are routed to supervisors, and operators learn to say "hold the line" or "one moment please" instead of "hang on."

Meeting performance standards based on these criteria does not typically lead to large rewards. A beginning operator usually earns about $22,000 a year working swing shifts that may begin at 8:30 A.M., noon, 2:00 P.M., 4:30 P.M., 8:30 P.M., or 2:00 A.M. Only the highest-rated operators have opportunities to be transferred, promoted, or given educational benefits.

Steve Buckley, training and development manager for MTC, knows that to change the fast and friendly MTC operator of the past to one who is fast and friendly but profitable as well is going to be a real challenge. Buckley has not figured out yet how to get the operators to conclude each transaction by saying "Thank you for using MTC." A recent clandestine supervisor survey revealed that fewer than 20% of the operators were using the requested reply. Buckley is also being pressured by the local union leaders who represent the telephone operators to reduce the job stress brought on by the high volume of people transactions and the constant, computer-assisted surveillance. One thing is for sure, however: Buckley must implement a plan for improvement.

CASE QUESTIONS

1. Can Buckley really change the behavior of the operators?
2. How can Buckley succeed in getting the operators to say, "Thank you for using MTC"? Should he involve the union in his attempts to do so?
3. Is computer monitoring the answer?
4. Should the operators really decide on the change?

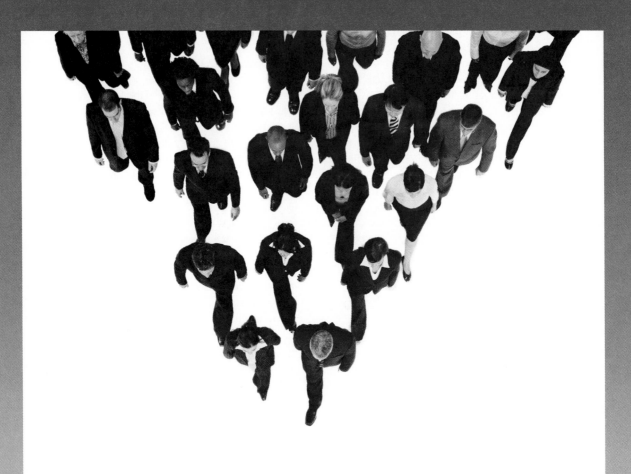

Understanding Unionization and Collective Bargaining

Learning Goals

After reading this chapter, you should be able to:

1 Explain the strategic importance of unionization and collective bargaining.

2 Describe the historical context and the current status of unions.

3 List the elements of the organizing campaign.

4 Explain the collective bargaining process.

5 Describe how labor agreements are negotiated.

6 Identify the modes of conflict resolution.

7 Describe the elements of contract administration.

8 Discuss two current issues in unionization and collective bargaining.

MANAGING HUMAN RESOURCES AT UNITED PARCEL SERVICE

Founded in 1907, United Parcel Service (UPS) is known worldwide for package delivery service. Operating in more than 200 countries, it's also a leading provider of specialized transportation and logistics services, including supply chain management. UPS's total revenues exceed $45 billion yearly. Its history of outstanding performance has landed it at the top of its industry in *Fortune*'s "100 Most Admired Companies."

The company's 410,000 employees (60,000 of whom are outside the United States) are represented by the Teamsters union. Thanks partly to the union, UPS employees are some of the most highly paid in their industry. Once people join UPS, they tend to stay; so the company benefits by having relatively low turnover costs.

For most of UPS's 100-year history, management and the teamsters have worked together in a productive, collaborative relationship guided by UPS founder Jim Casey's philosophy that "You can be a good Teamster and a good UPSer." The one exception was in August of 1997, when the union went on strike.

It appears that UPS learned from the strike experience of 1997. According to CEO Mike Eskew, labor and management understand that all parties need to work together in a collaborative partnership to make sure that all is well. Key to maintaining a positive relationship between the union and UPS are the ongoing efforts of Allen Hill, senior vice president of HR and public affairs, and Ken Hall, the Teamsters' head of its Parcel and Small Package Division. Through outreach on the Teamsters' Web site and area steward training programs, the Parcel and Small Package Division works to ensure that the security of a good Teamster contract is available to all members. Under the direction of Ken Hall, the division maintains an increasing number of staff charged with effectively serving UPS members throughout the United States.[1] ▲

THE STRATEGIC IMPORTANCE OF UNIONIZATION AND COLLECTIVE BARGAINING

As economic conditions continue to change in the twenty-first century, the union-management relationship will probably also change. Changes are likely to occur both in unionization efforts and in the bargaining relationships between existing unions and management. For example, the United Auto Workers (UAW) union is extending its efforts to unionize nonteaching employees in universities. The Teamsters are seeking to represent the workers of Federal Express.[2] To put into perspective these aspects of union-management relationships, this chapter describes the process of forming a union (unionization) and the characteristics of administering an agreement reached between the union and management (collective bargaining).

Unionization *is the effort by employees and outside agencies (unions or associations) to act as a single unit when dealing with management over issues relating to their work.* When recognized by the National Labor Relations Board (NLRB), a union has the legal authority to negotiate with the employer on behalf of employees—to improve wages, hours, and conditions of employment—and to administer the ensuing agreement.[3]

The core of union-management relations is collective bargaining. **Collective bargaining** *generally includes (1) the negotiation of work conditions that, when written up as the collective agreement, becomes the basis for employee-employer relationships on the job, and (2) activities related to interpreting and enforcing the collective agreement and resolving any conflicts arising from it.*[4]

The existence—or even the possibility of—a union can significantly influence how an employer manages its vital human resources. Unions can help employees get what they want—for example, high wages and job security—from their employers. But for a company's managers, unionization usually means giving up some control over workplace practices such as hiring new workers, making job assignments, and introducing automation or other new work methods. Work practices may be less efficient after unionization. Alternatively, unionization can result in increased workforce cooperation and the development of new strategies to help the company be more competitive! This is exactly what the United Steelworkers of America (USWA) union did for the Goodyear Tire and Rubber Company in 2003 and 2006.[5]

Unions obtain legal rights for their members that employees without union representation don't have. Thus, a union's presence pressures managers to consider employee reactions to a wide variety of decisions. These pressures are also felt by managers in nonunion companies who want to remain union-free. When employees feel their concerns are being ignored, the appeal of union representation is likely to increase.[6] Consequently, it may be no more expensive for a company to operate with unionized rather than nonunionized employees.[7]

When unions give wage concessions or cooperate in joint workplace efforts, such as teamwork programs, they can help employers remain profitable and competitive, thus ensuring their survival during especially difficult times.[8] Unions also can help identify workplace hazards and improve job security for their members.[9] Clearly, unions have important roles to play in addressing the strategic issues of a multinational company. These are described in more detail in the feature "Managing with Metrics: Unions' Involvement Enhances Competitiveness."[10]

FAST FACT

Unions are present in about 25% of Fortune's "100 Most Admired Companies."

Unions' Involvement Enhances Competitiveness

Costs are a critical metric in determining a company's competitiveness, and labor costs are no exception. When high costs interfere with a firm's financial performance, wage reductions agreed upon by unions and management can help lower costs. When the United Steelworkers union agreed to wage concessions for its members, it helped Goodyear Tire and Rubber survive and remain globally competitive. The wage concessions were agreed upon in exchange for a promise that the company would keep factories open in the United States and protect future retiree health care benefits. "Reaching agreement . . . on a contract that competitively positions Goodyear for the future is a huge achievement for everyone involved in the negotiation process," said Robert J. Keegan, chairman and chief executive officer. "The end result is Goodyear will be a stronger company, a stronger employer, and a stronger overall global competitor." Goodyear is now able to lower its labor costs and price its products more competitively.

At Boeing, the process of reducing costs is a long-term effort. Since 2000, Boeing and the International Association of Machinists have agreed to concessions that will result in a reduction of almost 20,000 union jobs. The union membership numbers will decline due in part to a decision to outsource a large chunk of the 7E7 assembly work to Asia and Europe. The decision to outsource this work will improve another key metric: operating margin. In exchange, Boeing said that it would build much of the new plane in Washington. Boeing also agreed to hand out bonuses of $3,000 to machinists in 2006 and 2007. Still Boeing's commercial plane division makes only a 7% operating margin, while Airbus makes 16.7%. Boeing and the union both understand that competing effectively against Airbus is essential to their long-term survival. To help improve Boeing's competitiveness, the company offered to work hand in hand with the union to end decades of bitter labor relations that sank employee morale to an all-time low. Boeing sees this new relationship as vital to keeping costs down and improving its operating margin over the next few years.

Unionization and Collective Bargaining within the Integrated HRM System

Exhibit 14.1 illustrates the general process of unionization and shows its relationship to other elements of the HRM system. As the story of UPS and Exhibit 14.1 illustrate, unionizing and collective bargaining activities often involve other HRM practices. In the UPS example, pensions and the use of part-time workers were important issues in the strike between the Teamsters and UPS. Other concerns that are important to both union leaders and members are job security, cost-of-living increases, working conditions, and health and safety.

Increasingly, unions are also concerned about training and education for their members.[11] They recognize that staying competitive in a global marketplace often requires companies to redesign work using the most current technologies available. When new technologies are introduced, workers usually need new skills. To stay employed, union members must therefore acquire the needed skills. Doing so often requires employers to provide additional training and education.

Unions also care about performance measurement and compensation practices that tie employee performance to pay. They want to ensure that these and other HRM activities are implemented with fairness and respect for each employee. Unions such as the Teamsters, the CWA, the USWA, and the UAW have also worked with companies such as UPS, Goodyear, and Boeing to provide and implement programs in safety and health.[12] Thus, unions often work with HR professionals as they design and help employers implement a variety

FAST FACT

In Seattle, the Communications Workers of America (CWA) teamed with Cisco to build a laboratory to house Web programming classes.

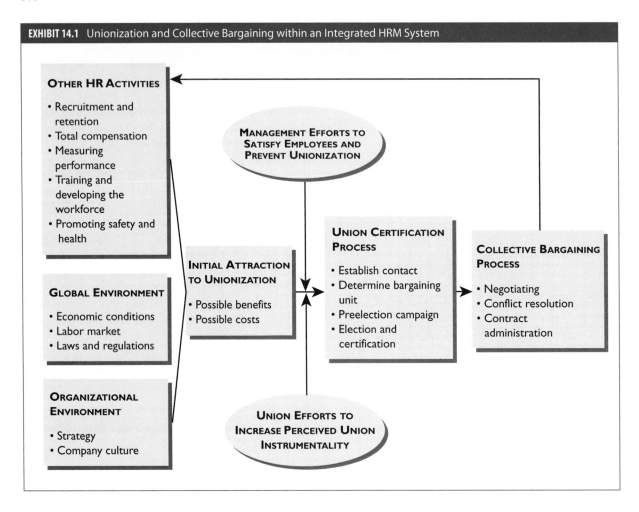

EXHIBIT 14.1 Unionization and Collective Bargaining within an Integrated HRM System

of HRM practices. Among the roles and responsibilities to be fulfilled are those shown in the feature "The HR Triad—Extended: Roles and Responsibilities in Unionization and Collective Bargaining."

As formal organizations, unions also use all of the practices of managing human resources described in this book to manage their own human resources. They need to plan for the union's long-term needs, recruit and retain their own employees, compensate those employees, and manage their performance. Unions are concerned about having a workforce that is diverse, well educated, and able to serve the needs of the membership. Thus, a union's internal HR department plays a vital role in the success of the union and the attainment of its own strategic objectives (e.g., increasing union membership).

THE HISTORICAL CONTEXT AND UNIONS TODAY

A better understanding of the attitudes and behaviors of both unions and management can be gained through a knowledge of past union-management relations.

A Brief History

The beginning of the labor union movement in the United States can be traced back to the successful attempt of journeyman printers to win a wage increase in 1778. By the 1790s, unions of shoemakers, carpenters, and

LINE MANAGERS	HR PROFESSIONALS	EMPLOYEES	UNIONS
• Know the laws and regulations that govern what can and can't be said to employees regarding unionization during an organizing campaign. • Understand why employees are likely to join a union. • Support the efforts of HR professionals in developing and implementing policies to support good working conditions. • Manage employees with respect and equality. • Participate in grievance procedures to resolve complaints fairly. • Work with HR professionals to develop an effective relationship with union representatives.	• Train line managers about the unionization rights of employees. • Develop HR policies to provide good working conditions. • Continually survey employees' attitudes so that management knows employees' views and opinions. • Work with line managers in dealing effectively with union representatives. • Develop mechanisms for effective grievance resolution and ensure managers and employees understand these procedures. • Be proactive in addressing employees' concerns before major conflicts erupt.	• Understand what unions do and how they function. • Express views on workplace conditions, wages, and working hours. • Bargain in good faith through union representatives with line managers and HR professionals. • Fulfill rights and responsibilities in the union contract. • Use mechanisms for grievances as appropriate. • Be aware of the issues management and labor leaders are discussing.	• Abide by laws and regulations governing legal union activities. • Strive to improve wages and working conditions for union members. • Offer to work with management to improve company profitability and survival. • Bargain with line managers and HR professionals. • Participate in development of effective grievance procedures. • Be willing to adapt to local conditions and changes in technology and economic conditions.

printers had appeared in Boston, Baltimore, New York, and other cities. The Federal Society of Journeymen Cordwainers, for example, was organized in Philadelphia in 1794, primarily to resist employers' attempts to reduce wages. Other issues of concern to these early unions were union shops (companies using only union members) and the regulation of apprenticeships to prevent the replacement of journeyman employees.

The early unions had methods and objectives that are still evident in unions today. Although there was no collective bargaining, the unions established a price below which members would not work. Strikes were used to enforce this rate. These strikes were relatively peaceful and for the most part successful.

One negative characteristic of early unions was their susceptibility to economic depressions. Until the late 1800s, most unions thrived in times of prosperity but died off during depressions. During difficult economic times, unions found it harder to convince workers to stand up against employers, who had the power to put them out of work completely. The weakness of unions at this time may have been related to their insularity. Aside from sharing information on strikebreakers (which are known as "scabs" to those who oppose them), the unions operated independently of each other.

Labor conditions went through several important changes by the end of the nineteenth century. Transportation systems (canals, railroads, and turnpikes) expanded the markets for products and increased worker mobility. As the economy and markets expanded, the cost of setting up a business increased; one consequence of this change was that craft workers found it more difficult to remain independent and be their own boss. Instead, they became skilled workers employed by a large business. Unionism found its start in these skilled occupations.

Unions continued to experience ups and downs that were tied to economic and legal conditions. Employers took advantage of economic depressions to combat unions: In "an all out frontal attack . . . they engaged in frequent lockouts, hired spies . . . summarily discharged labor 'agitators,' and [engaged] the services of strikebreakers on a widespread scale."[13] These actions, and the retaliations of unions, established a tenor of violence and lent a strong adversarial nature to union-management relations, the residual effects of which are still in evidence today.

In the twentieth century, several laws were passed that provided legitimacy, structure, and governance to the union movement. Some of the most significant laws were the Norris-LaGuardia Act of 1932, the National Labor Relations Act (or Wagner Act) of 1935, the Labor Management Relations Act (or Taft-Hartley Act) of 1947, the Labor Management Reporting and Disclosure Act (or Landrum-Griffin Act) of 1959, Executive Order 10988 of 1962, and the Civil Service Reform Act of 1978.

Today, the adversarial nature of the union-management relationship has been diminished to a certain extent by a more cooperative one. Strikes have become less frequent, and unions now rely more on collective bargaining as the primary method of negotiating with employers. These changes have been dictated in part by current trends in union membership, including the shifting distribution of the membership and changing industry dynamics such as the continuing shift away from traditional manufacturing jobs.

Decline in Membership

FAST FACT

New York and Alaska have the highest percentage of unionization at about 25%. North Carolina has the lowest at about 3%.

Union membership in the United States has declined steadily from its high of 35.5% of the workforce in 1945. In the mid-1950s, 35% of the workforce was unionized. In 1970, the percentage of unionized workers in the labor force was about 25%. In 2008, unions represented approximately 12% of all workers.

However, the rates of unionization differ dramatically in the private and public sectors.[14] In the public sector, the rate of unionization has held fairly steady at about 35%. Thus, in mostly public occupations (e.g., law enforcement, health care, firefighting, and education), rates of unionization are relatively high.

Exhibit 14.2 shows the steady decline in union representation in the private sector.

Contributing to the decline in union memberships has been the growth in service sector employment, high-technology jobs, and white-collar jobs, all of which historically have had low proportions of union members. Other contributing circumstances have included a decline in employment in industries that are highly unionized, improved human resource management practices, and the increased decertification of unions. To counter these trends, union leaders in the AFL-CIO and some other unions have increased their efforts to expand their membership base.[15]

" *Andy Stern, who leads the largest and fastest-growing union in the country, is determined to save the American worker.* "

Matt Bai
Journalist

Traditionally dominated by (mostly white) men, today's unions must also be responsive to the concerns of women and minorities. These populations are increasingly present in the workforce, and they provide the best opportunities for growth in union membership. In addition to including a greater variety of groups, the union movement has sought to include people from more diverse backgrounds in the grassroots of labor. It has expanded its organizing efforts in the South, increased efforts to organize construction and kitchen workers in

EXHIBIT 14.2 Declining Rate of Unionization in the U.S. Private Sector

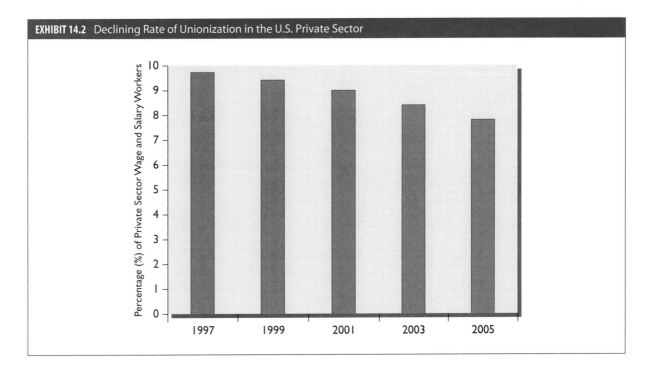

Las Vegas, signed up asbestos cleanup crews in New York, signed up more farm workers in California, and signed up more health care and property service workers nationwide. It is doing this with the help of a new crop of workers/ organizers who are young, ambitious, college-educated people with a passion for the union movement. The organizers of today understand that they need to know how a company operates, and they need to find workers who are unhappy with the status quo. With the real wages of many workers remaining stagnant or even falling, calls to organize may be heard by an increasing number of willing ears—especially those of white-collar workers.[16]

To gain organizational and financial strength, several unions have merged in recent years. For example, UNITE HERE was formed from a merger of the International Ladies' Garment Workers' Union (ILGWU), the Amalgamated Clothing Workers of America (ACWA), the Textile Workers Union of America (TWUA), and the Hotel Employees and Restaurant Employees International Union (HERE).[17] UNITE HERE is the union that helped to organize the widely publicized strike of blue-collar and office workers at Yale University in 2003. The strike closed down the student cafeteria and spurred about 100 faculty supporters of the strike to move their classes off campus to churches and government buildings. By the time the dispute was settled, workers had won a new contract that nearly doubled their pensions and guaranteed wage increases of 3% to 5% annually for eight years.[18]

Although mergers between unions may not increase membership directly, they generally improve the efficiency of union-organizing efforts and reduce costly jurisdictional disputes between unions. Increased organizational strength from mergers may also enable unions to cover industries and occupations previously underrepresented in union membership, such as health care and telecommunications workers.[19]

FAST FACT

Rates of unionization around the world:

- *Australia*   *35%*
- *Brazil*   *44%*
- *France*   *9%*
- *Germany*   *23%*
- *Japan*   *20%*
- *Mexico*   *43%*
- *Sweden*   *78%*
- *United Kingdom*   *29%*

EXHIBIT 14.3 Union Density by State

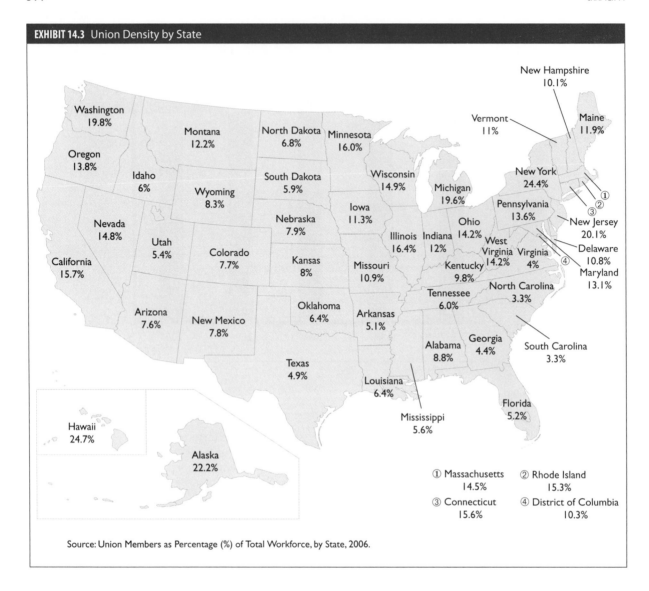

Source: Union Members as Percentage (%) of Total Workforce, by State, 2006.

Distribution of Membership

As Exhibit 14.3 shows, unionization levels vary by state.[20] States with relatively high levels of unionization include Alaska, Hawaii, Michigan, and New York; states with the lowest levels of unionization include Arizona, Arkansas, North Carolina, and South Carolina. All the states with low rates of unionization also have **right to work laws,** *which state that employees are not required to join the union as a condition of employment in a company that is already organized.* Twenty-two states have these laws and are referred to as right-to-work states.

Structure of American Unions

The basic unit of labor unions in the United States is the national (or international) union, a body that organizes, charters, and controls member locals. National unions develop the general policies and procedures by which locals operate, and they help locals in areas such as collective bargaining. National unions provide clout for locals because they control a large number of employees and can influence large organizations through national strikes or slowdown activities.

The umbrella organization for national unions is the **AFL-CIO,** *the American Federation of Labor and Congress of Industrial Organizations.* With about 10 million members, it represents about 80% of the total union membership in the United States. Recently, the size of the AFL-CIO has declined because of disagreements among union leaders. Rather than remain under the AFL-CIO umbrella, unions such as the Teamsters and UNITE HERE decided to drop out and create another umbrella organization.[21]

Every two years, the AFL-CIO holds a convention to develop policy and amend its constitution. Each national union is represented in proportion to its membership. Between conventions, an executive council (the governing body) and a general board direct the organization's affairs; a president is in charge of day-to-day operations.

The executive council's activities include evaluating legislation that affects labor and watching for corruption within the AFL-CIO. Standing committees are appointed to deal with executive, legislative, political, educational, organizing, and other activities. The department of organization and field services, for instance, focuses its attention on organizing activities.

At the heart of the labor movement are the 70,000 or so local unions. The locals represent the workers at the workplace. Most locals elect a president, a secretary-treasurer, and perhaps one or two other officers from the membership. It is at the local level that much of the union's day-to-day contact with managers and HR professionals takes place.

The larger locals hire a **business representative,** *who is a full-time employee hired to handle employee grievances and contract negotiations.* Locals also have a **steward,** *who is an employee elected by the employee's work unit to act as the union representative at the workplace and to respond to company actions against employees that may violate the labor agreement.* The steward protects the rights of workers by filing grievances when the employer has acted improperly.

How Unions Operate

The activities of union locals revolve around collective bargaining and grievance handling. In addition, locals hold general meetings, publish newsletters, and otherwise keep their members informed. Unless a serious problem exists, attendance at meetings is usually low, and the election of officers often draws votes from less than one-fourth of the membership.

At the two national headquarters of the AFL-CIO and Change to Win, committees work on a wide range of issues, including civil rights, job security, community service, economic policy, union-management cooperation, education, ethical practices, executive pay, housing, international affairs, legislation, public relations, health care, research, safety, Social Security, and veterans' affairs. A publications department produces literature for the membership and outsiders. National union headquarters also provide specialized services to regional and local bodies. People trained in organizing, strikes, legal matters, public relations, and negotiations are available to individual unions.

In addition to the AFL-CIO, national unions, such as the Teamsters, the CWA, the UAW, and the SEIU, are active in the political arena. Labor maintains a strong lobbying force in Washington, D.C. and is involved in political action committees at the state and local levels. The UAW lobbied in Washington to restrict car imports in an attempt to bolster U.S. automakers and increase jobs.

FAST FACT

Change to Win is the new labor federation that broke away from the AFL-CIO in 2005. Its big members include UNITE HERE and the Teamsters.

FAST FACT

The AFL-CIO's Office of Investment keeps track of CEO compensation levels. It believes that excessive CEO pay is a point around which it can rally the workers.

In Mexico, unions have the right to organize workers at a business, but only one union represents a given location. That is, all employees at a given location are covered by a single union. When a strike is called, the workplace is closed until the strike is settled; picket lines are unknown.

In case of a dispute, the burden of proof is always on the employer. Labor law is part of Mexico's constitution, and workers aren't allowed to renounce those rights. Therefore, any individual employment contract or collective agreement that limits constitutionally given rights is considered invalid.

Since the advent of NAFTA, union organizations in the United States have seen the development of positive relations with Mexico as a strategic opportunity and necessity. When companies such as General Electric and General Motors increased their operations in Mexico, the U.S. unions that were already active in these companies began providing support to the local unions in Mexico. U.S. unions have also attempted to work through NAFTA to improve wages and working conditions in Mexico. NAFTA legislation empowers the secretaries of labor in Canada,

the United States, and Mexico to impose fines on a country that fails to enforce its labor laws.

Approximately one-third of the Canadian labor force is unionized. About three-fourths of the union members are affiliated with the Canadian Labor Congress (CLC). As in the United States, the union local is the basic local unit. The CLC is the dominant labor group at the national level, with political influence comparable to that of the AFL-CIO.

The labor laws in Canada are similar to those in the United States, but with some noteworthy differences. For example, Canadian labor laws require frequent interventions by governmental bodies before a strike can take place. In the United States, government involvement is largely voluntary and infrequent. For the Canadian union movement as a whole, the trend toward concessionary bargaining to avoid layoffs and plant closings appears to be less evident than it is in the United States. In general, Canadian and U.S. labor groups are becoming increasingly autonomous. In the case of the UAW, the Canadian organization split off completely from the UAW and the two now operate independently of each other.[23]

It lobbied against the North American Free Trade Agreement (NAFTA) and for health care reform. To help their membership, unions are expanding their activities on all levels and in some cases working with other organizations to attain mutual goals. Unions are also trying to increase their effectiveness in their recruiting efforts and organizing campaigns. Descriptions of these activities in Mexico and Canada are offered in the feature "Managing Globalization: Unionization in Mexico and Canada."[22]

3
LEARNING GOAL

FAST FACT

Union salting refers to the practice of union organizers seeking employment in companies without disclosing their true backgrounds in order to establish a base for union organizing activities.

THE ORGANIZING CAMPAIGN

A major function of the NLRB is to conduct the process in which a union is chosen to represent employees. This is accomplished through a certification election to determine whether the majority of employees want the union to represent them. The process by which a single union is selected to represent all employees in a particular unit is crucial to the American system of collective bargaining. If a majority of those voting opt for union representation, all employees are bound by that choice, and the employer is obligated to recognize and bargain with the chosen union.

Because unions can acquire significant power, employers are usually anxious to keep them out. Adding to this potential union-management conflict is the possibility of competition and conflict between two or more unions that want to win certification by the same group of employees. The certification process has several stages, as outlined in Exhibit 14.4.[24]

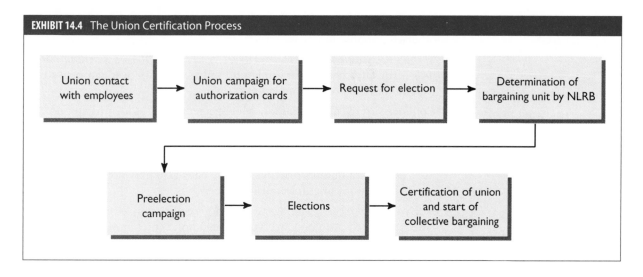

EXHIBIT 14.4 The Union Certification Process

Soliciting Employee Support

In the campaign to solicit employee support, unions traditionally attempt to contact the employees, obtain a sufficient number of authorization cards, and request an election from the NLRB.

Establishing Contact between the Union and Employees. Contact between the union and employees may be initiated by either party. National unions usually contact employees in industries or occupations in which they have an interest or are traditionally involved. The UAW, for example, has contacted nonunion employees in the new automobile plants that have been built in the southern United States by German and Japanese auto companies. Thus far, the unions have been relatively unsuccessful. The same is true at Wal-Mart.[25]

In other cases, employees may approach the union. The union is usually happy to oblige any employees interested in organizing, regardless of whether their reasons include low pay, poor working conditions, or other areas of dissatisfaction. U.S. workers are generally apathetic toward unions, however; so they are not likely to initiate contact with a union until their relationship with their employer has become very problematic.

Prohibited Actions. At the point that contact occurs between the union and employees, the company must be careful to avoid engaging in unfair labor practices. Accordingly, *employers should not*

- *Misrepresent the facts.* Any information management provides about a union or its officers must be factual and truthful.
- *Threaten employees.* It is unlawful to threaten employees with loss of their jobs or transfers to less desirable positions, income reductions, or loss or reductions of benefits and privileges. The use of intimidating language to dissuade employees from joining or supporting a union also is forbidden. In addition, supervisors may not blacklist, lay off, discipline, or discharge any employee because of union activity.
- *Promise benefits or rewards.* Supervisors may not promise a pay raise, additional overtime or time off, promotions, or other favorable considerations in exchange for an employee's agreement to refrain from joining a

FAST FACT

In 2000, the meat cutting department at one Wal-Mart voted to establish a union. Two weeks later, Wal-Mart disbanded its meat cutting departments.

union or signing a union card, to vote against union representation, or to otherwise oppose union activity.

- *Make unscheduled changes in wages, hours, benefits, or working conditions.* Any such changes are unlawful unless the employer can prove they were initiated before union activity began.
- *Conduct surveillance activities.* Management is forbidden to spy on employees' union activities, to request antiunion workers to do so, or to make any statements that give workers the impression that they are being watched. Supervisors also may not attend union meetings or question employees about a union's internal affairs. They also may not ask employees for their opinions of a union or its officers.
- *Interrogate workers.* Managers may not require employees to tell them who has signed a union card, voted for union representation, attended a union meeting, or instigated an organization drive.
- *Prohibit solicitation.* Employees have the right to solicit members on company property during their nonworking hours, provided this activity does not interfere with work being performed, and to distribute union literature in nonwork areas during their free time.[26]

Employers can and perhaps should

- Discuss the history of unions and make factual statements about strikes, violence, or the loss of jobs at plants that have unionized.
- Discuss their own experiences with unions.
- Advise workers about the costs of joining and belonging to unions.
- Remind employees of the company benefits and wages they receive without having to pay union dues.
- Explain that union representation won't protect workers against discharge for cause.
- Point out that the company prefers to deal directly with employees (not through a third party) in settling complaints about wages, hours, and other employment conditions.
- Tell workers that, in negotiating with the union, the company is not obligated to sign a contract or accept all the union's demands, especially those that aren't in its economic interests.
- Advise employees that unions often resort to work stoppages to press their demands and that such tactics can cost workers money.
- Inform employees of the company's legal right to hire replacements for workers who go out on strike for economic reasons.[27]

FAST FACT

Union leaders estimate that 70% of their new recruits now come from card check campaigns.

Authorization Cards and the Request for Elections. Once contact has been made, the union begins the campaign to collect sufficient authorization cards, or signatures of employees interested in having union representation. This campaign must be carried out within the constraints set by law. Traditionally, unions first had to obtain authorization cards from 30% of the employees before they could petition the NLRB for an election. (Procedures in the public sector are similar.) If the NLRB determined that there was indeed sufficient interest, it would schedule an election. If the union got more than 50% of the employees to sign authorization cards, it could petition the employer as the bargaining representative. Employers could refuse, whereupon the union petitioned the

NLRB for an election. Today, this same process can be carried out through a procedure known as **card checking,** *which is a procedure that grants a union recognition by a company when 50% of the employees have indicated that they are in favor of the union.*[28] Although not used extensively, the card checking procedure reduces the entire process by which employers come to recognize a union because it does not require holding a formal election.

It is legal for an employer to resist a union's card signing or card checking campaign, so many companies prohibit solicitation on their premises. However, it is not legal for employers to actively interfere with an employee's freedom of choice. Union representatives have argued that employers ignore the law prohibiting interference because the consequences of interfering are minimal and that by doing so they can effectively discourage unionism.

During a traditional union campaign and election process, it is important that the company not engage in unfair labor practices. Unfair labor practices, when identified, generally cause the election to be set aside. Severe violations by the employer can result in certification of the union as the bargaining representative, even if it has lost the election.

Determination of the Bargaining Unit

When a union gathers enough signatures under the traditional process to petition for an election, the NLRB identifies the **bargaining unit,** *which is the group of employees that will be represented by the union.* The bargaining unit must be truly appropriate and must not contain a mix of antagonistic interests or submerge the legitimate interests of a small group of employees in the interests of a larger group.[29]

To ensure the fullest freedom of collective bargaining, legal constraints and guidelines have been established for specifying the bargaining unit. Professional and nonprofessional groups can't be included in the same unit, and a craft unit can't be placed in a larger unit unless both units agree to it. Other issues the NLRB considers when defining the bargaining unit include the physical location(s) of employees, skill levels, the degree of company ownership, and the collective bargaining history.

From the union's perspective, the most desirable bargaining unit is one whose members are prounion and will help win certification. The unit also must have sufficient influence in the organization to give the union some power once it wins representation. Employers generally want a bargaining unit that's the least beneficial to the union; they want to maximize the likelihood of union failure in the election and minimize the power of the unit.

Preelection Campaign

After the bargaining unit has been determined, both union and employer embark on a **preelection campaign.** Unions claim to provide a strong voice for employees, emphasizing improvement in wages and working conditions and the establishment of a grievance process to ensure fairness. Employers emphasize the costs of unionization: dues, strikes, and loss of jobs. Severe violations of the legal constraints on behavior, such as the use of threats or coercion, are prevented by the NLRB, which watches the pre-election activity.

Election, Certification, and Decertification

Generally, elections are part of the process of determining whether unions will win the right to represent workers. Elections can also determine whether unions will *retain* the right to represent employees.

FAST FACT

Unions want the card check process to replace the traditional voting process entirely.

Election and Certification.

The NLRB conducts the certification election. The **certification election** *determines whether the union is recognized as the legal representative of the employees in the organization.* To unionize a workplace, at least 30% of workers must sign cards calling for an election. However, usually, to ensure a win, unions won't call an election unless they are sure that at least 50% will vote favorably.

Once a union has been certified, the employer is required to bargain with that union. If a majority of employees do not vote in favor of the union, another election can't be held for at least a year. Generally, about one-third to one-half of all certification elections result in a union being certified. The success rate of union elections is lower in large companies.

Using the less formal card check approach to organizing a group of workers is faster and less bureaucratic than holding formal elections."[30] A contract settlement between Verizon and the International Brotherhood of Electrical Workers gave Verizon employees the right to be represented by the union if 55% signed up through the cards, which they did.

Decertification Elections.

The NLRB also conducts **decertification elections** *that can remove a union from representation.* If 30% or more of the employees in an organization request a decertification election, it will be held. Decertification elections most frequently occur in the first year of a union's representation when the union is negotiating its first contract. During this period, union strength has not yet been established, and employees are readily discouraged if they don't see quick results from union representation. Also, if employees feel that their relationships with supervisors and managers deteriorate after the union is voted in, they may have second thoughts about having voted in favor of it.

Deciding to Join a Union

Unions were originally formed in response to the exploitation and abuse of employees by management. To understand the union movement today, we need to examine why employees decide to join unions and why they decide not to.

Several factors influence employees in deciding whether to join a union. In general, however, three conditions strongly influence employees who decide to join a union: dissatisfaction, lack of power, and union instrumentality.[31]

Dissatisfaction.

When an individual takes a job, certain conditions of employment (wages, hours, and type of work) are specified in the employment contract. In addition to the formal employment contract, an informal psychological contract also exists between employer and employee. The **psychological contract** *consists of an employee's unspecified expectations about reasonable working conditions, requirements of the work itself, the level of effort that should be expended on the job, and the nature of the authority the employer should have in directing the employee's work.*[32] These expectations are related to the employee's desire to satisfy certain personal preferences in the workplace. The degree to which the organization fulfills these preferences determines the employee's level of satisfaction. Dissatisfaction with the implicit terms and conditions of employment leads employees to attempt to improve their work situation, often through unionization. If management wants to make unionization less attractive to employees, it must make work conditions more satisfying.

Lack of Power.

Unionization is seldom the first recourse of employees who are dissatisfied with some aspect of their jobs. The first attempt to improve the work situation is usually made by an individual acting alone. Someone who has enough power or influence can effect the necessary changes without collaborating with others. The jobholder's amount of power is determined by how difficult it is to replace the person and how important or critical the job is to the overall success of the organization. A very talented employee who performs an essential task and who is difficult to replace may be able to persuade an employer to make significant changes that benefit the entire workforce. However, employees who can easily be replaced and those performing tasks that are not central to the strategic mission of the organization are not likely to be powerful enough to create change acting alone. For them collective action is more likely to be an effective way to influence the organization.[33]

Union Instrumentality. When employees are dissatisfied with aspects of a work environment—such as pay, promotion opportunity, treatment by supervisor, the job itself, and work rules—they may perceive a union as being able to help improve the situation. If they believe that the union may be able to help, they then weigh the value of the benefits to be obtained through unionization against unionization's costs, such as a lengthy organizing campaign and bad feelings between supervisors, managers, and other employees who don't want a union. Research suggests that employees' willingness to support a union is also affected by general attitudes about unions formed early in life.[34]

   Beliefs about unions in general and about the particular union to be voted on shape employees' perceptions of union instrumentality. **Union instrumentality** *is the value an employee feels a union would have, after weighing the costs and benefits against the likelihood of a union's being able to obtain the benefits.*[35] The more that employees believe a union can obtain positive work aspects, the more instrumental employees perceive the union to be in removing the causes of dissatisfaction. When the benefits exceed the costs and union instrumentality is high, employees are more likely to be willing to support a union.[36] After joining a union, employee commitment to the union influences how much they participate in union activities.[37] Exhibit 14.5 summarizes the factors that influence whether employees unionize.

THE COLLECTIVE BARGAINING PROCESS

Collective bargaining is a complex process in which union and management negotiators maneuver to win the most advantageous contract.[38] How the issues involved are settled depends on

- The quality of the union-management relationship.
- The processes of bargaining used by labor and management.
- Management's strategies in collective bargaining.
- The union's strategies in collective bargaining.

   The labor relations system is composed of three subunits—employees, management, and the union—with the government influencing interaction among the three. Employees may be managers or union members, and some union members are part of the union management system (local union leaders). Each of the three interrelationships in the system is regulated by specific federal statutes.

   Each group in the labor relations model typically has different goals. Workers are interested in improved working conditions, wages, and opportunities. Unions also are interested in these, as well as their own survival, growth, and acquisition

> 66 *I would leave the field before I was working for a union. Unions would create a wall between management and the workers. You would destroy creativity.* 99

Jordan Slott
Staff Engineer
Silicon Valley, CA

FAST FACT

Union workers' median weekly earnings: $781

Nonunion workers' median weekly earnings: $612

A 28% difference!

4
LEARNING GOAL

EXHIBIT 14.5 Factors That Influence Whether Employees Organize

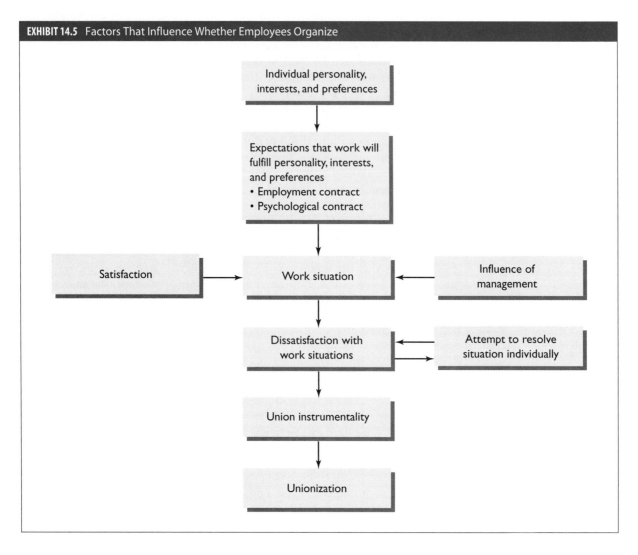

of power, which depend on their ability to maintain the support of the employees by providing for their needs. Management has overall organizational goals (e.g., increasing profits, market share, and growth rates) and also seeks to preserve managerial prerogatives to direct the workforce and to attain the personal goals of the managers (e.g., promotion or achievement). Government is interested in a stable and healthy economy, the protection of individual rights, and safety and fairness in the workplace. All of these factors influence the roles that these groups play.

Adversarial Relationship

When the goals of unions, management, and government are seen as competing, an adversarial relationship emerges, with labor and management each attempting to get a bigger cut of the pie, while government oversees its own interests. In an **adversarial relationship** *between union and management, the union's role is to gain concessions from management during collective bargaining and to preserve those concessions through the grievance procedure.* The union is an outsider and critic of the company.[39]

Historically, unions in the United States have played the adversary role in their interactions with management. Their focus has been on wages, hours, and working conditions as they attempted to get "more and better" from management. This approach worked well in economic boom times, but unions encountered difficulties when the economy wasn't as healthy. Recently, the threat of continued job losses and relentless competitive pressure to reduce costs has induced unions to reconsider their approach.

Cooperative Relationship

Some unions have begun to enter into collaborative efforts with employers.[40] For example, the USWA now works cooperatively with Goodyear Tire and Rubber. Together, labor and management are finding ways to restructure costs so that the tire industry can survive and keep jobs in the United States. Similarly, American Airlines believes that collaboration with unions can increase productivity, and the UAW is working with the automobile suppliers as well as the auto companies to help manage health care costs.[41]

A **cooperative relationship** *requires that union and management solve problems, share information, and integrate outcomes.* In a cooperative relationship, the union's role is that of a partner, not a critic. The union is jointly responsible with management for reaching a suitable solution to business challenges.

In the United States, cooperative agreements seem to be particularly fragile. One problem may be that neither partner—labor or management—has much experience with these relationships, which require that each side trust the other. Increasingly, managers recognize that the success of most of the programs they undertake to improve their organization depends on the acceptance of the unions present in the organization. Involving unions during the design of change initiatives is a good way to gain their acceptance. Although cooperative approaches are not typical in the United States, they have been built into labor relations in other countries, including Sweden, Germany, and now throughout the European Union.[42]

Bargaining Processes

As we have noted, unions negotiate and implement agreements with management through the process of collective bargaining. In this section, we describe in more detail five types of bargaining that can occur during contract negotiations:

1. Distributive.
2. Integrative.
3. Concessionary.
4. Continuous.
5. Intraorganizational.

Distributive Bargaining. Distributive bargaining takes place when the parties are in conflict over the issue—that is, when a specific outcome represents a gain for one party and a loss for the other. With **distributive bargaining,** *each party negotiates with the goal of achieving its own best possible outcome.* The process is outlined in Exhibit 14.6.[43]

On any particular issue, union and management negotiators each have three identifiable positions. The union has an *initial demand point,* which is generally more than it expects to get; a *target point,* which is its realistic assessment of what it may be able to get; and a *resistance point,* or the lowest acceptable level for the issue. Management has three similar points: an *initial offer point,* which is usually lower than the expected settlement; a *target point,*

" *A lot of times when [cooperative relationships] break down, it's not because of new economic circumstances. An individual can make a difference—a new plant manager, a new local president.* "

Douglas Fraser
Past President
United Auto Workers

" *When we renegotiated the United Auto Workers' contract in 2003, we had quite a few discussions with them so they would understand how they could achieve better rewards. And their productivity, in particular, has dramatically improved: it's up about 9 percent since 2003. Without that improvement, we would need millions of additional labor hours to get our product out the door. These employees have shared in the benefits of improved productivity.* "

Bob Lane
Chief Executive Officer
Deere & Company

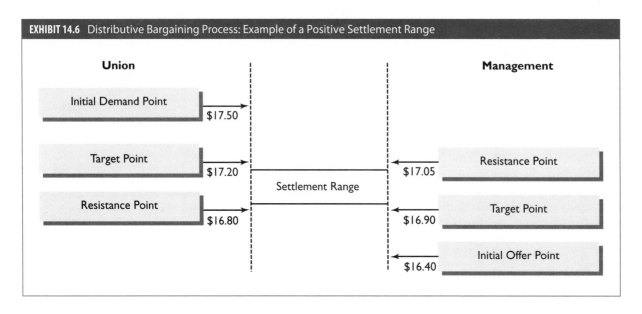

EXHIBIT 14.6 Distributive Bargaining Process: Example of a Positive Settlement Range

at which it would like to reach agreement; and a *resistance point,* or its upper acceptable limit.

If, as shown in Exhibit 14.6, management's resistance point is greater than the union's, a *positive settlement range* exists. If, however, management's resistance point is below the union's, a *negative settlement range,* or bargaining impasse, exists, and there is no common ground for negotiation.[44] For example, on the issue of wages, the union may have a resistance point of $16.80 an hour, a target of $17.20, and an initial demand point of $17.50. Management may offer $16.40 but have a target of $16.90 and a resistance point of $17.05. The positive settlement range is between $16.80 and $17.05, and this is where the settlement will likely be. However, only the initial wage demand and offer are made public at the beginning of negotiations.

The model shown in Exhibit 14.6 describes the process of bargaining for a single issue. In actual negotiations, several issues are negotiated simultaneously; so the process is more complex than depicted. Union concessions on one issue may be traded for management concessions on another. Because many issues are addressed simultaneously, the actual process of bargaining is quite complicated and dynamic.

Integrative Bargaining. When more than one issue needs to be resolved, integrative agreements may be pursued. **Integrative bargaining** *focuses on creative solutions that reconcile (integrate) the parties' interests and yield joint benefits.* It can occur only when negotiators have a so-called expanding-pie attitude—that is, when the two parties (union and management) have two or more issues and are willing to develop creative ways to satisfy both parties.[45]

Concessionary Bargaining. Distributive and integrative bargaining are the primary approaches to bargaining; concessionary bargaining often occurs within these two frameworks. With **concessionary bargaining**, *employers seek givebacks or concessions from the unions, promising job security in return.*

Concessionary bargaining may be prompted by severe economic conditions faced by employers. In the early 1990s, this type of bargaining was prevalent, especially in smokestack industries, such as automobiles, steel, rubber, and to some extent transportation. Concessions sought by management from the unions included wage freezes, wage reductions, outsourcing, layoffs, work rule changes or elimination, benefit reductions, increased productivity, and more hours of work for the same pay.[46] Two-tier wage systems were tried in some industries, but problems of inequity and lower worker morale offset much of the savings from lower labor costs.[47] In addition, the available evidence suggests that agreements arrived at through concessionary bargaining erode union solidarity, leadership credibility, and control, as well as union power and effectiveness.[48]

Continuous Bargaining. Due to the rapid rate of change in global and domestic environments, some labor and management negotiators are turning to continuous bargaining. With **continuous bargaining**, *joint committees with representatives from both labor and management meet on a regular basis to explore issues and solve problems of common interest.* Continuous bargaining committees have appeared in the retail food, over-the-road trucking, nuclear power, and men's garment industries.[49] Characteristics of continuous bargaining include

- Frequent meetings during the life of the contract.
- A focus on external events and problem areas rather than on internal problems.
- Use of the skills of outside experts in decision making.
- Use of a problem-solving (integrative) approach.[50]

The intention of continuous bargaining is to develop a union-management structure that's capable of adapting positively and productively to sudden changes in the environment. This approach is different from, but an extension of, the emergency negotiations that unions have insisted on when inflation or other circumstances have substantially changed the acceptability of the existing agreement. Continuous bargaining is a permanent arrangement intended to avoid the crises that often occur under traditional collective bargaining systems.

Intraorganizational Bargaining. Regardless of how negotiations between management and labor proceed, the bargaining teams from each side also engage in intraorganizational bargaining. During **intraorganizational bargaining**, *the representatives for labor and management confer with their respective constituents over changes in bargaining positions.* Management negotiators may have to convince management to change its position on an issue: for instance, to agree to a higher wage settlement. Union negotiators must eventually convince their members to accept the negotiated contract. They must be sensitive to the demands of the membership, but also be practical about can be achieved. When the membership votes on the proposed package, it will be strongly influenced by the opinions of the union negotiators.

NEGOTIATING THE AGREEMENT

Once a union is certified as the representative of a bargaining unit, it becomes the only party that can negotiate an agreement with the employer for all members of that work unit, whether they are union members or not. Technically, however, individuals in the unit can still negotiate with the employer for personal deals that give them more than the other members receive. Such deals are more likely if the agreement is silent on the issues involved in such a deal.

The union serves as a critical link between employees and employer. It is responsible to its members to negotiate for what they want, and it has the duty to represent all employees fairly. The quality of its bargaining is an important measure of union effectiveness.

Negotiating Committees

The employer and the union select their own representatives for the negotiating committee. When choosing its representatives, neither party is required to consider the wishes of the other. For example, management negotiators can't refuse to bargain with representatives of the union because they dislike them or don't think they are appropriate.

Union negotiating teams typically include representatives of the union local, often the president and other executive staff members. In addition, the national union may send a negotiating specialist—usually a labor lawyer—to work with the team. The negotiators selected by the union don't have to be members of the union or employees of the company. The general goal is to balance skill and experience in bargaining with knowledge and information about the specific situation.

At the local level, when a single bargaining unit is negotiating a contract, the company is usually represented by the manager and members of the labor relations or HR staff. Finance and production managers also may be involved. When the negotiations are critical, either because the bargaining unit is large or because the effect on the company is great, specialists such as labor lawyers may be included on the team.

In national negotiations, industrial relations or HR executives frequently head a team of specialists from corporate headquarters. Managers from critical divisions or plants within the company may also be included. Again, the goal is to have expertise along with specific knowledge about critical situations.

The Negotiating Structure

Most contracts are negotiated by a single union and a single employer. In some situations, however, different arrangements can be agreed on. Sometimes a single union negotiates with several similar companies (e.g., firms in the construction industry). At the local level, this is called multiemployer bargaining; at the national level, it is referred to as industrywide bargaining. Industrywide bargaining occurs in the railroad, coal, wallpaper, and men's suits industries. In 2003, the UAW engaged in multiemployer bargaining that led to the approval of similar new contracts with General Motors, Ford, and the Chrysler Group. After announcing that the union had reached the conclusion of its third deal in as many days, UAW President Ron Gettelfinger explained their objective, "Since the start of these negotiations, one of our goals has been to bring this industry together." GM's Chair and CEO Rick Wagoner agreed that the deals moved the industry in that direction. Improved coordination in the industry is considered important as U.S. automakers struggle to compete against foreign competition.[51]

Another arrangement involves several unions bargaining jointly with a single employer, which is called coordinated bargaining. Although not as common as multiemployer and industrywide bargaining, coordinated bargaining appears to be increasing, especially in the public sector. Coordinated bargaining and industrywide bargaining often result in pattern settlements, where similar wage rates are imposed on the companies whose employees are represented by the same union in a given industry.

The construction industry has a wide-area multicraft bargaining structure. This structure was a response to the employers' need to be more price-competitive and have fewer strikes and to the unions' desire to gain more control at the national level. The bargaining agreements cover a geographic region rather than a local company, and they cover several construction crafts simultaneously. This bargaining structure reduces the unions' ability to whipsaw employers. **Whipsawing** *occurs when one contract settlement is used as a precedent for the next, thus forcing the employer to get all contracts settled in order to have all the employees working.* As a result of whipsawing, an employer frequently agrees to more favorable settlements on all contracts, regardless of the conditions and merits of each one, just to keep all employees working.[52]

Preparation for Bargaining

Prior to the bargaining session, management and union negotiators need to develop the strategies and proposals they will use. These strategies reflect the objectives of the two sides.

Management Strategies. To prepare for union negotiations, management needs to complete four tasks:

1. Preparation of specific proposals for changes in contract language.
2. Determination of the general size of the economic package that the company expects to offer during the negotiations.
3. Preparation of statistical displays and supportive data that the company will use during negotiations.
4. Preparation of a bargaining book for use by company negotiators that compiles the information on issues that will be discussed, giving an analysis of the effect of each clause, its use in other companies, and other facts.[53]

The relative cost of pension contributions, pay increases, health benefits, and other bargaining provisions should be determined prior to negotiations. Other costs should also be considered. For instance, management might ask itself, "What is the cost of union demands for changes in grievance and discipline procedures or transfer and promotion provisions?" Management should also ask, "What might be some of the benefits of agreeing to the demands of the union?" Besides avoiding a strike, benefits might include improved productivity and an improved reputation as an employer of choice. The goal is to be as well prepared as possible by considering the implications and ramifications of the issues that will be discussed and by being able to present a strong argument for the position taken.

Union Strategies. Like management, unions need to prepare for negotiations by collecting information. Because collective bargaining is the major means by which a union can convince its members of its effectiveness and value, this is a critical activity. Unions collect information on the

*   Financial situation of the company and its ability to pay.
*   Attitude of management toward various issues, as reflected in past negotiations or inferred from negotiations in similar companies.
*   Attitudes and desires of the employees.

The first two types of information give the union an idea of what demands management is likely to accept. The third type of information provides a basis for predicting what members will accept as part of the final contract. For example, the union might ask, "Is a pension increase preferred over increased vacation or holiday benefits?" Membership preferences usually vary with the characteristics of the workers. Younger workers may prefer more holidays, shorter workweeks, and limited overtime, whereas older workers are more likely to be interested in pension plans, medical benefits, and overtime rules. The union can determine these preferences by using questionnaires and meetings to survey its members.

Issues for Negotiation

The **Labor Management Relations Act (LMRA)** *specifies the issues that can be discussed in collective bargaining sessions and establishes three categories of issues for negotiation: mandatory, permissive, and prohibited.*

Mandatory issues *are those that employers and employee representatives (unions) are obligated to meet and discuss; these are, according to the act, "wages, hours, and other terms and conditions of employment."* These issues affect management's ability to run the company efficiently and are central to the union's desire to protect jobs and workers' standing in their jobs.

Permissive issues *are those that are not specifically related to the nature of the job but still of concern to both parties.* For example, decisions about price, product design, and new jobs may be subject to bargaining if the parties agree to it. Permissive issues usually develop when both parties see that mutual discussion and agreement will be beneficial, which may be more likely in the context of a cooperative relationship. This is the case of the negotiation between the USWA union and Goodyear. Here the cooperative relationship enabled them to discuss the strategy of the company going forward. Management and union negotiators can't refuse to agree on a contract if they fail to settle a permissive issue.

Prohibited issues *concern illegal or outlawed activities, that is, issues that may not be discussed in collective bargaining sessions.* Examples of prohibited issues include the demand that an employer use only union-produced goods or, where it is illegal, that it employ only union members.

Total Compensation. Wage conflicts are a leading cause of strikes. Compensation-related difficulties arise because a wage increase is a direct cost to the employer, and a wage decrease is a direct cost to the employee. As discussed in Chapter 10, rates of pay are influenced by a variety of issues, including the going rate in an industry, the employer's ability to pay, the cost of living, and productivity. All of these subjects are often debated and discussed in negotiations.

Benefits and Services. Because the cost of benefits and services can run as high as 40% of the total cost of wages, it is a major concern in collective bargaining. Benefit provisions are very difficult to remove once they are in place, so management tends to be cautious about agreeing to them. Some commonly negotiated forms of benefits and services are pensions, paid vacations, retraining, paid holidays, sick leave, job security, health care and life insurance, dismissal or severance pay, and supplemental unemployment benefits. As Exhibit 14.7 shows, unionized employees are much more likely to have defined benefit plans and insurance for medical care, dental care, and vision care.[54] For employees with families, these benefits can be worth several thousand dollars per year.

Because health care costs have continued to rise over the past several years, as discussed in Chapter 12, they have become one of the main issues in collective bargaining agreements. Often the negotiations address the issue of how much of the cost increases will be paid by the employer versus employees. GE recently was subjected to a nationwide strike over this issue. The strike closed down 48 GE facilities in 23 states. GE had made a decision to raise health care copayments, which meant an increased cost to employees of about $300 per year. GE argued that it had the right to make this decision

---

FAST FACT

Health care costs for current workers and retirees, layoffs, outsourcing, and pension security are becoming more important bargaining issues than wages.

EXHIBIT 14.7 Coverage for Major Benefits

	Retirement Benefits			Health Care Benefits		
	Defined Plans (All)	Defined Benefit Plans	Defined Contribution Plans	Medical Care	Dental Care	Vision Care
All employees	49%	20%	40%	45%	32%	19%
Union	83%	72%	39%	60%	51%	37%
Nonunion	45%	15%	40%	44%	30%	17%

Note: Values indicate the percentage of workers participating in health care and retirement benefits, private industry, based on a 2003 survey of 2,984 private industry organizations.

unilaterally, but union leaders argued that such health benefit issues have always been negotiated. For GE, increasing health care costs threatened to damage its competitiveness—its costs had increased more than 50% in the previous five years. It expected employees to pay for some of the increases. According to some union experts, disputes such as the one at GE are likely to be increasingly common in the next few years. "Until the public policy crisis is resolved, we're going to have a much more chaotic labor relations process," predicted Tom Juravich, director of the Labor Relations Research Center at the University of Massachusetts Amherst.[55]

Hours of Employment. Organizations are required by federal labor law to pay overtime for work beyond 40 hours a week, but unions continually try to reduce the number of hours in the standard workweek to less than 40. Negotiations may focus on including the lunch hour in the eight-hour-day requirement or on providing overtime pay for time spent working longer than an eight-hour shift.

Institutional Issues. Some issues are not directly related to jobs but are nevertheless important to both employees and management. Institutional issues that affect the security and success of both parties include

- *Union security.* About two-thirds of the major labor contracts stipulate that employees must join the union after being hired into its bargaining unit. However, 22 states that traditionally have had low levels of unionization have passed right-to-work laws outlawing union membership as a condition of employment.

- *Checkoff.* Unions have attempted to arrange for the payment of dues through deductions from employees' paychecks. By law, employees must agree in writing to a dues checkoff. A large majority of union contracts contain a provision for this agreement.

- *Strikes.* The employer may insist that the union agree not to strike during the life of the contract, typically when a cost of living clause has been included. The agreement may be unconditional, allowing no strikes at all, or it may limit strikes to specific circumstances.

- *Managerial prerogatives.* More than half the agreements today stipulate that certain activities are the right of management. In addition, management in most companies argues that it has residual rights, meaning that rights not specifically limited by the agreement belong to management.

> *A lot of people don't understand the union. They look at their wages and think they're doing as well as they would with the union. But when the hotel closes or they have no place to go, they get nothing. If you're in a union, you still have all the money that went into a pension. You have benefits. You have security.*
>
> *Bernice Thomas*
> *Las Vegas Worker and Mother*
> *of Eight Children*

Administrative Issues. Administrative issues concern the treatment of employees at work. These issues include

- *Breaks and cleanup time.* Some contracts specify the time and length of coffee breaks and meal breaks for employees. In addition, jobs requiring cleanup may have a portion of the work period set aside for this procedure.

- *Job security.* Job security is perhaps the issue of greatest concern to employees and unions. Employers are concerned with a restriction on their ability to lay off employees. Changes in technology or attempts to subcontract work impinge on job security. Today companies are outsourcing more work to other companies with lower wage costs. They are also offshoring work to their own employees in other countries. Both of these actions put pressure on jobs in the United States. Thus, job security continues to be a primary issue for most unions.

- *Seniority.* Length of service is used as a criterion for many HR decisions in most collective agreements. Layoffs are usually determined by seniority—last-hired/first-fired. Seniority is also important in transfer and promotion decisions. The method of calculating seniority is usually specified to clarify the relative seniority of employees.

- *Discharge and discipline.* Termination and discipline are tough issues, and even when an agreement addresses these problems, many grievances are filed concerning the way they are handled.

- *Safety and health.* Although the Occupational Safety and Health Act specifically deals with worker safety and health, some contracts have provisions specifying that the company will provide safety equipment, first aid, physical examinations, accident investigations, and safety committees. Hazardous work may be covered by special provisions and pay rates. Often the agreement will contain a general statement that the employer is responsible for the safety of the workers, so that the union can use the grievance process when safety issues arise.

- *Production standards.* The level of productivity or performance of employees is a concern of both management and the union. Management is concerned with efficiency, and the union is concerned with the fairness and reasonableness of management's demands. Increasingly, both are concerned about total quality and the quality of work life.

- *Grievance procedures.* The contract usually outlines a process for settling disputes that may arise during its administration.

- *Training.* The design and administration of training and development programs and the procedure for selecting employees for training may also be bargaining issues. This is particularly important when the company is attempting to introduce new technologies and needs people with new competencies to perform the new jobs.

- *Duration of the agreement.* Agreements can last for one year or longer, with the most common period being three years.

Factors Affecting Bargaining

The preceding discussion suggests that negotiations proceed in a rational manner and end in resolution when a positive contract zone exists. Unfortunately, negotiators often fail to reach agreement, even when a positive contract zone exists.

To fully understand the negotiation process, it is important to examine the decision processes of negotiators. If the biases of negotiators can be identified, then prescriptive approaches and training programs can be developed to improve negotiations. The following are common cognitive or mental limitations exhibited in negotiator judgments.[56]

The Mythical Fixed Pie. All too frequently, negotiators believe that their interests automatically conflict with the other party's interests. In other words, what one side wins, the other side loses. In fact, most conflicts have more than one issue at stake, with the parties placing different values on the different issues. Consequently, the potential usually exists for integrative agreements. A fundamental task in training negotiators lies in identifying and eliminating this false fixed-pie assumption and preparing them to look for trade-offs between issues of different value to each side.

Framing. Research on decision making shows that the perspective people take when deciding whether to accept a settlement is affected by whether they feel they are winning or losing. Consider the following bargaining situation. The union claims that its members need a raise to $12 an hour and that anything less will represent a loss due to inflation. Management argues that the company can't pay more than $10 an hour and that anything more would impose an unacceptable loss. In this situation, $11 an hour is seen as a loss by both sides. If each side had the choice between settling at $11 an hour or going to binding arbitration, they would be likely to take the risk and move toward arbitration rather than settle. Changing the frame of the situation to a positive one, however, could result in a very different outcome. If the union viewed anything above $10 an hour as a gain, and if management viewed anything under $12 an hour as a gain, then a negotiated settlement at $11 an hour would be more likely.

As this example emphasizes, the frame (positive or negative) of negotiators can make the difference between settlement and impasse. One solution to impasses, then, is to train negotiators to alter their own frame of reference, as well as that of the other party, so that both sides can recognize when gains are possible.[57]

CONFLICT RESOLUTION

Although the desired outcome of collective bargaining is agreement on the conditions of employment, on many occasions, negotiators are unable to reach such an agreement at the bargaining table. In these situations, several alternatives are used to break the deadlock. The most dramatic response is a strike or lockout; indirect responses are also used, and third-party interventions such as mediation and arbitration are common as well.

Strikes and Lockouts

A **strike** *occurs when the union is unable to get management to agree to a demand it believes is critical and tells employees to refuse to work at the company. When management refuses to allow employees to work, the situation is called a* **lockout**. In 2003, a lockout by port operators and shipping lines was followed by an 11-day longshoremen's strike. When the longshoremen lockout occurred, the main issue was the introduction of computer technology to track cargo. Management wanted to introduce new technologies for scanning and tracking cargo, to modernize the ports and improve their efficiency. The International Longshore and Warehouse Union (ILWU) opposed the technology because it

FAST FACT

The longshoremen's lockout and strike caused a loss to the U.S. economy estimated at $1 billion.

feared the change would displace some of their members and create new jobs for nonunion workers. If they were going to agree to the new technology, the longshoremen wanted improved wages and benefits. Management ordered the lockout because, it said, the workers were engaging in a slowdown. A month later, an 11-day strike by the ILWU closed 29 ports around the country. The lockout and subsequent strike meant that ships were stranded at sea and unable to unload their cargo. Millions of dollars worth of agricultural cargo rotted, and many department stores were worried that they would not receive the merchandise they needed for the upcoming holiday season.[58]

Strong membership support for a strike strengthens the union negotiators' position. If the strike takes place, union members picket the employer, informing the public about the existence of a labor dispute and preferably, from the union's point of view, convincing it to avoid this company during the strike. Union members commonly refuse to cross the picket line of another striking union, which gives added support to the striking union.

Employers usually attempt to continue operations while a strike is in effect. They either run the company with supervisory personnel and people not in the bargaining unit or hire replacements for the striking employees. At the conclusion of the strike, employers will be expected to

1. Reinstate strikers in all the positions that remain unfilled, unless they have substantial business reasons for doing otherwise.

2. Establish a preferential hiring list for displaced strikers to facilitate their recall as new openings occur.

The success of a strike depends on its ability to cause economic hardship to the employer. Severe hardship usually causes the employer to concede to the union's demands.[59] Thus, from the union's point of view, the cost of the company's lack of production must be high. The union, therefore, actively tries to prevent replacement employees from working. Although the company can legally hire replacements, the union reacts strongly to the employment of scabs, as these workers are called, and the replacement employees may be a cause of increasingly belligerent labor relations. The hiring of replacement workers may reach a level where companies keep them even after the strike is settled—if it is settled at all. This tactic has given employers even more power in a strike situation. Thus, the union movement seeks a law to prevent replacement workers from becoming permanent workers.

The timing of the strike is also often critical. The union attempts to hold negotiations just before the employer has a peak demand for its product or services, when a strike will have the maximum economic effect.

Although strikes have been on the decline, they are costly to both the employer, who loses revenue, and to employees, who lose income. If a strike is prolonged, the cost to employers may never be fully recovered. This is why employers seek to avoid strikes. Moreover, the public interest is generally not served by strikes, which often are an inconvenience and can have serious consequences for the economy as a whole.

Slowdowns. Short of an actual strike, unions may invoke a work slowdown. At a Caterpillar plant, Lance Vaughan usually installed a set of small and large hoses on huge off-highway trucks—small hoses first, then the big hoses. But when a slowdown started, he began to install the big hoses first, and then reach awkwardly around them to attach the smaller hoses. The result was lost production time. Technically, Vaughan was just doing his job; the instructions

FAST FACT

The number of strikes involving more than 1,000 U.S. workers was 222 in 1960. In 2006, it was 20.

FAST FACT

At Caterpillar, workers engaged in a slowdown by just following what was written in their job descriptions.

furnished by Caterpillar's engineers actually described the inefficient procedure as the way to do it. Normally, Vaughan would have ignored such instructions and made a note to himself to tell the engineers to fix the mistake in the instructions. When the slowdown began, however, he stopped speaking up and began working according to the rules furnished by the company. "I used to give the engineers ideas," explained Vaughan, who had worked at Caterpillar for 20 years. "We showed them how to eliminate some hose clips and save money. And I recommended larger bolts that made assembly easier and faster, and were less likely to come loose."[60] At Caterpillar, the slowdown was referred to as an "in-plant" strategy. Regardless of the name, the result is the same: a reduction of work output, physically and mentally. Slowdowns can be more effective than actual strikes.

Primary Boycotts. Unions sometimes want to make the public more aware of their cause. To do so, they may engage in a primary boycott. For instance, a union that is striking a soda bottling company may set up an informational picket line at grocery stores that sell the bottler's products. It has generally been ruled that as long as the picket line is directed at the target of the strike—in this case, the bottling company—it constitutes a primary boycott and is legal. The picket line becomes illegal, however, when it tries to prevent customers from shopping at the grocery store. Interfering with the grocery store's business would be called a secondary boycott. Secondary boycotts are illegal because they can harm innocent third parties, such as the grocery store's employees.

Corporate Campaigns. In a corporate campaign, a union may ask the public and other unions to write letters to a company, requesting that it change the way it bargains with the union. Some unions are using their power as shareholders to influence companies' policies and practices (e.g., of reducing health care benefits of workers and outsourcing jobs to nonunion companies). Many unions manage the pension benefits of their members. Usually, they invest pension assets in corporate stocks—typically valuable assets that give the union considerable clout as a shareholder. In Cincinnati, Ohio, the area's construction unions own 5 million shares of Kroger stock. Kroger is also headquartered in Cincinnati. Using this financial clout, the construction unions picketed Kroger to protest its threat to cut health care benefits for Kroger employees. In this example, the construction unions were able to influence the employment conditions of other workers who did not belong to their unions because they controlled substantial shares in the grocery chain.[61]

Mediation

Mediation *is a procedure in which a neutral third party helps the union and management negotiators reach a voluntary agreement.*[62] Having no power to impose a solution, the mediator attempts to facilitate the negotiations between union and management. The mediator may make suggestions and recommendations and perhaps add objectivity to the often emotional negotiations. To have any success at all, mediators must have the trust and respect of both parties and have sufficient expertise and neutrality to convince the union and employer that they will be fair and equitable. The U.S. government operates the Federal Mediation and Conciliation Service (FMCS) to make experienced mediators available to unions and companies. The core of the FMCS mission is "Building Sound Labor-Management Relations through Mediation." The FMCS has been doing this for more than 50 years.

FAST FACT

The power of the arbitrator's decision was established by three Supreme Court decisions in 1960 referred to as the Steelworkers' Trilogy, and all involved the United Steelworkers.

Arbitration

Arbitration *is a procedure in which a neutral third party studies the bargaining situation, listens to both parties and gathers information, and then makes a determination that is binding on the parties.* The arbitrator, in effect, determines the conditions of the agreement.

In final offer arbitration, the arbitrator can choose between the final offer of the union and the final offer of the employer. The arbitrator can't alter these offers but must select one as it stands. The arbitrator chooses the offer that appears more fair. Losing the arbitration decision means settling for the other's offer, so each side is pressured to make as good an offer as possible. By contrast, in conventional arbitration, the arbitrator is free to fashion any award deemed appropriate.

Once the contract impasse is removed, union and management have an agreement. Abiding by it is the essence of contract administration; however, at times, arbitration will again be necessary—namely, when a grievance is filed. This type of arbitration is referred to as rights arbitration or grievance arbitration.

CONTRACT ADMINISTRATION

Once signed, the collective agreement becomes the contract that governs daily work life. That is, the daily operation and activities in the organization are subject to the conditions of the agreement. Because of the difficulty of writing an unambiguous agreement anticipating all the situations that will occur over its life, disputes will inevitably occur over the contract's interpretation and application. The most common method of resolving these disputes is a grievance procedure. Virtually all agreements negotiated today provide for a grievance process to handle employee complaints.

Grievance Procedures

Basically, a grievance is a charge that the union-management contract has been violated.[63] A grievance may be filed by the union for employees or by employers, although management rarely does so. The grievance process is designed to investigate the charges and to resolve the problem. Common sources of grievances are

- Outright violation of the agreement.
- Disagreement over facts.
- Dispute over the meaning of the agreement.
- Dispute over the method of applying the agreement.
- Argument over the fairness or reasonableness of actions.[64]

Grievance procedures typically involve several stages. The collective bargaining agreement specifies the maximum length of time that can elapse between the incident that is the subject of the dispute and the filing of a grievance on that incident. The most common grievance procedure, shown in Exhibit 14.8,[65] involves the following four steps:

Step 1. An employee who feels that the labor contract has been violated usually contacts the union steward, and together they discuss the problem with the supervisor. If the problem is simple and straightforward, it is often resolved at this level.

Step 2. If agreement cannot be reached at the supervisor level, or if the employee is not satisfied, the complaint can enter the second step of the grievance

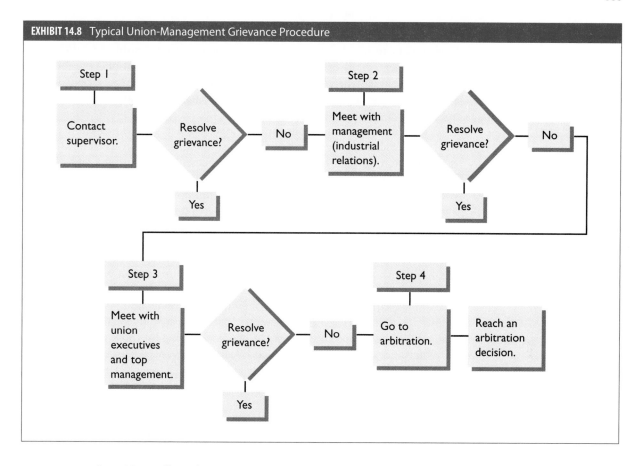

EXHIBIT 14.8 Typical Union-Management Grievance Procedure

procedure. Typically, a human resource representative of the company now seeks to resolve the grievance.

Step 3. If the grievance is sufficiently important or difficult to resolve, it may be taken to the third step. Although contracts vary, they usually specify that top-level management and union executives be involved at this stage. These people have the authority to make the major decisions that may be required to resolve the grievance.

Step 4. If a grievance cannot be resolved at the third step, an arbitrator will likely need to consider the case and reach a decision. The arbitrator is a neutral, mutually acceptable individual who may be appointed by the FMCS or some private agency. The arbitrator holds a hearing, reviews the evidence, and then rules on the grievance. The decision of the arbitrator is usually binding.

Because the cost of arbitration is shared by the union and employer, some incentive exists to settle the grievance before it goes to arbitration. An added incentive in some cases is the requirement that the loser pay for the arbitration. The expectation behind these incentives is that the parties will screen or evaluate grievances more carefully because pursuing a weak grievance to arbitration will be expensive.

Occasionally, the union will call a strike over a grievance. This may happen when the issue at hand is so important that the union feels that it cannot wait for the slow arbitration process. Such an "employee rights" strike may be legal; however, *if a contract specifically forbids strikes during the tenure of the collective bargaining agreement, a strike is not legal and is called a* **wildcat strike**. Wildcat strikes are not common because most grievances are settled through arbitration.

Grievance Issues

Grievances can be filed over any workplace issue that is subject to the collective agreement, or they can be filed over the interpretation and implementation of the agreement itself. The most common type of grievance reaching the arbitration stage involves discipline and discharge, although many grievances are filed over other issues.

Absenteeism can be grounds for discharge, and a grievance procedure may be used to determine whether the absenteeism in question is excessive. Insubordination is either failure to do what the supervisor requests or the outright refusal to do it. If the supervisor's orders are clear, explicit, and legal, and if the employee is warned of the consequences, discipline for refusal to respond is usually acceptable. The exception is when the employee feels that the work endangers health.

Because seniority is typically used to determine who is laid off, bumped from a job to make way for someone else, or rehired, its calculation is of great concern to employees. Seniority is also used as one of the criteria to determine eligibility for promotions and transfers; so management must be careful in this area to avoid complaints and grievances.

Compensation for time away from work, vacations, holidays, or sick leave is also a common source of grievances. Holidays cause problems because special pay arrangements often exist for people working on those days.

Wage and work schedules may also lead to grievances. Disagreements often arise over the interpretation or application of the agreement relating to such issues as overtime pay, pay for reporting, and scheduling. Grievances have been filed over the exercise of such management rights as the right to introduce technological changes, use subcontractors (outsource), or change jobs in other ways. This type of behavior may also be the source of charges of unfair labor practices, since these activities may require collective bargaining.

The Taft-Hartley Act gives unions the right to file grievances on their own behalf if they feel their rights have been violated. It also gives unions access to information necessary to process the grievance or to make sure the agreement is not being violated. In addition, unions may file grievances for violations of union shop or checkoff provisions. On the other hand, employees have the right to present their *own* grievances on an individual basis, and the employer can resolve such grievances without the union's presence. The only qualifying items are that adjustments cannot abrogate the collective agreement and the union must be given an opportunity to participate in the grievance proceedings at some point prior to the adjustment.

Occasionally, other activities prompt grievances. Wildcat strikes or behavior that functions as a strike (e.g., mass absences from work) can result in a management grievance. Increasingly, outsourcing, offshoring, and the hiring of replacement workers are issues resulting in grievances.

Management Procedures

Management can significantly affect the grievance rate by adopting proper procedures for taking action against an employee. One of the most important procedures involves that of discipline and discharge. The issue of just cause and fairness is central to most discipline grievances. Employers must ensure that the employee is adequately warned of the consequences, that the rule involved is related to operation of the company, that a thorough investigation is undertaken, and that the penalty is reasonable. In areas outside of discipline and discharge, management can avoid grievance problems by educating supervisors and managers about labor relations and about the conditions of the collective agreement. It has been found that supervisors with labor knowledge are an important factor in the reduction of grievances.

Union Procedures

The union has an obligation to its members to provide them with fair and adequate representation and to process and investigate grievances brought by its members speedily. Thus, it should have a grievance handling procedure that aids in effectively processing grievances without being guilty of unfair representation. Unfair representation, according to the NLRB, is usually related to one of four types of union behavior:

1. *Improper motives.* The union cannot refuse to process a grievance because of the employee's race or gender or because of the employee's attitude toward the union.

2. *Arbitrary conduct.* Unions cannot dismiss a grievance without investigating its merits.

3. *Gross negligence.* The union cannot recklessly disregard the employee's interests.

4. *Union conduct after filing the grievance.* The union must process the grievance to a reasonable conclusion.[66]

Because the employer can also be cited for unfair representation, management should attempt to maintain a fair grievance process. Company labor relations managers should avoid taking advantage of union errors in handling grievances so that such actions do not affect fair representation.

Another important influence on the grievance process is the union steward. Since the union steward is generally the first person to hear about an employee's grievance, the steward has substantial influence on the grievance process. A steward can either encourage an employee to file a grievance, suggest that the problem is really not a grievance, or informally resolve the problem outside the grievance procedure. The personalities of stewards may, in fact, influence the number of grievances filed.[67] Because stewards are selected from the ranks of employees and may have little knowledge of labor relations, the union should train them to improve their effectiveness. The company can also be liable in a fair representation suit and therefore should support such training.

Metrics for Assessing the Collective Bargaining Process

The effectiveness of the entire collective bargaining process can be measured by the extent to which each party attains its goals, but this approach has its difficulties. Because goals are incompatible in many cases and can therefore lead to conflicting estimates of effectiveness, a more useful measure may be the quality of the system used to resolve conflict. Conflict is more apparent in the collective bargaining process, where failure to resolve the issues typically leads to strikes. Another measure of effectiveness is the success of the grievance process, or the ability to resolve issues developing from the bargaining agreement.

Effectiveness of Negotiations. Because the purpose of negotiations is to achieve an agreement, the agreement itself can be used as an overall measure of bargaining effectiveness. A healthy and effective bargaining process encourages the discussion of issues and problems and their subsequent resolution at the bargaining table. Thus, joint programs for productivity and quality-of-work-life improvements can be regarded as successes resulting from effective union-management relations.

The amount of effort required to reach an agreement is another measure of how well the process is working. Some indications of this effort are the duration of negotiations, the outcome of member ratification votes, the frequency and duration of strikes, the use of mediation and arbitration, the need for government intervention, and the quality of union-management relations (whether conflict or cooperation exists).

Effectiveness of Grievance Procedures. The success of a grievance procedure may be judged differently depending on whose perspective one takes. Management may view the number of grievances filed and the number settled in its favor as measures of effectiveness. A small number of grievances filed or a large portion settled in its favor would be indications of success. From the union perspective, however, a large number of grievances filed and a small number settled in favor of the company may indicate success.

Other metrics for gauging grievance procedure effectiveness are the level in the grievance procedure at which grievances are usually settled; the frequency of strikes or slowdowns during the term of labor agreements; the rates of absenteeism, turnover, and sabotage; and the necessity for government intervention.

The success of arbitration is often judged by the acceptability of the decisions, the satisfaction of the parties, the degree of innovation, and the absence of bias in either direction. The effectiveness of any third-party intervention rests in part on how successfully strikes are avoided, because the purpose of such intervention is precisely to avert this extreme form of conflict resolution.

8

L E A R N I N G   G O A L

CURRENT ISSUES

There are two current issues that are particularly important for unions today, namely whether it is possible to have a global union and union involvement in social accountability.

Global Unions

Major topics that some union leaders are dealing with concern how to build membership, reform U.S. health care policy to boost the competitiveness of employers, and create labor-management partnerships that might let companies off-load their health care, pensions, and training to unions. While each of these topics is important, the overarching issue to labor leaders, such as the SEIU's president Andy Stern, is the image of a global union. This was reflected in the theme of a recent convention of a worldwide federation of unions representing up to 17 million workers: "Imagine a Global Union."[68] Stern believes that a global union is both necessary and possible.

> *The challenge in America is not to stop globalization. The real question is how, in the long term, can the jobs that remain in America become decent-paying jobs?*
>
> Andy Stern
> President
> Service Employees
> International Union (SEIU)

I honestly think that what we're going to see happen in the next ten years, if not sooner, is a convergence of a global labor movement, a global corporate-responsibility movement, and nongovernmental organizations. In the end, we're all dealing with the same sets of concerns, and, more important, with the same grouping of multinational employers. Before, we shared a sense of purpose, but we really didn't share employers. When you look at the corporate-responsibility movement, clearly a lot of those issues relate to work, and there are hundreds if not thousands of NGOs around the world that are dealing with business and multinational corporations. So I think we're on the cusp of another convergence trend. As employers and employees get "divorced," people have seven or ten jobs in a lifetime, and an employer is not responsible for your work life. We need to build new organizations that can help people, and on the global level that will require joint efforts by unions, NGOs, and corporate-responsibility groups.

And already, there are signs of this happening according to Andy Stern:

> We are beginning to build a network of different unions around the world, developing a common set of proposals to deal with global employers and a common set of responses if global employers aren't particularly interested in these proposals.

Social Accountability

Under the label of social accountability are a variety of employment issues, including sweat shops, unfair labor conditions, child labor, labor supply chains, and contract factories. One U.S. multinational company that is deeply involved in this current issue is Nike. Like many large multinationals, it must address labor issues in its own factories and in so-called contract factories, to which Nike outsources the production of its footwear and apparel. The contract factories are at the beginning of the supply chain for Nike's products that we all see in stores today. Initially, Nike was less involved in the working conditions of these factories than they are today. When stories of sweat shop conditions and use of child labor went public, Nike became increasingly aware and involved. According to the company:[69]

> Nike's approach to labor conditions in our contract factories is evolving. We've evolved from a focus on our own Code of Conduct to advocating common standards across the industry. We've evolved from outsourcing labor monitoring to relying on a trained team of internal monitors and support for common monitoring platforms such as the Fair Labor Association. We are evolving from a focus on monitoring to a focus on capacity building. We are evolving from an exclusive focus on factory floor impact to an exploration of ways to help change the industry through transparency and multi-stakeholder collaborations.
>
> These changes are driven by awareness that structural issues endemic to the global footwear, apparel and equipment industries affect an individual company's ability to change conditions in particular factories.[70]

In other words, Nike is trying to make its suppliers and their contract factories more socially accountable to its code of conduct, which reflects the positions and concerns of other organizations such as the Fair Labor Association, the AFL-CIO, and the ILO. Nike does this with monitoring of its contract factories. But this, according to Nike, is complex and requires constant attention:

> Our monitoring processes provide us with clear issues arising inside factories. What they do not tell us, however, is how those issues are affected by events of external factors. For example, in trying to reduce excessive overtime, we can focus on more effective policing of factories to achieve compliance. But simply focusing on policing does not address the root cause and might take resources away from engaging in broader discussions about why workers in some cases want extra hours. Those are the discussions that may lead to greater and more lasting changes. This kind of root cause analysis requires active listening and engagement in the broader dialogue with civil society, institutions and businesses around supply chain working conditions.[71]

What Nike and other multinational companies are trying to do is build social accountability into the operations of its contractors. Conversely, organizations such as the AFL-CIO and SEIU are trying to build social accountability into the operations of Nike and the other multinationals.[72]

Andy Stern envisions a global union that would address this very current and critical issue. Even if such a union never exists, multinational corporations are likely to feel continued pressure to staff their locations with managers who are transparent, fair, and respectful. For HR professionals, this provides an important opportunity to engage in staffing and training activities that respond to the growing demand to build businesses that are socially accountable and financially profitable.[73]

CHAPTER SUMMARY WITH LEARNING GOALS

1 STRATEGIC IMPORTANCE. Line managers and HR professionals need to know as much as possible about unionization because the stakes are substantial. Unions and employers can work together to benefit all stakeholders. Companies like UPS and Deere & Company demonstrate every day that this is possible.

2 HISTORICAL CONTEXT AND THE CURRENT STATUS. Unions and management have operated as adversaries because many of their goals are in conflict. Conflict is detrimental to both management and unions. Effective labor relations reduce such conflict. Although cooperation is not widespread, it may become the dominant style of union-management relations in the future. Its effects are particularly apparent in collective bargaining, contract negotiation, and grievance processing.

3 ELEMENTS OF THE ORGANIZING CAMPAIGN. Unionization may be attractive to employees who are dissatisfied with their working conditions and to those who feel powerless to change conditions. By correcting unsatisfactory working conditions or by not allowing them to occur in the first place, organizations reduce the likelihood of unionization. However, once a union-organizing campaign begins, a company cannot legally stop it without engaging in unfair labor practices. The unionization campaign includes soliciting employee support, determining the bargaining unit, and the election itself.

4 COLLECTIVE BARGAINING PROCESS. As economic conditions in the world have changed substantially, so have union-management relations. Collective bargaining is a process for unions and management to address employees' concerns without disruptive strikes. Increasingly, managers recognize that cooperative relationships can improve their company's competitiveness. Unions see cooperative relationships as instrumental in protecting the jobs and incomes of their members. These relationships in turn can influence the five types of bargaining that can occur during contract negotiations.

5 NEGOTIATING THE AGREEMENT. Labor and management each select a bargaining committee to negotiate the new agreement. The negotiations may be (1) between a single union and a single company or multiple companies or (2) between multiple unions and a single company. Bargaining issues are mandatory, permissive, or prohibited. The issues can be grouped into wage, benefits and services, institutional, and administrative issues.

6 MODES OF CONFLICT RESOLUTION. When negotiators are unable to reach an agreement at the bargaining table, three alternatives are a strike and/or lockout, mediation, and arbitration. In the United States, strikes and lockouts have declined dramatically as employers and unions seek to avoid work stoppages and the interruption of goods and services to customers. Mediation and arbitration have become more common ways to resolve conflicts and differences.

7 ELEMENTS OF CONTRACT ADMINISTRATION. Almost all labor contracts outline procedures for handling employee complaints. The most common grievance is related to discipline and discharge, although wages, promotions, seniority, vacations, holidays, and management and union rights are also sources of complaints. The effectiveness of the collective bargaining process is usually assessed by measures of how well the process is working.

⚠ **CURRENT ISSUES.** Two important current issues in unionization and collective bargaining are (1) the development of global unions and (2) social accountability. Global unions represent the attempt by unions around the world to coordinate their activities. This seems to be particularly necessary in dealing with multinational corporations that have operations in a variety of countries. Social accountability can be encouraged and monitored by these global unions as well as by traditional single-country unions. Further efforts can help improve safety and health conditions, use of child labor, and compensation levels.

TERMS TO REMEMBER

Adversarial relationship	Lockout
AFL-CIO	Mandatory issues
Arbitration	Mediation
Bargaining unit	Permissive issues
Business representative	Preelection campaign
Card checking	Prohibited issues
Certification election	Psychological contract
Collective bargaining	Right-to-work law
Concessionary bargaining	Steward
Continuous bargaining	Strike
Cooperative relationship	Union instrumentality
Decertification elections	Unionization
Distributive bargaining	Union salting
Integrative bargaining	Whipsawing
Intraorganizational bargaining	Wildcat strike
Labor and Management Relations Act	

QUESTIONS FOR DISCUSSION AND REFLECTIVE THINKING

1. Describe how a strike by the Teamsters against UPS would affect that company's various stakeholders. Would the timing of the strike make a difference? Explain.
2. Union membership has been declining in the United States for many years. What do you think are the major reasons for this?
3. Despite the fact that union membership is relatively low, many people believe that the fear of unionization serves to ensure that employers treat employees well. Do you agree or disagree with this view? Why?
4. Describe the actions that an employer may take when a union attempts to organize the workforce. What employer actions are prohibited?
5. Distinguish mediation from arbitration. How does a grievance procedure differ from interest arbitration? What is final offer arbitration?

PROJECTS TO EXTEND YOUR LEARNING

1. **Integration and Application.** Before continuing, review the cases of Southwest Airlines and Lincoln Electric at the end of this book. Then answer the following questions.

    a. Compare and contrast Lincoln Electric and Southwest Airlines with regard to the following.
- Views of management regarding union representation of their workers.
- Views of employees regarding union representation.
- Consequences of these views for cooperation and conflict between employees and management.

    b. What changes in the environment or the company might lead Lincoln Electric's employees to become more interested in unionization? How likely do you think such changes are to occur?

2. **Using the Internet.** Go online and learn more about the many different unions in the U.S., and the history of unionization and collective bargaining.

    a. Learn about several union organizations by visiting their home pages, which contain a wealth of information:
- USWA (www.uswa.org).
- AFL-CIO (www.aflcio.org).
- UAW (www.uaw.org).
- CWA (www.cwa-union.org).
- AFSCME (www.afscme.org).
- SEIU (www.seiu.org).

    b. Learn about labor union history and the development and structure of unions by visiting the Web site of the George Meany Center at www.aflcio.org.

    c. Learn more about patterns of union membership in the United States from the Web sites of the AFL-CIO (www.aflcio.org) and the Bureau of Labor Statistics (www.bls.gov).

    d. Learn more about mediation from the Federal Mediation and Conciliation Service at www.fmcs.gov.

    e. Learn more about government's role in labor relations at www.dol.gov/dol/topic/labor-relations/index.htm.

    f. For information about union rates around the world and to learn more about global unions, visit the International Labour Organization's Web site at www.ilo.org, and that of the Global Union at www.union-network.org.

3. **Experiential Activity.** A good way to learn more about union activities in your local area is to talk to people who are involved. Before you begin this activity, be sure to learn what you can using some of the online resources listed above.

Activity

Step 1. Begin by identifying one or two local organizations in which a union is present. Then try to talk to the union steward, the business representative, and at least two union members. Try to get answers to the following questions.

    a. What are the names of the local unions in these organizations?

    b. Is the local affiliated with a larger national organization? If yes, how?

    c. Who is included the bargaining unit(s)?

    d. How long has the union been present in the organization? If the union was certified within the past two or three years, try to find someone who can tell you what it was like to go through the campaign and election process.

    e. Has the union held a strike in the past five years? If yes, find someone who can tell you what it was like to go on strike.

    f. What issues are of greatest concern to the members of this union?

Step 2. Write a brief summary describing what you have learned, and if your instructor indicates it is appropriate, prepare a 5-minute report to present to your classmates.

CASE STUDY
THE UNION'S STRATEGIC CHOICE

Maria Dennis sits back and thoughtfully reads through the list of strategies that the union's committee gave her this morning. If her union is to rebuild the power it has lost over the past few years, it's time to take drastic action. If the union continues to decline as it has during the last few years, it won't be able to represent the members who voted for it to be their exclusive bargaining representative.

Dennis was elected at her union's convention to be the international president of the Newspaper Workers International Union (NWIU). At the time, she knew it would not be an easy job, although she looked forward to taking on a new challenge. But she had no idea just how difficult it would be to get the union back on its feet again.

The NWIU was founded in the late 1890s and was made up of newspaper typographers who were responsible for such tasks as setting type on linotype machines, creating the layout of newspapers, proofing articles, and printing newspapers. Members of the union typically completed a six-year apprenticeship, learning all the different tasks involved in the printing process. Before 1960, printing professionals were considered the elite of the industrial workforce. The craft demanded that typographers be literate at a time when even some people in the middle and upper classes were not. Furthermore, printing was a highly skilled, highly paid craft.

Since the 1980s, however, the union has declined. Literacy is no longer a unique characteristic, and automation has led to a deskilling of the craft. The introduction of video display terminals, optical character recognition scanners, and computerized typesetting has eliminated substantial compositor work, and the demand for skilled union workers has been reduced. The union experienced its peak membership of 120,000 in 1975. During the 1980s, membership began a substantial decline, and in 2006, the total membership was less than 40,000. The reduced membership has resulted in other problems for the union. First, fewer members mean fewer dues, which are the union's main source of revenue. Consequently, the union is having some serious financial problems and is being forced to cut some of its services to members.

Second, the union is experiencing a significant loss in bargaining power with newspaper management. In the past, the printers were fairly secure in their jobs because there was a good demand in the labor market for individuals who could run the complicated printing equipment. But the recent switch to automation has eliminated many jobs and has also made it possible for employers to easily replace union employees. Anyone can be trained in a short time to use the new printing equipment. Therefore, if union members decide to strike for better wages, hours, and working conditions, management could easily, and legally, find replacements for them. In essence, the union is unable to fulfill its main mission, which is to collectively represent the employees who voted for it.

To solve the current crisis, Dennis is considering five options:

1. Implement an associate member plan through which any individual can join the union for a fee of $50 a year. Although these members would not be fully represented on the job, they would get an attractive package of benefits, such as low-cost home, health, and auto insurance.

2. Attempt some cooperative labor-management relations programs, such as getting member representation on newspaper boards of directors or employee participation programs in the workplace.

3. Put more effort into political action. For example, lobby for labor law reform or for new laws more favorable to unions. Initiate action that would result in harsher penalties against employers that practice illegal union-avoidance activities, such as threatening to move the business if a union is voted in or firing prounion employees.

4. Appeal to community leaders to speak out in favor of the union to improve public relations, to help recruit new members, and to encourage employers to bargain fairly when negotiating with the union.

5. Search for another union with which the printing professionals might merge, thus increasing their membership, strengthening their finances, increasing their bargaining power, and obtaining economies of scale.

Dennis realizes that each of these options could have both positive and negative results and is unsure which strategy, if any, she should recommend for the union to pursue. In less than three hours, however, she will have to present the list to the council with her recommendations.

CASE QUESTIONS

1. What are the strengths and weaknesses of each strategy?
2. What strategies could be employed to get new bargaining units?
3. What other types of services could the union offer to its members?
4. What would be your final recommendation? Justify your response.

Source: K. Stratton-Devine, University of Alberta.

INTEGRATIVE CASE
SOUTHWEST AIRLINES

The tale of two men, one airline and one cocktail napkin…"Let's start our own airline," Rollin W. King said to his friend Herb Kelleher in a bar years ago. "Convince me," Herb replied. Rollin drew a triangle connecting Texas's major cities on a cocktail napkin. He said, "We could offer fares so low people would fly instead of drive." Herb paused, placed his drink on the napkin, and then spoke, "Rollin, you're crazy. Let's do it."[1]

Introduction

Southwest Airlines is currently facing a multitude of challenges to its historically successful business strategy that have created concerns about its ability to grow in the future. These challenges are both external and internal. External challenges include leaner competitors, higher gas prices, and limited growth opportunities. Internally the company faces challenges such as reducing costs, keeping its unique culture intact, changes in the leadership of the company, and continually finding excellent talent. Southwest's talent is selected very carefully, and at the same time is compensated very competitively, resulting in relatively low labor costs for the company. The continued access to and availability of talent has a direct impact on Southwest's operating strategy of being the cheapest and most efficient airline, which in turn depends on highly motivated employees who deliver outstanding customer service.

Southwest's cofounder and former CEO and chairman, Herb Kelleher, created a unique culture that has been sustained for more than 37 years. He is the figurehead that embodies the company's greatest strengths. The unique culture that Kelleher championed and helped create has been able, thus far, to sustain the company's recruitment and retention goals for the types of employees it targets. Employee ownership has been used extensively to tie the fortunes of the company with those responsible for it and to retain employees who might otherwise turn to Southwest's competitors. Employee satisfaction, along with the recognition that Southwest is one of the best companies for attracting, developing, and retaining talented people, makes it a well-oiled industry leader.

The question is whether Southwest can continue its profitability, outstanding level of customer service, and reputation for being low cost, on time, and safe in the context of a limited pool of market talent, which is at the heart of its competitive advantage. Can the company maintain its low turnover rate even though the demand for skilled labor has put significant pressures on the recruitment and retention of employees? Can the firm continue to spend so much time and money on staffing and training and remain competitive and equally profitable while all these external conditions apply pressure on its business?

In addition to these questions, all of the external environmental issues, such as increased direct competition, increased gas prices, increased cost pressures, and the change from a short-haul airline to a longer-haul airline, will have an impact on the future growth and success of the company. The strategies that have been so successful in the past will have to be modified to allow the company to grow into other markets, and these modifications will come with all their accompanying challenges. The key to these challenges may be the company's understanding and appreciation of its people.

Background

Few industries have experienced the turmoil faced by the U.S. domestic airline business during the past three decades. Once characterized by high wages, stable prices, and choreographed competition, the industry changed swiftly and dramatically when deregulation took effect in 1978. Several of the strongest and greatest airlines (e.g., Pan Am, Eastern) disappeared through mergers or bankruptcies. Strikes and disruptions interfered with companies' attempts to reduce costs. New competitors aggressively swooped into the marketplace; the majority failed. The industry is again in a period of high demand and expanding profitability. Despite the volatile conditions and many organizational failures, one carrier grew and prospered throughout this entire period: Southwest Airlines.

Southwest was controversial from its inception. Although the Texas Aeronautics Commission approved Southwest's petition to fly on February 20, 1968, the nascent airline was locked

Source: Ari Ginsberg and Richard Freedman prepared the original version of this case with the research assistance of Bill Smith. It is used here with their permission. They thank Myron Uretsky, Eric Greenleaf, and Bethany Gertzog for their valuable comments and suggestions. They also appreciate the careful review, corrections, and helpful recommendations made by Susan Yancey of Southwest Airlines on an earlier version. The case is intended to serve as the basis for class discussion rather than to illustrate either effective or ineffective handling of an administrative situation. A glossary of their key terms appears in Appendix SA.1. Some interesting facts about Southwest Airlines are shown in Appendix SA.2.

The case was updated in 2007 by Susan E. Jackson, Randall S. Schuler, and Steve Werner. Materials to update this case were taken from Southwest's Web site, Southwest's annual reports, Southwest's reports to shareholders, numerous articles, and the case materials of a team composed of Megha Channa, Olympia Cicchino, Shirish Grover, Mohini Mukherjee, and Drew Von Tish, all students in the Rutgers University Master's of HRM program; the materials are used with their permission. Additional materials and insights were provided by Kristin Nordfors and the students at the GSBA Zurich. We thank the Southwest Officers Joe Harris and Jeff Lamb for graciously agreeing to interviews.

in legal battles for three years because competing airlines—Braniff, TransTexas, and Continental—fought through political and legal means to keep it out of the market. Through the efforts of Herb Kelleher, a New York University law school graduate, Southwest finally secured the support of both the Texas Supreme Court and the U.S. Supreme Court, and began service June 18, 1971 to Houston, Dallas, and San Antonio.

Southwest emerged from these early legal battles with its now famous underdog fighting spirit. The company built its initial advertising campaigns around a prominent issue of the time as well as its airport location. Thus "Make Love, Not War" became the airline's theme, and the company became the Love airline. Fittingly, *LUV* was chosen as the company's stock ticker symbol. Southwest went on to see successful growth through three distinct periods. The Proud Texan period (1971–1978) saw the establishment of a large-city service network within its home state of Texas. Because it did not engage in interstate commerce, the fledgling carrier was not subject to many federal regulations, particularly those imposed by the Civil Aeronautics Board (CAB). The second phase, Interstate Expansion (1978–1986), was characterized by the opening of service to 14 other states. Interstate expansion was made possible by, and thus coincided with, the deregulation of the domestic airline industry. The most recent phase, National Achievement (1987–present), has been a time of considerable growth, distinguished recognition, and success.

The External Environment of the Airline Industry

The competitive environment in which Southwest operates can be subdivided into customer segments, competitor groups, and passenger service segments.

The two major categories of passengers are (1) leisure travelers, who tend to be quite price-sensitive, and (2) business travelers, who are more concerned with convenience. To satisfy the different needs of these groups, airlines present a wide variety of services, depending on their strategy. For example, airlines differ by geographical coverage; some specialize in short-haul service while others provide a vast network of interconnected long- and short-haul flights on a global basis through a network of strategic alliances.

The U.S. airlines can be generally categorized into three major competitor groups based on geographical coverage. First are the national airlines such as American Airlines, Delta, United, America West, Southwest, JetBlue, AirTran, and Continental. Second are the regionals, which include Frontier Airlines, Spirit Airlines, and Alaska Airlines. Third are the commuter or feeder carriers, most of which operate as extensions of the major carriers. Some of these include Atlantic Coast Airlines (operating as United Express), Atlantic Southeast Airlines (operating as Delta's Business Express), Ted, Song, and numerous others, some of which change quickly. These airlines can be further

categorized into (1) traditional carriers with business and coach classes and (2) low-fare/low-frills, single-class carriers.

They also differ in how their routes are structured within the territories they serve. The two extremes are point-to-point and hub-and-spoke. The former is characterized by direct service between two points. The latter is characterized by complex and coordinated routes and by schedule structures that channel passengers from numerous far-flung airports (the spokes) through a central airport (the hub). The hub itself has many costly infrastructure requirements (baggage handling systems, large terminals, maintenance facilities, and parts inventories). For companies that rely on a network, like a hub-based airline or telephone company, competitive advantage accrues from economies of scope (i.e., the geographic reach of the network). Economies of scope do not necessarily complement economies of scale, and in fact they are often achieved at the expense of scale economies and vice versa. Thus, although the hub-and-spoke system is driven by economies of scope, either strategy—hub-and-spoke or point-to-point—has its own inherent costs and organizational implications.[2]

Passenger service can also be characterized in terms of breadth. An airline may choose to provide a broad gamut of services including meals, advance seat assignments, and frequent flier programs (full service), or it can offer only Spartan services (no frills). A further differentiation is the number of service classes offered. Most airlines have two classes of service, first class and coach. Some offer three classes: first-class, business, and coach (United and American on select flights). Others offer only coach (Southwest), and a few offer only first class (Midwest Airlines). In addition to the direct cost of providing differentiated service, amenities such as first-class seating and in-flight meals indirectly affect the cost structure of an airline by limiting the number of seats its aircraft can hold.

Competitive Environment

The Airline Deregulation Act of 1978 redefined the industry by eliminating the ability of the government to set fares, allocate routes, and control entry into and exit from markets. Unfortunately, most airlines were hamstrung by high cost structures, including exorbitant labor costs, and highly inefficient planes and infrastructure facilities. After the complete removal of entry and price controls by 1980, competition intensified considerably as new entrants cherry-picked the large carriers' most profitable routes. This led to an extended period of severe industry shakeout and consolidation.

Structural Characteristics

The industry's structural characteristics make it a tough place to be very profitable. In fact, if one were to total the profits and losses of all airlines since the industry was deregulated, the number would be negative. The overall industry is not highly concentrated, although it has become more so since deregulation. Nevertheless, most discrete markets are served by a limited number of carriers. In the oligopolistic markets in which most airlines compete, the pricing actions of one company affect the profits of all competitors. Intense price wars have been a frequent event in the industry. Because competition varies from route to route, a carrier can dominate one market, be dominated in another, and face intense rivalry in a third. As a result of the hub-and-spoke system, airlines face head-to-head competition with more carriers in more markets.

Suppliers tend to have relatively high bargaining power. Certain unions are in a position to shut down airlines. Airplane manufacturers (Boeing, Airbus) have considerable power in altering the terms of purchase for planes. Furthermore, the business is capital intensive and requires very large expenditures for airplanes and other infrastructure.

If the industry is so difficult, why are there new entrants such as Virgin America, which entered in August 2007? Because despite difficult economics, the industry is still attractive to new entrants. There are few substitutes for long-haul air travel. In addition, most of the incumbents have high cost structures that are exceedingly difficult to improve significantly. Carrier failures and downsizing have also created a large supply of relatively new used aircraft, and the cost of acquiring aircraft is reduced further by the practice of aircraft leasing. Given high debt levels and low profitability in comparison to other industries, most airlines, including Southwest, have begun to lease their planes rather than purchase them. In light of high debt and low profits, the depreciation tax shield is not as valuable to the airlines. By leasing, carriers can sell that tax shield to the leasing company, actually creating value for the carrier. As a result, entry barriers are not as high as one would expect in other capital-intensive industries.

Furthermore, new entrants generally gain significant cost advantage by securing lower labor costs because they are not burdened by the unfavorable union contracts that affect many older airlines. Many of the union contracts agreed to by the major airlines call for higher pay and contain work rule provisions that reduce labor productivity. In addition, new entrants are sometimes able to gain favorable terms by purchasing the excess capacity of other airlines, such as training and maintenance.

Profitability

To survive and profit in this tough environment, airlines attempt to manipulate three main variables:

1. Cost, calculated as total operating expenses divided by available seat miles (ASM).
2. Yield, calculated as total operating revenues divided by the number of revenue passenger miles (RPM).
3. Load factor, calculated as the ratio between RPMs and ASMs, which measures capacity utilization.

Thus, profitability, defined as income divided by ASM, is computed as:

$$\text{Profitability} = (\text{Yield} \times \text{Load factor}) - \text{Cost}$$

The major airlines have faced intensive competition from low-priced airlines for the past 10–15 years. Though these low-priced airlines expanded the market for air travel, they also placed great downward pressure on the prices of the majors, thereby reducing their yields. To compete, the majors engaged in great cost-cutting efforts.

September 11, 2001, substantially affected the profitability of the industry. With the added costs of increased security, initial decreases in passengers, and dramatic increases in fuel costs, the industry did not achieve profitability again until 2006. Profitability of the industry was attained again in large part because the large carriers laid off 38% of the workforce, more than 170,000 workers over those five years. Further, pay was frequently reduced for those not laid off, often through bankruptcies.[3]

Outlook

The outlook for the airline industry is currently positive compared to the five years following September 11, 2001. Most carriers have brought costs under control (although frequently through bankruptcies). The number of passengers have returned to pre-9/11 levels. Passengers have grown accustomed to the increased security measures put in place. In fact, the industry had its first profitable year in 2006.

Despite these improvements, there are several threats to the industry as a whole. The first is a number of external factors that could raise costs industrywide. Rising costs lead to higher fares, which reduce the number of travelers. Further increases in gas prices, labor unions wanting back the concessions that they gave up during the lean times, rising interest rates, or additional changes in government regulations could substantially increase costs. Second, there are a number of external factors unrelated to costs that could reduce customer demand. Changing economic conditions, technology failures, and perceived safety issues such as increases in actual or perceived terrorist activity could substantially reduce the number of airline passengers.

Numerous airlines shed their financial obligations through bankruptcies in the last few years. United Airlines, ATA, US Airways, Northwest Airlines, and Delta Airlines have recently emerged or are still currently protected by bankruptcy proceedings. Because the airlines emerging from bankruptcy are more competitive, the competitiveness of the industry itself is now more intense. This increased intensity has affected the plans of many in the industry. Smaller airlines such as AirTran Airways, JetBlue, and Frontier have reduced their growth plans. Further, a number of airlines have shown interest in consolidation through mergers.[4]

Southwest Airlines' Mission and Objectives

Southwest Airlines' mission focuses to an unusually great degree on customer service and employee commitment. According to its annual report, the mission of Southwest Airlines is "dedication to the highest quality of Customer Service delivered with a sense of warmth, friendliness, individual pride, and Company Spirit." Indeed, Southwest proudly proclaims, "We are a company of People, not planes. That is what distinguishes us from other airlines and other companies." In many respects, the vision that separates Southwest from many of its competitors is the degree to which it is defined by a unique partnership with, and pride in, its employees. As stated in its Annual Report:

> At Southwest Airlines, People are our most important asset. Our People know that because that's the way we treat them. Our People, in turn, provide the best Customer Service in the airline industry. And that's what we are in business for—to provide Legendary Customer Service. We start by hiring only the best People, and we know how to find them. People want to work for a "winner," and because of our success and the genuine concern and respect we have for each of our Employees, we have earned an excellent reputation as a great place to work. As a result, we attract and hire the very best applicants. Once hired, we train, develop, nurture, and, most important of all, support our People! In other words, we empower our Employees to effectively make decisions and to perform their jobs in this very challenging industry.

The airline's goal is to deliver a basic service very efficiently and safely. This translates into a number of fundamental objectives. A central pillar of its approach is to provide safe, low-price transportation in conjunction with maximum customer convenience. The airline provides a high frequency of flights with consistent on-time departures and arrivals. Southwest's employees also aspire to make this commodity service a fun experience. Playing games is encouraged, such as, "Guess the weight of the gate agent." The fun spirit is tempered so that it is never in poor taste and does not alienate business travelers.

Southwest Airlines' Strategy

Southwest Airlines is categorized as a low-fare/no-frills airline. However, its current size and importance have led most analysts to consider it to be one of the major airlines despite its fit in the low-fare segment. In a fundamental sense, Southwest's business-level strategy is to be the cheapest and most efficient operator in specific domestic regional markets, while continuing to provide its customers with a high level of convenience and service leveraged from its highly motivated employees. Essentially, Southwest's advantage is that although it is low-cost, it still has a good safety reputation and a high level of customer service.

Cost Leadership

Southwest operates as the lowest-cost major airline in the industry. The airline devised a number of clever stratagems to achieve this low-cost structure. For example, by serving smaller, less congested secondary airports in larger cities, which tend to have lower gate costs and landing fees, Southwest can maintain schedules cheaply and easily. Southwest's approach is also facilitated by its focus on the U.S. Southwest and other locations with generally excellent weather conditions, which leads to far fewer delays. Moreover, by following a point-to-point strategy, Southwest need not coordinate flight schedules into connecting hubs and spokes, which dramatically reduces scheduling complexity and costs. The fact that Southwest uses only one type of aircraft, the Boeing 737, also reduces costs. Recently, Southwest's timely usage of fuel hedges saved the company more than $2 billion in fuel costs since 2000. Fuel hedges are currently in place through 2012.

Fleet Composition

Southwest has the simplest fleet composition among the major airlines. The company flies only Boeing 737 planes. Southwest currently owns or leases approximately 500 planes and has firm orders for another 100 planes from Boeing through 2012. The company also has options or purchase rights on an additional 168 planes through 2014. In choosing the fuel-efficient 737, Southwest developed a close relationship with Boeing that enabled it to receive comparatively favorable purchase terms. Although Southwest flies a number of model variations of the 737, the cockpits of the entire fleet are standardized. Therefore, any pilot can fly any plane, and any plane can be deployed on any route. In addition to helping capture scale economies at a much smaller size than its larger competitors, the homogeneous fleet composition reduces the complexities of training, maintenance, and service. It is difficult to calculate the large savings associated with this approach, but they exist in almost all operating areas including scheduling, training, aircraft deployment and use, wages and salaries, maintenance, and spare parts inventories.

Route Structure

Historically, Southwest has specialized in relatively short-haul flights and has experienced considerable threat from providers of ground transportation (cars, trains, and buses) because the buyers of these short-haul services tend to be quite price sensitive. Southwest has widened the market for air travel by attracting large numbers of patrons who previously relied on ground transportation. Emphasis on short-haul flights has also allowed them to pare costly services such as food, which passengers demand on longer flights. Passengers are provided with only an "extended snack": pretzels, peanuts, and a beverage.

Southwest entered the Philadelphia market in 2004. Within six months, the number of passengers flying between Chicago

Midway and Philadelphia more than doubled and the average fare declined 35%. Historically, Southwest's entry into new markets has reduced fares by an average of 65% and increased passenger traffic at least 30%. Some markets have seen traffic increase by as much as 500% after Southwest entered them. This increase in traffic and decrease in fares is now recognized as the Southwest Effect.[5]

Turnaround Time

Its route structure has helped Southwest to experience the most rapid aircraft turnaround time in the industry (15–20 minutes versus an industry average of 55 minutes). Interestingly, Southwest's 20 Minute Turnaround can be traced directly to the carrier's first days of operation in Texas when financial pressures forced the company to sell one of the four Boeing 737s it had purchased for its initial service. Having only three planes to fly three routes necessitated very rapid turnaround.

Rapid turnaround time is essential for short-haul flights because airplanes are airborne for a smaller percentage of time than on long-haul flights. Faster turnaround also allows Southwest to fly more daily segments with each plane, which in turn increases its assets' turnover. Their ability to maintain this practice is being challenged by heightened security requirements, but so far they seem to be doing well. Short turnaround time is supported by Southwest's compensation practices. Pilots get paid only for the time they are actually flying, not for the time the pilots and their aircraft sit at a gate.

Gates

Access to gates is often a constraining factor in the ability of airlines to expand because major airports have a limited numbers of gates and most are already taken by other airlines. An emphasis on less crowded secondary airports has alleviated this problem for Southwest; the airline purchases or leases gates at airports, as opposed to renting the gates of other airlines, thus enabling it to use its own ground crews. Recently, Southwest has been experimenting with entering primary airports and even the hubs of other airlines. Since 2004, Southwest has entered Philadelphia, Pittsburgh, Washington, Denver, and San Francisco.[6]

Connections

Southwest historically did not offer connections to other airlines, simplifying its ground operations. However, this limited access for many passengers, particularly for international flights. Thus, in 2005 Southwest began its first code-sharing arrangement with ATA Airlines. This allows each airline to market and sell the other's flights, allowing connections. A new computer system introduced in 2009 provides the capability to offer connections to the Caribbean right away and Europe in the near future.[7]

Fare Structure

Southwest also controls costs through its simplified fare structure. While Southwest's major competitors have complex fare structures and use computers and artificial intelligence programs to maximize passenger revenues, Southwest offers no special business or first-class seating. Rather, they generally offer a regular coach fare and a limited number of discounted coach fares. There are no requirements to stay over a Saturday night.

The simplified fare structure allows the majority of the Southwest's customers (over 70%) to book their own ticket through Southwest's Web site (www.southwest.com). This reduces labor costs related to reservations and commissions.

Labor

Labor is the largest cost component of airlines despite the heavy capital investment demanded in the industry. Southwest's labor costs are roughly 35% of revenues and 40% of all expenses. This represents about 5 cents per seat mile.[8] Southwest currently has 10 collective bargaining agreements in place, which cover about 87% of Southwest's employees. Given the ability of unions to bring carrier operations to a halt, it is not surprising that they wield considerable power. The International Association of Machinists and Aerospace Workers represents customer service and reservation employees; the Transportation Workers of America (TWU) represents flight attendants as well as ramp, operations, provisioning, and freight agents; the Southwest Airline Pilots' Association (SWAPA) represents pilots; and the International Brotherhood of Teamsters (IBT) represents stock clerks and flight simulator technicians. Mechanics and appearance technicians are represented by the Aircraft Mechanics Fraternal Association (AMFA), training instructors are represented by the Southwest Airlines Professional Instructor Association (SWAPIA), and flight dispatchers are represented by Southwest Airlines Employee Association (SAEA).

In an industry where unions and management have often been at war—and where unions have the power to resist essential changes—the quality of their relationship is a crucial issue. Appendix SA.3 reports an interview with Joe Harris, the vice president of labor and employee relations, who discusses the relationship between Southwest and the unions. Southwest has never had a strike, lockout, layoffs, or pay cuts. Instead, when Southwest seeks to reduce labor costs, as it did in 2004 and 2007, it offers highly paid employees lucrative buyouts. Southwest's CEO, Gary C. Kelly, meets with union leaders quarterly to discuss finances and strategy. Southwest's base pay has historically been at or below market, with numerous opportunities to share in company success through variable pay programs including profit sharing and a stock purchase plan. However, currently Southwest's pay packages are generally at or above the market because of the drastic cuts in salaries by other airlines. Southwest has the highest level of benefits in the U.S. airline industry. Compensation and benefits will be described in greater detail later.

Customer Service

Southwest's approach to customer service is one of its core strategies. Its Positively Outrageous Service (POS) is different from the customer service associated with other major airlines. Service is provided with friendliness, caring, warmth, and company spirit; the staff goes out of their way to be helpful. This approach to service leverages Southwest's outstanding relationship with its employees. Call Southwest and a person rather than a computer will answer. If your flight has problems, you are likely to get a letter in a few days from Southwest's Senior Manager of Proactive Customer Communications apologizing and explaining what happened.[9] However, this stellar customer service does not include costly amenities like reserved seats or food service, and it offers only very limited automatic baggage rechecking. By emphasizing flight frequency and on-time performance, Southwest has redefined the concept of quality air service. This unusual approach has allowed Southwest to differentiate its service while maintaining its cost leadership strategy.

Growth

Despite its remarkable growth in a very competitive industry, Southwest has not emphasized growth as an objective. Since its inception, Southwest has grown at a very constant rate, usually between 10 and 15% a year. Its controlled growth philosophy as been a key to its success.[10] The inability to manage rapid growth has been blamed for the failure of many carriers, including Braniff, PeopleExpress, and ValuJet. The five years following September 11, 2001 were probably the most difficult five-year period in airline history, with numerous bankruptcies and an astounding number of layoffs. During that period Southwest's revenues increased more than 60%. However, Southwest has needed to modify some its previous strategies to maintain growth. The introduction of code sharing and moving into primary airports, as mentioned, are recent examples.

The Internal Environment of Southwest Airlines

Southwest, like most airlines, is a formal and centralized organization. Organizationally, Southwest is structured according to functions. The nature of operations in the airline business is quite mechanical. That is, airline operations naturally aim for efficiency and consistency. They are not spontaneous; they value clocklike behavior. Planes must be in certain places at certain times and must be operated safely and efficiently. Safety itself requires following very rigorous procedures to ensure proper maintenance and training. The reputation of an airline can be seriously damaged by only one or two serious accidents. Therefore, the organization of Southwest is characterized by a high degree of formalization and standardization.

How has Southwest Airlines maintained high levels of customer and employee satisfaction in the context of a functional organization? The company uses a number of mechanisms to allow employee participation. The fundamental concept is the notion of a "loose-tight" design. In the context of tight rules and procedures, employees are encouraged to take a wide degree of leeway. The company maintains rather informal job descriptions and decentralizes decision making regarding customer service. So while there is very high standardization regarding operations, it is low with respect to customer service. Employees are empowered to do what is necessary to satisfy customers. Flight attendants are allowed to improvise cabin instructions and use their judgment in addressing passengers' needs. The company management operates with an informal open-door policy that allows employees to circumvent the formal hierarchy. Employees are encouraged to try things, knowing they will not be punished.

Size

Southwest operates about 500 Boeing 737s in more than 60 cities and employs over 33,000 people. Nevertheless, Southwest is still substantially smaller than the largest major airlines. For example, American Airlines has over 75,000 employees and United has over 55,000. Yet Southwest carries more passengers in the United States than any other airline, and its market value is greater than all the other major airlines' combined.

Adaptability

Southwest has been a very nimble organization, quick to take advantage of market opportunities. For example, when American Airlines and USAir scaled back their California operations, Southwest quickly took over the abandoned gates, acquired more planes, and now has a substantial percentage of the California market. Southwest's recent expansions into big hubs like Philadelphia, Denver, and Pittsburgh were in response to opportunities created by competitors reducing service there. Southwest's adaptability is well described by Rita Bailey, formerly Southwest's HR director. She believes the company sees itself "as a speedboat circling around the slow cruise ships."[11]

Technology

Like all airlines, Southwest is a very heavy user of computer-related technology. This technology supports all activities from scheduling to reservations to general operations support. Their network supports a reservation system that has enabled Southwest to be the first carrier to offer ticketless travel on all of its flights. More than 90% of Southwest's customers choose the ticketless option, which eliminates the costs of printing and processing paper tickets. It is estimated that it costs an airline from $15 to $30 to produce and process a single paper ticket. The ticketless system offers significantly improved customer service by eliminating lines at ticket counters.

Over the last few years Southwest has spent tens of millions of dollars on new technology to automate and improve various functions. Southwest recently developed an automated boarding pass system with Dell computers. Southwest has also invested in a system that links ground and air technology, thereby automating flight information that can be used externally, internally, and operationally. This information is displayed on new liquid crystal flat panel monitors in airports.[12]

Marketing activities explicitly build on the Internet as a primary marketing channel. Southwest was the first carrier to host a Web site (www.southwest.com), which was deemed Best Airline Website by *Air Transport World*. In 2005, Southwest launched an Internet feature called Ding!, which notifies subscribers, with visual and audio alerts on their computers, about short-term localized special fares. The introduction of Ding! helped Southwest earn *Airline Business* magazine's 2005 Strategy Award for Marketing.

Management

Southwest's chief executive officer (CEO) is Gary C. Kelly, who is under contract to lead the firm until 2011. Two people who were with Southwest from the beginning have recently stepped down from leadership positions. Colleen C. Barrett was president and in charge of such key functions as marketing, sales, advertising, human resources, customer relations, and governmental affairs. Cofounder and former CEO, Herb Kelleher, was until recently chairman of the board. Both retired from their leadership positions in 2008 but will remain with the company until 2013.[13] Although no longer a leader of the firm, Herb Kelleher still embodies Southwest's culture.

What set Herb Kelleher apart was his charismatic nature. His friendly, participative, deeply involved, and caring approach was and is revered throughout the organization. A very large number of employees know the chairman, and he is reputed to know thousands of them by name. Kelleher's management style, which had been described as a combination of Sam Walton's thriftiness and Robin Williams's wackiness,[14] seems to have been consistent right from the beginning. Direct, visible, and, some would say, even bizarre, he has attended company parties dressed in drag and appeared in a company ad as Elvis. Kelleher is reputed to have engaged people in conversations for hours, at all hours, about company and industry issues, often with a drink in his hand. He almost always seems ready for a party, and this fun-oriented atmosphere pervades the organization.

Culture

The most distinguishing feature of Southwest Airlines is its culture. All of Southwest's employees receive a card from their employer on their birthday, the date of their anniversary, Thanksgiving, and Christmas. Halloween costume contests, poem contests, and chili cook-offs are common. When competitors and outside observers describe Southwest, they tend to focus on its cultural attributes. Herb Kelleher made the development and maintenance of culture one of his primary duties. The culture permeates the entire organization and sends clear signals about the behavior expected at Southwest. In 1991 Colleen Barrett set up a company culture committee, composed of people from all geographic areas and levels of the company. The committee, which meets four times a year, is charged with preserving and enhancing the company culture. The committee also raises funds to reward employee teams who just need a boost or who have worked especially hard. Flight crews might be surprised with snacks or with help cleaning their planes. One program created by the committee is called the Heroes of the Heart program. It is used to honor employees who are rarely seen by customers but who are unsung heroes. A subcommittee selects one group who shows outstanding effort in serving and supporting other employees. The group is honored with a party, gets a mention in the newsletter and in-flight magazine, and has their name painted on one of SWA's Heroes of the Heart–designated aircrafts. The culture creates a sense of family and mission.[15]

The culture also stresses the importance of having fun at work. Humor is a significant aspect of the work environment. Such attributes are believed by senior management to enhance a sense of community, trust, and spirit and to counterbalance the stress and pressures of the mechanistic demands of airline operations. One excerpt from Southwest's "The Book on Service: What Positively Outrageous Service Looks Like at Southwest Airlines" is rather instructive:

> "Attitude breeds attitude...." If we want our customers to have fun, we must create a fun-loving environment. That means we have to be self-confident enough to reach out and share our sense of humor and fun—with both our internal and external customers. We must want to play and be willing to expend the extra energy it takes to create a fun experience with our customers.

This approach certainly contributes significantly to the lowest employee turnover rate in the industry (about 5%) and the highest level of consumer satisfaction.

Another characteristic is the cooperative relationship among employee groups. This can be an advantage in functional structures, which are notorious for generating coordination problems. In other airlines, work procedures clearly demarcate job duties. However, at Southwest everyone pitches in regardless of the task. Stories abound of pilots helping with baggage and of employees going out of their way to help customers. In one particularly bizarre story, an agent babysat a passenger's dog for two weeks so that the customer could take a flight on which pets were not allowed. Employee cooperation affects the bottom line. When pilots help flight attendants clean the aircraft and check in passengers at the gate, turnaround time, a cornerstone of the low-cost structure, is expedited.

Forged over 30 years, Southwest's culture has been a source of sustainable competitive advantage. A Bankers Trust analyst put it this way:

> Southwest has an indefinably unique corporate culture and very special management/employee relationship that has taken years to cultivate. Employees have long had a significant stake in the company; employee ownership and employee contribution to wealth creation are not ideas that are alien to the workforce of Southwest Airlines since it is emphatically not "just a job." The pilots are well compensated relative to the industry average, and they understand that. The challenge was to find creative ways to tie together the fortunes of the company with those responsible for it without risk or destruction of shareholder value . . . and, unlike the employee groups at other major airlines, the Southwest pilots understand that.[16]

Despite all of the freedom that the culture permits, in some areas the company also employs very stringent controls. Perhaps the best example is that Herb Kelleher himself had to approve all expenditures over $1,000!

Human Resource Management at Southwest Airlines

At Southwest Airlines the human resource function is called the People Department. According to the department's mission statement: "[R]ecognizing that our people are the competitive advantage, we deliver the resources and services to prepare our people to be winners, to support the growth and profitability of the company, while preserving the values and special culture of Southwest Airlines." The crucial importance of human resources to the strategy of Southwest has made the People Department more organizationally central to the company than its counterparts are at its competitors. See Appendix SA.4 for an interview with Jeff Lamb, vice president of people and leadership development, for more information about Southwest's HR practices. The importance of HR is reflected in every human resource function. Recruiting, selection, training, performance management, compensation, benefits, and labor relations all support Southwest's strategy and culture.

Recruiting

Given Southwest's reputation as a great place to work, it generally receives many applications for each job opening. For example in 2006, the company hired 3,633 people, but received over 280,000 applications. Thus, less than 2% of applicants are actually hired. In theory, the odds of getting into Harvard are higher.[17] One could safely say that Southwest's reputation and unique employee-friendly culture make up its greatest recruiting tool. The time and money spent on the recruiting and selection process has resulted in a turnover rate of 5%, the lowest in the industry. Traditionally,

an HR department in most companies does not do much to endear itself to finance. However, Southwest's CEO, Gary Kelly, is convinced that investing in hiring is vital. "If you are not going to work hard to get people who are a good fit, it will hurt you. For example, we have never had a strike. What airline is even close to being able to say that?"

Selection

Southwest publicly explains almost every detail of the practices it uses to select employees. In theory, any company could attempt to copy the process and claim it as their own, but it would probably fail for a number of reasons. First, Southwest expends much more energy and time on the process than most companies do. To find the right people, they spend the money up front on the selection process in the belief that it becomes worthwhile over time. So not every company would be willing or able to make that type of investment. Second, Southwest's selection process matches the unique culture of the company. This process is best described by Herb Kelleher:

> We like mavericks—people who have a sense of humor. We look for attitude. We'll train you on whatever you need to do, but the one thing we can't do is change inherent attitudes. Other companies don't value attitude. They don't pay all that much attention to it. They don't make it a priority. I've been with companies where they have an opening, and you know what they consider the function of the personnel department? To plug a hole as quickly as they possibly can. That's quite different from what we do in many cases. Some years ago our VP of the People Department told me they had interviewed 34 people for a ramp agent position in Amarillo, Texas, and she was a little embarrassed about the amount of time it was taking and the implied cost of it, and my answer was: if you have to interview 134 people to get the right attitude on the ramp in Amarillo, Texas, do it.[18]

What does Southwest look for in the selection process? The approach places great emphasis on hiring based on attitude. The search is for something that Southwest considers to be elusive and important: a blend of energy, humor, team spirit, and self-confidence. These key predictors are used by Southwest to indicate how well applicants will perform and fit in with its own unique culture. The process can take up to six weeks before anybody is hired. About 20% of recruits fail to make it through the training period at the University for People in Dallas.

Selection: The Process

The People Department at Southwest enjoys an extremely important role in its selection and placement process. This kind of centralized process helps the organization, as the applicants have to go to one place and specialists trained in selection techniques can assist in the process of deciding which candidates should be hired and where they ought to be placed. Southwest keeps the line managers and other employees involved in the process, and doing so benefits the company for a number of reasons. Employees who get the opportunity to contribute in the selection of their team members become more committed to helping them succeed, and the process also gives them a sense of urgency. The involvement of all levels of management and employees along with the HR department in the selection and placement process helps Southwest build a strong network of employees, who can then successfully forward the organization's mission of providing the right attitude and service to its customers.

The People Department has sound procedures in place for any level of selection, be it in the form of personality tests, interviews, or other assessments. The selection and placement decisions, however, are ultimately made by a combined panel of line managers and specialized representatives from the People Department. These decisions seem to be made with the full participation of present employees in the spirit of true partnership. The People Department is responsible for designing the process and is largely responsible for attracting, helping in the selection and placement of, and retaining a strong set of employees.

All applications go through the People Department, and prospective candidates are then interviewed and tested for *aptitude and attitude* by a panel of interviewers in keeping with a consistent process developed by the HR function. Once selection decisions are made, the placement of the right individual in the right position is once again done with the involvement of all levels of employees from that department, along with specialists.

The selection process has enabled Southwest to maintain a strong, unified culture in the face of enormous growth and to groom management talent within the company. This is reflected at the senior management level, where promotions within the ranks have led to most positions being occupied by insiders, some of them having started their careers in entry-level positions.

Selection: Personality Test as a Selection Technique

The predictors most stringently used for the selection of employees are personality and values. How does Southwest identify applicants with the desired personality and values? One way is its use of a personality test to rate candidates (on a scale from one to five) on seven separate traits.[19] The seven areas evaluated include cheerfulness, optimism, decision-making skills, team spirit, communication, self-confidence, and self-starter skills. Anything less than a three is considered cause for rejection. With this methodology, the airline has chosen to use a multiple-hurdles approach where an applicant must exceed fixed levels of proficiency on all of the predictors to be accepted. With this approach a higher rating in one area will not compensate for a lower score on one of the other predictors. Southwest

believes in these seven predictors and that failing to make the grade in even one will guarantee that the person will be unsuccessful on the job. The process of selection based on the seven predictors applies to everyone from pilots to mechanics. In the words of Libby Sartain, "we would rather go short and work overtime than hire one bad apple."[20]

Selection: The Interview as a Selection Technique

In addition to the evaluation of the seven predictors, Southwest uses other methods in the selection process. The process, as at most companies, includes a number of interviews, depending on the job. For example, a panel of representatives from the People Department and the Inflight Department first interviews the candidates for flight attendant jobs. Before the selection process is finished, the candidates also have one-on-one interviews with a recruiter or supervisor from the hiring department and a peer. The selection is highly systematic, and a multiple-hurdles approach combined with a good interview design help to ensure that only the best candidates get selected. The selection of candidates who fit the organizational culture of Southwest is undoubtedly critical to its success.

The interviewers look for team-oriented people with matching prior work experiences. A common theme in screening all candidates has to do with people skills. The easiest way to get into trouble at Southwest is to offend another employee. Even when pilots are interviewed, the airline goes out of its way to find candidates who lack an attitude of superiority and who seem likely to treat coworkers with respect. Southwest's system for selecting its people is time intensive but based on a history of bringing in people who fit into the culture of the company.[21]

Southwest developed its interview process in collaboration with Development Dimensions International, a consulting firm that specializes in designing sound selection procedures. The procedures at Southwest Airlines adhere to the basic principles of good interview design: structured questions, systematic scoring, multiple interviewers, and interviewer training. The questions are tailored to the specific needs and requirements of each job, as well as to attributes like judgment and decision-making skills. Questions frequently focus on past behaviors, such as "Describe a situation in which you handled a crisis at work" or "Give an example of when you were able to change a coworker's attitude about something."

Selection: Other Selection Techniques

In addition to personality tests and interviews, Southwest uses a number of unique and clever techniques to assess applicants. Applicants' attitudes are assessed from the moment they call for an application. When someone calls for an application, managers jot down anything memorable about the conversation, whether good or bad. When applicants are flown out for an interview, they are given special tickets, so that all Southwest employees know this is a recruit. Again, anything memorable about the applicant, whether they were particularly friendly or complaining throughout the flight, is noted and passed to HR. At the interview site, Southwest asks applicants to speak in front of large groups of other applicants, but the speaker isn't the only one being evaluated. Those in the audience are being watched to see if they are attentive and interested or bored and distracted. Southwest recruiter Michael Burkhardt sums up the technique, "We want to see how they interact with people when they think they're not being evaluated." [22]

Training

In an organization where attitudes, culture, and fit are so important, it is natural that the company places such a great emphasis on socialization and training. Just as McDonald's has its Hamburger University, Southwest has its University for People. The training of new hires is focused on building relational competence as well as functional expertise. Each new hire receives one to two weeks of classroom training and two to three weeks of on-the-job training. Orientation includes ample exposure to Southwest's culture, featuring videos such as "Keeping the Spirit Alive," which includes Herb Kelleher dressed as Elvis and Southwest legends such as the idea for the airline on the cocktail napkin.

Training is very broadly focused so that new employees understand the jobs of the other Southwest staffers they may have to interact with. This helps employees understand how their job fits and how they can support others, consistent with the team aspect of the culture. To further this understanding, Southwest has a number of programs such as Day in the Field and Walk a Mile that allow employees to spend a day working in other departments or jobs.[23]

Everyone at Southwest has a responsibility for self-improvement and training. Once a year, all Southwest employees, including all senior management, are required to participate in training programs designed to reinforce shared values. Except for flight training, which is regulated and certified, all training is done on the employee's own time. Nonetheless, the training department operates at full capacity, seven days a week. The fun spirit of Southwest emerges in graduates very early.

Labor Relations

The importance of labor relations cannot be underestimated in a company that is about 87% unionized. Thus, the pay and benefits of most employees are specified through the collective bargaining process. Here again Kelleher's unusual abilities emerged. Somehow he was able to convince union members and officials to identify with the company and closely tie employee fortunes with the company's. Largely due to Herb Kelleher, the relationship between Southwest and the unions have been generally collaborative, signaling trust and a willingness to compromise. The unions and the firm share the goal of wanting secure long-term commitments. This was evident by the unusually long 10-year contract signed with the pilots in

1995. When the flight attendants' contract negotiations became unusually combative in 2004, Kelleher, who was no longer CEO, stepped in and negotiated a generous contract. Larry Parker, then CEO, quit shortly afterward, and Gary Kelly took the reigns of the company.[24]

With Gary Kelly at the helm, Southwest now finds itself in the unusual position of being a pay leader coming into contract negotiations. Southwest's long-term contracts, coupled with many other airlines getting pay cuts through concessions and bankruptcies, have resulted in Southwest's often being a pay leader as current contracts expire. With most contracts needing to be renewed in the next five years, time will tell if the historically cooperative relationships will result in unions' being willing to make concessions consistent with the new industry standards.

Compensation

Unlike the current situation, Southwest historically has paid its employees at or somewhat below the market in base pay, with plenty of opportunities for above-market pay through a number of different variable pay programs. These included profit sharing and stock purchase plans. Southwest introduced the first profit-sharing plan in the airline industry. Since profits are directly affected by costs, this pay program clearly supports Southwest's low-cost strategy. The program began with a cash component and a portion tied to a retirement account, but it is currently completely tied to a retirement account. This is consistent with Southwest's view of long-term employee relationships.

Southwest's stock purchase plan allows employees to purchase stock shares from payroll deductions at a discount. The profit-sharing payout can also be invested in Southwest stock. Southwest employees own around 8% of the company's stock. The airline's current stock price is prominently displayed at each Southwest facility to keep employees abreast of the value of their ownership.

Southwest also uses recognition to reward their employees. These awards occur at the local and corporate level. They are clearly supported by top management and are unquestionably tied to Southwest's strategy and culture. There are numerous programs in addition to the Heroes of the Heart, including the President's Award and the Winning Spirit Award. The awards in these programs and others are given to employees who perform at a high level consistent with Southwest's strategy and culture. The awards can come with plaques, monetary payments, photos taken during the awards ceremony, photos of the award winner with the CEO, and mention in the company newsletter. When customers send in letters raving about great service, managers attach a smiley face sticker, frame the letter, and hang it in the office. Each department has an agent of the month award, which can lead to an agent of the quarter award. Agents of the quarter receive plaques and an award luncheon. Employees who demonstrate exemplary service are celebrated in pictures and stories in the corporate newsletter, *Luv Lines*, as well as in the halls of headquarters. Five-dollar meal vouchers are frequently given as spot awards for exemplary behavior.[25]

Also noteworthy is that, in an era when chief executive pay has escalated to huge amounts, Southwest's company officers do not get the perks (e.g., cars or club memberships) often enjoyed by their counterparts in comparable organizations, and they even stay in the same hotels as flight crews. Southwest has refused to compete for executive talent based on salary. Like lower-level employees, company executives tend to get salaries below or at the market, but through stock ownership their monetary gains are closely tied to the company's financial future.

Benefits

Southwest provides one of the most attractive benefits packages in the industry. Employees receive medical insurance, dental insurance, vision coverage, life insurance, long-term disability insurance, dependent care, adoption assistance, and mental health assistance. Most of these are at no cost. Employees and their family fly free on Southwest and at a discount on other carriers. Then, of course, there are the numerous parties. Another benefit is being part of the so-called Southwest Family. Southwest lets employees know how much they are valued by helping them in times of need, be it with financial assistance or something else. Finally, one of Southwest's most prized benefits is job security. Because Southwest has never had a layoff, employees realize that job security is an important benefit provided by Southwest and few other airlines.[26]

Performance Management

As would be expected, Southwest employees' evaluations are based partly on demonstrating the Southwest Spirit of outrageous customer service. Managers who give an employee superior performance ratings must include documentation of actual examples of exemplary customer service that warranted the rating. However, most performance measures used at Southwest are broader and more cross-functional than a manager's judgment. This motivates cooperation rather than competition, consistent with Southwest's culture. At other airlines, delays are attributed to specific units such as fueling, cleaning, or baggage handling. At Southwest, delays are tied to the entire team or process, reducing blame shifting, and encouraging employees to assist other functions when needed. At most other airlines, the purpose of performance measurement is to provide accountability, frequently in connection with punitive implications. At Southwest, performance measurement is used as a performance management tool to foster cooperation, learning, and improvement.[27]

To promote employee awareness of the effects of their efforts on the company's bottom line, *LUV Lines* reports breakeven volumes per plane. Note that this measure is also a group

rather than individual measure. The newsletter also informs employees not only of Southwest's issues, but of competitor news as well. Southwest shares detailed business information every quarter with its employees, under the label of Knowing the Score. The financials are explained in simple terms such as how costs have affected net income and the employees' profit sharing. The belief is that informed employees are better equipped to make decisions.

Southwest Airlines Performance Indicators

Many different criteria can be used to evaluate Southwest's success in achieving its basic objectives. Certainly Southwest's different constituencies look at its performance in different ways. Southwest takes particular pride in the following accomplishments:

- Over 35 years of safe, reliable operations.
- Consistently number one in fewest customer complaints in the Department of Transportation's Air Travel Consumer Report.
- Named in *BusinessWeek* magazine's first list of "Customer Service Champs" in March 2007.
- Consistently in the top five of *Fortune* magazine's list of "100 Best Companies to Work For" (until Southwest stopped participating in 2000).
- Named by *BusinessWeek* magazine as one of the 50 best places to launch a career.
- Consistently in *Fortune* magazine's list of "America's Top Ten Most Admired Corporations."
- Consistently in *Business Ethics* magazine's list of "100 Best Corporate Citizens."
- Thirty-four years of profitability.
- Consistent financial success that provides thousands of jobs in the aerospace industry.
- A route system that has grown to 63 cities in 32 states, carrying more than 90 million customers on around 500 Boeing 737 aircraft.
- A passenger volume consisting of more domestic passengers and departures than any other U.S. airline in 2007.

No issue is more important than safety and security. One needs only to study the checkered history of ValuJet or Air Florida to see what one catastrophic crash can do to an airline when the airline is perceived to have been at fault. Meanwhile, Southwest maintains a 35-year safety record and is generally acknowledged to be one of the world's safest airlines.

Customer Service

Of course, Southwest's customers remain one of the company's main constituencies. Despite its no-frills orientation, Southwest consistently receives the highest rankings for customer satisfaction. This is achieved through the successful management of customer expectations. By emphasizing low price and consistency, Southwest has successfully re-defined the concept of quality airline service. For example, Southwest has consistently been one of the best airlines with respect to customer service as measured by the Department of Transportation (DOT) Air Travel Consumer Reports. It has frequently been rated as having the highest on-time record, best baggage handling, and fewest customer complaints. In March 2007, *BusinessWeek* named Southwest as one of the Customer Service Champs.

Employee Satisfaction

Given its mission, employee satisfaction is another important indicator of company success. Personnel are a crucial determinant of organizational performance throughout the industry. Southwest's culture and how it treats its employees has consistently made it an employer of choice. Further, Southwest's corporate reputation for being both ethical and socially responsible makes its employees proud to be a member of the Southwest family.

However, Southwest's employees are not only satisfied; they are productive. Southwest employees are the most productive in the industry. A single agent usually staffs gates, where competitors commonly use two or three. Ground crews are composed of six or fewer employees, about half the number used by other carriers. Despite the lean staffing, planes are turned around in half the time of many rivals. Southwest also has one of the lowest personnel turnover ratios in the industry. Employee satisfaction and productivity can largely be attributed to Southwest's culture, but a history of management–labor harmony is also likely to have played a part.

As noted, labor relations is an important determinant of company survival. With the emphasis today on cost containment, however, Southwest may find it more challenging, as time goes on, to maintain harmonious relations with the unions given that the 2004 agreement with the flight attendants included a raise of 31% over the contract's six years and that pilots are currently the highest paid in the industry.[28] On the other hand, Southwest has had generally peaceful and cooperative labor relations throughout most of its history.

Continued Profitability

Southwest's high customer service, productive employees, and low-cost strategy have consistently led to profitability in an industry that has frequently lost money. Despite its low-cost structure, Southwest is not able to control all costs. One advantage that larger, broader-scope carriers can enjoy is a relatively limited exposure to fuel price volatility. Their broader scope can allow them to take advantage of geographic differences in fuel prices, but they do not always have the financial resources to hedge against future price increases. Southwest's aggressive fuel hedges has made the difference between being profitable or not in many recent quarters. Southwest (like JetBlue) also has

the advantage of a younger and more fuel-efficient fleet than its larger competitors.

Steady Growth

Southwest's steady growth over numerous years is now evident in its market share, another indicator of an organization's performance. By this criterion, Southwest also ranks at the top of the industry. For example, it consistently ranks first in market share in 90 of its top 100 city-pair markets, and overall has 65% of total market share in those markets. Because of the Southwest Effect, the carrier gains this share by growing the size of each of its markets; this is achieved by means of a fare structure that is on average noticeably lower than that of the majors.

The Challenges Ahead

Southwest Airlines is no Johnny-come-lately. Its basic strategy of consistent low-cost, no-frills, high-frequency, on-time air transportation with friendly service is a recipe that has been refined over more than 36 years. It has worked for the company in periods of catastrophic losses for the industry as well as in times of abundance. Southwest has been able to compete successfully with both the major airlines and those that have been formed to copy its formula. Nevertheless, there are numerous challenges ahead. As already noted, many of these challenges apply to the industry as a whole. But there are also challenges ahead that are more specific to Southwest.

Controlling Costs

Although controlling costs is an important challenge for all airlines, Southwest's situation is unique. It has been so good at controlling costs for so long that there is less room for cost savings than in other airlines. Southwest's cost advantage due to fuel hedges will be substantially reduced over the next few years. Also, Southwest's commitment to not having layoffs and pay cuts may lead to sustained increases in labor costs compared to other airlines. Of course, one way to offset increased costs is to increase revenue.

Increasing Revenue

Southwest is exploring many options to increase revenue. These include assigned seating for a nominal charge, increasing the scope of its cargo services, increasing sales for ancillary services such as hotel rooms, rental cars, and vacation packages on its Web site, and introducing charges for incidentals.[29] Many of these options mean changing the way Southwest has been doing business since its inception. Thus there is considerable risk in adopting them. Another way to increase revenue is to increase the size of the airline through growth.

Future Growth

Southwest will eventually saturate its historic niche. The company currently flies into 63 airports with more than 3,300 flights per day. Its old strategy of focusing on good climates and smaller, less congested airports has contributed to Southwest's low costs. Many believe that poor weather conditions can affect Southwest's ability to maintain on-time performance and can significantly affect operations down the line. This is magnified by a schedule based on a rapid turnaround, which leaves little leeway for flight delays. Southwest entered and then left the Denver market when bad weather forced an unacceptable number of delays and canceled flights.

This puts a limit on growth because there are only a finite number of markets that can satisfy these criteria. Thus, Southwest has begun to enter markets in poorer climates and to introduce longer-haul flights. Providence, Rhode Island, and Philadelphia, Pennsylvania, two of the newer locations, are not good weather locations.[30] There are about 56 airports in good weather locations with populations of over 100,000. Southwest currently serves 36. It is unclear how much demand for point-to-point service exists in the remaining 20.

If Southwest decides to introduce food services as an amenity for longer-haul flights, it would require galleys and onboard services that would significantly boost the cost of operation of those airplanes. Longer flights also result in fewer flights per day and may serve to drive down yield. A mixture of galleyed and nongalleyed aircraft will also make fleet scheduling less flexible. Furthermore, there will be a greater need for functions in the organization responsible for new elements such as national marketing, the frequent flyer program, interline agreements, new geographic operations, and possibly food services.

Southwest apparently recognizes the potential saturation of its historic markets and the limited number of attractive short-haul markets. Therefore, it has expanded into some longer-haul markets. Longer-haul markets provide not only avenues for future growth, but also potentially higher margins. On average, the company's cost per ASM is about 9 cents. However, on its longer routes, costs can be as low as half that.

Expansion into international travel is also an option. Its code sharing agreement with ATA will help make this more feasible, as will its new computer system. This would be an entry into a new area for Southwest, which will require new capabilities, including managing foreign employees and dealing with exchange rate risk.

People and culture also are major concerns to further expansion. Southwest is highly selective; it consequently needs a large pool of applicants to find a few people good enough for the culture. With labor shortages across the country, it may be difficult to attract large pools of applicants. Without the selectivity, Southwest may not be able to get the human resources it needs to differentiate itself from others. The unique culture of Southwest helps make the company really fly, but this is being called into question by such events as the 2004 contract negotiations with the flight attendants. As companies expand, particularly in size and geographic location, they often find that it becomes increasingly more difficult to maintain the same culture. No doubt, the new leadership will have its hands full in maintaining the culture and the cost levels that have been so critical to Southwest's success.

Competition

During the last several years, the gap between Southwest and the rest of the majors has narrowed as other carriers have attempted to emulate Southwest's formula. Some of the larger traditional airlines have developed lowered-cost short-haul divisions. For example, both United and Delta have introduced an "airline within an airline" to lower costs for short-haul flights. These separate divisions may hire their own pilots and ground support at much lower costs under separate contractual relations with unions. Under these arrangements, pilots can often be employed for less than half the cost of the parent airline.[31]

At the same time, Southwest has adopted many of the features that the majors use to support their large networks. As Southwest has grown in scope, it has introduced national advertising, including NFL sponsorship; a frequent flyer program, including a branded credit card; and interline and marketing agreements with international carriers. The carrier's average stage length has also increased over the last several years. Southwest has now expanded into geographic markets and climates that are not as compatible with its original fair-weather, low-congestion strategy. Its flights now compete head to head with some of the major carriers.

Continental, America West, United's Ted, and Delta's Song seem to be some of Southwest's strongest competitors, in addition to AirTran and JetBlue.[32] JetBlue, under the leadership of David Neeleman, the opposite in personality from Herb Kelleher, is fast becoming a no-frills airline for Southwest to take seriously. It has a philosophy similar to Southwest's; for example, it has just one type of plane, the Airbus A320, and doesn't serve meals. It does, however, let passengers pick their seats and has leather upholstery, free satellite TV, and a frequent flyer program. JetBlue recently received a great deal of negative publicity when it had a thousand delayed flights and stranded hundreds of passengers on tarmacs for several hours due to an ice storm. Nevertheless, the company worked hard to regain customer support, spending millions on flight vouchers for disgruntled passengers. Southwest cannot afford to ignore this ambitious airline.[33] The industry has watched Southwest's tremendous success for almost four decades; it's not surprising that a number of competitors have emerged, and will continue to emerge, that try to copy it.

APPENDIX SA.1 Glossary of Terms

ARC	Airline Reporting Corporation, an organization owned by the airlines that serves as a clearinghouse for processing airline tickets.
ASM	Available seat mile. One ASM is one sellable seat, flown for one mile. For example, a 138-seat Boeing 737 traveling 749 miles from LGA to ORD (LaGuardia to O'Hare) represents 103,362 ASMs.
Class of service	The fare level at which a ticket is sold. This does not refer to the cabin in which the passenger flies. For example, a United Airlines' availability display shows the following classes of service for coach: Y B M H Q V. By subdividing coach into classes, airlines can control inventory and manage yield.
Code share	An interline agreement by which two carriers are able to apply their flight numbers to the same plane. This often includes an interline connection. For example, American Airlines and South African Airlines code-share on SAA's flight to JHB (Johannesburg). The flight has an AA flight number and an SAA flight number. AA can sell it as an American Airlines flight.
CRS	Computer reservation system. Allows airlines and travel agents to reserve and sell seats on airline flights. CRS companies include Apollo, Sabre, System One, and Worldspan.
Direct flight	Any flight designated by a single flight number. Direct flights can include multiple stops and even changes of aircraft. For example, Pan Am Flight 1 at one time made 11 stops as it flew "around the world" direct from LAX to JFK.
Full fare	Designated as "full Y." The undiscounted first class, business, or coach fare. For domestic fares, this is used to calculate the level of discounted fares. Full Y is rarely paid for domestic flights, but is common on international flights when inventory is scarce.
Interline agreement	Any of various agreements between carriers. Common interline agreements concern the transfer of baggage, the endorsement and acceptance of tickets, and joint airfares (e.g., a passenger flies USAir from Albany to JFK and then SAS to Copenhagen).
Inventory	The number of seats available for each class of service for a given flight. For example, a USAir flight may have no K inventory available (seats to sell at K class fare levels), although higher-priced H seats may be available. Both seats are in coach.
Load factor	The percentage of ASMs that are filled by paying passengers. Can be calculated by dividing RPMs by ASMs.
O&D	Origin and destination. The originating and terminating airports of an itinerary segment. Connection points are not counted in O&Ds. This is different from city-pair, which refers to the origination and termination of a flight segment. For example, for a passenger traveling on NW from HPN (White Plains) to SMF (Sacramento), the O&D market is HPN–SMF. The city-pairs flown will be HPN–DTW and DTW–SMF (White Plains–Detroit, Detroit–Sacramento).
Restricted fare	Any fare that has restrictive rules attached to it. Common restrictions include Saturday night stayover, advance purchase, day/time of travel, non-refundability, and class of service. Generally, lower fares have greater restrictions.
RPM	Revenue passenger mile. One passenger paying to fly one mile. For example, a passenger who pays to fly from LGA to ORD represents 749 RPMs. The class of service and fare paid are not considered in calculating RPMs.
Stage length	The length of a flight segment. For example, the stage length between LGA and ORD is 749 miles.
Unrestricted fare	A fare with no restrictions. Often, this is not the full fare. For example, American's Y26 fare is an unrestricted fare, but it is still lower than the full Y fare.
Yield	Measured as revenue per RPM.

APPENDIX SA.2 Southwest Airlines Fast Facts

- Southwest has never had a layoff.
- Southwest serves over 60 million cans of soda, juices, and water annually.
- Southwest's shortest daily flight is 133 miles, between Fort Myers and Orlando.
- If you had purchased $1,000 worth of stock in Southwest airlines in 1972 it would now be worth more than $1,000,000.
- Southwest adopted the first profit-sharing plan in the U.S. airline industry in 1973.
- Southwest received over 280,000 resumes in 2006, and hired 3,363 new employees.
- Southwest has never had a strike or lockout.
- All of the employees who started with the company in 1971 are now millionaires.
- Southwest serves over 100 million bags of peanuts and pretzels annually.
- About 87% of Southwest's employees are unionized.
- Southwest's longest daily flight is 2,510 miles between Oakland and Philadelphia.
- Over 2,000 of Southwest's employees have spouses who are also Southwest employees.
- Southwest has been profitable for more than 34 consecutive years.
- Employees own about 8% of Southwest's stock.

APPENDIX SA.3 Interview with Joe Harris, Vice President, Labor and Employee Relations

Question 1: Tell me about labor and employee relations at Southwest Airlines.

Well, let me give you some background. I've practiced labor and employment law for 39 years. I was with the National Labor Relations Board and then I went into private practice, representing management. Southwest Airlines was one of my clients, whom I represented for 34 years. I wouldn't work for another company, because I embrace the notion of positive relations between unions and management, which is what Southwest does. Arbitrators have told me that they've never seen anything like it. Southwest management and unions will enter a room with hugs and laughs, then it may get heated for a while, and then when it's all over there's more hugs and laughs.

Question 2: What is Southwest's philosophy regarding employees and unions?

Labor relations at Southwest is based on its relationship with its employees. If you look at our mission statement, you will see what portion of it is devoted to employees and customers. Our primary concern is employees, then customers and shareholders. If we treat employees with dignity and respect, and highly value them, then we must do the same with the unions that represent them.

Question 3: Why do you think other American firms have had so much difficulty in achieving this type of cooperative relationship with unions?

I think most management has an inordinate fear of unions. It's almost universal. They are fearful to get a union representing their employees and they are fearful of the union once it's in. They go to great lengths to stop unions from representing their employees. That has never been the case at Southwest. The first president of Southwest was Lamar Muse. Very early on, Lamar and Herb agreed that they would not fight the labor unions. Lamar's reason was economic. He believed that there were financial reasons to work together with the union, and that in the long-term it would benefit the company financially. Herb's reason was philosophical. He believed that this was the right thing to do. So the collaborative nature of the relationship between Southwest and the unions was established early in Southwest's history. I helped negotiate the first contract between Southwest and a union in August of 1973 and Southwest's philosophy was present then. That philosophy sustains us and is still prevalent. It started from the top leaders and is still supported by the top leaders today.

Question 4: How have unions affected Southwest's success?

I think this question was best answered by the Carl Kuwitzky who is president of the union representing our pilots. In the August 2007 edition of the newsletter of the Southwest Airlines' Pilots' Association, he said, "The goodwill of the pilot corps is the cornerstone for the success of Southwest Airlines' past, present, and future. Never underestimate the value of our goodwill. With it we will have mutually assured success. Without it, we will have mutually assured destruction…just like we see in the graveyard of airline-labor relations of the past." He speaks to the issue of how the positive relationship between unions and management has been critical to Southwest's success, and I agree with his sentiments.

Question 5: What challenges do you see ahead for Southwest Airlines in general and with respect to employee and labor relations?

I believe Southwest's greatest challenge ahead is keeping costs under control. Fuel costs are a large component of our costs. Even small changes in fuel cost add up to big numbers. The benefits we've gotten from hedging can't last forever, so fuel costs are definitely an issue. Rising fuel costs then put pressure on other costs. Salaries and labor costs are our greatest costs, so we have to keep those in line. However, we understand that employees need to buy shoes for their kids and pay the bills. All the other airlines have lowered labor costs through bankruptcies or givebacks. We've never done that at Southwest. So the challenge is to take care of employees while still remaining a viable competitor. We've got to be smart and figure out a way to do that.

—Joe Harris, vice president, labor and employee relations (August 30, 2007),
Southwest Airlines

APPENDIX SA.4 Interview with Jeff Lamb, Vice President, People and Leadership Development

Question 1: Tell me about the HR practices at Southwest Airlines.

I've been here for two and a half years. It's well-known that we hire for attitude and train for skill. Our HR practices were well established and very successful when I got here, thus I was very cautious in making any changes. However, we are hiring lots of people, so we have to be more efficient. So we looked at a few things about selection that could make a difference. We know that we want to continue hiring people that fit our culture, but many thought that Southwest's culture was indefinable. Yet we have to define it to be able to select based on it. So we came up with what we thought were the core values. We came up with three. They are first, a warrior spirit, which captures the idea of working hard, being the underdog, being a fighter. Second, a servant's heart, which means putting others first, being altruistic, and having proactive customer service. Third, a fun-loving attitude. Of course we also value getting excellent results.

   A key indicator of the success of our HR practices is the involvement of front-line employees. Employees are empowered to make decisions and they contribute to HR decisions. We use interview teams, which include recruiters and front-line employees. When employees love the company and love working for Southwest, they want to get involved and help choose whom they are going to work with. Employees do call recruiters and let them know how applicants treated them at the gate. We are not going to hire someone who was rude to our employees. This empowerment also relates to other areas of HR. For example, our relationship with unions is more guidelines than strict rules. Our employees don't want their hands tied. They are like owners. They want pay for performance. They want to have the freedom to create and innovate.

APPENDIX SA.4 Interview with Jeff Lamb, Vice President, People and Leadership Development (*continued*)

Question 2: What is Southwest's philosophy guiding various HR practices?

It's our mission statement. We have a general mission statement and a mission statement to employees. We are one of the few companies that has that. We are an employer of choice. It's an awesome privilege and responsibility to help create the place that will continue to be a great place to work for the next 30 years. We've hired one-third of our workforce over the last three years. There is always the possibility that the culture could get diluted. We are trying to make sure that doesn't happen. We focus on retention, leadership development, and culture. We have a program called onboarding—it's a training program for employees in their first year. The program is aimed to improve retention by communicating what is great at Southwest and by communicating internal best practices. We have extensive new hire orientations and a new online orientation to help employees learn the Southwest way.

However, we also have to focus on costs. We've reduced staffing costs 56% per hire over the last two years. We've done this by investing in new technology, revamping our processes, and working closely with internal customers. For example, we had a retention problem for baggage loaders on the ramp in Baltimore from summer of 2005 to summer of 2006. We hired 167 people and were only able to retain 11. We worked with the Baltimore crew, created a retention champion position, and carved out a team to focus on the situation. At Southwest we are still below 5% in turnover, which is tremendous for this industry.

Question 3: How do your HR practices fit with each other?

The system works together to allow employees the freedom to create and innovate and to allow leaders to recognize them for it. We have tremendous recognition programs, probably quadruple what other companies do. Although it's simplistic, it really just little things, like random acts of kindness. When your daughter graduates from college and gets a gift from the president, it's something. There's not a leader here who would think twice about taking the team bowling this afternoon as a reward for a team accomplishment. But rewards go beyond recognition. We pay at or above the market. We value our employees and take a paternalistic attitude toward benefits, which tend to be tied to tenure. We have a tremendous retirement plan. We match 7.3% for our 401(k)s and also offer a profit-sharing plan, which has paid out over many years. We have a great history of providing stock options.

Performance management also reflects our value of employees. We have what we call loving feedback. It celebrates successes, it lets people know how they're doing, but it's also honest. Employees are happier to get negative feedback than no feedback at all. Our feedback system really has two fronts. The first is based on metrics, such as daily luggage-handling performance. The other front is the conversation, the person-to-person discussion that frequently occurs.

Question 4: How has selection and development affected Southwest's success?

Very few companies have a business methodology of putting their people first. Our view is that happy employees lead to happy customers, which create happy shareholders. Thus our strong people practices put the employee first, then the customer and shareholder. When you stand behind your employees, that reverberates throughout the organization. It builds fierce loyalty. Our recent survey of employees showed an incredible level of employee satisfaction. Putting the employees first is hard. When things get tight, it's tempting to cut training and other things that matter to the employees.

Question 5: What challenges do you see ahead for Southwest Airlines in general and with respect to selection and development?

One challenge that has to be on our radar is the impending labor shortage. When you look at the numbers, the upcoming retirements, it could create difficulties. You can't be a large organization today and not have it on your radar. So what we're doing is like the fuel hedging, we're doing people hedging. We're focusing on retention and development. Retention is critical. Even with our very low turnover rate, below 5%, that means we need 1,700 employees next year just to replace those that leave. Assuming a one-year salary cost of replacing them, which is conservative, you're talking about $55 million. When we charge on average $100 per flight and make, let's say $10 on each one, that's a lot of flights we have to sell just to cover those costs.

Some would say that maintaining our culture is a challenge. I think it is critically important, but I think all the mechanics are in place. We're treating people like we would want to be treated, letting them know they are valued.

Of course another challenge is costs. We strive to be have the lowest costs and the best customer service. We're using a lot of metrics to achieve this. The language of business is numbers and you need to know how you're doing. HR has to add value. HR needs to be efficient in what it does, or you can't go asking other departments to be efficient. We have to be competitive to be one of the best places to work.

—Jeff Lamb, vice president, people and leadership development (August 30, 2007), Southwest Airlines

THE LINCOLN ELECTRIC COMPANY

People are our most valuable asset. They must feel secure, important, challenged, in control of their destiny, confident in their leadership, be responsive to common goals, believe they are being treated fairly, have easy access to authority and open lines of communication in all possible directions. Perhaps the most important task Lincoln employees face today is that of establishing an example for others in the Lincoln organization in other parts of the world. We need to maximize the benefits of cooperation and teamwork, fusing high technology with human talent, so that we here in the USA and all of our subsidiary and joint venture operations will be in a position to realize our full potential.

George Willis, former chief executive officer
The Lincoln Electric Company

Introduction

Today, the Lincoln Electric Company, under the leadership of John Stropki, is the world leader in the design, development, and manufacture of arc-welding products, robotic arc-welding systems, and plasma and oxyfuel cutting equipment. The company also has a leading global position in the brazing and soldering alloys market. Headquartered in Cleveland, Ohio, Lincoln has more than 33 manufacturing locations, including operations, manufacturing alliances, and joint ventures in 19 countries and a worldwide network of distributors and sales offices covering more than 160 countries, including China, India, and Brazil. The company's U.S. market share (for arc-welding products) is estimated at more than 40%.[1]

The Lincoln incentive management plan has been well-known for many years. Many college management texts make reference to the Lincoln plan as a model for achieving higher worker productivity. Certainly, the firm has been successful according to the usual measures.

James F. Lincoln died in 1965 and there was some concern, even among employees, that the management system would fall into disarray, that profits would decline, and that year-end bonuses might be discontinued. Quite the contrary, since Lincoln's death, the company appears as strong as ever. Each year, except the recession years 1982 and 1983, has seen high profits and bonuses. In 1995, Lincoln Electric's centennial, sales for the first time surpassed $1 billion. While there was some employee discontent about relatively flat bonuses in 1995, employee morale and productivity remain very good.[2] Employee turnover is almost nonexistent except for retirements. Lincoln's market share is stable. The historically high stock dividends continue. Today, sales exceed $2 billion and employees number about 9,000.

A Historical Sketch

In 1895, after being "frozen out" of the depression-ravaged Elliott-Lincoln Company, a maker of Lincoln-designed electric motors, John C. Lincoln, took out his second patent and began to manufacture his improved motor. He opened his new business, unincorporated, with $200 he had earned redesigning a motor for young Herbert Henry Dow, who later founded the Dow Chemical Company.

Started during an economic depression and cursed by a major fire after only one year in business, the company grew, but hardly prospered, through its first quarter century. In 1906, John C. Lincoln incorporated the business and moved from his one-room, fourth-floor factory to a new three-story building he erected in east Cleveland. He expanded his workforce to 30 and sales grew to over $50,000 a year. John preferred being an engineer and inventor rather than a manager, though, and it was to be left to another Lincoln to manage the company through its years of success. In 1907, after a bout with typhoid fever forced him from Ohio State University in his senior year, James F. Lincoln, John's younger brother, joined the fledgling company. In 1914 he became the active head of the firm, with the titles of general manager and vice president. John remained president of the company for some years but became more involved in other business ventures and in his work as an inventor.

One of James Lincoln's early actions was to ask the employees to elect representatives to a committee that would advise him on company operations. This Advisory Board has met with the chief executive officer every two weeks since that time. This was only the first of a series of innovative personnel policies that have, over the years, distinguished Lincoln Electric from its competitors.

The first year the Advisory Board was in existence, working hours were reduced from 55 per week, then standard, to 50 hours a week. In 1915, the company gave each employee a paid-up life insurance policy. A welding school, which continues today, was begun in 1917. In 1918, an employee bonus plan was attempted. It was not continued, but the idea was to resurface later.

The Lincoln Electric Employees' Association was formed in 1919 to provide health benefits and social activities. This

Source: This case was originally prepared by Arthur Sharplin and appears in R. S. Schuler and P. D. Buller (eds.), *Cases in Management, Organizational Behavior and Human Resource Management*, 7th ed. (Cincinnati, OH: South-Western, 2006). It is adapted here by R. S. Schuler and used with the permission of the authors. For more on Lincoln's global business, see D. Briscoe, R. S. Schuler, and L. Claus, *International Human Resource Management*, 3rd ed. (London: Routledge, 2008).

organization continues today and has assumed several additional functions over the years. In 1923, a piecework pay system was in effect, employees got two weeks' paid vacation each year, and wages were adjusted for changes in the Consumer Price Index. Approximately 30% of the common stock was set aside for key employees in 1914. A stock purchase plan for all employees was begun in 1925.

The board of directors voted to start a suggestion system in 1929. The program is still in effect, but cash awards, a part of the early program, were discontinued several years ago. Now suggestions are rewarded by "additional points" that affect year-end bonuses.

The legendary Lincoln bonus plan was proposed by the Advisory Board and accepted on a trial basis in 1934. The first annual bonus amounted to about 25% of wages. There has been a bonus every year since then. The bonus plan has been a cornerstone of the Lincoln management system, and recent bonuses have approximated annual wages.

By 1944, Lincoln employees enjoyed a pension plan, a policy of promotion from within, and continuous employment. Base pay rates were determined by formal job evaluation and a merit rating system was in effect.

In the prologue of James F. Lincoln's last book, Charles G. Herbruck writes regarding the foregoing personnel innovations:

> They were not to buy good behavior. They were not efforts to increase profits. They were not antidotes to labor difficulties. They did not constitute a "do-gooder" program. They were an expression of mutual respect for each person's importance to the job to be done. All of them reflect the leadership of James Lincoln, under whom they were nurtured and propagated.

During World War II, Lincoln prospered as never before. By the start of the war, the company was the world's largest manufacturer of arc-welding products. Sales of about $4,000,000 in 1934 grew to $24,000,000 by 1941. Productivity per employee more than doubled during the same period. The Navy's Price Review Board challenged the high profits. And the Internal Revenue Service questioned the tax deductibility of employee bonuses, arguing they were not "ordinary and necessary" costs of doing business. But the forceful and articulate James Lincoln was able to overcome the objections.

Certainly since 1935, and probably for several years before that, Lincoln's productivity has been well above the average for similar companies. The company claims levels of productivity more than twice those for other manufacturers from 1945 onward. Information available from outside sources tends to support these claims.

Company Philosophy

James F. Lincoln was the son of a Congregational minister, and Christian principles were at the center of his business philosophy.

The confidence that he had in the efficacy of Christ's teachings is illustrated by the following remark taken from one of his books:

> The Christian ethic should control our acts. If it did control our acts, the savings in cost of distribution would be tremendous. Advertising would be a contact of the expert consultant with the customer, in order to give the customer the best product available when all of the customers' needs are considered. Competition then would be in improving the quality of products and increasing efficiency in producing and distributing them; not in deception, as is now too customary. Pricing would reflect efficiency of production; it would not be a selling dodge that the customer may be sorry he accepted. It would be proper for all concerned and rewarding for the ability used in producing the product.

There is no indication that Lincoln attempted to evangelize his employees or customers—or the general public for that matter. Neither the former chairman of the board and chief executive, George Willis, nor his predecessor, Donald F. Hastings, mentioned the Christian gospel in their speeches and interviews. The company motto, "The actual is limited, the possible is immense," is prominently displayed, but there is no display of religious slogans, and there is no company chapel.

Attitude toward the Customer

James Lincoln saw the customer's needs as the raison d'etre for every company. He wrote, "When any company has achieved success so that it is attractive as an investment, all money usually needed for expansion is supplied by the customer in retained earnings. It is obvious that the customer's interests, not the stockholder's, should come first." In 1947 he said, "Care should be taken . . . not to rivet attention on profit. Between 'How much do I get?' and 'How do I make this better, cheaper, more useful?' the difference is fundamental and decisive." Willis, too, ranked the customer as management's most important constituency. This is reflected in Lincoln's policy to "at all times price on the basis of cost and at all times keep pressure on our cost. . . ." Lincoln's goal, often stated, is "to build a better and better product at a lower and lower price." James Lincoln said, "It is obvious that the customer's interests should be the first goal of industry."

This priority, and the priority given to other groups, is reflected in the vision, missions, and values statements and the set of goals shown in Appendix LE.1.

Attitude toward Stockholders

Stockholders are given last priority at Lincoln. This is a continuation of James Lincoln's philosophy: "The last group to be considered is the stockholders who own stock because they think it will be more profitable than investing money in any other way." Concerning division of the largesse produced by incentive management, he wrote, "The absentee stockholder also will get his share, even if undeserved, out of the greatly increased profit that the efficiency produces."

Attitude toward Unionism

There has never been a serious effort to organize Lincoln employees. While James Lincoln criticized the labor movement for "selfishly attempting to better its position at the expense of the people it must serve," he still had kind words for union members. He excused abuses of union power as "the natural reactions of human beings to the abuses to which management has subjected them." Lincoln's idea of the correct relationship between workers and managers is shown by this comment: "Labor and management are properly not warring camps; they are parts of one organization in which they must, and should, cooperate fully and happily."

Beliefs and Assumptions about Employees

If fulfilling customer needs is the desired goal of business, then employee performance and productivity are the means by which this goal can best be achieved. The Lincoln attitude toward employees, reflected in the following comments by James Lincoln, is credited by many with creating the success the company has experienced:

> He is just as eager as any manager is to be part of a team that is properly organized and working for the advancement of our economy. He has no desire to make profits for those who do not hold up their end in production, as is true of absentee stockholders and inactive people in the company.
>
> If money is to be used as an incentive, the program must provide that what is paid to the worker is what he has earned. The earnings of each must be in accordance with accomplishment.
>
> Status is of great importance in all human relationships. The greatest incentive that money has, usually, is that it is a symbol of success. The resulting status is the real incentive. Money alone can be an incentive to the miser only.
>
> There must be complete honesty and understanding between the hourly worker and management if high efficiency is to be obtained.

These beliefs and assumptions have helped shaped Lincoln's human resource objectives. These are shown in Appendix LE.2.

Lincoln's Business

Arc welding has been the standard joining method in shipbuilding for decades. It is the predominant way of connecting steel in the construction industry. Most industrial plants have their own welding shops for maintenance and construction. Manufacturers of tractors and all kinds of heavy equipment use arc welding extensively in the manufacturing process. Many hobbyists have their own welding machines and use them for

making metal items such as patio furniture and barbecue pits. The popularity of welded sculpture as an art form is growing.

While advances in welding technology have been frequent, arc-welding products, in the main, have hardly changed. Lincoln's Innershield process is a notable exception. This process, described later, lowers welding cost and improves quality and speed in many applications.

The company's share of the U.S. arc-welding products market appears to have been about 40% for many years. The welding products market has grown somewhat faster than the level of industry in general. The market is highly price competitive, with variations in prices of standard items normally amounting to only a percentage point or two. Lincoln's products are sold directly by its engineering-oriented sales force and indirectly through its distributor organization.

The other major welding process, flame welding, has not been competitive with arc welding since the 1930s. However, plasma arc welding, a relatively new process that uses a conducting stream of superheated gas (plasma) to confine the welding current to a small area, has made some inroads, especially in metal tubing manufacturing, in recent years. Major advances in technology that will produce an alternative superior to arc welding in the next decade or so appear unlikely. Also, it seems likely that changes in the machines and techniques used in arc welding will be evolutionary rather than revolutionary.

It is also reasonable to observe that Lincoln Electric's business objectives, shown in Appendix LE.3, are likely to change in an evolutionary rather than a revolutionary way.

Products

The company is primarily engaged in the manufacture and sale of arc-welding products: electric welding machines and metal electrodes. Lincoln also produces electric motors ranging from 0.5 horsepower to 200 horsepower. Motors constitute about 8–10% of total sales. Several million dollars have recently been invested in automated equipment that will double Lincoln's manufacturing capacity for 0.5- to 20-horsepower electric motors. The electric welding machines, some consisting of a transformer or motor and generator arrangement powered by commercial electricity and others consisting of an internal combustion engine and generator, are designed to produce 30 to 1,500 amperes of electrical power. This electrical current is used to melt a consumable metal electrode with the molten metal being transferred in superhot spray to the metal joint being welded. Very high temperatures and hot sparks are produced, and operators usually must wear special eye and face protection and leather gloves, often along with leather aprons and sleeves. Lincoln and its competitors now market a wide range of general-purpose and specialty electrodes for welding mild steel, aluminum, cast iron, and stainless and special steels. Most of these electrodes are designed to meet the standards of the American Welding Society, a trade association. They are thus essentially the same in size and composition from one manufacturer to another. Every electrode manufacturer has a limited number of unique products, but these typically constitute only a small percentage of total sales.

Welding electrodes are of two basic types: coated stick electrodes and coiled wire. Coated "stick" electrodes, usually 14 inches long and smaller than a pencil in diameter, are held in a special insulated holder by the operator, who must manipulate the electrode to maintain a proper arc width and pattern of deposition of the metal being transferred. Stick electrodes are packaged in 6- to 50-pound boxes.

Thin coiled wire is designed to be fed continuously to the welding arc through a gun held by the operator or positioned by automatic positioning equipment. The wire is packaged in coils, reels, and drums weighing from 14 to 1,000 pounds and may be solid or flux cored.

For more information on products visit the Web site at http://www.lincolnelectric.com.

Manufacturing Process

The main plant is in Euclid, Ohio, a suburb on Cleveland's east side. There are no warehouses. Materials flow from the half-mile-long dock on the north side of the plant through the production lines to a very limited storage and loading area on the south side.

Materials used on each workstation are stored as close as possible to the workstation. The administrative offices, near the center of the factory, are entirely functional. A corridor below the main level provides access to the factory floor from the main entrance near the center of the plant. *Fortune* declared the Euclid facility one of America's ten best managed factories.

Another Lincoln plant, in Mentor, Ohio, houses some of the electrode production operations, which were moved from the main plant. Electrode manufacturing is highly capital intensive. Metal rods purchased from steel producers are drawn down to smaller diameters, cut to length, and coated with pressed-powder flux (for stick electrodes) or plated with copper (for conductivity) and put into coils or spools for wire. Lincoln's Innershield wire is hollow and filled with a material similar to that used to coat stick electrodes. As mentioned earlier, this represented a major innovation in welding technology when it was introduced. The company is highly secretive about its electrode production processes, and outsiders are not given access to the details of those processes.

Lincoln welding machines are made on a series of assembly lines. Gasoline and diesel engines are purchased partially assembled, but practically all other components are made from basic industrial products, for example, steel bars and sheets and bar copper conductor wire.

Individual components, such as gasoline tanks for engine-driven welders and steel shafts for motors and generators, are made by numerous small "factories within a factory." The shaft for a certain generator, for example, is made from raw steel bar by one operator who uses five large machines, all running continuously. A saw cuts the bar to length, a digital lathe machines different sections to varying diameters, a special mining machine cuts a slot for the keyway, and so forth until a finished shaft is produced. The operator moves the shafts from machine to machine and makes necessary adjustments. Another operator punches, shapes, and paints sheet metal cowling parts. One assembles steel laminations onto a rotor shaft, then winds, insulates, and tests the rotors. Finished components are moved by crane operators to the nearby assembly lines. Many of these processes continue to be automated to enhance plant efficiency. To further enhance efficiencies across all areas of the company, Lincoln Electric launched its Six Sigma program. Since 2000, Lincoln has completed more than 200 projects in its U.S. and Canadian facilities, resulting in a savings of more than $10 million. Among their employees they have trained more than 160 Red Belts, 70 Black Belts, and one Master Black Belt. To date, Six Sigma initiatives have been rolled out in the United States, Canada, Mexico, and Asia.

Worker Performance and Attitude

Exceptional worker performance at Lincoln is a matter of record. The typical Lincoln employee earns about twice as much as other factory workers in the Cleveland area. Yet the company's labor cost per sales dollar is well below industry averages. Worker turnover is practically nonexistent except for retirements and departures by new employees. Turnover is less than 4% for employees who have been on the jobs for at least 18 months.[3]

Sales per Lincoln factory employee currently exceed $150,000. An observer at the factory quickly sees why this figure is so high. Each worker is proceeding busily and thoughtfully about the task at hand. There is no idle chatter. Most workers take no coffee breaks. Many operate several machines and make a substantial component unaided. The supervisors are busy with planning and record keeping duties and hardly glance at the people they "supervise." The manufacturing procedures appear efficient: no unnecessary steps, no wasted motions, no wasted materials. Finished components move smoothly to subsequent workstations. Appendix LE.4 includes summaries of interviews with employees.

Organizational Structure

Lincoln has never allowed development of a formal organization chart. The objective of this policy is to ensure maximum flexibility. An open-door policy is practiced throughout the company, and personnel are encouraged to take problems to the persons most capable of resolving them. Once, Harvard Business School researchers prepared an organization chart reflecting the implied relationships at Lincoln. The chart became available within the company, and present management feels that had a disruptive effect. Therefore, no organizational chart appears in this case.

Perhaps because of the quality and enthusiasm of the Lincoln workforce, routine supervision is almost nonexistent. A typical production supervisor, for example, supervises as many as 100 workers, a span of control that does not allow more than infrequent worker-supervisor interaction.

Position titles and traditional flows of authority do imply something of an organizational structure, however. For example, the vice president of sales and the vice president of the electrode division report to the president, as do various staff assistants such as the director of human resources and the director of purchasing.

Using such implied relationships, it has been determined that production workers have two or, at most, three levels of supervision between themselves and the president.

Human Resource Policies and Practices

As mentioned earlier, it is Lincoln's remarkable human resource policies and practices that are credited by many with the company's success.

Recruitment and Selection

Every job opening is advertised internally on company bulletin boards, and any employee can apply for any job so advertised. External hiring is permitted only for entry-level positions. Selection for these jobs is done on the basis of personal interviews; there is no aptitude or psychological testing. A committee consisting of vice presidents and supervisors interviews candidates initially cleared by the personnel department. Final selection is made by the supervisor who has a job opening. Nonetheless, it is increasingly desirable that factory workers have some advanced mathematical skills and understand the use of computers. Consequently, Lincoln's expansion is becoming increasingly dependent on getting employees qualified to work in the Lincoln environment within the famous incentive system.[4]

Job Security

In 1958 Lincoln formalized its guaranteed continuous employment policy, which had already been in effect for many years. There have been no layoffs since World War II. Since 1958, every worker with over two years' longevity has been guaranteed at least 30 hours per week, 49 weeks per year.

The policy has never been so severely tested as during the 1981 to 1983 recession. As a manufacturer of capital goods, Lincoln's business is highly cyclical. In previous recessions the company was able to avoid major sales declines. However, sales plummeted 32% in 1982 and another 16% the next year. Few companies could withstand such a revenue collapse and remain profitable. Yet Lincoln not only earned profits, but no employee was laid off and year-end incentive bonuses continued. To weather the storm, management cut most of the nonsalaried workers back to 30 hours a week for varying periods of time. Many employees were reassigned, and the total workforce was

slightly reduced through normal attrition and restricted hiring. Many employees grumbled at their unexpected misfortune, probably to the surprise and dismay of some Lincoln managers. However, sales and profits—and employee bonuses—soon rebounded.

Performance Evaluations

Each supervisor formally evaluates subordinates twice a year using the cards shown in Exhibit LE.1. The employee (nonmanagement) performance criteria of quality, dependability, ideas, and cooperation, and "output are considered to be independent of each other. Marks on the cards are converted to numerical scores that are forced to average 100 for each evaluating supervisor. Individual merit rating scores normally range from 80 to 110. Any score over 110 requires a special letter to top management. These scores (over 110) are not considered in computing the required 100-point average for each evaluating supervisor.

Suggestions for improvements often result in recommendations for exceptionally high performance scores. Supervisors discuss individual performance marks with the employees concerned. Each warranty claim is traced to the individual employee whose work caused the defect. The employee's performance score may be reduced, or the worker may be required to repay the cost of servicing the warranty claim by working without pay.

Performance evaluation for managerial and all salaried employees is conducted using six criteria or competencies. These include (1) leadership/ownership, (2) decision making and judgment, (3) results orientation, (4) teamwork/commitment, (5) quality and customer focus, and (6) creativity/innovation. The evaluation is conducted on a semiannual basis using a conventional graphic rating format. For each of these criteria, the employees must establish goals based on the strategic needs of the company. Employees are provided feedback and coaching at least once a year for performance improvement and development. Evaluation results influence merit pay and bonus decisions.

Compensation

Basic wage levels for jobs at Lincoln are determined by a wage survey of similar jobs in the Cleveland area.[5] These rates are adjusted quarterly in accordance with changes in the Cleveland area wage index. Insofar as possible, base wage rates are translated into piece rates. Today the average Lincoln factory worker earns the equivalent of approximately $17 an hour versus the average $14.25 manufacturing wage in the Cleveland area. Practically all production workers and many others—for example, some forklift operators—are paid by piece rate. Once established, piece rates are never changed unless a substantive change in the way a job is done results from a source other than the worker doing the job.

In December of each year, a portion of annual profits is distributed to employees as bonuses. Incentive bonuses

EXHIBIT LE. 1 Merit Rating Cards

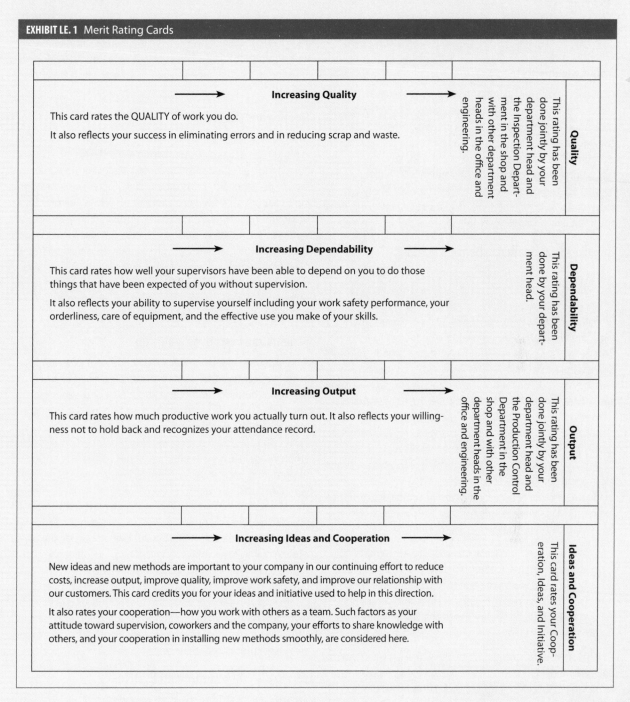

Quality

Increasing Quality

This card rates the QUALITY of work you do.

It also reflects your success in eliminating errors and in reducing scrap and waste.

This rating has been done jointly by your department head and the Inspection Department in the shop and with other department heads in the office and engineering.

Dependability

Increasing Dependability

This card rates how well your supervisors have been able to depend on you to do those things that have been expected of you without supervision.

It also reflects your ability to supervise yourself including your work safety performance, your orderliness, care of equipment, and the effective use you make of your skills.

This rating has been done by your department head.

Output

Increasing Output

This card rates how much productive work you actually turn out. It also reflects your willingness not to hold back and recognizes your attendance record.

This rating has been done jointly by your department head and the Production Control Department in the shop and with other department heads in the office and engineering.

Ideas and Cooperation

Increasing Ideas and Cooperation

New ideas and new methods are important to your company in our continuing effort to reduce costs, increase output, improve quality, improve work safety, and improve our relationship with our customers. This card credits you for your ideas and initiative used to help in this direction.

It also rates your cooperation—how you work with others as a team. Such factors as your attitude toward supervision, coworkers and the company, your efforts to share knowledge with others, and your cooperation in installing new methods smoothly, are considered here.

This card rates your Cooperation, Ideas, and Initiative.

since 1934 have averaged about 90% of annual wages. Individual bonuses are proportional to merit rating scores. For example, assume the amount set aside for bonuses is 80% of total wages paid to eligible employees. A person whose performance score is 95 will receive a bonus of 76% of annual wages. While these percentages have often resulted in high total compensation, some employees believe that their bonuses are not rising fast enough, despite rising profits. This reflects the firm's decision to use profits to expand the operations rather than put them into higher bonuses. It also reflects the fact that more workers today are sharing in a bonus pool that is only a little higher than in many years in the 1980s.[6]

Vacations

The company is shut down for two weeks in August and two weeks during the Christmas season. Vacations are taken during these periods. For employees with over 25 years of service, a fifth week of vacation may be taken at a time acceptable to superiors.

Work Assignments

Management has the authority to transfer workers and to switch between overtime and short time as required. Supervisors have undisputed authority to assign specific parts to individual workers, who may have their own preferences due to variations in piece rates. During the 1982–1983 recession, 50 factory workers volunteered to join sales teams and fanned out across the country to sell a new welder designed for automobile body shops and small machine shops. The result: $10 million in sales and a hot new product.

Employee Participation in Decision Making

Thinking of participative management usually evokes a vision of a relaxed, nonauthoritarian atmosphere. This is not the case at Lincoln. Formal authority is quite strong. "We're very authoritarian around here," says Willis. James F. Lincoln placed a good deal of stress on protecting management's authority. "Management in all successful departments of industry must have complete power," he said. "Management is the coach who must be obeyed. The men, however, are the players who alone can win the game." Despite this attitude, there are several ways in which employees participate in management at Lincoln.

Richard Sabo, former assistant to the chief executive officer, relates job enlargement/enrichment to participation. He said, "The most important participative technique that we use is giving more responsibility to employees. We give a high school graduate more responsibility than other companies give their foremen." Management puts limits on the degree of participation that is allowed, however. In Sabo's words:

> When you use "participation," put quotes around it. Because we believe that each person should participate only in those decisions he is most knowledgeable about. I don't think production employees should control the decisions of the chairman. They don't know as much as he does about the decisions he is involved in.

The Advisory Board, elected by the workers, meets with the chairman and the president every two weeks to discuss ways of improving operations. As noted earlier, this board has been in existence since 1914 and has contributed to many innovations. The incentive bonuses, for example, were first recommended by this committee. Every employee has access to Advisory Board members, and answers to all Advisory Board suggestions are promised by the following meeting. Willis, Hastings, and Stropki are quick to point out, though, that the Advisory Board only recommends actions. "They do not have direct authority," Willis says, "and when they bring up something that management thinks is not to the benefit of the company, it will be rejected."

Under the early suggestion program, employees were awarded one-half of the first year's savings attributable to their suggestions. Now, however, the value of suggestions is reflected in performance evaluation scores, which determine individual incentive bonus amounts.

Training and Education

Production workers are given a short period of on-the-job training and then placed on a piecework pay system. Lincoln does not pay for off-site education, unless very specific company needs are identified. The idea behind this latter policy, according to Sabo, is that everyone cannot take advantage of such a program, and it is unfair to expend company funds for an advantage to which there is unequal access. Recruits for sales jobs, already college graduates, are given on-the-job training in the plant followed by a period of work and training at one of the regional sales offices. Today, Lincoln Electric conducts a large number of training programs. Visit their Web site to review them all and you may be very impressed!

Benefits and Executive Perquisites

A medical plan and a company-paid retirement program have been in effect for many years. A plant cafeteria, operated on a breakeven basis, serves meals at about 60% of usual costs. The Employees' Association, to which the company does not contribute, provides disability insurance and social and athletic activities. The employee stock ownership program has resulted in employee ownership of about 50% of the common stock. Under this program, each employee with more than two years of service may purchase stock in the corporation. The price of these shares is established at book value. Stock purchased through this plan may be held by employees only. Dividends and voting rights are the same as for stock that is owned outside the plan. Approximately 75% of the employees own Lincoln stock.

As to executive perquisites, there are none—crowded, austere offices, no executive washrooms or lunchrooms, and no reserved parking spaces. Even the top executives pay for their own meals and eat in the employee cafeteria. If the CEO arrives late due to a breakfast speaking engagement, he has to park far away from the factory entrance.

Financial Policies

James F. Lincoln felt strongly that financing for company growth should come from within the company—through initial cash investment by the founders, through retention of earnings, and through stock purchases by those who work in the business. He saw the following advantages of this approach:

1. Ownership of stock by employees strengthens team spirit. "If they are mutually anxious to make it succeed, the future of the company is bright."
2. Ownership of stock provides individual incentive because employees feel that they will benefit from company profitability.

3. "Ownership is educational." Owner-employees "will know how profits are made and lost; how success is won and lost. There are few socialists in the list of stockholders of the nation's industries."

4. "Capital available from within controls expansion." Unwarranted expansion would not occur, Lincoln believed, under his financing plan.

5. "The greatest advantage would be the development of the individual worker. Under the incentive of ownership, he would become a greater man."

6. "Stock ownership is one of the steps that can be taken that will make the worker feel that there is less of a gulf between him and the boss. Stock ownership will help the worker to recognize his responsibility in the game and the importance of victory."

Until 1980, Lincoln Electric borrowed no money. Even now, the company's liabilities consist mainly of accounts payable and short-term accruals. The unusual pricing policy at Lincoln was succinctly stated by Willis: "At all times price on the basis of cost and at all times keep pressure on our cost." This policy resulted in the price for the most popular welding electrode then in use going from 16 cents a pound in 1929 to 4.7 cents in 1938. According to Dr. C. Jackson Grayson of the American Productivity Center in Houston, Texas, Lincoln's prices increased only one-fifth as fast as the Consumer Price Index from 1934 to about 1970. This resulted in a welding products market in which Lincoln became the undisputed price leader for the products it manufactures. Not even the major Japanese manufacturers, such as Nippon Steel for welding electrodes and Saka Transformer for welding machines, were able to penetrate this market.

Substantial cash balances accumulated each year preparatory to paying the year-end bonuses. Modest success with international expansion put some pressure on what was basically a conservative financial philosophy. However, the company borrowed money in 1992 to pay for employee bonuses in the United States. In 1995 Lincoln issued $119 million of new stock. This sale created greater public ownership. As a consequence, Don Hastings, then CEO, remarked that the company must now consider not only the employees but also its shareholders, customers, and suppliers.[7] For more current financial information, visit Lincoln's Web site. Its 10-K Report and Annual Report contain a great deal of useful information.

How Well Does Lincoln Serve Its Stakeholders?

Lincoln Electric differs from most other companies in the importance it assigns to each of the groups it serves. Hastings identifies these groups, in the order of priority ascribed to them, as: (1) customers, (2) employees, and (3) stockholders. As suggested, the 1995 stock issue increased the salience of the stockholders.

Certainly the firm's customers have fared well over the years. Lincoln prices for welding machines and welding electrodes are acknowledged to be the lowest in the marketplace. Quality has consistently been high. The cost of field failures for Lincoln products was recently determined to be a remarkable 0.04% of revenues. The Fleetweld electrodes and the SA-200 welders have been the standard in the pipeline and refinery construction industry, where price is hardly a criterion, for decades. A Lincoln distributor in Monroe, Louisiana, says that he has sold several hundred of the popular AC-225 welders, which are warranted for one year, but has never handled a warranty claim.

Perhaps the best served of all of management's constituencies have been the employees. Not the least of their benefits, of course, are the year-end bonuses, which effectively double an already average compensation level. The foregoing description of the personnel program and the comments in Appendix LE.4 further illustrate the desirability of a Lincoln job.

While stockholders were relegated to a secondary status by James F. Lincoln, they have done very well indeed. Recent dividends exceeded $11 a share and earnings per share have approached $30. In January 1980, the price of restricted stock, committed to employees, was $117 a share. By 1989, the stated value, at which the company will repurchase the stock if tendered, was $201. A check with the New York office of Merrill Lynch at that time revealed an estimated price on Lincoln stock of $270 a share, with none being offered for sale. Technically, this price applies only to the unrestricted stock owned by the Lincoln family, a few other major holders, and employees who have purchased it on the open market. Risk associated with Lincoln stock, a major determinant of stock value, is minimal because of the small amount of debt in the capital structure, because of an extremely stable earnings record, and because of Lincoln's practice of purchasing the restricted stock whenever employees offer it for sale. The 1995 stock sale has changed this situation dramatically. The stock now trades freely on the NASDAQ stock exchange (symbol: LECO).

Management Quality

It is easy to believe that the reason for Lincoln's success is the excellent attitude of the employees and their willingness to work harder, faster, and more intelligently than other industrial workers. However, Sabo suggests that appropriate credit be given to Lincoln executives, whom he credits with carrying out the following policies:

1. Management has limited research, development, and manufacturing to a standard product line designed to meet the major needs of the welding industry.

2. New products must be reviewed by manufacturing and all producing costs verified before being approved by management.

3. Purchasing is challenged not only to procure materials at the lowest cost, but also to work closely with engineering and manufacturing to ensure that the latest innovations are implemented.

4. Manufacturing supervision and all personnel are held accountable for reduction of scrap, energy conservation, and maintenance of product quality.

5. Production control, material handling, and methods engineering are closely supervised by top management.

6. Management has made cost reduction a way of life at Lincoln, and definite programs are established in many areas, including traffic and shipping, where tremendous savings can result.

7. Management has established a sales department that is technically trained to reduce customer welding costs. This sales approach and other real customer services have eliminated nonessential frills and resulted in long-term benefits to all concerned.

8. Management has encouraged education, technical publishing, and long-range programs that have resulted in industry growth, thereby ensuring market potential for the Lincoln Electric Company.

Sabo writes, "It is in a very real sense a personal and group experience in faith—a belief that together we can achieve results which alone would not be possible. It is not a perfect system and it is not easy. It requires tremendous dedication and hard work. However, it does work and the results are worth the effort."

Going Global

As stated in the beginning of this case, Lincoln Electric has production sites in 19 other countries and distribution and sales offices in more than 160 countries. As Lincoln Electric has increased its global presence, it has learned just how much it can use the same philosophy of managing human resources. The company has learned that countries have important legal, cultural, and political conditions that can influence the effectiveness and applicability of some of their practices and that the company needs to either adapt to them or locate in places where the differences with the United States are more modest. This process of learning, however, was not necessarily easy or without some cost. During the late 1980s and early 1990s, Lincoln expanded rapidly, sometimes by acquiring existing companies, sometimes by joint ventures, and sometimes by establishing a new facility. Lincoln's top management assumed that there would be enough people around the world who would take to the Lincoln system as much as do the employees in Cleveland. They learned that this assumption was not always valid and as a consequence they had to close some facilities. As a result of top management's relatively limited international experience, the 1990s proved to be very challenging, costly, and humbling times. (See the letter from the CEO to the shareholders in Exhibit LE.2.) Donald Hastings has described these times in great detail in his article entitled "Lincoln Electric's Harsh Lessons from International Expansion," in the *Harvard Business Review* (May–June 1999): 163–178. Their experiences are reflected today in the missions and values statements of the company shown in Appendix LE.1. The global business environment continues to be a major growth opportunity for Lincoln Electric, both in terms of global production and exports from the United States. In 2006, Lincoln Electric received the President's E Star Award for Exports in recognition of its achievement in supporting export growth in the U.S. business community. With continued growth in the emerging markets, Lincoln is continuing to grow organically and through acquisitions.

APPENDIX LE.1   Vision, Missions, and Values Statements of the Lincoln Electric Company[9]

Vision Statement

Lincoln Electric will be the undisputed world leader in the arc-welding industry as measured by global sales volume, while simultaneously aiming to maximize shareholder value.

We will be the leader in supplying the finest quality welding and cutting products. In order to accomplish this, we will continue our emphasis on being the industry's lowest cost producer, on providing applications expertise and solutions for our customers, and on developing new and innovative technology that responds to customer needs with value-added products and services.

Mission Statement

Total Solutions. We will be driven by customer satisfaction and become known as the supplier of choice in our industries. We will strive to exceed customer expectations. We will be a solutions company, not simply a supplier of equipment or consumables.

Expertise. We will be differentiated from our competitors by technology, quality, applications engineering, sales and marketing expertise.

Global. We will be global, with over 40% of our total sales coming from outside North America. We will have cost-competitive manufacturing facilities located worldwide, where appropriate, to best serve our customers' needs.

Principles. We will base our human resources systems on our proven principles reflective of our core values and our commitment to attract, reward, develop, and motivate high-quality people. They will reflect the global scope of our business while demonstrating responsibility and flexibility with respect to cultural diversity and statutory and regional business realities.

Stakeholders. Our emphasis on continuous improvement in all aspects of our business will enable us to reward our shareholders and employees.

Responsibility. We will continually strive to be environmentally responsible and support the communities where we operate and the industries in which we participate.

Values Statement

Our Core Values. As a responsible and successful company in partnership with our customers, distributors, employees, shareholders, suppliers, and our host communities, we pledge ourselves to conduct our business in accordance with these core values:

- Respond to our customers' needs and expectations with quality, integrity, and value.
- Recognize people as our most valuable asset.
- Maintain and expand the Lincoln Incentive Management philosophy.
- Practice prudent and responsible financial management.
- Strive continually to be environmentally responsible.
- Support communities where we operate and industries in which we participate.

To Realize Our Mission and Support Our Core Values, We Have Established the Following Goals:

Respond to Our Customers' Needs and Expectations with Quality, Integrity, and Value

- Assure value through innovative, functional, and reliable products and services in all the markets we serve around the world.
- Exceed global standards for products and service quality.
- Provide our customers with personalized technical support that helps them achieve improvements in cost reduction, productivity, and quality.
- Lead the industry in aggressive application of advanced technology to meet customer requirements.
- Invest constantly in creative research and development dedicated to maintaining our position of market leadership.
- Achieve and maintain the leading market share position in our major markets around the world.

Recognize People As Our Most Valuable Asset

- Maintain a safe, clean, and healthy environment for our employees.
- Promote employee training, education, and development, and broaden skills through multidepartmental and international assignments.
- Maintain an affirmative action program and provide all employees with opportunities for advancement commensurate with their abilities and performance regardless of race, religion, national origin, sex, age, or disability.
- Maintain an environment that fosters ethical behavior, mutual trust, equal opportunity, open communication, personal growth, and creativity.
- Demand integrity, discipline, and professional conduct from our employees in every aspect of our business and conduct our operations ethically and in accordance with the law.
- Reward employees through recognition, "pay for performance," and by sharing our profits with incentive bonus compensation based on extraordinary achievement.

(continued)

APPENDIX LE.1 Vision, Missions, and Values Statements of the Lincoln Electric Company (*continued*)

Maintain and Expand the Lincoln Incentive Management Philosophy

Promote dynamic teamwork and innovation as the most profitable and cost-effective way of achieving:

- A committed work ethic and positive employee attitudes throughout the company.
- High-quality, low-cost manufacturing.
- Efficient and innovative engineering.
- Customer-oriented operation and administration.
- A dedicated and knowledgeable sales and service force.
- A total organization responsive to the needs of our worldwide customers.

Practice Prudent and Responsible Financial Management

- Establish attainable goals, strategic planning, and accountability for results that enhance shareholder value.
- Promote the process of employee involvement in cost reductions and quality improvements.
- Recognize profit as the resource that enables our Company to serve our customers.

Strive Continually to Be Environmentally Responsible

- Continue to pursue the most environmentally sound operating practices, processes, and products to protect the global environment.
- Maintain a clean and healthy environment in our host communities.

Support Communities Where We Operate and Industries in Which We Participate

- Invest prudently in social, cultural, educational, and charitable activities.
- Contribute to the industries we serve and society as a whole by continuing our leadership role in professional organizations and education.
- Encourage and support appropriate employee involvement in community activities.

APPENDIX LE.2 Lincoln Electric's HR Objectives

What Are the HR Objectives of Lincoln Electric?

- To maintain and expand the Lincoln Incentive Management Philosophy
- To recognize people as [the company's] most valuable asset
- To promote training, education, and development that broaden employee skills
- To maintain an affirmative action program and provide all employees with opportunities for advancement commensurate with their abilities and performance regardless of race, religion, national origin, sex, age, or disability

---

APPENDIX LE.3 Lincoln Electric's Business Objectives

Business Objectives of Lincoln Electric

- To be a global leader in price and quality and serve the customers first
- To achieve and retain global leadership as a total quality supplier of superior products and services
- To respond to our customers with quality, integrity, and value
- To practice prudent and responsible financial management
- To strive continually to be environmentally responsible
- To support communities where we operate and industries in which we participate
- To maintain an environment that fosters ethical behavior, mutual trust, equal opportunity, open communication, personal growth, and creativity
- To promote feedback
- To demand integrity, discipline, and professional conduct from our employees in every aspect of our business and conduct operations ethically and in accordance with the law
- To reward employees through recognition, pay for performance, and by sharing profits with incentive bonus compensation based on extraordinary achievement as a means of motivation
- To promote dynamic teamwork and innovation

APPENDIX LE.4   Employee Interviews

Following are typical questions and answers from employee interviews. In order to maintain each employee's personal privacy, fictitious names have been given to the interviewees.

Interview 1

Betty Stewart, a 52-year-old high school graduate who had been with Lincoln 13 years, was working as a cost accounting clerk at the time of the interview.

Q: What jobs have you held here beside the one you have now?

A: I worked in payroll for awhile, and then this job came open and I took it.

Q: How much money did you make last year, including your bonus?

A: I would say roughly around $25,000, but I was off for back surgery for awhile.

Q: You weren't paid while you were off for back surgery?

A: No.

Q: Did the Employees' Association help out?

A: Yes. The company doesn't furnish that, though. We pay $8 a month into the Employees' Association. I think my check from them was $130 a week.

Q: How was your performance rating last year?

A: It was around 100 points, but I lost some points for attendance for my back problem.

Q: How did you get your job at Lincoln?

A: I was bored silly where I was working, and I had heard that Lincoln kept their people busy. So I applied and got the job the next day.

Q: Do you think you make more money than similar workers in Cleveland?

A: I know I do.

Q: What have you done with your money?

A: We have purchased a better home. Also, my son is going to the University of Chicago, which costs $13,000 a year. I buy the Lincoln stock, which is offered each year, and I have a little bit of gold.

Q: Have you ever visited with any of the senior executives, like Mr. Willis or Mr. Hastings?

A: I have known Mr. Willis for a long time.

Q: Does he call you by name?

A: Yes. In fact, he was very instrumental in my going to the doctor that I am going to with my back. He knows the director of the clinic.

Q: Do you know Mr. Hastings?

A: I know him to speak to him, and he always speaks, always. But I have known Mr. Willis for a good many years. When I did Plant Two accounting I did not understand how the plant operated. Of course you are not allowed in Plant Two, because that's the electrode division. I told my boss about the problem one day, and the next thing I knew Mr. Willis came by and said, "Come on, Betty, we're going to Plant Two." He spent an hour and a half showing me the plant.

Q: Do you think Lincoln employees produce more than those in other companies?

A: I think with the incentive program the way that it is, if you want to work and achieve, then you will do it. If you don't want to work and achieve, you will not do it no matter where you are. Just because you are merit rated and have a bonus, if you really don't want to work hard, then you're not going to. You will accept your 90 points or 92 or 85 because even with that you make more money than people on the outside.

Q: Do you think Lincoln employees will ever join a union?

A: I don't know why they would.

Q: So you say that money is a very major advantage?

A: Money is a major advantage, but it's not just the money. It's the fact that having the incentive, you do wish to work a little harder. I'm sure that there are a lot of men here who, if they worked some other place, would not work as hard as they do here. Not that they are overworked—I don't mean that—but I'm sure they wouldn't push.

Q: Is there anything that you would like to add?

A: I do like working here. I am better off being pushed mentally. In another company if you pushed too hard you would feel a little bit of pressure, and someone might say, "Hey, slow down, don't try so hard." But here you are encouraged, not discouraged.

(continued)

APPENDIX LE.4 Employee Interviews (*continued*)

Interview 2

Ed Sanderson, a 23-year-old high school graduate who had been with Lincoln four years, was a machine operator in the electrode division at the time of the interview.

Q: How did you happen to get this job?

A: My wife was pregnant, and I was making three bucks an hour and one day I came here and applied. That was it. I kept calling to let them know I was still interested.

Q: Roughly, what were your earnings last year including your bonus?

A: $45,000.

Q: What have you done with your money since you have been here?

A: Well, we've lived pretty well and we bought a condominium.

Q: Have you paid for the condominium?

A: No, but I could.

Q: Have you bought your Lincoln stock this year?

A: No, I haven't bought any Lincoln stock yet.

Q: Do you get the feeling that the executives here are pretty well thought of?

A: I think they are. To get where they are today, they had to really work.

Q: Wouldn't that be true anywhere?

A: I think more so here because seniority really doesn't mean anything. If you work with a guy who has 20 years here, and you have two months and you're doing a better job, you will get advanced before he will.

Q: Are you paid on a piece-rate basis?

A: My gang does. There are nine of us who make the bare electrode, and the whole group gets paid based on how much electrode we make.

Q: Do you think you work harder than workers in other factories in the Cleveland area?

A: Yes, I would say I probably work harder.

Q: Do you think it hurts anybody?

A: No, a little hard work never hurts anybody.

Q: If you could choose, do you think you would be as happy earning a little less money and being able to slow down a little?

A: No, it doesn't bother me. If it bothered me, I wouldn't do it.

Q: Why do you think Lincoln employees produce more than workers in other plants?

A: That's the way the company is set up. The more you put out, the more you're going to make.

Q: Do you think it's the piece rate and bonus together?

A: I don't think people would work here if they didn't know that they would be rewarded at the end of the year.

Q: Do you think Lincoln employees will ever join a union?

A: No.

Q: What are the major advantages of working for Lincoln?

A: Money.

Q: Are there any other advantages?

A: Yes, we don't have a union shop. I don't think I could work in a union shop.

Q: Do you think you are a career man with Lincoln at this time?

A: Yes.

Interview 3

Roger Lewis, a 23-year-old Purdue graduate in mechanical engineering who had been in the Lincoln sales program for 15 months, was working in the Cleveland sales office at the time of the interview.

Q: How did you get your job at Lincoln?

A: I saw that Lincoln was interviewing on campus at Purdue, and I went by. I later came to Cleveland for a plant tour and was offered a job.

Q: Do you know any of the senior executives? Would they know you by name?

A: Yes, I know all of them—Mr. Hastings, Mr. Willis, Mr. Sabo.

APPENDIX LE.4 Employee Interviews (*continued*)

Q: Do you think Lincoln sales representatives work harder than those in other companies?

A: Yes. I don't think there are many sales reps for other companies who are putting in 50- to 60-hour weeks. Everybody here works harder. You can go out in the plant, or you can go upstairs, and there's nobody sitting around.

Q: Do you see any real disadvantage of working at Lincoln?

A: I don't know if it's a disadvantage, but Lincoln is a Spartan company, a very thrifty company. I like that. The sales offices are functional, not fancy.

Q: Why do you think Lincoln employees have such high productivity?

A: Piecework has a lot to do with it. Lincoln is smaller than many plants, too; you can stand in one place and see the materials come in one side and the product go out the other. You feel a part of the company. The chance to get ahead is important, too. They have a strict policy of promoting from within, so you know you have a chance. I think in a lot of other places you may not get as fair a shake as you do here. The sales offices are on a smaller scale, too. I like that. I tell someone that we have two people in the Baltimore office, and they say, "You've got to be kidding." It's smaller and more personal. Pay is the most important thing. I have heard that this is the highest-paying factory in the world.

Interview 4

Jimmy Roberts, a 47-year-old high school graduate who had been with Lincoln 17 years, was working as a multiple drill press operator at the time of the interview.

Q: What jobs have you had at Lincoln?

A: I started out cleaning the men's locker room in 1967. After about a year I got a job in the flux department, where we make the coating for welding rods. I worked there for seven or eight years and then got my present job.

Q: Do you make one particular part?

A: No, there are a variety of parts I make—at least 25.

Q: Each one has a different piece rate attached to it?

A: Yes.

Q: Are some piece rates better than others?

A: Yes.

Q: How do you determine which ones you are going to do?

A: You don't. Your supervisor assigns them.

Q: How much money did you make last year?

A: $53,000.

Q: Have you ever received any kind of award or citation?

A: No.

Q: Was your rating ever over 110?

A: Yes. For the past five years, probably, I made over 110 points.

Q: Is there any attempt to let the others know . . . ?

A: The kind of points I get? No.

Q: Do you know what they are making?

A: No. There are some who might not be too happy with their points and they might make it known. The majority, though, do not make it a point of telling other employees.

Q: Would you be just as happy earning a little less money and working a little slower?

A: I don't think I would, not at this point. I have done piecework all these years, and the fast pace doesn't really bother me.

Q: Why do you think Lincoln productivity is so high?

A: The incentive thing—the bonus distribution. I think that would be the main reason. The paycheck you get every two weeks is important too.

Q: Do you think Lincoln employees would ever join a union?

A: I don't think so. I have never heard anyone mention it.

Q: What is the most important advantage of working here?

A: Amount of money you make. I don't think I could make this type of money anywhere else, especially with only a high school education.

Q: As a black person, do you feel that Lincoln discriminates in any way against blacks?

A: No. I do not think any more so than any other job. Naturally, there is a certain amount of discrimination, regardless of where you are.

(*continued*)

APPENDIX LE.4   Employee Interviews (*continued*)

Interview 5

Joe Trahan, a 58-year-old high school graduate who had been with Lincoln 39 years, was employed as a working supervisor in the tool room at the time of the interview.

Q: Roughly what was your pay last year?

A: Over $56,000, salary, bonus, stock dividends.

Q: How much was your bonus?

A: About $26,000.

Q: Have you ever gotten a special award of any kind?

A: Not really.

Q: What have you done with your money?

A: My house is paid for, and my two cars. I also have some bonds and the Lincoln stock.

Q: What do you think of the executives at Lincoln?

A: They're really top-notch.

Q: What is the major disadvantage of working at Lincoln Electric?

A: I don't know of any disadvantage at all.

Q: Do you think you produce more than most people in similar jobs with other companies?

A: I do believe that.

Q: Why is that? Why do you believe that?

A: We are on the incentive system. Everything we do, we try to improve to make a better product with a minimum of outlay. We try to improve the bonus.

Q: Would you be just as happy making a little less money and not working quite so hard?

A: I don't think so.

Q: Do you think Lincoln employees would ever join a union?

A: I don't think they would ever consider it.

Q: What is the most important advantage of working at Lincoln?

A: Compensation.

Q: Tell me something about Mr. James Lincoln, who died in 1965.

A: You are talking about Jimmy Sr. He always strolled through the shop in his shirtsleeves. Big fellow. Always looked distinguished. Gray hair. Friendly sort of guy. I was a member of the Advisory Board one year. He was there each time.

Q: Did he strike you as really caring?

A: I think he always cared for people.

Q: Did you get any sensation of a religious nature from him?

A: No, not really.

Q: And religion is not part of the program now?

A: No.

Q: Do you think Mr. Lincoln was a very intelligent man, or was he just a nice guy?

A: I would say he was pretty well educated. A great talker—always right off the top of his head. He knew what he was talking about all the time.

Q: When were bonuses for beneficial suggestions done away with?

A: About 18 years ago.

Q: Did that hurt very much?

A: I do not think so, because suggestions are still rewarded through the merit rating system.

Q: Is there anything you would like to add?

A: It's a good place to work. The union kind of ties other places down. At other places, electricians only do electrical work, carpenters only do carpentry work. At Lincoln Electric we all pitch in and do whatever needs to be done.

Q: So a major advantage is not having a union?

A: That's right.

EXHIBIT LE. 2 Letter from the CEO

To Our Shareholders:

Each of you is aware that your company faced enormous challenges in 1993. Those challenges required a focused, creative and positive leadership approach on the part of your management team. As I write this, first quarter 1994 results indicate that the domestic economy is continuing its upward surge. Because of the many tough decisions we had to make in 1993, we are now poised to take advantage of an improved economic climate. Even though much of my personal time has been devoted to overseeing the situation in Europe, excellent results are being achieved in the U.S.A. and Canada.

During 1993, a thorough strategic assessment of our foreign operations led to the conclusion that Lincoln Electric lacked the necessary financial resources to continue to support 21 manufacturing sites. We did not have the luxury of time to keep those plants operating while working to increase our sales and profitability. As a result, with the endorsement of our financial community, the Board of Directors approved management's recommendation to restructure operations in Europe, Latin America, and Japan.

The restructuring included closing the Messer Lincoln operations in Germany; reducing employment throughout Lincoln Norweld, which operates plants in England, France, the Netherlands, Spain, and Norway; and closing manufacturing plants in Venezuela, Brazil, and Japan. The result was a workforce reduction totaling some 770 employees worldwide. We are not abandoning these markets by any means. Rather, the restructuring will allow us to retain and increase sales while relieving us of the high costs associated with excess manufacturing capacity. Now that the restructuring has been accomplished, we operate fifteen plants in ten countries. This capacity will be adequate to supply the inventory needed to support our customers and an increasingly aggressive marketing strategy. We are internationally recognized for outstanding products and service, and we have been certified to the international quality standard ISO-9002.

It was not easy for Lincoln Electric to eliminate manufacturing capacity and jobs. However, I must point out that the overseas companies were given repeated opportunities to turn their performance around. In all fairness, no one anticipated the depth of the recession that continues to devastate Europe, and particularly Germany. But we could not, in good conscience, risk both the continuous erosion of shareholder value and the jobs of our dedicated U.S. employees by remaining unprofitable in these manufacturing operations.

For the second year in the history of this company, it was necessary to take restructuring charges that resulted in a consolidated loss. The restructuring charge totaled $70,100,000 ($40,900,000 after tax), and contributed to a consolidated net loss for 1993 of $38,100,000, compared to a $45,800,000 consolidated loss in 1992.

In 1993 our U.S. and Canadian operations achieved outstanding results with increased levels of sales and profitability and a significant gain in market share. We made a huge step forward by concentrating on the "Top Line" to meet one of our major goals—manufacturing and selling $2.1 million worth of product from our Ohio company each billing day from June 1 through the end of the year. Our Canadian company also made significant contributions with a 38% increase in sales. The bottom line automatically moved into greater profitability.

These impressive gains were not made without sacrifice. Lincoln manufacturing people voluntarily deferred 614 weeks of vacation, worked holidays, and many employees worked a seven-day-a-week schedule to fill the steady stream of orders brought in by the sales department as we capitalized on an emerging domestic economy that we felt was being largely ignored by our major competitors.

This remarkable achievement would never have been possible without the expert management of your President and Chief Operating Officer Frederick W. Mackenbach. His leadership consistently inspired our employees and management team alike. The U.S. company's extraordinary performance encouraged the Board of Directors to approve a gross bonus of $55 million, and to continue the regular quarterly dividend payment throughout the year. As you know, the usual course of action for a company reporting a consolidated loss is to cut or defer bonuses and dividends. That these were paid is a tribute to our Board and their steadfast belief in the long-range, proven benefits of the Incentive Management System.

Thinking in the long term is critical to our progress in a world that too often seems to demand instant solutions to complex problems. Your Chairman, your Board, and your management team are determined to resist that impulse. Currently, Lincoln people around the world are working diligently to formulate a Strategic Plan that will carry this company into the next century. An important element of this business plan will be our new state-of-the-art motor manufacturing facility, which is on schedule. Furthermore, we have strengthened our international leadership with the addition of executives experienced in global management to our Board and to key management posts.

While your company is indeed emerging from a very challenging period in its history, we project excellent results for 1994, with strong sales, increased profits, and the benefits of those developments accruing to shareholders, customers, and employees. As the year proceeds, we will be looking forward to our Centennial in 1995. I am confident that you and I will enjoy celebrating that event together.

Sincerely,
Donald E. Hastings
Chairman and Chief Executive Officer [Retired May 1997]

POSTSCRIPT: In Lincoln Electric's centennial year, 1995, sales topped $1 billion for the first time. It was also the year that Hastings eliminated the two-tier wage plan that was instituted in 1993. Under this plan, new hires started at 75% of the normal pay rate. This plan increased the turnover among the new hires and was regarded as unfair by senior workers.[8] According to one of them, "If an individual shows he can handle the workload, he should be rewarded."

ENDNOTES

Chapter 1

1 R. Levering and M. Moskowitz, "100 Best Companies to Work For 2007—In Good Company," *Fortune* (January 22, 2007): 94–96; R. Levering and M. Moskowitz, "The 100 Best Companies to Work For," *Fortune* (January 8, 2001): 148–168; R. Levering and M. Moskowitz, "The 100 Best Companies to Work For," *Fortune* (January 12, 2004): 56–78; adapted from C. A. O'Reilly III and J. Pfeffer, *Hidden Value: How Great Companies Achieve Extraordinary Results with Ordinary People* (Boston: Harvard Business School Press, 2000): 49–77; D. B. Turban and D. M. Cable, "Firm Reputation and Applicant Pool Characteristics," *Journal of Organizational Behavior* 24 (2003): 733–751; S. Bates, "Seven Organizations Win Double Honors as Great Places to Work," www.shrm.org/hrnews_published/articles/CMS_005603.asp (September 30, 2003).

2 For a recent discussion, see T. M. Jones, W. Felps, and G. A. Bigley, "Ethical Theory and Stakeholder-Related Decisions: The Role of Stakeholder Culture," *Academy of Management Review* 32(1) (2007): 137–155.

3 R. S. Kaplan and D. P. Norton, "Measuring the Strategic Readiness of Intangible Assets," *Harvard Business Review* (February 2004): 52–63.

4 N. Wong, "Let Spirit Guide Leadership," *Workforce* (February 2000): 33–36; C. Handy, "A Better Capitalism," *Across the Board* (April 1998): 16–22.

5 T. M. Welbourne and A. O. Andrews, "Predicting the Performance of Initial Public Offerings: Should Human Resource Management Be in the Equation?" *Academy of Management Journal* 39 (1996): 891–919.

6 D. Whitford, "A Human Place to Work," *Fortune* (January 8, 2001): 108–120.

7 L. Grant, "Happy Workers, Happy Returns," *Fortune* (January 12, 1998): 81. Also see B. Schneider, P. J. Hanges, D. B. Smith, and A. N. Salvaggio, "Which Comes First: Employee Attitudes or Organizational Financial and Market Performance?" *Journal of Applied Psychology* 88(5) (2003): 836–851; G. E. Fryzell and J. Wang, "The Fortune Corporation 'Reputation' Index: Reputation for What?" *Journal of Management* 20 (1994): 1–14.

8 J. K. Harter, F. L. Schmidt, and T. L. Hayes, "Business-Unit-Level Relationship Between Employee Satisfaction, Employee Engagement, and Business Outcomes: A Meta-Analysis," *Journal of Applied Psychology* 87(2) (2002): 268–279. For a recent review, see B. E. Becker and M. A. Huselid, "Strategic Human Resources Management: Where Do We Go From Here?" *Journal of Management* 32(6) (2006): 898–925. For descriptions of other studies that show the linkage between managing human resources and organizational effectiveness, see J. Bae and J. Lawler, "Organizational and HRM Strategies in Korea: Impact on Firm Performance in an Emerging Economy," *Academy of Management Journal* 43(3) (2000): 502–517; B. E. Becker and M. A. Huselid, "High Performance Work Systems and Firm Performance: A Synthesis of Research and Managerial Implications," in G. Ferris (ed.), *Research in Personnel and Human Resources Management* (Greenwich, CT: JAI Press, 1998); and the entire volume of the *Academy of Management Journal*'s "Special Research Forum on Human Resource Management and Organizational Performance," 39(4) (August 1996).

9 Based on data presented in B. E. Becker, M. A. Huselid, and D. Ulrich, *The HR Scorecard: Linking People, Strategy, and Performance* (Boston: Harvard Business School Press, 2001).

10 A. Wilkinson, G. Godfrey, and M. Marchington, "Bouquets, Brickbats and Blinkers: Total Quality Management and Employee Involvement in Practice," *Organization Studies* 18(5) (1997): 799–819.

11 A. Wilkinson, G. Godfrey, and M. Marchington, *Human Capital Management: The CFO's Perspective* (New York: Mercer, 2003).

12 J. W. Johnson, "Linking Employee Perceptions of Service Climate to Customer Satisfaction," *Personnel Psychology* 49 (1996): 831–846.

13 D. A. Schuler and M. Cording, "A Corporate Social Performance—Corporate Financial Performance Behavioral Model for Consumers," *Academy of Management Review* 31(3) (2006): 540–558; R. Abelson, "Welcome Mat Is Out for Gay Investors," *The New York Times* (September 1, 1996): Section 3: 1, 7.

14 S. Bates, "Getting Engaged," *HRMagazine* (February 2004): 44–51.

15 M. A. Friedman, "Friedman Doctrine: The Social Responsibility of Business Is to Increase Its Profits," *The New York Times Magazine* (September 13, 1970): 32ff.

16 J. Brugmann and C. K. Prahalad, "New Social Compact," *Harvard Business Review* (February 2007): 80–90.

17 W. R. Scott, "The Adolescence of Institutional Theory," *Administrative Scientific Quarterly* (1987): 493–511; L. G. Zucker, "Institutional Theories of Organization," *Annual Review of Sociology* (1987): 443–464; J. W. Meyer and B. Rowan, "Institutionalized Organizations: Formal Structure as Myth and Ceremony," *American Journal of Sociology* (1977): 340–363.

18 To learn how researchers attempt to measure corporate social performances, see D. Kirkpatrick, "Looking for Profits in Poverty," *Fortune* (February 5, 2001): 175–176; B. M. Ruf, K. Muralidhar, and K. Paul, "The Development of a Systematic, Aggregate Measure of Corporate Social Performance," *Journal of Management* 24(1) (1998): 119–133.

19 R. Levering and M. Moskowitz, "Fortune 100 Best Companies to Work for 2007—In Good Company" *Fortune* (January 29, 2007): 94–114; L. Uchitelle, *The Disposable American* (New York: Knopf, 2006); E. Frauenheim, "Studies: More Workers Look to Switch Jobs," *Workforce Management* (February 13, 2006): 12.

20 G. Weber, "Preserving the Counter Culture," *Workforce Management* (February 2005): 28–34.

21 E. E. Lawler III, *The Ultimate Advantage: Creating the High Involvement Organization* (San Francisco: Jossey-Bass, 1992); E. E. Lawler III, S. A. Mohrman, and G. E. Ledford, *Employee Involvement in America: An Assessment of Practices and Results* (San Francisco: Jossey-Bass, 1992).

22 E. E. Lawler III, et al., *Employee Involvement and Total Quality Management* (San Francisco: Jossey-Bass, 1992); D. R. Denison, *Corporate Culture and Organizational Effectiveness* (New York: John Wiley, 1990).

23 J. Barney, "Firm Resources and Sustained Competitive Advantage," *Journal of Management* 17(1) (1991): 99–120. See also A. A. Lado, N. G. Boyd, P. Wright, and M. Kroll, "Paradox and Theorizing Within the Resource-Based View," *Academy of Management Review* 31(1) (2006): 115–131.

24 D. P. Shuit, "That Sartain Touch," *Workforce Management* (August 2003): 42–45; B. Leonard, "Ready to Soar," *HRMagazine* (January 2001): 52–56; W. Zellner, "Southwest: After Kelleher, More Blue Skies," *BusinessWeek* (April 2, 2001): 45.

25 D. K. Dutta, J. P. Guthrie, and P. M. Wright, "Human Resource Management and Labor Productivity: Does Industry Matter?" *Academy of Management Journal* 48(1) (2005): 135–145.

26 D. P. Shuit, "People Problems on Every Aisle," *Workforce Management* (February 2004): 26–34.

27 E. R. Demby, "The Insider: Benefits," *Workforce Management* (February 2004): 57–59.

28 For an example of a study that demonstrates the value of aligning human resources with strategic needs, see B. C. Skaggs and M. Youndt, "Strategic Positioning, Human Capital, and Performance in Service Organizations: A Customer Interaction Approach," *Strategic Management Journal* 25 (2004): 85–99.

29 For a detailed case description of HR professionals taking on strategic roles, see R. W. Quinn and W. Brockbank, "The Development of Strategic Human Resource Professionals at BAE Systems," *Human Resource Management* (45)(3) (Fall 2006): 477–494.

30 W. Brockbank, *Human Resource Competency Toolkit* (Alexandria, VA: Society for Human Resource Management/University of Michigan/Global Consulting Alliance, 2003). See also M. E. Graham and L. M. Tarbell, "The Importance of the Employee Perspective in the Competency Development of Human Resource Professionals," *Human Resource Management* 45(3) (Fall 2006): 337–355; B. S. Bell, S. Lee, and S. K. Yeung, "The Impact of E-HR on Professional Competency in HRM: Implications for the Development of HR Professionals," *Human Resource Management* 45(3) (Fall 2006): 295–308.

31 C. Brewster, E. Farndale, and J. van Ommeren, "HR Competencies and Professional Standards," *World of Federation Personnel Management Associations* (June 2000).

32 B. Leonard, "Gallup: Workplace Bias Still Prevalent," *HRMagazine* (February 2006): 34; A. K. Monrad, P. Prasad, *Handbook of Workplace Diversity* (Thousand Oaks, CA: Sage, 2006).

33 D. R. Briscoe, E. Claus, and R. S. Schuler, *International Human Resource Management*, 3rd ed. (London: Routledge, 2008); N. Adler and S. Bartholomew, "Managing Globally Competent People," *Academy of Management Executive* 6 (1992): 52–65.

34 C. Gomez, "The Influence of Environmental, Organizational, and HRM Factors on Employee Behaviors in Subsidiaries: A Mexican Case Study of Organizational Learning," *Journal of World Business* 39 (2004): 1–11.

35 R. Berenbeim, *Universal Conduct: An Ethics and Compliance Benchmarking Survey* (New York: The Conference Board: 2006).

36 "J. M. Smucker Co.," *Workforce Management* (March 13, 2006): 19.

37 For a recent review, see L. K. Treviño, G. R. Weaver, and S. J. Reynolds, "Behavioral Ethics in Organizations: A Review," *Journal of Management* 32 (2006): 951–990.

38 M. Huselid, B. Becker, and R. Beatty, *The Workforce Scorecard* (Boston: Harvard Business School Press, 2005); B. Becker, M. Huselid, and D. Ulrich, *The HR Scorecard* (Boston: Harvard Business School Press, 2001); also see www.metrus.com.

39 C. Salter, "She's Got Their Number," *Fast Company* (February 2007): 100–103, 108.

40 *Ibid.*

41 H. G. Gueutal and D. L. Stone, *The Brave New World of eHR* (Indianapolis: Jossey-Bass, 2005).

42 R. Cardy and J. Miller, "eHR and Performance Management: A Consideration of Positive Potential and the Dark Side," in H. G. Gueutal and D. L. Stone, *The Brave New World of eHR* (Indianapolis: Jossey-Bass, 2005).

43 P. Evans, V. Pucik, and J. L. Barsoux, *The Global Challenge. Frameworks for International Human Resource Management* (Boston: McGraw Hill, 2002); M. Gottfredson and K. Aspinall, "Innovation Versus Complexity: What Is Too Much of a Good Thing?" *Harvard Business Review* (November 2005): 62–73; *9th Annual Global CEO Survey: Globalisation and Complexity.* (New York: Pricewaterhousecoopers, 2006); L. Bryan and M. Zanini, "Strategy in an Era of Global Giants," *McKinsey Quarterly* (Fall 2005, 4): 25–36.

44 *Ibid.*

Chapter 2

1 "Face Value: Green Revolutionary," *The Economist* (April 7, 2007): 66; R. L. Boehm, "Leading Change: An Interview with the CEO of Deere & Company," *The McKinsey Quarterly Web Exclusive* (December 2006), www.mckinseyquarterly.com; John Deere Web site, www.deere.com (September 4, 2007).

2 Based on Mercer HR Consulting, "Cost-Cutting Shifts the Terrain," *Workforce Management* (December 2003): 86. Mercer Web site accessed at www.mercerHR.com.

3 S. Diesenhouse, "To Save Factories, Owners Diversify," *The New York Times* (November 30, 2003): BU5.

4 More details about trends in offshoring can be found in H. Scullion and D. Collings, *Global Staffing* (London: Routledge: 2006); J. Schramm, "Offshoring: SHRM Research Report," *Workplace Visions* 2 (2004): 1–8.

5 R. Miller and P. Engardio, "The Job Drain: Is It China's Fault?" *BusinessWeek* (October 13, 2003): 32–35.

6 G. Smith and C. Lindblad, "A Tale of What Free Trade Can and Cannot Do," *BusinessWeek* (December 22, 2003): 66–72; T. Stundza, "Trade Approaches $600 Billion," *Purchasing* (March 9, 2000): 70; see also http://www.exportvirginia.org/FastFacts/FastFacts_2007/ff_nafta_2007.pdf (September 12, 2007).

7 P. Krugman, "Toyota, Moving Northward," *The New York Times* (July 25, 2005): A19.

8 J. Schramm, "Does Europe Matter?" *Workplace Visions* (January 2004): 1–7.

9 C. H. Conde, "China and ASEAN in Services Pact," *The New York Times* (January 15, 2007): C2; based on information provided at the ASEAN home page, www.aseansec.org/home.htm (January 20, 2004).

10 N. Rogovsky, "Socially Sensitive Enterprise Restructuring" (Geneva: ILO, 2005), accessed at http://www.ilo.org/global/About_the_ILO/Media_and_public_information/Press_releases/lang—en/WCMS_075541/index.htm.

11 P. W. Hurst and W. C. Mills, "Ethical Behavior," accessed at www.ispi.org (November–December 2005).

12 K. Lucenko, "Strategies for Growth," *Across the Board* (September 2000): 63; I. M. Jawahar and G. L. McLaughlin, "Toward a Descriptive Stakeholder Theory: An Organizational Life Cycle Approach," *Academy of Management Review* 26 (2001): 397–414.

13 F. Hansen, "Balancing the Global Workforce," *Workforce Management* (December 11, 2006): 44–67.

14 R. S. Schuler, S. E. Jackson, and Y. Luo, *Managing Human Resources in Cross-Border Alliances* (London: Routledge: 2004); American Staffing Association (www.staffingtoday.net); "An Army of Surplus Labor," *Workforce Management* (December 2003): 96.

15 R. S. Schuler and S. E. Jackson, "HR Issues in Mergers and Acquisitions," *European Management Journal* (June 2001): 59–73.

16 For a discussion, see J. M. Shaver, "A Paradox of Synergy: Contagion and Capacity Effects in Mergers and Acquisitions," *Academy of Management Review* 31(4): 962–976.

17 R. S. Schuler, S. E. Jackson, and Y. Luo, *Managing Human Resources in Cross-Border Alliances* (London: Routledge: 2004); J. Bower, "Not All M & A's Are Alike—and That Matters," *Harvard Business Review* (March 2001): 93–101.

18 R. S. Schuler, S. E. Jackson, and Y. Luo, *Managing Human Resources in Cross-Border Alliances* (London: Routledge: 2004). For a full discussion of reasons for failure, see M. A. Hitt, R. D. Ireland, and R. E. Hoskisson, *Strategic Management: Competitiveness and Globalization* (Cincinnati, OH: Thompson South-Western, 2007).

19 R. S. Schuler, S. E. Jackson, and Y. Luo, *Managing Human Resources in Cross-Border Alliances* (London: Routledge: 2004).

20 R. S. Schuler, S. E. Jackson, and Y. Luo, *Managing Human Resources in Cross-Border Alliances* (London: Routledge: 2004).

21 R. S. Schuler, S. E. Jackson, and Y. Luo, *Managing Human Resources in Cross-Border Alliances* (London: Routledge: 2004). See also Emerge International, accessed at www.emergeinternational.com (accessed September 4, 2007).

22 For a detailed discussion of labor market trends and their implications for human resource management, see P. Coy and J. Ewing, "Where Are All the Workers?" *BusinessWeek* (April 9, 2007): 28–31; H. Scullion and D. Collings, *Global Staffing* (London: Routledge, 2006).

23 Corporate Leadership Council, "Managing the Workforce Planning Process" (August 2004); Hewitt International Report (October 2003); A. Bernstein, "Too Many Workers? Not for Long," *BusinessWeek* (May 2002): 126–130; D. Patel, *Workplace Forecast: A Strategic Outlook 2002–2003* (Alexandria, VA: SHRM Research, 2002); D. Patel, "Globalization," *Workplace Visions* 5 (2002): 1–8; for a contrarian's point of view, see A. Overbolt, "The Labor-Shortage Myth," *Fast Company* (August 2004): 23–24.

24 Based on data from the Bureau of Labor Statistics (www.bls.gov/emp). Also see projections made by the American Education Services (www.educationplanner.com).

25 For a detailed analysis of labor shortages, see E. Porter, "Coming Soon: The Vanishing Work Force," *The New York Times* (August 29, 2004): Section 3, 1; P. Coy, "Old, Smart, Productive," *BusinessWeek* (June 27, 2005): 78–86; R. Herman, T. Olivo, and J. Gioia, *Impending Crisis: Too Many Jobs, Too Few People* (Winchester, VA: Oakhill Press, 2003).

26 G. E. Gibson, Jr., A. Davis-Blake, K. E. Dickson, and B. Mentel, "Workforce Demographics Among Project Engineering Professionals—Crisis Ahead?" *Journal of Management in Engineering* (October 2003): 173–182.

27 A. Overholt, "The Hippest City in the USA?: Des Moines," *Fast Company* (October 2003): 96–98.

28 A. T. Mosisa, "The Role of Foreign-Born Workers in the U.S. Economy," *Monthly Labor Review* (May 2002): 3–14.

29 J. Barron, "88 Keys, Many Languages, One Proud Name: Workers at Steinway Reflect the Changing Face of New York," *The New York Times* (October 6, 2003): B1; also visit Steinway's Web site at www.steinway.com.

30 D. R. Briscoe, E. Claus, and R. S. Schuler, *International Human Resource Management*, 3rd ed. (London: Routledge, 2008); P. Christopher Earley and S. Ang, *Cultural Intelligence: Individual Interactions Across Cultures* (Stanford, CA: Stanford University Press, 2003); J. Hooker, *Working Across Cultures* (Stanford, CA: Stanford University Press, 2003).

31 J. Murray, "IBM Moves to Promote Offshoring," *IT Week* (May 19, 2005), Vnunet.com at www.vnunet.com; C. Hawn, "Offshore Storm: The Global Razor's Edge," *Fast Company* (February 2004): 27; W. M. Bulkeley, "IBM Data Give Rare Look at Sensitive 'Offshoring' Plans," *CNN Money* (January 19, 2004), money.cnn.com/services/ticherkeadlines/for5/200401190053DOIWJONESONLINE.

32 L. R. Gomez-Mejia and S. Werner, *Global Compensation* (London: Routledge, 2008); "Slow Growth Shapes Policies," *Workforce Management* (December 2003): 136. Chart based on data from the Bureau of Labor Statistics.

33 National Center for Education Statistics, *Trends in International Mathematics and Science Study, 1999* (February 12, 2004), accessed at nces.ed.gov/timss/results.asp. See also A. M. Konrad and J. R. Deckop, "Human Resource Management Trends in the United States: Challenges in the Midst of Prosperity," *International Journal of Manpower* (August 2001).

34 S. Rosen, J. Simon, J. R. Vincent, W. McLeod, M. Fox, and D. M. Thea, "AIDS Is Your Business," *Harvard Business Review* (February 2003): 80–87, accessed at http://hbswk.hbs.edu/archive/3338.html.

35 For detailed discussions of the HR issues faced by employers in Africa, including those associated with HIV/AIDS, see K. Kamoche, Y. Debrah, F. Horwitz, and G. N. Muuka, *Managing Human Resources in Africa* (London: Routledge, 2004).

36 See D. R. Briscoe, E. Claus, and R. S. Schuler, *International Human Resource Management,* 3rd ed. (London: Routledge, 2008).

37 Based on descriptions in G. Apfelthaler, H. J. Muller, and R. R. Rehder, "Corporate Global Culture as a Competitive Advantage: Learning from Germany and Japan in Alabama and Austria," *Journal of World Business* 37 (2002): 108–118.

38 B. Kabanoff and J. P. Daly, "Values Espoused by Australian and U.S. Organizations," *Applied Psychology: An International Review* 49(2) (2000): 284–314.

39 C. L. Ahmadjian and P. Robinson, "Safety in Numbers: Downsizing and the Deinstitutionalization of Permanent Employment in Japan," *Administrative Science Quarterly* (December 2001): 623–654.

40 R. Tung and V. Worm, "East Meets West: Northern European Expatriates in China," *Business and the Contemporary World* 9 (1997): 137–148; and N. Rogovsky and R. S. Schuler, "Managing Human Resources Across Cultures," *Business and the Contemporary World* 9 (1997): 63–75.

41 M. Javidan and R. J. House, "Cultural Acumen for the Global Manager: Lessons from Project GLOBE," *Organizational Dynamics* 29(4) (2001): 289–305; R. J. House, P. J. Hanges, M. Javidan, P. W. Dorfman, and V. Gupta, *Culture, Leadership, and Organizations: The GLOBE Study of 62 Societies* (Thousand Oaks, CA: Sage, 2004). For extensive descriptions of these generations and suggestions for managing them, see "Connecting Across the Generations in the Workplace," *Deloitte Talent Market Series: Volume 1* (2005); "Generational Talent Management—Strategies to Attract and Engage Generation Y in the U.S. Banking & Securities Industries," *Deloitte Report* (2006); "Who Are the Millenials? a.k.a. Generation Y," *Deloitte Report* (2005).

42 Z. Aycan, R. Kanungo, M. Mendonca, K. Yu, J. Deller, G. Stahl, and A. Kurshid, "Impact of Culture on Human Resource Management Practices: A 10-Country Comparison," *Applied Psychology: An International Review* 49 (2000): 192–221. For detailed descriptions of these differences, see P. R. Sparrow, C. Brewster, and H. Harris, *Globalizing Human Resource Management* (London: Routledge, 2004); P. Budhwar, *Managing Human Resources in Asia-Pacific* (London: Routledge, 2004); H. H. Larsen and W. Mayrhofer, *Managing Human Resources in Europe* (London: Routledge, 2006); M. Elvira and A. Dávila, *Managing Human Resources in Latin America* (London: Routledge, 2005).

43 E. F. Stone-Romero, D. L. Stone, and E. Salas, "The Influence of Culture on Role Conceptions and Role Behavior in Organizations," *Applied Psychology: An International Review* 52(3) (2003): 328–362; R. W. Brislin and E. S. Kim, "Cultural Diversity in People's Understanding and Uses of Time," *Applied Psychology: An International Review* 52(3) (2003): 363–382.

44 C. Robert, T. M. Probst, J. J. Martoccio, F. Glasgow, and J. J. Lawler, "Empowerment and Continuous Improvement in the United States, Mexico, Poland, and India: Predicting Fit on the Basis of Dimensions of Power Distance and Individualism," *Journal of Applied Psychology* 85 (2000): 643–658.

45 K. L. Newman and S. D. Nollen, "Culture and Congruence: The Fit Between Management Practices and National Culture," *Journal of International Business Studies* (1996): 753–776.

46 D. A. Wren, *The Evolution of Management Thought* (New York: John Wiley, 1994).

47 A. Berstein, "Low-Skilled Jobs: Do They Have to Move?" *BusinessWeek* (February 26, 2001): 94.

48 N. D. Schwartz, "Down and Out in White-Collar America," *Fortune* (June 23, 2003): 79–83; R. B. Reich, "High-Tech Jobs Are Going Abroad! But That's Okay," www.washingtonpost.com (November 2, 2003).

49 Adapted from C. Sulter, "On the Road Again," *Fast Company* (January 2002): 58.

50 W. F. Cascio, "Managing a Virtual Workplace," *Academy of Management Executive* 14(3) (2000): 81–90; see also A. J. Walker, "Visions of the Future: The Workforce of the Future," *IHRM Journal* (October–December 2000): 8–12.

51 A. Taylor III, "A Tale of Two Factories," *Fortune* (September 18, 2006): 118–126; C. Huff, "Framing a New Culture," *Workforce Management* (May 8, 2006): 28–36; "H&R Block: Aligning and Communicating Values to Enhance Organizational Culture," *Corporate Leadership Council* (August 2004). The Corporate Leadership Council Web page is accessed at www.corporateleadershipcouncil.com.

52 C. L. Bernick, "When Your Culture Needs a Makeover," *Harvard Business Review* (June 2001): 53–64.

53 P. Babcock, "Is Your Company Two-Faced?" *HRMagazine* (January 2004): 43–52.

54 J. F. Budd, Jr., "A Vision of a Mission," *Across the Board* (July–August 2001): 8.

55 B. Schlender, "Ballmer Unbound," *Fortune* (January 26, 2004): 117–124.

56 Refer to the Web site of Deere & Company: www.deere.com.

57 L. Soupata, "Integration Versus Extraction Mentality: Sustainable Development on a Global Scale," speech given on June 4, 2003, www.pressroom.ups.com/execforum/speeches/speech/text/0,1403,481,00.html.

58 R. Levering and M. Moskowitz, "The 100 Best Companies to Work For," *Fortune* (January 12, 2004): 57–78.

59 L. C. Lancaster and D. Stillman, *When Generations Collide* (New York: Harper Business, 2002); T. Gutner, "A Balancing Act for Gen X Women," *BusinessWeek* (January 21, 2002): 82; W. G. Bennis and R. J. Thomas, *Geeks and Geezers: How Era, Values and Defining Moments Shape Leaders* (Boston: Harvard Business School Press, 2002); C. Loughlin and J. Barling, "Young Workers' Work Values, Attitudes, and Behaviors," *Journal of Occupational and Organizational Psychology* 74 (2001): 543–558.

60 B. Burlingham, "What's Your Culture Worth?" *Inc.* (September 2001): 133; B. Burlingham, *A Stake in the Outcome* (New York: Doubleday, 2002).

61 S. Wetlaufer, "Common Sense and Conflict: An Interview with Disney's Michael Eisner," *Harvard Business Review* (January–February 2000): 113–124.

62 C. Daniels, "The Most Powerful Black Executives in America," *Fortune* (July 22, 2002): 60–80; visit www.deloitte.com for more information on diversity.

63 S. Foley, D. L. Kidder, and G. N. Powell, "The Perceived Glass Ceiling and Just Perceptions: An Investigation of Hispanic Law Associates," *Journal of Management* 28 (2002): 471–496.

64 S. N. Mehta, "What Minorities Really Want," *Fortune* (July 10, 2000): 181–186; E. LaBlanc, L. Vanderkam, and K. Vella-Zarb, "America's Best 50 Companies for Minorities," *Fortune* (July 10, 2000): 190–200.

65 K. H. Griffeth and M. R. Hebl, "The Disclosure Dilemma for Gay Men and Lesbians: 'Coming Out' at Work," *Journal of Applied Psychology* 87 (2002): 1191–1199.

66 This definition is adapted from the one provided by M. A. Hitt, R. D. Ireland, and R. E. Hoskisson, *Strategic Management: Competitiveness and Globalization* (Cincinnati, OH: Thompson South-Western, 2007).

67 R. S. Kaplan and D. P. Norton, *Strategy Maps: Converting Intangible Assets into Tangible Outcomes* (Boston: Harvard Business School Press, 2004).

68 R. S. Kaplan and D. P. Norton, "Having Trouble with Your Strategy? Then Map It," *Harvard Business Review* (September–October 2000): 167–176; B. E. Becker, M. A. Huselid, and D. Ulrich, *The HR Scorecard: Linking People, Strategy and Performance* (Boston: Harvard Business School Press, 2001).

69 R. Forrester, "Empowerment: Rejuvenating a Potent Idea," *Academy of Management Executive* 14(3) (2000): 67–73.

70 Adapted from H. W. Lane, M. B. Brechu, and D. T. A. Wesley, "Mabe's President Luis Berrondo Avalos on Teams and Industry Competitiveness," *Academy of Management Executive* 13(3) (1999): 8–10, and www.mabe .com.mx (May 2007); see also N. Athanassiou, W. F. Crittenden, L. M. Kelly, and P. Marquez, "Founder Centrality Effects on the Mexican Family Top Management's Group. Firm Culture, Strategic Vision and Goals, and Firm Performance," *Journal of World Business* 37 (2002): 139–150.

71 B. Schneider, S. A. Young, and W. H. Macey, "Corporate Service Intelligence: What It Is, Why It Is Important, How to Measure It, and How to Make It Happen," Valero Corp. Working Paper 2005, *MIT Sloan Management Review* 47(3) (Spring 2006): 5; B. Schneider, "Services Management," in W. B. Rouse (ed.), *Enterprise Transformation: Understanding and Enabling Fundamental Change* (New York: John Wiley, 2006), 161–173; B. Schneider, S. S. White, *Service Quality: Research Perspectives* (Thousand Oaks, CA: Sage, 2004); B. Schneider, M. W. Ehrhart, D. E. Mayer, J. Saltz, K. A. Niles-Jolly, "Understanding Organizational–Customer Links in Service Settings," *Academy of Management Journal* (48): 1017–1032.

72 B. L. Kirkman, B. Rosen, C. B. Gibson, P. E. Tesluk, and S. O. McPherson, "Five Challenges to Virtual Team Success: Lessons from Sabre, Inc.," *Academy of Management Executive* 16(3) (2002): 67–79; for more suggestions about leading virtual teams, see the entire issue of *Organizational Dynamics* 31(4) (2003), which is devoted to this topic.

73 S. E. Ante, "The New Blue," *BusinessWeek* (March 17, 2003): 80–88; S. E. Ante and I. Sager, "IBM's New Boss," *BusinessWeek* (February 11, 2002), accessed at www.businessweek.com/magazine/content/02_06/ b3769001.htm (April 25, 2003).

74 A. Aston, "Who Will Run the Plants?" *BusinessWeek* (January 22, 2007): 78; A. Fisher, "Retain Your Brains," *Fortune* (July 24, 2006): 49–50; D. W. DeLong, *Lost Knowledge: Confronting The Threat of an Aging Workforce* (Oxford: Oxford University Press: 2004); A. Fisher, "Have You Outgrown Your Job?," *Fortune* (August 21, 2006): 46–56; "Special Report: The Aging Workforce," *The Economist* (February 18, 2006): 65–67; "How to manage an aging workforce," *The Economist* (February 18, 2006): 11; "Insurance and Pensions," *Knowledge@Wharton*, knowledge.wharton.upenn.edu (accessed January 27, 2005); J. Garten, "Keep Boomers on the Job," *BusinessWeek* (November 14, 2005): 162; E. Frauenheim, "False Alarm," *Workforce Management* (October 9, 2006): 22–26; "The Aging of the U.S. Workforce: Employer Challenges and Responses," *Ernst & Young Report* (January 2006).

75 "Older Workers—Some Best Practices and Strategies for Engaging and Retaining Older Workers," statement of Comptroller General of the United States David M. Walker, United States Government Accountability Office, testimony given before the U.S. Senate Special Committee on Aging (February 28, 2007).

76 "The New Titans, A Survey of the World Economy," *The Economist* (September 16, 2006).

77 M. Arndt and G. Smith, "Emerging Giants," *BusinessWeek* (July 31, 2006).

78 T. L. Friedman, *The World Is Flat: A Brief History of the Twenty-First Century* (New York: Farrar, Straus and Giroux, 2005).

79 R. S. Schuler and I. Tarique, "International Human Resource Management: A Thematic Update and Suggestions for Future Research," *International Journal of Human Resource Management* (May 2007); M. A. Hitt, L. Tihanyi, T. Miller, and B. Connelly, "International Diversification: Antecedents, Outcomes, and Moderators," *Journal of Management* 32(6) (December 2006): 831–867.

80 *Ibid.*

81 W. Zellner, "Lessons from a Faded Levi Strauss," *BusinessWeek* (December 15, 2003): 44; K. Schoenberger, "Tough Jeans, a Soft Heart and Frayed Earnings," *The New York Times* (June 25, 2000): Section 3: 1, 12, 13; J. Makower, *Beyond the Bottom Line: Putting Social Responsibility to Work for Your Business and the World* (New York: Simon & Schuster, 1994).

Chapter 3

1 The authors thank Bill Maki for his descriptions of the Weyerhaeuser transformation process. See also www.weyerhaeuser.com for more historical and contemporary information.

2 J. Collison and C. Frangos, *Aligning HR with Organization Strategy Survey* (Alexandria, VA: Society for Human Resource Management, 2002); M. Beer and N. Nohria, "Cracking the Code of Change," *Harvard Business Review* (May–June 2000): 133–141.

3 S. F. Gale, "For ERP Success, Create a Culture Change," *Workforce* (September 2002): 80–83.

4 C. H. Deutsch, "Paper Jam at FedEx Kinko's," *The New York Times* (May 5, 2007): C1, C4.

5 Radical change is also referred to as discontinuous or fundamental change, retrofitting, transformation, and change and reinvention. Incremental change is also referred to as evolutionary change. See E. E. Lawler III and C. G. Worley, *Built to Change: How to Achieve Sustained Organizational Effectiveness* (San Francisco: Jossey-Bass, 2006).

6 M. Langley, "Inside Mulally's 'War Room': A Radical Overhaul of Ford," *The Wall Street Journal* (December 22, 2006): A1; G. Colvin, "Managing in Chaos," *Fortune* (October 2, 2006): 76–82; R. Gupta and J. Wendler, "Leading Change: An Interview with the CEO of P&G," *The McKinsey Quarterly Web Exclusive*, www.mckinseyquarterly.com (July 2005).

7 M. Beer and N. Nohria, *Breaking the Code of Change* (Boston: Harvard Business School Press, 2000); R. A. Johnson, "Antecedents and Outcomes of Corporate Refocusing," *Journal of Management* 22 (1996): 439–483.

8 Adapted from T. Lowry, "Can MTV Stay Cool?" *BusinessWeek* (February 20, 2006): 51–60; J. Hibbard, "Electronic Media: Judy McGrath" *Television Week* (April 10, 2006): 36; www.viacom.com/MTVnetwork (May 5, 2007).

9 "Improving Strategic Planning: A McKinsey Survey," *McKinsey Quarterly Survey of Business Executives* (July–August 2006); P. J. Brews and M. R. Hunt, "Learning to Plan and Planning to Learn: Resolving the Planning School/Learning School Debate," *Strategic Management*

Journal 20 (1999): 889–913; A. Van De Ven, H. Angle, and M. S. Poole, *Research on the Management Innovation* (Oxford University Press, 2000).

10 Adapted from S. E. Jackson and R. S. Schuler, "Turning Knowledge into Business Advantage," *Financial Times* (January 15, 2001): Mastering Management supplement. Copyright held by S. E. Jackson and R. S. Schuler. Used with permission.

11 J. Chatman, C. A. O'Reilly III, V. Chan, "Cisco Systems: Developing a Human Capital Strategy," *California Management Review* 47(2) (Winter 2005): 137–167.

12 "More Companies Turn to Workforce Planning to Boost Productivity and Efficiency," *The Conference Board*, available at www.conference-board .org (August 7, 2006); P. J. Robertson, D. R. Roberts, and J. I. Porras, "Dynamics of Planned Change: Assessing Empirical Support for a Theoretical Model," *Academy of Management Journal* 36 (1993): 619–663.

13 R. S. Schuler, S. E. Jackson, and Y. Luo, *Managing Human Resources in Cross-Border Alliances* (London: Routledge, 2004); Corporate Executive Board, *M&A Communications—Toward a Common Culture* (Washington, DC: Corporate Executive Board, 2002); Corporate Executive Board, *Best Practices in Acquiring Companies* (Washington, DC: Corporate Executive Board, 2002); J. Birkinshaw, H. Bresman, and L. Hakanson, "Managing the Post-Acquisition Integration Process: How the Human Integration and Task Integration Processes Interact to Foster Value Creation," *Journal of Management Studies* 37 (2000): 395–425; M. L. Marks and P. H. Mirvis, "Making Mergers and Acquisitions Work: Strategic and Psychological Preparation," *Academy of Management Executive* 15(2) (2000): 80–92. See also Emerge International (www.emergeinternational.com) for more tips on cultural integration.

14 K. Troy, *Change Management: Striving for Customer Value: A Research Report* (New York: The Conference Board, 1996).

15 S. P. Kirn, A. J. Rucci, M. A. Huselid, and B. E. Becker, "Strategic Human Resource Management at Sears," *Human Resource Management* 38 (1999): 329–336; A. J. Rucci, S. P. Kirn, and R. T. Quinn, "The Employee-Customer-Profit Chain at Sears," *Harvard Business Review* (January–February 1998): 82–97.

16 Adapted from R. S. Schuler, S. E. Jackson, and J. Storey, "HRM and Its Link with Strategic Management," in J. Storey (ed.), *Human Resource Management: A Critical Text* (London: Blackwell, 2001), 137–159.

17 For example, see "More Companies Turn to Workforce Planning to Boost Productivity and Efficiency," *The Conference Board*, available at www.conference-board.org (August 7, 2006); M. Baer and M. Frese, "Innovation Is Not Enough: Climates for Initiative and Psychological Safety, Process Innovations, and Firm Performance," *Journal of Organizational Behavior* 24 (2003): 45–68; K. M. B. Gravenhorst, R. A. Werkman, and J. J. Boonstra, "The Change Capacity of Organizations: General Assessment and Five Configurations," *Applied Psychology: An International Review* 52(1) (2003): 83–105.

18 "Improving Strategic Planning: A McKinsey Survey," *McKinsey Quarterly Survey of Business Executives* (July–August 2006); S. Fegley, *2006 Strategic HR Management: Survey Report* (Alexandria, VA: Society for Human Resource Management, 2006).

19 D. Creedman, "Six Easy Pieces," *Workforce Management* (May 2005): 59–62.

20 J. Kirby, "Reinvention with Respect: An Interview with Jim Kelly of UPS," *Harvard Business Review* (November 2001): 116–123; M. Beer and N. Nohria, "Cracking the Code of Change," *Harvard Business Review* (May–June 2000): 133–141.

21 J. W. Hedge, W. C. Borman, and S. E. Lammlein, *The Aging Workforce* (Washington, DC: American Psychological Association, 2006).

22 J. Collison and C. Frangos, *Aligning HR with Organization Strategy Survey* (Alexandria, VA: Society for Human Resource Management, 2002); P. J. Brews and M. R. Hunt, "Learning to Plan and Planning to Learn: Resolving the Planning School/Learning School Debate," *Strategic Management Journal* 20 (1999): 889–913. See also J. Waclawski and A. H. Church, *Organizational Development: Data Driven Methods for Change* (San Francisco: Jossey-Bass, 2002).

23 "Leading Change: An Interview with the CEO of P&G," *The McKinsey Quarterly Web Exclusive*, available at www.mckinseyquarterly.com (July 2005).

24 J. R. Stengel, A. L. Dixon, and C. T. Allen, "Listening Begins at Home," *Harvard Business Review* (November 2003): 106–117; R. Berner, "How A. G. Lafley Is Revolutionizing a Bastion of Corporate Conservatism," *BusinessWeek* (July 7, 2003): 52–63.

25 M. Meyers, "Panel Unconvinced of a Baby-Boom Bust," *Star Tribune* (July 11, 2006): D1.

26 D. Phillips, "Freight-Car Congestion Is Worrying Union Pacific," *The New York Times,* (March 31, 2004): C1, C4.

27 For more information about this survey and about the Malcolm Baldrige Award, visit the Web site of the National Institute of Standards and Technology at www.quality.nist.gov.

28 B. Mike and J. W. Slocum, Jr., "Slice of Reality: Changing Culture at Pizza Hut and Yum! Brands, Inc.," *Organizational Dynamics* 32(4) (2003): 319–330.

29 T. M. Begley and D. P. Boyd, "Articulating Corporate Values Through Human Resource Policies," *Business Horizons* (July–August 2000): 8–12.

30 N. Adler, L. Brody, and J. Osland, "The Women's Global Leadership Forum: Enhancing One Company's Global Leadership Capability," *Human Resource Management* 39(2–3) (Summer–Fall 2000): 209–225.

31 R. S. Kaplan and D. P. Norton, *The Strategy-Focused Organization: How Balanced Scorecard Companies Thrive in the New Business Environment* (Boston: Harvard Business Press, 2000); B. E. Becker, M. A. Huselid, and D. Ulrich, *The HR Scorecard: Linking People, Strategy, and Performance* (Boston, MA: Harvard Business School Press, 2001); C. Creelman, "Mark Huselid and the HR Balanced Scorecard," HR.com, available at www .hr.com/Hrcom/index.cfm/WeeklyMag/ (February 20, 2001).

32 M. A. West, C. Borrill, J. Dawson, J. Scully, M. Carter, S. Anelay, M. Patterson, and J. Waring, "The Link Between the Management of Employees and Patient Mortality in Acute Hospitals," *International Human Resource Management* 13 (December 2002): 1299–1310.

33 A. Farham, "Worst Airline?" *Forbes* (June 11, 2001): 105–115; G. Bethune and S. Huler, *From Worst to First: Behind the Scenes of Continental's Remarkable Comeback* (New York: John Wiley, 1999); M. Maynard, "Chief Executive of Continental to Step Down," *The New York Times* (January 17, 2004): E1.

34 For data about the types of HR metrics used most often, see S. Fegley, *2006 Strategic HR Management: Survey Report* (Alexandria, VA: Society for Human Resource Management, 2006).

35 For more discussion about HR metrics, see J. Fitz-Enz, *ROI of Human Capital: Measuring the Economic Value of Employee Performance* (New York: AMACOM, 2000); B. E. Becker, M. A. Huselid, and D. Ulrich, *The HR Scorecard* (Boston: Harvard Business School Press, 2001).

36 M. Hammers, "SunTrust Bank Combines 28 Recruiting and Screening Systems into One," *Workforce Management* (November 2003): 59–60. Also visit SunTrust's Web site at www.suntrust.com.

37 H. Fischer and K. D. Mittorp, "How HR Measures Support Risk Management: The Deutsche Bank Example," *Human Resource Management* 41 (2002): 477–490.

38 J. Chatman, C. A. O'Reilly III, and V. Chan, "Cisco Systems: Developing a Human Capital Strategy," *California Management Review* 47(2) (Winter 2005): 137–167.

39 M. Conlin, "Where Layoffs Are a Last Resort," *BusinessWeek* (October 8, 2001): 42.

40 W. J. Baumol, A. S. Blinder, and E. N. Wolff, *Downsizing in America: Reality, Causes, and Consequence* (New York: Russell Sage Foundation, 2003).

41 R. L. Knowdell, E. Branstead, and M. Moravec, *From Downsizing to Recovery—Strategic Transition Options for Organizations and Individuals* (Palo Alto, CA: CPP Books, 1994).

42 E. Zimmerman, "Why Deep Layoffs Hurt Long-Term Recovery," *Workforce* (November 2001): 48–53. A detailed discussion of internal labor markets can be found in L. T. Pinfield and M. F. Berner, "Employment Systems: Toward a Coherent Conceptualization of Internal Labor Markets," *Research in Personnel and Human Resource Management* 12 (1994): 41–78.

43 D. Greenlees, "Filipinos Are Taking More Calls in Outsourcing Boom," *The New York Times* (November 24, 2006): C4.

44 P. Engardio, "The Future of Outsourcing," *BusinessWeek* (January 30, 2006): 50–64; D. Farrel, N. Kaka, and S. Sturze, "Ensuring India's Offshoring Future," *The McKinsey Quarterly*, available at www.mckinseyquarterly .com (2005).

45 M. Frase-Blunt, "Call Centers Come Home," *HRMagazine* (January 2007): 85–89; L. G. Klaff, "An Ever-Changing Workforce Management Landscape," *Workforce Management*, available at www.workforce.com (December 2006); S. E. Ante, "Shifting Work Offshore? Outsourcer Beware," *BusinesssWeek* (January 12, 2004): 36–37 ; A. Meisler, "Think Globally, Act Rationally," *Workforce Management* (January 2004): 40–45; F. Vogelstein, "Silicon Valley's Hiring! (and Firing)," *Fortune* (June 23, 2003): 86.

46 P. Cappelli, "Labor Shortage? What Labor Shortage?" *HRMagazine* (October 2003): 12; D. P. Lepak, R. Takeuchi, and S. A. Snell, "Employment Flexibility and Firm Performance: Examining the Interaction Effects of Employment Mode, Environmental Dynamism, and Technological Intensity," *Journal of Management* 29(5) (2003): 681–703; M. C. Kernan and P. J. Hanges, "Survivor Reactions to Reorganization: Antecedents and Consequences of Procedural, Interpersonal, and Informational Justice," *Journal of Applied Psychology* 87(5) (2002): 916–928; "Companies Continue to Increase Staff Size," *HRMagazine* (January 2001): 35–36; "To Cut or Not to Cut," *The Economist* (February 10, 2001): 61–62; S. Kuczynski, "Help! I Shrunk the Company," *HRMagazine* (June 1999): 40–45.

47 F. Hansen, "Balancing the Global Workforce," *Workforce Management* (December 11, 2006): 44–67; P. Sparrow and C. Brewster, "Human Resource Strategy in an International Context," in W. M. Harris (ed.) *International Human Resource Management* (Amsterdam: Elsevier, 2006).

48 Adapted from S. L. Davis, "Assessment as Organizational Strategy," in R. Jeanneret and R. Silzer (eds.), *Individual Psychological Assessment: Predicting Behavior in Organizational Settings* (San Francisco: Jossey-Bass, 2001).

49 K. M. B. Gravenhorst, R. A. Werkman, and J. J. Boonstra, "The Change Capacity of Organizations: General Assessment and Five Configurations,"

Applied Psychology: An International Review 52(1) (2003): 83–105; L. Herscovitch and J. P. Meyer, "Commitment to Organizational Change: Extension of a Three-Component Model," *Journal of Applied Psychology* 87(3) (2002): 474–487; R. Silzer, "Shaping Organizational Leadership: The Ripple Effect of Assessment," in R. Jeanneret and R. Silzer (eds.), *Individual Psychological Assessment: Predicting Behavior in Organizational Settings* (San Francisco: Pfeiffer, 1998).

50 P. E. Figge, *Plan Closings—A Practical Guide* (Alexandria, VA: Society for Human Resource Management, 2003); see also W. F. Cascio, "Strategies for Responsible Restructuring," *Academy of Management Executive* 16(3) (2002): 80–91.

51 C. Wanberg and J. Banas, "Predictors and Outcomes of Openness to Changes in a Reorganizing Workplace," *Journal of Applied Psychology* 85(1) (2000): 132—142.

52 J. Jones, D. Aguirre, and M. Calderone, "10 Principles of Change Management," *Strategy+Business*, available at www.strategy-business .com (accessed February 15, 2005); G. Hamel, "Reinvent Your Company," *Fortune* (June 12, 2000): 99–118.

53 D. Ulrich, S. Kerr, and R. N. Ashkenas, *The GE Work-Out* (New York: McGraw-Hill, 2002); R. H. Schaffer, *Rapid Results: How 100-Day Projects Can Build the Capacity for Large-Scale Change* (San Francisco: Jossey-Bass, 2005).; D. Fisher, "Koch Industries: Mr. Big," *Forbes* (March 13, 2006): 100–104. See also the Georgia-Pacific Web site at www.gp.com (September 5, 2007)

54 S. Oreg, "Resistance to Change: Developing an Individual Differences Measure," *Journal of Applied Psychology* 88(4) (2003): 680–693; L. Gardenswartz and A. Rowe, "Overcoming Resistance to Your Diversity Initiative," *MOSAICS: SHRM Focuses on Workplace Diversity* 8(4) (October 2002): 3, 5; W. Echikson, "Nestlé: An Elephant Dances," *BusinessWeek e.Biz* (December 11, 2000): 44–48; R. Maurer, *Beyond the Wall of Resistance* (Austin, TX: Bard Books, 1996).

55 R. Kanter, "The Ten Deadly Mistakes of Wanna-Dots," *Harvard Business Review* (January 2001): 91–100; J. Kerstetter, "Peoplesoft's Hard Guy," *BusinessWeek* (January 15, 2001): 76–77; K. Skoldberg, "Tales of Change," *Organization Science* 5 (1994): 219–238.

56 T. Petzinger, Jr., "Georg Bauer Put Burden of Downsizing into Employees' Hands," *The Wall Street Journal* (May 10, 1996): B1.

57 M. C. Kernan and P. J. Hanges, "Survivor Reactions to Reorganization: Antecedents and Consequences of Procedural, Interpersonal, and Informational Justice," *Journal of Applied Psychology* 87(5) (2002): 916–928; S. Bates, "Middle Managers Anxious to Bolt Firms," *HRMagazine* (October 2003): 12; E. S. Barnes, "Even in a Bad Economy, Hypertherm Just Says No to Pink Slips," *Workforce Management* (July 2003): 96–99.

58 Research shows change initiatives are more often undertaken earlier in the careers of executives and less likely to occur later; for example, see M. Baer and M. Frese, "Innovation Is Not Enough: Climates for Initiative and Psychological Safety, Process Innovations, and Firm Performance," *Journal of Organizational Behavior* 24 (2003): 45–68; D. Miller and J. Shamsie, "Learning Across the Life Cycle: Experimentation and Performance Among the Hollywood Studio Heads," *Strategic Management Journal* 22 (2001): 724–745.

59 J. W. Dean, Jr., P. Brandes, and R. Dharwadkar, "Organizational Cynicism," *Academy of Management Review* 23(1998): 341–352; A. E. Reichers, J. P. Wanous, and J. T. Austin, "Understanding and Managing Cynicism About Organizational Change," *Academy of Management Executive* 11(1997): 48.

60 E. W. Morrison, "When Employees Feel Betrayed: A Model of How Psychological Contract Violation Develops," *Academy of Management Review* 22 (1997): 226–256; E. M. Mervosh, "Downsizing Dilemma," *Human Resource Executive* (February 1997): 50–53.

61 D. M. Schweiger, J. M. Ivancevich, and F. R. Power, "Executive Actions for Managing Human Resources Before and After Acquisition," *Academy of Management Executive* 1(2) (1986): 127–138.

62 G. Koretz, "Downsizing's Painful Effects," *BusinessWeek* (April 13, 1998): 23.

63 H. Axel, *HR Review: Implementing the New Employment Compact* (New York: The Conference Board, 1997).

64 J. P. Kotter, "Leading Change: Why Transformation Efforts Fail," *Harvard Business Review* (March–April 1995): 59–67.

65 S. Hamm, "A Passion for the Plan," *BusinessWeek* (August 21–28, 2006): 92–94; "A Survey of Talent," *The Economist* (October 7, 2006): 3–20; R. Athey, "It's 2008: Do You Know Where Your Talent Is?" *Deloitte Research* (2004).

66 "The Wholly Sustainable Enterprise: A Lean, Green, Earning Machine," available at www.deloitte.com (accessed January 16, 2007). See also see the Special Report by P. Engardio, "Beyond The Green Corporation," *BusinessWeek* (January 29, 2007): 50–64.

67 "HP's approach to supply chain social and environmental responsibility," HP Global Citizenship Report, available at www.hp.com (accessed January 29, 2007).

68 "AWB Awards Companies for Environmental Excellence," AWB Press Release, www.awb.org (accessed October 26, 2005). See the Deloitte Web site (www.deloitte.com) and "Weyerhaeuser's 2005 Sustainability Report," www.weyerhaueser.com (accessed January 10, 2007).

Chapter 4

1 Case developments, available at www.walmartclass.com/walmartclass_casedevelopments.html (February 7, 2007); J. Birger, "The Unending Woes of Lee Scott," *Fortune* (January 22, 2007): 120–122; A. Bernstein, "Wal-Mart Vs. Class Actions," *BusinessWeek* (March 21, 2005): 73–74; L. Featherstone, *Selling Women Short* (New York: Basic Books, 2004); C. Daniels, "Women vs. Wal-Mart," *Fortune* (July 21, 2003): 79–82; R. Zeilberger, "Is Wal-Mart Unfair to Its Female Employees: And Why They'll Still Work There," *DiversityInc* (December 2003–January 2004): 89–92.

2 S. Naumann and N. Bennett, "A Case for Procedural Justice Climate: Development and Test of a Multilevel Model," *Academy of Management Journal* 43 (2000): 881–889; J. Greenberg, "Looking Fair vs. Being Fair: Managing Impressions of Organizational Justice," in B. M. Staw and L. L. Cummings (eds.), *Research in Organizational Behavior*, vol. 12 (Greenwich, CT: JAI Press, 1990): 111–157.

3 M. Konovsky, "Understanding Procedural Justice and Its Impact on Business Organizations," *Journal of Management* 26 (2000): 489–511; W. C. Kim and R. Maugorgne, "Fair Process: Managing in the Knowledge Economy," *Harvard Business Review* (July–August 1997): 65–75.

4 J. C. Morrow, P. C. Morrow, and E. J. Mullen, "Intraorganizational Mobility and Work-Related Attitudes," *Journal of Organizational Behavior* 17 (1996): 363–374.

5 M. Conlin and W. Zellner, "Is Wal-Mart Hostile to Women?" *BusinessWeek* (July 16, 2001): 58–59; see also R. Garonzik, J. Brockner, and P. Siegel, "Identifying International Assignees at Risk for Premature Departure: The Interactive Effect of Outcome Favorability and Procedural Fairness," *Journal of Applied Psychology* 85 (2000): 13–20.

6 T. Simons and Q. Roberson, "Why Managers Should Care About Fairness: The Effects of Aggregate Justice Perceptions on Organizational Outcomes," *Journal of Applied Psychology* 88(3) (2003): 432–443.

7 J. A. Colquitt, D. E. Conlon, M. J. Wesson, C. Porter, and K. Y. Ng, "Justice at the Milennium: A Meta-Analytic Review of 25 Years of Organizational Justice Research," *Journal of Applied Psychology* 86 (2001): 425–445; H. Schroth and P. Shah, "Procedures: Do We Really Want to Know Them? An Examination of the Effects of Procedural Justice on Self-Esteem," *Journal of Applied Psychology* 85 (2000): 462–471; R. Cropanzano (ed.), *Justice in the Workplace: From Theory to Practice* (Mahwah, NJ: Lawrence Erlbaum Associates, 2000); see also D M. Rousseau, V. T. Ho, and J. Greenberg, "I-deals: Idiosyncratic Terms in Employment Relationships," *Academy of Management Review* 31 (2006): 977–994.

8 For example, see M. L. Williams, M. A. McDaniel, and N. T. Nguyen, "A Meta-Analysis of the Antecedents and Consequences of Pay Level Satisfaction," *Journal of Applied Psychology* 91 (2006): 392–413.

9 D. M. Mansour-Cole and S. G. Scott, "Hearing It Through the Grapevine: The Influence of Source, Leader-Relations, and Legitimacy on Survivors' Fairness Perceptions," *Personnel Psychology* 51 (1998): 25–53.

10 C. Lee, K. Law, and P. Bobko, "The Importance of Justice Perceptions on Pay Effectiveness: A Two-Year Study of a Skill-Based Pay Plan," *Journal of Management* 25 (1999): 851–873; M. P. Miceli, "Justice and Pay System Satisfaction," in R. Cropanzano (ed.), *Justice in the Workplace* (Mahwah, NJ: Lawrence Erlbaum Associates, 2000); R. L. Heneman, D. B. Greenberger, and S. Strasser, "The Relationship Between Pay-for-Performance Perceptions and Pay Satisfaction," *Personnel Psychology* 41 (1988): 745–761; M. P. Miceli et al., "Predictors and Outcomes of Reactions to Pay-for-Performance Plans," *Journal of Applied Psychology* 76 (1991): 508–521.

11 H. C. Triandis, "Cross-Cultural Industrial and Organizational Psychology," in H. C. Triandis, M. D. Dunnette, and L. M. Hough (eds.), *Handbook of Industrial and Organizational Psychology*, vol. 4 (Palo Alto, CA: Consulting Psychologists Press, 1994), 103–172.

12 R. Cropanzano, ed., *Justice in the Workplace* (Mahwah, NJ: Lawrence Erlbaum Associates, 2000).

13 S. Greenhouse and M. Barbaro, "Costco Bias Suit Is Given Class-Action Status," *The New York Times* (January 12, 2007): C9.

14 J. A. Colquitt, R. A. Noe, and C. L. Jackson, "Justice in Teams: Antecedents and Consequences of Procedural Justice Climate," *Personnel Psychology* 55 (2002): 83–109.

15 M. A. Korsgaard, S. E. Brodt, and E. M. Whitener, "Trust in the Face of Conflict: The Role of Managerial Trustworthy Behavior and Organizational Context," *Journal of Applied Psychology* 87(2) (2002): 312–319.

16 J. A. Colquitt, "On the Dimensionality of Organizational Justice: A Construct Validation of a Measure," *Journal of Applied Psychology* 86 (2001): 386–400.

17 B. B. Dunford and D. J. Devine, "Employment At-Will and Employee Discharge: A Justice Perspective on Legal Action Following Termination," *Personnel Psychology* 51 (1998): 903–934; C. E. Rusbult, et al., "Impact of Exchange Variables on Exit, Voice, Loyalty and Neglect: An Integrative Model of Responses to Declining Job Satisfaction," *Academy of Management Journal* 31 (1998): 599–627; J. Brockner and B. Wiesenfeld, "An Integrative Framework for Explaining Reactions to Decisions:

Interactive Effects of Outcomes and Procedures," *Psychological Bulletin* 120 (1996): 189–208; A. Davis-Blake, J. P. Broschak, and E. George, "Happy Together? How Using Nonstandard Workers Affects Exit, Voice, and Loyalty Among Standard Workers," *Academy of Management Journal* 46 (2003): 475–485.

18 T. R. Tyler and S. L. Blader, *Cooperation in Groups: Procedural Justice, Social Identity and Behavioral Engagement* (New York: Taylor & Francis, 2000).

19 S. Foley, D. L. Kidder, and G. N. Powell, "The Perceived Glass Ceiling and Justice Perceptions: An Investigation of Hispanic Law Associates," *Journal of Management* 28(4) (2002): 471–496; M. Elovainio, M. Kivimaki, and K. Helkama, "Organizational Justice Evaluations, Job Control Land Occupational Strain," *Journal of Applied Psychology* 86 (2001): 418–424; D. B. McFarlin and P. D. Sweeney, "Distributive and Procedural Justice as Predictors of Satisfaction with Personal and Organizational Outcomes," *Academy of Management Journal* 35 (1992): 626–637.

20 J. B. Olson-Buchanan and W. R. Boswell, "The Role of Employee Loyalty and Formality in Voicing Discontent," *Journal of Applied Psychology* 87(6) (2002): 1167–1174.

21 L. M. Roth, "Women on Wall Street: Despite Diversity Measures, Wall Street Remains Vulnerable to Sex Discrimination Charges," *Academy of Management Perspectives* (February 2007): 24–35.

22 For a review of research on discrimination, see B. M. Goldman, B. A. Gutek, and J. H. Stein, "Employment Discrimination in Organizations: Antecedents and Consequences," *Journal of Management* 32(6) (2006): 786–830; R. L. Dipboye and A. Colella, *Discrimination at Work* (Mahwah, NJ: Lawrence Erlbaum Associates, 2005).

23 This discussion is based mostly on R. E. Ringleb and H. A. Meiners, *Legal Environment of Business* (Cincinnati, OH: South-Western, 2001). Useful overviews also appear in R. D. Arvey and R. H. Faley, *Fairness in Selecting Employees*, 2nd ed. (Reading, MA: Addison-Wesley, 1988); and A. Gutman, *Law and Personnel Practices* (Newbury Park, CA: Sage, 1993).

24 J. Ledvinka, "Government Regulation and Human Resources," in A. Howard (ed.), *The Changing Nature of Work* (San Francisco: Jossey-Bass, 1995).

25 C. Edwards, "Coming Out in Corporate America," *BusinessWeek* (December 15, 2003): 64–72.

26 For a more detailed discussion of relevant federal and state laws and regulations, see B. A. Lee and D. R. Sockell, "Regulation of the HRM Function," in J. B. Mitchell, M. A. Zaidi, and D. Lewin (eds.), *The Human Resource Management Handbook* (Greenwich, CT: JAI Press, 1997), 199–232.

27 H. R. Fox and L. P. Karunaratne, "EEOC Updates on Sexual Discrimination," *The Industrial-Organizational Psychologist* (January 2001): 150–151; McAfee and Taft, *Age Discrimination in the Workplace* (Alexandria, VA: SHRM, 1999); P. E. Varca and P. Pattison, "Evidentiary Standards in Employment Discrimination: A View Toward the Future," *Personnel Psychology* 46 (1993): 239.

28 E. Porter, "UBS Ordered to Pay $29 Million in Sex Bias Lawsuit," *The New York Times* (April 7, 2005): C4.

29 A. Abramson and M. Silverstein, "Images of Aging in America 2004," AARP and the University of Southern California (March 2006).

30 U.S. Equal Employment Opportunity Commission "Disability Discrimination," available at www.eeoc.gov/types/ada.html (February 28, 2007).

31 J. Lewis, "New Jersey: Far-Reaching Civil Unions Law Passes," available at www.shrm.org (January 5, 2007).

32 G. M. Davis, "The Family and Medical Leave Act: 10 Years Later," *Legal Report* (July–August 2003): 1–8. For a summary of other key areas of developing state legislation, see J. Schramm, "State Public Policy and Its Impact on HR," *Workplace Visions* (3) (2004): 1–8.

33 L. Lau, "Minimum Wage, Record Retention, Major Change," *HRMagazine* (September 2007): 35.

34 Source: U.S. Equal Employment Opportunity Commission, available at www.eeoc.gov/stats/charges.html (February 12, 2007).

35 MasudaFunai, "EEOC Recoveries and Claims Lower in 2005," available at www.masudafunai.com/eng/legalupdates (December 30, 2005); K. Crawford, "EEOC Complaints Down, Fines Up," CNNMoney.com, available at http://money.cnn.com (February 15, 2005).

36 J. Pont, "Ruling Gives a New Basis for Age-Bias Claims," *Workforce Management* (May 2005): 20–22.

37 M. Orey, "Fear of Firing," *BusinessWeek* (April 23, 2007): 52–62; M. Conlin, "Revenge of the 'Managers,'" *BusinessWeek* (March 12, 2001): 60–62; L. Guernesy, "The Web: New Ticket to a Pink Slip," *The New York Times* (December 16, 1999): G1, 8; M. W. Walsh, "More Than Just a Wrongful Termination," *The New York Times* (January 31, 2001): G1; "Policy Guide: What Constitutes 'Good Cause' for Firing?" *Bulletin to Management* 49(3) (January 22, 1998): 24; "How Employers Can Use Employment-at-Will Disclaimers Effectively," *Fair Employment Practices Guidelines* (November 10, 1997): 6–8; "A Pledge of Job Security Can Alter At-Will Status," *Bulletin to Management* (August 14, 1997); S. A. Youngblood and L. Bierman, "Due Process and Employment-at-Will: A Legal and Behavioral Analysis," in K. M. Rowland and G. R. Ferris (eds.), *Research in Personnel and Human Resources Management* (Greenwich, CT: JAI Press, 1985): 185–230.

38 D. R. Briscoe and R. S. Schuler, *International Human Resource Management: Policy and Practice in Global Enterprises,* 2nd ed. (London: Routledge, 2004).

39 N. Rogovsky, R. S. Schuler, and L. K. Yoke, "Socially Sensitive Enterprise Restructuring: Country Context and Examples in Asia," *International Labour Office and Asian Productivity Organization* (2007).

40 F. Hansen and R. Chu, "Balancing the Global Workforce," *Workforce Management* (December 11, 2006): 44–67.

41 E. H. James and L.P. Wooten, "Diversity Crises: How Firms Manage Discrimination Lawsuits," *Academy of Management Journal* 49(6) (2006): 1103–1118.

42 See M. E. Gordon and G. E. Fryxell, "The Role of Interpersonal Justice in Organizational Grievance Systems," in R. Cropanzano (ed.), *Justice in the Workplace: From Theory to Practice* (Mahwah, NJ: Lawrence Erlbaum Associates, 2000).

43 R. Ganzel, "Second-Class Justice?" *Training* (October 1997): 84–96; A. J. Conti, "Alternative Dispute Resolution: A Court-Backed, Mandatory Alternative to Employee Lawsuits," *Fair Employment Practices Guidelines* (October 10, 1997): 1–15; P. Feuille and J. T. Delaney, "The Individual Pursuit of Organizational Justice: Grievance Procedures in Nonunion Workplaces," *Research in Personnel and Human Resources Management* 10 (1992): 187–232.

44 "Grievance Procedure: Overview of the Four Step Plan," www.co.pinellas.fl.us/persnl/emp-elations/grievance.htm (February 28, 2007).

45 W. R. Boswell and J. B. Olson-Buchanan, "Experiencing Mistreatment at Work: The Role of Grievance Filing, Nature of Mistreatment, and Employee Withdrawal," *Academy of Management Journal* 47 (2004):

129–139; C. Gopinath and T. Becker, "Communication, Procedural Justice, and Employee Attitudes: Relationships Under Conditions of Divestiture," *Journal of Management* 26 (2000): 63–83; M. T. Miklave, "Why 'Jury' Is a Four Letter Word," *Workforce* (March 1998): 56–64; K. Aquino, R. F. Griffeth, D. G. Allen, and P. W. Hom, "Integrating Justice Constructs into the Turnover Process: A Test of a Referent Cognitions Model," *Academy of Management Journal* 40 (1997): 1208–1227; M. Schminke, M. L. Ambrose, and T. W. Noel, "The Effect of Ethical Frameworks on Perceptions of Organizational Justice," *Academy of Management Journal* 40 (1997): 1190–1207; S. P. Schappe, "Bridging the Gap Between Procedural Knowledge and Positive Employee Attitudes: Procedural Justice as Keystones," *Group and Organization Management* 21(3) (September 1996): 337–364.

46 V. C. Smith, "Sign of the Times," *Human Resource Executive* (April 1997): 57–63; S. Caudron, "Blow the Whistle on Employment Disputes," *Workforce* (May 1997): 51–57; R. Furchgott, "Opposition Builds to Mandatory Arbitration at Work," *The New York Times* (July 20, 1997): F11; "Employee Relations," *HR Reporter* 14(12) (December 1997): 1–12; "NASD Votes to Nix Mandatory Arbitration," *Fair Employment Practices* (August 21, 1997): 99.

47 M. Barrier, "The Mediation Disconnect," *HRMagazine* (May 2003): 54–58; M. M Clark, "EEOC's Efforts to Expand Mediation Gain Momentum," *HRMagazine* (May 2003): 32, 34; P. Salvatore, "Mediation and Arbitration of Employment Law Claims," *Legal Report* (March–April 2001): 7–8; see also R. J. Weinstein, *Mediation in the Workplace: A Guide for Training, Practice, and Administration* (Westport, CT: Quorum Books, 2000).

48 G. Flynn, "High Court Weighs in on Arbitration," *Workforce* (June 2001): 100–101; M. Meece, "The Very Model of Conciliation," *The New York Times* (September 6, 2000): C1; D. Casey and B. Lee, "Mandatory Arbitration Clauses in Individual Employment Contracts: Enhancing Fairness and Enforceability," *Employee Relations Law Journal* 25 (Winter 1999): 57–75; G. Glynn, "Mandatory Binding Arbitration—Ensure Your Plan Is Usable," *Workforce* (June 1997): 121–127.

49 M. L. Bickner and C. Feigenbaum, "Developments in Employment Arbitration," *Dispute Resolution Journal* (January 1997): 234–251; S. Caudron, "Blow the Whistle on Employment Disputes," *Workforce* (May 1997): 51–57.

50 B. P. Sunoo, "Hot Disputes Cool Down in Online Mediation," *Workforce* (January 2001): 48–52.

51 L. Lawrence, "Coca-Cola Agrees to Record Discrimination Settlement," *HR News* (January 2001): 1, 4, 8.

52 "Rooting Out Racism," *BusinessWeek Online*, available at www .businessweek.com/reprints/00-02/b3663022.htm; *Texaco Task Force Report on Equality and Fairness Issues: Third Annual Report (2000)*, available at http://www.texaco.com; A. Bryant, "How Much Has Texaco Changed? A Mixed Report Card on Anti-Bias Efforts," *The New York Times* (November 2, 1997): 3-1, 3-16, 3-17; V. C. Smith, "Texaco Outlines Comprehensive Initiatives," *Human Resource Executive* (February 1997): 13; and "Texaco's Workforce Diversity Plan," as reprinted in *Workforce* (March 1997): supplement.

53 L. Bean, "What Happened to Diversity's Bad Boys? Texaco, Denny's, Coca-Cola," *DiversityInc* (October–November 2003): 111–116.

54 S. Fegley, "2006 Workplace Diversity and Changes to the EEO-1 Process," *SHRM Research* (October 2006). For a recent discussion of discimination research, see R. L. Dipboye and A. Colella (eds.), *Discrimination at Work* (Mahwah, NJ: Lawrence Erlbaum Associates, 2007).

55 C. E. Helfat, D. Harris, and P. J. Wolfson, "The Pipeline to the Top: Women and Men in the Top Executive Ranks of U.S. Corporations," *Academy of Management Perspectives* (November 2006): 42–64.

56 A. Pomeroy, "She's Still Lovin' It!" *HRMagazine* (December 2006): 58–61.

57 K. Hudon, "Wal-Mart Presses Suppliers to Enhance Their Diversity," *The Wall Street Journal* (February 23, 2007): A12.

58 "Toppling a Taboo: Businesses Go 'Faith-Friendly'," http://knowledge .wharton.upenn.edu (January 24, 2007); M. Gunther, "Queer Inc.," *Fortune* (December 11, 2006): 94–110; J. Kahn, "Diversity Trumps the Downturn," *Fortune* (July 9, 2001): 114–116.

59 S. Fegley, "2006 Workplace Diversity and Changes to the EEO-1 Process—Survey Report," *SHRM Research* (October 2006): *SHRM Survey Report on the Impact of Diversity Initiatives on the Bottom Line,* www .shrm.org/surveys (May 2001); see also T. Kochan, K. Bezrukova, R. Ely, S. Jackson, A. Joshi, K. Jehn, J. Leonard, D. Levine, and D. Thomas, "The Effects of Diversity on Business Performance: Report of the Diversity Research Network," *Human Resource Management* 42(1) (Spring 2003): 3–21.

60 www.dardenrestaurants.com (June 2006); "World's Largest Casual Dining Company Honors Its Best Suppliers with Top Award," *Fortune* (May 22, 2006); see also V. Liberman, "Tough Issues," *Across the Board,* May–June 2002, 22–29.

61 "Is There a Business Case for Diversity? Yes—But It's Not in the Numbers," http://knowledge.wharton.upenn.edu (January 10, 2007); K. Donovan, "Pushed by Clients, Law Firms Step Up Diversity Efforts," *The New York Times* (July 21, 2006).

62 J. P. Johnson III, "SHRM White Paper: Creating a Diverse Workforce," Society for Human Resource Management, www.shrm.org/hrresources/ whitepapers_published (December 13, 2003); www.mwhglobal.com (February 28, 2007).

63 T. Kochan, K. Bezrukova, R. Ely, E. S. Jackson, A. Joshi, K. Jehn, J. Leonard, D. Levine, and D. Thomas, "The Effects of Diversity on Business Performance: Report of the Diversity Research Network," *Human Resource Management Journal* 42 (2003): 3–22.

64 S. Din, "Radio Station Loses Ads After Racial Slurs," *The Star-Ledger* (May 11, 2005): 19.

65 For a discussion of color discrimination, see P. Mirza, "Where Is Color Discrimination Headed?" *HRMagazine* (December 2003): 64–67. See also G. Maatman, Jr. (ed.), *Worldwide Guide to Termination, Employment Discrimination, and Workplace Harassment Laws* (Chicago: Baker & McKenzie/CCH, 2001); K. Schneider, R. Hitlan, and P. Radhakrishnan, "An Examination of the Nature and Correlates of Ethnic Harassment Experiences in Multiple Contexts," *Journal of Applied Psychology* 85 (2000): 3–12.

66 For a recent review, see J. L. Berdahl, "Harrassment Based on Sex: Protecting Social Status in the Context of Gender Hierarchy," *Academy of Management Review* 32 (2000): 641–658; R. F. Gregory, *Unwelcome and Unlawful: Sexual Harassment in the American Workplace* (Ithaca: Cornell University Press: 2004); "A Question of Ethics," *Bulletin to Management* (July 9, 1992): 211.

67 K. S. Robinson, "American Muslims Report Discrimination After Sept. 11 Terrorist Attacks," *Society for Human Resource Management* (October 2002): 17; S. Saulny, "Muslim Workers Claim Bias at the Plaza," *The New York Times* (October 1, 2003): B3.

68 J. L. Berdahl and C. Moore, "Workplace Harassment: Double Jeopardy for Minority Women," *Journal of Applied Psychology* 91(2) (2006): 426–436.

69 A. M. Townsend, M. E. Whitman, and R. J. Aalberts, "What's Left of the Communications Decency Act?" *HRM Magazine* (June 1998): 124–127.

70 P. McGeehan, "Two Analysts Leave Salomon in Smut Case," *The Wall Street Journal* (March 31, 1998): C1, C25.

71 J. Steinhauer, "If the Boss Is Out of Line, What's the Legal Boundary?" *The New York Times* (March 27, 1997): D1, D4; "Reasonable Woman Standard Gains Ground," *Fair Employment Practices Guidelines* (June 25, 1993): 4.

72 K. M. Jarin and E. K. Pomfert, "New Rules for Same Sex Harassment," *HRM Magazine* (June 1998): 115–123.

73 N. A. Bowling and T. A. Beehr, "Workplace Harassment from the Victim's Perspective: A Theoretical Model and Meta-Analysis," *Journal of Applied Psychology* 91(5) (2006): 998–1012.

74 T. J. Elkins, "New HR Challenges in the Dynamic Environment of Legal Compliance," in S. Werner (ed.), *Managing Human Resources in North America: Current Issues and Perspectives* (London: Routledge, 2007): 44–58; W. K. Turner and C. S. Thrutchley, "Employment Law and Practices Training: No Longer the Exception—It's the Rule," *Legal Report* (July–August 2002): 1–8; "Preventing Sexual Harassment: Helpful Advice and Another Reason," *Fair Employment Practices* (February 19, 1998): 21; M. Raphan and M. Heerman, "Eight Steps to Harassment-Proof Your Office," *HR Focus* (August 1997): 11–12. For details about how to investigate harassment complaints, see A. Oppenheimer and C. Pratt, "Investigating Workplace Harassment," *HRMagazine* (September 2002): 135–136.

75 L. R. Offermann and A. B. Malamut, "When Leaders Harass: The Impact of Target Perceptions of Organizational Leadership and Climate on Harassment Reporting and Outcomes," *Journal of Applied Psychology* 87(5) (2002): 885–893.

76 K. S. Robinson, "Employees Engaging in Deceptive Behaviors at Alarming Rates," *HR News* (September 2000): 22.

77 M. M. Clark, "Corporate Ethics Programs Make a Difference, But Not the Only Difference," *HRMagazine* (July 2003): 36.

78 For detailed information about state and federal privacy laws, see D. Safon and Worklaw Network, *Workplace Privacy: Real Answers and Practical Solutions* (Toronto: Thomson, 2000).

79 B. Roberts, "Avoiding the Perils of Electronic Data," *HRMagazine* (January 2007): 72–77; A. Smith, "Federal Rules Define Duty to Preserve Work E-Mails," *HRMagazine* (January 2007): 27, 36.

80 R. Zeidner, "Employees Don't 'Get' Electronic Storage," *HRMagazine* (January 2007): 36.

81 For a critique of employer monitoring practices, see F. S. Lane III, *The Naked Employee* (New York: AMACOM, 2004). See also E. Eddy, D. Stone, and E. Stone-Romero, "The Effects of Information Management Policies on Reactions to Human Resource Information Systems: An Integration of Privacy and Procedural Justice Perspectives," *Personnel Psychology* 52 (1999): 335–358; J. Lipson, "HR Struggles with Fine Lines of Workplace Privacy," *HR News* (March 2001): 15, 19; D. Saton and Worklaw Network, *Workplace Privacy: Real Answers and Practical Solutions* (Toronto: Thompson, 2000).

82 J. Smerd, "Screener Sees Drop in Positive Tests; Presence of Meth Falls," *Workforce Management* (July 17, 2006): 3–4.

83 M. R. Frone, "Prevalence and Distribution of Illicit Drug Use in the Workforce and in the Workplace: Findings and Implications from a U.S. National Survey," *Journal of Applied Psychology* 91(4) (2006): 856–869; D. Ahmy, "Aiming for a Drug-Free Workplace," *The New York Times* (May 10, 2007): C6.

84 J. Marquez, "On-Site Blood Testing Raises Privacy Issues," *Workforce Management* (January 16, 2006): 10.

85 M. Schoeff, Jr., "Mixed Outlook for Genetics, Card-Check Bills," *Workforce Management* (February 26, 2007): 8; T. Raphael, "Testing Issue Still Unsettled," *Workforce* (June 2001): 19. For more information on the status of genetic testing and to learn about state laws that are applicable, see www.genome.gov.

86 "Wireless Incorporated," *The Economist* (April 28, 2007) 15–17; R. Zeidner, "Using Chips to Track Workers Discouraged," *HRMagazine* (April 2007): 34.

87 D. Robb, "Restricting Data Flow," *HRMagazine* (April 2003): 97–99.

88 M. J. Gelfand, M. Higgins, L. H. Nishii, J. L. Raver, A. Dominguez, F. Murakami, S. Yamaguchi, and M. Toyama, "Culture and Egocentric Perceptions of Fairness in Conflict and Negotiation," *Journal of Applied Psychology* 87(5) (2002): 833–845; S. Wasti, M. Bergman, T. Glomb, and F. Drasgow, "Test of the Cross-Cultural Generalizability of a Model of Sexual Harassment," *Journal of Applied Psychology* 85 (2000): 766–778; W. A. Carmell, "U.S. Law Heads Abroad," *International HR Update* (July 1998): 5.

89 Adapted from H. Feldman and A. Osland, "The United Way and Boy Scouts of America: Controversy in Portland, Oregon," in P. F. Buller and R. S. Schuler (eds.), *Managing Organizations and People,* 7th ed. (Mason, OH: Thomson South-Western, 2006). Used with permission.

Chapter 5

1 IBM Case Studies, accessed at www-306.ibm.com (June 2006); L. Berlin, *The Man Behind the Microchip: Robert Noyce and the Invention of Silicon Valley* (New York: Oxford University Press, 2005); S. F. Gale, "For ERP Success, Create a Culture Change," *Workforce* (September 2002): 83–88.

2 P. R. Sackett and R. M. Laczo, "Job and Work Analysis," in D. R. Ilgen and R. J. Klimoski (eds.), *Handbook of Psychology: Industrial and Organizational Psychology* (New York: John Wiley, 2003): 21–37; J. I. Sanchez and E. L. Levine, "The Analysis of Work in the 20th and 21st Centuries," in N. Anderson, S. S. Ones, H. K. Sinangil, and C. Viswesvaran (eds.), *Handbook of Industrial, Work and Organizational Psychology* (London: Sage, 2001): 70–90.

3 D. Rodriguez, "Developing Competency Models to Promote Integrated Human Resource Practices," *Human Resource Management* 41(3) (Fall 2002): 309–324; see J. Shippmann, R. Ash, M. Batitista, L. Carr, L. Eyde, B. Hesketh, J. F. Kehoe, K. Pearlman, E. Prien, and J. I. Sanchez, "The Practice of Competency Modeling," *Personnel Psychology* 53 (2000): 703–740; S. B. Parry, "The Quest for Competencies," *Training* (July 1996): 48–56.

4 D. Rahbah-Daniels, M. L. Erickson, and A. Dalik, "Here to Stay: Taking Competencies to the Next Level," *World at Work Journal* (First Quarter 2001): 70–77.

5 C. Sulter, "On the Road Again," *Fast Company* (January 2002): 58; "Lessons on Leadership: Follow These Leaders," *Fortune* (December 12, 2005); accessed at www.hoovers.com/yellow (June 2006); A. Zuckerman, "What Every Executive Needs to Know About Trucking

Trends," *WorldTrade Magazine*, available at www.worldtrademag.com (September 10, 2007).

6 T. Hindle, "The New Organization," *The Economist* (January 21, 2006): 21.

7 E. Brynjolfsson, A. A. Renshaw, and M. V. Alstyne, "The Matrix of Change," *Sloan Management Review* (Winter 1997): 37–54; M. Hammer and J. Champy, *Reengineering the Corporation* (New York: HarperCollins, 1993); M. Hammer, *Beyond Reengineering: How the Process-Centered Organization Is Changing Our Lives* (New York: HarperBusiness, 1996); J. Champy, *Reengineering Management: The Mandate for New Leadership* (New York: HarperBusiness, 1996).

8 J. Guaspari, "Dispatch from the Front: A Shining Example," *Across the Board* (May–June 2002): 67–68; M. E. Ruquest, "National Grange Mutual Rated No. 1 in Business Ease by Agents, Workers," *National Underwriter* (December 15, 2003): 9; M. E. Ruquest, "Making Things Easier for Agents," *National Underwriter, P & C* (May 10, 2004): 21.

9 For a complete discussion of job analysis, see M. T. Brannick, E. L. Levine, and F. P. Morgeson, *Job and Work Analysis*, 2nd ed. (Thousand Oaks, CA: Sage, 2007).

10 The essence of the Civil Rights Acts of 1964 and 1991, the Equal Opportunity in Employment Act of 1972, and various court decisions is that employment decisions are to be made on the basis of whether the individual is able to perform the job. Chapter 7 expands on the job relatedness of selection procedures.

11 "Objective Employee Appraisals and Discrimination Cases," *Fair Employment Practices* (December 6, 1990): 145–146.

12 M. M. Harris, "Practice Network: ADA and I-O Psychology," *The Industrial-Organizational Psychologist* 36(1) (1998): 33–37; "Job Analyses and Job Descriptions Under ADA," *Fair Employment Practices* (April 22, 1993): 45; see also K. Tyler, "Looking for a Few Good Workers?" *HRMagazine* (December 2000): 129; B. P. Sunoo, "Accommodating Workers with Disabilities," *Workforce* (February 2001): 86–93; E. Tahmincioglu, "Job Aides Open Doors for Those Who Can't," *The New York Times* (January 24, 2001): G1.

13 N. E. McDermott, "Independent Contractors and Employees: Do You Know One When You See One?" *Legal Report* (November–December, 1999): 1–4.

14 R. Lieber, "The Permatemps Contretemps," *Fast Company* (August 2000): 198–214.

15 J. Myers, "Cast Adrift at Microsoft." *SourceMagazine.com,* accessed at www.computersourcemag.com/articles (April 2003); D. Richman, "Microsoft 'Permatemps' Win, High Court Refuses Appeal," *Seattle Post-Intelligencer,* accessed at http://seattlepi.nwsource.com/business/msft111.shtml (January 11, 2000).

16 S. Bates, "A Tough Target: Employee or Independent Contractor?" *HRMagazine* (June 2001): 69–74.

17 G. Capaldo, L. Iandoli, and G. Zollo, "A Situationalist Perspective to Competency Management," *Human Resource Management,* 45(3) (Fall 2006): 429–448.

18 L. J. Pollack, C. Simons, H. Romero, and D. Hausser, "A Common Language for Classifying and Describing Occupations: The Development, Structure, and Application of the Standard Occupational Classification," *Human Resource Management* 41(3) (Fall 2002): 297–307.

19 For more detailed discussions, see M. T. Brannick and E. L. Levine, *Job Analysis: Methods Research, and Applications for Human Resource Management in the New Millennium* (Mahwah, NJ: Lawrence Erlbaum Associates, 2007); R. E. Ployhart, B. Schneider, and N. Schmitt, *Staffing Organizations: Contemporary Practice and Theory* (Mahwah, NJ: Lawrence Erlbaum Associates, 2006).

20 J. S. Schippmann, *Strategic Job Modeling: Working at the Core of Integrated Human Resources* (Mahwah, NJ: Lawrence Erlbaum Associates, 1999).

21 L. H. Markus, H. D. Cooper-Thomas, and K. N. Allpress, "Confounded by Competencies? An Evaluation of the Evolution and Use of Competency Models," *New Zealand Journal of Psychology* (34)(2) (July 2005): 117–126; D. Rodriguez, "Developing Competency Models to Promote Integrated Human Resource Practices," *Human Resource Management* 41(3) (Fall 2002): 309–324.

22 P. R. Sackett and R. M. Laczo, "Job and Work Analysis," in D. R. Ilgen and R. J. Klimoski (eds.), *Handbook of Psychology: Industrial and Organizational Psychology* (New York: John Wiley, 2003).

23 For additional information about competency modeling, see J. S. Schippmann et al., "The Practice of Competency Modeling," *Personnel Psychology* 53 (2000): 703–740; D. D. DuBois, "Competency Modeling," in D. G. Langdon, K. S. Whiteside, and M. M. McKenna (eds.), *Intervention Resource Guide: 50 Performance Improvement Tools* (San Francisco: Jossey-Bass, 1999): 106–111.

24 Equal Employment Opportunity Commission, "Uniform Guidelines on Employee Selection Procedures," *Federal Register* 43 (1978): 38290–38315; J. Ledvinka and V. G. Scarpello, *Federal Regulation of Personnel and Human Resource Management*, 2nd ed. (Boston: Kent Publishing, 1990).

25 Detailed discussions of issues related to creating job families are provided in J. Colhan and G. K. Burger, "Constructing Job Families: An Analysis of Quantitative Techniques Used for Grouping Jobs," *Personnel Psychology* 48 (1995): 563–586; M. K. Garwood, L. E. Anderson, and B. J. Greengart, "Determining Job Groups: Application of Hierarchical Agglomerative Cluster Analysis in Different Job Analysis Situations," *Personnel Psychology* (1991): 743–762; J. C. Hogan, "Structure of Physical Performance in Occupational Tasks," *Journal of Applied Psychology* 76 (1991): 495–507.

26 L. Sierra, "The Next Generation of Broadbanding: Insurance Company Overhauls Hierarchy with CareerBanding," *ACA News* (February 1998): 21–24; see also D. Gilbert and K. S. Abosch, *Improving Organizational Effectiveness Through Broadbanding* (Scottsdale, AZ: American Compensation Association, 1996).

27 V. M. Catana, W. Darr, and C. A. Campbell, "Performance Appraisal of Behavior-Based Competencies: A Reliable and Valid Procedure," *Personnel Psychology* (60) (2007): 210–230.

28 L. E. Baranowski and L. E. Anderson, "Examining Rater Source Variation in Work Behavior to KSA Linkages," *Personnel Psychology* (58) (2005): 1041–1054; C. V. Iddekinge, D. J. Putka, P. H. Raymark, and C. E. Edison, Jr., "Modeling Error Variance in Job Specification Ratings: The Influence of Rater, Job, and Organization-Level Factors," *Journal of Applied Psychology* 90(2) (2005): 323–334; F. P. Morgeson, K. Delaney-Klinger, M. S. Mayfield, P. Ferrara, and M. A. Campion, "Self-Presentation Processes in Job Analysis: A Field Experiment Investigating Inflation in Abilities, Tasks, and Competencies," *Journal of Applied Psychology* 89(4) (2004): 674–686. For a detailed discussion of how to maximize accuracy in job analysis results, see E. C. Dierdorff and M. A. Wilson, "A Meta-Analysis of Job Analysis Reliability," *Journal of Applied Psychology* 88(4) (2003): 635–646; J. I. Sanchez and E. L. Levine, "Accuracy or Consequential Validity: Which Is the Better Standard for Job Analysis Data?" *Journal of*

Organizational Behavior 21 (2000): 809–818; F. P. Morgenson and M. A. Campion, "Accuracy in Job Analysis: Toward an Inference Based Model," *Journal of Organizational Behavior* 21 (2000): 819–827; R. J. Harvey and M. A. Wilson, "Yes, Virginia, There Is an Objective Reality in Job Analysis," *Journal of Organizational Behavior* 21 (2000): 829–854.

29 M. K. Lindell, C. S. Clause, C. J. Brandt, and R. S. Landis, "Relationship Between Organizational Context and Job Analysis Task Ratings," *Journal of Applied Psychology* 83 (1998): 769–776; F. J. Landy and J. Vasey, "Job Analysis: The Composition of SME Samples," *Personnel Psychology* 44 (1991): 27–50.

30 F. P. Morgeson, K. D-Klinger, M. S. Mayfield, P. Ferrara, and M. A. Campion, "Self-Presentation Process in Job Analysis: A Field Experiment Investigating Inflation in Abilities, Tasks, and Competencies," *Journal of Applied Psychology* 89(4) (2004): 674–686.

31 R. D. Arvey, "Sex Bias in Job Evaluation Procedures," *Personnel Psychology* 39 (1986): 315–335; A. P. O'Reilly, "Skill Requirements: Supervisor-Subordinate Conflict," *Personnel Psychology* 26 (Spring 1973): 75–80.

32 J. I. Sanchez and E. I. Levine, "Accuracy or Consequential Validity: Which Is the Better Standard for Job Analysis Data?" *Journal of Organizational Behavior* 21 (2000): 809–818; J. Shippmann, *Strategic Job Modeling: Working at the Core of Integrated Human Resources* (Mahwah, NJ: Lawrence Erlbaum Associates, 1999).

33 L. E. Baranowski and L. E. Anderson, "Examining Rating Source Variation in Work Behavior to KSA Linkages," *Personnel Psychology* 58(4) (2005): 1041–1054.

34 D. E. Bowen and D. A. Waldman, "Customer-Driven Employee Performance," in D. R. Ilgen and E. D. Pulakos (eds.), *The Changing Nature of Work Performance: Implications for Staffing, Personnel Actions and Development* (San Francisco: Jossey-Bass, 1999).

35 F. C. Lager, *Ben & Jerry's: The Inside Scoop* (New York: Crown Trade Paperbacks, 1994).

36 A. W. Mathews, "New Gadgets Trace Truckers' Every Move," *The Wall Street Journal* (July 14, 1997): B1, B2.

37 W. C. Howell, "Human Factors in the Workplace," in M. D. Dunnette and L. M. Hough (eds.), *Handbook of Industrial Organizational Psychology*, vol. 2 (Palo Alto, CA: Consulting Psychologists Press, 1991): 209–270.

38 Information about O*NET is provided by the Department of Labor at www.doleta.gov/programs/onet/. See also N. G. Peterson, et al., "Understanding Work Using the Occupational Information Network (O*NET): Implications for Practice and Research," *Personnel Psychology* 54 (2001): 451–492. For more information on the description of occupations, see L. J. Pollack, C. Simons, H. Romero, and D. Hausser, "A Common Language for Classifying and Describing Occupations: The Development, Structure, and Application of the Standard Occupational Classification," *Human Resource Management* 41(3) (Fall 2002): 297–307.

39 For an example describing how O*NET was used by the U.S. Navy, see R. Reiter-Palmon, M. Brown, D. L. Sandall, C. Buboltz, and T. Nimps, "Development of an O*NET Web-Based Job Analysis and Its Implementation in the U.S. Navy: Lessons Learned," *Human Resource Management Review* 16 (2006): 294–309; N. G. Peterson, M. D. Mumford, W. C. Borman, P. R. Jeanneret, and E. A. Fleishman (eds.), *An Occupational Information System for the 21st Century: The Development of O*NET* (Washington, DC: American Psychological Association, 1999).

40 The PAQ is published by Consulting Psychologists Press. Our description of the PAQ and its development is based on E. J. McCormick, P. R. Jeanneret, and R. C. Mecham, "A Study of Job Characteristics and Job Dimensions as Based on the Position Analysis Questionnaire," *Journal of Applied Psychology* 56 (1972): 347–367; and E. J. McCormick and J. Tiffin, *Industrial Psychology*, 6th ed. (Englewood Cliffs, NJ: Prentice-Hall, 1994).

41 For additional discussion of the PAQ, see E. T. Cornelius III, A. S. DeNisi, and A. G. Blencoe, "Expert and Naive Raters Using the PAQ: Does It Matter?" *Personnel Psychology* (Autumn 1984): 453–464; E. J. McCormick, A. S. DeNisi, and B. Shaw, "Use of the Position Analysis Questionnaire for Establishing Job Component Validity of Tests," *Journal of Applied Psychology* 64 (1979): 51–56.

42 W. W. Tornow and P. R. Pinto, "The Development of a Managerial Job Taxonomy: A System for Describing, Classifying, and Evaluating Executive Positions," *Journal of Applied Psychology* 61 (1976): 410–418.

43 J. I. Sanchez and S. L. Fraser, "On the Choice of Scales for Task Analysis," *Journal of Applied Psychology* 77 (1992): 545–553; M. A. Wilson and R. J. Harvey, "The Value of Relative Time-Spent Ratings in Task-Oriented Job Analysis," *Journal of Business and Psychology* 4 (1990): 453–461.

44 J. C. Flanagan, "The Critical Incident Technique," *Psychological Bulletin* 51 (1954): 327–358.

45 I. L. Goldstein, *Training in Organizations: Needs Assessment, Development, and Evaluation* (Pacific Grove, CA: Brooks/Cole, 1993).

46 R. J. Harvey, "Job Analysis," in M. D. Dunnette and L. M. Hough (ed.), *Handbook of Industrial and Organizational Psychology*, vol.2 (Mountain View, CA: Davies-Black, 1991).

47 E. A. Fleishman and M. D. Mumford, "Ability Requirement Scales," in S. Gael, (ed.), *The Job Analysis Handbook for Business, Industry, and Government*, vol. 2 (New York: John Wiley, 1988).

48 J. S. Schippman, *Strategic Job Modeling: Working at the Core of Integrated Human Resources*; for more details about PROFILOR, visit the home page of Personnel Decisions Inc., available at www.pdi-corp. com/offerings/profilor_managers.asp.

49 R. M. Guion, *Assessment, Measurement, and Prediction for Personnel Decisions* (Mahway, NJ: Lawrence Erlbaum Associates, 1998); P. H. Raymark, M. J. Schmit, and R. M. Guion, "Identifying Potentially Useful Personality Constructs for Employee Selection," *Personnel Psychology* 50 (1997): 723–736.

50 Experts disagree about the usefulness of leadership competency models. For a discussion of the issues, see G. P. Hollenbeck, M. W. McCall, Jr., and R. F. Silzer. "Leadership Competency Models," *The Leadership Quarterly*, 2006, 17: 398–413.

51 J. S. Shippmann, R. A. Ash, et al., "The Practice of Competency Modeling," *Personnel Psychology*, 53 (2000): 703–740.

52 A. Barrett, "Star Search," *BusinessWeek* (October 10, 2005): 68–78.

53 R. B. Morgan and J. E. Smith, *Staffing the New Workplace: Selecting and Promoting Quality Improvement* (Milwaukee: ASQC Quality Press, 1996); K. P. Carson and G. L. Stewart, "Job Analysis and the Sociotechnical Approach to Quality: A Critical Examination," *Journal of Quality Management* 1 (1996): 49–64.

54 R. Lieber, "The Permatemps Contretemps," *Fast Company* (August 2000): 198–214; W. Bridges, *Job Shift: How to Prosper in a Workplace Without Jobs* (Reading, MA: Addison-Wesley, 1995).

55 C. Joinson, "Refocusing Job Descriptions," *HRMagazine* (January 2001): 67–72; J. I. Sanchez, "From Documentation to Innovation: Reshaping Job Analysis to Meet Emerging Business Needs," *Human Resource Management Review* 4(1) (1994): 51–74.

56 N. B. Kurland and T. D. Egan, "Telecommuting: Justice and Control in the Virtual Organization," *Organizational Science* 10 (1999): 500–513.

57 "Small Groups, Big Ideas," *Workforce Management* (February 26, 2006): 22–27; A. Deutschman. "The Fabric of Creativity," *Fast Company* (December 2004): 54–62.

Chapter 6

1 A. Fisher, "Playing for Keeps," *Fortune* (January 29, 2007): 85; "It's 2008: Do You Know Where Your Talent Is?" *Deloitte Research* (2004): 8; B. Turchin, "SAS Profile—Going Its Own Way," *Software Business* (January–February 2004), available at www.SoftwareBusinessOnline.com; G. C. Rappleye, Jr., "How High Is Humanizing Human Resources?" *Workforce* (March 2001); the SAS Institute Web site, available at www.sas.com (March 2001).

2 E. Frauenheim, "Valero Energy: Optimas Award Winner for Innovation," *Workforce Management* (August 8, 2006), available at www.workforce.com.

3 "Valero Jumps to No. 3 On Fortune's List of 'America's 100 Best Companies to Work For' in America," (January 9, 2006) Valero Energy Corporation, Web site, available at www.valero.com/NewsRoom/NewsReleases/NR_20060109.htm.

4 A. Lowe, "Click Here for Nursing Jobs," *HRMagazine* (May 2004): 101–103.

5 See Staffing.org, available at www.staffing.org, and "An Army of Surplus Labor," *Workforce Management* (December 2003): 98.

6 C. Huff, "Heroic Measures," *Workforce Management* (March 2005): 51–52.

7 T. Henneman, "Jack in the Box Going Upmarket in Benefits as Well as at Its Eateries," *Workforce Management* (March 2005): 76–77; see also the National Restaurant Association Educational Foundation Web site, available at www.nraef.org (May 2006).

8 "Does Hiring Minorities Hurt?" *BusinessWeek* (September 14, 1998): 26.

9 M. Hammers, "Almost Curtains," *Workforce Management* (August 2003): 54–55.

10 J. S. MacNeil, "Hey, Look Us Over," *Growth* (October 2002): 146.

11 G. Ruiz, "What Young Graduates Want," *Workforce Management*, accessed at www.workforce.com (June 5, 2006).

12 "2006 Winner—Service—Infosys Technologies," *Workforce Management* (March 13, 2006), accessed at www.workforce.com.

13 "Winning Strategies for a Global Workforce," *Towers Perrin Global Workforce Study* (2006), accessed at the Tower Perrin Web site: http://www.towersperrin.com/tp/jsp/hrservices_html.jsp?webc=203/global/spotlight/spotlight_gws.htm.

14 P. Buckley, K. Minette, D. Joy, and J. Michaels, "The Use of an Automated Employment Recruiting and Screening System for Temporary Professional Employees: A Case Study," *Human Resource Management Journal* 43 (2004): 233–241.

15 R. Zeidner, "Now Hear This!" *HRMagazine* (January 2007): 37.

16 J. Pont, "Honeywell Blog Aimed at Young Job Candidates," *Workforce Management* (September 2005): 32.

17 V. J. Hoffman and G. M. Davis, "OFCCP's 'Internet Applicant' Definition Requires Overhaul of Recruiting and Hiring Policies," *SHRM Legal Report* (January–February 2006): 1–5.

18 J. Alsever, "Chiquita Cleans Up Its Act," *Fortune* (November 27, 2006): 73.

19 D. Schoeneman, "Can Google Come Out to Play?" *The New York Times* (December 31, 2006): Section 9(1).

20 For detailed reviews of research that addresses this and other aspects of recruiting, see S. Rynes and D. Cable, "Recruiting Research in the 21st Century: Moving to a Higher Level," in W. C. Borman, D. R. Ilgen, and R. J. Klimoski (eds.), *Handbook of Psychology, vol. 12: Industrial and Organizational Psychology* (Hoboken, NJ: John Wiley, 2003); J. A. Breaugh and M. Starke, "Research on Employee Recruitment: So Many Studies, So Many Remaining Questions," *Journal of Management* 26(3) (2000): 405–434; A. E. Barber, *Recruiting Employees: Individual and Organizational Perspectives* (Thousand Oaks, CA: Sage, 1998).

21 K. Holland, "Inside the Minds of Your Employees," *The New York Times* (January 28, 2007): 18.

22 J. Reingold, "For the Class of 2000, the Sellers' Market Intensifies," *BusinessWeek* (May 8, 2000): 54; H. Axel, *HR Executive Review: Competing as an Employer of Choice* (New York: The Conference Board, 1996).

23 K. Holland, "Inside the Minds of Your Employees," The Corner Office (February 21, 2007), accessed at http://blogs.bnet.com/ceo/?p=269.

24 K. D. Carlson, M. L. Connerley, and R. L. Mecham III, "Recruitment Evaluation: The Case for Assessing the Quality of Applicants Attracted," *Personnel Psychology* 55 (2002): 4614–4690.

25 C. Joinson, "Capturing Turnover Costs," *HRMagazine* (July 2000): 107–119; B. Davidson, "The Importance of Cost Per Hire," *Workforce* (January 2001): 32–34.

26 R. T. Cober, D. J. Brown, L. M. Keeping, and P. E. Levy, "Recruitment on the Net: Do Organizational Web Site Characteristics Influence Applicant Attraction?" *Journal of Management* 30 (2004): 6236–6246.

27 P. R. Sparrow. "Globalization of HR at Function Level: Four Case Studies of the International Recruitment and Selection Process," *International Journal of Human Resource Management* 18(5) (2007): 845–867.

28 J. Marquez, "Deloitte Touche Tohmatsu: Optimas Award Winner for Global Outlook," *Workforce Management* (August 8, 2006), available at www.workforce.com.

29 For suggestions about how to avoid such problems, see I. Kotlyar, "If Recruitment Means Building Trust, Where Does Technology Fit In?" *Canadian HR Reporter* (October 7, 2002): 21–24.

30 A. Van Vianen, "Person-Organization Fit: The Match Between Newcomers' and Recruiters' Preferences for Organizational Cultures," *Personnel Psychology* 53 (2000): 113–149; T. A. Judge and D. M. Cable, "Applicant Personality, Organizational Culture, and Organizational Attraction," *Personnel Psychology* 50 (1997): 359–394; A. M. Saks and B. E. Ashforth, "A Longitudinal Investigation of the Relationships Between Job Information Sources, Applicant Perceptions of Fit, and Work Outcomes," *Personnel Psychology* 50 (1997): 395–426; R. W. Griffeth,

P. W. Hom, L. S. Fink, and D. J. Cohen, "Comparative Tests of Multiple Models of Recruiting Sources Effects," *Journal of Management* 23 (1997): 19–36.

31 R. M. Fernandez and N. Weinberg, "Sifting and Sorting: Personal Contacts and Hiring in a Retail Bank," *American Sociological Review* 17 (December 1997): 883–902.

32 F. Hansen, "Employee Referral Programs, Selective Campus Recruitment Could Touch Off Bias Charges," *Workforce Management* (June 26, 2006), accessed at www.workforce.com.

33 "The World of Work," *The Economist* (January 6, 2007), 57–58.

34 M. N. Martinez, "Get Job Seekers to Come to You," *HRMagazine* (August 2000): 45–51.

35 S. Baker and M. Kripalani, "Will Outsourcing Hurt America's Supremacy?" *BusinessWeek* (March 1, 2004): 84–94; D. Kirkpatrick, "Rage Against Off-Shoring Is Off Target," *Fortune* (February 23, 2004): 66; A. B. Fisher, "Think Globally, Save Your Job Locally," *Fortune* (February 23, 2004): 60.

36 For a detailed discussion of immigration and employment issues, see F. Hansen, "Employee Referral Programs, Selective Campus Recruitment Could Touch Off Bias Charges," *Workforce Management* (June 26, 2006), accessed at www.workforce.com.

37 J. Shapiro, P. Morrow, and I. Kessler, "Serving Two Organizations: Exploring the employment relationship of contracted employees," *Human Resource Management* 45(4) (2006): 561–583; J. Zappe, "Temp-to-Hire Is Becoming a Full-time Practice at Firms," *Workforce Management* (June 2005): 82–85; E. George and P. Chattopadhyay, "One Foot in Each Camp: The Dual Identification of Contract Workers," *Administrative Quarterly* 50 (2005): 68–99; L. Lawrence, "Microsoft 'Permatemp' Settlement Seen as Warning to Employers," *HR News* (February 2001): 8.

38 P. Cappelli, "Making the Most of Online Recruiting," *Harvard Business Review* (March 2001): 139–146.

39 P. Sellers, "A Kinder, Gentler Lehman Brothers," *Fortune* (January 22, 2007): 36–38; J. Anderson, "The Fork in the Road," *The New York Times* (August 6, 2006).

40 D. S. Chapman, K. L. Uggerslev, S. A. Carroll, K. A. Piasentin, and D. A. Jones, "Applicant Attraction to Organizations and Job Choice: A Meta-Analytic Review of the Correlates of Recruiting Outcomes," *Journal of Applied Psychology* 90(5) (2005): 928–944; K. H. Ehrhart and J. C. Ziegert, "Why Are Individuals Attracted to Organizations?" *Journal of Management* 31(6) (2005): 901–919.

41 W. R. Boswell, M. V. Roehling, M. A. LePine, and L. M. Moynihan, "Individual Job-Choice Decisions and the Impact of Job Attributes and Recruitment Practices: A Longitudinal Field Study," *Human Resource Management* 42(1) (Spring 2003): 23–37; B. R. Dineen, S. R. Ash, and R. A. Noe, "A Web of Applicant Attraction: Person-Organization Fit in the Context of Web-Based Recruitment," *Journal of Applied Psychology* 87(4) (2002): 723–734; V. Corwin, T. B. Lawrence, and P. J. Frost, "Five Strategies of Successful Part-Time Work," *Harvard Business Review* (July–August 2001): 121–127.

42 L. Gerdes, "The Best Places to Launch a Career," *BusinessWeek* (Sept. 24, 2007): 49–60; C. Collins, "The Interactive Effects of Recruitment Practices and Product Awareness on Job Seekers' Employer Knowledge and Application Behaviors," *Journal of Applied Psychology* 92(1) (2007): 180–190; C. J. Collins and C. K. Stevens, "The Relationship Between Early Recruitment-Related Activities and the Application Decisions of New Labor-Market Entrants: A Brand Equity Approach to Recruitment," *Journal of Applied Psychology* 87(6) (2002): 1121–1133.

43 M. Boyle, "Happy People, Happy Returns," *Fortune* (January 23, 2006): 100; D. B. Turban and D. M. Cable, "Firm Reputation and Applicant Pool Characteristics," *Journal of Organizational Behavior* 24 (2003): 733–751.

44 P. Sellers, "The Recruiter," *Fortune* (November 27, 2006): 87–89.

45 B. Parus, "The Sky's the Limit in Online Recruiting," *Workspan* (January 2001): 54–56; P. Cappelli, "Making the Most of On-Line Recruiting," *Harvard Business Review* (March 2001): 139–146.

46 D. B. Turban and T. W. Dougherty, "Influences of Campus Recruiting on Applicant Attraction to Firms," *Academy of Management Journal* 35 (1992): 739–765.

47 S. D. Maurer, V. Howe, and T. W. Lee, "Organizational Recruiting as Marketing Management: An Interdisciplinary Study of Engineering Graduates," *Personnel Psychology* 45 (1992): 807–833.

48 C. K. Stevens, "Antecedents of Interview Interactions, Interview Ratings, and Applicants' Reactions," *Personnel Psychology* 51 (1998): 54–85.

49 P. J. Kiger, "Search and Employ," *Workforce Management* (June 2003): 656–658.

50 K. G. Wheeler and T. M. Mahoney, "The Expectancy Model in the Analysis of Occupational Preference and Occupational Choice," *Journal of Vocational Behavior* 19 (1981): 113–122.

51 A. M. Konrad, J. E. Ritchie, Jr., P. Lieb, and E. Corrigall, "Sex Differences and Similarities in Job Attribute Preferences: A Meta-Analysis," *Psychological Bulletin* 126(4) (2000): 593–641.

52 A. E. Barber, M. J. Wesson, Q. Roberson, and M. S. Taylor, "A Tale of Two Job Markets: Organizational Size and Its Effects on Hiring Practices and Job Search Behavior," *Personnel Psychology* 52 (1999): 841–867.

53 C. K. Stevens and A. L. Kristof, "Making the Right Impression: A Field Study of Applicant Impression Management During Job Interview," *Journal of Applied Psychology* 80 (1995): 587–606.

54 R. D. Bretz, Jr., and T. A. Judge, "Realistic Job Previews: A Test of the Adverse Self-Selection Hypothesis," *Journal of Applied Psychology* 83 (1998): 230–337.

55 R. C. Barnett and D. T. Hall, "How to Use Reduced Hours to Win the War for Talent," *Organizational Dynamics* 29(3) (2001): 192–210; S. F. Gate, "Formalized Flextime: The Perk That Brings Productivity," *Workforce* (February 2001): 39–42; S. Branch, "MBAs: What They Really Want," *Fortune* (March 16, 1998): 167; N. Munk, "Organization Man," *Fortune* (March 16, 1998): 63–74; T. A. Stewart, "Gray Flannel Suit?" *Fortune* (March 16, 1998): 76–82.

56 M. W. Walsh, "Money Isn't Everything," *The New York Times* (January 30, 2001): G10.

57 E. Olson, "Some Web Job Site Put Out 'Gray Hair Welcome' Signs," *The New York Times* (January 14, 2007).

58 P. W. Hom, R. W. Griffeth, L. Palich, and J. S. Bracker, "Revisiting Met Expectations as a Reason Why Realistic Job Previews Work," *Personnel Psychology* 52 (1999): 97–112; P. W. Hom, R. W. Griffeth, L. E. Palich, and J. S. Bracker, "An Exploratory Investigation into Theoretical Mechanisms Underlying Realistic Job Previews," *Personnel Psychology* 51 (1998): 421–451.

59 J. P. Wanous, R. D. Poland, S. L. Premack, and K. S. Davis, "The Effects of Met Expectations on Newcomer Attitudes and Behaviors: A Review and Meta-Analysis," *Journal of Applied Psychology* 77(3) (1992): 288–297; J. M. Phillips, "Effects of Realistic Job Previews on Multiple Organizational Outcomes: A Meta-Analysis," *Academy of Management Journal* (1999): 156–172.

60 A. M. Saks, "A Psychological Process Investigation for the Effects of Recruitment Source and Organization Information on Job Survival," *Journal of Organizational Behavior* 15 (1994): 225–244.

61 R. D. Gatewood, M. A. Gowan, and G. J. Lautenschlager, "Corporate Image, Recruitment Image, and Initial Choice Decisions," *Academy of Management Journal* 36 (1993): 414–427.

62 C. R. Williams, C. E. Labig, Jr., and T. H. Stone, "Recruitment Sources and Posthire Outcomes for Job Applicants and New Hires: A Test of Two Hypotheses," *Journal of Applied Psychology* 78 (1993): 163–172.

63 J. S. Leonard, "The Impact of Affirmative Action Regulation on Employment," *Journal of Economic Perspectives* 3 (1990): 47–63.

64 IBM provided this information, which is also described in the company's various recruiting materials.

65 P. M. Wright, S. R. Ferris, J. S. Hiller, and M. Kroll, "Competitiveness Through Management of Diversity: Effects of Stock Price Valuation," *Academy of Management Journal* 38 (1995): 272–286.

66 G. M. Combs, S. Nadkarni, and M. W. Combs, "Implementing Affirmative Action Plans in Multinational Corporations," *Organizational Dynamics* 34(4) (2005): 346–360.

67 M. E. Heilman and V. B. Alcott, "What I Think You Think of Me: Women's Reactions to Being Viewed as Beneficiaries of Preferential Selection," *Journal of Applied Psychology* 86 (2001): 574–582; M. E. Heilman, C. J. Block, and P. Stathatos, "The Affirmative Action Stigma of Incompetence: Effects of Performance Information Ambiguity," *Academy of Management Journal* 40 (1997): 603–625.

68 D. A. Harrison, D. A. Kravitz, D. M. Mayer, L. M. Leslie, and D. L. Arey, "Understanding Attitudes Toward Affirmative Action Programs in Employment: Summary and Meta-Analysis of 35 Years of Research," *Journal of Applied Psychology* 91(5) (2006): 1013–1036; R. Cropanzano, J. E. Slaughter, and P. D. Bachiochi, "Organizational Justice and Black Applicants' Reactions to Affirmative Action," *Journal of Applied Psychology* 90(6) (2005): 1168–1184; D. R. Avery, "Reactions to Diversity in Recruitment Advertising—Are Differences Black and White?" *Journal of Applied Psychology* 88(4) (2003): 672–679.

69 For a full review of this and other research on affirmative action, see D. A. Kravitz, D. A. Harrison, M. E. Turner, E. L. Levine, W. Chaves, M. T. Brannick, D. L. Denning, C. J. Russell, and M. A. Conrad, *Affirmative Action: A Review of Psychological and Behavioral Research* (Bowling Green, OH: Society for Industrial and Organizational Psychology, 1997).

70 D. A. Kravitz and S. L. Klineberg, "Reactions to Two Versions of Affirmative Action Among Whites, Blacks, and Hispanics," *Journal of Applied Psychology* 85 (2000): 597–611.

71 J. E. Slaughter, E. F. Sinar, and P. D. Bachiochi, "Black Applicants' Reactions to Affirmative Action Plans: Effects of Plan Content and Previous Experience with Discrimination," *Journal of Applied Psychology* 87(2) (2002): 333–344.

72 U.S. Department of Labor, *A Report on the Glass Ceiling Initiative* (Washington, DC: U.S. Department of Labor, 1991).

73 A. C. Glebbeek and E. H. Bax, "Is High Turnover Really Harmful? An Empirical Test Using Company Records," *Academy of Management Journal* 47 (2004): 2772–2786.

74 J. D. Shaw, N. Gupta, and J. E. Delery, "Alternative Conceptualizations of the Relationship Between Voluntary Turnover and Organizational Performance," *Academy of Management Journal* 48(1) (2005): 50–68.

75 Hundreds of studies have examined the reasons for voluntary employee turnover. A detailed discussion is beyond the scope of this chapter. Interested readers can begin to learn more by consulting I. Huang, H. Lin, and C. Chuang, "Constructing Factors Related to Worker Retention," *International Journal of Manpower* 27(5) (2006): 491–508; J. D. Shaw, M. K. Duffy, J. L. Johnson, and D. E. Lockhart, "Turnover, Social Capital Losses, and Performance," *Academy of Management Journal* 48(4) (2005): 594–606; K. W. Mossholder, R. P. Settoon, and S. C. Henagan, "A Relational Perspective on Turnover: Examining Structural, Attitudinal, and Behavioral Predictors," *Academy of Management Journal* 48(4) (2005): 607–618; C. P. Maertz, Jr., and R. W. Griffeth, "Eight Motivational Forces and Voluntary Turnover: A Theoretical Synthesis with Implications for Research," *Journal of Management* 30 (2004): 676–683; R. W. Griffeth, P. W. Hom, and S. Gaertner, "A Meta-Analysis of Analysis of Antecedents and Correlates of Employee Turnover: Update, Moderator Tests, and Research Implications for the Next Millennium," *Journal of Management* 26(3) (2000): 463–488.

76 W. S. Harman, T. W. Lee, T. R. Mitchell, W. Felps, and B. P. Owens, "The Psychology of Voluntary Employee Turnover," *Current Directions in Psychological Science* 16(1) (2007): 51–54.

77 "Disconnect Between Employers, Employees Threatens Loss of Key Workers, Watson Wyatt Finds," Watson Wyatt Worldwide Web site, accessed at www.watsonwyatt.com (January 10, 2007).

78 J. McGriger, "Balance and Balance Sheets," *Fast Company* (May 2004): 96–97.

79 L. Uchitelle, *The Disposable American: Layoffs and Their Consequences* (New York: Alfred A. Knopf, 2006).

80 D. Leonhardt, "3,400 Layoffs Send a Message to Millions," *The New York Times* (April 4, 2007): C1.

81 A. Bernstein, "Too Many Workers? Not for Long," *BusinessWeek* (May 2002): 126–130.

82 J. Mueller and H. Liao, "Workforce Reduction and Job-Seeker Attraction: Examining Job Seekers' Reactions to Firm Workforce-Reduction Policies," *Human Resource Management* 45(4) (2006): 583–603.

83 D. Rigby, "Look Before You Lay Off," *Harvard Business Review* (April 2002): 20–21.

84 E. Zimmerman, "Why Deep Layoffs Hurt Long-Term Recovery," *Workforce* (November 2001): 48–53; for a more detailed discussion, see K. P. DeMeuse and M. L. Marks (eds.), *Resizing the Organization: Managing Layoffs, Divestitures, and Closings* (San Francisco: Jossey-Bass, 2002).

85 "Keeping the Crew," *Human Resource Executive* (January 2004): 8–12.

86 W. J. Baumol, A. S. Blinder, and E. N. Wolff, *Downsizing in America: Reality, Causes, and Consequences* (New York: Russell Sage Foundation, 2003).

87 F. Hansen, "A Permanent Strategy for Temporary Hires," *Workforce Management* (February 26, 2007): 25–30.

88 Deloitte Research, "How Manufacturing Companies Can Beat the Coming Talent Crisis: It's 2008. Do You Know Where Your Talent Is?" Deloitte Development LLC (2004), accessed at http://www.deloitte.com/dtt/article/0,1002,sid%253D2222%2526cid%253D100632,00.html.

89 M. Herbst, "Click for Foreign Labor," *BusinessWeek* (January 15, 2007): 71; Society for Human Resource Management, "HR Issues Update," ComPartners NewsManager, accessed at www.newsmanager.commpartners.com/shrm/2007-02-09/html (February 10, 2007); M. Aitken, G. Ratliff, C. Lange, and L. Shotell, "Electronic Employment Verification: What's Required Now and What's In-Store for HR Professionals?" Society for Human Resource Management, accessed at www.shrm.org/government (December 2006).

Chapter 7

1 S. F. Gale, "Three Companies Cut Turnover with Tests," *Workforce Management* (April 2002): 66–69.

2 B. Roberts, "Crunching the Numbers," *HRMagazine* (October 2003): 63–68.

3 T. Murphy and S. Zandvakili, "Data- and Metrics-Driven Approach to Human Resource Practices: Using Customers, Employees, and Financial Metrics," *Human Resource Management* 39(1) (Spring 2000): 93–105.

4 D. E. Terpstra and E. J. Rozell, "The Relationship of Staffing Practices to Organizational Level Measures of Performance," *Personnel Psychology* 46 (1993): 27–48.

5 For a discussion of developments in the use of staffing metrics, including Dell's practices, see C. Winkler, "Quality Check: Better Metrics Improve HR's Ability to Measure—and Manage—the Quality of HIrex," *HRMagazine* (May 2007): 93–98; for detailed discussions of utility analysis, see W. R. Cascio, *Costing Human Resources: The Financial Impact of Behavior in Organizations* (Cincinnati, OH: South-Western, 2000); E. F. Cabrera and N. S. Raju, "Utility Analysis: Current Trends and Future Directions," *International Journal of Selection and Assessment* 9 (2001): 92–102.

6 For a review of some challenges facing HR professionals, see R. E. Ployhart, "Staffing in the 21st Century: New Challenges and Strategic Opportunities," *Journal of Management* 32 (2006): 868–887.

7 For detailed discussions of selection processes, see N. Anderson, F. Lievens, K. van Dam, and A. M. Ryan, "Future Perspectives on Employee Selection: Key Directions for Future Research and Practice," *Applied Psychology: An International Review* 53 (2004): 501; K. Pearlman and M. F. Barney, "Selection for a Changing Workforce," in J. F. Kehoe (ed.), *Managing Selection in Changing Organizations: Human Resource Strategies* (San Francisco: Jossey-Bass, 2000): 3–72.

8 J. Zappe, "Recruiting Firms Setting Up Shop in Second Life," *Workforce Management* (March 26, 2007): 4.

9 For more complete discussions, see R. M. Guion and S. Highhouse, *Essentials of Personnel Assessment and Selection* (Mahwah, NJ: Lawrence Erlbaum Associates, 2006); R. E. Ployhart, B. Schneider, and N. W. Schmitt, *Staffing Organizations* (Mahwah, NJ: Lawrence Erlbaum Associates, 2006).

10 M. M. Lombard and R. W. Eichinger, "High Potentials as High Learners," *Human Resource Management* (Winter 2000): 321–329; H. G. Heneman III and T. A. Judge, *Staffing Organizations* (New York: McGraw-Hill-Irwin, 2002).

11 A. J. Vinchur, J. S. Schippmann, F. S. Switzer, III, and P. L. Roth, "A Meta-Analytic Review of Predictors of Job Performance for Salespeople," *Journal of Applied Psychology* 83 (1998): 586–597; D. E. Bowen and D. A. Waldman, "Customer-Driven Employee Performance," in D. R. Ilgen and E. D. Pulakos (eds.), *The Changing Nature of Performance* (San Francisco: Jossey-Bass, 1999): 154–191.

12 R. G. Jones, M. J. Stevens, and D. L. Fischer, "Selection in Team Contexts," in J. F. Kehoe (ed.), *Managing Selection in Changing Organizations: Human Resource Strategies* (San Francisco: Jossey-Bass, 2000), 210–241; G. Neuman and J. Wright, "Team Effectiveness: Beyond Skills and Cognitive Ability," *Journal of Applied Psychology* 84(3) (1999): 376–389; M. Stevens and M. A. Campion, "Staffing Work Teams: Development and Validation of a Selection Test for Teamwork Settings," *Journal of Management* 25 (1999): 207–228.

13 G. A. Neuman and J. Wright, "Team Effectiveness: Beyond Skills and Cognitive Ability," *Journal of Applied Psychology* 84 (1999): 376–389; S. Taggar, "Individual Creativity and Group Ability to Utilize Creative Resources: A Multilevel Model," *Academy of Management Journal* 45 (2002): 315–330.

14 G. Colvin, "Why Dream Teams Fail," *Fortune* (June 12, 2006): 87–92.

15 A. Edmondson, R. Bohmer, and G. Pisano, "Speeding Up Team Learning," *Harvard Business Review* (October 2001): 125–132.

16 D. P. Shuit, "Magic for Sale," *Workforce Management* (September 2004): 35–40; "Walt Disney Tops BusinessWeek's Inaugural 'Best Places to Launch a Career,'" Walt Disney Company press release (September 7, 2006), accessed at corporate.disney.go.com/careers/pdfs/disney_businessweek.pdf (September 12, 2007); V. C. Smith, "Spreading the Magic," *Human Resource Executive* (December 1996): 28–31.

17 D. Koeppel, "Those Low Grades in College May Haunt Your Job Search," *The New York Times* (December 31, 2006): Section 10, 1.

18 J. Romeo, "Answering the Call," *HRMagazine* (October 2003): 81–84; G. Nicholson, "Automated Assessments for Better Hires," *Workforce Management* (December 2000): 102–109.

19 McDaniel, M.A. (in press), "Validity Generalization as a Test Validation Approach," in S. M. McPhail (ed.) *Alternative Validation Strategies*; K. R. Murphy, *Validity Generalization: A Critical Review* (Mahwah, NJ: Lawrence Erlbaum Associates, 2003).

20 For a discussion of validity generalization and other related approaches, see C. C. Hoffman and S. M. McPhail, "Exploring Options for Supporting Test Use in Situations Precluding Local Validation," *Personnel Psychology* 51 (1998): 987–1003.

21 See F. L. Schmidt and J. E. Hunter, "The Validity and Utility of Selection Methods in Personnel Psychology: Practical and Theoretical Implications of 85 Years of Research Findings," *Psychological Bulletin* 124 (1998): 262–274.

22 Based on data presented in B. O'Leary, M. L. Lindholm, R. A. Whitford, and S. F. Freeman, "Selecting the Best and Brightest: Leveraging Human Capital," *Human Resource Management* (Fall 2002): 325–340; F. L. Schmidt and J. E. Hunter, "The Validity and Utility of Selection Methods in Personnel Psychology: Practical and Theoretical Implications of 85 Years of Research Findings," *Psychological Bulletin* 124 (1998): 262–274.

23 C. Boutelle, "New Principles Encourage Greater Accountability for Test Users and Developers," *Industrial-Organizational Psychologist* 41(3) (2004): 20–21.

24 A. Aston, "Who Will Run the Plants?" *BusinessWeek* (January 22, 2007): 78.

25 S. Hays, "Kinko's Dials into Automated Applicant Screening," *Workforce* (November 1999): 71–73.

26 For a review of recent research findings, see R. E. Ployhart, "Staffing in the 21st Century: New Challenges and Strategic Opportunities," *Journal of Management* 32(6) (December 2006): 868–897.

27 D. G. Lawrence, et al., "Design and Use of Weighted Application Blanks," *Personnel Administrator* (March 1982): 53–57, 101.

28 C. J. Russell, et al., "Predictive Validity of Biodata Items Generated from Retrospective Life Experience Essays," *Journal of Applied Psychology* 75(5) (1990): 569–580; H. R. Rothstein, et al., "Biographical Data in Employment Selection: Can Validities Be Made Generalizable?" *Journal of Applied Psychology* 75(2) (1990): 175–184.

29 M. Dean, C. J. Russell, and P. Muchinsky, "Life Experiences and Performance Prediction: Toward a Theory of Biodata," *Research in Personnel and Human Resource Management* 17 (1999): 245–281; G. Stokes, M. D. Mumford, and W. Owens (eds.), *Biodata Handbook: Theory, Research, and Use of Biographical Information for Selection and Performance Prediction* (Palo Alto, CA: Consulting Psychologists Press, 1994).

30 P. J. Taylor and B. Small, "Asking Applicants What They Would Do Versus What They Did Do: A Meta-Analytic Comparison of Situational and Past Behavior Employment Interview Questions," *Journal of Occupational and Organizational Psychology* 75 (2002): 277–294; M. D. Mumford, D. P. Costanza, M. S. Connelly, and J. E. Johnson, "Item Generation Procedures and Background Data Scales: Implications for Construct and Criterion-Related Validity," *Personnel Psychology* 49 (1996): 361–398; A. T. Dalessio and T. A. Silverhart, "Combining Biodata Test and Interview Information: Predicting Decisions and Performance Criteria," *Personnel Psychology* 47 (1994): 303–319.

31 F. A. Mael and B. E. Ashforth, "Loyal from Day One: Biodata, Organizational Identification, and Turnover Among Newcomers," *Personnel Psychology* 48 (1995): 309–333; R. D. Gatewood and H. S. Field, *Human Resource Selection* (Orlando, FL: Dryden, 1994).

32 M. McManus and M. Kelly, "Personality Measures and Biodata: Evidence Regarding Their Incremental Predictive Value in the Life Insurance Industry," *Personnel Psychology* 52 (1999): 137–148; K. Carlson, S. Scullen, F. L. Schmidt, H. R. Rothstein, and F. Erwin, "Generalized Biographical Data Validity Can Be Achieved Without Multi-Organizational Development and Keying," *Personnel Psychology* 52 (1999): 731–755.

33 S. Hansell, "Google Answer to Filling Jobs Is an Algorithm," *The New York Times* (January 3, 2007): A1, C9.

34 R. Folger and R. Cropanzano, *Organizational Justice and Human Resource Management* (Thousand Oaks, CA: Sage, 1998); F. A. Mael, M. Connerley, and R. A. Morath, "None of Your Business: Parameters of Biodata Invasiveness," *Personnel Psychology* 49 (1996): 613–650.

35 A. Hedger, "Taking a Strategic View of Employee Screening," *Workforce Management* (March 26, 2007): 43–52.

36 P. Babcock, "Spotting Lies," *HRMagazine* (October 2003): 46–52.

37 T. B. Stivarius, J. Skonberg, R. Fliegel, R. Blumberg, R. Jones, and K. Mones, "Background Checks: Four Steps to Basic Compliance in a Multistate Environment," *Legal Report* (March–April 2003): 1–8; M. A. Nusbaum, "When a Reference Is a Tool for Snooping," *The New York Times* (October 19, 2003): 12; S. Romero and M. Richtel, "Second Chance," *The New York Times* (March 5, 2001): C1; L. Walley and M. Smith, *Deception in Selection* (New York: John Wiley, 1998); E. A. Robinson, "Beware— Job Seekers Have No Secrets," *Fortune* (December 29, 1997): 285; "Positive Reference Leads to Claim of Negligence," *Fair Employment Practices Guidelines* 430 (April 25, 1997): 1; "Supreme Court Decision Possible Setback to Employee Reference," *Human Resource Executive* (April 1997): 8.

38 K. Gurchiek, "Web to Figure More Prominently in Sizing Up Applicants," Society for Human Resource Management, accessed at www.shrm.org (January 2, 2007).

39 J. F. Salgado, N. Anderson, S. Moscoso, C. Bertua, F. D. Fruyt, and J. P. Rolland, "A Meta-Analytic Study of General Mental Ability Validity for Different Occupations in the European Community," *Journal of Applied Psychology* 88(6) (2003): 1068–1081; M. A. Nusbaum, "When a Reference Is a Tool for Snooping," *The New York Times* (October 19, 2003): 12; F. L. Schmidt and J. E. Hunter, "The Validity and Utility of Selection Methods in Personnel Psychology: Practical and Theoretical Implications of 85 Years of Research Findings," *Psychological Bulletin* 124 (1998): 262–274.

40 E. A. Fleishman and M. K. Quaintance, *Taxonomies of Human Performance* (New York: Academic Press, 1984).

41 R. L. Roth, C. Bevier, P. Bobko, F. S. Switzer III, and P. Taylor, "Ethnic Group Differences in Cognitive Ability in Employment and Educational Settings: A Meta-Analysis," *Personnel Psychology* 54 (2001): 297–330; N. Schmitt, C. S. Clause, and E. D. Pulakos, "Subgroup Differences Associated with Different Measures of Some Common Job-Relevant Constructs," in C. R. Cooper and I. T. Roberson (eds.), *International Review of Industrial/Organizational Psychology*, vol. 11 (1996): 115–140. For a discussion of some alternatives to cognitive ability testing, see S. Zedeck and I. L. Goldstein, "The Relationship Between I/O Psychology and Public Policy: A Commentary," in J. F. Kehoe (ed.), *Managing Selection in Changing Organizations: Human Resource Strategies* (San Francisco: Jossey-Bass, 2000), 371–396.

42 S. Greengard, "Gimme Attitude," *Workforce Management* (July 15, 2003): 56–60, accessed at http://www.workforce.com/section/06/ feature/23/47/86/index.html; R. T. Hogan, J. C. Hogan, and B. W. Roberts, "Personality Measurement and Employment Decisions," *American Psychologist* 51 (1996): 469–477; R. T. Hogan, "Personality and Personality Measurement," in M. D. Dunnette and L. M. Hough (eds.), *Handbook of Industrial and Organizational Psychology* (Palo Alto, CA: Consulting Psychologists Press, 1991): 873–890.

43 J. M. Collins and D. H. Gleaves, "Race, Job Applicants, and the Five-Factor Model of Personality: Implications for Black Psychology, Industrial/Organizational Psychology, and the Five-Factor Theory," *Journal of Applied Psychology* 83 (1998): 531–544; R. R. McCrae and P. T. Costa, Jr., "Personality Trait Structure as a Human Universal," *American Psychologist* 52 (1997): 509–535; L. M. Hough and R. J. Schneider, "Personality Traits, Taxonomies, and Applications in Organizations," in K. R. Murphy (ed.), *Individual Differences and Behavior in Organizations* (San Francisco: Jossey-Bass, 1996): 31–88.

44 N. M. Dudley, K. A. Orvis, J. E. Lebiecki, and J. M. Cortina, "A Meta-Analytic Investigation of Conscientiousness in the Prediction of Job Performance: Examining the Intercorrelations and the Incremental Validity of Narrow Traits," *Journal of Applied Psychology* 91(1) (2006): 40–57; D. Bartram, "The Great Eight Competencies: A Criterion-Centric Approach to Validation," *Journal of Applied Psychology* 90(6) (2005): 1185–1203; T. A. Judge, D. Heller, and M. K. Mount, "Five-Factor Model of Personality and Job Satisfaction: A Meta-Analysis," *Journal of Applied Psychology* 87 (2002): 53–541; P. Caligiuri, "The Big Five Personality

Characteristics as Predictors of Expatriate's Desire to Terminate the Assignment and Supervisor-Rated Performance," *Personnel Psychology* 53 (2000): 67–88.

45 HR News Staff, "Reassess Personality Tests After Court Case," *HRMagazine* (September 2005): 30, 32.

46 R. Strauss, "When the Resume Is Not to Be Believed," *The New York Times* (September 12, 2006): G2.

47 K. R. Murphy, *Honesty in the Workplace* (Pacific Grove, CA: Brooks/Cole, 1993); D. S. Ones, C. Viswesvaran, and F. L. Schmidt, "Comprehensive Meta-Analysis of Integrity Test Validities: Findings and Implications for Personnel Selection and Theories of Job Performance," *Journal of Applied Psychology* 78 (1993): 679–703; W. J. Camara and D. L. Schneider, "Integrity Tests: Facts and Unresolved Issues," *American Psychologist* 49 (1994): 112–119; J. M. Collins and F. L. Schmidt, "Personality, Integrity, and White Collar Crime: A Construct Validity Study," *Personnel Psychology* 46 (1993): 295–311.

48 The Conference Board, "Are They Really Ready to Work?" (New York: The Conference Board, 2006).

49 J. B. Olson-Buchanan, F. Drasgow, P. J. Moberg, A. D. Mead, P. A. Keenan, and M. A. Donovan, "Interactive Video Assessment of Conflict Resolution Skills," *Personnel Psychology* 51 (1998): 1–24; J. A. Weekley and C. Jones, "Video-Based Situational Testing," *Personnel Psychology* 50 (1997): 25–49.

50 P. L. Roth, P. Bobko, and L. A. McFarland, "A Meta-Analysis of Work Sample Test Validity: Updating and Integrating Some Classic Literature," *Personnel Psychology* 58 (2005): 1009–1037; R. L. Griffith, *A Closer Examination of Applicant Faking Behavior* (Greenwich, CT: Information Age Publishing, 2006); W. L. Grubb III, M. A. McDaniel, "The Fakability of Bar-On's Emotional Quotient Inventory Short Form: Catch Me If You Can," *Human Performance* 20(1) (2007): 43–59.

51 N. J. Kolk, M. P. Born, and H. V. D. Flier, "The Transparent Assessment Center: The Effects of Revealing Dimension to Candidates," *Applied Psychology: An International Review* 52 (2003): 648–668; M. Damitz, D. Manzey, M. Kleinmann, and K. Severin, "Assessment Center for Pilot Selection: Construct and Criterion Validity and the Impact of Assessor Type," *Applied Psychology: An International Review* 52 (2003): 193–212; D. J. Woehr and W. Arthur, Jr., "The Construct-Related Validity of Assessment Center Ratings: A Review and Meta-Analysis of the Role of Methodological Factors," *Journal of Management* 29 (2003): 231–258.

52 J. N. Zall, "Assessment Centre Methods," in P. J. D. Drenth, H. Thierry, and C. J. DeWolff (eds.), *Handbook of Work and Organizational Psychology, vol. 3: Personnel Psychology* (Basingstoke, UK: Taylor & Francis, 1998); D. R. Briscoe, "Assessment Centers: Cross-Cultural and Cross-National Issues," *Journal of Social Behavior and Personality* 12 (1997): 261–270; A. C. Spychalski, M. A. Quinnones, B. A. Gaugler, and K. Pohley, "A Survey of Assessment Center Practices in Organizations in the United States," *Personnel Psychology* 5 (1997): 71–90.

53 L. M. Donahue, D. M. Truxillo, J. M. Cornwell, and M. J. Gerrity, "Assessment Center Construct Validity and Behavioral Checklists," *Journal of Social Behavior and Personality* 12(5) (1997): 85–108; B. B. Gaugler, et al., "Meta-Analysis of Assessment Center Validity," *Journal of Applied Psychology* 72 (1987): 493–511.

54 D. R. Briscoe, "Assessment Centers: Cross-Cultural and Cross-National Issues," *Journal of Social Behavior and Personality* (Special Issue) (1997): 261–270; C. C. Hoffman and G. C. Thornton III, "Examining Selection Utility Where Competing Predictors Differ in Adverse Impact," *Personnel Psychology* 50 (1997): 455–470.

55 R. A. Posthuma, F. P. Morgeson, and M. A. Campion, "Beyond Employment Interview Validity: A Comprehensive Narrative Review of Recent Research and Trends over Time," *Personnel Psychology* 55 (2002): 1–81; B. P. Sunoo, "How Fun Flies at Southwest Airlines," *Personnel Journal* (June 1995): 62–71. For a detailed discussion of employment interviews, see R. W. Eder and M. M. Harris (eds.), *The Employment Interview Handbook* (Thousand Oaks, CA: Sage, 1999).

56 J. Burnett and S. J. Motowidlo, "Relations Between Different Sources of Information in the Structured Selection Interview," *Personnel Psychology* 51 (1998): 963–983; CCH Incorporated, "20 Factors to Determine Worker Status," *Workforce Extra* (November 1999): 1–2; J. Cortina, N. Goldstein, S. Payne, H. Davidson, and S. Gilliland, "The Incremental Validity of Interview Scores Above Cognitive Ability and Conscientiousness Scores," *Personnel Psychology* 53 (2000): 325–351.

57 W. Tsai, C. Chen, and S. Chiu, "Exploring Boundaries of the Effects of Applicant Impression Management Tactics in Job Interviews," *Journal of Management* 31(1) (February 2005): 108–125; R. W. Eder and M. M. Harris, *The Employment Interview Handbook* (London: Sage, 2000); E. D. Pulakos and N. Schmitt, "Experience-Based and Situational Interview Questions: Studies of Validity," *Personnel Psychology* 48 (1995): 289–308; M. A. Campion, D. K. Palmer, and J. E. Campion, "A Review of Structure in the Selection Interview," *Personnel Psychology* 50 (1997): 655–702; M. A. McDaniel, et al., "The Validity of Employment Interviews: A Comprehensive Review and Meta-Analysis," *Journal of Applied Psychology* 79 (1994): 599–616; S. J. Motowidlo, et al., "Studies of the Structured Behavioral Interview," *Journal of Applied Psychology* 77 (1992): 571–587.

58 J. M. Sacco, C. R. Scheu, A. M. Ryan, and N. Schmitt, "An Investigation of Race and Sex Similarity Effects in Interviews: A Multilevel Approach to Relational Demography," *Journal of Applied Psychology* 88 (2003): 852–865; D. S. Ones and N. Anderson, "Gender and Ethnic Group Differences on Personality Scales in Selection: Some British Data," *Journal of Occupational and Organizational Psychology* 75 (2002): 255–276; A. I. Huffcutt and P. L. Roth, "Racial Group Difference in Employment Interview Evaluations," *Journal of Applied Psychology* 83 (1998): 179–189; C. T. Kulick, L. Roberson, and E. A. Perry, "The Multiple-Category Problem: Category Activation and Inhibition in the Hiring Process," *Academy of Management Review* 32 (2007): 529–548.

59 P. J. Taylor and B. Small, "Asking Applicants What They Would Do Versus What They Did Do: A Meta-Analytic Comparison of Situational and Past Behavior Employment Interview Questions," *Journal of Occupational and Organizational Psychology* 75 (2002): 277–294. For more discussion, see G. P. Latham, "The Situational Interview," in R. W. Eder and M. M. Harris (eds.), *The Employment Interview Handbook* (Thousand Oaks, CA: Sage, 1999), 159–178; S. J. Motowidlo, "Asking About Past Behavior Versus Hypothetical Behavior," in R. W. Eder and M. M. Harris (eds.), *The Employment Interview Handbook* (Thousand Oaks, CA: Sage, 1999), 179–190.

60 L. Fogli and K. Whitney, "Assessing and Changing Managers for New Organizational Roles," in R. Jeanneret and R. Silzer (eds.), *Individual Psychological Assessment: Predicting Behavior in Organizational Settings* (San Francisco: Jossey-Bass, 1998).

61 M. A. McDaniel, N. S. Hartman, D. L. Whetzel, and W. L. Grubb III, "Situational Judgment Tests, Response Instructions and Validity: A Meta-Analysis," *Personnel Psychology* (in press).

62 G. Nyfield and H. Baron, "Cultural Context in Adapting Selection Practices Across Borders," in J. F. Kehoe (ed.), *Managing Selection in Changing Organizations: Human Resource Strategies* (San Francisco: Jossey-Bass, 2000): 242–268; A. M. Ryan, L. McFarland, H. Baron, and

R. Page, "An International Look at Selection Practices: Nation and Culture as Explanations for Variability in Practice," *Personnel Psychology* 52 (1999): 359–391.

63 T. Lin, G. H. Dobbins, and J. L. Farh, "A Field Study of Race and Age Similarity Effects on Interview Ratings in Conventional and Situational Interviews," *Journal of Applied Psychology* 77 (1992): 363–371; see also A. J. Prewett-Livingston, H. S. Field, J. G. Veres III, and P. M. Lewis, "Effects of Interview Ratings in a Situational Panel Interview," *Journal of Applied Psychology* (1996): 178–186.

64 E. D. Pulakos, N. Schmitt, D. Whitney, and M. Smith, "Individual Differences in Interviewer Ratings: The Impact of Standardization, Consensus Discussion, and Sampling Error on the Validity of a Structured Interview," *Personnel Psychology* 49 (1996): 85–102.

65 D. M. Cable and T. A. Judge, "Interviewers' Perceptions of Person-Organization Fit and Organizational Selection Decisions," *Journal of Applied Psychology* 82 (1997): 546–561; C. M. Marlowe, S. Schneider, and C. E. Nelson, "Gender and Attractiveness Biases in Hiring Decisions: Are More Experienced Managers Less Biased?" *Journal of Applied Psychology* 81 (1996): 11–21.

66 C. K. Stevens, "Antecedents of Interview Interactions, Interviewers' Ratings, and Applicants' Reactions," *Personnel Psychology* 51 (1998): 55–85.

67 Data collected by Staffing.org, Inc.

68 M. Bolch, "Lights, Camera…Interview!" *HRMagazine* (March 2007): 99–102.

69 "EEOC Issues Final Guidance for Medical Examinations under ADA," *Fair Employment Practices Guidelines* (January 25, 1996): 5; "Past Accommodations Do Not Always Determine the Future," *Fair Employment Practices Guidelines* 436 (July 25, 1997): 1; A. Bryant, "Seeing What Really Matters," *The New York Times* (December 24, 1997): D1, D4; R. R. Faden and N. E. Kass, "Genetic Screening Technology: Ethical Issues in Access to Tests by Employers and Health Insurance Companies," *Journal of Social Issues* 49 (1993): 75–88.

70 S. Sonnenberg, "Can HR Legally Ask the Questions That Applicants with Disabilities Want to Be Asked?" *Workforce Management* (August 2002): 42–44. For a detailed discussion of providing accommodation for people with disabilities, see W. J. Campbell and M. E. Reilly, "Accommodations for Persons with Disabilities," in J. F. Kehoe (ed.), *Managing Selection in Changing Organizations: Human Resource Strategies* (San Francisco: Jossey-Bass, 2000), 319–367.

71 F. P. Alvarez, "Disability Management Law Grows Up: Examining the Supreme Court's Recent ADA and FMLA Rulings," *Legal Report* (September–October 2002): 1–8; D. D. Hatch and J. E. Hall, "Disabled Must Compete on Equal Basis," *Workforce Management* (2000): 109.

72 A. Meisler, "Negative Results," *Workforce Management* (October 2003): 35–40.

73 G. Nyfield and H. Baron, "Cultural Context in Adapting Selection Practices Across Borders," in J. F. Kehoe (ed.), *Managing Selection in Changing Organizations: Human Resource Strategies* (San Francisco: Jossey-Bass, 2000): 242–268; A. M. Ryan, L. McFarland, H. Baron, and R. Page, "An International Look at Selection Practices: Nation and Culture as Explanations for Variability in Practice," *Personnel Psychology* 52 (1999): 359–391.

74 D. S. Chapman, K. L. Uggerslev, and J. Webster, "Applicant Reactions to Face-to-Face and Technology-Mediated Interviews: A Field Investigation," *Journal of Applied Psychology* 88 (2003): 944–953; C. J. Collins and C. K. Stevens, "The Relationship Between Early Recruitment-Related Activities and the Application Decisions of New Labor-Market Entrants: A Brand Equity Approach to Recruitment," *Journal of Applied Psychology* 87 (2002): 1121–1133; D. M. Truxillo, T. N. Bauer, M. A. Campion, and M. E. Paronto, "Selection Fairness Information and Applicant Reactions: A Longitudinal Field Study," *Journal of Applied Psychology* 87 (2002): 1020–1031; A. M. Ryan and R. E. Ployhart, "Applicants' Perceptions of Selection Procedures and Decisions: A Critical Review and Agenda for the Future," *Journal of Management* 26(3) (2000): 565–606.

75 R. E. Ployhart, A. M. Ryan, and M. A. Bennett, "Explanations for Selection Decisions: Applicants' Reactions to Informational and Sensitivity Features of Explanations," *Journal of Applied Psychology* 84(1) (1999): 87–106.

76 T. Bauer, D. M. Truxillo, R. Sanchez, J. Craig, P. Ferrara, and M. A. Campion, "Applicant Reactions to Selection: Development of the Selection Procedural Justice Scale," *Personnel Psychology* 54 (2001): 387–420; D. Chan, N. Schmitt, J. M. Sacco, and R. P. DeShon, "Understanding Pretest and Posttest Reaction to Cognitive Ability and Personality Tests," *Journal of Applied Psychology* 83 (1998): 471–485.

77 D. Chan, "Racial Subgroup Difference in Predictive Validity Perceptions on Personality and Cognitive Ability Tests," *Journal of Applied Psychology* 82 (1997): 311–320; D. Chan, N. Schmitt, R. P. DeShon, C. S. Clause, and K. Delbridge, "Reactions to Cognitive Ability Tests: The Relationships Between Race, Test Performance, Face Validity Perceptions, and Test-Taking Motivation," *Journal of Applied Psychology* 82 (1997): 300–310.

78 F. Hansen, "Keeping Interviews on Point to Stay Out of Legal Hot Water," *Workforce Management* (August 14, 2006): 44–45.

79 S. F. Gale, "Putting Job Candidates to the Test," *Workforce Management* (2004): 91; see Rynes, "Who's Selecting Whom? Effects of Selection Practices on Applicants' Attitudes and Behavior," in N. Schmitt and W. C. Borman (eds.), *Personnel Selection in Organizations* (San Francisco: Jossey-Bass, 1993), 240–274.

80 A. Rodriguez and F. Prezant, "Better Interviews for People with Disabilities," *Workforce* (August 2002): 38–42.

81 R. Thompson, "Marriott HR Exec Speaks about Successes, Challenges of His Job," *HR News* (December 1999): 1–2, 37.

82 W. F. Cascio, "Reconciling Economic and Social Objectives in Personnel Selection: Impact of Alternative Decision Rules," *New Approaches to Employee Management: Fairness in Employee Selection* 1 (1992): 61–86; M. E. Baehr, et al., "Proactively Balancing the Validity and Legal Compliance of Personal Background Measures in Personnel Management," *Journal of Business and Psychology* 8 (Spring 1994): 345–354; S. E. Maxwell and R. D. Arvey, "The Search for Predictors with High Validity and Low Adverse Impact: Compatible or Incompatible Goals?" *Journal of Applied Psychology* 78 (1993): 433–437.

83 L. Micco, "California Bans Employment Bias Based on Genetic Testing," *HR News* (August 1998): 13.

84 For an excellent discussion of legal issues, see J. C. Sharf and D. P. Jones, "Employment Risk Management," in J. F. Kehoe (ed.), *Managing Selection in Changing Organizations: Human Resource Strategies* (San Francisco: Jossey-Bass, 2000): 271–318.

85 Society for Industrial and Organizational Psychology, *Principles for the Validation and Use of Personnel Selection Procedures*, 4th ed. (Bowling Green, OH: Society for Industrial and Organizational Psychology, 2003).

86 To learn more about how subtle discrimination can limit opportunities for women to develop their international competencies, see K. Tyler, "Don't Fence Her In," *HRMagazine* (March 2001): 70–77; *Passport to Opportunity: U.S. Women in Global Business,* research report (New York: Catalyst, 2000).

87 For discussions about how the design of selection procedures can affect adverse impact, see R. P. DeShon, M. R. Smith, D. Chan, and N. Schmitt, "Can Racial Difference in Cognitive Test Performance Be Reduced by Presenting Problems in a Social Context?" *Journal of Applied Psychology* 83 (1998): 438–451; K. Hattrup, J. Rock, and C. Scalia, " The Effects of Varying Conceptualizations of Job Performance on Adverse Impact, Minority Hiring, and Predicted Performance," *Journal of Applied Psychology* 82 (1997): 656–664; P. R. Sackett and J. E. Ellington, "The Effects of Forming Multi-Predictor Composites on Group Differences and Adverse Impact," *Personnel Psychology* 50 (1997): 707–722.

88 For other methods, see S. B. Morris and R. E. Lobsenz, "Significance Tests and Confidence Intervals for Adverse Impact Ratios," *Personnel Psychology* 53 (2000): 89–111.

89 R. Kopp, *The Rice Paper Ceiling: Breaking Through Japanese Corporate Culture* (New York: Stone Bridge Press, 1994).

90 D. R. Briscoe and R. S. Schuler, *International Human Resource Management,* 2nd ed. (London: Routledge, 2004).

91 C. Daily, S. Certo, and D. R. Dalton, "International Experience in the Executive Suite: The Path to Prosperity?" *Strategic Management Journal* 21 (2000): 515–523; M. Dalton, C. Ernst, J. Deal, and J. Leslie, *Success for the New Global Leader* (Greensboro, NC: Center for Creative Leadership, 2002).

92 To learn more about how culture affects hiring practices, see A. M. Ryan, L. McFarland, H. Baron, and R. Page, "An International Look at Selection Practices: Nation and Culture as Explanations for Variability in Practice," *Personnel Psychology* 52 (1999): 359–391; H. Scullion and M Linehan, *Global Staffing* (London: Routledge, 2005).

Chapter 8

1 C. Lachnit, "Hire Right: Do It the Ritz Way," *Workforce Management* (April 2002): 16; B. Lampton, "My Pleasure: The Ritz-Carlton Hotel," *Expert* (2003): 3, accessed at www.expertmagazine.com June 2006); additional information obtained from the company Web site, accessed at www .ritzcarlton.com; P. Hemp, "My Week as a Room-Service Waiter at the Ritz," *Harvard Business Review* (June 2002): 50–62.

2 "Four Employers Score with Programs to Develop, Retain Skilled Workforces," *BNA Bulletin to Management* (October 14, 1999): 321; for an extended discussion of the strategic importance of training and development, see S. Tannenbaum, "A Strategic View of Training and Learning," in K. Kraiger (ed.), *Creating, Implementing and Managing Effective Training and Development: State-of-the-Art Lessons for Practice* (San Francisco: Jossey-Bass, 2002): 10–52.

3 "SHRM—BNA Survey No. 63: Human Resource Activities, Budgets & Staffs, 1997–1998," *Bulletin to Management* (June 18, 1998): 2; "High-Technology Firms Lead the Way in Training," *Bulletin to Management* (February 5, 1998): 376; "1997 Industry Report," *Training* (October 1998): 33–65. Also see the American Society for Training & Development (ASTD) 2003 State of the Industry Report, accessed at http://www.astd .org/astd.

4 R. J. Grossman, "Developing Talent," *HRMagazine* (January 2005): 40–46.

5 L. G. Klaff, "An Ever-Changing Workforce Management Landscape Path," *Workforce Management* (December 2006), accessed at www .workforce.com. Also visit the Web site of ASTD at www.astd.org.

6 P. Kiger, "Health Partners Delivers Training That Works," *Workforce* (November 2002): 60–64.

7 Adapted from C. Huff, "Accent on Training," *Workforce Management* (March 2005): 54; see also E. Frauenheim, "Culture of Understanding," *Workforce Management* (November 2005): 26–30.

8 E. Zimmerman, "Better Training Is Just a Click Away," *Workforce* (January 2001): 36–42.

9 "Ethical Practice 2006: J. M. Smucker & Co.," *Workforce Management* (March 13, 2006): 19.

10 V. I. Sessa and M. London, *Continuous Learning in Organizations* (Mahwah, NJ: Lawrence Erlbaum Associates, 2006).

11 S. E. Jackson, M. Hitt, and A. S. DeNisi (eds.), *Managing Knowledge for Sustained Competitive Advantage* (San Francisco: Jossey-Bass/Pfeiffer, 2003).

12 M. Albert, "Managing Change at HP Lab: Perspectives for Innovation, Knowledge Management, and Becoming a Learning Organization," *The Business Review, Cambridge* (Summer 2006: 17–22.

13 L. Rubis, "Manager Training Helped Company Digest Big Bite," *HRMagazine* (December 2000): 61–62.

14 M. Silberman (ed.), *2006 ASTD Organization Development & Leadership Sourcebook* (Alexandria, Virginia: ASTD Press, 2006).

15 R. R. Ritti, *The Ropes to Skip and the Ropes to Know: Studies in Organizational Behavior*, 5th ed. (Columbus, OH: Grid Publishing, 1997).

16 L. Rubis, "Cultural Consistency amid Change at Analytic Graphics," *HRMagazine* (July 2005): 58–59; "Best Small & Medium Companies to Work for in America," Great Place to Work Institute (August 2006), www .greatplacetowork.com.

17 M. Johnson, "Use Anti-Harassment Training to Shelter Yourself from Suits," *HRMagazine* (October 1999): 77–81.

18 G. P. Hollenbeck, M. W. McCall, Jr., and R. F. Silzer, "Theoretical and Practitioner Letters—Leadership Competency Models," *The Leadership Quarterly* 17 (2006): 398–413.

19 S. J. Wells, "Who's Next?" *HRMagazine* (November 2003): 45–50.

20 D. P. Shuit, "Magic for Sale," *Workforce Management* (September 2004): 35–40.

21 W. Arthur Jr., W. Bennett, Jr., P. S. Edens, and S. T. Bell, "Effectiveness of Training in Organizations: A Meta-Analysis of Design and Evaluation Features," *Journal of Applied Psychology* 88(2) (2003): 234–245; J. S. Callahan, D. S. Kiker, and T. Cross, "Does Method Matter? A Meta-Analysis of the Effects of Training Method on Older Learner Trainer Performance," *Journal of Management* 29(5) (2003): 663–680.

22 R. J. Grossman, "IBM's HR Takes a Risk," *HRMagazine* (April 2007): 54–59.

23 S. Hays, "HR Strategies Help Push New Razor to Number One," *Workforce* (February 1999): 92–93; Industry Report 1998, "Who Gets Trained? Where the Money Goes," *Training* (October 1998): 55–67.

24 T. J. Maurer and B. A. Tarulli, "Investigation of Perceived Environment, Perceived Outcome, and Person Variables in Relationship to Voluntary

Development Activity by Employees," *Journal of Applied Psychology* 79 (1994): 3–14. See also L. A. Hill, *Becoming a Manager: Mastery of a New Identity* (Cambridge, MA: Harvard Business School Press, 1992); T. A. Scandura, "Dysfunctional Mentoring Relationships and Outcomes," *Journal of Management* 24 (1998): 449–467.

25 G. T. Chao, et al., "Organizational Socialization: Its Content and Consequences," *Journal of Applied Psychology* 79 (1994): 730–743; E. W. Morrison, "Newcomer Information Seeking: Exploring Types, Modes, Sources, and Outcomes," *Academy of Management Journal* 36 (1993): 557–589; C. Ostroff and S. W. J. Kozlowski, "Organizational Socialization as a Learning Process: The Role of Information Acquisition," *Personnel Psychology* 45 (1992): 849–874.

26 T. A. Stewart, "Brain Power: Who Owns It . . . How They Profit from It," *Fortune* (March 17, 1997): 105–110.

27 R. Zemke, "How to Do a Needs Assessment When You Think You Don't Have Time," *Training* (March 1998): 38–44; "Lifelong Learning and the Skills Shortage: Policy Guide," *Bulletin to Management* (November 27, 1997): 384; "Technology and Training: A Dynamic Duo," *Bulletin to Management* 48(10) (March 6, 1997): 80; L. Saari, et al., "A Survey of Management Training and Education Practices in U.S. Companies," *Personnel Psychology* 41 (1988): 731–745.

28 Adapted from I. L. Goldstein, *Training: Program Development and Evaluation* (Monterey, CA: Brooks/Cole, 1986): 8; for a more fully elaborated description of needs analysis, see I. L. Goldstein and J. K. Ford, *Training in Organizations*, 4th ed. (Belmont, CA: Wadsworth, 2002).

29 P. J. Kiger, "At USA Bank, Promotions and Job Satisfaction Are Up," *Workforce* (March 2001): 54–55.

30 For more information about diagnosing the learning climate, see S. I. Tannenbaum, "Enhancing Continuous Learning: Diagnostic Findings from Multiple Companies," *Human Resource Management* 36 (1997): 437–452.

31 D. A. Ready and J. A. Conger, "Why Leadership-Development Efforts Fail," *MIT Sloan Management Review* (Spring 2003): 83–88; I. F. Kesner, "Leadership Development: Perk or Priority?" *Harvard Business Review* (May 2003): 29–38; R. Larsson, K. R. Brousseau, M. J. Driver, M. Holmqvist, and V. Tranovskaya, "International Growth Through Cooperation: Brand-Driven Strategies, Leadership, and Career Development in Sweden," *Academy of Management Executive* 17(1) (2003): 7–24; K. Beavan, T. Lockhart, and K. Michaelson, "Leadership Development on the Job," in *2003 Handbook of Business Strategy* (New York: Thomson Media, 2002); D. B. Neary and D. A. O'Grady, "The Role of Training in Developing Global Leaders: A Case Study at TRW, Inc.," *Human Resource Management* (Summer–Fall 2000): 185–193. For extensive views on leadership development, see the Special Issue of *Harvard Business Review*, "Inside the Mind of the Leader" (January 2004). For a detailed discussion of the 3M leadership competency model, see M. Alldredge and K. Nilan, "3M's Leadership Competency Model: An Internally Developed Solution," *Human Resource Management* 39(2–3) (Summer–Fall 2000): 133–145; see also M. Dalton, C. Ernst, J. Deal, and J. Leslie, *Success for the New Global Managers* (San Francisco: Jossey-Bass, 2003).

32 T. J. Maurer, E. M. Weiss, and F. G. Barberite, "A Model of Involvement in Work-Related Learning and Development Activity: The Effects of Individual, Situational, Motivational, and Age Variables," *Journal of Applied Psychology* 88(4) (2003): 707–724; for more discussion of the advantages and disadvantages of basic assessment techniques, see I. L. Goldstein, "Training in Work Organizations," *Handbook of Industrial and Organizational Psychology* 2 (1991): 507–620.

33 S. O'Mahony and B. A. Bechky, "Stretchwork: Managing the Career Progression Paradox in External Labor Markets," *Academy of Management Journal* 49(5) (2006): 918–941.

34 Modified from J. K. Ford and R. A. Noe, "Self-Assessed Training Needs: The Effects of Attitudes Toward Training, Managerial Level and Function," *Personnel Psychology* 40 (1987): 39–53.

35 J. Conner and C. A. Smith, "Developing the Next Generation of Leaders: A New Strategy for Leadership Development at Colgate-Palmolive," in E. M. Mone and M. London (eds.), *HR to the Rescue: Case Studies of HR Solutions to Business Challenges* (Houston, TX: Gulf, 1998).

36 W. Byham, "Bench Strength," *Across the Board* (February 2000): 35–41.

37 R. Neil Olson and E. A. Sexton, "Gender Differences in the Returns to and the Acquisition of On-the-Job Training," *Industrial Relations* 35 (January 1996): 59; S. G. Baugh, M. J. Lankau, and A. Terri, "An Investigation of the Effects of Protégé Gender on Responses to Mentoring," *Journal of Vocational Behavior* 49 (1996): 309–323; P. J. Ohlott, M. N. Ruderman, and C. D. McCauley, "Gender Differences in Managers' Developmental Job Experiences," *Academy of Management Journal* 37 (1994): 46–67.

38 D. Brady, "Crashing GE's Glass Ceiling," *BusinessWeek* (July 28, 2003): 76–77; G. H. Harel, S. S. Tzafrir, and Y. Baruch, "Achieving Organizational Effectiveness Through Promotion of Women into Managerial Positions: HRM Practice Focus," *International Journal of Human Resource Management* 14(2) (March 2003): 247–263; Staff, "Delta Air Will Give School Grant to Train Minorities as Pilots," *The Wall Street Journal* (January 10, 2001): A6.

39 D. B. Sloan, "Identifying and Developing High Potential Talent: A Succession Management Methodology," *Industrial-Organizational Psychologist* (2000): 80–90.

40 J. Colquitt, J. LePine, and R. Noe, "Toward an Integrative Theory of Training Motivation: A Meta-Analytic Path Analysis of 20 Years of Research," *Journal of Applied Psychology* 85(5) (2000): 678–707.

41 See, for example, B. Ragins and J. Cotton, "Mentor Functions and Outcomes: A Comparison of Men and Women in Formal and Informal Mentoring Relationships," *Journal of Applied Psychology* 84(4) (1999): 529–550.

42 R. T. Sparrowe and R. C. Liden, "Two Routes to Influence: Integrating Leader-Member Exchange and Social Network Perspectives," *Administrative Science Quarterly* 50 (2005): 505–535. See the Special Issue of *Harvard Business Review*, "Inside the Mind of the Leader" (January 2004); D. B. Neary, "Creating a Company-Wide, Online, Performance Management System: A Case Study at TRW Inc.," *Human Resource Management* 41(4) (Winter 2002): 491–498; C. H. Deutsch, "An Apparent Heir at Xerox," *The New York Times* (June 1, 2003): 2.

43 J. Marquez, "Goldman Sachs: Optimas Award Winner for General Excellence," *Workforce Management* (March 26, 2007): 23.

44 B. Groysberg and S. Snook, *The Pine Street Initiative at Goldman Sachs* (Boston, MA: Harvard Business School Publishing, 2006).

45 J. Black and H. Gregersen, "High Impact Training: Forging Leaders for the Global Frontier," *Human Resource Management* 39(2–3) (Summer–Fall 2000): 173–184.

46 A. J. Towler and R. L. Dipboye, "Effects of Trainer Expressiveness, Organization, and Trainee Goal Orientation on Training Outcomes," *Journal of Applied Psychology* 86 (2001): 664–673.

47 R. J. Sternberg and E. L. Grigorenko, "Are Cognitive Styles Still in Style?" *American Psychologist* 52 (July 1997): 700–712; K. Kraiger, J. K. Ford, and E. Salas, "Application of Cognitive, Skill-Based, and Affective Theories of Learning Outcomes to New Methods of Training Evaluation," *Journal of Applied Psychology* 78 (1993): 311–328.

48 C. Lachnit, "Hire Right: Do It the Ritz Way," *Workforce* (April 2002): 16.

49 T. Minton-Eversole and K. Gurchiek, "New Workers Not Ready for Prime Time," *HRMagazine* (December 2006): 28, 34.

50 J. Strandberg, "Training for a Technology Upgrade," *Training* (November 1997): 36–38.

51 L. Heuring, "Six Sigma in Sight," *HRMagazine* (March 2004): 76–80.

52 B. Leonard, "Taking HR to the Next Level," *HRMagazine* (July 2003): 57–63. See also S. Kugel, "Foreign Workers Assessing What a New Bill Will Mean," *The New York Times* (February 24, 2004): 4.

53 L. Rubis, "Show and Tell," *HRMagazine* (April 1998): 110–117.

54 H. W. Marsh, G. E. Richards, and J. Barnes, "Multidimensional Self-Concepts: The Effects of Participation in an Outward Bound Program," *Journal of Personality and Social Psychology* 50 (1986): 195–204; H. W. Marsh, G. E. Richards, and J. Barnes, "A Long-Term Follow-Up of the Effects of Participation in an Outward Bound Program," *Personality and Social Psychology Bulletin* 12 (1987): 465–492.

55 See the Special Issue of *Harvard Business Review,* "Inside the Mind of the Leader," (January 2004); J. Laabs, "Emotional Intelligence at Work," *Workforce Management* (July 1999): 68–71; D. Goleman, *Working with Emotional Intelligence* (New York: Bantam Books, 1998); C. Cherniss and D. Goleman (eds.), *The Emotionally Intelligent Workplace* (San Francisco: Jossey-Bass, 2001).

56 E. White, "What Would You Do? Ethics Courses Get Context," *The Wall Street Journal* (June 12, 2006): B3; C. Huff, "Framing a Culture" *Workforce Management* (May 9, 2006): 28–36.

57 R. DeRouin, B. A. Fritzsche, and E. Salas, "E-Learning in Organizations," *Journal of Management* 31(6) (December 2005): 920–940.

58 T. Sitzmann, K, Kraiger, D. Stewart, and R. Wisher, "The Comparative Effectiveness of Web-Based and Classroom Instruction: A Meta-Analysis," *Personnel Psychology* 59 (2006): 623–664.

59 For a full discussion of the conditions required for effective OJT, see I. L. Goldstein and K. J. Ford, *Training in Organizations,* 4th ed. (Belmont, CA: Wadsworth, 2003); see also J. D. Facteau, G. H. Dobbins, J. E. A. Russell, R. T. Ladd, and J. D. Kudisch, "The Influence of General Perceptions of the Training Environment on Pretraining Motivation and Perceived Training Transfer," *Journal of Management* 21 (1995): 1–25; P. J. Ohlott, C. D. McCauley, and M. N. Ruderman, *Developmental Challenge Profile: Learning from Job Experiences* (Greensboro, NC: Center for Creative Leadership, 1993).

60 "Delta Air Will Give School Grant to Train Minorities as Pilots," *The Wall Street Journal* (January 10, 2001): A6; D. Stamps, "Will School-to-Work, Work?" *Training* (June 1996): 72–81.

61 C. McCauley, *The Job Challenge Profile: Participant Workbook* (San Francisco: Jossey-Bass, 1999).

62 A. Murrell, F. Crosby, and R. Ely, *Mentoring Dilemmas: Developmental Relationships Within Multicultural Organizations* (Mahway, NJ: Lawrence Erlbaum Associates, 1999); M. Higgins and K. E. Kram, "Reconceptualizing

Mentoring at Work: A Developmental Network Perspective," *Academy of Management Executive* 25(2) (2001): 264–288; S. L. Willis and S. S. Dubin (eds.), *Maintaining Professional Competence: Approaches to Career Enhancement, Vitality and Success Throughout a Work Life* (San Francisco: Jossey-Bass, 1990); J. A. Schneer and F. Reitman, "Effects of Employment Gaps on the Careers of M.B.A.'s: More Damaging for Men Than for Women?" *Academy of Management Journal* 33 (1990): 391–406; J. H. Greenhaus, S. Parasuraman, and W. M. Wormley, "Effects of Race on Organizational Experiences, Job Performance Evaluations and Career Outcomes," *Academy of Management Journal* 33 (1990): 64–86.

63 C. Kathy, "Newsmaker Profile: John Thompson: Man with a Plan," *San Francisco Chronicle* (January 29, 2002): 14; A. Saita, "Profile: John Thompson" *InformationSecurity* (February 2003), www.infosecuritymag .techtarget.com03 (accessed July 2006); H. K. Chang, "Execution and Customer Focus are Leadership Keys, Says Symantec's Thompson," address given at Stanford Graduate School of Business (March 2005), www.gsb.stanford.edu (accessed July 2006); C. Taylor, "John Thompson: Symantec, U.S.," *Time Magazine—Europe* (July 19, 2004), www.time .com (accessed July 2006); L. Hooper, "John Thompson, Symantec," *CRN* (November 11, 2005), www.crn.com (accessed July 2006); K. McLaughlin, "Thompson Outlines Symantec's 2006 Strategy," *CRN* (May 8, 2006), www.crn.com (accessed July 2006); "The 50 Who Matter Now," *Business 2.0* (July 2006): 83–98.

64 L. Deen, "One on One with Grace Lieblein," *Hispanic Engineer & Information Technology Online* (June 2006), www.hispanicengineer .com.

65 For tips on getting a mentor, see M. Heffernan and S.-N. Joni, "Of Protégés and Pitfalls," *Fast Company* (August 2005): 81–83.

66 The Economist Intelligence Unit, *The CEO's Role in Talent Management* (New York: The Economist, 2006).

67 S. Overman, "Mentors Without Borders," *HRMagazine* (March 2004): 83–86.

68 C. H. Deutsch, "A New Kind of Whistle-Blower: Company Refines Principles of Coaching and Teamwork," *The New York Times* (May 7, 1999): C1; B. Filipczak, "The Executive Coach: Helper or Healer?" *Training* (March 1998): 30–36.

69 S. R. Davis, J. H. Lucas, and D. R. Marcotte, "GM Links Better Leaders to Better Business," *Workforce Management* (April 1998): 62–68.

70 C. L. Cole, "Boeing U.," *Workforce Management* (October 2000): 62–68; T. Stewart, "See Jack. See Jack Run," *Fortune* (December 27, 1999): 284–290; J. Spiegel Arthur, "Virtual U.," *Human Resource Executive* (March 19, 1998): 44–46.

71 A. M. Saks and M. Belcourt, "An Investigation of Training Activities and Transfer of Training in Organizations," *Human Resource Management* 45(4) (2006): 629–648.

72 E. F. Holton III and T. T. Baldwin (eds.), *Improving Learning Transfer* (San Francisco: Jossey-Bass, 2003); for a detailed list of conditions that support transfer, see L. Burke and T. T. Baldwin, "Workforce Training Transfer: A Study of the Effect of Relapse Prevention Training and Transfer Climate," *Human Resource Management* 38(3) (Fall 1999): 227–242.

73 I. Speizer, "McDonald's Consistency Begins with an Education at Hamburger University," *Workforce Management*, www.workforce.com (January 2, 2007).

74 R. Becker, "Taking the Misery Out of Experiential Training," *Training* (February 1998): 78–88; M. Hequet, "Games That Teach," *Training* (July

1995): 53–58; T. A. Stewart, "The Dance Steps Get Trickier All the Time," *Fortune* (May 26, 1997): 157–160; G. C. Thornton III and J. N. Cleveland, "Developing Managerial Talent Through Simulation," *American Psychologist* (February 1990): 190–199; W. M. Bulkeley, "The World of Work Is a Keystroke Away for Students in Computer-Simulated Jobs," *The Wall Street Journal* (May 7, 1996): B1, B2.

75 For an excellent description of the many uses and issues of assessment centers, see the entire special issue, R. E. Riggio and B. T. Mayes (eds.), "Assessment Centers: Research and Applications," *Journal of Social Behavior and Personality* 12 (1997): 1–331.

76 P. Schinzler, "Sharing the Wealth," *BusinessWeek e-Biz* (March 2001): 36–40.

77 D. P. Shuit, "Sound the Retreat," *Workforce Management* (September 2003): 39–48.

78 K. Hafner, "Welding Kitchen Knives and Honing Office Teamwork Skills," *The New York Times* (January 13, 2007): C1.

79 For a review of related research, see J. A. Cannon-Bowers, L. Rhodenizer, E. Salas, and C. Bowers, "A Framework for Understanding Pre-Practice Conditions and Their Impact on Learning," *Personnel Psychology* 51 (1998): 291–310.

80 M. A. Quinones, "Pretraining Context Effects: Training Assignment as Feedback," *Journal of Applied Psychology* 80 (1995): 226–238; V. L. Huber, "A Comparison of Goal Setting and Pay as Learning Incentives," *Psychological Reports* 56 (1985): 223–235; V. L. Huber, "Interplay between Goal Setting and Promises of Pay-for-Performance on Individual and Group Performance: An Operant Interpretation," *Journal of Organizational Behavior Management* 7 (1986): 45–64.

81 P. J. Taylor, D. F. Russ-Eft, and D. W. L. Chan, "A Meta-Analytic Review of Behavior Modeling Training," *Journal of Applied Psychology* 90(4) (2005): 692–709.

82 Taylor, Russ-Eft, and Chan, op. cit.

83 G. May and W. Kahnweiler, "The Effect of a Mastery Practice Design on Learning and Transfer in Behavior Modeling Training," *Personnel Psychology* 53 (2000): 353–373.

84 V. L. Huber, Interplay Between Goal Setting and Promises of Pay-for-Performance: An Operant Interpretation," *Journal of Organizational Behavior Management* 7 (3–4) (1986): 45–64; J. D. Eyring, D. Steele Johnson, and D. J. Francis, "A Cross-Level Units-of-Analysis Approach to Individual Differences in Skill Acquisition," *Journal of Applied Psychology* 78 (1993): 805–814; P. Christopher Earley, "Self or Group? Cultural Effects of Training on Self-Efficacy and Performance," *Administrative Science Quarterly* 39 (1994): 89–117.

85 B. Ragins and J. Cotton, "Mentor Functions and Outcomes: A Comparison of Men and Women in Formal and Informal Mentoring Relationships," *Journal of Applied Psychology* 84(4) (1999): 529–550; V. L. Huber, G. P. Latham, and E. A. Locke, "The Management of Impressions Through Goal Setting," in R. A. Giacalone and P. Rosenfield (eds.), *Impression Management in the Organization* (Mahwah, NJ: Lawrence Erlbaum Associates, 1989).

86 P. Hogan, M. Hakel, and P. Decker, "Effects of Trainee-Generated vs. Trainer-Provided Rule Codes on Generalization in Behavioral Modeling Training," *Journal of Applied Psychology* 71 (1986): 469–473.

87 W. W. Tornow and M. London, "Maximizing the Value of 360-Degree Feedback: A Process for Successful Individual and Organizational Development," *Center for Creative Leadership* (March 1998); D. E. Coates, "Don't Tie 360 Feedback to Pay," *Training* (September 1998): 68–78.

88 J. E. Driskell, C. Copper, and A. Moran, "Does Mental Practice Enhance Performance?" *Journal of Applied Psychology,* 79 (1994): 481–492.

89 J. F. Brett and D. VandeWalle, "Goal Orientation and Goal Content as Predictors of Performance in a Training Program," *Journal of Applied Psychology* 84(6) (1999): 863–873; C. Frayne and G. P. Latham, "The Application of Social Learning Theory to Employee Self-Management of Attendance," *Journal of Applied Psychology* 72 (1987): 387–392.

90 See M. J. Waller, "The Timing of Adaptive Group Responses to Nonroutine Events. *Academy of Management Journal* 42 (1999): 127–137.

91 A. P. J. Ellis, J. R. Hollenbeck, D. R. Ilgen, C. O. L. H. Porter, B. J. West, and H. Moon, "Team Learning: Collectively Connecting the Dots," *Journal of Applied Psychology* 88(5) (2003): 821–835; B. L. Kirkman, B. Rosen, C. B. Gibson, P. E. Tesluk, and S. O. McPherson, "Five Challenges to Virtual Team Success: Lessons from Sabre, Inc.," *Academy of Management Executive* 16(3) (2002): 67–79; E. E. Salas, C. S. Brown, and J. A. Cannon-Bowers, "What We Know About Designing and Delivering Team Training: Tips and Guidelines," in K. Kraiger (ed.), *Creating, Implementing and Managing Effective Training and Development: State-of-the-Art Lessons for Practice* (San Francisco: Jossey-Bass, 2002): 234–262; E. E. Salas, J. A. Cannon-Bowers, and E. Eden, *Improving Teamwork in Organizations: Applications of Resource Management and Training* (Mahwah, NJ: Lawrence Erlbaum Associates, 2001); R. A. Guzzo and M. W. Dickson, "Teams in Organizations: Recent Research on Performance and Effectiveness," *Annual Review of Psychology* 47 (1996): 307–308; J. Cannon-Bowers, S. A. Tannebaum, E. Salas, and C. Volpe, "Defining Competencies and Establishing Team Training Requirements," *Team Effectiveness and Decision Making* (2000): 333–380.

92 H. Campbell, "Adventures in Teamland: Experiential Training Makes the Lesson Fun," *Personnel Journal* (May 1996): 56–62; see also J. P. Meyer, "Four Territories of Experience: A Developmental Action Inquiry Approach to Outdoor-Adventure Experiential Learning," *Academy of Management Learning and Education* 2(4) (2003): 352–363.

93 J. W. Dean, Jr., and M. P. Sharfman, "Does Decision Process Matter? A Study of Strategic Decision Making Effectiveness," *Academy of Management Journal* 39 (1996): 368–396; P. W. Mulvey, J. F. Viega, and P. M. Elsass, "When Teammates Raise a White Flag," *Academy of Management Executive* 10 (1996): 40–49; R. L. Priem, D. A. Harrison, and N. K. Muir, "Structured Conflict and Consensus Outcomes in Group Decision Making," *Journal of Management* 21 (1995): 691–710.

94 For a review of research on cross-cultural training, see D. P. S. Bhawuk and R. W. Brislin, "Cross-Cultural Training: A Review," *Applied Psychology: An International Review* 49 (2000): 162–191.

95 For reviews, see D. Chrobot-Mason and M. A. Quinones, "Training for a Diverse Workforce," in K. Kraiger (ed.), *Creating, Implementing and Managing Effective Training and Development: State-of-the-Art Lessons for Practice* (San Francisco: Jossey-Bass, 2002): 117–159; S. E. Jackson and A. Joshi, "Research on Domestic and International Diversity in Organizations: A Merger That Works?" in *International Handbook of Work and Organizational Psychology,* vol. 2 (Thousand Oaks, CA: Sage, 2001); see also T. F. Pettigrew, "Intergroup Contact Theory, "*Annual Review of Psychology* 49 (1998): 65–85.

96 S. L. Rynes and B. A. Rosen, "A Field Survey of Factors Affecting the Adoption and Perceived Success of Diversity Training," *Personnel Psychology* 48 (1995): 247–270.

97 E. Frauenheim, "Crossing Cultures," *Workforce Management* (November 21, 2005): 26–32.

98 N. R. Lockwood, "Leadership Development: Optimizing Human Capital for Business Success," *SHRM Research Report* (Alexandria, VA: Society for Human Resource Management, 2006).

99 Adapted from M. Javidan, P. W. Dorfman, M. S. de Loupe, and R. J. House, "In the Eye of the Beholder: Cross Cultural Lessons in Leadership from GLOBE," *Academy of Management Perspectives* (February 2006): 67–90. See also D. Nilsen, B. Kowske, and K. Anthony, "Managing Globally," *HRMagazine* (August 2005): 11–15.

100 Adapted from J. Marquez, "Companies Send Employees on Volunteer Projects Abroad to Cultivate Leadership Skills," *Workforce Management* (November 2005): 50–52.

101 R. J. Kramer, *Developing Global Leaders: Enhancing Competencies and Accelerating the Expatriate Experience.* (New York: The Conference Board, 2005).

Chapter 9

1 D. B. Neary, "Creating a Company-Wide, Online Performance Management System: A Case Study at TRW, Inc.," *Human Resource Management Journal* 41 (2002): 491–498.

2 For a thorough review, see R. D. Arvey and K. R. Murphy, "Performance Evaluation in Work Settings," *Annual Review of Psychology* 49 (1998): 141–168.

3 J. C. Kovac, "The Performance-Management Process," *Workspan* (October 2006): 96; R. Greenberg and L. Lucid, "Four Principles of Performance Leadership," *Workspan* (September 2004): 42–45.

4 WorldatWork, Sibson, and Synygy, "The State of Performance Management," *WorldatWork Survey Brief,* www.worldatwork.org (accessed August 2005).

5 For detailed discussions of work motivation theory and research, see P. Steel and C. J. Konig, "Integrating Theories of Motivation," *Academy of Management Review* 31 (2006): 889–913; A. S. DeNisi and R.D. Pritchard, "Performance Appraisal, Performance Management and Improving Individual Performance: A Motivational Framework," *Management and Organization Review* 2 (2006): 253–277; R. M. Steers, R. T. Mowday, and D. L. Shapiro, "The Future of Work Motivation Theory," *Academy of Management Review* 29 (2004): 379–387; E. A. Locke and G. P. Latham, "What Should We Do About Motivation Theory? Six Recommendations for the Twenty-First Century," *Academy of Management Review* 29 (2004): 388–403.

6 A. D. Staijkovic and F. Luthans, "Self-Efficacy and Work-Related Performance: A Meta-Analysis," *Psychological Bulletin* 124(2) (1998): 240–261; W. Van Erde and H. Thierry, "Vroom's Expectancy Models and Work-Related Criteria: A Meta-Analysis," *Journal of Applied Psychology* 81 (1996): 575–586.

7 D. Fenn, "Personnel Best," *Inc.* (February 2000): 75–83.

8 P. Steel and C. J. Konig, "Integrating Theories of Motivation," *Academy of Management Review* 31 (2006): 889–913.

9 D. H. Lindsley, D. J. Brass, and J. B. Thomas, "Efficacy-Performance Spirals: A Multilevel Perspective," *Academy of Management Review* 20 (1995): 645–678.

10 E. A. Locke, "Motivation, Cognition, and Action: An Analysis of Studies of Task Goals and Knowledge," *Applied Psychology: An International*

Review 49 (2000): 408–429; E. A. Locke and G. P. Latham, *A Theory of Goal Setting and Task Performance* (Englewood Cliffs, NJ: Prentice-Hall, 1990).

11 E. D. Pulakos, *Performance Management* (Alexandria, VA: SHRM Foundation, 2004); A. Ozias, "Exploring the Role of Performance Management," *Workspan* (June 2003).

12 WorldatWork, Sibson, and Synygy, "The State of Performance Management," *WorldatWork Survey Brief,* www.worldatwork.org (accessed August 2005).

13 K. Gagne, "One Day at a Time: Using Performance Management to Translate Strategy into Results," *Workspan* (February 2002).

14 P. Sellers, "Pepsi Opens a Second Front," *Fortune* (August 8, 1994): 71–76; J. R. Fulkerson and R. S. Schuler, "Managing Worldwide Diversity at Pepsi-Cola International," in S. E. Jackson (ed.), *Diversity in the Workplace: Human Resources Initiatives* (New York: Guilford Publications, 1992).

15 A. Park and P. Burrows, "What You Don't Know About Dell," *BusinessWeek* (November 2003): 76–84; see www.dell.com.

16 B. Burlingham, "What's Your Culture Worth? *Inc.* (September 2001): 133; B. Burlingham, A *Stake in the Outcome* (New York: Doubleday, 2002); www.setpointusa.com/value.asp (accessed June 28, 2007).

17 P. Gooderham, O. Nordhaug, and K. Ringdal, "National Embed-dedness and Calculative Human Resource Management in US Subsidiaries in Europe and Australia," *Human Relations* 59 (2006): 1491–1513; H. Shih, Y. Chiang, and I. Kim., "Expatriate Performance Management from MNEs of Different National Origins," *International Journal of Manpower* 26 (2005): 157–176.

18 S. B. Malos, "Current Legal Issues in Performance Appraisal," in J. W. Smither (ed.), *Performance Appraisal: State of the Art in Practice* (San Francisco: Jossey-Bass, 1998): 49–94.

19 A. S. DeNisi and R. D. Pritchard, "Performance Appraisal, Performance Management and Improving Individual Performance: A Motivational Framework," *Management and Organization Review* 2 (2006): 253–277; M. S. Taylor, M. K. Renard, and K. B. Tracy, "Managers' Reactions to Procedurally Just Performance Management Systems," *Academy of Management Journal* 41 (1998): 565–579; L. M. Keeping and P. E. Levy, "Performance Appraisal Reactions: Measurement, Modeling, and Method Bias," *Journal of Applied Psychology* 85(5) (2000): 708–723.

20 G. Ruiz, "Performance Management Underperforms," *Workforce Management* (June 26, 2006): 47–49.

21 N. P. Mero, R. M. Guidice, and A. L. Brownlee, "Accountability in a Performance Appraisal Context: The Effect of Audience and Form of Accounting on Rater Response and Behavior," *Journal of Management* 33 (2007): 223–252; J. Kochanski and A. Sorensen, "Managing Performance Management," *Workspan* (September 2005): 21–26; E. E. Lawler III and M. McDermott, "Current Performance Management Practices: Examining the Varying Impacts," *WorldatWork Journal* (Second Quarter 2003); C. O'Neill and L. Holsinger, "Effective Performance Management Systems: 10 Key Design Principles," *WorldatWork Journal* (Second Quarter 2003); C. M. Ellis, "Improving the Impact of Performance Management," *Workspan* (February 2002).

22 K. Tyler, "Performance Art," *HRMagazine* (August, 2005); K. Tyler, "One Bad Apple," *HRMagazine* (December 2004).

23 D. G. Bachrach, B. C. Powell, E. Bendoly, and R.G. Richey, "Organizational Citizenship Behavior and Performance Evaluations: Exploring the Impact of Task Interdependence," *Journal of Applied Psychology* 91 (2006): 193–201; D. Kiker and S. J. Motowdlo, "Main and

Interaction Effects of Task and Contextual Performance on Supervisory Reward Decisions," *Journal of Applied Psychology* 84(4) (1999): 602–609; T. D. Allen and M. C. Rush, "The Effects of Organizational Citizenship Behavior on Performance Judgments: A Field Study and a Laboratory Experiment," *Journal of Applied Psychology* 83 (1998): 247–260.

24 W. C. Borman and S. J. Motowidlo, "Expanding the Criterion Domain to Include Elements of Contextual Performance," in N. Schmitt and W. C. Borman, *Personnel Selection in Organizations* (San Francisco: Jossey-Bass, 1993), 71–99.

25 H. S. Field and W. H. Holley, "The Relationship of Performance Appraisal System Characteristics to Verdicts in Selected Employment Discrimination Cases," *Academy of Management Journal* (1982): 392–406.

26 H. L. Jackson and D. S. Ones, "Counterproductive Leader Behavior," in S. Werner (ed.), *Managing Human Resources in North America: Current Issues and Perspectives* (London: Routledge, 2007), 114–125; R. Posthuma, M. A. Campion, and A. L. Vargas, "Predicting Counterproductive Performance Among Temporary Workers: A Note," *Industrial Relations* 44 (2005): 550–555.

27 S. L. Rynes, B. Gerhart, and L. Parks, "Personnel Psychology: Performance Evaluation and Pay for Performance," *Annual Review of Psychology* 56 (2005): 571–600.

28 See the Payless ShoeSource Code of Ethics, accessed at www .payless.com/Images/2006_Code_Of_Ethics.pdf; K. Gagne, "One Day at a Time: Using Performance Management to Translate Strategy into Results," *Workspan* (February, 2002).

29 Based on J. P. Campbell, et al., "A Theory of Performance," in N. Schmitt and W. C. Borman (eds.), *Personnel Selection in Organizations* (San Francisco: Jossey-Bass, 1993): 35–70; E. D. Pulakos, S. Arad, M. A. Donovan, and K. E. Plamondon, "Adaptability in the Workplace: Development of a Taxonomy of Adaptive Performance," *Journal of Applied Psychology* 85 (2000): 612–624.

30 G. Ruiz, "Performance Management Underperforms," *Workforce Management* (June 26, 2006): 47–49.

31 D. K. Lindo, "Can You Answer Their Questions?: The Proper Way of Conducting Performance Appraisals," *Supervision* 68 (January 1, 2007): 20–22.

32 V. U. Druskat and S. Wolff, "Effects and Timing of Development Peer Appraisals in Self-Managing Work Groups," *Journal of Applied Psychology* 84(1) (1999): 38–74.

33 D. J. Woehr, M. K. Sheehan, and W. Bennett, Jr., "Assessing Measurement Equivalence Across Rating Sources: A Multitrait-Multirater Approach," *Journal of Applied Psychology* 90 (2005): 592–600; L. E. Atwater, and J. F. Brett, "Antecedents and Consequences of Reactions to Developmental 360° Feedback," *Journal of Vocational Behavior* 66 (2005): 532–548.

34 J. W. Smither, M. London, and R. R. Reilly, "Does Performance Improve Following Multisource Feedback?: A Theoretical Model, Meta-Analysis, and Review of Empirical Findings," *Personnel Psychology* 58 (2005): 33–66; C. Viswesvaran, D. S. Ones, and F. L. Schmidt, "Comparative Analysis of the Reliability of Job Performance Ratings," *Journal of Applied Psychology* 81 (1996): 557–574.

35 G. P. Latham, J. Almost, S. Mann, & C. Moore, "New Developments in Performance Management," *Organizational Dynamics*, 34 (2005): 77–87.

36 S. J. Ashford, "Self-Assessments in Organizations: A Literature Review and Integrative Model," *Research in Organizational Behavior* 11

(1989): 133–374; T. H. Shore, L. M. Shore, and G. C. Thornton III, "Construct Validity of Self- and Peer Evaluations of Performance Dimensions in an Assessment Center," *Journal of Applied Psychology* 77 (1992): 42–54; J. L. Farh, G. H. Dobbins, and B. S. Cheng, "Cultural Relativity in Action: A Comparison of Self-Ratings Made by Chinese and U.S. Workers," *Personnel Psychology* 44 (1991): 129–147.

37 J. Dulebohn and G. Ferris, "The Role of Influence in Perceptions of Performance Evaluations' Fairness," *Academy of Management Journal* 42(3) (1999): 288–303; B. D. Cawley, L. M. Keeping, and P. E. Levy, "Participation in the Performance Appraisal Process and Employee Relations: A Meta-Analytic Review of Field Investigations," *Journal of Applied Psychology* 83 (1998): 615–633.

38 G. P. Latham, J. Almost, S. Mann, and C. Moore, "New Developments in Performance Management," *Organizational Dynamics*, 34 (2005): 77–87; F. J. Yammarino and L. E. Atwater, "Do Managers See Themselves as Others See Them? Implications of Self-Other Rating Agreement for Human Resources Management," *Organizational Dynamics* (Spring 1997): 35–44.

39 R. Jelley and R. Goffin, "Can Performance-Feedback Accuracy Be Improved? Effects of Rater Priming and Rating-Scale Format on Rating Accuracy," *Journal of Applied Psychology* 86(1) (2001): 134–144; L. E. Atwater, C. Ostroff, F. J. Yammarino, and J. W. Fleenor, "Self-Other Agreement: Does It Really Matter?" *Personnel Psychology* 51 (1998): 577–598.

40 For a complete review of international differences in performance management, see A. Varma, P. S. Budhwar, and A. DeNisi, *Global Performance Management* (London: Routledge, 2008).

41 J. L. Farh, G. H. Dobbins, and C. S. Cheng, "Cultural Relativity in Action: A Comparison of Self-Ratings Made by Chinese and U.S. Workers," *Personnel Psychology* 44 (1991): 129–147.

42 T. H. Shore, L. M. Shore, and G. C. Thornton III, "Construct Validity of Self- and Peer Evaluations," *Journal of Applied Psychology* 77 (1992): 42–54; R. Saavedra and S. K. Kwun, "Peer Evaluation in Self-Managing Work Groups," *Journal of Applied Psychology* 78 (1993): 450–462.

43 T. J. Maurere, N. S. Raju, and W. C. Collins, "Peer and Subordinate Performance Appraisal Measurement Equivalence," *Journal of Applied Psychology* 83 (1998): 693–702.

44 G. P. Latham, J. Almost, S. Mann, and C. Moore, "New Developments in Performance Management," *Organizational Dynamics*, 34 (2005): 77–87.

45 J. Greenberg, C. E. Aston-James, and N. M. Ashkanasy, "Social Comparison Processes in Organizations," *Organizational Behavior and Human Decision Processes* 102 (2007): 22–41.

46 M. Goldsmith, "To Help Others, Start with Yourself," *Fast Company* (March 2004): 100.

47 D. Antonioni and H. Park, "The Relationship Between Rater Affect and Three Sources of 360-Degree Feedback Ratings," *Journal of Management* 27 (2001): 479–495; D. Antonioni, "The Effects of Feedback Accountability on Upward Appraisal Ratings," *Personnel Psychology* 47 (1994): 349–360.

48 A. J. Walker and J. Smither, "A Five-Year Study of Upward Feedback: What Managers Do with Their Results Matters," *Personnel Psychology* 52 (1999): 393–423.

49 P. A. Heslin and G. P. Latham, "The Effect of Upward Feedback on Managerial Behavior," *Applied Psychology: An International Review* 53 (2004): 23–37.

50 C. F. Seifer, G. Yukl, and R. A. McDonald, "Effects of Multisource Feedback and a Feedback Facilitator on the Influence Behaviors of Managers Toward Subordinates," *Journal of Applied Psychology* 88 (2003): 561–569.

51 G. Huet-Cox, T. Nielsen, and E. Sundstrom, "Get the Most from 360-Degree Feedback: Put It on the Internet," *HRMagazine* (May 1999): 92–103; R. Lepsinger and A. D. Lucia, *The Art and Science of 360° Feedback* (San Francisco: Pfeiffer, 1997).

52 F. Luthans and S. J. Peterson, "360-Degree Feedback with Systematic Coaching: Empirical Analysis Suggests a Winning Combination," *Human Resource Management* 3(42) (Fall 2003): 243–256.

53 L. E. Atwater, J. F. Brett, and A. C. Charles, "Multisource Feedback: Lessons Learned and Implications for Practice," *Human Resource Management* 46(2) (2007): 285–307; G. Toegel and J. A. Conger, "360-Degree Assessment: Time for a Reinvention," *Academy of Management Learning and Education* 2 (2003): 297–311; R. Lepsinger and A. Lucia, "360 Degree Feedback and Performance Appraisal," *Training* 34 (1997): 62–70.

54 K. Holland, "Performance Reviews: Many Need Improvement," *The New York Times* (September 10, 2006): B3–B4; J. McGregor, "The Struggle to Measure Performance," *BusinessWeek* (January 9, 2006): 26–28; S .E. Scullen, P. K. Bergey, and L. Aiman-Smith, "Forced Distribution Rating Systems and the Improvement of Workforce Potential: A Baseline Simulation," *Personnel Psychology* 58 (2005): 1–32; S. Bates, "Forced Ranking," *HRMagazine* (June 2004): 63–68; M. O'Malley, "Forced Ranking: Proceed Only with Great Caution," *WorldatWork Journal* (First Quarter 2003).

55 V. M. Catano, W. Darr, and C. A. Campbell, "Performance Appraisal of Behavior-Based Competencies: A Reliable and Valid Procedure," *Personnel Psychology* 60 (2007): 201–230.

56 E. Harmon, S. C. Hensel, and T. E. Lukes, "Measuring Performance in Services," *The McKinsey Quarterly* (March 28, 2006).

57 K. R. Murphy and J. I. Constans, "Behavioral Anchors as a Source of Bias in Rating," *Journal of Applied Psychology* (November 1987): 573.

58 Adapted from V. L. Huber, *Validation Study for Electronics Maintenance Technical Positions* (Washington, DC: Human Resource Development Institute, AFL-CIO, 1991).

59 "Busch's Performance Evaluations," *Workforce Management Archive* (July 30, 2003), accessed at www.workforce.com/archive/article/23/42/03.php.

60 G. Ruiz, "Performance Management Underperforms," *Workforce Management* (June 26, 2006): 47–49.

61 E. A. Locke, "Motivation, Cognition, and Action: An Analysis of Studies of Task Goals and Knowledge," *Applied Psychology: An International Review* 49 (2000): 408–429; E. A. Locke and G. P. Latham, *A Theory of Goal Setting and Task Performance* (Englewood Cliffs, NJ: Prentice-Hall, 1990).

62 A. S. DeNisi and K. Williams, "Cognitive Approaches to Performance Appraisal," in G. R. Ferris and K. M. Rowland (eds.), *Research in Personnel and Human Resource Management* (Greenwich, CT: JAI Press, 1988): 109–156; A. S. DeNisi, T. P. Cafferty, and B. M. Meglino, "A Cognitive View of the Appraisal Process: A Model and Research Propositions," *Organizational Behavior and Human Performance* 33 (1984): 360–396.

63 K. F. E. Wong and J. Y. Y. Kwong, "Effects of Rater Goals on Rating Patterns: Evidence from an Experimental Field Study," *Journal of Applied Psychology* 92 (2007): 577–585; J. Reb and R. Cropanzano, "Evaluating Dynamic Performance: The Influence of Salient Gestalt Characteristics on Performance Ratings," *Journal of Applied Psychology* 92 (2007): 490–499; T. A. Judge and G. R. Ferris, "Social Context of Performance Evaluation Decisions," *Academy of Management Journal* 36 (1993): 80–105.

64 A. S. DeNisi and K. Williams, "Cognitive Approaches to Performance Appraisal," in G. R. Ferris and K. M. Rowland (eds.), *Research in Personnel and Human Resource Management* (Greenwich, CT: JAI Press, 1988): 109–156; D. R. Ilgen and J. M. Feldman, "Performance Appraisal: A Process Focus," in B. Staw and L. Cummings (eds.), *Research in Organizational Behavior* (Greenwich, CT: JAI Press, 1983): 141–197.

65 K. F. E. Wong and J. Y. Y Kwong, "Between-Individual Comparisons in Performance Evaluation: A Perspective from Prospect Theory," *Journal of Applied Psychology* 90 (2005): 284–294; T. R. Kurtzberg, C. E. Naquin, and L. Y. Belkin, "Electronic Performance Appraisals: The Effects of E-Mail Communication on Peer Ratings in Actual and Simulated Environments," *Organizational Behavior and Human Decision Processes* 98 (2005): 216–226.

66 C. E. Lance, J. A. LaPointe, and A. M. Stewart, "A Test of the Context Dependency of Three Causal Models of Halo Rater Error," *Journal of Applied Psychology* 79 (1994): 332–340; J. S. Kane, H. J. Bernardin, P. Villanova, and J. Peyrefitte, "Stability of Rater Leniency: Three Studies," *Academy of Management Journal* 38 (1995): 1036–1051.

67 R. L. Dipboye, "Some Neglected Variables in Research on Discrimination in Appraisals," *Academy of Management Review* (January 1985): 118–125; B. R. Nathan and R. A. Alexander, "The Role of Inferential Accuracy in Performance Rating," *Academy of Management Review* (January 1985): 109–117.

68 F. Lievens and J. I. Sanchez, "Can Training Improve the Quality of Inferences Made by Raters in Competency Modeling?: A Quasi-Experiment," *Journal of Applied Psychology* 92 (2007): 812–819; B. B. Baltes, C. B. Bauer, and P. A. Frensch, "Does a Structured Free Recall Intervention Reduce the Effect of Stereotypes on Performance Ratings and by What Cognitive Mechanism?" *Journal of Applied Psychology* 92 (2007): 151–164; R. F. Martell and D. P. Evans, "Source-Monitoring Training: Toward Reducing Rater Expectancy Effects in Behavioral Measurement," *Journal of Applied Psychology* 90 (2005): 956–963.

69 G. P. Latham, J. Almost, S. Mann, and C. Moore, "New Developments in Performance Management," *Organizational Dynamics*, 34 (2005): 77–87; P. A. Heslin, G. P. Latham, and D. VandeWalle, "The Effect of Implicit Person Theory on Performance Appraisals," *Journal of Applied Psychology* 90 (2005): 842–856; H. J. Bernadin, M. B. Buckley, C. Tyler, and D. S. Wiese, "A Reconsideration of Strategies in Rater Training," *Research in Personnel and Human Resource Management* 18 (2000): 221–274.

70 K. R. Murphy and J. N. Cleveland, *Understanding Performance Appraisal: Social, Organizational, and Goal-Based Perspectives* (Thousand Oaks, CA: Sage Publications, 1995).

71 M. K. Mount, M. R. Sytsma, J. Fisher Hazucha, and K. E. Holt, "Rater-Ratee Race Effects in Developmental Performance Ratings of Managers," *Personnel Psychology* 50 (1997): 51.

72 K. R. Murphy, "Difficulties in the Statistical Control of Halo," *Journal of Applied Psychology* 67 (1982): 161–164; L. Hirshhord, *Meaning in the New Team Environment* (Reading, MA: Addison-Wesley, 1991); K. R. Murphy and J. N. Cleveland, *Understanding Performance Appraisal: Social, Organizational, and Goal-Based Perspectives* (Thousand Oaks, CA: Sage Publications, 1995).

73 K. S. Lyness and M. E. Heilman, "When Fit Is Fundamental: Performance Evaluations and Promotions of Upper-Level Female and Male Managers," *Journal of Applied Psychology* 91 (2006): 777–785; R. F. Martell and M. R. Borg, "A Comparison of the Behavioral Rating Accuracy of Groups and Individuals," *Journal of Applied Psychology* 78 (1993): 43–50.

74 J. Marquez, "Communicating Beyond Ratings Can Be Difficult," *Workforce Management* (April 24, 2006): S5; S. B. Silverman, C. E. Pogson, and A. B. Cober, "When Employees at Work Don't Get it: A Model for Enhancing Individual Employee Change in Response to Performance Feedback," *Academy of Management Executive* 19 (2005): 135–147; M. London, *Job Feedback: Giving, Seeking, and Using Feedback for Performance Improvement,* 2nd ed. (Mahwah, NJ: Lawrence Erlbaum Associates, 2003).

75 M. D. Cannon and R. Witherspoon, "Actionable Feedback: Unlocking the Power of Learning and Performance Improvement," *Academy of Management Executive* 19 (2005): 120–134.

76 V. L. Huber, P. Podsakoff, and W. D. Todor, "An Investigation of Biasing Factors in the Attributions of Subordinates and Their Supervisors," *Journal of Business Research* 4 (1986): 83–97.

77 C. D. Lee, "Feedback, Not Appraisal," *HRMagazine* (November 2006); J. T. Rich, "The Solution for Employee Performance Mismanagement," *Workspan* (February 2002); K. Renk, "I Want My TV," *Awards & Incentives* (2000): 158–162; K. Kirkland and S. Manoogian, *Ongoing Feedback: How to Get It, How to Use It* (Greensboro, NC: Center for Creative Leadership, 1998).

78 J. D. Elicker, P. E. Levy, and R. J. Hall, "The Role of Leader-Member Exchange in the Performance Appraisal Process," *Journal of Management* 32 (2006): 531–551.

79 G. S. Alder and M. L. Ambrose, "An Examination of the Effect of Computerized Performance Monitoring Feedback on Monitoring Fairness, Performance, and Satisfaction," *Organizational Behavior and Human Decision Processes* 97 (2005): 161–177; L. E. Atwater, D. A. Waldman, D. Atwater, and P. Cartier, "An Upward Feedback Field Experiment: Supervisors' Cynicism, Reactions, and Commitment to Subordinates," *Personnel Psychology* 53 (2000): 275–297.

80 T. Cook and M. R. Dixon, "Performance Feedback and Probabilistic Bonus Contingencies Among Employees in a Human Service Organization," *Journal of Organizational Behavior* Management, 25 (2005): 45–63; M. M. Kennedy, "So How'm I Doing?" *Across the Board* (June 1997): 53–54.

81 R. Ilies and T. A. Judge, "Goal Regulation Across Time: The Effects of Feedback and Affect," *Journal of Applied Psychology* 90 (2005): 453–467.

82 A. Bandura, *Principles of Behavior Modification* (New York: Holt, Rinehart & Winston, 1969); R. W. Beatty and C. E. Schneier, "A Case for Positive Reinforcement," *Business Horizons* 2 (April 1975): 57–66.

83 S. B. Silverman, C. E. Pogson, and A. B. Cober, "When Employees at Work Don't Get it: A Model for Enhancing Individual Employee Change in Response to Performance Feedback," *Academy of Management Executive* 19 (2005): 135–147.

84 B. P. Sunoo, "This Employee May Be Loafing, Can You Tell? Should You Tell?" *Personnel Journal* (December 1996): 54–62; "Jury Awards Manager Accused of Theft $25 Million," *Bulletin to Management* (March 27, 1997): 97; P. Carbonara, "Fire Me. I Dare You!" *Inc.* (March 1997): 58–64.

85 C. Winkler, "Peak Performance: Technology Helps Measure and Manage Employee Performance," *HRMagazine* (January 2007); P. Loucks, "Automation Makes Pay-for-Performance Work," *Workspan* (October 2006): 53–55; A. J. Cohen and M. E. Hall, "Automating Your Peformance and Competency Evaluation Process," *WorldatWork Journal* (Third Quarter 2005): 64–71; D. Robb, "Building a Better Workforce," *HRMagazine* (October 2004).

86 R. Morgan, "Making the Most of Performance Management Systems," *Compensation and Benefits Review* (2006): 22–27; F. Lampron and L. Koski, "Implementing Web-Enabled Performance Management," *Workspan* (January, 2004).

87 S. Chan, "New Scanners for Tracking City Workers," *The New York Times* (January 23, 2007):B1–B6.

88 D. S. Mohl, "Balancing Employer Monitoring and Employee Privacy," *Workspan* (September 2006): 68–70; D. S. Onley, "Technology Gives Big Brother Capability," *HRMagazine* (July 2005).

89 The situation described is based on C. Fishman, "Engines of Democracy," *Fast Company* (October 1999): 175–202.

Chapter 10

1 D. Brill and K. Kish, "Success at Synapse: Investing in People Reaps Big Dividends for a Small Company," *Journal of Organizational Excellence* 24 (2005): 65–73, accessed at www.synapsegroupinc.com (July 1, 2007) .

2 J. D. Shaw, "Competitive Advantage Through HRM," *Managing Human Resources in North America: Current Issues and Perspectives* (London: Routledge, 2007), 100–113; WorldatWork Compensation Advisory Board, "The Changing Role of Compensation," *WorldatWork Survey Brief* (April 2005).

3 C. Garvey, "Philosophizing Compensation," *HRMagazine* (January 2005).

4 D. E. Terpstra and A. L. Honoree, "Employees' Responses to Merit Pay Inequity," *Compensation and Benefits Review* (January–February 2005): 51–58; L. M. Roth, "Because I'm Worth It? Understanding Inequality in a Performance-Based Pay System," *Sociological Inquiry* 76 (2006): 116–139.

5 P. D. Sweeney and D. B. McFarlin, "Wage Comparisons with Similar and Dissimilar Others," *Journal of Occupational Organizational Psychology* 78 (2005): 113–141; M. Williams, M. A. McDaniel, and N. T. Nguyen, "A Meta-Analysis of the Antecedents and Consequences of Pay Level Satisfaction," *Journal of Applied Psychology* 91 (2006): 392–413.

6 R. L. Heneman, "Pay Satisfaction," *The Blackwell Encyclopedia of Management: Human Resource Management,* 2nd ed. (Malden, MA: Blackwell Publishing, 2005), 274.

7 C. O. Trevor and D. L Wazeter, "A Contingent View of Reactions to Objective Pay Conditions: Interdependence Among Pay Structure Characteristics and Pay Relative to Internal and External Referents," *Journal of Applied Psychology* 91(6) (2006): 1260–1275; J. S. Adams, "Toward an Understanding of Equity," *Journal of Abnormal and Social Psychology* 67 (1963): 422–436.

8 A. S. Tsui, J. L. Pearce, L. W. Porter, and A. M. Tripoli, "Alternative Approaches to the Employee–Organization Relationship: Does Investment in Employees Pay Off?" *Academy of Management Journal* 40 (1997): 1089–1121; D.A. Rodriguez, F. Targa, and M. H. Belzar, "Pay Incentives and Truck Driver Safety: A Case Study," *Industrial and Labor Relations Review* 59 (2006): 205–225.

9 D. B. McNatt, M. Glassman, and R. B. McAfee, "Pay Inversion Versus Pay for Performance: Can Companies Have Their Cake and Eat It

Too?" *Compensation and Benefits Review* (March–April 2007): 27–35; D. E. Terpstra and A. L. Honoree, "Employees' Responses to Merit Pay Inequity," *Compensation and Benefits Review* (January–February 2005): 51–58; S. C. Currall, A. J. Towler, T. A. Judge, and L. Kohn, "Pay Satisfaction and Organizational Outcomes," *Personnel Psychology* 58 (2005): 613–640; B. Kuvaas, "Work Performance, Affective Commitment, and Work Motivation: The Roles of Pay Administration and Pay Level," *Journal of Organizational Behavior* 27 (2006): 365–385.

10   J. Greenberg, "Losing Sleep Over Organizational Justice: Attenuating Insomniac Reactions to Underpayment Inequity with Supervisory Training in Interactional Justice," *Journal of Applied Pscychology* 91 (2006): 58–69.

11   J. Newman, "Compensation Lessons from the Fast-Food Trenches," *Workspan* (March 2007): 23–26; D. Kadlec, "Where Did My Raise Go?" *Time* (May 26, 2003): 44–54; I. Polyak, "Money Talks, But Is Anyone Listening?" *Workforce Management* (August 2003): 26.

12   F. Hansen, "Workplace Trends," *Compensation & Benefits Review* (March–April 2006): 13–14.

13   F. Hansen, "A New Way to Pay," *Workforce Management* (October 24, 2005): 33–40.

14   A. G. Tekleab, K. M. Bartol, and W. Lui, "Is it Pay Levels or Pay Raises That Matter to Fairness and Turnover?" *Journal of Organizational Behavior* 26 (2005): 899–921.

15   M. A. Edwards, "The Law and Social Norms of Pay Secrecy," *Berkeley Journal of Employment & Labor Law* 26 (2005): 41–63.

16   A. Parsons, "6 HR Communication Trends You Need to Know About," *Workspan* (April 2007): 47–50; A. Colella, R. L. Paetzold, A. Zardhoohi, and M. J. Wesson, "Exposing Pay Secrecy," *Academy of Management Review*, 32 (2007): 55–71; S. Vallas, "Communication Is the Key to Total Rewards Success," *Workspan* (October 2006): 25–27.

17   "Should Companies Disclose Salary Structures?" *Workspan* (August 2005): 10–12.

18   D. Scalise, "Happy Workers," *Hospital and Health Networks* (March 2006): 28–30.

19   K. K. Merriman, "A Fairness Approach to Market-Based Pay," *Workspan* (March 2006): 49–50; S. Werner and D. Ones, "The Determinants of Perceived Pay Inequities: The Effects of Comparison Other Characteristics and Pay-System Communication," *Journal of Applied Social Psychology* 20 (2000): 1300–1329.

20   A. Markels, "Blank Check," *The Wall Street Journal* (April 9, 1998): R11.

21   WorldatWork and Buck Consultants, "The State of Electronic Communications in Compensation and Human Resources," *World at Work Survey Brief* (October, 2005).

22   F. L. Giancola, "Using Advertising Principles to Sell Total Rewards," *Compensation and Benefits Review* (Sept./Oct. 2006): 35–39.

23   M. Makri and L. R. Gomez-Mejia, "Executive Compensation: Something Old, Something New," *Managing Human Resources in North America: Current Issues and Perspectives* (London: Routledge, 2007).

24   J. S. Lublin, "The Pace of Pay Gains, a Survey Overview," *The Wall Street Journal* (April 9, 2007): R1; "In the Money: A Special Report on Executive Pay," *The Economist* (January 20, 2007): S1–S20; R. Kirkland and D. Burke, "The Real CEO Pay Problem," *Fortune* (July 10, 2006): 78–86; D. Brady, "No Hair Shirts, But Still…," *BusinessWeek* (May 1, 2006): 36–38;

"2005 Trends in CEO Pay," *AFL-CIO Paywatch,* accessed at www.aflcio .org/paywatch/ (October 5, 2006); H. L. Tosi, Jr., S. Werner, J. R. Katz, and L. R. Gomez-Mejia, "How Much Does Performance Matter? A Meta-Analysis of CEO Pay?" *Journal of Management* 26(2) (2000): 301–339.

25   J. S. Lublin, "Ten Ways to Restore Investor Confidence in Compensation," *The Wall Street Journal* (April 9, 2007): R1; J. Sasseen, "A Better Look at the Boss's Pay," *BusinessWeek* (February 26, 2007): 44; T. J. Elkins, "New HR Challenges in the Dynamic Environment of Legal Compliance," *Managing Human Resources in North America: Current Issues and Perspectives* (London: Routledge, 2007); A. Tergesen, "How Much Are Execs Really Paid?" *BusinessWeek* (March 20, 2006): 96–98; A. Borrus, "At the SEC, an Eye on Salaries," *BusinessWeek* (January 18, 2006): 11.

26   M. Herbst, "The Elite Circle of $1 CEOs," *BusinessWeek Online* (May 11, 2007): 11; J. McGregor, "Dollar-a-Year (or Less) Men," *BusinessWeek* (April 23, 2007): 9; S. Appleton, "After Rejecting Pay, Some CEOs Find Less Can Be More," *The Wall Street Journal* (March 12, 2007): B1.

27   D. Brady, "Charm Offensive," *BusinessWeek* (June 26, 2006): 76–80; R. Kirkland and D. Burke, "The Real CEO Pay Problem," *Fortune* (July 10, 2006): 78–86; D. Brady, "No Hair Shirts, But Still…," *BusinessWeek* (May 1, 2006): 36–38;

28   B. Grow, "Home Depot's CEO Cleans Up," *BusinessWeek,* (May 25, 2006): 11.

29   Y. Yanadori and J. H. Marler, "Compensation Strategy: Does Business Strategy Influence Compensation in High Technology Organizations?" *Strategic Management Journal* 27 (2006): 559–570.

30   T. Martin, "Can Compensation Impact the Bottom Line?" *Workspan* (February 2004); B. Hill and C. Tande, "Total Rewards: The Employment Value Proposition," *Workspan* (October 2006): 19–22.

31   E. Frauenheim, "IBM's People Chief: A Leader in Leadership," *Workforce Management* (May 21, 2007): 1,20–23; R. K. Platt, "The Big Picture at Big Blue: Total Rewards at IBM," *Workspan* (August 2000): 27; W. Fox, "Staying a Step Ahead of the Competition with Outstanding Total Compensation," *ACA News* (October 1998): 20–22.

32   S. Werner, "Concluding Thoughts," *Managing HR in North America: Current Issues and Perspectives* (London: Routledge, 2007).

33   B. Parus, "Effective Rewards Support Culture Change," *Workspan* (November 2002).

34   R. A. Guzzo, R. D. Jette, and R. A. Katzell, "The Effects of Psychologically Based Intervention Programs on Worker Productivity: A Meta-Analysis," *Personnel Psychology* 38 (1985): 275–291.

35   P. Kaihla, "Best-Kept Secrets of the World's Best Companies," *Business 2.0* (April 1, 2006).

36   R. F. Stolz, "Keeping the Crew," *Human Resource Executive* (December 2003): 8–12.

37   J. M. Pappas and K. E. Flaherty, "The Moderating Role of Individual-Difference Variables in Compensation Research," *Journal of Managerial Psychology* 21 (2006): 19–35.

38   M. A. Thompson, "Border Crossing: Canadian Talent Heading South," *ACA News* (May 2001): 33–37.

39   J. D. Shaw, "Competitive Advantage Through HRM," *Managing Human Resources in North America: Current Issues and Perspectives* (London: Routledge, 2007).

40 E. Zimmerman, "The Joy of Flex," *Workforce Management* (March 2004): 38–40.

41 N. H. Woodward, "Entry-Level Gulf Coast Workers Are Elusive," *HRMagazine* (January 2006): 26–27.

42 V. Infante, "The Future of the Minimum Wage?" *Workforce* (March 2001): 29; "Myth and the Minimum Wage," *BusinessWeek* (October 12, 1998): 6.

43 M. D. Brenner, "The Economic Impact of the Boston Living Wage Ordinance," *Industrial Relations* 44 (2005): 59–83l; "The High Cost of Low Prices," *BusinessWeek* (December 6, 2003): 168.

44 B. Klaas, "Outsourcing and HRM," *Managing HR in North America: Current Issues and Perspectives* (London: Routledge, 2007).

45 Bureau of Labor Statistics, "Employer Costs for Employee Compensation," *BLS Report* (March 2007), accessed at www.bls.gov/ncs/ect/home.htm (accessed September 17, 2007).

46 S. R. Mehta, "The Law of One Price and a Theory of the Organization: A Ricardian Perspective on Interindustry Wages," *RAND Journal of Economics* 29 (1998): 137–156.

47 M. Arai, "Wages, Profits, and Capital Intensity: Evidence from Matched Worker-Organization Data," *Journal of Labor Economics* 21 (2003): 593–618; J. E. Pearce, "Tenure, Unions, and the Relationship Between Employer Size and Wages," *Journal of Labor Economics* 8 (1990): 251–269.

48 U.S. Bureau of Labor Statistics, "Union Affiliation of Employed Wage and Salary Workers by Occupation," accessed at www.bls.gob/news.release/union2.t03.htm (July 2007).

49 U.S. Department of Labor, "General Information on the Fair Labor Standards Act," accessed at www.dol.gov/esa/regs/compliance/whd/mwposter.htm (October 2006).

50 W. Koeniger, M. Leonardi, and L. Nunziata, "Labor Market Institutions and Wage Inequality," *Industrial and Labor Relations Review* 60 (2007): 340–356; A. Smith, "Governors OK Minimum Wage Increases," *HRMagazine* (June 2006): 42; E. S. Povich, "Who's Afraid of the Minimum Wage," *Fortune Small Business* (August 2006); P. Bacon, Jr., "Wage-ing Battle," *Time* (July 17, 2006): 10; D. Neumark, M. Schweitzer, and W. Wascher, "The Effects of Minimum Wages on the Distribution of Family Incomes," *The Journal of Human Resources* 40 (2005):867–894.

51 M. M. Clark, "Preparations Suggested for Final Overtime Regs," *HRMagazine* (February 2004): 25–26.

52 G. Flynn, "Pizza as Pay? Compensation Gets Too Creative," *Workforce Management* (August 1998): 91–96.

53 A. L. Honoree and D. C. Wyld, "The New FLSA Regulations and the Sales Force: Who Is Entitled to Overtime Pay," *Compensation and Benefits Review* (January–February 2006): 29–36; D. E. Alpert and D. Gerard, "FLSA Update: What You Need to Know," *Workspan* (April 2005): 38–41; Department of Labor, "FairPay Fact Sheet by Exemption Under the FLSA," accessed at www.dol.gov/esa/regs/compliance/whd/fairpay/fs17a_overview.htm (September 17, 2006).

54 F. Hansen, "UBS Agrees to Pay $89 Million to Settle Financial Adviser's Claims," *Compensation and Benefits Review* (May–June 2006): 10–11; "$42.5 Million Settlement for Wage Claims by Financial Advisers," *Workspan* (May 2006): 84; "More Than 3,000 Brokers Would Share in $37 Million Settlement," *Workspan* (November 2005).

55 U.S. Department of Labor, "General Information on the Fair Labor Standards Act," accessed at www.dol.gov/esa/regs/compliance/whd/mwposter.htm (September 17, 2006).

56 "How Widespread Is the Gender Pay Gap?" *HR Focus* (June 2006): 3–5.

57 Y. Besen and M. S. Kimmel, "At Sam's Club, No Girls Allowed: The Lived Experience of Sex Discrimination," *Equal Opportunities International* 25 (2006): 172–187; J. Ramey, "Court Weighs Wal-Mart Motion to Dismiss Class Action," *Supermarket News* (August 15, 2005); A. Bernstein, "Wal-Mart Vs. Class Actions," *BusinessWeek* (March 21, 2005); D. Ackman, "Wal-Mart and Sex Discrimination by the Numbers," *Forbes* (June 23, 2004); W. Zellner, "No Way to Treat a Lady," *BusinessWeek* (March 3, 2003).

58 J. A. Fossum, "Comparable Worth," *The Blackwell Encyclopedia of Management: Human Resource Management*, 2nd ed. (Malden, MA: Blackwell Publishing, 2005), 63; J. P. Rudin and K. Byrd, "U.S. Pay Equity Legislation: Sheep in Wolves Clothing," *Employee Responsibilities and Rights Journal* 13 (2003): 183–190.

59 S. Adams and D. Neumark, "When Do Living Wages Bite?" *Industrial Relations* 44 (2005): 164–179; S. Adams and D. Neumark, "The Effects of Living Wage Laws: Evidence from Failed and Derailed Living Wage Campaigns," *Journal of Urban Economics* 58 (2005): 177–202.

60 S. Greenhouse, "Maryland Is First State to Require Living Wage," *The New York Times*, (May 9, 2007): A21.

61 K. Muilenburg and G. Singh, "The Modern Living Wage Movement," *Compensation and Benefits Review* (January–February 2007): 21–28; D. Fairris, "The Impact of Living Wages on Employers: A Control Group Analysis of the Los Angeles Ordinance," *Industrial Relations* 44 (2005): 84–105; M.Reich, P. Hall, and K. Jacobs, "Living Wage Policies at the San Francisco Airport: Impacts on Workers and Businesses," *Industrial Relations* 44 (2005): 106–138.

62 G. Washburn and D. Mihalopoulos, "Daley Vetoes Big Box Law," *Chicago Tribune* (September 12, 2006): A1; J. Caplan and E. Ferkenhoff, "A Big-Box Battle," *Time* (August 21, 2006): 51; R. Freeman, "Fighting for Other Folks' Wages: The Logic and Illogic of Living Wage Campaigns," *Industrial Relations* 44 (2005): 14–31.

63 Y. Yanadori and J. H. Marler, "Compensation Strategy: Does Business Strategy Influence Compensation in High-Technology Organizations?" *Strategic Management Journal* 27 (2006): 559–570; T. Martin, "Can Compensation Impact the Bottom Line?" *Workspan* (February 2004).

64 E. E. Lawler III, "Becoming a Key Player in Business Strategy," *Workspan* (January 2006): 10–12; P. Gilles, "Building a Foundation for Effective Pay Systems," *Workspan* (September 2001).

65 Bureau of Labor Statistics, "Employer Costs for Employee Compensation," *BLS Report* (March 2007), accessed at www.bls.gov/ncs/ect/home.htm (September 17, 2007).

66 W. F. Cascio, "Decency Means More Than 'Always Low Prices': A Comparison of Costco to Wal-Mart's Sam's Club," *Academy of Management Perspectives* 20 (August 2006): 26–37.

67 S. Fournier, "Keeping Line Managers in the Know," *ACA News* (March 2000).

68 A. P. Cilmi, "Managers: The Critical Link in a Successful Rewards and Recognition Program," *Workspan* (November 2005): 19–22.

69 L. Grensing-Pophal, "Communication Pays Off," *HRMagazine* (May 2003): 77–80.

70 J. D. Shaw, N. Gupta, and J. E. Delery, "Pay Dispersion and Workforce Performance: Moderating Effects of Incentives and Interdependence," *Strategic Management Journal* 23 (2002): 491–512; P. Gilles, "Enhancing the Participatory Process of Compensation Design," *ACA News* (May 1998): 27–29.

71 T. J. Keaveny, "Job Evaluation Administrative Issues," *The Blackwell Encyclopedia of Management: Human Resource Management*, 2nd ed. (Malden, MA: Blackwell Publishing, 2005), 205.

72 J. C. Kovak, "Valuing Internal Hierarchy Using Nonquantitative Evaluation Methods," *Workspan* (June 2006): 75; D. B. Balkin, "Ranking Job Evaluation Method," *The Blackwell Encyclopedia of Management: Human Resource Management*, 2nd ed. (Malden, MA: Blackwell Publishing, 2005), 307.

73 M. C. Bloom, "Classification Job Evaluation Method," *The Blackwell Encyclopedia of Management: Human Resource Management*, 2nd ed. (Malden, MA: Blackwell Publishing, 2005), 57.

74 WorldatWork, "Quick Question: What Type of Job Evaluation System Do You Use?" (June 2004), accessed at www.worldatwork.org/ (October 18, 2006).

75 K. Gilbert, "The Role of Job Evaluation in Determining Equal Value in Tribunals: Tool, Weapon, or Cloaking Device?" *Employee Relations* 27 (2005): 7–19.

76 "Structure of the FES," www.opm.gov (accessed October 18, 2006).

77 T. van Sliedregt, O. F. Voskuijl, and H. Theirry, "Job Evaluation Systems and Pay Grade Structures: Do They Match?" *International Journal of Human Resource Management* 12 (2001): 1313–1324.

78 F. Hilling, "Job Evaluation Is Here to Stay," *WorldatWork Journal* 12 (Third Quarter, 2003): 14–21.

79 C. Bacca, "Clarifying Competencies: Powerful Tools for Diving Business Success," *Workspan* (March 2006): 44–56; D. J. Cira and E. R. Benjamin, "Competency-Based Pay: A Concept in Evolution," *Compensation and Benefits Review* (September–October 1998): 21–29.

80 P. K. Zingheim and J. R. Schuster, "Reassessing the Value of Skill Based Pay," *WorldatWork Journal* 11 (Third Quarter, 2002): 72–77.

81 H. Risher, "There is a Need for Agreement on Competencies," *Workspan* (January 2007): 60–61.

82 H. Risher, "Second-Generation Banded Salary Systems," *WorldatWork Journal* (First Quarter 2007): 20–28; J. C. Kovac, "Broadbanding: Creating a Flat Organization, "*Workspan* (November 2006): 67; M. A. Mazer, "Variable Competency Banding: Combining Variable Pay, Competencies, and Broadbanding," *Workspan* (May 2004); G. A. Stoskopf, "Choosing the Best Salary Structure for Your Organization," *WorldatWork Journal* 11 (Fourth Quarter, 2002): 28–36.

83 J. A. Green and R. W. Keuch, "Contribution-Driven Competency-Based Pay," *ACA Journal* (Autumn 1997): 62–71.

84 K. S. Abosch and B. L. Hmurovic, "A Traveler's Guide to Global Broadbanding," *ACA Journal* (Summer 1998): 38–46.

85 B. Parus, "Broadbanding Highly Effective, Survey Shows," *ACA News* (July–August 1998): 40–41; see also M. Enos and G. Limoges, "Broad-Banding: Is That Your Company's Final Answer?" *WorldatWork Journal* (Fourth Quarter 2000): 61–68.

86 G. E. Ledford, "Three Case Studies on Skill-Based Pay: An Overview," *Compensation and Benefits Review* (April 1990): 11–23.

87 J. H. Dulebohn and S. E. Werling, "Compensation Research Past, Present, and Future," *Human Resource Management Review* 17 (2007): 191–207.

88 J. Marquez, "Lawsuits Could Raise Scrutiny of Pay Surveys," *Workforce Management* (July 31, 2006): 12; J. C. Kovac, "Avoiding Anti-Trust Litigation When Conducting Salary Surveys," *Workspan* (April 2005): 71.

89 C. H. Fay and M. Tare, "Market Pricing Concerns," *WorldatWork Journal* (Second Quarter 2007): 61–69; G. Stern and Y. Borcia, "10 Tips for Becoming Survey Savvy," *Workspan* (February 2007): 27–28.

90 "Occupational Pay Relatives," Bureau of Labor Statistics (December 2005), accessed at www.bls.gov/ncs/ocs/home.htm (October 2006).

91 J. C. Kovac, "Geographic Differentials," *Workspan* (February 2006): 83.

92 M. Reilly and L. Audi, "Does It Still Make Sense to Use Geographic Pay Rates?" *Workspan* (December 2006).

93 Learn more about The Clayton Wallis Company and see examples of other benchmark job descriptions by visiting www.compensation-online .com/cwmain.htm. K. Lemaire, "Competency-Based Pay: A Practitioner's Guide," in C. H. Fay, M. A. Thompson, and D. Knight, *The Executive Handbook on Compensation* (New York: Free Press, 2001), 486–495.

94 J. C. Kovac, "Setting Rates of Pay: Compensation Philosophy," *Workspan* (March 2007).

95 G. A. Stoskopf, "Choosing the Best Salary Structure for Your Organization," *WorldatWork Journal* 11 (Fourth Quarter, 2002).

96 For a thorough overview of this topic, see L. R. Gomez-Mejia and S. Werner (eds.), *Global Compensation* (London: Routledge, 2008).

97 F. Hansen, "Many Countries, One System," *Workforce Management* (October 23, 2006): 28; R. White, "A Strategic Approach to Building a Consistent Rewards Program," *Compensation and Benefits Review* (July–August 2005): 23–40; F. Hansen, "Centralized Compensation Structures Are Increasing," *Compensation and Benefits Review* (January–February 2005): 8–10.

98 WorldatWork, "Global Compensation Practices," Survey Brief (September 2004).

99 U.S. Department of Labor, "A Chartbook of International Comparisons," accessed at www.dol.gov/asp/media/reports/chartbook/ chartbook_jun06.pdf (October 2006); J. J. Martocchio, *Strategic Compensation*, 3rd ed. (Upper Saddle River, NJ: Pearson Prentice Hall, 2004); G. T. Milkovich and J. M Newman, *Compensation*, 8th ed. (New York: McGraw-Hill/Irwin, 2005); D. Brown, "The Third Way: The Future of Pay and Rewards Strategies in Europe," *WorldatWork Journal* (Second Quarter 2000); S. E. Gross and M. Edelstein, "Paying the Price of Global Expansion," *Workspan* (September 2006): 43–46; M. Uzcategui and F. Diez, "A Journey Through Compensation in Latin America," *WorldatWork Journal* (First Quarter 2005): 59–70.

100 J. Marquez, "McDonald's Rewards Program Leaves Room for Some Local Flavor," *Workforce Management* (April 10, 2006): 26.

101 Society of Human Resource Management, "SHRM Special Expertise Panels 2005 Trends Report," accessed at www.shrm.org/trends (October 30, 2006); Society of Human Resource Management, "SHRM Special Expertise Panels 2006 Trends Update," accessed at www.shrm.org/ trends (October 30, 2006).

102 B. Gault and V. Lovell, "The Costs and Benefits of Policies to Advance Work/Life Integration," *American Behavioral Scientist* 49 (2006): 1152–1164.

103 S. Fegley, *2006 Benefits Survey* (Alexandria, VA: SHRM/SHRM Foundation, 2006).

104 Society of Human Resource Management, "SHRM Special Expertise Panels 2006 Trends Update," accessed at www.shrm.org/trends (October 30, 2006).

105 J. Vaslow and F. Lampron, "Nintendo Case Study: Before and After Automated Compensation Management," *Workspan* (November 2006): 35–37.

Chapter 11

1 See the USPS Web site, accessed at www.usps.com (July 1, 2007); J. Schuster, P. Weatherhead, and P. Zingheim, "Pay for Performance Works: The United States Postal Service Presents a Powerful Business Case," *WorldatWork Journal* (First Quarter 2006): 24–31. Also see the Annual Progress Reports of the USPS and track their progress on the Strategic Transformation Plan, 2006–2010.

2 K. Whitehouse, "More Companies Offer Packages Linking Pay Plans to Performance," *The Wall Street Journal* (December 13, 2005): B6.

3 Workforce Management Staff, "No Real Money on the Table," *Workforce Management* (December 2003): 115.

4 O. Gottschalg and M. Zollo, "Interest Alignment and Competitive Advantage," *Academy of Management Review* 32(2) (2007): 418–437; L. de Swardt, T. Veldsman, and G. Roodt, "Toward an Empirically Validated Variable Pay Methodology," *WorldatWork Journal* (Fourth Quarter 2006): 7–17.

5 M. V. Russo and N. S. Harrison, "Organizational Design and Environmental Performance: Clues from the Electronics Industry," *Academy of Management Journal* 48(4) (2005): 582–593.

6 P. Shafer and V. Fischetti, "Rewarding Your Way to Double-Digit Growth," *WorldatWork Journal* (Fourth Quarter 2005): 6–15.

7 D. Brown and M. West, "Rewarding Service? Using Reward Policies to Deliver Your Customer Service Strategy," *WorldatWork Journal* (Fourth Quarter 2005): 22–31.

8 J. Sammer, "CA Restatement a Cautionary Tale on Designing, Monitoring Sales Compensation Programs," *Workforce Management* (July 31, 2006): 36–37.

9 C. B. Cadsby, F. Song, and F. Tapon, "Sorting and Incentive Effects of Pay for Performance: An Experimental Investigation," *Academy of Management Journal* 50(2) (2007): 387–405.

10 M. J. Ducharme, P. Singh, and M. Podolsky, "Exploring the Links Between Performance Appraisals and Pay Satisfaction," *Compensation and Benefits Review* (September–October 2005): 46–52.

11 N. Byrnes, "Avon Calling—Lots of New Reps," *BusinessWeek* (June 2, 2003): 53–54.

12 P. Digh, "The Next Challenge: Holding People Accountable," *HRMagazine: Diversity Agenda* (October 1998): 63–69; S. N. Mehta, "Diversity Pays," *The Wall Street Journal* (April 11, 1996): R12.

13 L. Summers, "Integrated Pay for Performance: The High-Tech Marriage of Compensation Management and Performance Management," *Compensation and Benefits Review* (January–February 2005): 18–25; P. K. Zingheim and J. R. Schuster, "The Next Decade for Pay and Rewards," *Compensation and Benefits Review* (January–February 2005): 26–32.

14 Recognition Professionals International, "Glossary of Terms," accessed at www.recognition.org (January 30, 2007).

15 S. J. Peterson and F. Luthans, "The Impact of Financial and Nonfinancial Incentives on Business-Unit Outcomes over Time," *Journal of Applied Psychology* 91 (2006): 156–165.

16 K. M. Kroll, "Let's Get Flexible," *HRMagazine* (April 2007): 97–100; S. Harris, "What's the Perceived Value of Your Incentives?" *Workspan* (February 2007): 21–25; S. L. Rynes, B. Gerhart, and K. A. Minette, "The Importance of Pay in Employee Motivation: Discrepencies Between What People Say and What They Do," *Human Resource Management* (Winter 2004): 381–394; S. Ladika, "Rewarding Exempt Employees," *HRMagazine* (September 2006).

17 P. K. Zingheim and J R. Schuster, "Revisiting Effective Incentive Design: Still the Major ROI Reward Opportunity," *WorldatWork Journal* (First Quarter 2005): 50–58.

18 S. Rubenfeld and J. David, "Multiple Employee Incentive Plans: Too Much of a Good Thing?" *Compensation and Benefits Review* (March–April 2006): 35–39.

19 J. Fried, "Skin in the Game," *Inc.* (July 2006): 33–36.

20 A. C. Daniels, "The Leader's Role in Pay Systems and Organizational Performance," *Compensation and Benefits Review* (May–June 2006): 56–60; K. Bradsher, "Efficiency on Wheels," *The New York Times* (June 16, 2000): C1, 8.

21 D. Brown and M. West, "Rewarding Service," *WorldatWork Journal* (Fourth Quarter 2005): 22–31.

22 B. Hensel, Jr., "Continental Says Thanks a Hundredfold," *Houston Chronicle* (December 11, 2006): 1.

23 B. Gerhart, "Designing Reward Systems: Balancing Result and Behaviors," in C. H. Fay, M. A. Thompson, and D. Knight, *The Executive Handbook on Compensation: Linking Strategic Rewards to Business Performance* (New York: Free Press, 2001): 214–237.

24 C. Gomez, B. Kirkman, and D. Shapiro, "The Impact of Collectivism and In-Group/Out-Group Membership on the Evaluation Generosity of Team Members," *Academy of Management Journal* 43(6) (2000): 1097–1106; F. Moussa, "Determinants, Process, and Consequences of Personal Goals and Performance," *Journal of Management* 26(6) (2000): 1259–1285; P. M. Wright, et al., "Productivity and Extra-Role Behavior: The Effects of Goals and Incentives on Spontaneous Helping," *Journal of Applied Psychology* 78 (1993): 374–381.

25 P. Buchenroth, "Driving Performance: Making Pay Work for the Organization," *Compensation and Benefits Review* (May–June 2006): 30–35.

26 Hay Group, *The Hay Report: Compensation and Benefits for 1998 and Beyond* (New York: The Hay Group, 1998).

27 J. V. Simons, "Case Study: A Nonprofits Scorecard Comes of Age," *Workspan* (December 2006).

28 Results reported in "No Real Money on the Table," *Workforce Management* (December 2003): 115. For more details, go to the Mercer Web site (http://www.mercerhr.com).

29 J. Kiska, "Customer Satisfaction Pays Off," *HRMagazine* (February 2004): 87–93; E. E. Lawler III, "Reward Practices and Performance Management System Effectiveness," *Organizational Dynamics* 32(4) (2003): 396–404; S. J. Berman, "Using the Balance Scorecard in Strategic Compensation," *ACA News* (June 1998): 16–19.

30 J. B. Wood, "Customer Satisfaction and Loyalty," *ACA Journal* (Summer 1998): 48–60.

31 J. Fierman, "The Perilous New World of Fair Pay," *Fortune* (June 13, 1994): 58–59.

32 R. D. Banker, S-Y Lee, G. Potter, and D. Srinivasan, "Contextual Analysis of Performance Impacts of Outcome-Based Incentive Compensation," *Academy of Management Journal* 39 (1996): 920–948.

33 J. R. Deckop, R. Mangel, and C. Cirka, "Getting More Than You Pay for: Organizational Citizenship Behavior and Pay-for-Performance Plans," *Academy of Management Journal* 41 (1999): 420–428; G. D. Jenkins, Jr., A. Mitra, N. Gupta, and J. D. Shaw, "Are Financial Incentives Related to Performance? A Meta-Analytic Review of Empirical Research," *Journal of Applied Psychology* 83 (1998): 777–787.

34 For an excellent set of articles, see *Human Resource Management Journal* 43 (Spring 2004); E. Deci, R. Koestner, and R. Ryan, "A Meta-Analytic Review of Experiments Examining the Effects of Extrinsic Rewards on Intrinsic Motivation," *Psychological Bulletin* 125(6) (1999): 627–668; R. Eisenberger and J. Cameron, "Detrimental Effects of Reward," *American Psychologist* 51 (November 1996): 1153–1166.

35 "Policy Guide: Incentive Pay Can Bring Many Rewards," *Bulletin to Management* (June 5, 1997): 184; "Policy Guide: Employers Use Pay to Lever Performance," *Bulletin to Management* (August 21, 1997): 272.

36 M. Frase-Blunt, "What Goes Up May Come Down," *HRMagazine* (August 2001): 85–90.

37 T. Fang and J. S. Heywood, "Output Pay and Ethnic Wage Differentials: Canadian Evidence," *Industrial Relations* 45 (2006): 173–193; J. S. Heywood and P. L. O'Halloran, "Racial Earnings Differentials and Performance Pay," *The Journal of Human Resources* 40 (2005): 435–452.

38 W. Arulampalam, A. L. Booth, and M. L. Bryan, "Is There a Glass Ceiling over Europe? Exploring the Gender Pay Gap Across the Wage Distribution," *Industrial and Labor Relations Review* 60 (2007): 163–186.

39 A. Joshi, H. Liao, and S. E. Jackson, "Cross-Level Effects of Workplace Diversity on Sales Performance and Pay," *Academy of Management Journal* 49(3) (2006): 459–481; R. Sharpe, "As Leaders, Women Rule," *BusinessWeek* (November 20, 2000): 75–84.

40 J. Sotherlund and C. Gokturk, "Paying for Performance: Walking a Legal Fine Line," *Workspan* (January 2007): 38–40.

41 B. Cherry, "Recent Trends in Equity Compensation," *Workspan* (January 2007): 21–22; P. Babcock, "Options to Stock Options," *HRMagazine* (April 2006); L. Zong, "The Changing Requirements for Equity Compensation," *WorldatWork Journal* (Second Quarter 2006): 24–33.

42 D. Scott, T. D. McMullen, and R. S. Sperling, "The Fiscal Management of Compensation Programs," *WorldatWork Journal* 14(3) (2005): 13–25.

43 J. Sammer, "Figuring Incentive Plans' ROI," *HRMagazine* (July 2006); T. E. Weinberger, "Evaluating the Effectiveness of Incentive Plan Design within Company Constraints," *Compensation and Benefits Review* (November/December 2005): 27–33.

44 W. Jenkins and M. C. Fina, "Health Care Organizations Attract, Retain, and Motivate Through Recognition Programs," *Workspan* (June 2007): 31–34; T. Gentry, "Re-Engineering Recognition," *Workspan* (February 2007): 47–48; WorldatWork, "Trends in Employee Recognition 2005," *WorldatWork Survey Brief* (May 2005).

45 A. P. Cilmi, "Managers: The Critical Link in a Successful Rewards and Recognition Program," *Workspan* (November 2005): 19–22.

46 J. Flaherty, "Suggestions Rise from the Floors of U.S. Factories," *The New York Times* (April 18, 2001): C1, 7.

47 J. Wiscombe, "Rewards Get Results," *Workforce Management* (April 2002): 42–48.

48 C. Huff, "Recognition That Resonates," *Workforce Management* (September 11, 2006): 25–27; WorldatWork, "Trends in Employee Recognition 2005," *WorldatWork Survey Brief* (May 2005).

49 C. Huff, "So Plastic: Gift Cards Are Most Popular Incentive," *Workforce Management* (September 11, 2006): 30.

50 A. L. Overhalt, "Cuckoo for Customers," *Fast Company* (June 2004): 86–87.

51 R. L. Heneman, "Merit Pay," in C. H. Fay, M. A. Thompson, and D. Knight (eds.), *The Executive Handbook on Compensation: Linking Strategic Rewards to Business Performance* (New York: Free Press, 2001).

52 Workspan Staff?, "Back to Basics: Merit Matrix," *Workspan*, (September 2005): 67.

53 F. Hansen, "Money Transfer," *Workforce Management* (October 23, 2006): 23–25.

54 S. J. Wells, "No Results, No Raise," *HRMagazine* (May 2005): 77–80.

55 "Real Wages Decline Across the Board," *Workforce Management* (December 12, 2005): 56–66.

56 K.Chou, "Pay for Performance: On Life Support," *Workspan* (September 2005): 29–37; H. Risher, "Pay for Performance: Alive and Well," *Workspan* (September 2005): 29–37.

57 B. Sonsin, "A Pat(ent) on the Back," *HRMagazine* (March 2000): 107.

58 D. C. Johnston, "Agents Say Fast Audits Hurt I.R.S.," *The New York Times* (January 12, 2007): C1, 4.

59 E. A. Fong and H.L.Tosi, Jr., "Effort, Performance, and Conscientiousness: An Agency Theory Perspective," *Journal of Management* 33(2) (2007): 161–179; A. Cox, "The Outcomes of Variable Pay Systems: Tales of Multiple Costs and Unforeseen Consequences," *International Journal of Human Resource Management* 16 (2005):1475–1497.

60 W. B. Abernathy, "Linking Performance Scorecards to Profit-Indexed Performance Pay," *ACA News* (April 1998): 23–25.

61 M. Bolch, "Rewarding the Team," *HRMagazine* (February 2007); C. Garvey, "Steer Teams with the Right Pay," *HRMagazine* (May 2002); S. E. Gross and S. P. Leffler, "Team Pay," in C. H. Fay, M. A. Thompson, and D. Knight (eds.), *The Executive Handbook on Compensation: Linking Strategic Rewards to Business Performance* (New York: Free Press, 2001), 465–485; D. B. Balkin and E. F. Montemayor, "Explaining Team-Based Pay: A Contingency Perspective Based on the Organizational Life Cycle, Team Design, and Organizational Learning Literatures," *Human Resource Management Review* 10(3) (2000): 249–269.

62 J. Davis, "Retaining Your Hot Skills Employees—Use Dollars AND Sense," *ACA Journal* (First Quarter 2000): 47–56; B. Nelson, "Does One Reward Fit All?" *Workforce Management* (February 1997): 67–70.

63 M. Akdere and T. Yilmaz, "Team Performance Based Compensation Plans: Implications for Human Resources and Quality Improvement from Agency Theory Perspective," *International Journal of Human Resources Development and Management* 6(1) (2006): 77–91.

64 S. C. Carr, M. R. Hodgson, D. H. Vent, and I. P. Purcell, "Pay Diversity Across Work Teams: Doubly De-Motivating Influences?" *Journal of Managerial Psychology* 20(5) (2005): 417–439.

65 R. Masternak and M.A. Camuso, "Gainsharing and Lean Six Sigma—Perfect Together," *WorldatWork Journal* (First Quarter 2005): 42–49.

66 J. B. Arthur and L. Aiman-Smith, "Gainsharing and Organizational Learning: An Analysis of Employee Suggestions over Time," *Academy of Management Journal* 44 (2001): 737–754.

67 K. Paulsen and D. Westman, "Using Gainsharing to Motivate Generation X," *ACA News* (July–August 1999): 44–48; T. M. Welbourne and L. R. Gomez Mejia, "Gainsharing: A Critical Review and a Future Research Agenda," *Journal of Management* 21 (1995): 559–609.

68 P. Kaihla, "Best-Kept Secrets of the World's Best Companies," *Business 2.0* (April 2006).

69 D. Scott, P. Davis, and C. Cockburn, "Scanlon Principles and Processes," *WorldatWork Journal* (First Quarter 2007): 29–36; D-O Kim, "Factors Influencing Organizational Performance in Gainsharing Programs," *Industrial Relations* 35 (April 1996): 227.

70 J. Pellet, "Profit Potential," *Entrepreneur* (January 2006): 59.

71 M. Magnan and S. St-Onge, "The Impact of Profit Sharing on the Performance of Financial Services Firms," *Journal of Management Studies* 42(4) (2005): 761–791.

72 J. M. Pappas and K. E. Flaherty, "The Moderating Role of Individual-Difference Variables in Compensation Research," *Journal of Managerial Psychology* 21 (2006): 1–35; T. Begley and C. Lee, "The Role of Negative Affectivity in Pay-at-Risk Reactions: A Longitudinal Study," *Journal of Applied Psychology* 90(2) (2005): 382–388.

73 "A Tricky Business," *The Economist* (June 30, 2001): 55–56.

74 WorldatWork, "Key Sales Incentive Plan Practices," *WorldatWork Survey Brief* (April 2005).

75 M. Boyle, "Best Buy's Giant Gamble," *Fortune* (April 3, 2006).

76 J. Sammer, "Weighing Pay Incentives," *HRMagazine* (June 2007): 64–68; J. Stoeckmann, "Change on the Horizon: An Analysis of Sales Compensation Practices," *Workspan* (April 2007): 41–44.

77 WorldatWork, "Key Sales Incentive Plan Practices," *WorldatWork Survey Brief* (April 2005).

78 K. Bonamici, "Hot Starbucks to Go," *Fortune* (January 26, 2004): 60–74; W. J. Duncan, "Stock Ownership and Work Motivation," *Organizational Dynamics* 30(1) (2001): 1–11.

79 T. Francis, "Inside Eileen Fisher's Employee Stock Plan," *The Wall Street Journal* (January 22, 2007): B1.

80 A. N. Stuart, "Taking Stock of SARs," *CFO* (April 2006): 13.

81 N. Byrnes, "Which Is Better—Stock or Options?" *BusinessWeek* (July 21, 2003): 25; Bureau of Labor Statistics, "BLS Reports on Non-Executive Employee Stock Options," *Workspan* (January 2001): 13.

82 Based on D. G. Goodall, "Global Employee-Based Equity Plans—Can They Work for Your Company?" in C. Reynolds (ed.), *Guide to Global Compensation and Benefits* (San Diego, CA: Harcourt, 2001), 121–158; G. Paulin, "Using Stock to Retain Key Employees," *WorldatWork Journal* (Third Quarter 2000): 45–51.

83 C. E. Devers, R. M. Wiseman and R. M. Holmes, Jr., "The Effects of Endowment and Loss Aversion in Managerial Stock Option Valuation," *Academy of Management Journal* 50 (2007): 191–208; N. Byrnes, "Which Is Better—Stock or Options?" *BusinessWeek* (July 21, 2003): 25; P. Sparrow, "The Psychological Consequences of Employee Ownership: On the Role of Risk, Reward, Identity and Personality," *Trends in Organizational Behavior* 8 (2001): 79–90.

84 D. Delves, "Stock Options: Underused and Underwater," *Workforce* (January 2003): 50–54; L. Lavelle, "When Good Options Go Bad," *BusinessWeek E.Biz* (December 11, 2000): 96–98.

85 F. L. Aenlle-Rocha, "Stock Option Backdating: What It Means for Your Company," *Workspan* (May 2007): 36–38; J. Fox, "Self-Deal? CEOs? Nahhh…," *Fortune* (November 27, 2006): 95–96; A. Lashinsky, "Options Gone Wild!" *Fortune* (July 10, 2006): 50.

86 P. Dvorak, "Theory and Practice: Tweaking the Stock-Option Grant," *The Wall Street Journal* (April 30, 2007): B3; L. Zong, "The Changing Requirements of Equity Compensation," *WorldatWork Journal* (Second Quarter 2006): 24–33.

87 J. Markoff and D. Leonhardt, "Microsoft Will Award Stock, Not Options, to Employees," *The New York Times* (July 9, 2003): 1, 4; S. Kershaw, "For Newer Microsoft Employees, a Sense of Redress," *The New York Times* (July 10, 2003): 1, 4; P. J. Kiger, "Microsoft Leads the Way in Opting Out of Options," *Workforce Management* (August 2003): 74–76.

88 L. R. Gomez-Mejia and S. Werner (eds.), *Global Compensation* (London: Routledge, 2008); D. J. Chichelli, "Global Sales Compensation," *Workspan* (May 2007): 49–52; A. Katsoudas, S. Olsen, and P. Weems, "New Trends in Global Equity Rewards," *Workspan* (March 2007): 29–33; S. Trotman and S. Ross, "Rationalizing Global Incentive Pay Plans: Look at the Big Picture," *Workspan* (October 2005): 31–33; D. R. Briscoe and R. S. Schuler, *International Human Resource Management*, 2nd ed. (London: Routledge, 2004).

89 I. Bjorkman, C. F. Fey, and H. J. Park, "Institutional Theory and MNC Subsidiary HRM Practices: Evidence from a Three-Country Study," *Journal of International Business Studies* 38 (2007): 430–446; "Global Pay for Performance," *HRMagazine* (April 2006); R. J. Long and J. L. Shields, "Performance Pay in Canadian and Australian Firms: A Comparative Study," *International Journal of Human Resource Management* 16(10) (2005): 1783–1811.

90 D. G. Goodall, "Global Employee-Based Equity Plans—Can They Work for Your Company?" in C. Reynolds (ed.), *Guide to Global Compensation and Benefits*, 2nd ed. (San Diego, CA: Harcourt, 2001), 121–158.

91 K. M. Kacmar, "Ethics and HRM," in S. Werner (ed.), *Managing Human Resources in North America: Current Issues and Perspectives* (London: Routledge, 2007).

92 M. Benz and B. S. Frey, "Corporate Governance: What Can We Learn from Public Governance?" *Academy of Management Review* 32 (2007): 92–104; D. J. Denis, P. Hanouna, and A. Sarin, "Is There a Dark Side to Incentive Compensation?" *Journal of Corporate Finance* 12 (2006): 467–488.

93 J. R. Deckop, K. K. Merriman, and S. Gupta, "The Effects of CEO Pay Structure on Corporate Social Performance," *Journal of Management* 32(3) (2006): 329–342; L. S. Mahoney and L. Thorne, "Corporate Social Responsibility and Long-Term Compensation: Evidence from Canada," *Journal of Business Ethics* 57 (2005): 241–253.

94 E. M. Matsumura and J. Y. Shin, "Corporate Governance Reform and CEO Compensation: Intended and Unintended Consequences," *Journal* *of Business Ethics* 62 (2005): 101–113; "Fat Cats Feeding," *The Economist* (October 11, 2003): 64–66.

95 B. Hill, "New Rules: Paying for Performance," *Workspan* (May 2006): 44–52; H. Chen, Y. Hsieh, "Key Trends of the Total Reward System in the 21st Century," *Compensation and Benefits Review* (November–December 2006): 64–70.

96 E. White, "Employer's Increasingly Favor Bonuses to Raises," *The Wall Street Journal* (August 28, 2006): B3.

Chapter 12

1 See the Steelcase Web site, accessed at www.steelcase.com (June 28, 2007); also personal communication with Libby Child, manager, managed claims and disability nanagement services, Steelcase.

2 Metlife's 2005/2006 Employee Benefits Trend Survey, accessed at www.metlife.com.

3 Bureau of Labor Statistics, "Employer Costs for Employee Compensation (March, 2007), accessed at www.bls.gov/ncs/ect/home .htm (July 10, 2007).

4 J. Martocchio, "The Cost of Employee Benefits," in S. Werner (ed.), *Managing Human Resources in North American: Current Issues and Perspectives* (London: Routledge, 2007).

5 J. Martocchio, "The Cost of Employee Benefits," in S. Werner (ed.), *Managing Human Resources in North American: Current Issues and Perspectives* (London: Routledge, 2007); "Benefits Costs Reach Crisis Stage," *Workforce Management* (December 2003): 119.

6 A. Fisher, "Playing for Keeps," *Fortune* (January 22, 2007): 85–92.

7 "Benefits Help Retention in Two-Thirds of Cases," *Employee Benefits* (September 2004): 12.

8 S. Miller, "Employers Underestimate Retention Risk over Health, Retirement Benefits," *SHRM Compensation and Benefits Library*, accessed at www.shrm.com (September 2006).

9 "Why You Should Consider Elder-Care Benefits as a Retention Tool," *HR Focus* (May 2006): 5–6.

10 "Age Is So Often a State of Mind," *Employee Benefits* (August 2006): 4–5; G. A. Stoskopf, "Using Total Rewards to Attract and Retain Health Care Employees," *WorldatWork Journal* (Third Quarter 2004): 16–25.

11 A. Lashinsky, "Search and Enjoy," *Fortune* (January 22, 2007):70–82.

12 S.Fegley, *2006 Benefits Survey* (Alexandria, VA: SHRM/SHRM Foundation, 2006).

13 "Employer Costs for Employee Compensation—March 2007," Bureau of Labor Statistics, U.S. Department of Labor, accessed at www .bls.gov/ncs/ect/home.htm.

14 S. Fegley, *2006 Benefits Survey* (Alexandria, VA: SHRM/SHRM Foundation, 2006); R. Pear, "Health Spending at a Record Level," *The New York Times* (January 9, 2004): A1, A16.

15 "Employer Costs for Employee Compensation—March 2007," Bureau of Labor Statistics, U.S. Department of Labor, accessed at www .bls.gov/ncs/ect/home.htm.

16 J. G. Kilgour, "Public Sector Pension Plans in California: How Big Is the Problem?" *Compensation and Benefits Review* (March–April 2007): 4–26; J. G. Kilgour, "The Debate Concerning State and Local Pension

Plans," *WorldatWork Journal* (Second Quarter 2007): 48–60; J. Revell, "The $366 Billion Outrage," *Fortune* (May 31, 2004): 130–141.

17 "National Compensation Survey: Employee Benefits in Private Industry in the U.S., March 2006," Bureau of Labor Statistics, U.S. Department of Labor, accessed at www.bls.gov/ncs/ect/home.htm; K. Blanton,"Health Care Costs Dog Small Firms," *Boston Globe* (July 7, 2004): D1, D8; E. L. Andrews, "Health Care Heights: Soaring Rates Leave Little Companies in a Bind," *The New York Times* (February 24, 2004): G1, G8.

18 S. Fegley, *2006 Benefits Survey* (Alexandria, VA: SHRM/SHRM Foundation, 2006).

19 A. Lashinsky, "Search and Enjoy," *Fortune* (January 22, 2007): 70–82.

20 J. C. Kovac, "Social Secuity," *Workspan* (June 2005): 71; R. Kuttner, "Social Security: Finally, An Honest Debate," *BusinessWeek* (March 15, 2004): 24; see the Web site of the U.S. Department of Labor, Bureau of Labor Statistics, accessed at www.bls.gov.

21 E. Eckholm, "Overhauls Proposed in Benefits for Jobless," *The New York Times* (September 14, 2006): A21; P. Carroll, "Integrated Benefits Plans Offer Companies Key Advantages," *ACA News* (March 2000): 29–32.

22 See statistics at the Occupational Safety & Health Administration Web site, accessed at www.osha.gov.

23 M. P. McQueen, "The Growing Appeal of Disability Insurance," *The Wall Street Journal* (December 19, 2006): D1; M. Athavale and S. M. Avila, "Large Deductible Workers' Compensation Plans," *Compensation and Benefits Review* (November–December 2006): 20–25.

24 Libby Child, personal conversation with authors (April 7, 2001).

25 See the FLMA fact sheet at www.dol.gov/esa; J. C. Kovac, "Family and Medical Leave Act," *Workspan* (June 2007): 76; G. M. Davis, "The Family and Medical Leave Act: 10 Years Later," *Legal Report* (July–August 2003): 1, 8.

26 S. Fegley, *2006 Benefits Survey* (Alexandria, VA: SHRM/SHRM Foundation, 2006); "FMLA Perspectives and Practices," *WorldatWork Survey Brief* (April 2005).

27 R. Kuttner, "The Great American Pension-Fund Robbery," *BusinessWeek* (September 8, 2003): 24.

28 C. Hirschman, "Fiduciary Fitness," *HRMagazine* (September 2003): 60–64; S. Bates, "More U.S. Firms offer Pension Investment Advice," accessed at www.shrm.org/hrnews_published/articles/CMS_005681 .asp (October 7, 2003); J. Revell, "CEO Pensions: The Latest Way to Hide Millions," *Fortune* (April 28, 2003): 68–69.

29 K. Chu, "401(k), Employers Get Creative to Get Workers to Participate," *USA Today* (August 7, 2006): 1B–2B; C. Hirschman, "Autopilot 401(k)s Gain Altitude," *HRMagazine* (December 2005); P. J. Kiger, "New Hope for Troubled Retirement Plans," *Workforce Management* (October 2003): 53–56.

30 L. Gomes, "HPs Pension Switch Signals End to Era of Cozy Retirements," *The Wall Street Journal* (March 14, 2007): B1; C. Hirschman, "Coupling Financial Advice to Your Retirement Plan," *HRMagazine* (March 2007): 80–88; J. Sammer, "Sage Advice," *HRMagazine* (November 2006); J. Marquez, "Getting Employees in the Game," *Workforce Management* (August 28, 2006): 27–29; J. Marquez, "IBM Shift Sets High Standard for Firms Freezing Pensions," *Workforce Management* (January 16, 2006): 3–4; C. Hirschman, "Autopilot 401(k)s Gain Altitude," *HRMagazine*, (December 2005); J. Morris, "The Changing Pension Landscape," *Compensation and*

Benefits Review (September–October 2005): 30–35; J. Marquez, "IBM Strives for the Security of Defined-Benefit Programs as It Shifts Focus to 401(k)s," *Workforce Management* (June 2005): 79–80; H. Gleckman, "A Nest Egg That's a No-Brainer," *BusinessWeek* (April 25, 2005): 108–110.

31 "National Compensation Survey: Employee Benefits in Private Industry in the U.S., March 2006," Bureau of Labor Statistics, U.S. Department of Labor, accessed at www.bls.gov/ncs/ect/home.htm; "Benefit Costs Reach Crisis Stage," *Workforce Management* (December 2003): 128.

32 L. G. Kraft, "The Insider: Retirement," *Workforce Management* (July 2004): 57–58.

33 W. Updegrave, "Why You Don't Want to Be a Company Man," *Money Magazine* (June 1, 2006).

34 M. Chester, D. Dodds, and T. Walker, "The ERISA Copycat Phenomenon," *Compensation and Benefits Review* (November–December 2005): 34–46.

35 S. Block, "Hybrid Plans: Easier to Offer Now," *USA Today* (August 7, 2006): 4B; "Cash Balance Plans Conversions Actually Increase Employer Costs, Study Reveals," *HRMagazine* (May 2004): 32, 38.

36 S. Block, "Hybrid Plans: Easier to Offer Now," *USA Today* (August 7, 2006): 4B; J. VanDerhei, "The Controversy of Traditional vs. Cash Balance Plans," *ACA News* (Fourth Quarter 1999): 7–26.

37 M. W. Walsh, "Unresolved on Pensions," *The New York Times* (January 17, 2007): C1–C8; M. W. Walsh, "Court Rules for IBM on Pension," *The New York Times* (August 8, 2006): C1–C10; S. Miller, "IBM Wins Appeal in Cash Balance Pension Case: Another Spur for Conversions," accessed at www.shrm.com/rewards (August 2006); U.S. Department of Labor, "Frequently Asked Questions about Cash Balance Plans," accessed at www.dol.gov/ebsa/faqs/faq_consumer_Cashbalanceplans.html (March 12, 2007).

38 J. C. Kovac, "All You Need to Know About ERISA," *Workspan* (May 2005): 88; U.S. Department of Labor, accessed at www.dol.gov/ebsa/faqs/faq_consumer_pension.html.

39 D. Halonen, "PBGC Budget Report Shows the Sky Isn't Falling After All," *Pensions and Investments* (November 11, 2006); *PBGC Annual Management Report* (November 2006), accessed at www.pbgc.com; *Pension Insurance Data Book 2005* (Summer 2006), accessed at www.pbgc.com; M. Schoeff, Jr., "Pension Benefit Guaranty Corp.," *Workforce Management* (March 13, 2006): 24.

40 J. Blasi, D. Kruse, and A. Bernstein, *In the Company of Owners* (New York: Basic Books, 2003).

41 T. J. Bartl, "The Pension Protection Act's Impact on Total Rewards Professionals," *Workspan* (October 2006): 88–90; Department of Labor, accessed at www.dol.gov/EBSA/pensionreform.html.

42 S. Fegley, *2006 Benefits Survey* (Alexandria, VA: SHRM/SHRM Foundation, 2006).

43 M. Freudenheim, "Health Care Costs Rise Twice as Much as Inflation," *The New York Times* (September 27, 2006): C1–C7; National Coalition on Health Care, "Facts on Health Care Costs," accessd at www.nchc.org (March 27, 2007).

44 "Employer Health Benefits 2006 Survey," The Kaiser Family Foundation and Health Research and Educational Trust, 2006.

45 J. C. Kovac, "Health Care," *Workspan* (November, 2004): 77.

46 B. J. Feder, "Deere Sees a Future in Health Care," *The New York Times* (July 1, 1994): D1; J. J. Laabs, "Deere's HMO Turns Crisis into Profit," *Personnel Journal* (October 1992): 82–89.

47 J. C. Kovac, "Health Care," *Workspan* (November, 2004): 77; "Benefit Costs Reach Crisis Stage," *Workforce Management* (December 2003): 122; T. Lieberman, "HMO or PPO: Are You in the Right Plan?" *Consumer Reports* (October 2001): 27–29.

48 J. C. Kovac, "Health Care," *Workspan* (November, 2004): 77.

49 T. Lerche, "The Impact of Consumer-Directed Health Plans with Integrated Health-Improvement Services," *WorldatWork Journal* (Second Quarter 2007): 5–22; C. Calvert, "Consumer-Driven Health Care: Why Do Companies Take the Plunge?" *Workspan* (January 2007): 51–53; J. C. Kovac, "Consumer-Driven Health Care," *Workspan* (April 2004).

50 S. J. Wells, "Will Employees Orchestrate Their Health Care?" *HRMagazine* (December 2006); M. T. Bond, M. E. Dobeck, and D. E. Knapp, "Using Health Saving Accounts to Provide Low-Cost Health Care," *Compensation and Benefits Review* (March–April 2005): 29–32; S. Neeleman, "Making Health Savings Accounts Work," *Compensation and Benefits Review* (March–April 2005): 33–35;

51 C. Fruitrail and V. Wedin, "Creating Better Health Care Consumers: A Case Study," *Compensation and Benefits Review* (September–October 2006): 40–45; L. Sanicola and K. Ickes, "Instituting a Full Replacement Health Savings Account," *Workspan* (January 2006): 44–46.

52 C. Fuoco-Karasinski, "Building More Fit Employees," *Workspan* (April 2007): 65–67; M. R. Dufresne, and D. Anderson, "Consumer-Driven Health Care: Is It a Silver Bullet?" *Workspan* (February 2007): 31–33; S. Fegley, *2006 Benefits Survey* (Alexandria, VA: SHRM/SHRM Foundation, 2006); "FMLA Perspectives and Practices," *WorldatWork Survey Brief* (April 2005); H. Gleckman and J. Carey, "An Apple a Day—On the Boss," *BusinessWeek* (October 14, 2002): 122–124; B. Kirsch, "Working Well," *Human Resource Executive* (May 5, 1998): 45–47.

53 J. G. Altonji and E. Usui, "Work Hours, Wages, and Vacation Leave," *Industrial and Labor Relations Review* 60(3) (2007): 408–428; C. Fritz and S. Sonnentag, "Recovery, Well-Being, and Performance-Related Outcomes: The Role of Workload and Vacation Experiences," *Journal of Applied Psychology* 91(4) (2006): 936–945; "National Compensation Survey: Employee Benefits in Private Industry in the U.S., March 2006," Bureau of Labor Statistics, U.S. Department of Labor, accessed at www.bls.gov/ncs/ect/home.htm.

54 R. W. Geisel, "Going into Leave Debt," *HRMagazine* (September 2005).

55 World Tourist Organization, www.tia.org.; D. R. Briscoe and R. S. Schuler, *International Human Resource Management*, 2nd ed. (London: Routledge, 2004).

56 F. Giancola, "Making Sense of Sabbaticals," *Workspan* (July 2006): 39–41; M. Bolch, "Time to Refocus," *HRMagazine* (May 2006); S. Fegley, *2006 Benefits Survey* (Alexandria, VA: SHRM/SHRM Foundation, 2006).

57 C. Navarro and C. Bass, "The Case for Automating Absence Management," *Workspan* (February 2007): 59–61.

58 D. J. Thompson, "The Seven Levers of Change for Work/Life Effectiveness," *WorldatWork Journal* (First Quarter 2007): P. Wang and F. O. Walumbwa, "Family Friendly Programs, Organizational Commitment, and Work Withdrawal: The Moderating Role of Transformational Leadership," *Personnel Psychology* 60(2) (2007): 397–427; 54–61; N. R. Lockwood, "Work/Life Balance: Challenges and Solutions," *SHRM Research Quarterly* 2 (2003): 1–10.

59 P. L. Perrewe, "The Changing Family and HRM," in S. Werner (ed.), *Managing Human Resources in North America: Current Issues and Perspectives* (London: Routledge, 2007), 60–71; S.Fegley, *2006 Benefits Survey* (Alexandria, VA: SHRM/SHRM Foundation, 2006); K. S. Robinson, "Employers Increase Work/Life Programs," *HRMagazine* (March 2004): 32; S. Feeney, "Employees Find a Field of Family-Friendly Benefits in Des Moines," *Workforce Management* (July 2003): 81–83; J. Perry-Smith and T. Blum, "Work-Family Human Resource Bundles and Perceived Organizational Performance," *Academy of Management Journal* 43(6) (2000): 1107–1117.

60 R. M. Johnson, "U.S. Telework Trends: Working from Anywhere," *Workspan* (May 2007): 74–76; S. Flannery, "Telecommuting: Issues to Consider When Your Employees Take the Office Home," *Workspan* (April 2007): 5–62.

61 K. Gurchiek, "Give Us Your Sick," *HRMagazine* (January 2007); N. Vogel, "Meeting Special Needs: A Benefit That Adds Value for Both Employees and Employers," *Compensation and Benefits Review* (March–April 2006): 57–61; K. Tyler, "Gone Camping," *HRMagazine* (January 2006); N. H. Woodward, "Helping Workers Pay College Costs," *HRMagazine* (August 2005); R. W. Geisel, "School's in at Work," *HRMagazine* (June 2005).

62 P. J. Kiger, "A Case for Child Care," *Workforce Management* (April 2004): 34–40.

63 B. Mulcahy, "Why You Should be Caring for Your Company's Caregivers," *Workspan* (June 2007): 37–39; K. Rose, "Elder Care: A Responsibility That Requires a Collaborative Effort," *WorldatWork Journal* (Second Quarter 2006): 60–69; S. Fegley, *2006 Benefits Survey* (Alexandria, VA: SHRM/SHRM Foundation, 2006); N. R. Lockwood, "The Aging Workforce," *2003 Research Quarterly* (Alexandria, VA: SHRM): 1–10.

64 P. Weaver, "Long-Term Planning: Long-Term-Care Insurance Avaiable Through Employers Is Broadening Its Reach," *HRMagazine* (May 2007): 85–90.

65 M. Hammers, "'Family-Friendly' Benefits Prompt Non-Parent Backlash," *Workforce Management* (August 2003): 77–79; T. J. Rothauser, J. A. Gonzalez, N. E. Clarke, and L. L. O'Dell, "Family-Friendly Backlash—Fact or Fiction? The Case of Organizations' On-Site Child Care Centers," *Personnel Psychology* 51 (1998): 685–706; A. Hayashi, "Mommy-Track Backlash," *Harvard Business Review* (March 2001): 33–42.

66 M. Conlin, "Unmarried America" *BusinessWeek* (October 2003): 106–116.

67 J. C. Kovac, "Domestic Partner Benefits," *Workspan* (February 2007): 108; R. W. Geisel, "Responding to Changing Ideas of Family," *HRMagazine* (August 2004): 89–98.

68 F. Ivery, "Tuition-Aid Programs Are an Integral Part of Career Development," *Workspan* (January 2007): 29–31; M. Bolch, "Bearing Fruit," *HRMagazine* (March 2006).

69 G. S. Benson, D. Finegold, and S. A. Mohrman, "You Paid for the Skills, Now Keep Them: Tuition Reimbursement and Voluntary Turnover," *Academy of Management Journal* 47 (2004): 315–331.

70 C. Hirschman, "Employees' Choice," *HRMagazine* (February 2006).

71 R. Levering and M. Moskowitz, "In Good Company," *Fortune* (January 22, 2007): 94–114; D. Cadrain, "Just Desserts," *HRMagazine* (March 2005).

72 P. Babcock, "Find What Workers Want," *HRMagazine* (April 2005); M. Frase-Blunt, "Time to Redo Your Benefits?" *HRMagazine* (December 2002); L. Gaughan, J. Kasparek, J. Hagens, and J. Young, "The Employee as Customer," *Workspan* (September 2000).

73 J. C. Decker, A. Joshi, and J. J. Martocchio, "Employee Benefits as Context for Intergenerational Conflict," *Human Resource Management Review* 17 (2007): 208–220; "Do Employees Prefer Health Care or More Pay?" *Workspan* (February 2007): 19; R. R. Feinsod and T. O. Davenport, "The Aging Workforce: Challenge or Opportunity?" *WorldatWork Journal* (Third Quarter 2006): 14–23; M. Frase-Blunt, "Time to Redo Your Benefits?" *HRMagazine* (December 2002).

74 J. Ewing, "Revolt of the Young," *BusinessWeek* (September 22, 2003): 48; J. Dulebohn, B. Murray, and M. Sun, "Selection Among Employer-Sponsored Pension Plans: The Role of Individual Differences," *Personnel Psychology* 53 (2000): 405–432.

75 A. Cohen, "Decision Support in the Benefits Consumer Age," *Compensation and Benefits Review* (March–April 2006): 46–51; C. Hirschman, "Employees' Choice," *HRMagazine* (February 2006); V. Gieseke, "Key Considerations in Automating Health and Welfare Benefits Administration," *Compensation and Benefits Review* (November–December 2005): 56–63; M. Levy, "The ABCs of Cafeteria Plans," *Workspan* (June 2002).

76 D. Ackley, "Communication: The Key to Putting the Benefit Back into Benefits," *Workspan* (February 2006): 32–34; "Ideas on Improving Benefits Communication with Employees," *HR Focus* (December 2005): 11–13.

77 A. Parsons and K. Groh, "The New Road to Effective Communications," *Compensation and Benefits Review*, (July–August 2006): 57–62; L. Grenshing-Pophal, "Now Hear This," *HRMagazine* (June 2006); S. Marcotte, "Wired Workforce: The State of Electronic Communications in Total Rewards," *Workspan* (March 2006): 21–24.

78 M. Kisilevitz, S. Debgupta, and D. Metz, "Improving Employee Benefits Behavior Through Effective Communication," *WorldatWork Journal* (First Quarter 2006): 52–61.

79 J. Schramm, "SHRM Workplace Forecast 2006–2007," *SHRM Report* (June 2006).

80 National Coalition on Health Care, "Facts on Health Care Costs," accessed at www.nchc.org (March 27, 2007); M. Freudenheim, "Workers Feel Pinch of Rising Health Costs," *The New York Times* (October 22, 2003): C1, C2.

81 K. Staloch, "How Your Company Can Save Money Without Cutting Pharmacy Benefits," *Workspan* (June 2007): 51–54; E. Pezalla, "Employer Strategies for Managing New Prescription Drugs," *Workspan* (January 2007: 46–49; R. Epstein, "Current Trends in Drug Spending," *Workspan* (December 2006); K. Roberts, "50 Ideas for Controlling Health-Care Costs," *Workspan* (January 2006): 32–35; M. E. Medland, "Shaving Health Costs," *HRMagazine* (June 2005); J. Weber, M. Arndt, and L. Cohen, "America, This Is Really Gonna Hurt," *BusinessWeek* (September 17, 2001): 46–48.

82 B. Liddick, "Going the Distance for Health Savings," *HRMagazine* (March 2007); M. Conlin, "Get Healthy—or Else," *BusinessWeek* (February 26, 2007): 58–69.

83 J. McCracken, "UAW May Run Some Retiree Benefits: GM, Ford Explore Moving Obligation for Health Care," *The Wall Street Journal* (January 23, 2007): A3; Kaiser/Hewiit, "Retiree Health Benefits Examined," *Kaiser/Hewitt 2006 Survey on Retiree Health Benefits* (December 2006); C. Loomis, "The Tragedy of General Motors," *Fortune* (February 20, 2006).

Chapter 13

1 "Ergo Activities Make John Deere Workplaces Safer," accessed at www.deere.com (September 11, 2006); E. Tahmincioglu, "Battling Job-Related Aches and Pains," *The New York Times* (January 3, 2001): G1; J. Barling and M. R. Frone, "Occupational Injuries: Setting the Stage," in J. Barling and M. R. Frone (eds.), *The Psychology of Workplace Safety* (Washington, DC: American Psychological Association: 2004), 3–14; M. J. Burke and S. A. Sarpy, "Improving Worker Safety and Health Through Interventions," in D. A. Hofmann and L. E. Tetrick (eds.), *Health and Safety in Organizations: A Multilevel Perspective* (San Francisco: Jossey-Bass, 2003), 56–90.

2 J. C. Quick and L. E. Tretrick (eds.), *Handbook of Occupational Health Psychology* (Washington, DC: American Psychological Association [APA], 2003).

3 "New Health and Safety Issues," Steelcase, accessed at www.steelcase.com (January 15, 2004).

4 R. J. Grossman, "Space: Another HR Frontier," *HRMagazine* (September 2002): 29–34; R. Grossman, "Back with a Vengeance," *HRMagazine* (August 2001): 36–46; S. Greenhouse, "Ergonomics Report Cites Job Injuries," *The New York Times* (January 18, 2001): C6; R. Grossman, "Make Ergonomics," *HRMagazine* (April 2000): 36–42; M. Conlin, "Is Your Office Killing You?" *BusinessWeek* (June 5, 2000): 114–124; M. Minehan, "OSHA Ergonomics Regs Draw Immediate Fire," *HR News* (January 2001): 1, 3; K. Tyler, "Sit Up Straight," *HRMagazine* (September 1998): 121–128.

5 M. J. Burke, S. A. Sarpy, P. E. Tesluk, and K. Smith-Crowe, "General Safety Performance: A Test of a Grounded Theoretical Model," *Personnel Psychology* 55 (2002): 429–457; T. DeGroot and D. S. Kiker, "A Meta-Analysis of the Non-Monetary Effects of Employee Health Management Programs," *Human Resource Management* 42(1) (Spring 2003): 53–69.

6 C. A. Heaney, "Worksite Health Interventions: Targets for Change and Strategies for Attaining Them," in J. C. Quick and L. E. Tetrick (eds.), *Handbook of Occupational Health Psychology* (Washington, DC: American Psychological Association [APA], 2003), 305–324; J. Lein, S. Markowitz, M Fahs, and P. Landrigan, *Costs of Occupational Injuries and Illnesses* (Ann Arbor: University of Michigan Press, 2000); R. Shindledecker, "Health and the Bottom Line," *Workspan* (September 2000): 6–8; W. Altman, "Health and Safety Commission Chair Bill Callaghan on 'Good Health Is Good Business,'" *Academy of Management Executive* 14(2) (May 2000): 8–11; J. Quick, J. Gavin, C. L. Cooper, and J. D. Quick, "Executive Health: Building Strength, Managing Risks," *Academy of Management Executive* 14(2) (May 2000): 34–46; W. Atkinson, "Safety—at a Price," *HRMagazine* (November 1999): 52–59; M. Arndt, "It Pays to Tell the Truth," *BusinessWeek* (June 5, 2000): 128–130; R. Grossman, "Out with the Bad Air . . . ," *HRMagazine* (October 2000): 37–45; L. Grensing-Pophal, "Clearing the Air," *HRMagazine* (August 2000): 64–70.

7 R. J. Grossman, "Back with a Vengence," *HRMagazine* (August 2001): 36–46; W. Atkinson, "Is Workers' Comp Changing?" *HRMagazine* (July 2000): 50–61; U. Lundberg, I. Dohns, B. Melin, L. Sandsjö, G. Palmerud, T. Kadefors, M. Elkström, and D. Parr, "Psychophysiological Stress Responses, Muscle Tension, and Neck and Shoulder Pain Among Supermarket Cashiers," *Journal of Occupational Health Psychology* 4(3) (1999): 245–255; V. Infante, "The Irony of Ergonomic Regulation," *Workforce Management* (January 2001): 26; P. Leigh, S. Markowitz, M. Fahs, and P. Landrigan, *Cost of Occupational Injuries and Illnesses* (Ann Arbor: University of Michigan Press, 2000).

8 "Healthy Vision Month Observed in May," *NIH News*, accessed at www.healthyvision2010.org/hvm/pr.asp (May 1, 2006); "The Importance of Eye Protection for Work and Recreation," American Optometric Association, accessed at www.aoa.org/documents/eye-safety.ppt#20 (January 8, 2007).

9 F. Willis, "Carpal Tunnel Syndrome," *Modern Drug Discovery* 4(3) (March 2001): 19–20, accessed at http://pubs.acs.org/subscribe/journals/mdd/v04/i03/html/03health.html (January 8, 2007).

10 W. Atkinson, "The Carpal Tunnel Conundrum," *Workforce Management* (September 2002): 17.

11 "Our Mission Statement," accessed at www.benjerry.com (January 2, 2007); W. Atkinson, "The Carpal Tunnel Conundrum," *Workforce Management* (September 2002): 17; also from Ben and Jerry's *Annual Reports* 1992–2000; G. Smith, "A Famous Brand on the Rocky Road," *BusinessWeek* (November 17, 2000): 54; "Ben & Jerry's Sacred Cow," CNN (December 3, 1999); B. Cohen and J. Greenfield, *Ben & Jerry's Double Dip* (New York: Simon & Schuster, 1997).

12 V. M. Kelly, "Living, Breathing, Working" *AFT On Campus* (December 2006–January 2007): 10–12.

13 D. L. Nelson and B. L. Simmons, "Health Psychology and Work Stress: A More Positive Approach," in J. C. Quick and L. E. Tetrick (eds.), *Handbook of Occupational Health Psychology* (Washington, DC: American Psychological Association [APA], 2003), 97–120.

14 *Mental Health and Work: Impact, Issues and Work Practices*, (Geneva: World Health Organization and International Labour Organisation, 2000), 1, 33, accessed at www.who.int/mental_health/media/en/712.pdf (accessed September 21, 2007).

15 "National Census of Fatal Occupational Injuries in 2005", Bureau of Labor Statistics, http://www.bls.gov/news.release/pdf/cfoi.pdf (August 10, 2006).

16 T. V. Riper, "America's Most Dangerous Jobs," accessed at http://www.msnbc.msn.com/id/15640339 (November 14, 2006).

17 "The NRA Should Hold Its Fire," Ideas Editorials, *BusinessWeek* (August 15, 2005); R. J. Grossman, "Bulletproof Practices," *HRMagazine* (November 2002): 34–42.

18 "Workplace Illnesses and Injuries in 2005," Bureau of Labor Statistics, accessed at www.bls.gov/news.release/pdf/osh.pdf (October 19, 2006).

19 K. Gurchiek, "Study Finds Eye-Opening Cost Associated with Fatigued Workers," accessed at www.shrm.org (January 30, 2007); J. B. Bennett, R. F. Cook, and K. R. Pelletier, "Toward an Integrated Framework for Comprehensive Organizational Wellness: Concepts, Practices, and Research in Workplace Health Promotion," in J. C. Quick and L. E. Tetrick (eds.), *Handbook of Occupational Health Psychology* (Washington, DC: American Psychological Association [APA], 2003), 69–96; M. J. Smith, B. T. Karsh, P. Carayon, and F. T. Conway, "Controlling Occupational Safety and Health Hazards," in J. C. Quick and L. E. Tetrick (eds.), *Handbook of Occupational Health Psychology* (Washington, DC: American Psychological Association [APA], 2003), 35–68; M. Budman, "Counting the Costs," *Across the Board* (March–April 2002): 38–40.

20 For detailed discussions, see "Coming Clean: Drug and Alcohol Testing in the Workplace," *World of Work* 57 (September 2006): 33; J. Barling and M. R. Frone (eds.), *The Psychology of Workplace Safety* (Washington, DC: American Psychological Association [APA], 2004), and D. A. Hofmann and L. E. Tetrick (eds.), *Health and Safety in Organizations* (San Francisco: Jossey-Bass, 2003). Also see P. J. Kiger, "Healthy, Wealthy and Wise," *Workforce Management* (July 2003): 40–42.

21 C. Brotherton, "The Role of External Policies in Shaping Organizational Health and Safety," in D. A. Hofmann and L. E. Tetrick (eds.), *Health and Safety in Organizations: A Multilevel Perspective* (San Francisco: Jossey-Bass, 2003), 372–396; J. D. Shaw and J. E. Delery, "Strategic HRM and Organizational Health," in D. A. Hofmann and L. E. Tetrick (eds.), *Health and Safety in Organizations: A Multilevel Perspective* (San Francisco: Jossey-Bass, 2003), 233–260; D. A. Hofmann and L. E. Tetrick, "The Etiology of the Concept of Health: Implications for 'Organizing' Individual and Organizational Health," in D. A. Hofmann and L. E. Tetrick (eds.), *Health and Safety in Organizations: A Multilevel Perspective* (San Francisco: Jossey-Bass, 2003), 1–28.

22   N. H. Woodward, "Making Safety Job No. 1," *HRMagazine* (January 2007): 60–65; N. R. Lockwood, "Safety Training in the Workplace," *SHRM Research* (February 2005); S. Adams, "Costs Drive Safety Training Needs," *HRMagazine* (January 2003).

23   For a full discussion, see R. R. Sinclair and L. E. Tetrick, "Pay and Benefits: The Role of Compensation Systems in Workplace Safety," in J. Barling and M. R. Frone (eds.), *The Psychology of Workplace Safety* (Washington, DC: American Psychological Association [APA], 2004), 181–201.

24   M. Villano, "Financial Side Effects of On-the-Job Injuries," *The New York Times* (December 10, 2006): 11; K. Roberts, "Using Workers' Compensation to Promote a Healthy Workplace," in D. A. Hofmann and L. E. Tetrick (eds.), *Health and Safety in Organizations: A Multilevel Perspective* (San Francisco: Jossey-Bass, 2003), 341–371; A. G. Lipold, "The Soaring Costs of Workers' Comp," *Workforce Management* (February 2003): 42–48.

25   G. Kranz, "Transitional Duty Pays Off for Employers, Charities, and Injured Workers," *Workforce Management* (December 2003): 75–77.

26   E. K. Kelloway, "Labor Unions and Occupational Safety: Conflict and Cooperation," in J. Barling and M. R. Frone (eds.), *The Psychology of Workplace Safety* (Washington, DC: American Psychological Association [APA], 2004), 249–264.

27   G. R. Gray, D. W. Myers, and P. S. Myers, "Collective Bargaining Agreements: Safety and Health Provisions," *Monthly Labor Review* (May 1998): 13–35.

28   For a discussion about weapons policies that promote safety, see R. J. Grossman, "Weapons Policies Under Fire," *HRMagazine* (September 2007): 53–58.

29   J. Barling and M. R. Frone (eds.), *The Psychology of Workplace Safety* (Washington, DC: American Psychological Association [APA], 2004); D. Zohar, "Safety Climate: Conceptual and Measurement Issues," in J. C. Quick and L. E. Tetrick (eds.), *Handbook of Occupational Health Psychology* (Washington, DC: American Psychological Association [APA], 2003), 123–142; P. Tesluk and N. R. Quigley, "Group and Normative Influences on Health and Safety: Perspectives from Taking a Broad View on Team Effectiveness," in D. A. Hofmann and L. E. Tetrick (eds.), *Health and Safety in Organizations: A Multilevel Perspective* (San Francisco: Jossey-Bass, 2003), 131–172; D. Zohar, "A Group-Level Model of Safety Climate: Testing the Effect of Group Climate on Microaccidents in Manufacturing Jobs," *Journal of Applied Psychology* 85(4) (2000): 587–596.

30   "Out of Disaster Comes a Call for Creating a 'Safety Culture,'" *Workforce Management* (April 23, 2007): 1–4; "Company CEOs Accept Award at NSC's 94th Annual Congress and Expo," accessed at www.nsc .org (November 6, 2006).

31   Research on organizational cultures and safety often focuses on the development of a positive safety climate. For a detailed discussion,

see M. Griffin and A. Neal, "A Study of the Lagged Relationships Among Safety Climate, Safety Motivation, Safety Behavior, and Accidents at the Individual and Group Levels," *Journal of Applied Psychology* 91(4) (2006): 946–953; T. Katz-Navon, E. Naveh, and Z. Stern, "Safety Climate in Health Care Organizations: A Multidimensional Approach," *Academy of Management Journal* 48(6) (2005): 1075–1089; A. Neal and M. A. Griffin, "Safety Climate and Safety at Work," in J. Barling and M. R. Frone (eds.), *The Psychology of Workplace Safety* (Washington, DC: American Psychological Association [APA], 2004), 15–34; "Report Finds Safer Workplaces in U.S.," *HRMagazine* (March 2004): 28.

32   D. A. Hofmann and F. P. Morgesen, "The Role of Leadership in Safety," in J. Barling and M. R. Frone (eds.), *The Psychology of Workplace Safety* (Washington, DC: American Psychological Association [APA], 2004), 159–180.

33   J. Barling, C. Loughlin, and E. K. Kelloway, "Development and Test of a Model Linking Safety-Specific Transformational Leadership and Occupational Safety," *Journal of Applied Psychology* 87(3) (2002): 488–496; see also D. Zohar, "The Influence of Leadership and Climate on Occupational Health and Safety," in D. A. Hofmann and L. E. Tetrick (eds.), *Health and Safety in Organizations: A Multilevel Perspective* (San Francisco: Jossey-Bass, 2003), 201–232.

34   D. Barstow and L. Bergman, "A Family's Fortune, a Legacy of Blood and Tears," *The New York Times* (January 9, 2003): A1, A20, A21; D. Barstow and L. Bergman, "Deaths on the Job, Slaps on the Wrist," *The New York Times* (January 10, 2003): A1, A16, A17; "Frontline: A Dangerous Business," PBS (2003).

35   L. E. Tetrick and J. C. Quick, "Prevention at Work: Public Health in Occupational Settings," in J. C. Quick and L. E. Tetrick (eds.), *Handbook of Occupational Health Psychology* (Washington, DC: American Psychological Association [APA], 2003), 3–18; J. B. Bennett, R. F. Cook, and K. R. Pelletier, "Toward an Integrated Framework for Comprehensive Organizational Wellness: Concepts, Practices, and Research in Workplace Health Promotion," in J. C. Quick and L. E. Tetrick (eds.), *Handbook of Occupational Health Psychology* (Washington, DC: American Psychological Association [APA], 2003), 69–96; M. J. Burke, S. A. Sarpy, P. E. Tesluk, and K. Smith-Crowe, "General Safety Performance: A Test of a Grounded Theoretical Model," *Personnel Psychology* 55 (2002): 429–457.

36   M. J. Smith, B. T. Karsh, P. Carayon, and F. T. Conway, "Controlling Occupational Safety and Health Hazards," in J. C. Quick and L. E. Tetrick (eds.), *Handbook of Occupational Health Psychology* (Washington, DC: American Psychological Association [APA], 2003), 35–68; K. S. Robinson, "Learn to Keep the Workplace Healthy: Toxic Mold Dangerous to Both Employees and Businesses," *Society for Human Management* (October 2002): 7, 11.

37   N. Stein, "Son of a Chicken Man," *Fortune* (May 13, 2002): 137–146.

38   "Workplace Illnesses and Injuries in 2005," Bureau of Labor Statistics, accessed at www.bls.gov/news.release/pdf/osh.pdf (October 19, 2006); "National Census of Fatal Occupational Injuries in 2005," Bureau of Labor Statistics, accessed at www.bls.gov/news.release/pdf/cfoi.pdf (August 10, 2006), 3.

39   "Working Overtime Increases Risk of Workplace Injuries More Than Job Hazard, U.S. Study Finds," *Insurance Journal*, accessed at www.insurancejournal.com/news/national/2005/08/18/58572.htm (August 18, 2005).

40   *OSHA 2003–2008 Strategic Management Plan*, accessed at www .osha.gov (January 8, 2004).

41 N. C. Tompkins, "The Federal Hazard Communication Standard: The Employee 'Right To Know' Law," SHRM white paper, accessed at www.shrm.org (August 1994, revised November 1996, reviewed November 2002); "Six Need-to-Know Tips for a Safe Workplace," *Business and Legal Reports* (January 6, 2004), accessed at www2.hrnext.com.

42 M. J. Burke, S. A. Sarpy, P. E. Tesluk, and K. Smith-Crowe, "General Safety Performance: A Test of a Grounded Theoretical Model," *Personnel Psychology* 55 (2002): 429–457; see also M. J. Burke and S. A. Sarpy, "Improving Worker Safety and Health Through Interventions," in D. A. Hofmann and L. E. Tetrick (eds.), *Health and Safety in Organizations: A Multilevel Perspective* (San Francisco: Jossey-Bass, 2003), 56–90.

43 "Firefighters Report Increase in Lung Illness from World Trade Center Dust," *American College of Chest Physicians* (May 10, 2007), accessed at www.sciencedaily.com/releases/2007.

44 F. Meilinger, "OSHA Signs Letter of Agreement with Mexico," OSHA announcement, accessed at www.osha.gov (July 21, 2004).

45 "HIV/AIDS and Work: Global Estimates, Impact on Children and Youth, and Response?" International Labour Organization, accessed at www.ilo.org (2006), xi, xii.

46 *Global Compact Policy Dialogue on HIV/AIDS* (Geneva: International Labour Organization [ILO], 2003).

47 E. Tahmincioglu, "Ergonomics Is Back on the Radar Screen for Both Business and Regulators," *Workforce Management* (July 2004): 59–61.

48 For a detailed discussion of safety and health hazards, see M. J. Smith, B. T. Karsh, P. Carayon, and F. T. Conway, "Controlling Occupational Safety and Health Hazards," in J. C. Quick and L. E. Tetrick (eds.), *Handbook of Occupational Health Psychology* (Washington, DC: American Psychological Association [APA], 2003), 35–68; D. A. Hofmann and L. E. Tetrick, "The Etiology of the Concept of Health: Implications for 'Organizing' Individual and Organizational Health," in D. A. Hofmann and L. E. Tetrick (eds.), *Health and Safety in Organizations: A Multilevel Perspective* (San Francisco: Jossey-Bass, 2003), 1–28; K. Sparks, B. Faragher, and C. L. Cooper, "Well-Being and Occupational Health in the 21st Century Workplace," *Journal of Occupational and Organizational Psychology* 74 (2001): 489–509.

49 N. R. Kleinfield, "Diabetics in the Workplace Confront a Tangle of Laws," *The New York Times* (December 26, 2006): A1; H. Ernst, "The Diabetes Explosion," *Fortune* (December 11, 2006): 122; J. Smerd, "Aggressive Prescription for Controlling Diabetes," *Workforce Management* (July 17, 2006): 41–44.

50 M. R. Frone, "Predictors of Work Injuries Among Employed Adolescents," *Journal of Applied Psychology* 83 (1998): 565–576.

51 A. D. Eschtruth, S. A. Sass, and J. P. Aubry, "Employers Lukewarm About Retaining Older Workers" (Boston: Center for Retirement Research at Boston College, May 2007); *The Business Case for Workers Age 50+* (New York: Towers Perrin, 2005); "Facing Middle-Age Injuries," *CNN* (July 18, 2000): 1–3.

52 U.S. Department of Labor and the Bureau of Labor Statistics, accessed at http://www.llstats.bls.gov (January 8, 2004); E. Esen, *SHRM Workplace Violence Survey* (Alexandria, VA: Society for Human Resource Management, 2004); S. A. Baron, S. Hoffman, and J. Merrill, *When Work Equals Life: The Next Stage of Workplace Violence* (San Francisco: Pathfinder, 2000); T. D. Schneid, *Occupational Health Guide to Violence in the Workplace* (Chelsea, MI: Lewis Publishers, 1998).

53 E. F. Sygnature and G. A. Toscano, "Work-Related Homicides: The Facts," *Compensation and Working Condition* (Spring 2000): 3–8.

54 "Occupational Violence," National Institute for Occupational Safety and Health, accessed at www.cdc.gov/niosh/injury/traumaviolence.html (January 8, 2007); A. Benedict, 2006 Weapons in the Workplace Survey Report, SHRM Research (November 2006); N. R. Lockwood, "Workplace Violence Prevention," SHRM Research (February 2005).

55 M. M. LeBlanc and E. K. Kelloway, "Predictors and Outcomes of Workplace Violence and Aggression," *Journal of Applied Psychology* 87(3) (2002): 444–453; S. C. Douglas and M. J. Martinko, "Exploring the Role of Individual Differences in Predicting Workplace Aggression," *Journal of Applied Psychology* 86(4) (2001): 547–559; J. H. Neuman and R. A. Baron, "Workplace Violence and Workplace Aggression: Evidence Concerning Specific Forms, Potential Causes and Preferred Targets," *Journal of Management* 24(3) (1998): 391–419; G. R. VanderBos and E. Q. Bulatao (eds.), *Violence on the Job: Identifying Risks and Developing Solutions* (Washington, DC: American Psychological Association [APA], 1996); A. M. O'Leary-Kelly, R. W. Griffin, and D. J. Glew, "Organization-Motivated Aggression: A Research Framework," *Academy of Management Review* 21 (1996): 225–253.

56 C. L. Cooper, P. Dewe, and M. O'Driscoll, "Employee Assistance Programs," in J. C. Quick and L. E. Tetrick (eds.), *Handbook of Occupational Health Psychology* (Washington, DC: American Psychological Association [APA], 2003), 289–304.

57 R. Valliere, "Spate of Murders Spurred Postal Service to Radically Change Handling Violence," *Occupational Safety and Health Reporter* 34(31) (July 29, 2004): 785–786.

58 Visit the Web sites of the U.S. Department of Labor and the Bureau of Labor Statistics, the National Safety Council, and the National Center for Health Statistics for the latest information.

59 See the OSHA Website (www.osha.gov) for its 2003–2008 "Strategic Management Plan."

60 For a comprehensive review of research on the consequences of work design, see S. E. Humphrey, J. D. Nahrgang, F. P. Morgeson, "Integrating Motivational, Social and Contextual Work Design Features: A Meta-Analytic Summary and Theoretical Extension of the Work Design Literature," *Journal of Applied Psychology* 92 (2007): 1332–1356.

61 S. Sonnentag and F. R. H. Zijlstra, "Job Characteristics and Off-Job Activities as Predictors of Need for Recovery, Well-Being, and Fatigue," *Journal of Applied Psychology* 91(2) (2006): 330–350; J. R. Hackman and G. R. Oldham, *Work Redesign* (Reading, MA: Addison-Wesley, 1980); G. Dodd and D. C. Ganster, "The Interactive Effects of Variety, Autonomy, and Feedback on Attitudes and Performance," *Journal of Organizational Behavior* 17 (1996): 329–347; R. W. Renn and R. J. Vandenberg, "The Critical Psychological States: An Underrepresented Component in Job Characteristics Model Research," *Journal of Management* 21 (1995): 279–303; S. P. Brown and T. W. Leigh, "A New Look at Psychological Climate and Its Relationship to Job Involvement, Effort, and Performance," *Journal of Applied Psychology* 81 (1996): 358–368.

62 J. Barling, E. K. Kelloway, and R. D. Iverson, "High-Quality Work, Job Satisfaction, and Occupational Injuries," *Journal of Applied Psychology* 88(2) (2003): 276–283.

63 S. K. Parker, N. Turner, and M. A. Griffin, "Designing Healthy Work," in D. A. Hofmann and L. E. Tetrick (eds.), *Health and Safety in Organizations: A Multilevel Perspective* (San Francisco: Jossey-Bass, 2003), 91–130.

64 D. H. Shapiro, Jr., C. E. Schwartz, and J. A. Astin, "Controlling Ourselves, Controlling Our World," *American Psychologist* 51 (December 1996): 1213–1230; J. Schaubroeck and D. E. Merritt, "Divergent Effects of Job Control on Coping with Work Stressors: The Key Role of Self-Efficacy," *Academy of Management Journal* 40 (1997): 738–754.

65   T. Thoerell, "To Be Able to Exert Control over One's Own Situation: A Necessary Condition for Coping with Stressors," in J. C. Quick and L. E. Tetrick (eds.), *Handbook of Occupational Health Psychology* (Washington, DC: American Psychological Association [APA], 2003), 201–219.

66   This summary is based on the excellent review provided by C. S. Smith, L. M. Sulsky, and W. E. Ormond, "Work Arrangements: The Effects of Shiftwork, Telework, and Other Arrangements," in D. A. Hofmann and L. E. Tetrick (eds.), *Health and Safety in Organizations: A Multilevel Perspective* (San Francisco: Jossey-Bass, 2003), 261–284; see also C. S. Smith, S. Folkard, and J. A. Fuller, "Shiftwork and Working Hours," in J. C. Quick and L. E. Tetrick (eds.), *Handbook of Occupational Health Psychology* (Washington, DC: American Psychological Association [APA], 2003), 163–220.

67   G. Florkowski, *Managing Global Legal Systems* (London: Routledge, 2006); C. S. Smith, S. Folkard, and J. A. Fuller, "Shiftwork and Working Hours," in J. C. Quick and L. E. Tetrick (eds.), *Handbook of Occupational Health Psychology* (Washington, DC: American Psychological Association [APA], 2003): 163–183.

68   J. R. B. Halbesleben and W. M. Bowler, "Emotional Exhaustion and Job Performance: The Mediating Role of Motivation," *Journal of Applied Psychology* 92(1) (2007): 93–106; C. Dormann and J. de Jonge, "Stressors, Resources, and Strain at Work: A Longitudinal Test of the Triple-Match Principle," *Journal of Applied Psychology* 91(5) (2006): 1359–1374; A. Zacharatos, J. Barling, and R. D. Iverson, "High-Performance Work Systems and Occupational Safety," *Journal of Applied Psychology* 90(1) (2005): 77–93. A useful booklet for employers interested in understanding job stress is NIOSH Working Group, *Stress at Work* (Cincinnati, OH: NIOSH, undated).

69   G. E. Hardy, D. Woods, and T. D. Wall, "The Impact of Psychological Distress on Absence from Work," *Journal of Applied Psychology* 88(2) (2003): 306–314.

70   For a review of research on the health consequences of modern office technology, see M. D. Coovert and L. F. Thompson, "Technology and Workplace Health," in J. C. Quick and L. E. Tetrick (eds.), *Handbook of Occupational Health Psychology* (Washington, DC: American Psychological Association [APA], 2003), 221–242.

71   A. Griffiths and F. Munir, "Workplace Health Promotion," in D. A. Hofmann and L. E. Tetrick (eds.), *Health and Safety in Organizations: A Multilevel Perspective* (San Francisco: Jossey-Bass, 2003), 316–340; "Please, Somebody! Open a Window!" *BusinessWeek* (January 18, 1999): 8.

72   M. Friedman and R. Rosenman, *Type A Behavior and Your Heart* (New York: Alfred A. Knopf, 1974); for a review of more recent research on the relationship between personality and personal health and well-being, see P. E. Spector, "Individual Differences in Health and Well-Being in Organizations," in D. A. Hofmann and L. E. Tetrick (eds.), *Health and Safety in Organizations: A Multilevel Perspective* (San Francisco: Jossey-Bass, 2003), 29–55.

73   B. Kallestad, "Bad bosses common, problematic," *Seattle Post-Intelligencer* (January 1, 2007).

74   P. M. Le Blanc, W. B. Schaufeli, M. C. W. Peters, and T. W. Taris, "Take Care! The Evaluation of a Team-Based Burnout Intervention Program for Oncology Care Providers," *Journal of Applied Psychology* 92(1) (2007): 213–227; A. Shirom, "Job-Related Burnout: A Review," in J. C. Quick and L. E. Tetrick (eds.), *Handbook of Occupational Health Psychology* (Washington, DC: American Psychological Association [APA], 2003): 245–264.

75   L. A. Witt, M. C. Andrews, and D. S. Carlson, "When Conscientiousness Isn't Enough: Emotional Exhaustion and Performance Among Call Center Customer Service Representatives," *Journal of Management* 30 (2004): 149–160.

76   M. Maslach and M. P. Leiter, *The Truth About Burnout: How Organizations Cause Personal Stress and What to Do About It* (San Francisco: Jossey-Bass, 1997); R. Cropanzano, D. E. Rupp, and Z. S. Byrne, "The Relationship of Emotional Exhaustion to Work Attitudes, Job Performance, and Organizational Citizenship Behaviors," *Journal of Applied Psychology* 88(1) (2003): 160–169; C. L. Cordes and T. W. Dougherty, "A Review and Integration of Research on Job Burnout," *Academy of Management Review* 18 (1993): 621–656.

77   N. H. Woodward, "Making Safety Job No. 1," *HRMagazine* (January 2007): 60–65; C. Murphy, "The CEO Workout," *Fortune* (July 10, 2006): 43–44; L. Grensing-Pophal, "Health Education Turns Proactive," *HRMagazine* (April 2005): 101–104; M. W. Walsh, "Keeping Workers Safe, But at What Cost?" *The New York Times* (December 20, 2000): G1; L. Miller, "People on the Move Are Going Back to Driving School," *The Wall Street Journal* (May 20, 1997): A1; "Safety: A Quick Pay-Off, a Long-Term Commitment," *HR Reporter* (October 1990): 6; R. Pater, "Safety Leadership Cuts Costs," *HRMagazine* (November 1990): 46–47.

78   M. Arndt, "How O'Neill Got Alcoa Shining," *BusinessWeek* (February 5, 2001): 39.

79   T. Bland and P. Forment, "Navigating OSHA's Ergonomics Rule," *HRMagazine* (February 2001): 61–67; M. Moss, "For Older Employees, On-the-Job Injuries Are More Often Deadly," *The Wall Street Journal* (June 17, 1997): A1; D. P. Levin, "The Graying Factor," *The New York Times* (February 20, 1994): 3-1, 3-3.

80   "Some Ergonomic Tips Toward Healthy and Effective Offices," Steelcase Web site, accessed at www.steelcase.com (January 15, 2004).

81   J. R. Hollenbeck, D. R. Ilgen, and S. M. Crampton, "Lower Back Disability in Occupational Settings: A Review of the Literature from a Human Resource Management View," *Personnel Psychology* 45 (1992): 247–278.

82   S. Bates, "Industry Ergonomic Guidelines 'Not Standards in Disguise,' OSHA Official Says," *HRMagazine* (September 2003): 34.

83   N. Turner and S. K. Parker, "The Effect of Teamwork on Safety Processes and Outcomes," in J. Barling and M. R. Frone (eds.), *The Psychology of Workplace Safety* (Washington, DC: American Psychological Association [APA], 2004), 35–62.

84   J. A. Adkins and H. M. Weiss, "Program Evaluation: The Bottom Line in Organizational Health," in J. C. Quick and L. E. Tetrick (eds.), *Handbook of Occupational Health Psychology* (Washington, DC: American Psychological Association [APA], 2003), 399–416; K. DeRango and L. Franzini, "Economic Evaluations of Workplace Health Interventions: Theory and Literature Review," in J. C. Quick and L. E. Tetrick (eds.), *Handbook of Occupational Health Psychology* (Washington, DC: American Psychological Association [APA], 2003), 417–430; M. J. Burke and S. A. Sarpy, "Improving Worker Safety and Health Through Interventions," in D. A. Hofmann and L. E. Tetrick (eds.), *Health and Safety in Organizations: A Multilevel Perspective* (San Francisco: Jossey-Bass, 2003), 56–90.

85   D. Hellriegel, S. E. Jackson, and J. W. Slocum, Jr., *Management,* 11th ed. (Cincinnati, OH: South-Western, 2008).

86   T. Minton-Eversole, "Impact of Genetic Information in Workplace Explored," *HR News* (September 2000): 1, 15; K. Ridder, "Genetic Testing Raises Fears of Workplace Bias," *Dallas Morning News* (April 26, 1998):

8H; S. Greengard, "Genetic Testing: Should You Be Afraid? It's No Joke," *Workforce Management* (July 1997): 38–44.

87 L. Koss-Feder, "Slowing Down the Treadmill, with Help," *The New York Times* (June 29, 2003): 10; J. D. Holloway, "Keeping Employees Healthy and Happy," *Monitor on Psychology* (December 2003): 32–33.

88 A. Weintraub, "I Can't Sleep," *BusinessWeek* (January 26, 2004): 66–74; M. Frese, "Social Support as a Moderator of the Relationship Between Work Stressors and Psychological Dysfunctioning: A Longitudinal Study with Objective Measures," *Journal of Occupational Health Psychology* 4(3) (1999): 179–192; E. Diener, E. Suh, R. Lucas, and H. Smith, "Subjective Well-Being: Three Decades of Progress," *Psychological Bulletin* 125(2) (1999): 276–302.

89 R. E. Quillian-Wolever and M. Wolever, "Stress Management at Work," in J. C. Quick and L. E. Tetrick (eds.), *Handbook of Occupational Health Psychology* (Washington, DC: American Psychological Association [APA], 2003), 355–375.

90 K. Tyler, "Cut the Stress: With HR-Provided Training, Employees Can Learn How to Avoid What Makes Them Tense," *HRMagazine* (May 2003): 101–106; D. Etzion, D. Eden, and Y. Lapidot, "Relief from Job Stressors and Burnout: Reserve Service as a Respite," *Journal of Applied Psychology* 83 (1998): 577–585; M. Westman and D. Eden, "Effects of Vacation on Job Stress and Burnout: Relief and Fade Out," *Journal of Applied Psychology* 82 (1997): 516–527.

91 J. Wojcik, "Firm to Charge Employees for Unhealthy Ways," *Workforce Management* (July 23, 2007): 6; J. Marquez, "Multinationals Bring Wellness Plans to Europe," *Workforce Management* (October 9, 2006): 14–16; M. Schoeff, Jr., "UPS Employees Get Advice from Health Coaches," *Workforce Management* (August 28, 2006): 14; N. H. Woodward, "Is an on-site exercise facility or an off-site reimbursement program better for your organization?" *HRMagazine* (June 2005): 79–84.

92 A. Meisler, "All Aboard," *Workforce Management* (July 2004): 30–32.

93 N. Hellmich, "Heavy Workers, Hefty Price," accessed at www.usatoday.com (September 11, 2005).

94 M. Conlin, "Get Healthy—or Else," *BusinessWeek* (February 26, 2007): 58–69; R. J. Grossman, "Countering a Weight Crisis," *HRMagazine* (March 2004): 42–50; J. C. Erfurt, A. Foote, and M. A. Heirich, "The Cost-Effectiveness of Worksite Wellness Programs for Hypertension Control, Weight Loss, Smoking Cessation and Exercise," *Personnel Psychology* 45 (1992): 5–27.

95 K. Zernike, "Fight Against Fat Shifting to the Workplace," *The New York Times* (October 12, 2003): A1, A26. For more on Union Pacific, visit www.up.com.

96 For an illustration of how to estimate the ROI for the active management of several diseases, see M. Hammers, "More Care, Less Cost," *Workforce Management* (March 2004): 55–58.

97 "Health Effects of Cigarette Smoking," Fact Sheet, National Center for Chronic Disease Prevention and Health Promotion, Tobacco Information and Prevention Source (TIPS), accessed at www.cdc.gov (December 2006).

98 J. B. Thelen, "Smelling Smoke," *HRMagazine* (December 2006): 105–111; A. Griffiths and F. Murnir, "Workplace Health Promotion," in D. A. Hofmann and L. E. Tetrick (eds.), *Health and Safety in Organizations: A Multilevel Perspective* (San Francisco: Jossey-Bass, 2003), 316–340.

99 S. Rosen, J. Simon, J. R. Vincent, W. MacLeod, M. Fox, and D. M. Thea, "AIDS Is Your Business," *Harvard Business Review* (February 2003): 81–87.

100 "Guidance for Protecting Employees Against Avian Flu," U.S. Department of Labor, Occupational Safety & Health Administration, accessed at www.osha.gov (January 16, 2007).

101 "Emergency Preparedness for Business," National Institute for Occupational Safety and Health, accessed at www.cdc.gov (January 16, 2007); "Hurricane eMatrix," U.S. Department of Labor, Occupational Safety & Health Administration, accessed at www.osha.gov (January 16, 2007). Also see Fgi World (www.fgiworld.com).

102 D. R. Briscoe, E. Claus, and R. S. Schuler, *International Human Resource Management*, 3rd ed. (London: Routledge, 2008).

103 Kroll Web site, accessed at www.kroll.com (January 16, 2007).

Chapter 14

1 See the United Parcel Service Web site (www.ups.com) and the Teamsters Web site (www.teamsters.com), accessed June 28, 2007; M. Hammers, "Wanted: Part-Timers with Class," *Workforce Management* (January 2003): 27–29; R. J. Grossman, "Trying to Heal the Wounds," *HRMagazine* (September 1998): 85–92; D. A. Tosh, "After the UPS Strike," *ACA News* (October 1997): 11–14.

2 For details, go to www.teamsters.com and www.fedexwatch.org.

3 For a more extensive discussion of unionization and the entire union-management relationship, see W. H. Holley, Jr., K. M. Jennings, and R. S. Wolters, *The Labor Relations Process*, 8th ed. (Mason, OH: South-Western, 2004); P. F. Clark, *Building More Effective Unions* (Ithaca, NY: ILR Press, 2000); J. A. Fossum, *Labor Relations: Development, Structure, Process*, 8th ed. (New York: Irwin McGraw-Hill, 2002).

4 For an overview and in-depth discussion of collective bargaining, see G. Chaison, *Unions in America* (New York: Sage: 2006); H. C. Katz and T. A. Kochan, *An Introduction to Collective Bargaining and Industrial Relations* (New York: Irwin McGraw-Hill, 2003).

5 DiGiTAL50.com, "USW Ratifies Agreement with Goodyear; Pact Provides Company Substantial Cost Savings," *The Goodyear Tire & Rubber Company* (January 3, 2007), accessed at www.digital50.com; M. R. Kropko, "Goodyear Workers Vote on Contract," *The Star-Ledger* (December 28, 2006): 53; D. Welch, "What Goodyear Got from Its Union," *BusinessWeek* (October 20, 2003): 148–149.

6 D. Welch, "Can the UAW Stay in the Game?" *BusinessWeek* (June 10, 2002): 78–79.

7 G. Chaison, "Unions in America," in J. A. Fossum, *Labor Relations: Development, Structure, Processes*, 8th ed. (New York: McGraw-Hill, 2002); H. Katz and T. A. Kochan, *An Introduction to Collective Bargaining and Industrial Relations* (New York: Irwin McGraw-Hill, 2003).

8 M. Arndt, "Salvation from the Shop Floor," *BusinessWeek* (February 3, 2003): 100–101; D. Hakin, "Tough Times Force UAW to Employ New Strategy," *The New York Times* (September 17, 2003): C1, C15; M. France, "After the Shooting Stops," *BusinessWeek* (March 12, 2001): 98–99; J. Nee, P. Kennedy, and D. Langham, "Increasing Manufacturing Effectiveness Through Joint Union/Management Cooperation," *Human Resource Management* 38(1) (Spring 1999): 77–85; D. A. Tosh, "After the UPS Strike," *ACA News* (October 1997): 11–14; M. J. Koch and G. Hundley, "The Effects of Unionism on Recruitment and Selection Methods," *Industrial Relations* 36(3) (July 1997): 349.

9 D. Welch, "The UAW: Using Trade-Offs to Gain Traction," *BusinessWeek* (September 8, 2003): 80–81.

10 M. R. Kropko, "Goodyear Workers Vote on Contract," D. Welch, "What Goodyear Got from Its Union," M. Dunlop, "Boeing Union's Windfall Arrives," *Herald* (November 30, 2006); S. Holmes, "Boeing Putting Out the Labor Fires," *BusinessWeek* (December 29, 2003): 43; P. Elstrom, "Needed: A New Union for the New Economy," *BusinessWeek* (September 4, 2000): 48; T. A. Kochan and P. Osterman, *The Mutual Gains Enterprise: Forging a Winning Partnership Among Labor, Management, and Government* (Boston: Harvard Business School Press, 1994).

11 See the AFL-CIO Web site (www.afl-cio.org) and the CWA Web site (www.cwa-union.org).

12 See the AFL-CIO Web site (http://www.afl-cio.org) and the United Steelworkers Web site (www.uswa.org).

13 A. A. Sloane and F. Witney, *Labor Relations*, 10th ed. (Englewood Cliffs, NJ: Prentice-Hall, 2000); see also R. O. Wright, *Chronology of Labor in the United States* (Jefferson, NC: McFarland, 2003).

14 S. Greenhouse, "Sharp Decline in Union Members in '06," *The New York Times* (January 26, 2007): A17; H. S. Farber, "Union Membership in the United States: The Divergence Between the Public and Private Sectors," Working paper #503, Princeton University (September 2005); U.S. Bureau of Labor Statistics, accessed at www.bls.gov.

15 S. Greenhouse, "The New Face of Solidarity," *The New York Times* (June 16, 2006): C1; M. Bai, "The New Boss," *The New York Times Magazine* (January 30, 2005): 38; U.S. Bureau of Labor Statistics, accessed at www.bls.gov.

16 R. Kirkland, "The New Face of Labor," *Fortune* (October 16, 2006): 123–132; M. Richtel, "Unions Struggle as Communications Industry Shifts," *The New York Times* (June 1, 2005): C1; S. Greenhouse, "Between Union Leader and His Protégé: Tension over Direction of Labor Movement," *The New York Times* (December 5, 2004): 34; Web site of the AFL-CIO, accessed at www.afl-cio.org; C. Daniels, "Watch for Rallies in the Valley," *Fortune* (April 2, 2001): 36.

17 A. Meisler, "Who Will Fold First?" *Workforce Management* (January 2004): 28–33; the UNITEHERE Web site, accessed at www.unitehere.org (October 21, 2004).

18 A. Meisler, "Unions Take Employers to School," *Workforce Management* (October 2003): 21–22.

19 L. T. Mendonca, "Shaping Up the Labor Movement: An Interview with the Head of the Service Employees International Union," *The McKinsey Quarterly* 1 (October 4, 2006); S. Greenhouse, "Amid Difficulties, Leaders of Labor See Opportunity," *The New York Times* (September 5, 2005): A7; S. Greenhouse, "2 Large Industrial Unions Plan to Merge," *The New York Times* (January 12, 2005): A18; D. Welch, "A Breakthrough for Labor," *BusinessWeek* (August 2, 2004): 86–87.

20 C. D. Gifford, *Directory of U.S. Labor Organizations, 2005 Edition* (Washington, DC: BNA Books, 2005); Bureau of Labor Statistics, Union affiliation of employed wage and salary workers by state, accessed at www.bls.gov/news.release/union2.t05.htm.

21 A. Bernstein, "Checking In? First Pass the Picket Line," *BusinessWeek* (February 20, 2006): 39; S. Greenhouse, "2 Major Construction Unions Plan to Leave A.F.L.-C.I.O.," *The New York Times* (February 15, 2006): A16; S. Greenhouse, "Unions Resume Debate Over Merging and Power," *The New York Times* (November 18, 2004): A28.

22 B. Simon, "A Cross-Border Battle of Auto Unions Heats Up," *The New York Times* (April 15, 2004): W1; For a detailed comparison of the United States and Canada, see S. M. Lipset and N. M. Meltz, *The Paradox of American Unionism: Why Americans Like Unions More Than Canadians*

Do But Join Much Less (Ithaca, NY: ILR Press, 2004); see also G. Gori, "Strike at VW Mexico Ends Unusually," *The New York Times* (September 6, 2001): W1; S. Greenhouse, "In U.S. Unions, Mexico Finds Unlikely Ally on Immigration," *The New York Times* (July 19, 2001): A1, A21; M. Maynard, "Canada Vote May Bring Union to Japan Carmaker," *The New York Times* (July 6, 2001): C1, C11.

23 For a more detailed discussion of labor relations in other countries, see M. Morley, *Global Industrial Relations* (London: Routledge, 2006).

24 Prepared for this chapter by William D. Todor, professor of human resource management, The Ohio State University.

25 A. Bianco, "No Union, Please, We're Wal-Mart," *BusinessWeek* (February 13, 2006): 78–81; S. Greenhouse, "How Do You Drive Out a Union? South Carolina Factory Provides a Textbook Case," *The New York Times* (December 14, 2004): A30. For an interesting description of attempts that are being made to organize Wal-Mart, see C. Daniels, "Up Against the Wal-Mart," *Fortune* (May 17, 2004): 112–120.

26 W. B. Gould, *A Primer on American Labor Law* (Cambridge: MIT Press: 2004); M. Bryant and R. Gilson, "Unions Can Organize Temporary Employees Along with Regular Workforce," *Legal Report* (November–December 2000): 7–8; G. Flynn, "When the Unions Come Calling," *Workforce Management* (November 2000): 82–87.

27 D. P. Twomey, *Labor Law and Legislation*, 7th ed. (Cincinnati, OH: South-Western, 1985); J. Hoerr, "The Strange Bedfellows Backing Workplace Reform," *BusinessWeek* (April 20, 1990): 57. See also R. Koenig, "Quality Circles Are Vulnerable to Union Tests," *The Wall Street Journal* (March 28, 1990): B1; L. E. Hazzard, "A Union Says Yes to Attendance," *Personnel Journal* (November 1990): 47–49.

28 D. Leonhardt, "Worthy Goal of Flawed Bill: Aiding Unions," *The New York Times* (June 27, 2007): C1; S. Greenhouse, "Employers Sharply Criticize Shift in Unionizing Method to Cards from Elections," *The New York Times* (March 11, 2006): A9.

29 J. G. Getman, S. B. Goldberg, and J. B. Herman, *Union Representation Elections: Law and Reality* (New York: Russell Sage, 1976), 72.

30 Greenhouse, *Ibid*; A. Meisler, "Board Deals unions a Bad hand," *Workforce Management* (July 2004): 26; A. Meisler, "Who Will Fold First?" *Workforce Management* (January 2004): 28–33; S. Romero, "Accord Is Reached for Most Workers in Phone Walkout," *The New York Times* (August 21, 2003): A1, A19.

31 G. Chaison, "Unions in America," in J. A. Fossum, *Labor Relations: Development, Structure, Processes*, 8th ed. (New York: McGraw-Hill, 2002); H. H. Tan and S. Aryee, "Antecedents and Outcomes of Union Loyalty: A Constructive Replication and an Extension," *Journal of Applied Psychology* 87(4) (2002): 715–722.

32 S. Greenhouse, "The First Unionization Vote by Dot-Com Workers Is Set," *The New York Times* (January 9, 2001): C4; C. Hirschman, "Overtime Overload," *HRMagazine* (December 2000): 84–92; M. Conlin, "Labor Laws Apply to Dot-Coms? Really?" *BusinessWeek* (February 26, 2001): 96–98.

33 A. Ritter, "Are Unions Worth the Bargain?" *Personnel* (February 1990): 12–14.

34 P. Bamberger, A. Kluger, and R. Suchard, "The Antecedents and Consequences of Union Commitment: A Meta-Analysis," *Academy of Management Journal* 42(3) (1999): 304–318.

35 S. Greenhouse, "New Labor Group Beginning Drive for Higher Pay," *The New York Times* (April 22, 2006): A11; S. A. Youngblood, A. DeNisi, J. L. Molleston, and W. H. Mobley, "The Impact of Work Attachment,

Instrumentality Beliefs, Perceived Labor Union Image, and Subjective Norms on Union Voting Intentions and Union Membership," *Academy of Management Journal* (1984): 576–590.

36 H. Katz and T. A. Kochan, *An Introduction to Collective Bargaining and Industrial Relations* (New York: Irwin McGraw-Hill, 2003).

37 C. J. Fullagar, D. G. Gallagher, P. F. Clark, and A. E. Carroll, "Union Commitment and Participation: A 10-Year Longitudinal Study," *Journal of Applied Psychology* 89 (2004): 730–737.

38 For more details about collective bargaining, see G. Chaison, "Unions in America," in J. A. Fossum, *Labor Relations: Development, Structure, Processes*, 8th ed. (New York: McGraw-Hill, 2002); P. F. Clark, J. Delaney, and A. Frost, *Collective Bargaining in the Private Sector* (Champaign, IL: Industrial Relations Research Association, 2003).

39 For a detailed discussion of grievance procedures, see BNA Editors, *Grievance Guide,* 11th ed. (Washington, DC: BNA Books, 2003); R. Peterson and D. Lewin, "Research on Unionized Grievance Procedures: Management Issues and Recommendations," *Human Resource Management* 39(4) (Winter 2000): 395–406; W. Zellner, "Congestion at the Bargaining Table, Too," *BusinessWeek* (March 19, 2001): 46.

40 T. Kosdrosky, "Auto Supplier Beats Detroit's Odds," *The Wall Street Journal* (May 10, 2007): A10.

41 M. Maynard, "UAW Pact with Dana Suggests Softer Stance," *The New York Times* (July 7, 2007): C1–C3; J. Bailey, "Anger Management at American Air," *The New York Times* (July 23, 2006): 3-1.

42 M. J. Morley, P. Gunnigle, and D. G. Collings, *Global Industrial Relations* (New York: Routledge: 2006); A. Fox, "To Consult and Inform," *HRMagazine* (October 2003): 87–91; C. Hirschman, "When Operating Abroad, Companies Must Adopt European-Style HR Plan," *HR News* (March 2001): 1, 6; R. Meredith, "Saturn Union Votes to Retain Its Cooperative Company Pact," *The New York Times* (March 12, 1998): D1, D4.

43 Adapted from R. Walton and R. B. McKersie, *A Behavioral Theory of Labor Negotiations* (New York: McGraw-Hill, 1965), 43.

44 J. A. Fossum, *Labor Relations: Development, Structure, Processes*, 8th ed. (New York: McGraw-Hill, 2002).

45 L. L. Thompson, *The Mind and Heart of the Negotiator,* 2nd ed. (Upper Saddle River, NJ: Prentice-Hall, 2003); M. H. Bazerman, *Judgment in Managerial Decision Making* (New York: John Wiley, 1986); M. H. Bazerman, T. Magliozzi, and M. A. Neale, "The Acquisition of an Integrative Response in a Competitive Market," *Organizational Behavior and Human Decision Processes* 34 (1985): 294–313.

46 S. Greenhouse, "Unions Finding That Employers Want More Concessions," *The New York Times* (July 11, 2003): A12.

47 M. Winerip, "A Union Standing Fast Now Stands to Lose," *The New York Times* (June 12, 1996): A16; K. Jennings and E. Traynman, "Two-Tier Plans," *Personnel Journal* (March 1988): 56–58.

48 M. Winerip, "A Union Standing Fast Now Stands to Lose," *The New York Times* (June 12, 1996): A16; K. Jennings and E. Traynman, "Two-Tier Plans," *Personnel Journal* (March 1988): 56–58; W. Zellner, "What Was Don Carty Thinking?" *BusinessWeek* (May 5, 2003): 32.

49 A. A. Sloane and F. Witney, *Labor Relations*, 10th ed. (Englewood Cliffs, NJ: Prentice-Hall, 2000).

50 J. A. Fossum, "Labor Relations," in S. T. Carroll and R. S. Schuler, *Human Resource Management in the 1980s* (Washington, DC: Bureau of National Affairs Inc., 395–396.

51 M. Maynard, "No Retreat, No Surrender (They Hope)," *The New York Times* (June 18, 2006): 3-1; D. Welch, "The UAW Isn't Buying Detroit's Blues," *BusinessWeek* (June 6, 2005): 38–40; "G. M. Accord Finishes Talks for U.A.W.," *The New York Times* (September 19, 2003): C1, C6.

52 P. Hartman and W. Franke, "The Changing Bargaining Structure in Construction: Wide-Area and Multicraft Bargaining," *Industrial and Labor Relations Review* (January 1980): 170–184.

53 A. A. Sloane and F. Witney, *Labor Relations*, 10th ed. (Englewood Cliffs, NJ: Prentice-Hall, 2000), 59.

54 "Benefit Costs Reach Crisis Stage," *Workforce Management* (December 2003): 118–130.

55 D. Stires, "The Breaking Point," *Fortune* (March 3, 2003): 104–112.

56 M. H. Bazerman and M. A. Neale, "Heuristics in Negotiation: Limitations to Effective Dispute Resolution," in M. H. Bazerman and R. J. Lewick (eds.), *Negotiating in Organizations* (Thousand Oaks, CA: Sage, 1983): 51–67; R. E. Walton and R. B. McKersie, *A Behavioral Theory of Labor Negotiations* (New York: McGraw-Hill, 1965).

57 M. A. Neale, V. L. Huber, and G. Northcraft, "The Framing of Negotiations: Contextual Versus Task Frame," *Organizational Behavior and Human Decision Processes* 39 (1987): 228–241.

58 S. Greenhouse, "Both Sides See Gains in Deal to End Port Labor Dispute," *The New York Times* (November 25, 2003): A14.

59 C. Giambusso, "Delta's Labor Troubles: View from the Cockpit," *The New York Times* (January 7, 2001): BU6; W. Zellner, "Up Against the Wal-Mart," *BusinessWeek* (March 13, 2000): 76–78; E. Zimmerman, "HR Lessons from a Strike," *Workforce Management* (November 2000): 36–42.

60 D. Weimer, "A New Cat on the Hot Seat," *BusinessWeek* (March 9, 1998): 56–61; A. Bernstein, "Why Workers Still Hold a Weak Hand," *BusinessWeek* (March 2, 1998): 98; "Tentative Deal Reached by Caterpillar and the UAW," *Bulletin to Management* 49(7) (February 19, 1998): 49.

61 A. Bernstein, A. Borrus, and C. Palmeri, "Labor Sharpens Its Pension Sword," *BusinessWeek* (November 24, 2003): 62–63; A. Meisler, "A High-Stakes Union Fight: Who Will Fold First?" *Workforce Management* (January 2004): 28–38.

62 S. Briggs, "Labor/Management Conflict and the Role of the Neutral," in R. S. Schuler, S. A. Youngblood, and V. L. Huber (eds.), *Personnel and Human Resource Management*, 3rd ed. (St. Paul, MN: West, 1988).

63 K. E. Boroff and D. Lewin, "Loyalty, Voice, and Intent to Exit a Union Firm: A Conceptual and Empirical Analysis," *Industrial and Labor Relations Review* 51(1) (October 1997): 50–63; S. Slichter, J. Healy, and E. Livernash, *The Impact of Collective Bargaining on Management* (Washington, DC: Brookings, 1960), 694.

64 B. Bemmels and J. R. Foley, "Grievance Procedure Research: A Review and Theoretical Recommendations," *Journal of Management* 22(3) (1996): 359–384.

65 Prepared by William D. Todor for this chapter.

66 National Labor Relations Board, Memorandum 79–55 (July 7, 1979).

67 D. R. Dalton and W. D. Todor, "Manifest Needs of Stewards: Propensity to File a Grievance," *Journal of Applied Psychology* (December 1979): 654–659.

68 L. T. Mendonca, "Shaking Up the Labor Movement: An Interview with the Head of the Service Employees International Union," *McKinsey Quarterly*, accessed at www.mckinseyquarterly.com (2006 Number 1);

W. N. Cooke, "Multinationals, Globalisation, and Industrial Relations," in M. J. Morley, P. Gunnigle, and D. G. Collings (eds.), in *Global Industrial Relations* (New York: Routledge: 2006). For more information about UNI (or the Global Union), the Union Network International, visit their Web site at www.union-network.org.

69 D. Roberts and P. Engardio, "Secrets, Lies, and Sweatshops," *BusinessWeek* (November 27, 2006): 50–58; K. D. Ewing, "International Labour Standards," in M. J. Morley, P. Gunnigle, and D. G. Collings in *Global Industrial Relations* (New York: Routledge: 2006).

70 "Evolution: Shifting Our Approach to Labor Compliance," accessed at www.nike.com (December 29, 2006).

71 "Evolution: Shifting Our Approach to Labor Compliance," accessed at www.nike.com (December 29, 2006); L. T. Mendonca, "Shaking Up the Labor Movement: An Interview with the head of the Service Employees International Union," *McKinsey Quarterly*, accessed at www.mckinseyquarterly.com (2006 Number 1).

72 *2007 Corporate Social Responsibility: United States, Australia, India, China, Canada, Mexico and Brazil: A Pilot Study*, (Alexandria, VA: Society for Human Resource Management, 2007).

73 Jack and Suzy Welch, "Avoiding Strikes-and Unions," *BusinessWeek* (January 15, 2007): 92.

Integrative Case Study: Southwest Airlines

1 K. Brooker, "The Chairman of the Board Looks Back," *Fortune* (May 28, 2001): 63–76.

2 M. Maynard, "Get Out the Glue for a New Business Model," *The New York Times* (July 11, 2004): Section 3-1, 3-3; W. Zellner and M. Arndt, "Can Anything Fix the Airlines?" *BusinessWeek* (April 7, 2003): 52–53; P. Coy, "The Airlines: Caught Between a Hub and a Hard Place," *BusinessWeek* (August 5, 2002): 83.

3 M. Trottman, and S. Carey, "Unfriendly Skies: As Pay Falls, Airlines Struggle to Fill Jobs," *The Wall Street Journal* (May 16,2007): A1; J. Bailey, "As Airlines Surge, Pilots Want Share," *The New York Times* (January 30, 2007): C1/C10; B. Gimbel, "Southwest's New Flight Plan," *Fortune* (May 16, 2005): 93–98.

4 Southwest Airlines' Form 10-K, Annual Report to Shareholders for Fiscal Year Ended December 21, 2006, accessed at www.southwest.com (July 19, 2007).

5 J. H. Gittell, *The Southwest Airlines Way* (New York: McGraw-Hill, 2003).

6 S. McCartney, "Southwest Makes Inroads at Hubs," *The Wall Street Journal* (May 1, 2007): D3.

7 Associated Press, "Southwest Closer to Offering Overseas Links," *Houston Chronicle* (June 20, 2007): D3; W. Zellner, "Dressed to Kill… Competitors," *BusinessWeek* (February 21, 2005): 60–61.

8 Southwest's 2006 Annual Report and 2006 Form 10-K, accessed at www.southwest.com/investor_relations/swaar06.pdf (July 12, 2007).

9 J. Bailey, "Airlines Learn to Fly on a Wing and a Apology," *The New York Times* (March 17, 2007): 1/21; A. Kadet, "Touch-Tone Trouble," *Smart Money* (February 2007): 120.

10 D. Field, "On the Offensive," *Airline Business* (February 2006): 28–29; J. H. Gittell, *The Southwest Airlines Way* (New York: McGraw-Hill, 2003).

11 "Southwest Airlines Advocates Honesty and Thrills at Work," *Personnel Today* (February 1, 2005): 3.

12 D. Field, "On the Offensive," *Airline Business* (February 2006): 28–29.

13 J. Bailey, "Co-Founder of Southwest Airlines to Retire as Chairman Next Year," *The New York Times* (July 20, 2007): C4.

14 K. Brooker, "Can Anyone Replace Herb?" *Fortune* (April 17, 2000): 186–192.

15 M. Cohn, "Southwest's Rise Tests Funky, Upstart Culture: Imperatives of Growth May Force Airline to Change," *Baltimore Sun* (November 19, 2006); J. McKay, "Southwest's Culture Includes Cards, Contests," *Pittsburgh Post Gazette* (January 6, 2005); P. Singh, "Strategic Reward Systems at Southwest Airlines," *Compensation and Benefits Review* (March–April 2002): 28–33.

16 K. Jones, "Herb's Flight Plan," *Texas Monthly* (March 1999); W. Zellner, "Southwest: After Kelleher, More Blue Skies," *BusinessWeek* (April 2, 2001): 45.

17 J. H. Gittell, "Paradox of Coordination and Control," *California Management Review* (Spring 2000): 101–117.

18 "CEO Profile of Herb Kelleher," *Chief Executive Magazine* (March 2000).

19 P. Carbonara, "Hire for Attitude, Train for Skill," *Fast Company* (August 1996): 73–78.

20 *Ibid.*

21 J. H. Gittell, "Paradox of Coordination and Control," *California Management Review* (Spring 2000): 101–117.

22 M. V. Copeland, "Best-Kept Secrets of the World's Best Companies," *Business 2.0* (April 2007): 82–96.

23 J. Martin, "Dancing with Elephants," *Fortune Small Business* (October 2004): 84–92; J. H. Gittell, *The Southwest Airlines Way* (New York: McGraw-Hill, 2003).

24 B. Gimbel, "Southwest's New Flight Plan," *Fortune* (May 16, 2005): 93–98.

25 D. L. Rhoades, "Growth, Customer Service, and Profitability, Southwest Style," *Managing Service Quality* 16(5) (2006): 538–547; J. H. Gittell, *The Southwest Airlines Way* (New York: McGraw-Hill, 2003); P. Singh, "Strategic Reward Systems at Southwest Airlines," *Compensation and Benefits Review* (March–April 2002): 28–33.

26 S. J. Miles and W. G. Mangold, "Positioning Southwest Airlines Through Employee Branding," *Business Horizons* (April 2005): 535–545; P. Singh, "Strategic Reward Systems at Southwest Airlines," *Compensation and Benefits Review* (March–April 2002): 28–33.

27 D. L. Rhoades, "Growth, Customer Service, and Profitability, Southwest Style," *Managing Service Quality* 16(5) (2006): 538–547; J. H. Gittell, *The Southwest Airlines Way* (New York: McGraw-Hill, 2003).

28 J. Bailey, "As Airlines Surge, Pilots Want Share," *The New York Times* (January 30, 2007): C1–C10; J. Helyar, "Southwest Finds Trouble in the Air," *Fortune* (August 9, 2004): 38; M. Trottman, "Spirit of Fun and Hard Work Is Clouded by Picketing and Employee Complaints," *The Wall Street Journal* (July 11, 2003): 1.

29 D. Reed, "Are Extra Fees in Southwest's Future?" *USA Today* (March 26, 2007): 1B.

30 M. Maynard, "In Philadelphia, Southwest Is Trying the Front Door," *The New York Times* (January 31, 2004): C1, C14.

31 W. Zellner, "Cute New Planes, Same Old Problems," *BusinessWeek* (March 1, 2004): 42; M. Maynard, "The East Joins the Low-Fare Bazaar,"

The New York Times (February 8, 2004): 1, 11; C. Haddad, "Getting Down and Dirty with the Discounters," *BusinessWeek* (October 28, 2002): 76–78.

32 B. Grow, "Don't Discount This Discounter," *BusinessWeek* (May 24, 2004): 84–85; W. Zellner, "Coffee, Tea, or Bile? Resentful Airline Workers Could Hobble Turnaround Plans," *BusinessWeek* (June 2, 2003): 56–58; W. Zellner, "Strafing the Big Boys Again," *BusinessWeek* (June 23, 2003): 36; W. Wells, "Lord of the Skies," *Forbes* (October 14, 2002): 130–137; M. Arndt and W. Zellner, "American Draws a Bead on JetBlue," *BusinessWeek* (June 24, 2002): 48; R. C. Ford, "David Neeleman, CEO of JetBlue Airways, on People = Strategy = Growth," *Academy of Management Executive* (May 2004): 139–143; L. Zuckerman, "JetBlue, Exception Among Airlines, Is Likely to Post a Profit," *The New York Times* (November 7, 2001): C3; E. Wong, "Airline's New Diet Has Rivals Watching," *The New York Times* (January 12, 2003): Section 3: 1, 11; E. Wong, "Delta Answer to JetBlue Is Set to Fly Next Week," *The New York Times* (April 12, 2003): C1–2.

33 MSNBC, "JetBlue Snafu Could Cost 30 Million or More," (February 20, 2007), accessed at http://www.msnbc.msn.com/id/17237319/ (July 19, 2007); M. Maynard, "Virgin Plans to Build Its New Discount Air Carrier in U.S. from Scratch," *TheNew York Times* (June 8, 2004): C2; W. Zellner, "Is JetBlue's Flight Plan Flawed?" *BusinessWeek* (February 16, 2004): 72–75; M. Wells, "Lord of the Skies," *Forbes* (October 14, 2002): 130–138.

Integrative Case Study: Lincoln Electric

1 See the company's Web site for more current information on all issues and topics addressed in this case (http://www.lincolnelectric.com).

2 T. W. Gerdel, "Lincoln Electric Experiences Season of Worker Discontent," *Plain Dealer* [Cleveland] (December 10, 1995): 1-C.

3 Z. Schiller, "A Model Incentive Plan Gets Caught in a Vise," *BusinessWeek* (January 22, 1996): 89, 92.

4 R. Narisetti, "Job Paradox Manufacturers Decry a Shortage of Workers While Rejecting Many," *The Wall Street Journal* (September 8, 1995): A4.

5 Z. Schiller, "A Model Incentive Plan Gets Caught in a Vise," *BusinessWeek* (January 22, 1996): 89, 92.

6 T. W. Gerdel, "Lincoln Electric Experiences Season of Worker Discontent," *Plain Dealer* [Cleveland] (December 10, 1995): 1-C.

7 *Ibid.*

8 R. M. Hodgetts, "A Conversation with Donald F. Hastings of the Lincoln Electric Company," *Organizational Dynamics* (Winter 1997): 68–74; M. Gleisser, "Lincoln CEO's Formula: Mutual Trust and Loyalty," *Plain Dealer* [Cleveland] (June 22, 1996): 2-C.

9 Visit the Lincoln Web site at www.lincolnwelders.com/corporate/about/vision.asp.

NAME INDEX

A

Aalberts, R. J., 586
Abelson, R., 576
Abernathy, W. B., 608
Abosch, K. S., 587, 606
Abramson, A., 584
Ackley, D., 612
Ackman, D., 605
Adams, Eula, 59
Adams, J. S., 603
Adams, S., 603, 605, 614
Adamson, Jim, 258
Addabbo, Joseph, Jr., 348
Adkins, J. A., 616
Adler, N., 577, 581
Adolf, Mary M., 193
Aenlle-Rocha, F. L., 609
Aguirre, D., 582
Ahmadjian, C. L., 579
Ahmy, D., 586
Aiman–Smith, L., 602, 609
Aitken, M., 592, 606
Akdere, M., 608
Albert, M., 596
Alcott, V. B., 591
Alder, G. S., 601, 603
Alexander, R. A., 602
Alldredge, M., 597
Allen, C. T., 581
Allen, D. G., 585
Allpress, K. N., 587
Almost, J., 601, 602
Alpert, D. E., 605
Alsever, J., 589
Alstyne, M. V., 587
Altman, W., 613
Altonji, L. G., 611
Alvarez, F. P., 595
Ambrose, M. L., 585, 603
Anderson, Brad, 360
Anderson, D., 611
Anderson, J., 590
Anderson, L. E., 587, 588
Anderson, N., 586, 592, 593, 594
Andrews, A. O., 576

Andrews, E. L., 610
Andrews, M. C., 616
Anelay, S., 581
Anesta, Michael A., 48
Ang, S., 578
Angle, H., 581
Ante, S. E., 580, 582
Anthony, K., 600
Antonioni, D., 599, 601
Apfelthaler, G., 579
Appleton, S., 604
Aquino, K., 585
Arad, S., 601
Arai, M., 605
Arey, D. L., 591
Arndt, M., 580, 612, 613, 616, 617, 620, 621
Arthur, J. B., 609
Arthur, J. Spiegel, 598
Arthur, W., Jr., 594, 596
Arulampalam, W., 608
Arvey, R. D., 584, 588, 595, 600
Aryee, S., 618
Ash, Mary Kay, 345
Ash, R. A., 586, 588
Ash, S. R., 590
Ashford, S. J., 601
Ashforth, B. E., 589, 593
Ashkanasy, N. M., 601
Ashkenas, R. N., 582
Aspinall, K., 577
Astin, J. A., 615
Aston, A., 580, 593
Aston–James, C. E., 601
Athanassiou, N., 580
Athavale, M., 610
Athey, R., 583
Atkins, Betsy S., 5
Atkinson, W., 613
Atwater, D., 603
Atwater, L. E., 601, 602, 603
Aubry, J. P., 615
Audi, L., 606
Augustinho, Carl, 488
Austin, J. T., 582

Avery, D. R., 591
Avery, Paul, 229
Avila, S. M., 610
Axel, H., 583, 589
Aycan, Z., 579
Ayub, Tahir, 307

B

Babcock, P., 579, 593, 608, 612
Bacca, C., 606
Bachiochi, P. D., 591
Bachrach, D. G., 600
Bacon, P., Jr., 605
Bae, J. 576
Baehr, M. E., 595
Baer, M., 581, 582
Bai, M., 512, 618
Bailey, J., 618, 619, 620
Baker, S., 590
Bakke, Dennis, 486
Baldwin, T. T., 598
Balkin, D. B., 606, 608
Ball, John, 412
Balmer, Steven A., 47, 426
Baltes, B. B., 602
Bamberger, P., 618
Banas, J., 582
Bandura, A., 603
Banker, R. D., 606, 608
Baranowski, L. E., 587, 588
Barbaro, M., 583
Barber, A. E., 589, 590
Barberite, F. G., 597
Barling, J., 579, 613, 614, 615, 616
Barnes, E. S., 582
Barnes, J., 598
Barnett, R. C., 590
Barney, J., 577
Barney, M. F., 592
Baron, H., 594, 595, 596
Baron, S. A., 615
Barrett, A., 588
Barrier, M., 585
Barron, J., 578

Barsoux, J. L., 577
Barstow, D., 614
Bartholomew, S., 577
Bartl, T. J., 609, 611
Bartol, K. M., 604
Bartram, D., 593
Baruch, Y., 597
Bass, C., 611
Bates, S., 576, 582, 587, 602, 610, 616
Batitista, M., 586
Bauer, C. B., 602
Bauer, T. N., 595
Baugh, S. G., 597
Baumol, W. J., 582, 591
Bax, E. H., 591
Bazerman, M. H., 619
Bean, L., 585
Beatty, R., 577, 603
Beavan, K., 597
Bechky, B. A., 597
Becker, B., 576, 577, 580, 581, 598
Becker, R., 598
Becker, T., 585
Beddia, Paul J., 400
Beehr, T. A., 586
Beer, M., 580, 581
Begley, T. M., 581, 609
Belcourt, M., 598
Belkin, L. Y., 602
Bell, B. S., 577
Bell, S. T., 596
Belzar, M. H., 603
Bemick, C. L., 577
Bemmels, B., 619
Bendoly, E., 600
Benedict, A., 615
Benjamin, E. R., 606
Bennett, J. B., 613, 614
Bennett, M. A., 595
Bennett, N., 583
Bennett, W., Jr., 596, 601
Bennis, W. G., 579
Benson, G. S., 612
Benz, M., 607, 609

Berdahl, J. L., 585, 586
Berenbeim, R., 22, 577
Bergey, P. K., 602
Bergman, L., 614
Bergman, M., 586
Berlin, L., 586
Berman, S. J., 407, 607
Bernanke, Ben, 64
Bernardin, H. J., 602
Berner, M. F., 582
Berner, R., 581
Bernick, C. L., 579
Bernstein, A., 578, 583, 591, 605, 611, 618, 619
Bernstein, D., 589
Berstein, A., 579
Bertua, C., 593
Besen, Y., 605
Bethune, Gordon, 91, 92, 581
Bevier, C., 593
Bezos, Jeffrey, 6, 230
Bezrukova, K., 585
Bhawuk, D.P.S., 599
Bianco, A., 618
Bickner, M. L., 585
Bierman, L., 584
Bigley, G. A., 576
Bingham, Charley, 311
Birger, J., 583
Birkinshaw, J., 581
Bjorkman, L., 609
Black, J., 597
Blader, S. L., 584
Blamberger, P., 616
Bland, T., 616
Blanton, K., 610
Blasi, J., 611
Blencoe, A. G., 588
Blinder, A. S., 582, 591
Block, C. J., 591
Block, S., 611
Bloom, M. C., 606
Blum, T., 612
Blumberg, R., 593
Bobko, P., 583, 593, 594
Bock, Laszlo, 250
Boehm, Rodger L., 101, 577
Boet–Whitaker, Carl, 358
Bohmer, R., 592
Bolch, M., 595, 608, 611, 612
Boman, W. C., 599
Bonamici, K., 609
Bond, M. T., 611
Boonstra, J. J., 581, 582
Booth, A. L., 608
Borcia, Y., 606
Borg, M. R., 603
Borman, W. C., 581, 588, 589, 595, 601
Born, M. P., 594
Boroff, K. E., 619
Borrill, C., 581

Borrus, A., 604, 619
Bosack, Leonard, 3
Boswell, W. R., 584, 590
Bottoms, Ken, 218
Boussard, Gerard, 81
Boutelle, C., 592
Bowen, D. E., 588, 592
Bowers, C., 598
Bowie, Carol, 427
Bowler, W. M., 616
Bowling, N. A., 586
Boyd, D. P., 581
Boyd, N. G., 577
Boyle, M., 590, 609
Bracker, J. S., 590
Bradsher, K., 607
Brady, D., 595, 597, 602, 604
Brandes, P., 582
Brandt, C. J., 588
Brannick, M. T., 587, 591
Branstead, E., 582
Brass, D. J., 600
Breaugh, J. A., 589
Brechu, M. B., 580
Brenner, M. D., 605
Bresman, H., 581
Brett, J. F. , 597, 599, 601, 602
Bretz, R. D., Jr., 590
Brews, P. J., 580, 581
Brewster, C., 577, 579, 582
Bridges, William, 181, 588
Briggs, S., 619
Brill, D., 603
Briscoe, D. R., 577, 578, 579, 584, 594, 596, 609, 611, 617
Brislin, R. W., 579, 599
Brockbank, W., 577
Brockner, J., 583
Brodt, S. E., 583
Brody, L., 581
Brooker, K., 620
Broschak, J. P., 584
Brotherton, C., 613
Broussard, Gerard, 17
Brousseau, K. R., 597
Brown, C. S., 599
Brown, D. J., 589
Brown, D., 606, 607
Brown, Jeff, 282
Brown, M., 588
Brown, S. P., 615
Brownlee, A. L., 600
Brugmann, J., 576
Brush, Donald, 110–111
Bryan, L., 577, 608
Bryan, M. L., 608
Bryant, A., 585, 595
Bryant, M., 618
Brynjolfsson, L., 587
Buboltz, C., 588

Buchenroth, P., 389, 607
Buckley, M. B., 602
Buckley, P., 589
Buckley, Steve, 505
Budd, J. F., Jr., 579
Budhwar, P., 579, 601
Budman, M., 613
Bulatao, E. Q., 615
Bulkeley, W. M., 578, 599
Buller, P. F., 586
Burger, G. K., 587
Burke, D., 604
Burke, L., 598
Burke, M. J., 614, 615, 616
Burkhardt, Michael, 551
Burlingham, B., 579, 600
Burnett, J., 594
Byham, W., 91, 595, 597
Byrd, K., 605
Byrne, Z. S., 616
Byrnes, N., 607, 609

C

Cable, D. M., 576, 589, 590, 595
Cabrera, E. F., 592
Cadrain, D., 612
Cadsby, C. B., 607
Cafferty, T. P., 602
Calderone, M., 582
Caligiuri, P., 593
Callahan, J. S., 596
Calvert, C., 611
Camara, W. J., 594
Cameron, J., 608
Campbell, C. A., 587, 602
Campbell, H., 599
Campbell, J. P., 601
Campbell, W. J., 595
Campion, J. E., 594
Campion, M. A., 587, 588, 592, 594, 595, 601
Camuso, M.A., 609
Cannon, M. D., 603
Cannon–Bowers, J. A., 599
Capaldo, G., 587
Caplan, J., 605
Cappelli, P., 582, 590
Carayon, P., 613, 614, 615
Carbonara, P., 603, 620
Cardy, R., 577
Carey, J., 611
Carey, S., 620
Carlson, D. S., 616
Carlson, K. D., 589, 593
Carmell, W. A., 586
Carnegie, Andrew, 315
Carr, L., 586
Carr, S. C., 609
Carroll, A. E., 619
Carroll, P., 610
Carroll, S. A., 590

Carroll, S. T., 619
Carson, K. P., 588
Carter, M., 581
Cartier, P., 603
Cascio, W. F., 579, 582, 592, 595, 605
Casey, D., 585
Catano, V. M., 587, 602
Caudron, S., 585
Cawley, B. D., 601
Certo, S., 596
Chaison, G., 615, 616, 617, 618, 619
Chambers, Jeff, 189, 331
Chambers, John, 3, 4, 18, 77
Champy, J., 587
Chan, D. W. L., 599
Chan, D., 595, 596
Chan, S., 601, 603
Chan, V., 581, 582
Chang, H. K., 598
Chao, G. T., 595, 597
Chapman, D. S., 590, 595
Charles, A. C., 602
Chatman, J., 581, 582
Chattopadhyay, P., 590
Chaves, W., 591
Chen, C., 594
Chen, H., 610
Cheng, B. S., 601
Cherniss, C., 598
Cherry, B., 608
Chester, M., 609, 611
Chiang, Y., 600
Chichelli, D. J., 609
Chiu, S., 594
Chizen, Bruce, 295
Chou, K., 608
Chrobot–Mason, D., 599
Chu, K., 610
Chu, R., 584
Chuang, C., 591
Church, A. H., 581
Cilmi, A. P., 603, 605, 606, 608
Cira, D. J., 606
Cirka, C., 608
Clark, M. M., 585, 586, 605
Clark, P. F., 617, 619
Clarke, N. E., 612
Claus, E., 577, 578, 579, 617
Clause, C. S., 588, 593, 595
Cleveland, J. N., 599, 602
Coates, D. E., 599
Cober, A. B., 603
Cober, R. T., 589
Cockburn, C., 609
Cohen, A. J., 603, 612
Cohen, B., 613
Cohen, Debra J., 464, 590
Cohen, L., 612
Cohn, M., 618, 620

Cole, C. L., 596, 598
Colella, A., 584, 585, 604
Colhan, J., 587
Collings, D., 577, 578, 619, 620
Collins, C. J., 590, 595
Collins, J. M., 593, 594
Collins, W. C., 601
Collison, J., 580, 581
Colquitt, J. A., 583, 597
Colvin, G., 580, 592
Combs, G. M., 591
Combs, M. W., 591
Conde, C. H., 578
Conger, J. A., 597, 602
Conlin, M., 582, 583, 584, 612, 613, 617, 618
Conlon, D. E., 583
Connelly, B., 580
Connelly, M. S., 593
Conner, J., 597
Connerley, M. L., 589, 593
Conover, John, 27
Conrad, M. A., 591
Constans, J. I., 602
Conti, A. J., 584
Conway, F. T., 613, 614, 615
Cook, R. F., 613, 614
Cook, T., 603
Cooke, W. N., 618, 620
Coonradt, Chuck, 417
Cooper, C. L., 593, 613, 615
Cooper–Thomas, H. D., 587
Coovert, M. D., 616
Copeland, M. V., 620
Copper, C., 599
Cordes, C. L., 616
Cording, M., 576
Cornelius, E. T., III., 588
Cornwell, J. M., 594
Corrigall, E., 590
Cortina, J. M., 593, 594
Corwin, V., 590
Coss, David, 368
Costa, P. T., Jr., 593
Costanza, D. P., 593
Cotton, J., 597, 599
Coughlin, Tom, 113
Couturiaux, Paris, 325
Cox, A., 608
Coy, P., 578, 620
Craig, J., 595
Crampton, S. M., 616
Crawford, K., 584
Creedman, D., 581
Creelman, C., 581
Crittenden, W. F., 580
Cropanzano, R., 583, 584, 591, 593, 602, 616
Crosby, F., 598
Cross, T., 596

Cummings, L. L., 583, 602
Currall, S. C., 604

D

Daily, C., 596
Dale, James, 150
Dalessio, A. T., 593
Dalik, A., 586
Dalton, D. R., 596, 619
Dalton, Francie, 320
Dalton, M., 596, 597
Daly, J. P., 579
Damitz, M., 594
Daniels, A. C., 607
Daniels, C., 579, 583, 607, 618
Daniels, Jim, 220
Darr, W., 587, 602
Darwin, Charles, 76
Davenport, T. O., 612
David, J., 607
Davidson, Diane, 181
Davidson, H., 594
Dávila, A., 579
Davis, G. M., 584, 589, 610
Davis, J., 608
Davis, K. S., 591
Davis, P., 609
Davis, S. L., 582
Davis, S. R., 598
Davis–Blake, A., 578, 584
Dawson, J., 581
de Jonge, J., 616
De Luque, M. S., 600
de Swardt, L., 607
Deal, J., 596, 597
Dean, J. W., Jr., 582, 599
Dean, M., 593
Debgupta, S., 612
Debrah, Y., 578
Deci, E., 608
Decker, J. C., 612
Decker, P., 599
Deckop, J. R., 578, 608, 609
Deen, L., 598
DeGroot, T., 613
Delaney, J. T., 584, 619
Delaney–Klinger, K., 587
Delbridge, K., 595
Delery, J. E., 591, 606, 614
Dell, Michael, 320
Deller, J., 579
DeLong, D. W., 580
Delves, D., 609
Demby, E. R., 577
DeMeuse, K. P., 591
Deming, W. Edwards, 421
Denis, D. J., 609
DeNisi, A. S., 588, 596, 600, 601, 602, 618
Denison, D. R., 577
Denning, D. L., 591

Dennis, Maria, 543
DeRango, K., 616
DeRouin, R., 596, 598
Deshon, R. P., 595, 596
Deutsch, C. H., 580, 597, 598
Deutschman, A., 589
Devers, C. E., 609
Devine, D. J., 583
Dewe, P., 615
DeWolff, C. J., 594
Dharwadkar, R., 582
Dickson, K. E., 578
Dickson, M.W., 599
Diener, E., 617
Dierdorff, E. C., 587
Diesenhouse, S., 577
Diez, F., 606
Digh, P., 607
Din, S., 585
Dineen, B. R., 590
Dipboye, R. L., 584, 585, 587, 602
Dixon, A. L., 581
Dixon, M. R., 603
Dixon, Mark, 261
Dobbins, G. H., 595, 598, 601
Dobeck, M. E., 611
Dodd, G., 615
Dodds, D., 611
Dohns, I., 613
Dominguez, A., 586
Donahue, L. M., 594
Donovan, K., 585
Donovan, M. A., 594, 601
Dorfman, P. W., 579, 600
Dormann, C., 616
Dougherty, T. W., 590, 616
Douglas, S. C., 615
Dow, Herbert Henry, 558
Drasgow, F., 586, 594
Drenth, P. J. D., 594
Driskell, J. E., 597, 599
Driver, M. J., 597
Druskat, V. U., 601
Dubin, S. S., 598
DuBois, D. D., 587
Ducharme, M. J., 607, 620
Dudley, N. M., 593
Duffy, M. K., 591
Dufresne, M. R., 611
Dukes, Betty, 113, 120, 126
Dulebohn, J., 601, 606, 612
Duncan, Emily, 137
Duncan, Russell, 393
Duncan, W. J., 609
Dunford, B. B., 583
Dunlop, M., 618
Dunnette, M. D., 583, 588, 593
Dutta, D. K., 577
Dvorak, P., 609

E

Earley, P. Christopher, 578, 599
Echikson, W., 582
Eckholm, E., 610
Eddy, E., 586
Edelstein, M., 606
Edelsten, Mark, 387
Eden, D., 617
Eden, E., 599
Edens, P. S., 596
Eder, R. W., 594
Edge, Judy H., 420
Edison, C. E., Jr., 587
Edmondson, A., 592
Edwards, C., 584
Edwards, M. A., 604
Egan, T. D., 589
Ehrhart, K. H., 590
Ehrhart, M. G., 580
Eichinger, R. W., 592
Eisenberger, R., 608
Eisner, Michael, 59
Elicker, J. D., 603
Elkins, T. J., 586, 604
Elkström, M., 613
Ellington, J. E., 596
Elliot, Lee, 193
Ellis, A. P. J., 597, 599
Ellis, C. M., 600
Elovainio, M., 584
Elsass, P. M., 599
Elstrom, P., 618
Elvira, M., 579
Ely, R., 585, 598
Engardio, P., 577, 582, 583, 620
Enos, M., 606
Epstein, R., 612
Erfurt, J. C., 617
Erickson, M. L., 586
Ernst, C., 596, 597
Ernst, H., 615
Eschtruth, A. D., 615
Esen, E., 615
Eskew, Mike, 507
Etzion, D., 617
Evans, D. P., 577, 602
Everitt, David C., 65
Ewing, J., 578, 612
Ewing, K. D., 620
Eyde, L., 586
Eyring, J. D., 599

F

Facteau, J. D., 598
Faden, R. R., 595
Fahs, M., 613
Faley, R. H., 584
Famdale, E., 575
Fang, T., 608
Faragher, B., 615
Farber, H. S., 618

Farh, J. L., 595, 601
Farham, A., 581
Farndale, E., 577
Farrel, D., 582
Fay, C. H., 606, 607, 608
Featherstone, L., 583
Feder, B. J., 611
Feeney, S., 612
Fegley, S., 581, 585, 607, 610, 611, 612
Feigenbaum, C., 585
Feinsod, R. R., 612
Feldman, H., 586
Feldman, J. M., 602
Felps, W., 576, 591
Fenn, D., 600
Ferkenhoff, E., 605
Fernandez, R. M., 590
Ferrara, P., 587, 588, 595
Ferris, G. R., 576, 584, 601, 602
Ferris, S. P., 591
Feuille, P., 584
Fey, C. F., 609
Field, D., 618, 620
Field, H. S., 593, 595, 601
Fields, Mitch, 505
Fierman, J., 608
Figge, P. E., 582
Filipczak, B., 598
Fina, M. C., 608
Finegold, D., 612
Fink, L. S., 590
Fischer, D. L., 592
Fischer, H., 582
Fischetti, V., 607
Fisher, A., 580, 589, 590, 610
Fisher, D., 582
Fisher, Kim, 3
Fishman, C., 603
Fitz–Enz, J., 581
Flaherty, J., 608
Flaherty, K. E., 604, 609
Flanagan, J. C., 588
Flannery, S., 612
Fleenor, J. W., 601
Fleishman, E. A., 588, 593
Fliegel, R., 593
Flier, H. V. D., 594
Florkowski, G., 614, 616
Flynn, G., 585, 605, 618
Fogli, L., 594
Foley, J. R., 619
Foley, S., 579, 584
Folger, R., 593
Folkard, S., 616
Fong, E. A., 608
Foote, A., 617
Ford, Henry, 51, 143
Ford, J. K., 595, 597, 598
Ford, R. C., 621

Forment, P., 616
Forrester, R., 580
Fossum, J. A., 603, 605, 617, 618, 619
Fournier, S., 605
Fox, A., 619
Fox, H. R., 584
Fox, J., 609
Fox, M., 578, 617
Fox, W., 604
France, M., 617
Francis, D. J., 599
Francis, T., 609
Frangos, C., 580, 581
Franke, W., 619
Franklin, Deb, 195
Franzini, L., 616
Frase-Blunt, M., 582, 608, 612
Fraser, Douglas, 523
Fraser, S. L., 588
Frauenheim, E., 577, 580, 589, 596, 600, 604
Frayne, C., 599
Freeman, R., 605
Freeman, S. F., 592
Frensch, P. A., 602
Frese, M., 581, 582, 617
Freudenheim, M., 609, 611, 612
Frey, B. S., 609
Fried, J., 607
Friedman, M., 8, 576, 616
Friedman, T. L., 54, 580
Fritz, C., 611
Fritzsche, B. A., 598
Frone, M. R., 586, 613, 614, 615, 616
Frost, A., 619
Frost, P. J., 590
Fruitrail, C., 611
Fruyt, F. D., 593
Fryxell, G. E., 576, 584
Fulkerson, J. R., 600
Fullagar, C. J., 617, 619
Fuller, J. A., 616
Fuoco-Karasinski, C., 611
Furchgott, R., 585

G

Gael, S., 588
Gaertner, S., 591
Gagne, K., 600, 601
Gale, S. F., 580, 586, 590, 592, 595
Gallagher, D. G., 619
Ganster, D. C., 615
Ganzel, R., 584
Gardner, Jonathon, 364
Garonzik, R., 583
Garten, J., 580
Garvey, C., 603, 608

Garwood, M. K., 587
Gates, Bill, 57
Gatewood, R. D., 591, 593
Gaughan, L., 612
Gaugler, B. B., 594
Gault, B., 606
Gavin, J., 613
Gazzara, Kevin, 305
Geisel, R. W., 611, 612
Gelfand, M. J., 586
Gentry, T., 608
George, E., 584, 590
Gerard, D., 605
Gerdel, T. W., 619, 621
Gerdes, L., 590
Gerhart, B., 601, 607
Gerrity, M. J., 594
Getman, J. R., 618
Gettelfinger, Ron, 526
Giacalone, R. A., 599
Giambusso, C., 619
Giancola, F. L., 604, 611
Giannone, Adrienne, 412
Gibson, C. B., 580, 599
Gibson, G. E., Jr., 578
Gieseke, V., 612
Gifford, C. D., 618
Gilbert, D., 587
Gilbert, K., 606
Gilbreth, Frank and Lillian, 166
Gilles, P., 605, 606
Gilliland, S., 594
Gilson, R., 618
Gimbel, B., 620
Ginacola, F., 609
Gioia, J., 578
Gittell, J. H., 618, 620
Glasgow, F., 579
Glassman, M., 603
Gleaves, D. H., 593
Glebbeek, A. C., 591
Gleckman, H., 611
Gleisser, M., 621
Glew, D. J., 615
Glomb, T., 586
Glynn, G., 585
Godfrey, G., 576
Goffin, R., 601
Gokturk, C., 608
Goldberg, S. B., 618
Goldman, B. M., 584
Goldsmith, M., 599, 601
Goldstein, I. L., 588, 593, 597, 598
Goldstein, N., 594
Goleman, D., 598
Gomes, L., 610
Gomez, C., 577, 607
Gomez, L., 608
Gomez–Mejia, L. R., 578, 604, 606, 609

Goodall, D. G., 609
Gooderham, P., 600
Goodnight, Jim, 189
Gopinath, C., 585
Gordon, M. E., 584
Gordon, Wayne, 487
Gori, G., 618
Gossas, Peter, 103
Gottfredson, M., 577
Gottschalg, O., 607
Gould, Andrew, 179
Gould, W. B., 618
Gow, Anthony, 58
Gowan, M. A., 591
Graham, M. E., 577
Grant, L., 576
Gravenhorst, K. M. B., 581, 582
Gray, G. R., 614
Grayson, C. Jackson, 565
Green, J. A., 606
Greenberg, J., 583, 601, 604
Greenberg, R., 600
Greenberger, D. B., 583
Greenfield, J., 613
Greengard, S., 593, 617
Greengart, B. J., 587
Greenhaus, J. H., 598
Greenhouse, S., 583, 605, 613, 618, 619
Greenlees, D., 582
Gregersen, H., 597
Gregory, R. F., 585
Grensing–Pophal, L., 603, 605, 613, 616
Griffeth, K. H., 579
Griffeth, R. W., 585, 589, 590, 591
Griffin, M. A., 614, 615
Griffin, R. W., 615
Griffith, R. L., 594
Griffiths, A., 614, 616, 617
Grigorenko, E. L., 598
Groh, K., 612
Gross, S. E., 606, 608
Grossman, R. J., 596, 613, 614, 617
Grow, B., 604, 621
Groysberg, B., 597
Grubb, W. L., III, 594
Guaspari, J., 587
Gubanich, Kathleen C., 275, 362
Guernesy, L., 584
Gueutal, H. G., 577
Guichiek, K., 610
Guidice, R. M., 600
Guion, R. M., 588
Gunnigle, P., 619, 620
Gunther, M., 585
Gupta, N., 591, 606, 608
Gupta, R., 580

Gupta, S., 609
Gupta, V., 579
Gurchiek, K., 593, 598, 612, 613
Gutek, B. A., 584
Guthrie, J. P., 577
Gutman, A., 584
Gutner, T., 579
Guzzo, R. A., 599, 604

H

Hackman, J. R., 615
Haddad, C., 620
Hafner, K., 597, 599
Hagens, J., 612
Hakanson, L., 581
Hakel, M., 599
Hakin, D., 617
Halbesleben, J. R. B., 614, 616
Hall, D. T., 590
Hall, J. E., 595
Hall, Ken, 507, 528
Hall, M. E., 603
Hall, P., 605
Hall, R. J., 603
Halligan, Ron, 242, 248
Halonen, D., 611
Hamel, G., 582
Hamm, S., 583
Hammer, M., 587
Hammers, M., 582, 589, 612, 617
Hammond, Chuck, 317
Handy, C. 576
Hanges, P. J., 576, 579, 582
Hanion, Karen, 347
Hanouna, P., 609
Hansell, S., 593
Hansen, F., 578, 582, 584, 590, 591, 595, 604, 605, 606, 608
Hansens, E., 603
Hardy, G. E., 616
Harel, G. H., 597
Harman, W. S., 591
Harmon, E., 602
Harrington–Mackin, Deborah, 249
Harris, D., 585
Harris, H., 579
Harris, M. M., 582, 587, 594
Harris, S., 607
Harrison, D. A., 591, 599
Harrison, N. S., 607
Hart, Peter, 413
Harter, J. K., 576
Hartman, N. S., 594
Hartman, P., 619
Harvey, R. J., 588
Hastings, Donald, 621
Hatch, D. D., 595
Hattrup, K., 596

Hausser, D., 587, 588
Hawn, C., 578
Hayashi, A., 612
Hayes, T. L., 576
Hays, S., 593, 596
Hazucha, J. Fisher, 602
Hazzard, L. E., 618
Healy, J., 619
Heaney, C. A., 613
Hebl, M. R., 579
Hedge, J. W., 581
Hedger, A., 593
Heerman, M., 586
Heffernan, M., 598
Heilman, M. E., 591, 603
Heirich, M. A., 617
Helfat, C. E., 585
Helkama, K., 584
Heller, D., 593
Hellman, M. F., 589
Hellmich, N., 617
Hellriegel, D., 616
Helyar, J., 620
Hemp, P., 596
Henagan, S. C., 591
Heneman, H. G., III, 592
Heneman, R. L., 583, 603, 608
Henneman, T., 589
Hensel, B., Jr., 607
Hensel, S. C., 602
Hequet, M., 598
Herbst, M., 592, 604
Herman, J. B., 618
Herman, R., 578
Herscovitch, L., 582
Hesketh, B., 586
Heslin, P. A., 601, 602
Heuring, L., 598
Heywood, J. S., 608
Hibbard, J., 580
Higgins, Andrew, 409
Higgins, M., 586, 598
Highhouse, S., 592
Hill, Allen, 455
Hill, B., 416, 604, 610
Hill, Jennifer, 184, 187
Hiller, J. S., 591
Hilling, F., 606
Hilts, Maureen, 337
Hindle, T., 587
Hirschman, C., 610, 612, 618, 619
Hirshhord, L., 602
Hitchcock, Darcy, 344
Hitlan, R., 585
Hitt, M. A., 578, 580, 596
Hmurovic, B. L., 606
Ho, V. T., 583
Hockaday, Irv, 20
Hodgetts, R. M., 621
Hodgson, M. R., 609
Hoerr, J., 618

Hoffman, C. C., 592, 594
Hoffman, S., 615
Hoffman, V. J., 589
Hofmann, D. A., 613, 614, 615, 616, 617
Hofstede, Geert, 52
Hogan, J. C., 587
Hogan, P., 599
Hogan, R. T., 593
Holland, K., 589, 602
Hollenbeck, G. P., 588, 596
Hollenbeck, J. R., 599, 616
Holley, W. H., 601, 617
Holloway, J. D., 617
Holmes, R. M. , Jr., 609
Holmqvist, M., 597
Holsinger, L., 600
Holt, K. E., 602
Holton, E. F., III, 596, 598
Hom, P. W., 585, 590, 591
Honeycut, Bradley, 437
Honoree, A. L., 603, 604, 605
Hooker, J., 578
Hooper, L., 598
Hoover, Deborah K., 359
Horwitz, F., 578
Hoskisson, R.E., 578, 580
Hough, L. M., 583, 588, 593
House, R. J., 579, 600
Howard, A., 584
Howe, Maria, 432
Howe, V., 590
Howell, W. C., 588
Hsieh, Y., 610
Huang, I., 591
Huber, V. L., 599, 602, 603, 619
Hudon, K., 585
Huet–Cox, G., 602
Huff, C., 579, 589, 596, 598, 608
Huffcutt, A. I., 594
Huler, S., 581
Humphrey, S. E., 615
Hundley, G., 617
Hunt, Edie, 209
Hunt, M. R., 580, 581
Hunter, J. E., 592
Hurst, P. W., 578
Huselid, M., 576, 577, 580, 581
Hutcherson, Patricia, 290

I

Iandoli, L., 587
Ickes, K., 611
Iddekinge, C. V., 587
Ilgen, D. R., 586, 587, 588, 589, 592, 599, 602, 616
Ilies, R., 603
Immelt, Jeffrey R., 360
Infante, V., 605, 613

Ireland, R. D., 578, 580
Ivancevich, J. M., 583
Iverson, R. D., 615, 616
Ivery, F., 612

J

Jackson, C. L., 583
Jackson, H. L., 601
Jackson, S. E., 578, 581, 585, 596, 599, 600, 608, 616
Jacobs, K., 605
James, E. H., 584
Jarin, K. M., 586
Javidan, M., 579, 600
Jawahar, I. M., 578
Jeanneret, P. R., 588
Jeanneret, R., 582, 594
Jeffrey, Galina, 343
Jehn, K., 585
Jelley, R., 601
Jenkins, G. D., Jr., 608
Jenkins, W., 608
Jennings, K. M., 617
Jennings, K., 619
Jette, R. D., 604
Jobs, Steve, 287
Johnson, D. Steele, 599
Johnson, J. F., 593
Johnson, J. L., 591
Johnson, J. P., III, 585
Johnson, J. W., 576
Johnson, Jim, 116, 117
Johnson, Lyndon B., 125
Johnson, M., 596
Johnson, R. A., 580
Johnson, R. M., 612
Johnston, D. C., 608
Joinson, C., 589
Jonas, Hank, 347
Jones, C., 594
Jones, D. A., 590
Jones, D. P., 595
Jones, J., 582
Jones, K., 620
Jones, R. G., 592
Jones, R., 593
Jones, T. M., 576
Joni, S –N., 598
Joseph, Bradley, 495
Joshi, A., 585, 599, 608, 612
Joy, D., 589
Judge, T. A., 589, 590, 592, 593, 595, 602, 603, 604
Juravich, Tom, 529

K

Kabanoff, B., 579
Kacmar, K. M., 609
Kadefors, T., 613
Kadet, A., 620
Kadlec, D., 604

Kahn, J., 585
Kahnweiler, W., 599
Kaihla, P., 604, 609
Kaka, N., 582
Kalinowski, Walter, 202
Kallestad, B., 616
Kamoche, K., 578
Kane, J. S., 602
Kanter, R., 582
Kanungo, R., 579
Kaplan, R. S., 576, 580, 581
Karsh, B. T., 613, 614, 615
Karunaratne, L. P., 584
Kasparek, J., 612
Kass, N. E., 595
Kathy, C., 598
Katsoudas, A., 609
Katz, H. C., 617, 619
Katz, J. R., 604
Katzell, R. A., 604
Katz-Navon, T., 614
Keaveny, T. J., 606
Keegan, Robert J., 509
Keenan, P. A., 594
Keeping, L. M., 589, 600, 601
Kehoe, J. F., 586, 592, 593, 594, 595
Kelleher, Herb, 6, 95, 544, 548, 551
Kellner, Larry, 92
Kelloway, E. K., 614, 615
Kelly, Gary C., 546, 548, 551
Kelly, L. M., 580
Kelly, M., 593
Kelly, V. M., 613
Kennedy, John F., 505
Kennedy, M. M., 603
Kennedy, P., 617
Kernan, M. C., 582
Kerr, S., 582
Kershaw, S., 609
Kerstetter, J., 582
Kesner, I. F., 597
Kessler, I., 590
Keuch, R. W., 606
Khan, Elisan, 140
Kidder, D. L., 579, 584
Kiger, P. J., 590, 596, 597, 609, 610, 612, 613
Kiker, D. S., 596, 600, 613
Kilgour, J. G., 610
Kim, D-O, 609
Kim, E. S., 579
Kim, I., 600
Kim, S. P., 578
Kim, W. C., 583
Kimmel, M. S., 605
Kirby, J., 581
Kirch, Kent, 203
Kirkland, K., 603
Kirkland, R., 604, 618
Kirkman, B. L., 580, 599, 607

Kirkpatrick, D., 576, 590
Kirn, S. P., 581
Kirsch, B., 611
Kish, K., 603
Kisilevitz, M., 612
Kiska, J., 607
Kivimaki, M., 584
Klaas, B., 605
Klaff, L. G., 582, 596
Kleinfield, N. R., 615
Kleinmann, M., 594
Klimoski, R. J., 586, 587, 589
Klineberg, S. L., 591
Kluger, A., 618
Knapp, D. E., 611
Knight, D., 607, 608
Knight, Joe, 321
Knowdell, R. L., 582
Koch, M. J., 617
Kochan, T. A., 617, 618, 619
Kochan, T., 585
Kochanski, J., 600
Koenig, R., 618
Koeniger, W., 605
Koeppel, D., 592
Koestner, R., 608
Kohn, Alfie, 410
Kohn, L., 604
Kolk, N. J., 594
Kongaard, M. A., 581
Konig, C. J., 600
Konovsky, M., 583
Konrad, A. M., 578, 590
Kopp, R., 596
Kopp, Wendy, 209
Koretz, G., 583
Korsgaard, M. A., 583
Kosdrosky, T., 619
Koski, L., 603
Koss-Feder, L., 617
Kotlyar, I., 589
Kotter, J., 104, 583
Kovac, J. C., 600, 606, 610, 611, 612
Kowske, B., 600
Kozlowski, S. W. J., 597
Kraft, L. G., 611
Kraiger, K., 596, 598, 599
Kram, K. E., 598
Kramer, R. J., 600
Kranz, G., 614
Kravitz, D. A., 591
Kripalani, M., 590
Kristof, A. L., 590
Kroll, K. M., 607
Kroll, M., 577, 591
Kropko, M. R., 617, 618
Krug, Dan, 420
Kruse, D., 611
Kuczynski, S., 582
Kudisch, J. D., 598

Kugel, S., 598
Kulik, C. T., 594
Kurland, N. B., 589
Kurshid, A., 579
Kurtin, Ronnie, 462
Kurtzberg, T. R., 602
Kuttner, R., 610
Kuvaas, B., 604
Kwong, J. Y. Y., 602
Kwun, S. K., 601

L
Laabs, J. J., 598, 611
Labig, C. E., Jr., 591
Lachnit, C., 596, 598
Laczo, R. M., 586, 587
Ladd, R. T., 598
Ladika, S., 607
Lado, A. A., 577
Lafley, A. G., 84
LaGalbo, Joe, 164
Lager, F. C., 588
Lamb, Jeff, 557
Lammlein, S. E., 581
Lamp, Jeff, 221
Lampron, F., 603, 607
Lampton, B., 596
Lancaster, L. C., 579
Lance, C. E., 602
Landis, R. S., 588
Landrigan, P., 613
Landy, F. J., 588
Lane, Bob, 35, 36, 272, 473, 523
Lane, F. S., III, 586
Lane, H. W., 580
Langdon, D. G., 587
Lange, C., 592
Langham, D., 617
Langley, M., 580
Lankau, M. J., 597
Lapidot, Y., 617
LaPointe, J. A., 602
Larsen, H. H., 579
Larsson, R., 597
Lashinsky, A., 609, 610
Latham, G. P., 594, 599, 600, 601, 602
Lau, L., 584
Lautenschlager, G. J., 591
Lavelle, L., 609
Lavin, Carol, 56
Law, K., 583
Lawler, E. E., III, 577, 580, 600, 605, 607
Lawler, J., 576, 579
Lawrence, D. G., 593
Lawrence, L., 585, 590
Lawrence, T. B., 590
Le Blanc, P. M., 616
Leaonhardt, D., 589
Lebiecki, J. E., 593

LeBlanc, E., 579
LeBlanc, M. M., 615
Leche, T., 609
Ledford, G. E., 577, 606
Ledvinka, J., 584, 587
Lee, B. A., 584, 585
Lee, C. D., 603
Lee, C., 583, 603, 609
Lee, Joe R., 114
Lee, S., 577
Lee, S-Y, 608
Lee, T. W., 590, 591
Leffler, S. P., 608
Leigh, P., 613
Leigh, T. W., 615
Lein, J., 613
Leiter, M. P., 616
Lemaire, K., 606
Leonard, B., 577, 598
Leonard, J. S., 591
Leonard, J., 585
Leonardi, M., 605
Leonhardt, D., 591, 609, 618
Lepak, D. P., 582
LePine, J., 597
LePine, M. A., 590
Lepsinger, R., 602
Lerche, T., 611
Lerner, Sandy K., 3
Leslie, J., 596, 597
Leslie, L. M., 591
Levering, R., 576, 577, 579, 612
Levin, D. P., 616
Levine, D., 585
Levine, E. L., 586, 587, 588, 591
Levinson, A., 63, 443
Levy, M., 612
Levy, P. E., 589, 600, 601, 603
Lewick, R. J., 619
Lewin, D., 584, 619
Lewis, J., 584
Lewis, P. M., 595
Lewis, Peter B., 356
Liao, H., 591, 608
Liberman, V., 585
Liddick, B., 612
Liden, R. C., 597
Lieb, P., 590
Lieber, R., 587, 588
Lieberman, T., 611
Lievens, F., 592, 602
Limoges, G., 606
Lin, H., 591
Lin, T., 595
Lincoln, James F., 558, 564
Lincoln, John C., 558
Lindblad, C., 578
Lindell, M. K., 588
Lindholm, M. L., 592

Lindo, D. K., 601
Lindsley, D. H., 600
Linehan, M., 596
Lipold, A. G., 614
Lipset, S. M., 618
Lipson, J., 586
Livernash, E., 619
Lobsenz, R. E., 596
Locke, E. A., 599, 600, 602
Lockhart, D. E., 591
Lockhart, T., 597
Lockwood, N. R., 600, 611, 612, 614, 615
Loeb, Michael, 355
Lombard, M. M., 592
London, M., 596, 597, 599, 601, 603
Long, R. J., 609
Loomis, C., 612
Loucks, P., 603
Loughlin, C., 579, 614
Lovell, V., 606
Lowe, A., 589
Lowry, T., 580
Lublin, J. S., 604
Lucas, J. H., 598
Lucas, R., 617
Lucenko, K., 578
Lucia, A. D., 602
Lucid, L., 600
Lui, W., 604
Lukes, T. E., 602
Lundberg, U., 613
Luo, Y., 578, 581
Luthans, F., 600, 602, 607
Lyness, K. S., 603

M
Maatman, G., Jr., 585
MacDonald, Randy, 209, 360
Macey, W. H., 580
Mackey, John P., 360
MacLeod, W., 617
MacNeil, J. S., 589
Mael, F. A., 593
Maertz, C. P., Jr., 591
Magliozzi, T., 619
Magnan, M., 609
Mahoney, L. S., 609
Mahoney, T. A., 590
Makower, J., 580
Makri, M., 604
Malamut, A. B., 586
Malos, S. B., 600
Mangel, R., 608
Mangold, W. G., 620
Mann, S., 601, 602
Manoogian, S., 603
Mansour-Cole, D. M., 583
Manzey, D., 594
Marchington, M., 576
Marcotte, D. R., 598

Marcotte, S., 612
Markels, A., 604
Markham, Bill, 116
Markoff, J., 609
Markowitz, S., 613
Marks, M. L., 581, 591
Markus, L. H., 587
Marler, J. H., 604, 605
Marlowe, C. M., 595
Marquez, J., 586, 589, 597, 600, 603, 606, 610, 611, 617
Marquez, P., 580
Marsh, H. W., 598
Martell, R. F., 602, 603
Martin, Edward, 167
Martin, J., 620
Martin, T., 604, 605
Martinez, M. N., 590
Martinko, M. J., 615
Martocchio, J. J., 579, 606, 610, 612
Maslach, M., 616
Masternak, R., 609
Mathews, A. W., 588
Matsumura, E. M., 609
Maugorgne, R., 583
Maurer, Rick, 344, 582
Maurer, S. D., 590
Maurer, T. J., 596, 597, 601
Maxwell, S. E., 595
May, G., 599
Mayer, D. M., 580, 591
Mayes, B. T., 599
Mayfield, M. S., 587, 588
Maynard, M., 581, 618, 619, 620, 621
Mayrhofer, W., 579
Mazer, M. A., 606
McAfee, R. B., 603
McCall, M. W. Jr., 588, 596
McCartney, S., 620
McCauley, C. D., 597, 598
McCauley, C., 598
McCormick, Ernest J., 169, 588
McCracken, J., 612
McCrae, R. R., 593
McDaniel, M. A., 583, 592, 594, 603
McDermott, M., 600
McDermott, N. E., 587
McDonald, R. A., 602
McFarland, L. A., 594, 595, 596
McFarlin, D. B., 584, 603
McGeehan, P., 586
McGrath, Judy, 76
McGregor, J., 602, 604
McGriger, J., 591
McKay, J., 620
McKenna, M. M., 587

McKersie, R. B., 619
McLaughlin, G. L., 578
McLaughlin, K., 598
McLeod, W., 578
McManus, M., 593
McMullen, T. D., 608
McNatt, D. B., 603
McNerney, James, 283
McPhail, S. M., 592
McPherson, S. O., 580, 599
Mead, A. D., 594
Mecham, R. C., 588
Mecham, R. L., III, 589
Medland, M. E., 612
Meece, M., 585
Meglino, B. M., 602
Mehler, Mark, 191
Mehta, S. N., 579, 607
Mehta, S. R., 605
Meilinger, F., 615
Meiners, H. A., 584
Meisler, A., 582, 595, 617, 618, 619
Melin, B., 613
Meltz, N. M., 618
Mendonca, L. T., 616, 617
Mendonca, M., 579
Mentel, B., 578
Meredith, R., 619
Mero, N. P., 600
Merrill, J., 615
Merriman, K. K., 604, 609
Merritt, D. E., 615
Mervosh, E. M., 582
Metz, D., 612
Meyer, J. P., 582, 599
Meyer, J. W., 576
Meyers, M., 581
Micco, L., 595
Miceli, M. P., 583
Michaels, J., 589
Michaelson, K., 597
Mihalopoulos, D., 605
Mike, B., 581
Miklave, M. T., 585
Miles, S. J., 620
Milkovich, G. T., 606
Miller, D., 582
Miller, J., 577
Miller, Kim, 114, 117
Miller, L., 616
Miller, R., 360, 577
Miller, S., 610, 611
Miller, T., 580
Mills, W. C., 578
Minehan, M., 613
Minette, K. A., 589, 607
Minton-Eversole, T., 598, 614
Mirvis, P. H., 581
Mirza, P., 585
Mitchell, Mike, 32–33

Mitchell, T. R., 591
Mitra, A., 608
Mittorp, K. D., 582
Moberg, P. J., 594
Mobley, W. H., 618
Mohl, D. S., 603
Mohrman, S. A., 577, 612
Molleston, J. L., 618
Mone, E. M., 597
Mones, K., 593
Monrad, A. K., 577
Montemayor, E. F., 608
Moon, H., 599
Mooneyhan, Codey, 490
Moore, C., 586, 601, 602
Moore, Jim, 286
Moran, A., 599
Moran, Frank, 219
Morath, R. A., 593
Moravec, M., 582
Morgan, R. B., 588
Morgan, R., 603
Morgesen, F. P., 614
Morgeson, F. P., 587, 588, 594, 615
Morley, M. J., 618, 619, 620
Morridge, John, 3
Morris, J., 610
Morris, S. B., 596
Morrison, E. W., 583, 597
Morrow, J. C., 583
Morrow, P. C., 583, 590
Moscoso, S., 593
Mosisa, A. T., 578
Moskowitz, M., 576, 577, 579, 612
Moss, M., 616
Mossholder, K. W., 591
Motowidlo, S. J., 594, 600, 601
Mott, Richard, 270
Mount, M. K., 593, 602
Moussa, F., 607
Mowday, R. T., 600
Moynihan, L. M., 590
Muchinsky, P., 593
Mueller, J., 591
Muilenburg, K., 605
Muir, N. K., 599
Mulcahy, B., 612
Mullen, E. J., 583
Muller, H. J., 579
Mulvey, P. W., 599
Mumford, M. D., 588, 593
Munir, F., 616, 617
Munk, N., 590
Murakami, F., 586
Muralidhar, K., 576
Murnir, F., 617
Murphy, C., 616
Murphy, K. R., 592, 593, 594, 600, 602

Murphy, T., 592
Murray, B., 612
Murray, J., 578
Murray, Michael, 479
Murrell, A., 598
Muuka, G. N., 578
Myers, D. W., 614
Myers, J., 587
Myers, Maurice, 496
Myers, P. S., 614

N

Nadkarni, S., 591
Nahrgang, J. D., 615
Naquin, C. E., 602
Narisetti, R., 621
Nathan, B. R., 602
Naumann, S., 583
Navarro, C., 611
Naveh, E., 614
Neal, A., 614
Neale, M. A., 619
Neary, D. B., 597, 600
Nee, J., 617
Neeleman, S., 611
Nelson, B., 608
Nelson, C. E., 595
Nelson, D. L., 613
Nelson, Kent C., 284
Nelson, Sharon, 142
Neuman, G. A., 592
Neuman, J. H., 615
Neumark, D., 605
Newman, Harry, 40
Newman, J. M., 604, 606
Newman, K. L., 579
Ng, K.Y., 583
Nguyen, N. T., 583, 603
Nicholson, G., 592
Nielsen, T., 602
Nilan, K., 597
Niles-Jolly, K. A., 580
Nilsen, D., 600
Nimps, T., 588
Nishii, L. H., 586
Nixon, Richard M., 125
Noe, R. A., 583, 590, 597
Noel, T. W., 585
Nohria, N., 580, 581
Nollen, S. D., 579
Nordhaug, O., 600
Northcraft, G., 619
Norton, D. P., 576, 580, 581
Norvell, Larry, 150
Nunziata, L., 605
Nusbaum, M. A., 593
Nyfield, G., 594, 595

O

O'Dell, L. L., 612
O'Driscoll, M., 615
O'Grady, D. A., 597

O'Halloran, P. L., 608
O'Leary-Kelly, A. M., 615
O'Malley, M., 602
Odle, Stephanie, 113, 120
Offermann, L. R., 586
Ohlott, P. J., 597, 598
Oldham, G. R., 615
O'Leary, B., 592
Olivo, T., 578
Olsen, S., 609
Olson, E., 590
Olson, R. Neil, 597
Olson-Buchanan, J. B.,
    584, 594
O'Mahony, S., 597
O'Neill, C., 600
O'Neill, Paul, 494
Ones, D. S., 586, 594, 601,
    604
Onley, D. S., 603
Oppenheimer, A., 586
Option, Dave, 246
Oreg, S., 582
O'Reilly, C. A., III, 576,
    581, 582
O'Reilly, A. P., 588
Orey, M., 584
Orfalea, Paul, 75
Ormond, W. E., 616
Orvis, K. A., 593
Osland, A., 586
Osland, J., 581
Osterman, P., 618
Ostroff, C., 597, 601
Otto, Larry, 151
Overhalt, A. L., 608
Overholt, A., 578, 606
Overman, S., 598
Owens, B. P., 591
Owens, W., 593

P

Pace, Dave, 10
Paetzold, R. L., 604
Page, R., 595, 596
Palich, L. E., 590
Palmer, D. K., 594
Palmeri, C., 619
Palmerud, G., 613
Palmisano, Sam, 63
Pappas, J. M., 604, 609
Parasuraman, S., 598
Park, A., 600
Park, H. J., 609
Parker, Larry, 551
Parker, S. K., 615, 616
Parks, Jack, 471
Parks, L., 601
Paronto, M. E., 595
Parr, D., 613
Parry, S. B., 586
Parsons, A., 604, 612

Parus, B., 590, 604, 606
Patel, D., 578
Pater, R., 616
Patterson, M., 581
Pattison, P., 584
Paul, K., 576
Paulin, G., 609
Paulsen, K., 609
Payne, S., 594
Pear, R., 610
Pearce, J. E., 605
Pearce, J. L., 603
Pearlman, K., 586, 592
Pellet, J., 609
Pelletier, K. R., 613, 614
Perrewe, P. L., 612
Perry, E. A., 594
Perry-Smith, J., 612
Pescuric, Alice, 299
Peters, M. C. W., 616
Peterson, N. G., 588
Peterson, R., 619
Peterson, S. J., 602, 607
Pettigrew, T. F., 599
Petzinger, T., Jr., 582
Peyrefitte, J., 602
Pezalla, E., 612
Pfeffer, J., 576
Pham, Thuy, 254
Phillips, D., 289, 581
Phillips, J. M., 591
Piasentin, K. A., 590
Pinfield, L. T., 582
Pinto, P. R., 588
Pisano, G., 592
Plamondon, K. E., 601
Platt, R. K., 604
Ployhart, R. E., 587, 592,
    593, 595
Podolsky, M., 607
Podsakoff, P., 603
Pogson, C. E., 603
Pohley, K., 594
Poland, R. D., 591
Pollack, L. J., 587, 588
Polyak, I., 604
Pomeroy, A., 585
Pomfert, E. K., 586
Pont, J., 584, 589
Poole, M. S., 581
Porras, J. I., 581
Porter, C. O. L. H., 599
Porter, C., 583
Porter, E., 578, 584
Porter, L. W., 603
Posthuma, R. A., 594, 601
Potter, G., 608
Poulson, Cherly, 438
Povich, E. S., 605
Powell, B. C., 600
Powell, G. N., 579, 584
Power, F.R., 583

Prahalad, C. K., 576
Prasad, P., 577
Pratt, C., 586
Premack, S. L., 591
Prewett-Livingston, A. J., 595
Prezant, F., 595
Priem, R. L., 599
Priem, Windle, 302
Prien, E., 586
Pritchard, R. D., 600
Probst, T. M., 579
Pruitt, Dave, 184
Pucik, V., 577
Pucik, Viado, 29
Pulakos, E. D., 588, 592, 593,
    594, 595, 600, 601
Purcell, I. P., 609
Putka, D. J., 587

Q

Quaintance, M. K., 593
Quick, J. C., 613, 614, 615,
    616, 617
Quigley, N. R., 614
Quillian-Wolever, R. E., 617
Quinn, R. T., 581
Quinones, M. A., 594, 599

R

Radhakrishnan, P., 585
Ragins, B., 597, 599
Rahbah-Daniels, D., 586
Rainville, Mike, 486
Raju, N. S., 592, 601
Ramey, J., 605
Ranson, John, 315
Raphael, T., 586
Raphan, M., 586
Rappleye, G. C., Jr., 589
Ratliff, G., 592
Raver, J. L., 586
Raymark, P. H., 587, 588
Ready, D. A., 597
Reb, J., 602
Redman, Jay, 7
Reed, D., 620
Rehder, R. R., 579
Reich, M., 605
Reich, R. B., 579
Reichers, A. E., 582
Reilly, M. E., 595, 606
Reilly, R. R., 601
Reingold, J., 589
Reiter-Palmon, R., 588
Reitman, F., 598
Renard, M. K., 600
Renk, K., 603
Renn, R. W., 615
Renshaw, A. A., 587
Revell, J., 610
Reynolds, C., 609
Reynolds, S. J., 577

Rhoad, Laura, 488
Rhoades, D. L., 620
Rhodenizer, L., 599
Rich, J. T., 603
Richards, G. E., 598
Richards, Susan, 405
Richey, R. G., 600
Richman, D., 587
Richtel, M., 593, 618
Ridder, K., 616
Rigby, D., 591
Riggio, R. E., 599
Ringdal, K., 600
Ringleb, R. E., 584
Riper, T. V., 611
Risher, H., 606, 608
Ritchie, J. E., Jr., 590
Ritter, A., 618
Ritti, R. R., 596
Robb, D., 586, 603
Roberson, L., 594
Roberson, Q., 583, 590
Robert, C., 579
Roberts, B. W., 593
Roberts, B., 586, 592
Roberts, D. R., 581
Roberts, D., 620
Roberts, K., 612, 614
Robertson, I. T., 593
Robertson, P. J., 581
Robinson, E. A., 593
Robinson, K. S., 585, 586,
    612, 614
Robinson, P., 579
Robinson, Sandra, 418
Robinson, Teri, 210
Rock, J., 596
Rodriguez, A., 595
Rodriguez, D. A., 603
Rodriguez, D., 586, 587
Roehling, M. V., 590
Rogovsky, N., 579, 584
Rolland, J. P., 593
Romeo, J., 592
Romero, H., 587, 588
Romero, S., 593, 618
Roodt, G., 607
Rose, K., 612
Rosen, B., 580, 599
Rosen, S., 578, 617
Rosenfield, P., 599
Rosenman, R., 616
Ross, S., 609
Roth, L. M., 584, 603
Roth, P. L., 592, 593, 594
Rothauser, T. J., 612
Rothstein, H. R., 593
Rousseau, D. M., 583
Rowan, B., 576
Rowe, A., 582
Rowland, K. M., 584, 602
Rozell, E. J., 592

Rubel, Matt, 328
Rubenfeld, S., 607
Rubis, L., 596, 598
Ruckley, P., 587
Ruderman, M. N., 597, 598
Rudin, J. P., 605
Ruf, B. M., 576
Rugala, Eugene A., 488
Ruiz, G., 589, 600, 601, 602
Rupp, D. E., 616
Ruquest, M. E., 587
Rusbult, C. E., 583
Russ-Eft, D. F., 599
Russell, C. J., 591, 593
Russell, J. E. A., 598
Russo, M. V., 607
Ryan, A. M., 592, 594,
    595, 596
Ryan, R., 608
Rynes, S. L., 589, 599,
    601, 607

S

Saari, L., 597
Saavedra, R., 601
Sacco, J. M., 594, 595
Sackett, P. R., 586, 587, 596
Safon, D., 586
Sager, I., 580
Saita, A., 598
Saks, A. M., 589, 591, 598
Saks, A., 589, 591, 598
Salas, E., 579, 598, 599
Salgado, J. F., 593
Salisbury, Dallas, 450
Salter, C., 577
Saltz, J., 580
Salvaggio, A. N., 576
Salvatore, P., 585
Sammer, J., 607, 608,
    609, 610
Sanchez, Dave, 92
Sanchez, J. I., 586, 587, 588,
    589, 602
Sanchez, R., 595
Sandall, D. L., 588
Sandsjö, L., 613
Sanicola, L., 611
Sarin, A., 609
Sarpy, S. A., 613, 614,
    615, 616
Sass, S. A., 615
Sasseen, J., 604
Saton, D., 586
Saulny, S., 585
Saunier, Anne, 330
Scalia, C., 596
Scalise, D., 604
Scarpello, V. G., 587
Schaffer, R. H., 582
Schappe, S. P., 585

Schaubroeck, J., 615
Schaufeli, W. B., 616
Scheu, C. R., 594
Schiller, Z., 621
Schinzler, P., 599
Schippmann, J. S., 587, 592
Schlender, B., 579
Schmidt, F. L., 576, 592, 593,
    594, 601
Schminke, M., 585
Schmit, M. J., 588
Schmitt, N. W., 587, 592,
    593, 594, 595, 596, 601
Schneer, J. A., 598
Schneid, T. D., 615
Schneider, B., 576, 580,
    587, 592
Schneider, D. L., 594
Schneider, K., 585
Schneider, R. J., 593
Schneider, S., 595
Schneier, C. E., 603
Schoeff, M., Jr., 586, 611, 617
Schoenberger, K., 580
Schoeneman, D., 589
Schramm, J., 577, 578,
    584, 612
Schroth, H., 583
Schuler, D. A., 576
Schuler, R. S., 577, 578, 579,
    580, 581, 584, 586, 596,
    600, 609, 611, 617, 619
Schultz, Howard, 4, 10, 12,
    424, 454
Schuster, J. R., 606, 607
Schwartz, C. E., 615
Schwartz, N. D., 579
Schweiger, D. M., 583
Schweitzer, M., 605
Scott, D., 608, 609
Scott, S. G., 583
Scott, W. R., 576
Scullen, S. E., 593, 602
Scullion, H., 577, 578, 596
Scully, J., 581
Seifer, C. F., 602
Sellers, P., 590, 600
Sessa, V. I., 596
Settoon, R. P., 591
Severin, K., 594
Sexton, E. A., 597
Shafer, P., 607
Shah, P., 583
Shamsie, J., 582
Shapiro, D. H., Jr., 615
Shapiro, D. L., 600, 607
Shapiro, J., 590
Sharf, J. C., 595
Sharfman, M. P., 599
Sharpe, R., 608
Shaver, J. M., 578
Shaw, B., 588

Shaw, J. D., 591, 603, 604,
    606, 608, 614
Sheehan, M. K., 601
Shelley, Bill, 461
Shih, H., 600
Shin, J. Y., 609
Shindledecker, R., 613
Shippmann, J. S., 586, 588
Shirom, A., 616
Shore, L. M., 601
Shore, T. H., 601
Shotell, L., 592
Shuit, D. P., 577, 592,
    596, 599
Siebel, Tom, 408
Siegel, P., 583
Sierra, L., 587
Silberman, M., 596
Silverhart, T. A., 593
Silverman, S. B., 603
Silverman, S.R., 601
Silverstein, M., 584
Silzer, R. F., 588
Silzer, R., 582, 594
Simmons, B. L., 613
Simon, B., 618
Simon, J., 578, 617
Simons, C., 587, 588
Simons, J. V., 607
Simons, T., 583
Sims, Paula, 352–353
Sinangil, H. K., 586
Sinar, E. F., 591
Sinclair, R. R., 614
Sinegal, James, 118, 370
Singh, G., 605
Singh, P., 607, 620
Sitzmann, T., 598
Skaggs, B. C., 577
Skags, B. R., 575
Skoldberg, K., 582
Skonberg, J., 593
Slaughter, J. E., 591
Slichter, S., 619
Sloan, D. B., 597
Sloane, A. A., 618, 619
Slocum, J. W., Jr., 581, 616
Slott, Jordan, 521
Small, B., 593, 594
Smerd, J., 586, 615
Smith, A., 586, 605
Smith, Andrew, 57
Smith, C. A., 597
Smith, C. S., 616
Smith, D. B., 576
Smith, Fred, 275
Smith, G., 578, 580, 613
Smith, H., 617
Smith, J. E., 588
Smith, M. J., 613, 614, 615
Smith, M. R., 593, 595, 596
Smith, Susan M., 6

Smith, V. C., 585, 592
Smith-Crowe, K., 613, 614, 615
Smither, J. W., 600, 601
Smolenski, Eric, 234
Snell, S. A., 582
Snook, S., 597
Sockell, D. R., 584
Song, F., 607
Sonnentag, S., 611, 615
Sonsin, B., 608
Sorensen, A., 600
Sotherlund, J., 608
Soupata, L., 58, 579
Sparks, K., 615
Sparrow, P. R., 579, 582, 589, 609
Sparrowe, R. T., 597
Spector, P. E., 616
Speizer, I., 598
Sperling, R. S., 608
Spychalski, A. C., 594
Srinivasan, D., 608
Stabile, Vincent, 251
Stahl, G., 579
Staijkovic, A. D., 600
Staloch, K., 612
Stamps, D., 598
Starke, M., 589
Stathatos, P., 591
Staw, B. M., 583, 602
Steel, P., 600
Steers, R. M., 600
Stein, J. H., 584
Stein, N., 614
Steinhauer, J., 586
Stengel, J. R., 581
Stengel, Jim, 85
Stern, Andrew, 9, 538
Stern, G., 606
Stern, Z., 614
Sternberg, R. J., 598
Stevens, C. K., 590, 595
Stevens, M. J., 592
Stewart, A. M., 602
Stewart, D., 598
Stewart, G. L., 588
Stewart, T. A., 590, 597, 598, 599
Stiffler, Mark, 410
Stillman, D., 579
Stires, D., 619
Stivarius, T. B., 593
Stoeckmann, J., 609
Stokes, G., 593
Stolz, R. F., 604
Stone, D. L., 577, 579, 586
Stone, T. H., 591
Stone-Romero, E. F., 579, 586
St-Onge, S., 609
Storey, J., 581
Stoskopf, G. A., 606, 610

Strandberg, J., 598
Strasser, S., 583
Strauss, R., 594
Stuart, Mary Kim, 323
Stundza, T., 578
Sturze, S., 582
Suchard, R., 618
Suh, E., 617
Sulsky, L. M., 616
Sulter, C., 579, 586
Summers, L., 607
Sun, M., 612
Sundstrom, E., 602
Sunoo, B. P., 585, 587, 594, 603
Sweeney, P. D., 584, 603
Switzer, F. S., III, 592, 593
Sygnature, E. F., 615
Sytsma, M. R., 602

T

Taggar, S., 592
Tahmincioglu, E., 587, 613, 615
Takeuchi, R., 582
Tan, H. H., 618
Tande, C., 604
Tannebaum, S. A., 599
Tannenbaum, S. I., 596, 597
Tapon, F., 607
Tarbell, L. M., 577
Tare, M., 606
Targa, F., 603
Tarique, I., 580
Taris, T. W., 616
Tarulli, B. A., 596
Taylor, A., III, 579
Taylor, C., 598
Taylor, Johnny C., 240
Taylor, M. S., 590, 600
Taylor, P. J., 593, 594, 599
Tergesen, A., 604
Terpstra, D. E., 592, 603, 604
Terri, A., 597
Tesluk, P. E., 580, 599, 613, 614, 615
Testa, Russ, 418
Tetrick, L. E., 613, 614, 615, 616, 617
Tharp, Charles, 37
Thea, D. M., 578, 617
Theirry, H., 606
Thelen, J. B., 617
Thierry, H., 594, 600
Thoerell, T., 616
Thomas, Bernice, 530
Thomas, D., 585
Thomas, J. B., 600
Thomas, R. J., 579
Thompson, D. J., 611
Thompson, L. F., 616
Thompson, L. L., 619

Thompson, M. A., 604, 606, 607, 608
Thompson, R., 595
Thomson, Todd S., 7
Thornton, G. C., III, 594, 599, 601
Thrutchley, C. S., 586
Tiffin, J., 588
Tihanyi, L., 580
Todor, W. D., 603, 618, 619
Toegel, G., 602
Tompkins, N. C., 615
Tornow, W. W., 588, 599
Toscano, G. A., 615
Tosh, D. A., 617
Tosi, H. L., Jr., 604, 608
Towler, A. J., 597, 604
Townsend. A. M., 586
Toyama, M., 586
Tracy, K. B., 600
Tranovskaya, V., 597
Traynman, E., 619
Trevino, L. K., 577
Trevor, C. O., 603
Triandis, H. C., 583
Tripoli, A. M., 603
Trotman, S., 609
Trottman, M., 620
Troy, K., 581
Troyan, Ken, 103
Truxillo, D. M., 594, 595
Tsai, W., 594
Tsui, A. S., 603
Tung, R., 579
Turban, D. B., 576, 590
Turchin, B., 589
Turner, M. E., 591
Turner, N., 615, 616
Turner, W. K., 586
Twomey, D. P., 618
Tyler, C., 602
Tyler, K., 587, 596, 600, 612, 613, 617
Tyler, P., 593
Tyler, T. R., 584
Tzafrir, S. S., 597

U

Uchitelle, L., 577, 591
Uggerslev, K. L., 590, 595
Ulrich, D., 576, 577, 580, 581, 582
Updegrave, W., 611
Usui, E., 611
Uzcategui, M., 606

V

Valentine, Don, 3
Vallas, S., 604
Valliere, R., 615
Van Dam, K., 592
Van De Ven, A., 581

Van Eerde, W., 600
Van Ommeren, J., 577
van Sliedregt, T., 606
Van Vianen, A., 589
Vandenberg, R. J., 615
VanderBos, G. R., 615
VanDerhei, J., 611
Vanderkam, L., 579
VandeWalle, D., 599, 602
Varca, P. E., 584
Vargas, A. L., 601
Varma, A., 601
Vasella, Daniel, 4
Vasey, J., 588
Vaslow, J., 607
Vaughan, Lance, 532
Veldsman, T., 607
Vella-Zarb, K., 579
Velte, Lisa, 275
Vent, D. H., 609
Veres, J. G., III, 595
Viega, J. F., 599
Vilano, M., 612
Villanova, P., 602
Vincent, J. R., 578, 617
Vinchur, A. J., 592
Viswesvaran, C., 586, 594, 601
Vogel, N., 612
Vogelstein, F., 582
Volpe, C., 599
Voris, Janet, 184
Voskuijl, O. F., 606

W

Waclawski, J., 581
Wagoner, Rick, 526
Waldman, D. A., 588, 592, 603
Walker, A. J., 579, 601
Walker, David M., 580
Walker, Jay, 355
Walker, M., 143
Walker, T., 611
Wall, T. D., 616
Waller, M. J., 599
Walley, L., 593
Walsh, M. W., 584, 590, 611, 616
Walton, R., 619
Walton, Sam, 548
Walumbwa, F. O., 611
Wanberg, C., 582
Wang, J., 576
Wang, P., 611
Wanous, J. P., 582, 591
Waring, J., 581
Wascher, W., 605
Washburn, G., 605
Wasti, S., 586
Wazeter, D. L., 603
Weatherhead, P., 607

Weaver, G. R., 577
Weaver, P., 612
Weber, G., 577
Weber, J., 612
Weber, Lisa, 397
Webster, J., 595
Wedin, V., 611
Weekley, J. A., 594
Weems, P., 609
Weimer, D., 619
Weinberg, N., 590
Weinberger, T. E., 608
Weinstein, R. J., 585
Weintraub, A., 617
Weiss, E. M., 597
Weiss, H. M., 616
Welbourne, T. M., 576, 609
Welch, D., 617, 618, 619
Welch, Jack, 14, 620
Welch, Suzy, 14, 620
Wells, M., 621
Wells, S. J., 596, 608, 611
Wells, W., 621
Wendler, J., 580
Werkman, R. A., 581, 582
Werling, S. E., 606
Werner, S., 578, 586, 601,
    604, 606, 609, 610, 612
Wesley, D. T. A., 580
Wesson, M. J., 583, 590, 604
West, B. J., 599
West, M. A., 581, 607
Westman, D., 609
Westman, M., 617
Wetlaufer, S., 579
Wheeler, K. G., 590

Whetzel, D. L., 594
White, E. , 598, 610
White, F., 596
White, R., 606
White, S. S., 580
Whitehouse, K., 607
Whitener, E. M., 583
Whiteside, K. S., 587
Whitford, D., 576
Whitford, R. A., 592
Whitman, M. E., 586
Whitney, D., 595
Whitney, K., 594
Wiese, D. S., 602
Wiesenfeld, B., 583
Wildertrotter,
    Maggie, 134
Wilkinson, A., 576
Williams, C. R., 591
Williams, K., 602
Williams, M. L., 583, 603
Williams, Robin, 548
Willis, F., 613
Willis, George, 558, 564
Willis, S. L., 598
Wilson, M. A., 587
Winerip, M., 619
Winkler, C., 592, 603
Wiscombe, J., 608
Wiseman, Jim, 270
Wiseman, R. M., 609
Wisher, R., 598
Wisnefsky, Eric, 335
Witherspoon, R., 603
Witney, F., 618, 619
Witt, L. A., 616

Woehr, D. J., 594, 601
Wojcik, J., 617
Wolever, M., 617
Wolff, E. N., 582, 591
Wolff, S., 601
Wolfson, P. J., 585
Wolters, R. S., 617
Wonderlic, Charles, Jr., 230
Wong, E., 621
Wong, K. F. E., 602
Wong, K., 600
Wong, N., 576
Wood, J. B., 608
Woodward, N. H., 605, 612,
    614, 616, 617
Woods, D., 616
Wooten, L. P., 584
Worley, C. G., 580
Worm, V., 579
Wormley, W. M., 598
Wren, D. A., 579
Wright, J., 592
Wright, P. M., 577, 591, 607
Wright, R. O., 618
Wyld, D. C., 605

Y

Yamaguchi, S., 586
Yammarino, F. J., 601
Yanadori, Y., 604, 605
Yang, Jerry, 56
Yeung, S. K., 577
Yilmaz, T., 608
Yoke, L. K., 584
Youndt, M., 577
Young, A., 578

Young, J., 612
Young, Mary B., 80
Young, S. A., 580
Youngblood, S. A., 584,
    618, 619
Yu, K., 579
Yukl, G., 602

Z

Zacharatos, A., 616
Zall, J. N., 594
Zandvakili, S., 592
Zanini, M., 577
Zappe, J., 590, 592
Zardhoohi, A., 604
Zarrella, Ron, 246
Zedeck, S., 593
Zeidner, R., 586, 589
Zeilberger, R., 583
Zellner, W., 577, 580, 583,
    605, 619, 620, 621
Zemke, R., 597
Zernike, K., 617
Ziegert, J. C., 590
Zijlstra, F. R. H., 615
Zimmerman, E., 582, 591,
    596, 605, 619
Zingheim, P. K., 606, 607
Zohar, D., 614
Zollars, Bill, 155
Zollo, G., 587
Zollo, M., 607
Zong, L., 608, 609
Zucker, L. G., 576
Zuckerman, A., 586
Zuckerman, L., 621

SUBJECT INDEX

A

Ability tests, 246
Absence, 471
Absolute standards appraisals, 336–338
Accidents
  occupational, 486–487
  prevention, 494–495
Accountability, 101
  of managers, 325
Accounting
  Financial Accounting Standards Board (FASB), 411
  performance-based pay, 411–412
Accuracy
  rating, improving, 341–342
  rewards, rating, 342
  of self-appraisals, 332
Acquisitions, 45–46
  elements of planning, 78
  training, 274–275
Action plans, 107
  implementing, 101–105
Active participation, training, 300
Activities for managing human resources, 16–19
Adjustments, compensation, 385–387
Administration
  benefit programs, 463–465
  contracts, 534–538
Administrative agencies, 125–128
Adobe Systems, company culture, 57
Advanced Financial Solutions, recruiting/retaining employees, 195
Advanced Micro Devices, selection decisions, 236
Advantages
  of customized job analysis, 173

of learning formats, 292
of team incentives, 420
Adversarial collective bargaining relationships, 522–523
Affective outcomes, 290–291
Affirmative action programs (AAPs), 213–216
  voluntary programs, 260
Aflac, compensation, 358
AFL-CIO, 512, 515
Age Discrimination in Employment Act of 1967 (ADEA), 121–122
Aging workforce, 63–64
Agreements
  negotiating, 525–531
  settlement, 134
AIDS, 48–50, 484, 500–501
Alberto-Culver Company, company culture, 56
Alcan, health and safety, 479–480
Alcohol and testing, 253–254
Alignment
  performance management, 318
  planning, 17, 74–78
Alliance partners, 9
Amalgamated Clothing Workers of America (ACWA), 513
American Express, labor costs in India, 49
American Psychological Association (APA), 257
Americans with Disabilities Act of 1990 (ADA), 122–123, 157
Analysis
  behavioral cause-and-effect models, 90–91
  competency modeling, 173–179
  demographic needs, 285–286

ergonomic, 167
job. See Job analysis
needs, 283
organizational, 84–85, 282–283
personnel, 283–284
Position Analysis Questionnaire (PAQ), 169–170
questionnaires, 172–173
Analytical Graphics, training and development, 275
Anniversary approach, 331
Anticipatory change, 76
Antidiscrimination training principles, 277
Appeals, grievances, 132
Applicants
  job applicant assessment, 244–254
  recruiting. See Recruiting
  rejecting, 212–213
  selection decisions, perspective of, 254–256
Application blank, 244
Appraisals, 156. See also Performance
  360-degree, 334–335, 352–353
  absolute standards, 336–338
  formats, 335–340
  legally defensible, 322
  norm-referenced, 335–336
  peer, 333
  performance, 331–335. See also Performance
  problem behavior, 346–347
  results-based, 338–340
  self-appraisal, 332–333
  timely, rewarding, 342
Arbella Insurance, compensation, 361
Arbitration, 132–133, 534
Asia-Pacific Economic Cooperation (APEC), 42

Assertiveness, 52
Assessment, 107
  centers, 249–250, 298
  external/organizational environments, 82–91
  intervention effectiveness, 496–497
  job applicant, 244–254
  personal history, 244
  techniques, 237, 238–241
  of the twenty-first-century workforce, 248
Assistance
  displaced employees, 221
  supervisors, 294–296
Association of Southeast Asian Nations (ASEAN), 40, 41
AT&T, job analysis, 179
Attitude surveys, 285
Attracting employees with performance-based pay, 398–399
Au Bon Pain, performance measurements, 327
Auditing employee usage, 466
Authorization cards, unions, 518–519
Automation
  of compensation, 389
  performance management, 347
Automobile Club d'Italia (ACI), 158
Avoiding layoffs, 221
Avon, performance-based pay, 402
Awards
  length-of-service, 412
  multiple, 415
  recognition, 403, 412–415
  spot, 413–414
  for suggestions, 414

B

Baby Boomer generation, retirement, 453

Background verification, 245

Baja Beach Club, privacy, 144

Barclaycard International, recruiting, 202

Barden Bearings, managing human resources, 110–111

Bargaining units, 519

Basic Pilot program, 222

Bausch & Lomb, integrity tests, 247

Behavior
  absolute standards appraisals, 336–338
  anchored rating scales, 337–338
  cause-and-effect models, 90–91
  ethics, 291
  for global leaders, 306
  modeling, 300
  modification, 496
  performance measurements, 326–327
  of recruiters, 210–211

Behavioral observed scales (BOS), 338

Benchmark jobs, 380–381

Benefit programs, 10, 435
  administration of, 463–465
  automation of, 389
  compensation. See Compensation
  costs, 441
  current issues, 465–467
  defined benefit plans, 447–448
  developmental, 463
  external environments, 441–442
  health and safety, 478
  health care, 453–457
  integrated HRM systems, 439–444
  legal considerations, 451–453
  mandatory protection program, 445–447
  organizational environments, 442–444
  overview of, 436–439
  paid leave, 457–459
  triad (HR), 444–445
  unions, 528
  USA Motors, 471
  voluntary protection programs, 447–453
  work/life, 459–462

Benefits of safe and healthy workplaces, 474

Ben & Jerry's Homemade Ice Cream
  carpal tunnel syndrome (CTS), 474, 475
  health and safety, 479–480
  observations, 165

Best Buy, executive compensation, 360

Best Forest Products Company, 57

Bloomingdales, diversity management, 136

Boeing, unions, 509

Bona fide occupational qualifications (BFOQ), 260

Bottom-line HR metrics, 92–93

Boycotts, 533

Boy Scouts of America case study, 150–151

Broadbanding, 377

Burger King, recruiting/retaining employees, 193–194

Burnout, job, 492–494

Business board games, 298

Business objectives, benefit programs, 438–439

Business planning, aligning, 81–82

Business strategies, 37, 60–63, 66
  compensation, implementing, 360–361
  customer service, 61–62
  innovation, 63
  low cost, 61

Business travel benefits, 463

Byrd v. Ronayne (1995), 332

C

Cadbury Schweppes, recruiting/retaining employees, 199

Calculating utility, 231–232

Canada, unionization in, 516

Canadian Labor Congress (CLC), 516

Cancer, 489

Candidates
  job applicant assessment, 244–254
  selecting, 242–244. See also Selection decisions

Careers
  paths, 162–163
  planning discussions, 285

Carl Buddig & Company, 204

Carpal tunnel syndrome (CTS), 474
  Ben & Jerry's, 475

Case management, 466

Case studies
  360-degree appraisals, 352–353
  aligning HR at SBC, 32–33
  Barden Bearings, 110–111
  City Hospital, 266–267
  Defense Systems, Inc. (DSI), 226–227
  Forest Products Company (FPC), 311
  HITEK Information Services, 184–187
  Howe 2 Ski Stores, 432–433
  Levi Strauss & Company, 70–71
  Lincoln Electric Company, 560–575
  Midwest Telephone Company (MTC), 505
  Newspaper Workers International Union (NWIU), 543
  Southwest Airlines, 544–559
  State Bank, 393
  United Way/Boy Scouts of America, 150–151
  USA Motors, 471

Cash balance plans, 451

Cash rewards, 397

Caterpillar, unions, 532

Cendant Mortgage, performance management, 314, 325

Centers, assessment, 249–250, 298

Central American Free Trade Agreement (CAFTA), 41

CEOs (chief executive officers)
  succession planning, 98
  view of human resources, 36

Certification, unions, 516, 519–521

Change
  anticipatory, 76
  degree of, 75–76
  facilitating, 101–105
  organizational, types of, 75–77
  overview of, 78–82
  performance management, 318
  planning, 17
  planning for, 74–78
  resistance to, managing, 103
  timing of, 76–77

Checks, background, 245

Chevron
  downsizing, 84
  HR forecasts, 86

Child care services, 460–461

Children's Hospital Boston, 420

China, labor costs, 48

Chrysler Group
  collective bargaining, 526
  team development, 302

Cingular Wireless, 137

Circuit City, layoffs, 220

Cirque du Soleil, host-country nationals (HCNs), 262

Cirrus Logic, selection decisions, 235

Cisco Systems
  compensation, 358
  external labor markets, 202
  human resources (HR), managing, 3

City Hospital, selection decisions, 266–267

Civil Rights Act of 1964 (Title VII), 121

Civil Service Reform Act (1978), 512

Classification, job classification method, 373

Clear instructions, 299

Code of ethics, 22

Cognitive knowledge, 288–289

Collective bargaining, 19, 507. See also Unions
  agreements, negotiating, 525–531
  conflict resolution, 531–534
  contract administration, 534–538
  current issues, 538–540
  integrated HRM systems, 509–510
  metrics, 537–538
  overview of, 508–510
  processes, 521–525

Combined distribution plans, 422

Commissions, 423–424

Commitment, employee, 10

Common themes, 24–28

Communication, 101
  of benefit programs, 464–465
  compensation, 358–359
  fairness, 120. See also Fairness
  Federal Hazard Communication Standard, 482

Communications Workers of America (CWA), 509

Communities-of-practice, 273–274
Community Internship Program, 9
Community relations, 8–9
Company culture, 56–60, 66
  health and safety, 479
  mission, 57–58
  subcultures, 58–60
  values, 58
  vision, 57
Company reputation, 199
Compensation, 10, 11, 355
  adjustments, 385–387
  automation of, 389
  benefits. *See* Benefit programs
  business strategies, implementing, 360–361
  communication, 358–359
  competency-based pay structure, 385
  current issues, 389
  development of total, 18
  executives, 359–360
  external environments, 364–365
  globalization, 387–388
  individual pay equity, 386
  integrated HRM systems, 361–370
  internal pay structure, designing, 384–385
  internal value of jobs, establishing, 372–379
  legal constraints, 365–369
  legal protection, 156
  minimum wage, 366–367
  monetary and nonmonetary, 361–362
  multiple pay structures, 378–379
  organizational environments, 369–370
  organizational pay policies, setting, 383–384
  overview of, 356–361
  pay levels, setting, 379–384
  performance-based pay, 18, 400. *See* Performance-based pay
  salary budget surveys, 386
  single pay structures, 378–379
  skill-based pay, 378, 385
  social considerations, 365–369
  State Bank, 393
  total cost of benefit programs, 441
  triad (HR), 370–372
  unemployment, 445–446

vacations, 458
  workers', 446
Compensatory approach, 242
Competencies
  building, 304–305
  for global firms, 21–22
  job evaluation, 377–378
  modeling, 17
  pay structure, 385
Competency modeling, 153–154
  3M, 178
  analysis, 173–179
  current issues, 179–181
  health and safety, 477–478
  independent contractors, 157–158
  information collection methods, 165–166
  inventories, 179
  legal protection, 156–158
  overview of, 154–159
  sources of information used, 163–165
  strategic change, 155–156
  terminology, 159–163
  training and development, 277–278
Competition
  cost versus knowledge, 39
  employees, recruiting/retaining, 193–194
  improving, 270–271
  union involvement to enhance, 509
  United States labor market, 47–48
Competitive advantage, creating, 11–14
Complexity, managing, 28–29
Compliance, 113. *See also* Legal compliance
Computer technologies, 54. *See also* Technologies
Concessionary bargaining, 524–525
Conflict resolution, 531–534
Consent decrees, 214
Consequences
  of country cultures, 53
  of selection decisions, 232
  of unsafe and unhealthy workplaces, 474
Consistency, training, 301
Constraints, training, 283
Consumer-driven medical plans, 455–456
Content of the discussion, feedback, 344–345
Content validation, 237
Continental Airlines, linking objectives, 91–92

Contingent workers, 44
  recruiting, 207
Continuous bargaining, 525
Contracts
  administration, 534–538
  employment, 129–130
Control over work, 490
Conventional medical insurance plans, 453–454
ConWay, performance management, 314
Cooking events, 299
Cooperative collective bargaining relationships, 523
Coordination
  of benefits, 466
  of plans and timetables, 80
Corporate campaigns, 533
Corporate cultures, 13
Corporate reputations, building, 209–210
Corporate universities, 297
Costco, organizational environment compensation, 370
Costs
  benefit programs, 441
  benefit programs, controlling, 436–437
  of health and safety, 476–477
  labor, 48–50
  labor, reducing, 193
  performance-based pay, 398
  of selection decisions, 230–231
Country cultures, 37, 50–53, 66, 83
  consequences of, 53
  dimensions of, 52–53
Courts, setting disputes, 133–134
Coworker relations deteriorates, 493–494
Credit Suisse, diversity management, 137
Criteria
  behavior, 326
  of interest, establishing, 236
  multiple, 328
  related validation, 237
  results, performance measurements, 327
  trait-based, 326
  weighting, 328–329
Crowley Maritime Corporation, 414
Cultures
  awareness training, 303
  differences, 117

differences, self-appraisals, 332–333
  of fairness, creating, 134–135
  multiculturalism, managing, 327
  performance-driven, 320–323
Current distribution plans, 422
Current issues, 66
  benefit programs, 465–467
  compensation, 389
  external environments, 63–65
  fairness and legal compliance, 143–145, 146
  health and safety, 501
  job analysis, 179–181
  performance, 347–348
  performance-based pay, 427–429
  planning, 105–106
  recruiting, 221–223
  retaining employees, 221–223
  selection decisions, 261–262
  training and development, 303–307
  unions, 538–540
Customers
  employee fairness, 114–115
  importance of human resources (HR), 6–7
  job analysis, 165
  performance measurements, 334
  training for, 272
Customer service
  business strategies, 61–62
  improving, 271–272
  performance measurements, 327
Customized job analysis, 171–173, 177–179
Cynicism, 103

D

Dannon Yogurt, health and safety programs, 478
Darden Restaurants, diversity management, 137, 138
Data analysis, 466
Data I/O Corporation, performance-based pay, 414
Data Protection Directive, 145
Death (in the workplace), 476
Decertification, unions, 519–521
Decline, 44–45

Decline of job analysis, 180
Deere & Company
    company culture, 58
    external/organizational
        environments, 36
    globalization, 39
    health and safety,
        479–480
    health maintenance
        organizations (HMOs),
        454
    human resources, managing,
        35, 473
Defense Systems, Inc. (DSI),
    226–227
Deferred compensation plans,
    422
Defined benefit plans,
    447–448
Defined contribution plans,
    IBM, 449
Dell, Inc., performance
    management, 320
Deloitte Touche Tohmatsu,
    recruiting, 203
Delphi, HR forecasts, 86
Demographic needs analysis,
    285–286
Depersonalization, 492
Design choices for
    performance-based pay,
    402–410
Deutsche Bank, HR metrics
    for, 93–94
Development. *See also*
    Training
    compensation, 363–364
    of competitive workforces,
        18, 269. *See also*
        Workforce
    conditions for effective,
        286–288
    current issues, 303–307
    e-learning, 292–293
    evaluating, 278–279
    Forest Products Company
        (FPC), 311
    global leadership,
        305–307
    within integrated HRM
        systems, 275–279
    learning objectives, stating,
        288–291
    maximizing, 299–301
    needs, 281–286
    on-the-job training (OJT),
        293–296
    overview of, 270–275
    personal development plans,
        310
    program formats, selecting,
        291–299

    of skills, 10
    teams, 302–304
    of total compensation, 18
    triad (HR), 280–281
Developmental benefit
    programs, 463
Diagnosis of feedback, 344
Dimensions of country
    cultures, 52–53
Direct index approach,
    338–339
Disability insurance, 446
Disadvantages
    of customized job analysis,
        173
    of learning formats, 292
    of team incentives, 420
Discrimination
    antidiscrimination training
        principles, 277
    based on sexual orientation,
        121
    detection of, 257–259
    lawsuits, 135
    practices, defending,
        259–260
Diseases
    occupational, 489
    prevention, 497
Disney, company culture, 59
Disputes, settling, 131–134,
    146
Distributive bargaining, 523
Distributive justice, 117
Diversity, management
    initiatives, 135–139
Domestic partner benefit and
    services, 461–462
Domino's Pizza, performance
    management, 334
Dow, HRIM, 55–56
Downsizing, 44
    Chevron, 84
    Defense Systems, Inc. (DSI),
        226–227
Drug and alcohol testing,
    253–254
DuPont
    compensation, 358
    401(k)s, 450
DynMcDermott, health and
    safety, 479

E

Earnings-at-risk pay, 404,
    422–426
Economic benefits of diversity,
    137–139
Economic globalization, 37,
    39–42, 66, 82
Economic Recovery Tax Act
    of 1981, 452

Economic utility, 230
    calculating, 231–232
Effectiveness
    of diversity initiatives,
        evaluating, 137
    intervention, 496–497
    performance-based pay, 412
    training and development,
        279, 286–288
Efficiency, 11
eHR, 28
80% rule, 258–259
Elder care services, 461
e-learning, 292–293
Elections
    request for union, 518–519
    union processes, 519–521
Electronic documents, privacy,
    143
Electronic media, recruiting,
    202–203
Elements
    of a job description, 163
    of organizational
        environments, 37
Eligibility rules, performance-
    based pay, 406
Eli Lilly
    career planning discussions,
        285
    stock options, 425
Email, privacy, 143
Emotional exhaustion, 492
Employability, 11
Employee Assistance Programs
    (EAPs), 325, 457
Employee Relations Program,
    196
Employee Retirement Income
    Security Act of 1974
    (ERISA), 442, 452
Employees, 10–11
    action plans, involvement
        in, 101
    benefits. *See* Benefit
        programs; Services
    compensation, 372
    displaced, assisting, 221
    engagement, 7
    fairness, overview of,
        116–120
    gay, lesbian, bisexual, and
        transgender (GLBT),
        120
    opinions, 87–89
    part-time, 208
    performance-based pay,
        398–399
    performance-based pay,
        acceptance of, 410–411
    performance management,
        324

    recommendations, 12
    recruiting. *See* Recruiting
    referrals, 203–204
    responsibility sharing, 24
    retaining. *See* Retaining
        employees
    retaining qualified, 17
    roles, external/
        organizational
        environments, 38
    satisfaction, 317
    selection, 17–18. *See also*
        Selection decisions
    shortages, planning for, 96
    as source of added value, 12
    support for, 325
    support for unions,
        soliciting, 517–519
    surveys, 87–88
    training and development,
        280–281
    who are rare, 12–13
Employee stock option plans,
    450–451
Employee stock ownership
    plans (ESOPs), 424
Employer Information Report
    (EEO-1), 213
Employers, cost of benefit
    programs, 441
Employment
    contracts, 129–130
    foreign nationals, 207
Employment-at-will,
    128–131
    limitations to, 129
Empowerment, feelings
    of, 10
Enron, ethics, 429
Enterprise Resource Planning
    (ERP), 74
Equal Employment
    Opportunity Commission
    (EEOC), 113, 126, 213
    *Technical Assistance Manual
        on Employment
        Provisions*, 257
Equal Pay Act, 367–368
Equity, individual pay, 386
Ergonomics, 167, 495
Ernst & Young
    benefit programs, 440
    computer technology, 54
Errors, rating, 341
Ethics
    behavior, 291
    code of, 22
    managing, 27
    performance-based pay,
        427–429
    recruiting, 211–213
    training, 272

workforce, screening for, 248
EU (European Union)
    privacy in, 145
    regional trade zones, 40
Evaluation. *See also* Appraisals
    compentency-based job, 377–378
    objectives of job, 372–373
    performance, 318
    performance-based pay, 412
    training development, 278–279
Evart Glass Plant (Chrysler Group), 302
Executive Order 10988 of 1962, 512
Executive orders, 125
Executives
    CEOs. *See* CEOs
    compensation, 359–360
    education programs, 297
Expatriates, selection decisions, 261
Expectancy, 315–316
Expenses. *See also* Costs
    employees, recruiting/retaining, 191–192
External environments, 14–16, 36–39
    benefit programs, 441–442
    compensation, 364–365
    current issues, 63–65
    health and safety, 480–481
    performance-based pay, 402
    performance management, 319–323
    scanning, 82–91
External equity, 385–386
External labor markets, 201–207
External market pay rates, determining, 379–382
ExxonMobil, business strategies, 60

F

Factories, technologies in, 53–54
Failure of mergers and acquisitions, 45–46
Fairchild Semiconductor
    alignment, planning for, 74–75
    human resources, managing, 153–154
    job analysis, 155
Fair content, 255
Fair Labor Association, 539
Fair Labor Standards Act (FLSA), 366–367

Fairness, 13, 113
    culture of, creating, 134–135
    current issues, 143–145
    disputes, settling, 131–134
    employees' view of, 116–120
    employment-at-will, 128–131
    international operations, 130–131
    layoffs, 130
    legal means to ensure, 120–128
    overview of, 114–116
    pay, 356
    perceptions of, 146
    proactive approaches to, 134–143
    reciprocation, 142–143
    selection decisions, 256
Fairview Health Systems, consumer-driven medical plans, 455
Family and Medical Leave Act of 1993 (FMLA), 125, 442, 446–447
Fatal occupational injuries, 481
Fear, 103
Federal contractors, 213–214
Federal guidelines for selection decisions, 257
Federal Hazard Communication Standard, 482
Federal laws, 121–123
Federal Mediation and Conciliation Service (FMCS), 133, 533
Federal Society of Journeymen Cordwainers, 511
Federated Department Stores, 136
FedEx
    corporate cultures, 13–14
    performance management, 314
FedEx Kinko's, 75
Feedback, 13
    content of the discussion, 344–345
    follow-up, 345–346
    legally defensible, 322
    performance, 343–347
    performance-based pay, 400–401
    perspectives, differing, 343–344
    preparation, 344
    timing, 344
    training, 300–301

Females, breaking the glass ceiling, 216–217
Financial Accounting Standards Board (FASB), 411
Financial services industry, outsourcing, 96
Flexibility of benefit programs, 464
Flexible Work Options (FWO) program, 363
Flextime, 460
Focal-point approach, 330–331
Focus groups, 89
Focus on behavior, interviews, 250–251
Follow-up, feedback, 345–346
Forced distribution method, 335–336
Ford Motor Company
    collective bargaining, 526
    company culture, 59
Forecasts
    human resources (HR), 85–87
    statistical, 87
Foreign nationals, recruiting, 206–207
Foreign workers in the United States, 222–223
Forest Products Company (FPC), 311
Formal course, 298
Formats
    appraisals, 335–340
    rating scales, 342
Forms, 175–177
    401(k)s, 450
    403(b)s, 449
Frameworks for managing human resources, 14–19
Framing, 531
Freedom to Compete award (EEOC), 135
Frequency of performance reviews, 330
Frustration, 488
Future orientation, 52

G

Gainsharing plans, 421
Games, business board, 298
GAO (Government Accountability Office), 451
Gates Energy Products, 274
Gay, lesbian, bisexual, and transgender (GLBT) employees, 120
GE (General Electric)
    360-degree appraisals, 334–335, 352–353

business strategies, 61
Canada and Mexico, unionization in, 516
compensation, 360
feedback, timing, 344
labor costs in India, 49
selection decisions, 237
Gender differentiation, 52
General health examinations, 253
General Mills
    performance measurements, 333–334
    privacy, 144
General Motors (GM)
    Canada and Mexico, unionization in, 516
    collective bargaining, 526
    health care services, 467
Genetech, labor markets, 197
Genetic testing and screening, 253
GeoEngineers, Inc., performance-based pay, 405
Georgia-Pacific, improvement process teams, 102
GlaxoSmithKline, broadbanding, 377
Global firms, competencies for, 21–22
Globalization, 37, 39–42, 66, 82
    compensation, 387–388
    health and safety, 483–485
    leadership training and development, 305–307
    managing, 26–27
    performance-based pay, 426–427
    privacy issues, 145
    recruiting, 203
    unions, 538–539
    vacations, 458
Global labor market, 48–50
Global labor shortage, 221–222
Global Leadership and Organizational Behavior Effectiveness (GLOBE), 52
Global Professional in Human Resources (GPHR), 22
Global selection decisions, legal considerations, 260
Global workforce planning, 105
Goals
    performance management, 317–318
    training, 282
Goodyear, unions, 509

Google
  benefit programs, 443
  stock options, 425
Gore-Tex fabrics, teamwork,
    181
Grades, pay, 377, 384–385
Grants, stock, 424
Graphic rating scales, 337
Great Depression, 95
Green-circled, pay equity,
    386–387
Grievances
  hearings, 132
  procedures, 131–132,
    534–538
Groups
  focus, 89
  interviews, 166
Growth, rapid, 43–44

H

Harassment policies, 138–142
Hard Rock Cafe International,
    465
Harrah's, consumer-driven
    medical plans, 455
Hay Group, compensation, 383
Hay Guide–Chart Profile, 374
Hazards in the workplace,
    478, 486–494. *See also*
    Safety
Health
  current issues, 501
  external environments,
    480–481
  globalization, 483–485
  hazards in the workplace,
    486–494
  improving, 494–501
  integrated HRM systems,
    476–485
  job burnout, 492–494
  laws, 481–483
  medical tests, 252–254
  Midwest Telephone
    Company (MTC), 505
  organizational
    environments, 479–480
  overview of, 474–476
  triad (HR), 485–486
  workplace stressors,
    491–492
Health and safety committees,
    495–496
Health care, 18–19, 453–457.
    See also Benefit programs
  Employee Assistance
    Programs (EAPs), 457
  insurance, 10
  medical insurance plans,
    453–456
  wellness programs, 456–457

Health maintenance
    organizations (HMOs),
    454
Hearings, grievance, 132
Hewitt and Associates,
    broadbanding, 377
Hewlett-Packard (HP)
  401 (k)s, 450
  business planning, aligning,
    81–82
  communities-of-practice,
    273–274
  supply chain management,
    106
  virtual workforce, 55
History of unions, 510–516
HITEK Information Services,
    job descriptions at,
    184–187
HIV/AIDS, 48–50, 484,
    500–501
Home Depot
  executive compensation,
    360
  living wage laws, 368–369
Honesty in recruiting, 212
Honeywell, recruiting/
    retaining employees, 199
Hospital utilization programs,
    466
Host-country nationals
    (HCNs), 261–262
Hotel Employees and
    Restaurant Employees
    International Union
    (HERE), 513
Howe 2 Ski Stores, incentive
    pay, 432–433
HR professionals
  benefit programs, 444
  compensation, 371
  Occupational Information
    Network (O*NET),
    168
  performance management,
    324–325
  roles, external/
    organizational
    environments, 38
  selection decisions, 233–234
  training and development,
    281
Human assets, 5
Humane orientation, 52
Human resource information
    management (HRIM),
    55–56
Human resource management
    (HRM) systems, 17. *See
    also* Managing human
    resources
  benefit programs, 439–444

compensation, 361–370
  employees, recruiting/
    retaining, 196–199
  health and safety, 476–485
  in learning organizations,
    77
  performance-based pay,
    399–402
  performance management,
    319–323
  selection decisions, 234–236
  training and development,
    275–279
  unionization, 509–510
Human resources (HR)
  action plans, 107
  competencies for global
    firms, 21–22
  current issues, 28–29
  definition of, 14
  forecasts, 85–87
  managing, 3
  metrics, 91–94. *See also*
    Metrics
  objectives, 91–94
  planning, 17, 73, 107. *See
    also* Planning
  planning, elements of,
    78–80
  plans, 80, 107
  plans, developing, 94–101
  professionals, 20–24
  recruiting, 211. *See also*
    Recruiting
  strategic importance of,
    4–11
  timetables, 80, 94, 99–101
Hyundai Motor America,
    137

I

IBM
  401(k)s, 450
  business strategies, 63
  compensation, 360
  defined contribution plans,
    448–449
  globalization, compensation
    in context of, 387
  labor costs, 48
  selection decisions, 236
  skill shortage in U.S., 47
  training and development,
    279
  virtual workforce, 55
Immigration, 483
  reform, 222–223
Implementation of
    performance-based pay,
    410–412
Improshare gainsharing plan,
    421

Incentive pay, 404, 418–422.
    See also Performance-
    based pay
  Howe 2 Ski Stores,
    432–433
Incumbents, job, 164
Independent contractors, 44
  legal protection, 157–158
India, labor costs, 49
Individual incentives, 419
Individual interviews, 166
Individual pay equity, 386
Industrial Revolution, 105
Industry capital intensity, 365
Industry conditions,
    compensation, 364–365
Industry dynamics, 37, 43–46,
    66, 83
Industry life cycles, 43–45
Industry unionization, 365
Inflation, effect on benefit
    programs, 442
Informal discussions, 131
Information collection
    methods, 165–166
Information technology (IT)
  labor costs, 49
  virtual workforce, 55
Infosys BPO, improving
    customer service, 271
In-group collectivism, 52
Initiatives, diversity
    management, 135–139
Innovation, business
    strategies, 63
Institutional collectivism, 52
Instrumentality
  question, 316–317
  unions, 521
Insurance programs, 10. *See
    also* Benefit programs
  disability, 446
Intangible human assets, 5–6
Integrated HRM systems
  benefit programs and
    services, 439–444
  compensation, 361–370
  employees, recruiting/
    retaining, 196–199
  health and safety, 476–485
  performance-based pay,
    399–402
  performance management,
    319–323
  training and development
    within, 275–279
  unionization, 509–510
Integrative bargaining, 524
Integrity tests, 247–249
Interactional justice, 118–119
Interactive video training
    (IVT), 297

Internal environments, performance management, 319–323
Internal equity, 385–386
Internal labor market, 199, 200–201
Internal pay structure, designing, 384–385
Internal transfers, 97
International Labor Organization (ILO), 42, 484
International Ladies' Garment Workers Union (ILGWU), 513
International Longshore and Warehouse Union (ILWU), 531–532
International operations, legal compliance, 130–131
Internet
  e-learning, 292–293
  external environments, searching, 68
  recruiting, 204
Interpersonal skills, 289–290
Interpretation of questionnaires, 172–173
Internal value of jobs, establishing, 372–379
Intervention effectiveness, assessing, 496–497
Interviews, 166, 250–252
  focus on behavior, 250–251
  multiple, 251–252
  Southwest Airlines, 250
  structure of, 250
  systematic scoring, 251
  Trader Joe's, 250
  trained interviewers, 252
Intraorganizational bargaining, 525
Inventories
  competency modeling, 179
  talent, 200–201
Investors, importance of human resources to, 4–6

J

J. M. Smucker & Company, ethics, 273
Jack in the Box, recruiting/ retaining employees, 193–194
Jamestown Advanced Products, Inc., 333
JC Penney, 401(k)s, 450
Job analysis, 17, 153–154
  current issues, 179–181
  customized, 171–173, 177–179
  decline of, 180

health and safety, 477–478
independent contractors, 157–158
information collection methods, 165–166
legal protection, 156–158
overview of, 154–159
sources of information used, 163–165
standardized approaches, 166–170, 174–177
strategic change, 155–156
teamwork, 181
terminology, 159–163
training and development, 277–278
triad (HR), 158–159
Job applicants
  assessment, 244–254
  selection decisions, perspective of, 254–256
Job-based pay
  grades and ranges, 384–385
  structures, 373
Jobs
  benchmark, 380–381
  burnout, 492–494
  characteristics theory, 489
  classification method, 373
  compentency-based job evaluation, 377–378
  definition of, 159–161
  description, elements of, 163
  descriptions, 161–162, 184–187
  enrichment, 156
  evaluation, objectives of, 372–373
  fairs, 196, 205–206
  incumbents, 164
  Internal value of jobs, establishing, 372–379
  natural time span of, 331
  needs analysis, 283
  objectives of evaluation, 372–373
  poorly designed, 489–491
  postings, 200
  ranking method, 373
  training, 10
Johnson, Lyndon B., 125
Joining unions, 520–521
Joint ventures, 9
JPMorgan Chase, stress management, 497
JPS Health Network, recruiting, 191

K

Kemper Insurance, compensation, 361
Kinko's. See FedEx Kinko's

Knowledge
  cognitive, 288–289
  management, 272–274
  tests, 246–247
Korean War, 441
Kroger, unions, 533
Kyphon, Inc., competitiveness, 270–271

L

Labor costs, 48–50
  performance-based pay, 397–398
  reducing, 193
Labor force, fairness, 114
Labor Management Relations Act of 1947 (LMRA), 512, 528
Labor Management Reporting and Disclosure Act (1959), 512
Labor markets, 37, 46–50, 66, 83, 197
  comparisons, 258
  compensation, 364
  global, 48–50
  United States, 46–48
Labor Relations Research Center, 529
Lag policy, 383
Landrum-Griffin Act, 512
Language skills, 290
Laws, 8
  compensation, 365–369
  discrimination, prohibiting, 256–257
  to ensure fairness, 120–128
  fairness, 114
  federal, 121–123
  health and safety, 481–483
  right to work, 514
  state, 123–125
Lawsuits, discrimination, 135
Layoffs, 13, 95–96
  legal compliance, 130
  managing, 220–221
  unexpected, 116
Leadership
  development plans, 99
  health and safety, 479–480
Lead policy, 383
Learning
  knowledge management and, 272–274
  objectives, stating, 288–291
  organizations, 77–78
Legal compliance, 8, 113
  current issues, 143–145
  disputes, settling, 131–134
  employment-at-will, 128–131

feedback, 322
international operations, 130–131
layoffs, 130
overview of, 114–116
termination, 129
training and development, 277
Legal considerations
  of performance-based pay, 411–412
  retirement plans, 451–453
  in selection decisions, 256–260
Legal constraints, compensation, 365–369
Legal institutions, 83
Legal means to ensure fairness, 120–128
Legal precedents, 128
Legal protection
  independent contractors, 157–158
  job analysis, 156–158
Legal trends, recruiting/ retaining employees, 199
Length-of-service awards, 412–413
Levi Strauss & Company case study, 70–71
Lifestyle information, access to, 144
Limitations to employment-at-will, 129
Lincoln Electric Company
  benefit programs, 443
  case study, 560–575
  performance-based pay, 398, 399, 401, 403
  performance management, 314
Line managers, 20
  employees, retaining/ recruiting, 195
  roles, external/ organizational environments, 38
  selection decisions, 233–234
Line-of-sight, 406
Living wage laws, 368–369
L.L. Bean, recruiting, 207
Lockouts, 531–532
Low-cost business strategies, 61
Low pay, 357–358
Low-performance situations, 343
Low personal accomplishment, 493
Lucent Technologies, selection decisions, 235

M

Macy's, diversity
    management, 136
Malcolm Baldrige Award, 87,
    88, 269
Management
    diversity initiatives,
        135–139
    resistance to change, 103
    risk, metrics for, 94
    supply chain, 106
    Total Quality Management
        (TQM), 87
Management by objectives
    (MBO), 339–340
Management Position
    Description
    Questionnaire (MPDQ),
    170
Managers
    accountability of, 325
    benefit programs, 444
    compensation, 371
    line, 20
    performance management,
        323–324
    stress, 492
    support for, 325
    training and development,
        280
Managing complexity, 28–29
Managing ethics, 27
Managing globalization,
    26–27
Managing human resources, 3
    activities for, 16–19
    Barden Bearings, 110–111
    Cisco Systems, 3
    common themes, 24–28
    Deere & Company, 35, 473
    Fairchild Semiconductor,
        153–154
    framework for, 14–19
    Levi Strauss & Company,
        70–71
    Outback Steakhouse, 229
    Ritz-Carlton Hotel
        Company, 269
    roles, 25
    SAS Institute, 189
    Steelcase, 435
    strategic importance of,
        4–11
    Synapse Group, Inc., 355
    TRW, 313
    United Parcel Service (UPS),
        507
    United States Postal Service
        (USPS), 395
    Wal-Mart, 113
    Weyerhaeuser Company,
        73

Managing knowledge,
    272–274
Managing layoffs, 220–221
Managing multiculturalism,
    26, 327
Managing performance. See
    Performance
Managing teams, 25
Managing with metrics,
    27–28, 180
Mandatory issues, 528
Mandatory protection
    programs, 440, 445–447
Mape Landmark Woodcraft,
    health and safety, 486
Market pay policies,
    establishing, 382–383
Market rates, setting pay
    levels, 379–384
Markets, labor, 197. See also
    Labor markets
Mass production technologies,
    53–54
Mastery, training, 300
Match policy, 383
Maximizing training and
    development, 299–301
McDonald's
    diversity management,
        135, 136
    employees, recruiting/
        retaining, 193–194
    globalization, compensation
        in context of, 388
    off-site training, 298
Measurements
    performance, 326–329,
        400–401, 416. See also
        Performance
    performance-based pay,
        406–409
Mediation, 132–133, 533
Medical information, access
    to, 144
Medical insurance plans,
    453–456
Medical tests, 252–254
    drug and alcohol testing,
        253–254
    general health
        examinations, 253
    genetic testing and
        screening, 253
MedStar Health,
    compensation, 358
Memory aids, providing,
    342
Mental health, 475–476
Mentoring, 294–296
Mercedes-Benz
    Credit Corporation, 103
    location in Alabama, 51

Merck Pharmaceuticals,
    company culture, 57
Mergers, 45–46
    elements of planning, 78
    training, 274–275
Merit pay, 403, 416
Merrill Lynch
    Fair Labor Standards Act
        (FLSA), 367
    performance management,
        343
    reputations, building, 209
Methods
    forced distribution,
        335–336
    information collection,
        165–166
    job classification, 373
    job ranking, 373
    point factor rating, 374–377
    recruiting, 199–208
Metrics
    behavioral cause-and-effect
        models, 90–91
    bottom-line HR, 92–93
    collective bargaining,
        537–538
    for Deutsche Bank, 93–94
    human resources (HR),
        91–94
    human resources (HR)
        planning, 78–80
    managing with, 27–28, 180
    objectives, matching, 92–94
    for SunTrust Bank, 93
Mexico
    health and safety
        considerations, 483
    unionization in, 516
Microsoft
    company culture, 57
    independent contractors,
        157
    job analysis, 179
    stock options, 426
Midwest Telephone Company
    (MTC), 505
Minimum wage, 366–367
Mirage Resorts, rejecting
    applicants, 212
Missed promotions, 116
Mission statements, 57–58
Misunderstandings, 103
Mix, pay, 362–363
Models, behavioral cause-and-
    effect, 90–91
Modification, behavior, 496
Monetary compensation,
    361–362
Monitoring
    performance, 318, 349
    safety and health, 494

Montgomery Watson Harza
    (MWH), 137, 139
Morgan Stanley, harassment
    policies, 140
Motivation
    enhancing, 315–317
    factors that influence, 316
    performance-based pay,
        398–399
Motorola
    360-degree appraisals,
        334–335
    compensation, 360
    performance-based pay, 418
MTV Networks, planning for
    change, 77
Multiculturalism, managing,
    26, 327
Multinational corporations
    (MNCs), 8
Multiple awards, 415
Multiple criteria, 328
Multiple-hurdles approach,
    242
Multiple interviews, 251–252
Multiple pay structures,
    378–379
Multiple raters, using,
    342–343
Multiple source evaluations,
    334–335
Multiple stakeholders, 4
Muslims, harassment of, 140
Mythical fixed pie, 531

N

National Business Ethics
    Survey, 142
National Center for Health
    Statistics, 476
National Institute for
    Occupational Safety and
    Health (NIOSH), 482
National Labor Relations Act
    (Wagner Act) of 1935,
    512
National Labor Relations
    Board (NLRB), 126, 128,
    508, 519
Natural time span of jobs, 331
Needs
    demographic needs analysis,
        285–286
    job needs analysis, 283
    organizational needs
        analysis, 282–283
    person needs analysis,
        283–284
    self-assessed training,
        284–285
    training and development,
        281–286

Negative settlement range, 524
Negotiating collective bargaining agreements, 525–531
New Balance, computer technology, 54
Newspaper Workers International Union (NWIU), 543
Nike, unions, 539
Nintendo of America, compensation, 389
Nixon, Richard M., 125
NJ 101.5, 137
Nondiscrimination, 157
Nonfatal workplace injuries, 481
Nonmonetary compensation, 361–362
Nonqualified plans, 447
Norm-referenced appraisals, 335–336
Norris-LaGuardia Act of 1932, 512
North American Free Trade Agreement (NAFTA), 40, 483

O

Objectives
  of benefit programs and services, 437
  human resources (HR), 91–94
  management by objectives (MBO), 339–340
  metrics, matching, 92–94
  performance-based pay, 396–397
  planning, 78–80
  strategic business objectives, linking to, 91–92
Observations, 165–166
Obsession, 488
Occupational accidents, 486–487
Occupational diseases, 489
Occupational Information Network (O*NET), 167–169
Occupational Safety and Health Act of 1970
Occupational Safety and Health Administration (OSHA), 126, 127, 481–483
Occupational Safety and Health Review Commission (NIOSH), 482
Occupations, definition of, 159–161

Offshoring, 97
Off-site training, 297–299
Off-the-job paid leaves, 457–459
Oncale v. Sundown Offshore Service Inc. (1998), 140
On-site training, 296–297
On-the-job training (OJT), 293–296
Open-door policies, 13
Opinions, employees, 87–89
Options, stock, 404, 425
Organizational analysis, 84–85
Organizational change, types of, 75–77
Organizational environments, 14–16, 36–39
  benefit programs, 442–444
  compensation, 369–370
  health and safety, 479–480
  performance-based pay, 401
  scanning, 82–91
Organizational needs analysis, 282–283
Organizational pay policies, setting, 383–384
Organizational redesign, 155–156
Organizing campaigns, unions, 516–521
Outback Steakhouse, managing human resources, 229
Outdoor training, 299
Outsourcing, 96
Owners, importance of human resources to, 4–6

P

Paid leave, 457–459
Participants in performance, 331–335
Part-time employees, 208
Pay. *See also* Compensation and benefits, 10
  earnings-at-risk, 404, 422–426
  fairness, 356
  grades, 377, 384–385
  incentive, 418–422
  levels, setting, 379–384
  low, 357–358
  merit, 403
  mix, 362–363
  performance, linking to, 417–418
  performance-based. *See* Performance-based pay
  secrecy, 358
  variable pay, shift toward, 429

Payless ShoeSource, performance measurements, 328
Payne v. Western & A.R.R., Co. (1884), 128
Peer appraisals, 333
Pella, 95
Pension Benefit Guaranty Corporation (PBGC), 452
Pentagon, attack on, 95
Perceptions of fit, 211
Performance, 313
  appraisals, formats, 335–340
  behavioral cause-and-effect models, 90–91
  compensation, 363–364
  current issues, 347–348
  deficiencies, causes of, 345
  deteriorates, 493
  feedback, 343–347
  focal-point approach, 330–331
  goals, 317–318
  health and safety, effect on, 478
  integrated HRM systems, 319–323
  internal/external environments, 319–323
  legal protection, 156
  management, 18
  management, overview of, 314–318
  measuring, 326–329, 400–401, 416
  monitoring, 318, 349
  orientation, 52
  participants, 331–335
  pay, linking to, 417–418
  performance-based pay, 18
  problem behavior, 346–347
  rating errors, 341
  rating processes, 340–343
  rewards, linking to, 409–410
  timing, 329–331
  training, maintaining after, 301
  triad (HR), 323–325
Performance-based pay
  accounting, 411–412
  current issues, 427–429
  design choices for, 402–410
  earnings-at-risk pay, 422–426
  effectiveness, 412
  ethics, 427–429
  external environments, 402
  globalization, 426–427
  implementation, 410–412
  incentive pay, 418–422

integrated HRM systems, 399–402
  legal considerations, 411–412
  measurements, 406–409
  organizational environments, 401
  overview of, 396–399
  recognition awards, 412–415
  rewards, 404–406, 416–417
  taxes, 411–412
  triad (HR), 402
  types of, 403–404
Performance-driven cultures, 320–323
Permatemps, 157
Permissive issues, 528
Personal development plans, 310
Personal history assessment, 244
Personality-Related Position Requirements Form (PPRF), 175–177
Personality tests, 247
Personal services, 463
Personal traits, performance measurements, 326
Person needs analysis, 283–284
Personnel Decisions International (PDI), 286
Perspective of job applicants, 254–256
Pfizer, stock options, 425
Pharm Tech, broadbanding, 377
Phases in HR planning for alignment and change, 79
Physical (violent) actions, 488
Physiological-physical conditions, 477
Planning
  action plans, implementing, 101–105
  for alignment and change, 74–78
  business planning, aligning with, 81–82
  current issues, 105–106
  Enterprise Resource Planning (ERP), 74
  global workforce, 105
  human resources (HR), 17, 107
  leadership development plans, 99
  overview of, 78–82
  performance-based pay, 400–401

Planning (*continued*)
performance management, 318
personal development, 310
staffing, 98
succession, 98
training, 98–100, 277–278
Plante & Moran, reducing turnover, 219
Point factor rating method, 374–377
Point of service (POS) plans, 455
Policies, 16–17
harassment, 138–142
market pay policies, establishing, 382–383
organizational pay policies, setting, 383–384
Political landscape, 37, 66, 82
Poorly designed jobs, 489–491
Position Analysis Questionnaire (PAQ), 169–170
Positions, definition of, 159–161
Positive settlement range, 524
Postings, job, 200
Power distance, 52
PPG Industries, goals, 318
Practices, 16–17
Predictors
measures of, 242
reliable, 241–242
selecting, 237–238
valid, 237–241
Preelection campaigns, 519
Preferred provider organizations (PPOs), 454–455
Preparation for feedback, 344
Prescription drug management, 466
Prevention
accidents, 494–495
diseases, 497
harassment, 141
PricewaterhouseCoopers (PwC), 306–307
Primary boycotts, 533
Primary care physicians (PCPs), 454
Principal Financial Group, 47
Privacy
in the EU (European Union), 145
in the global context, 145
in the United States, 143–145
Privacy Act of 1974, 143
Private employment agencies, 205

Proactive approaches to fairness, 134–143, 146
Problem behavior, appraisals, 346–347
Procedural justice, 117–118
Processes
collective bargaining, 521–525
selection decisions, fairness of, 256
Procter & Gamble (P&G)
360-degree appraisals, 334–335
behavioral cause-and-effect models, 90–91
child care services, 460–461
leadership development plans, 99
organizational analysis, 84
training and development, 278
training plans, 99
Productivity, 5
based on compensation, 361
benefit programs, 436
employees, recruiting/ retaining, 191–192
enhancing, 315–317
Professional in Human Resources (PHR), 21
Profiles, Hay Guide–Chart Profile, 374
Profitability
importance of human resources on, 5
improving, 11
Profit sharing plans, 13, 422, 450–451
Program formats, selecting training and development, 291–299
Prohibited issues, 528
Promotions
missed, 116
systems, 10, 13
Prudential
domestic partner benefits and services, 461
off-site training, 298
Public employment agencies, 204–205

Q
Qualified plans, 447
Quality
job design, 489
Total Quality Management (TQM), 87, 289
of work, 10
Questionnaires, 166
creating, 171–172

Management Position Description Questionnaire (MPDQ), 170
Position Analysis Questionnaire (PAQ), 169–170
Quid pro quo harassment, 140

R
Rackspace, performance-based pay, 415
Ranges, pay, 384–385
Ranking
jobs, 373
straight, 335
Rapid growth, 43–44
Raters
multiple, using, 342–343
training, 342
Rating
accuracy, improving, 341–342
errors, 341
point factor rating method, 374–377
processes, performance, 340–343
Rating scales, 336
behaviorally anchored, 337–338
formats, 342
graphic, 337
Ratios, industry capital intensity, 365
Reactions
to harassment, 140
to unjust treatment, 119–120
Reader's Digest, consumer-driven medical plans, 455
Realistic previews, 212
Recalls, 207–208
Reciprocation of fairness, 142–143
Recognition awards, 403, 412–415
Recruiting, 17, 189
applicant's perspective, 208–211
benefit programs, importance of, 437–438
contingent workers, 207
current issues, 221–223
electronic media, 202–203
employee referrals, 203–204
ethics, 211–213
experience of, 210–211
external labor markets, 201–207
foreign nationals, 206–207

honesty in, 212
improving, 270
within integrated HRM systems, 196–199
internal labor markets, 200–201
L.L. Bean, 207
overview of, 190–195
public employment agencies, 204–205
sources and methods, 199–208
training and development, 278
U.S. Postal Service, 199
walk-in applicants, 202
Red-circled, pay equity, 387
Reengineering, 156
Reference checks, 245
Referrals from employees, 203–204
Refocusing plans, 104–105
Regional trade zones, 40–42
Regulations, 8. *See* Laws
compensation, 365–369
discrimination, prohibiting, 256–257
health and safety, 481–483
Rehires, 207–208
Reinforcers, 301
Rejecting applicants, 212–213
Reliable predictors, 241–242
Relocation assistance, 463
Renewal, 44–45
Reputations, building, 209–210
Request for union elections, 518–519
Research and development, 9
Resolution of disputes online, 133
Resources
Enterprise Resource Planning (ERP), 74
learning organizations, 77–78
training, 283
Respect, showing, 104
Responsibilities
for employee benefits and services, 444
employees, recruiting/ retaining, 194
to ensure fairness and legal compliance, 115
external/organizational environments, 38
health and safety, 485
job analysis, 158–159
for managing human resources, 25
performance-based pay, 403

performance management, 324
planning, alignment, and change, 83
selection decisions, 232–236
sharing, 24
of total compensation, 371
in training and development, 281
in unionization, 511
Results
criteria (performance measurements), 327
results-based appraisals, 338–340
selection decisions, fairness of, 256
Retaining employees, 17, 189, 217–221
benefit programs, importance of, 437–438
compensation issues, 357
current issues, 221–223
improving, 270
within integrated HRM systems, 196–199
overview of, 190–195
performance-based pay, 398–399
Retention, definition of, 190
Retirement plans
health care services, 466–467
legal considerations, 451–453
types of, 448
Return on investment (ROI), 230
Revenge, 119
Reviewing plans, 104–105
Reviews, performance, 330
Revising plans, 104–105
Rewards, 416–417
accuracy, rating, 342
performance, linking to, 409–410
performance-based pay, 404–406
Right to work laws, 514
Risk
earnings-at-risk pay, 404, 422–426
management, metrics for, 94
Ritz-Carlton Hotel Company
company culture, 57
human resources, managing, 269
on-the-job training (OJT), 293
Roadblocks (feedback), removing, 344–345

Roles
analysis, 181. See also Job analysis
for employee benefits and services, 444
employees, recruiting/retaining, 194
to ensure fairness and legal compliance, 115
external/organizational environments, 38
health and safety, 485
for HR professionals, 21
job analysis, 158–159
for managing human resources, 25
performance-based pay, 403
performance management, 324
planning, alignment, and change, 83
selection decisions, 232–236
of total compensation, 371
in training and development, 281
in unionization, 511
Rosenbluth International, selection decisions, 234
Rowe v. General Motors (1972), 157
Rucker gainsharing plan, 421
Rules
80%, 258–259
eligibility, performance-based pay, 406

S

Sabre Holdings, business strategies, 62
Safety
aging workforce, effect on, 487
current issues, 501
external environments, 480–481
globalization, 483–485
hazards in the workplace, 486–494
improving, 494–501
integrated HRM systems, 476–485
job burnout, 492–494
laws, 481–483
Midwest Telephone Company (MTC), 505
organizational environments, 479–480
overview of, 474–476
programs, 10, 18–19
triad (HR), 485–486
workplace stressors, 491–492

Salaries. See Compensation
Salting, unions, 516
Sampling, work, 165
Sarbanes-Oxley Act of 2002 (SOX), 360
SAS Institute
child care services, 460–461
human resources, managing, 189
internal labor market, 200–201
Satisfaction
customers, 6–7
employees, 10, 317
Scana, external labor markets, 202
Scanlon gainsharing plan, 421
Scanning, 78, 107
external environments, 82–91
organizational environments, 82–91
Schedules
flextime, 460
vesting, 425
Schering Plough, 193–194
Schlumberger
competency inventories, 179
metrics, managing with, 180
Scoring interviews, 251
Screening
for ethics, 248
genetic testing and, 253
Sears, compensation, 360
Second Life, 236
Secrecy, pay, 358
Securities and Exchange Commission (SEC), 360
Selection decisions
current issues, 261–262
discriminatory practice, defending, 259–260
expatriates, 261
job applicant assessment, 244–254
legal considerations in, 256–260
legal protection, 156
overview of, 230–236
perspective of job applicants, 254–256
process, designing, 236–244
training and development, 278
triad (HR), 232–236
Selection systems, 10, 17–18
Self-appraisal, 332–333
Self-assessed training needs, 284–285
Self-reinforcement, 301

Semper International, selection decisions, 236
Seniority, 260
Senior Professional in Human Resources (SPHR), 21
September 11, 2001, 95, 140
Service Employees International Union (SEIU), 9, 515
Services, 435. See also Benefit programs
health and safety, 478
integrated HRM systems, 439–444
overview of, 436–439
unions, 528
Setpoint, performance management, 321
Settlement
agreements, 134
disputes, 131–134, 146
Sexual harassment, 140. See also Harassment policies
Sexual orientation, discrimination, 121
Sharing, profit, 422
Shift work, 490–491
Sick leave, 10, 471. See also Benefit programs
Single pay structures, 378–379
Skill-based pay, 378, 385
Skills, 289
development of, 10
interpersonal, 289–290
language, 290
shortage, United States, 46–47
Slowdowns, 532–533
SMART, 318
Smoking cessation programs, 500
Snap-On, privacy, 144
Social Accountability International (SAI), 42
Social accountability of unions, 539–540
Social considerations, compensation, 365–369
Social Security Act, 204–205, 445
Social Security Insurance
eligibility for, 442
legal considerations, 451
as a mandatory protection program, 445
Society
importance of human resources (HR), 7–9
and the law, 114
Society for Human Resource Management (SHRM), 21

Society for Industrial and Organizational Psychology (SIOP), 257
Solomon Smith Barney, harassment policies, 140
Sources
of information used, job analysis, 163–165
recruiting, 199–208
Southwest Airlines
case study, 544–559
corporate cultures, 13–14
HR plans, developing, 95
interviews, 250
layoffs, avoiding, 221
performance management, 314
Spot awards, 413–414
Staffing
metrics, 93. See also Metrics
planning, 98
Stakeholders, 4
Standardized approaches to job analysis, 166–170, 174–177
Standards
Federal Hazard Communication Standard, 482
Financial Accounting Standards Board (FASB), 411
selection decisions, 257
Starbucks
benefit programs, 443, 444
globalization, compensation in context of, 387
retirement savings programs, 450
State Bank, compensation, 393
State laws, 123–125
Statistical forecasts, 87
Steelcase, managing human resources, 435
Stock appreciation rights (SARs), 424
Stock grants, 424
Stock options, 404, 425
Stock ownership, 424–426
Straight commissions, 423–424
Straight ranking, 335
Strategic business objectives, linking HR objectives, 91–92
Strategic change, job analysis, 155–156
Strategic objectives
achieving, 18
performance-based pay, 396–397

Strategic planning, 81. See also Planning
Strategies, recruiting/retaining employees, 190–191
Stress
management, 497–499
in the workplace, 491–492
Strikes, 531–532
wildcat, 535
Structure
competency-based pay structure, 385
internal pay structure, designing, 384–385
of interviews, 250
skill-based pay structure, 385
Studies
case. See Case studies
time-and-motion, 166–167
Subcultures, 58–60
Subject matter experts (SMEs), 163
Subordinates, performance measurements, 333–334
Succession planning, 98
Suggestions, awards for, 414
SunTrust Bank, HR metrics for, 93
Supervisors
assistance, 294–296
job analysis, 164
performance measurements, 332
Supplier Diversity Program (Wal-Mart), 136
Suppliers, 9
Supply chain management, 106
Surveys
attitude, 285
employees, 87–88
salary budget, 386
Sustainability, 105–106
Sustainable competitive advantage, 11
Symantec, mentoring, 294
Synapse Group, Inc., managing human resources, 355
Systematic scoring, interviews, 251

T

Taft-Hartley Act (1947), 512
Talent. See also Employees
inventories, 200–201
pool, 98
timetables for developing, 100–101
Tangible human assets, 5–6

Target, living wage laws, 368–369
Task-focused job analysis, 160
Taxes
benefit programs, 442
performance-based pay, 411–412
Teach for America, 209
Teams
building, 10
incentives, 420
job analysis, 181
managing, 25
reasons for, 26
training and development, 302–304
Technical Assistance Manual on Employment Provisions (EEOC), 257
Technologies, 37, 53–56, 66
computer, 54
employees, recruiting/retaining, 198
factories, 53–54
health and safety, 480–481
human resource information management (HRIM), 55–56
implementing new, 271
knowledge management, 272–273
mass production, 53–54
performance, monitoring, 349
virtual workforce, 54–55
Temporary workers, 157
Tenneco, performance-based pay, 401
Termination, legal compliance, 129
Terminology, job analysis, 159–163
Terrorism, 95, 140
Testing
ability tests, 246
drug and alcohol, 253–254
integrity tests, 247–249
knowledge tests, 246–247
medical tests, 252–254
personality tests, 247
written tests, 246–249
Texas Instruments (TI), focus groups, 89
Textile Workers Union of America (TWUA), 513
The Conference Board, 79
Threats, verbal, 488
3M
business strategies, 61
competency modeling, 178
HR plans, developing, 97

Timberland, company culture, 58
Time-and-motion studies, 166–167
Time frames, performance-based pay, 408–409
Timetables, 80, 107
developing, 94, 99–101
for developing talent, 100–101
Time Warner, business strategies, 60
Timing
of change, 76–77
feedback, 344
performance measurements, 329–331
Title VII (Civil Rights Act of 1964), 121
Total compensation, 356–361
compensation. See Compensation
development of, 18
Total Quality Management (TQM), 87, 289
Trader Joe's, interviews, 250
Trained interviewers, 252
Trained job analysts, 164
Training, 10, 18, 269
acquisitions, 274–275
climate for, 282–283
compensation, 363–364
conditions for effective, 286–288
consistency, 301
cultural awareness, 303
current issues, 303–307
for customers, 272
e-learning, 292–293
evaluating, 278–279
feedback, 300–301
Forest Products Company (FPC), 311
global leadership, 305–307
health and safety, 478
within integrated HRM systems, 275–279
interactive video training (IVT), 297
learning objectives, stating, 288–291
legal protection, 156
maximizing, 299–301
mergers, 274–275
needs, 281–286
on-site, 296–297
on-the-job training (OJT), 293–296
outdoor, 299
overview of, 270–275
performance, maintaining after, 301

planning, 98–100
program formats, selecting, 291–299
raters, 342
teams, 302–304
triad (HR), 280–281
Transfers, internal, 97
Triad (HR), 19–24
 benefit programs, 444–445
 compensation, 370–372
 employees, recruiting/ retaining, 194–195
 fairness and legal compliance, 115–116
 health and safety, 485–486
 job analysis, 158–159
 performance-based pay, 402
 performance management, 323–325
 planning process, 82
 selection decisions, 232–236
 training and development, 280–281
TRW
 human resources, managing, 313
 multiculturalism, managing, 327
 performance management, 314
Turnover, 437. *See also* Retaining employees
 reasons for, 217–218
 reducing, 218–219
Twenty-first-century workforce, assessment, 248
Tyco, performance-based pay, ethics, 429
Types
 of harassment, 139–142
 of organizational change, 75–77
 of performance-based pay, 403–404
 of retirement plans, 448

U
Uncertainty avoidance, 52
Unemployment compensation, 445–446
Unexpected layoffs, 116
Uniform Guidelines on Employee Selection Procedures (1978), 257
Unilever
 global leaders, building, 89
 performance-based pay, 401
Unionization, 83, 365, 507. *See also* Unions

integrated HRM systems, 509–510
 overview of, 508–510
Union Pacific Railroad
 HR forecasts, 86
 wellness programs, 499
Unions, 9, 19
 AFL-CIO, 512
 agreements, negotiating, 525–531
 Amalgamated Clothing Workers of America (ACWA), 513
 Communications Workers of America (CWA), 509
 conflict resolution, 531–534
 contract administration, 534–538
 current issues, 538–540
 globalization, 538–539
 health and safety, 478–479
 history of, 510–516
 Hotel Employees and Restaurant Employees International Union (HERE), 513
 instrumentality, 521
 International Ladies' Garment Workers Union (ILGWU), 513
 International Longshore and Warehouse Union (ILWU), 531–532
 joining, 520–521
 monetary benefits, effect on, 442
 Newspaper Workers International Union (NWIU), 543
 organizing campaigns, 516–521
 salting, 516
 Service Employees International Union (SEIU), 9, 515
 social accountability, 539–540
 Textile Workers Union of America (TWUA), 513
 United Auto Workers (UAW), 508, 515, 517
 United Steelworkers of America (USWA), 508
United Auto Workers (UAW), 508, 515, 517
United States
 foreign workers in the, 222–223
 labor markets, 46–48
 privacy in, 143–145

United States Postal Service (USPS)
 human resources, managing, 395
 performance-based pay, 398, 401, 402
 recruiting, 199
 variable pay, 429
 violence (in the workplace), 488–489
United States v. City of Chicago (1990), 157
United Stationers, training plans, 98
United Steelworkers of America (USWA), 508
United Way case study, 150–151
UNITE HERE, 513
Unit incentives, 421–422
Universities, corporate, 297
University of Michigan Business School, 20
Unjust treatment, reactions to, 119–120
UPS (United Parcel Service)
 360-degree appraisals, 334–335
 Community Internship Program, 9
 human resources, managing, 507
 privacy, 144
 time-and-motion studies, 166
 unions, 509
 wellness programs, 456
U.S. Department of Transportation (DOT), 92
U.S. Training and Employment Service, 204
U.S. Treasury Bonds, 451
USA Bank, training goals, 282
USA Motors, benefit programs, 471

V
Vacations, 10, 458
Valassis Communications, 405
Valence question, 317
Valero Energy
 employees, recruiting, 192
 internal labor market, 200–201
Validity generalization, 237
Valid predictors, 237–241
Values
 company culture, 58
 of selection decisions, 231
Vanguard Group, compensation, 362

Variable pay, 397
 shift toward, 429
Verbal threats, 488
Verification, background, 245
Vesting schedules, 425
Video, interactive video training (IVT), 297
Violence (in the workplace), 476, 488–489
Virtual workforce, 54–55
 Sabre Holdings, 62
Vision, company culture, 57
Voluntary affirmative action programs, 214–215, 260
Voluntary protection programs, 440, 447–453
Volunteerism, 8–9

W
W. L. Gore, selection decisions, 236
Wages, 10. *See also* Compensation
Walk-in applicants, 202
Wal-Mart
 benefit programs, 440
 diversity management, 136, 137–138
 Equal Pay Act, 368
 globalization, compensation in context of, 387
 hiring costs, 363
 human resources, managing, 113
 living wage laws, 368–369
 organizational environment, 16
 organizational environment compensation, 370
 privacy, 144
Walt Disney, selection decisions, 237
Wegmans Food Markets, 16
Weighting criteria, 328–329
Weight loss programs, 500
Wellness programs, 456–457, 499
Wendy's, consumer-driven medical plans, 455
Westell Technologies, privacy, 144
Weyerhaeuser Company
 communication during restructuring, 103
 ethical behavior, 291
 human resources, managing, 73
 leadership development plans, 99
 organizational change, 76
Whipsawing, 527

Whole Foods, compensation, 359
Wildcat strikes, 535
Wilderness trips, 299
Win-win situations, creating, 11
Worker Adjustment and Retraining Act of 1988 (WARN), 100
Worker-focused job analysis, 160
Workers' compensation, 446
Workforce, 44. *See also* Labor markets
  aging of, 63–64

capable, obtaining, 230
development of competitive, 269
global planning, 105
planning process (HP), 82
virtual, 54–55, 62
Workforce Management magazine, 272
Working Woman, 209
Work/life benefit programs, 459–462
Work pacing, 490
Workplace safety and health. *See* Health; Safety
Work sampling, 165

Work simulations, 249
Worldcom, performance-based pay, ethics, 429
World Federation of Personnel Management Associations (WFPMA), 22
World Health Organization (WHO), 484
World Trade Center, attack on, 95
World Trade Organization (WTO), 42
World War II, 441
Worldwide operations, 39–40

Worthington Industries, selection decisions, 237
Written complaints, 131–132
Written tests, 246–249

X

Xerox, timetables, 99

Y

Yellow Freight, computer technology, 54